PUNCTUATION PASSPORT

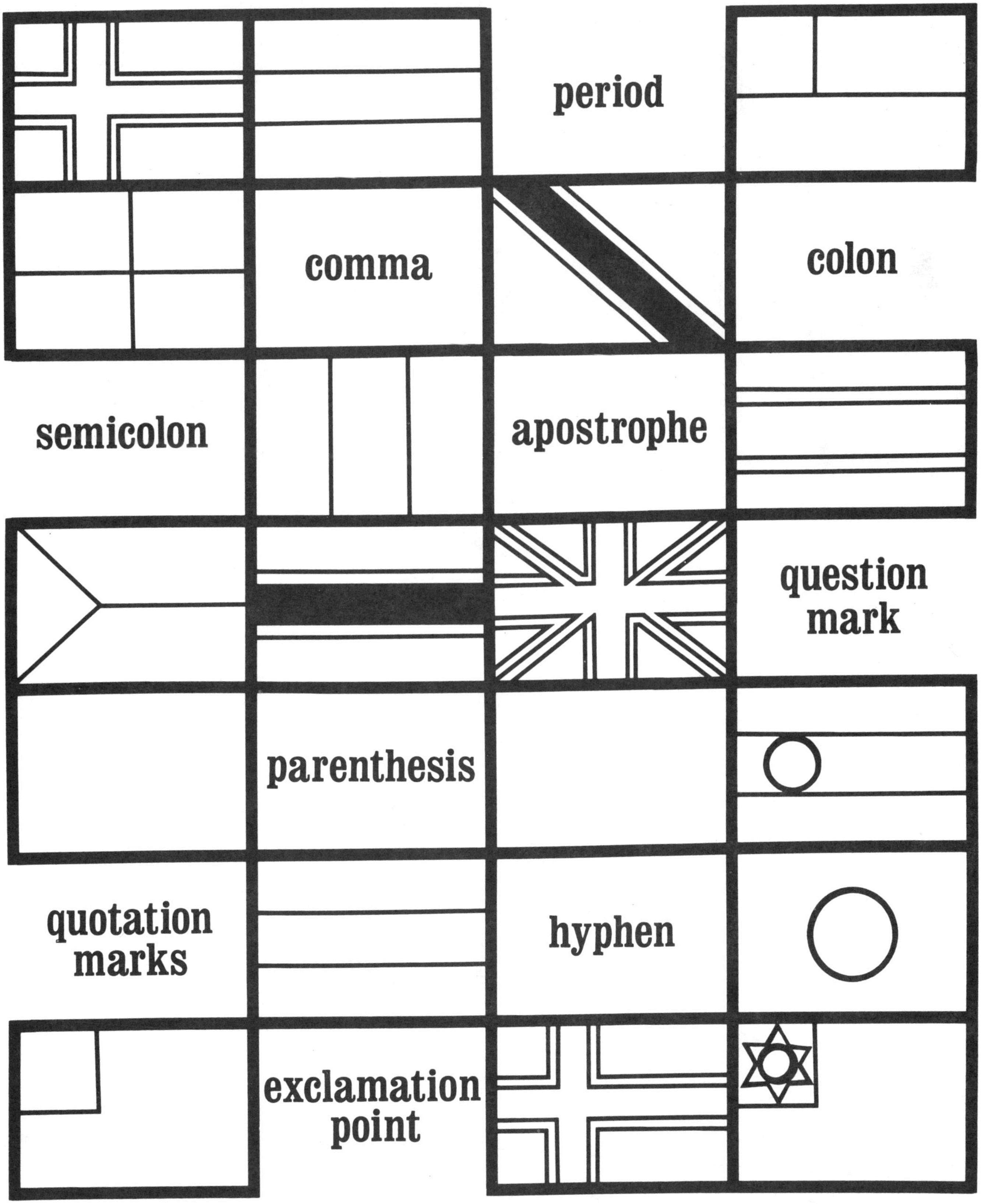

GRADES 4-8 • WRITTEN & ILLUSTRATED BY BEV ARMSTRONG

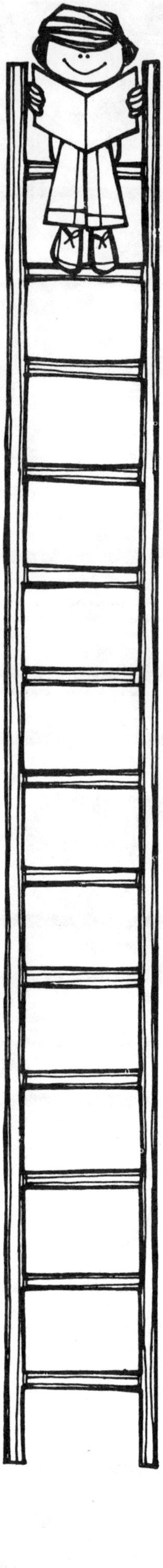

THE LEARNING WORKS

P.O. BOX 6187 SANTA BARBARA, CALIF. 93111

TABLE OF CONTENTS

PERIODS

GREECE 

NAME ____________________

CRACK THE CODE

Use a period after a sentence that is a statement or a command.

Polybius, an ancient Greek, developed this code, which uses numbers in place of letters. The code for each letter is a double number: the number to its left, and the number above it. For example, A = 11, B = 12, G = 22, R = 43, and X = 54. Both Y and Z = 55; by decoding the other letters in a word containing the number 55, you should be able to figure out whether the 55 stands for Y or Z (example: 55 35 35 = ZOO, 55 15 44 = YES).

Translate the message below. Be sure to put a period at the end of each sentence. (Hint: there are six sentences.)

	1	2	3	4	5
1	A	B	C	D	E
2	F	G	H	I	J
3	K	L	M	N	O
4	P	Q	R	S	T
5	U	V	W	X	Y/Z

22 43 15 15 13 15 23 11 44 33 11 34 55 24 44 32 11 34 14 44 11 34 14

33 35 51 34 45 11 24 34 44 45 23 15 33 11 24 34 13 43 35 41 44 11 43 15

35 32 24 52 15 44 11 34 14 22 43 11 41 15 44 33 11 34 55 21 11 43 33 15 43 44

11 32 44 35 43 11 24 44 15 44 23 15 15 41 11 34 14 22 35 11 45 44 45 23 15

53 24 34 45 15 43 44 11 43 15 32 35 34 22 11 34 14 13 35 32 14

44 51 33 33 15 43 44 24 34 22 43 15 15 13 15 13 11 34 12 15 52 15 43 55

23 35 45 45 23 15 43 15 24 44 32 24 45 45 32 15 43 11 24 34

THE PUNCTUATION PASSPORT

NAME ______________________

ABBREVIATION ROUNDUP

Use a <u>period</u> after an abbreviation.

An abbreviation is a shortened form of a word. The abbreviations for these twenty words are written on the cattle in the picture at the bottom of the page. Write each abbreviation next to the word that it stands for. "Round up" each cow as you use it by drawing a circle around it. The first one is done for you.

1. Road Rd.
2. Mountains ________
3. January ________
4. August ________
5. North ________
6. Street ________
7. Monday ________
8. Bridge ________
9. Highway ________
10. University ________
11. December ________
12. Court ________
13. Avenue ________
14. Hospital ________
15. National ________
16. Boulevard ________
17. October ________
18. Post Office ________
19. Friday ________
20. Island ________

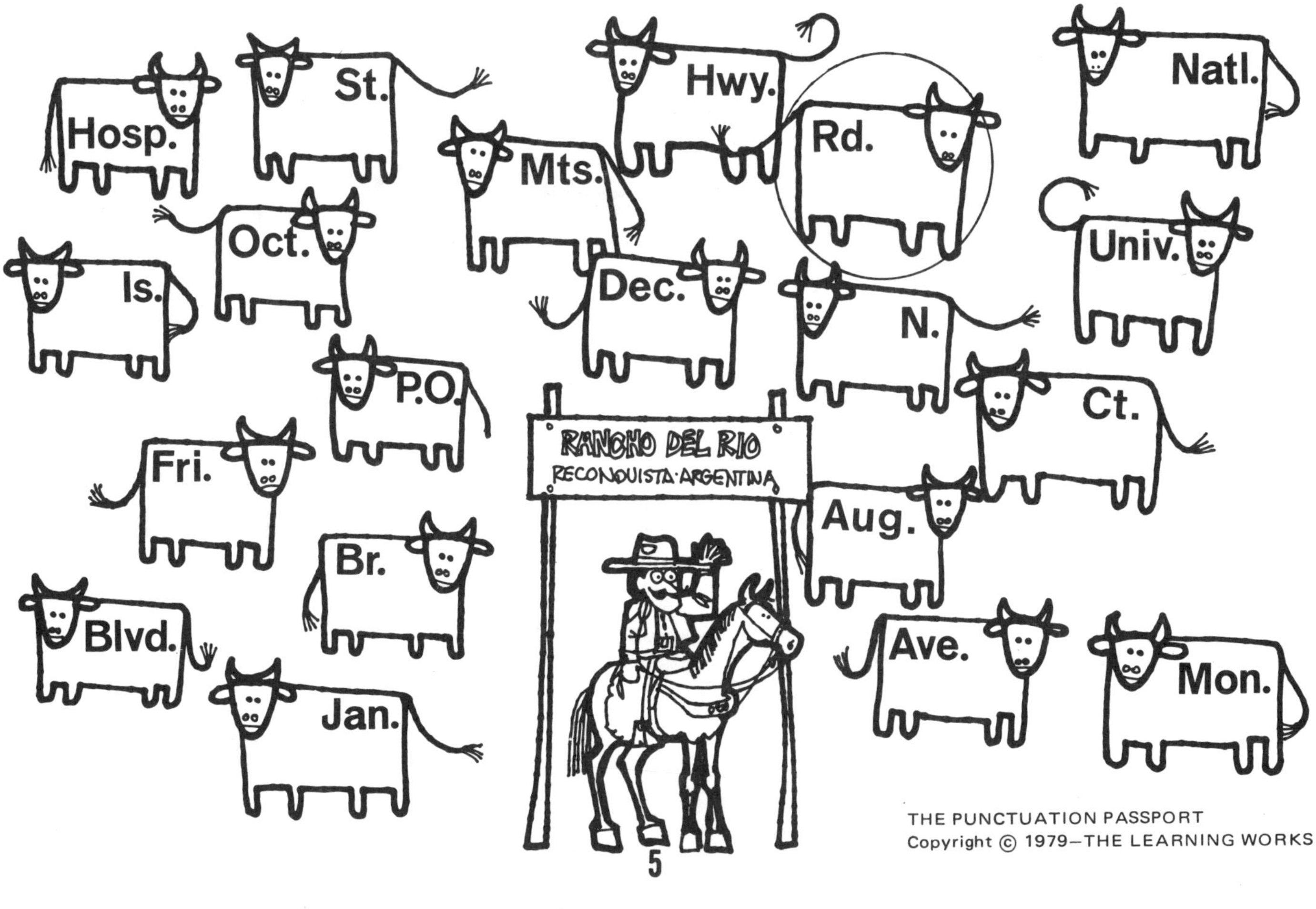

NAME ______________________

TAG THE BAGS

Use a period after an initial or an abbreviation in a title or name.

You have brought a tour group to Canada, where the participants are ready to enjoy their various hobbies. Add the missing periods to the names on the baggage tags. Draw a line from each tag to the suitcase containing things which that person will need. Use your dictionary if you need help with the words in the suitcases.

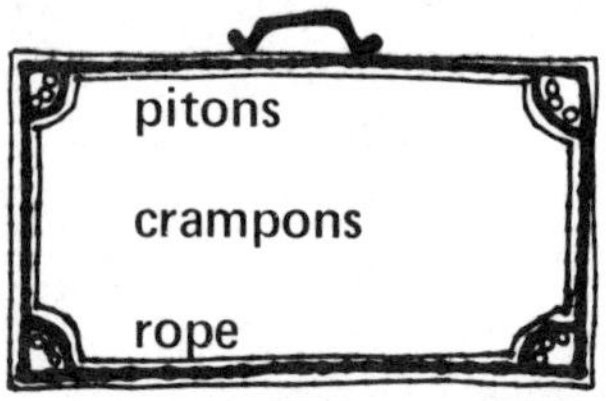

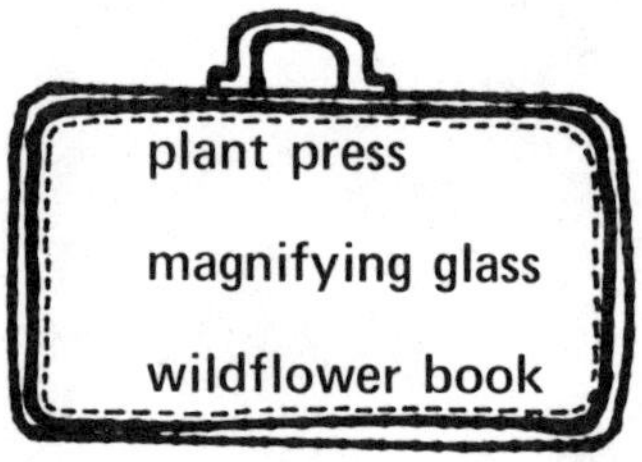

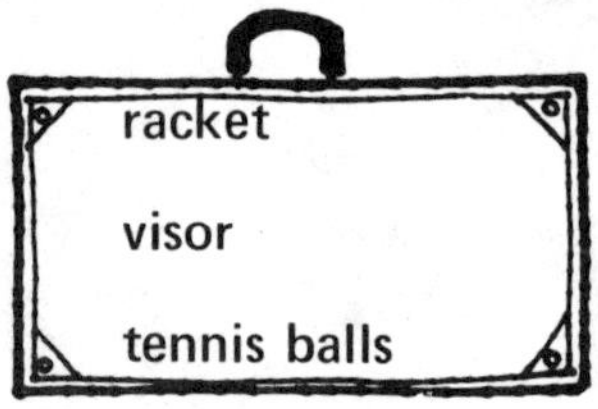

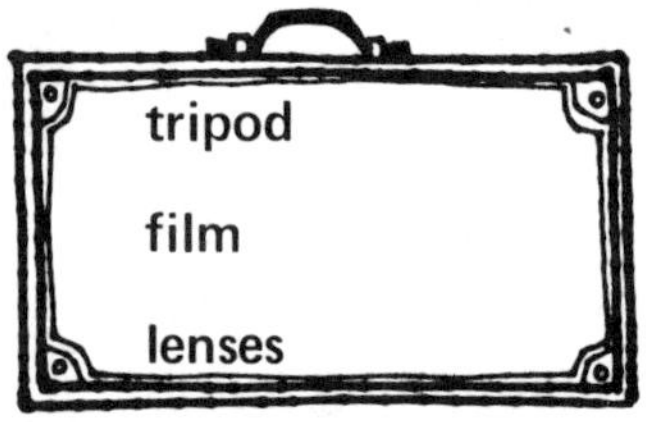

GOV C L CARR
tennis player

DR S N WILSON
bird watcher

MRS J B GARST
rock climber

SEN M C ANDERSON
stamp collector

MS R WILLIAMS
skier

REV E L GRAY
painter

DR R RODRIGUEZ
botanist

MR B R BENSON
photographer

CAPT C B ROSS
backpacker

LT R RIDER
fisherman

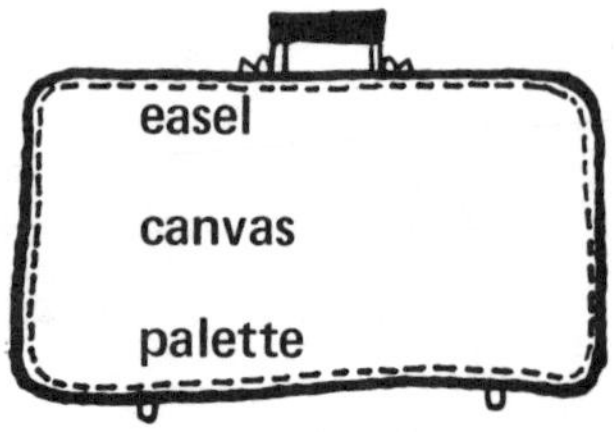

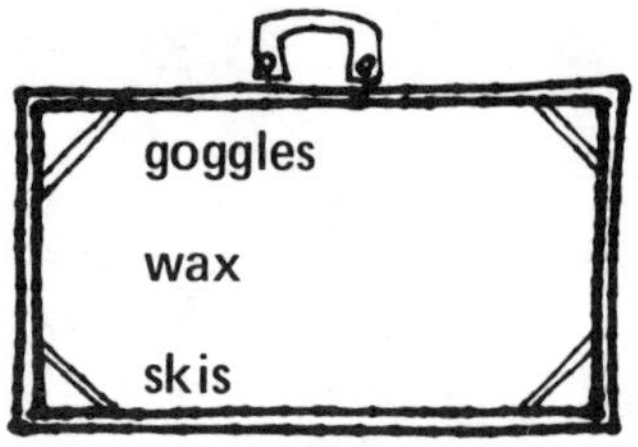

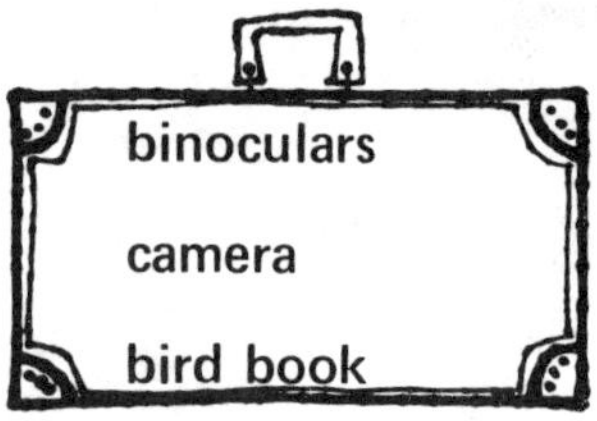

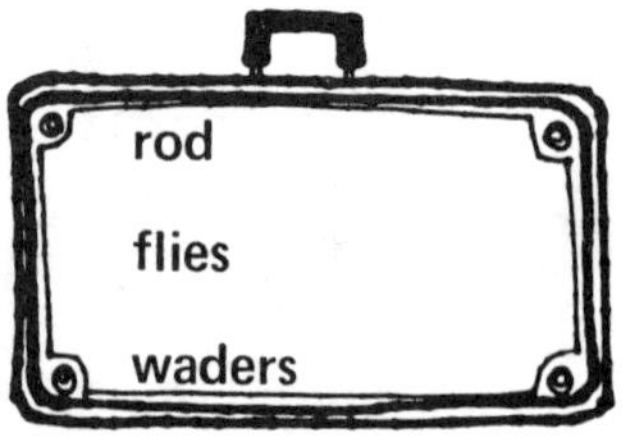

THE NETHERLANDS

NAME ______________________

COMMAS AND CARNATIONS

Use a comma between words in a series.

Pam, Sally, Doris, Beth, Lisa, and Chris went to a Dutch flower market. Each girl bought three kinds of flowers whose names began with the same letter as her own name. Figure out which flowers each girl bought. Write them after the names below. Don't forget the commas! The first sentence is done for you.

1. Pam bought pansies, poppies, and petunias.
2. Sally bought ______________________
3. Doris bought ______________________
4. Beth bought ______________________
5. Lisa bought ______________________
6. Chris bought ______________________

AUSTRALIA 

NAME______________________

HOPPING AROUND AUSTRALIA

> Use a <u>comma</u> between the name of a city or town and the name of a state or country. Also use a <u>comma</u> to set off a state or country from the rest of the sentence.

Pretend that you are a pilot exploring the isolated towns of Australia's "outback." Look at the map and choose the towns that sound most interesting to you. Then visit them in an imaginary journey, filling out the pilot's diary below.

In each blank space write the name of a town and the territory in which it is located. (Australia's territories are like our states. Territory names are written in large letters on the map.) Remember to put commas between the names of the towns and the territories. The first one is done for you.

Beginning at Wee Waa, New South Wales, chart your course on the map.

I took off from *Wee Waa, New South Wales,* into a clear and cloudless sky. A few hours later, I saw the town of ______________________ below me. I was glad to arrive in ______________________ by nightfall. The next morning, I took off for ______________________. My second stop that day was ______________________. I intended to get to ______________________ that night, but strong winds blew me off course and I wound up in ______________________ instead. Then I asked how to get to ______________________ and took off in that direction. However, there were dust storms in the area, so I went to ______________________ instead.

NAME ____________________

PERU 

LLAMA PROBLEMS

> A comma is used in direct address, to set off the name of a person (or animal) being spoken to.

Imagine that you are trying to herd these llamas down a long, narrow trail in the Andes Mountains. Llamas are good, strong pack animals, but they can be stubborn and mischievous. Sometimes they spit, bite, or kick. They may stop to eat along the trail, roll over on their packs, or lie down and refuse to move. If you were giving one command to each of these llamas, what would you say? Write your commands below in sentence form, including a llama's name in each sentence. Remember to set off the names with commas. The first one has been done for you.

1. Pigre, hurry up!
2. ____________________
3. ____________________
4. ____________________
5. ____________________
6. ____________________
7. ____________________
8. ____________________
9. ____________________

SAUDI ARABIA

NAME____________________

DATES WITH A CAMEL

Use a <u>comma</u> between the day and year in a date.

Help fill the camel's bag with "dates." Write the dates on the lines. Remember to put commas between the days and the years. The first one is done for you.

1. March 4, 1963
the fourth day of March, 1963

2. ____________________
the first day of August, 1980

3. ____________________
today's date

4. ____________________
the tenth day of the last month of 1911

5. ____________________
next Saturday's date

6. ____________________
the fifteenth day of July, 1894

7. ____________________
the first day of the year 2000

8. ____________________
the thirtieth day of May, 1975

9. ____________________
April Fool's Day, 1955

10. ____________________
your birthdate (day, month, and year)

COMMAS

FINLAND 

NAME ____________________

FISHING FINNS

Use a comma to set off "yes" and "no" at the beginning of a sentence.

Which of these Finnish fishermen have caught fish? Their lines are tangled, so look carefully. Complete the sentences below, remembering to add a comma after "yes" or "no." The first one is done for you.

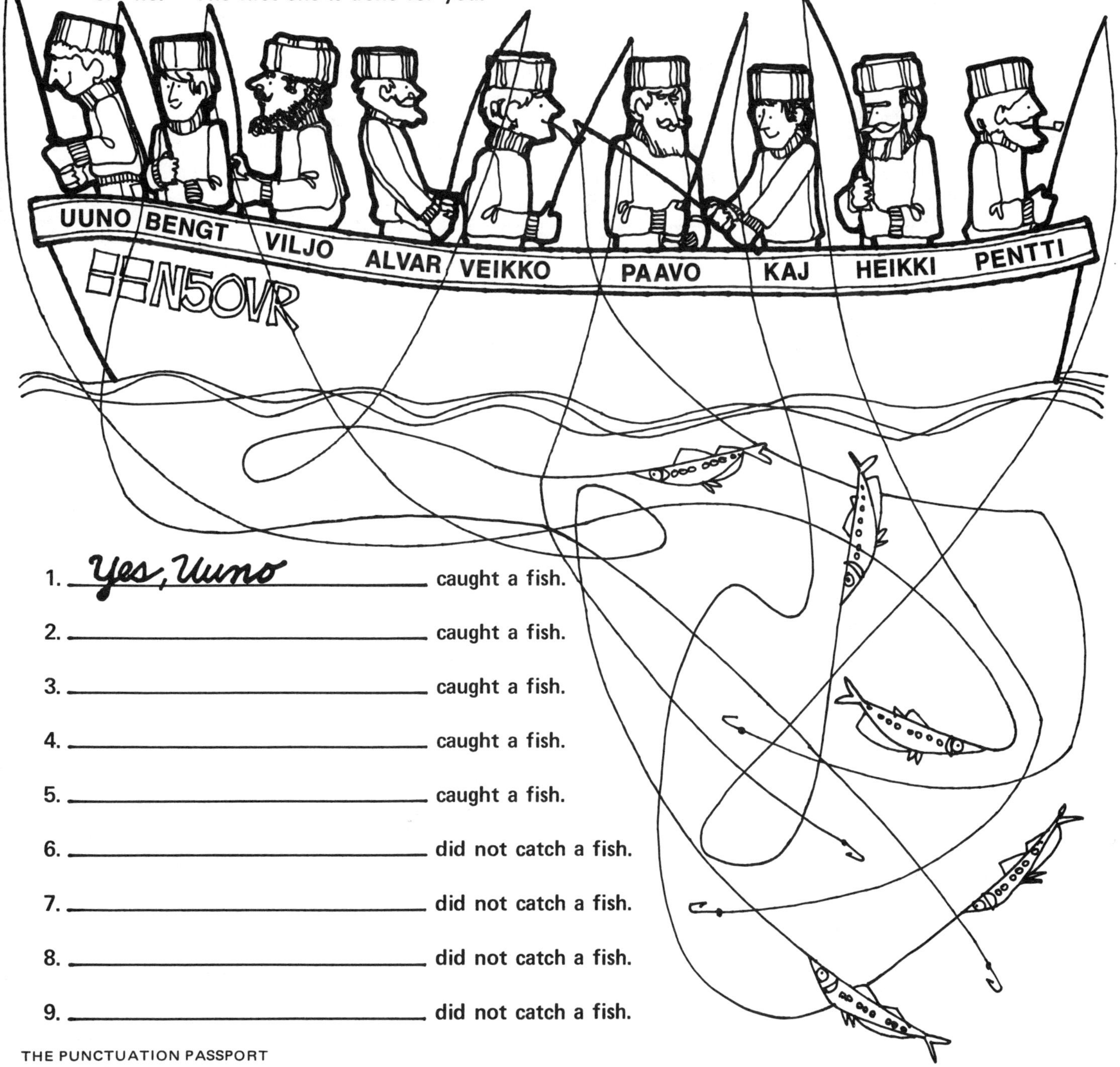

1. *Yes, Uuno* caught a fish.
2. ____________________ caught a fish.
3. ____________________ caught a fish.
4. ____________________ caught a fish.
5. ____________________ caught a fish.
6. ____________________ did not catch a fish.
7. ____________________ did not catch a fish.
8. ____________________ did not catch a fish.
9. ____________________ did not catch a fish.

MEXICO

NAME ____________________

COOLING OFF IN CUERNAVACA

Use a comma before a conjunction when it joins two complete sentences. These words are often used as conjunctions: and, but, or, nor, so.

It's a hot day in Cuernavaca, Mexico, and the little ice cream store by the main square is crowded. In each sentence below, find the conjunction and put a comma in front of it.

1. I would like a chocolate ice cream cone and my friend would like lemon.
2. I was going to try mango ice cream but I think I'll have strawberry instead.
3. Should I have two scoops of coconut or should I try one of coconut and one of mint?
4. I've never had a chance to try papaya ice cream before so I think I'll get some.
5. I can't figure out what flavor this pink ice cream is nor can I identify the green kind.
6. Watermelon ice cream sounds weird but I'm going to have some.
7. I can't decide what flavors to get so why don't you get in line ahead of me?
8. Stand by the sign in front of the store and I will take your picture.
9. Do you think that pineapple and peach would taste good together or do you think I should get pineapple and vanilla?
10. I will never challenge you to an ice cream-eating contest again nor will I ever eat more than six scoops at once!

ITALY

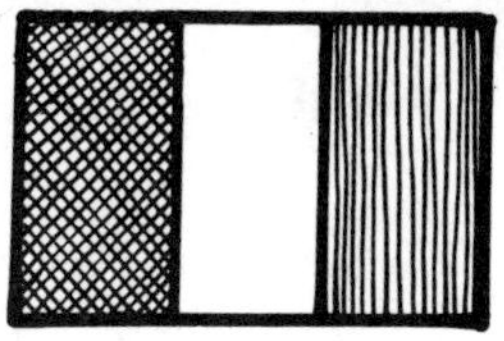

NAME ______________________

FORTUNE TELLING TIME

Use a comma between a quotation and the rest of the sentence unless a question mark or exclamation point is needed.

Ten tourists visited the fortune teller at an Italian circus. Make up a fortune for each person. Write the fortunes on the lines. Put a comma and quotation mark after each fortune. The first one is done for you.

1. "You are going to be very rich," said the fortune teller to Nancy.
2. "You will marry someone who is ____________________ she told Richard.
3. "Next year you are going to lose ____________________ Madam Mystery said to Mrs. Wilson.
4. "You will have good luck until ____________________ she pointed out to Brad.
5. "Sometime soon you will win ____________________ announced the fortune teller to Mrs. Anderson.
6. "You should be careful, because you are about to ____________________ said Madam Mystery to Mr. Brown.
7. "Tomorrow you will meet someone who ____________________ she stated to Christopher.
8. "Your life will be long and ____________________ she told Lisa.
9. "You will be happy next month because ____________________ ____________ explained the fortune teller to Mr. Sanchez.
10. "On your fortieth birthday you will ____________________ she announced to Michael.

NAME________________________

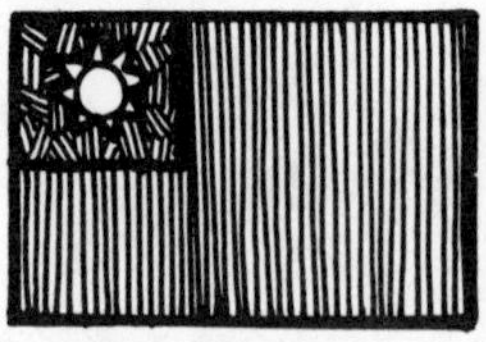

GO FLY A KITE!

Long introductory clauses and prepositional phrases are set off from the main phrase by a <u>comma</u>.

Each of these sentences needs a comma after the introductory clause or phrase. Check the box by the word that the comma should follow. Put the comma in the sentence where it belongs. The first one is done for you.

1. Over twenty thousand years ago, Chinese armies sent men up in large kites to spy on enemy troops.
   A. ☐ thousand, B. ☑ ago, C. ☐ armies,

2. On islands of the South Pacific fishermen use kites to carry their lines far out over the water.
   A. ☐ islands, B. ☐ Pacific, C. ☐ fishermen,

3. When the bridge across Niagara Falls was built a kite carried the rope that pulled the first cable over the river.
   A. ☐ bridge, B. ☐ Falls, C. ☐ built,

4. In the year 1752 Benjamin Franklin conducted his famous experiment with a kite and key.
   A. ☐ 1752, B. ☐ Franklin, C. ☐ experiment,

5. Three years before Franklin's experiment two Scottish scientists used kites with thermometers to measure the temperatures of clouds.
   A. ☐ years, B. ☐ experiment, C. ☐ scientists,

6. While other people traveled English country roads in carts pulled by horses George Pocock zipped along in a lightweight kite-pulled cart that he had developed.
   A. ☐ roads, B. ☐ carts, C. ☐ horses,

7. Early in this century kites carrying special instruments were used to record weather conditions.
   A. ☐ century, B. ☐ instruments, C. ☐ used,

8. During the first World War enemy camps were photographed by cameras mounted on kites.
   A. ☐ War, B. ☐ camps, C. ☐ photographed,

9. When wireless radio was first being developed kites were used to lift aerials and transmit radio signals.
   A. ☐ radio, B. ☐ developed, C. ☐ used,

10. On the ninth day of the ninth month people in China celebrate Kite's Day by flying thousands of colorful kites.
    A. ☐ month, B. ☐ China, C. ☐ Day,

RUSSIA

NAME ______________________

POLAR BEAR PARENTHESES

Parentheses enclose parts of a sentence that could be left out, such as explanations or comments.

Here are some examples of how parentheses are used:

1. Polar bears are found in the Arctic, on the coasts of the Soviet Union (Russia), Alaska, Canada, and Greenland.
2. Male polar bears weigh 900–1500 pounds (420–700 kilograms).
3. The mother polar bear stays with her cub (or cubs) for at least ten months.
4. In the spring, polar bears like to eat grass, seaweed, moss, and berries (cranberries, bilberries, and crowberries).
5. Polar bears live for up to 35 years in captivity (probably less in the wild).

Add parentheses where they are needed in each of these sentences.

1. Polar bears can run surprisingly fast 18 miles per hour on the slippery ice.
2. Male polar bears may hibernate during the darkest part of the year November, December, and January.
3. Animals eaten by polar bears include seals especially ringed seals , fish, and birds.
4. Newborn polar bear cubs are only ten or twelve inches twenty-five or thirty centimeters long.
5. A heavy layer of fat up to three inches thick helps keep these bears warm.
6. Polar bears are strong swimmers; they have been seen swimming great distances over 150 miles from land.
7. Polar bear cubs are born during the winter November–January in caves that the mother bears have dug in the snow.
8. Polar bears are sometimes carried out to sea on drifting ice floes large pieces of floating ice.

NAME______________________

WHAT A WILD SAFARI !

Use an exclamation point after a sentence or a quotation that shows strong feeling.

As your photographic safari pushes through the Tanzanian wilderness, complete the following exclamatory sentences. Be sure to end each one with an exclamation point.

Example: I really hope to see a *herd of giraffes!*

1. The gorilla is going to____________________
2. Here comes an enormous____________________
3. Hey! That monkey took my____________________
4. Run for your lives! I see____________________
5. Watch out for the____________________
6. Wow! That rhinoceros is____________________
7. Oh, no! I forgot to bring my____________________
8. This giant snake is about to____________________
9. I wish I____________________
10. Ssh! I think I see____________________
11. What a terrific picture of____________________
12. My camera was just eaten by____________________

INDIA

NAME ______________________________

TOURING THE TAJ MAHAL

Use a question mark after a sentence that asks a question.

Imagine that you are a tour guide taking a group to see the Taj Mahal in India. The sentences below are things that the people in your group are saying. Some are questions and some are not. Put a question mark at the end of each sentence that asks a question, and a period at the end of each sentence that does not.

When was the Taj Mahal built

Wasn't it started in 1630

It took 20,000 workers twenty years to build it

What are those four towers called

Those are minarets, aren't they

The marble that this is made of was brought from Makrana, 250 miles away

Are the shah and his wife actually buried here

What does this writing on the wall say

Shah Jahan built the Taj Mahal for his wife, Mumtaz-I-Mahal

Who designed it

Did you see these carved flowers

Craftsmen came from all over Asia and Europe to work on this monument

How long is the reflecting pool in front

The dome is 120 feet high – over thirty-six meters

I'd like to know how much it would cost to build this today

Is it true that the shah planned to erect another building like this across the river

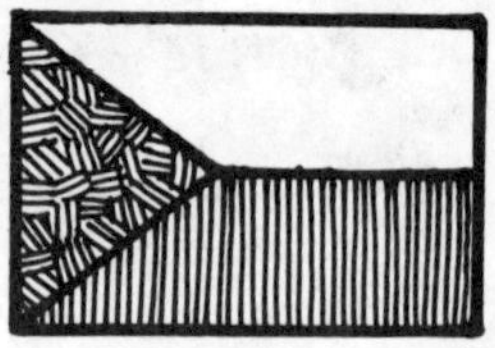

NAME__________________________

CZECHOSLOVAKIAN CHECKUP

The hyphen is used at the end of a line when a word is broken and is continued on the next line. Words are divided by syllables. Example: win - dow is divided correctly; wi - ndow is not.

Hidden in the puzzle below is a map of Czechoslovakia. Look at the words in the map. Some are divided correctly (between syllables) and some are not. Shade in the areas with the words that are divided correctly. This will form the shape of Czechoslovakia. Use your dictionary if you need help.

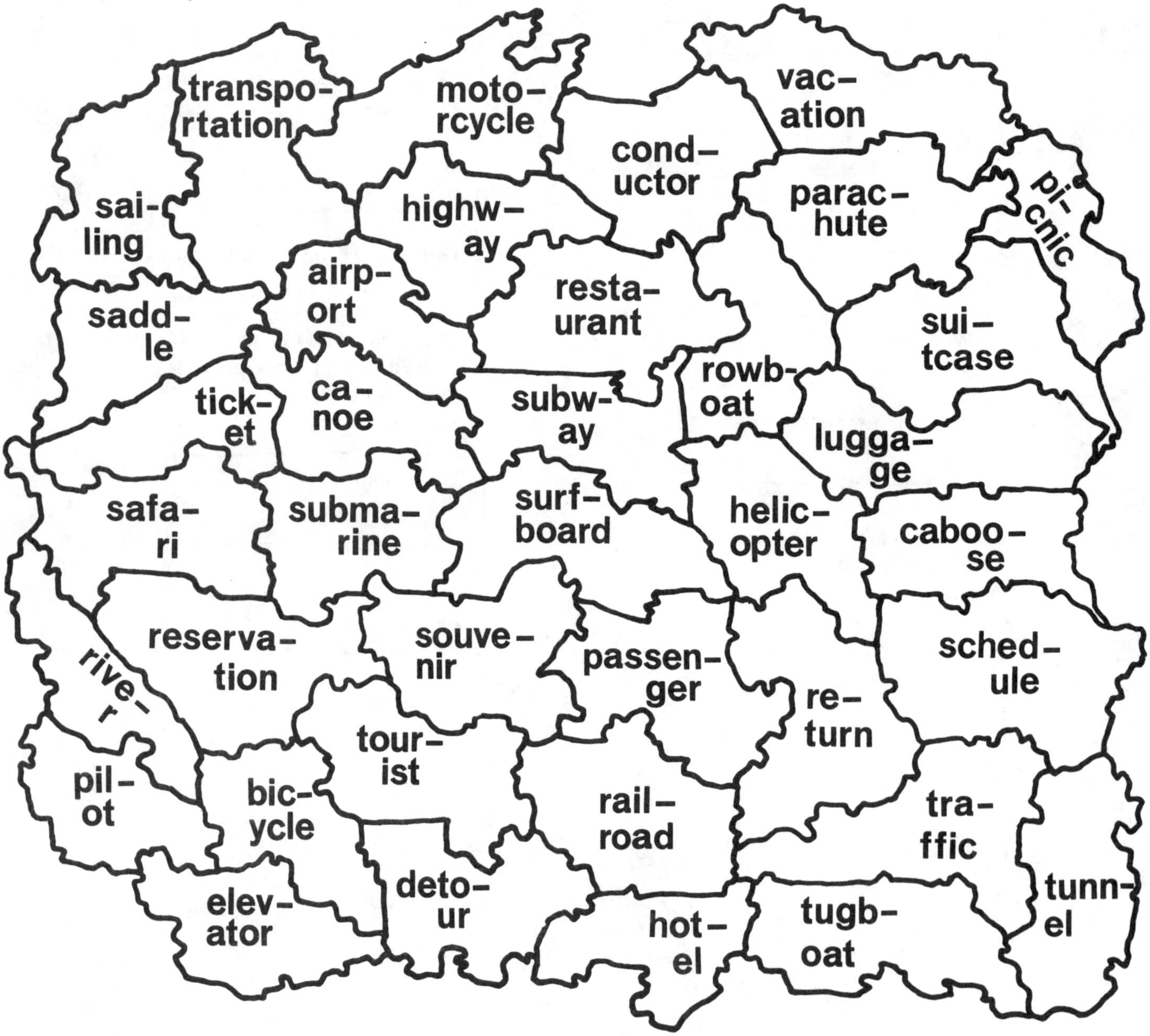

GUATEMALA

NAME ____________________

BARTER FOR A BLANKET

A contraction is a combination of two words with one or more letters omitted. When writing a contraction, use an apostrophe to show where the letters have been left out.

Fill in the contractions in the conversation below. The first one has been done for you. Don't forget the apostrophes!

"That's (That is) really a nice blanket." "Yes — ________ (would not) you like to buy it?"

"I ________ (do not) know. ________ (What is) the price?" "________ (I am) asking only fifty quetzales."

"Fifty quetzales! It ________ (is not) worth that much." "You ________ (will not) find another one like it for less."

"Unless ________ (you will) sell it for twenty quetzales, ________ (I am) not interested."

"Twenty quetzales! Now ________ (who is) crazy? How about forty-five?"

"________ (It is) still too expensive. The most ________ (I would) pay is twenty-five."

"Twenty-five! ________ (Can not) you see how well made it is? It took my wife a week to weave it, and ________ (she will) be mad if I ________ (do not) charge at least forty."

"If ________ (she is) mad, ________ (that is) not my problem. ________ (I will) buy a blanket somewhere else. I ________ (can not) pay more than thirty-five."

"Look, since I ________ (have not) sold anything yet today, ________ (I will) lower the price to thirty-eight quetzales. ________ (It is) my final offer. Take it or leave it."

"________ (You are) almost down to my final offer: thirty-five."

"That ________ (is not) enough! ________ (Who is) going to tell my wife this ________ (blanket is) worth only that much?"

"You are, I guess. Good-bye — ________ (I have) got to go now."

"Wait, wait! ________ (You would) pay thirty-seven quetzales, ________ (would not) you?"

"________ (Let us) make a deal: how about thirty-six?" "Sold!"

JAPAN

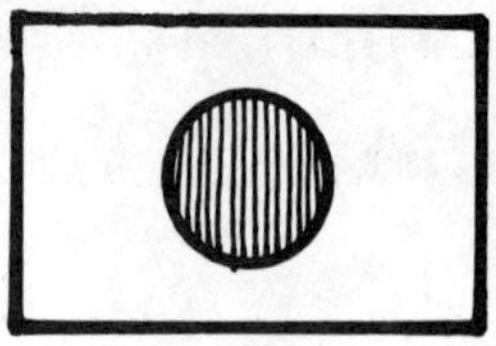

NAME________________________

WHOSE SHOES ?

Add an apostrophe and "s" to single nouns to show ownership. These nouns are called singular possessive nouns.

A tour bus has stopped at a Japanese tea house, and the tourists have left their shoes outside while going in for tea. Each pair of shoes is labeled with the owner's name. Can you match the shoes to the descriptions below? Write the person's name as a possessive noun. The first one is done for you.

1. Willem's shoes are made of wood.
2. ________________ shoes have many buttons.
3. ________________ shoes have high heels.
4. ________________ shoes have buckles.
5. ________________ shoes are very small.
6. ________________ shoes have fur trim.
7. ________________ shoes are tennis shoes.
8. ________________ shoes have curly toes.
9. ________________ shoes have very thick soles.
10. ________________ shoes have spikes.

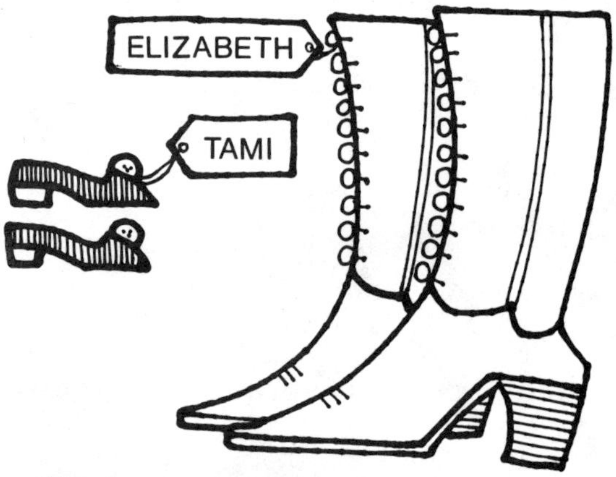

NAME__________________________

NEW ZEALAND ZOO

Add an apostrophe to plural nouns ending in "s" to show ownership.

It's feeding time at the zoo. Here is a list of what the keepers will serve to the animals. Rewrite each phrase so that the animals' names are plural possessive nouns. The first one is done for you.

1. hay for the camels — *the camels' hay*
2. meat for the tigers ____________________
3. shrimp for the flamingos ____________________
4. squid for the seals ____________________
5. bananas for the toucans ____________________
6. worms for the hedgehogs ____________________
7. peanuts for the squirrels ____________________
8. sunflower seeds for the parrots ____________________
9. eggs for the armadillos ____________________
10. tomatoes for the iguanas ____________________
11. potatoes for the porcupines ____________________
12. fish for the puffins ____________________
13. grapes for the opossums ____________________
14. lettuce for the turtles ____________________
15. grain for the peacocks ____________________

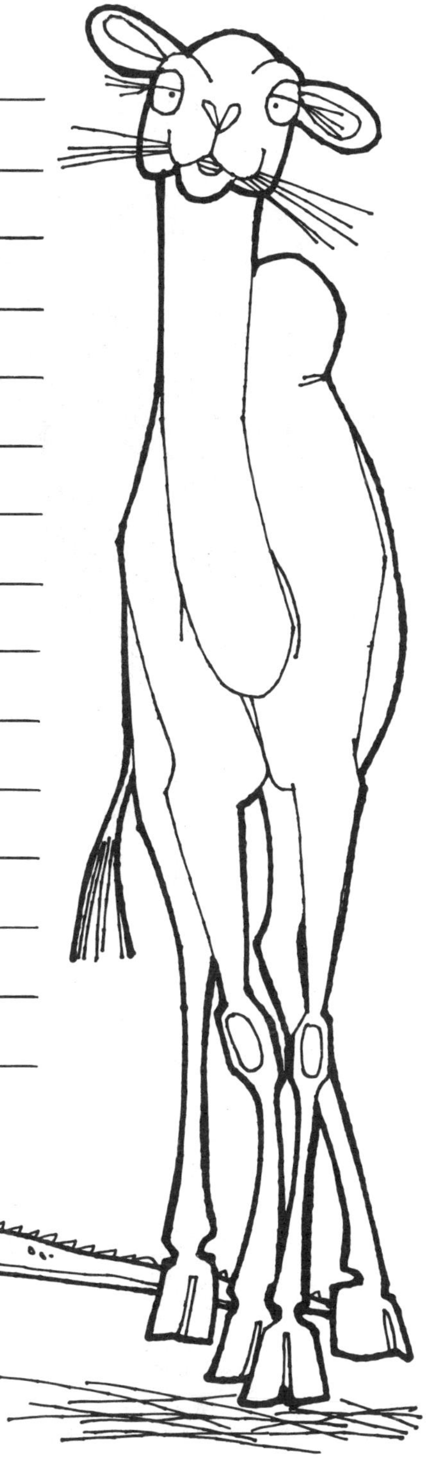

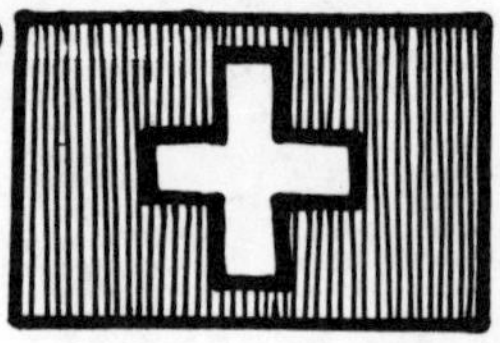

NAME________________________

THE CUCKOO CUCKOO CLOCK

Use a colon after the greeting of a business letter, at the beginning of a list of things in a sentence, and to separate hours and minutes when writing times.

Fourteen colons are missing from these letters. Can you write them in the spaces where they belong?

Dear Sir

Last week I bought this cuckoo clock from you. So far, it has made the following mistakes at 8 00 it cuckoos once, at 10 30 it cuckoos three times, at 3 15 it cuckoos nine times, and at 12 00 it is silent.

This is very confusing, and I want to have the clock repaired or replaced.

Sincerely,
Rolf Reutemann

Dear Mr. Reutemann

We have had no luck in repairing your clock. We tried to fix it, but now it cuckoos six times at 4 00 and eleven times at 4 15. Since the clock can't be fixed, we will do one of these three things for you refund your money, send a new clock, or send this cuckoo cuckoo clock back to you.

Sincerely,
Hans Hessen

Dear Mr. Hessen

Believe it or not, I want you to send the cuckoo cuckoo clock back to me! I miss having it surprise me by cockooing seven times at 2 00 or once at 11 15 or thirteen times at 6 30. I'll buy another clock that tells correct time, and just keep the cuckoo cuckoo to listen to. Thank you for trying to help.

Sincerely,
Rolf Reutemann

FRANCE

NAME ____________________

A TOUR OF THE TOWER

A semicolon is used in a compound sentence between two principal clauses that are not joined by a conjunction. Example: Eiffel designed the tower for the Paris Exhibition; it was finished in March, 1889.

The semicolons are missing from these compound sentences. Put a semicolon in each sentence in the place where it belongs.

1. For many years, the Eiffel Tower was the tallest structure in the world it stands on the Champs de Mars in Paris.

2. Alexandre Gustave Eiffel designed the tower he also built the structure for the Statue of Liberty and designed locks for the Panama Canal.

3. The tower was completed on March 31, 1889 it took two years, two months, and two days to build.

4. Eiffel drew detailed plans for the tower they showed where each of the 12,000 parts would go.

5. The tower is made from wrought iron it weighs over 6,300 metric tons and is held together by 2½ million rivets.

6. Elevators and subways lead to the platforms and to the top there are 1,792 steps and each of the three elevators holds 63 people.

7. From the top of the tower you can see for over fifty miles during World War I it was used as a military observation tower.

8. The tower is about 300 meters tall on top is a twenty-meter television antenna.

9. The French weather bureau uses the Eiffel Tower as a weather reporting station and laboratory there is scientific equipment in a room at the top.

10. It cost a million dollars to build the Eiffel Tower in the first year a million dollars' worth of tickets were sold to people visiting the tower.

PANAMA

NAME ____________________

PICK A PARROT

> Use quotation marks before and after a quotation.

These parrots from Panama have been taught to talk. Copy what each parrot says on the lines below, using the first sentence as a guide. Put a comma after the word "says" and put quotation marks around what the parrot says. Make sure that the first quotation mark comes after the comma, and the second quotation mark comes after the period or question mark.

1. Pico says, "Pass the crackers."
2. Risa says ____________________
3. Tictac says ____________________
4. Rojo says ____________________
5. Grito says ____________________
6. Yoyo says ____________________
7. Rubio says ____________________
8. Boba says ____________________

REVIEW

SOUTH AFRICA

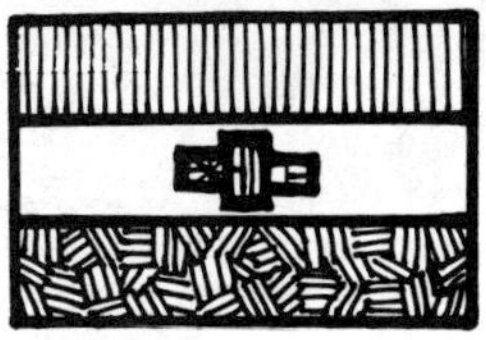

NAME ______________________

DIAMONDS !

Some of the punctuation marks in the sentences below have been replaced by diamond shapes. Read each sentence carefully, and write the missing punctuation marks in the diamonds. To check your work, cross off each diamond in the box as you use it.

1. India and Brazil were the first major diamond-producing countries ◇ later ◇ in 1867) diamonds were discovered in South Africa.

2. Eighty percent of the world ◇ s diamonds are now produced by three countries ◇ the Republic of South Africa, Russia, and Zaire.

3. Wow ◇ Did you know that the first large diamond found in South Africa was picked up by a farmer ◇ s child ◇

4. Yes ◇ some diamonds have been found in the United States.

5. Even in a diamond mine, diamonds aren ◇ t easy to find ◇ thirty-five million pounds of rock must be crushed to get a pound of diamonds.

6. Industrial diamonds ◇ sometimes called "bort") are used to saw, drill, and shape glass ◇ metal ◇ and ceramics ◇

7. Diamonds are formed under great pressure ◇ sometimes, when the rock around a dia ◇ mond is broken, the diamond explodes.

8. We usually think of diamonds as being shiny jewels ◇ but before they are cut and polished they look like dull, grayish rocks ◇

9. Diamonds are priced according to size, cutting, perfection, and color ◇ yellow, brown, pink, blue, violet, or green).

10. Dad ◇ did you know that meteorites contain microscopic diamonds ◇

11. The largest diamond ever found (the Cullinan ◇ weighed over one and one-fourth pounds.

12. Diamonds got their name from the Greek word "adamas ◇ ◇ which means "unconquerable."

13. On April 25 ◇ 1980 ◇ Dr ◇ R ◇ D ◇ Jones and I will visit a factory in Atlanta ◇ Georgia, to see how diamonds are made into jewelry.

? . " , ' (, , . , – , ; ' (, , ! . ; , (? ,) : ' ; .

PUNCTUATION PASSPORT

Name ______________________ **Departure date** ______________

☐ **GREECE**

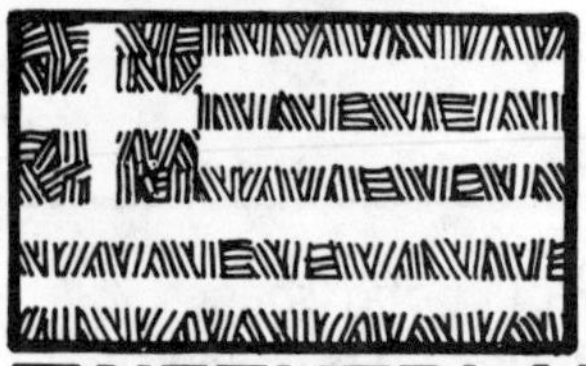

☐ **ARGENTINA**

☐ **CANADA**

☐ **NETHERLANDS**

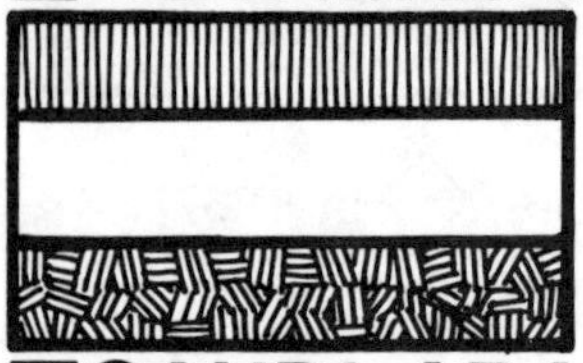

☐ **AUSTRALIA**

☐ **PERU**

☐ **SAUDI ARABIA**

☐ **FINLAND**

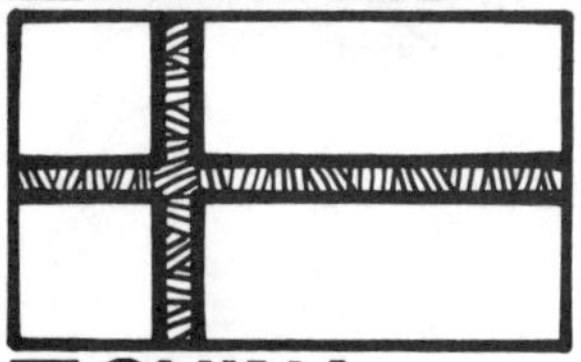

☐ **MEXICO**

☐ **ITALY**

☐ **CHINA**

☐ **RUSSIA**

☐ **TANZANIA**

☐ **INDIA**

☐ **CZECHOSLOVAKIA**

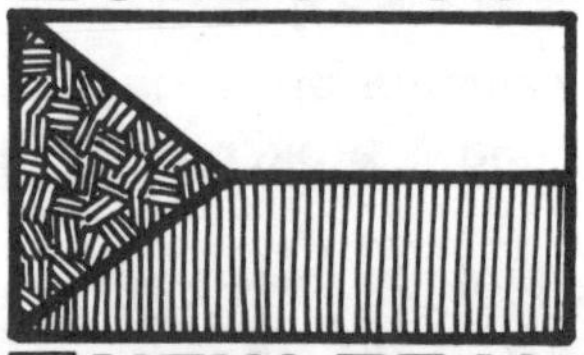

☐ **GUATEMALA**

☐ **JAPAN**

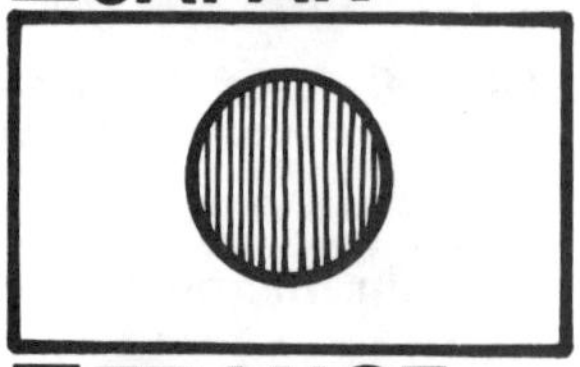

☐ **NEW ZEALAND**

☐ **SWITZERLAND**

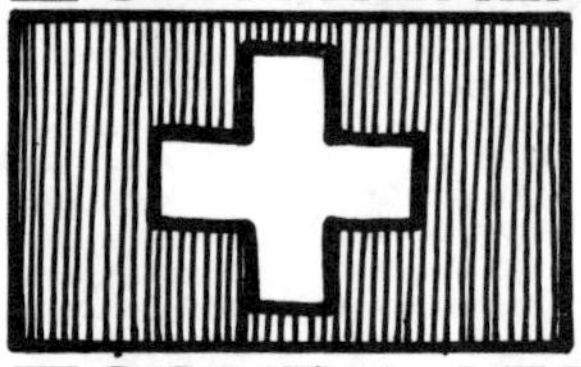

☐ **FRANCE**

☐ **PANAMA**

☐ **SOUTH AFRICA**

Official signature ______________________

ANSWERS

Page 4. Crack the Code

Greece has many islands and mountains. The main crops are olives and grapes. Many farmers also raise sheep and goats. The winters are long and cold. Summers in Greece can be very hot. There is little rain.

Page 5. Abbreviation Roundup

1. Road – Rd.
2. Mountains – Mts.
3. January – Jan.
4. August – Aug.
5. North – N.
6. Street – St.
7. Monday – Mon.
8. Bridge – Br.
9. Highway – Hwy.
10. University – Univ.
11. December – Dec.
12. Court – Ct.
13. Avenue – Ave.
14. Hospital – Hosp.
15. National – Natl.
16. Boulevard – Blvd.
17. October – Oct.
18. Post Office – P.O.
19. Friday – Fri.
20. Island – Is.

Page 6. Tag the Bags

GOV. C.L. CARR – racket, etc.
DR. S.N. WILSON – binoculars, etc.
MRS. J.B. GARST – pitons, etc.
SEN. M.C. ANDERSON – hinges, etc.
MRS. R. WILLIAMS – goggles, etc.
REV. E.L. GRAY – easel, etc.
DR. R. RODRIGUEZ – plant press, etc.
MR. B.R. BENSON – tripod, etc.
CAPT. C.B. ROSS – canteen, etc.
LT. R. RIDER – rod, etc.

Page 7. Commas and Carnations (Flower names may be in different order within sentences.)

1. Pam bought pansies, poppies, and petunias.
2. Sally bought sunflowers, snapdragons, and sweet peas.
3. Doris bought dahlias, daffodils, and daisies.
4. Beth bought buttercups, bluebells, and begonias.
5. Lisa bought lilacs, lilies, and lobelias.
6. Chris bought crocuses, camellias, and carnations.

Page 8. Hopping around Australia

Answers will vary. Check for commas between names of towns and territories.

Page 9. Llama Problems

Answers will vary. Check for commas after names of llamas.

Page 10. Dates with a Camel

1. March 4, 1963
2. August 1, 1980
3. Answers will vary.
4. December 10, 1911
5. Answers will vary.
6. July 15, 1894
7. January 1, 2000
8. May 30, 1975
9. April 1, 1955
10. Answers will vary.

Page 11. Fishing Finns (Order in which names are listed may vary.)

1. Yes, Uuno caught a fish
2. Yes, Alvar caught a fish.
3. Yes, Paavo caught a fish.
4. Yes, Viljo caught a fish.
5. Yes, Pentti caught a fish.
6. No, Bengt did not catch a fish.
7. No, Veikko did not catch a fish.
8. No, Kaj did not catch a fish.
9. No, Heikki did not catch a fish.

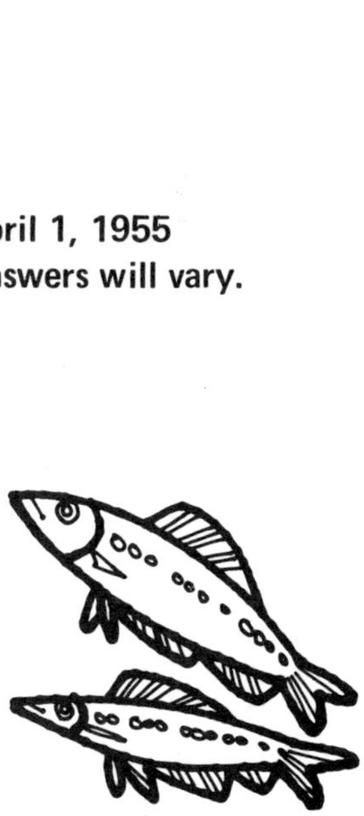

Page 12. Cooling Off in Cuernavaca

1. cone, and
2. cream, but
3. coconut, or
4. before, so
5. is, nor
6. weird, but
7. get, so
8. store, and
9. together, or
10. again, nor

Page 13. Fortune Telling Time

Answers will vary. Make sure that commas come before quotation marks.

Page 14. Go Fly a Kite!

1. B 2. B 3. C 4. A 5. B 6. C 7. A 8. A 9. B 10. A

Page 15. Polar Bear Parentheses

1. (18 miles per hour)
2. (November, December, and January)
3. (especially ringed seals)
4. (twenty-five or thirty centimeters)
5. (up to three inches thick)
6. (over 150 miles)
7. (November—January)
8. (large pieces of floating ice)

Page 16. What a Wild Safari!

Answers will vary. Sentences should each end with an exclamation point.

Page 17. Touring the Taj Mahal

1. question mark
2. question mark
3. period
4. question mark
5. question mark
6. period
7. question mark
8. question mark
9. period
10. question mark
11. question mark
12. period
13. question mark
14. period
15. period
16. question mark

Page 18. Czechoslovakian Checkup

Correctly hyphenated words: ticket, safari, reservation, canoe, submarine, surfboard, souvenir, tourist, passenger, railroad, return, schedule

Page 19. Barter for a Blanket

That's, wouldn't, don't, What's, I'm, isn't, won't, you'll, I'm, who's, It's, I'd, Can't, she'll, don't, she's, that's, I'll, can't, haven't, I'll, It's, You're, isn't, Who's, blanket's, I've, You'd, wouldn't, Let's

Page 20. Whose Shoes?

1. Willem's
2. Elizabeth's
3. Lucy's
4. Pam's
5. Tami's
6. Nick's
7. Hans's
8. Olga's
9. Alex's
10. Scott's

Page 21. New Zealand Zoo

1. the camels' hay
2. the tigers' meat
3. the flamingos' shrimp
4. the seals' squid
5. the toucans' bananas
6. the hedgehogs' worms
7. the squirrels' peanuts
8. the parrots' sunflower seeds
9. the armadillos' eggs
10. the iguanas' tomatoes
11. the porcupines' potatoes
12. the puffins' fish
13. the opossums' grapes
14. the turtles' lettuce
15. the peacocks' grain

Page 22. The Cuckoo Cuckoo Clock

Sir:, mistakes:, 8:00, 10:30, 3:15, 12:00, Reutemann:, 4:00, 4:15, you:, Hessen:, 2:00, 11:15, 6:30

Page 23. A Tour of the Tower

1. world; it
2. tower; he
3. 1889; it
4. tower; they
5. iron; it
6. top; there
7. miles; during
8. tall; on
9. laboratory; there
10. tower; in

Page 24. Pick a Parrot

Answers will vary. Check positions of commas, quotation marks, periods, and question marks.

Page 25. Diamonds!

1. 
2. 
3. 
4. 
5. 
6. 
7. 
8. 
9. 
10. 
11. 
12. 
13. 

period.

* Use a period after a sentence that is a statement or command.
* Use a period after an abbreviation.
* Use a period after an initial.

comma,

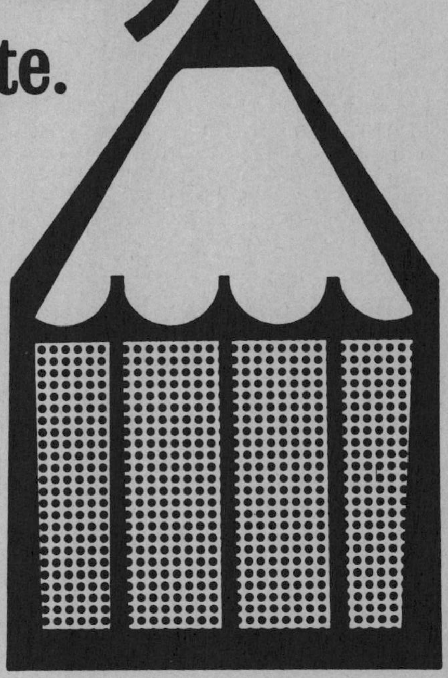

* Use a comma between the day and year in a date.
* Use a comma between words in a series.
* Use a comma to set off "yes" and "no" at the beginning of a sentence.
* Use a comma between the name of a city and the name of a state or country. Also use a comma to set off a state or country from the rest of the sentence.
* Use a comma before a conjunction when it joins two complete sentences.
* Use a comma in direct address to set off the name of a person being spoken to.
* Use a comma between a quotation and the rest of the sentence unless a question mark or exclamation point is needed.
* Use commas after long phrases and clauses.

(parentheses)

* Parentheses enclose parts of a sentence that could be left out, such as explanations or comments.

exclamation point!

* Use an exclamation point after a sentence or a quotation that shows strong feeling.

question mark?

* Use a question mark after a sentence that asks a question.

hy-
phen

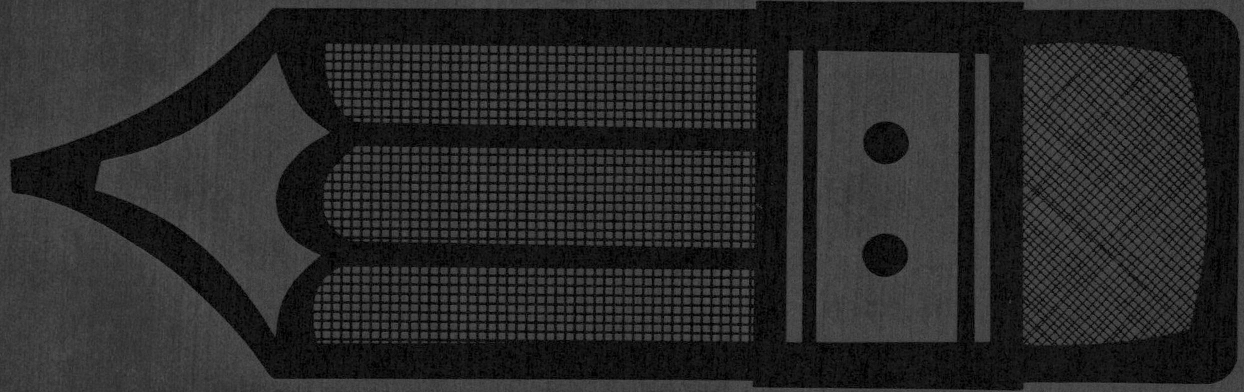

*The hyphen is used at the end of a line when a word is broken and is continued on the next line. Words are divided by syllables.

apostrophe’

* Use an apostrophe to show that one or more letters have been left out of a word.
* Add an apostrophe and “s” to single nouns to show ownership.
* Add an apostrophe to plural nouns ending in “s” to show ownership.

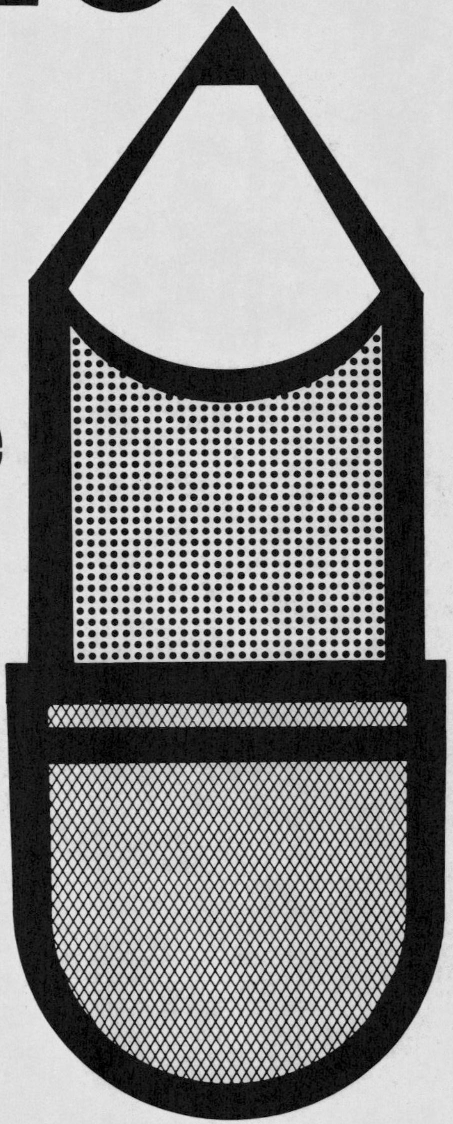

colon:

- * Use a colon after the greeting of a business letter.
- * Use a colon at the beginning of a list of things in a sentence.
- * Use a colon to separate hours and minutes when writing times.

semicolon;

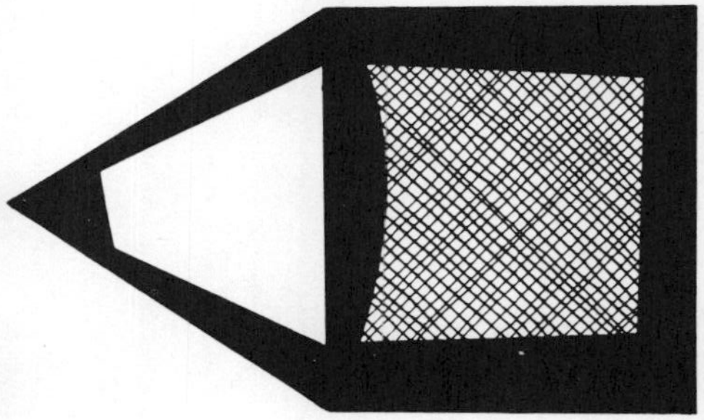

* The semicolon is used in a compound sentence between two principal clauses that are not joined by a conjunction.

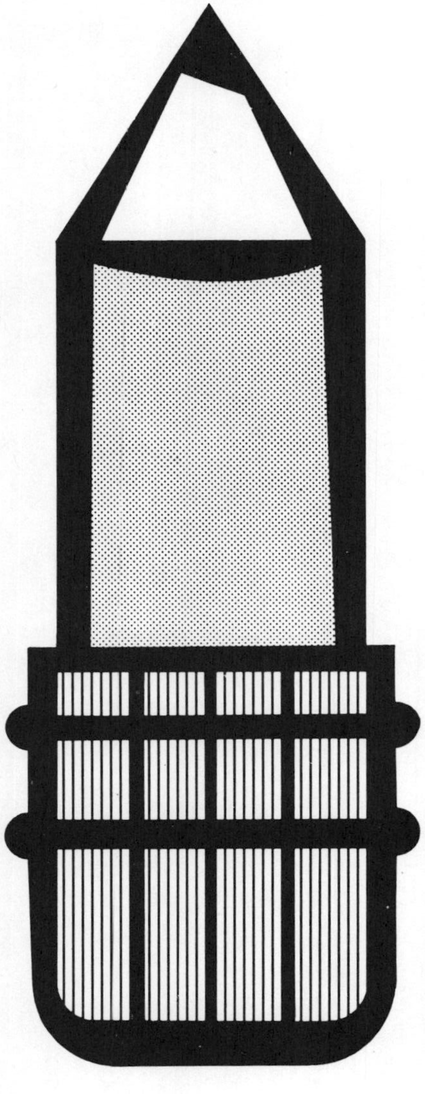

“quotation marks”

* Use quotation marks before and after a quotation.

Occupational Therapy TOOLKIT

Patient Handouts and Treatment Guides
7th Edition

Physical Disabilities
Chronic Conditions
Geriatrics

Written and Illustrated by
Cheryl A. Hall, Occupational Therapist

Hallen House Publishing
Timonium, Maryland

Occupational Therapy Toolkit: Patient Handouts and Treatment Guides, 7th Edition

Published online: 7/1997. Published as an eBook and print book: 8/2007.
Revised, updated and expanded: 10/2008, 9/2009, 9/2010, 7/2012, 8/2013, 4/2018.

ISBN-13: 978-1-948726-00-9

Disclaimer

The information contained in the Occupational Therapy Toolkit: Patient Handouts and Treatment Guides 7th edition is intended as an educational resource for use by occupational therapists, occupational therapy assistants, occupational therapy students or, occupational therapy assistants students only. The ideas expressed are by no means the only approach to a given diagnosis; it is neither complete nor exhaustive, and does not cover all disabilities, diseases, ailments, physical conditions or their management or treatment.

The information is not intended to convey medical, healthcare or other advice for any specific individual. The information is not intended as a substitute for appropriate clinical decision-making. The occupational therapist, occupational therapy assistant, or occupational therapy student is responsible for providing appropriate therapy based on an individual client's needs and goals.

The materials are not intended as medical advice for the public. Should you have any healthcare or disability questions or concerns, please consult a physician for an appropriate referral to Occupational Therapy.

The materials are believed to be accurate and timely. There is no warranty or guarantee concerning the accuracy or reliability of the content of *Occupational Therapy Toolkit: Patient Handouts and Treatment Guides 7th Edition*

Citation - APA Format

Hall, C. A. (2018). *Occupational therapy toolkit: patient handouts and treatment guides* (7th ed.). Timonium, MD: Hallen House Publishing.

Please Note: There are Limits on the Permission to Reproduce

The Occupational Therapy Toolkit print book is protected by copyright.

Permission to make and distribute photocopies of the handouts is only granted to one OT, OT student, OTA, or OTA student for their individual patients/clients only. The Occupational Therapy Toolkit header and the copyright information must be retained on each page. The treatment guides cannot be photocopied.

The OT Toolkit print book cannot be purchased or used by a business. Multiple persons are not allowed to use or make photocopies from the OT Toolkit print book.

The OT Toolkit print book cannot be duplicated or reproduced in its entirety; the pages, text, and images cannot be extracted, or modified.

Thank you,

Cheryl

Cheryl Hall, OT
cheryl@ottoolkit.com
www.ottoolkit.com

Occupational Therapy TOOLKIT

Treatment Guides - Section 1
Arranged Alphabetically in Document

Occupational Therapy TOOLKIT

Treatment Guides - Section 1
Arranged Alphabetically in Document

Conditions and Diseases

Occupational Therapy TOOLKIT

Treatment Guides - Section 1

Arranged Alphabetically in Document

Conditions and Diseases

Occupational Therapy TOOLKIT

ADL and Mobility Handouts - Section 2

Arranged Alphabetically in Document

Occupational Therapy TOOLKIT

ADL and Mobility Handouts - Section 2
Arranged Alphabetically in Document

Bed Mobility

Dressing

Dressing with One Hand

Occupational Therapy TOOLKIT

ADL and Mobility Handouts - Section 2
Arranged Alphabetically in Document

Occupational Therapy TOOLKIT

ADL and Mobility Handouts - Section 2

Arranged Alphabetically in Document

Occupational Therapy TOOLKIT

Educational Handouts - Section 3

Arranged Alphabetically in Document

Occupational Therapy TOOLKIT

Educational Handouts - Section 3
Arranged Alphabetically in Document

Occupational Therapy TOOLKIT

Educational Handouts - Section 3
Arranged Alphabetically in Document

Occupational Therapy TOOLKIT

Therapeutic Exercise Handouts - Section 4

Arranged Alphabetically in Document

Occupational Therapy TOOLKIT

Therapeutic Exercise Handouts - Section 4
Arranged Alphabetically in Document

Occupational Therapy TOOLKIT

Therapeutic Exercise Handouts - Section 4
Arranged Alphabetically in Document

Occupational Therapy TOOLKIT

Therapeutic Exercise Handouts - Section 4
Arranged Alphabetically in Document

Bibliography is available at www.ottoolkit.com/pdfs/bibliography.pdf

Occupational Therapy TOOLKIT

Action Tremor

Action tremors include:

- Postural tremors occur when a limb or the body is held voluntarily against gravity. Postural tremors affect reaching, sitting posture, and standing posture.
- Kinetic tremors occur during task performance and affect drinking, eating, writing, typing, buttoning, and grooming.
- Intention tremor occurs with purposeful movement toward a target.
- Task-specific tremors occur when performing highly skilled, goal-oriented tasks such as handwriting or speaking.
- Isometric tremor occurs during a voluntary contraction not accompanied by movement such as holding a dumbbell in the same position.

(Tremor Fact Sheet NINDS, 2016)

Impairments and Functional Limitations:
ADL, IADL, productivity and leisure impairment
Minimal or no tremor present at rest
Other conditions - essential tremor, neurological conditions (multiple sclerosis, stroke, traumatic brain injury, amyotrophic lateral sclerosis, Parkinson's disease, Alzheimer's disease, and Huntington's disease)

Assessments:
Archimedes spirals
Finger-nose-finger test
Observation of functional task performance

Occupational Therapy Intervention:
ADL, IADL, productivity and leisure training incorporating adaptive equipment and/or task modifications to compensate for tremor and/or reduce the amplitude of the tremors.

- Writing (weighted pens, voice recorders)
- Eating and drinking (weighted utensils, non-slip matting, and weighted plates, avoid difficult foods such as peas and spaghetti)
- Grooming and dressing (wrist weights, magnetic clasp on jewelry)
- Computer use (change mouse settings, voice recognition software)

Determine what factors (time of day, certain activities) increase the tremor using a daily log of activities.

Retrain hand dominance if appropriate.

Educate in body/arm stabilization to reduce amplitude of tremors during functional tasks.

Action Tremor

Occupational Therapy Intervention:
Provide therapeutic activities and exercises to strengthen core and proximal muscles.

Teach stress management and relaxation techniques (progressive muscle relaxation, deep breathing, self-hypnosis, guided imagery, tai chi, yoga and meditation).

Educate patient and caregivers about tremors and the availability of community resources. Encourage participation in support groups.

Patient and Caregiver Handouts:

Activities of Daily Living

Activities of Daily Living (ADL)
- Bathing and Showering
- Dressing
- Feeding, Eating, and Swallowing
- Functional Mobility
- Grooming and Oral Hygiene
- Rest and Sleep
- Sexual Activity
- Toileting

Instrumental Activities of Daily Living (IADL)
- Care for others/pets
- Clothing Care
- Community Mobility
- Driving
- Financial and Mail Management
- Functional Communication
- Health Management
- Home and Yard Maintenance
- Meal Preparation
- Medication Management
- Shopping

Leisure and Social Activities
Work/Volunteer Activities

Assessments:
Assessment of Motor and Process Skills (AMPS) (Fisher et al., 1993)
Community Mobility Assessment (Brewer et al., 1998)
Functional Independence Measure (Granger et al., 1986)
Kitchen Task Assessment (Baum et al., 1993)
Kohlman Evaluation of Living Skills (Kohlman-Thompson et al., 1992)
Performance Assessment of Self-Care Skills (Rogers & Holmes et al., 1989)
Rabideau Kitchen Evaluation Revised (Neistadt et al., 1994)
Safety Assessment of Function and Environment for Rehabilitation (Oliver et al., 1993)

Occupational Therapy Intervention:
Apply different approaches for solving ADL and IADL difficulties.

- Remediate underlying limitations to safety and independence: physical impairments (muscle weakness, impaired hand function, limited ROM, paralysis, incoordination, impaired balance, fatigue, dyspnea, abnormal tone, tremor), sensory impairment (impaired sensation, low vision, hard of hearing, vestibular, pain), behavioral, cognition, perception.

Activities of Daily Living

Occupational Therapy Intervention:

- Train in compensatory techniques. (Safety techniques, one-handed techniques, pacing, energy conservation, joint protection, low vision techniques, cognitive/perceptual compensation. Step-by-step instructions, task segmentation, task sequencing, backward chaining, verbal and physical cueing, hand-over-hand guiding).
- Train in the use of adaptive equipment and assistive devices.
- Provide environmental modifications and adaptations.
- Instruct in task modification (change the task, eliminate part or the entire task, or have someone else do part or the entire task).

Train in safe and efficient functional mobility (sit to stand, bed mobility skills, transfers, standing, ambulation, and wheelchair mobility) during ADL and IADL tasks.

Provide caregiver/family education and training.

Grading Levels of ADL and IADL Independence

- Independent (no equipment, no physical assistance)
- Modified Independent (needs equipment and/or increased time)
- Supervision (set-up and/or supervision, no physical assistance is required)
- Contact Guard (occasional physical hands-on assistance for safety)
- Minimal Assistance (individual performs ≥ 75% of task)
- Moderate Assistance (individual performs 50-74% of task)
- Maximal Assistance (individual performs 25-49% of task)
- Dependent (individual performs ≤ 24% of task)

Ideas to consider when documenting ADL and IADL

- Task performed
- Position for the activity
- Adaptive equipment used
- Task modifications utilized
- Level of independence and physical assistance required
- Level of cues was required (verbal, visual, and tactile)
- Major limiting factors (sequencing, balance, fatigue, safety)
- Compensatory strategies used (joint protection, pacing, energy conservation)
- Ability to plan, initiate, organize, sequence, and complete the tasks
- Ability to perform safely, consistently and efficiently

Adhesive Capsulitis

Impairments and Functional Limitations:
Difficulty reaching overhead, behind head and behind back
Muscle weakness
ROM loss
Pain
Impaired posture
Co-occurring conditions - stroke, Parkinson's disease, cervical disc disease, diabetes, thyroid disorders, biceps tendonitis, rotator cuff pathologies, complex regional pain syndrome

Occupational Therapy Intervention:
Adaptive equipment and/or task modifications to prevent pain and compensate for limited ROM during reaching overhead, behind head and behind back. Some activities include fastening a bra in the back, putting on a belt, reaching for a wallet in the back pocket, reaching for a seatbelt, combing the hair, lifting weighted objects.

Provide therapeutic activities and exercises.

Phase 1 "Pre-Freezing and Phase 2 "Freezing"

- Joint mobilization
- Pain-free shoulder ROM (pendulum exercises, pulley, PROM, AAROM, AROM)
- Pain-free shoulder stretches
- Isometric strengthening
- AROM of the elbow, wrist, and hand

Phase 3 "Frozen"

- Progressive low load, prolonged shoulder stretching
- End-range joint mobilization with distraction and capsular stretching
- Rotator cuff exercises, scapular exercises and resistive band exercises

Phase 4 "Thawing" pain diminishes, joint motion and strength returns

- Continue joint mobilization
- Continue shoulder stretching and strengthening exercises
- Muscle reeducation to regain normal GH and scapulothoracic biomechanics

Instruct in pain self-management

- Coordinate medication peak with exercise and activity.
- Use superficial heat and cold.
- Use deep (diaphragmatic) breathing and other relaxation techniques.
- Transcutaneous electric nerve stimulation (TENS)

Adhesive Capsulitis

Occupational Therapy Intervention:
Instruct in joint protection techniques.

- Practice good body mechanics and posture.
- Take frequent breaks.
- Modify activities that cause symptoms.
- Instruct in injury prevention to decrease recurrence.

Patient and Caregiver Handouts:

Occupational Therapy TOOLKIT

Alzheimer's Disease and Related Dementias - Early Stage

Impairments and Functional Limitations:

Function - decreased initiation, planning and organization of daily activities; with complex tasks such as meal planning, medication management, managing finances and driving

Cognition - forgetful, impaired attention span, impaired judgment, impaired decision making, confused about time but not about places or persons, misplaces items, forgets appointments, gets lost in familiar area, mild word-finding difficulty, needs repetition to learn

Behavior - depression, anxiety and apathy

Assessments:

Allen Cognitive Lacing Screen (ACLS-5) (Riska-Williams et al., 2007)
Cognitive Performance Test (CPT) (Burns et al., 2015)
Executive Functional Performance Test (Baum et al., 2003)
Performance Assessment of Self-Care Skills (PASS) (Rogers & Holm 1989)
Routine Task Inventory-Expanded (RTI-E) (Allen 1989, Katz 2006)

Stages, Measures and Expected Scores:

Functional Assessment Staging (FAST) = 4 (Reisburg 1982)
Mini Mental States Examination (MMSE) = 20-25 (Folstein 1974)

Occupational Therapy Intervention:

ADL, IADL, productivity and leisure training

- Provide treatment that matches the cognitive abilities of the patient.
- Maximize safety and independence by simplifying the activities, structuring the environment and providing adaptive equipment.
- Provide visual cues such as directional signs, label on drawers and closets, and written directions for using common household items and appliances.
- Recommend safety equipment in the bathroom.
- Assist patient and caregiver in developing a structured schedule of self-care, activities and rest/sleep.
- Address ability to drive safely. Provide referral to driving rehab specialist and/or explore alternative transportation options.

Provide physical exercise and activities to maintain ROM, strength and endurance and provide cognitive stimulation. Choose activities that reflect the person's interest, cognitive capacity and physical abilities.

Train in the use of compensatory strategies for memory and organization. Develop a memory notebook.

Occupational Therapy TOOLKIT

Alzheimer's Disease and Related Dementias - Early Stage

Occupational Therapy Intervention:
Provide education about fall risk and prevention strategies.

Assist in the creation of a "Life Story" notebook. Include photos and narratives about friends and family members, key life events, rituals, routines, education, placed lived and traveled, work history, military history, pets, favorite foods, hobbies and pastimes. Place related objects in a "Life Story" box.

Complete a comprehensive, performance-based home/work assessment. Recommend and/or provide modifications, adaptive equipment and/or assistive technology. Provide specific interventions for cognitive impairments.

Educate in wellness (smoking cessation, healthy eating, physical activity and exercise, stress management and relaxation, good sleep habits, social engagement and intellectual stimulation).

Educate patient and caregivers about Alzheimer's disease and community resources. Provide educational materials to the caregiver about stress management and caring for their own health. Encourage participation in support groups.

Patient and Caregiver Handouts:
Putty Exercises 683
Upper Body Exercises - Hand Weights 765
Upper Body Strength Activities 773

Additional Treatment Guides
Cognition 56
Health Management 115

Occupational Therapy TOOLKIT

Alzheimer's Disease and Related Dementias - Mid Stage

Impairments and Functional Limitations:

Function - requires assistance with self-care, neglects hygiene and eating, unable to perform IADLs safely due to poor judgment, has problems with apraxia and agnosia, changes in posture, gait and balance

Cognition - disoriented, confused, forgets names of close family members, aphasia, anomia, able to recall the past, able to respond to instructions

Behavior - agitation, wandering, anxiety, physical and verbal aggression, psychosis, inappropriate behavior, resistant to care, hallucinations, suspiciousness or paranoia, irritable, socially withdrawn, rummaging and hoarding, repetitive questioning, sleep issues and sundowning

Assessments:

Allen Cognitive Lacing Screen (ACLS-5) (Riska-Williams et al., 2007)
Executive Functional Performance Test (Baum et al., 2003)
Performance Assessment of Self-Care Skills (PASS) (Rogers & Holm 1989)
Routine Task Inventory-Expanded (RTI-E) (Allen 1989, Katz 2006)

Stages, Measures and Expected Scores:

Functional Assessment Staging (FAST) = 5-6e (Reisburg 1982)
Mini Mental States Examination (MMSE) = 10-19 (Folstein 1974)

Occupational Therapy Intervention:

ADL and leisure training

- Provide activities that match the cognitive abilities of the patient in an error- free environment.
- Maximize safety and independence through simplifying the activities, structuring the environment and providing adaptive equipment.
- Provide task segmentation and step-by-step instructions with cues.
- Cueing hierarchy
    1. Verbal cue - ask open-ended questions. "What is this?" (show a hairbrush).
    2. Verbal cue - provide two choices. "Is this a hairbrush or deodorant?"
    3. Verbal cue - use directive cue. "This is a hairbrush."
    4. Visual cue - demonstrate brushing hair or use pictures.
    5. Tactile cue - provide hand-over-hand guiding.
- Assist patient and caregiver in developing a structured schedule of self-care, activities and rest/sleep.
- Develop activity/occupation centers throughout the environment for the patient to engage safely in meaningful activities. When possible, engage all the senses: vision, hearing, taste, smell, movement and touch.

Alzheimer's Disease and Related Dementias - Mid Stage

Occupational Therapy Intervention:
Train in safe and efficient functional mobility (sit to stand, bed mobility skills, transfers, wheelchair mobility, ambulation and stairs).

- Train in the safe and correct use of assistive devices and adaptive equipment (walkers, canes, sliding boards, bed transfer handles, leg lifters, wheelchairs) as appropriate.

Provide physical exercise and activities to maintain ROM, strength and endurance and provide cognitive stimulation. Choose activities that reflect the person's interests, cognitive capacity and physical abilities.

Provide education about fall risk and prevention strategies. Provide alternatives to physical restraints.

Assist caregivers in managing challenging behaviors.

Complete a comprehensive, performance-based home assessment. Recommend and/or provide modifications, adaptive equipment and/or assistive technology. Provide specific interventions for cognitive impairments.

- Eliminate triggers for stress and agitation. Remove mirrors if they cause delusions or hallucinations. Increase lighting to minimize shadows.
- Prevent injuries
  - Slips, trips, and falls - see the Fall Risk Assessment and Prevention Treatment Guide.
  - Burns - remove lighters and matches, restrict smoking, disable stove/oven, lower water temperature
  - Poisoning - place locks on cabinets, refrigerators, and freezers, secure garbage, remove poisonous plants and items that look like food such as artificial fruit and pet food, lock up laundry and cleaning supplies, chemicals, poisons, and medications
  - Cuts - replace glass shower doors, disable garbage disposal, lock up sharp objects and breakable objects
  - Electrocution - unplug or store electrical appliances in the kitchen and bathroom, childproof electrical outlets
  - Other - lock up firearms, lock up power tools, restrict access to car
- Limit wandering. Secure doors and windows, control access to stairs, storage areas, basements, garages and home offices, install door alarms
- Provide safe areas for wandering and safe access to outdoors.

Alzheimer's Disease and Related Dementias - Mid Stage

Occupational Therapy Intervention:
Educate patient and caregivers about Alzheimer's disease and community resources. Provide educational materials to the caregiver about stress management and caring for their own health. Encourage participation in support groups.

Patient and Caregiver Handouts:

Additional Treatment Guides:

Alzheimer's Disease and Related Dementias - Late Stage

Impairments and Functional Limitations:
Function - dependent with ADLs, incontinent, bed-bound or chair-fast, dysphasia
Cognition - severe impairment of all cognitive functions, no recognition of family members, no verbal ability, may use non-verbal communication such as eye contact, crying, groaning, may respond to sounds, tastes, smells, and touch, may interpret and uses basic body language
Behavior - agitation and aggression
Potential complications - falls, contractures, skin breakdown, aspiration pneumonia

Stages, Measures and Expected Scores:
Functional Assessment Staging (FAST) = 7a-7f (Reisburg 1982)
Mini Mental States Examination (MMSE) = 0-9 (Folstein 1974)

Occupational Therapy Intervention:
ADL training

- Provide treatment that matches the cognitive abilities of the patient.
- Train in grooming and self-feeding tasks using adaptive equipment and/or hand-over-hand guiding, as appropriate.
- Modify food textures and consistencies.
- Provide sensory stimulation (vision, hearing, taste, smell, movement and touch).
- Train in the safe and correct use of assistive devices and adaptive equipment.

Instruct caregiver in PROM exercises, positioning in bed and chair, positioning when eating/feeding, correct lifting and turning techniques, transfer techniques and adaptive equipment (bedside commode, wheelchair, seating cushion, patient lifts).

Educate caregivers about Alzheimer's disease and community resources. Provide educational materials about stress management and caring for their own health. Encourage participation in support groups.

Patient and Caregiver Handouts:
Check Your Skin 379
Passive Range of Motion 651
Position in Bed to Reduce Pressure 460

Additional Treatment Guides:
Feeding, Eating, and Swallowing 87
Grooming and Oral Hygiene 109

Amputation of the Lower Limb

Impairments and Functional Limitations:
ADL, IADL, productivity and leisure impairment
Functional mobility impairment
Impaired strength - upper and lower body
Limited activity tolerance and endurance
Residual limb pain and hypersensitivity
Phantom pain and/or phantom sensation
Impaired balance
Fall risk with fear of falling
Altered body image
Co-occurring conditions - diabetes, cancer, peripheral vascular disease, depression, chronic kidney disease, low back pain
Potential complications - DVT's, joint contractures, wound infection, neuromas, skin breakdown, hip and/or knee contractures

Occupational Therapy Intervention:
ADL, IADL, productivity and leisure training

- Train with and without the prosthesis.
- Recommend and/or provide adaptive equipment and task modifications to compensate for impaired balance and strength.
- Instruct in pacing and energy conservation strategies.

Train in safe and efficient functional mobility (sit to stand, bed mobility skills, transfers, standing, ambulation and wheelchair mobility) during ADL and IADL tasks.

- Train with and without the prosthesis.
- Train in the use of adaptive mobility equipment: (Hospital bed, lift chair, standard wheelchair/electric wheelchairs, seating cushions, transfer boards, hydraulic patient lifts, bed rails, and trapeze).
- Train in transfer methods (stand-pivot, sit-pivot, transfer board, forward/ backward transfers).
- Instruct in pressure relief.

Provide functional balance activities to increase balance confidence with ADL tasks. Use graded activities in sitting and standing, supported and unsupported, with and without prosthesis.

Pre-prosthetic readiness of the residual limb

- Instruct in skin inspection of the residual limb and the remaining limb. Use a long-handled mirror.

Amputation of the Lower Limb

Occupational Therapy Intervention:

Pre-prosthetic readiness of the residual limb (continued)

- Prevent contractures.
    - AKA - hip flexors, abductors, and external rotators
    - BKA - hip and knee flexion (promote lying prone in bed, avoid pillows under the residual limb, instruct in proper positioning, provide knee immobilizer)
- Manage residual limb pain (proper fitting prosthesis, ultrasounds, TENS, superficial heat and cold, relaxation techniques).
- Manage phantom pain/sensation (education, proper fitting prosthesis, relaxation techniques, superficial heat and cold, Mirror Box Therapy, biofeedback, TENS).
- Reduce hypersensitivity (desensitization techniques).

Provide UE and core activities and exercises to increase strength specifically for scapular depressors, elbow extensors and wrist extensors (overhead pulley, chair push-ups and depression blocks).

Prosthetic training

- Instruct in donning and doffing prosthesis, gel liner or socks.
- Teach management of sock ply.
- Instruct in the care of the prosthesis and sock hygiene.

Complete a comprehensive, performance-based home/work assessment. Recommend and/or provide modifications, adaptive equipment and/or assistive technology.

Provide education about fall risk and prevention strategies.

Educate patient and caregivers about the availability of community resources. Encourage participation in support groups.

Patient and Caregiver Handouts:

Occupational Therapy TOOLKIT

Amputation of the Lower Limb

Patient and Caregiver Handouts:

Additional Treatment Guides:

Amputation of the Upper Limb

Impairments and Functional Limitations:
ADL, IADL, work and leisure impairment
Functional mobility impairment
Impaired strength - upper and lower body
Limited activity tolerance and endurance
Residual limb pain and hypersensitivity
Phantom pain and/or phantom sensation
Altered body image
Co-occurring conditions - depression, anxiety, cancer, diabetes, traumatic brain injury
Potential complications - wound infection, heterotopic ossification, neuroma, skin breakdown

Outcome Measures:
Assessment for Capacity of Myoelectric Control (Linder et al., 2015)
Activities Measure of Upper Limb Amputees (Resnik et al., 2013)
Orthotics and Prosthetics User Survey (Heinemann et al., 2003)
Trinity Amputation and Prosthesis Experience Scales (Gallagher et al., 2000)

Occupational Therapy Intervention - Pre-Prosthetic Stage:
ADL and IADL training without prosthesis

- Teach one-handed ADL techniques. Recommend and/or provide adaptive equipment and task modifications to compensate for limb loss.
- Retrain hand dominance (if appropriate).
- Instruct in pacing and energy conservation strategies.
- Instruct in body mechanics and body symmetry during activities.

Train in safe and efficient functional mobility (sit to stand, bed mobility skills, transfers, standing, ambulation and wheelchair mobility) during ADL and IADL tasks.

Manage the residual limb.

- Provide incision site and wound care as appropriate. Once healed provide scar management (moist heat, scar massage, silicone gel at night, desensitization).
- Provide edema control, stump conditioning and stump shaping. Instruct in the use of a shrinker or figure eight elastic bandage wrapping.
- Provide progressive weight bearing into the residual limb.
- Manage residual limb pain (proper fitting prosthesis, ultrasounds, TENS, superficial heat and cold, relaxation techniques).
- Manage phantom pain/sensation (education, relaxation techniques, compression garments, superficial heat and cold, Mirror Box Therapy, biofeedback, TENS).
- Reduce hypersensitivity (desensitization techniques).

Amputation of the Upper Limb

Occupational Therapy Intervention - Pre-Prosthetic Stage (continued):
Provide active ROM and stretching exercises and home program to increase and/or maintain residual limb ROM. Progress when medically allowed to resistive strengthening (scapular stabilization, shoulder girdle, elbow and wrist as appropriate).

Provide exercises and activities to improve trunk stability, core strengthening, contra-lateral limb and lower extremity strength and endurance.

Provide education about prosthetic devices. Options include body-powered/ conventional prosthetic devices, external powered/myoelectric prosthetic devices, hybrid prosthetic devices, passive functional/cosmetic prosthetic devices, and adaptive/recreational prosthetic devices. Not using a prosthetic device is also an option.

Provide myoelectric site testing and training (external powered).

Train in the upper body motions required for controlling the prosthesis terminal devices and/or elbow (body-powered).

Occupational Therapy Intervention - Basic Prosthetic Training:
Instruct in caring for the residual limb (skin hygiene, sock or liner hygiene, progressive wearing schedule and inspection of residual limb before and after wearing the prosthesis).

Instruct in caring for the prosthesis and terminal device (operation of components, cleaning, maintenance, charging batteries, upgrading the software).

Instruct in wearing the prosthesis (don/doff prosthesis, don/doff liner/sleeve or socks, apply lubricants/powders, remove/apply harness, manage the vacuum/suction sealing device, properly align the residual limb with the electrodes, change terminal devices).

Provide training in using the terminal device and prosthetic components to reach, grasp, carry and release objects of various sizes, shapes, weights and densities.

Train in ADL and IADL, leisure, work and driving, using prosthesis. Teach body symmetry and body mechanics.

Provide adjustments and modifications to the prosthesis and terminal device, as needed.

Educate patient and caregivers about the availability of community resources. Encourage participation in support groups.

Occupational Therapy TOOLKIT

Amputation of the Upper Limb

Patient and Caregiver Handouts:

Amyotrophic Lateral Sclerosis

Impairments and Functional Limitations:
ADL, IADL, productivity and leisure impairment
Functional mobility impairment
Upper motor neuron signs (spasticity, hyperflexia, pathological reflexes)
Lower motor neuron signs (muscle weakness, muscle atrophy, fasciculations, hypoflexia, hypotonicity, muscle cramps)
Bulbar signs (dysarthria, dysphagia, sialorrhea (excessive saliva), pseudobulbar palsy)
Respiratory symptoms (nocturnal respiratory difficulty, exertional dyspnea, accessory muscle overuse, paradoxical breathing)
Other symptoms (fatigue, weight loss, cachexia, tendon shortening, joint contractures)
Co-occurring conditions - adhesive capsulitis, depression, anxiety
Not affected (eye muscles, bowel and bladder control, sexual function, sight, hearing, smell, taste, and touch, cognition and intellect)

Rating Scales:
Amyotrophic Lateral Sclerosis Functional Rating Scale (Cedarbaum et al., 1999)

Occupational Therapy Intervention:
ADL, IADL, productivity and leisure training

- Use adaptive equipment and task modifications to compensate for weakness.
- Button hook, zipper pull, built up for pens, utensils and toothbrushes, electric toothbrushes, key holders, jar openers, padded bathroom safety equipment, grab bars, dressing equipment, telephone aides, environmental control unit, computer modifications, mobile arm supports and suspension slings
- Educate on strategies to manage fatigue and conserve energy.
- Address ability to drive safely. Refer to driving rehab specialist and/or explore alternative transportation options.

Train in safe and efficient functional mobility (sit to stand, bed mobility skills, transfers, standing, ambulation and wheelchair mobility) during ADL and IADL tasks.

- Train in the use of adaptive mobility equipment - sliding boards, ramps, hospital beds, bed rails, trapeze, lift chairs, transfer boards, hydraulic patient lifts.
- Provide a fully equipped power wheelchair with tilt, recline, power elevating leg rests, air or gel cushion, adjustable armrests, soft headrest, modified controls, ventilator support. Anticipate the progression of the disease. Refer to a Seating and Mobility Specialist (SMS).

Provide devices to support weak joints - wrist cock-up, arm sling, cervical collar, resting hand splint.

Instruct in positioning for comfort and ADL participation, in wheelchair and in bed.

Amyotrophic Lateral Sclerosis

Occupational Therapy Intervention:
Provide therapeutic activities and exercises to maintain strength and ROM.

- For mild weakness, provide light resistive exercises only for muscles graded 3+/5 and above, followed by stretching exercises. Decrease or discontinue resistance if fasciculations occur.
- If an exercise program produces cramps, muscle soreness, fatigue or weakness lasting longer than 30 minutes, it is too strenuous. Avoid excessive use of accessory muscles or heavy breathing. Monitor breathing with a pulse oximeter; use the modified Borg Scale to rate fatigue.
- As weakness progresses, provide assisted ROM and stretching exercises and instruct caregiver to perform passive ROM and stretching exercises.

Provide pain management techniques.

- Modalities (heat, ice, ultrasound)
- Deep tissue massage, myofascial release

Complete a comprehensive, performance-based home/work assessment. Recommend and/or provide modifications, adaptive equipment and/or assistive technology.

Provide education regarding fall risk and prevention strategies.

Teach strategies to incorporate wellness and health management routines into daily activities.

Educate patient and caregivers about ALS, community resources. Encourage participation in support groups. Provide educational materials to the caregiver about stress management and caring for their own health.

Patient and Caregiver Handouts:
Exercise Tips for Amyotrophic Lateral Sclerosis 571
Passive Range of Motion 651
Splint/Brace Instructions 475
Stress Management 477
Tips to Conserve Energy 482
Upper Body Exercises - Hand Weights 765
Upper Body Strength Activities 773

Additional Treatment Guides:
Health Management 115

Ankylosing Spondylitis

Impairments and Functional Limitations:
ADL, IADL, work and leisure impairment
Functional mobility impairment
Pain, stiffness and inflammation with limited ROM and/or fusion of the spine and sacroiliac, may progress to hips, knees or shoulders.
Restricted ROM of chest wall due to fusion of the costovertebral joints
Muscle weakness
Impaired balance
Fatigue
Other symptoms and conditions - vertebral fractures, spinal stenosis, spondylitic heart disease, joint replacements

Occupational Therapy Intervention:
ADL, IADL, work and leisure training

- Train in the use of adaptive equipment to compensate for pain and limited ROM in the spine (lower body dressing, workplace modifications, adapted driving).
- Train in safe and efficient functional mobility (sit to stand, bed mobility skills, transfers, standing, ambulation and wheelchair mobility) during ADL and IADL tasks. Train in the use of adaptive mobility equipment as appropriate.
- Instruct in pacing and energy conservation strategies, body mechanics and good posture.

Instruct in pain self-management strategies.

- Coordinate medication peak with exercise and activity.
- Superficial heat and cold
- Deep (diaphragmatic) breathing and other relaxation techniques
- Positioning devices (seat cushions, back supports, pillows)
- Instruct in using a pain journal.
- Utilize the problem solving process to identify ways to manage pain.

Teach strategies to manage fatigue and conserve energy.

- Assess using the Fatigue Impact Scale (Fisk et al., 1994).
- Teach pacing and energy conservation strategies.
- Balance self-care, productivity, play and rest.
- Encourage good sleep hygiene.
- Encourage keeping a fatigue journal.
- Utilize the problem solving process to identify ways to manage fatigue.

Ankylosing Spondylitis

Occupational Therapy Intervention:
Complete a comprehensive, performance-based home/work/leisure assessment. Recommend and/or provide home/work/leisure and activity modifications.

Provide education about fall risk and prevention strategies.

Teach strategies to incorporate wellness and health management routines into daily activities.

Educate patient and caregivers about ankylosing spondylitis and the availability of community resources. Encourage participation in support groups.

Patient and Caregiver Handouts:

Additional Treatment Guides

Apraxia

Apraxia is a cognitive disorder of purposeful and skilled movement of previously learned skills.

Ideational apraxia is the impaired ability to conceptualize a task, to know what object to use and how to use it, and/or how to sequence or organize the steps to complete the task.

Ideomotor apraxia is the impaired ability to plan or complete motor actions. The kinesthetic memory required to carry out the movement is lost. The patient knows WHAT to do, but not HOW to do it.

Assessments:
Pantomime on command

- Transitive movements (familiar actions with objects, such as brushing teeth)
- Intransitive movements (symbolic movements without objects, such as the sign for "crazy", "okay", "good-bye")

Imitate the performance of transitive, intransitive, and novel meaningless movements.
Gesture in response to seeing and holding actual tools

Occupational Therapy Intervention:

- Cognitive Strategy Training
    - Teach internal and external compensatory strategies (self-verbalization, verbal cues, physical assistance, list of written steps, pictures, or video recording).
- Errorless Learning
    - Errors are prevented during functional activities by providing physical support (such as hand-over-hand guiding), cuing or parallel demonstration.

Patient and Caregiver Handouts:
Tips to Improve Motor-Planning 493

Balance

Impairments and Functional Limitations:
Muscle weakness (specifically quadriceps, ankle dorsiflexors, ankle plantar flexors)
Limited range of motion in the lower extremities
Slowed reaction time
Reduced processing of sensory information (proprioceptive/somatosensory, visual and vestibular)
Disequilibrium
Cognitive impairment

Assessments and Rating Scales:
Berg Balance Scale (Berg 1995)
Gait Speed Test (Guralnik et al., 1994)
Modified Clinical Test of Sensory Integration on Balance (Shumway-Cook 1986)
Multi-Directional Reach Test (Newton et al., 1997)
Sitting Balance Scale (Medley, Thompson et al., 2011)
Tinetti Balance and Gait Evaluation (Tinetti 1986)
Trunk Impairment Scale (Verheyden et al., 2004)

Occupational Therapy Intervention:
Provide a multi-component balance training program.

- Ensure patient safety during training to prevent falls and injuries.
- Incorporate balance exercises into everyday activities.
- Incorporate balance exercises during regular strength training, stretching, and endurance routines.
- Perform balance training first (when combined with resistance and flexibility activities). Recommend 10-15 minutes, three days a week.

Provide progressive challenges to balance.

- Static balance control in sitting, half kneeling, tall kneeling, standing, tandem standing, single leg standing, lunging and squatting
- Dynamic balance control while on a moving surface (therapy ball, wobble board, mini trampoline)
- Challenge postural reactions
    - Ankle strategy
    - Hip strategy
    - Stepping strategy
    - Weight shift strategy
    - Suspensory strategy

Balance

Occupational Therapy Intervention:
Progress balance activities and exercises by challenging the visual system (low lighting, wear sunglasses indoors, eyes closed), the proprioceptive/somatosensory system (unstable surfaces such as foam pads, therapy ball, mini trampoline, balance disc, wobble board, Biomechanical Ankle Platform System (BAPS), Bosu ball trainer, ambulation on an uneven surface), and the vestibular systems (gaze stability exercises).

Provide dual-tasking balance challenges combining a balance exercise with another form of physical activity (ball kick, ball toss, arm or leg exercises), a cognitive task (count backward from 100 by 3's, recite the alphabet backwards, or name the presidents) or by adding external distractions (noise, people, music).

Utilize interactive video games (Wii-Fit, Wii-Sport, Kinect) and brain fitness programs (Mindfit) to challenge balance.

Patient and Caregiver Handouts:
Balance Exercise Guidelines 519
Balance Exercises - Sitting 520
Balance Exercises - Standing 523
Core Exercise Guidelines 545
Core Exercises - Back Muscles 546
Core Exercises - Pelvic Muscles 549
Core Exercises - Stomach Muscles 550
Exercise Ball Guidelines 564
Exercise Ball - Back Muscles 565
Exercise Ball - Pelvic Muscles 567
Exercise Ball - Stomach Muscles 569

Additional Treatment Guides:
Dizziness 75
Therapeutic Exercise 195

Bathing and Showering

Bathing and showering includes obtaining and using supplies, turning water on and off, regulating water temperature, washing, rinsing, and drying all body parts and hair, achieving and maintaining bathing position and maintaining adequate hygiene. Bathing can take place in a shower, tub, in front of a sink, at bedside or in bed.

Impairments and Functional Limitations:
Impaired shoulder strength and/or ROM
Impaired hand strength, ROM, sensation and/or coordination
Impaired LE function
Limited activity tolerance and endurance
Impaired balance
Pain
Visual perceptual and cognitive impairment

Occupational Therapy Intervention:
Apply different approaches for solving difficulties with bathing and showering.

- Remediate underlying limitations to safety and independence: physical impairments (muscle weakness, impaired hand function, limited ROM, paralysis, incoordination, impaired balance, fatigue, dyspnea, abnormal tone, tremor), sensory impairment (impaired sensation, low vision, hard of hearing, vestibular, pain), behavioral, cognition, perception.
- Train in compensatory techniques (safety techniques, one-handed techniques, pacing, energy conservation, joint protection, body mechanics, breathing techniques, low vision techniques, cognitive/perceptual compensation, using step-by-step instructions, task segmentation, task sequencing, backward chaining, verbal and physical cueing, hand-over-hand guiding).
- Train in the use of adaptive equipment and assistive devices (bathtub thermometer, built-up bath brush, hand held shower, hand wash mitt, long handled brush, shower chair, bath bench, padded bath bench, leg lifter, non-slip bathmat, grab bars).
- Provide environmental modifications and adaptations (hang towel racks lower, hang shower caddy lower, replace turn faucets with lever style, adjust back legs of the shower chair lower to keep hips back in the chair, install grab bars, install tub cutout).
- Instruct in activity modification.
    - Change the task (use hand towels instead of heavier bath towels, trade bar soap for liquid soap in plastic pump bottles).
    - Eliminate part or all of the task (shower every other day instead of daily, eliminate the need to stand by sitting to bathe).
    - Have someone else do part or the entire task (hairdresser for shampoo, help to wash feet and back).

Bathing and Showering

Occupational Therapy Intervention:
Train in safe and efficient functional mobility (sit to stand, bed mobility skills, transfers, standing, ambulation, and wheelchair mobility) during bathing and showering tasks.

Provide caregiver/family education and training.

Patient and Caregiver Handouts:

Biceps Tendonitis

Impairments and Functional Limitations:
Anterior shoulder pain during shoulder flexion and lifting activities that involve elbow flexion
Pain may occur after being immobile during the night.
Weakness of shoulder muscles
Co-occurring conditions - rotator cuff pathology

Provocative Tests:
Palpation of the bicipital groove
Yergason's Test

Occupational Therapy Intervention:
Recommend and/or provide adaptive equipment and task modification to compensate for limited overhead activities and lifting.

Instruct in pain self-management strategies.
- Coordinate medication peak with exercise and activity.
- Apply superficial cold.
- Practice deep (diaphragmatic) breathing and other relaxation techniques.

Provide physical agent modalities (ultrasound, heat before stretching and cold pack after stretching) to decrease pain and inflammation and to improve participation in ADL tasks.

Provide neck and shoulder stretching activities and exercise. When pain-free, progress to strengthening of the shoulder.

Patient and Caregiver Handouts:

Breast Cancer - Pre and Postoperative Management

Surgical procedures include radical, modified or simple mastectomies, lymph node dissection, and breast reconstruction.

Impairments and Functional Limitations:
ADL, IADL, productivity and leisure impairment
Impaired ROM and strength of trunk and upper extremity
Post-op pain and edema
Potential secondary complications - nerve damage, lymphedema

Occupational Therapy Preoperative Intervention:

- Baseline measurements (ROM, strength, sensation, and limb measurements)
- Provide education about post-operative activity limitations, precautions and exercise.
- Instruct in good posture during activities.
- Educate about lymphedema prevention or risk factor reduction.
- Teach strategies to incorporate wellness and health management routines into daily activities.
- Educate about breast cancer and the availability of community resources. Encourage participation in support groups.

Occupational Therapy Postoperative Intervention:
ADL, IADL, productivity and leisure training

- Treat underlying limitations to safety and independence.
- Recommend and/or provide adaptive equipment as needed. Train in lower body ADL equipment following reconstructive surgery involving abdominal muscles.
- Instruct in good posture during activities.
- Instruct in protective use of affected arm for the first 2 weeks. Avoid overuse, avoid sleeping on the same side as the surgery, avoid lifting more than 5 pounds, keep tasks below 90-degrees of shoulder motion. Instruct to elevate arm several times a day to manage post-op edema. *Unless otherwise instructed by surgeon.*

Train in safe and efficient functional mobility (sit to stand, bed mobility skills, transfers, ambulation and wheelchair mobility) during ADL and IADL tasks.

Pain self-management

- Coordinate medication peak with exercise and activity.
- Teach stress management and relaxation techniques.
- Use pillows to help arm and shoulder relax in sitting and lying down.
- Instruct in good posture during activities.

Breast Cancer - Pre and Postoperative Management

Occupational Therapy Postoperative Intervention:
Provide graded UE activities and exercises. *Follow the referring surgeon's specific guidelines for ROM and progression of exercises.*

- AROM exercises starting 2-3 days after surgery. Progress exercises until full ROM restored. Begin strengthening 4-6 weeks after surgery.
- Instruct in deep (diaphragmatic) breathing exercises and lateral expansion.
- Instruct in a walking program.

Provide surgical scar management at 3-4 weeks post surgery (mobilization, massage, desensitization, stretching exercises).

Provide education about lymphedema prevention and risk factor reduction.

Patient and Caregiver Handouts:

Arm Measurement	369
Deep (Diaphragmatic) Breathing	393
Edema (Swelling) Control of the Arm(s)	408
Good Posture	416
Mastectomy Exercises	627
Scar Massage	471
Tips to Prevent Lower Body Lymphedema	501
Walking Guidelines	784

Additional Treatment Guides:

Cancer	34
Health Management	115

Burn Injury

Impairments and Functional Limitations:
Outcomes will vary with the type of burn, extent/size of burn, depth of burn, joints/body areas involved, secondary injuries and pre-existing conditions.

ADL, IADL, productivity and leisure impairment
Functional mobility impairment
Muscle weakness
Limited range of motion at risk for contractures and hypertrophic scarring
Limited activity tolerance
Impaired respiratory status
Impaired integument
Sensory loss
Pain
Edema
Impaired body image, self esteem
Post-traumatic stress disorder, depression, anxiety
Complications - hypovolemic shock, inhalation injury, renal failure, compartment syndrome, infection, heterotopic ossification, limb loss, peripheral neuropathies

Rating Scales:
Lund and Browder Chart (Hettiaratchy et al., 2004)
Vancouver Scar Scale (Sullivan et al., 1990)

Occupational Therapy Intervention - Acute Care Phase:
Medical intervention includes pain management, ongoing wound debridement and wound care, surgical procedures (escharotomy, fasciotomy, skin grafting, amputations) and infection control.

Prevent ROM loss, prevent contractures and reduce edema.

- Provide anti-deformity positioning using static splinting and positioning devices.
- Provide positioning, compression and AROM for edema control.
- Provide splints to immobilize joints post-surgery.
- Provide passive ROM to all joints. Preferably, during medicated dressing changes. If patient is alert, encourage active and active-assisted ROM. Exercise contraindications include exposed tendons or joints, post-grafting, infection.
- Educate patient and caregivers in all aspects of care.

Once medically cleared, progress ADLs, sitting and standing tolerance, transfers and ambulation using adaptive equipment and modifications as needed. Before mobility, apply compression wraps over lower extremity dressings to improve pain control and vascular response.

Burn Injury

Occupational Therapy Intervention - Rehabilitation Phase:
Medical intervention - surgical release of scar contractures, reconstructive or plastic surgery

ADL, IADL, productivity and leisure training

- Recommend and/or provide adaptive equipment to compensate for ROM loss.
- Instruct in donning and doffing compression garments and splints, or teach patient to accurately instruct and direct others.
- Instruct in managing skin care which includes monitoring skin for pressure areas/breakdown, scar massage, moisturizing and sun protection.
- Instruct in concealing and corrective cosmetics.

Train in safe and efficient functional mobility (sit to stand, bed mobility skills, transfers, standing, ambulation and wheelchair mobility) during ADL and IADL tasks.

Provide an individualized progressive exercise and activity program to improve strength, flexibility and endurance. Incorporate increased physical activity into daily routine. Monitor cardiovascular status.

Instruct in range of motion exercises and gentle prolonged stretching.

- Modalities prior to stretching (thermotherapy, paraffin, hydrotherapy)
- Manual therapy techniques (massage, mobilization)
- Continue positioning and/or splints (static, dynamic) as needed

Provide burn scar management.

- Scar massage
- Desensitization techniques
- Pressure garments and silicone gel sheeting

Prevent or manage edema.

- Compression garment or wrapping
- Position body part in elevation
- Active self-range of motion exercises in elevation

Instruct in pain self-management strategies.

- Coordinate medication peak with exercise and activity.
- Deep (diaphragmatic) breathing and other relaxation techniques
- Transcutaneous electric nerve stimulation (TENS)
- Pacing and energy conservation
- Coping strategies

Burn Injury

Occupational Therapy Intervention - Community Reintegration Phase:
Teach strategies for handling social challenges (answering questions, dealing with unkind remarks or reactions) and provide opportunities to participate in community re-entry outings.

Complete a comprehensive, performance-based home/work/leisure/driving assessment. Recommend and/or provide modifications, adaptive equipment and/or assistive technology.

Teach strategies to incorporate wellness and health management routines into daily activities.

Educate patient and caregivers about burns, community resources. Encourage participation in support groups.

Patient and Caregiver Handouts:

Additional Treatment Guides:

Occupational Therapy TOOLKIT

Cancer

Impairments will vary with type, location and stage of the cancer, treatment received (chemotherapy, hormone therapy, surgery, radiation, immunotherapy, bone marrow transplant), and pre-cancer medical, functional, social, and psychological status.

Impairments and Functional Limitations:
ADL, IADL, productivity and leisure impairment
Functional mobility impairment
Impaired ROM, strength of trunk, lower and upper extremities, postural imbalance (due to deconditioning, pain, scar formation post-surgery/radiation)
Pain (pre-existing pain, postoperative pain, nerve compressions from tumors, changes in body posture, side effect from all treatments)
Chemotherapy-induced peripheral neuropathy (foot-drop, impaired fine motor function)
Lymphedema of the upper or lower extremity (side effect of surgery and/or radiation, increased risk with breast cancer, vulvar cancer, uterine cancer, prostate cancer, lymphoma or melanoma)
Bone fractures (increased risk with lung, prostate, breast, thyroid, multiple myeloma, or renal cancers)
Fatigue - unrelieved by rest, persistent, interferes with function (side-effect chemotherapy or radiation)
Dyspnea
Impaired balance, fall risk (side effect of chemotherapy)
Cognitive changes "chemo-brain" (side effect of chemotherapy, radiation or brain metastasis)
Dysarthria and dysphasia
Bowel and bladder dysfunction
Immunocompromised
Changes in self-esteem and body image
Depression and anxiety

Assessments and Rating Scales:
Canadian Occupational Performance Measure (Law et al., 2014)

Occupational Therapy Intervention:
ADL, IADL, productivity and leisure training

- Treat underlying limitations to safety and independence.
- Recommend and/or provide adaptive equipment and task modification.
- Instruct in good posture during activities.

Train in safe and efficient functional mobility (sit to stand, bed mobility skills, transfers, standing, ambulation and wheelchair mobility) during ADL and IADL tasks.

Cancer

Occupational Therapy Intervention:
Instruct in pain self-management strategies.

- Coordinate medication peak with exercise and activity.
- Apply superficial heat and cold.
- Teach stress management and relaxation techniques.
- Use positioning devices (seat cushions, back supports, pillows).
- Instruct in using a pain journal.
- Utilize the problem solving process to identify ways to manage pain.

Provide surgical scar management at 3-4 weeks post surgery (mobilization, massage, desensitization, stretching exercises).

Provide an individualized, slowly progressive exercise program that includes aerobic, strengthening and flexibility activities.

Teach strategies to manage fatigue and conserve energy.

- Assess using the Fatigue Impact Scale (Fisk et al., 1994).
- Teach pacing and energy conservation strategies.
- Balance self-care, productivity, play and rest.
- Encourage good sleep hygiene.
- Encourage keeping a fatigue journal.
- Utilize the problem solving process to identify ways to manage fatigue.
- Encourage participation in a paced aerobic exercise program.
- Encourage healthy eating. Refer to dietician as needed.

Provide a fall prevention program that includes balance, coordination and agility training and education about fall risk and prevention strategies. Provide functional balance activities to increase balance confidence with ADL tasks.

Instruct in compensation techniques for peripheral neuropathy.

Teach compensatory techniques for cognitive impairment.

Complete a comprehensive, performance-based home assessment. Recommend and/or provide home modifications, adaptive equipment and/or assistive technology.

Occupational Therapy TOOLKIT

Cancer

Occupational Therapy Intervention:
Prevent lymphedema.

- Educate about lymphedema prevention or risk factor reduction, skin care.
- Obtain baseline measurements of arms/legs and measure periodically.
- Achieve or maintain healthy body weight.

Manage lymphedema using Complete Decongestive Therapy (CDT) (performed by a certified lymphedema therapist).

- Provide manual lymph drainage (MLD) and teach self-MLD.
- Instruct in deep breathing and relaxation techniques.
- Provide multilayer bandaging to decrease lymphedema following MLD.
- Provide compression garments to maintain reduction of lymphedema after MLD and multilayer bandaging.
- Home program for AROM, stretching and low-intensity strengthening exercises performed while wearing compression garments.
- Instruct in donning and doffing compression garments, wearing schedule, care of garments and garment replacement timeframes.

Teach strategies to incorporate wellness and health management routines into daily activities.

Educate patient and caregivers about cancer the availability of community resources. Encourage participation in support groups.

Patient and Caregiver Handouts:

Additional Treatment Guides:

Cancer

Additional Treatment Guides:

Cardiac Disease

Conditions include cardiomyopathy, congestive heart failure (CHF), coronary artery disease (CAD) and valvular heart disease.

Impairments and Functional Limitations:
ADL, IADL, productivity and leisure impairment
Functional mobility impairment
Limited activity tolerance and endurance
Limited sitting and standing tolerance
Lower extremity edema
Dyspnea with functional activities
Urge incontinence
Fall risk
Depression

Occupational Therapy Intervention:
ADL, IADL, productivity and leisure training

- Recommend and/or provide adaptive equipment.
- Instruct patient in donning and doffing support stockings.
- Reinforce weighing self. Assess if patient can access a scale safely, has a system to record weight and can recall weight guidelines.
- Reinforce dietary instructions during kitchen management.
- Assess safe and easy access of toilet and BSC when taking diuretics.
- Teach patient and caregivers about the safe use of oxygen during ADL and mobility (fire safety, managing O2 lines, care and correct use of oxygen equipment, carrying portable O2).
- Reinforce medication management. Assist patient in developing a system to remember medications (pillbox, telephone reminders, lists, pictures).

Instruct in pursed lip breathing applied during ADL tasks.

Assess and monitor blood pressure, heart rate, respiratory rate and oxygen saturations and perceived rate of exertion in response to functional activities and exercise.

Teach strategies to manage fatigue and conserve energy.

- Assess using the Fatigue Impact Scale (Fisk et al., 1994).
- Teach pacing and energy conservation strategies.
- Balance self-care, productivity, play and rest.
- Encourage good sleep hygiene.
- Encourage keeping a fatigue journal.
- Utilize the problem solving process to identify ways to manage fatigue.

Cardiac Disease

Occupational Therapy Intervention:
Train in safe and efficient functional mobility (sit to stand, bed mobility skills, transfers, standing, ambulation and wheelchair mobility) during ADL and IADL tasks.

- Teach patient to position self in bed on pillows or a wedge to ease breathing.
- Instruct patient to elevate legs to reduce edema. Modify recliner chair handle by using a length of PVC pipe to provide leverage. Attach a strap to a footstool to pull into position.

Provide progressive activities and low resistive exercises to improve strength and endurance. Avoid isometric exercises.

Teach stress management and relaxation techniques.

Provide education about fall risk and prevention strategies.

Complete a comprehensive, performance-based home assessment. Recommend and/or provide modifications, adaptive equipment and/or assistive technology.

Teach strategies to incorporate wellness and health management routines into daily activities.

Educate patient and caregivers about cardiac disease and the availability of community resources. Encourage participation in support groups.

Patient and Caregiver Handouts:
Edema (Swelling) Control of the Leg(s) 409
Fatigue Journal 412
Pursed Lip Breathing 470
Put On and Take Off Support Stockings 300
Putty Exercises 683
Stress Management 477
Tips to Conserve Energy 482
Tips to Conserve Energy with Meal and Home Management 483
Tips to Conserve Energy with Self Care Tasks 484
Upper Body Exercises - Hand Weights 765
Upper Body Strength Activities 773

Additional Treatment Guides:
Health Management 115

Therapist Resources:
Cardiac Precautions for Exercise 375

Occupational Therapy TOOLKIT

Cardiac Surgery

Coronary artery bypass graft (CABG), valve replacement or repair

Impairments and Functional Limitations:
ADL, IADL, productivity and leisure impairment
Functional mobility impairment
Limited ROM
Impaired upper extremity strength
Limited activity tolerance and endurance
Dyspnea
Pain
Edema - lower extremity
Depression
Co-occurring conditions - rotator cuff injury

Occupational Therapy Intervention:
ADL, IADL, productivity and leisure training

- Recommend and/or provide adaptive equipment and task modifications to reduce the need to bend forward, twist or overreach (don/doff bra, toilet hygiene, shoes and socks, support stockings).
- Instruct in pacing and energy conservation strategies.
- Instruct in sternal precautions during ADL tasks.
- Reinforce dietary instructions during kitchen management.

Train in safe and efficient functional mobility (sit to stand, bed mobility skills, transfers, standing, ambulation and wheelchair mobility) during ADL and IADL tasks, while adhering to sternal precautions.

Instruct in balancing rest and activity, signs and symptoms of overworking the heart, self-pulse monitoring, Rated Perceived Exertion (RPE) Scale and progression of activities.

Assess and monitor blood pressure, heart rate, respiratory rate and oxygen saturations and perceived rate of exertion in response to functional activities and exercise.

Teach stress management and relaxation techniques.

Complete a comprehensive, performance-based home assessment. Recommend and/or provide modifications, adaptive equipment and/or assistive technology.

Cardiac Surgery

Occupational Therapy Intervention:
Teach strategies to incorporate wellness and health management routines into daily activities.

Educate patient and caregivers about cardiac disease and the availability of community resources. Encourage participation in support groups.

Patient and Caregiver Handouts:

Additional Treatment Guides:

Therapist Resources:

Carpal Tunnel Syndrome - Conservative Management
Median Nerve Compression at the Wrist

Impairments and Functional Limitations:
Pain and paresthesias along median nerve distribution
Impaired grip and pinch strength, and fine motor coordination
Atrophy of the thenar muscles
Rotator cuff and scapular weakness
Co-occurring conditions - obesity, arthritis, hypothyroidism, diabetes

Provocative Tests/Outcome Measures:
Flick Sign (Gunnarsson et al., 1997)
Manual Ability Measure (Chen & Bode 2010)
Michigan Hand Outcome Questionnaire (Chung et al., 1998)
Disabilities of the Arm, Shoulder, and Hand (Beaton et al., 2001)

Occupational Therapy Intervention:
Recommend and/or provide adaptive equipment and task modifications to compensate for pain and weakness (tying shoes, buttoning shirts, using a key in a lock, holding cane or walker, writing).

Provide a custom wrist splint in neutral, wear 24 hours a day. Instruct how to don/doff, wear schedule and hygiene.

Instruct in joint protection techniques.

- Practice good body mechanics and posture.
- Avoid repetitive hand and wrist motion.
- Perform activities with wrist in neutral.
- Take frequent breaks.
- Modify activities that cause symptoms.
- Instruct in injury prevention to decrease recurrence.

Provide UE therapeutic activities and exercises.

- Hand and wrist stretching
- Tendon and median nerve glides
- Progress to hand and wrist strengthening exercises once symptoms are relieved
- Rotator cuff and scapular strengthening

Provide pain and edema management.

- Low-intensity ultrasound
- Carpal mobilization
- Elastic therapeutic tape

Carpal Tunnel Syndrome - Conservative Management
Median Nerve Compression at the Wrist

Occupational Therapy Intervention:
Instruct in pain self-management strategies

- Coordinate medication peak with exercise and activity.
- Apply superficial cold.
- Practice deep (diaphragmatic) breathing and other relaxation techniques.
- Instruct in using a pain journal.
- Utilize the problem solving process to identify ways to manage pain.

Provide sensory re-education intervention.

- Teach sensory compensatory techniques.
- Provide sensory stimulation techniques.

Patient and Caregiver Handouts:

Occupational Therapy TOOLKIT

Carpal Tunnel Syndrome - Postoperative Management
Median Nerve Decompression at the Wrist

Impairments and Functional Limitations:
Post-op pain and edema
Impaired grip and pinch strength, and fine motor coordination
Rotator cuff and scapular weakness
Co-occurring conditions - obesity, arthritis, hypothyroidism, diabetes

Assessments and Rating Scales:
Manual Ability Measure (Chen & Bode 2010)
Michigan Hand Outcome Questionnaire (Chung et al., 1998)
Disabilities of the Arm, Shoulder, and Hand (Beaton et al., 2001)

Occupational Therapy Intervention:
Recommend and/or provide adaptive equipment and task modifications to compensate for pain and weakness (tying shoes, buttoning shirts, using a key in a lock, holding cane or walker, writing).

Progression depends on co-morbidities, surgical procedure performed, stage of healing, and postoperative complications. *Follow the referring surgeon's specific guidelines for progression.*

Stage 1: Protection
- No lifting, carrying or resistive activities until cleared by surgeon.
- Provide a pre-fabricated wrist splint in neutral or with 15-degrees of extension. Instruct how to don/doff, wear schedule and hygiene.
- Provide pain and edema management.
- Provide AROM exercises of uninvolved joints.
- Instruct in tendon and median nerve glides.
- Teach joint protection techniques.

Stage 2: Active Motion
- Continue treatment as described above.
- Progress AROM exercises.
- Provide scar management.

Stage 3: Strengthening
- Progress strengthening.

Occupational Therapy TOOLKIT

Carpal Tunnel Syndrome - Postoperative Management
Median Nerve Decompression at the Wrist

Patient and Caregiver Handouts:

Cervical Stenosis, Myelopathy and Radiculopathy

Conditions include central disc herniation, degenerative disc disease, and spinal tumors.

Impairments and Functional Limitations:
ADL, IADL, productivity and leisure impairment
Functional mobility impairment
Impaired fine motor coordination
Pain
Paresthesia or hypesthesia
Impaired strength
Impaired balance
Abnormal reflexes
Urinary and/or bowel incontinence

Occupational Therapy Intervention:
ADL, IADL, productivity and leisure training

- Recommend and/or provide adaptive equipment and task modifications to compensate for limitations in neck and upper extremities.
- Instruct how to don/doff neck brace/collar, wearing schedule and hygiene.
- Recommend and/or provide adaptive equipment and task modifications to compensate for weak grasp and sensory loss (buttonhook, built-up pen, rubber bands or non-slip drawer liner placed around utensils, grooming containers, cups, rubber gloves to provide grip for opening doorknobs, jars).
- Instruct in body mechanics and postural training avoiding cervical extension Instruct in pacing and energy conservation strategies.
- Modify computer (the position of the monitor should encourage a neutral cervical posture, use of a slanted writing board, document holder, bookstand, and telephone headset).
- Address ability to drive safely. Refer to driving rehab specialist and/or explore alternative transportation options.

Train in safe and efficient functional mobility (sit to stand, bed mobility skills, transfers, standing, ambulation and wheelchair mobility) during ADL and IADL tasks.

Provide an individualized exercise program that includes neck stretching and isometric exercises progressing to isotonic neck strengthening, upper limb strengthening and flexibility. Goal is to improve neck strength and mobility without increasing symptoms.

Instruct in pain self-management.

- Coordinate medication peak with exercise and activity.
- Apply superficial heat and cold.
- Practice deep (diaphragmatic) breathing and other relaxation techniques.

Occupational Therapy TOOLKIT

Cervical Stenosis, Myelopathy and Radiculopathy

Occupational Therapy Intervention:
Provide education about fall risk and prevention strategies.

Complete a comprehensive, performance-based home assessment. Recommend and/or provide modifications, adaptive equipment and/or assistive technology.

Patient and Caregiver Handouts:

Additional Treatment Guides:

Cervical Spine Surgery

Impairments and Functional Limitations:
ADL, IADL, productivity and leisure impairment
Functional mobility impairment
Impaired fine motor coordination
Pain
Paresthesia or hypesthesia
Impaired strength
Impaired balance
Abnormal reflexes
Urinary and/or bowel incontinence
Fall risk
Co-occurring conditions - osteoarthritis, rheumatoid arthritis
Potential complications - dysphagia, laryngeal nerve injury

Occupational Therapy Intervention:
ADL, IADL, productivity and leisure training

- Recommend and/or provide adaptive equipment and task modifications to prevent bending, lifting or twisting. Shower chair, grab bars, non-slip mat, hand held shower, long bath sponge, raised toilet seat, bedside commode, leg lifter, reacher, sock aid, shoehorn, elastic shoelaces, dressing stick.
- Recommend and/or provide adaptive equipment and task modifications to compensate for weak grasp and sensory loss (buttonhook, built-up pen, rubber bands or non-slip drawer liner placed around utensils, grooming containers, cups, rubber gloves to provide grip for opening doorknobs, jars).
- Instruct how to don/doff neck brace/collar, wearing schedule and hygiene.
- Instruct in pacing and energy conservation strategies.
- Instruct in good posture and body mechanics.

Train in safe and efficient functional mobility (sit to stand, bed mobility skills, transfers, standing, ambulation and wheelchair mobility) while adhering to cervical spine precautions.

Instruct in spinal surgery precautions as ordered by the surgeon. *Always follow the referring surgeon's protocol.*

Instruct in pain self-management strategies.

- Coordinate medication peak with exercise and activity.
- Apply superficial cold.
- Practice deep (diaphragmatic) breathing and other relaxation techniques.

Occupational Therapy TOOLKIT

Cervical Spine Surgery

Occupational Therapy Intervention:
Provide an individualized upper body ROM and strengthening exercise program. Progression depends on co-morbidities, surgical procedure performed, stage of healing, and postoperative complications. *Follow the referring surgeon's specific guidelines for progression.*

Provide education about fall risk and prevention strategies.

Complete a comprehensive, performance-based home assessment. Recommend and/or provide home and activity modifications.

Patient and Caregiver Handouts:

Additional Treatment Guides:

Chronic Obstructive Pulmonary Disease

Conditions include emphysema, chronic bronchitis, asthma and bronchiectasis

Impairments and Functional Limitations:
ADL, IADL, productivity and leisure impairment
Functional mobility impairment
Limited range of motion (chest and shoulders)
Muscle weakness
Impaired balance
Limited activity tolerance and endurance
Dyspnea at rest and with functional activities
Memory impairment
Co-occurring conditions - stress incontinence, cubital tunnel syndrome, depression and anxiety, heart disease, hypertension, lung cancer

Stages of COPD
Mild - FEV1 is equal or greater than 80 percent
Moderate - FEV1 is between 50 and 79 percent
Severe - FEV1 is between 30 to 49 percent
Very Severe - FEV1 is less than 30 percent

Occupational Therapy Intervention:
ADL, IADL, productivity and leisure IADL training

- Recommend and/or provide adaptive equipment and task modifications to compensate limited activity tolerance and dyspnea, and to reduce the need to stand, bend and reach.
- Teach patient and caregivers about the safe use of oxygen during ADL and mobility (fire safety, managing O2 lines, care and correct use of oxygen equipment, carrying portable O2).
- Reinforce dietary instructions during kitchen management.
- Instruct in medication management.

Teach strategies to manage fatigue and conserve energy.

- Assess using the Fatigue Impact Scale (Fisk et al., 1994).
- Teach pacing and energy conservation strategies.
- Balance self-care, productivity, play and rest.
- Encourage good sleep hygiene.
- Encourage keeping a fatigue journal.
- Utilize the problem solving process to identify ways to manage fatigue.

Occupational Therapy TOOLKIT

Chronic Obstructive Pulmonary Disease

Occupational Therapy Intervention:
Train in safe and efficient functional mobility (sit to stand, bed mobility skills, transfers, standing, ambulation and wheelchair mobility) during ADL and IADL tasks.

Provide graded UE and trunk activities and progressive resistive therapeutic exercises that incorporate breathing techniques. Provide breathing and stretching exercise that incorporates breathing techniques and teach coordination of breathing during ADL tasks.

Instruct in pursed lip breathing and slow, relaxed, deep breathing. Instruct in heart rate and dyspnea self-monitoring with application to functional tasks. Instruct in respiratory panic strategies.

Assess and monitor blood pressure, heart rate, respiratory rate and oxygen saturations and perceived rate of exertion in response to functional activities and exercise.

Complete a comprehensive, performance-based home assessment. Recommend and/or provide modifications, adaptive equipment and/or assistive technology.

Teach stress management and relaxation techniques to control anxiety.

Provide a fall prevention program that includes balance, coordination and agility training and education about fall risk and prevention strategies. Provide functional balance activities to increase balance confidence with ADL tasks.

Teach strategies to incorporate wellness and health management routines into daily activities.

Educate patient and caregivers about COPD, community resources. Encourage participation in support groups. Refer to Outpatient Pulmonary Rehab as appropriate. Provide educational materials to the caregiver about stress management and caring for their own health.

Patient and Caregiver Handouts:

Arm Cycle	518
Breathing Distress - Causes and Tips to Prevent	373
Breathing Distress Control	374
Controlled Cough	381
Fatigue Journal	412
Postural Drainage Positions	465
Posture Exercises	676

Occupational Therapy TOOLKIT

Chronic Obstructive Pulmonary Disease

Patient and Caregiver Handouts:

Additional Treatment Guides:

Chronic/Persistent Pain Syndrome

Impairments and Functional Limitations:
ADL, IADL, productivity and leisure impairment
Impaired functional mobility
Antalgic gait
Chronic pain (localized or generalized)
Deconditioned
Chronic fatigue
Sleep problems
Cognitive difficulty including impaired memory and concentration
Depression, anxiety, social isolation, emotional instability, anger
Co-occurring conditions include headaches, arthritis, spinal stenosis, osteoporosis, repetitive stress injuries, back pain, whiplash injuries, degenerative joint disorders, complex regional pain syndrome, shingles, fibromyalgia, myofascial pain syndrome, neuropathies, and multiple surgeries

Assessments and Rating Scales:
Chronic Pain Coping Inventory (Jensen et al., 1991)
Coping Strategies Questionnaire (Robinson et al., 1997)
Fear Avoidance Beliefs Questionnaire (Waddell et al., 1993)
Geriatric Pain Measure (Ferrell et al., 2000)
Pain Catastrophizing Scale (Sullivan et al., 1995)
Pain Self Efficacy Questionnaire (Nicholas et al., 1989)
West Haven Yale Multidimensional Pain Inventory (Kerns et al., 1985)

Occupational Therapy Intervention:
ADL, IADL, productivity and leisure training
- Recommend and/or provide adaptive equipment and task modifications to allow participation in tasks without increasing pain.
- Instruct in good posture and body mechanics during ADL tasks.
- Teach pacing of activities.

Train in safe and efficient functional mobility (sit to stand, bed mobility skills, transfers, standing, ambulation and wheelchair mobility) during ADL and IADL tasks.

Teach strategies to manage fatigue and conserve energy.
- Assess using the Fatigue Impact Scale (Fisk et al., 1994).
- Teach pacing and energy conservation strategies.
- Balance self-care, productivity, play and rest.
- Encourage good sleep hygiene.
- Encourage keeping a fatigue journal.
- Utilize the problem solving process to identify ways to manage fatigue.

Chronic/Persistent Pain Syndrome

Occupational Therapy Intervention:
Provide an individualized exercise program that includes endurance, strengthening, and flexibility activities. Proceed slowly without exacerbating pain. Include a graded walking program, aquatic therapy, yoga, qigong, and tai chi.

Instruct in pain self-management strategies.
- Provide education about the pain cycle.
- Coordinate medication peak with exercise and activity.
- Apply superficial heat and cold.
- Practice deep (diaphragmatic) breathing and other relaxation techniques.
- Use self-massage techniques (foam rollers, tennis ball, rolling massage stick).
- Transcutaneous electric nerve stimulation (TENS).
- Use positioning devices (seat cushions, back supports, pillows, splints).
- Instruct in using a pain journal.
- Utilize the problem solving process to identify ways to manage pain flares.

Complete a comprehensive, performance-based home/work assessment. Recommend and/or provide modifications, adaptive equipment and/or assistive technology.

Teach strategies to incorporate wellness and health management routines into daily activities.

Educate patient and caregivers about pain neuroscience education and the availability of community resources. Encourage participation in support groups.

Patient and Caregiver Handouts:

Body Mechanics	371
Deep (Diaphragmatic) Breathing	393
Fatigue Journal	412
Good Posture	416
Pain Journal	456
Posture Exercises	676
Stress Management	477
Stretch Band Exercises - Arms	749
Superficial Cold & Heat	480
Tips to Conserve Energy	482
Upper Body Exercises - Hand Weights	765

Additional Treatment Guides:

Heath Management	115
Rest and Sleep	166

Occupational Therapy TOOLKIT

Clothing Care

Clothing care includes washing items by hand, transporting laundry, sorting clothes, opening and pouring laundry detergent, operating washing machine, moving wet clothes to dryer, operating dryer, cleaning lint filter, removing clothes from dryer, hanging up clothes to dry, setting up ironing board, ironing, folding clothes, hanging up clothes in closet, putting clothes away, mending clothes.

Impairments and Functional Limitations:
Impaired shoulder strength and/or ROM
Impaired hand strength, ROM, sensation and/or coordination
Impaired LE function
Limited activity tolerance and endurance
Impaired balance
Pain
Visual perceptual impairment
Cognitive impairment

Occupational Therapy Intervention:
Apply different approaches for solving difficulties with clothing care.

- Remediate underlying limitations to safety and independence: physical impairments (muscle weakness, impaired hand function, limited ROM, paralysis, incoordination, impaired balance, fatigue, dyspnea, abnormal tone, tremor), sensory impairment (impaired sensation, low vision, hard of hearing, vestibular, pain), behavioral, cognition, perception.
- Train in compensatory techniques (safety techniques, one-handed techniques, pacing, energy conservation, joint protection, body mechanics, breathing techniques, low vision techniques, cognitive/perceptual compensation).
- Train in the use of adaptive equipment and assistive devices (laundry cart, reacher/tongs or spaghetti server to retrieve clothes from washer and dryer)
- Provide environmental modifications and adaptations (sufficient lightening, store supplies within easy and safe reach, low vision modifications to control panel, relocate laundry appliances, lower closet rods, and lower clothes drying lines).
- Instruct in activity modification.
    - Change the task (transfer wet clothes into dryer a few items at a time, use smaller containers for detergent, wash smaller loads, sit to iron, sort clothes, pre-treat stains, and fold laundry).
    - Eliminate part or the entire task (wear clothes made of easy care fabrics).
    - Have someone else do part or the entire task (get help to fold large items, use a laundry service).

Provide caregiver/family education and training.

Occupational Therapy TOOLKIT

Cognition

Hierarchy of Cognitive Skills
Basic cognitive skills (alertness, attention, memory)
Praxis
Language and communication
Executive functions (the skills and abilities needed to accomplish goal-directed activities, such as initiating, planning, prioritizing, organization, sequencing, shifting to next step or task, problem-solving, decision-making, considering consequences, judgment, time management, working memory, regulating thinking and behaviors)

Cognitive Assessments and Screens:
Allen Cognitive Lacing Screen (ACLS-5) (Riska-Williams 2007)
Arnadottir OT-ADL Neurobehavioral Evaluation (A-ONE) (Arnadottir 1990)
Cognitive Assessment of Minnesota (CAM) (Rustad et al 1993)
Executive Function Performance Test (EFPT) (Baum et al., 2003)
The Kettle Test (Hartman-Maeir et al., 2005)
Loewenstein Occupational Therapy Cognitive Assessment (LOTCA) (Katz et al., 1989)
Montreal Cognitive Assessment (MoCA) (Nasreddine et al., 2005)
Multiple Errands Test-R (Morrison et al., 2013)
Routine Task Inventory-Expanded (RTI-E) (Allen 1989, Katz 2006)
The Test of Everyday Attention (TEA) (Robertson et al 1994)
The Trail Making Test (Reitan & Wolfson 1995)

Occupational Therapy Intervention:
Arousal/Alertness

- Provide sensory (tactile, auditory, and visual) stimulation.
    - Use familiar and meaningful controlled stimulation (favorite foods, music, voices).
    - Once arousal is achieved, follow through with a functional activity (Example: use a warm washcloth to elicit arousal, and then proceed with grooming task).
- Provide vestibular stimulation.
    - Rolling, bending, reaching, PNF patterns, sit to stand activities

Attention

- Provide opportunities to practice maintaining attention during focused tasks.
- Use a timer.
- Adapt the environment (reduce clutter, teach organizational strategies, keep items in consistent places, return items when finished).
- Instruct on ways to minimize distractions (focus on one thing, find a quiet place, close the curtains, turn off the TV or radio).

Occupational Therapy Intervention:
Memory

- Teach external memory aids/devices (follow a routine, use reminders, let someone or something else remember).
- Teach internal memory aids (store information into memory more efficiently, use memory tricks).
- Use errorless learning and spaced retrieval techniques during ADL tasks.
    - Select activities or activity components that match the individual's cognitive capabilities.
    - Make sure person is clear about what is expected.
    - Break the task into smaller parts and teach the parts separately.
    - Anticipate problems and correct in advance.
    - Guide through a task and then gradually decrease the cues given.
- Cueing hierarchy.
    - Verbal cue - ask open-ended questions. "What is this?" (show a hairbrush)
    - Verbal cue - provide two choices. "Is this a hairbrush or deodorant?"
    - Verbal cue - use a directive cue. "This is a hairbrush."
    - Visual cue - demonstrate brushing hair or use pictures.
    - Tactile cue - provide hand-over-hand guiding.
- Adapt the environment to support cognitive function.
    - Teach organizational strategies.
    - Reduce triggers for stress and agitation.
    - Prevent injuries (slip and falls, burns, poisoning, cuts, electrocution).
    - Control wandering (secure doors and windows, control access to stairwells, storage areas, basements, garages, home offices).

Apraxia - see separate treatment guide

Executive Functions

- Task-specific training (verbal self-instruction)
- Adapt the environment to support cognitive function (reduce distractions, use checklists, cueing devices, random alerting tones).
- Use specific approaches to intervention.
    - Cognitive Orientation to Daily Occupational Performance (Polatajko & Mandich, 2004)
    - Neurofunctional Approach (Giles 1993)
    - Dynamic Interactional Model (Toglia 2005)

Cognition

Occupational Therapy Intervention:
All Cognitive Areas
Strengthen residual cognitive abilities.

Educate in wellness (smoking cessation, healthy eating, physical activity and exercise, stress management and relaxation, good sleep habits).

Educate caregivers about the nature of cognitive impairments. Educate caregivers how to provide cognitive support (cueing methods and strategies) during functional tasks. Make recommendations on amount of care the person needs.

Patient and Caregiver Handouts:

Additional Treatment Guides:

Therapist Resources:

Community Mobility

Passenger in vehicle (car, taxi, van, SUV, truck, shuttle, para-transit services, bus, train, subway, plane), arranging transportation, maneuvering on a bus/train/plane, transferring in and out of vehicle, fastening seatbelt, storing mobility devices, transporting purchased items

Pedestrian (with or without assistive devices including canes, walkers, crutches, manual wheelchairs, electric wheelchairs, power assist wheelchairs, scooters), accessing elevators/escalators, opening and closing doors, moving through doorways, crossing the street safely, negotiating obstacles, climbing stairs and curbs, moving up and down ramps, slopes, and curb cuts, transporting items purchased, various weather conditions

Impairments and Functional Limitations:
Impaired physical function
Limited activity tolerance and endurance
Pain
Vision loss
Perceptual impairment
Cognitive impairment

Assessments:
Power-Mobility Indoor Driving Assessment (Dawson et al., 1995)

Occupational Therapy Intervention:
Apply different approaches for solving difficulties with community mobility.

- Remediate underlying limitations to safety and independence: physical impairments (muscle weakness, impaired hand function, limited ROM, paralysis, incoordination, impaired balance, fatigue, dyspnea, abnormal tone, tremor), sensory impairment (impaired sensation, low vision, hard of hearing, vestibular, pain), behavioral, cognition, perception.
- Train in compensatory techniques (safety techniques, low vision techniques, cognitive/perceptual compensation).
- Train in the use of adaptive equipment and modifications (wheeled cart, car transfer handle, seat belt assist).
- Instruct in task modification (bank and shop by mail, delivery services).

Patient and Caregiver Handouts:
Car Transfers 225

Complex Regional Pain Syndrome Type I

Formally known as Reflex Sympathetic Dystrophy (RSD)

Impairments and Functional Limitations:
Difficulty using the affected UE with functional tasks
Severe pain
Hyperesthesia
Sudomotor changes (edema, sweating changes)
Decreased range of motion and/or strength
Trophic changes (hair, nails, skin)
Vasomotor changes
Other conditions - stroke, peripheral nerve injury

Medical Treatment:
Psychotherapy including cognitive behavior therapy
Medications (pain medicines, corticosteroids, bone loss medicines, and antidepressants)
Other treatments (sympathetic nerve-blocking, intravenous ketamine, spinal cord stimulation)

Occupational Therapy Intervention:
Prevention

- Control the first signs of edema.
- Provide scapular mobilization.
- Instruct in correct handling of the arm during mobility and ADLs.
- Avoid shoulder flexion over 90° without scapular gliding.
- Avoid overhead pulleys.
- Train patient and caregivers in positioning in bed and chair.
- Train patient and caregivers in care of the affected extremity.

Treatment

- Edema control
- Pain-free PROM, self-ROM and AROM activities
- Scapular mobilization
- Progressive weight bearing
- Transcutaneous electric nerve stimulation (TENS)
- Ultrasound
- Tactile desensitization
- Graded motor imagery
- Mirror therapy

Complex Regional Pain Syndrome Type I

Occupational Therapy Intervention:
Educate patient and caregivers about CRPS-1 and the availability of community resources. Encourage participation in support groups.

Patient and Caregiver Handouts:

Additional Treatment Guides:

Cubital Tunnel Syndrome - Conservative Management
Ulnar Nerve Compression at the Elbow

Impairments and Functional Limitations:
Pain and paresthesias medial elbow, ulnar hand, 4th and 5th fingers
Impaired strength, ROM, and coordination ulnar side of hand
Rotator cuff and scapular weakness
Surgery is frequently required

Provocative Tests:
Wadsworth Elbow Flexion Test (Wadsworth et al., 1995)
Tinel's Sign (Tinel 1915)
Upper Limb Tension Test (Butler et al., 1987)

Occupational Therapy Intervention:
Recommend and/or provide adaptive equipment and task modifications to reduce pain and compensate for weak grasp and incoordination. Modify carrying purses/handbags, holding phone, sleep posture, reading posture, driving posture, ADL and work ergonomics.

Provide positioning at night in 30°-60° of elbow flexion using towel wrapped around the elbow or a static anterior elbow splint. Provide gel pads to protect the elbow from pressure.

Provide UE therapeutic activities and exercises.
- Ulnar nerve glides
- AROM to uninvolved joints
- Elbow and forearm stretching activities and active exercise to increase ROM
- Progress to elbow and forearm strengthening activities and exercises once symptoms are relieved.

Provide pain management.
- Pulsed ultrasound
- Phonophoresis
- Elastic therapeutic tape

Instruct in pain self-management strategies.
- Coordinate medication peak with exercise and activity.
- Superficial cold
- Deep (diaphragmatic) breathing and other relaxation techniques
- Pain journal
- Problem solving process to identify ways to manage pain

Cubital Tunnel Syndrome - Conservative Management
Ulnar Nerve Compression at the Elbow

Occupational Therapy Intervention:
Instruct in joint protection techniques.

- Practice good body mechanics and posture.
- Avoid prolonged/repetitive elbow flexion/extension and flexion/pronation.
- Reduce or stop vibration.
- Avoid resting the elbows on hard surfaces.
- Take frequent breaks.
- Modify activities that cause symptoms.
- Instruct in injury prevention to decrease recurrence.

Patient and Caregiver Handouts:

Body Mechanics	371
Elbow, Forearm and Wrist Active Range of Motion	555
Elbow, Forearm and Wrist Strength Exercises	557
Elbow, Forearm and Wrist Stretches	559
Exercise Tips for Orthopedic Conditions	577
Good Posture	416
Median Nerve Glides	632
Pain Journal	456
Shoulder and Rotator Cuff Exercises Free Weight	712
Superficial Cold	480

Cubital Tunnel Syndrome - Postoperative Management
Ulnar Nerve Decompression at the Elbow

Impairments and Functional Limitations:
Post-op pain and edema
Impaired hand strength, ROM, and coordination
Rotator cuff and scapular weakness

Assessments and Rating Scales:
Manual Ability Measure (Chen & Bode 2010)
Michigan Hand Outcome Questionnaire (Chung et al., 1998)
Disabilities of the Arm, Shoulder, and Hand (Beaton et al., 2001)

Occupational Therapy Intervention:
Recommend and/or provide adaptive equipment and task modifications to reduce pain and compensate for weak grasp and incoordination. Modify carrying purses/handbags, holding phone, sleep posture, reading posture, driving posture, ADL and work ergonomics.

Progression depends on co-morbidities, surgical procedure performed, stage of healing, and postoperative complications. *Follow the referring surgeon's specific guidelines for progression.*

Stage 1: Protection

- No lifting, carrying or resistive activities until cleared by surgeon.
- Provide a long arm splint with elbow flexed to 70°-90°, forearm and wrist in neutral. Instruct how to don/doff, wear schedule and hygiene.
- Provide pain and edema management.
- Provide AROM exercises of uninvolved joints.
- Instruct in ulnar nerve glides.
- Teach joint protection techniques.

Stage 2: Active Motion

- Continue treatment as described above.
- Progress AROM exercises.
- Provide scar management.

Stage 3: Strengthening

- Progress strengthening.
- Add rotator cuff and scapular strengthening.

Cubital Tunnel Syndrome - Postoperative Management
Ulnar Nerve Decompression at the Elbow

Patient and Caregiver Handouts:

Depression

Clinical Manifestations:
Physical - unplanned and significant increase or decrease in weight, sleeping too much or too little, fatigue or loss of energy, psychomotor agitation or retardation, decline in personal hygiene
Cognitive - impaired motivation, inability to concentrate or focus, loss of interest in activities previously enjoyed, lack of future planning
Behavioral - depressed mood most of the time, feelings of guilt and worthlessness, recurrent thoughts of death or suicide

Risk Factors:
Stressful life events, examples include recent bereavement, personal injury or illness, chronic pain, divorce or separation, change in the health of a family member, retirement
Previous history of depression and/or suicide attempt(s)
Family history of major depressive disorder
Certain medicines or combination of medicines - anticonvulsants, anti-inflammatory drugs, antibiotics, Parkinson's drugs, antipsychotic medications, cardiovascular medications, hormones, sedatives, anxiolytics, stimulants, chemotherapy
Substance abuse
Living alone, being socially isolated or lacking a supportive social network
Damage to body image from amputation, SCI, burns, cancer surgery
Fear of death
Poor eating habits (may be a result of depression or due to B12 deficiency)
Lack of physical mobility

Medical Management:
Psychopharmacology
Electro Convulsive Therapy
Psychotherapy (cognitive-behavioral therapy (CBT), mindfulness-based cognitive therapy (MBCT), interpersonal psychotherapy, reminiscence therapy, brief problem-solving treatment)
Depression care management through evidence-based depression programs such as IMPACT, PEARLS and Healthy IDEAS

Assessments and Rating Scales:
Beck Depression Inventory (BDIII) (Beck et al., 1996)
Canadian Occupational Performance Measure (Law et al., 2014)
Cornell Scale for Depression in Dementia (Alexopoulos et al., 1999).
Geriatric Depression Scale (GDS) (Yesavage et al., 1983)
Occupational Performance History Interview-II (Kielhofner et al., 2004)
Patient Health Questionnaire 9 (PHQ9) (Bian et al., 2010)
Revised Interest Checklist (Scaffa 2002)

Depression

Occupational Therapy Intervention:
Therapeutic Use of Self (Mosey 1986)
- Develop a trusting relationship.
- Be fully present and engaged with the patient.
- Listen to and do not dismiss their experience of suffering.
- Provide extrinsic motivation and verbal reinforcement.
- Provide opportunities to succeed.

ADL, IADL, work and leisure training
- Treat underlying limitations to safety and independence.
- Encourage patient to carry out ADL routines.
- Assist in setting and following a realistic daily schedule, balancing self-care, productivity and leisure.
- Reinforce medication management. Assist patient in developing a system to remember antidepressant medications (pillbox, telephone reminders, lists).
- Instruct in good sleep habits.
- Address ability to shop and prepare meals.
- Teach strategies to incorporate wellness and health management routines into daily activities.

Provide psychosocial support.
- Reinforce psychotherapy and cognitive behavioral strategies.
- Facilitate life-review writing.

Promote social participation by encouraging involvement in social groups and meaningful leisure activities. Teach the use of email and social media networking sites.

Provide therapeutic exercises and activities. Incorporate increased physical activity into daily routine. Encourage participation in social exercise (walk with a friend, classes).

Encourage use of full spectrum bulbs, spending time near a sunny window or outdoors.

Educate patient and caregivers about depression and the availability of community resources. Encourage participation in support groups.

Patient and Caregiver Handouts:
Anxiety Journal 368
Daily Journal 382
Hip and Knee Exercises - Seated 615
Stress Management 477

Depression

Patient and Caregiver Handouts:

Additional Treatment Guides

De Quervain's Syndrome - Conservative Management

Impairments and Functional Limitations:
Pain and edema, along the distal wrist, at the radial styloid
Impaired grip and pinch strength
Impaired fine motor coordination
Rotator cuff and scapular weakness
Co-occurring conditions - diabetes, arthritis, acute trauma

Provocative Tests/Outcome Measures:
Disabilities of the Arm, Shoulder, and Hand (Beaton et al., 2001)
Finkelstein Test (Finkelstein 1930)
Manual Ability Measure (Chen & Bode 2010)
Michigan Hand Outcome Questionnaire (Chung et al., 1998)

Occupational Therapy Intervention:
Recommend and/or provide adaptive equipment and task modification to minimize ulnar deviation at the wrist and substitute power grip for pinch (tie shoes, button shirts, open jars, cut with scissors, needlework, use a key in a lock, hold cane or walker, write).

Provide a forearm-based thumb spica splint, removed only during AROM exercises. Instruct how to don/doff, wear schedule and hygiene.

Instruct in joint protection techniques.
- Practice good body mechanics and posture.
- Avoid repetitive motion.
- Take frequent breaks.
- Modify activities that cause symptoms.
- Instruct in injury prevention to decrease recurrence.

Provide UE therapeutic activities and exercises.
- Gentle ROM and hand/wrist stretching
- Progress to hand and wrist strengthening exercises, once symptoms are relieved.
- Add rotator cuff and scapular strengthening.

Instruct in pain self-management.
- Coordinate medication peak with exercise and activity.
- Use ice massage over radial wrist.
- Practice deep (diaphragmatic) breathing and other relaxation techniques.
- Stretch neck muscles.

De Quervain's Syndrome - Conservative Management

Patient and Caregiver Handouts:

De Quervain's Syndrome - Postoperative Management

Impairments and Functional Limitations:
Pain and edema at base of thumb
Impaired grip and pinch strength
Impaired fine motor coordination
Rotator cuff and scapular weakness
Co-occurring conditions - diabetes, arthritis, acute trauma

Outcome Measures:
Disabilities of the Arm, Shoulder, and Hand (Beaton et al., 2001)
Manual Ability Measure (Chen & Bode 2010)
Michigan Hand Outcome Questionnaire (Chung et al., 1998)

Occupational Therapy Intervention:
Recommend and/or provide adaptive equipment and task modifications to compensate for weak grasp and pinch.

Provide therapeutic activities and exercises. Progression depends on co-morbidities, surgical procedure performed, stage of healing, and postoperative complications. *Follow the referring surgeon's specific guidelines for progression.*

Stage 1: Protection
- No lifting, carrying or resistive activities until cleared by surgeon.
- Provide a forearm-based thumb spica splint, worn for 2-3 weeks. Instruct how to don/doff, wear schedule and hygiene.
- Provide pain and edema management.
- Gentle AROM exercises
- Teach joint protection techniques.

Stage 2: Active Motion
- Continue treatment as described above.
- Progress AROM exercises.
- Provide scar management.

Stage 3: Strengthening
- Progress strengthening.

De Quervain's Syndrome - Postoperative Management

Patient and Caregiver Handouts:

Diabetes - Type 2

Impairments and Functional Limitations:
ADL, IADL, productivity and leisure impairment
Functional mobility impairment
Muscle weakness
Limited activity tolerance and endurance
Impaired fine motor coordination
Peripheral neuropathy
Low vision due to diabetic retinopathy
Co-occurring conditions - retinopathy, heart disease, chronic kidney disease, PVD, stroke, peripheral neuropathy, lower extremity amputations, diabetic hand/shoulder syndrome, Charcot arthropathy

Occupational Therapy Intervention:
ADL, IADL, productivity and leisure training

- Recommend and/or provide adaptive equipment.
- Instruct in foot care and foot safety. Teach daily foot inspection and hygiene using an inspection mirror. Teach patient to perform monofilament screening for protective sensation loss.
- Reinforce healthy eating while planning and preparing meals.
- Instruct in pacing and energy conservation strategies.
- Teach compensatory techniques and safety measures for sensory deficits. Test bath/dish water temperature using the intact extremity or a thermometer. Lower the water heater temperature to 120°F (48°C). Avoid cuts and burns in kitchen. Avoid using heating pads on impaired extremities. Wear gloves to prevent frostbite. Avoid going barefoot. Wear sunscreen to prevent sunburn. Use intact hand to handle sharp kitchen utensils. Use vision to compensate for sensory loss. Perform skin checks.
- Provide compensation techniques and adaptive devices for vision loss, sensory loss and/or one-handed use, filling insulin syringes, taking oral medications, monitoring blood glucose, reading food labels, measuring controlled portions.

Train in safe and efficient functional mobility (sit to stand, bed mobility skills, transfers, wheelchair mobility, ambulation and stairs).

Provide an individualized exercise program that includes endurance, strengthening, and flexibility activities. Goal is to lower blood sugar levels, improve insulin sensitivity, and strengthen the heart.

- Monitor blood sugar 30 minutes before and immediately after exercising. A safe pre-exercise blood sugar range is 100 to 250 mg/dL. During exercise monitor for signs of low blood sugar, if blood sugar drops below 70 mg/dL, stop exercising and eat 15 to 20 grams of fast-acting carbohydrate.

Occupational Therapy TOOLKIT

Diabetes - Type 2

Occupational Therapy Intervention:
Treat diabetic hand and/or shoulder syndrome (limited joint mobility/stiff hand, Duyputren's contracture, stenosing tenosynovitis/trigger finger, carpal/cubital/radial tunnel syndromes, and adhesive capsulitis). Review applicable treatment guides.

Provide education about fall risk and prevention strategies.

Complete a comprehensive, performance-based home/work assessment. Recommend and/or provide modifications, adaptive equipment and/or assistive technology.

Reinforce the American Association of Diabetic Educators 7 *Self Care Behaviors.* (1) healthy eating, (2) being active, (3) healthy coping, (4) problem solving, (5) risk reduction, (6) monitoring (blood pressure, blood glucose, weight, activity, foot inspections and eye exams) (7) taking medication. The American Diabetes Assoc recommends A1C < 7%, blood pressure < 130/80 and LDL < 100. Consult with a Certified Diabetic Educator.

Teach strategies to incorporate wellness and health management routines into daily activities.

Educate patient and caregivers about diabetes and the availability of community resources. Encourage participation in support groups.

Patient and Caregiver Handouts:

Don't Let a Fall Get You Down - Booklet	395
Exercise Tips for Diabetes	573
Foot Care and Foot Safety	413
Putty Exercises	683
Stress Management	477
Stretch Band Exercises - Arms	749
Tips to Conserve Energy	482
Upper Body Exercises - Hand Weights	765
Upper Body Strength Activities	773

Additional Treatment Guides

Amputation of the Lower Limb	13
Fall Risk Assessment and Prevention	84
Health Management	115
Low Vision and Blindness	127
Peripheral Neuropathy	160

Dizziness

Impairments and Functional Limitations:
Gaze instability
Postural instability
Gait disorders
Physical de-conditioning
Difficulty with transitional movements (rolling, supine to sit, sit to stand, walking with certain head movements)
Difficulty moving quickly
Difficulty with dual task performance
Depression
Fall risk
Fear of falling

Symptoms and Causes of Dizziness:

- Vertigo - A sensation that the surroundings are spinning or moving exacerbated by head movement. Symptoms are episodic and paroxysmal and include nystagmus and nausea. Conditions include benign paroxysmal positional vertigo (BPPV), labyrinthitis, vestibular neuritis, head trauma, acoustic neuroma, and Meniere's disease.

- Disequilibrium - Unsteadiness, imbalance, or loss of equilibrium without an abnormal sensation in the head. Symptoms are typically worse in the dark. Symptoms usually occur during walking and disappear with sitting or lying down. Conditions include poor vision, de-conditioning, Parkinson's disease, peripheral neuropathy, effect of poly-pharmacy and drug interactions.

- Presyncope/syncope - Feeling of losing consciousness or blacking out. Cardiovascular in nature and include arrhythmias, myocardial infarction, carotid artery stenosis, supraventricular tachycardia and orthostatic hypotension.

- Lightheadedness - Vague symptoms, possibly feeling disconnected with the environment. Conditions include anxiety disorders, depression, hyperventilation syndrome and the effects of taking multiple medication and drug interactions.

Assessments:
Dizziness Handicap Inventory (Jacobson et al., 1990)
Vertigo Handicap Questionnaire (Yardley et al., 1992)
Vertigo Symptom Scale (Yardley et al., 1992)

Dizziness

Occupational Therapy Intervention:
Vertigo
- Vestibular Rehabilitation Therapy (VRT) provided by specially trained OT or PT.
- VRT is an exercise-based treatment program designed to promote vestibular adaptation and substitution.
- VRT includes canalith repositioning procedures, vertigo habituation exercises, gaze stabilization exercises, balance retraining, home safety, ADL and functional mobility training, fall prevention and patient education about the condition.

Disequilibrium
- Therapeutic exercises to increase strength, flexibility, endurance and balance.
- Train in safe and efficient functional mobility (sit to stand, bed mobility skills, transfers, standing, ambulation and wheelchair mobility) during ADL and IADL tasks.
- Fall prevention (include recommendations for good night lighting, sitting with ADLs, installing grab bars and railings)
- Modify environment to decrease noise, visual clutter, and need to perform multiple tasks at one time.

Presyncope/syncope
- Reinforce education regarding replacement of fluids, rising slowly from lying or sitting positions, sleeping with the head of the bed elevated, increasing salt intake and participating in regular exercise.

Lightheadedness
- Instruct in pursed lip breathing and stress management.

Educate patient and caregivers about dizziness and the availability of community resources. Encourage participation in support groups.

Patient and Caregiver Handouts:
Don't Let a Fall Get You Down - Booklet 395
Pursed Lip Breathing 470
Stress Management 477

Additional Treatment Guides
Balance 24
Fall Risk Assessment and Prevention 84
Functional Mobility 103
Home Safety and Modification 118
Therapeutic Exercise 195

Dressing

Dressing includes selecting appropriate clothing for the time of day, weather, and occasion. Obtain clothing from closets and drawers. Dress and undress using open-front garments (shirt/blouse, robe, sweater, jacket, winter coat), pullover garments (sweatshirt, t-shirt, sweater), bra, pants, skirts, suspenders, necktie, scarf, gloves, underwear, socks, pantyhose, nylons, shoes, boots, slippers, support and anti-embolism stockings. Open and close fasteners, (snaps, buttons, hooks, zippers, Velcro). Managing personal devices (hearing aids, eyeglasses, contacts, AFO, hand splint, back brace, slings, and prosthetics).

Impairments and Functional Limitations:
Impaired shoulder strength and/or ROM
Impaired hand strength, ROM, sensation and/or coordination
Impaired LE function
Limited activity tolerance and endurance
Impaired sitting balance
Impaired standing balance
Pain
Visual perceptual impairment
Cognitive impairment

Occupational Therapy Intervention:
Apply different approaches for solving difficulties with dressing.

- Remediate underlying limitations to safety and independence. Physical impairments (muscle weakness, impaired hand function, limited ROM, paralysis, incoordination, impaired balance, fatigue, dyspnea, abnormal tone, tremor), sensory impairment (impaired sensation, low vision, hard of hearing, vestibular, pain), behavioral, cognition, perception.
- Train in compensatory techniques (safety techniques, one-handed techniques, pacing, energy conservation, joint protection, body mechanics, breathing techniques, low vision techniques, cognitive/perceptual compensation, step-by-step instructions, task segmentation, task sequencing, backward chaining, verbal and physical cueing, hand-over-hand guiding).
- Train in the use of adaptive equipment and assistive devices (buttonhook, Velcro closures on shoes, elastic shoelaces, long handled shoehorn, dressing stick, reacher, sock aid, zipper pull, loops on pants, loops on socks, labeling system for identifying clothes, and specialized clothing).
- Provide environmental modifications and adaptations (avoid storing items on the floor, lower closet poles, organize clothes within easy reach, and label drawers using picture or words).

Dressing

Occupational Therapy Intervention:
Apply different approaches for solving difficulties with dressing (continued).

- Instruct in activity modification.
    - Change the task (place the weaker extremity into the garment first, dress in a supine position).
    - Eliminate part or all of the task (choose garments that are easy to put on and remove such as: elastic waist pants, loose fitting tops, pullover tops, suspenders instead of a belt, Velcro shoes, slip on shoes, front hook bra, sports bra, camisole).
    - Have someone else do part or the entire task.

Train in safe and efficient functional mobility (sit to stand, bed mobility skills, transfers, standing, ambulation, and wheelchair mobility) during dressing tasks.

Provide caregiver/family education and training.

Patient and Caregiver Handouts:

Occupational Therapy TOOLKIT

Dressing

Patient and Caregiver Handouts:

Driving

Driver of a vehicle (car, van, SUV, or truck) with or without structural modifications, adapted driving equipment, or both. Transfer to and out of vehicle, fasten and unfasten seatbelt, adjust mirrors, start ignition, operate controls, open and close car doors, trunk, and hood, store wheelchairs and ambulation devices, pump gas. Has the physical, cognitive and perception abilities for driving.

Impairments and Functional Limitations:
Impaired physical function
Vision loss
Perceptual impairment
Cognitive impairment
Medication side effects (sedation, hypoglycemia, blurred vision, hypotension, dizziness, syncope or loss of coordination)

Assessments:
Generalist - Reviews driving and community mobility goals and needs on the initial evaluation, make referrals to a driving specialist. Available screening tools include:

- AAA Roadwise Review
- Driving Decisions Workbook, UM Transportation Research Institute
- Fitness-to-Drive Screening Measure, University of Florida
- Physician's Guide to Assessing and Counseling Older Drivers, American Medical Association
- Trail Making Test - Part A and B
- Useful Field of Vision Test (Wood et al., 2014)
- Vision - contrast sensitivity

Driving specialist - Provides a comprehensive evaluation including clinical and behind-the-wheel assessments.

- OT-Driver Off Road Assessment (OT-DORA) Battery (Unsworth et al., 2011)

Occupational Therapy Intervention:
Apply different approaches for solving difficulties.

- Remediate underlying limitations to safety and independence. Physical impairments (muscle weakness, impaired hand function, limited ROM, paralysis, incoordination, impaired balance, fatigue, dyspnea, abnormal tone, tremor), sensory impairment (impaired sensation, low vision, hard of hearing, vestibular, pain), behavioral, cognition, perception.
- Provide education and training to improve driving ability.
    - AAA Mature Driver Safety Course
    - CarFit
    - AARP Driver Safety Online Course

Driving

Occupational Therapy Intervention:

- Train in compensatory techniques. One-handed techniques and low vision compensation.
- Train in the use of adaptive equipment and modifications.
  - Simple (key extenders, leveraging devices, swivel seat cushion, seat cushion, leg lifter, steering wheel covers, extendable visors, handy bar, seat belt adapters, car lifts and carrying devices for a wheelchair or a scooter).
  - Complex - recommended and trained by a Driver Rehab Specialist (hand controls for the brakes and accelerator, pedal extenders, left-foot accelerator pedal, panoramic mirrors, convex mirrors, steering wheel knobs, turn-signal crossovers).
- Instruct in task modification (change the task, eliminate part or all of the task or have someone else do part or the entire task).
  - Modifying when and how to drive (only on back roads, during daylight, avoid left-turns, not during rush hour, or bad weather).
  - Exploring alternative transportation options (rides with family and friends, taxicabs, para-transit services, public transportation, walk).

Patient and Caregiver Handouts:

Epicondylitis - Conservative Management

Lateral epicondylitis, also called tennis elbow
Medial epicondylitis, also called golfer's elbow

Impairments and Functional Limitations:
Pain at the lateral or medial epicondyle and respective muscle origins
Muscle weakness especially for gripping
Co-occurring conditions - diabetes, arthritis, rotator cuff pathology, de Quervain's tenosynovitis, and carpal tunnel syndrome

Provocative Tests/Outcome Measures:
Disabilities of the Arm, Shoulder, and Hand (Beaton et al., 2001)
Lateral epicondylitis - pain increases with resisted wrist extension and radial deviation
Medial epicondylitis - pain increases with resisted wrist flexion or forearm pronation
Patient-Rated Tennis Elbow Evaluation (PRTEE) (MacDermid 2005)

Occupational Therapy Intervention:
Recommend and/or provide adaptive equipment and task modifications to prevent pain and avoid repetitive elbow, forearm and wrist motion. Activities that cause pain include making a fist, gripping a doorknob, lifting heavy objects, typing, using computer mouse and keyboard, painting, carpentry, knitting, sports such as tennis and golf.

Provide a forearm band (counter-force brace) during activity. Instruct to wear the forearm band distal to the flexor or extensor muscle group origin. Elbow sleeves worn at rest. Consider a wrist splint as needed for extremely symptomatic patients.

Provide pain management.
- Ultrasound
- Soft tissue mobilization, friction massage
- Elastic therapeutic tape

Instruct in pain self-management strategies.
- Coordinate medication peak with exercise and activity.
- Apply superficial cold.
- Practice deep (diaphragmatic) breathing and other relaxation techniques.
- Instruct in using a pain journal.
- Utilize the problem solving process to identify ways to manage pain.
- Stretch neck muscles.

Epicondylitis - Conservative Management

Occupational Therapy Intervention:
Instruct in joint protection techniques.
- Practice good body mechanics and posture.
- Avoid repetitive upper extremity motion.
- Take frequent breaks.
- Modify activities that cause symptoms.
- Instruct in injury prevention to decrease recurrence.

Provide therapeutic activities and exercises.
- Start with gentle elbow/forearm/wrist stretching.
- Progress to elbow/forearm/wrist strengthening when pain-free.
- Add rotator cuff and scapula strengthening.

Patient and Caregiver Handouts:

Fall Risk Assessment and Prevention

Health risk factors include low vision, chronic medical conditions (arthritis, stroke, Parkinson's disease, CHF), postural hypotension, taking four or more medications, recent illness, or admission to hospital, cognitive impairment, dizziness, muscle weakness, balance problems, walking difficulty, and foot disorders.

Environmental risk factors include unsafe floor coverings, lack of handrails on stairs, poor lighting, clutter on the floor, unsafe furniture, throw rugs, slippery surfaces in bathroom, lack of grab bars.

Behavioral risk factors include fear of falling, lack of concentration, carrying something while using stairs, not using the handrails, wearing unsuitable footwear, physical inactivity, climbing on chairs to reach high items, rushing to answer the phone or to the bathroom, wearing clothing that are too long, taking high-risk medications (psychotropic, cardiovascular meds, diuretics, hypnotics, antidepressants, anti-anxiety), using a mobility device that is in poor condition or is not the correct height.

Assessments:
Activities-specific Balance Confidence Scale (ABC) (Powell et al., 1995)
Beers List of Potentially Inappropriate Medications for the Elderly
Berg Balance Scale (Berg 1989) [risk score 0-20 = high, 21-40 = medium, 41-56 = low]
Foot screening (footwear, protective sensation, pain)
Four Step Square (Dite et al., 2007) [≥ 15 seconds = increased risk]
Functional Reach (Duncan 1990) [6-10 inches = moderate risk, 0-6 inches =high risk]
Gait Speed (Fritz 2010) [< 4.5 meters/sec.]
Geriatric Depression Scale (Parmelee & Katz 1990)
Home Safety and Performance Assessment
Measurement of ROM, flexibility, muscle strength
Mini Mental States Examination (MMSE) (Folstein 1975)
Modified Falls Efficacy Scale (MFES) (Hill et al., 1996) [< 8 = increased risk]
One Leg Stand [≤ 12 seconds]
Sensory assessment
Tandem Stand [≤ 30 seconds]
Timed Get Up and Go (TUG) (Podsiadlo et al., 1991) [≥ 15 seconds = increased risk]
Tinetti Assessment Tool (Tinetti 1986) [< 19 of 28]
Vestibular assessment
Vital signs

Occupational Therapy Intervention:
Provide a multi-factorial fall intervention program that includes the following:

Provide education about the factors that increase risk for falling and how to analyze falls.

Fall Risk Assessment and Prevention

Occupational Therapy Intervention:
Treat underlying limitations to safety and independence - physical (strength, hand function, ROM, coordination, balance, endurance, abnormal tone), sensory (tactile, vision, hearing, vestibular, pain), behavioral, cognition and/or perception.

Train ADL, IADL, productivity and leisure and functional mobility tasks with emphasis on safety, balance confidence and fall prevention.

- Train in safe use of mobility devices and ensure correct fit and condition.
- Train in low vision techniques as appropriate.
- Instruct in safe footwear and clothing. Choose shoes that are well fitting and supportive, have a thin, textured and slip-resistance sole, secure with laces or Velcro closures, and have a low, broad heel. Avoid shoes without heel support, shoes with thick soles, loose slip-ons that are not supportive or secure, and avoid heels greater than 1 inch. Avoid robes, gowns, and pants that are too long. Avoid wide sleeves and loose pockets that may catch on handrails ends, cabinet knobs or doorknobs.

Provide therapeutic exercises to improve balance and strength. Instruct to incorporate physical activity into daily routine.

Provide functional balance activities to increase balance confidence and reduce fear of falling.

Educate about the common triggers for falls and prevention strategies.

Teach how to fall safely (keep elbows and knees bent not rigid, protect your head, land on muscle, roll with the fall), and how to recover from a fall.

Educate in modifying behavioral risk factors.

Recommend protective items as appropriate. (Helmet, hip protectors, knee pads, and elbow pads).

Assess for foot problems and evaluate protective foot sensation using a Semmes Weinstein 10-gram (5.07) monofilament. Refer to podiatrist if needed.

Educate about the relationship between taking four or more medications and/or high-risk medications and falls. Recommend a medication review by a physician or pharmacist.

Complete a comprehensive, performance-based home assessment. Recommend home and activity modifications.

Occupational Therapy TOOLKIT

Fall Risk Assessment and Prevention

Patient and Caregiver Handouts:

Additional Treatment Guides:

Therapist Resources:

Feeding, Eating, and Swallowing

Feeding or pre-oral phase includes anticipation, salivation, positioning self for feeding, setting-up the meal, using utensils and tableware (fork, spoon, knife, cup, glassware, mug, bottle, plate, bowl), bringing soft food, solid food and liquids to the mouth with fingers or utensils, eating and drinking adequate amount, finishes meal in a reasonable period of time

Eating or oral phase includes removing food from utensils using the lips, sealing lips to keeps food/liquid in mouth, chewing, forming food into a bolus, moving the bolus to the back of the tongue

Swallowing or pharyngeal phase involuntary control as the bolus moves into the throat and triggers the swallow reflex. The vocal cords close, the larynx rises and the epiglottis closes over airway

Esophageal phase involuntary control as the bolus move down the esophagus to the stomach

Impairments and Functional Limitations:

Impaired hip, trunk, neck, shoulder strength, ROM, sensation and/or coordination
Impaired elbow, wrist, hand strength, ROM, sensation and/or coordination
Impaired facial, lip, tongue, jaw, throat muscle strength, ROM, sensation, and/or coordination
Limited activity tolerance, endurance and/or respiratory capacity
Visual perceptual impairment
Cognitive impairment
Loss of taste and smell
Loss of teeth
Dry mouth
Delayed or absent swallow reflex, reduced pharyngeal peristalsis, unilateral pharyngeal weakness, reduced laryngeal elevation and/or closure, cricopharyngeal dysfunction
Co-occurring conditions include stroke, head injury, ALS, MS, cerebral palsy, Parkinson's disease, dementia, head and neck cancer, COPD, GERD, malnutrition, aspiration pneumonia, dehydration

Assessments:

Oral stage - bedside examination
Pharyngeal and esophageal stage - Fiber-optic Endoscopic Evaluation of Swallow or Videofluoroscopic Swallowing Study

Feeding Intervention - Pre-oral Phase

- Remediate underlying limitations to safety and independence. Physical impairments (muscle weakness, impaired hand function, limited ROM, paralysis, incoordination, impaired balance, fatigue, dyspnea, abnormal tone, tremor), sensory impairment (impaired sensation, low vision, hard of hearing, vestibular, pain), behavioral, cognition, perception.

Feeding, Eating, and Swallowing

Feeding Intervention - Pre-oral Phase (continued)

- Provide environmental modifications and adaptations (contrast tableware and surface, avoid busy patterns and clutter, adjust table heights, provide a quiet environment and minimize distractions, adequate lighting with reduced glare, food that is visually appealing, discourage talking while eating).
- Train in the use of adaptive equipment and assistive devices (adapted cups or mugs, long straws, straw holders, u-cuff, cylindrical foam, non-slip matting, scoop dish, plate guard, positioning supports, overhead sling).
- Instruct to wear eyeglasses and hearing aids during mealtime.
- Instruct in proper positioning for safe swallowing and self-feeding.
- Train in compensatory feeding techniques (one-handed techniques, pacing, energy conservation, joint protection, low vision techniques, cognitive/perceptual compensation, step-by-step instructions, task segmentation, task sequencing, backward chaining, verbal and tactile cueing, hand-over-hand guiding).
- If fatigue is a factor, eat the largest meal early in the day or eat several small meals during the day. Chop or mince solid foods.
- Instruct patient and/or caregiver in performing proper oral hygiene after each meal.
- Train caregiver on how to feed another person safely. Instruct caregiver in the signs and symptoms of aspiration.

Eating Intervention - Oral Phase (performed by therapists with advanced training)

- Facial, lip, jaw, tongue, and tongue-base muscle strengthening and ROM exercises.
- Modify food textures and thicken liquids.
- Train in strategies to reduce residual food in the mouth (tongue sweep, alternate solids/liquids, alternate cold/hot foods, multiple swallow, place food on unimpaired side, smaller food amount, slow down rate of eating).

Swallowing Intervention - Pharyngeal Phase (performed by therapists with advanced training)

- Provide thermal-tactile oral stimulation techniques.
- Provide neuromuscular electrical stimulation (NMES).
- Instruct in head and neck postures (head back, chin tuck, head rotated toward involved side, head tilt away from involved side, side-lying).
- Instruct in airway protection strategies (post-swallow throat clearing, double swallow, supraglottic swallow, super supraglottic swallow, Mendelsohn maneuver, effortful swallow).
- Provide exercises for vocal fold adduction.
- Instruct in Shaker head lift exercise.

Occupational Therapy TOOLKIT

Feeding, Eating, and Swallowing

Patient and Caregiver Handouts:

Additional Treatment Guides:

Occupational Therapy TOOLKIT

Financial and Mail Management

Managing finances and mail includes recognizes coins and bills, manipulating coins and bills, make and receive change, simple addition and subtraction, writing checks, balancing checkbook, depositing and withdrawing money, using ATM machine, using online banking, paying bills, budgeting, estimating cost, accessing mailbox, carrying letters and packages, opening letter and packages, using objects (scissors, ruler, paper clips, stapler, pencil sharpener), tasks are performed timely.

Impairments and Functional Limitations:
Impaired hand strength, ROM, sensation and/or coordination
Visual perceptual impairment
Cognitive impairment

Occupational Therapy Intervention:
Apply different approaches for solving difficulties with managing finances.

- Remediate underlying limitations to safety and independence. Physical impairments (muscle weakness, impaired hand function, limited ROM, paralysis, incoordination, impaired balance, fatigue, dyspnea, abnormal tone, tremor), sensory impairment (impaired sensation, low vision, hard of hearing, vestibular, pain), behavioral, cognition, perception.
- Train in compensatory techniques (safety techniques, one-handed techniques, low vision techniques, cognitive/perceptual compensation).
- Train in the use of adaptive equipment and assistive devices (low vision aids, using a reacher to pick up the newspaper, moving the location of the mailbox).
- Instruct in activity modification.
  - Change the task (use online banking, read the newspaper online).
  - Eliminate part or the entire task (automatic deposits, bank by mail).
  - Have someone else do part or the entire task (let someone else manage finances and mail).

Fracture of the Elbow (Radial Head, Olecranon and/or Distal Humerus)

Impairments and Functional Limitations:
ADL, IADL, productivity and leisure impairment
Functional mobility impairment
Muscle weakness
Limited elbow ROM
Pain and edema
Weight bearing restrictions
Potential complications - elbow flexion contracture, ulnar nerve damage, heterotopic ossification

Assessments:
Disabilities of the Arm, Shoulder, and Hand (Beaton et al., 2001)
Michigan Hand Outcome Questionnaire (Chung et al., 1998)
Patient-Rated Elbow Evaluation (MacDermid & Michlovitz 2006)

Occupational Therapy Intervention:
ADL, IADL, productivity and leisure training

- Train in one-handed techniques and adherence to weight-bearing restrictions during ADL tasks.
- Recommend and/or provide adaptive equipment and task modifications to compensate for non-use of affected arm.

Train in safe and efficient functional mobility (sit to stand, bed mobility skills, transfers, standing, ambulation and wheelchair mobility) with adherence to upper extremity weight bearing restrictions.

Provide activities and exercises for all uninvolved joints to prevent loss of ROM and strength.

Provide orthotic as indicated. Instruct how to don/doff, wear schedule and hygiene.

Once fracture is stable, provide progressive elbow and forearm activities and exercises. Progression depends on co-morbidities, type of injury, stage of healing, surgical intervention, and complications. *Follow the referring physician's specific guidelines for progression.*

Provide pain management and edema control techniques.

- PAM's as indicated
- Compression, elevation, massage
- Manual Edema Mobilization

Fracture of the Elbow
(Radial Head, Olecranon and/or Distal Humerus)

Occupational Therapy Intervention:
Instruct in pain self-management.
- Coordinate medication peak with exercise and activity.
- Apply superficial cold.
- Practice deep (diaphragmatic) breathing and other relaxation techniques.
- Gently stretch neck muscles.
- Position arm properly.

Complete a comprehensive, performance-based home assessment. Recommend and/or provide modifications, adaptive equipment and/or assistive technology.

Provide education about fall risk and prevention strategies.

Patient and Caregiver Handouts:

Additional Treatment Guides:

Therapist Resources:

Fracture of the Hip (Proximal Femur)

Surgical repair - open reduction with internal fixation (ORIF) or hip arthroplasty

Impairments and Functional Limitations:
ADL, IADL, productivity and leisure impairment
Functional mobility impairment
Muscle weakness
Limited hip ROM
Pain and edema
Weight bearing restrictions
Co-occurring conditions - osteoarthritis, osteoporosis, metastatic cancer
Potential complications - fall risk, DVT's

Occupational Therapy Intervention:
ADL, IADL, productivity and leisure training

- Apply weight bearing restrictions.
- Adaptive equipment training for toileting, bathing and LE dressing (including anti-embolism stockings) to compensate for restricted hip ROM. (Shower chair, grab bars, non-slip mat, hand-held shower, long bath sponge, raised toilet seat, bedside commode, leg lifter, reacher, sock aid, shoe horn, elastic shoelaces, dressing stick, walker bag or tray).

Train in safe and efficient functional mobility (sit to stand, bed mobility skills, transfers, standing, ambulation and wheelchair mobility) with adherence to weight bearing restrictions.

- Instruct in safe walker use and transporting items.
- Monitor cardiac status during ambulation. Amount of energy required to perform limited weight bearing is 30 to 50% greater than normal ambulation.

Provide therapeutic activities and exercises.

- Strengthen upper body for walker/cane usage.
- Progress sitting and standing tolerance during ADLs and mobility
- Increase balance confidence with ADL tasks.

Complete a comprehensive, performance-based home assessment. Recommend and/or provide modifications, adaptive equipment and/or assistive technology.

Provide education about fall risk and prevention strategies.

Patient and Caregiver Handouts:
Upper Body Exercises - Hand Weights 765

Fracture of the Hip (Proximal Femur)

Additional Treatment Guides:

Therapist Resources:

Fracture of the Shoulder (Proximal Humerus)

Involves the articular surface, greater tuberosity, less tuberosity and/or surgical neck

Impairments and Functional Limitations:
ADL, IADL, productivity and leisure impairment
Functional mobility impairment
Muscle weakness
Limited shoulder ROM
Pain and edema
Immobilization and weight bearing restrictions
Co-occurring conditions - arthritis, osteoporosis
Potential complications - nerve injury, rotator cuff injury, fall risk

Occupational Therapy Intervention:
ADL, IADL, productivity and leisure training

- Train in one-handed techniques and adaptive equipment while adhering to immobilization and weight bearing restrictions.
- Instruct in axillary hygiene, donning and doffing of shoulder sling/immobilizer and cryotherapy, and proper arm positioning during sitting and supine.

Train in safe and efficient functional mobility (sit to stand, bed mobility skills, transfers, standing, wheelchair mobility, ambulation and stairs) while adhering to shoulder immobilization and weight bearing restrictions.

Provide activities and exercises for all uninvolved joints to prevent loss of ROM and strength.

Once fracture is stable, provide progressive shoulder activities and exercises to increase ROM and strength. Progression depends on co-morbidities, type of injury, stage of healing, surgical intervention, and complications. *Follow the referring physician's specific guidelines for progression.*

Instruct in pain self-management.

- Coordinate medication peak with exercise and activity.
- Apply superficial cold.
- Practice deep (diaphragmatic) breathing and other relaxation techniques.

Complete a comprehensive, performance-based home assessment. Recommend and/or provide modifications, adaptive equipment and/or assistive technology.

Provide education about fall risk and prevention strategies.

Occupational Therapy TOOLKIT

Fracture of the Shoulder (Proximal Humerus)

Patient and Caregiver Handouts:

Additional Treatment Guides:

Therapist Resources:

Fracture of the Wrist (Distal Radius)

Colles' fracture - radial and dorsal displacement
Smith's fracture - volar displacement

Impairments and Functional Limitations:
ADL, IADL, productivity and leisure impairment
Functional mobility impairment
Muscle weakness
Limited wrist ROM
Pain and edema
Immobilization and weight bearing restrictions
Potential complications - carpal tunnel syndrome, triangular fibrocartilage complex lesions, extensor tendons rupture, regional complex pain syndrome

Assessments and Rating Scales:
Disabilities of the Arm, Shoulder, and Hand (Beaton et al., 2001)
Manual Abilities Measure (MAM) (Chen & Bode 2010)

Occupational Therapy Intervention:
ADL, IADL, productivity and leisure training with one-handed techniques and adaptive equipment with adherence to weight bearing restrictions

Train in safe and efficient functional mobility (sit to stand, bed mobility skills, transfers, standing, ambulation and wheelchair mobility) with adherence to weight bearing restrictions.

While Immobilized:

- Control edema and pain.
- Provide activities and exercises for all uninvolved joints to prevent loss of ROM and strength (neck, shoulder, elbow, fingers).
- Encourage normal arm swing when walking.

Once Cast Removed:

- Provide wrist splint per surgeon protocol.
- Provide thermal modalities (moist heat, paraffin) and joint mobilization.
- Once fracture is stable, provide progressive wrist and forearm activities and exercises. Progression depends on co-morbidities, type of injury, stage of healing, surgical intervention, and complications. *Follow the referring physician's specific guidelines for progression.*
- Provide scar management (moist heat, scar massage, silicone gel at night, desensitization).

Fracture of the Wrist (Distal Radius)

Occupational Therapy Intervention:
Complete a comprehensive, performance-based home assessment. Recommend and/or provide modifications, adaptive equipment and/or assistive technology.

Provide education about fall risk and prevention strategies.

Patient and Caregiver Handouts:

Additional Treatment Guides:

Therapist Resources:

Occupational Therapy TOOLKIT

Frailty and Debility

Impairments and Functional Limitations:
ADL, IADL, productivity and leisure impairment
Functional mobility impairment
Slow walking speed
Muscle weakness
Limited activity tolerance and endurance
Impaired balance
Impaired vision and hearing
Chronic pain
Advanced age, 80+
Co-occurring conditions - functional decline, falls, fear of falling, delirium, dementia, dizziness, depression, incontinence, sleep disorders, malnutrition, dehydration, pressure ulcers, sarcopenia, hypothermia, and hyperthermia

Assessments:
6 Minute Walk Test (Enright et al., 1998)
Berg Balance Scale (Berg 1989)
Geriatric Depression Scale (Parmelee & Katz 1990)
Mini Mental State Exam MMSE (Folstein 1975)
Nutrition Screening Initiative (White et al., 1992)
Physical Performance Test (Lusardi et al., 2004)
Timed 10-Meter Walk Test (Bohannon et al., 1996)

Occupational Therapy Intervention:
ADL, IADL, productivity and leisure training

- Treat underlying limitations to safety and independence - physical (strength, hand function, ROM, coordination, balance, endurance, abnormal tone), sensory (tactile, vision, hearing, vestibular, pain), behavioral, cognition and/or perceptual.
- Address nutritional health - oral health, ability to feed self, ability to shop, access kitchen, prepare nutritious meals and get adequate hydration. Encourage to eat with others.
- Address ability to drive safely. Provide referral to driving rehab specialist and/or explore alternative transportation options.

Train in safe and efficient functional mobility (sit to stand, bed mobility skills, transfers, standing, ambulation and wheelchair mobility) during ADL and IADL tasks.

- Train in the safe and correct use of assistive devices and adaptive equipment (walkers, canes, sliding boards, bed transfer handles, leg lifters, wheelchairs) as appropriate.

Frailty and Debility

Occupational Therapy Intervention:
Provide an individualized exercise program that includes progressive endurance, strengthening and flexibility activities.

Recommend the use of an activity tracker.
Instruct patient and caregiver in a written home exercise program.

Provide functional balance activities to increase balance confidence with ADL tasks.

Provide pain management.

Provide a fall prevention program that includes balance, coordination and agility training and education about fall risk and prevention strategies.

Complete a comprehensive, performance-based home assessment. Recommend and/or provide modifications, adaptive equipment and/or assistive technology.

Educate about the negative effects of prolonged sitting and bed rest. Educate regarding hypothermia and hyperthermia prevention.

Patient and Caregiver Handouts:
Balance Exercise Guidelines 519
Balance Exercises - Sitting 520
Balance Exercises - Standing 523
Hip and Knee Exercises - Seated 615
Putty Exercises 683
Stretch Band Exercises - Arms 749
Upper Body Exercises - Hand Weights 765
Walking Guidelines 784

Additional Treatment Guides:
Activities of Daily Living 3
Balance 24
Chronic/Persistent Pain Syndrome 53
Fall Risk Assessment and Prevention 84
Functional Mobility 103
Home Safety and Modification 118
Pressure Ulcers 164
Rest and Sleep 166
Therapeutic Exercise 195
Urinary Incontinence 205

Functional Communication

Functional speaking includes verbally communicating basic needs.
Functional writing includes holding a pen/pencil/stylus, signing name on documents, writing cards and letters, addressing envelopes, maintaining an address book and calendar, writing checks, completing doctor office forms or job applications, writing grocery, shopping lists and to-do lists, writing in a journal, word puzzles.
Functional reading includes seeing the print, holding reading material, obtaining information from medicine labels, food labels, cooking instructions, the newspaper, phone book, TV guide, street signs, the mail, a menu, maps, appliance controls, TV remote.
Functional hearing includes one-to-one conversations, hearing the phone, doorbell, alarm clock, smoke/CO2 detector low battery alert and alarm.
Using communication devices - Telephone use includes obtaining and dialing phone numbers, using emergency numbers (911, 311), managing emergency response systems, holding the phone, phone placement, answering the phone on time. Computer/tablet/ cell phone use includes powering on and off, using keyboard and mouse, viewing the screen, using programs and apps, charging device. Augmentative and alternative communication systems

Impairments and Functional Limitations:
Impaired hand strength, ROM, sensation and/or coordination
Visual perceptual impairment
Cognitive impairment
Aphasia, dysarthria

Occupational Therapy Intervention:
Apply different approaches for solving difficulties with functional communication.

- Remediate underlying limitations to safety and independence. Physical impairments (muscle weakness, impaired hand function, limited ROM, paralysis, incoordination, impaired balance, fatigue, dyspnea, abnormal tone, tremor), sensory impairment (impaired sensation, low vision, hard of hearing, vestibular, pain), behavioral, cognition, perception.
- Train in compensatory techniques (one-handed techniques, low vision techniques, cognitive/perceptual compensation, step-by-step instructions, sign language and gestures).
- Train in the use of adaptive equipment and assistive devices.
    - Speaking (low tech and high tech devices, augmentative & alternative communication systems, typewriters, keyboards)
    - Writing (individual writing aids, voice-activated tape recorders)
    - Reading (magnifiers, large-print books, reading machines, adequate lighting, page-turners, book holders, audio books)

Functional Communication

Occupational Therapy Intervention:

- Train in the use of adaptive equipment and assistive devices (continued).
  - Telephone (use cordless phone or cell phone, large buttons and numbers, one-touch dialing, speakerphones, headsets, receiver holder, handset amplifier, captioned telephone).
  - Computer/tablet/cell phone (typing sticks, screen magnifiers, large print keyboard, voice recognition software, mouth stick, head pointer).
- Instruct in activity modification.
  - Provide modification to computer/tablet/cell phone by accessing the keyboard and mouse settings and accessibility/ease of access features.

Additional Treatment Guides:

Handwriting 113

Functional Mobility

Functional mobility is moving from one position or place to another during everyday activities and includes:

Bed mobility - Move upward in supine, move downward in supine, move side to side in supine, bridge, roll from supine to side-lying, roll from side lying to supine, maintain side lying, roll from supine to prone, roll from prone to supine, move from supine to long sitting, move from supine to sit at edge of bed, move from sit at edge of bed to supine, scoot along the edge of bed, tolerate sitting at edge of bed. Perform all bed mobility tasks to the right/left side or strong/weak side.

Transfers - Sit-to-stand, stand-to-sit, stand-pivot transfers, sit-pivot transfers, slide board transfers, dependent, mechanical lift transfers. Transfers to and from all surfaces (bed, chair, wheelchair, tub, toilet, shower, floor, and car). Perform all transfers to the right/left side or strong/weak side.

Ambulation - With or without assistive devices (cane, crutch, walker) and/or orthotic or prosthetic device. Walk forward, walk backward, side stepping, turn in place, turn to the left, turn to the right, turn in a circle, tandem walk, braid walking, walk on even and uneven terrain, walk on soft terrain (grass, sand, gravel), change speed, change direction, walk up ramp, walk down ramp, manage curb cuts, manage hills, manage slopes to the right and left, open and close doors, negotiate over/around obstacles, ascend and descend stairs (step-by-step and step-over-step) ascend and descend curbs, negotiate elevators and escalators.

Manual wheelchair mobility - Lock brakes, manage footrests, manage armrests, propel forward, propel backward, stops, turn to the left, turn to the right, 180-degree turn, 360-degree turn, negotiate obstacles, open and close doors, move through doorways, move over thresholds, move up and down ramps, ascend and descend curbs and slopes. Advanced skills include move over uneven terrain, move over soft terrain (grass, sand, gravel), perform stationary wheelies, turn in place while performing a wheelie, descend inclines, curbs and stairs from wheelie position, fold and unfold wheelchair.

Power wheelchair or scooter mobility - Manage controls, manage footrests, manage armrests, move forward, move backward, stops, turn to the left, turn to the right, 180-degree turn, 360-degree turn, negotiate obstacles, open and close doors, move through doorways, move over thresholds, move up and down ramps, able to charge battery.

Reach from sitting and standing positions. Reach forward, backward, up overhead, to the side, and to the floor.

Carry objects during mobility tasks.

Impairments and Functional Limitations:

Impaired strength, tone, sensation, coordination and/or ROM
Limited activity tolerance and endurance
Impaired balance
Pain

Impairments and Functional Limitations: continued
Dyspnea
Visual perceptual and cognitive impairment

Occupational Therapy Intervention:
Apply different approaches for solving difficulties with functional mobility.
- Remediate underlying limitations to safety and independence. Physical impairments (muscle weakness, impaired hand function, limited ROM, paralysis, incoordination, impaired balance, fatigue, dyspnea, abnormal tone, tremor), sensory impairment (impaired sensation, low vision, hard of hearing, vestibular, pain), behavioral, cognition, perception.
- Train in compensatory techniques (safety techniques, one-handed techniques, energy conservation, joint protection, weight-shifting/repositioning, body mechanics, low vision techniques, cognitive/perceptual compensation, step-by-step instructions, task segmentation, task sequencing, verbal and physical cueing).
- Provide and train in the use of adaptive equipment and assistive devices. ane, crutches, walker, rollators, manual wheelchair, power-assist wheelchairs, motorized scooters, power wheelchair, transfer board, walker basket or tray, leg lifter, bed handle, bedside commode, bed support frame, satin bed sheets to reduce friction, toilet safety frame, raised toilet seat, bed/chair riser, transfer belt, shower chair/bench, overhead transfer systems, rolling commode chair).
- Provide environmental modifications and adaptations (ramps, stair glides, raise/lower height of bed, chair or sofa, use a firmer mattress, place solid support under sofa/chair cushions, remove shower doors, widen doorways).
- Instruct in activity modification.
    - Change the task (take the stairs one-step at a time, scoot up/down the stairs on bottom).
    - Eliminate part or the entire task (use bedside commode, use stair glide).
    - Have someone else do part or the entire task (mechanical lift transfers).

Provide caregiver/family education and training in body mechanics, proper transfer techniques. Encourage participation in an exercise program.

Patient and Caregiver Handouts:
Adaptive Equipment

Occupational Therapy TOOLKIT

Functional Mobility

Patient and Caregiver Handouts:

Ambulation

Bed Mobility

Stairs

Functional Mobility

Patient and Caregiver Handouts:

Transfers

Occupational Therapy TOOLKIT

Generalized Anxiety Disorder

Clinical Manifestations:
Body reactions - nervous, restless, fatigue, muscle tension, pounding, racing or abnormal heartbeat, sweaty palms
Thoughts - racing or unwanted thoughts, poor concentration, irrational fear of being out of control or of the unknown, fearful thoughts about the future/reoccurrence of an illness
Behaviors - hypervigilant, excessive or unreasonable worry, difficulty sleeping/relaxing, avoid situations that cause anxiety, disrupts all activities
Emotions - feeling irritable or anger, feeling fearful, feeling apprehension or dread
Co-occurring - depression, chronic conditions, substance abuse

Medical Treatment:
Psychopharmacology
Psychotherapy - including cognitive-behavioral treatment (CBT),
Mindfulness-based cognitive- behavioral therapy (M-CBT), social skills training

Assessments and Rating Scales:
Canadian Occupational Performance Measure (Law et al., 2014)
Generalized Anxiety Disorder (GAD-7) (Spitzer et al., 2006)

Occupational Therapy Intervention:
Therapeutic Use of Self (Mosey 1986).

- Develop a trusting relationship.
- Be fully present and engaged with the patient.
- Listen to and do not dismiss their experience of suffering.
- Provide extrinsic motivation and verbal reinforcement.
- Provide opportunities to succeed.

ADL, IADL, productivity and leisure training

- Treat underlying limitations to safety and independence.
- Assist in setting and following a realistic daily schedule, balancing self-care, productivity and leisure.
- Reinforce medication management. Assist patient in developing a system to remember medications (pillbox, telephone reminders, lists).
- Instruct in good sleep habits.
- Teach strategies to incorporate wellness and health management routines into daily activities.

Provide psychosocial support.

- Reinforce psychotherapy and cognitive behavioral strategies.

Generalized Anxiety Disorder

Occupational Therapy Intervention:
Teach strategies for managing anxiety.

- Encourage the use of an anxiety journal.
- Assist patient to plan for situations that may trigger anxiety.
- Teach patent to identify and challenge unhealthy thoughts.
- Assist patient in developing strategies to reduce anxiety.
- Teach action planning, SMART goals and problem solving.
- Teach stress management and relaxation techniques.

Promote social participation by encouraging involvement in social groups and meaningful leisure activities. Teach the use of email and social media networking sites.

Provide therapeutic exercises and activities. Incorporate increased physical activity into daily routine. Encourage participation in social exercise (walk with a friend, classes).

Educate patient and caregivers about anxiety disorders and the availability of community resources. Encourage participation in support groups.

Patient and Caregiver Handouts:
Anxiety Journal 368
SMART Goals 472
SMART Goals - Action Plan 473
Stress Management 477

Additional Treatment Guides
Depression 66
Health Management 115
Medication Management 135
Rest and Sleep 166

Grooming and Oral Hygiene

Grooming includes obtaining and using supplies, removing body hair (using razors, tweezers, lotions, etc.), applying and removing make-up, washing, drying, combing/brushing, styling head and facial hair, caring for finger and toenails, applying body lotion, applying deodorant, blowing nose. Oral hygiene includes obtaining and using supplies, opening toothpaste and mouthwash, using toothpaste and mouthwash, flossing, brushing teeth/dentures/partials, removing and reinserting dentures/partials.

Impairments and Functional Limitations:
Impaired trunk, UE strength and/or ROM
Impaired hand strength, ROM, sensation and/or coordination
Limited activity tolerance and endurance
Impaired sitting and/or standing balance
Visual perceptual and/or cognitive impairment

Occupational Therapy Intervention:
Apply different approaches for solving difficulties with grooming and oral hygiene.

- Remediate underlying limitations to safety and independence. Physical impairments (muscle weakness, impaired hand function, limited ROM, paralysis, incoordination, impaired balance, fatigue, dyspnea, abnormal tone, tremor), sensory impairment (impaired sensation, low vision, hard of hearing, vestibular, pain), behavioral, cognition, perception.
- Train in compensatory techniques (safety techniques, one-handed techniques, pacing, energy conservation, joint protection, body mechanics, breathing techniques, low vision techniques, cognitive/perceptual compensation, step-by-step instructions, task segmentation, task sequencing, backward chaining, verbal and physical cueing, hand-over-hand guiding).
- Train in the use of adaptive equipment and assistive devices (floss holder, water flosser, nailbrush with suction cup base, long handled lotion applicator, long handled combs and brushes, inspection mirror, cylindrical foam tubing, magnifying mirror, universal cuff).
- Provide environmental modifications and adaptations (lower the bathroom sink, store items within reach, sit to perform tasks).
- Instruct in task modification.
    - Change the task (use electric toothbrush, hold item and move head).
    - Eliminate part or all of the task (short haircut eliminates the need to style hair, put toothpaste in mouth instead of on toothbrush).
    - Have someone else do part or the entire task (have hair done professionally, podiatrist to cut toenails).

Patient and Caregiver Handouts:

Guillain-Barré Syndrome

Impairments and Functional Limitations:
Progressive ascending flaccid weakness that is bilateral and symmetrical. Degree of muscle weakness can range from mild limb paresis to total flaccid paralysis of the limb, trunk, respiratory, oropharyngeal, oculomotor and facial muscles
Fatigue
Pain
Impaired sensation including loss of proprioception, paresthesias (numbness, tingling, crawling skin) and hypersensitivity to light touch
Autonomic dysfunction including fluctuations in blood pressure, cardiac arrhythmias and urinary retention
Depression and anxiety

Occupational Therapy Intervention - Acute Stage:
Educate patient and caregiver in preventing contractures, pressure ulcers and DVT's.

- Teach skin inspection, pressure relief, and positioning in bed and chair.
- Re-position every 2 hours.
- Obtain bed overlays, pressure-relieving mattress, and seating or wheelchair cushions.
- Provide support for weak joints (wrist cock-up, arm sling, cervical collar, resting hand splint, armrests, pillows, trays, foot drop splints).
- Provide gentle passive ROM and stretching exercises.

Instruct patient and caregivers in safe transfer techniques.

Pain management
    Therapeutic modalities (TENS, moist heat pack)
    Desensitization and sensory reeducation interventions

Occupational Therapy Intervention - Recovery Stage:
ADL, IADL, productivity and leisure training using adaptive equipment and task modifications to compensate for weakness

Train in safe and efficient functional mobility (sit to stand, bed mobility skills, transfers, standing, ambulation and wheelchair mobility) during ADL and IADL tasks. Train in the use of adaptive mobility equipment as appropriate. Refer to a Seating and Mobility Specialist (SMS) as appropriate.

Occupational Therapy Intervention - Recovery Stage (continued):
Teach strategies to manage fatigue and conserve energy.

- Assess using the Fatigue Impact Scale (Fisk et al., 1994).
- Teach pacing and energy conservation strategies.
- Balance self-care, productivity, play and rest.
- Encourage good sleep hygiene.
- Encourage keeping a fatigue journal.
- Utilize the problem solving process to identify ways to manage fatigue.

Provide therapeutic activities and exercises when the patient begins to recover sensation and motor control.

- Progress from AAROM to AROM to resistive
- Teach proprioceptive neuromuscular facilitation (PNF) techniques.
- Observe for muscle substitutions.

Provide functional balance activities to increase balance confidence with ADL tasks.

- Graded activities in sitting and standing, supported and unsupported

Provide a fall prevention program that includes balance, coordination and agility training and education about fall risk and prevention strategies.

Complete a comprehensive, performance-based home/work assessment. Recommend and/or provide modifications, adaptive equipment and/or assistive technology.

Educate patient and caregivers about Guillain-Barré Syndrome and the availability of community resources. Encourage participation in support groups.

Patient and Caregiver Handouts:

Occupational Therapy TOOLKIT

Guillain-Barré Syndrome

Additional Treatment Guides:

Handwriting

Handwriting includes understanding and interpreting letters and words, obtaining and using supplies (pens, pencils, paper, and writing surface), achieving and maintaining good position of body in chair, arms on the table and correct grasp on pen/pencil, producing legible writing.

Everyday writing tasks includes signing name, writing cards and letters, addressing envelopes, maintaining an address book and calendar, writing checks, filling out doctor office forms, job applications, taking notes and exams in class, taking phone messages, making grocery, shopping lists and to-do lists, journaling, word puzzles.

Impairments and Functional Limitations:
Impaired shoulder stability
Impaired trunk control
Limited activity tolerance and endurance
Impaired fine and gross motor coordination
Impaired grip and pinch strength, ROM, sensation
Low vision
Impaired visual motor control
Visual perceptual impairment
Cognitive impairment
Speech and language disorders

Assessments:
Obtain a pre-disability handwriting sample (i.e. address book, shopping list).
Have the person write 10 to 15 lines from the sample.
Compare the two and document:

- Legibility and letter formation (form and slant), spacing of letters and words, proportional size and height of letters
- Quality of the pen/pencil lines, pressure of pen on the paper
- Control of the writing instrument (pressure on the pen, grasp and isolated finger movements, arm slides left to right and top to bottom of paper)
- Speed of performance
- Endurance for writing
- Position for writing

Occupational Therapy Intervention:
Apply different approaches for solving difficulties with handwriting.

- Remediate underlying limitations. Physical (UE and core strength, ROM, hand function, fine, gross and visual motor coordination, balance, endurance, abnormal tone), sensory (tactile, vision, hearing, vestibular, pain), behavioral, cognition, perception

Handwriting

Occupational Therapy Intervention:

- Train in compensatory techniques, (one-handed techniques, pacing, energy conservation, joint protection, low vision techniques, verbal and physical cueing, hand-over-hand guiding, hand dominance retraining).
- Instruct in good positioning during writing tasks.
    - Posture - seated in a chair, feet flat on the floor, back supported, elbows, hips and knees are at 90-degree angles
    - Writing surface - vertical slant of about 20-degrees
    - Arm placement - the body weight is shifted to the non-writing arm, the writing hand is resting on the paper, and the non-writing arm stabilizes the paper
    - Paper placement - at an angle of about 15° in line with the writing arm
    - Functional grasps include tripod grasp (pen held between thumb and first two fingers), quadrupod grasp (pen held between thumb and first three fingers), adapted tripod grasp (pen held between thumb, index finger and the middle finger)
- Train in the use of adaptive equipment and assistive devices. Raised line paper, various pens and pencils (felt-tip, roller ball, soft lead, different diameters and shapes), various grips and built-ups (triangle grip, Stetro grip, crossover grip, rubber bands, masking tape), weighted pen or wrist weight, Pencil Pal, Handi-Writer, clipboards, slant boards, Dycem, magnifier, using a ruler to guide writing, red marker to mark edge.
- Provide environmental modifications and adaptations. Minimize distractions, alter seating, adjust slant and height of writing surface, provide good lighting.
- Instruct in task modification.
    - Change the task - change pen grip, use print instead of script.
    - Eliminate part or the entire task - use computer, voice recorder, type using a computer or virtual keyboard.

Patient and Caregiver Handouts:

Health Management

Assessments:
36-Item Short Form Survey Instrument (SF-36) (Rand et al., 2014)
Pizzi Health and Wellness Assessment (Pizzi 2001)
Pizzi Healthy Weight Management Assessment (Pizzi 2013)

Occupational Therapy Intervention:
Identify barriers to health management (depression, lacks readiness to change, language barrier, low health literacy, multiple chronic conditions, knowledge deficit, lack of transportation, socioeconomic issues, ineffective coping skills, mental status).

Promote health and wellness.

- Eat healthy foods while following dietary recommendations.
- Control and/or lose weight.
- Incorporate physical activity and exercise into daily routines.
- Prioritize good sleep.
- Manage stress.
- Balance self-care, productivity, rest, social, and leisure activities.
- Strengthen social support network.
- Quit smoking.
- Limit caffeine and alcohol.

Teach strategies to incorporate healthy habits and routines into daily activities.

Educate patient and caregivers about chronic health condition.

- Manage and monitor the signs and symptoms of the condition (dyspnea, pain, fatigue, hypo/hyperglycemia, anxious thoughts).
- Use measurement tools and record results (blood glucose monitor, blood pressure monitor, pulse oximetry, symptom journals).
- Prevent secondary complications (skin breakdown, UTI's).
- Reinforce strategies to reduce exacerbations/reoccurrence/hospital readmissions.
    - Avoid infections (cover face with mask, avoid close contact with people who have a cold or flu, use proper and frequent hand washing).
    - Take medications as directed.
    - Know the early signs and symptoms of illness/exacerbation.
- Instruct patient in performing tasks and treatments specific to managing the condition (measure food portions, adhere to medication regimen, skin inspection, weight shifts, elevating legs, weighing self, testing blood sugar, diabetic foot care, breathing techniques, pacing, energy conservation, joint protection techniques, body mechanics, posture).

Health Management

Occupational Therapy Intervention:
Educate patient and caregivers about chronic health condition (continued).

- Train in the use of adaptive equipment, assistive devices, and technology (talking scales, talking blood pressure monitors, pre-filled pill organizers, automatic pill dispensers, medication reminder watch, eye drop devices, magnifier for syringes and prescription bottles, weekly pill organizers, cell phone/tablet/computer apps).

Reinforce partnership with caregiver and health care providers.

- Make, keep, and participate in healthcare appointments. Utilize a daily planner/calendar.
- Communicate effectively with caregivers and health care providers.
- Collaborate with health care providers regarding goals and treatments.
- Organize and maintain medical records include test results, medical history, list of medication, logbooks of measurements (glucose, blood pressure).

Explore why the patient may not be adhering to their health management.

- Assess readiness to change using Transtheoretical Model Stages of Change.
- Teach use of specific tools (SMART Goals, Action Plans).
- Assist to develop problem solving skills (define problem, brainstorm possible solutions, pick a solution, implement solution, review the results).
- Implement problem-solving strategies to overcome barriers to health and wellness.
- Provide information on community resources. Encourage participation in support groups.

Patient and Caregiver Handouts:

Health Care Team	235
SMART Goals	472
SMART Goals - Action Plan	473
Tips for Making and Keeping Health Care Visits	332

Additional Treatment Guides

Medication Management	135

Home and Yard Maintenance

Home maintenance includes cleaning personal areas next to the bed or chair, dusting, cleaning the toilet, tub/shower and sink, gathering and taking out trash, replacing trashcan liners, cleaning spills, mopping/sweeping the floor, washing and drying dishes, loading and unloading dishwasher, cleaning countertops and appliances, light vacuuming, changing sheets, making the bed, watering plants, making small repairs, changing light bulbs, replacing batteries in smoke detector, flashlights and other devices, cleaning windows, cleaning/replacing furnace filters.
Yard maintenance includes sweeping sidewalk/porch/driveway, trimming bushes, mowing/watering the yard, weeding, raking leaves, shoveling snow, arranging for help if necessary.

Impairments and Functional Limitations:
Impaired shoulder strength and/or ROM
Impaired hand strength, ROM, sensation and/or coordination
Impaired LE function
Pain
Limited activity tolerance and endurance
Impaired balance

Occupational Therapy Intervention:
Apply different approaches for solving difficulties with home and yard maintenance.

- Remediate underlying limitations to safety and independence. Physical impairments (muscle weakness, impaired hand function, limited ROM, paralysis, incoordination, impaired balance, fatigue, dyspnea, abnormal tone, tremor), sensory impairment (impaired sensation, low vision, hard of hearing, vestibular, pain), behavioral, cognition, perception.
- Train in compensatory techniques (safety techniques, one-handed techniques, pacing, energy conservation, joint protection, body mechanics, breathing techniques, low vision techniques, cognitive/ perceptual compensation).
- Train in the use of adaptive equipment and assistive devices (reacher to pick up items from floor, built-up and long handled cleaning equipment, aerosol can holder, front load washer and dryer).
- Instruct in activity modification.
    - Change the task (divide each room into smaller areas and tackle each section, break up chores over the whole week, doing a little each day).
    - Eliminate part or the entire task (use paper towels to eliminate extra laundry, sit when possible).
    - Have someone else do part or the entire task (hire a housekeeping service, repairperson, gardener).

Patient and Caregiver Handouts:
Tips to Conserve Energy with Meal and Home Management 483

Home Safety and Modification

Impairments and Functional Limitations:
ADL and mobility impairment
Impaired strength and ROM
Impaired hand function
Impaired balance
Low vision
Cognitive deficits

Assessments:
Home Environmental Assessment Protocol HEAP (Gitlin et al., 2002)
Safety Assessment of Function and Environment SAFER (Backman et al., 2002)
Westmead Home Safety Assessment (Clemson et al., 1997)

Occupational Therapy Intervention:
Complete a comprehensive, performance-based home assessment with the patient and their family/caregiver. Assess home accessibility, slip and trip hazards, lighting, fire safety. Evaluate how patient interacts with the environment during ADL and IADL activities.

Teach the patient and family/caregiver how to recognize and resolve potential safety hazards in the home.

Provide low cost, simple changes:

- Remove trip and slip hazards inside and outside the home from stairs and pathways (clutter, throw rugs, mats and runners, electric cords, low furniture, newspapers, shoes, bedcovers).
- Provide nightlights, flashlights, bathmats or decals, carpet tape, battery operated lights, non-slip strips for steps.
- Adjust equipment to make it safer (adjust height of walker, bedside commode, shower chair, move walker wheels to inside).
- Rearrange furniture and lighting sources. Add lighting.
- Organize cabinets and closets.
- Remove fire hazards (overloaded outlets, clutter on the stovetop, blocked exits). Install smoke detectors. Change batteries in smoke detectors.

Recommend and provide resources for obtaining assistive technology:

- Simple adaptive equipment (reacher, sock aid, bed and chair risers, walker tray, bed rails, hand-held showerhead)
- Durable medical equipment (raised toilet seat, shower chair, electric lift chair, hospital bed, bedside commode)
- Personal emergency response system

Home Safety and Modification

Occupational Therapy Intervention:
Recommend structural modifications for architectural barriers.

- Construct ramp, install grab bars, install handrails on inside or outside stairs, convert bathtubs to showers, add easy-to-reach electrical outlets, add lighting on stairs and in closets, install light switches at the top and bottom of stairs, repair flooring, carpet, stairs, windows, walkways, remove doors from bathroom, closets or shower, install stair-lifts, install swing-hinges, widen doorways, lower countertops and cabinets.
- Identify funding sources and community resources.

Instruct in modifying risk-taking behaviors during ADL and IADL activities.

- Examples of risk taking behaviors include: carrying something while using stairs, not using the stair handrails, wearing unsuitable footwear, climbing on chairs to reach high items, rushing to answer the phone or to the bathroom, wearing clothing that are too long, wearing reading glasses on the stairs, not turning on lights, using towel bar for support, standing to put on pants.

Provide additional interventions for cognitive impairments (as appropriate).

- Eliminate triggers for stress and agitation. Remove mirrors if they cause delusions or hallucinations. Increase lighting to minimize shadows.
- Prevent injuries.
    - Slips, trips, and falls - see the Fall Risk Assessment and Prevention Treatment Guide.
    - Burns - remove lighters and matches, restrict smoking, disable stove/oven, lower water temperature.
    - Poisoning - place locks on cabinets, refrigerators, and freezers, secure garbage, remove poisonous plants and items that look like food such as artificial fruit and pet food, lock up laundry and cleaning supplies, chemicals, poisons, and medications.
    - Cuts - replace glass shower doors, disable garbage disposal, lock up sharp objects and breakable objects.
    - Electrocution - unplug or store electrical appliances in the kitchen and bathroom, childproof electrical outlets.
    - Other - lock up firearms, lock up power tools, restrict access to car.
- Limit wandering. Secure doors and windows, control access to stairs, storage areas, basements, garages, and home offices, install door alarms.
- Provide safe areas for wandering, safe access to outdoors.

Home Safety and Modification

Occupational Therapy Intervention:
Provide additional interventions for hearing loss (as appropriate).

- Make auditory signals louder (add amplifying device to telephone, TV).
- Replace auditory signals with visual or physical signals (flashing light attached to doorbell, telephone or timer, a strobe light attached to smoke alarm, TDD, activate closed caption on televisions, alarm clocks that vibrate the bed).
- Decrease background noise and echoes (install insulating materials around noisy appliances like dishwashers and washing machines, install insulating materials on floors, use fabric window coverings).

Provide additional interventions for low vision (as appropriate).

- Control glare and shadows. Use lampshades, light filtering shades, mini blinds, and sheer curtains inside. Use sunglasses, visor, or hat outdoors.
- Improve lighting. Turn on lights, use task lighting for grooming, reading, and food prep, flashlight for portable task lightening, nightlights, motion sensors or timers that automatically turn on lights, full spectrum bulbs, higher wattage bulbs, reflective tape around doorknobs and light switches. Try various light levels to establish the best for each task.
- Provide color and contrast. Choose solid colors instead of patterns. Use bright colors to provide contrast between an object and the background (dinner plates from placemat, chopping board from foods, wall sockets/light switches from the wall, bathmat from tub, door from the wall, stair handrail from the wall). Wrap grab bars with brightly colored electrical tape, paint the edges of stairs, paint door thresholds, use colored acetate sheets for reading.
- Modify telephones, thermostats, and appliances with tactile markings.

Assess follow-through on recommendations, teach safe use of adaptive equipment, durable medical equipment, personal emergency response systems, and structural modifications.

Additional Treatment Guides:
Fall Risk Assessment and Prevention 84

Therapist Resource:
Home Safety and Performance Assessment 423

Huntington's Disease

Impairments and Functional Limitations:
ADL, IADL, productivity and leisure impairment
Functional mobility impairment
Gait impairments -slow speed, decreased stride length, increased variability
Progressive movement disorders - chorea, akathisia, dystonia, akinesia, and bradykinesia
Muscle weakness
Rigidity and spasticity
Pain
Fatigue
Impaired balance
Impaired posture and trunk control
Impaired fine motor coordination
Respiratory dysfunction
Dysphagia/dysarthria
Cognitive and perceptual impairment include lack of initiation, lack of insight, impaired memory, impaired executive functions, word finding difficulty, anosognosia.
Behavioral symptoms including personality changes (irritability, apathy, antisocial attitudes, intermittent explosive disorder, anxiety, impulsiveness, aggression, hostility) change in sexual behavior, restlessness and agitation, depression and suicide risk, increased risk for alcohol and drug dependency, manic episodes, psychosis (delusions, paranoia, hallucinations, obsessions)
Other symptoms and conditions - incontinence, weight loss, risk of falls

Rating Scale:
Unified Huntington's Disease Rating Scale (UHDRS)

Occupational Therapy Intervention:
ADL, IADL, productivity and leisure training

- Recommend and/or provide adaptive equipment and task modifications to compensate for impaired UE function, balance and postural control. (Built up handles, non-spill cups, non-slip matting, unbreakable dishes, bath mitt, shower chair).
- Maximize safety and independence through simplifying the activities, structuring the environment, and providing adaptive equipment.
- Train in pacing and energy conservation techniques.
- Teach proper positioning during ADLs using supportive seating, bracing elbows on table or against sides.
- Assist patient and caregiver in developing a consistent, structured schedule of self-care, activities and rest/sleep.

Huntington's Disease

Occupational Therapy Intervention:
Train in safe and efficient functional mobility (sit to stand, bed mobility skills, transfers, standing, ambulation and wheelchair mobility) during ADL and IADL tasks.

- Train in the use of adaptive mobility equipment - rollator, wheelchair (may need to pad), seating systems, hydraulic patient lifts.

Provide physical exercise and activities to maintain ROM, strength, coordination and endurance and provide cognitive stimulation. Choose activities that reflect the person's interest, cognitive capacity and physical abilities.

Provide functional balance activities to increase balance confidence with ADL tasks. Recommend safety equipment (elbow and knee protectors, helmet or soft head protector).

Provide training and education about fall risk and prevention strategies.

Provide cognitive and perceptual training in the use of compensatory strategies.

Assist caregivers in managing challenging behaviors.

Complete a comprehensive, performance-based home assessment. Recommend and/or provide modifications (including padding doorways, hard surfaces and sharp edges, placing mattress on floor, removing breakables, stabilizing furniture), adaptive equipment and/or assistive technology.

Educate patient and caregivers about Huntington's disease, community resources. Encourage participation in support groups. Provide educational materials to the caregiver about stress management and caring for their own health.

Additional Treatment Guides:

Joint Contractures

Impairments and Functional Limitations:
ADL and mobility impairment
Loss of joint range of motion
Pain
Spasticity
Potential complication - pressure ulcers and/or compromised skin integrity
Co-occurring conditions - pressure ulcers, stroke, arthritis, joint infections, diabetes, Parkinson's disease, Alzheimer's disease, heterotopic ossification

Occupational Therapy Intervention:
Prevention:

- Instruct in daily active and/or passive range of motion through full range.
- Manage spasticity.
- Provide continuous passive motion devices.
- Instruct in pain control.
- Instruct in positioning and good posture.
- Provide splints to support weak joints.
- Instruct in hygiene to improve skin integrity and reduce risk for breakdown.

Treatment:

- Consult with physician about medical control of pain and spasticity.
- Provide modalities prior to stretching (thermotherapy, ultrasound, paraffin, hydrotherapy).
- Provide manual therapy techniques (massage, mobilization).
- Instruct in range of motion exercises (passive, active-assist and/or active).
- Instruct in passive or active static stretching. Hold between 5 and 60 seconds and perform 4 times a day.
- Provide proprioceptive neuromuscular facilitation (PNF) stretching techniques.
- Provide spring-assisted dynamic progressive splints and/or serial casts/splints.
- Monitor skin blanching to avoid compromising vascularity.
- Provide techniques and/or equipment to compensate for limitations.

Patient and Caregiver Handouts:
Passive Range of Motion 651
Superficial Heat 481

Additional Treatment Guides:
Pressure Ulcers 164
Therapeutic Exercise 195

Occupational Therapy TOOLKIT

Kidney Disease

Impairments and Functional Limitations:
ADL, IADL, productivity and leisure impairment
Functional mobility impairment
Impaired strength
Limited activity tolerance and endurance
Fatigue
Pain
Co-occurring conditions - diabetes, hypertension

Occupational Therapy Intervention:
ADL, IADL, productivity and leisure training

- Recommend and/or provide adaptive equipment.
- Reinforce dietary instructions during kitchen management.
- Instruct in pacing and energy conservation strategies.

Reinforce instructions about care and protection of dialysis access site.

- Avoid sleep on the side with the dialysis access site.
- Wear clothes that are loose fitting.
- Do not carry heavy objects.
- Avoid blood pressure, IV medications and injections in the arm with the dialysis access site.

Teach strategies to manage fatigue and conserve energy.

- Assess using the Fatigue Impact Scale (Fisk et al., 1994).
- Teach pacing and energy conservation strategies.
- Balance self-care, productivity, play and rest.
- Encourage good sleep hygiene.
- Encourage keeping a fatigue journal.
- Utilize the problem solving process to identify ways to manage fatigue.

Provide UE therapeutic exercises and activities to improve strength and endurance.

- Begin with very low intensity and progress slowly.
- Monitor for hypotension before, during and after exercise.
- Instruct to not exercise with fever, or if dialysis is missed. Recommend exercising on non-dialysis days, or before dialysis. Blood pressure may be too low after dialysis.

Complete a comprehensive, performance-based home assessment. Recommend and/or provide modifications, adaptive equipment and/or assistive technology.

Occupational Therapy TOOLKIT

Kidney Disease

Occupational Therapy Intervention:
Provide a fall prevention program that includes balance, coordination and agility training and education about fall risk and prevention strategies. Provide functional balance activities to increase balance confidence with ADL tasks.

Teach strategies to incorporate wellness and health management routines into daily activities.

Patient and Caregiver Handouts:

Exercise Tips for Renal Conditions	579
Fatigue Journal	412
Putty Exercises	683
Stress Management	477
Tips to Conserve Energy	482
Upper Body Exercises - Hand Weights	765

Additional Treatment Guides:

Diabetes - Type 2	73
Fall Risk Assessment and Prevention	84
Health Management	115
Home Safety and Modification	118

Leisure and Social Activities

Impairments and Functional Limitations:
Impaired shoulder strength and/or ROM
Impaired hand strength, ROM, sensation and/or coordination
Impaired LE function
Limited activity tolerance and endurance
Impaired balance
Pain
Visual perceptual and cognitive impairment

Assessments:
Activities Card Sort (Baum et al., 2008)
Canadian Occupational Performance Measure (Law et al., 2014)
Modified Interest Checklist (Kielhofher & Neville 1983)

Occupational Therapy Intervention:
Explore past, current and future leisure interests.

Instruct in activity balancing for self-care, productivity, leisure/play, and rest.

Apply different approaches for solving difficulties with leisure participation.
- Remediate underlying deficits. Physical (strength, hand function, ROM, coordination, balance, endurance, abnormal tone), sensory (tactile, vision, hearing, vestibular, pain), behavioral, cognition, perception.
- Train in compensatory techniques (safety techniques, one-handed techniques, energy conservation, joint protection, low vision techniques, cognitive/perceptual compensation, step-by-step instructions, task segmentation, task sequencing, backward chaining, verbal and physical cueing, hand-over-hand guiding).
- Train in the use of adaptive equipment and assistive devices (large print books, magnifiers, large print cards, cardholders, book holders, large handled garden tools, raised flowerbeds, books on tape).
- Provide environmental modifications and adaptations (increase task lighting, modifications to radio and TV, modifications to electronic devices, transportation options in order to attend leisure activities).

Patient and Caregiver Handouts:
Leisure Activities 434

Occupational Therapy TOOLKIT

Low Vision and Blindness

Impairments and Functional Limitations:
ADL, IADL, productivity and leisure impairment
Functional mobility impairment
Impaired vision

- Diabetic retinopathy causes blurry vision, irregular patches of vision loss, loss of peripheral and/or central vision.
- Glaucoma causes loss of peripheral vision and difficulty in low light conditions.
- Cataracts cause blurry vision, sensitivity to light and glare and difficulty with contrast sensitivity and color identification.
- Macular degeneration causes loss of central vision, deceased ability to see fine detail and distorted vision.

Fall risk with fear of falling
Co-occurring conditions - Charles Bonnet Syndrome, diabetes, depression

Assessments:
Assess how vision loss is affecting occupational performance.
Canadian Occupational Performance Measure (Law et al., 2014)

Occupational Therapy Intervention:
Teach compensation techniques for vision loss during daily living skills, communication skills and mobility.

- Facilitate use of remaining vision:
    - Instruct in strategies to facilitate the use of remaining vision (eccentric viewing techniques, scanning and page-orientation techniques).
- Provide adaptations so less vision is required:
    - Train in the use of optical devices that enlarge objects.
        - Near optical devices for close work, such as reading and sewing (hand magnifiers, stand magnifiers, reading glasses)
        - Distance optical devices for activities such as attending movies and sporting events, reading street signs, and identifying numbers on buses and trains (binoculars and hand-held telescopes, spectacle-mounted telescopes).
    - Train in the use of non-optical devices so less vision is required (enlarged clocks, timers, phone keys, large print books and playing cards, CCTV, electronic reading machines, computer magnification software).
    - Train in the use of non-optical devices that provide contrast (bold-lined paper, bold-lined black pen, writing guides, colored acetate sheets).

Occupational Therapy Intervention:
Teach compensation techniques for vision loss during daily living skills, communication skills and mobility (continued).

- Provide adaptations so no vision is required:
  - Train in the use of non-visual devices to facilitate the use of other senses (audio books, radio information services, tape recorders, talking watches and tactile markings, talking glucose monitor, talking scale, talking blood pressure cuff, smart phones, voice assistants such as Google Home, Apple's Siri and Amazon Alexa).
  - Facilitate the development of the other senses and memory to compensate for vision loss.

Train in safe and efficient functional mobility.

- Teach systematic horizontal and vertical scanning of the environment to locate stationary items and moving items. Train with or without optical devices.
- Instruct patient in indoor mobility techniques (upper body protection, lower body protection and trailing).
- Instruct caregivers to be a sighted guide.
- Teach wayfinding in the home.
- Refer to an Orientation & Mobility Specialist.

Complete a comprehensive, performance-based home assessment. Recommend and/or provide modifications, adaptive equipment and/or assistive technology. Provide specific interventions for low vision.

- Control glare and shadows. Use lampshades, light filtering shades, mini blinds, and sheer curtains inside. Use sunglasses, visor or hat outdoors.
- Improve lighting. Turn on the lights; use task lighting for grooming, reading and food prep, flashlight for portable task lightening, nightlights, motion sensors or timers that automatically turn on lights, full spectrum bulbs, higher wattage bulbs, reflective tape around doorknobs and light switches. Try various light levels to establish the best for each task.
- Provide color and contrast. Choose solid colors instead of patterns. Use bright colors to provide contrast between an object and the background such as dinner plates and mat, chopping board and foods, wall sockets/light switches and the wall, bathmat and tub, door and the wall, stair handrail and the wall. Wrap grab bars with brightly colored electrical tape, paint the edges of stairs, paint door thresholds, colored acetate sheets for reading.
- Modify telephones, thermostats, and appliances with tactile markings.

Provide a fall prevention program that includes balance, coordination and agility training and education about fall risk and prevention strategies.

Occupational Therapy TOOLKIT

Low Vision and Blindness

Occupational Therapy Intervention:
Educate patient and caregivers about low vision and the availability of community resources. Encourage participation in support groups.

Patient and Caregiver Handouts:

Additional Treatment Guides

Therapist Resources:

Lumbar Stenosis

Conditions include central disc herniation, degenerative disc disease, and spinal tumors

Impairments and Functional Limitations:
ADL, IADL, productivity and leisure impairment
Functional mobility impairment
Gait deviations
Back pain (exacerbated by prolonged sitting, back extension and downhill walking, relieved by bending forward, side lying and sitting)
Paresthesia
Muscle weakness
Reflex changes
Impaired balance
Limited activity tolerance and endurance
Co-occurring conditions - sciatica, fall risk, urinary incontinence, sexual dysfunction

Occupational Therapy Intervention:
ADL, IADL, productivity and leisure training

- Treat underlying impairments that limit safety and independence.
- Recommend and/or provide adaptive equipment and task modifications to avoid pain and maintain the spine in relative lumbar flexion.
- Instruct in applying good posture and body mechanics during ADLs.
- Instruct in donning and doffing back support and/or brace.
- Instruct in pacing and energy conservation strategies.

Train in safe and efficient functional mobility (sit to stand, bed mobility skills, transfers, standing, ambulation and wheelchair mobility) during ADL and IADL tasks.

Provide UE therapeutic exercises and activities to improve strength and endurance.

Provide education about fall risk and prevention strategies.

Complete a comprehensive, performance-based home/work assessment. Recommend and/or provide modifications, adaptive equipment and/or assistive technology.

Patient and Caregiver Handouts:

Lumbar Spine Surgery

Surgical approaches include simple decompression (lumbar laminectomy, laminotomy, or foraminotomy) or decompression with lumbar fusion

Impairments and Functional Limitations:
ADL, IADL, productivity and leisure impairment
Functional mobility impairment
Restricted lumbar ROM
Impaired balance
Muscle weakness
Pain
Co-occurring conditions - osteoarthritis, fall risk
Potential complications - DVT, spinal cord injury, sexual dysfunction

Occupational Therapy Intervention:
ADL, IADL, productivity and leisure training with adherence to lumbar spine precautions

- Recommend and/or provide adaptive equipment and task modifications to prevent bending, lifting or twisting (shower chair, grab bars, non-slip mat, hand held shower, long bath sponge, raised toilet seat, bedside commode, leg lifter, reacher, sock aid, shoe horn, elastic shoelaces, dressing stick).
- Instruct in how to don/doff spinal orthosis, wearing schedule and hygiene.
- Instruct in pacing and energy conservation strategies.
- Instruct in body mechanics and good posture.

Train in safe and efficient functional mobility (sit to stand, bed mobility skills, transfers, standing, ambulation and wheelchair mobility) during ADL and IADL tasks with adherence to lumbar spine precautions.

Instruct in spinal surgery precautions as ordered by the surgeon (limit sitting to 20 minutes at a time, sit in reclined position, no bending, twisting or lifting over 10 pounds). Typically applies to laminectomy, laminotomy and discectomy, but not to fusion. *Always follow the referring surgeon's protocol.*

Instruct in pain self-management.

- Coordinate medication peak with exercise and activity.
- Apply superficial cold.
- Practice deep (diaphragmatic) breathing and other relaxation techniques.
- Use positioning devices.

Lumbar Spine Surgery

Occupational Therapy Intervention:
Provide education about fall risk and prevention strategies.

Complete a comprehensive, performance-based home assessment. Recommend and/or provide modifications, adaptive equipment and/or assistive technology.

Patient and Caregiver Handouts:

Additional Treatment Guides:

Meal Preparation

Meal preparation includes menu planning, following recipes, reading food labels and cooking instructions, knowledge of diet, obtaining supplies (upper and lower cabinets, drawers, pantry and refrigerator), using appliances (stovetop, oven, microwave, crock pot, toaster, toaster oven, coffee maker), preparing food, opening packages (jars, boxes, bottles, cans, cartons), using tools (spatula, can opener, grater, peeler, measuring cups and spoons, knifes, mixer, blender), pouring hot and cold liquids, transferring hot/cold items, setting and clearing the table, cleaning up the work area wrapping/unwrapping food in foil/plastic wrap, using food storage bag and safe food handling.

Impairments and Functional Limitations:
Impaired shoulder strength and/or ROM
Impaired hand strength, ROM, sensation and/or coordination
Impaired LE function
Limited activity tolerance and endurance
Impaired balance
Pain
Visual perceptual impairment
Cognitive impairment

Assessments:
Kitchen Task Assessment (Baum et al., 1993)
Rabideau Kitchen Evaluation Revised (Neistadt et al., 1994)

Occupational Therapy Intervention:
Apply different approaches for solving difficulties with meal preparation and clean up.

- Remediate underlying limitations to safety and independence. Physical impairments (muscle weakness, impaired hand function, limited ROM, paralysis, incoordination, impaired balance, fatigue, dyspnea, abnormal tone, tremor), sensory impairment (impaired sensation, low vision, hard of hearing, vestibular, pain), behavioral, cognition, perception.
- Train in compensatory techniques (safety techniques, one-handed techniques, pacing, energy conservation, joint protection, body mechanics, breathing techniques, low vision techniques, cognitive/perceptual compensation, step-by-step instructions, task segmentation, task sequencing, backward chaining, verbal and physical cueing, hand-over-hand guiding).
- Train in the use of adaptive equipment and assistive devices (material to stabilize bowls and cutting boards, large handled tools, rolling cart, walker basket, low vision aids, adaptive cutting board, lightweight dishes, pot and pans, appliances that replace manual tools such as food processors, salad shooter, electric can opener, electric jar opener, electric teakettles).

Occupational Therapy TOOLKIT

Meal Preparation

Occupational Therapy Intervention:

- Provide environmental modifications and adaptations (rearrange cabinet so items are between knee and shoulder level, use a chair in work area for rest, use turntables, install slide-out shelving for easier access, install a food disposer to minimize trash, tactile markings, color-coded markings, faucet turners).
- Instruct in activity modification.
    - Change the task (use microwave, toaster oven for cooking, allow items to cool off before transporting).
    - Eliminate part or the entire task (buying pre-cut vegetables or prepared meals, frozen dinners, eat at the kitchen counter).
    - Have someone else do part or the entire task (meals delivery service, grocery delivery service).

Levels of Meal Preparation:

- Simple task cold (bottled drink, pudding cup, granola bar, yogurt)
- Multi task cold (sandwich, cereal with milk, lettuce salad, fruit salad, smoothie)
- Simple task hot using the stovetop, microwave, toaster, toaster oven, coffee maker or electric kettle (canned soup, frozen dinner, toast, tea, coffee, eggs)
- Multi task hot using the stovetop, crock-pot or oven (spaghetti, chili, soup, cookies, lasagna, baked chicken, bread)

Patient and Caregiver Handouts:

Adaptive Equipment for Meal Prep	216
Manage Kitchen Tasks with a Walker	258
Manage Kitchen Tasks with a Wheelchair	260
Meal Prep with One Hand	262
Tips to Conserve Energy with Meal and Home Management	483

Occupational Therapy TOOLKIT

Medication Management

Medications include prescription and over-the-counter medication (oral, eye drops, skin creams, injections, inhalants, and oxygen). Medication management includes obtaining a prescription, understanding the purpose of the medication, understanding potential side effects, reading and understanding the information in the prescription label, taking the correct medication in the prescribed quantity and at the prescribed time, ordering new medication and refills from pharmacy in a timely manner, opening and closing the containers, removing pills from containers, dispensing eye drops and inhalants, managing syringes, applying creams. Managing medical devices that deliver medications: (syringes, portable/home oxygen concentrators/tanks, and nebulizers).

The occupational therapist role in medication management is a supportive one to the prescriber, pharmacist, and nursing. Occupational therapists do not prescribe medication, recommend medication, fill medication boxes, or administer medication.

Impairments and Functional Limitations:
Impaired hand strength, ROM, sensation, pain and/or coordination
Visual perceptual impairment
Cognitive or psychological impairment
Non-adherence
Multiple medications

Assessments:
ManageMed Screen (MMS) (Robnett et al., 2004)
Montreal Assessment of Cognition (MoCA) (Nasreddine et al., 2005)
Pillbox Test (Zartman et al., 2013)
Screening for Self-Medication Safety Post Stroke (S-5) (Kaizer et al., 2010)

Occupational Therapy Intervention:
Apply different approaches for solving medication management difficulties.

- Remediate underlying limitations to safety and independence. Physical impairments (muscle weakness, impaired hand function, limited ROM, paralysis, incoordination, impaired balance, fatigue, dyspnea, abnormal tone, tremor), sensory impairment (impaired sensation, low vision, hard of hearing, vestibular, pain), behavioral, cognition, perception.
- Train in compensatory techniques (one-handed techniques, low vision techniques, cognitive/perceptual compensation, using step-by-step instructions, medication lists, reminder notes, integrate task into existing routines).
- Train in the use of adaptive equipment, assistive devices and technology (pre-filled pill organizers, automatic pill dispensers, medication reminder watch, eye drop devices, magnifier for syringes and prescription bottles, weekly pill organizers, cell phone/tablet/computer apps).

Medication Management

Occupational Therapy Intervention:
Apply different approaches for solving medication management difficulties.

- Provide environmental modifications and adaptations (adequate lighting, color-coded bottles, large-print medication labels, uncluttered, quiet environment).
- Instruct in activity modification.
    - Change the task (non-child resistant packaging).
    - Eliminate part or the entire task (pre-filled insulin syringes, arrange for delivery via courier or mail service).
    - Have someone else do part or the entire task (text messaging or telephone call reminders, delegate the task to another person).

Explore why the patient may not be adhering to their prescribed medication routine.

- Assess readiness to change using Transtheoretical Model Stages of Change.
- Teach use of specific tools (SMART Goals, Action Plans).
- Assist to develop problem solving skills (define problem, brainstorm possible solutions, pick a solution, implement solution, review the results).
- Implement problem solving strategies to overcome barriers to medication compliance and management.
- Provide information on community resources. Encourage participation in support groups.

Provide education about understanding the information that accompanies the medication.

Provide caregiver/family education and training.

Patient and Caregiver Handouts:
SMART Goals 472
SMART Goals - Action Plan 473

Additional Treatment Guides
Cognition 56
Health Management 115

Mild Cognitive Impairment (MCI)

Amnestic MCI primarily affects memory. A person may start to forget important information that he or she would previously have recalled easily, such as appointments, conversations or recent events. (Alzheimer's Association 2013)

Nonamnestic MCI primarily affects thinking skills (executive functions). A person may have difficulty making sound decisions, judging time or sequencing of the steps needed to complete a complex task. Cognitive changes are serious enough to notice, but the changes are not severe enough to interfere with daily life or independent function. (Alzheimer's Association 2013)

Other conditions that can affect cognition - delirium, medication side effects, vitamin B-12 deficiencies, high blood pressure, depression, fatigue, sleep disturbances.

Assessments:
Brief Cognitive Assessment Tool (Mansbach et al., 2012)
Canadian Occupational Performance Measure (Law et al., 2014)
Everyday Cognitive Questionnaire (Farias et al., 2008)
Executive Function Performance Test (Baum et al., 2003)
Weekly Planning Calendar Activity (Toglia et al., 2015)

Occupational Therapy Intervention:
Provide cognitive remediation tasks and compensation techniques during complex IADLs (medication management, money management, meal preparation, work and driving).

Educate patient and caregivers in MCI and the availability of community resources. Encourage participation in support groups.

Promote lifestyle changes/wellness (smoking cessation, healthy eating, controlling chronic conditions, physical activity and exercise, stress management and relaxation, good sleep habits, engaging in social and cognitive activities).

Additional Treatment Guides

Cognition	56
Depression	66
Driving	80
Health Management	115
Medication Management	135

Occupational Therapy TOOLKIT

Morbid Obesity - Person of Size

Body mass index (BMI) of 35 or higher

Impairments and Functional Limitations:
ADL, IADL, productivity and leisure impairment
Functional mobility impairment
Limited activity tolerance and endurance
Dyspnea with functional activities
Musculoskeletal pain
Co-occurring conditions - depression, anxiety, heart disease, neuropathies, stasis and pressure ulcers, sleep disorders, diabetes, stroke, chronic kidney disease, osteoarthritis, bariatric surgery, incontinence, lymphedema, cellulitis, heat intolerance

Occupational Therapy Intervention:
ADL, IADL, productivity and leisure training

- Recommend and/or provide adaptive equipment. Make adaptations to adaptive equipment to compensate for larger size (larger sock aid, extensions on bath brushes, extensions on toileting aids, extra long shower hose, remove back from shower chair, toilet bidet).
- Instruct in pacing and energy conservation strategies.
- Instruct in balancing self-care, productivity, play and rest.
- Provide online and catalog clothing resources.
- Assist in improving community access through car modification or public transportation.

Train in safe and efficient functional mobility (sit to stand, bed mobility skills, transfers, standing, ambulation and wheelchair mobility) during ADL and IADL tasks.

- Provide resources for accessible furniture (lift chair) and DME (bedside commode, hospital bed, wheelchairs, mechanical lifts) that will accommodate larger size and weight range.
- Train caregivers in safe transfers and lifts.

Provide UE therapeutic exercises and activities to improve strength and endurance.

Instruct in the prevention and control of lymphedema.

Complete a comprehensive, performance-based home assessment. Recommend and/or provide modifications, adaptive equipment and/or assistive technology.

Teach strategies to incorporate weight loss strategies, wellness and health management routines into daily activities.

Morbid Obesity - Person of Size

Occupational Therapy Intervention:
Educate patient and caregivers about weight loss and the availability of community resources. Encourage participation in support groups.

Patient and Caregiver Handouts:

Additional Treatment Guides:

Multiple Sclerosis

Impairments and Functional Limitations:
ADL, IADL, productivity and leisure impairment
Functional mobility impairment
Muscle weakness
Spasticity
Fatigue
Impaired pulmonary function
Impaired balance
Impaired posture and trunk control
Impaired coordination
Action tremor
Paresthesias
Pain (neuropathic and nociceptive)
Dizziness and vertigo
Impaired vision (problems with visual acuity, contrast sensitivity, color vision, and depth perception, diplopia, oscillopsia)
Cognitive impairment
Other symptoms and conditions - depression, bladder and bowel dysfunction, urinary tract infections, heat intolerance, dysarthria, dysphonia, dysphagia, seizures, pressure sores, sexual dysfunction, contractures, disuse atrophy, risk of falls, osteoporosis

Rating Scale:
Multiple Sclerosis Quality of Life Inventory (MSQLI) (Fischer et al., 1999)

Occupational Therapy Intervention:
ADL, IADL, productivity and leisure training

- Recommend and/or provide adaptive equipment and task modifications to compensate for impaired coordination, strength and endurance.
- Provide low vision compensation techniques and adaptive devices.
- Address ability to drive safely. Provide referral to driving rehab specialist and/or explore alternative transportation options.

Train in safe and efficient functional mobility (sit to stand, bed mobility skills, transfers, standing, ambulation and wheelchair mobility) during ADL and IADL tasks.

- Train in the use of adaptive mobility equipment - hospital beds, lift chairs, standard wheelchair/electric wheelchairs, seating cushions, transfer boards, hydraulic patient lifts. Refer to a Seating and Mobility Specialist (SMS).

Multiple Sclerosis

Occupational Therapy Intervention:
Teach strategies to manage fatigue and conserve energy.

- Assess using the Modified Fatigue Impact Scale for MS (Fisk et al., 1994)
- Teach pacing and energy conservation strategies.
- Balance self-care, productivity, play and rest.
- Encourage good sleep hygiene.
- Encourage keeping a fatigue journal.
- Utilize the problem solving process to identify ways to manage fatigue.

Provide therapeutic activities and exercises to improve ROM, strength and endurance.

- Strengthening exercises, progress slowly using sub-maximal resistance and frequent repetitions
- Stretching program to decrease spasticity and prevent contractures
- Aquatic therapy (ideal water temperature is 85-degrees or lower)
- Avoid fatigue and avoid increasing core body temperature

Instruct in cooling strategies. Use fans and air conditioners, drink chilled fluids, take cool showers/baths, avoid direct sunlight, use an umbrella, close the curtains/shades, wear layered clothing that can be removed, store cooling packs in the refrigerator and apply them on wrists and neck, wear a cooling vest.

Instruct in pain self-management strategies.

- Teach relaxation techniques.
- Use self-massage techniques (foam rollers, tennis ball, rolling massage stick).
- Transcutaneous electric nerve stimulation (TENS).

Teach compensatory techniques and safety measures for sensory deficits. Test bath/dish water temperature using the intact extremity or a thermometer. Lower the water heater temperature to 120°F (48°C). Avoid cuts and burns in kitchen. Avoid using heating pads on impaired extremities. Wear gloves to prevent frostbite. Avoid going barefoot. Wear sunscreen to prevent sunburn. Use intact hand to handle sharp kitchen utensils. Use vision to compensate to sensory loss. Perform skin checks.

Provide positioning splints as appropriate.

- Resting splint at night for weak finger and wrist extensors
- Wrist cock-up splints during functional tasks for weak wrist extensors.

Provide functional balance activities to increase balance confidence with ADL tasks.

- Graded activities in sitting and standing, supported and unsupported

Occupational Therapy TOOLKIT

Multiple Sclerosis

Occupational Therapy Intervention:
Teach compensation techniques for tremors.

Provide training and education about fall risk and prevention strategies.

Complete a comprehensive, performance-based home assessment. Recommend and/or provide modifications, adaptive equipment and/or assistive technology.

Teach stress management and relaxation techniques (progressive muscle relaxation, deep breathing, self-hypnosis, guided imagery, tai chi, yoga and meditation).

Provide cognitive retraining and training in the use of compensatory strategies.

Teach strategies to incorporate wellness and health management routines into daily activities.

Educate patient and caregivers about multiple sclerosis, community resources. Encourage participation in support groups. Provide educational materials to the caregiver about stress management and caring for their own health.

Patient and Caregiver Handouts:

Additional Treatment Guides:

Myasthenia Gravis - Generalized

Impairments and Functional Limitations:
ADL, IADL, productivity and leisure impairment
Functional mobility impairment
Fluctuating muscle weakness and fatigue of voluntary muscle groups (ocular, oropharyngeal, facial, neck, shoulder, intercostals, diaphragm, trunk, hip, upper and lower limbs). Proximal weakness is greater than distal weakness. Weakness and fatigue increases with activity and improves with rest.
Limited activity tolerance and endurance
Dyspnea
Impaired vision due to blurred or double vision, reduced ocular movement
Dysarthria
Dysphagia and difficulty chewing
Depression and anxiety
Co-occurring conditions include thyroid disease, lupus, rheumatoid arthritis and diabetes.
Factors that can exacerbate symptoms of MG and can result in myasthenic crisis include fatigue, systemic illness (especially viral respiratory infections), hypothyroidism or hyperthyroidism, emotional stress and upset, extreme heat, over or under medication, some medications and herbal supplements that affect neuromuscular transmission, smoking.

Rating Scale:
Myasthenia Gravis Activities of Daily Living Profile (Wolfe et al., 1999)

Occupational Therapy Intervention:
ADL, IADL, productivity and leisure training
- Recommend and/or provide adaptive equipment and task modifications to compensate for impaired proximal muscle weakness and fatigue.
- Provide low vision compensation techniques and adaptive devices.
- Address ability to drive safely. Provide referral to driving rehab specialist and/or explore alternative transportation options.

Teach strategies to manage fatigue and conserve energy.
- Assess using the Fatigue Impact Scale (Fisk et al., 1994).
- Teach pacing and energy conservation strategies.
- Balance self-care, productivity, play and rest.
- Encourage good sleep hygiene.
- Encourage keeping a fatigue journal.
- Utilize the problem solving process to identify ways to manage fatigue.

Myasthenia Gravis - Generalized

Occupational Therapy Intervention:
Teach stress management and relaxation techniques.

Train in safe and efficient functional mobility (sit to stand, bed mobility skills, transfers, standing, ambulation and wheelchair mobility) during ADL and IADL tasks.

Provide therapeutic activities and exercises to improve ROM, strength, endurance and balance.

- Exercise is appropriate for stable patients only.
- Emphasize large muscle groups. Walking, stationary bike, arm cycle, light free weights, swimming with caution.
- Exercise at a low to moderate intensity.
- Coordinate exercise programs with PT and Speech to avoid fatigue.
- Avoid fatigue and avoid increasing core body temperature.

Instruct in cooling strategies. Use fans and air conditioners, drink chilled fluids, take cool showers/baths, avoid direct sunlight, use an umbrella, close the curtains/shades, wear layered clothing that can be removed, store cooling packs in the refrigerator and apply them on wrists and neck, wear a cooling vest.

Complete a comprehensive, performance-based home/work assessment. Recommend and/or provide home/work modifications, adaptive equipment and/or assistive technology.

Provide education about fall risk and prevention strategies.

Teach strategies to incorporate wellness and health management routines into daily activities.

Educate patient and caregivers about myasthenia gravis and the availability of community resources. Encourage participation in support groups.

Patient and Caregiver Handouts:
Exercise Tips for Myasthenia Gravis 576
Fatigue Journal 412
Putty Exercises 683
Stress Management 477
Tips to Conserve Energy 482
Upper Body Exercises - Hand Weights 765
Upper Body Strength Activities 773

Myasthenia Gravis - Generalized

Additional Treatment Guides:

Myocardial Infarction

Impairments and Functional Limitations:
ADL, IADL, productivity and leisure impairment
Functional mobility impairment
Limited activity tolerance and endurance
Dyspnea
Muscle weakness
Lower extremity edema
Depression
Co-occurring conditions - angina, coronary artery disease, bypass surgery

Occupational Therapy Intervention:
ADL, IADL, productivity and leisure training

- Recommend and/or provide adaptive equipment to reduce strain during lower body ADLs.
- Instruct patient in donning and doffing support stockings.
- Reinforce dietary instructions during kitchen management.
- Instruct in pacing and energy conservation strategies.
- Teach patient to position self in bed on pillows or wedge to ease breathing.
- Instruct patient to elevate legs to reduce edema. Modify recliner chair handle using a length of PVC pipe to provide leverage, attach a strap to a footstool to ease pulling it into position.

Train in safe and efficient functional mobility (sit to stand, bed mobility skills, transfers, wheelchair mobility, ambulation and stairs).

Teach patient and caregivers about the safe use of oxygen during ADL and mobility (fire safety, managing O2 lines, care and correct use of oxygen equipment, carrying portable O2).

Instruct in UE active ROM exercises to prevent stiffness and as a warm-up to walking exercise.

Instruct in balancing rest and activity, signs and symptoms of over working, self-pulse monitoring, Rated Perceived Exertion (RPE) Scale, and progression of activities.

Assess and monitor blood pressure, heart rate, respiratory rate and oxygen saturations and perceived rate of exertion in response to functional activities and exercise.

Teach stress management and relaxation techniques.

Myocardial Infarction

Reinforce lifestyle changes (smoking cessation, healthy eating to reduce cholesterol, blood pressure and/or blood sugar, weight loss and control, physical activity and exercise, stress management, good sleep habits).

Patient and Caregiver Handouts:

Edema (Swelling) Control of the Leg(s)	409
How to Check Your Heart Rate	429
Stress Management	477
Tips to Conserve Energy	482
Tips to Conserve Energy with Meal and Home Management	483
Tips to Conserve Energy with Self Care Tasks	484

Additional Treatment Guides:

Cardiac Disease	38
Cardiac Surgery	40
Health Management	115

Osteoarthritis - Conservative Management

Impairments and Functional Limitations:
ADL, IADL, productivity and leisure impairment
Functional mobility impairment
Limited UE and LE ROM
Impaired hand function
Muscle weakness
Limited activity tolerance and endurance
Joint pain, stiffness and inflammation that increase with activity
Postural changes
Impaired balance
Co-occurring conditions - joint replacements, joint contractures, fall risk

Assessments:
Manual Ability Measure (MAM) (Chen & Bode 2010)

Occupational Therapy Intervention:
ADL, IADL, productivity and leisure training

- Train in the use of adaptive equipment to improve grasp (built-ups), improve ease of performance (electric can opener), compensate for range of motion loss (dress stick), compensate for weak/absent muscle (universal cuff, jar opener), prevent stress on joints (lever door handle), prevent prolonged grasp (book holder, Dycem), prevent accidents (bath seat, nonskid rugs).
- Instruct in pacing, energy conservation, joint protection, good posture and body mechanics.
- Instruct in balancing self-care, productivity, play and rest.

Train in safe and efficient functional mobility (sit to stand, bed mobility skills, transfers, standing, ambulation and wheelchair mobility) during ADL and IADL tasks.

Provide an individualized exercise program that includes low-impact, low-intensity endurance, strengthening, and flexibility activities. Goal is to maintain strength and joint mobility. Use yoga blocks, wrap foam around weights, use weight lifting gloves to improve grip.

- Acute flare-ups - instruct in performing gentle passive or active ROM exercises 3-4 times daily followed by icing for 15 minutes.
- Non-acute joints - instruct in the use of superficial heat, gentle isometric strengthening in pain free range.

Provide splints to rest inflamed joints, maintain correct joint alignment, improve functional control and support weak or painful joints.

Osteoarthritis - Conservative Management

Occupational Therapy Intervention:
Instruct in pain self-management strategies.

- Coordinate medication peak with exercise and activity.
- Apply superficial heat and cold.
- Practice deep (diaphragmatic) breathing and other relaxation techniques.
- Use self-massage techniques (foam rollers, tennis ball, rolling massage stick).
- Use positioning devices (seat cushions, back supports, pillows, splints).
- Instruct in using a pain journal.
- Utilize the problem solving process to identify ways to manage pain.

Provide pain management.

- Transcutaneous electrical nerve stimulation (TENS)
- Manual therapy techniques (massage, myofascial and soft tissue mobilization)
- Elastic therapeutic tape

Complete a comprehensive, performance-based home assessment. Recommend and/or provide modifications, adaptive equipment and/or assistive technology.

Provide education about fall risk and prevention strategies.

Teach strategies to incorporate wellness and health management routines into daily activities.

Educate patient and caregivers about arthritis and the availability of community resources. Encourage participation in support groups. Encourage participation in community, evidence-based exercise programs: (Active Living Every Day, Arthritis Foundation Aquatic Program, Arthritis Foundation Exercise Program, Enhance Fitness, Fit and Strong, Walk with Ease).

Patient and Caregiver Handouts:

Deep (Diaphragmatic) Breathing	393
Exercise Tips for Arthritis	572
Joint Protection for Arthritis	431
Pain Journal	456
Splint/Brace Instructions	475
Superficial Cold & Heat	480
Tips to Conserve Energy	482
Upper Body Active Range of Motion	758

Additional Treatment Guides:

Health Management	115

Osteoporosis

Impairments and Functional Limitations:
ADL, IADL, productivity and leisure impairment
Functional mobility impairment
Analgesic gait
Gait changes (COG forward)
Muscle weakness
Postural changes
Limited activity tolerance and endurance
Back and neck pain
Impaired balance (frequent fallers, poor balance reactions, fear of falling)
Co-occurring conditions - fractures in the vertebrae, femur and radius

Occupational Therapy Intervention:
ADL, IADL, productivity and leisure training

- Recommend and/or provide adaptive equipment and task modifications to minimize spinal flexion and trunk rotation.
- Instruct in pacing, energy conservation, good posture, and body mechanics.
- Reinforce dietary instructions during kitchen management.

Train in safe and efficient functional mobility (sit to stand, bed mobility skills, transfers, standing, ambulation and wheelchair mobility) during ADL and IADL tasks.

Provide light resistive UE activities and exercises to improve strength and endurance.

Provide functional balance activities to increase balance confidence with ADL tasks.

Instruct in pain self-management strategies.

- Coordinate medication peak with exercise and activity.
- Apply superficial heat and cold.
- Practice deep (diaphragmatic) breathing and other relaxation techniques.
- Use positioning devices (seat cushions, back supports, pillows, splints).
- Instruct in using a pain journal.
- Utilize the problem solving process to identify ways to manage pain.

Provide education about fall risk and prevention strategies.

Complete a comprehensive, performance-based home assessment. Recommend and/or provide modifications, adaptive equipment and/or assistive technology.

Osteoporosis

Occupational Therapy Intervention:
Promote wellness by reinforcing lifestyle changes (smoking cessation, follow a regular exercise plan that includes weight-bearing, achieve and maintain ideal body weight through healthy eating, develop good sleep habits, increase intake of calcium and vitamin D, minimize caffeine and alcohol intake).

Teach strategies to incorporate health management routines into daily activities.

Patient and Caregiver Handouts:

Additional Treatment Guides:

Occupational Therapy TOOLKIT

Palliative Care and Hospice

Impairments and Functional Limitations:
Premature dependence in ADL, IADL, productivity and leisure
Functional mobility impairment
Limited activity tolerance and endurance
Pain

Assessments:
Canadian Occupational Performance Measure (Law et al., 2014)

Occupational Therapy Intervention:
The focus is on comfort and quality of life through engagement in occupations.

ADL, IADL, leisure and productivity participation

- Assist in maintaining independence for as long as possible, and then move to interdependence and finally to dependence as functional status declines.
- Recommend and/or provide adaptive equipment and task modifications to reduce the effort or time required for an activity.
- Provide education on pacing, energy conservation, breathing techniques and activity balancing.
- Provide meaningful occupations to help the patient prepare for death.
    - Completing personal projects
    - Telling one's life story with photos and journaling
    - Writing letters to give to family and friends after the patient has died.
    - Creating remembrances through writing poems, stories, cards, family recipes, artwork, music or giving away belongings

Train in safe and efficient functional mobility (sit to stand, bed mobility skills, transfers, standing, ambulation and wheelchair mobility) during ADL and IADL tasks.

- Train in the use of adaptive mobility equipment - hospital beds, lift chairs, standard wheelchair/electric wheelchairs, seating cushions, transfer boards, hydraulic patient lifts.
- Train caregivers in safe handling techniques that minimizes stress and pain.

Complete a comprehensive, performance-based home assessment. Recommend and/or provide modifications, adaptive equipment and/or assistive technology.

Provide education about fall risk and prevention strategies.

Minimize deformity and contractures.

- Train patient and caregivers in positioning in chair and bed.
- Provide active and/or passive range of motion exercises.

Occupational Therapy TOOLKIT

Palliative Care and Hospice

Occupational Therapy Intervention:
Instruct in pain self-management strategies.

- Coordinate medication peak with exercise and activity.
- Apply superficial heat and cold.
- Practice deep (diaphragmatic) breathing and other relaxation techniques.
- Use self-massage techniques (foam rollers, tennis ball, rolling massage stick).
- Transcutaneous electric nerve stimulation (TENS).
- Use positioning devices (seat cushions, back supports, pillows, splints).
- Instruct in using a pain journal.
- Utilize the problem solving process to identify ways to manage pain.

Patient and Caregiver Handouts:

Parkinson's Disease - Early Stage
Hoehn and Yahr Stages 1 to 2.5

Impairments and Functional Limitations:
Motor symptoms are minimal and may include a slight tremor, fatigue, stiffness in the shoulders and hips, changes in posture and gait.
Difficulty with cognitively demanding IADLs (work related tasks, medication management, financial management, meal management, shopping).

Assessments and Rating Scales:
Canadian Occupational Performance Measure (Law et al., 2014)
Executive Function Performance Test (EFPT) (Baum et al., 2003)
Modified Hoehn and Yahr Staging
Modified Schwab and England Activities of Daily Living (Factor et al., 2002)
Parkinson's Disease Questionnaire PDQ-39 (Jenkinson et al., 2008)
Performance Assessment of Self-Care Skills (PASS) (Rogers & Holm 1989)
Unified Parkinson's Disease Rating Scale (Fahn et al., 1987)

Occupational Therapy Intervention:
ADL, IADL, work and leisure training
- Promote full participation in occupations.
- Instruct in proper posture during ADLs.

Teach strategies to manage fatigue and conserve energy.
- Assess using the Fatigue Impact Scale (Fisk et al., 1994).
- Teach pacing and energy conservation strategies.
- Balance self-care, productivity, play and rest.
- Encourage good sleep hygiene.
- Encourage keeping a fatigue journal.
- Utilize the problem solving process to identify ways to manage fatigue.

Provide graded therapeutic activities and exercises to improve ROM and strength, coordination, prevent contractures, improve posture, and promote extension.

Teach strategies to improve handwriting and computer skills.

Provide cognitive retraining and instruct in compensatory strategies.

Evaluate home, work and leisure environments and recommend safety and future equipment needs.

Teach strategies to incorporate wellness and health management routines into daily activities.

Parkinson's Disease - Early Stage
Hoehn and Yahr Stages 1 to 2.5

Occupational Therapy Intervention:
Educate patient and caregivers about Parkinson's disease and the availability of community resources. Encourage participation in support groups.

Patient and Caregiver Handouts:

Additional Treatment Guides:

Parkinson's Disease - Mid Stage
Hoehn and Yahr Stage 3-4

Impairments and Functional Limitations:
ADL, IADL, productivity and leisure impairment
Functional mobility impairment
Gait characterized by start hesitation, shuffling gait, reduced walking speed, festination and freezing episodes.
Fall risk with fear of falling
Motor symptoms (TRAP)
- Tremors - resting tremors and action tremors
- Rigidity - cramping and soreness of muscles, fatigue, contracted muscles, back and neck pain, stooped posture, loss of arm swing when walking, reduced trunk flexibility, shuffling of the feet, impaired dexterity and coordination, micrographia
- Akinesia - slowness of movements, incomplete movement, difficulty initiating movements and sudden stopping of ongoing movement, reduced eye blinking, reduce facial expression, dysarthria
- Postural instability - forward head, rounded shoulders, increased thoracic kyphosis, increased flexion of the trunk, and bending of the knees

Neuropsychiatric symptoms (impaired cognition, depression, apathy, anxiety, psychosis, hallucinations, delusions, impulse control)
Autonomic dysfunction (orthostatic hypotension, constipation, bladder dysfunction, excessive sweating, heat intolerance, drooling, dysphagia)
Sleep dysfunction (excessive daytime sleepiness, insomnia, REM sleep behavior disorder, restless leg syndrome)
Sensory changes (taste, smell and vision)

Assessments and Rating Scales:
Canadian Occupational Performance Measure (Law et al., 2014)
Modified Schwab and England Activities of Daily Living (Factor et al., 2002)
Modified Hoehn and Yahr Staging
Parkinson's Disease Questionnaire PDQ-39 (Jenkinson et al., 2008)
Performance Assessment of Self-Care Skills (PASS) (Rogers & Holm 1989)
Unified Parkinson's Disease Rating Scale (Fahn et al., 1987)

Occupational Therapy Intervention:
ADL, IADL, productivity and leisure training
- Provide training during medication "on" time.
- Encourage focused attention and concentration on tasks, minimize distractions, educate on avoiding multi-tasking and teach cognitive strategies (internal and external cues).
- Break tasks down into steps and teach each step multiple times before adding the next step.

Parkinson's Disease - Mid Stage
Hoehn and Yahr Stage 3-4

Occupational Therapy Intervention:
ADL, IADL, productivity and leisure training

- Recommend and/or provide adaptive equipment and task modifications to compensate for fatigue, tremors and bradykinesia during tasks. Electric warming tray to keep food hot, inner lip plates, weighted cutlery, loose fitting clothes, Velcro closers on shoes, pull over tops, toileting and bathing equipment.
- Teach strategies to improve handwriting and computer skills.
- Assist patient and caregiver in developing a structured schedule of self-care, activities and rest/sleep.

Train in safe and efficient functional mobility (sit to stand, bed mobility skills, transfers, standing, ambulation and wheelchair mobility) during ADL and IADL tasks.

- Encourage focused attention and concentration on tasks, minimize distractions, educate on avoiding multi-tasking and teach cognitive strategies (internal and external cues).
- Break tasks down into steps and teach each step before adding the next step.
- Train in the use of adaptive mobility equipment - hospital beds, lift chairs, standard wheelchair/electric wheelchairs (with tilt-in-space option), transfer boards, hydraulic patient lifts, leg lifter, bed rails.

Teach strategies to manage fatigue and conserve energy.

- Assess using the Fatigue Impact Scale (Fisk et al., 1994).
- Teach pacing and energy conservation strategies.
- Balance self-care, productivity, play and rest.
- Encourage good sleep hygiene.
- Encourage keeping a fatigue journal.
- Utilize the problem solving process to identify ways to manage fatigue.
- Encourage performance of activities during medication peak times.

Provide graded therapeutic activities and exercises to improve ROM and strength, coordination, prevent contractures, improve posture, and promote extension.

- Examples - Forced exercise (theracycle), LSVT BIG - whole body, large amplitude movements, Nintendo Wii, Dance for PD, Tai Chi, boxing, Nordic walking

Provide functional balance activities to increase balance confidence with ADL tasks.

- Graded activities in sitting and standing, supported and unsupported

Educate regarding the common triggers for falls and teach compensation strategies.

Parkinson's Disease - Mid Stage
Hoehn and Yahr Stage 3-4

Occupational Therapy Intervention:
Instruct in pain self-management strategies.

- Coordinate medication peak with exercise and activity.
- Apply superficial heat and cold.
- Practice deep (diaphragmatic) breathing and other relaxation techniques.
- Use positioning devices (seat cushions, back supports, pillows, splints).

Complete a comprehensive, performance-based home assessment. Recommend and/or provide modifications, adaptive equipment and/or assistive technology.

Provide cognitive retraining and instruct in compensatory strategies.

Teach strategies to incorporate wellness and health management routines into daily activities.

Educate patient and caregivers about Parkinson's disease, community resources. Encourage participation in support groups. Provide educational materials to the caregiver about stress management and caring for their own health.

Patient and Caregiver Handouts:
Cognitive Strategies to Improve Movement 380
Deep (Diaphragmatic) Breathing 393
Fatigue Journal 412
Good Posture 416
Parkinson's Disease Exercises 644
Passive Range of Motion 651
Posture Exercises 676
Putty Exercises 683
Stress Management 477
Tips to Conserve Energy 482
Tips to Manage Action Tremors 500
Writing Tips for Parkinson's 511

Additional Treatment Guides:
Activities of Daily Living 3
Cognition 56
Fall Risk Assessment and Prevention 84
Feeding, Eating, and Swallowing 87
Functional Mobility 103
Health Management 115

Occupational Therapy TOOLKIT

Parkinson's Disease - Late Stage
Hoehn and Yahr Stage 5

Impairments and Functional Limitations:
ADL dependent, incontinence
Significant posture, gait and balance deficits
May be bed/chair-bound
Pain
Dysphasia
Impaired communication
Impaired cognition
Agitation, anxiety, hallucinations, delusions
Other symptoms and conditions - falls, pressure ulcers, contractures, constipation

Occupational Therapy Intervention:
ADL training

- Provide grooming and self-feeding training with adaptive equipment and/or hand-over-hand guiding, as appropriate.
- Modify food textures and consistencies.
- Provide sensory stimulation (vision, hearing, taste, smell, movement and touch).

Instruct caregiver.

- Avoid ADLs, transfers or exercises when "off" or un-medicated.
- Teach passive ROM exercises with superficial heat and/or cold for pain relief.
- Instruct in proper positioning in bed and chair and when eating/feeding.
- Teach correct body mechanics while lifting, turning, and transferring.
- Provide education about fall risk and prevention strategies.
- Train in the safe and correct use of adaptive equipment (hospital beds, lift chairs, bedside commode, wheelchair, seating cushions, hydraulic patient lifts).

Educate caregivers about Parkinson's disease and community resources. Provide educational materials about stress management and caring for their own health, and encourage participation in support groups.

Patient and Caregiver Handouts:
Body Mechanics 371
Check Your Skin 379
Passive Range of Motion 651
Position in Bed to Reduce Pressure 460

Additional Treatment Guides
Joint Contractures 123

Peripheral Neuropathy

Impairments and Functional Limitations:
ADL, IADL, productivity and leisure impairment
Functional mobility impairment
Sensory changes in the distal extremities - may present as sensory pain (sharp, burning), sensory impairment (numbness, tingling) or both
Impaired hand function and fine motor coordination
Neuropathic pain
Muscle weakness
Impaired balance with a positive Rhomberg sign
Partial foot drop
Fall risk
Co-occurring conditions - diabetes, chemotherapy induced, Guillain-Barré, lupus, neuropathies, skin ulcers, chronic kidney or liver disease

Assessments:
Canadian Occupational Performance Measure (Law et al., 2014)

Occupational Therapy Intervention:
ADL, IADL, productivity and leisure training

- Recommend and/or provide adaptive equipment and task modifications to compensate for impaired hand function and sensory loss (grip pen, rubber bands or non-slip drawer liner placed around utensils, cups and containers, wearing rubber gloves with tasks to provide grip, button hooks, zipper pulls, Velcro or non-slip material placed on computer keys, change accessibility settings on computers/cell phones/tablets).
- Instruct in using vision to compensate for sensory impairment during hand tasks and mobility.
- Instruct to monitor skin on hands and feet for injury and areas of redness. Recommend supportive footwear.
- Teach compensatory techniques and safety measures for sensory deficits. Test bath/dish water temperature using the intact extremity or a thermometer. Lower the water heater temperature to 120°F/48°C. Avoid cuts and burns in kitchen. Avoid using heating pads on impaired extremities. Wear gloves to prevent frostbite. Avoid going barefoot. Wear sunscreen to prevent sunburn. Use intact hand to handle sharp kitchen utensils. Use vision to compensate for sensory loss. Perform skin checks.
- Provide education about fall risk and prevention strategies.

Provide therapeutic exercises and activities to improve active ROM and endurance (include tendon and nerve gliding exercises).

Peripheral Neuropathy

Occupational Therapy Intervention:
Provide desensitization and sensory re-education interventions.

Patient and Caregiver Handouts:

Additional Treatment Guides:

Post-Poliomyelitis Syndrome

Impairments and Functional Limitations:
ADL, IADL, productivity and leisure impairments
Functional mobility impairment
New or increased muscle weakness
New or increased muscle and joint pain
New or increased fatigue that is greater in the afternoon
Decreased muscle tone
Limited ROM - hips, ankles, cervical spine, shoulders, scoliosis, kyphosis
Impaired balance
Dyspnea
Cognitive dysfunction related to fatigue affecting memory and concentration
Co-occurring conditions - restrictive lung disease, cold intolerance, dysphagia, depression, carpal tunnel syndrome, cubital tunnel syndrome, sleep disorders, myofascial pain syndrome, osteoarthritis, fibromyalgia

Occupational Therapy Intervention:
ADL, IADL, productivity and leisure training

- Recommend and/or provide adaptive equipment and task modifications to compensate for muscle weakness, paralysis and ROM limitations.
- Address ability to drive safely. Provide referral to driving rehab specialist and/or explore alternative transportation options.

Train in safe and efficient functional mobility (sit to stand, bed mobility skills, transfers, standing, ambulation and wheelchair mobility) during ADL and IADL tasks.

Teach strategies to manage fatigue and conserve energy.

- Assess using the Fatigue Impact Scale (Fisk et al., 1994).
- Teach pacing and energy conservation strategies.
- Balance self-care, productivity, play and rest.
- Encourage good sleep hygiene.
- Encourage keeping a fatigue journal.
- Utilize the problem solving process to identify ways to manage fatigue.

Provide an individualized exercise program that includes endurance, strengthening and flexibility activities. Goal is to improve strength and endurance.

- Instruct to exercise with low-moderate intensity of short duration with regular rests and adequate time for muscles to recover. Do not exercise to the point of muscle fatigue, monitor for changes in endurance, muscle soreness or weakness.

Occupational Therapy TOOLKIT

Post-Poliomyelitis Syndrome

Occupational Therapy Intervention:
Provide functional balance activities to increase balance confidence with ADL tasks.

Instruct in pain self-management strategies.

- Coordinate medication peak with exercise and activity.
- Apply superficial cold.
- Practice deep (diaphragmatic) breathing and other relaxation techniques.
- Use positioning devices.
- Instruct in using a pain journal.
- Utilize the problem solving process to identify ways to manage pain.

Provide cognitive retraining and instruct in compensatory strategies.

Complete a comprehensive, performance-based home assessment. Recommend and/or provide modifications, adaptive equipment and/or assistive technology.

Provide education about fall risk and prevention strategies.

Teach strategies to incorporate wellness and health management routines into daily activities.

Educate patient and caregivers about post-poliomyelitis syndrome and the availability of community resources. Encourage participation in support groups.

Patient and Caregiver Handouts:

Exercise Tips for Post-Poliomyelitis Syndrome	578
Fatigue Journal	412
Pain Journal	456
Posture Exercises	676
Pursed Lip Breathing	470
Putty Exercises	683
Stress Management	477
Stretch Band Exercises - Arms	749
Superficial Cold	480
Superficial Heat	481
Tips to Conserve Energy	482
Upper Body Exercises - Hand Weights	765
Upper Body Strength Activities	773

Additional Treatment Guides:

Health Management	115

Pressure Ulcers

Also referred to as decubitus ulcers, pressure sores or bed sores

Risk Factors:
Impaired sensory perception
Incontinence
Immobility/inactivity
Pain
Impaired functional mobility including bed mobility, transfers, ambulation
Impaired ROM, strength, balance, tone
Altered skin integrity
Impaired circulation
Impaired nutrition and/or hydration

Rating Scales:
The Braden Scale (Braden 2005)

Occupational Therapy Intervention:
Sensory Perception

- Instruct in basic skin care using a mild soap and warm (not hot) water. Use moisturizer and avoid massage over bony prominences.
- Keep bed sheets and clothing free of wrinkles and food crumbs. Avoid leaving objects in the bed.
- Teach skin inspection with long handed mirror or web-camera specifically of the ischium, sacrum, greater trochanters, heels, and occiput.
- Instruct in weight shift while up in chair or wheelchair. Chair push-ups, leaning side to side or forward. Stand up if able and re-seat self.

Moisture

- Provide strategies to reduce sweating (fabric choices, use of fans).
- See Urinary Incontinence treatment guide.

Activity

- Encourage early mobilization. Provide bed mobility and transfer training.
- Recommend well-fitting shoes and/or protective footwear (post-op shoe, heel or forefoot weight-bearing shoe).
- Provide therapeutic exercise (P/AA/AROM), in supine, sitting and standing as appropriate.
- Manage pain.

Mobility

- Instruct in re-positioning every 2 hours in bed and every 15 minutes when sitting.

Pressure Ulcers

Occupational Therapy Intervention:
Mobility (continued)

- Instruct in good posture and positioning when sitting and lying. Use pillows and foam wedges to reduce pressure over bony prominences.
- Avoid raising the head of the bed more than 30°, unless medically contraindicated. Always raise the foot of the bed when raising the head.
- Avoid prolonged hip and knee flexion when in bed or sitting.
- Obtain bed overlays, pressure-relieving mattress and seating/wheelchair cushions (air, gel, foam or a combination). Use a pressure mapping system to obtain even pressure distribution.
- Support weak body parts with headrests, high backs, armrests, leg rests, a wheelchair tray, wedges and/or pillows.
- Provide treatment for spasticity and/or contractures.

Friction and Shear

- Avoid dragging the patient during transfers and repositioning. Use a 2-person lift with draw sheet or use a mechanical lift.
- Provide an over-head trapeze.
- Use a slide sheet or sheepskin mat on a transfer board.
- Recommend the use of satin bed sheets.
- Recommend wearing socks in bed to reduce friction on heels.

Nutrition

- Address patient's ability to feed themselves and access or prepare meals.
- Encourage good nutrition and hydration.

Patient and Caregiver Handouts:

Additional Treatment Guides:

Rest and Sleep

Impairments and Functional Limitations:
Decreased quality of life
Daytime sleepiness
Impaired memory and concentration
Fall risk

Characteristics of Sleep Problems:
Difficulty falling asleep
Difficulty telling the difference between night and day
Early morning awakening
Waking up often during the night

Factors Contributing to Sleep Problems:
Primary sleep disorders (circadian rhythm disorder, sleep apnea, restless leg syndrome, periodic limb movement disorder, REM-behavior disorder)
Musculoskeletal/arthritis pain
Neurological disease (e.g., Parkinson's disease, Alzheimer's disease)
Congestive heart failure
Reflux
Pulmonary disease
Over-active bladder
Psychiatric disorders (e.g., anxiety, depression, psychosis, dementia, delirium)
Medication adverse/side effects (antidepressants, caffeine, analgesics, diuretics)
Poor sleep habits (irregular sleep-wake times, daytime napping)
Environmental factors (noise, room temperature, too much light, uncomfortable mattress, unfamiliar environment, bedfellow habits)

Occupational Therapy Intervention:
Address pain, urinary incontinence, depression, anxiety.

Assist in establishing pre-sleep routines - regular bedtime and wake time, rituals to perform prior to going to bed.

Assess the sleep environment and provide modifications and adaptations as needed to promote healthy sleep.

- Address temperature and ventilation, positioning needs (pain, dyspnea, pressure relief), ability to manage bed covers, using CPAP machines, nighttime toileting safety, and need for adaptive equipment. Recommend sound machines to add white noise, blackout curtains and eye masks to limit light.

Rest and Sleep

Occupational Therapy Intervention:
Teach stress management and relaxation techniques (progressive muscle relaxation, deep breathing, self-hypnosis, guided imagery, tai chi, yoga and meditation).

Encourage daily physical activity. Instruct to incorporate increased physical activity into daily routine.

Reinforce lifestyle changes (smoking cessation, healthy eating to reduce cholesterol, blood pressure and/or blood sugar, weight loss and control, physical activity and exercise, stress management, good sleep habits).

Refer to a sleep disorder specialist as appropriate.

Patient and Caregiver Handouts:
Good Sleep Habits 418
Stress Management 477

Additional Treatment Guides:
Chronic/Persistent Pain Syndrome 53
Depression 66
Functional Mobility 103
Generalized Anxiety Disorder 107
Therapeutic Exercise 195
Urinary Incontinence 205

Rheumatoid Arthritis - Conservative Management

Impairments and Functional Limitations:
ADL, IADL, productivity and leisure impairment
Functional mobility impairment
Antalgic gait
Postural changes
Impaired balance
Systemic disease, characterized by periods of exacerbations and remissions
Morning stiffness that lasts longer than 1 hour
Limited activity tolerance and endurance
Joint contractures
Impaired strength
Impaired grip and pinch strength
Joint deformity and instability
Joint pain and swelling
Limited ROM
Impaired hand function, manipulation and dexterity
Fatigue
Co-occurring conditions - carpal tunnel syndrome, cervical myelopathy, rotator cuff tears, trochanteric bursitis, tendon reconstruction, joint replacement

Assessments:
Manual Ability Measure (MAM) (Chen & Bode 2010)

Occupational Therapy Intervention:
ADL, IADL, productivity and leisure training

- Train in the use of adaptive equipment to improve grasp (built-ups), improve ease of performance (electric can opener), compensate for ROM loss (dress stick), compensate for weak/absent muscle (universal cuff, jar opener), prevent stress on joints (lever door handle), prevent prolonged grasp (book holder, Dycem), prevent accidents (bath seat, nonskid rugs).
- Instruct in pacing, energy conservation, and joint protection.
- Instruct in balancing self-care, productivity, play and rest.

Train in safe and efficient functional mobility (sit to stand, bed mobility skills, transfers, standing, ambulation and wheelchair mobility) during ADL and IADL tasks.

- Adaptive mobility equipment - hospital beds, lift chairs, standard wheelchair/ electric wheelchairs, transfer boards, hydraulic patient lifts, leg lifter, bed rails

Rheumatoid Arthritis - Conservative Management

Occupational Therapy Intervention:
Provide an individualized exercise program that includes low-impact, low-intensity endurance, strengthening, and flexibility activities. Goal is to maintain strength and joint mobility. Use yoga blocks, wrap foam around weights, use weight lifting gloves to improve grip.

- Acute flare-ups - instruct in performing gentle passive or active ROM exercises 3-4 times daily followed by icing for 15 minutes.
- Non-acute joints - instruct in the use of superficial heat, gentle isometric strengthening in pain free range.

Instruct in joint protection, body mechanics and good posture.

- Positioning devices for bed and chair

Provide splints to rest inflamed joints, maintain joint alignment, improve functional control and support weak or painful joints.

- Nighttime static, static-progressive, or dynamic extension splinting for elbow contractures
- Resting hand splint for night use
- Wrist cock-up splint
- Thumb spica splint
- Figure of eight splint for swan neck deformities
- Reverse knucklebender or spring finger extension for boutonniere deformities
- Ulnar deviation splint

Provide pain management.

- Physical agents modalities (cryotherapy, hydrotherapy, ultrasound, thermotherapy)
- Manual therapy techniques (massage, mobilization)

Instruct in pain self-management strategies.

- Coordinate medication peak with exercise and activity.
- Apply superficial heat and cold.
- Practice deep (diaphragmatic) breathing and other relaxation techniques.
- Use positioning devices (seat cushions, back supports, pillows, splints).
- Instruct in using a pain journal.
- Utilize the problem solving process to identify ways to manage pain.

Complete a comprehensive, performance-based home assessment. Recommend and/or provide modifications, adaptive equipment and/or assistive technology.

Rheumatoid Arthritis - Conservative Management

Occupational Therapy Intervention:
Provide education about fall risk and prevention strategies.

Teach strategies to incorporate wellness and health management routines into daily activities.

Educate patient and caregivers about arthritis and the availability of community resources. Encourage participation in support groups. Encourage participation in community, evidence-based exercise programs: (Active Living Every Day, Arthritis Foundation Aquatic Program, Arthritis Foundation Exercise Program, Enhance Fitness, Fit and Strong, Walk with Ease).

Patient and Caregiver Handouts:

Body Mechanics	371
Exercise Tips for Arthritis	572
Good Posture	416
Joint Protection for Arthritis	431
Pain Journal	456
Splint/Brace Instructions	475
Stress Management	477
Superficial Cold	480
Superficial Heat	481
Tips to Conserve Energy	482
Upper Body Active Range of Motion	758

Additional Treatment Guides:

Chronic/Persistent Pain Syndrome	53
Health Management	115

Therapist Resources:

Arthritic Joint Changes and Deformities	370

Rotator Cuff Pathology - Conservative Management

Impairments and Functional Limitations:
Muscle weakness and atrophy of the rotator cuff, deltoid and scapulothoracic muscles
Impaired posture
Pain with activities above shoulder level
Painful arc (AROM between 60 and 100-degrees of abduction)
Limited AROM but not PROM unless there is adhesive capsulitis

Provocative Tests:
Drop-arm (Park et al., 2005)
Empty-can Supraspinatus (Park et al., 2005)
External Rotation/Infraspinatus Strength (Park et al., 2005)
Hawkins-Kennedy Impingement Test (Hawkins & Kennedy 1980)
Lift-off Subscapularis (Hertel et al., 1996)
Neer Impingement Sign (Gibson et al., 2005)
Simple Shoulder Test (UW Medicine)

Occupational Therapy Intervention:
Recommend and/or provide adaptive equipment and task modifications to compensate for shoulder pain and limited ROM.

Instruct patient to sleep with a pillow between the trunk and arm. Avoid sleeping with the arm overhead or tucked against the chest in internal rotation.

Provide pain management.

- Physical agents modalities (cryotherapy, ultrasound, E-stim, thermotherapy)
- Transcutaneous electrical nerve stimulation (TENS)
- Mobilization of the scapula and glenohumeral joints
- Elastic therapeutic tape

Instruct in joint protection techniques.

- Practice good body mechanics and posture.
- Take frequent breaks.
- Modify activities that cause symptoms.
- Instruct in injury prevention to decrease recurrence.

Instruct in pain self-management strategies.

- Coordinate medication peak with exercise and activity.
- Practice deep (diaphragmatic) breathing and other relaxation techniques.
- Instruct in using a pain journal.
- Stretch neck muscles.

Rotator Cuff Pathology - Conservative Management

Occupational Therapy Intervention:
Provide therapeutic activities and exercises.

- Acute phase: Provide shoulder stretching and ROM exercises. Strengthen uninvolved joints.
- When pain free, provide progressive shoulder stabilization and rotator cuff strengthening activities and exercises to improve posture, increase ROM and strength.

Patient and Caregiver Handouts:

Rotator Cuff Pathology - Postoperative Management

Impairments and Functional Limitations:
Functional mobility impairment
Muscle weakness and atrophy of the rotator cuff, deltoid and scapulothoracic muscles
Limited ROM
Post-op pain and edema
Potential complications - shoulder stiffness, failure to heal, infection, reflex sympathetic dystrophy, deep venous thrombosis

Occupational Therapy Intervention:
Recommend and/or provide adaptive equipment and task modifications to compensate for shoulder pain and limited ROM while adhering to movement precautions.

Instruct in axillary hygiene, movement precautions, donning and doffing of shoulder sling/immobilizer and cryotherapy unit. Instruct in positioning shoulder in sitting and supine.

Train in safe and efficient functional mobility (sit to stand, bed mobility skills, transfers, standing, ambulation and wheelchair mobility) during ADL and IADL tasks.

Provide therapeutic activities and exercises. Progression depends on co-morbidities, surgical procedure performed, stage of healing, and postoperative complications. *Follow the referring surgeon's specific guidelines for progression.*

Stage 1: Protection
- No lifting, carrying or resistive activities until cleared by surgeon.
- Provide pain and edema management.
- Provide AROM exercises of uninvolved joints.

Stage 2: Active Motion
- Continue treatment as described above.
- Progress AROM exercises

Stage 3: Strengthening
- Progress strengthening

Educate regarding fall risk and prevention strategies.

Patient and Caregiver Handouts:
Daily Tasks after Shoulder Surgery 392
Elbow, Wrist and Hand Active Exercises 563
Exercise Tips for Orthopedic Conditions 577

Occupational Therapy TOOLKIT

Rotator Cuff Pathology - Postoperative Management

Patient and Caregiver Handouts:

Additional Treatment Guides

Scleroderma/Systemic Sclerosis

Impairments and Functional Limitations:
ADL, IADL, productivity and leisure impairments
Functional mobility impairment
Muscle weakness
Restricted ROM (including claw hand deformity and impaired oral mobility)
Impaired fine motor coordination
Limited activity tolerance and endurance
Impaired body image
Co-occurring conditions - Raynaud's phenomena, ischemic ulcers (fingertips, knuckles, toes, lips nose and ears), carpal tunnel syndrome, cubital tunnel syndrome, renal disease, restrictive lung disease (pulmonary fibrosis and restricted ROM of chest wall), pulmonary hypertension, pericardial effusion, congestive heart failure, dysphagia, Sjögren syndrome (dry eyes and mouth), depression, gastrointestinal problems (impaired motility of the esophagus and the intestines), arthritis, renal disease

Occupational Therapy Intervention:
ADL, IADL, productivity and leisure training

- Recommend and/or provide adaptive equipment and task modifications to compensate for UE ROM loss, weakness, limited grasp and impaired fine motor.
- Dental care using pediatric toothbrush and adaptations for flossing
- Instruct in pacing, energy conservation, and joint protection.

Train in safe and efficient functional mobility (sit to stand, bed mobility skills, transfers, wheelchair mobility, ambulation and stairs).

- Train in the safe and correct use of assistive devices and adaptive equipment (walkers, canes, raised toilet seats, bed transfer handles, leg lifters, wheelchairs) as appropriate.
- Recommend footwear and orthotics.

Calcium deposits can form on the elbows, knees and ischial tuberosities (sitting bones). Recommend gel elbow pads, kneepads and seating cushions to prevent breakdown of the skin.

Provide graded UE therapeutic activities and exercises to maintain neck, shoulder, elbow, wrist, hand mobility, facial and TMJ mobility, and chest excursion.

- Provide facial exercise with emphasis on mouth opening. Monitor by measuring with a plastic ruler. Provide hand exercises with emphasis on web spaces and extension. Monitor that full ROM is being achieved during home program by using templates (for example trace around extended hand; make cardboard cutouts for finger flexion and neck extension; monitor web spaces using various lids. Use marks on the wall for shoulder flexion/abduction.

Scleroderma/Systemic Sclerosis

Occupational Therapy Intervention:
Instruct in postural exercises, deep (diaphragmatic) breathing and inspiratory muscle trainers to improve breathing pattern and chest wall strength and ROM.

Instruct in pain self-management strategies.

- Coordinate medication peak with exercise and activity.
- Apply superficial heat including paraffin.
- Practice deep (diaphragmatic) breathing and other relaxation techniques.
- Use self-massage techniques (foam rollers, tennis ball, rolling massage stick).
- Use positioning devices (seat cushions, back supports, pillows, splints).
- Instruct in using a pain journal.
- Utilize the problem solving process to identify ways to manage pain.

Teach strategies to manage fatigue and conserve energy.

- Assess using the Fatigue Impact Scale (Fisk et al., 1994).
- Teach pacing and energy conservation strategies.
- Balance self-care, productivity, play and rest.
- Encourage good sleep hygiene.
- Encourage keeping a fatigue journal.
- Utilize the problem solving process to identify ways to manage fatigue.

Complete a comprehensive, performance-based home assessment. Recommend and/or provide modifications, adaptive equipment and/or assistive technology.

Provide education about fall risk and prevention strategies.

Teach strategies to incorporate wellness and health management routines into daily activities.

Educate patient and caregivers about scleroderma and the availability of community resources. Encourage participation in support groups.

Patient and Caregiver Handouts:

Occupational Therapy TOOLKIT

Scleroderma/Systemic Sclerosis

Patient and Caregiver Handouts:

Additional Treatment Guides:

Sexual Expression and Activity

Sexual activity is engaging in activities that result in sexual satisfaction and/or meet relational or reproductive needs. (Occupational therapy practice framework: Domain and process, 3rd Edition, AOTA 2014)

Impairments and Functional Limitations:
Sexual dysfunction (diminished sex drive, painful or uncomfortable genital sensations, difficulty reaching orgasm, erectile dysfunction, vaginal dryness)
Physical impairments (muscle weakness, impaired hand function, limited ROM, paralysis, incoordination, impaired balance, fatigue, dyspnea, abnormal tone, tremor restrictions associated with joint replacements, surgery, cardiac disease)
Sensory impairments
Cognitive impairment
Bowel and/or bladder incontinence
Altered body image (amputation, burns, paralysis, arthritic joints)
Medication side effects
Relationship issues (discomfort with touching scars, fear of causing physical pain, performance anxiety, altered marital and family roles, fear of rejection, developing new sexual relationships)

Occupational Therapy Intervention:
Therapists providing sexuality intervention need to understand their own personal beliefs and attitudes about sexuality and be comfortable, knowledgeable and skilled in educating their patients about the subject.

Utilize a treatment framework, such as the PLISSIT model (Annon 1976).

Permission - give permission to express sexual concerns/issues and ask for permission to address sexual concerns/issues.
Limited **I**nformation - provide information about the effect the condition has on sexuality and sexual function.
Specific **S**uggestions - provide specific suggestions for sexual adaptations to the patient and their partner (if applicable).
Intensive **T**herapy - provide referral to specialists, psychologists, and/or sex therapists.

Apply different approaches for solving difficulties with sexual activity.

- Remediate underlying limitations to safety and independence. Physical impairments (muscle weakness, impaired hand function, limited ROM, paralysis, incoordination, impaired balance, fatigue, dyspnea, abnormal tone, tremor), sensory impairment (impaired sensation, low vision, hard of hearing, vestibular, pain), behavioral, cognition, perception.

Sexual Expression and Activity

Apply different approaches for solving difficulties with sexual activity (continued).

- Train in compensatory techniques (application of energy conservation, joint protection, body mechanics, breathing techniques, relaxation techniques).
- Train in adaptive equipment and assistive devices, (pillows and bolsters for positioning, sexual enhancement devices). Discuss safety related to using the wheelchair and/or shower equipment for sexual activity.
- Modify the activity.
    - Provide suggestions for preparatory activity (massage, warm bath, desensitization techniques, stretching exercises, relaxation techniques, plan activity at peak of pain medications or peak energy time).
    - Provide suggestions for positioning using pillows or other aides.
    - Provide suggestions in alternative positions to minimize spasticity, prevent pain, protect joints and joint replacements, protect paralyzed limbs, adhere to weight-bearing restrictions, and/or compensate for limited strength/ROM/sensation/endurance/amputations.
    - Provide suggestions for non-intercourse activity, when appropriate.

Encourage good communication between patient and partner. Assist patient in developing social skills that will promote relationships.

Provide information about safely resuming sexual activity post-surgery, post-injury, joint replacement, heart attack, stroke, or spinal cord injury.

Provide information about medical complications and risks associated with sexual activity (bowel and bladder care, catheter care, skin protection and inspection post-activity, autonomic dysreflexia in patients with spinal cord injury above T6, cardiac precaution, hip precautions, spinal precautions, protection against STD's). Instruct on when to notify physician.

Provide information about body mapping the erogenous zones and using all available senses for sexual enhancement.

Recommend participation in support groups, in person and online.

Shopping

Shopping (local errands, groceries, personal items, bank, library, dry cleaner, pharmacy, restaurant and online shopping) includes preparing shopping lists, selecting and purchasing items, managing shopping cart, selecting method of payment, completing money transaction, transporting purchases, putting away items purchased, arranging for home delivery.

Impairments and Functional Limitations:
Impaired shoulder strength and/or ROM
Impaired hand strength, ROM, sensation and/or coordination
Impaired LE function
Limited activity tolerance and endurance
Impaired balance
Visual perceptual impairment
Cognitive impairment

Occupational Therapy Intervention:
Apply different approaches for solving difficulties with shopping.

- Remediate underlying limitations to safety and independence. Physical impairments (muscle weakness, impaired hand function, limited ROM, paralysis, incoordination, impaired balance, fatigue, dyspnea, abnormal tone, tremor), sensory impairment (impaired sensation, low vision, hard of hearing, vestibular, pain), behavioral, cognition, perception.
- Train in compensatory techniques (safety techniques, one-handed techniques, pacing, energy conservation, body mechanics, breathing techniques, low vision techniques, cognitive/perceptual compensation).
- Train in the use of adaptive equipment and assistive devices (reacher, magnifying glass, personal shopping cart).
- Instruct in activity modification.
    - Change the task (ask the clerk to bag the groceries lightly, and pack cold and frozen food together, make several trips to bring the groceries into the house, take the cold and frozen foods first, rest, then return for the remainder).
    - Eliminate part or the entire task (arrange for home delivery of groceries and medications, shop on the internet and through catalogs).
    - Have someone else do part or the entire task (ask for help reaching high or low items, get help for carrying heavy items, arrange for home delivery).

Spinal Cord Injury
Paraplegia T1-S5

Impairments and Functional Limitations:
ADL, IADL, productivity and leisure impairment
Functional mobility impairment
Motor paralysis or paresis below level of injury
Sensory loss below level of injury
Low endurance and vital capacity due to intercostals paralysis (T1-12)
Spasticity
Bowel and bladder dysfunction
Sexual dysfunction
Co-occurring conditions with traumatic SCI - traumatic brain injury, multiple traumas
Co-occurring conditions with non-traumatic SCI - osteoarthritis, spinal stenosis, spinal tumors, transverse myelitis
Potential secondary complications - bradycardia (T1-6), autonomic dysreflexia (T1-6), orthostatic hypotension (T1-6), impaired temperature regulation, pain (musculoskeletal or neuropathic), upper extremity overuse syndromes (rotator cuff injury, tendinitis, entrapment neuropathies, osteoarthritis), contractures, pressure ulcers, heterotopic ossification, cardiovascular disease, UTI's, pulmonary embolism, DVT's, pneumonia, osteoporosis resulting in pathological LE fractures, depression, adjustment disorders

Assessments and Classification Scales:
American Spinal Injury Association (ASIA) Impairment Scale
International Standards for Neurological Classification of SCI (ISNCSCI)

Outcome Measures:
Canadian Occupational Performance Measure (Law et al., 2014)
Spinal Cord Independence Measure (SCIM) (Catz et al., 1997)

Functional Movements:

T1	Finger adduction/abduction
T1-12	Intercostals, abdominals and trunk
L2	Hip flexion/adduction
L3	Knee extension
L4	Hip abduction, ankle dorsiflexion
L5	Hip extension, toe extension
S1	Knee flexion, ankle plantar flexion
S2	Toe flexion

Occupational Therapy Intervention:
Functional limitations and activity outcomes based on complete level of injury. Incomplete spinal injuries, the presence of co-morbidities, the patient's weight and age will alter the expected level of function.

Spinal Cord Injury
Paraplegia T1-S5

Occupational Therapy Intervention:
Teach patient to accurately instruct and direct others in all aspects of their care (self-care, mobility, exercise, pulmonary care, positioning, signs and symptoms of secondary complications).

Provide ADL, IADL, productivity and leisure training, using adaptive techniques, custom modifications, adaptive equipment and assistive technology.

Expected outcomes typical for complete spinal cord injury

	T1-4	T5-9	T10-L2	L3-L4	L5-S5
Communication	Indep	Indep	Indep	Indep	Indep
Eating	Indep	Indep	Indep	Indep	Indep
Grooming	Indep	Indep	Indep	Indep	Indep
Dressing UE	Indep	Indep	Indep	Indep	Indep
Bathing UB	Indep	Indep	Indep	Indep	Indep
Dressing LE	Indep	Indep	Indep	Indep	Indep
Bathing LB	Indep	Indep	Indep	Indep	Indep
Bladder	Indep	Indep	Indep	Indep	Indep
Bowel	Indep	Indep	Indep	Indep	Indep
Light meal prep	Indep	Indep	Indep	Indep	Indep
Light Homemaking	Indep	Indep	Indep	Indep	Indep
Heavy Homemaking	Some A	Some A	Some A	Indep to some A	Indep
Driving car with hand controls	Indep	Indep	Indep	Indep	Indep
Load wheelchair into car	Some to total A	Some A	Indep	Indep	Indep

Train in the use of custom modifications and adaptive equipment.

- Bathing - padded tub bench or padded shower/commode chair, long-handled sponges, grab bars, hand-held showerhead
- Bowel and Bladder - padded toilet seat, suppository inserter, digital stimulators, hand mirrors, enema inserters
- Driving - hand controls, roof mounted wheelchair lift
- Homemaking - long-handled brush and broom, reaching aid, specific kitchen appliances and environmental modifications

Train in safe and efficient functional mobility (transfer techniques, bed mobility skills standing, and wheelchair mobility) during ADL and IADL tasks, based on level of injury.

Expected outcomes typical for complete spinal cord injury

	T1-4	T5-9	T10-L2	L3-4	L5-S5
Mat/bed mobility	Some A to indep	Independent	Independent	Independent	Independent
Transfers	Independent	Independent	Independent	Independent	Independent
Transfers - floor/car	Indep to some A	Independent	Independent	Independent	Independent
Manual WC	Some A to indep	Independent	Independent	Advanced skills. Uses part-time	Advanced skills. Uses part-time
Standing	Some A with standing frame	Indep with standing frame	Indep with KAFOs and AD	Indep with KAFOs/AFOs	Indep with or without AFOs
Ambulation	Not indicated	Not functional, may walk for exercise with assist using AD and KAFOs.	Indep with AD and KAFOs. Household only.	Indep with KAFOs/AFOs and AD. Household and community	Indep with or without cane and AFOs. Household and community

Spinal Cord Injury
Paraplegia T1-S5

Occupational Therapy Intervention:
Provide therapeutic activities and exercises for trunk and upper extremities.

- Avoid spinal ROM, and stretching/strengthening of the hip and truck muscles until fracture site is stabilized. *Always follow the surgeon's specific instructions.*
- Once cleared, progress ROM and stretching to improve flexibility, prevent contractures, and reduce spasticity.
- Provide progressive resistance training to improve strength and endurance in innervated muscles. Utilize FES and neuroprosthetics to improve strength and endurance in partially innervated muscles.
- Provide repetitious practice of functional movements to improve motor control.

Instruct in postural re-education.

- Provide and instruct in proper positioning in bed (supine, prone and side lying) and proper posture in wheelchair.
- Provide strengthening for posterior shoulder and trunk muscles, stretching for anterior shoulder and chest muscles.
- Reassess positioning needs periodically.

Instruct in pressure ulcer prevention.

- Inspect skin.
- Teach weight shifts from manual chair.
- If a pressure ulcer occurs, problem solve with the client to determine the cause and prevent reoccurrence.

Instruct in prevention of upper extremity overuse injuries in manual wheelchair users (rotator cuff pathology, tendinitis, entrapment neuropathies).

- Assess using Wheelchair User's Shoulder Pain Index.
- Educate patient about the risk of overuse injury.
- Treat upper extremity injuries and pain.
- Instruct in joint protection, pacing and energy conservation techniques.

Reinforce respiratory management (T1-8).

- Secretion removal (percussion, vibration, postural drainage)
- Inspiratory muscle training (breathing exercises, inspiratory muscle trainers)
- Cough training (assisted coughing techniques, abdominal electrical stimulation, abdominal binder)

Spinal Cord Injury
Paraplegia T1-S5

Occupational Therapy Intervention:
Teach strategies to incorporate wellness and health management routines into daily activities.

Community Reintegration:

- Provide a comprehensive, performance-based home/work/leisure/school assessment.
- Recommend and/or provide modifications, adaptive equipment and/or assistive technology.
- Assist with leisure and social participation intervention.
- Recommend vocational rehabilitation strategies to assist the return to work.
- Community mobility training, driving training

Educate patient and caregivers about preventing secondary complications, hiring and managing paid caregivers, and availability of community resources and peer support/support groups.

Patient and Caregiver Handouts:

Additional Treatment Guides:

Spinal Cord Injury
Tetraplegia/Quadriplegia C1-8

Impairments and Functional Limitations:
ADL, IADL, productivity and leisure impairment
Functional mobility impairment
Motor paralysis or paresis below level of injury
Sensory loss below level of injury
Respiratory dysfunction (ventilator dependent C1-3, weaning may be possible at C4)
Low endurance and vital capacity due to intercostals paralysis
Spasticity
Bowel and bladder dysfunction
Sexual dysfunction
Co-occurring conditions with traumatic SCI - traumatic brain injury, multiple traumas
Co-occurring conditions with non-traumatic SCI - osteoarthritis, spinal stenosis, spinal tumors, transverse myelitis
Potential secondary complications - bradycardia, autonomic dysreflexia, impaired temperature regulation, orthostatic hypotension, pain (musculoskeletal or neuropathic), upper extremity overuse syndromes (rotator cuff injury, tendinitis, entrapment neuropathies, osteoarthritis), contractures, pressure ulcers, heterotopic ossification, cardiovascular disease, UTI's, pulmonary embolism, DVT's, pneumonia, osteoporosis resulting in pathological LE fractures, depression, adjustment disorders

Assessments and Classification Scales:
American Spinal Injury Association (ASIA) Impairment Scale
International Standards for Neurological Classification of SCI (ISNCSCI)

Outcome Measures:
Capabilities of UE Instrument in Tetraplegia (CUE) (Marino et al., 1998)
Quadriplegic Index of Function (QIF) (Gresham et al., 1986)
Spinal Cord Independence Measure (SCIM) (Catz et al., 1997)

Functional Movements:

C1-3	Neck flexion, extension and rotation
C4	Scapular elevation, diaphragm
C5	Scapular adduction/abduction, shoulder flexion/abduction, elbow flexion
C6	Scapular protractor, shoulder extension/adduction, wrist extension
C7	Elbow extension, wrist flexion, finger extension, thumb adduction/ abduction
C8	Finger flexion, thumb flexion/extension

Spinal Cord Injury
Tetraplegia/Quadriplegia C1-8

Occupational Therapy Intervention: (requires advanced training)
Functional limitations and activity outcomes based on complete level of injury. Incomplete spinal injuries, the presence of co-morbidities, the patient's weight and age will alter the expected level of function.

Teach patient to accurately instruct and direct others in all aspects of their care (self-care, mobility, exercise, pulmonary care, positioning, signs and symptoms of secondary complications).

Provide ADL, IADL, productivity and leisure training, using custom modifications, adaptive equipment and assistive technology, based on level of injury.

Expected outcomes typical for complete spinal cord injury

	C1-4	C5	C6	C7-8
Communication	Indep after set-up	Indep after set-up	Independent	Independent
Hand function	None	None	Tenodesis	Tenodesis
Eating	Total assist	Indep after set-up	Independent	Independent
Grooming	Total assist	Some assist	Indep to some assist	Independent
Dressing UE	Total assist	Some assist	Independent	Independent
Bathing UB	Total assist	Total assist	Independent	Independent
Dressing LE	Total assist	Total assist	Some to total assist	Indep to some assist
Bathing LB	Total assist	Total assist	Some to total assist	Indep to some assist
Bladder	Total assist	Total assist	Some to total assist	Indep to some assist
Bowel	Total assist	Total assist	Some to total assist	Some to total assist
Light meal prep	Total assist	Total assist	Some assist	Independent
Light Homemaking	Total assist	Total assist	Total assist	Independent
Driving	Not indicated	Not indicated	Independent	Independent

Train in the use of custom modifications, adaptive equipment, high and low assistive technology.

- Communication - mouth stick (C1-5), head pointer (C1-5), typing stick (C5), telephone headset (C1-5), environmental control units (C1-5), voice control for mouse and keyboard functions (C1-5), audio books (C1-5), augmentative/alternative communication system (C1-3)
- Eating - long straws and straw holder (C1-5), dorsal long opponens with U-cuff (C5), mobile arm support (C5), scoop dish (C5), plate guard (C5-8), handled cup (C5), rocker knife (C6-8), dignity silverware (C6-7)
- Grooming - straps for hairbrush and razor (C5), built-up handles (C6-7)
- Dressing - Dycem gloves (C6-7), modified buttonhook (C6-7), loops on zippers, pants, socks (C6-7), Velcro on shoes (C6-7), specialized clothing (C6-7)
- Bathing - padded reclining shower/commode chair (C1-5), padded tub bench or padded shower/commode chair (C6-8), bath mitts (C6-7), adapted long-handled sponges (C6-8), grab bars (C6-8), hand-held shower (C6-8)
- Bowel and Bladder (C6-8) - suppository inserter, mirrors, enema inserters
- Driving - adaptive van (C5-8)

Spinal Cord Injury
Tetraplegia/Quadriplegia C1-8

Occupational Therapy Intervention:
Train in safe and efficient functional mobility (transfer techniques, bed mobility skills and wheelchair mobility) during ADL and IADL tasks, using customized modified adaptive equipment and assistive technology.

Expected outcomes typical for complete spinal cord injury

	C1-4	C5	C6	C7-8
Mat/bed mobility	Total assist	Some assist	Indep	Indep
Transfers - level	Total assist	Some assist	Indep to some assist	Indep
Transfers - uneven	Total assist	Total assist	Some to total assist	Indep to some assist
Transfers - floor	Total assist	Total assist	Some to total assist	Some to total assist
Manual WC - indoor	Total assist	Indep to some assist	Indep	Indep
Manual WC - outdoor	Total assist	Some to total assist	Some to total assist	Indep to some assist
Power WC	Indep	Indep	Indep	Indep
Standing	Total assist	Total assist	Total assist	Indep to some assist
Ambulation	Not indicated	Not indicated	Not indicated	Not indicated

- Bed mobility training: fully electric bed (C1-6), pressure relief mattress (C1-8), loop ladder (C5-6), suspended loops (C5-6)
- Sitting and standing tolerance - tilt table, hydraulic or standard standing frame (C1-8)
- Provide and train in the use of customized power wheelchair (C1-6). Modified controls (sip-n-puff, chin/head activation, joystick) power recline and/or tilt, head positioning, lateral trunk supports, wheelchair pressure relief cushion
- Provide and train in the use of customized manual wheelchair (C5-8). Lightweight, peg rim projections, high-pressure tires, adjust rear axle as far forward as possible, push gloves, pressure relief cushion
- Manual wheelchair training: even terrain (C-8), uneven terrain (C7-8), propelling forward/backward (C5-8), 360° turns (C5-8), popping into a wheelie (C6-8), ascending/descending curbs (C6-8)
- Transfer training: quad lift transfers (C1-5), mechanical lift (C1-8), pivot (C1-8), sliding board (C1-8), floor transfer (C7-8). Train in the use of adaptive mobility equipment: transfer board (over-wheel, curved or straight), mechanical patient lifts (self-sling, mobile or ceiling mounted)

Provide therapeutic activities and exercises for trunk and upper extremities.
- Until fracture site is stabilized, avoid head and neck ROM, shoulder ROM past 90°, stretching and strengthening of the shoulders and scapula muscles. *Always follow the surgeon's specific instructions.*
- ROM and stretching to improve flexibility, prevent contractures and reduce spasticity.
- Provide repetitious practice of functional movements to improve motor control.
- Provide progressive resistance training to improve strength and endurance in innervated muscles. Use FES and neuroprosthetics to improve strength and endurance in partially innervated muscles.

Spinal Cord Injury
Tetraplegia/Quadriplegia C1-8

Occupational Therapy Intervention:
Facilitate a functional tenodesis grasp (complete injuries at C6-8).

- Tenodesis splinting
- Tenodesis ranging
- Grasp/release retraining
- Active and/or resistive wrist extension exercises
- FES and neuroprosthetics

Provide hand splinting to maximize function, protect weak muscles and assist with ADL tasks.

- Intrinsic plus resting hand splints (C1-6), elbow extension splints at night and during shoulder exercises (C5-6), soft wrist positioning splints (C5), dorsal long opponens with u-cuff (C5), tenodesis splint (C6-7), thumb opponens splint (C6-7), dorsal long opponens (C6-7)

Instruct in postural re-education.

- Instruct in proper positioning in bed (supine, prone and side lying). Instruct in proper posture in wheelchair.
- Provide strengthening for posterior shoulder and trunk muscles and stretching for anterior shoulder and chest muscles.
- Reassess positioning needs periodically.

Instruct in pressure ulcer prevention.

- Skin inspection - caregiver performs (C1-4), independent with equipment (C5-8)
- Weight shifts using power tilt/recline wheelchair - independent (C1-6)
- Weight shifts from manual chair - caregiver performs (C1-4), hooks elbows and leans forward or to the side (C5-6), push-ups from armrests (C7-8)
- If a pressure ulcer occurs, problem solve with the client to determine the cause and prevent reoccurrence.

Reinforce respiratory management.

- Secretion removal (percussion, vibration, postural drainage)
- Inspiratory muscle training (breathing exercises, inspiratory muscle trainers)
- Cough training (assisted coughing techniques, abdominal electrical stimulation, abdominal binder)

Spinal Cord Injury
Tetraplegia/Quadriplegia C1-8

Occupational Therapy Intervention:
Instruct in prevention of upper extremity overuse injuries in manual wheelchair users (rotator cuff pathology, tendinitis, entrapment neuropathies).

- Assess with Wheelchair User's Shoulder Pain Index.
- Educate patient about the risk of overuse injury.
- Treat upper extremity injuries and pain.
- Instruct in joint protection, pacing and energy conservation techniques.

Teach strategies to incorporate wellness and health management routines into daily activities.

Community Reintegration:

- Provide a comprehensive, performance-based home/work/leisure/school assessment. Recommend and/or provide modifications, adaptive equipment and/or assistive technology.
- Assist with leisure and social participation intervention.
- Recommend vocational rehabilitation strategies to assist with return to work.
- Community mobility training, driving training (C5-8)

Educate patient and caregivers about preventing secondary complications, hiring and managing paid caregivers, and availability of community resources and peer support/support groups.

Patient and Caregiver Handouts:

Additional Treatment Guides:

Stroke

Impairments and Functional Limitations:
ADL, IADL, productivity and leisure impairment
Impaired functional mobility
Hemiparesis or hemiplegia of the upper and lower extremities
Spasticity
Impaired postural control and balance
Impaired coordination
Limited activity tolerance and endurance
Impaired sensation
Central post-stroke pain
Language disorders (aphasia, dysarthria, dyspraxia)
Dysphasia
Visual and perceptual impairment
Cognitive impairment
Behavioral disorders (depression, lability, low frustration tolerance, impulsivity)
Bladder and bowel dysfunction
Potential secondary complications - biomechanical shoulder pain (biceps tendonitis, rotator cuff pathology, adhesive capsulitis, complex regional pain syndrome), edema (upper and lower extremity), pressure ulcers, joint contractures, depression, DVT's, aspiration pneumonia, seizures, fall risk

Assessments and Rating Scales:
Arnadottir OT-ADL Neurobehavioral Evaluation (A-ONE) (Arnadottir 1990)
Assessment of Motor and Process Skills (AMPS) (Fisher et al., 1993)
Chedoke-McMaster Stroke Assessment Scale (Gowland et al., 1993)
Canadian Occupational Performance Measure (Law et al., 2014)
Modified Ashworth Scale (Bohannon & Smith 1987)
Stroke Impact Scale (Duncan et al., 1999)

Occupational Therapy Intervention:
ADL, IADL, productivity and leisure training

- Safely incorporate affected extremity with all activities.
- Use compensatory techniques (task modification, one-handed techniques, hand-over-hand guiding, task segmentation, end chaining).
- Recommend and/or provide adaptive equipment: Rocker knife, inner lip plates, holders for books or playing cards, stabilizing devices for activities that traditionally require two-handed performance (e.g., cutting vegetables, cleaning dentures), and keyboards adapted for one-handed computer use.
- Instruct in pacing and energy conservation strategies.

Train in safe and efficient functional mobility (sit to stand, bed mobility skills, transfers, standing, ambulation and wheelchair mobility) during ADL and IADL tasks.

Stroke

Occupational Therapy Intervention:
Provide functional posture and balance activities.

- Focus on stability, weight shifting, body awareness, trunk rotation & elongation.
- Have patient turn toward affected side when reaching.
- Set up room so the patient must physically move to their affected side.
- Provide reach-grasp-hold-release activities, in standing and sitting, with and without support.

Provide activities and exercises to uninvolved side to prevent loss of ROM and strength.

Restore function of the upper extremity. Use a variety of remedial approaches according to the needs of the patient.

- Provide early mobilization and positioning.
- Incorporate task-oriented/task specific training.
- Provide opportunities to use and move the arm throughout the day (use of ball bearing feeder, mobile arm support, overhead suspension sling, functional splinting such as wrist cock-up and dynamic finger extension splints).
- Provide modified constraint-induced movement therapy (mCIT) or constraint-induced movement therapy (CIMT).
- Instruct an arm and hand strengthening exercise program.
- Provide functional electrical stimulation (FES) for wrist extensors during functional tasks and/or shoulder subluxation.
- Instruct in a functional dynamic orthoses (SaeboFlex, SaeboReach).
- Use cognitive strategies (mirror therapy, mental imagery/practice, action observation).
- Provide sensory re-education intervention.
    - Avoid increasing spasticity.
    - Encourage use of extremity in functional tasks.
    - Provide weight-bearing activities.
    - Provide sensory stimulation activities.
    - Teach compensatory techniques and safety measures for sensory deficits. Test bath/dish water temperature using the intact extremity or a thermometer. Lower the water heater temperature to 120°F (48°C). Avoid cuts and burns in kitchen. Avoid using heating pads on impaired extremities. Wear gloves to prevent frostbite. Avoid going barefoot. Wear sunscreen to prevent sunburn. Use intact hand to handle sharp kitchen utensils. Use vision to compensate to sensory loss. Perform skin checks.

Occupational Therapy Intervention:
Restore function of the upper extremity. Use a variety of remedial approaches according to the needs of the patient (continued).

- Prevent or manage hand edema.
  - Teach active self-range of motion exercises in elevation.
  - Position hand in elevation
  - Use retrograde massage.
  - Use gentle grade 1-2 mobilizations for the hand and fingers.
  - Provide a compression garment.
- Manage spasticity.
  - Prevent contractures.
  - Provide PROM, SROM and stretching exercises.
  - Instruct in positioning in bed, chair and during mobility.
  - Select use of splinting to protect hand/wrist: resting hand splint for flaccid to mild tone, spasticity splint for moderate to high tone.
  - Post-Botox injections, provide strengthening/FES to antagonists, stretching and splinting
- Prevent or manage shoulder pain.
  - Avoid overaggressive therapy and overhead pulleys.
  - Mobilize and strengthen the scapula.
  - Position arm with cubital fossa facing up, 45° shoulder abduction and comfortable shoulder external rotation.
  - Provide firm support devices such as lap trays and arm troughs.
  - Range of motion exercises should not move the shoulder beyond 90-degrees of flexion and abduction unless there is upward rotation of the scapula and external rotation of the humeral head.
  - Manage acquired orthopedic conditions (biceps tendonitis, impingement syndrome, adhesive capsulitis, rotator cuff pathologies, CRPS-1).
  - Use functional electrical stimulation (FES) for shoulder subluxation.

Instruct patient and caregivers in care of the affected extremity.

- Prevent and control of edema.
- Teach passive ROM exercises.
- Teach self-ROM exercises.
- Protect and support the affected arm during bed mobility, transfers and ambulation using slings, a pocket, or hand hold and during wheelchair use by using a hemi tray or arm trough.
- Teach proper positioning in bed, chair and wheelchair.
- Instruct in care and use of positioning splints.

Teach compensatory strategies for perceptual deficits.

Stroke

Occupational Therapy Intervention:
Provide cognitive retraining and train in the use of compensatory strategies.

Provide education about fall risk and prevention strategies.

Community reintegration:

- Complete a comprehensive, performance-based home assessment. Recommend and/or provide modifications, adaptive equipment and/or assistive technology.
- Encourage leisure and social participation.
- Address ability to drive safely. Provide referral to driving rehab specialist and/or explore alternative transportation options.
- Recommend vocational rehabilitation strategies to assist with return to work if appropriate.

Teach strategies to incorporate wellness and health management routines into daily activities.

Educate patient and caregivers about stroke, availability of community resources. Encourage participation in support groups.

Patient and Caregiver Education Handouts:

Edema (Swelling) Control of the Arm(s)	408
Edema (Swelling) Control of the Leg(s)	409
In and Out of Bed - Toward Your Weaker Left Side	250
In and Out of Bed - Toward Your Weaker Right Side	252
Position in Bed - Left Side Weakness	458
Position in Bed - Right Side Weakness	459
Position Your Arm - Left Side Weakness	461
Position Your Arm - Right Side Weakness	462
Protect the Arm - Left Side Weakness	468
Protect the Arm - Right Side Weakness	469
Splint/Brace Instructions	475
Stress Management	477
Tips to Conserve Energy	482
Using a Front Wheel Walker (2 wheels)	503
Using a Wheelchair	509

Patient and Caregiver Exercise Handouts:

Balance Exercise Guidelines	519
Balance Exercises - Sitting	520
Balance Exercises - Standing	523
Fine Motor Activities	582

Occupational Therapy TOOLKIT

Stroke

Patient and Caregiver Exercise Handouts:

Additional Treatment Guides:

Therapeutic Exercise

Tests and Measurements:
Range of motion - goniometer
Aerobic - 6 Minute Walk Test, 2 Minute Step Test, Gait Speed Test, Physical Performance Test, Timed Up and Go Test, stress testing for high risk individuals.
Resistance - 1 Repetition Max test, 30 Second Chair Stand, grip strength, Manual Muscle Test.

Occupational Therapy Intervention:
Range of Motion: exercises that increase or maintain joint mobility, prevent contractures

- Passive ROM - movement performed by external forces such as another person, or device (continuous passive motion machine)
- Active-Assisted ROM - assistance provided by another body part, another person, or a device (dowel, finger ladder, or pulleys)
- Active ROM - movement performed actively, without external aid

Aerobic/Endurance Conditioning include activities that use large muscle groups and increase heart rate/breathing for an extended period. An endurance exercise program has four variables: frequency, intensity, duration, and type of activity.

- Perform aerobic exercises a minimum of 20-30 minutes a day, 3-5 days a week. Total daily exercise time can be cumulative (i.e. 10 minutes, 3 times a day). Exercise at a moderate to vigorous intensity. Include a 5-10 minute warm-up period consisting of total body movements and a 10-minute cool-down period consisting of total body movement and static stretches. *
- Gardening, mowing, raking, housework, cycling on a stationary bicycle, bicycling or walking outdoors, mall walking, Nordic walking, hiking, swimming, dancing, treadmill, elliptical trainer, sustained arm movement, stair climbing, rowing machines, arm cycling, arm ergometer, wheelchair pushing, wheelchair sports, boxing, low-impact aerobics, seated aerobics, water aerobics, exercise videos, community exercise programs, golfing without a cart

Resistive/Strengthening Exercise includes exercise and activities that build muscle strength, power, and endurance. A resistive exercise program has five variables: resistance, intensity, reps, sets, and frequency.

- Perform resistive exercises 2-3 times a week on nonconsecutive days. Exercise at a moderate to high intensity. Perform 8-10 exercises that target the major muscle groups, with 10-15 repetitions.*
- Inhale before the lift; spend two to three seconds on the concentric contraction while exhaling, and then four to six seconds for the eccentric contraction.
- Rest one to two minute between exercises

Therapeutic Exercise

Occupational Therapy Intervention:
Resistive Exercise (continued)

- Duration of the exercise program can be limited or indefinite (6 to 12 weeks are required for significant change in muscle strength and muscle endurance).
- Hand-held weights, cuff weights, resistive bands, open-kinetic-chain exercise, closed-kinetic-chain exercises, isometrics, PNF, Pilates, Yoga, Tai chi, body-weight exercises, medicine balls, stairs, rowing, machine circuit workout, exercise videos, community exercise programs, exercise programs for a specific conditions

Flexibility/Stretching includes techniques that stretch muscle length. Includes - static stretching, dynamic stretching, PNF, and joint mobilization/manipulation techniques

- Perform stretching exercises 3-7 times a week for at least 10 minutes. Stretch each major muscle group for 20-30 seconds, repeat 3-4 times.*
- Perform stretches following aerobic and strengthening exercises.
- Yoga, flexibility routines, mechanical stretching, assisted stretching

Balance Exercise - see separate treatment guide

*Recommendations based on the ACSM's Exercise Management for Persons with Chronic Disease and Disabilities.

Patient and Caregiver Handouts:
Range of Motion

Aerobic/Endurance Conditioning

Resistive Exercise

Occupational Therapy TOOLKIT

Therapeutic Exercise

Patient and Caregiver Handouts:
Resistive Exercise

Flexibility/Stretching

Other

Toileting

Toileting includes bowel and bladder continence, clothing management, obtaining toilet paper, flushing toilet, maintaining toileting position, maintaining hygiene (for females, wiping from front to back), washing hands, donning and removing incontinence briefs and pads, disposing of incontinence briefs and pads, managing menses, caring for catheters (external, indwelling, intermittent), caring for ostomies, using urinals and bedpans, using enemas and suppositories, performing bowel and bladder programs

Impairments and Functional Limitations:
Impaired UE/LE strength, ROM, sensation and/or coordination
Limited activity tolerance and endurance
Impaired balance
Pain
Visual perceptual impairment
Cognitive impairment

Occupational Therapy Intervention:
Apply different approaches for solving difficulties with toileting.

- Remediate underlying limitations to safety and independence. Physical impairments (muscle weakness, impaired hand function, limited ROM, paralysis, incoordination, impaired balance, fatigue, dyspnea, abnormal tone, tremor), sensory impairment (impaired sensation, low vision, hard of hearing, vestibular, pain), behavioral, cognition, perception.
- Train in compensatory techniques (safety techniques, one-handed techniques, pacing, energy conservation, joint protection, body mechanics, breathing techniques, low vision techniques, cognitive/perceptual compensation. Using step-by-step instructions, task segmentation, task sequencing, backward chaining, verbal and physical cueing, timed voiding).
- Train in the use of adaptive equipment and assistive devices (toilet aids, female and male urinals, raised toilet seat, toilet safety frame, bedside commode, grab bars, rolling commode, overhead transfer system).
- Provide environmental modifications and adaptations (move toilet paper within easy reach, keep an extra set of dressing tools in the bathroom, color toilet bowl water to make the water easier to see, install a higher toilet).
- Instruct in activity modification.
    - Change the task (men can sit to urinate, stand to flush toilet to avoid twisting).
    - Eliminate part or the entire task (use no-rinse hand cleaners to eliminate hand washing, use bedside commode to eliminate using the bathroom).
    - Have someone else do part or the entire task.

Toileting

Occupational Therapy Intervention:
Train in safe and efficient functional mobility (sit to stand, bed mobility skills, transfers, standing, ambulation, and wheelchair mobility) during toileting tasks.

Provide caregiver/family education and training.

Patient and Caregiver Handouts:

Therapist Resources:

Occupational Therapy TOOLKIT

Total Hip Replacement (Arthroplasty)

Impairments and Functional Limitations:
ADL, IADL, productivity and leisure impairment
Functional mobility impairment
Impaired lower extremity strength, ROM
Impaired endurance/tolerance for sitting/standing
Hip movement restrictions and/or weight bearing restrictions
Post-op pain and edema
Co-occurring conditions - femoral neck fracture, avascular necrosis, osteoarthritis, osteoporosis, rheumatoid arthritis
Potential complications - DVT, prosthesis dislocation, Trendelenburg gait, sciatic nerve injury, infection of surgical site or prosthesis, greater trochanteric pain syndrome, piriformis syndrome, fall risk

Occupational Therapy Intervention:
ADL, IADL, productivity and leisure training

- Apply hip dislocation precautions and/or weight bearing restrictions.
- Train in use of long handled adaptive equipment for toileting, bathing and LE dressing (including anti-embolism stockings) to compensate for restricted hip ROM, dislocation precautions and/or pain (shower chair, grab bars, non-slip mat, hand-held shower, long bath sponge, raised toilet seat, bedside commode, leg lifter, reacher, sock aid, shoehorn, elastic shoelaces, dressing stick, walker bag).

Train in safe and efficient functional mobility (sit to stand, bed mobility skills, transfers, standing, ambulation and wheelchair mobility) with adherence to hip ROM precautions and/or weight bearing restrictions. Instruct in safe walker use and transport of items.

Provide therapeutic activities and exercises.

- Strengthen upper body for walker/cane usage.
- Progress sitting and standing tolerance during ADLs and mobility
- Increase balance confidence with ADL tasks.

Complete a comprehensive, performance-based home assessment. Recommend and/or provide modifications, adaptive equipment and/or assistive technology.

Provide education about fall risk and prevention strategies.

Patient and Caregiver Handouts:

Car Transfer	225
Hip Dislocation Precautions - Posterior Approach	422
In and Out of Bed - Toward Your Left Side After Hip Surgery	240

Occupational Therapy TOOLKIT

Total Hip Replacement (Arthroplasty)

Patient and Caregiver Handouts:

Additional Treatment Guides:

Total Knee Replacement (Arthroplasty)

Impairments and Functional Limitations:
ADL, IADL, productivity and leisure impairment
Functional mobility impairment
Muscle weakness
Limited knee range of motion
Impaired endurance/tolerance for sitting/standing
Post-op pain and edema
Weight bearing restrictions
Co-occurring conditions - osteoarthritis, rheumatoid arthritis
Potential complications - DVT, infection of surgical site or prosthesis, knee flexion contracture, peroneal nerve palsy, patellar fracture, supracondylar fracture

Occupational Therapy Intervention:
ADL, IADL, productivity and leisure training

- Train in the use of adaptive equipment to compensate for knee ROM limitations and adhere to weight bearing restrictions if imposed. Walker bag, walker tray, shower chair, grab bars, non-slip mat, hand-held shower, long bath sponge, raised toilet seat, bedside commode, leg lifter, reacher, sock aid, shoehorn, elastic shoelaces, dressing stick.

Train in safe and efficient functional mobility (sit to stand, bed mobility skills, transfers, standing, ambulation and wheelchair mobility) during ADL and IADL tasks.

- Instruct in walker safety and transport of items.

Provide therapeutic activities and exercises.

- Strengthen upper body for walker/cane usage.
- Progress sitting and standing tolerance during ADLs and mobility
- Increase balance confidence with ADL tasks.

Complete a comprehensive, performance-based home assessment. Recommend and/or provide modifications, adaptive equipment and/or assistive technology.

Provide education about fall risk and prevention strategies.

Patient and Caregiver Handouts:
Upper Body Exercises - Hand Weights 765

Additional Treatment Guides:
Fall Risk Assessment and Prevention 84
Functional Mobility 103
Home Safety and Modification 118

Total Shoulder Replacement (Arthroplasty)

Impairments and Functional Limitations:
ADL, IADL, productivity and leisure impairment
Functional mobility impairment
Muscle weakness
Limited ROM
Shoulder movement restrictions and/or weight bearing restrictions
Post-op pain and edema
Co-occurring conditions - osteoarthritis, rheumatoid arthritis, osteonecrosis, rotator cuff repair, fractures of the humeral head
Potential complications - prosthetic loosening, glenohumeral instability, rotator cuff tears, nerve injury, and deltoid detachment

Outcome Measures:
American Shoulder and Elbow Surgeon's Shoulder Evaluation (Beaton et al., 1996)
Simple Shoulder Test (Lippitt et al., 1993)

Occupational Therapy Intervention:
ADL, IADL, productivity and leisure training

- Train in one-handed techniques and adaptive equipment while adhering to shoulder precautions.
- Instruct in axillary hygiene, shoulder precautions, donning and doffing of shoulder sling/immobilizer, cryotherapy unit, arm positioning in sitting and supine, signs and symptoms of wound infection.

Train in safe and efficient functional mobility (sit to stand, bed mobility skills, transfers, standing, ambulation and wheelchair mobility) during ADL and IADL tasks while adhering to shoulder precautions.

Provide progressive shoulder activities and exercises to increase ROM and strength. Progression depends on co-morbidities, surgical procedure performed, stage of healing, and postoperative complications. *Follow the referring surgeon's specific guidelines for progression.*

- Immediate Postoperative Phase
  - Passive exercises and active-assisted exercises
- Early Strengthening
  - Active exercises
- Moderate Strengthening
  - Strengthening exercises, light functional activities
- Advance Strengthening
  - Progressive home program

Occupational Therapy TOOLKIT

Total Shoulder Replacement (Arthroplasty)

Occupational Therapy Intervention:
Provide activities and exercises for all uninvolved joints to prevent loss of ROM and strength.

Instruct in pain self-management strategies

- Coordinate medication peak with exercise and activity.
- Apply superficial heat and cold.
- Practice deep (diaphragmatic) breathing and other relaxation techniques.

Educate regarding fall risk and prevention strategies.

Complete a comprehensive, performance-based home assessment. Recommend and/or provide home and activity modifications.

Patient and Caregiver Handouts:

Additional Treatment Guides:

Occupational Therapy TOOLKIT

Urinary Incontinence

Includes functional, urge, stress, mixed, and overflow urinary incontinence

Impairments and Functional Limitations:
Physical impairments that limit mobility, transfers, and clothing management
Cognitive impairment
Environmental limitations
Weak pelvic floor
Co-occurring conditions - diabetes, stroke, dementia, multiple sclerosis, Parkinson's disease, SCI, spinal stenosis, pulmonary disease
Potential complications - accelerated need for long-term care placement, social isolation fall risk, skin breakdown, depression

Occupational Therapy Intervention:
Treat underlying cognitive, physical and environmental limitations to safety and independence.

Provide toilet management training.

- Managing absorbent product (selection, don/doff, timely changing and disposal).
- Cleaning thoroughly after toileting (flushable wipes, instruct women to clean front to back).
- Teach managing clothing during toileting. Recommend clothing that is easy to remove.
- Toileting transfer with adaptive equipment (grab bars, raised seats)
- Provide alternatives to using a toilet (male and female urinals, bedpans and bedside commodes).

Instruct in implementing behavioral techniques.

- Scheduled toileting - functional UI
- Double voiding - overflow UI
- Urge suppression techniques - urge UI
- Prompted toileting - urge, stress and mixed UI
- Contract pelvic floor muscles before coughing or sneezing - stress UI

Instruct in exercise program - urge, stress and mixed UI.

- Pelvic floor muscle exercises (Kegel), with or without biofeedback, vaginal weight training and/or pelvic floor electrical stimulation
- Facilitory muscles exercises (transverse abdominis, hip adductor, hip abductor and gluteal contractions)
- Refer to a specialist as needed.

Urinary Incontinence

Patient and Caregiver Handouts:

Additional Treatment Guides:

Therapist Resources:

Vertebral Compression Fracture

Impairments and Functional Limitations:
ADL, IADL, productivity and leisure impairment
Functional mobility impairment
Gait changes (COG forward)
Postural changes (thoracic kyphosis)
Limited activity tolerance and endurance
Muscle weakness
Back pain that worsens with upright postures
Instability and problems with balance loss
Co-occurring conditions - osteoporosis, greater trochanteric pain syndrome, cancer, Paget's disease

Occupational Therapy Intervention:
ADL, IADL, productivity and leisure training

- Recommend and/or provide adaptive equipment and task modifications to avoid spinal flexion and trunk rotation.
- Train to don and doff back support brace.
- Instruct in pacing, energy conservation, good posture, and body mechanics.
- Reinforce dietary instructions during kitchen management.

Train in safe and efficient functional mobility (sit to stand, bed mobility skills, transfers, standing, ambulation and wheelchair mobility) during ADL and IADL tasks.

Instruct in body mechanics and good posture to minimize spinal flexion and trunk rotation.

Instruct in pain self-management strategies.

- Coordinate medication peak with exercise and activity.
- Apply superficial heat and cold.
- Practice deep (diaphragmatic) breathing and other relaxation techniques.
- Use positioning devices (seat cushions, back supports, pillows, splints).
- Instruct in using a pain journal.
- Utilize the problem solving process to identify ways to manage pain.

Provide education about fall risk and prevention strategies.

Complete a comprehensive, performance-based home assessment. Recommend and/or provide modifications, adaptive equipment and/or assistive technology.

Teach strategies to incorporate wellness and health management routines into daily activities.

Occupational Therapy TOOLKIT

Vertebral Compression Fracture

Patient and Caregiver Handouts:

Additional Treatment Guides:

Visual Perception

Visual Perception Includes:
Basic visual skills (visual acuity, visual fields, ocular motility)
Unilateral spatial neglect (personal, peri-personal and extra-personal neglect)
Visual perception (visual-motor integration, visual closure, spatial relations, figure-ground discrimination, visual sequencing, visual memory, form constancy)

Assessments:
Arnadottir OT-ADL Neurobehavioral Evaluation (A-ONE) (Arnadottir 1990)
Basic visual skills (Snellen eye chart, confrontation visual field exam)
Catherine Bergego Scale (unilateral spatial neglect) (Azouvi et al., 1996)
Line Bisection and Cancellation Tests (unilateral spatial neglect) (Wilson et al., 1987)
Motor Free Visual Perception Test (Colarusso et al., 2001)
Occupational Therapy Adult Perceptual Screening Test (Cooke et al., 2004)
Ontario Society of Occupational Therapists Perceptual Evaluation (Boys et al., 1988)
Rivermead Perceptual Assessment Battery (Whiting et al., 1985)

Occupational Therapy Intervention:
Visual Acuity
- Refer to a vision specialist for corrective lenses.
- Instruct to wear corrective lenses during activities.
- Modify the environment and tasks - use large print items, magnifiers, increase lighting, use contrast, decrease clutter.
- Teach compensation by using the remaining sensory systems.

Visual Fields
- Outline working areas for tasks (reading, sorting, or cooking).
- Teach compensation by turning the head.

Ocular Motility
- Oculo-motor exercises

Unilateral Spatial Neglect
- Put important objects and communicate on the *unaffected* side.
- Provide verbal cues to scan to the affected side.
- Provide visual cues in the affected space such as post-it notes or colored tape.
- Modify environment (reduce clutter, improve lighting, organize items).
- Trunk rotation activities
- Limb activation activities (such as constraint induced movement therapy)
- Neck/hand vibration during scanning activities
- Prism Glasses
- Eye patching over the "unaffected" eye
- Visual scanning activities
- Mental imagery (Lighthouse strategy)

Visual Perception

Occupational Therapy Intervention:

Visual-Motor Integration

- Functional activities that require eye-hand, eye-foot or eye-body coordination (fine motor tasks, ball kicking, tapping foot and clapping in time to music)

Figure-Ground Discrimination

- Provide activities that require finding items from a background (item in a cluttered drawer, a white sock on a white countertop, food in the refrigerator).
- Environmental adaptations (organize, minimize visual distractions and clutter, add color and contrast)

Visual Spatial Relations

- Use hand-over-hand guiding during functional tasks.
- Compensate by using sense of touch.
- Environmental adaptations (organize, minimize visual distractions and clutter, add color and contrast)
- Obstacle courses

Form Constancy

- Practice identifying object of similar shape, in different orientations.
- Compensate by using sense of touch.
- Environmental adaptations (organize, minimize visual distractions and clutter, add color and contrast, label items, keep frequently used items oriented correctly)

Patient and Caregiver Handouts:

Adaptive Equipment for Bathing

Item	Picture	Where to Buy
☐ Bath transfer bench	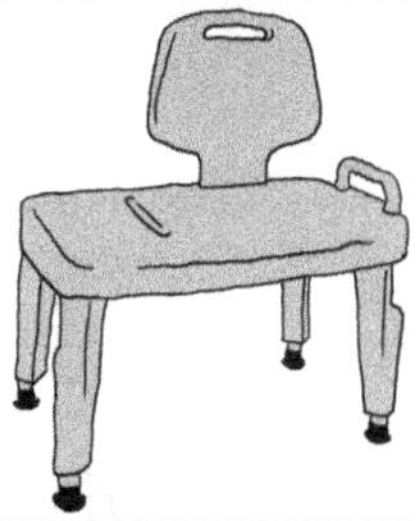	
☐ Bath seat	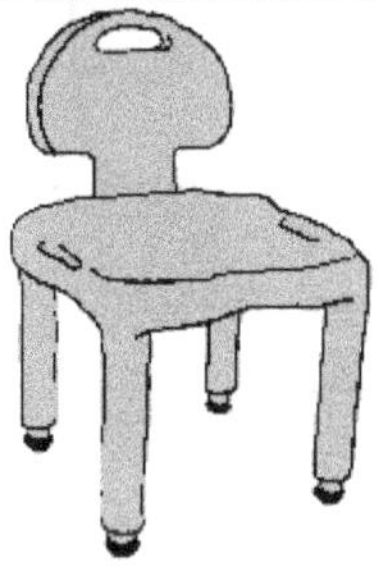	
☐ Shower seat		
☐ Round shower stool	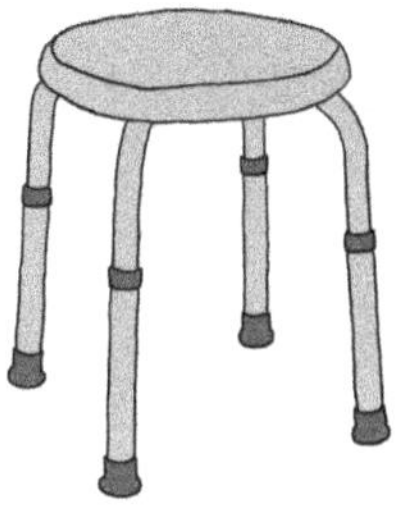	
☐ Shower stool with a seat that turns	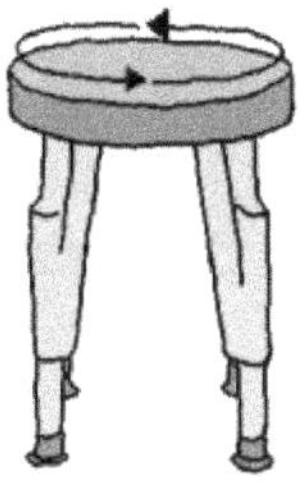	

Occupational Therapy TOOLKiT

Adaptive Equipment for Bathing

Item	Picture	Where to Buy
☐ Grab bar		
☐ Clamp-on tub rail	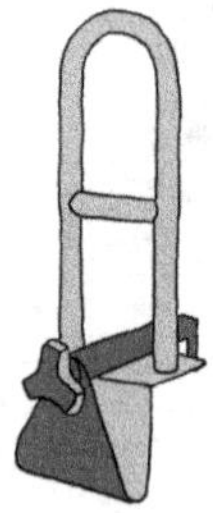	
☐ Non-slip bath mat	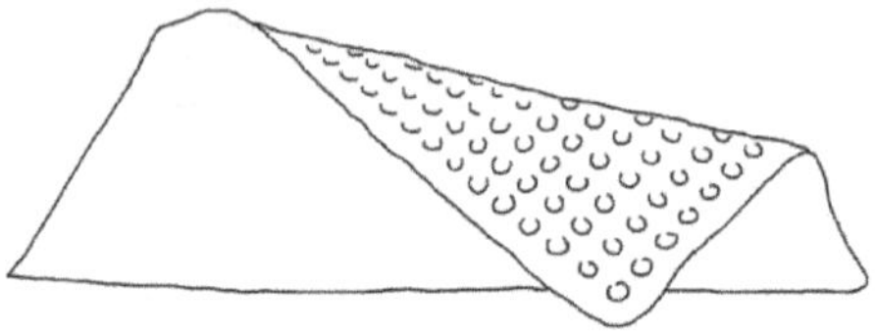	
☐ Handheld shower	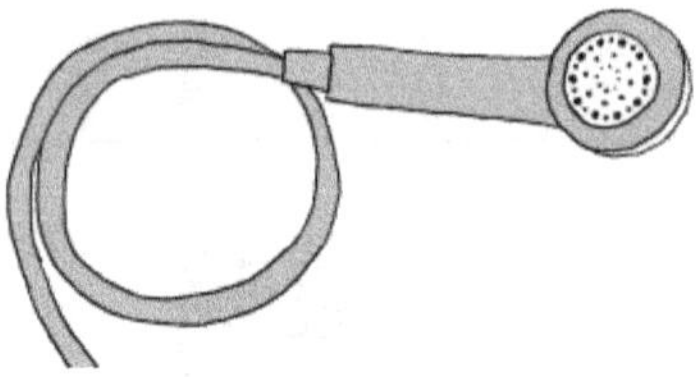	
☐ Long handle brush		
☐ Leg lifter		

Occupational Therapy TOOLKIT

Adaptive Equipment for Dressing

Item	Picture	Where to Buy
☐ Dressing stick		
☐ Soft sock aid	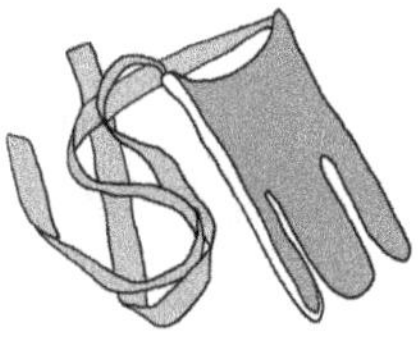	
☐ Hard sock aid		
☐ Reacher		
☐ Button hook	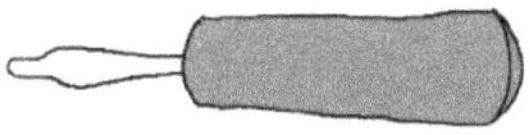	
☐ Long shoe horn		
☐ Stretch laces		
☐ Velcro for shoes and clothes		

Adaptive Equipment for Eating

Item	Picture	Where to Buy
☐ Cuff with slot	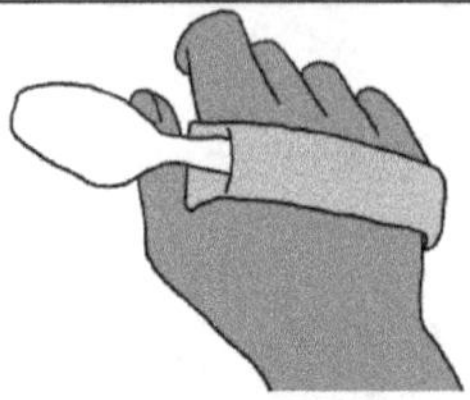	
☐ Built up spoon and fork		
☐ Angled spoon and fork		
☐ Weighted spoon and fork	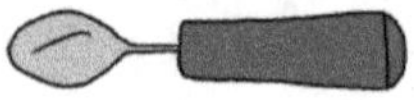	
☐ Rocker knife		
☐ Rolling knife		
☐ Inner lip plate	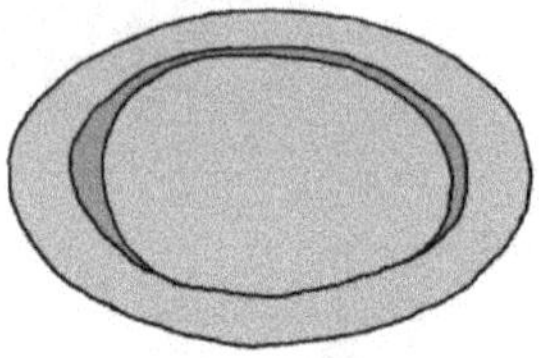	
☐ Nose cut-out cup	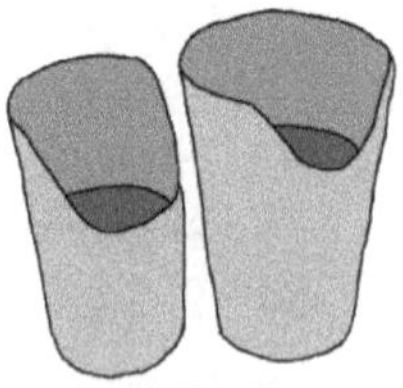	
☐ Mug with a lid		

Occupational Therapy TOOLKIT

Adaptive Equipment for Grooming and Mouth Care

	Item	Picture	Where to Buy
☐	Electric toothbrush	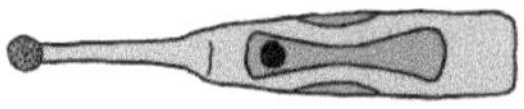	
☐	Dental floss holder		
☐	Nail brush with suction base	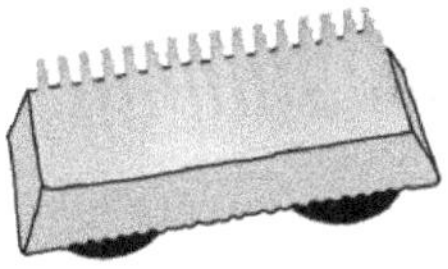	
☐	Long handle device to apply lotion		
☐	Long handle combs and brushes	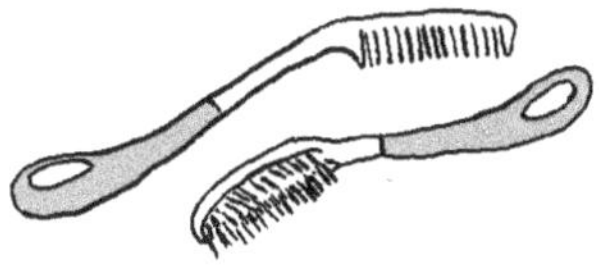	
☐	Long handle mirror	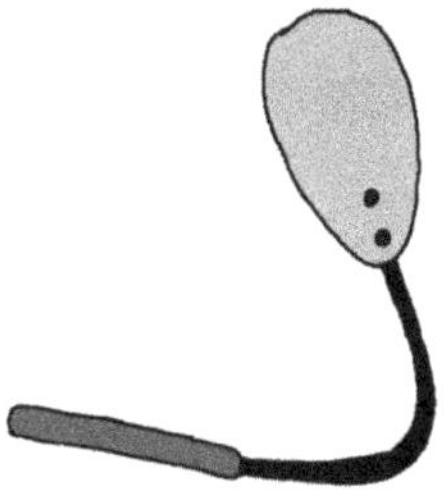	
☐	Foam tubing	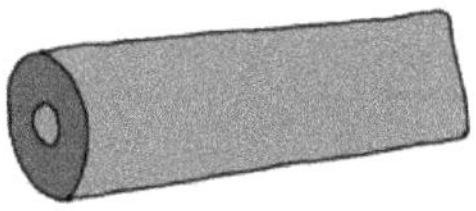	
☐	Non-slip drawer liner		

Occupational Therapy TOOLKIT

Adaptive Equipment for Meal Prep

Item	Picture	Where to Buy
☐ Cutting board	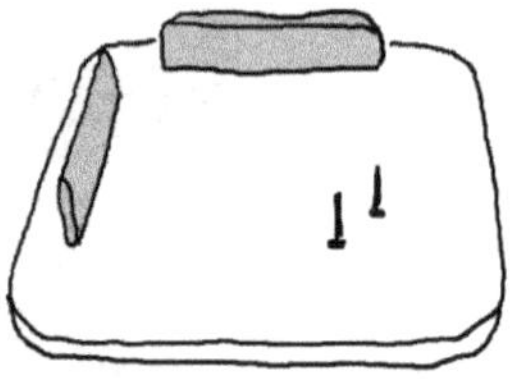	
☐ Scoop strainer	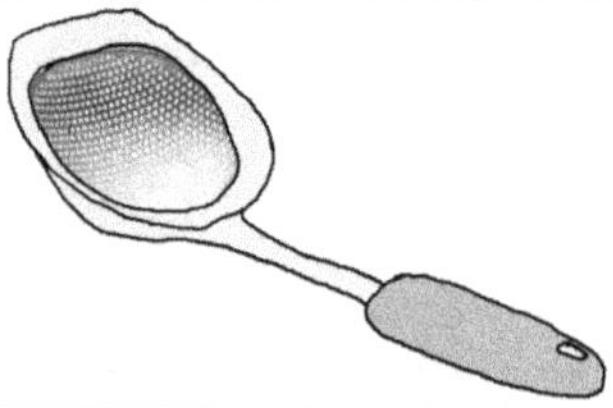	
☐ Can opener		
☐ Device to open jars	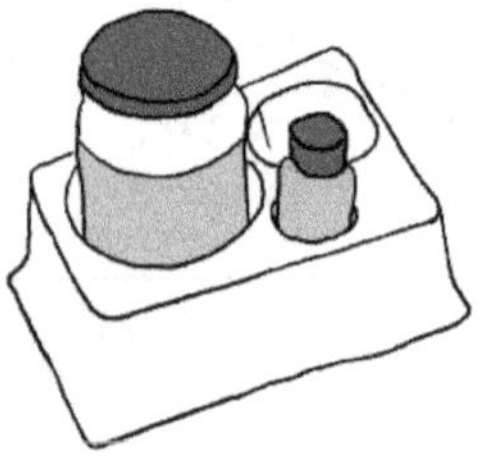	
☐ Scissors that stay open	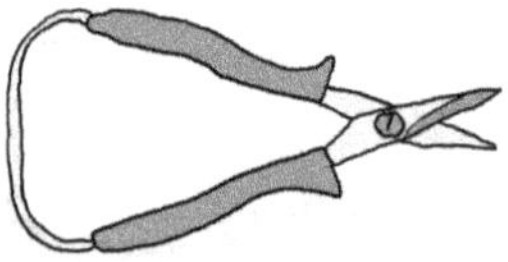	
☐ Peeler	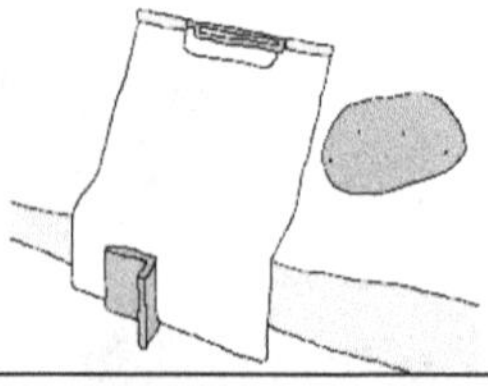	
☐ Pot holder	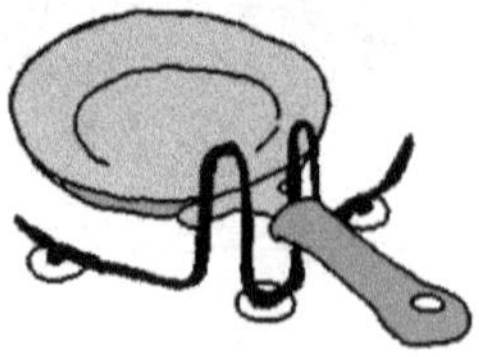	

Occupational Therapy TOOLKIT

Adaptive Equipment for Mobility

Item	Picture	Where to Buy
☐ Wheelchair	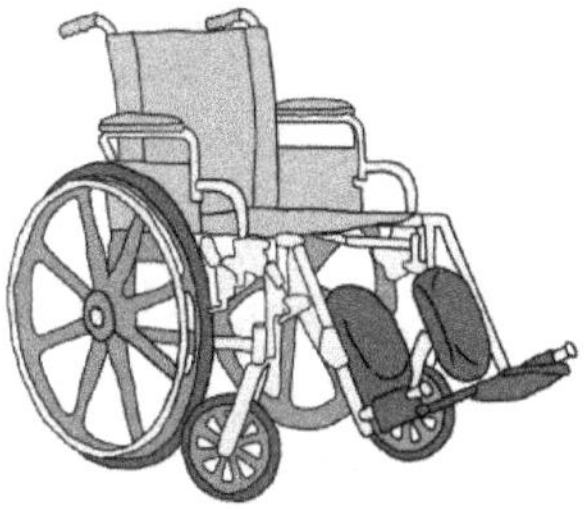	
☐ Transport chair	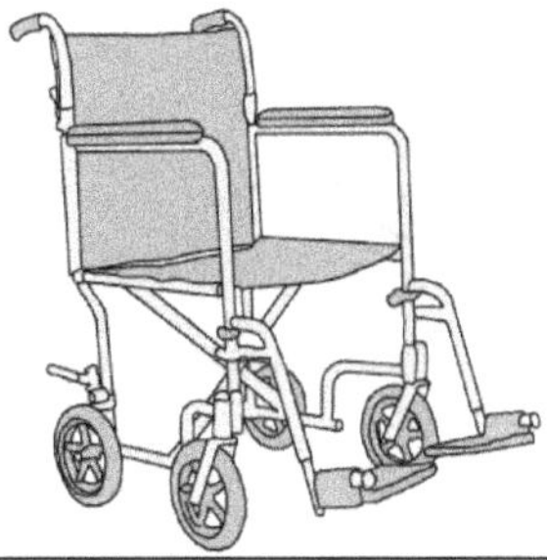	
☐ Standard walker	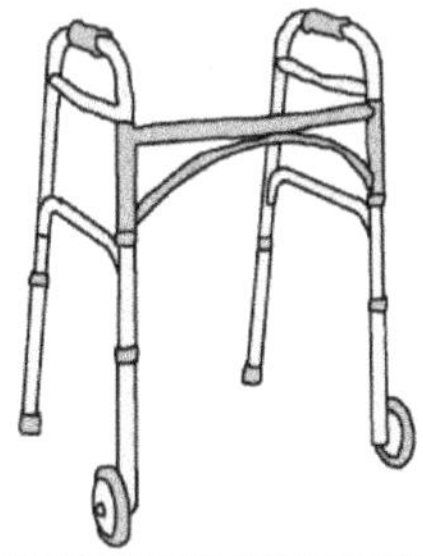	
☐ Walker skies	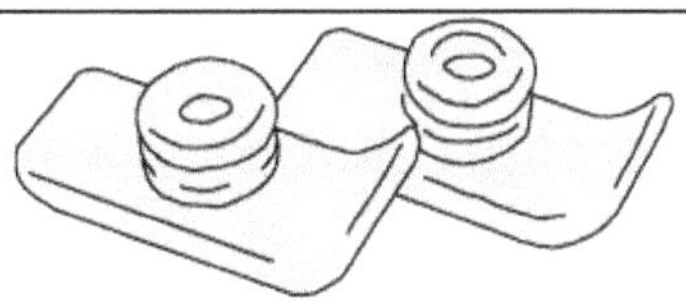	
☐ Rollator	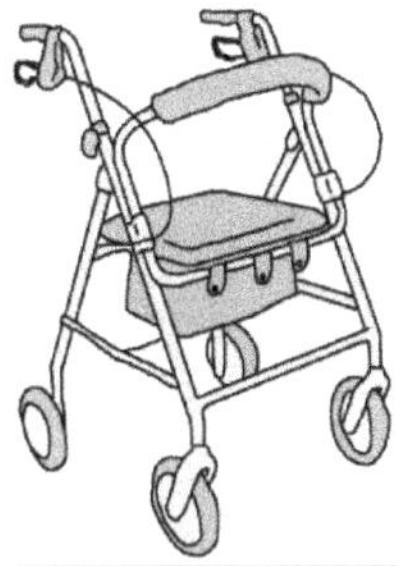	

Adaptive Equipment for Moving in Bed

Item	Picture	Where to Buy
☐ Over-bed trapeze	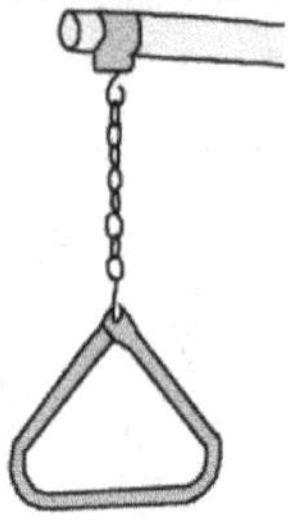	
☐ Bed ladder	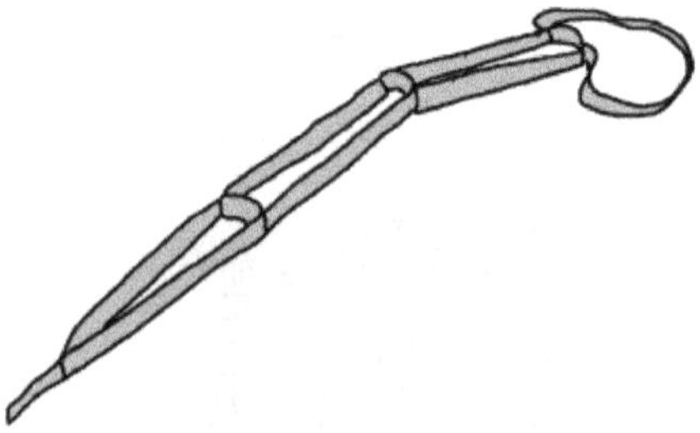	
☐ Blanket support frame	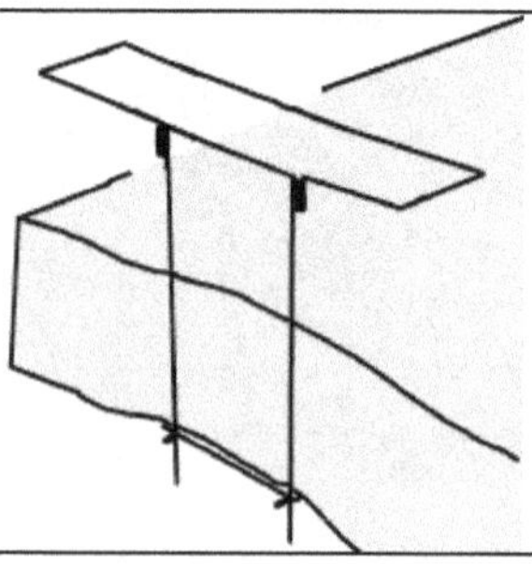	
☐ Leg lifter	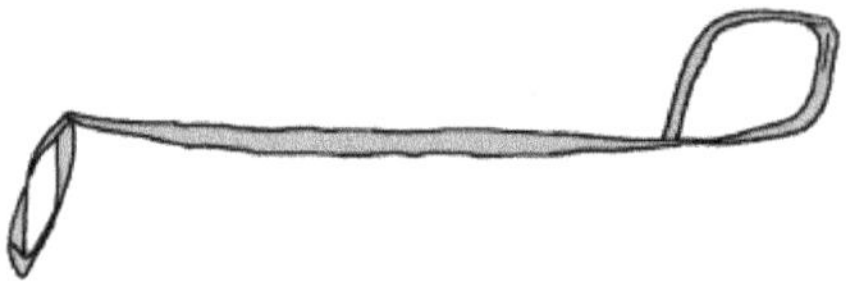	
☐ Bed handle	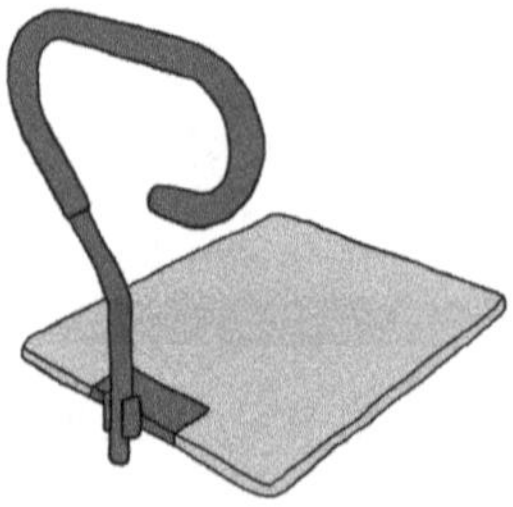	

Adaptive Equipment for Transfers

Item	Picture	Where to Buy
☐ Transfer board	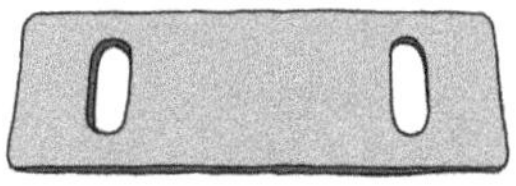	
☐ Bed and chair risers	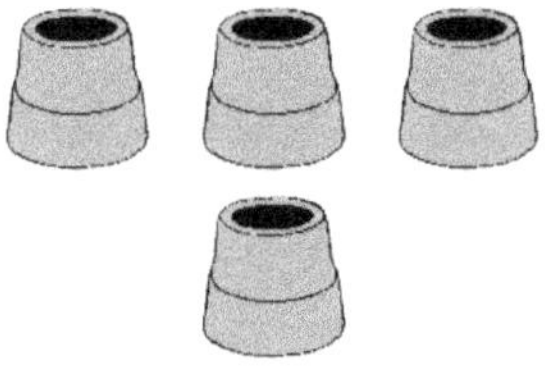	
☐ Transfer belt	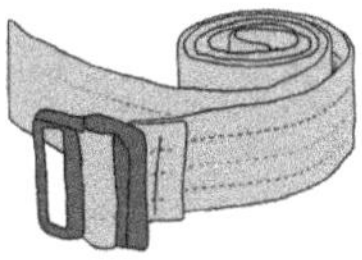	
☐ Lift chair	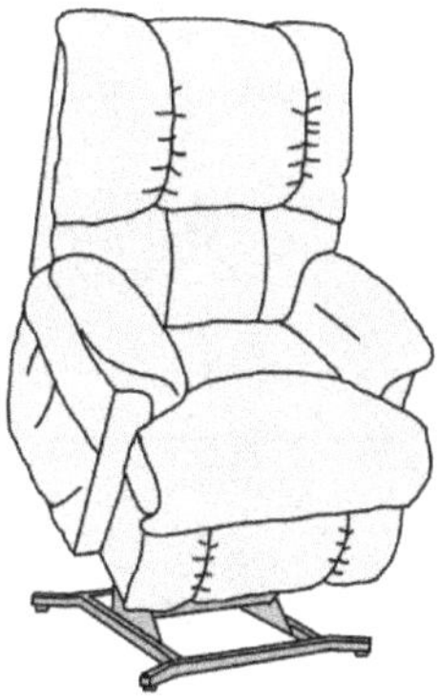	
☐ Patient lift	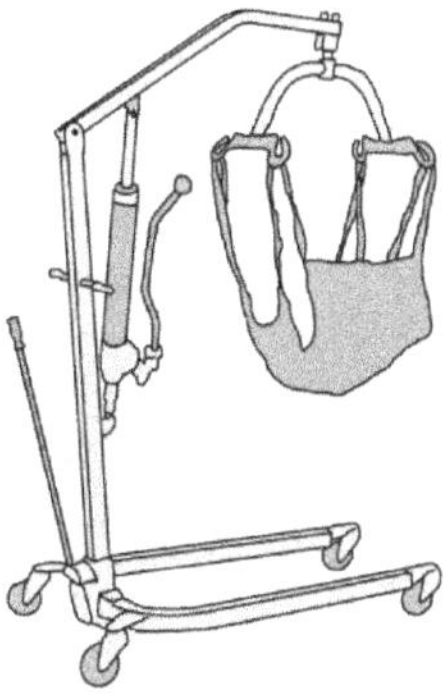	

Occupational Therapy TOOLKIT

Adaptive Equipment for Using the Bathroom

Item	Picture	Where to Buy
☐ Bedside commode		
☐ Toilet frame		
☐ Raised toilet seat without arms		
☐ Raised toilet seat with arms		
☐ Moist wipes	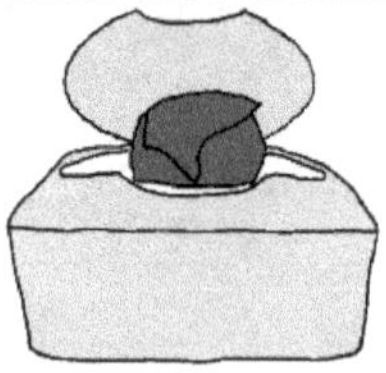	
☐ Wiping aid	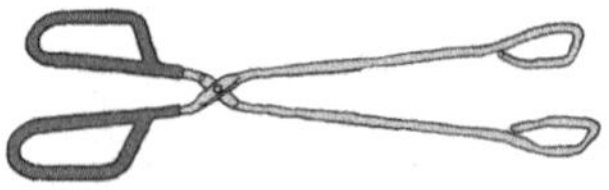	
☐ Urinals	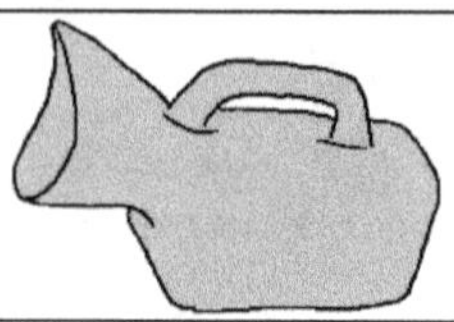	

Occupational Therapy TOOLKIT

Adaptive Equipment for Walking

Item	Picture	Where to Buy
☐ Hemi walker		
☐ Quad cane	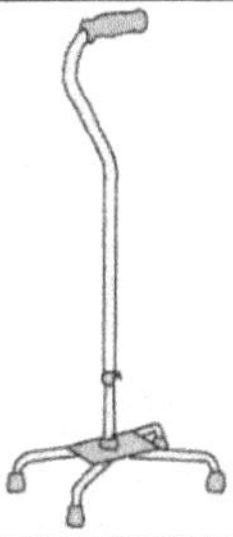	
☐ Straight cane		
☐ Tripod cane base	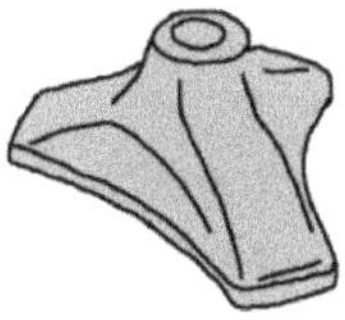	
☐ Walker tray	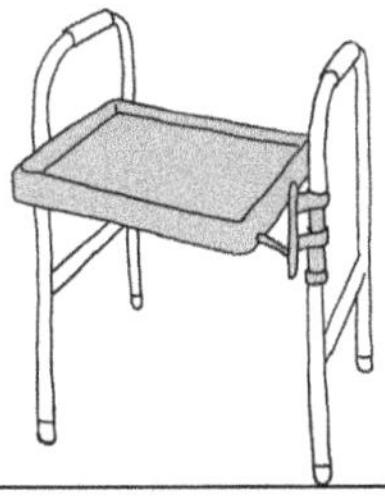	
☐ Walker basket		

Bathing Tips

- Allow enough time to bathe. It is not safe to rush when you are soapy and wet.
- Be sure the floor of the tub or shower is non-slip. If it is not, apply a non-slip bath mat.

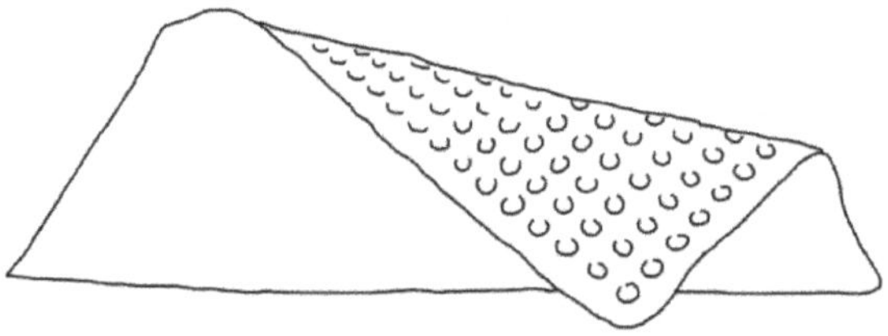

- If you use a cane, tell someone that you are in the shower.
If you use a walker, have someone in the bathroom ready to help if needed.
If you use a wheelchair, have someone help you transfer and bathe.
- If you cannot stand in the shower, use a shower seat or bath bench. Do not use a folding chair or lawn chair. They are unsafe and can make you fall.

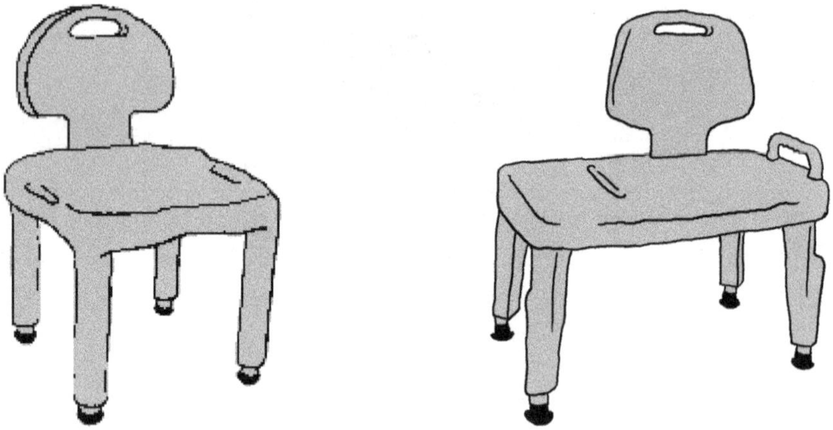

- Wear a medical alert button while you bathe.
- Lower the water heater to about 120°F (48°C) to prevent burns.

Bathing Tips

- Lower the shower caddy, so you can reach items when you sit to bathe.
- Lower the hooks on the back of the door. This will make the towels easy to reach.
- Place a bar of soap in a nylon stocking and tie to the shower chair. Use liquid soap in plastic pump bottles.
- Adjust the front legs of the shower chair or bench higher. This offsets the slope of the tub.
- Do not hold onto the soap dish, towel bars, or shower doors for support. Install grab bars on the wall where you enter. Also install one on the inside wall of the tub or shower stall.
- Use a towel or a leg lifter to lift your legs into the tub.
- Place non-slip treads on the tub where you step in. This will to keep your foot from slipping.
- Use a rubber mat to grip the faucets.
- If drying off is tiring, use hand towels or a terry cloth robe. Dry off before getting out of the tub.
- Finish drying by sitting on the toilet seat. Use a toilet seat cover, so you do not slip.

Bridging

1. Lie on your back. Bend your knees and place both feet flat. Rest your arms at your sides.

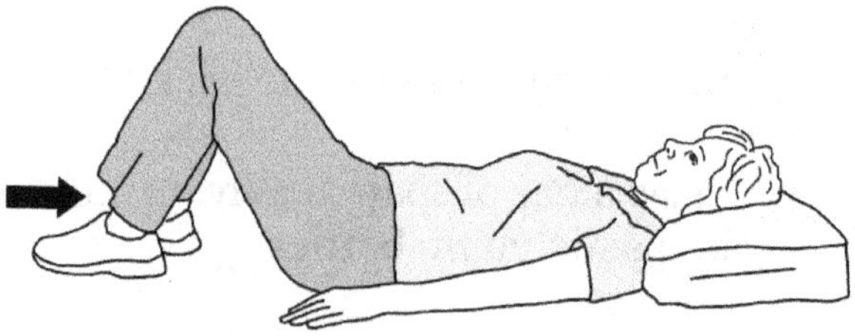

2. Press your feet and your arms into the bed. Lift your hips off the bed.

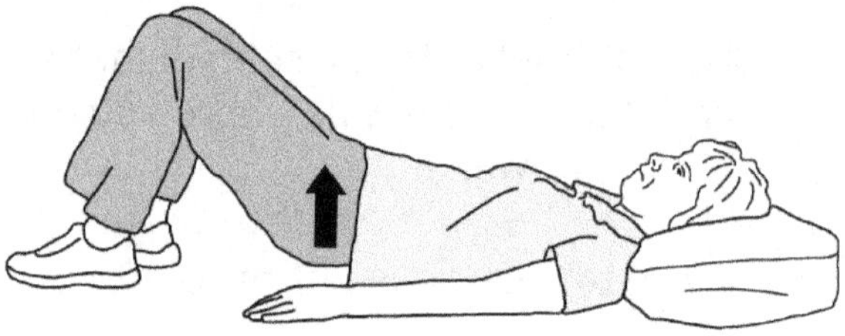

3. A caregiver can help by holding your knees.

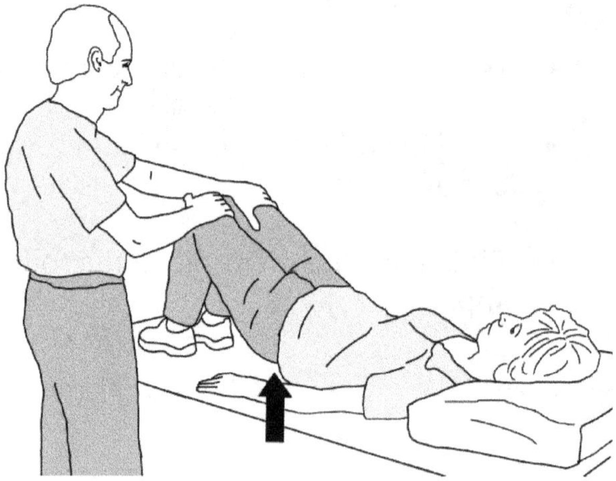

Car Transfer

1. Move the seat as far back as it will go. Use a cushion or pillow on the seat to raise it.

2. Move back until you feel the seat against your legs.

3. Place one hand on the dashboard and one hand on the back of the seat. Tuck your head and sit down.

4. Move back onto the seat as far as you can. Lift your legs into the car one at a time.

Reverse this process to exit the car.

Down a Curb or Single Step Using a Walker

Do not rush. Make sure you have your balance before stepping down.

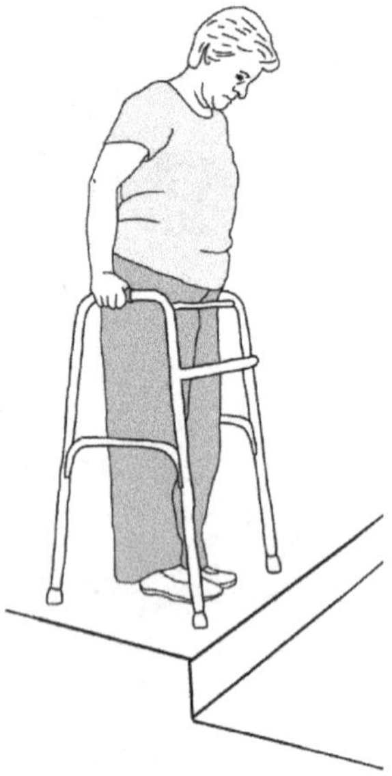

1. Walk up to the curb until the walker is near the edge. Step into the walker.

2. Lower the walker. Place all four legs of the walker onto the ground.

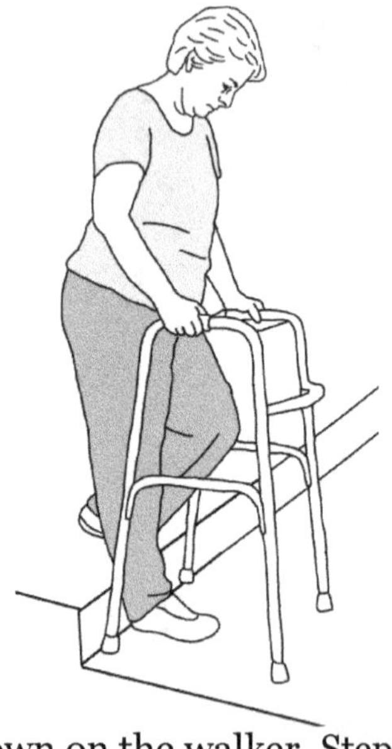

3. Push down on the walker. Step down with your weaker leg.

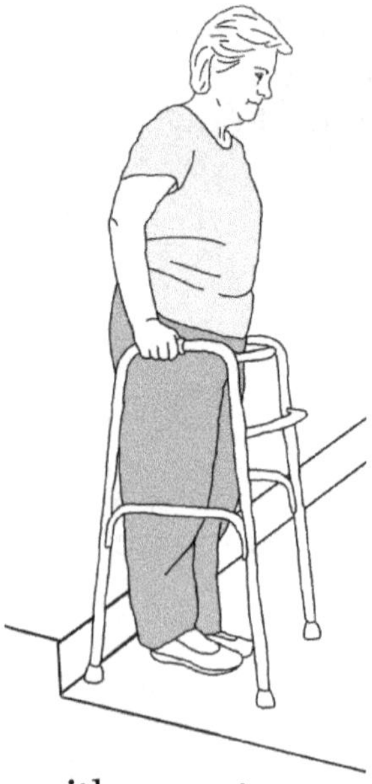

4. Step down with your stronger leg.

Up with the "good" and down with the "bad". This is an easy way to recall which leg to use first.

Down Steps with a Rail Using a Cane

Do not rush. Make sure you have your balance before using the stairs.

1. Hold on to the rail. Hold the cane in your other hand. This may be your weaker side or your stronger side.

2. Place the cane down on the first step.

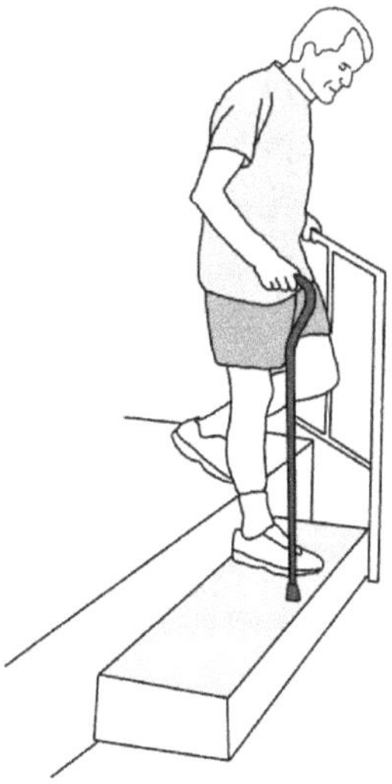

3. Step down with your weaker leg.

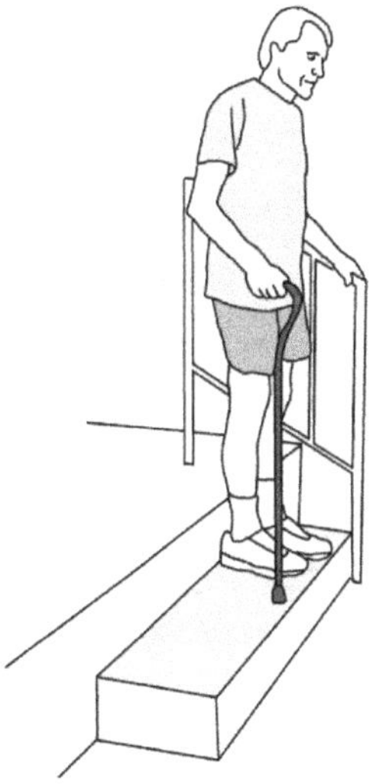

4. Step down with your stronger leg to the same step. Balance yourself. Repeat: cane, weaker leg, stronger leg, one step at a time.

Up with the "good" and down with the "bad". This is an easy way to recall which leg to use first.

Occupational Therapy TOOLKIT

Down Steps with a Rail Using a Closed Walker

Do not rush. Make sure you have your balance before using the stairs.

1. Fold the walker. Hold the rail. Place the walker to your side and down to the next step, along the riser.

2. Support your weight between the rail and the walker. Step down with your weaker leg.

3. Step down to the same step with your stronger leg. Balance yourself.

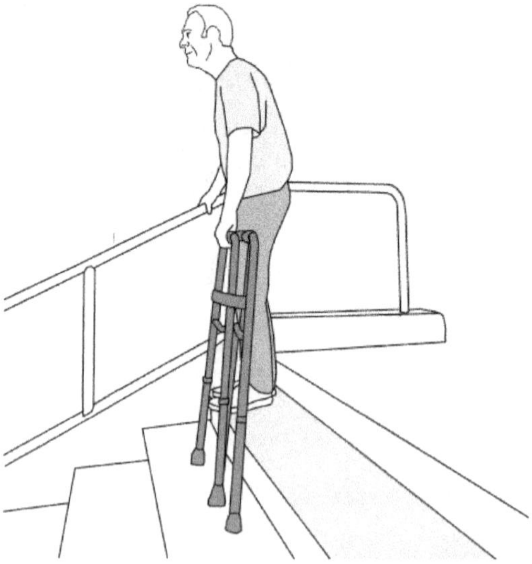

4. Repeat: walker, weaker leg, stronger leg, one step at a time.

Up with the "good" and down with the "bad". This is an easy way to recall which leg to use first.

Down Steps with a Rail Using an Open Walker

Do not rush. Make sure you have your balance before using the stairs.

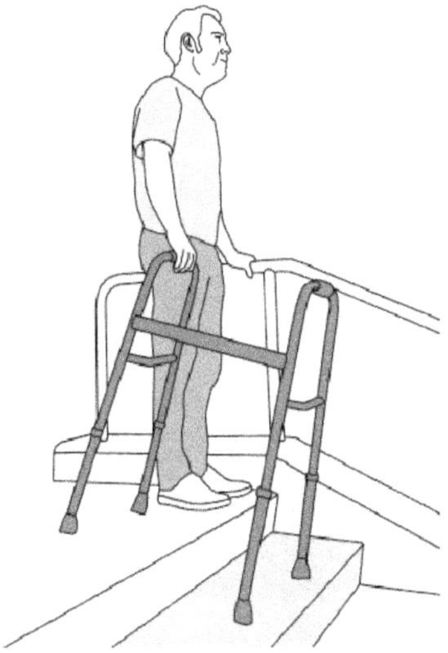

1. Hold the walker with one hand and the rail with your other hand. Turn the walker to the side. Put the front two legs of the walker on the next step down.

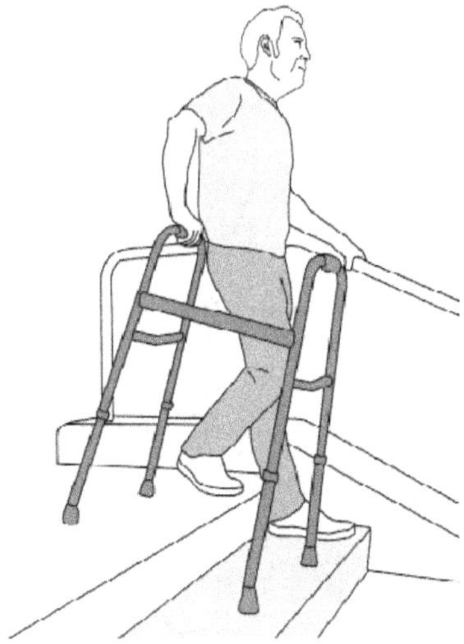

2. Support your weight between the rail and the walker. Step down with your weaker leg.

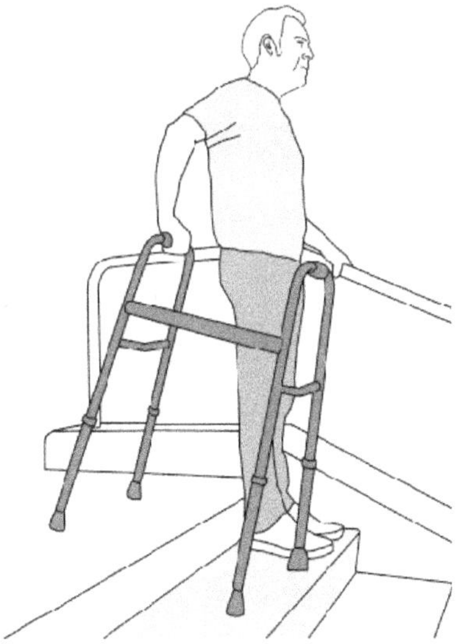

3. Step down to the same step with your stronger leg. Balance yourself.

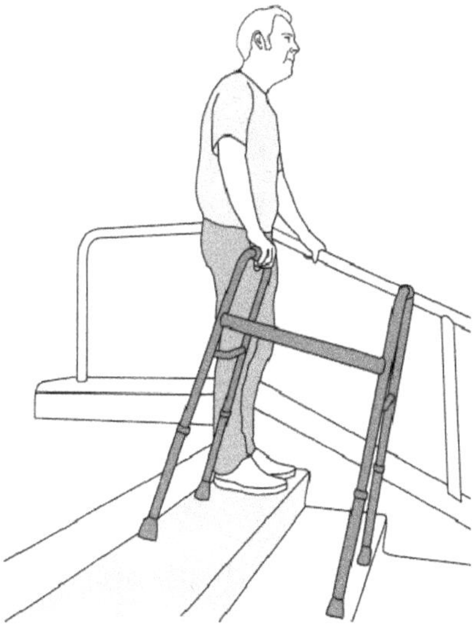

4. Repeat: walker, weaker leg, stronger leg, one step at a time.

Up with the "good" and down with the "bad". This is an easy way to recall which leg to use first.

Down Steps without a Rail Using a Cane

Do not rush. Make sure you have your balance before using the stairs.

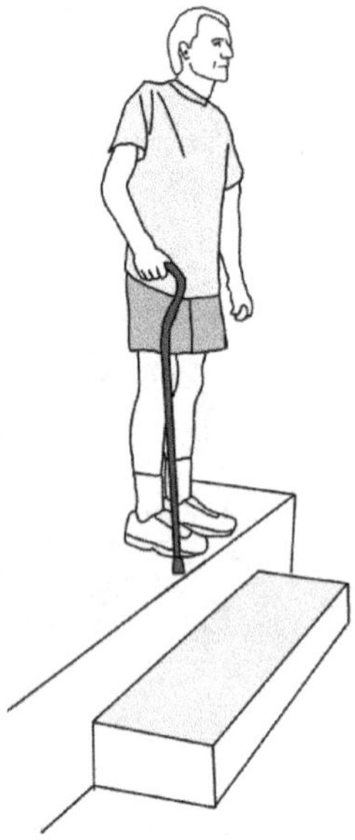

1. Hold the cane on your stronger side.

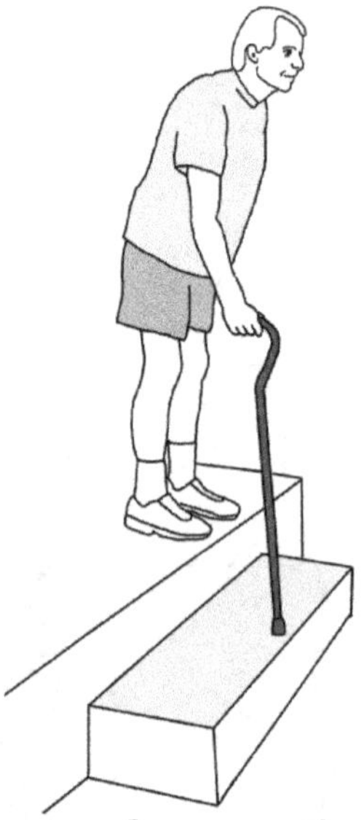

2. Place the cane down on the first step.

3. Step down with your weaker leg.

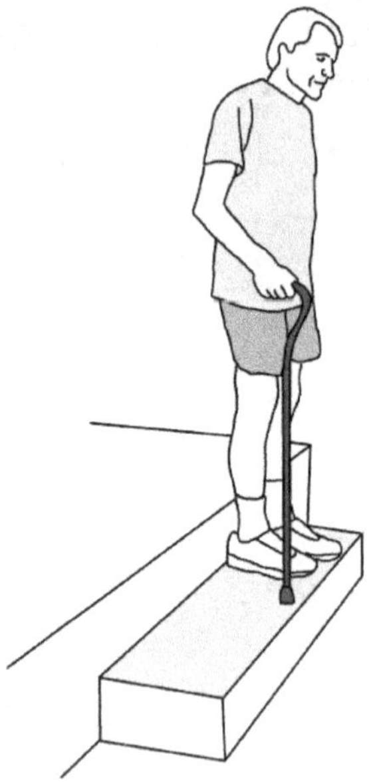

4. Step down with your stronger leg to the same step. Balance yourself. Repeat: cane, weaker leg, stronger leg, one step at a time.

Up with the "good" and down with the "bad". This is an easy way to recall which leg to use first.

Dressing Tips

Safety Tips

- Sit to get dressed in a chair with arms.
- Store items in easy to reach places.
- Do not store items on the floor. Do not leave dirty clothes on the floor.
- If you use a walker, carry items with a walker basket or tray.

Put On and Take Off a Shirt or Top

- Choose clothes that are easy to put on and take off.
- To take off an open front shirt, grab the collar. Pull the shirt over your head.

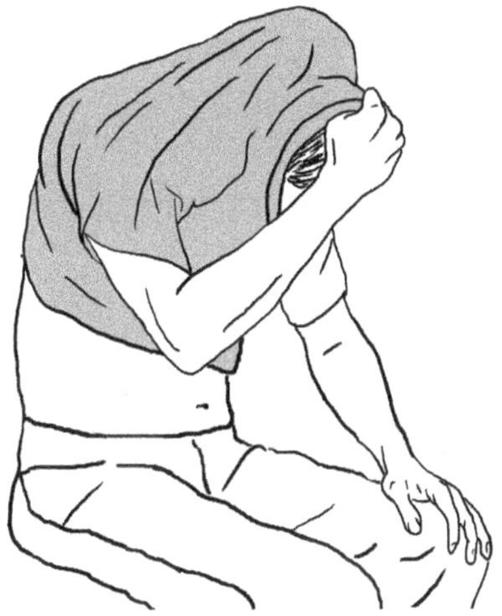

- If you have trouble with buttons, use a buttonhook. Select tops that go on over your head. Keep all the buttons closed except the top two. Pull the shirt on over your head.

Dressing Tips

Put On a Bra

- Hook the bra in the front and then move it to the back.
- Wear a sports bra or a tank top.
- Fasten a larger sized bra and put on over your head.

Put On and Take Off Pants

- Sit in a chair with arms to put on and take off pants.
- Put your weaker leg in the pant leg first.
- If you cannot reach your feet, cross one leg over your other leg, prop your leg up on the bed or use a dressing stick or reacher.

- Use a piece of non-slip fabric to hold your legs crossed.

Put On and Take Off Socks and Shoes

- Sit in a sturdy chair with arms to put on and take off socks and shoes.
- If you cannot reach your feet, cross one leg over your other leg, prop your leg up on the bed or use a sock aid and long shoehorn.

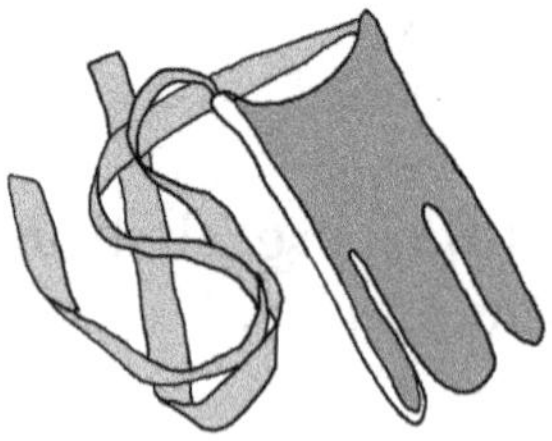

- If you cannot tie shoelaces, wear slip-on shoes. You can also use stretch laces or Velcro.
- Put on pants before you put on socks. Take off socks before taking off pants.

Get Down On the Floor

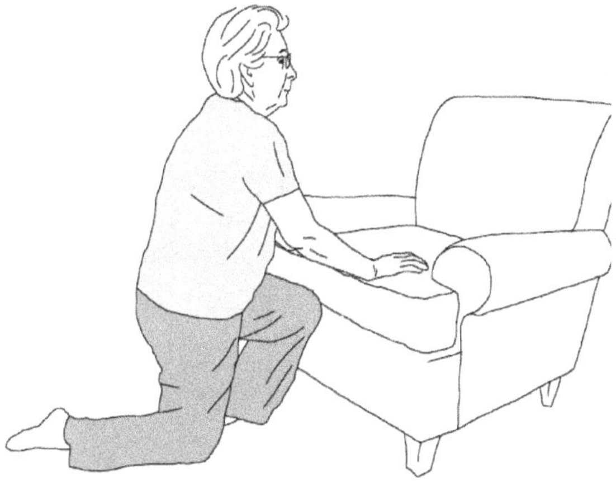

1. Place your hands on the seat of the chair.

2. Lower onto your weaker knee.

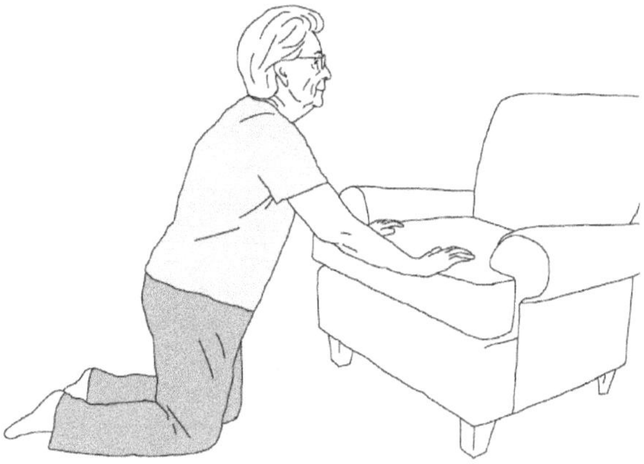

3. Place your other knee down.

4. Reach down to the floor and lower onto one hip. Sit back onto your bottom.

Get Up From the Floor

1. Get onto your hands and knees and crawl to a sturdy chair.

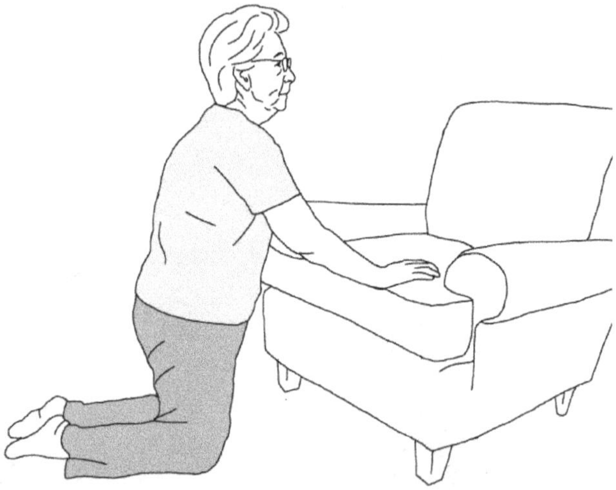

2. Kneel in front of the chair and place your hands on the seat.

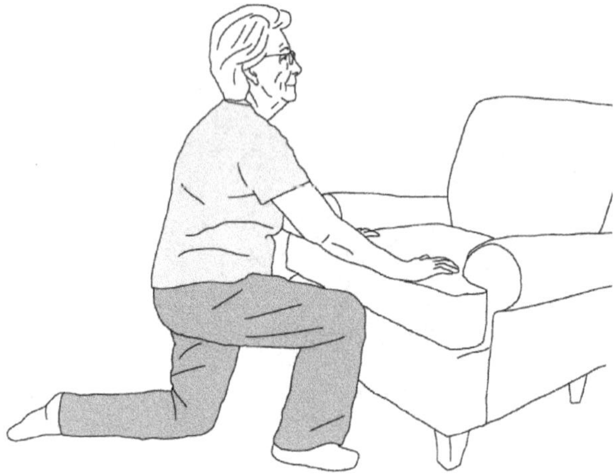

3. Lift your stronger leg and place your foot flat on the floor.

4. Lean onto the chair and push up to a stand using your legs and arms. Turn around and sit in the chair.

Occupational Therapy TOOLKIT

Health Care Team

Name	Purpose	Address	Phone	How Often
Dr. Smith	*Heart doctor*	*Main Street Clinic*	555-999-9999	*every month*

How to Install Grab Bars - Faucet on the Left

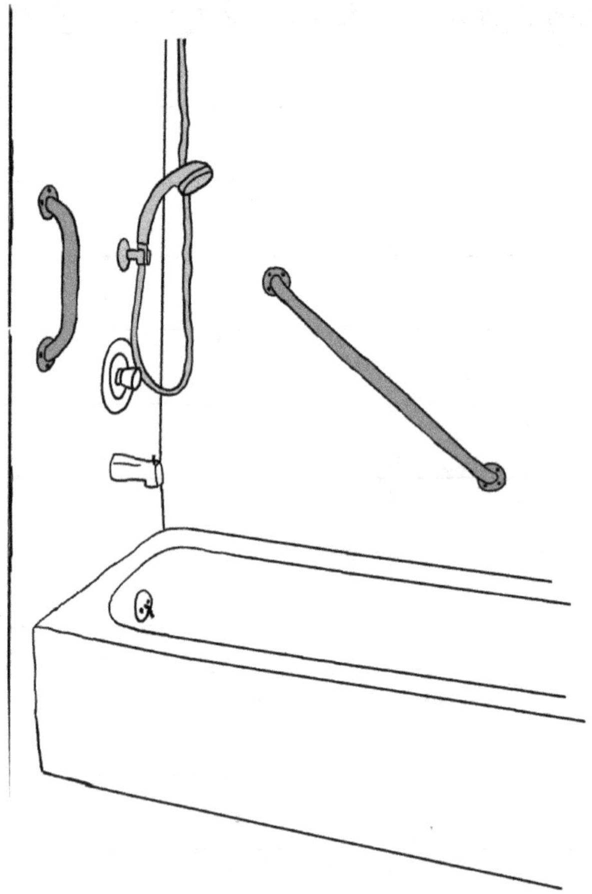

Hire a trained person to install the grab bars.

Install a grab bar on the inside wall of a tub or shower stall. Choose one that is 24 inches (60 cm) long. Install it at a 45° angle.

Add a second grab bar on the wall where you enter. It should be at least 12 inches (30 cm) long and placed up and down.

How to Install Grab Bars - Faucet on the Right

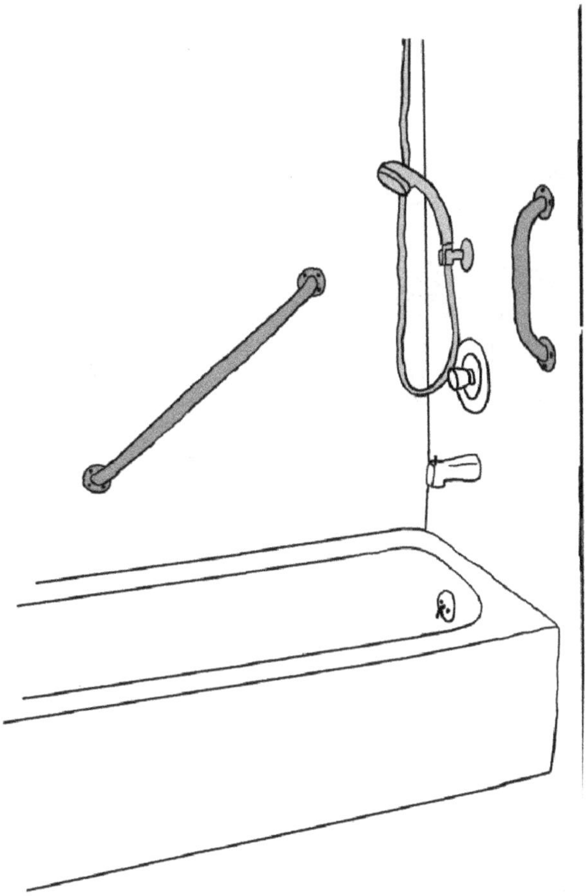

Hire a trained person to install the grab bars.

Install a grab bar on the inside wall of a tub or shower stall. Choose one that is 24 inches (60 cm) long. Install it at a 45° angle.

Add a second grab bar on the wall where you enter. It should be at least 12 inches (30 cm) long and placed up and down.

In and Out of Bed - Toward Your Left Side

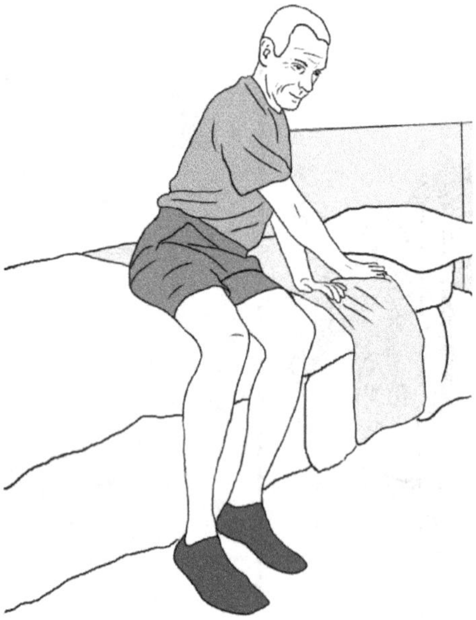

1. Sit back on the bed.

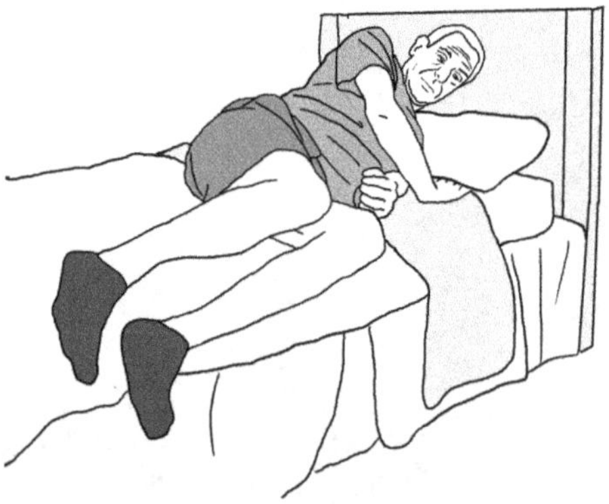

2. Lower onto your left elbow.

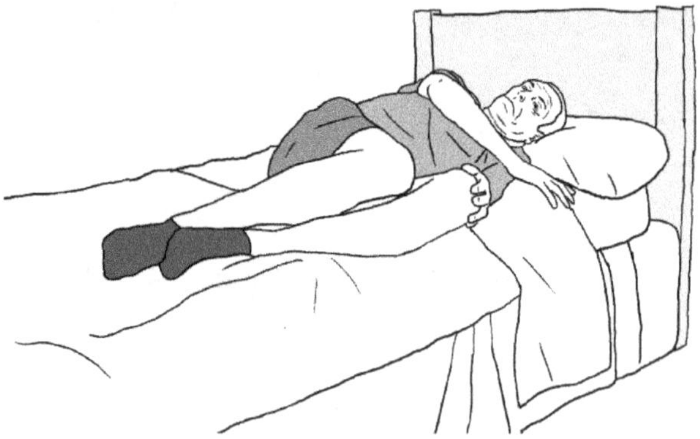

3. At the same time, lift your legs up onto the bed.

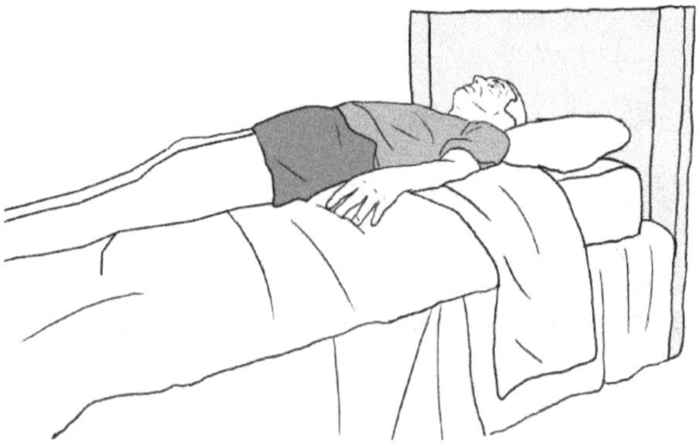

4. Roll onto your back.

1 of 2

In and Out of Bed - Toward Your Left Side

1. Bend both knees.

2. Reach across with your right arm and roll on your side.

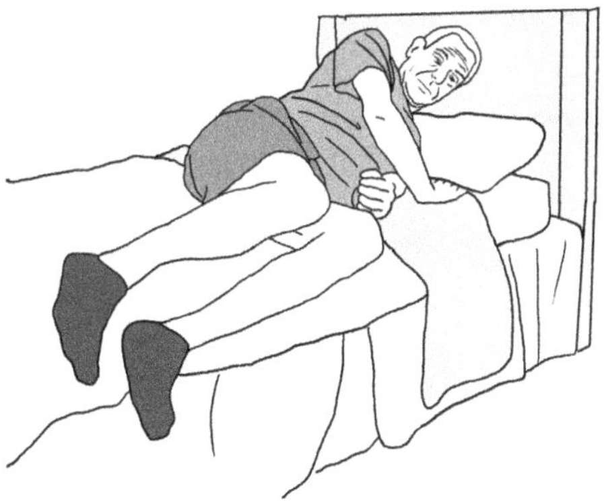

3. Push up from the bed using your arms.

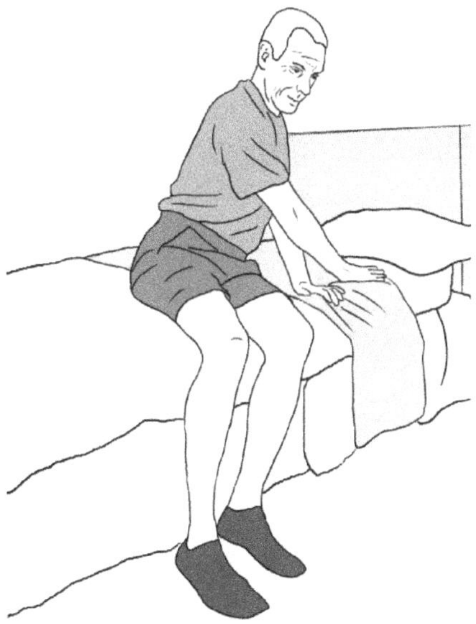

4. At the same time, lower your legs off the bed. Sit on the side of the bed for a few minutes before you stand up.

2 of 2

In and Out of Bed - Toward Your Left Side After Hip Surgery

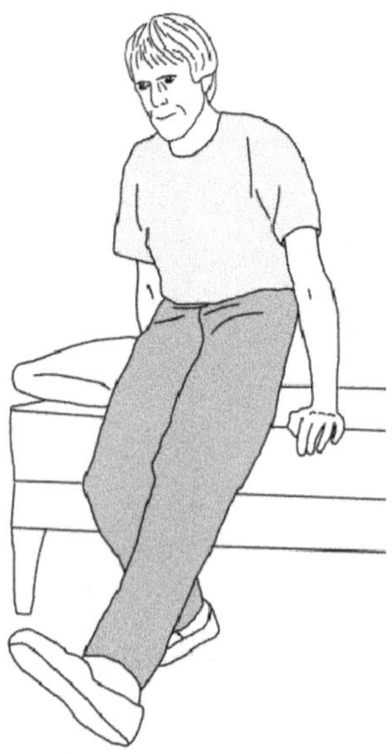

1. Move back until you feel the bed. Slide your affected leg forward. Reach for the bed, and sit down.

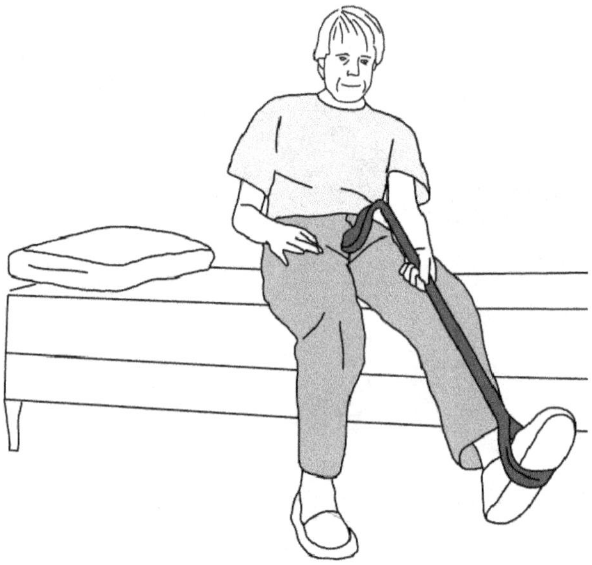

2. Lean back. Place the leg lifter on your affected leg. Lift your affected leg onto the bed.

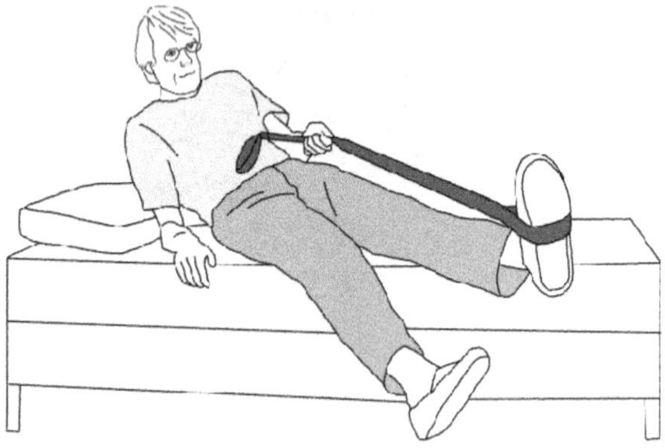

3. Move both legs onto the bed at the same time. Keep your legs about 12 inches (30 cm) apart.

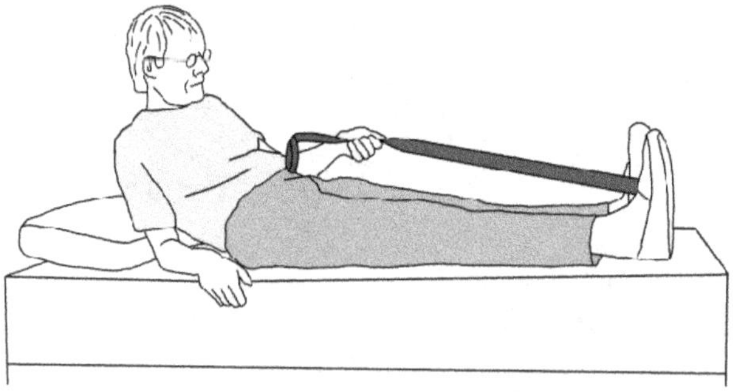

4. Use a wedge between your legs.

In and Out of Bed - Toward Your Left Side After Hip Surgery

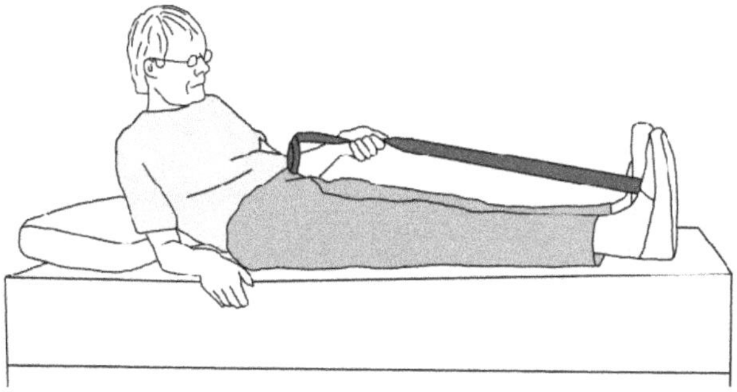

1. Place the leg lifter on your affected leg.

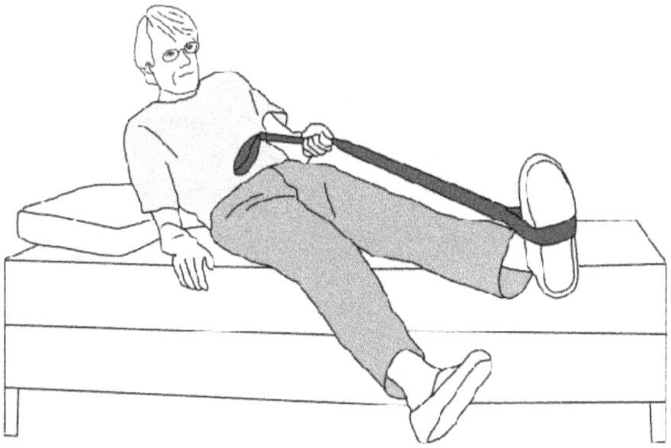

2. Move both legs off the bed at the same time. Keep your legs about 12 inches (30 cm) apart.

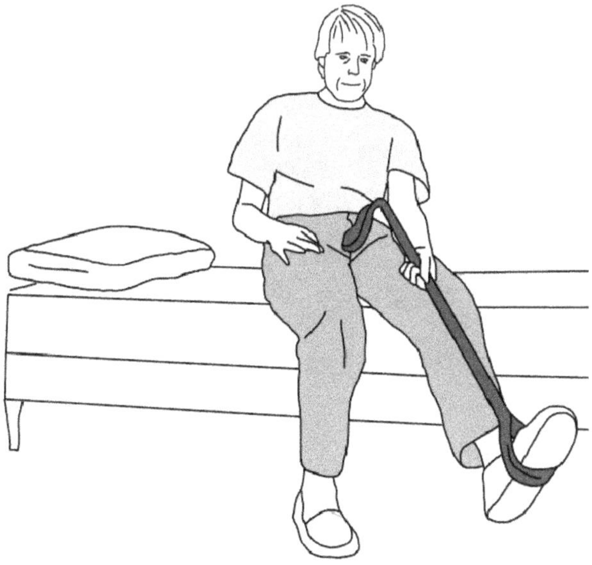

3. Keep leaning back. Lower your affected leg to the floor.

4. Sit on the side of the bed for a few minutes before you stand up.

Occupational Therapy TOOLKIT

In and Out of Bed - Toward Your Left Side
Log Rolling

1. Sit on the edge of the bed. Straighten your back and tighten your stomach.

2. Keep your back straight and your stomach muscles tight. Lower onto your left elbow. At the same time, move your legs onto the bed.

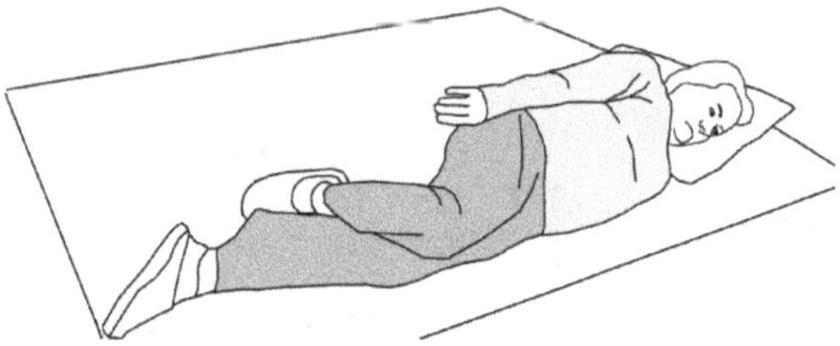

3. Keep your back straight and your stomach muscles tight.

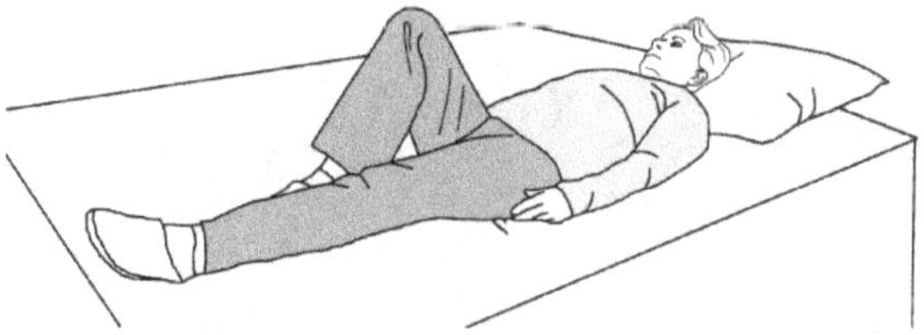

4. Log roll onto your back.

In and Out of Bed - Toward Your Left Side
Log Rolling

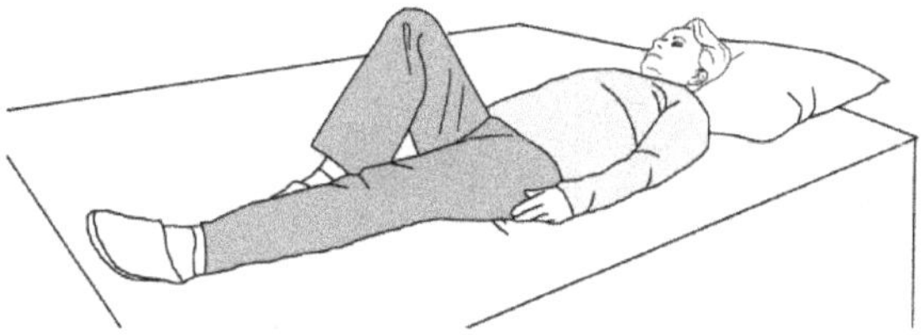

1. Bend your right leg.

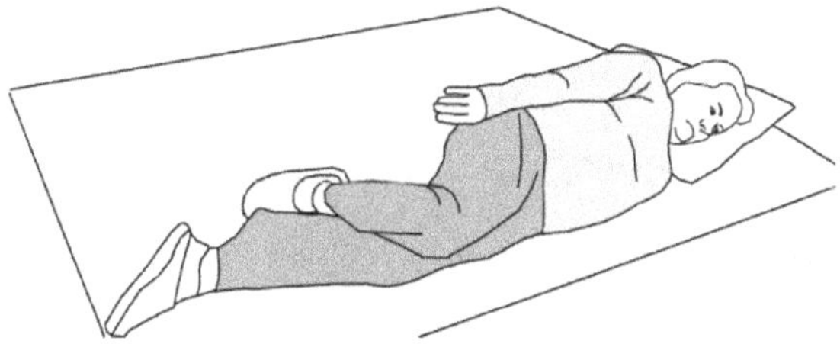

2. Keep your back straight and your head on the pillow. Use your right leg to log roll onto your left side.

3. Keep your back straight and your stomach muscle tight. Push up with your left arm. At the same time, lower your legs off the bed.

4. Sit on the side of the bed for a few minutes before you stand up.

In and Out of Bed - Toward Your Right Side

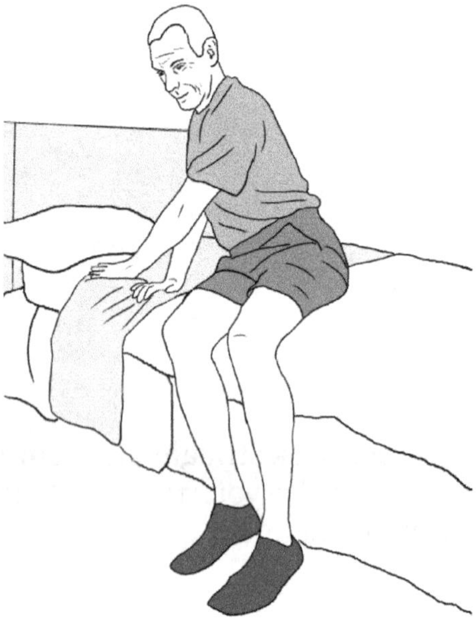

1. Sit back on the bed.

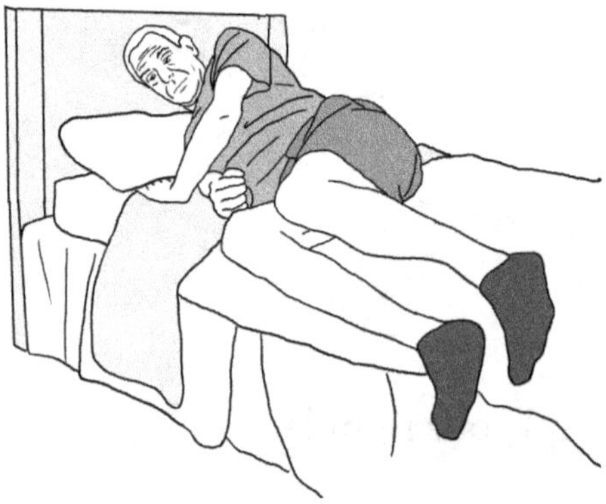

2. Lower onto your right elbow.

3. At the same time, lift your legs up onto the bed.

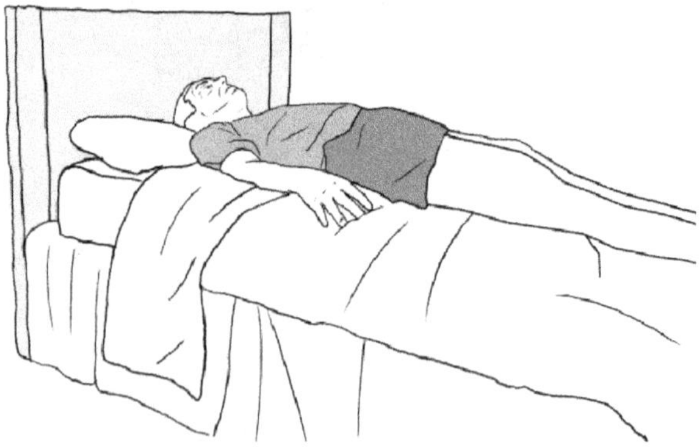

4. Roll onto your back.

In and Out of Bed - Toward Your Right Side

1. Bend both knees.

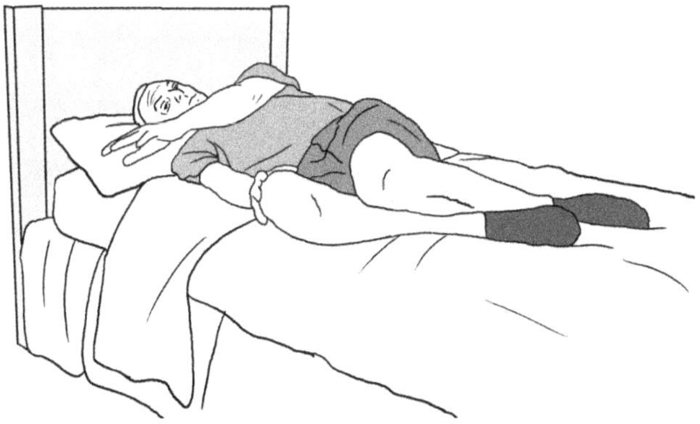

2. Reach across with your left arm and roll on your side.

3. Push up from the bed using your arms.

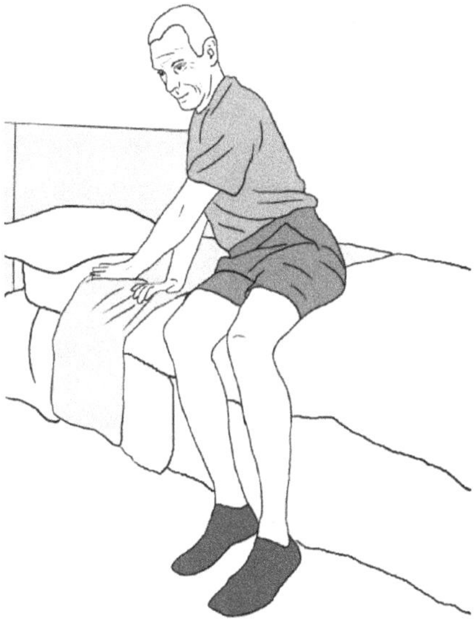

4. At the same time, lower your legs off the bed. Sit on the side of the bed for a few minutes before you stand up.

In and Out of Bed - Toward Your Right Side After Hip Surgery

1. Move back until you feel the bed. Slide your affected leg forward. Reach for the bed, and sit down.

2. Lean back. Place the leg lifter on your affected leg. Use it to lift your affected leg onto the bed.

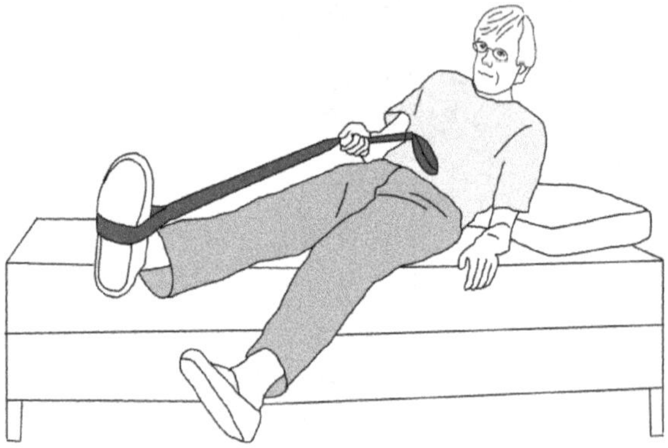

3. Move both legs onto the bed at the same time. Keep your legs about 12 inches (30 cm) apart.

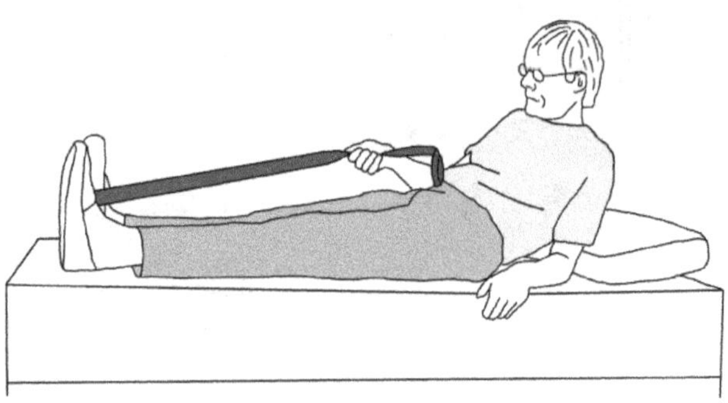

4. Use a wedge between your legs.

Occupational Therapy TOOLKIT

In and Out of Bed - Toward Your Right Side After Hip Surgery

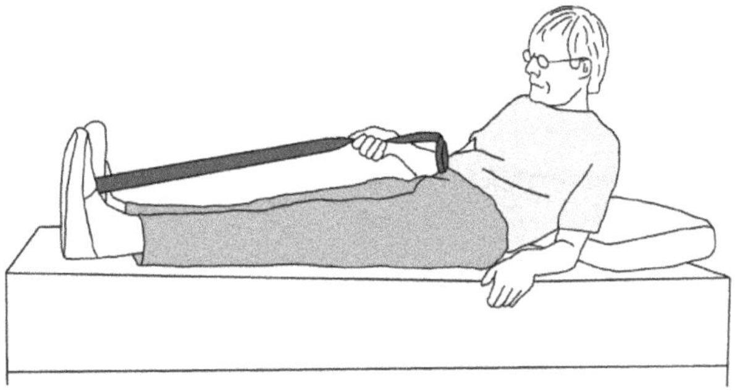

1. Place the leg lifter on your affected leg.

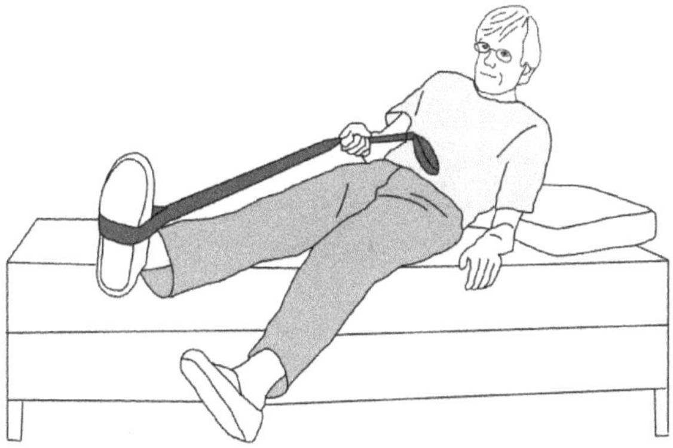

2. Move both legs off the bed at the same time. Keep your legs about 12 inches (30 cm) apart.

3. Lean back. Lower your affected leg to the floor.

4. Sit on the side of the bed for a few minutes before you stand up.

In and Out of Bed - Toward Your Right Side
Log Rolling

1. Sit on the edge of the bed. Straighten your back and tighten your stomach.

2. Keep your back straight and your stomach muscles tight. Lower onto your right elbow. At the same time, move your legs onto the bed.

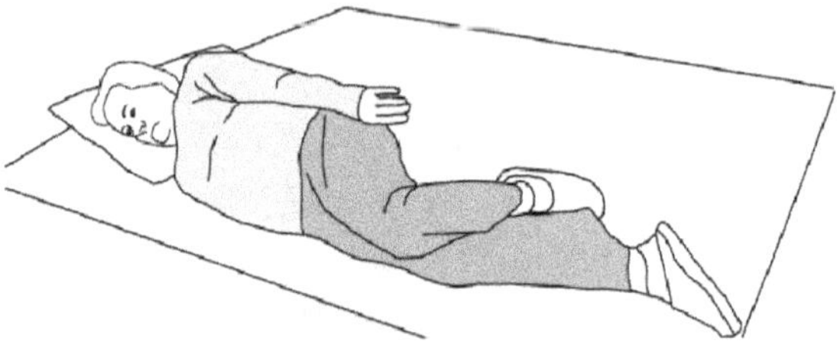

3. Keep your back straight and your stomach muscles tight.

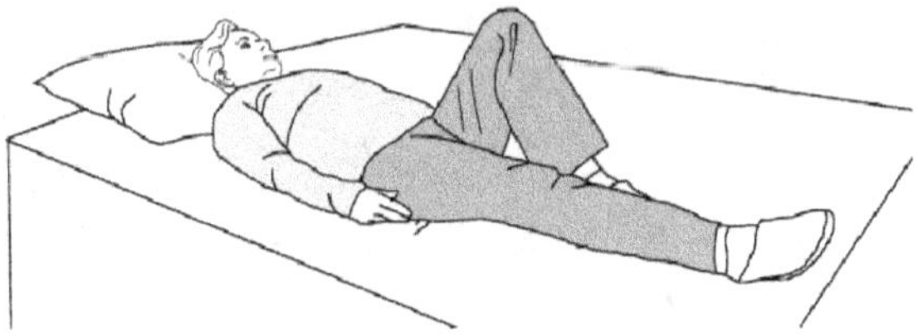

4. Log roll onto your back.

In and Out of Bed - Toward Your Right Side
Log Rolling

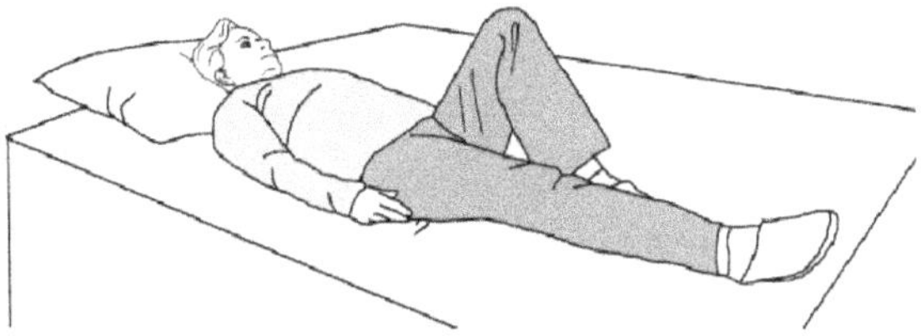

1. Bend your left leg.

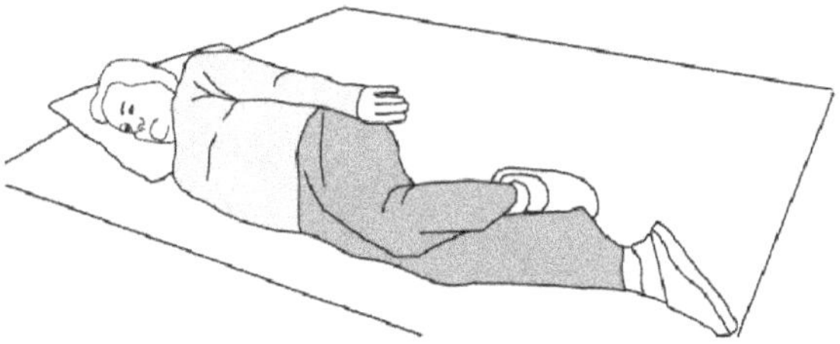

2. Keep your back straight and your head on the pillow. Use your left leg to log roll onto your right side.

3. Keep your back straight and your stomach muscle tight. Push up with your right arm. At the same time, lower your legs off the bed.

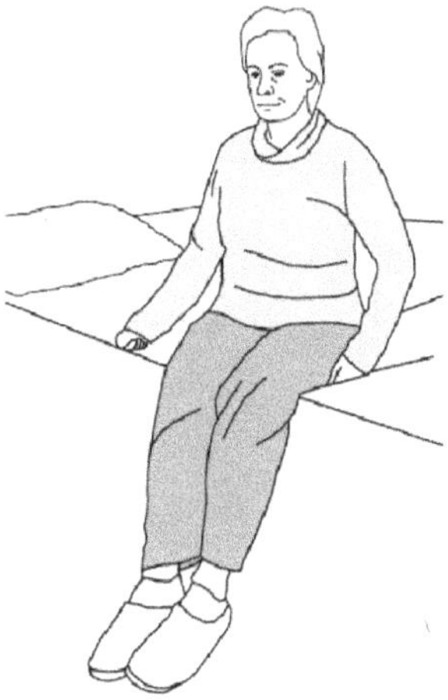

4. Sit on the side of the bed for a few minutes before you stand up.

In and Out of Bed - Toward Your Weaker Left Side

1. Sit back on the bed. Hook your right foot behind your left foot.

2. Lower yourself to the bed. At the same time, lift your legs onto the bed.

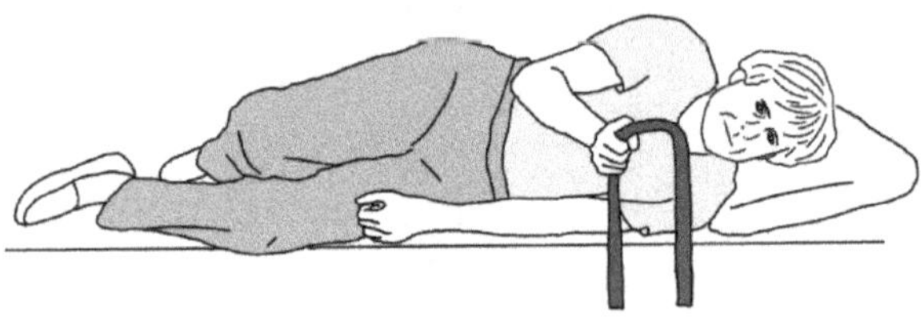

3. Push on the bed rail.

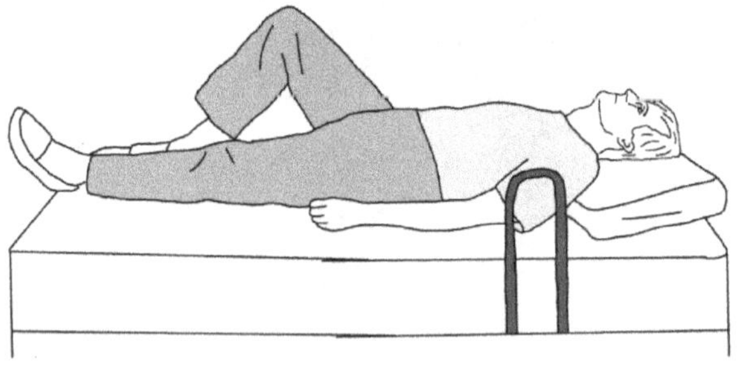

4. Roll onto your back.

1 of 2

In and Out of Bed - Toward Your Weaker Left Side

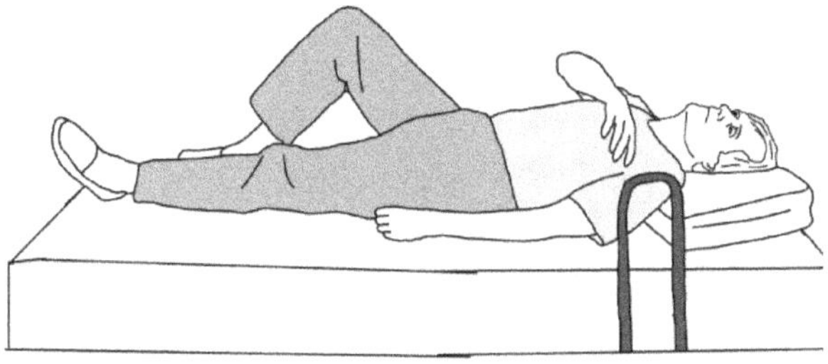

1. Lie on your back. Bend your right knee. Reach over for the bed rail.

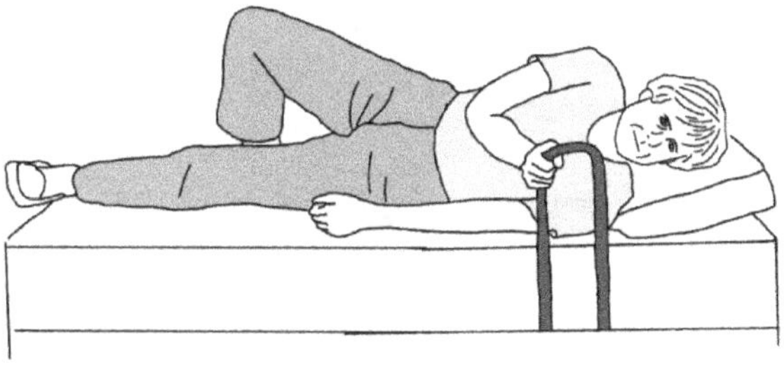

2. Push with your right foot as you pull on the bed rail. Roll onto your left side.

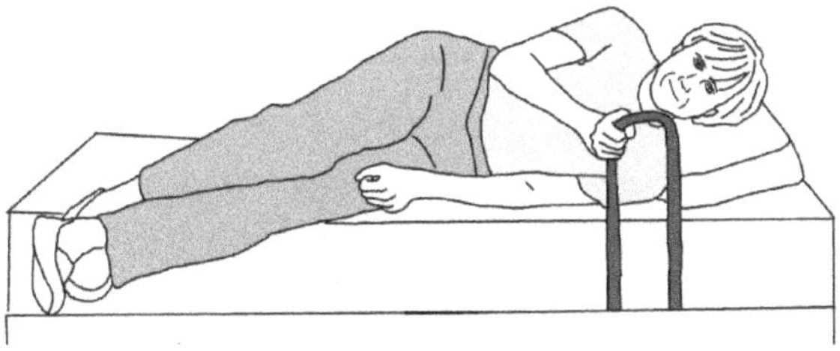

3. Hook your right foot behind your left foot. Push your left foot off the bed. At the same time, push up using your right arm.

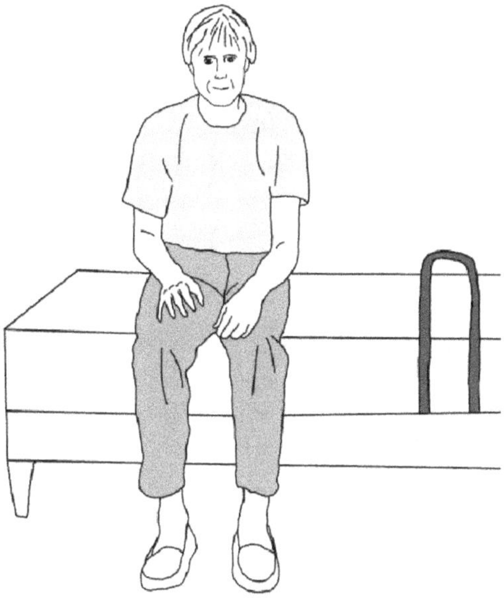

4. Sit on the side of the bed for a few minutes before you stand up.

In and Out of Bed - Toward Your Weaker Right Side

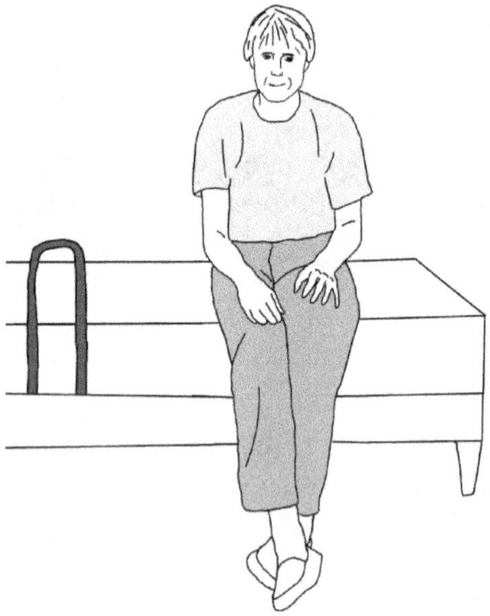

1. Sit back on the bed. Hook your left foot behind your right foot.

2. Lower yourself to the bed. At the same time, lift your legs onto the bed.

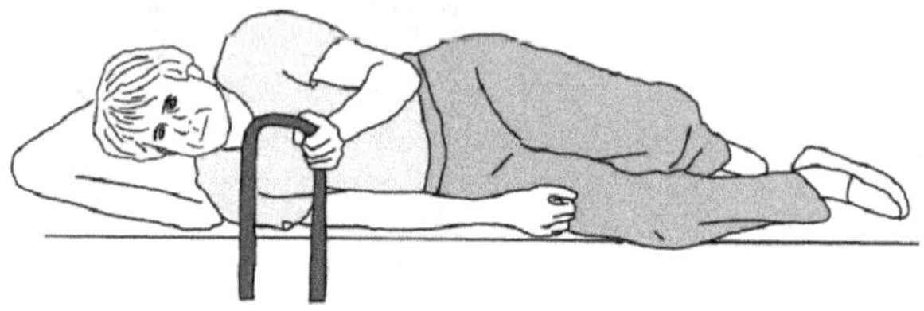

3. Push on the bed rail.

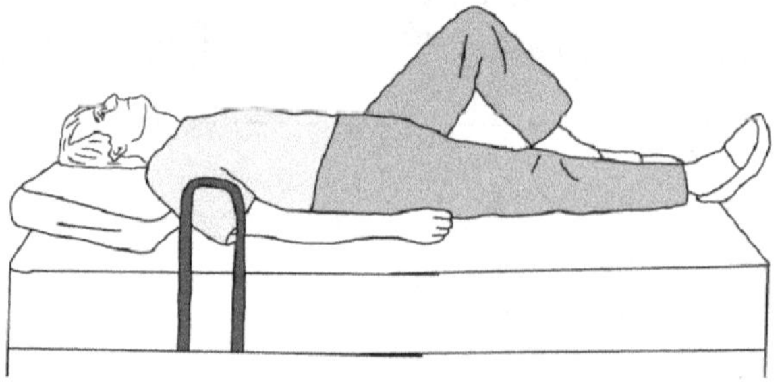

4. Roll onto your back.

In and Out of Bed - Toward Your Weaker Right Side

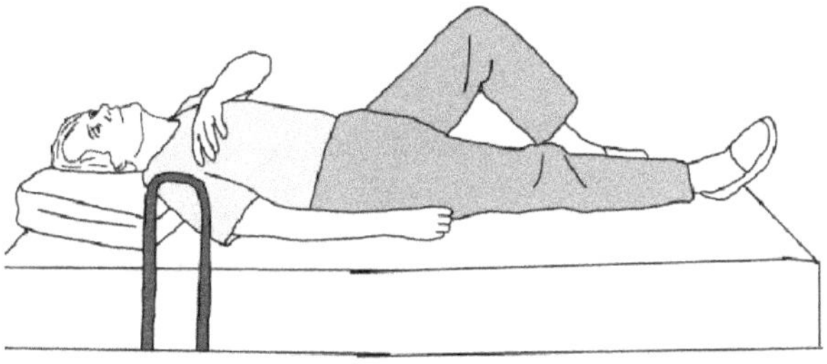

1. Lie on your back. Bend your left knee. Reach over for the bed rail.

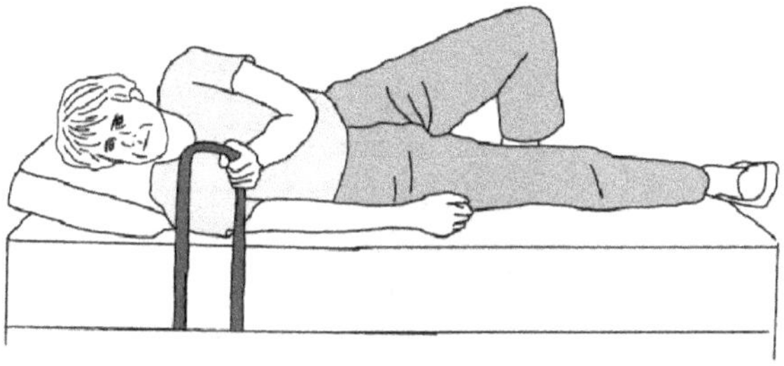

2. Push with your left foot as you pull on the bed rail. Roll onto your right side.

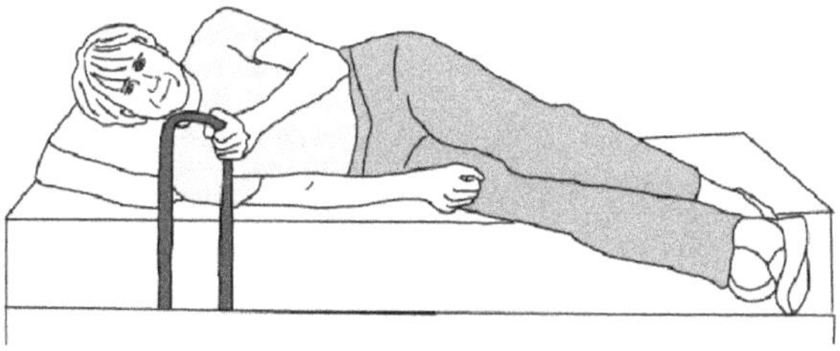

3. Hook your left foot behind your right foot. Push your right foot off the bed. At the same time, push up using your left arm.

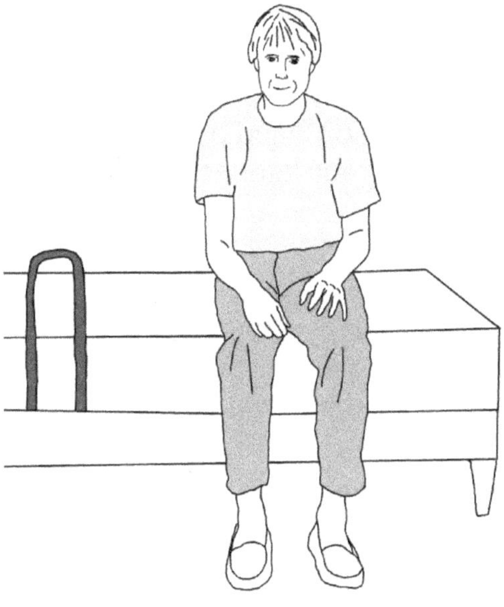

4. Sit on the side of the bed for a few minutes before you stand up.

In and Out of Bed with Help - Toward Their Left Side

Go over the steps. Ask the person if they are ready to move.

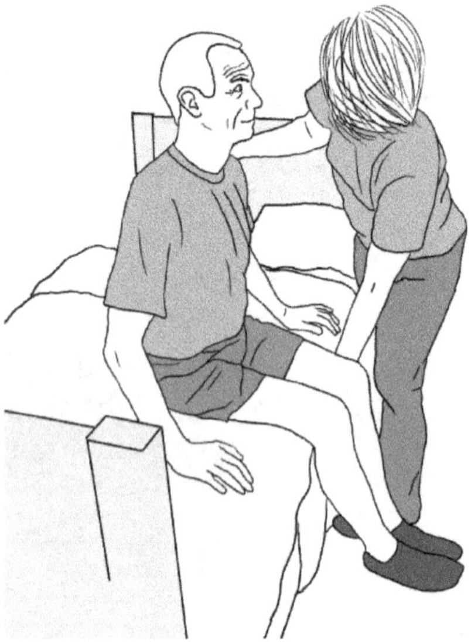

1. Place your right hand on the person's shoulder and your left hand under their knees.

2. Help the person lower onto their left side. At the same time, lift their legs onto the bed.

3. Help the person roll onto their back.

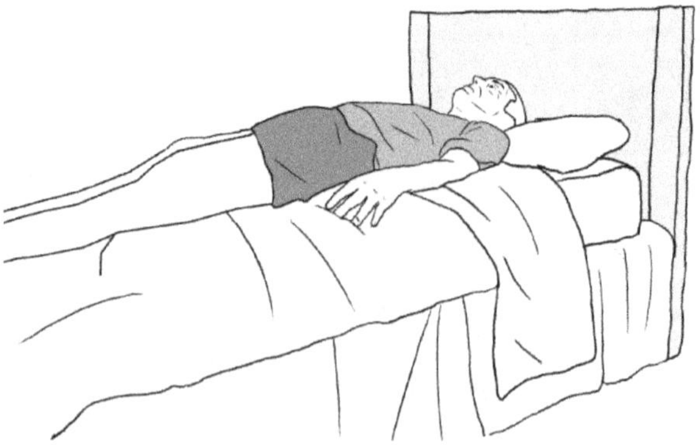

4. Straighten the person's legs.

In and Out of Bed with Help - Toward Their Left Side

Go over the steps. Ask the person if they are ready to move.

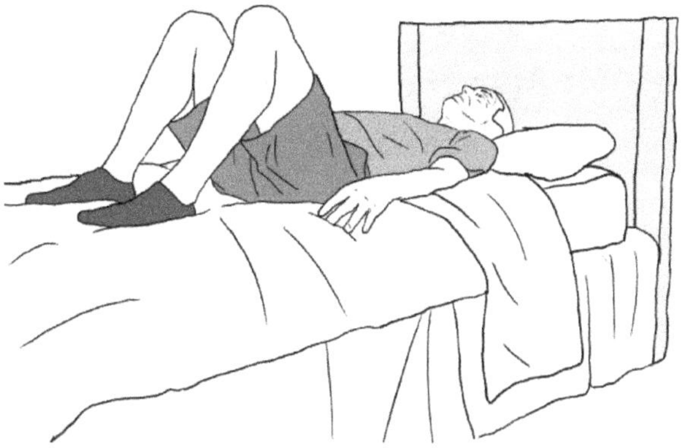

1. Help the person bend their knees.

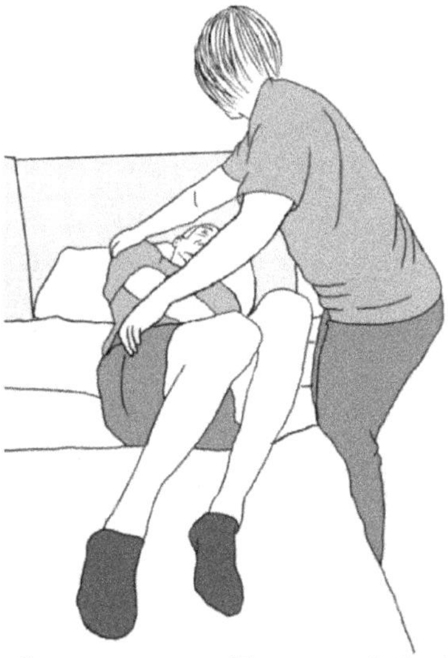

2. Help the person roll toward their left side. Place one hand on their right hip and the other on their right shoulder.

3. Swing both legs over the side of the bed. Place one hand under their left shoulder and your other hand on their right knee. Sit the person up.

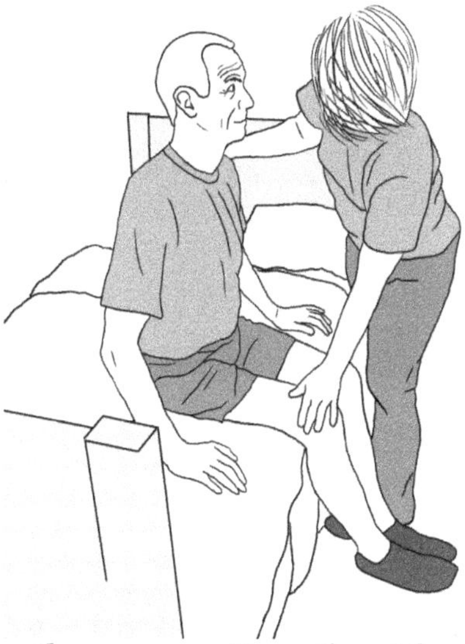

4. Have the person sit on the side of the bed for a few minutes before they stand up.

In and Out of Bed with Help - Toward Their Right Side

Go over the steps. Ask the person if they are ready to move.

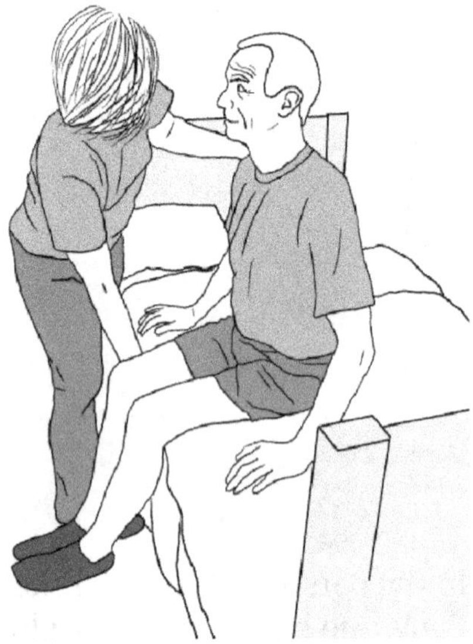

1. Place your right hand on the person's shoulder and your left hand under their knees.

2. Help the person lower onto their left side. At the same time, lift their legs onto the bed.

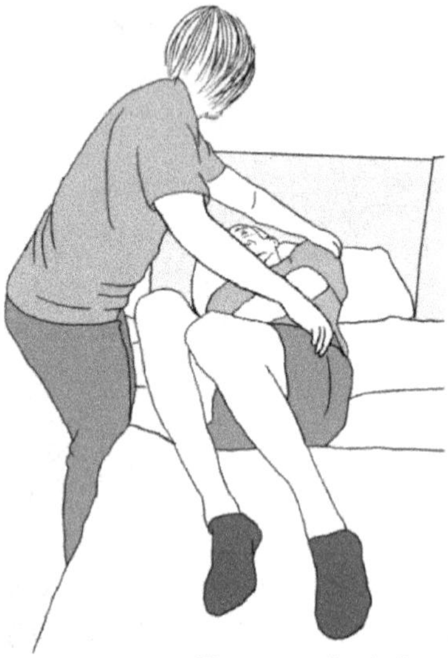

3. Help the person roll onto their back.

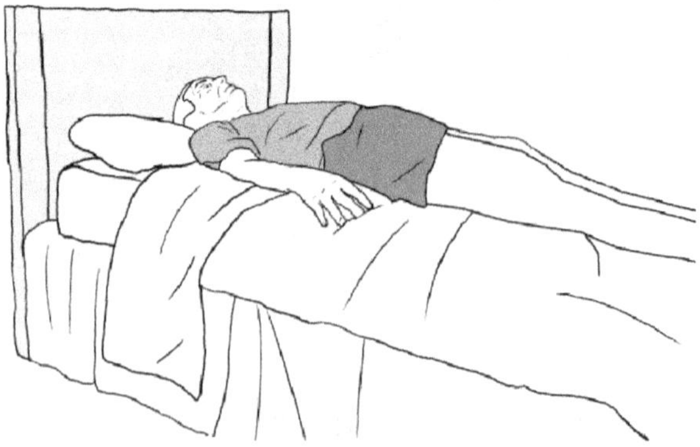

4. Straighten the person's legs.

In and Out of Bed with Help - Toward Their Right Side

Go over the steps. Ask the person if they are ready to move.

1. Help the person bend their knees.

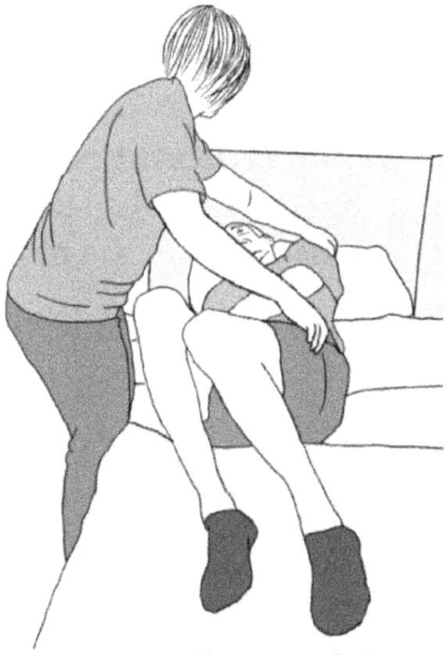

2. Help the person roll toward their right side. Place one hand on their left hip and the other on their left shoulder.

3. Swing both legs over the side of the bed. Place one hand under their right shoulder and your other hand on their left knee. Sit the person up.

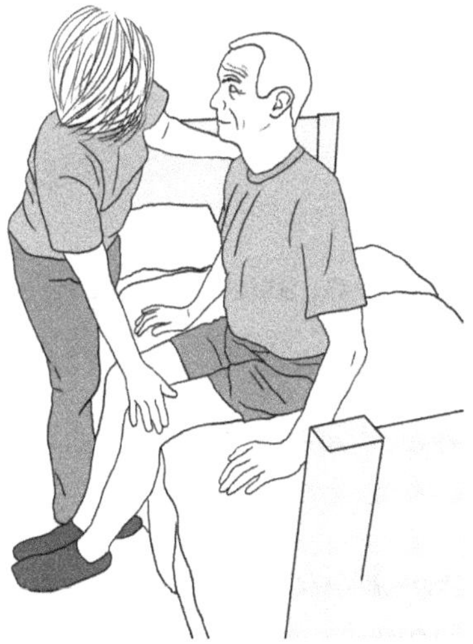

4. Have the person sit on the side of the bed for a few minutes before they stand up.

Manage Kitchen Tasks with a Walker

Safe in the kitchen
- Do not store paper or plastic in the oven.
- Keep the space near the oven and stove tidy.
- Use a non-slip rug in front of the sink to catch water drips.

Use the cupboards and refrigerator
- Put the items you use the most within easy reach.
- Use a turntable in the refrigerator and on the counter.

Use the oven, stove, and microwave
- Do not leave the kitchen when you are cooking.
- Use a toaster or slow cooker. They turn off on their own.
- Wait for hot items to cool off.
- Use a slotted spoon to drain pasta and other hot foods.

Move food and dishes to and from the table
- Move food to the table in a covered dish.
- Use a walker tray or basket to carry items.

Manage Kitchen Tasks with a Walker

Prepare food

- Sit to prepare and mix foods.
- Use the counter to slide pots and pans instead of lifting them.

Pour hot and cold liquids

- Pour liquids over the sink to catch any spills.
- Pour hot liquids after they cool down.

Clean up

- Limit the amount of trash. Use a garbage grinder. Empty the trash often.
- Use a reacher to pick up items dropped on the floor.

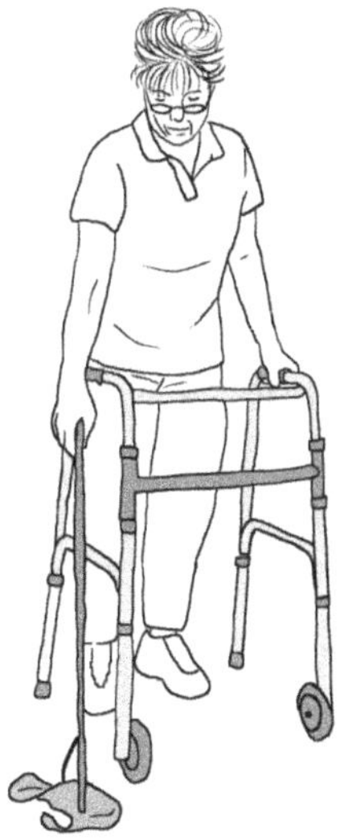

Occupational Therapy TOOLKIT

Manage Kitchen Tasks with a Wheelchair

Safe in the kitchen

- Do not store paper or plastic in the oven.
- Keep the space near the oven and stove tidy.
- Use a non-slip rug in front of the sink to catch water drips.

Use the cupboard and refrigerator

- Put the items you use the most within easy reach.
- Use a turntable in the refrigerator and on the counter.

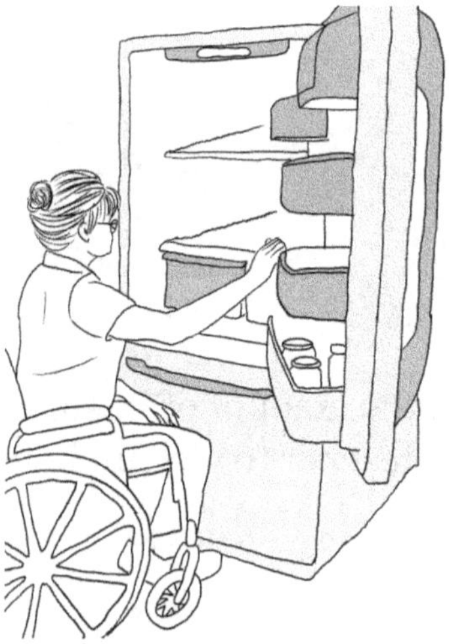

Use the oven, stove, and microwave

- Do not leave the kitchen when you are cooking.
- Use a toaster or slow cooker. They turn off on their own.
- Wait for hot items to cool off.
- Use a slotted spoon to drain pasta and other hot foods.

Manage Kitchen Tasks with a Wheelchair

Move food and dishes to and from the table

- Use a cookie sheet or lapboard to carry items.
- Carry food in a covered dish. Put them on your lap or tucked at the side. Use a thermos to carry liquids.
- Use the counter to slide pots instead of lifting them.

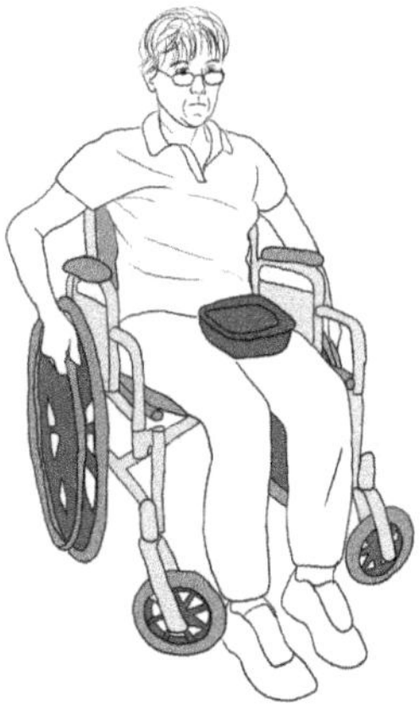

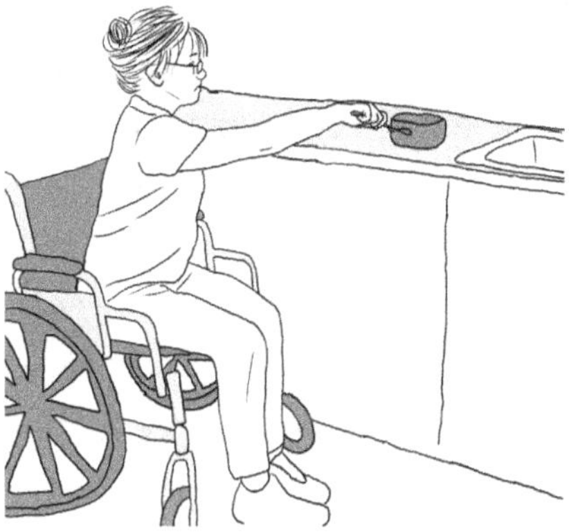

Pour hot and cold liquids

- Pour liquids over the sink to catch any spills.
- Pour hot liquids after they cool down.

Clean up

- Limit the amount of trash. Use a garbage grinder. Empty the trash often.
- Use a reacher to pick up items dropped on the floor.

2 of 2

Meal Prep with One Hand

Prepare

- Sit to prepare and mix foods, and wash dishes.
- Use recipes that are quick and easy to prepare.

Stir

- Use a rubber mat or wet towel under bowls. This will keep them from sliding.

Cut

- Buy pre-cut fresh fruit and vegetables.
- Use a cutting board with raised sides. This will keep food from falling off. Use nails in the cutting board to hold food.

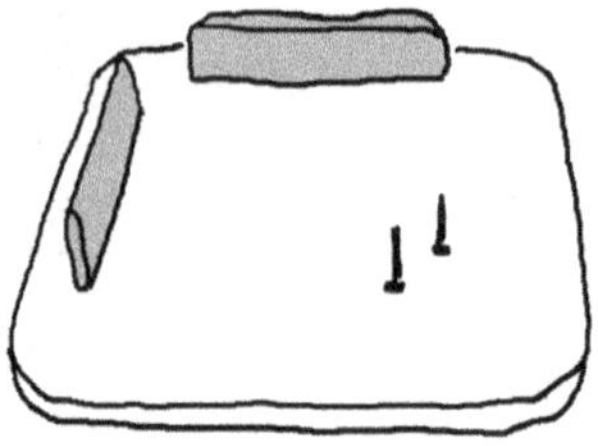

- Use a device for slicing, grating or dicing.
- Use a pizza cutter to cut soft foods.
- Stab a piece of food with a fork. Hold the fork with your weaker hand. Cut the food with a knife.

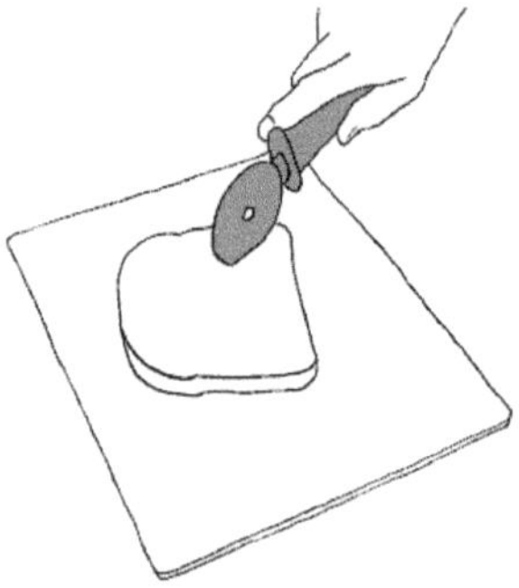

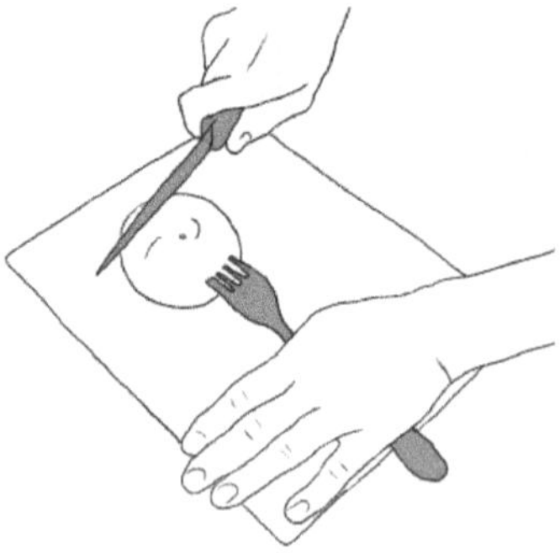

Meal Prep with One Hand

Peel

- Attach a suction cup brush to the side of the sink to scrub food clean.
- Use a peeler for one hand.

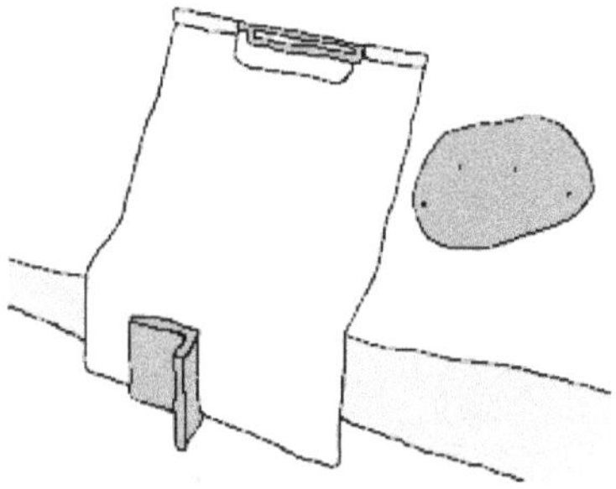

Spread

- Use the sides on the one-hand cutting board to keep bread from moving.

Open jars, cans, and packages

- Use a jar opener and can opener made for one hand.
- Use scissors made for one hand.

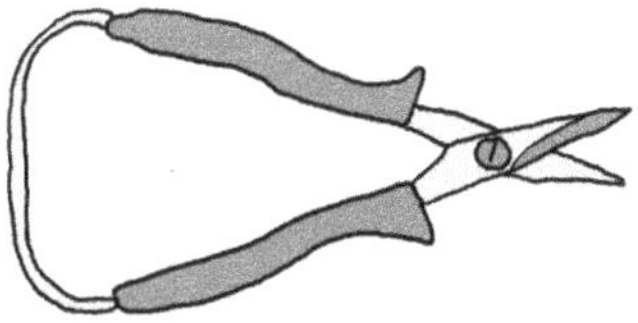

Pour hot and cold liquids

- Pour hot liquids after they cool down.
- Pour drinks in a cup placed in the sink. Any spills will be easy to rinse away.
- Use the counter to slide pots instead of lifting them.

Clean up

- Place a dish drainer in the sink. Use it to hold the dishes when washing. Use a second drainer to dry the dishes.
- Limit the amount of trash. Use a garbage grinder. Empty the trash often.

Move from One Side of the Bed to the Other

1. Lie on your back. Bend your knees and place both feet flat. Rest your arms at your sides.

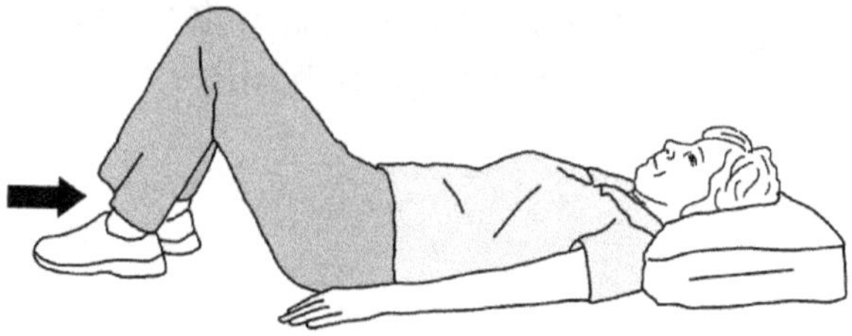

2. Press your feet and your arms into the bed. Lift your hips off the bed.

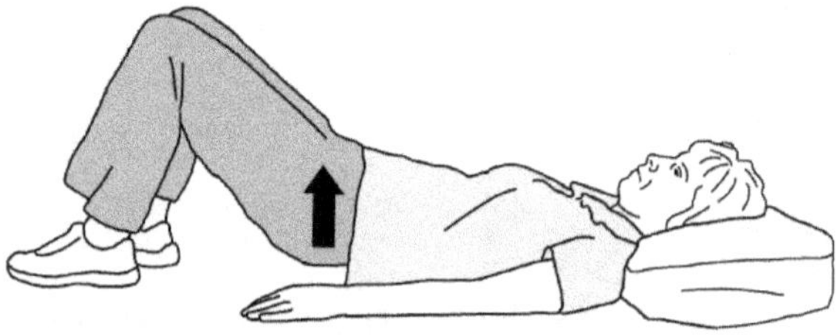

3. With your hips lifted, shift them to the side. Then lower your hips to the bed.

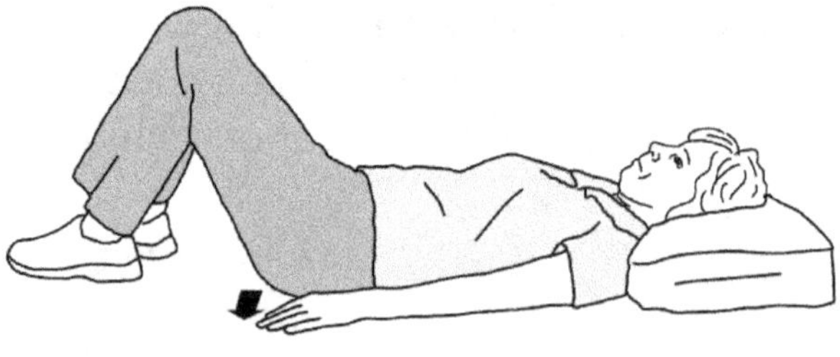

4. Lift your head and shoulders off the bed and shift them to the side.

A trapeze or side rails can help you move.

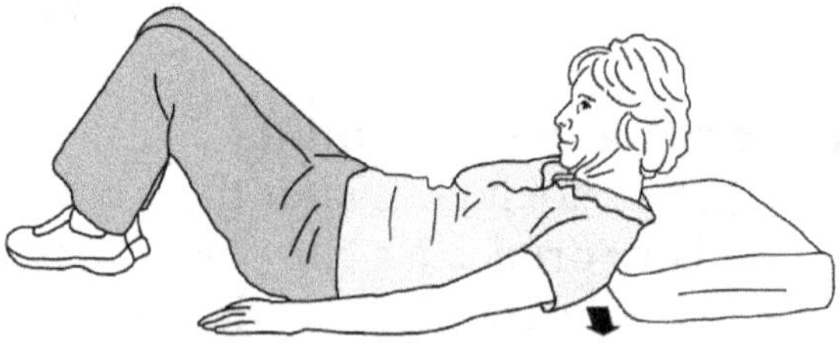

Move Up in Bed

1. Bend your knees. Bring your heels close to your bottom.

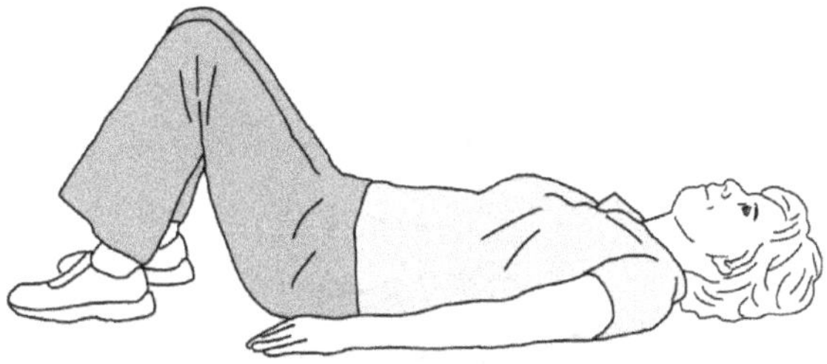

2. Rise onto both elbows.

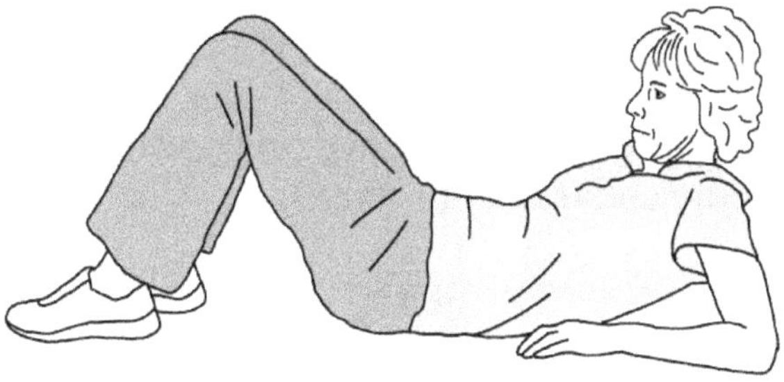

3. Push toward the head of the bed using your legs and arms.

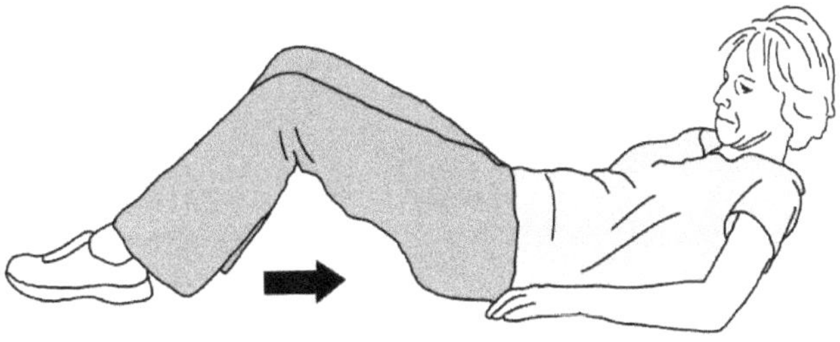

Put On a T-shirt with One Hand
Left Side Weakness

1. Place the shirt face down on your lap with the collar at your knees.

2. Gather the hole of the left sleeve and place on your lap.

3. Lean forward and place your left arm into the sleeve hole.

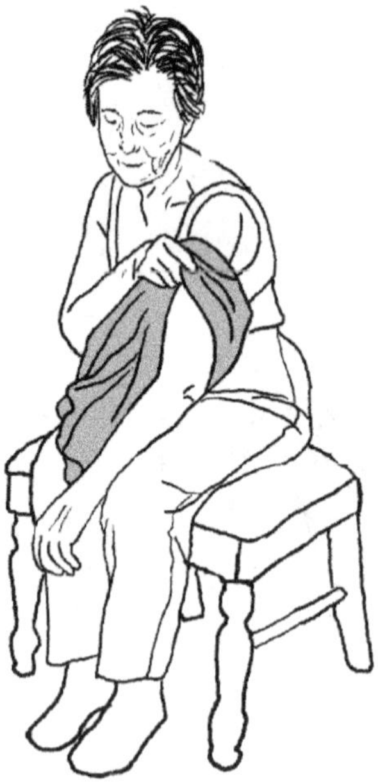

4. Pull the sleeve up your arm and over your elbow.

1 of 2

Put On a T-shirt with One Hand
Left Side Weakness

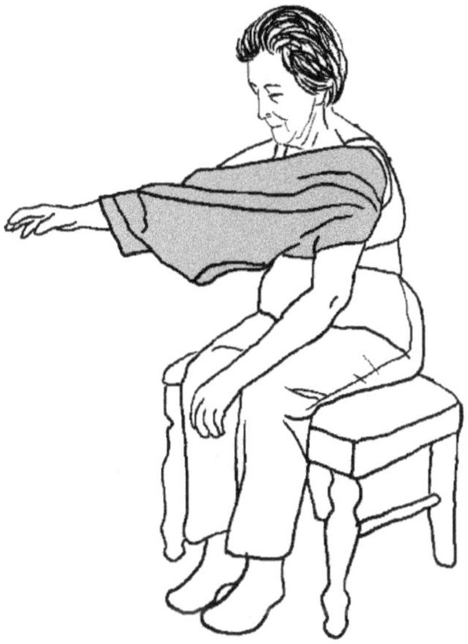

5. Place your right arm into the right sleeve hole.

6. Grasp the shirt and pull it over your head.

7. Push the shirt over your left shoulder.

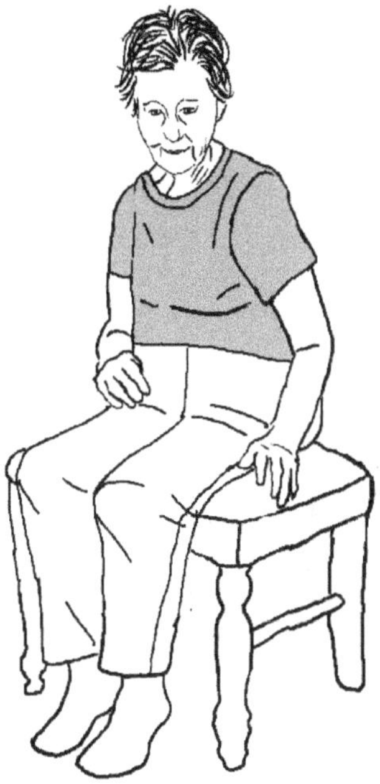

8. Adjust the shirt, by pulling it down in the front and the back.

2 of 2

Put On a T-shirt with One Hand
Right Side Weakness

1. Place the shirt face down on your lap with the collar at your knees.

2. Gather the hole of the right sleeve and place on your lap.

3. Lean forward and place your right arm into the sleeve hole.

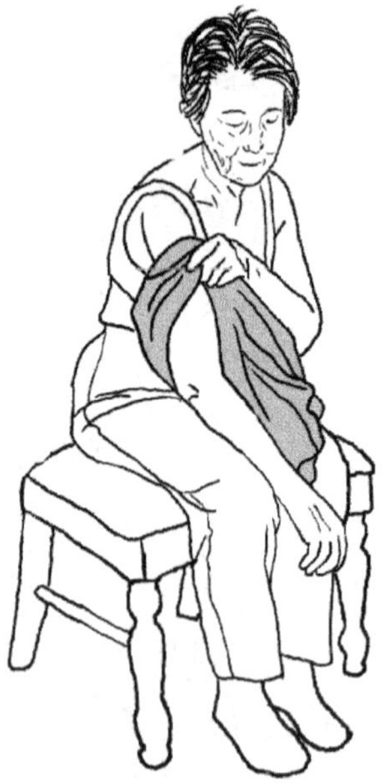

4. Pull the sleeve up your arm, over your elbow.

1 of 2

Put On a T-shirt with One Hand
Right Side Weakness

5. Place your left arm into the left sleeve hole.

6. Grasp the shirt and pull it over your head.

7. Push the shirt over your right shoulder.

8. Adjust the shirt, by pulling it down in the front and the back.

Put On an Open Front Shirt with One Hand
Left Side Weakness

1. Find the left sleeve. Lean forward and hang your left arm between your legs.

2. Move the sleeve up your left arm.

3. Move the shirt around your shoulders and back.

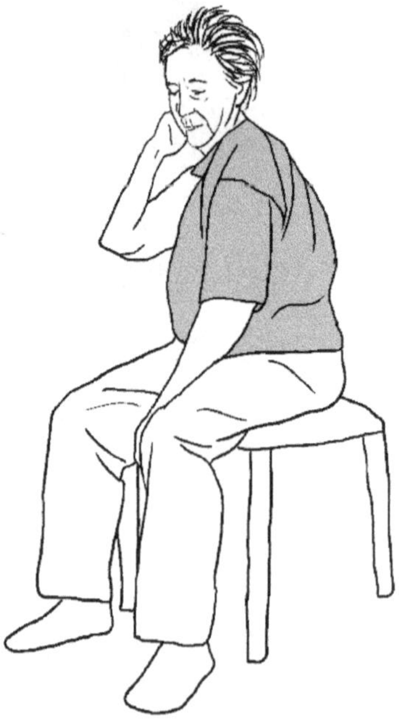

4. Grasp the collar and pull the shirt around your right shoulder.

Put On an Open Front Shirt with One Hand
Left Side Weakness

5. Place your right arm into the right sleeve.

6. Button the shirt.

2 of 2

Put On an Open Front Shirt with One Hand
Right Side Weakness

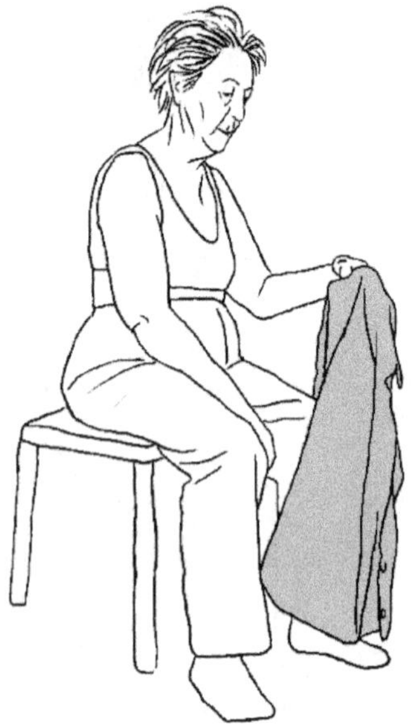

1. Find the right sleeve. Lean forward and hang your right arm in between your legs.

2. Move the sleeve up your right arm.

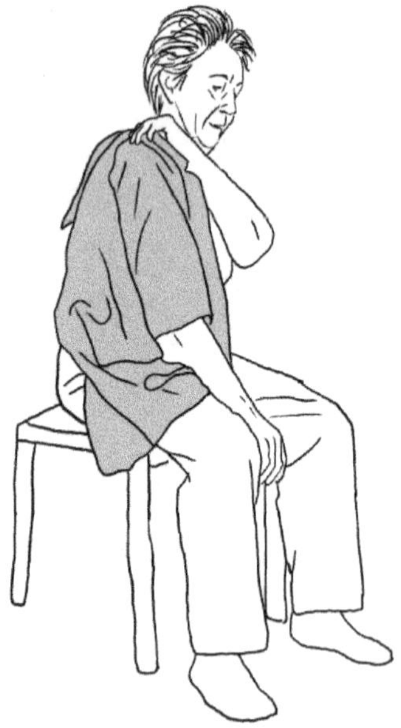

3. Move the shirt around your shoulder and back.

4. Grasp the collar and pull the shirt around your left shoulder.

1 of 2

Put On an Open Front Shirt with One Hand
Right Side Weakness

5. Place your left arm into the left sleeve.

6. Button the shirt.

Occupational Therapy TOOLKiT

Put On and Take Off a Bra with One Hand
Left Side Weakness

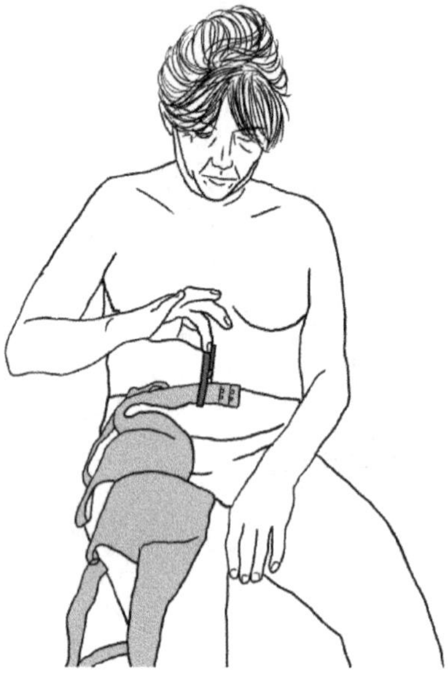

1. Clip the loop side of the bra to the pants.

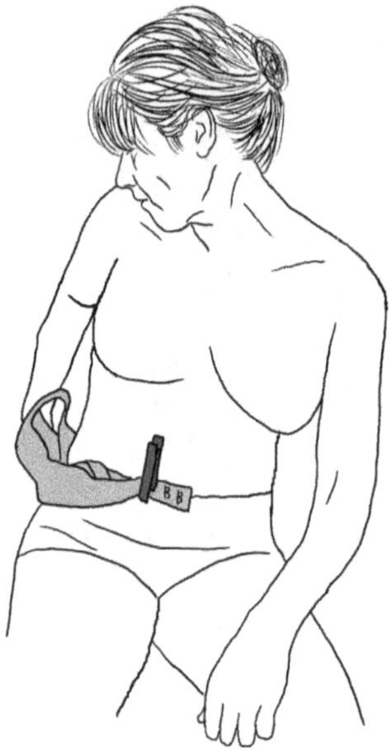

2. Move the bra behind your back around to your right side.

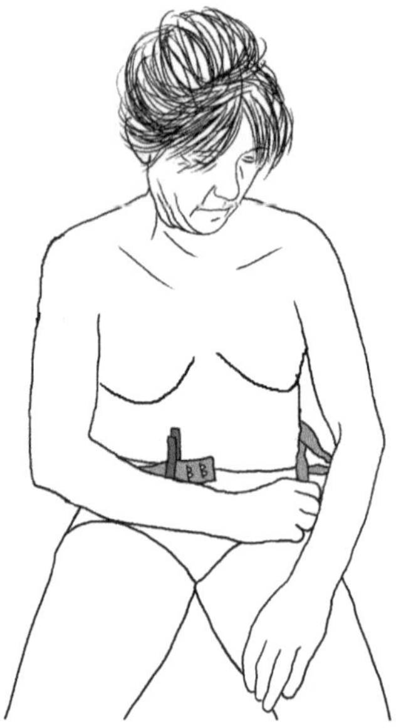

3. Reach back on your left side and pull the bra forward.

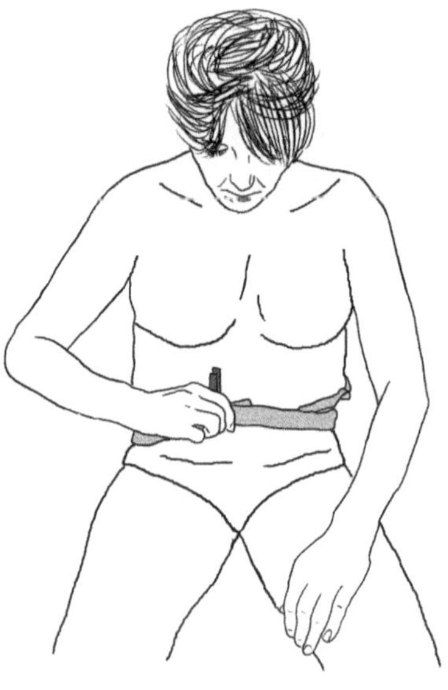

4. Hook the bra.

1 of 2

Occupational Therapy TOOLKIT

Put On and Take Off a Bra with One Hand
Left Side Weakness

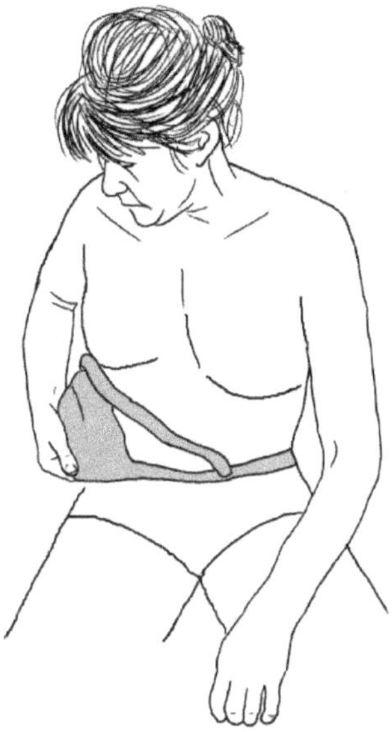

5. Remove clip and move the bra around your waist.

6. Place your left hand into the left shoulder strap.

7. Pull the left shoulder strap up onto your shoulder.

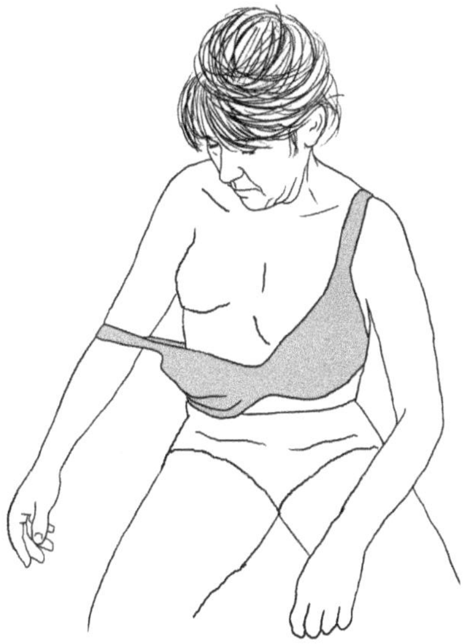

8. Put your right arm into the other bra strap. Reverse the steps to take off the bra.

Occupational Therapy TOOLKIT

Put On and Take Off a Bra with One Hand
Right Side Weakness

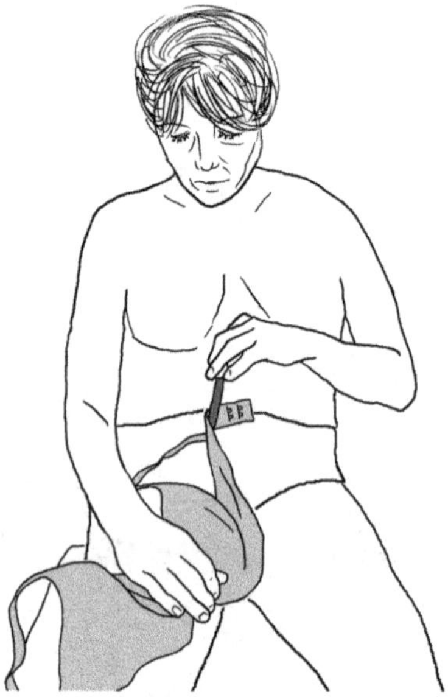

1. Clip the loop side of the bra to the pants.

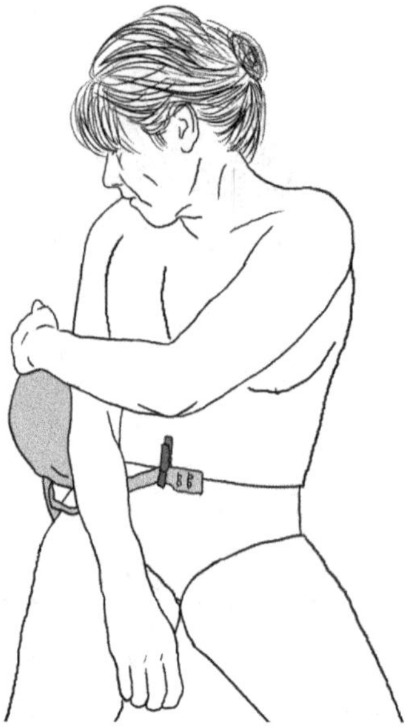

2. Move the bra behind your back around to your right side.

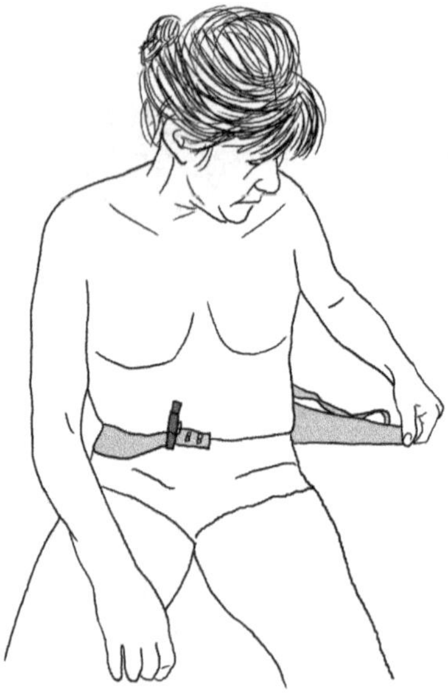

3. Reach back on your left side and pull the bra forward.

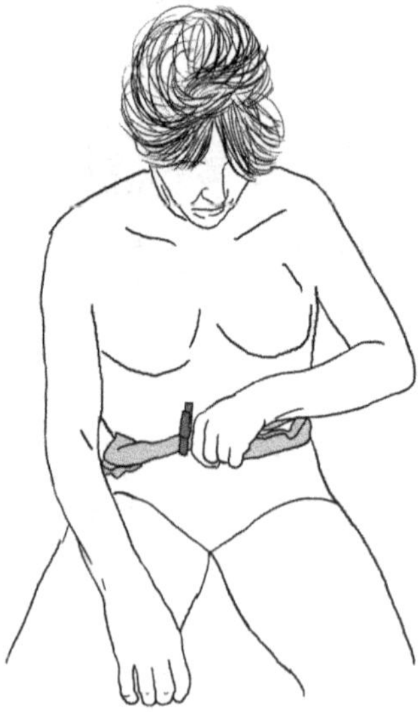

4. Hook the bra.

1 of 2

Put on and Take Off a Bra with One Hand
Right Side Weakness

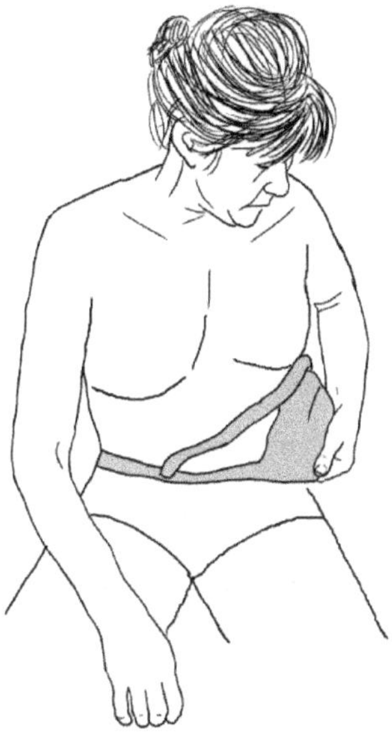

5. Remove clip and move the bra around your waist.

6. Place your right hand into the right shoulder strap.

7. Pull the right shoulder strap up onto your shoulder.

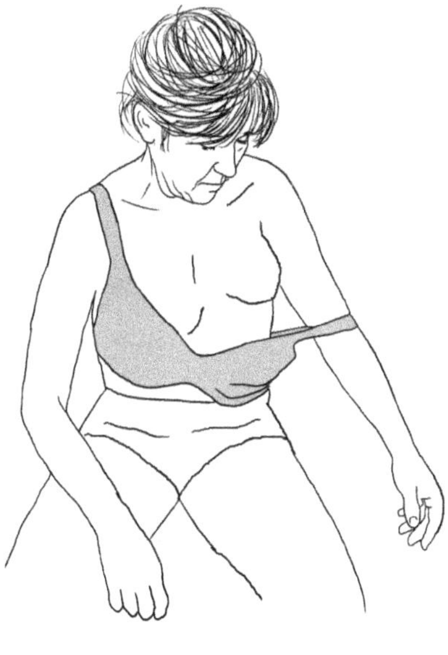

8. Put your left arm into the other bra strap. Reverse the steps to take off the bra.

2 of 2

Put On and Take Off a T-shirt
Arm-Head-Arm

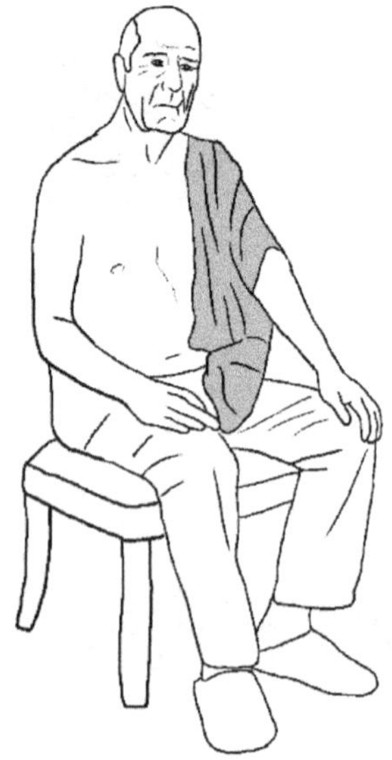

1. Place your weaker arm into the one sleeve.

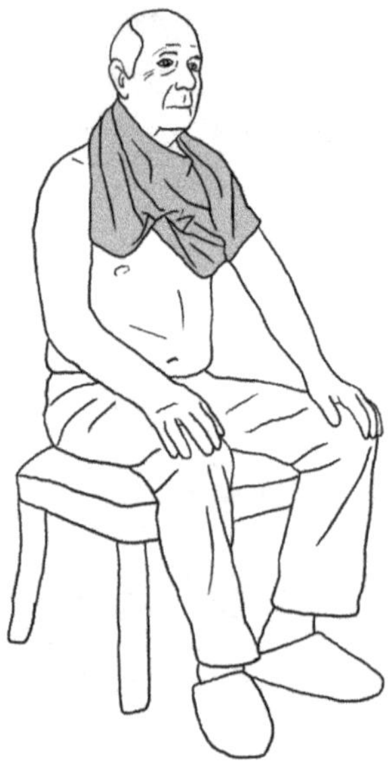

2. Pull the shirt over your head.

3. Place your stronger arm into the other sleeve.

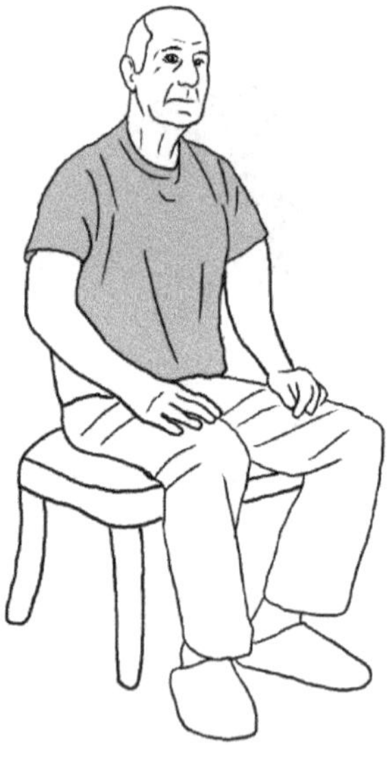

4. Pull shirt down and arrange. Reverse the steps to take off the shirt.

Put On and Take Off a T-shirt
Head-Arm-Arm

1. Place the shirt over your head.

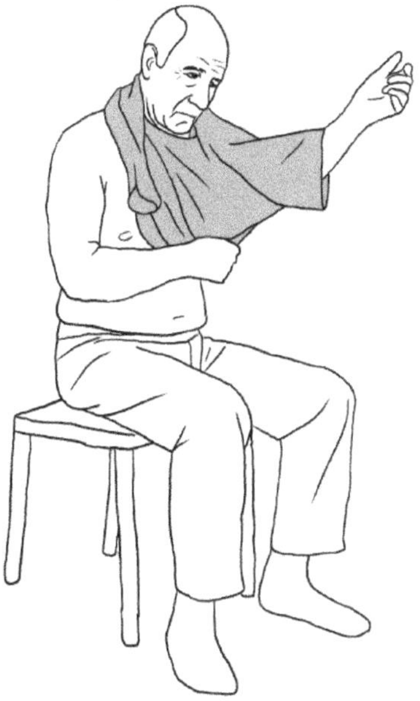

2. Put your weaker arm into one sleeve.

3. Put your stronger arm into the other sleeve.

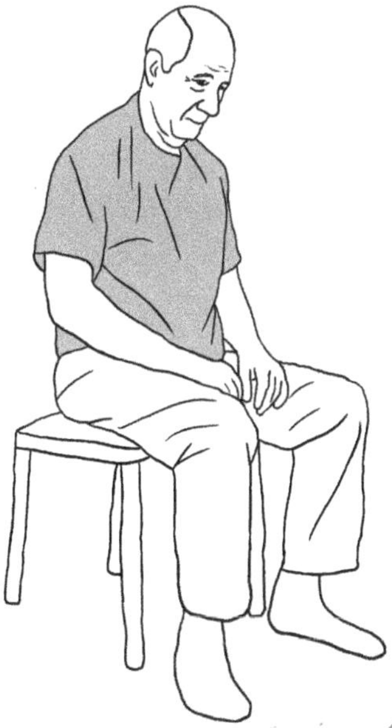

4. Pull the shirt down in front. Reverse the step to take off the shirt.

Put On and Take Off a T-shirt Using a Dressing Stick

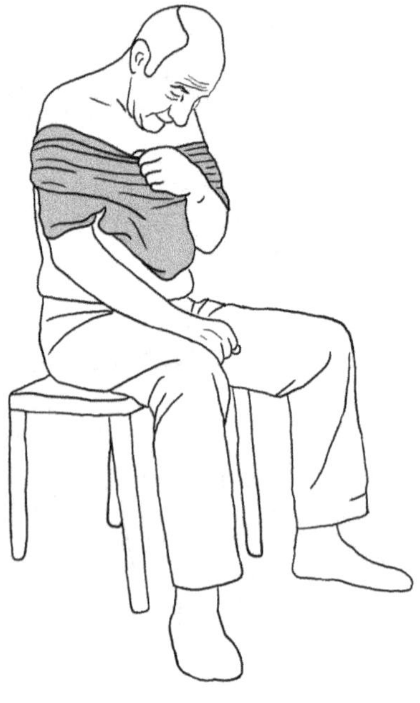

1. Put both arms in the sleeves.

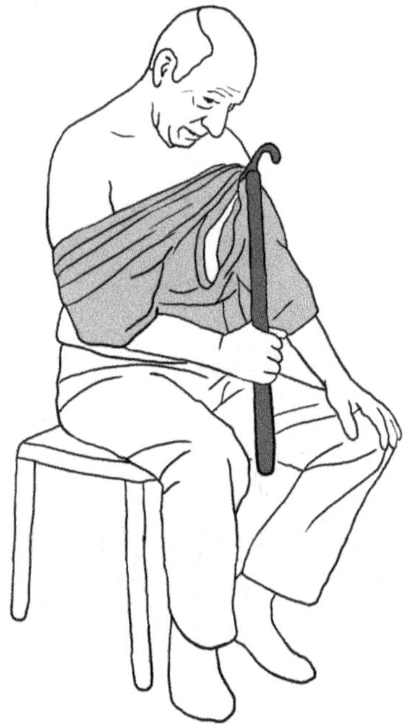

2. Place the hook of the dressing stick on the back of the collar.

3. Push the shirt up and over your head.

4. Pull the shirt down in front.

Put On and Take Off a T-shirt Using a Dressing Stick

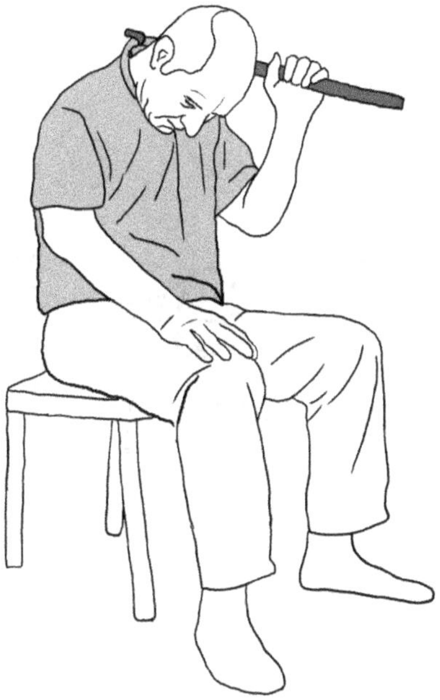

5. Hook the dressing stick on the collar behind your neck.

6. Pull the shirt off over your head.

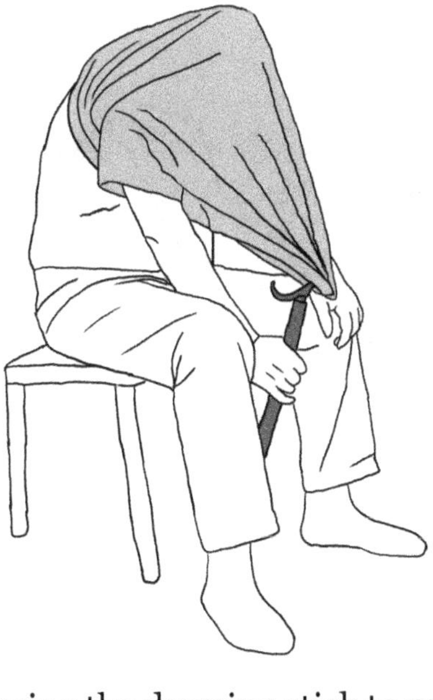

7. Keep using the dressing stick to pull the shirt off your head.

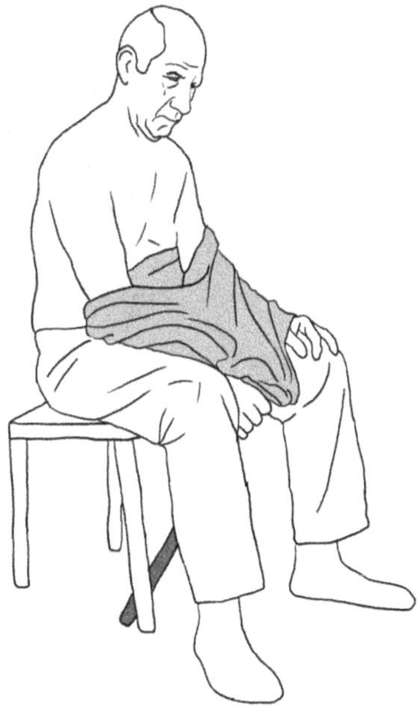

8. Remove the dressing stick from the collar and take the shirt off your arms.

Put On and Take Off an Ankle-Foot Brace (AFO)
Method 1 - Left Leg

Never wear the brace without a shoe. The brace is very smooth and you may slip.

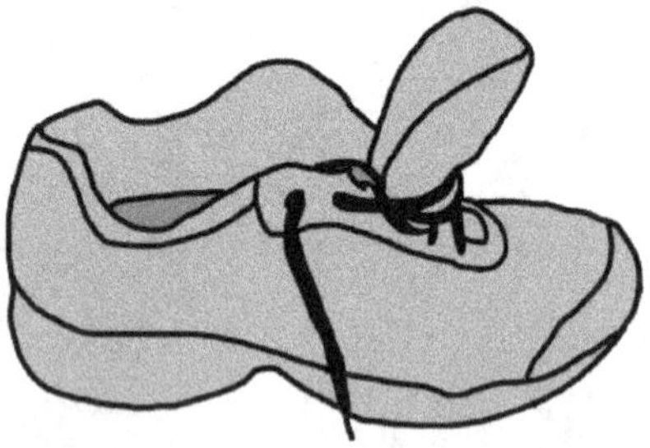

1. Loosen the laces or Velcro straps.

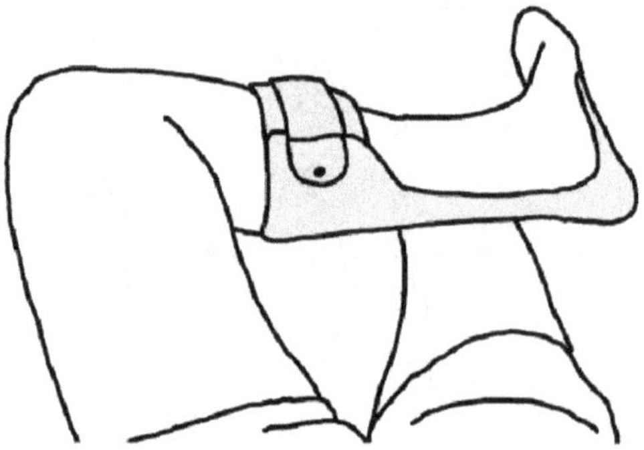

2. Place the brace on your leg and foot. Fasten the straps. Lift your foot to your other knee.

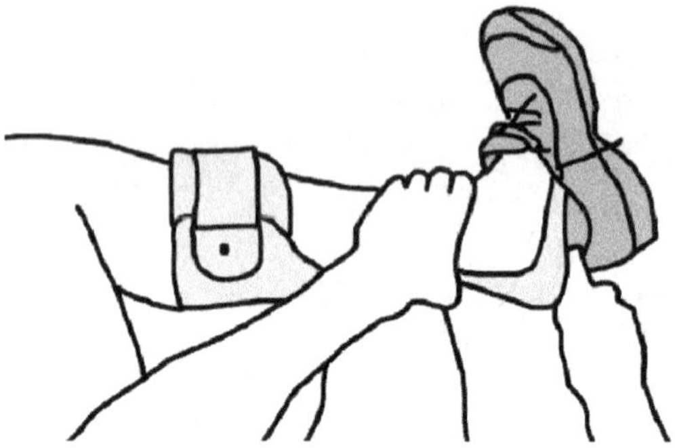

3. Hold your ankle and brace at the same time. Put the shoe over your foot and the brace.

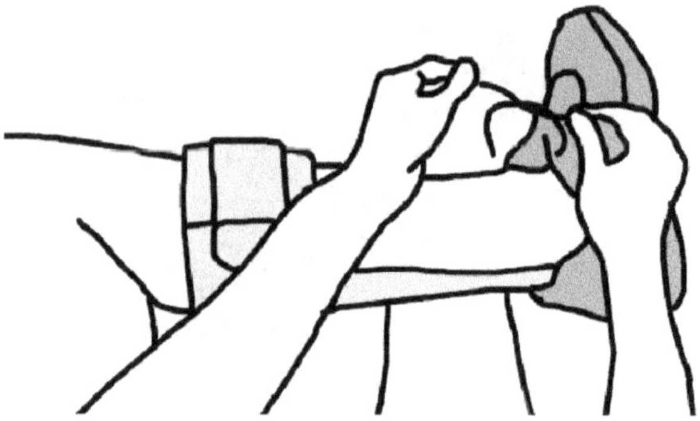

4. Adjust the straps. Tighten and fasten the laces or Velcro. Reverse the steps to take off the brace.

Put On and Take Off an Ankle-Foot Brace (AFO)
Method 1 - Right Leg

Never wear the brace without a shoe. The brace is very smooth and you may slip.

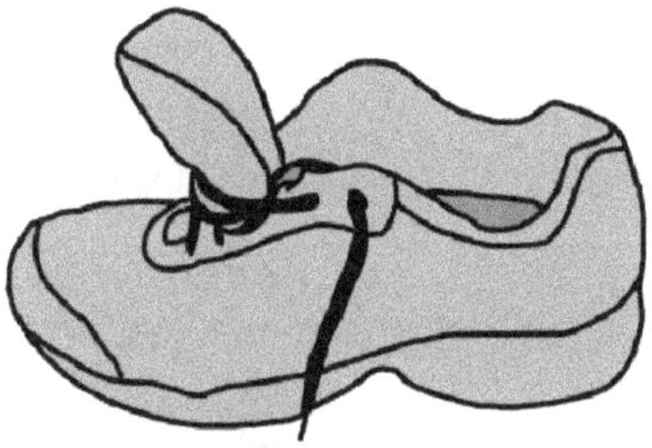

1. Loosen the laces or Velcro straps.

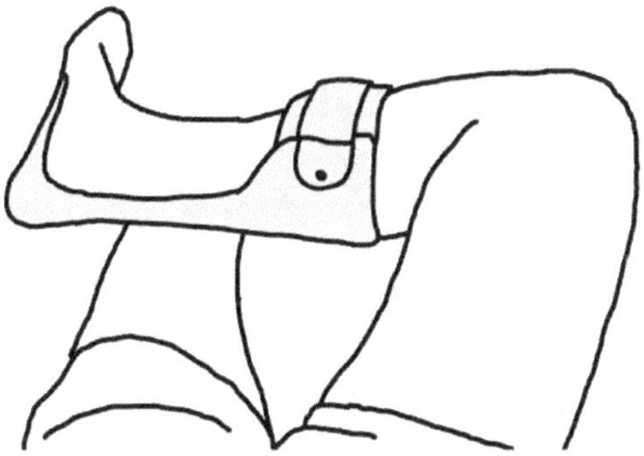

2. Place the brace on your leg and foot. Fasten the straps. Lift your foot to your other knee.

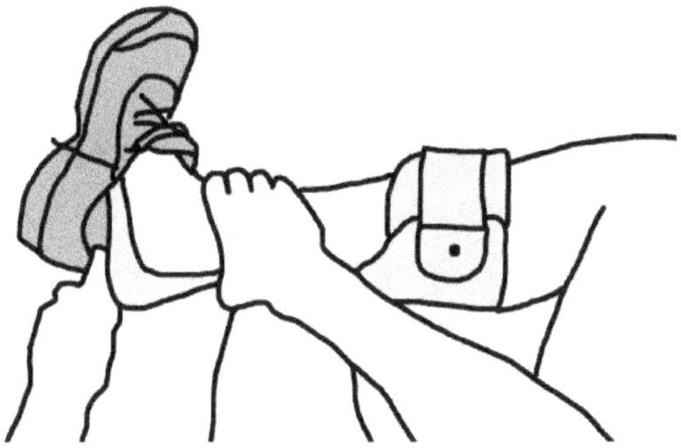

3. Hold your ankle and brace at the same time. Put the shoe over your foot and the brace.

4. Adjust the straps. Tighten and fasten the laces or Velcro. Reverse the steps to take off the brace.

Put On and Take Off an Ankle-Foot Brace (AFO)
Method 2 - Left Leg

Never wear the brace without a shoe. The brace is very smooth and you may slip.

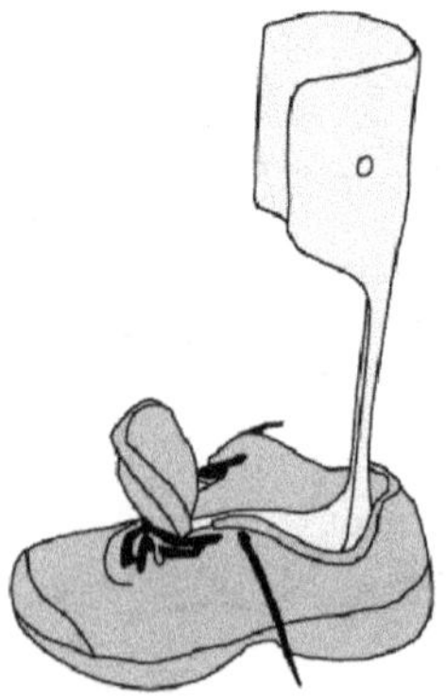

1. Loosen the laces or Velcro. Place the brace into the shoe.

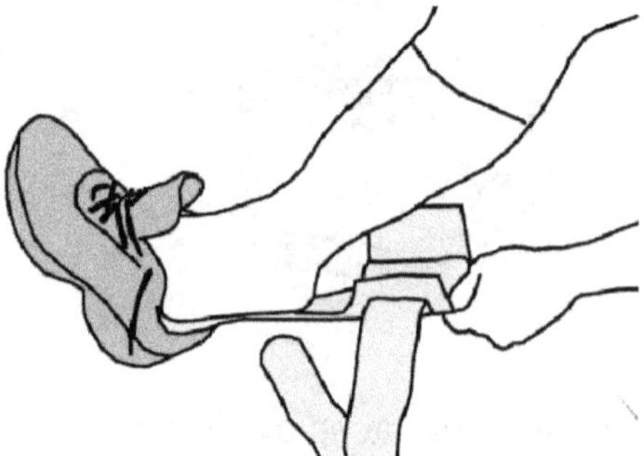

2. Slide your foot into the brace.

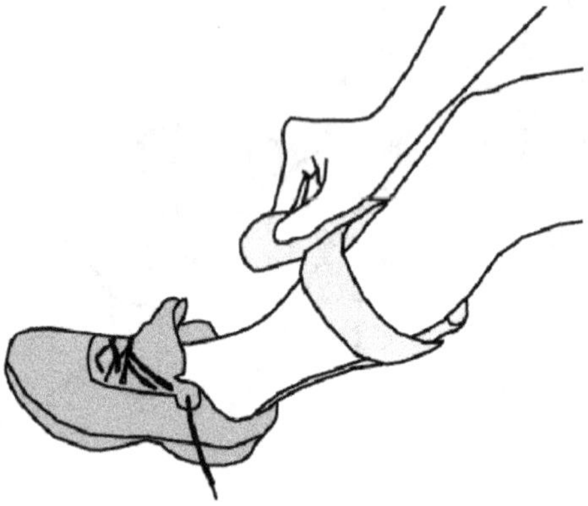

3. Fasten the straps.

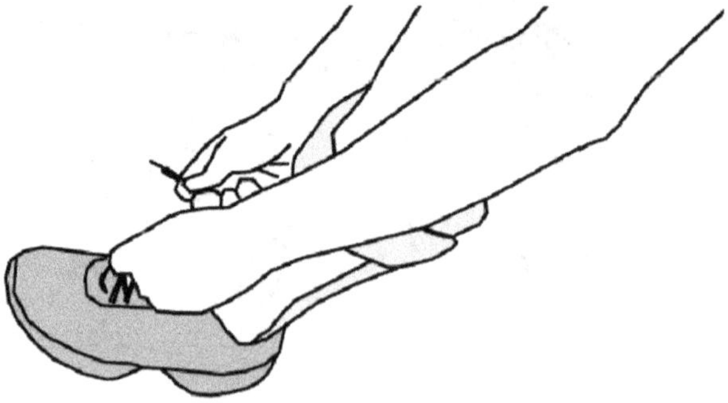

4. Tighten and fasten the laces or Velcro. Reverse the steps to take off the brace.

Occupational Therapy TOOLKIT

Put On and Take Off an Ankle-Foot Brace (AFO)
Method 2 - Right Leg

Never wear the brace without a shoe. The brace is very smooth and you may slip.

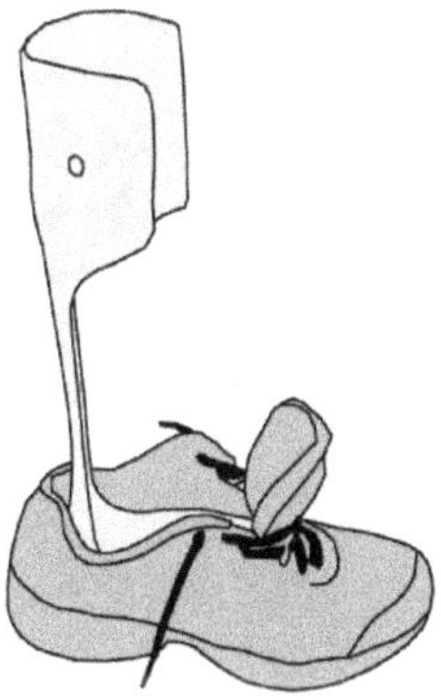

1. Loosen the laces or Velcro. Place the brace into the shoe.

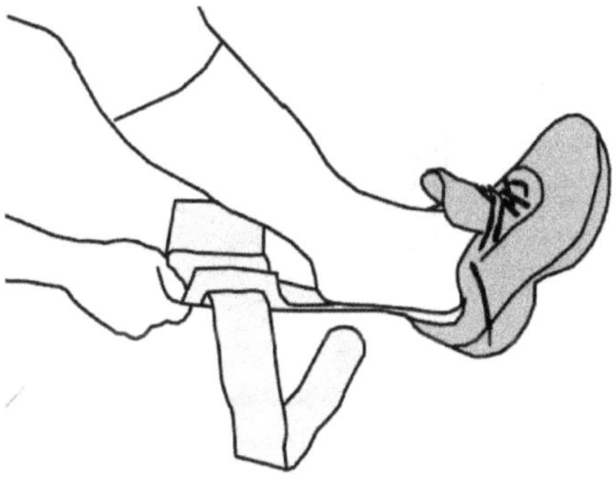

2. Slide your foot into the brace.

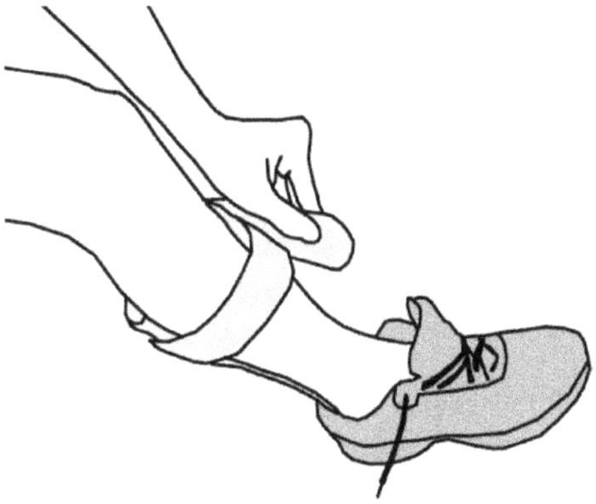

3. Fasten the straps.

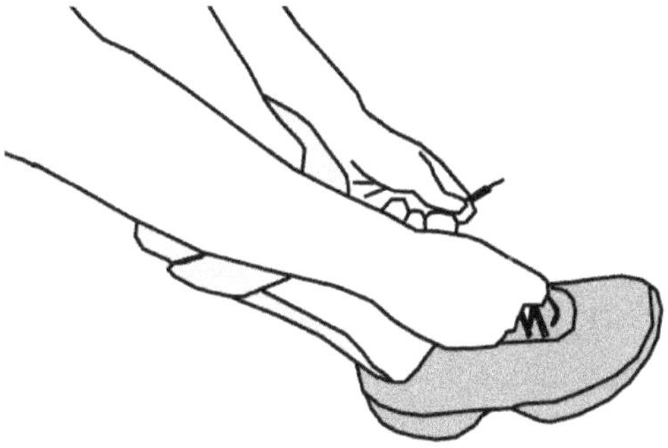

4. Tighten and fasten the laces or Velcro. Reverse the steps to take off the brace.

Put On and Take Off an Open Front Shirt
One Shoulder Drape

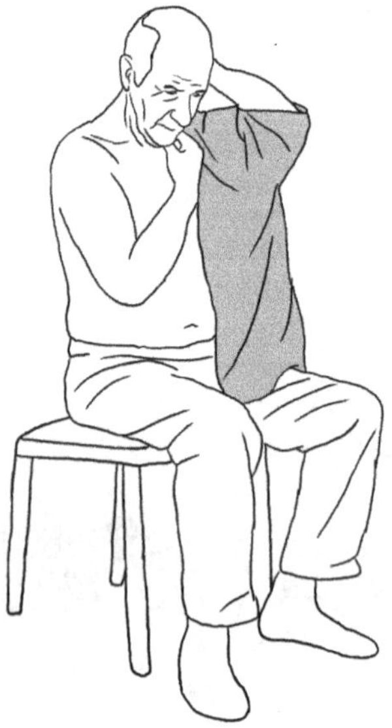

1. Put your stronger arm into one shirtsleeve first.

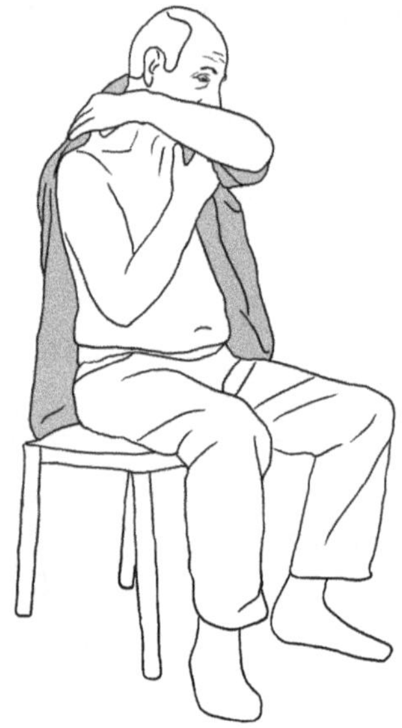

2. Reach around behind your neck and grasp the collar.

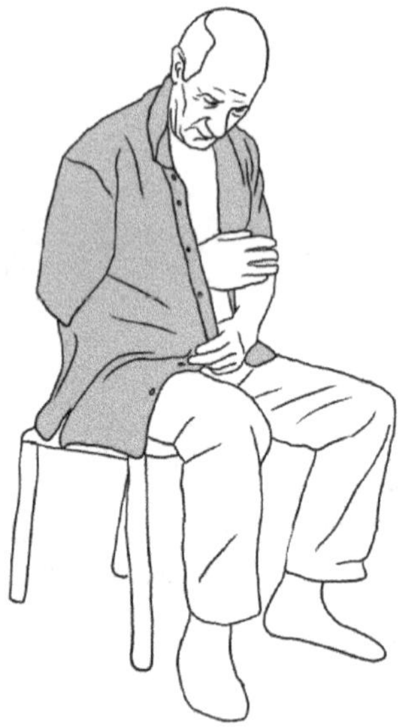

3. Drape the shirt over your weaker shoulder.

4. Push your weaker arm into the other sleeve. Reverse the steps to take off the shirt.

Put On and Take Off an Open Front Shirt
Two Shoulder Drape

1. Drape the shirt over both shoulders.

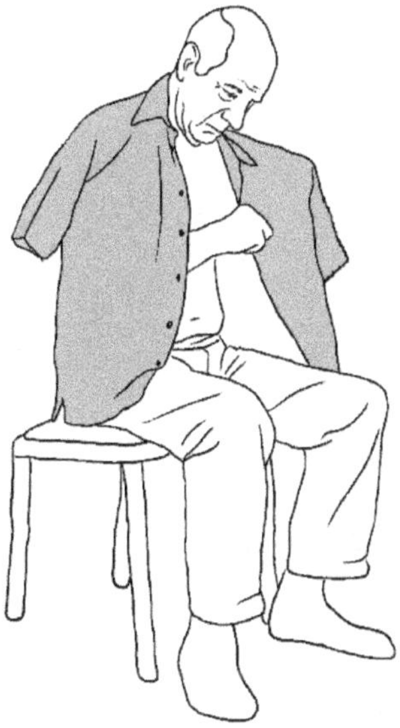

2. Place one arm into the sleeve.

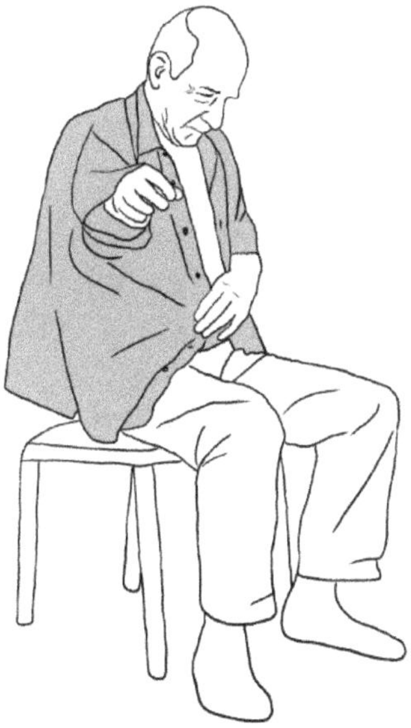

3. Place your other arm into the other sleeve.

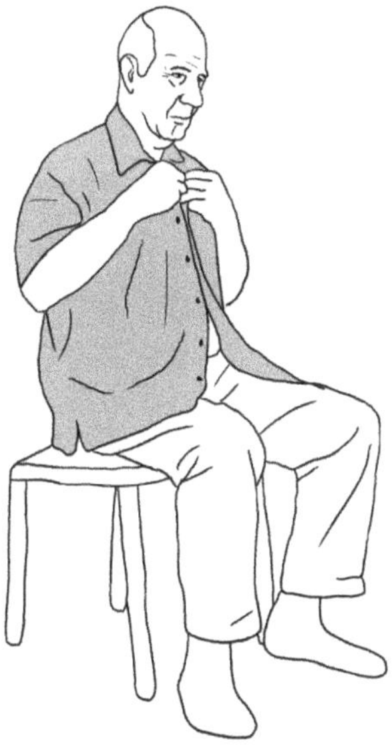

4. Arrange the shirt and button. Reverse the steps to take off the shirt.

Occupational Therapy TOOLKIT

Put On and Take Off an Open Front Shirt Using a Dressing Stick

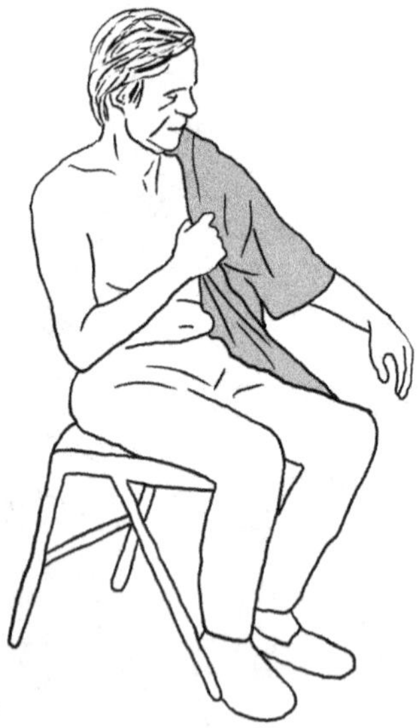

1. Place one arm into the shirt. Pull the sleeve up to your shoulder.

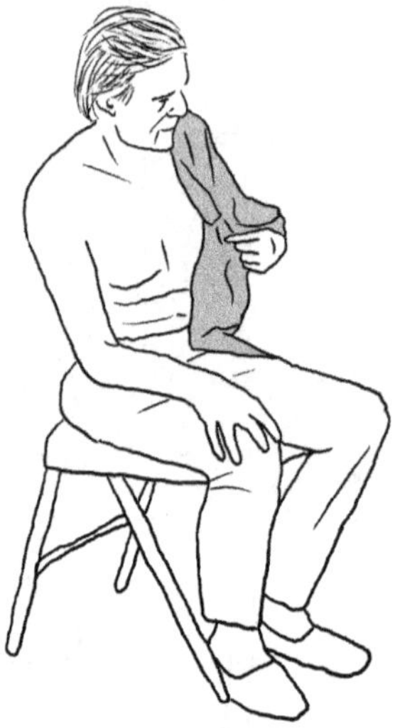

2. Pull the collar forward, until you see the other side of the shirt.

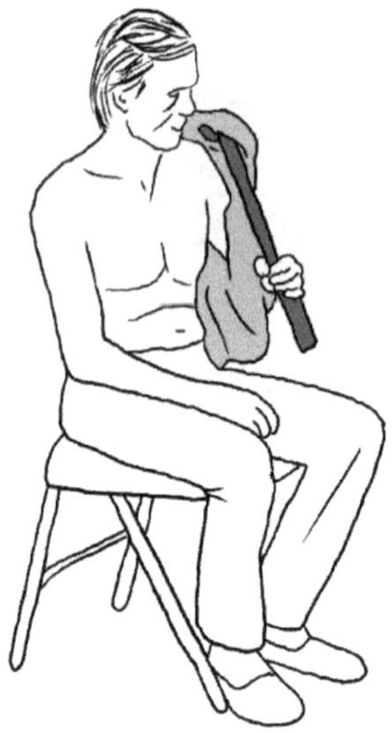

3. Hook the dressing stick at the collar.

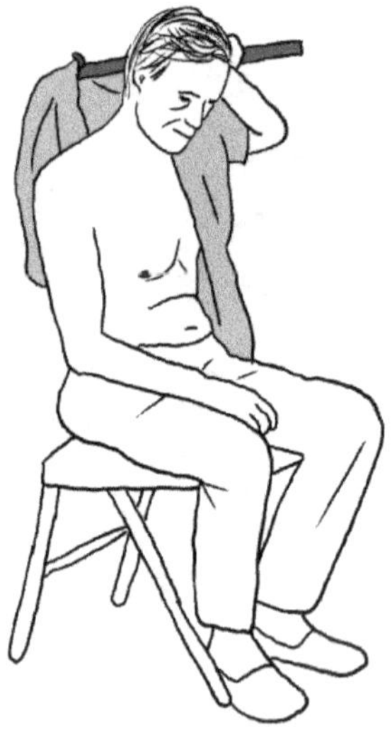

4. Using the dressing stick, move the shirt around behind your neck.

1 of 2

Put On and Take Off an Open Front Shirt Using a Dressing Stick

5. Pull the shirt forward over your other shoulder using the dressing stick.

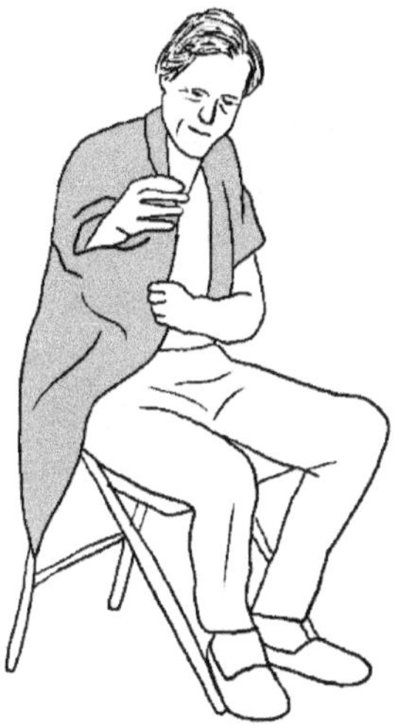

6. Place your arm into the sleeve.

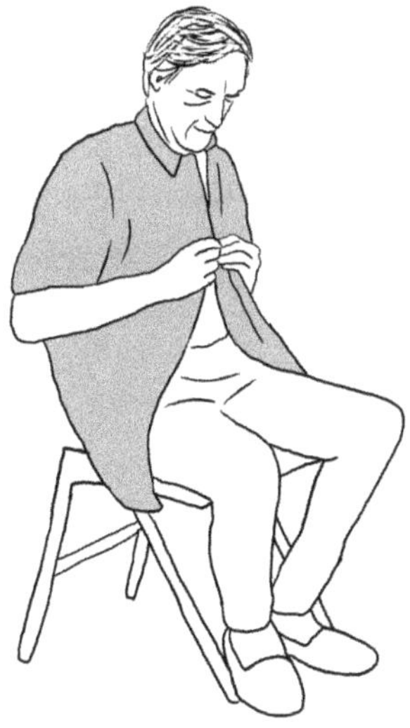

7. Adjust the shirt and button.

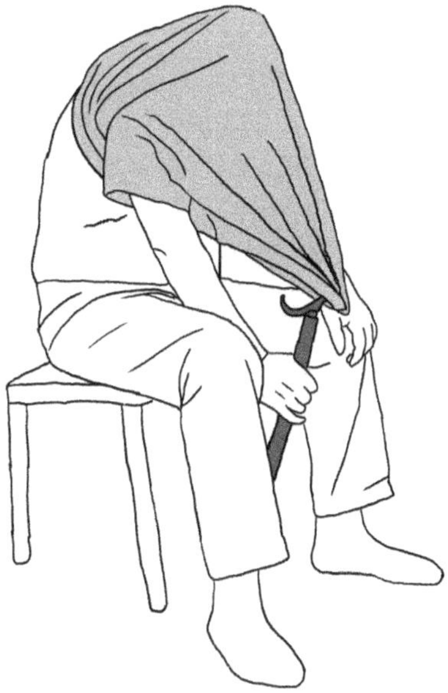

8. To take off the shirt, pull it over your head using the dressing stick.

Put On and Take Off Pants - Method 1

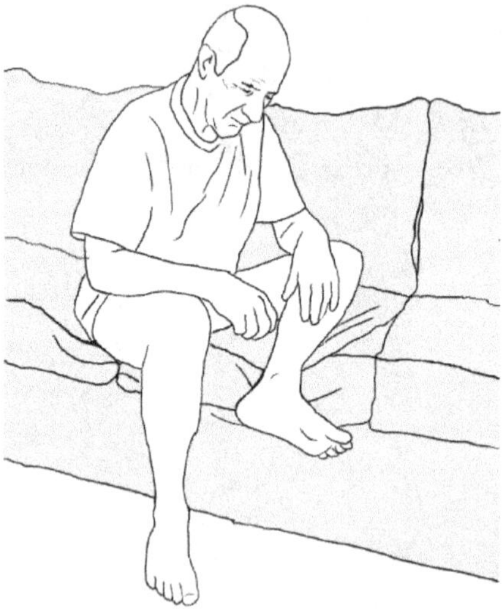

1. Lift your weaker leg up onto the bed or sofa.

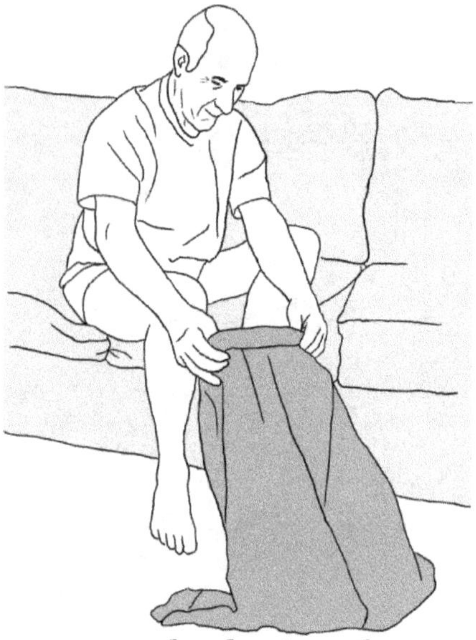

2. Place your weaker leg into the pants. Pull until you can see your foot.

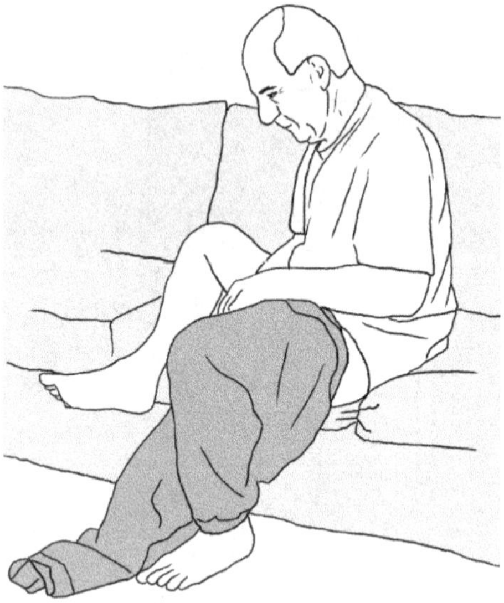

3. Turn and face the other way. Place your stronger leg up on the sofa or bed.

4. Place your stronger leg into the pants.

1 of 2

Put On and Take Off Pants - Method 1

5. Lean from one side to your other side and pull the pants over your hips. Reverse the steps to take off the pants.

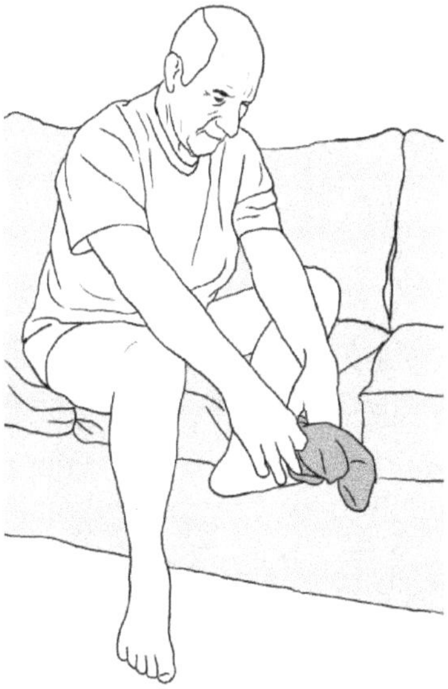

6. This method will also work to put on and take off shoes and socks.

Put On and Take Off Pants - Method 2

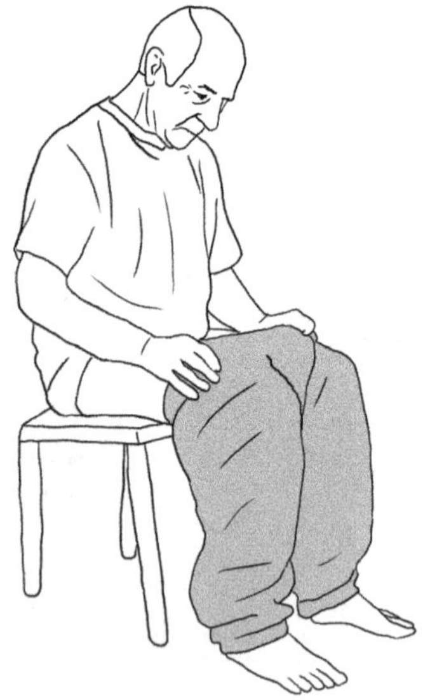

1. Stay seated. Put on the pants and pull them up over your knees.

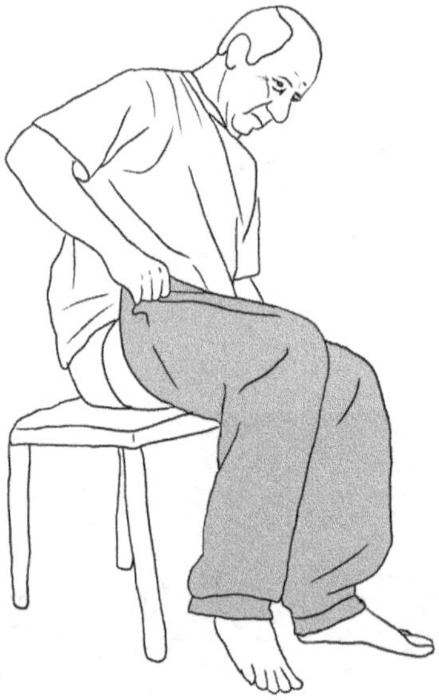

2. Lean to your side and pull the pants up over one hip.

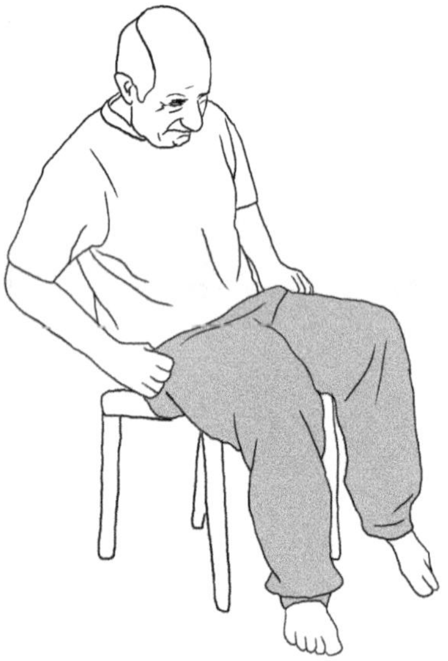

3. Lean to your other side and pull the pants up over your other hip. Repeat until the pants are up. Reverse the steps to take off the pants.

Occupational Therapy TOOLKIT

Put On and Take Off Pants, Socks, and Shoes Lying Down

1. Put your weaker leg into the pants first.

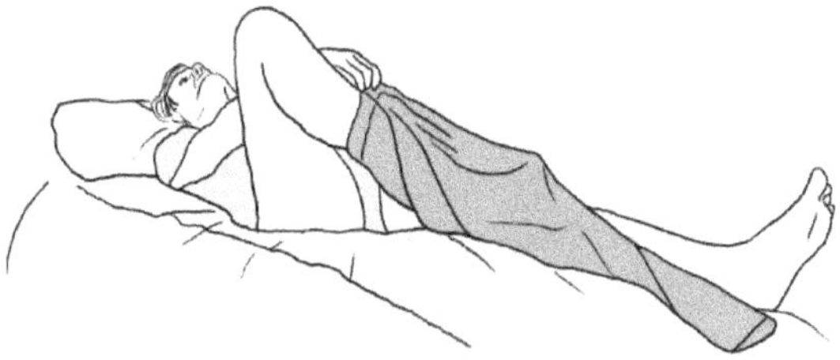

2. Put your stronger leg into the pants.

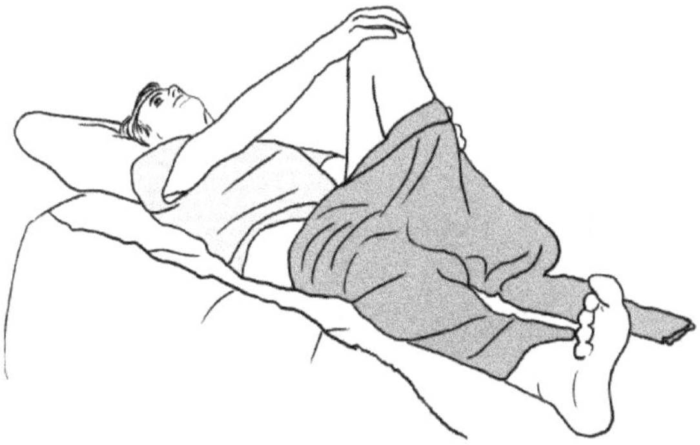

3. Log roll to one side and pull up the side of the pants.

4. Log roll to your other side and pull up the other side of the pants.

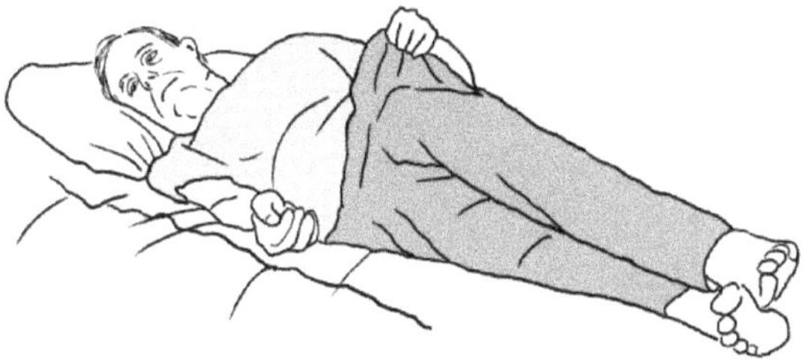

5. Lie on your back to put on the socks and shoes.

Reverse the steps to take off the shoes, socks and pants.

Put On and Take Off Pants, Socks, and Shoes Using a Stool

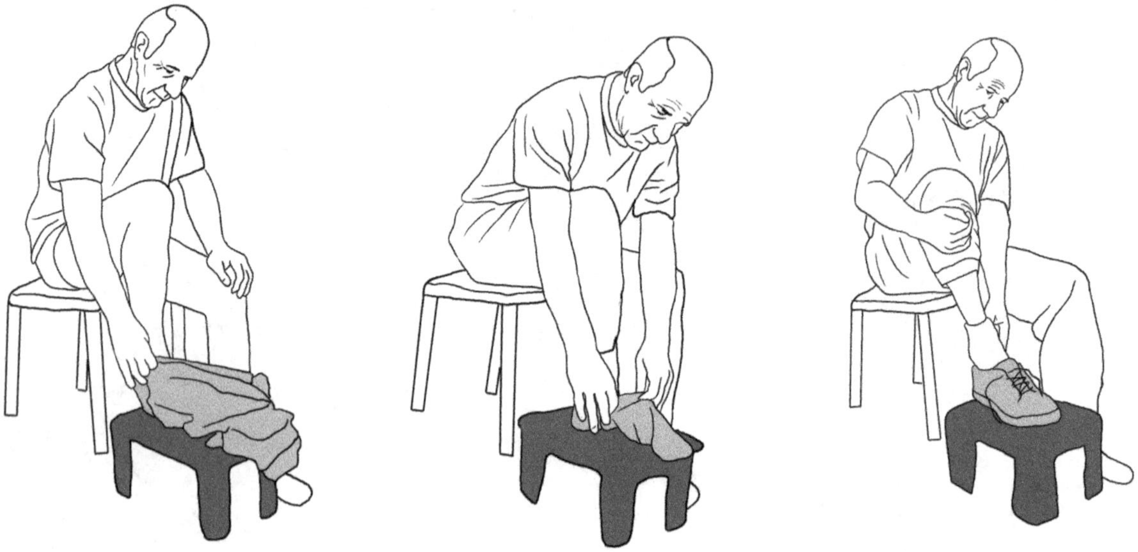

Use a stool to bring your foot closer.

Put On and Take Off Pants Using a Dressing Stick or Reacher

1. Use the dressing stick or reacher to lower the pants to the ground.

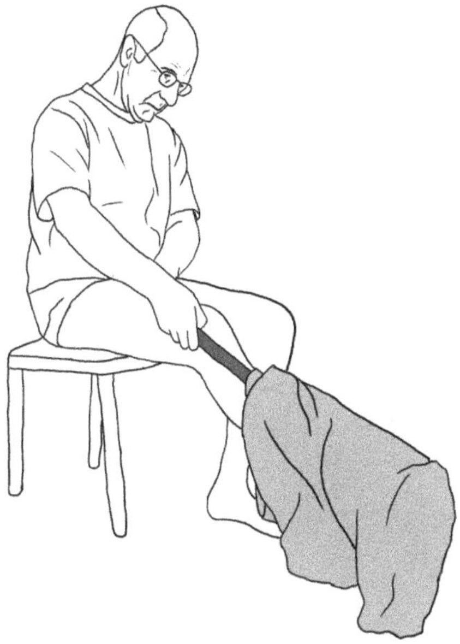

2. Put your weaker leg into the pants first.

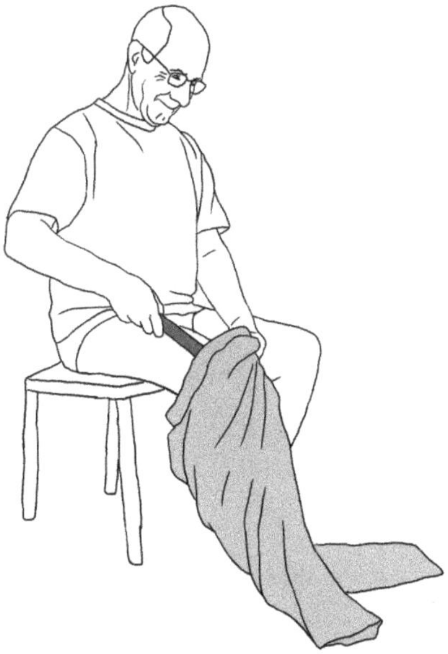

3. Pull the pants up your leg.

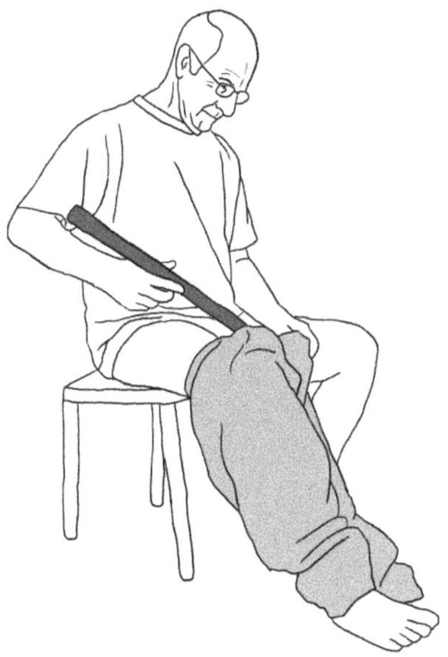

4. When you can reach the pants, remove the dressing stick or reacher. Pull the pant leg over your foot.

Put On and Take Off Pants Using a Dressing Stick or Reacher

5. Use the dressing stick or reacher to lower the pants back to the floor.

6. Put your other leg into the pants. Use the dressing stick or reacher to pull the pants up.

7. Pull the pants up over your knees and feet while still sitting.

8. Stand and pull the pants up.

Put On and Take Off Pants
Using a Dressing Stick or Reacher

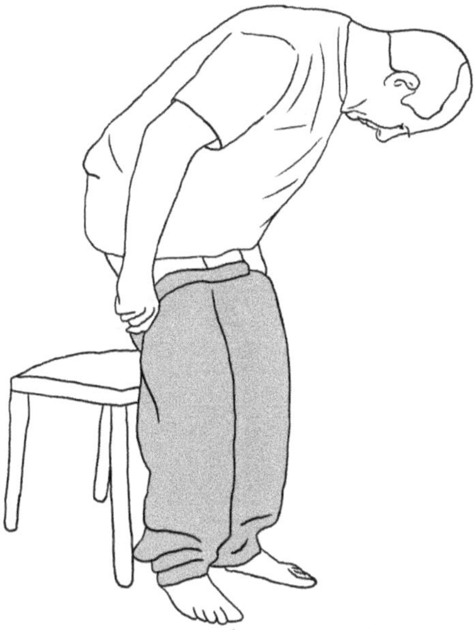

1. Sit and undo the pants. Stand up and lower the pants past your hips.

2. Sit down. Use the dressing stick or reacher to push the pants down.

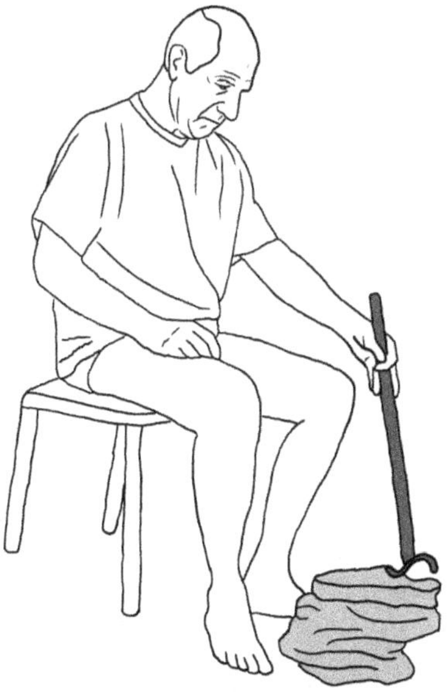

3. Take off the pants from your feet.

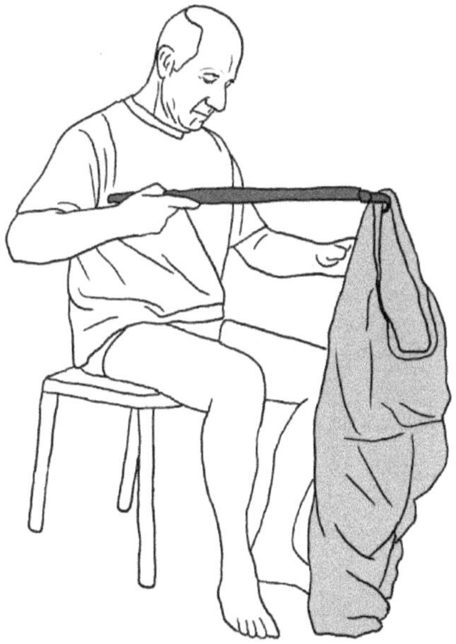

4. Use the dressing stick or reacher to pick the pants up off the floor.

Put On and Take Off Socks and Shoes Using Dressing Tools

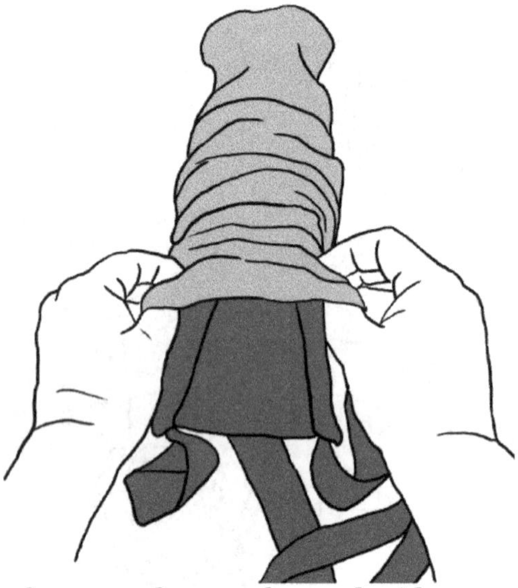

1. Gather a sock over the sock aid.

2. Hold onto the straps and lower the sock aid to the floor.

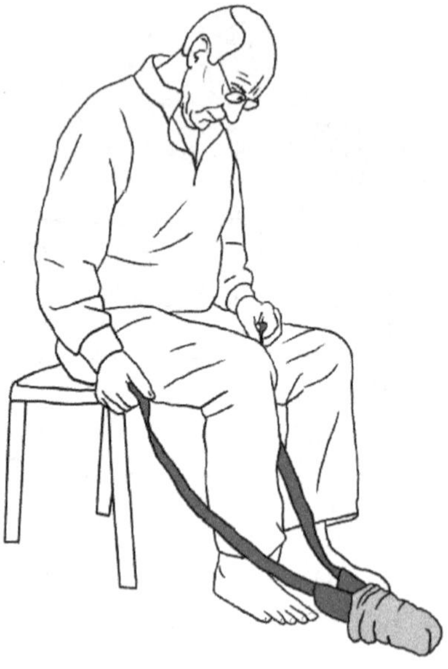

3. Place the sock aid in front of your foot.

4. Point your foot and pull the sock aid over your toes.

Put On and Take Off Socks and Shoes Using Dressing Tools

5. Lift your foot up and pull the sock aid out.

6. To take off the sock, use the dressing stick or reacher. Hook the back of the sock and push it off.

7. Wear slip-on shoes or replace the laces with stretch laces or Velcro. Use a long handled shoehorn to put shoes on.

8. Take off the shoe by using the dressing stick to push the shoe off your heel.

Occupational Therapy TOOLKiT

Put On and Take Off Support Stockings

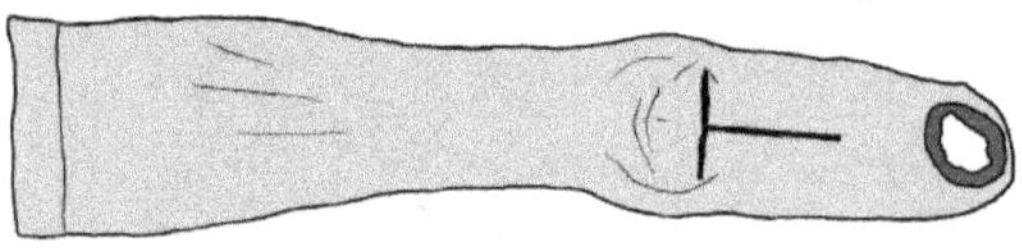

Turn the stockings inside out. Lay the stockings out flat, with the heel up. Mark each one, with a "T" using a Sharpie. You only need to do this once.

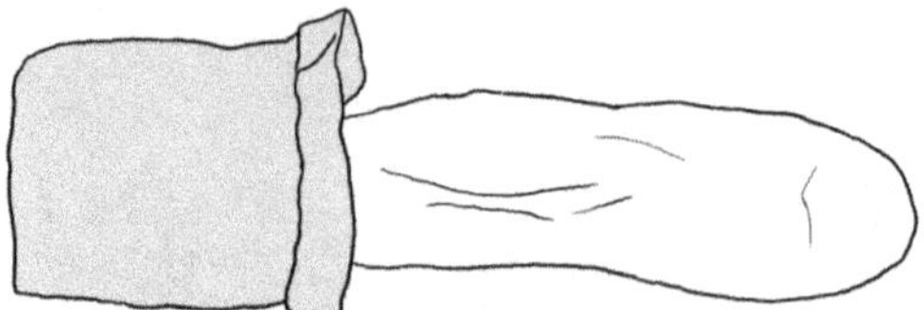

1. Start with the stockings right side out. Turn the stocking back onto itself until you get to the top of the "T".

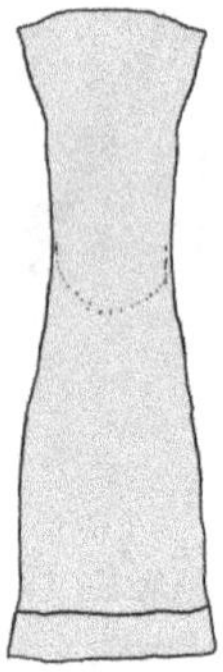

2. The toe of the stocking will fold inside.

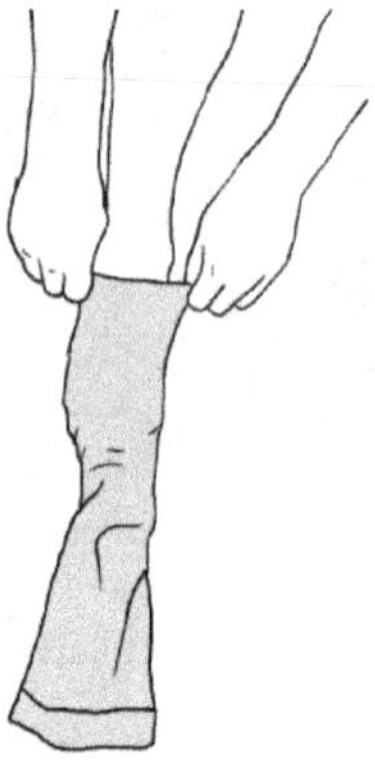

3. Find the bottom of the stocking, the down stroke of the "T". Line it up with the bottom of your foot.

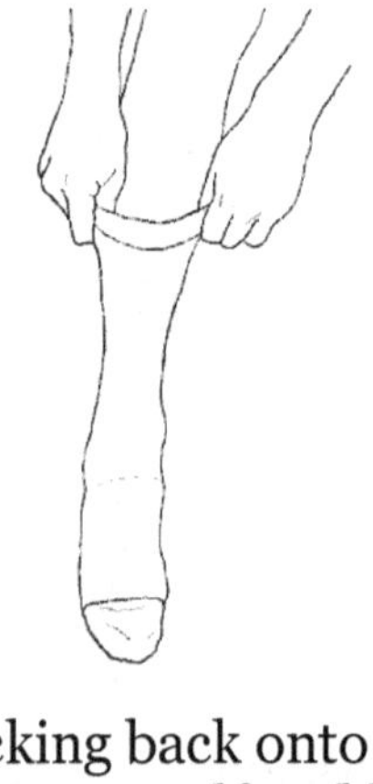

4. Pull the stocking back onto itself. Pull the stocking up your calf and knee. Smooth out the folds.

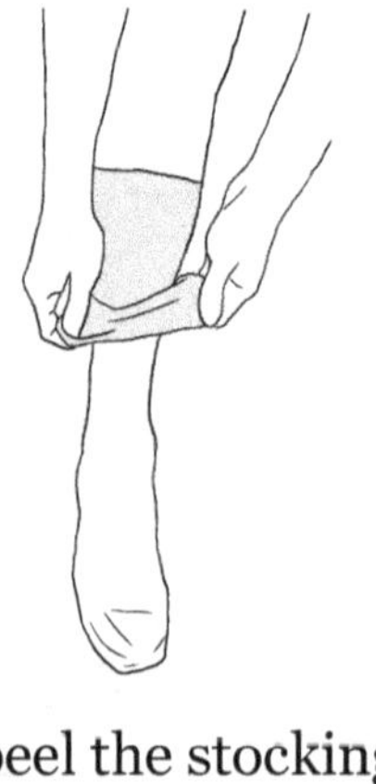

5. To remove, peel the stocking off inside out.

You may need to adjust the stockings during the day.

Occupational Therapy TOOLKIT

Put On Pants with One Hand
Left Side Weakness

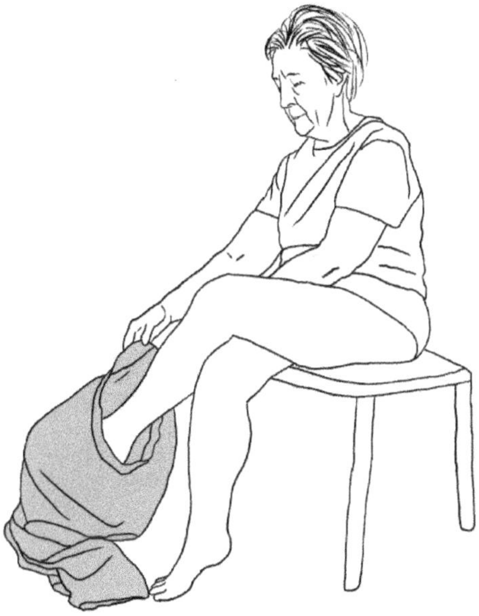

1. Cross your left leg over your right knee. Place the left pants leg over your left foot.

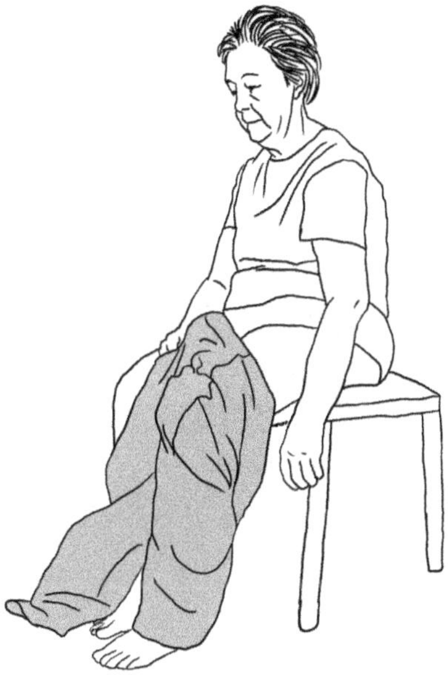

2. Pull the pants leg until you can see your foot.

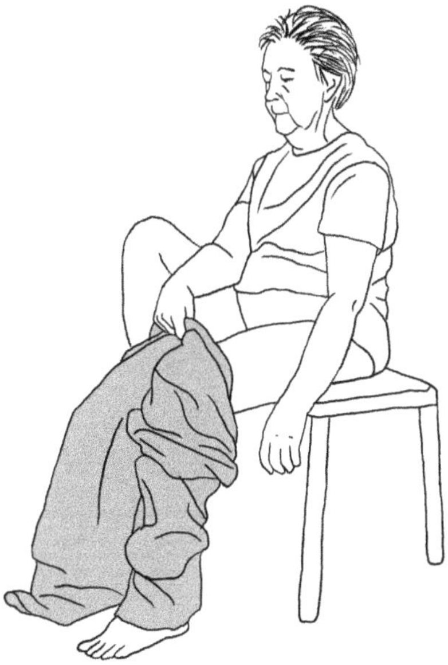

3. Place your right foot into the right leg of the pants.

4. Pull the pants up as far as you can.

Put On Pants with One Hand
Left Side Weakness

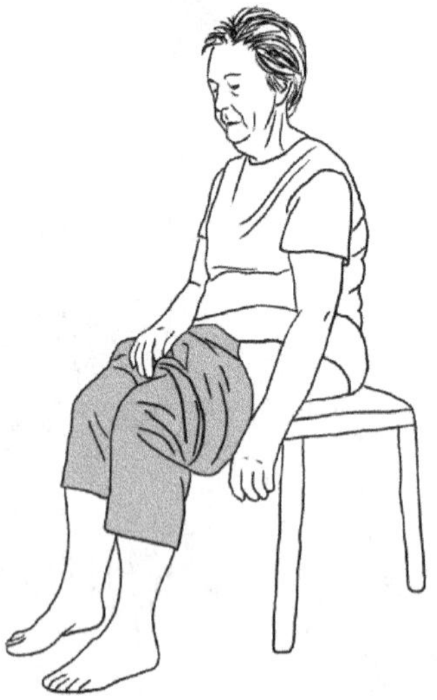

5. Pull the pant legs up over both knees. This will stop them from falling when you stand up.

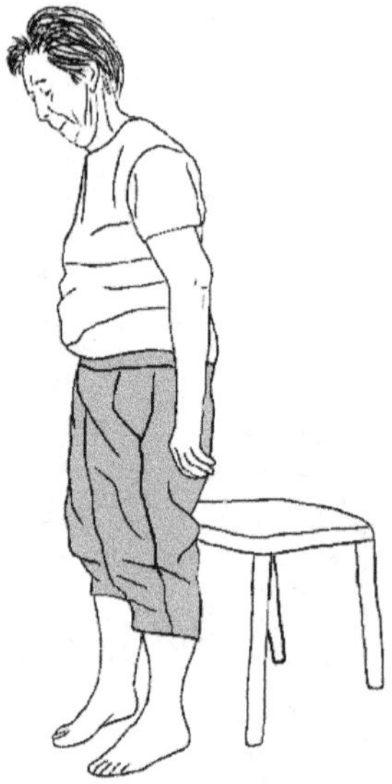

6. Stand and pull up the pants. Sit down to fasten the pants.

Options if you cannot stand.

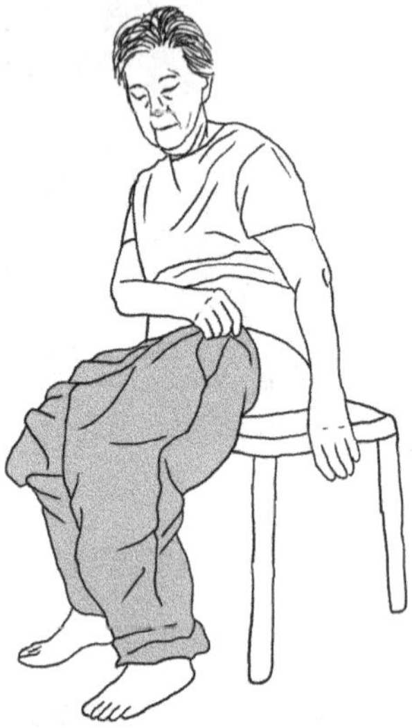

5. Stay seated and lean from one side to your other side.

6. Work the pants up over your hips.

2 of 2

Occupational Therapy TOOLKIT

Put On Pants with One Hand
Right Side Weakness

1. Cross your right leg over your left knee. Place the right pants leg over your right foot.

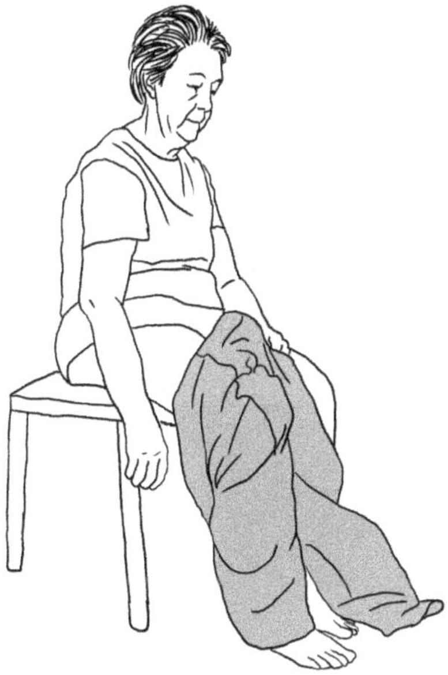

2. Pull the pants leg until you can see your foot.

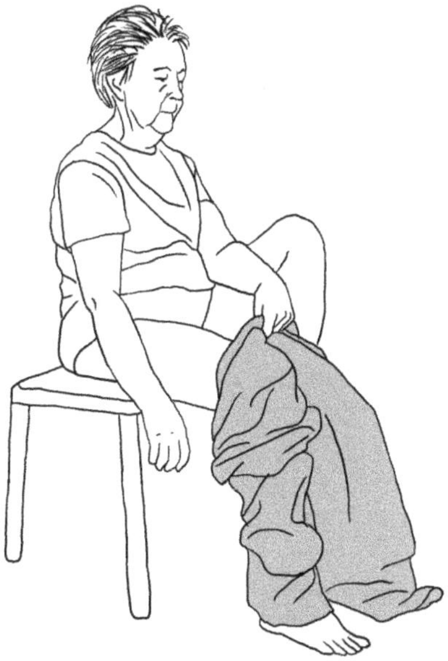

3. Place your left foot into the left leg of the pants.

4. Pull the pants up as far as you can.

1 of 2

Put On Pants with One Hand
Right Side Weakness

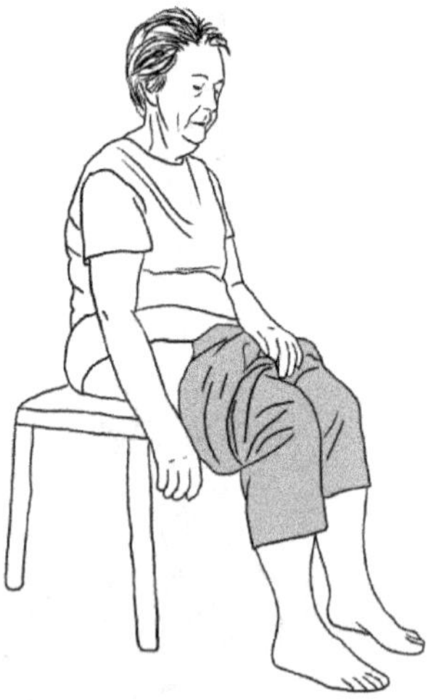

5. Pull the pant legs up over both knees. This will stop them from falling when you stand up.

6. Stand and pull up the pants. Sit down to fasten the pants.

Options if you cannot stand

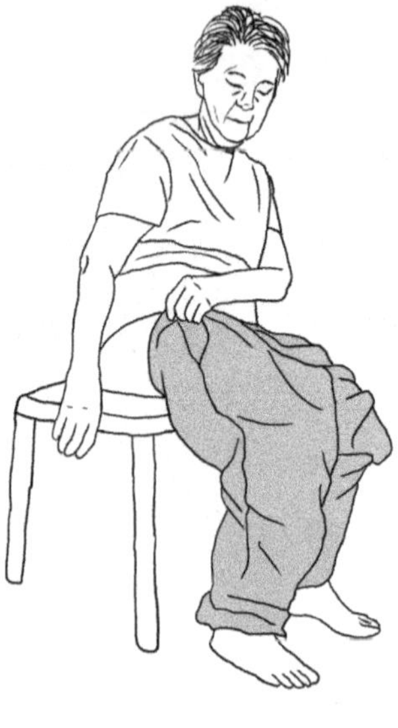

5. Stay seated and lean from one side to your other side.

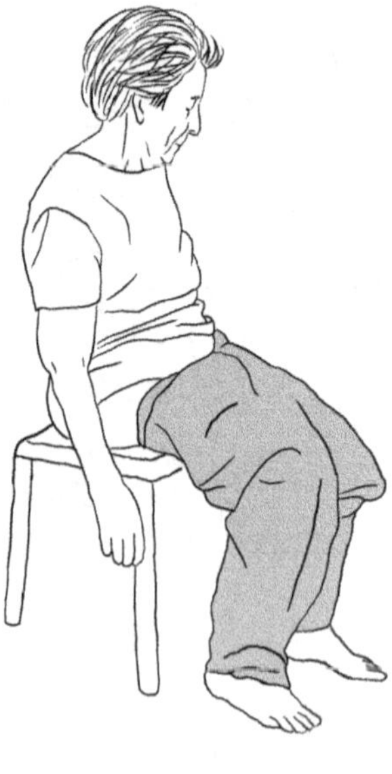

6. Work the pants up over your hips.

Put On Socks and Shoes with One Hand
Left Side Weakness

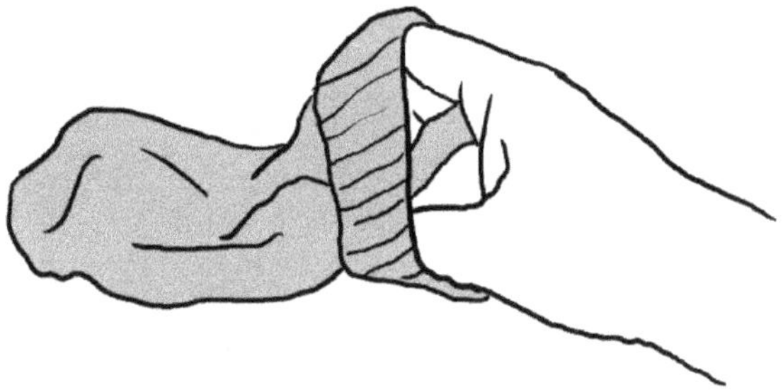

1. Use your right hand to spread the sock open.

2. Cross your left leg over your right knee. Place the sock over your foot.

3. Cross your left leg over your right knee. Place your foot into the shoe.

4. Wear slip-on shoes or replace the laces with stretch laces or Velcro.

Put On Socks and Shoes with One Hand
Right Side Weakness

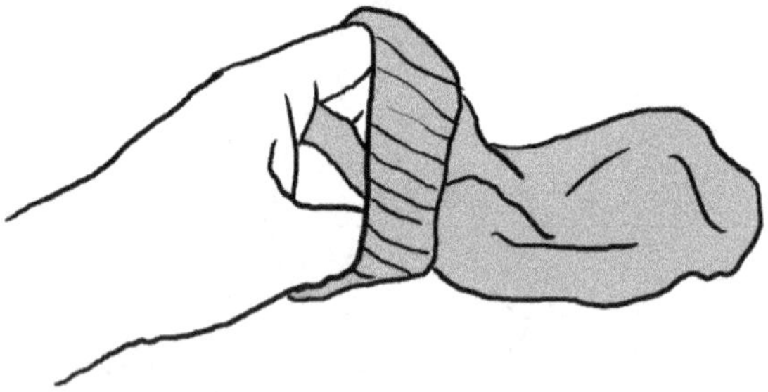

1. Use your left hand to spread the sock open.

2. Cross your right leg over your left knee. Put the sock over your foot.

3. Cross your right leg over your left knee. Place your foot into the shoe.

4. Wear slip-on shoes or replace the laces with stretch laces or Velcro.

Roll Onto Your Left Side

1. Lie on your back. Bend your right leg so your foot is flat on the bed. Reach your right arm toward the edge of the mattress or a bed handle.

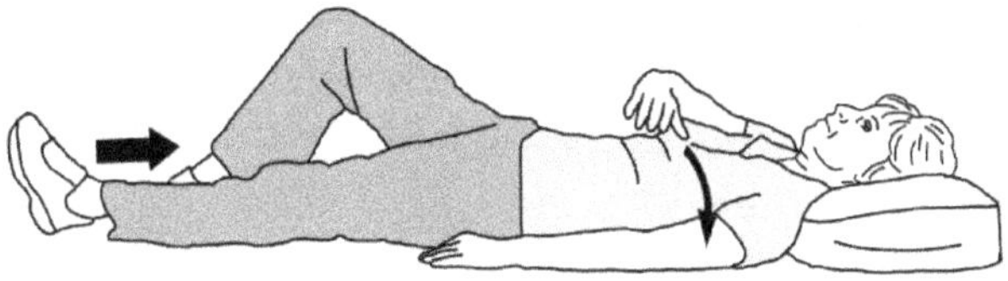

2. Use your right foot to push off. Pull on the bed handle or mattress. Roll onto your side.

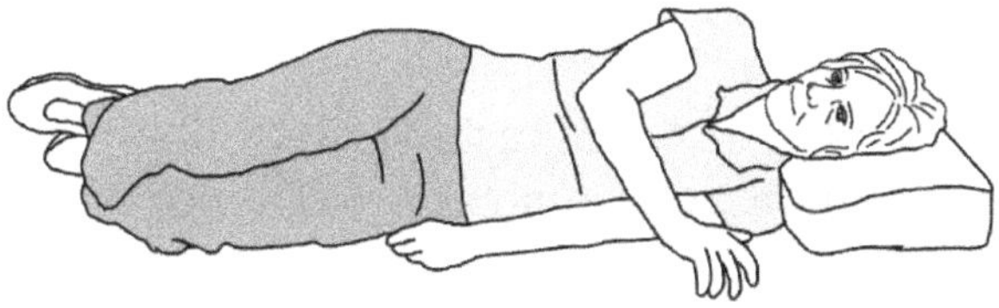

3. A caregiver can help by moving you from your shoulder and hip.

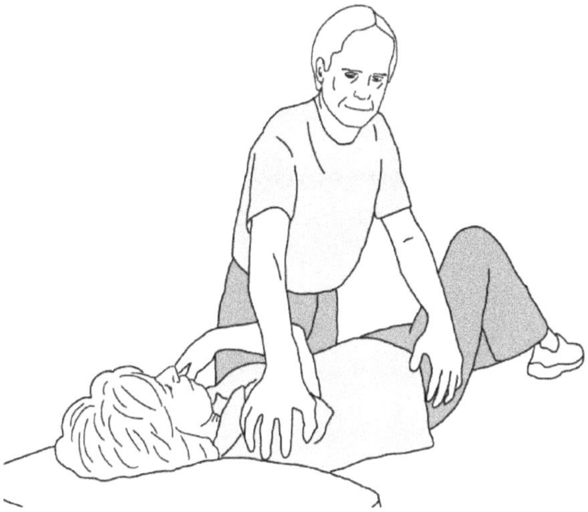

Roll Onto Your Right Side

1. Lie on your back. Bend your left leg so your foot is flat on the bed. Reach your left arm toward the edge of the mattress or a bed handle.

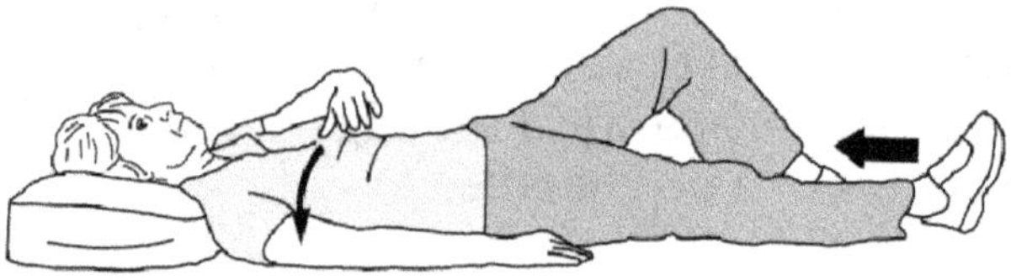

2. Use your left foot to push off. Pull on the bed handle or mattress. Roll onto your side.

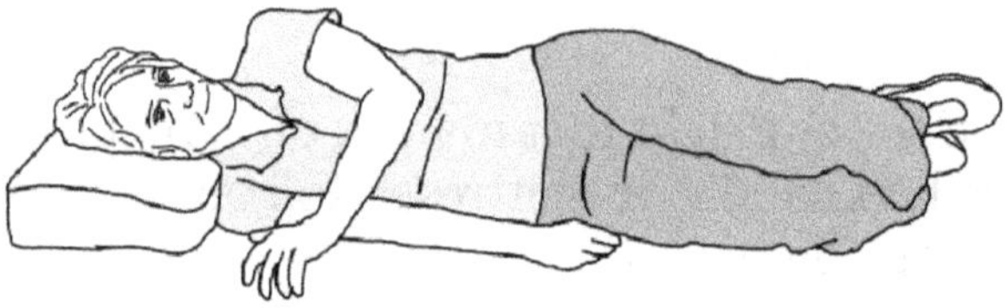

3. A caregiver can help by moving you from your shoulder and hip.

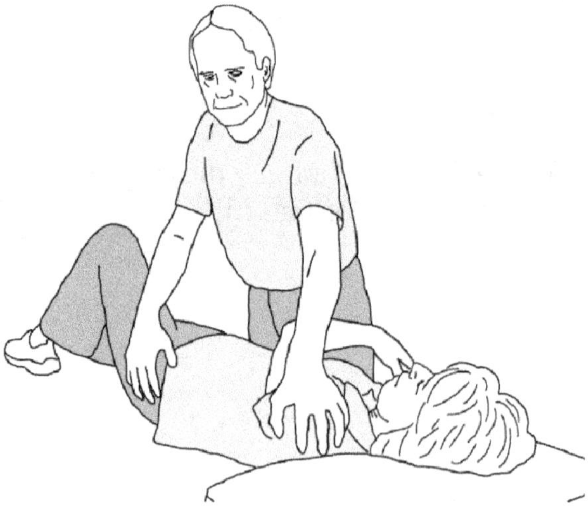

Occupational Therapy TOOLKIT

Sit-Pivot Transfer - Move to the Left
To and From a Wheelchair, Chair, Bed or Commode

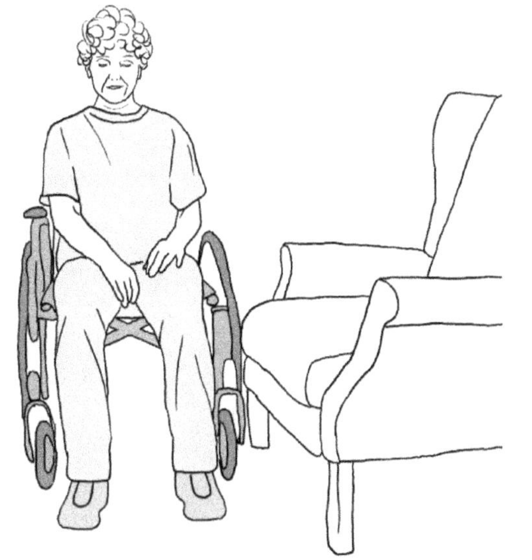

1. Try to transfer to your stronger side. Place the wheelchair next to the chair you are moving. Lock the brakes and remove the armrest and leg rest.

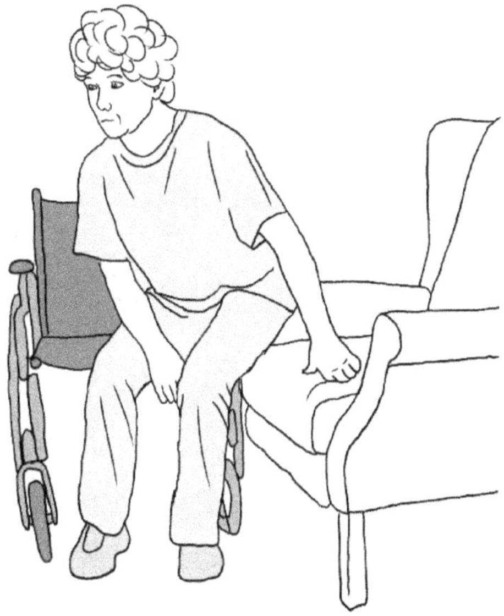

2. Reach over to the chair you are moving. Stand up just enough to clear your hips from the wheelchair.

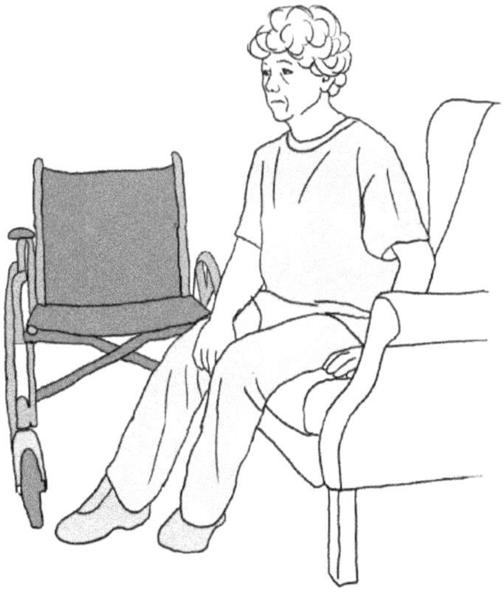

3. Slide over onto the chair.

4. Move your hips back into the chair.

Use this transfer when moving onto the commode, bed or back to the wheelchair.

Sit-Pivot Transfer - Move to the Right
To and From a Wheelchair, Chair, Bed or Commode

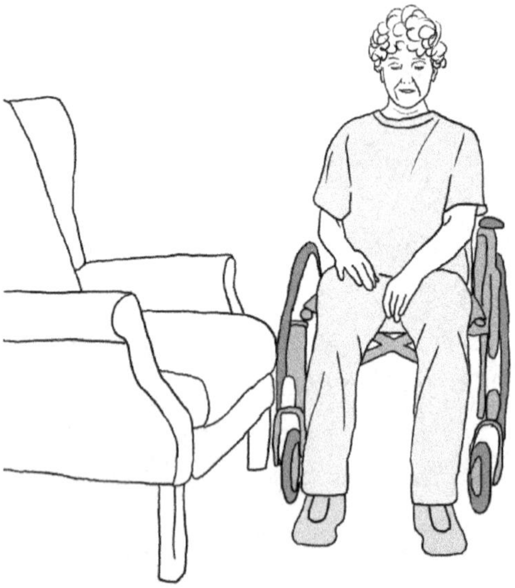

1. Try to transfer to your stronger side. Place the wheelchair next to the chair you are moving. Lock the brakes and remove the armrest and leg rest.

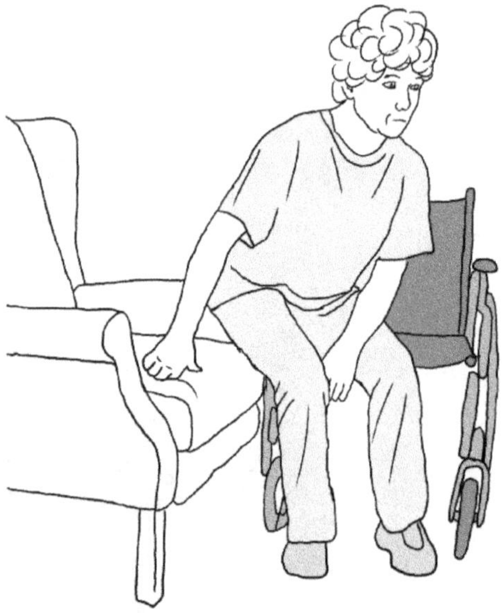

2. Reach over to the chair you are moving. Stand up just enough to clear your hips from the wheelchair.

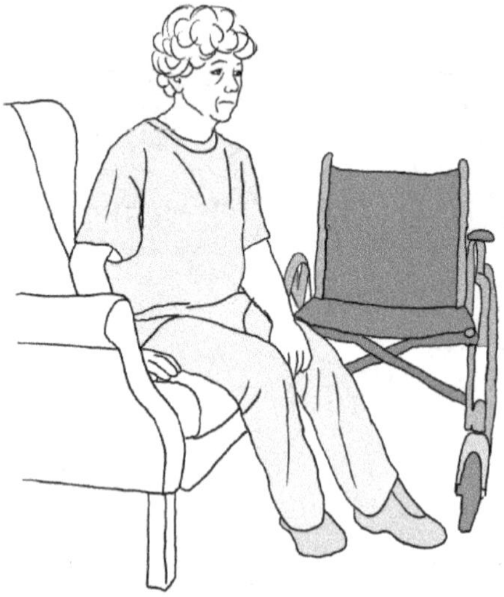

3. Slide over onto the chair.

4. Move your hips back into the chair.

Use this transfer when moving onto the commode, bed or back to the wheelchair.

Occupational Therapy TOOLKIT

Sit-Pivot Transfer with Help - Move to Their Left
To and From a Wheelchair, Chair, Bed or Commode

Go over the steps of the transfer. Ask the person if they are ready to move. Try to transfer to the person's stronger side.

1. Help the person scoot to the edge of the chair. Squat in front and grab the transfer belt. Keep your knees bent and your back straight.

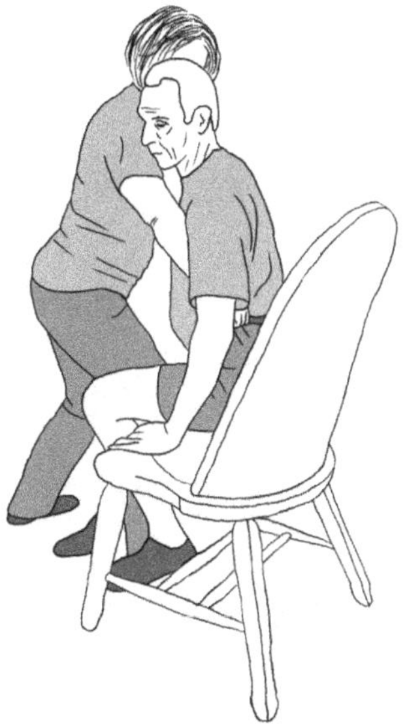

2. Block the weaker knee, in case it buckles. Rock the person forward, until their bottom lifts. The person can push up from the chair.

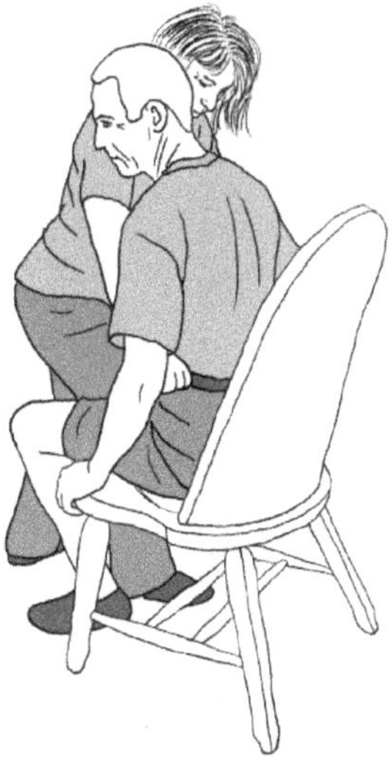

3. Swing the person to the other surface.

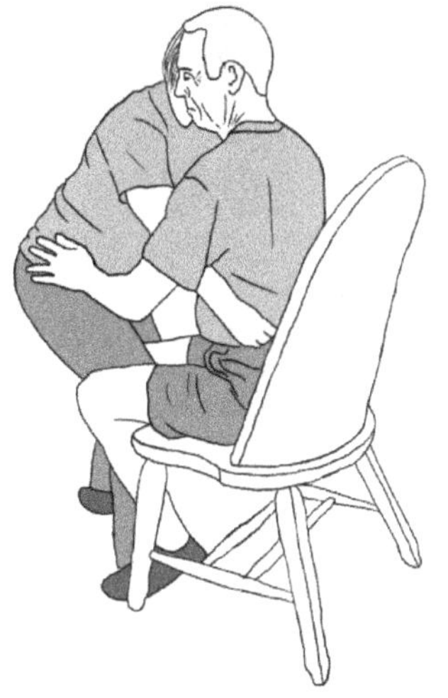

4. Do not twist your spine. You should end by facing the person.

Sit-Pivot Transfer with Help - Move to Their Right
To and From a Wheelchair, Chair, Bed or Commode

Go over the steps of the transfer. Ask the person if they are ready to move. Try to transfer to the person's stronger side.

1. Help the person scoot to the edge of the chair. Squat in front and grab the transfer belt. Keep your knees bent and your back straight.

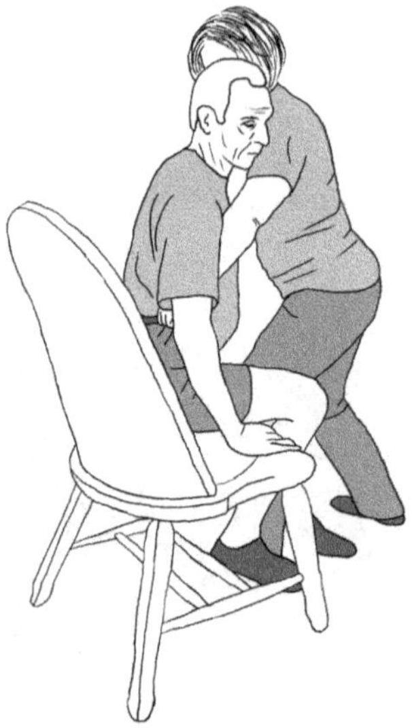

2. Block the weaker knee, in case it buckles. Rock the person forward, until their bottom lifts. The person can push up from the chair.

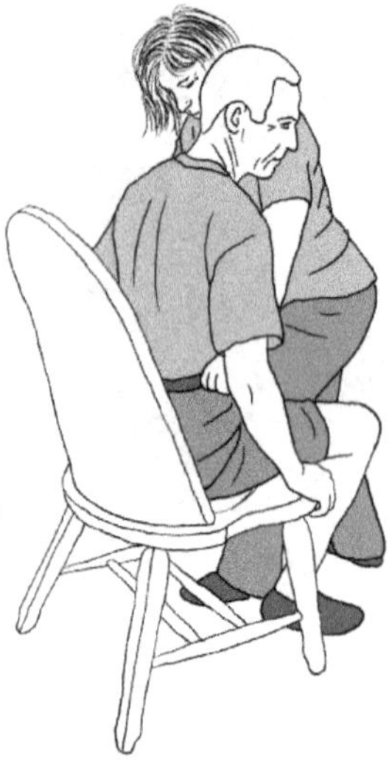

3. Swing the person to the other surface.

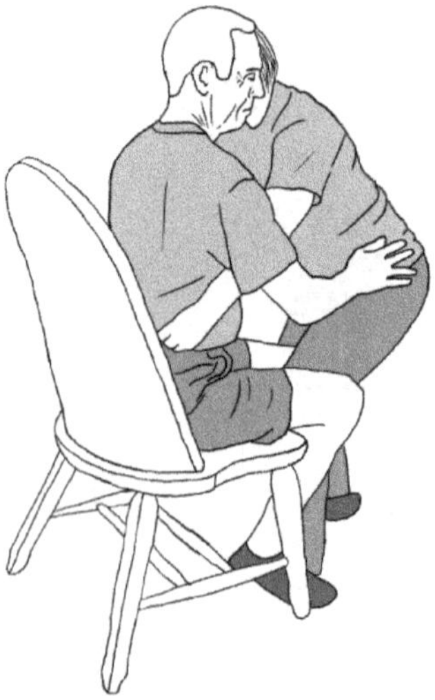

4. Do not twist your spine. You should end by facing the person.

Sitting Down
Wheelchair, Chair, Bed or Commode

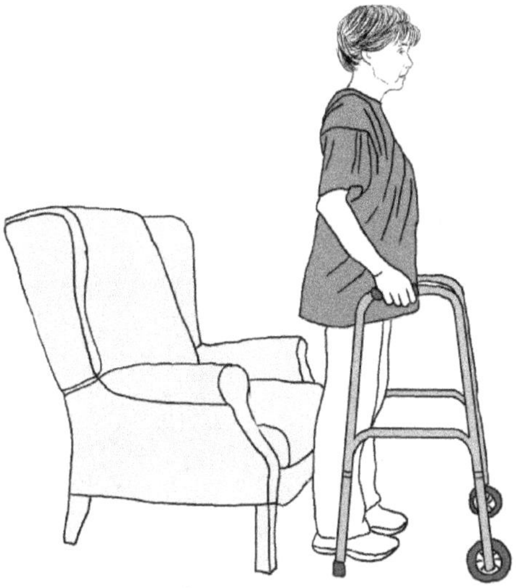

1. Move back until you feel the chair.

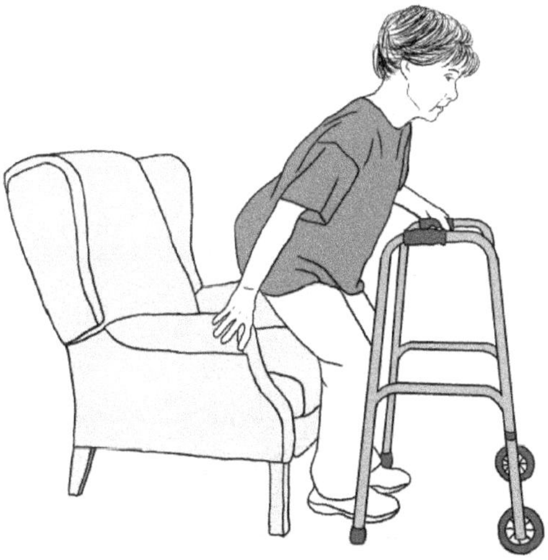

2. Bend forward at your hips. Reach back with one hand for the chair arm or edge of the chair. Reach back with your other hand.

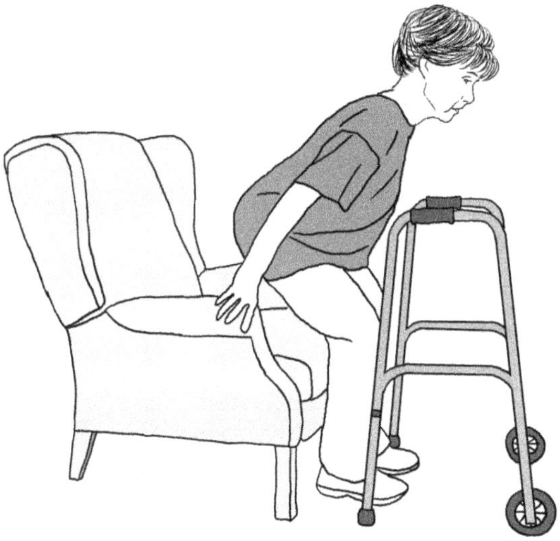

3. Sit down slowly. Try not to drop into the chair.

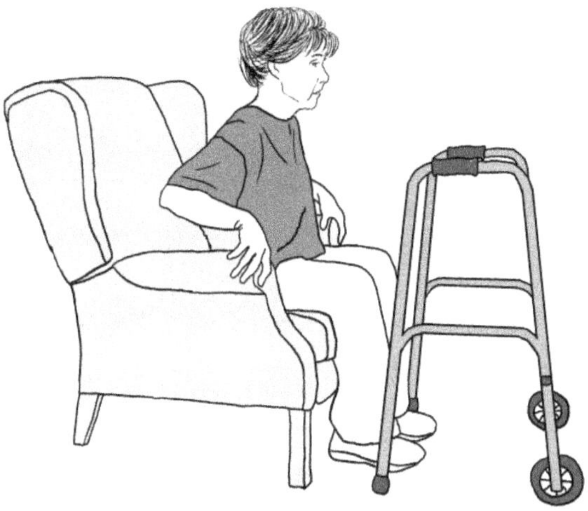

4. Slide back into the chair.

Sitting Down - After Hip Surgery
Wheelchair, Chair or Commode

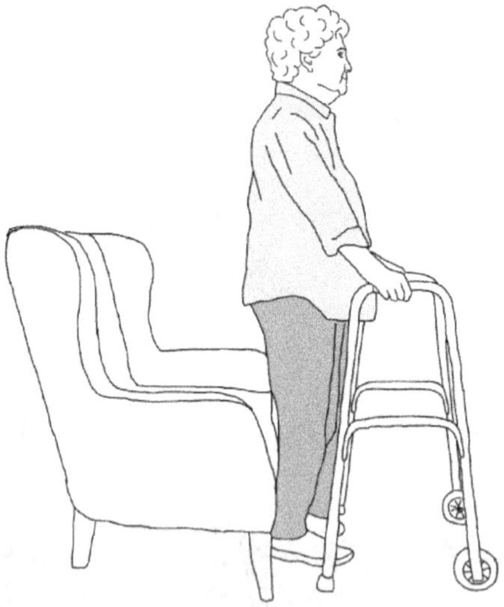

1. Move back until you feel the chair.

2. Slide your affected leg forward. Reach back with one hand for the chair arm or edge of chair. Reach back with your other hand.

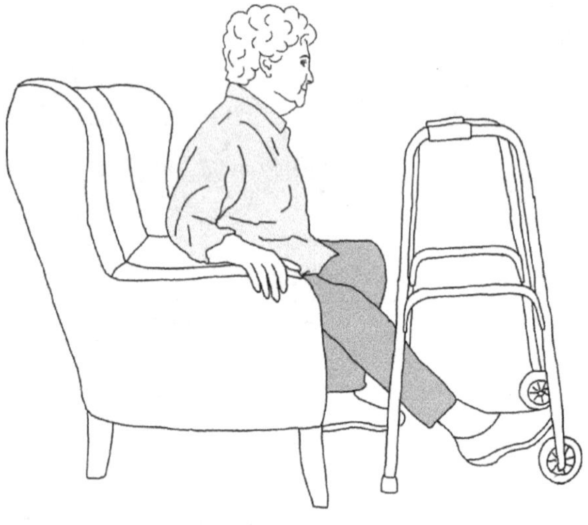

3. Sit down slowly. Keep your affected leg out in front. Try not to drop into the chair.

Occupational Therapy TOOLKIT

Standing Up
Wheelchair, Chair or Commode

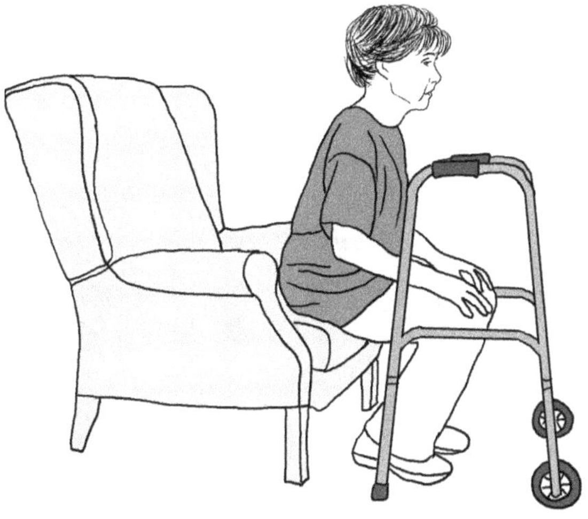

1. Scoot to the edge of the chair.

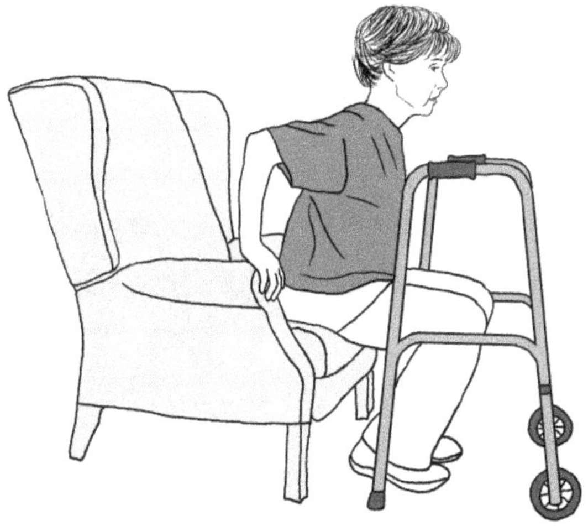

2. Pull your feet back. Lean forward with your "nose over toes".

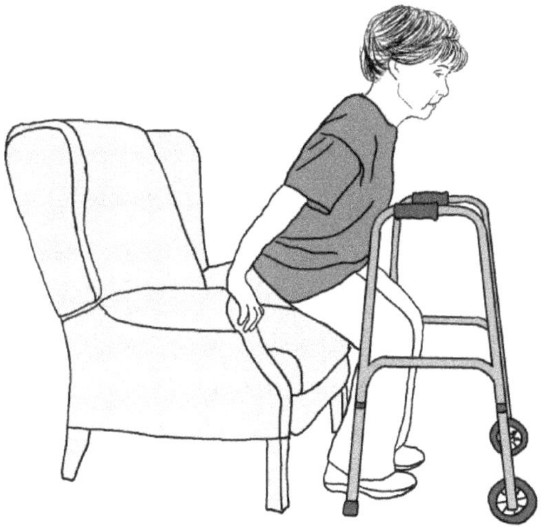

3. Push up from the chair arms. Do not pull up using the walker.

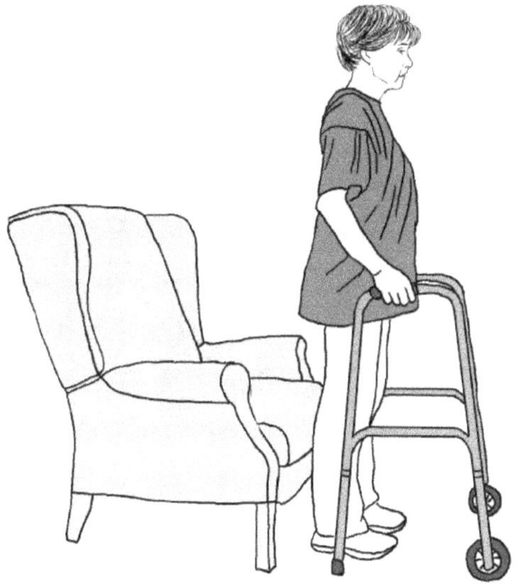

4. Make sure you have your balance before walking.

Standing Up - After Hip Surgery
Wheelchair, Chair or Commode

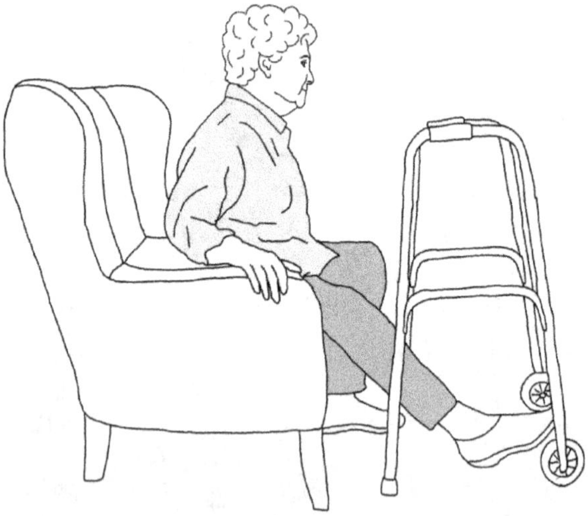

1. Scoot to the edge of the chair. Move your affected leg out in front. Pull your other foot back.

2. Keep your affected leg out in front. Push up from the chair arms. Do not pull up using the walker

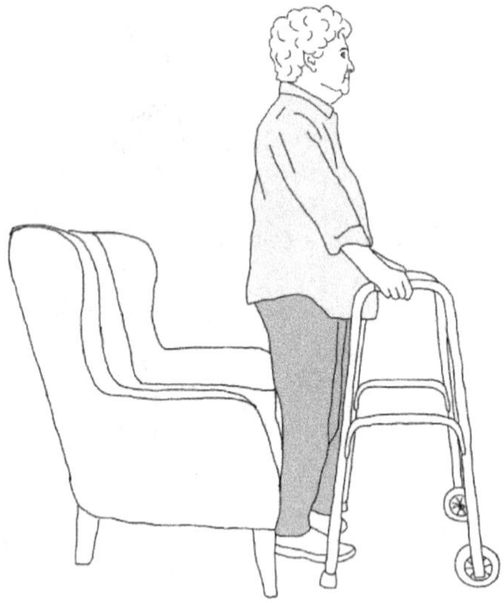

3. Make sure you have your balance before walking.

Standing Up with Help
Wheelchair, Chair, Bed or Commode

Go over the steps and ask the person if they are ready to stand.

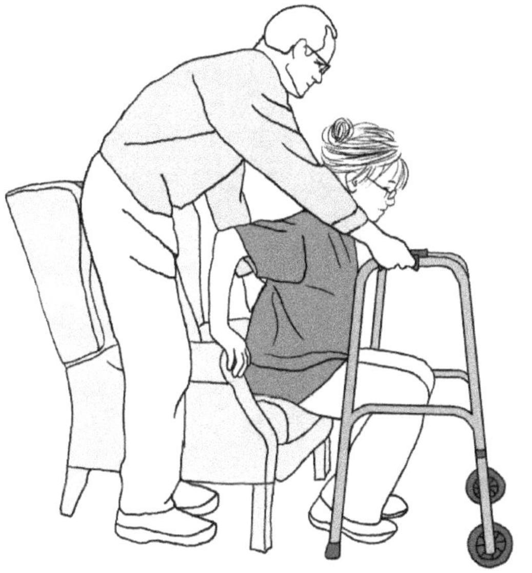

1. Stand on the person's weaker side. Hold onto the walker and the transfer belt. Help the person scoot to the edge of the chair.

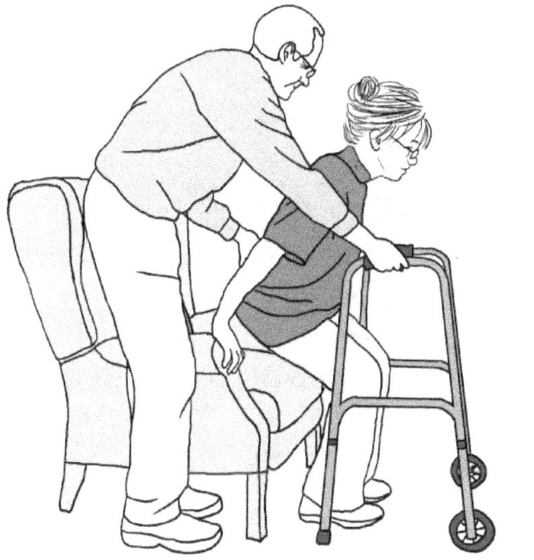

2. Help the person lean forward, "nose over toes." Help them push up from the chair arms.

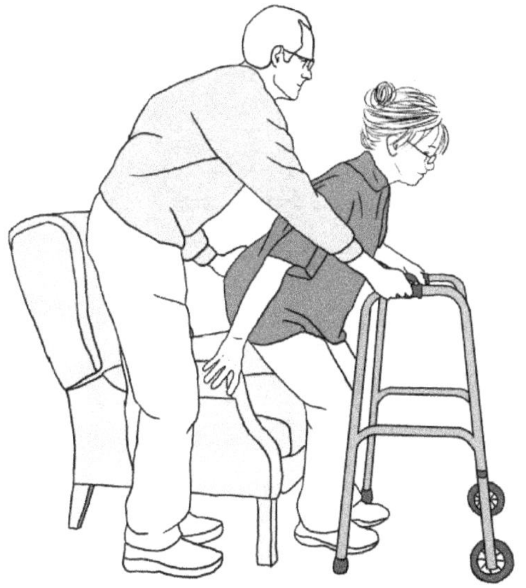

3. Help the person stand.

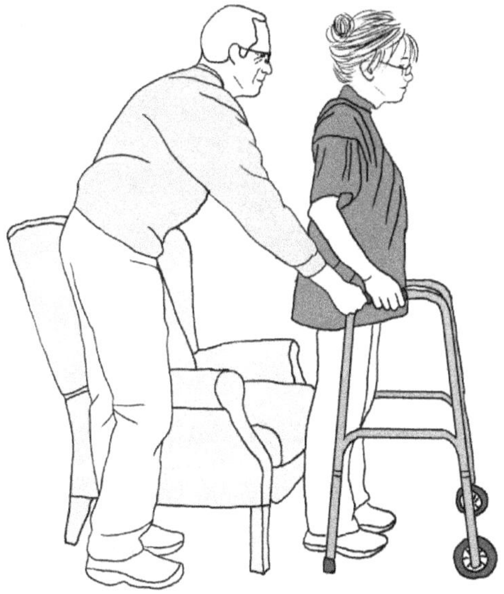

4. Make sure the person has their balance before walking.

Occupational Therapy TOOLKIT

Stand-Pivot Transfer with Help - Move to Their Left To and From a Wheelchair, Chair, Bed or Commode

Go over the steps of the transfer. Ask the person if they are ready to move. Try to transfer to the person's stronger side.

1. Help the person scoot to the edge of the chair. Squat in front and grab the transfer belt. Keep your knees bent and your back straight.

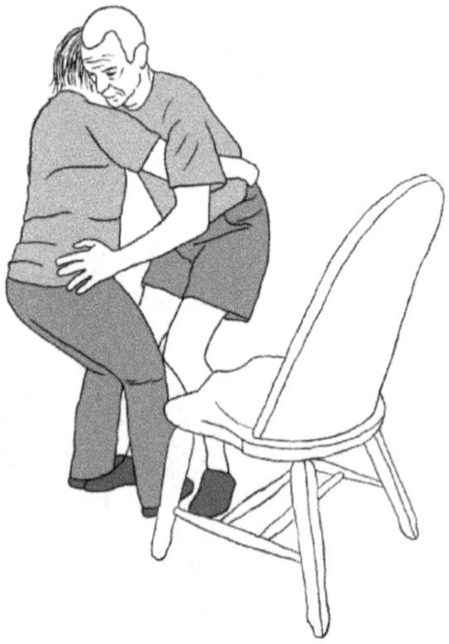

2. Block the weaker knee, in case it buckles. You will both stand at the same time. The person can push up from the chair.

3. Pull your hips toward their hips as you both stand up.

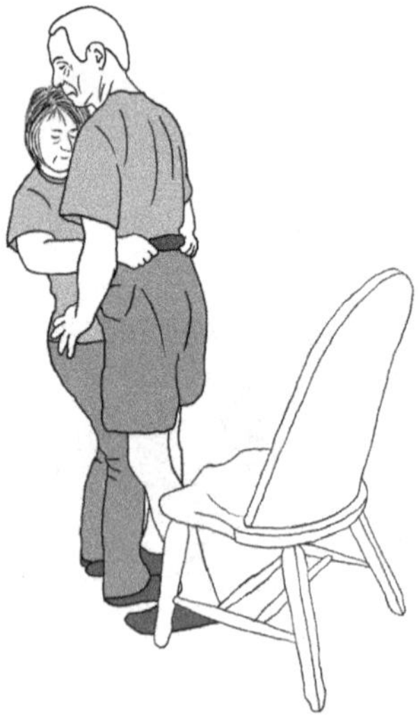

4. Take small steps, and move to the other surface.

1 of 2

Stand-Pivot Transfer with Help - Move to Their Left To and From a Wheelchair, Chair, Bed or Commode

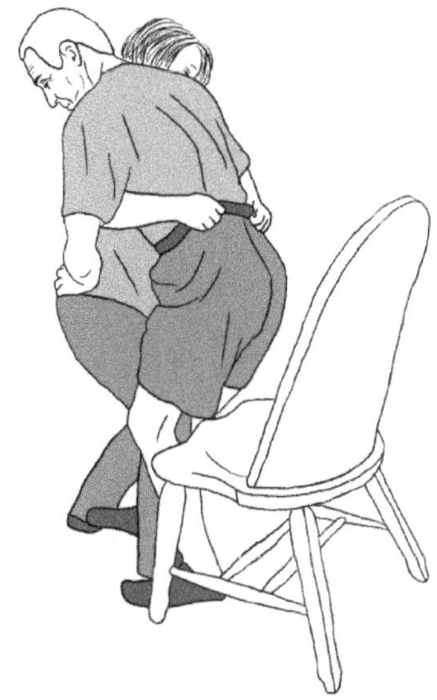

5. Block the weaker knee again and lower the person into the chair. Squat down with your knees bent and back straight.

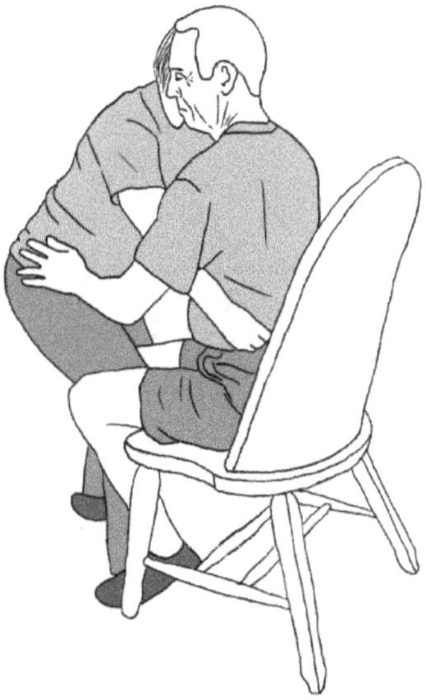

6. Help the person get their hips back into the chair.

Stand-Pivot Transfer with Help - Move to Their Right
To and From a Wheelchair, Chair, Bed or Commode

Go over the steps of the transfer. Ask the person if they are ready to move. Try to transfer to the person's stronger side.

1. Help the person scoot to the edge of the chair. Squat in front and grab the transfer belt. Keep your knees bent and your back straight.

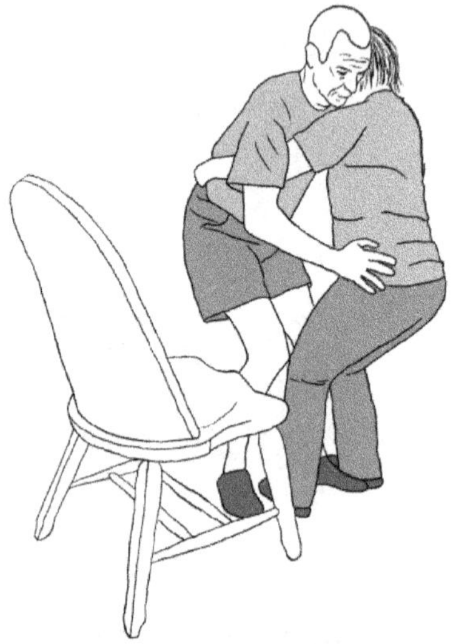

2. Block the weaker knee, in case it buckles. You will both stand at the same time. The person can push up from the chair.

3. Pull your hips toward their hips as you both stand up.

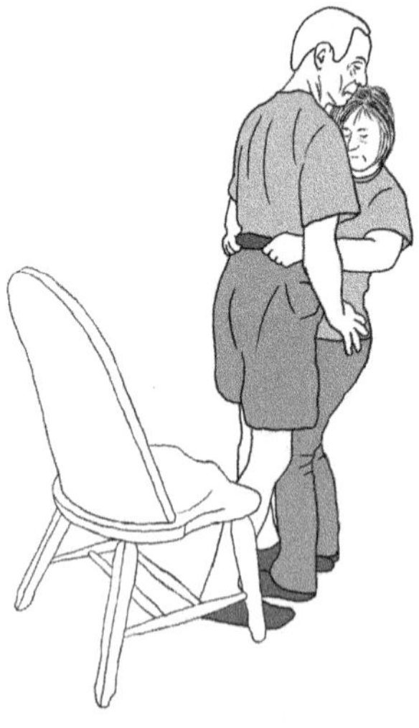

4. Take small steps, and move to the other surface.

Stand-Pivot Transfer with Help - Move to Their Right
To and From a Wheelchair, Chair, Bed or Commode

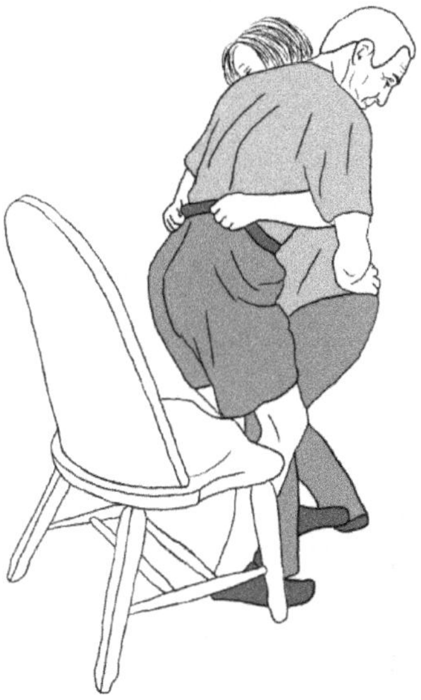

5. Block the weaker knee again and lower the person into the chair. Squat down with your knees bent and back straight.

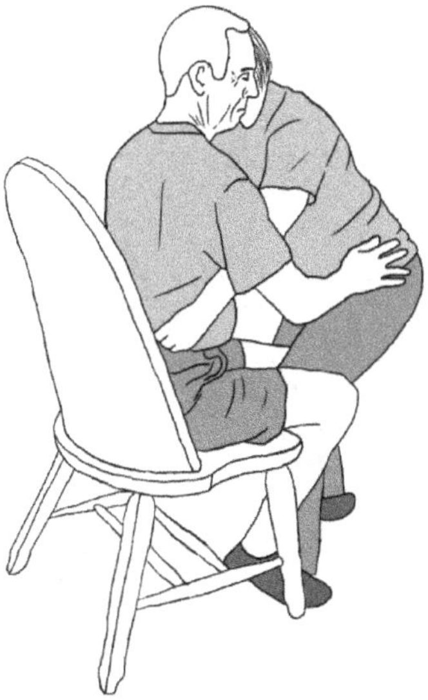

6. Help the person get their hips back into the chair.

Take Off a T-shirt with One Hand
Left Side Weakness

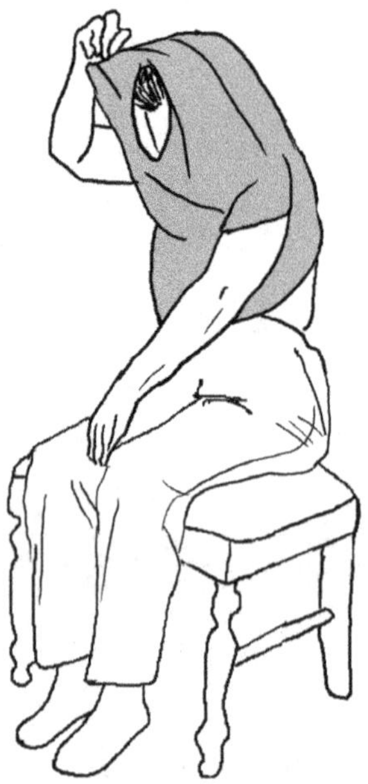

1. Grasp the collar of the shirt.

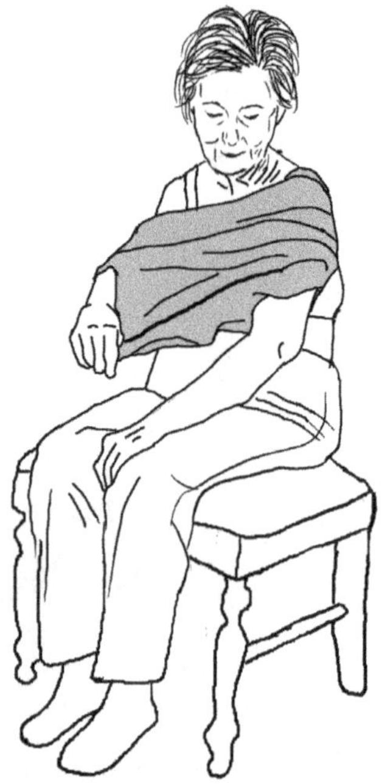

2. Pull the shirt over your head.

3. Use your right hand to push the shirt off your left arm.

4. Rub your right hand against your leg to remove the shirt from your right arm.

Take Off a T-shirt with One Hand
Right Side Weakness

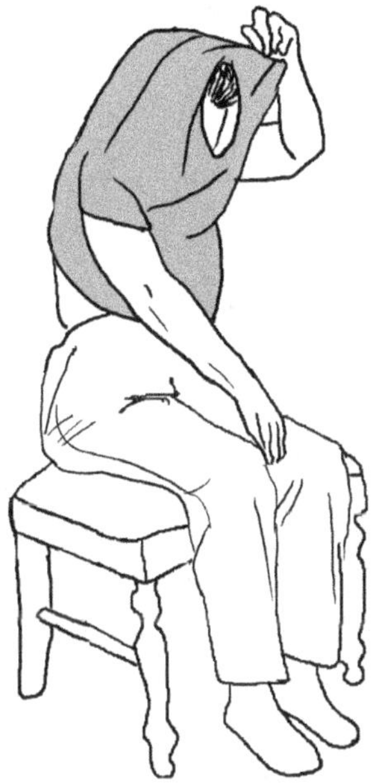

1. Grasp the collar of the shirt.

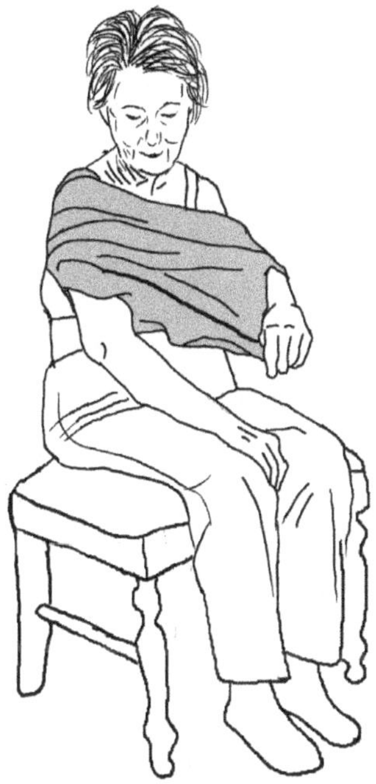

2. Pull the shirt over your head.

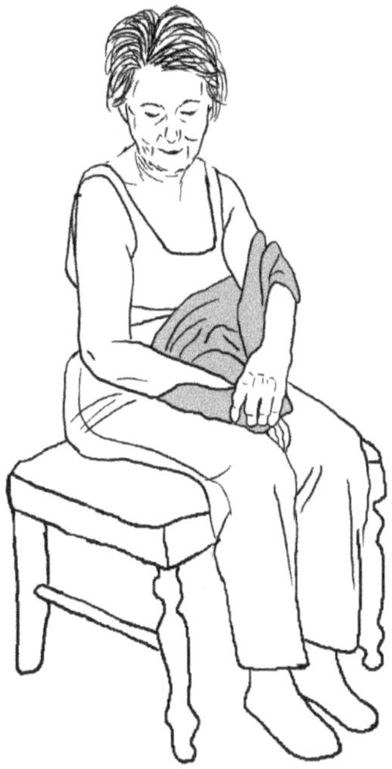

3. Use your left hand to push the shirt off your right arm.

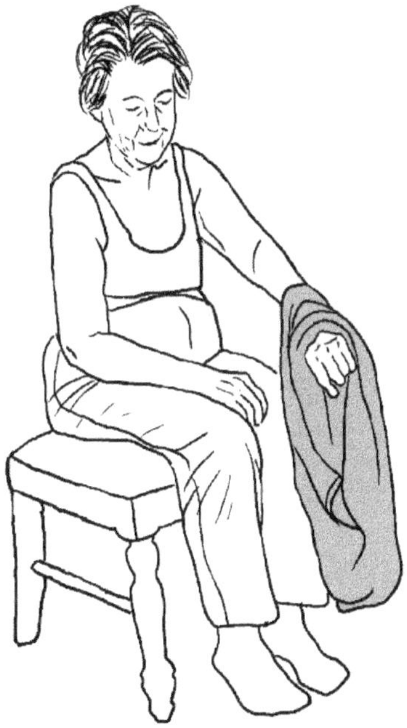

4. Rub your left hand against your leg to remove the shirt from your left arm.

Occupational Therapy TOOLKIT

Take Off an Open Front Shirt with One Hand
Left Side Weakness

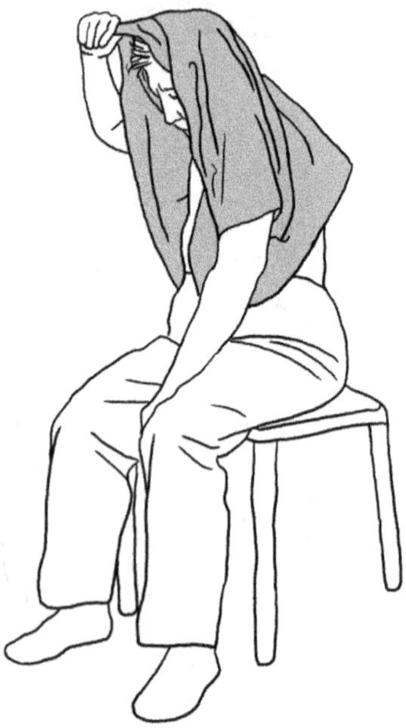

1. Open the shirt. Grasp the back of the collar.

2. Pull the shirt off over your head.

3. Take your left arm out of the sleeve.

4. Remove your right arm from the shirt by rubbing it against your leg.

Take Off an Open Front Shirt with One Hand
Right Side Weakness

1. Open the shirt. Grasp the back of the collar.

2. Pull the shirt off over your head.

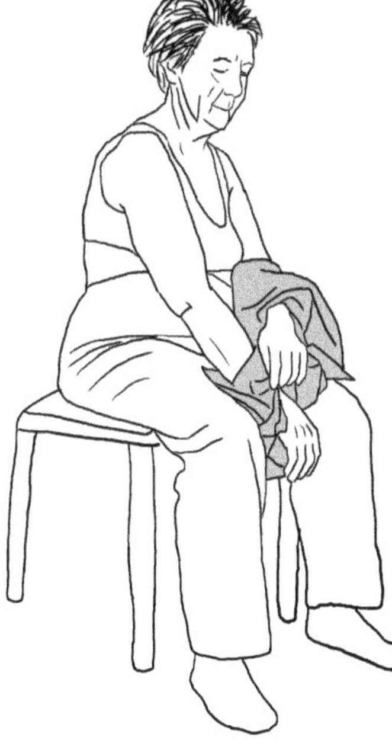

3. Remove your right arm from the sleeve.

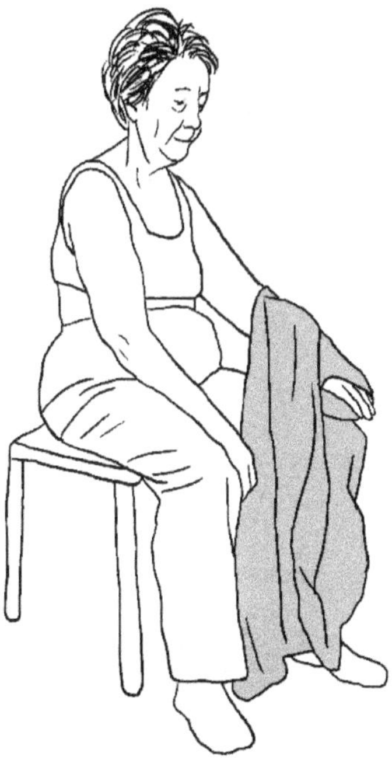

4. Remove your left arm from the shirt by rubbing it against your leg.

Occupational Therapy TOOLKIT

Take Off Pants with One Hand
Left Side Weakness

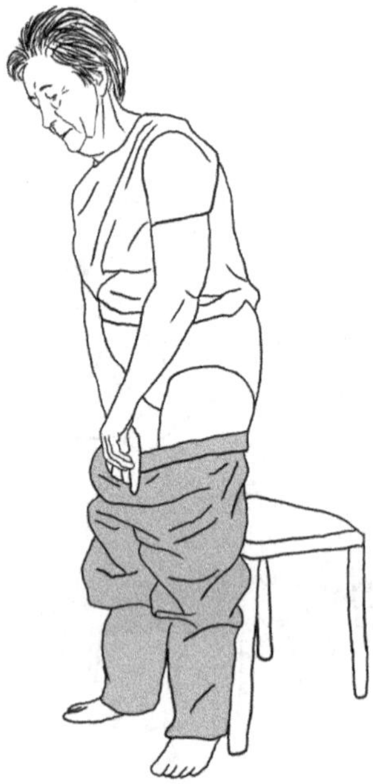

1. Open the pants while still seated. Stand and push the pants down past both hips.

2. Sit down.

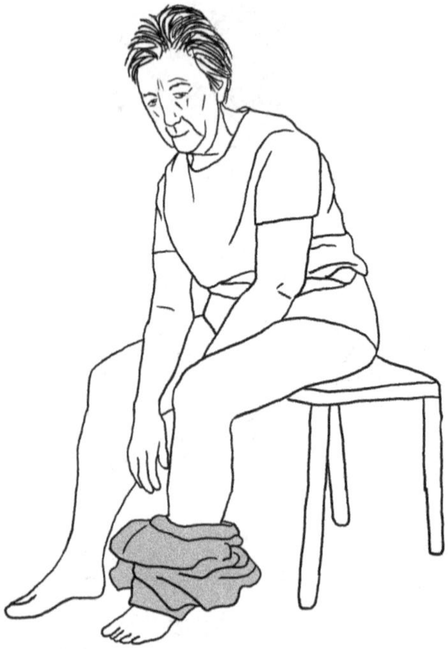

3. Remove the pants from your right leg.

4. Cross your left leg over your right and remove the pants from your left leg.

Take Off Pants with One Hand
Right Side Weakness

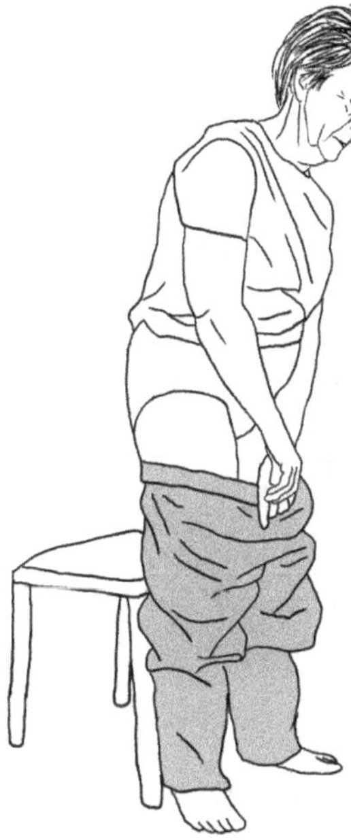

1. Open the pants while still seated. Stand and push the pants down past both hips.

2. Sit down

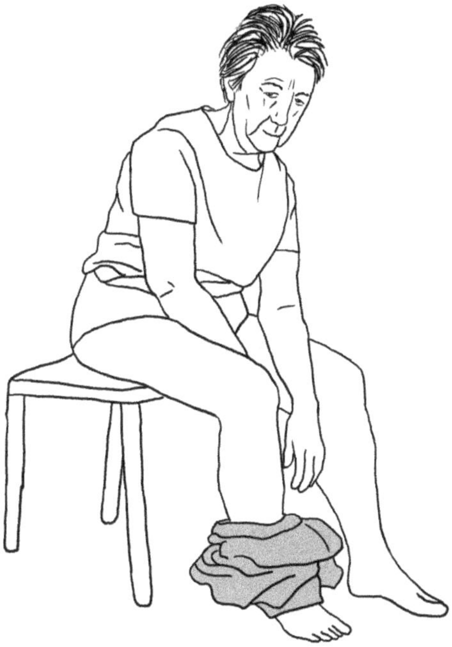

3. Remove the pants from your left leg.

4. Cross your right leg over your left and remove the pants from your right leg.

Tie Shoes with One Hand - Left Side Weakness
Prepare the Shoes

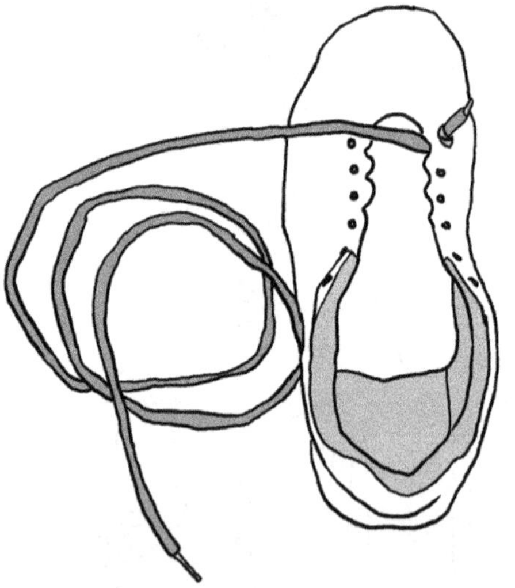

1. Place a knot at the end of the lace. Thread the lace through the last hole on the right side. Both shoes are the same.

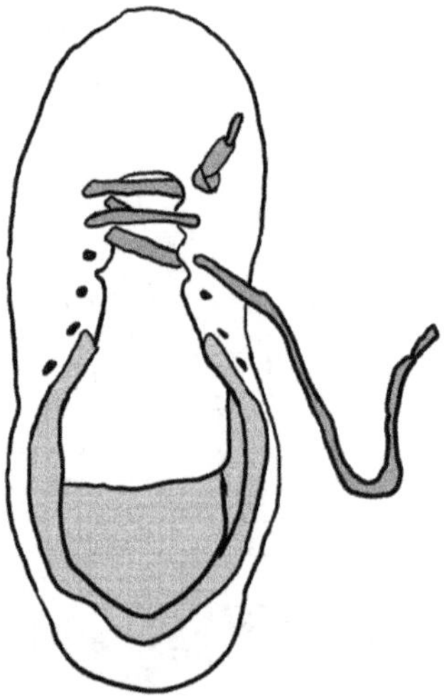

2. Lace the shoes. Thread the left side from the top.

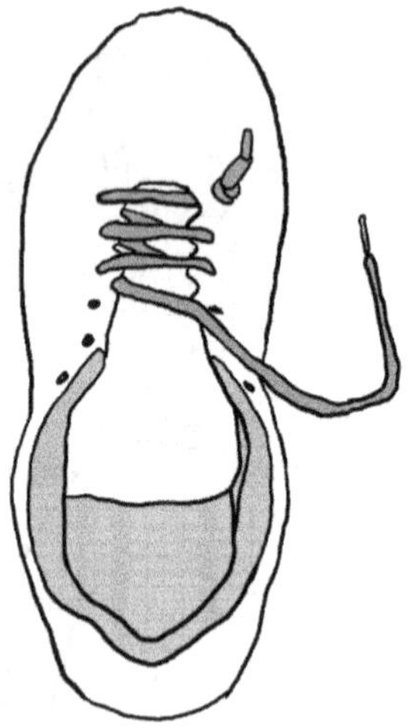

3. Thread the right side from the bottom.

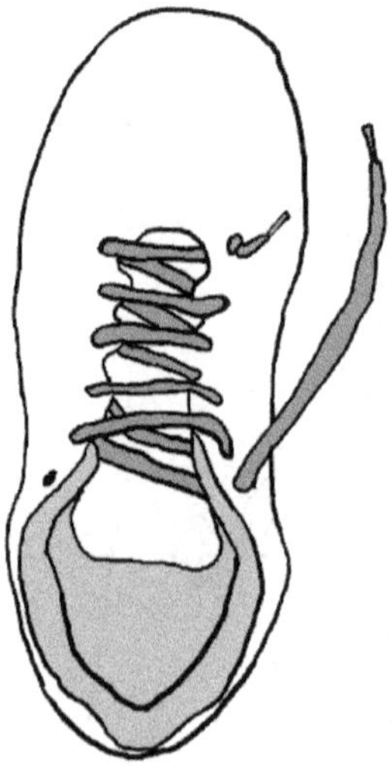

4. End on the last hole on the right side.

You will only need to prepare your shoes once.

Tie Shoes with One Hand
Left Side Weakness

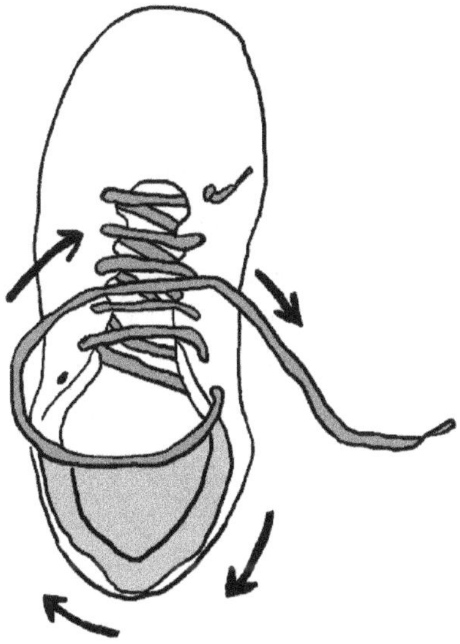

1. Hold onto the lace. Loop it around to the left. Both shoes are tied the same.

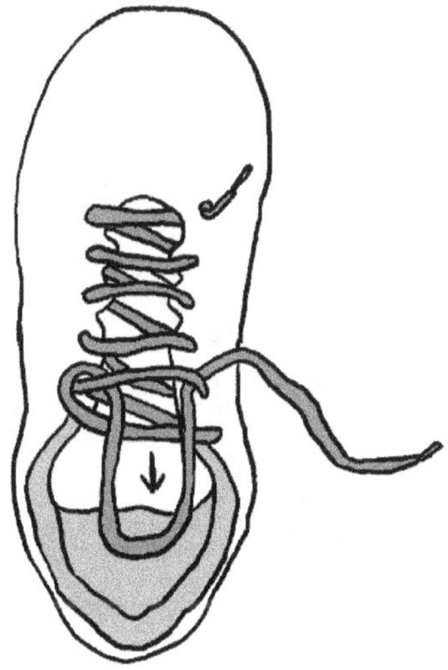

2. Push the loop up through the last lace that crosses over.

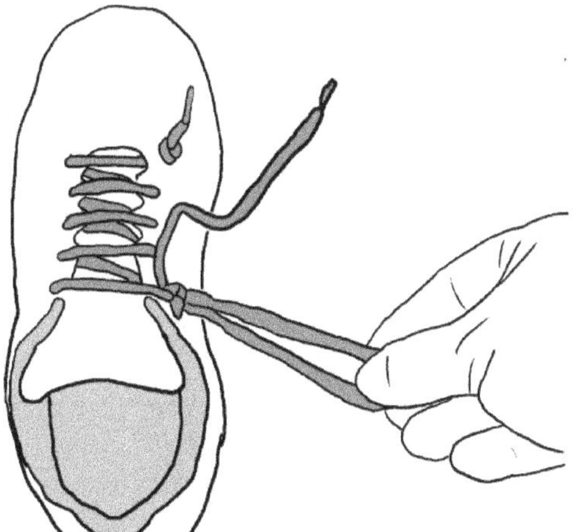

3. Pull the end of the loop to the right to tighten.

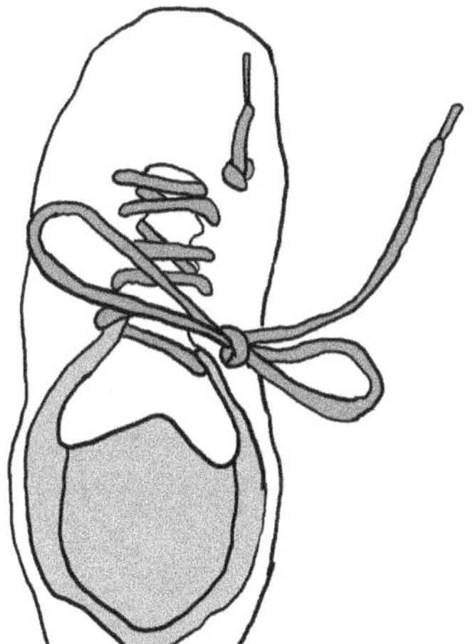

4. Put the end of the lace into the knot to make a second loop.

Tie Shoes with One Hand - Right Side Weakness
Prepare the Shoes

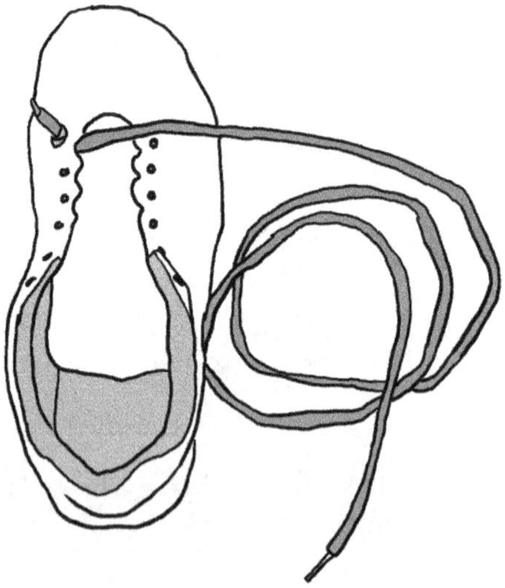

1. Place a knot at the end of the lace. Thread the lace through the last hole on the left side. Both shoes are the same.

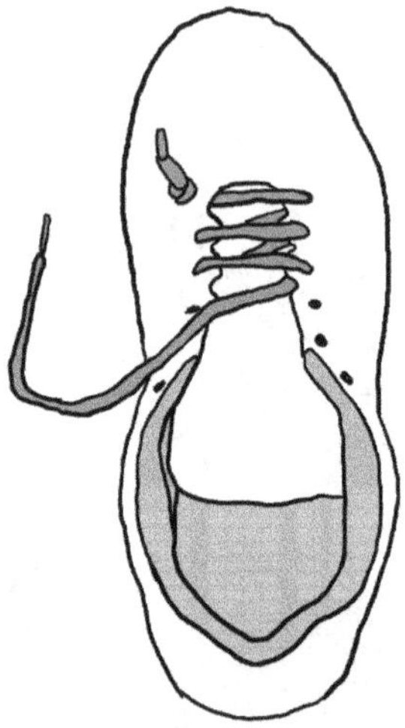

2. Lace the shoes. Thread the right side from the top.

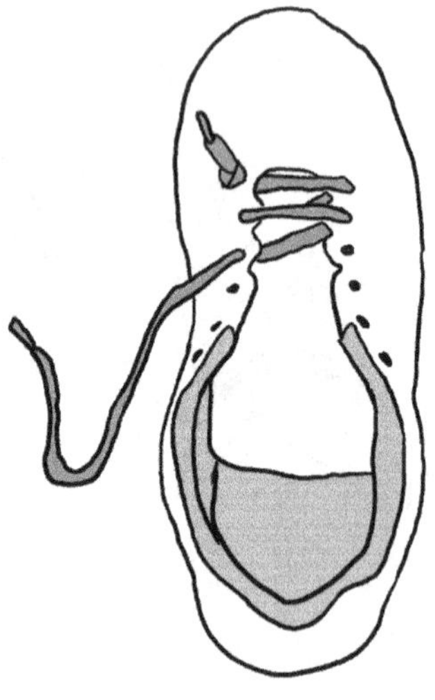

3. Thread the left side from the bottom.

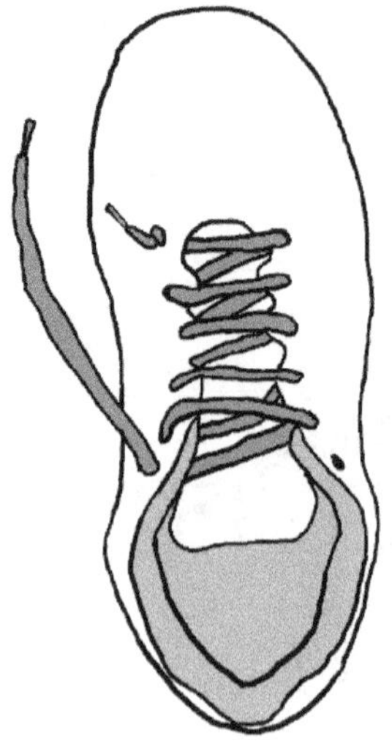

4. End on the last hole on the left side.

You will only need to prepare your shoes once.

Tie Shoes with One Hand
Right Side Weakness

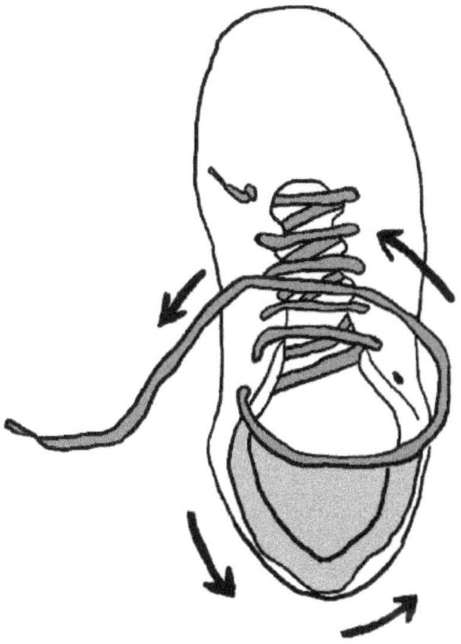

1. Hold onto the lace. Loop it around to the right. Both shoes are tied the same.

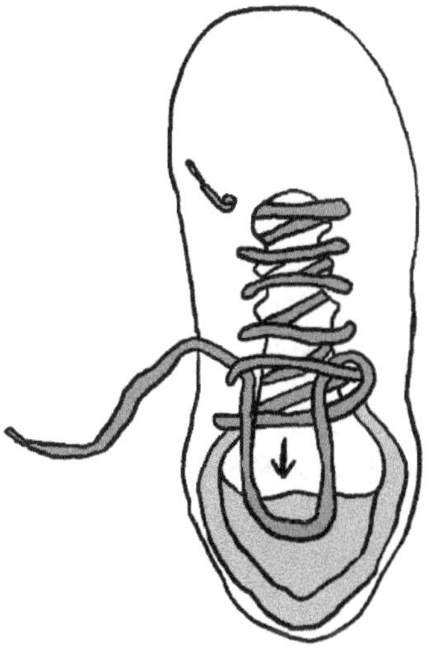

2. Push the loop up through the last lace that crosses over.

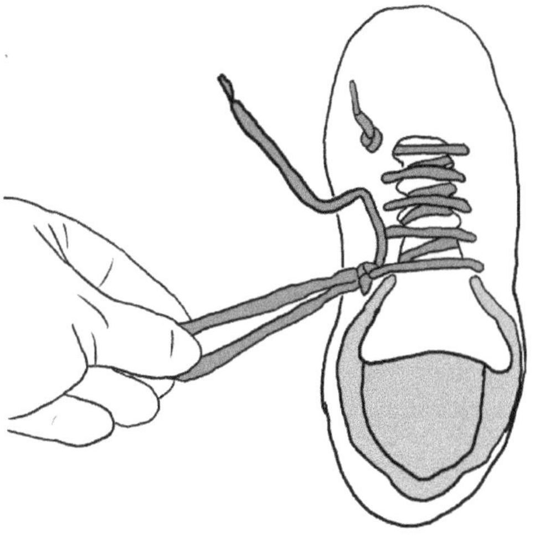

3. Pull the end of the loop to the left to tighten.

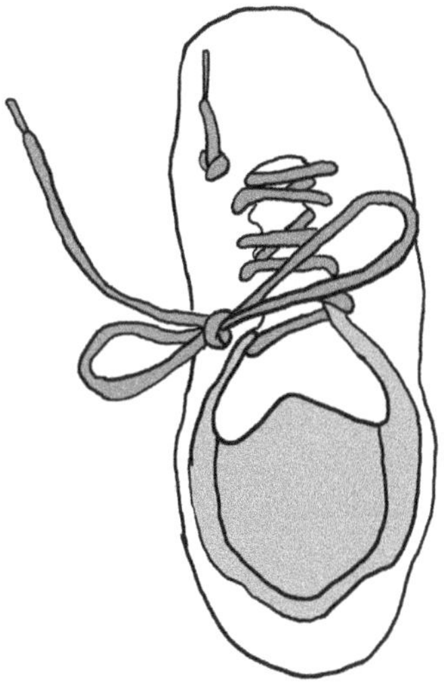

4. Put the end of the lace into the knot to make a second loop.

Tips for Making and Keeping Health Care Visits

- Place health care records in binder or a file on the computer.
- Write a list of all members of your health care team.
- Use only one calendar for all visits.
- Keep the calendar in a common place. Like the refrigerator or kitchen table.
- Write in pencil, so you can make changes.
- Avoid making visits for early in the morning or early in the month.
- Ask the doctor's office if they will remind you about your visits.
- Set alarms or alerts on a cell phone.

Tips for Using the Bathroom

Safety Tips

- A raised toilet seat will raise the height of the seat. A toilet frame will help you push up from the seat. A bedside commode over the toilet will do both.

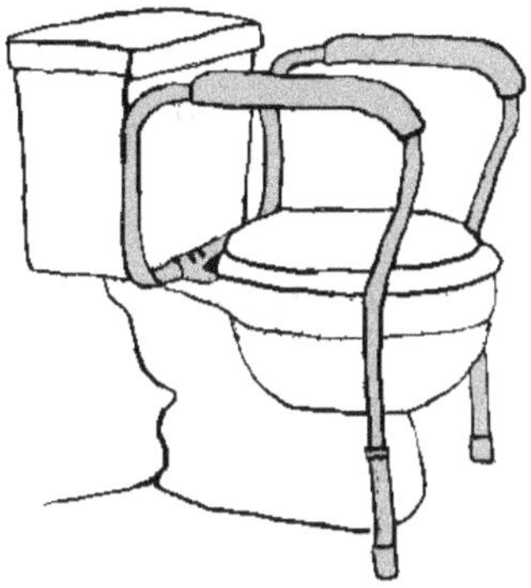

- The height of the toilet should allow you to touch your feet to the ground.
- If you cannot make it to the bathroom, use a bedside commode.
- Mark the legs of a toilet frame or bedside commode with colored tape. This will make it easy to see the legs.

Manage clothes

- Pull the pants up over your knees before standing. This will prevent them from falling to your ankles.

Tips for Using the Bathroom

Manage clothes

- Keep an extra set of dressing tools in the bathroom.
- Choose stretch waist pants that are easy to pull up and down.
- Remove long robes before going to the bathroom.

Clean up

- If you cannot reach the toilet paper, move the toilet paper.
- Use moist wipes to stay fresh between bathing.

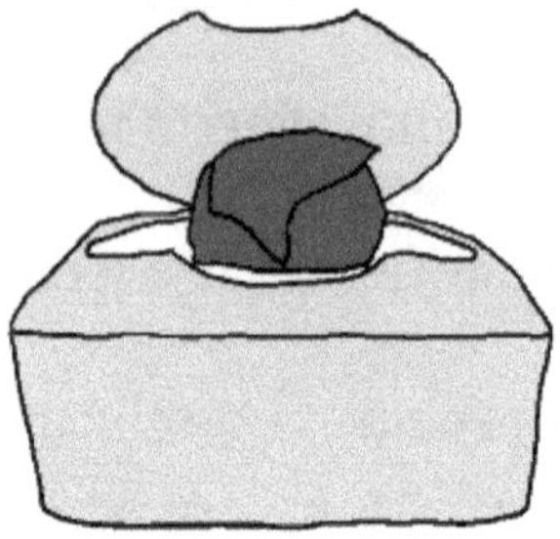

- A pair of tongs or a wiping aid can help you reach behind to wipe.

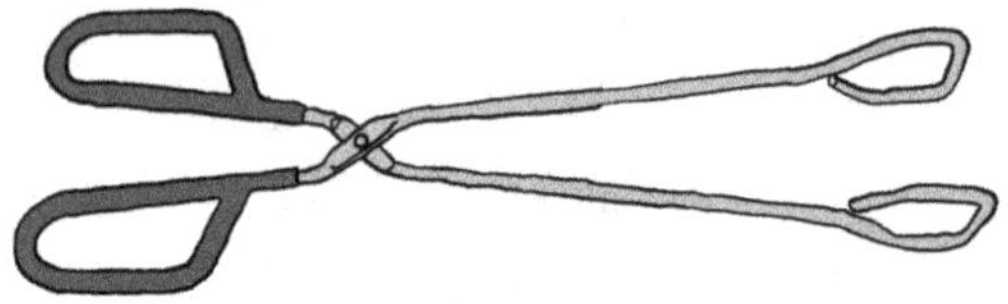

- Use a no rinse hand cleaner in the bathroom or next to the bedside commode.

2 of 2

Toileting Options
Therapist Resource

Toileting while in bed or at bedside.

- Use bedside commode (independent or with assistance).
- Use female/male urinal and/or bedpan (independent or with assistance).
- Use absorbent briefs or pads (independent or with assistance).
- Use internal or external catheter/colostomy.

Toileting while in the bathroom.

- Getting to the bathroom
    - Ambulate to bathroom (independent or with assistance).
    - Ambulate to bathroom using assistive device (independent or with assistance).
    - Use wheelchair or rolling commode to the bathroom (independent or with assistance).
    - Use overhead suspension system.
- Adaptive Equipment
    - Toilet only - standard height (14-15 inches)
    - Toilet only - chair height (16 - 17 inches)
    - Toilet (standard or chair height) with device
        - Grab bars only
        - Toilet safety frame only
        - BSC over existing toilet
        - Raised toilet seat only
        - Raised toilet seat plus grab bars
        - Raised toilet seat plus toilet safety frame
        - Raised toilet seat with push up handles
        - Rolling commode
- Modify use of the toilet.
    - Sitting to urinate (male)
    - Standing to urinate using a walker over toilet (male)
    - Sitting backwards (straddle)
    - Standing using urination device or urinal (male and female)

Transfer Board - Move to the Left
To and From a Wheelchair, Chair, Bed or Commode

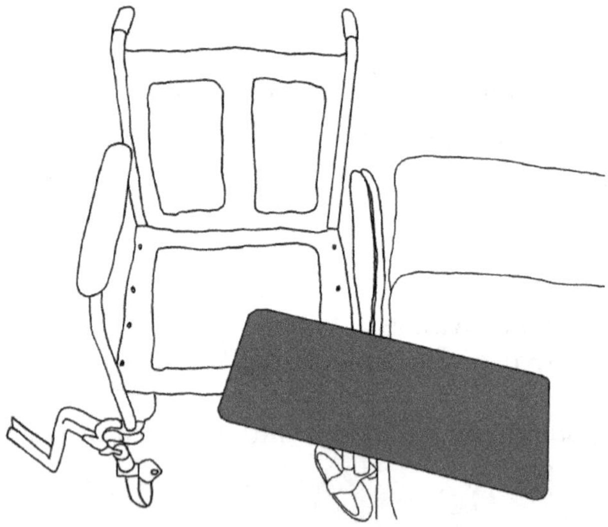

1. Try to transfer to your stronger side. Move the wheelchair next to the sofa or bed. Lock the brakes and remove the armrest and leg rest. Be sure the sofa or bed will not move during the transfer.

2. Lean to the right. Place the transfer board under your left hip.

3. Place your left hand flat on the transfer board and your other hand on the armrest. Lift your weight and move across the transfer board. A caregiver can help by guiding your legs.

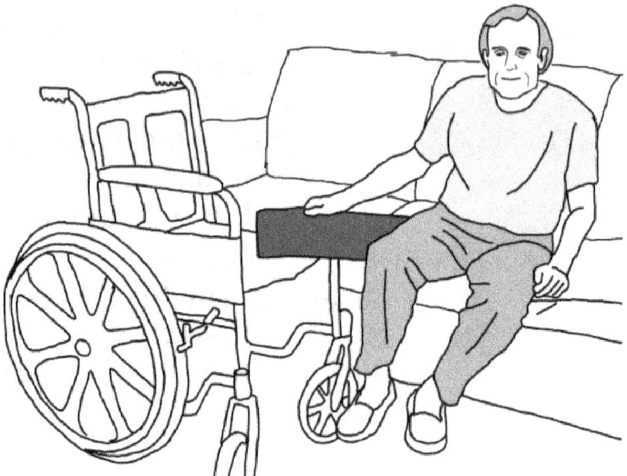

4. Move back in seat. Remove the transfer board.

Occupational Therapy TOOLKIT

Transfer Board - Move to the Right
To and From a Wheelchair, Chair, Bed or Commode

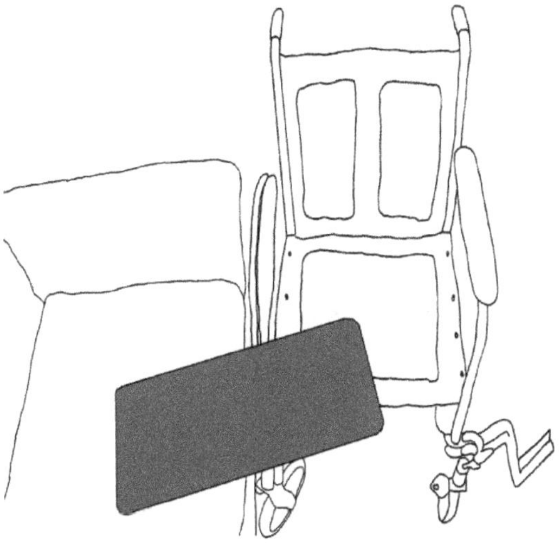

1. Try to transfer to your stronger side. Move the wheelchair next to the sofa or bed. Lock the brakes and remove the armrest and leg rest. Be sure the sofa or bed will not move during the transfer.

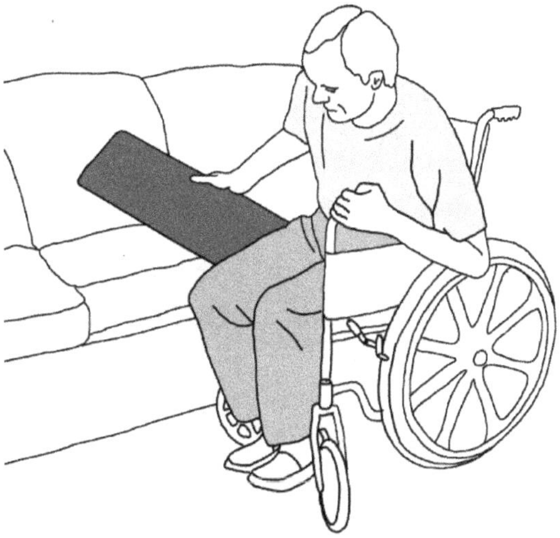

2. Lean to the left. Place the transfer board under your right hip.

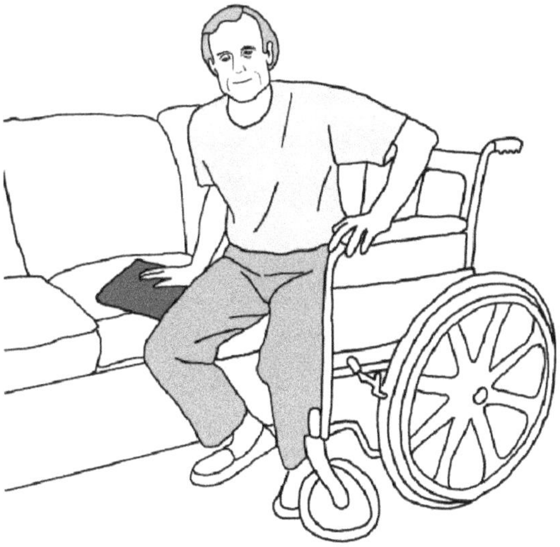

3. Place your right hand flat on the transfer board and your other hand on the armrest. Lift your weight and move across the transfer board. A caregiver can help by guiding your legs.

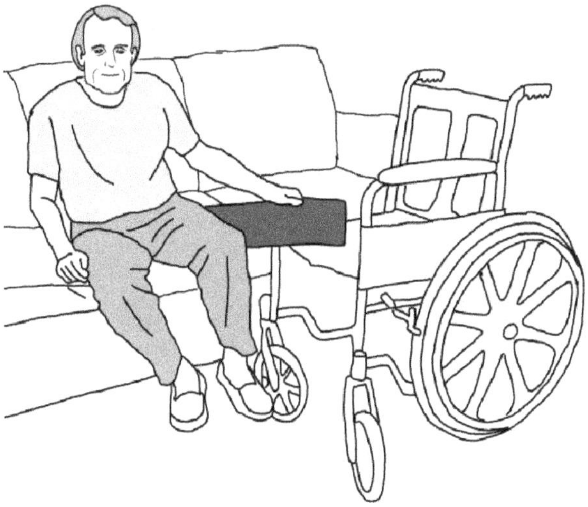

4. Move back in the seat. Remove the transfer board.

Occupational Therapy TOOLKIT

Transfer to Shower Chair (back up, turn left)

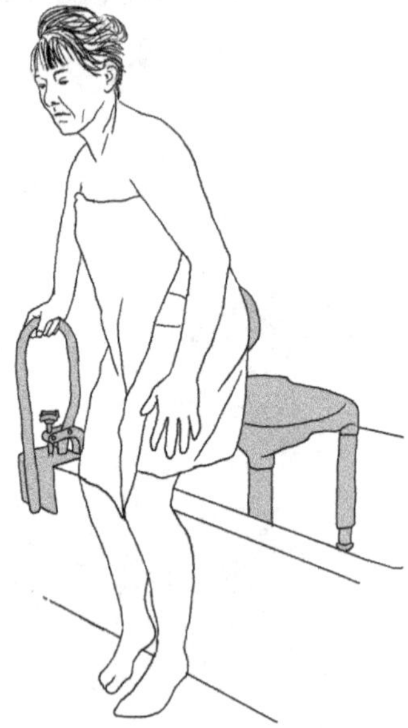

1. Move back until you feel the tub on the back of your legs.

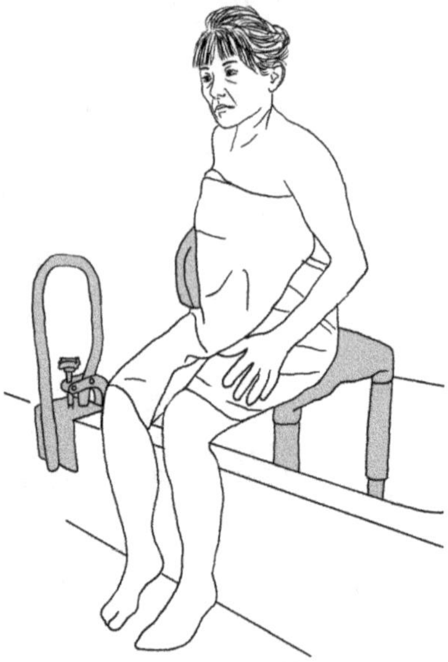

2. Reach back for the shower chair or a clamp-on tub rail. Sit down onto the seat and scoot back as far as you can.

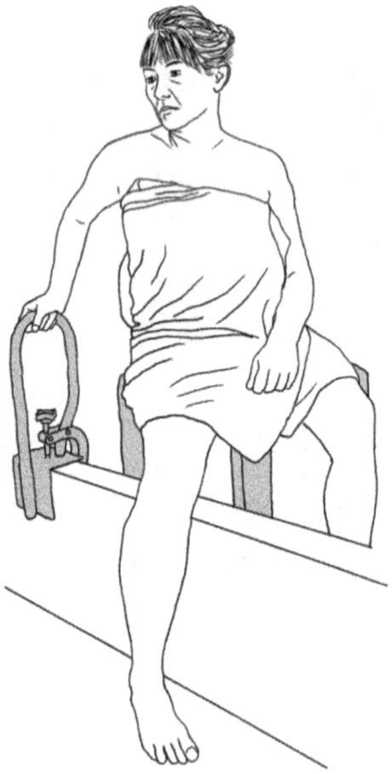

3. Turn your body to the left. Lift your left leg into the tub.

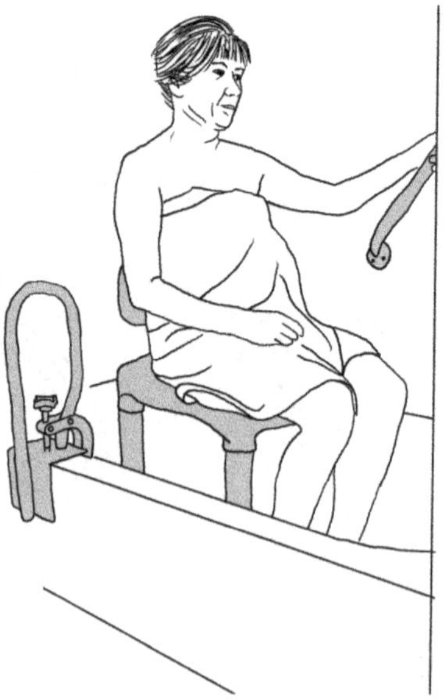

4. Scoot onto the seat. Lift your right leg into the tub. To get out, reverse the steps.

Transfer to Shower Chair (back up, turn right)

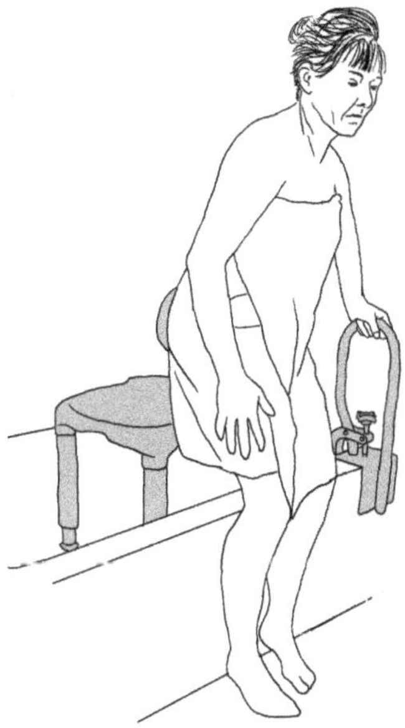

1. Move back until you feel the tub on the back of your legs.

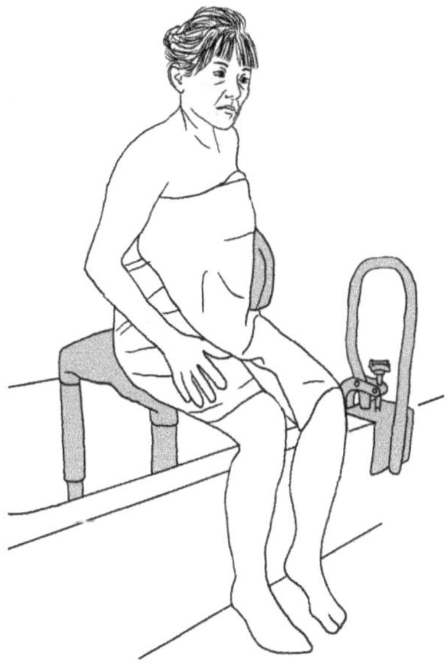

2. Reach back for the shower chair or a clamp-on tub rail. Sit down onto the seat and scoot back as far as you can.

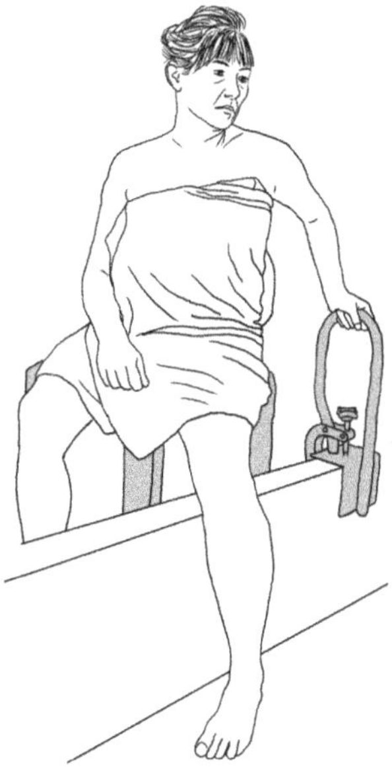

3. Turn your body to the right. Lift your right leg into the tub.

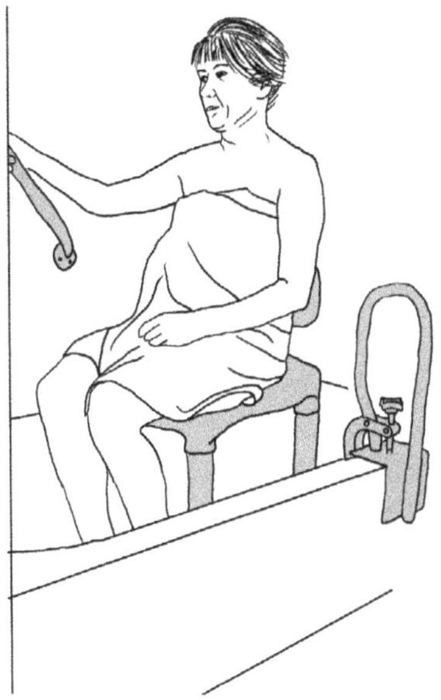

4. Scoot onto the seat. Lift your left leg into the tub. To get out, reverse the steps.

Transfer to Shower Chair (left leg, right leg, sit)

1. Face the wall and hold onto the grab bar.

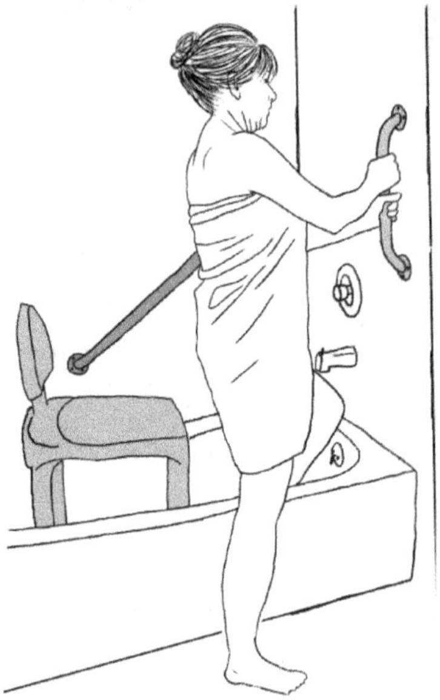

2. Step into the tub with your left leg.

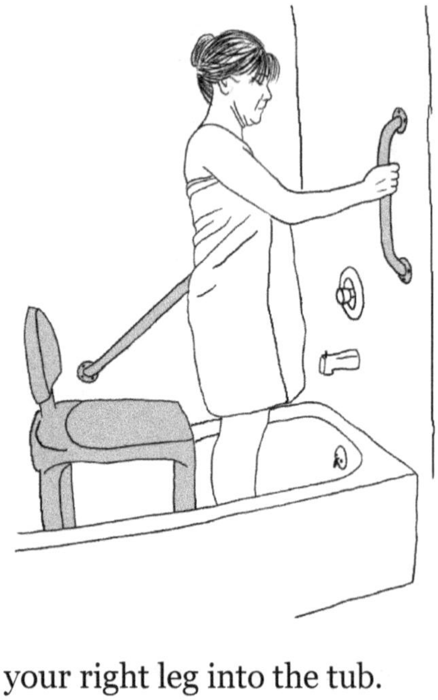

3. Lift your right leg into the tub.

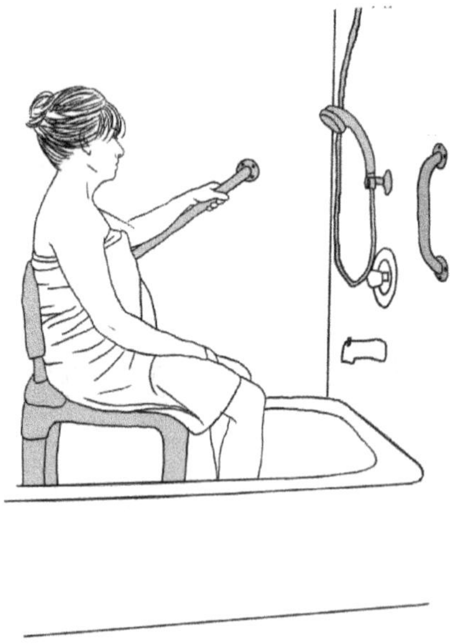

4. Sit down on the shower chair. Reverse the steps to get out.

Transfer to Shower Chair (right leg, left leg, sit)

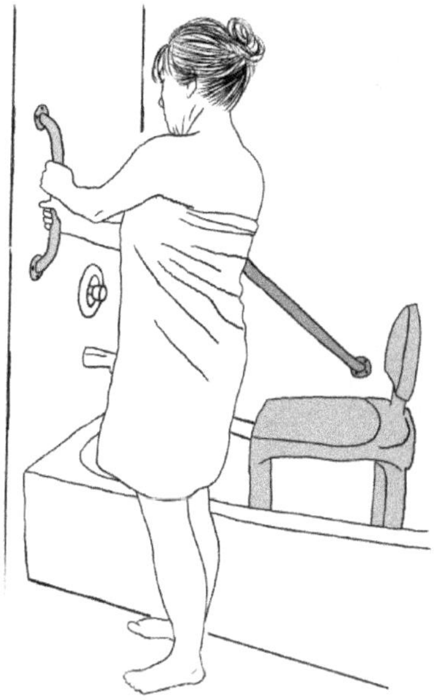

1. Face the wall and hold onto the grab bar.

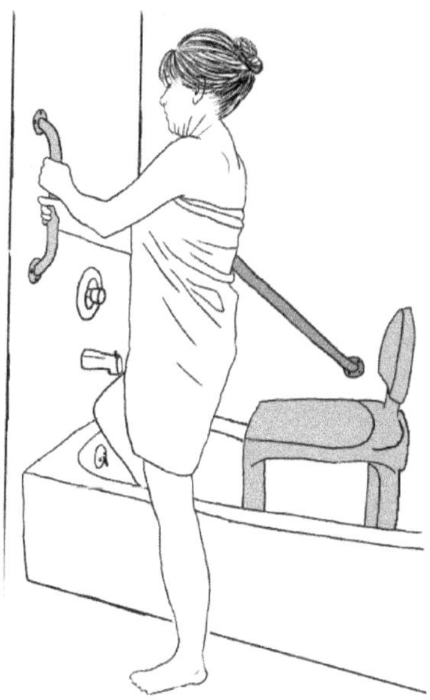

2. Step into the tub with your right leg.

3. Lift your left leg into the tub.

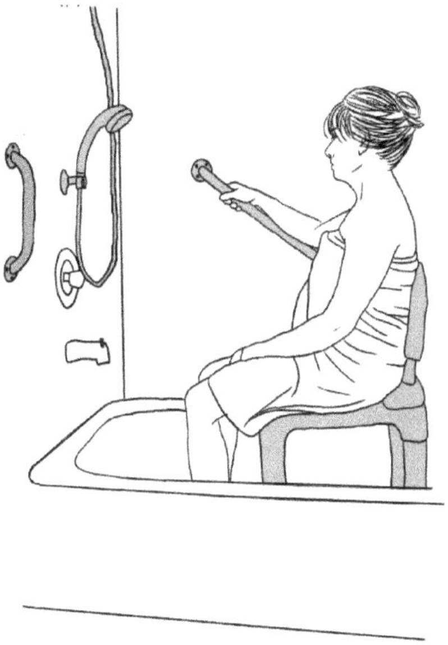

4. Sit down on the shower chair. Reverse the steps to get out.

Occupational Therapy TOOLKIT

Transfer to Shower Chair (left leg, sit, right leg)

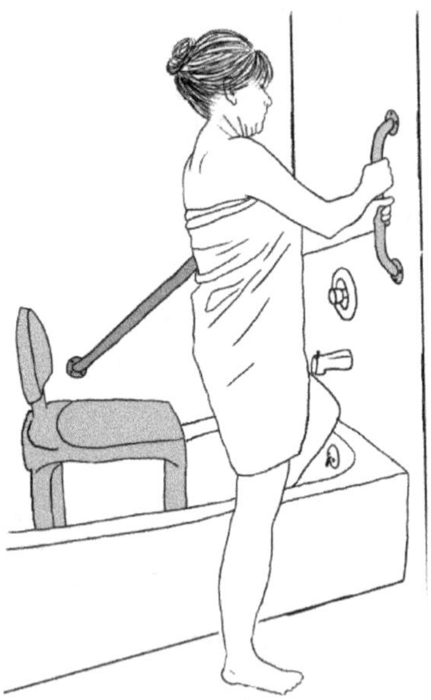

1. Face the wall and hold onto the grab bar. Step into the tub with your left leg.

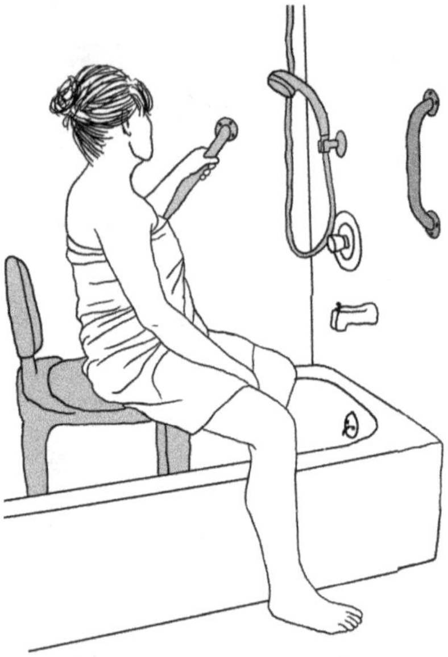

2. Sit on the shower chair.

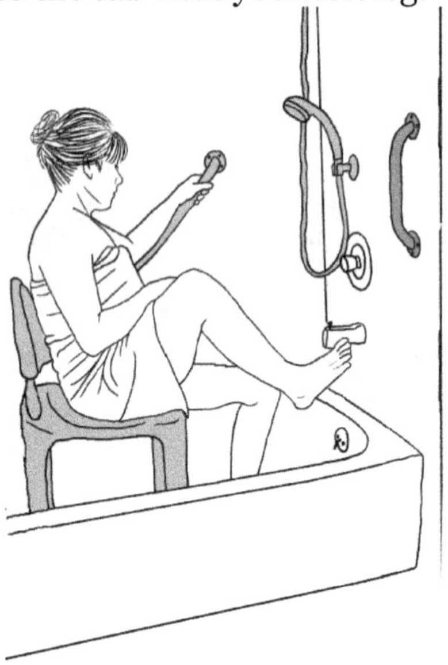

3. While you are sitting, lift your right leg into the tub.

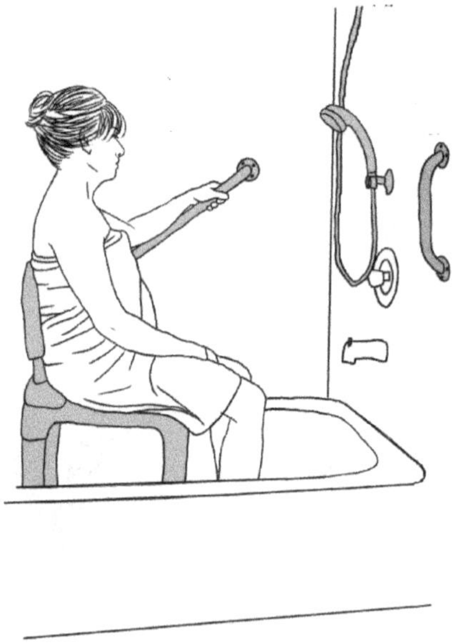

4. Reverse the steps to get out.

Transfer to Shower Chair (right leg, sit, left leg)

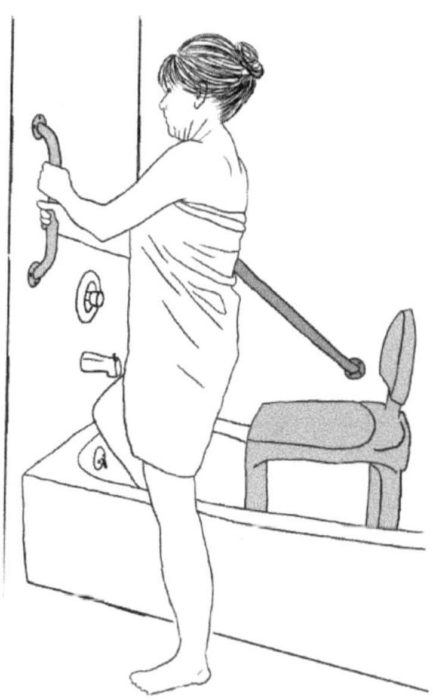

1. Face the wall and hold onto the grab bar. Step into the tub with your right leg.

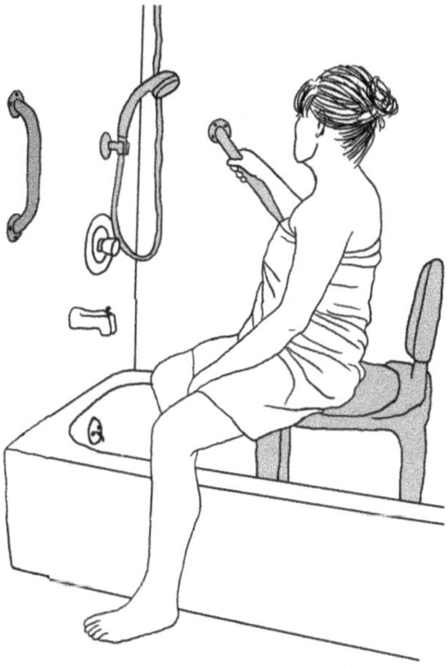

2. Sit on the shower chair.

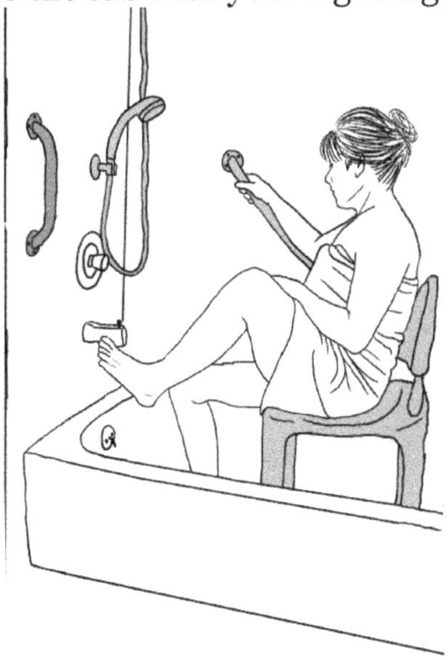

3. While you are sitting, lift your left leg into the tub.

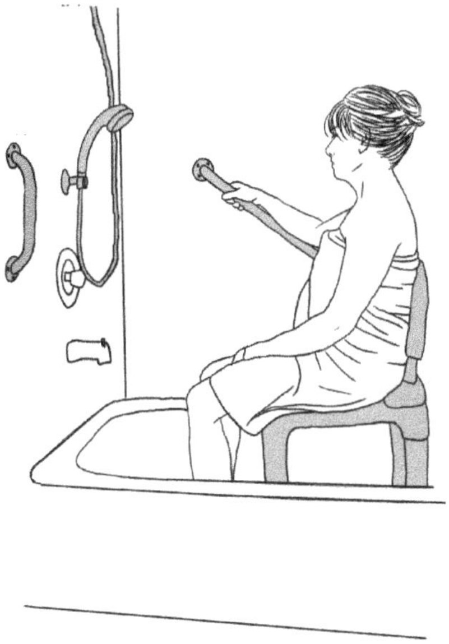

4. Reverse the steps to get out.

Transfer to Tub Bench - After Hip Surgery (back up, turn left)

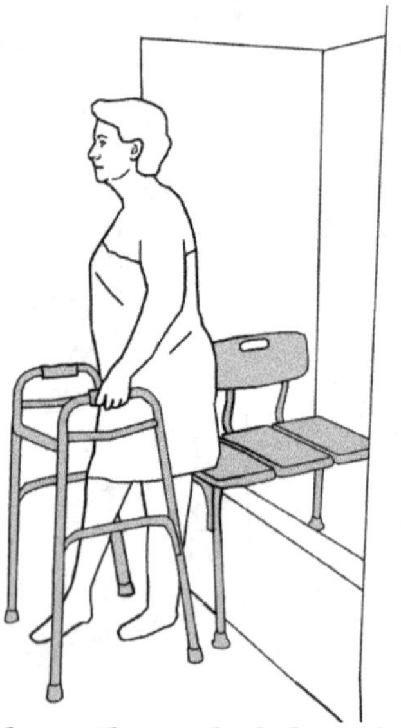

1. Move back until you feel the tub bench on the back of your legs.

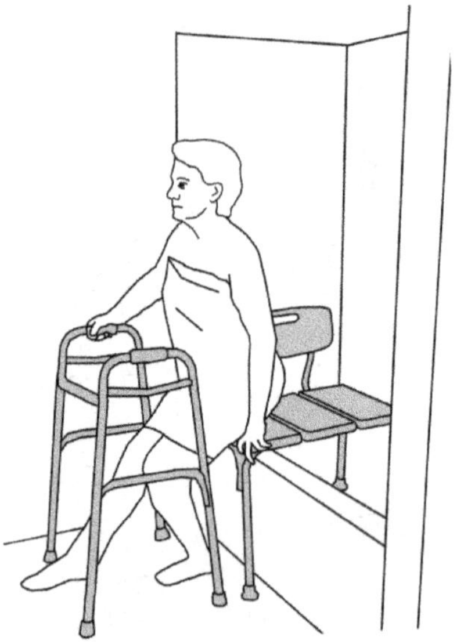

2. Slide your affected leg forward. Reach back for the tub bench and sit down. Scoot back as far as you can.

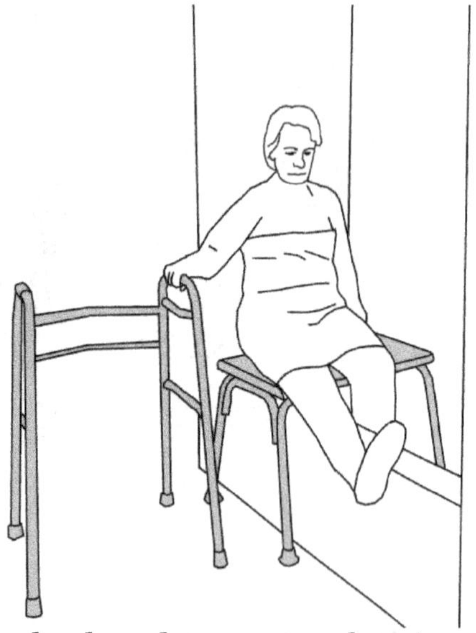

3. Lean back and move your legs into the tub. Turn the walker to the side for support.

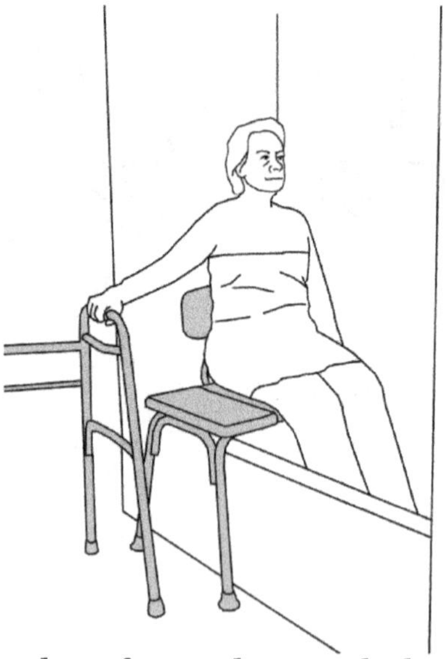

4. Do not lean forward to reach the faucets, stand and use a grab bar. Do not lean forward to wash your legs and feet, use a long handled brush. To get back out, reverse the steps.

Transfer to Tub Bench - After Hip Surgery (back up, turn right)

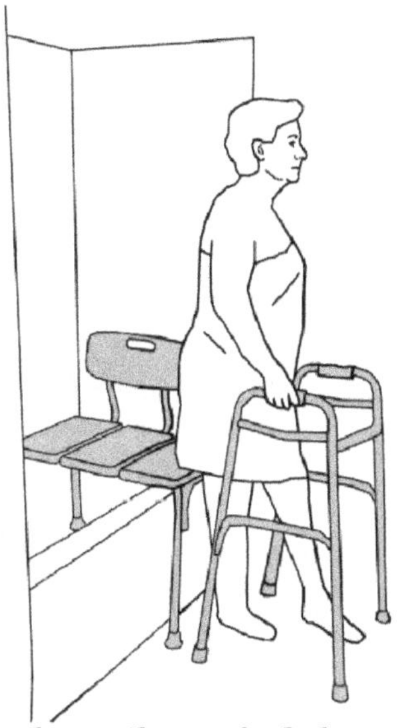

1. Move back until you feel the tub bench on the back of your legs.

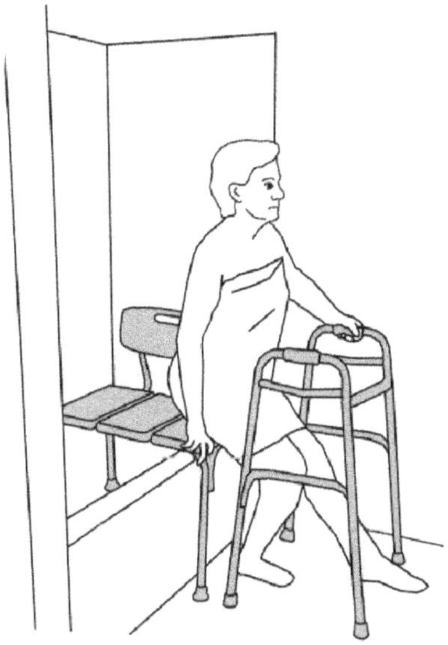

2. Slide your affected leg forward. Reach back for the tub bench and sit down. Scoot back as far as you can.

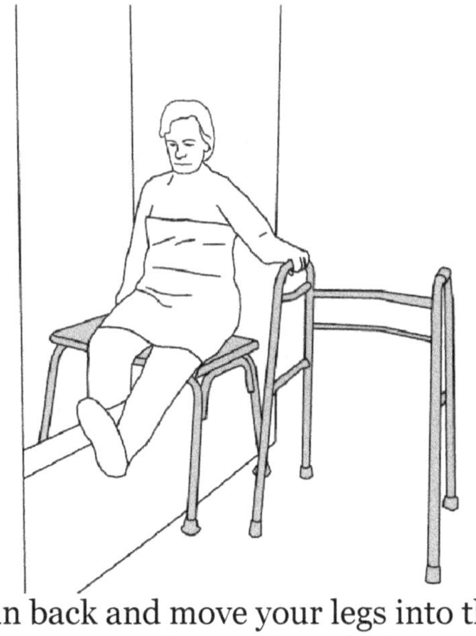

3. Lean back and move your legs into the tub. Turn the walker to the side for support.

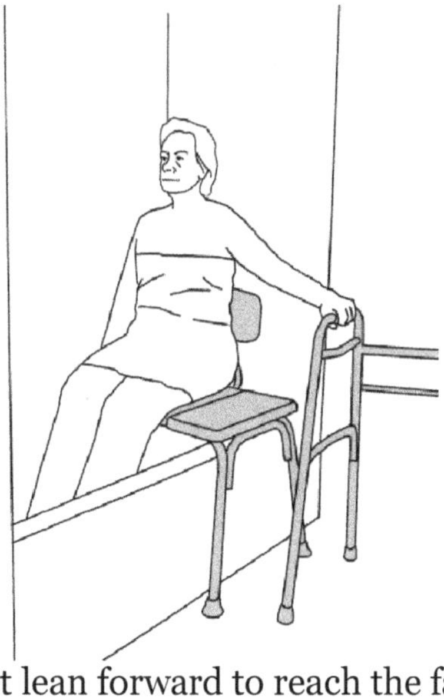

4. Do not lean forward to reach the faucets, stand and use a grab bar. Do not lean forward to wash your legs and feet, use a long handled brush. To get back out, reverse the steps.

Occupational Therapy TOOLKIT

Transfer to Tub Bench (back up, turn left)

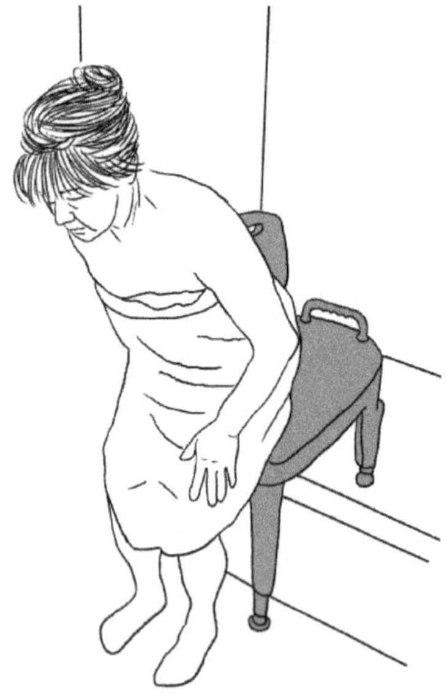

1. Back up to the tub bench until you feel it with your legs.

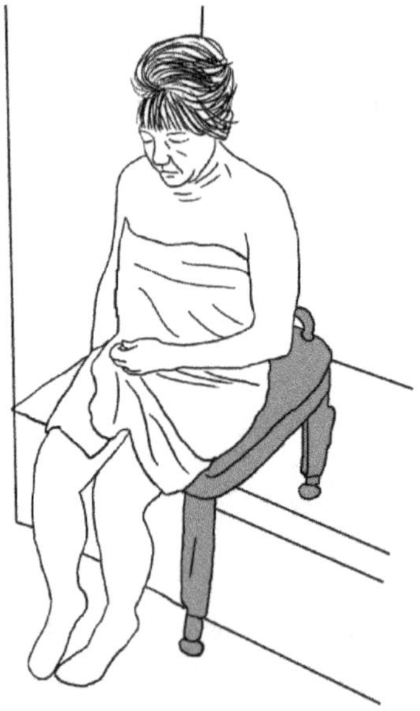

2. Reach back for the tub bench and sit down. Scoot back as far as you can.

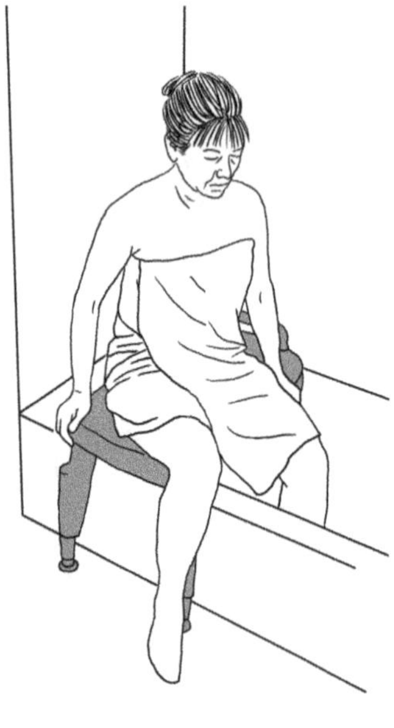

3. Turn your body to the left. Lift your left leg into the tub.

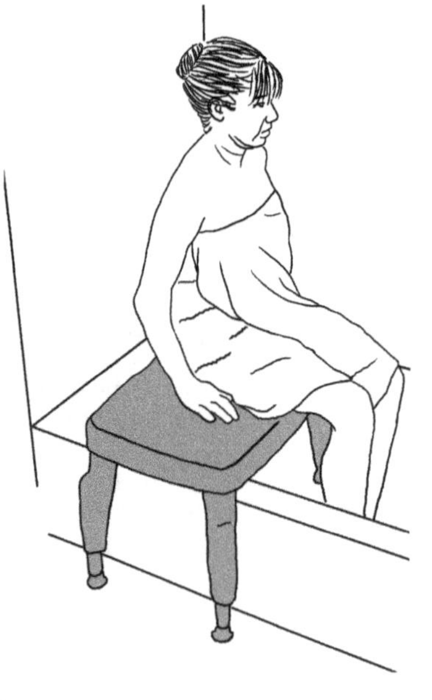

4. Scoot onto the seat. Lift your right leg into the tub. To get out, reverse the steps.

Transfer to Tub Bench (back up, turn right)

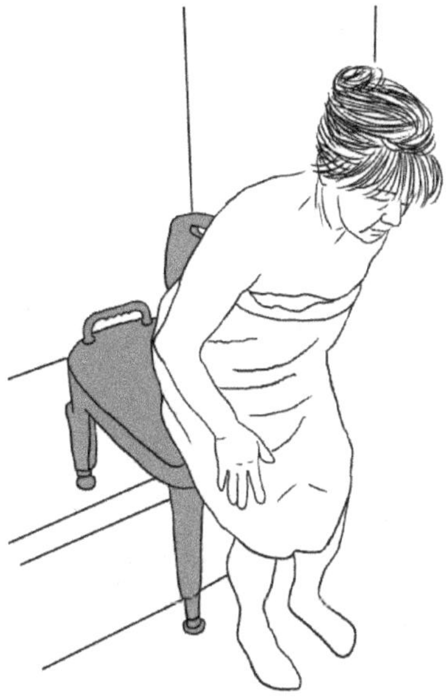

1. Back up to the tub bench until you feel it with your legs.

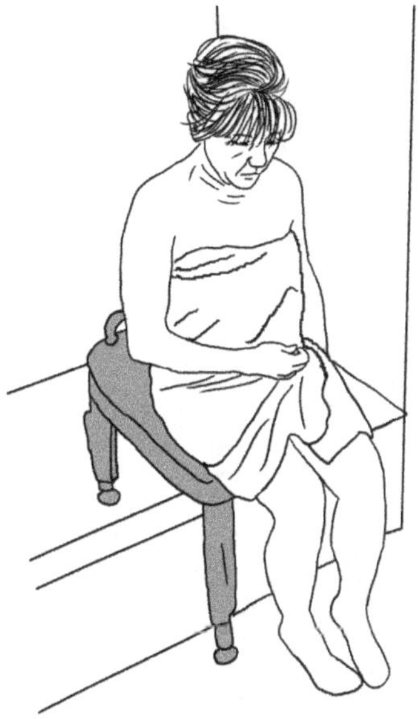

2. Reach back for the tub bench and sit down. Scoot back as far as you can.

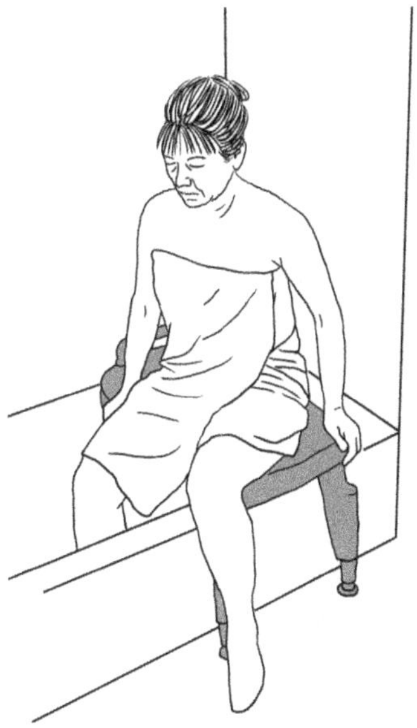

3. Turn your body to the right. Lift your right leg into the tub.

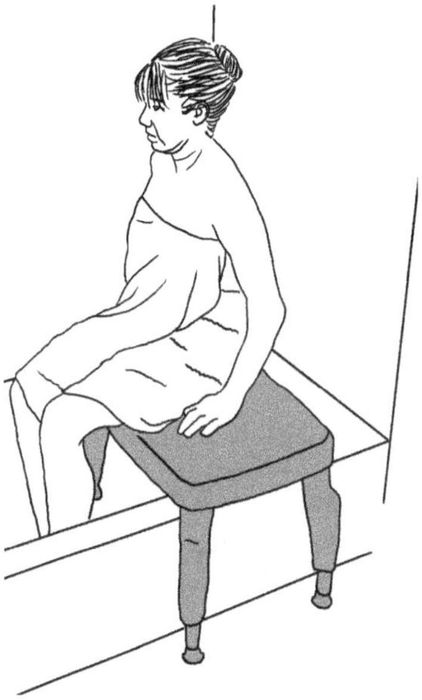

4. Scoot onto the seat. Lift your left leg into the tub. To get out, reverse the steps.

Transfer Wheelchair to Tub Bench - Move to the Left

1. Move the wheelchair close to tub bench. Lock the brakes.

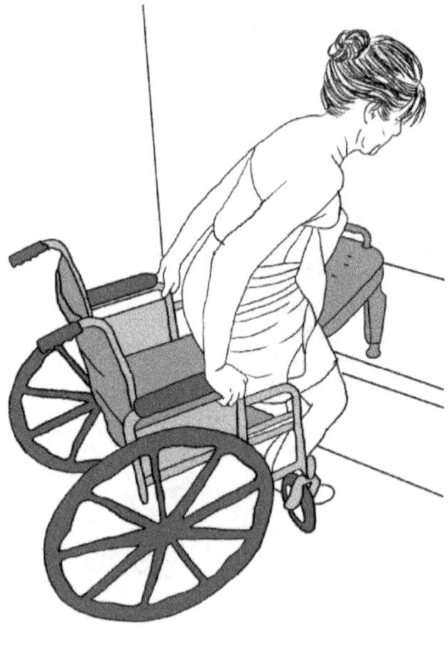

2. Pivot over to the tub bench.

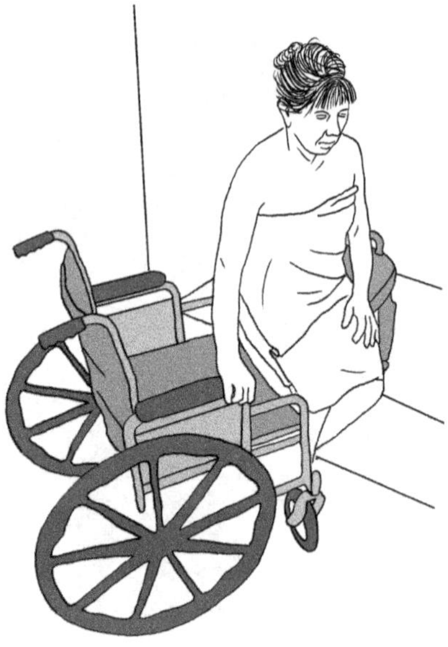

3. Sit on the tub bench.

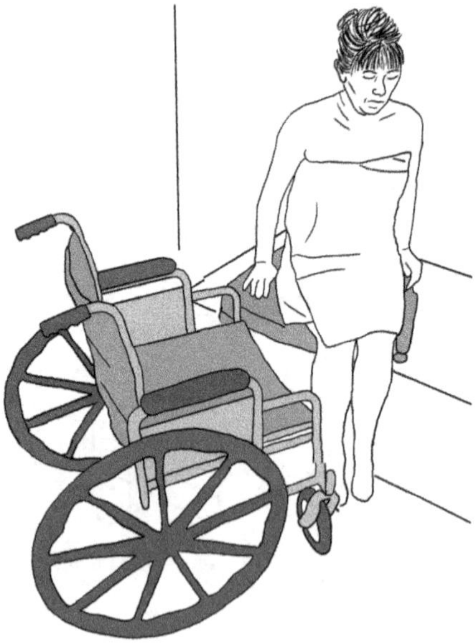

4. Scoot back onto the seat as far as you can.

Transfer Wheelchair to Tub Bench - Move to the Left

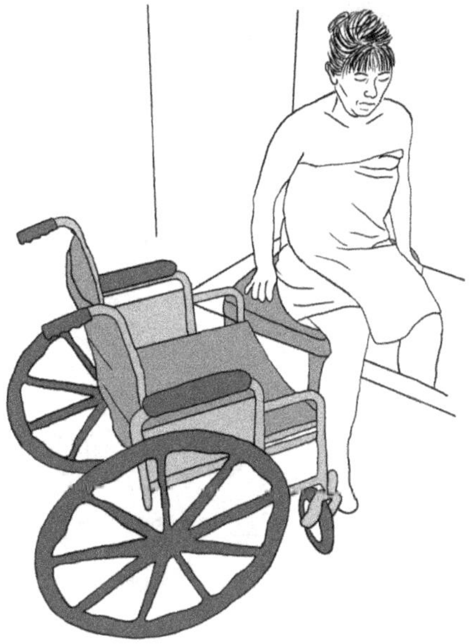

5. Lift your left leg into the tub.

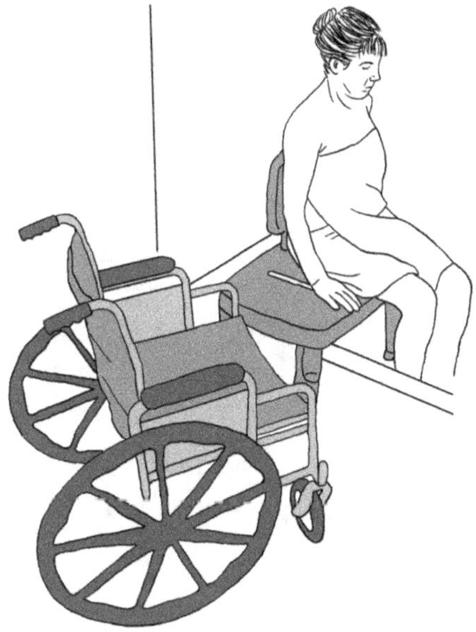

6. Scoot onto the seat. Lift your right leg into the tub. To get out, reverse the steps.

2 of 2

Transfer Wheelchair to Tub Bench - Move to the Right

1. Move the wheelchair close to the tub bench. Lock the brakes.

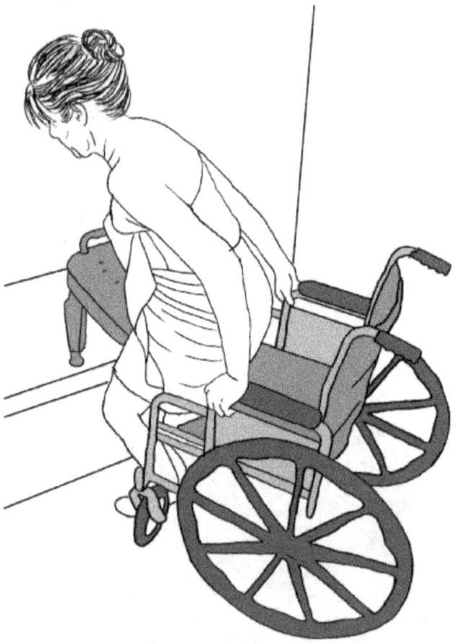

2. Pivot over to the tub bench.

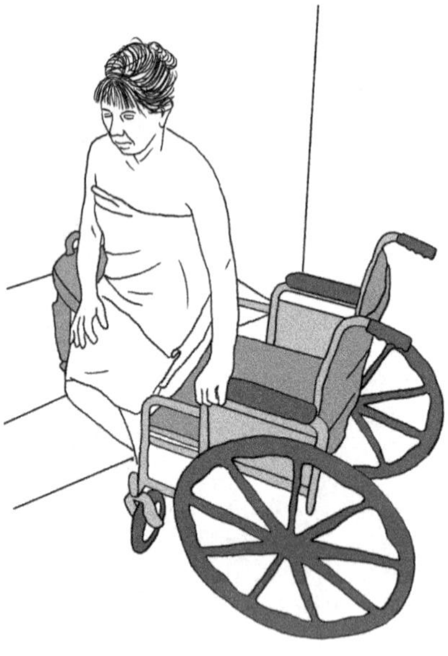

3. Sit on the tub bench.

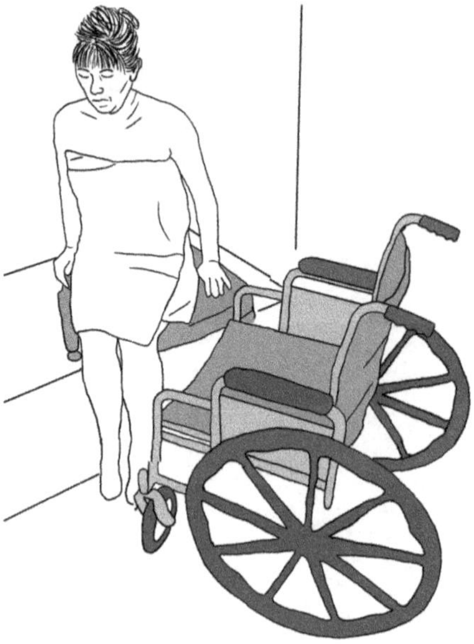

4. Scoot back onto the seat as far as you can.

1 of 2

Transfer Wheelchair to Tub Bench - Move to the Right

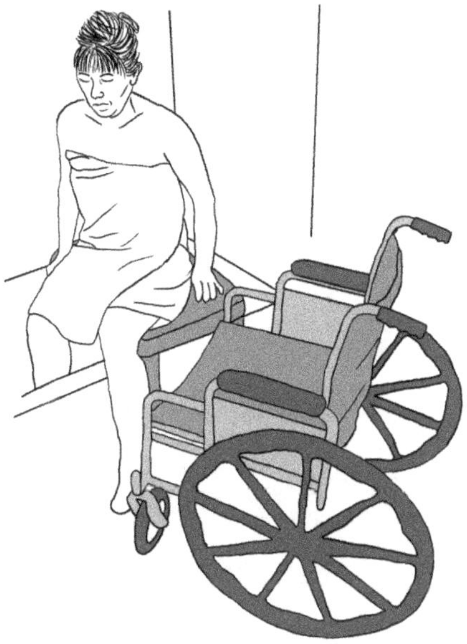

5. Lift your right leg into the tub.

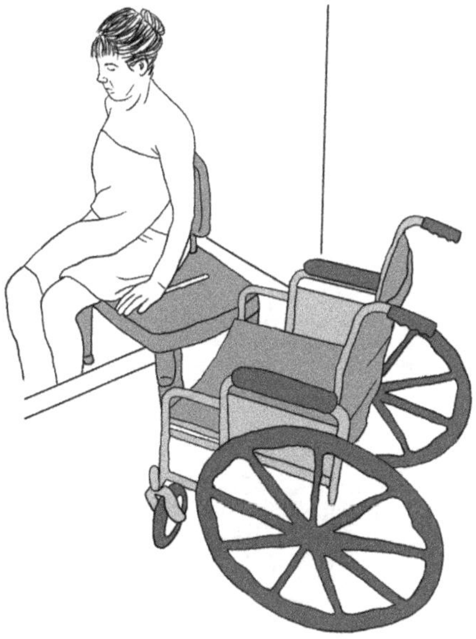

6. Scoot onto the seat. Lift your left leg into the tub. To get out, reverse the steps.

Up a Curb or Single Step Using a Walker

Do not rush. Make sure you have your balance before stepping up.

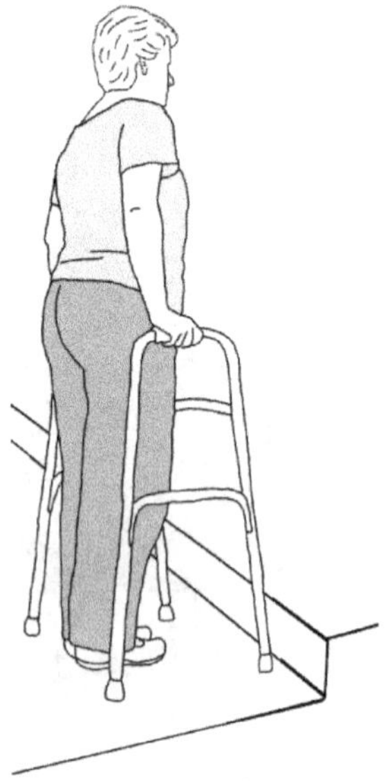

1. Walk up to the curb until the walker is near the edge. Step into the walker.

2. Lift the walker. Place all four legs of the walker up onto the curb.

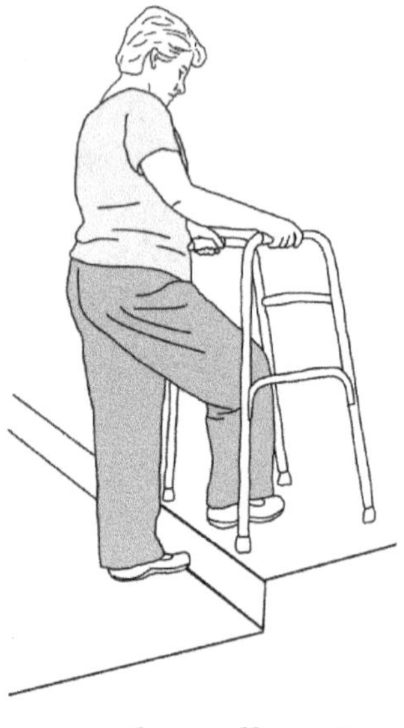

3. Push down on the walker. Step up with your stronger leg.

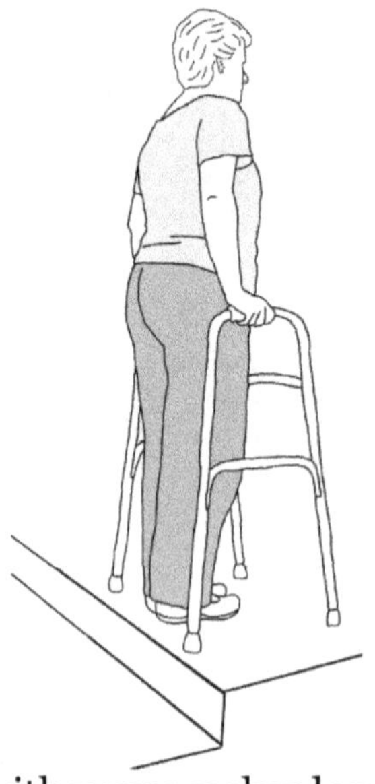

4. Step up with your weaker leg.

Up with the "good" and down with the "bad". This is an easy way to recall which leg to use first.

Occupational Therapy TOOLKIT

Up Steps with a Rail Using a Cane

Do not rush. Make sure you have your balance before using the stairs.

1. Hold on to the rail. Hold the cane in your other hand. This may be your weaker side or your stronger side.

2. Step up with your stronger leg to the first step.

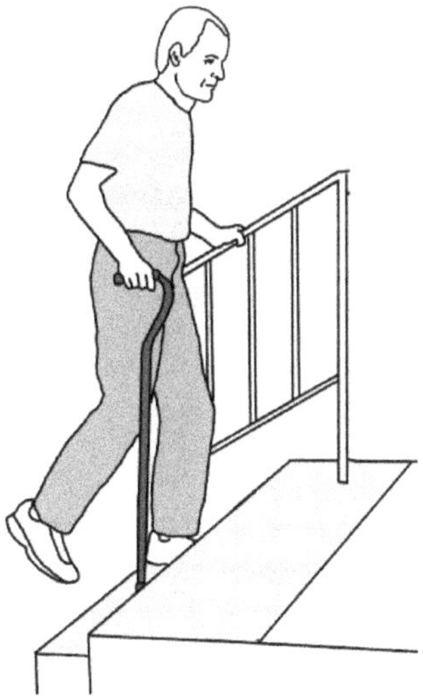

3. Step up with the cane and your weaker leg to the same step. Balance yourself.

4. Repeat: stronger leg, weaker leg with cane, one step at a time.

Up with the "good" and down with the "bad". This is an easy way to recall which leg to use first.

Occupational Therapy TOOLKIT

Up Steps with a Rail Using a Closed Walker

Do not rush. Make sure you have your balance before using the stairs.

1. Fold the walker. Hold the rail. Place the walker to your side and up to the next step, along the riser.

2. Support your weight between the rail and the walker. Step up with your stronger leg.

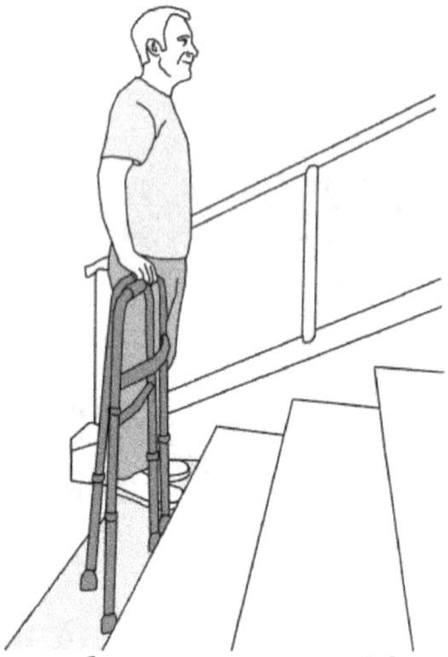

3. Step up to the same step with your weaker leg. Balance yourself.

4. Repeat: walker, stronger leg, weaker leg, one step at a time.

Up with the "good" and down with the "bad". This is an easy way to recall which leg to use first.

Up Steps with a Rail Using an Open Walker

Do not rush. Make sure you have your balance before using the stairs.

1. Hold the walker with one hand and the rail with your other hand. Turn the walker to the side. Put the front two legs of the walker on the next step up.

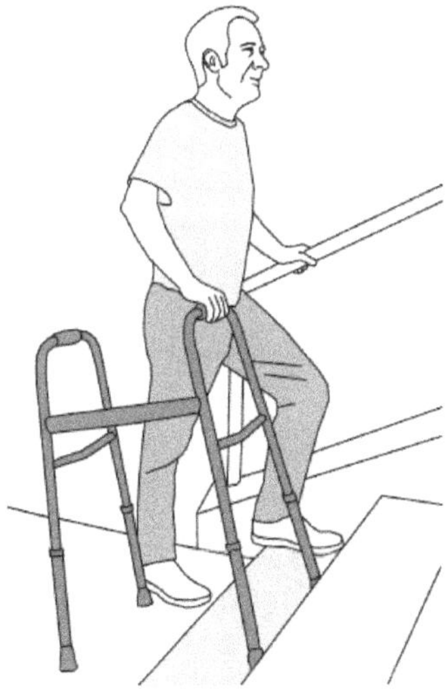

2. Support your weight between the rail and the walker. Step up with your stronger leg.

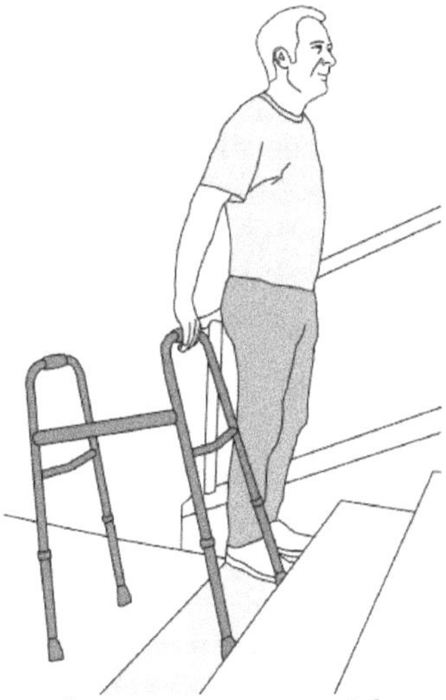

3. Step up to the same step with your weaker leg. Balance yourself.

4. Repeat: walker, stronger leg, weaker leg, one step at a time.

Up with the "good" and down with the "bad". This is an easy way to recall which leg to use first.

Up Steps without a Rail Using a Cane

Do not rush. Make sure you have your balance before using the stairs.

1. Hold the cane on your stronger side.

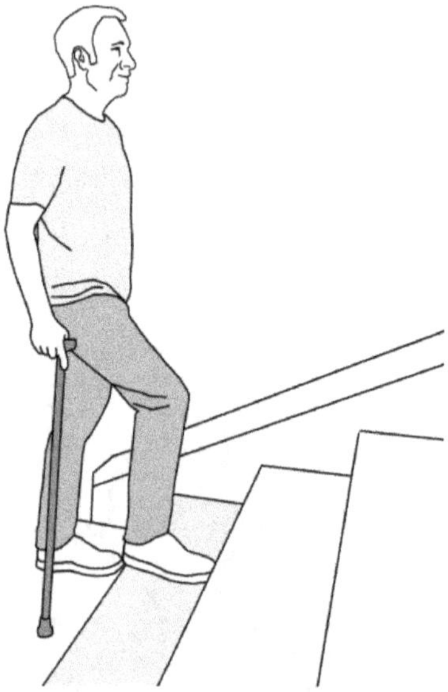

2. Step up with your stronger leg to the first step.

3. Step up with the cane and your weaker leg to the same step. Balance yourself.

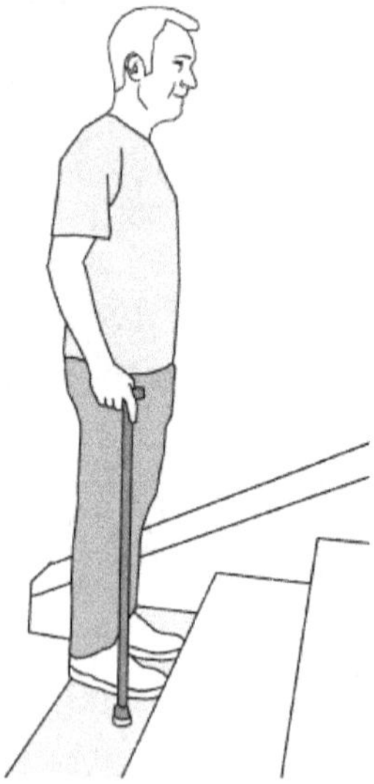

4. Repeat: stronger leg, weaker leg with cane, one step at a time.

Up with the "good" and down with the "bad". This is an easy way to recall which leg to use first.

Using a Buttonhook

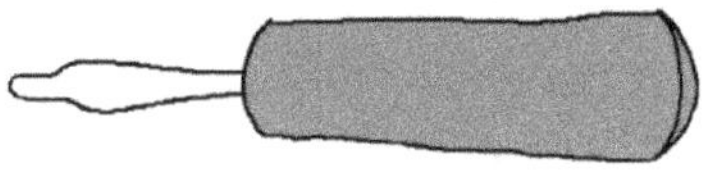

1. Insert the loop into the buttonhole.

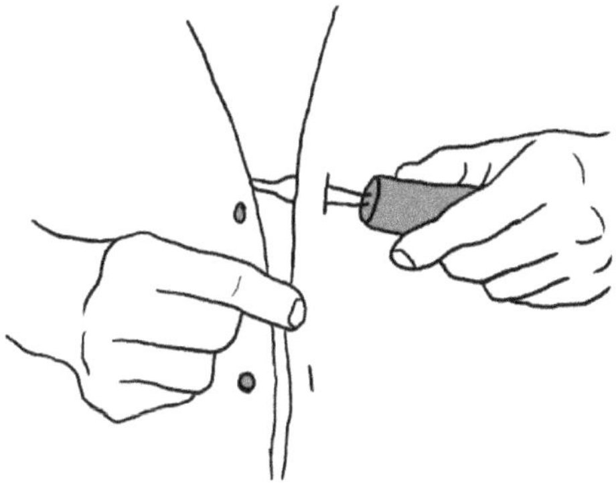

2. Hook the button with the loop.

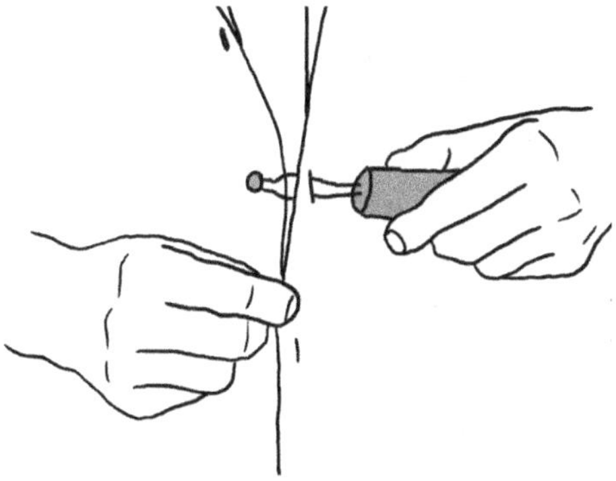

3. Pull the loop with the button through the buttonhole.

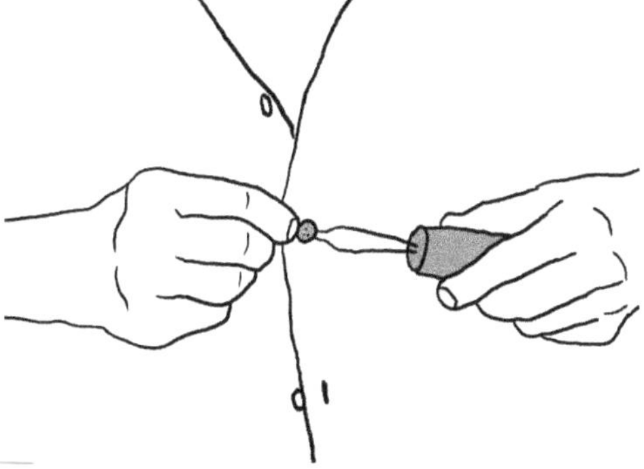

Walk with a Cane on the Stronger, Left Side

Hold the cane on your stronger, left side.

- Place the cane forward.
- Take a step with your weaker, right leg.
- Step forward with your stronger, left leg.
- Repeat: cane, right leg, left leg.

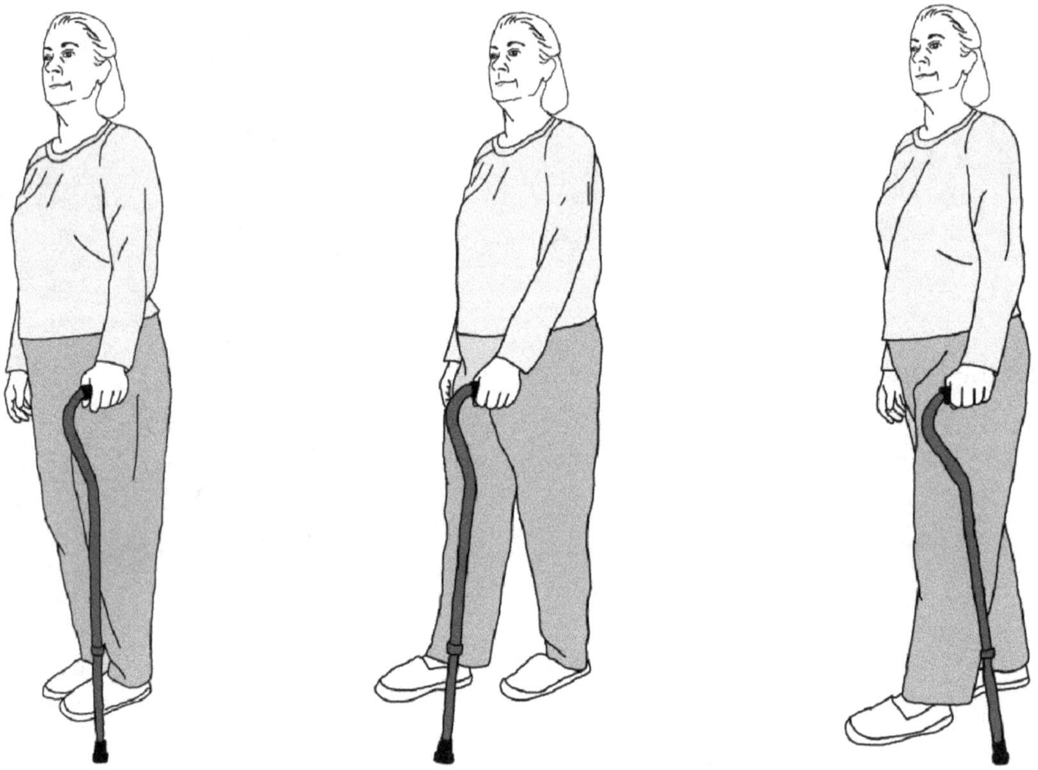

Walk with a Cane on the Stronger, Right Side

Hold the cane on your stronger, right side.

- Place the cane forward.
- Take a step with your weaker, left leg.
- Step forward with your stronger, right leg.
- Repeat: cane, left leg, right leg.

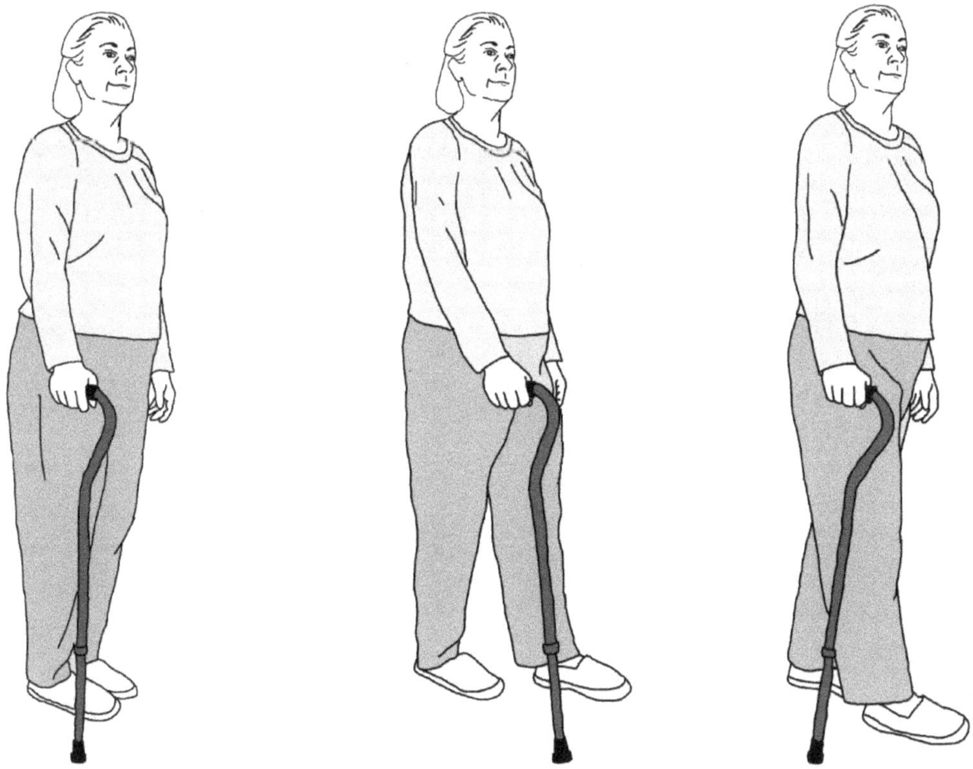

Walk with a Standard Walker
Full Weight Bearing (FWB)

You can put all your weight onto your affected leg. You should feel very little or no pain.

Stand up tall, tuck in your bottom and tighten your stomach muscles. Hold your head up and look ahead.

1. Lift the walker and move it forward. Place all four legs of the walker flat on the floor.

2. Step into the walker with your affected leg. Do not get too close to the front of the walker. You could lose your balance.

3. Take a step with your unaffected leg. Bring it a little ahead of your affected leg.

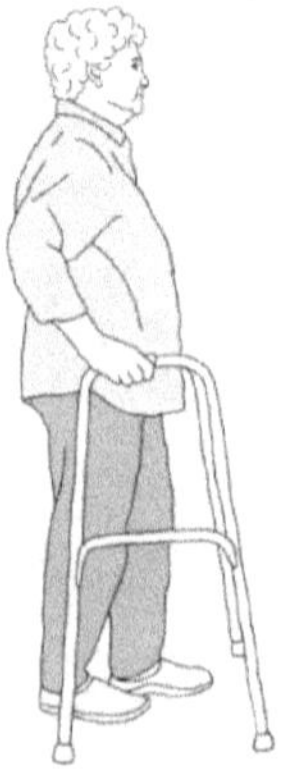

Repeat: walker, affected leg, unaffected leg.

Walk with a Standard Walker
Non-Weight Bearing (NWB)

You cannot put any weight onto your affected leg or let it touch the floor.

1. Stand up tall. Tuck in your bottom and tighten your stomach muscles. Hold your head up and look ahead. All your weight is on your unaffected leg.

2. Lift your walker and move it forward. All four legs of the walker must be flat on the floor.

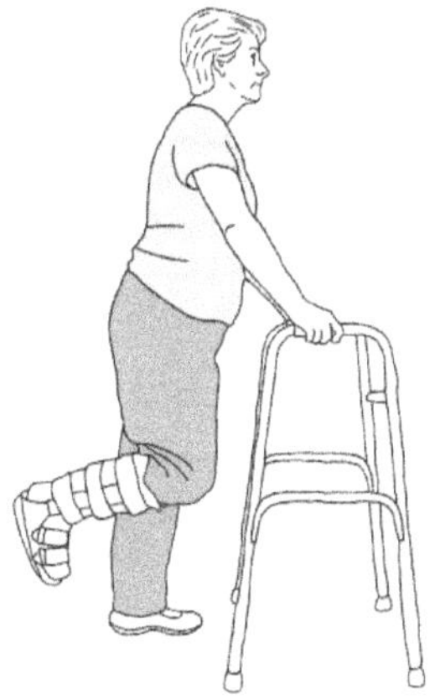

3. Push down on the walker with your arms. Hop onto your unaffected foot to the center of the walker. Do not hop too close to the front of the walker. If you are too close, you could lose your balance.

Repeat: walker, unaffected leg.

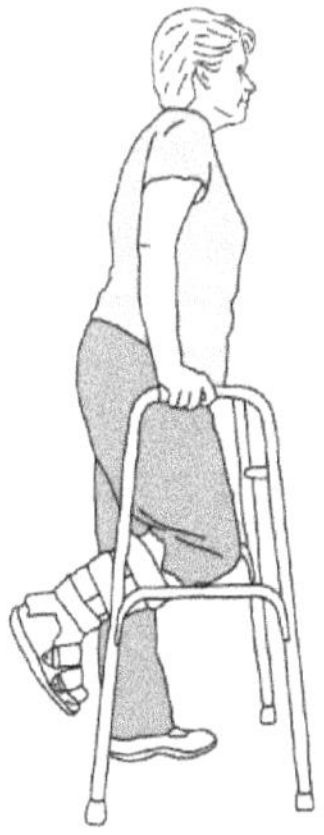

Walk with a Standard Walker
Partial Weight Bearing (PWB)

As your leg is healing, you may place a small amount of weight onto your affected leg. The range is between 30 - 50 percent of your weight.

Stand up tall, tuck in your bottom and tighten your stomach muscles. Hold your head up and look ahead.

1. Shift most of your weight onto your unaffected leg. Lift the walker and move it forward. All four legs of the walker must be flat on the floor.

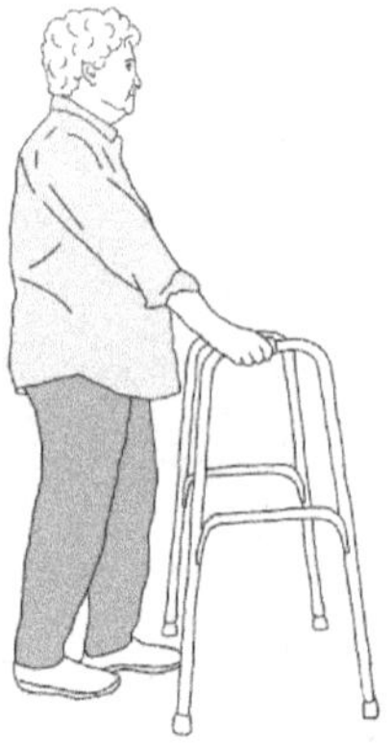

2. Step with your affected leg into the walker. Do not step too close to the front of the walker. If you are too close, you could lose your balance.

3. Use both arms to push down on the walker. This will keep some weight off your affected leg. Step forward with your unaffected leg into the center of the walker.

Repeat: walker, affected leg, unaffected leg.

Occupational Therapy TOOLKIT

Walk with a Standard Walker
Toe-Touch Weight Bearing (TTWB)

You can only touch the floor with your toe for balance. Do not place any weight onto your affected leg.

Stand up tall, tuck in your bottom and tighten your stomach muscles. Hold your head up and look ahead. All your weight is on your unaffected leg.

1. Lift the walker and move it forward. Place all four legs of the walker flat on the floor.

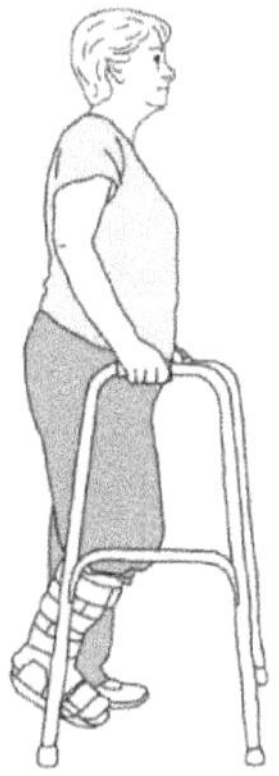

2. Move your affected foot forward into the walker. Only touch the ball of your foot on the floor for balance. Do not get too close to the front of the walker. If you are too close, you could lose your balance.

3. Push down on the walker with both arms. Support all your weight through your arms. Hop forward with your unaffected leg into the walker.

Repeat: walker, affected leg, unaffected leg

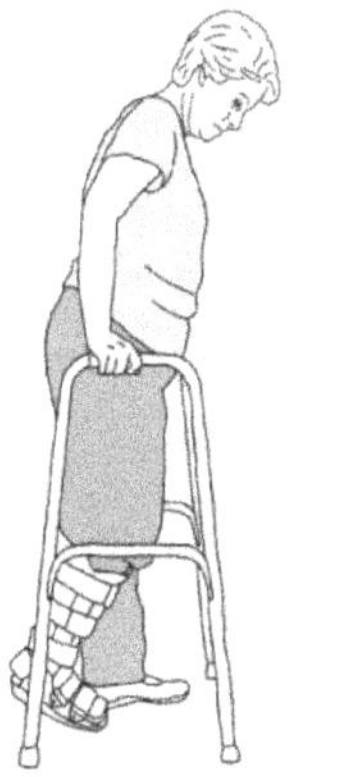

Walk with a Standard Walker
Weight Bearing as Tolerated (WBAT)

You can put 75-100 percent of your weight onto your affected leg. You should feel very little or no pain.

Stand up tall, tuck in your bottom and tighten your stomach muscles. Hold your head up and look ahead.

1. Lift the walker and move it forward. Place all four legs of the walker flat on the floor.

2. Step into the walker with your affected leg. Do not get too close to the front of the walker. You could lose your balance.

3. Support 0-25 percent of your weight through your arms. Take a step with your unaffected leg. Bring it a little ahead of the affected leg.

Repeat: walker, affected leg, unaffected leg.

Walk with a Wheeled Walker
Full Weight Bearing (FWB)

You can put all your weight onto your affected leg. You should feel very little or no pain.

Stand up, tuck in your bottom and tighten your stomach muscles. Hold your head up and look ahead.

1. Roll the walker forward.

2. Step into the walker with your affected leg. Do not get too close to the front of the walker. You could lose your balance.

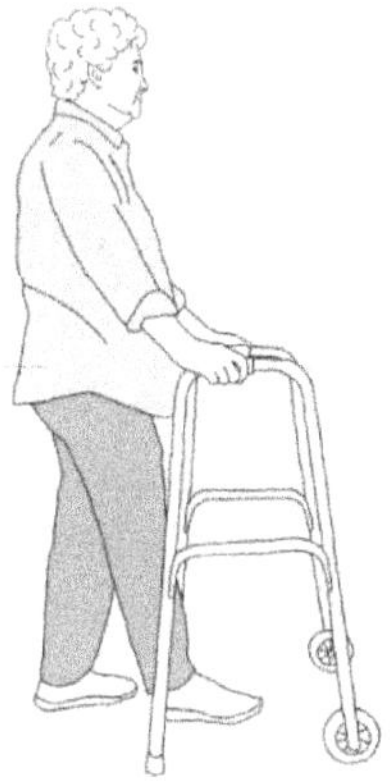

3. Take a step with your unaffected leg. Bring it a little ahead of your affected leg.

Repeat: walker, affected leg, unaffected leg

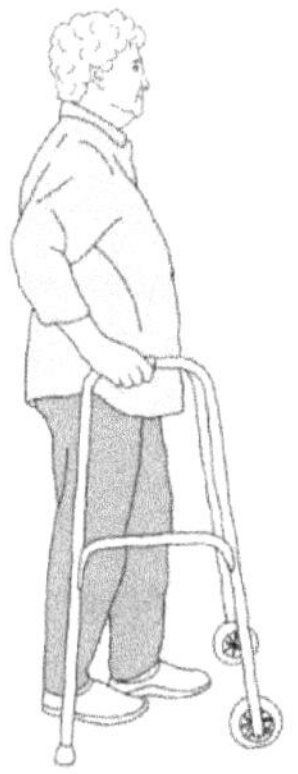

Walk with a Wheeled Walker
Weight Bearing as Tolerated (WBAT)

You can put 75-100 percent of your weight onto your affected leg. You should feel very little or no pain.

Stand up, tuck in your bottom and tighten your stomach muscles. Hold your head up and look ahead.

1. Roll the walker forward.

2. Step into the walker with your affected leg. Do not get too close to the front of the walker. You could lose your balance.

3. Support 0-25 percent of your weight through your arms. Take a step with your unaffected leg. Bring it a little ahead of your affected leg.

Repeat: walker, affected leg, unaffected leg

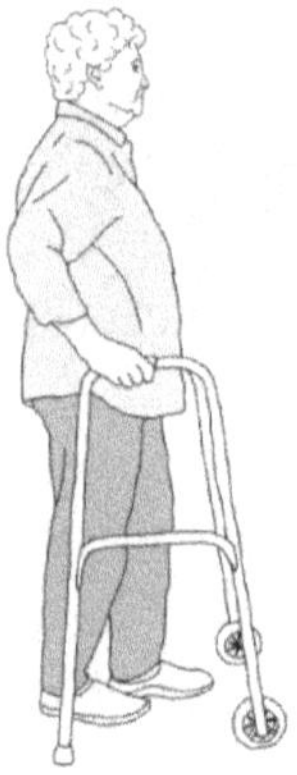

Wheelchair Mobility

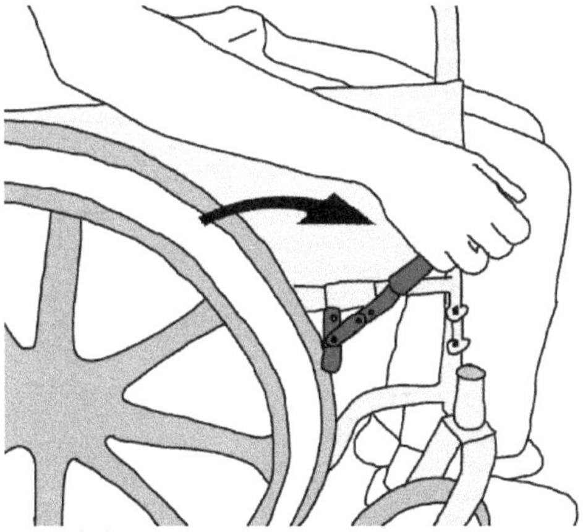

Lock the brakes when the wheelchair is not moving. Unlock the brakes before moving the wheelchair.

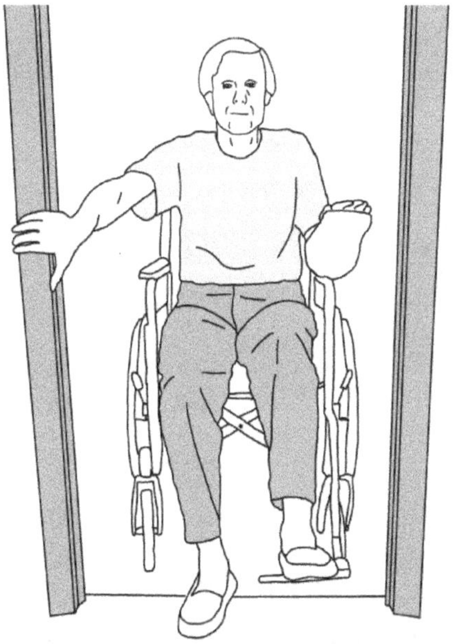

To move through a doorway, take your hand off the wheel. Place it on the frame. Use the frame to pull through the door.

To move the wheelchair forward, place your hand on the wheel rim. Push the wheel forward. Use your foot to pull you forward and to steer.

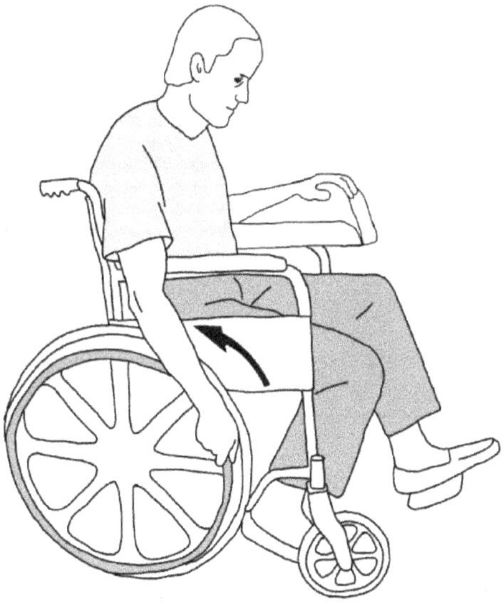

To move the wheelchair backward, place your hand on the wheel rim. Pull the wheel back. Use your foot to push you back and to steer.

Occupational Therapy TOOLKIT

Anxiety Journal

Date: ________________

What time did your anxiety start? ________________

How long did your anxiety last? ________________

On a scale of 1-10, rate your level of anxiety.

1	2	3	4	5	6	7	8	9	10
none									extreme

Describe the anxiety, how did it feel? Describe your thoughts, feelings and actions.

____

____

____

How did the anxiety affect you being able to do tasks or relate to others?

____

____

____

What (activity, feelings) happened before you felt anxious?

____

____

____

What did you do to reduce your anxiety and what was the result?

____

____

____

What could you have done differently?

____

____

____

Occupational Therapy TOOLKIT

Arm Measurements

Date	Upper arm ______ cm above elbow crease		Elbow crease		Forearm ______ cm below elbow crease		Wrist		Mid-hand	
	Left	Right	Left	Right	Left	Right	Left	Right	Left	Right

Record measurements in centimeters.

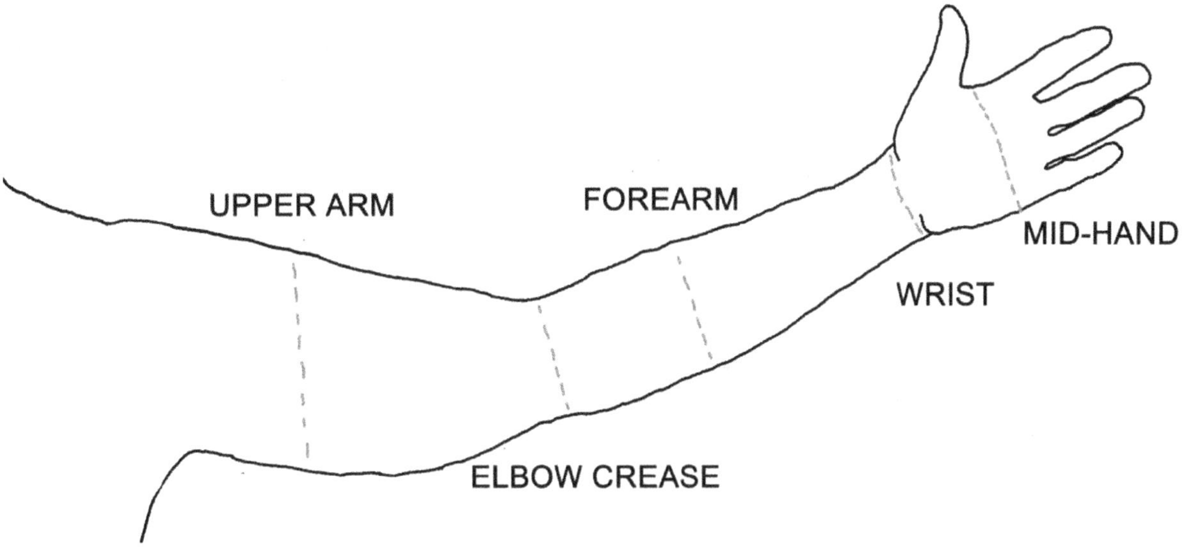

Arthritic Joint Changes and Deformities
Therapist Resource

Thumb

CM - dislocation and subluxation
MP - swan neck and Boutonniere
IP - swan neck and Boutonniere

Fingers

MCP - synovial hypertrophy, ulnar/radial deviation, instability, ankylosis, crepitation with motion, extensor tendon subluxation, extensor tendon rupture, intrinsic tightness, subluxation to dislocation
PIP - synovial hypertrophy, ulnar/radial deviation, instability, ankylosis, swan neck, Boutonniere, nodules, constrictive tenosynovitis
DIP - ankylosis, swan neck, Boutonniere, nodules, vasculitis

Wrist

Subluxation to dislocation, crepitation with motion, carpal tunnel syndrome, ankylosis, ulnar/radial deviation, tendon rupture, dislocation of ulnar styloid

Forearm

Limitation of supination range, limitation of pronation range, nodules on medial aspect of proximal forearm

Elbow

Flexion contractures, nodules on olecranon, ankylosis, crepitation with motion, cubital tunnel syndrome, instability

Shoulder

Crepitation with motion, synovial hypertrophy, restricted glenohumeral motion, muscle atrophy, weakness in rotator cuff muscles, ruptured bicep tendon

Cervical

Decreased range of motion or pain with range of motion, cervical myelopathy

Body Mechanics

Good body mechanics protect your back and neck. Good body mechanics includes good posture, limited bending and twisting, and good lifting and moving skills.

Good Posture (see handout).

Do Not Bend and Twist
Tasks that use bending include picking up an item off the floor; dressing and bathing your lower body; brushing your teeth at the sink; getting off the toilet.

- Use a reacher to pick up items.
- Store items used often at eye or waist level.
- Use dressing tools to put on shoes, socks, and pants.
- To brush your teeth, stand with your back straight and bend from your hips.
- To get up from the toilet, keep your back straight. Place one hand on the counter and your other hand on your thigh. Push up to stand up.
- Use a raised toilet seat.

Tasks that use twisting include reaching to the bedside table; reaching to the floor or table next to a chair or sofa; reaching for the toilet paper, and reaching to flush the toilet.

- Store items used often within reach.
- Move the toilet paper.
- Flush the toilet after you stand up.

Body Mechanics

Lift and Carry

- Use your legs instead your back.
- Keep your back straight. Squat down in front of the object.
- Pull in your hips and stomach to lift.
- Hold the object close to your body.
- To turn, rotate your whole body, not just your back.
- If the object is too heavy, ask someone to help you.

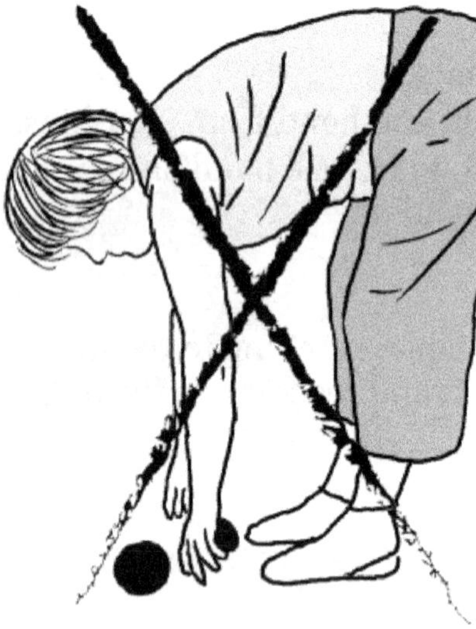

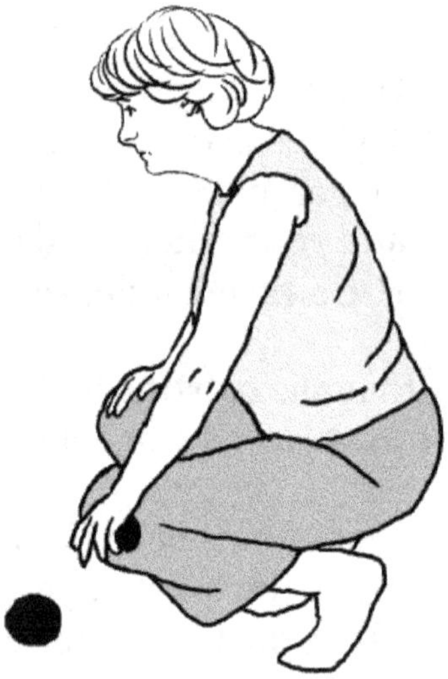

Push and Pull

- Use the weight of your body to help push or pull an object.
- Keep your feet apart and your back straight.
- If the object or person is too heavy, ask for help.

Breathing Distress
Causes and Tips to Prevent

Causes	Tips to Prevent
Doing too much	Know your limits. Use the tips to save your energy.
Infection or illness	Report these symptoms to the doctor right away. • More mucus than is normal. • Change in the color of mucus • Increase in coughing or wheezing • More shortness of breath than is normal. • Pain in the chest • Fever • Swelling at the ankles • Feeling very tired
Extreme weather changes	When it is cold outside, cover your nose and mouth with a scarf. This will help to warm the air before it reaches your lungs. On hot and humid days, stay indoors with the air on.
Using liquor or over- the-counter drugs	Talk with the doctor before using liquor or over-the-counter drugs.
Stressful events	Avoid events that may cause stress. Use the tools to help you relax.
Shallow breathing	Use the pursed lip. Use deep (diaphragmatic) breathing.
Coughing too hard	Use controlled cough. Drink plenty of fluids.

Occupational Therapy TOOLKIT

Breathing Distress Control

Try this method when you have the first symptoms of breathing distress.

1. Stay calm.
2. Sit down if you can.
3. Lean forward.
4. Relax your shoulders and your stomach muscles.
4. Begin pursed lip breathing; try to exhale as long as you can.
5. Add deep (diaphragmatic) breathing.

If symptoms do not improve, call the doctor for advice.

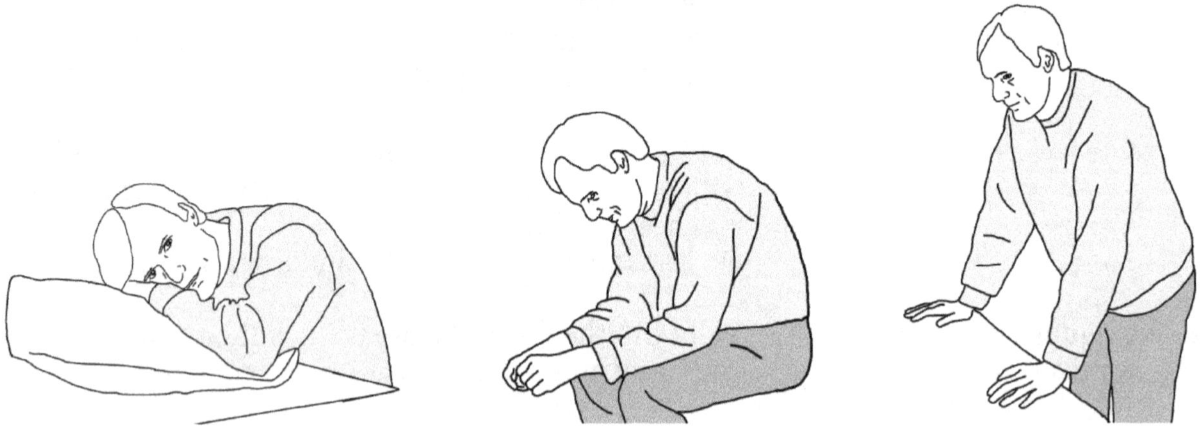

Cardiac Precautions for Exercise
Therapist Resource

If one of the following is present, stop therapy and contact the physician:

- SOB, chest pain, nausea and vomiting, diaphoresis (sweating), dizziness
- Staggering gait, ataxia
- Confusion or blank stare in response to questions
- Severe hypertension (systolic BP > 165, diastolic BP > 110)
- Severe and persistent hypotension (BP < 90, check parameters with MD)
- Resting heart rate > 130 BPM, < 40 BPM
- Inappropriate heart rate or BP changes with self-care activities (increase in HR of more than 20 BPM, or increase or decrease in systolic BP of more than 20 mmHg)
- Oxygen sat < 85%

Exercise contraindicated for the following:

- Uncontrolled atrial or ventricular arrhythmias
- Second or third degree heart block
- Recent embolism, either systemic or pulmonary
- Resting HR greater than 120 with a recent MI
- Resting HR greater than 130 with recent bypass surgery, cardiomyopathy, CHF, or valve surgery
- Thrombophlebitis
- Gross cardiac enlargement
- Resting or unstable angina
- Dissecting aneurysm
- Fever greater than 100°F (38°C)
- Primary, active pericarditis
- Severe aortic stenosis
- Uncontrolled CHF or HTN
- Uncontrolled diabetes mellitus (BS > 250 mg/dL)

Care of the Prosthesis and Lower Limb Coverings

Care of the Prosthesis

- Inspect the device every day. Look for cracks or rough edges.
- Wipe out the socket every day. Use a damp cloth and mild soap. Rinse with a clean, damp cloth. Dry the socket with a clean towel.
- When not in use, place the device on its side on the floor.

Care of the Limb Coverings

- Wash all limb coverings every day. Include ace wraps, shrinkers, socks, nylon sheaths, and gel liners.
- Use warm water and a mild soap. Rinse well.
- Roll in a towel to get rid of most of the water. Lie flat to dry.
- Be sure all limb coverings are clean and dry before using.

Care of the Prosthesis and Upper Limb Coverings

Care of the Prosthesis

- Inspect the device every day. Look for cracks or rough edges. Exam the prosthesis cables for cuts and areas of wear.
- Wipe out the socket every day. Use a damp cloth and a mild soap. Rinse with a clean, damp cloth. Dry the socket with a clean towel.
- Wash the harness when it becomes soiled. Clean and oil as needed.
- Replace the neoprene lining of the hook as needed.
- Hang up the device by the harness. Do not hang by the cable or cable strap.

Care of the Limb Coverings

- Wash all limb coverings every day. Include ace wraps, shrinkers, socks, nylon sheaths, and gel liners.
- Use warm water and a mild soap. Rinse well.
- Roll in a towel to get rid of most of the water. Lie flat to dry.
- Be sure all limb coverings are clean and dry before using.

Care of Your Residual Limb

Wash your residual limb every day. More often if needed.
- Use warm water and a mild, unscented soap.
- Only use lotions or other products that the doctor suggests.
- Do not shave your residual limb. This may cause ingrown hairs.

Inspect your residual limb every time you put on or remove the prosthesis.
- Use good lighting, and put on glasses, if you need them.
- Look at all parts your residual limb; the top and bottom, the sides and inside creases. Look for color changes (redness, bluing, white spots), rashes, blisters, cuts, sores or cracks in your skin. Use a long-handled mirror.
- Feel your residual limb for changes in temperature. It should feel warm all over without any hot spots. Feel for areas that are tender or swollen.
- Smell for any odors.
- If you notice changes, do not wear the prosthesis until you have contacted the doctor.

Protect your residual limb from pressure and rubbing.
- Use a clean sock or liner every time you put on the prosthesis. Apply them one at a time with the seams facing out. They should fit closely, without folds or wrinkles.
- Wear enough socks or liners to prevent movement within the prosthesis.
- Check the fit of the prosthesis throughout the day. Add or remove socks or liners as needed.
- Do not pad sore spots. Do not use band-aids and tape on your residual limb. This will add pressure between your skin and the prosthesis.
- Prevent swelling. Do not hang your residual limb off the edge of the bed or chair. Wear a shrinker or a stretch bandage when sleeping.
- Maintain your body weight. Weight changes will cause the prosthesis to fit poorly and lead to skin breakdown.

Occupational Therapy TOOLKIT

Checking Your Skin

Check your skin ______ times, every day. Use a long-handled mirror.

Look for redness, bruises, blisters, swelling, rashes or sores. If you notice any problems, contact the doctor. Keep pressure off the area, until the redness is gone or the sore has fully healed. Find out what caused the problem. Make changes so it does not happen again.

Areas at risk of skin damage

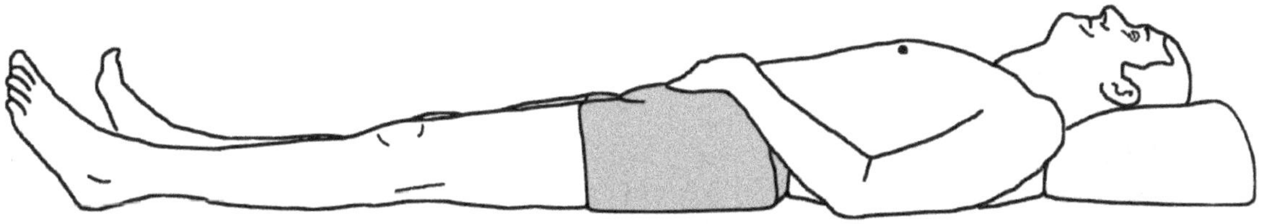

Heels   Sacrum   Elbows   Shoulder Blades   Back of Head

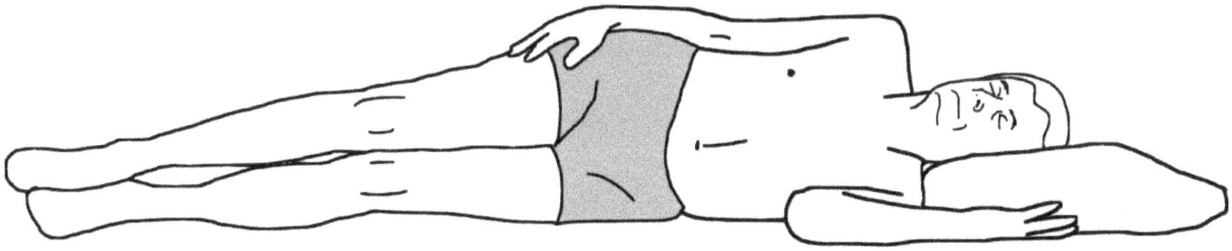

Ankle   Knees inside and outside   Hips   Ribs   Shoulder   Ear

---

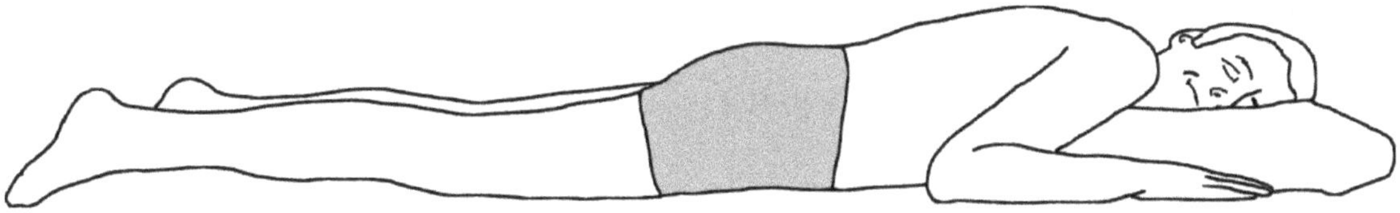

Toes   Knees   Penis   Hips   Breasts   Collar Bone   Cheeks

Notes: ____________________

____

____

____

Occupational Therapy TOOLKIT

Cognitive Strategies to Improve Movement

Cues You Think

- Begin all tasks by thinking, "I can" or "I will".
- Think about how you are going to move. Go over each step in your head. Think of the steps for drinking. "Reach forward, grasp cup, bend elbow, bring the cup to lips, tilt, drink, and swallow".
- Talk to yourself or aloud. Give yourself simple commands. For instance, if you shuffle when you walk say to yourself "Big Steps".
- During a freezing event, imagine a starting line on the floor and step over it.

Cues You Hear

- Have someone give you simple, short verbal cues. With walking, they can repeat "One, Two, One, Two" or "Left, Right, Left, Right" or "Big Steps".
- Use a metronome to help with start hesitation or freezing events. Focus on stepping in time to the beat. Set the beat-rate at 110-120 beats per minute for women and at 105-115 beats per minute for men.
- Move in time to the rhythm or to music.
- March in rhythm, while clapping, counting or tapping.

Cues You See

- If you have freezing episodes or trouble with turns, place colored tape on the floor as a guide. At turns, place them in a fan shape.
- Watch yourself in a mirror when getting dressed or doing other tasks.
- Watch someone else do the task.
- Write out the steps of a task on index cards. Read the cards to yourself, read them aloud or have someone else read them. Tackle one step at a time. Write out cue cards for tasks like eating, dressing, or bathing.

Controlled Cough

Controlled cough will help you move mucus from your lungs. It is good way to cough because it uses less effort. Coughing without control may cause the airways to spasm. Use the controlled cough after you use an inhaler or any time you need to cough.

1. Sit with both feet on the floor. Lean slightly forward. Relax your upper chest and shoulders.
2. Breathe slowly in through your nose.
3. Exhale through your mouth. Produce two or three short, sharp, controlled coughs or huffs. The first one or two will loosen the mucus and the last one will move the mucus up toward your mouth.
4. Keep breathing slowly in through your nose.
5. Repeat the controlled cough again. Exhale out through your mouth. Produce two or three short and sharp controlled coughs or huffs.
6. Spit mucus into a white tissue to check for color, amount and odor. Report any problems to the doctor.

Unless the doctor has said to limit fluids, drink plenty of fluid to thin mucus.

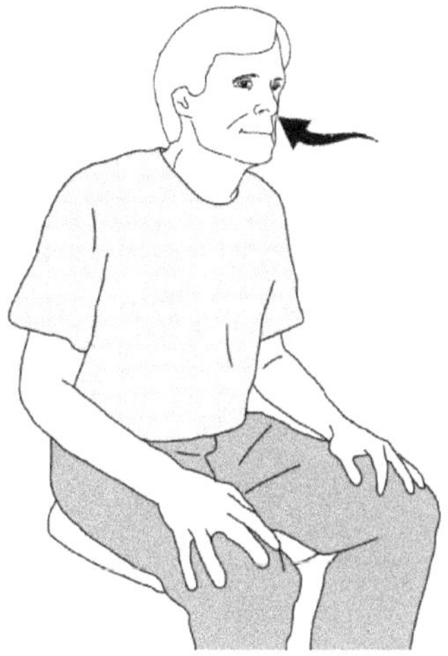

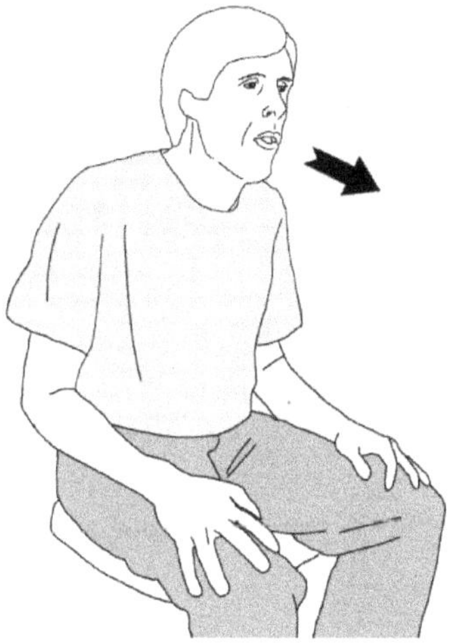

Daily Journal - Set Up

Choose a binder that has a clear panel on the front.

Add drawings, pictures or quotes to the cover sheet. Place in the front of the binder.

Add a calendar to the binder.

Label the sections:

- Personal Information
- Phone Numbers
- Monthly Calendar
- Daily Page
- Shopping Lists

Make copies of these pages:

- Personal Information (1 copy)
- Phone Numbers (2 copies)
- Daily Schedule (14 copies)
- Things to Recall about Today (14 copies)
- Shopping Lists (2 copies)

Fill out these pages:

- Personal Information
- Phone Numbers

Daily Journal - Tips for Using

Keep the journal and a pen with you.

Soon after you wake up, open the journal. Write the day and date on the left hand page of the Daily Schedule.

Check the Calendar and Daily Schedule for visits, alerts or medication times. Write them on the Daily Schedule.

Check off the items on the Daily Schedule that you complete.

Write" Things to Recall about Today" in your daily journal.

Add items to the shopping list.

Refer to the Daily Journal often.

Arrange to make copies of the journal pages before you run out.

Daily Schedule

Day

Month/Date

Year

Alerts, Visits Medications	
6 am	
7 am	
8 am	
9 am	
10 am	
11 am	
12 pm	
1 pm	
2 pm	
3 pm	
4 pm	
5 pm	
6 pm	
7 pm	
8 pm	
9 pm	
10 pm	

Things To Do Bills, Calls, Chores, Shopping	

Phone Numbers

Name	Phone Number	Relationship
		Medical doctor
		Pharmacy

Things to Remember about Today

Personal Information

Name:
Address:
Phone numbers:
In Case of Emergency:
Age and Date of Birth:
Medical History:

Shopping List

Daily Tasks after Back (Lumbar) Surgery

Safety Tips
- Keep pathways clear of objects, shoes, toys, scatter rugs or other items.
- Use a reacher to pick small objects up from the floor.
- Do not pull up on handrails, use only for guidance. Count the steps to help you keep track of when the last step is coming.

Showering
- Do not take tub baths or swim until cleared by the doctor.
- Do not shower until cleared by the doctor.
- Do not bend or twist when bathing. Use a long-handled bath sponge, hand held shower and a bath chair.

Dressing
- Do not twist or bend when getting dressed.
- Put on clothes while lying on your back.
- Do not bend at your waist. Bring one foot up to your other knee.
- Use long-handled dressing tools.

Using the Toilet
- Use a raised toilet seat or a bedside commode.
- Do not twist. Put the toilet paper within reach.
- Do not twist. Flush the toilet after standing.

Task at the Sink or Counter
- Stand with one foot in front of the other.
- Brace yourself with one hand on the counter.
- Bend at your hips and knees, not at your waist.

Meals
- Keep items within safe and easy reach on the counter and in the refrigerator.
- Use smaller bottles for milk and juice.
- Do not to lift items that weigh more than _____ lb/kg.

Notes:
- ______________________________
- ______________________________
- ______________________________
- ______________________________

Occupational Therapy TOOLKIT

Daily Tasks after Neck (Cervical) Surgery

Safety Tips
- Keep pathways clear of objects, shoes, toys, scatter rugs or other items.
- Use a reacher to pick small objects up from the floor.
- Do not pull up on handrails, use only for guidance. Count the steps to help you keep track of when the last step is coming.

Showering
- Do not take tub baths or swim until cleared by the doctor.
- Do not shower until cleared by the doctor. Wear the Philadelphia collar in the shower, if ordered.
- Do not bend or twist when bathing. Use a long-handled bath sponge, hand held shower and a bath chair.

Grooming
- Shave with an electric razor while lying on your back. In this position, you can remove the front part of the brace. Do not stand at the sink with the brace off.
- Use a cup to rinse your mouth, instead of spitting into the sink.

Dressing
- Do not twist or bend when getting dressed.
- Put on clothes while lying on your back.
- Do not bend at your waist. Bring one foot up to your other knee.
- Use long-handled dressing tools.

Using the Toilet
- Use a raised toilet seat or a bedside commode.
- Do not twist. Put the toilet paper within reach.
- Do not twist. Flush the toilet after standing.

Eating
- Use straws to drinks. Keep your neck aligned in neutral.
- Eat slowly and take small bites.
- Place a plate out away from your body to see the food. Raise the plate on a couple of books.
- Do not lean forward over the table or place your elbows on the table.

Meal Prep
- Keep items within safe and easy reach on the counter and in the refrigerator.
- Use smaller bottles for milk and juice.
- Do not to lift items that weigh more than _____ lb/kg.

Notes:
- ____
- ____

Daily Tasks after Open Heart Surgery

Washing Your Hair
- Use both arms at the same time to wash your hair.
- Bend your neck forward to make it easier.

Taking a Shower
- Use a shower chair to help you conserve energy.

Putting on a Shirt
- Put both your arms into the sleeves and then pull the shirt over your head.

Putting on Pants, Socks and Shoes
- For the first two weeks, do not reach past your knees.
- Use a dressing stick, sock aid and a long shoehorn.

Getting Out of Bed

Cross your arms over your chest. Roll over to your side. Drop both legs off the side. Use your trunk muscles to sit up.

Getting Out of a Chair

To stand, use your leg muscles. Use your arms only for balance.

Options to Avoid Lifting

Slide items along the counter.
Buy milk, juice in small bottles.
Keep items on easy-to-reach shelves.

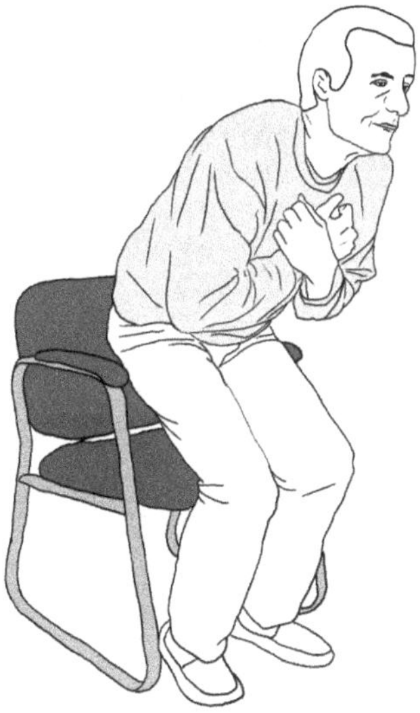

Daily Tasks after Shoulder Surgery

Follow precautions for _____ weeks.

Shoulder Sling

- Wear the shoulder sling most of the time. Only remove it to bath, dress and when doing your arm exercises.
- Place your elbow at a right angle. Keep your hand level with your elbow or a little higher.

Self-Care

- Remove the shoulder sling to bath and dress. Do not move your affected arm away from your body. Support your arm in the same position as the sling using some pillows.
- Bend over at your waist and let your affected arm passively come away from your body to wash under your arm.
- Dress your affected arm first and remove clothing from your affected arm last. Choose easy to put on clothes and shoes with Velcro or elastic closures.
- While in the sling, use your hand in front of your body. You can bend and straighten your elbow. Do not move your arm away from your body.
- Do not lean on your arm or bear weight on your affected arm. Do not use the affected arm to pull or push yourself up. Add a cushion to increase the height of the chair and the toilet by adding a raised toilet seat.
- Do not use your affected arm to reach behind your back. Do not tuck in a shirt or reach for toilet hygiene. Use a wiping aid to reach with your unaffected arm.

Sleeping

- Try to sleep while semi-reclined. Sleep in a chair that reclines or in a bed propped up on some pillows.
- To keep your affected arm in line with your body, wear the sling and put a pillow behind your elbow.

Notes:

- ______________________________
- ______________________________
- ______________________________
- ______________________________
- ______________________________
- ______________________________

Deep (Diaphragmatic) Breathing

Your diaphragm is a flat muscle that divides the chest and stomach. Using your diaphragm will increase the amount of oxygen that get into your lungs.

Locate your diaphragm

- Sit with back support. Loosen the waistband. Tilt your head forward a little. Relax your neck and shoulders.
- Place one hand on your stomach above your naval. Place your other hand on your chest.
- Find your diaphragm with a quick "sniff" or a few short pants. You will feel your diaphragm move with the hand on your stomach.

Practice deep (diaphragmatic) breathing

- Inhale deeply through your nose. Allow the hand on your stomach to rise. The hand on your chest should be still.
- Slowly exhale through pursed lips. Gently push with the hand that is on the stomach. The hand on your chest should be still.
- Practice your breathing during three, 10-minute sessions, every day.
- Stop if you feel dizzy or faint.

Occupational Therapy TOOLKIT

Desensitization

☐ Rub the tender (sensitive) areas with textures. Start with soft ones (cotton balls, velvet, and silk fabric). Progress to rougher textures (terry cloth, paper towels, and wool).

Use a fabric that is not pleasant, but not painful. Once you can bear the feeling, use the next texture.

Rub the texture in a circle for _____ seconds/minutes, _____ times a day.

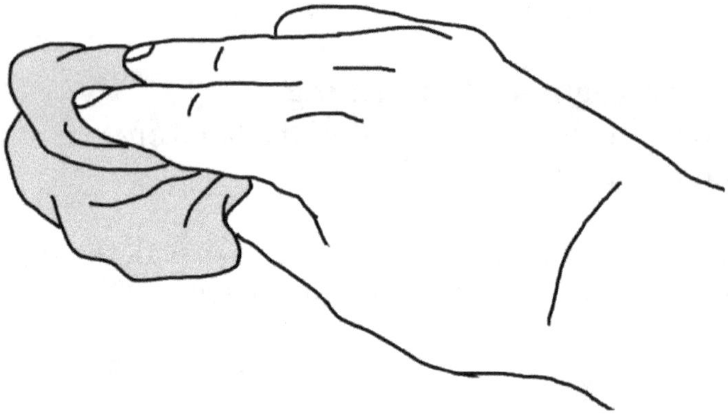

☐ Gently massage and apply pressure to the tender (sensitive) areas.

Massage for _____ seconds/minutes, _____ times a day.

☐ Gently tap the tender (sensitive) areas with your fingers.

Tap for _____ seconds/minutes, _____ times a day.

☐ Apply a small massager to the tender (sensitive) areas.

Vibrate for _____ seconds/minutes, _____ times a day.

Don't Let a Fall Get You Down

Tips to Lower the Risk For Falls

Don't Let a Fall Get You Down
Introduction

A fall is when a person, without meaning to, lands on the floor or ground.

Every person, old and young, is at risk for falling. 1 in 3 people over age 65 fall each year. As you age, the chance of getting hurt during a fall is much greater. You can prevent a fall. Falls do not have to be part of aging.

Falls can hurt you, make you less sure of yourself, make you afraid of falling and stop you from doing the things you enjoy.

What can I do to lower my fall risk?
Read this booklet and mark things about you, your home and your activities.

- Your Risk Factors
- Stay Active
- Create a Safe Home
- Be Safe Away From Home
- Feet, Footwear and Clothing
- Manage Your Health
- Know Your Medications
- Effect of a Fall
- If You Fall - What is next?

Review this booklet with your doctor, health care team and family.

Don't Let a Fall Get You Down
Your Risk Factors

Risk factors increase the chance of having a fall. The more risk factors you have, the higher the chance of falling. Most falls involve two or more risk factors. These risk factors combine to cause the fall. For example, having poor balance and walking on a slick surface. Some risk factors cannot change, like being over the age of 75. You can change many risk factors. Knowing our risk factors is the first step to lessen the risk of falls.

What can I do to lower my fall risk?
Check off the risk factors that apply to you. Read this booklet. Share what you learn with your family and your doctor.

- ☐ I am over the age of 75 years.
- ☐ I have low vision.
- ☐ I have arthritis, stroke, Parkinson's disease or heart disease.
- ☐ I take 4 or more medications every day.
- ☐ I take high-risk medications.
- ☐ I have dizziness.
- ☐ I have balance problems and/or problems with my walking.
- ☐ I have low blood pressure.
- ☐ I have had a recent illness and/or hospital stay.
- ☐ I have memory problems.
- ☐ I have weakness.
- ☐ I have foot problems.
- ☐ I fear falling.
- ☐ I carry items while using the stairs.
- ☐ I do not always use the handrails.
- ☐ I am not active.
- ☐ I rush to answer the phone.
- ☐ I wear clothing that is too long.
- ☐ I use a cane or walker that shows signs of wear or is not the correct height.
- ☐ I wear shoes or slippers that are unsafe.
- ☐ I climb on chairs to reach high items.
- ☐ I rush to the bathroom.
- ☐ My home has unsafe floor coverings.
- ☐ My home has poor lighting.
- ☐ I use unsafe furniture.
- ☐ My bathroom has slick surfaces.
- ☐ My stairs do not have handrails.
- ☐ I leave clutter on the floor.
- ☐ I use throw rugs in my home.
- ☐ My bathroom does not have grab bars.

Don't Let a Fall Get You Down
Stay Active

Active people are less likely to fall. If you do fall, you are less likely to be hurt. The more you sit, the greater the chance of falling and being hurt.

What can I do to lower my fall risk?
Talk with your doctor before start a new exercise program.

Take part in a moderate aerobic workout.

- Workout for at least 30 minutes, most days. The thirty minutes can be done in three 10-minute sessions.

- You should feel your heart rate and breathing increase. You should be able to talk, but not sing.

- Find something you enjoy. Try to walk, swim, dance, bowl, bike, or exercise with videos or in a class.

A good program also includes strength, balance, and stretching.

- Building strength will help you climb stairs, get out of a chair, and get in and out of a car.

  Work on your strength 2-3 times a week. Try hand weights, stretch bands, yoga, or exercise videos.

- Practice your balance throughout the day. Stand on one foot or stand with one foot in front of your other foot. Do this when you are brushing your teeth, washing the dishes or waiting in line.

  Work on your balance for 10-15 minutes, three days a week. Try Tai chi, non-contact boxing, dancing, balance ball, yoga.

- Stretch each day. This will help you reach, bend, stand up, and sit down with greater ease. You should stretch after aerobic and strength workouts.

Don't Let a Fall Get You Down
Create a Safe Home

More than 3 out of 4 falls occur in or around the home. Your home can put you at risk for a fall.

What can I do to lower my fall risk?
Conduct a walk-through of your home and yard. Look for problems that may lead to slips, trips or falls. With a few changes, you can decrease your risk of falling.

- Pay attention to the three major problems areas in the home.
    - Stairs
    - Bathroom
    - Bedroom
- Fix the most common hazards.
    - Pick up objects on the floor or ground.
    - Add grab bars in the bathroom.
    - Add hand rails on the stairs.
    - Increase lights inside and outside.
    - Put non-slip mats in the tub or shower.
- Use adaptive equipment.
    - Shower chair
    - Reacher
    - Bed and chair risers
- Remove hazards from the floor, pathways and stairs.
    - Remove throw rugs.
    - Move phone and lamp cords out of pathways.
    - Move sofas, chairs, table to allow clear pathways.
    - Remove hazards from walkways (leaves, moss, and ice).
    - Repair holes in walkways, wrinkles in carpet.
    - Never leave anything on the stairs.
- Move and do tasks with care.
    - Hold onto handrails and grab bars.
    - Do not rush, slow down and pick up your feet.
    - Do not climb on chairs or wobbly ladders.
    - Do not use chairs that have wheels.
    - Hold on to something steady when reaching for the floor.
    - Turn on the lights before going into a dark room. Use nightlights.
    - Remove your reading glasses before walking or using the stairs.
    - Do not leave items on the floor (shoes, the paper, books, blankets, pillows, phone cords, bedspreads, dirty clothes, pet toys, trash).
    - Never use your cell phone while walking.

Don't Let a Fall Get You Down
Be Safe Away From Home

Whether you are walking around the park or going to the store, falls can happen. You do not have any control over risks away from home so stay alert. Others may leave items in your path; your path may have hazards such as potholes, broken sidewalks, turned up mats, wet floors; there may not be handrails, grab bars, curb cuts, or ramps; the lighting may be poor.

What can I do to lower my fall risk?
Take your time, slow down, and be aware of the area. Focus your vision about six steps ahead. This will give yourself time to adjust your steps and avoid hazards.

Watch for items in your path. Boxes, trash, doormats, thresholds, uneven walkways, and tree roots can trip you.

Do not walk in crowded places. Shop when stores are not busy.

Be extra alert during and after stormy weather. Rain, snow, and ice can make the ground slick.

Use caution on stairs. Hold onto the handrail. Be aware that the step height may be higher or lower than normal.

Use a cane or walker in public. A walking aid will remind others to be more careful.

Keep a flashlight with you or use the flashlight feature on your phone. Light your path at night or in dark places like a movie theatre.

Call ahead and ask about the bathrooms, ramps, and lighting.

Ask for a tour when going to someone's home. Alert yourself to flooring changes, steps, and the bathroom location.

Plan before you travel. When flying, ask for assistance to and from the gate and plane. Have your ticket or money ready. Travel at non-peak times. When using local transit, ask the driver to wait until you are in your seat. Keep a hand free to hold on. Do not leave the seat when the vehicle is moving.

Occupational Therapy TOOLKIT

Don't Let a Fall Get You Down
Feet, Footwear and Clothing

Foot problems can be painful and affect your walking. Your feet can give you an early warning about health problems. Feet that are healthy and pain-free, help you stay active.

What can I do to lower my fall risk?

Feet

- Don't shuffle. Pick up your feet when you walk.
- Exercise your feet.
- Inspect your feet every day. Check for redness, blisters, cuts, sores, cracks, swelling or loss of feeling. If you notice any changes, call the doctor.
- See the doctor if you cannot cut your toenails.
- See the doctor if foot problems limit walking.
- Diabetes can cause sensory loss in your feet. Have your feet tested every year.

Footwear

- Choose shoes that have these features:
  - well-fitting
  - good support
  - lightweight
  - low, broad heel
  - thin, non-slip sole.
  - close with laces or Velcro
- Do not wear slip-on shoes, slippers, or walk without shoes.

Clothing

- Do not wear pants or dresses that are too long. Do not wear loose robes or let robe ties hang. Both can cause you to trip.
- Do not wear clothes with wide, open pockets. Do not wear clothes with sleeves are too long, too open or too wide. Both can catch doorknobs and stair rails.

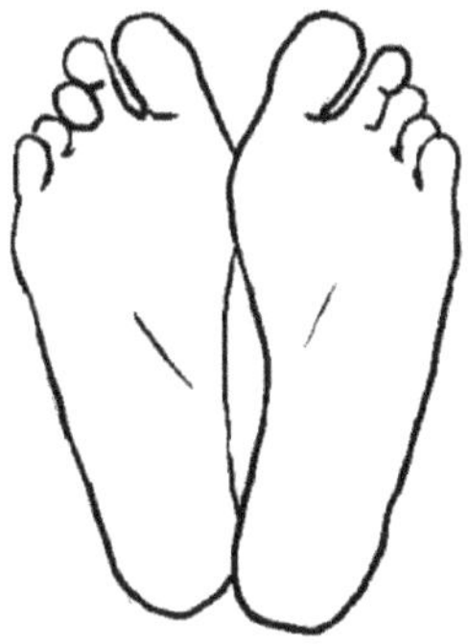

Don't Let a Fall Get You Down
Manage Your Health

Your health can put you at a higher risk for a fall. Osteoporosis causes bones to become weaken and fracture. Low blood pressure or a heart problem can cause you to be dizzy. Parkinson's disease, arthritis and stroke can affect your movement and reaction time. Diabetes can cause fainting if your blood sugar levels are low. Even a short-term illness can increase the risk of falling.

What can I do to lower my fall risk?
Have check-ups with the doctor to be sure you stay healthy.

Make the most of the doctor visits. Bring a list of questions and concerns. Repeat things back to the doctor in your words. Take notes. Bring a friend.

Keep your mind and body active.

Eat at least three meals every day. Enjoy eating from the five food groups. Drink plenty of water.

Have your eyesight tested at least once a year. More often if you have an eye condition.

Sitting or lying for more than 20 minutes can lower your blood pressure. When you get up you may feel dizzy. Sit on the edge of the bed or chair for a few minutes. Pump your ankles 10 times. Stand up. Pause for the count of 10. Take a slow, deep breath before you move.

If you have a fever, vomit or loose stools, you may become dehydrated. This can lead to weakness and a fall. Drink fluids, call the doctor, and arrange for in-home help.

Don't Let a Fall Get You Down
Know Your Medications

Some medications may increase the risk for falling.

- Medications that affect your brain. They may be used for sleep problems, anxiety, psychosis, seizures. depression, pain, motion sickness, nausea, and itching. They can cause sedation or drowsiness.
- Medications that lower blood pressure. They can cause a sudden drop in blood pressure. They can make you feel dizzy and faint.
- Medications that treat diabetes. They can cause low blood sugar. They can make you feel faint, and lightheaded.

What can I do to lower my fall risk?
Ask the doctor if you take any medications that may increase the risk for falling. If you are, ask if you can switch to a safer choice, lower the dose or stop taking the medicine. Do not stop any medication without talking to the doctor.

Take an active role in your health. Ask questions. Know what medications you are taking; what they are for; when to take them; and what the side effects are.

Keep an up-to-date medicine list with you and on the refrigerator. Review the list at all health care visits.

Ask the doctor or pharmacist before taking any over-the-counter medications or supplements.

Always take medications as directed. It may be easier to keep track if you use a pill box.

Talk to your doctor if you are worried about side effects or if your medication is not helping. Do not stop any medication without talking to the doctor.

Use only one pharmacy for all prescriptions. The pharmacist can review all the medications you take and tell the doctors about any concerns.

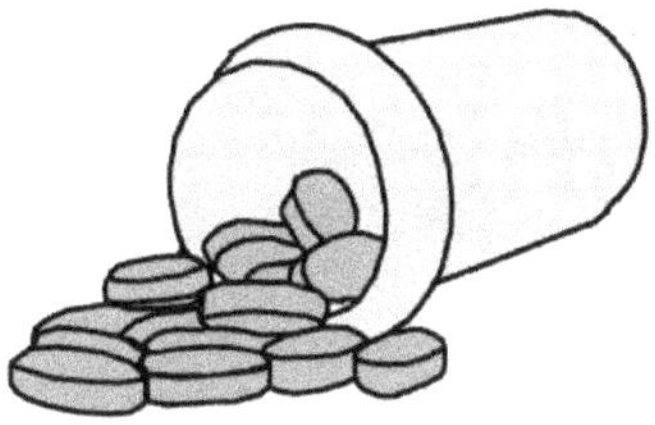

Don't Let a Fall Get You Down
Effects of a Fall

Three negative things can happen after a fall: physical injury, the fear of falling, and problems that result from not being able to get up from the floor.

Physical Injury
One in 10 falls will cause a severe injury.

What can I do to lower my fall risk?

Follow the tips given in this booklet. Stay active. Ask the doctor review all medications. Have your vision checked every year. Wear safe footwear. Remove tripping hazards at home. Add supports such as grab bars and handrails. Be careful and slow down.

Fear of Falling
Fear of falling is good when the task is high risk. Walking on ice is an example. We become more alert and careful.

Fear of falling is harmful when you do not trust your ability and you stop doing things.

What can I do to lower my fall risk?

- Talk to someone about your concerns.
- If you have a fall, fill out a *Post-Fall Survey*. Learn what caused the fall. Find out what you can do to reduce the chance of falling again.
- See a PT about a walking device.

Not Able to Get Up From the Floor
About half of the older adults who fall cannot get back up without help. The longer someone lays on the ground, the greater the risk of problems.

What can I do to lower my fall risk?

- Learn how to get up from the floor
- If you live alone, arrange to call someone daily at a set time.
- Carry a cell phone or a medical alert device.

Don't Let a Fall Get You Down
If You Fall - What's Next

No one plans to fall, but it is good to know what to do in case you do fall.

1. Do not panic. Take some slow, deep breaths. Take a minute to collect yourself. If you try to get up to quickly, you may do more harm.
2. Check if you are hurt.
3. If you are hurt or you cannot get off the floor, see the **Rest and Wait Plan**.
4. If you are not hurt and can get off the floor, see the **Up and About Plan**.

Rest and Wait Plan

1. Get help.
    - Use a cell phone or medical alert device.
    - Try to reach a phone and call emergency services at _____.
    - Attract someone's attention by banging on the wall or floor and shouting.
    - Crawl or slide to the front door and call for help.
2. Rest and wait for help to arrive.
3. If you lose control of your bladder, try to move away from the damp area.
4. Try not to stay in one place. Roll to the side and move your arms and legs. Keep pressure off any one area.

Up and About Plan

1. Roll onto your hands and knees and crawl to a sturdy chair.
2. Place your hands on the chair. Put your stronger foot flat on the floor.
3. Lean forward and put your weight onto your arms. Push up to with your legs and arms until you are standing.
4. Turn around and sit down. Rest there until you feel ready to stand.

Every Fall Needs Medical Help

Get medical help now if you are hurt in any way, but especially if you have a blow to your head, loss of alertness, signs of confusion or you take a blood thinner.

Make an appointment with the doctor if there is no injury. You want to know what caused the fall and what you can do to prevent another one. A fall may be the first sign of a medical problem.

Don't Let a Fall Get You Down
Post-Fall Survey

If you fall, you will want to know what caused the fall and what you can do to prevent another one. A fall may be the first sign of a medical problem. Please fill out this survey if you ever have a fall. Share it with your doctor, health care team and family.

1. What was the date and time of the fall? ______________________

2. Where did the fall occur? ______________________________________

3. Did you fall backward or forward? ________________________________

4. Did you have any symptoms before you fell (uneven heart rate, shortness of breath, chest pain, dizzy or faint)?
   ____
   ____

4. Did you pass out?
   ____

5. What was your mental state (alert, sleepy, confused)?
   ____
   ____

6. Have you had any recent changes in your medications? ______________
   If yes, list changes ____

7. What were you doing when you fell?
   ____
   ____

8. Were there any environmental or situational factors involved (clothing, shoes, rushing, furniture, rugs, cords, clutter)?
   ____
   ____
   ____

9. Could you get back up without help after falling? If you could not get up, how long was it before you received help? How did you call for help? _________
   ____

1 of 2

Don't Let a Fall Get You Down
Post-Fall Survey

10. Did you have any injuries? Did you see a doctor?

11. Since this fall, have you changed your actions in any way (avoided activities, made changes to your home)?

12. Since this fall how do you feel?

12. What could you have done to prevent this fall?

13. Comments

2 of 2

Edema (Swelling) Control of the Arm(s)

☐ Raise your arm above the level of your heart, as much as you can.

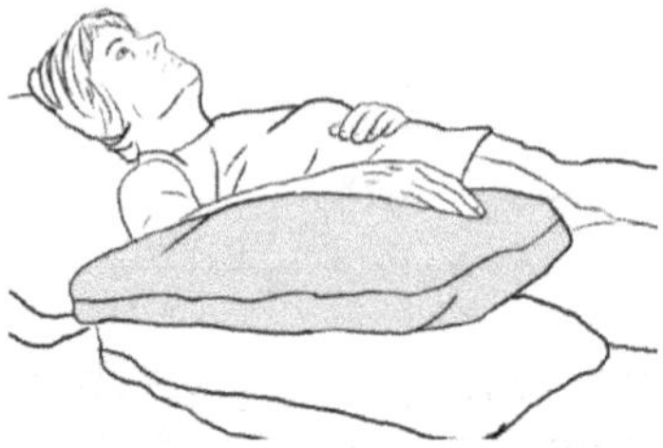

☐ Apply a cold pack to your shoulder-elbow-wrist-hand (circle). It should not be colder than 59° F (15°C).

Apply cold pack for _____ minutes, _____ times a day.

☐ Lightly massage your hand and arm with lotion. Start at your fingers and move up toward your shoulder.

Massage for _____ minutes, _____ times a day.

☐ Wear a compression sleeve or stockinet. Wear a compression glove with the seams facing out.

Wear the glove or stockinet _________________________.

☐ Apply elastic therapeutic tape to _________________________.

☐ Move your arm up and down as you squeeze a soft ball.

Repeat _____ times, _____ times a day.

Edema (Swelling) Control of the Leg(s)

☐ Keep your leg(s) up, as much as you can. Support your leg(s) with a pillow under your calf.

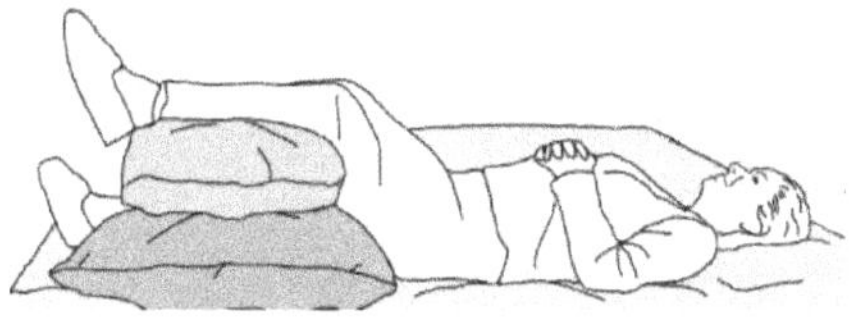

☐ Apply a cold pack to your hip-knee-ankle-foot (circle). It should not be colder than 59°F (15°C).

Apply cold pack for _____ minutes, _____ times a day.

☐ Lightly massage your foot and leg with lotion. Start at your foot and move up toward your hip.

Massage for _____ minutes, _____ times a day.

☐ Wear a compression stocking.

Wear the stocking __________________________.

☐ Apply elastic therapeutic tape to ____________________________________.

☐ Pump your ankles _________ times a day.

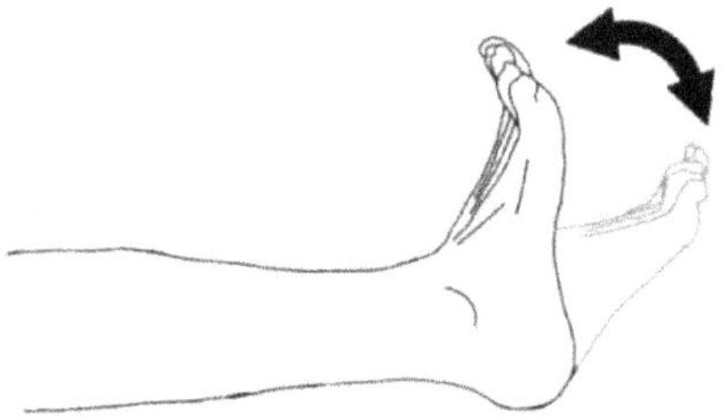

Fall Triggers and Tips to Prevent Falls
Therapist Resource

Fall Triggers	Examples	Tips to Prevent Falls
Being distracted when walking or moving between surfaces.	- Doing two tasks at the same time. - Walking and talking. - Walking and looking at a cell phone.	- Use your full attention and concentration. Practice mindfulness. - Carry items in pocket, a fanny pack or use a walker bag or walker tray. - Avoid non-essential talking. - If you need to speak, stop and hold onto something stable.
Hurrying or rushing while walking or moving between surfaces.	- Rushing to answer the phone. - Rushing to answer the doorbell. - Rushing to use the bathroom.	- Locate phone in more convenient location. Use a cell phone or portable phone. - Install intercom and camera system. - Use a voiding schedule. Move location by using a bedside commode.
Reaching down to the floor.	- Picking up dirty clothes, the newspaper or wiping up a spill.	- Do not place items on the floor. - Use long-handled reacher.
Reaching forward.	- Reaching for the light switch, reaching into a cupboard.	- Get close as you can to the task. - Hold onto counter or doorframe for stability.
Reaching up.	- Reaching up to a cupboard or closet shelf, hanging up clothes.	- Get close as you can to the task. - Stand with your feet shoulder-width apart and place one foot a step forward. - Hold onto counter or doorframe for stability.
Closing eyes while standing.	- Closing eyes to wash your face and or hair.	- Sit on a shower chair or bench to wash your face and/or hair. - Hold onto a grab bar.

Fall Triggers and Tips to Prevent Falls
Therapist Resource

Fall Triggers	Examples	Tips to Prevent Falls
Standing on one foot.	- Putting on pants, socks, or shoes. - Washing feet. - Stepping over the tub or shower edge.	- Sit on a sturdy armchair to place pants over your feet and to put on socks and shoes. - Sit on a shower chair or bench to wash your feet. - Hold onto a grab bar.
Walking backwards.	- Opening doors (cupboard, stove, etc.). - Stepping back to get out of the way of something or someone. - Backing in to a chair.	- Stand to side to open a door. - Take slow steps, sideways. 
Changing direction or turning.	- Turning to sit into a chair, the commode or on the bed. - Turning around after getting an item from the refrigerator, closet or cupboard. - Turning around at the end of a hallway.	- Do not reach for the armrest before turning fully. - When turning to sit down, step around slowly and with purpose. 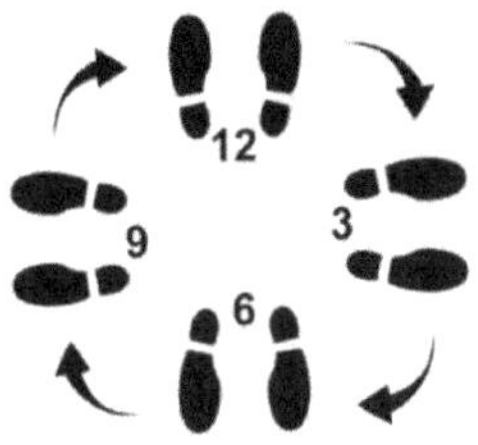 - Stop and focus on stepping feet in an arc, instead of a pivot turn. 

Occupational Therapy TOOLKIT

Fatigue Journal

Date: ________________________ Activity: ___________________________________

What time did the task start? ___________ How long did the task last? ___________

On a scale of 1-10, rate your level of fatigue **before** the activity.

1	2	3	4	5	6	7	8	9	10

None extreme

On a scale of 1-10, rate your level of fatigue **after** the activity.

1	2	3	4	5	6	7	8	9	10

None extreme

How long did it take to recover? _________________

What can you do to conserve energy and reduce fatigue?

____

____

____

Date: ________________________ Activity: ___________________________________

What time did the activity start? _________ How long did the activity last? _________

On a scale of 1-10, rate your level of fatigue **before** the activity.

1	2	3	4	5	6	7	8	9	10

None extreme

On a scale of 1-10, rate your level of fatigue **after** the activity.

1	2	3	4	5	6	7	8	9	10

None extreme

How long did it take to recover? _________________

What can you do to conserve energy and reduce fatigue?

____

____

____

Foot Care and Foot Safety

Check Your Feet

- Check your feet every day. Use good lighting and use your glasses. If you cannot check your feet, ask for help.
- Feel your feet for changes in temperature. Your feet should feel warm all over and not have any hot spots. Feel for areas that are tender or swollen.
- Look at all parts of your feet: the top and bottom, the sides and heels, the toes and toenails and between each toe. Look for color changes, blisters, cuts, sores, cracks. Use a hand mirror to view all areas.
- If you notice any changes, contact the doctor.

Protect Your Feet

- Always keep your feet clean and dry.
- If you swim, protect your feet with Vaseline and swim shoes.
- Do not walk without shoes at home or outside.
- Do not use tape, band-aids, cushion pads, or other products on your feet. Unless okay with the doctor.
- Always check the water temperature using your elbow before getting in the bath or shower.
- Do not use hot water bottles, hot or cold packs, heating pads or heat lamps near your feet. Unless okay with the doctor.
- Loosen the blankets at the bottom of the bed to reduce pressure on your toes.

Skin Care

- Wash your feet and toes every day.
- Use a mild soap and warm water. Rinse well.
- Do not soak your feet for more than a few minutes.
- Pat your feet dry with a soft towel. Dry between your toes.
- Use lotion on your feet and legs. Do not use lotion between your toes.

Nail care.

- Cut toenails straight across.
- Use a nail file to smooth the corners of your nails.
- Do not cut your skin around your nail bed.
- Have the doctor treat ingrown toenails, calluses or corns.
- Have your toenails cut by a doctor if you have trouble seeing your feet, cannot reach your toes, or if you have thick toenails.

Foot Care and Foot Safety

Socks

- Do not wear shoes without socks.
- Select seamless, well-fitting socks that wick away moisture.
- Change socks every day, more often if your feet perspire.
- Do not wear socks that are too tight and leave marks on your skin.
- Do not wear socks that are too loose and bunch up inside the shoes.
- Avoid socks that have mends, holes or thick seams.

Shoes

- Wear shoes that fit well and allow plenty of room for your toes.
- Do not wear pointed-toe shoes, open-toe shoes, sandals, flip flops, high heels or hard soles.
- Inspect shoes every day. Look for cracks in the soles, wrinkles in the lining or objects inside the shoes.
- Do not use pads, insoles or inserts in shoes.
- Do not lace shoes too tight or too loose. You should be able to fit a finger between the shoe and your heel.
- Rest your feet, remove shoes and put your feet up.

New Shoes

- Buy shoes late in the day, when your feet are largest.
- Shoes should fit well when you buy them.
- Select a full-service shoe store and have your feet measured.
- Try on both the right and left shoe. If your feet are not the same size, buy for your larger foot.

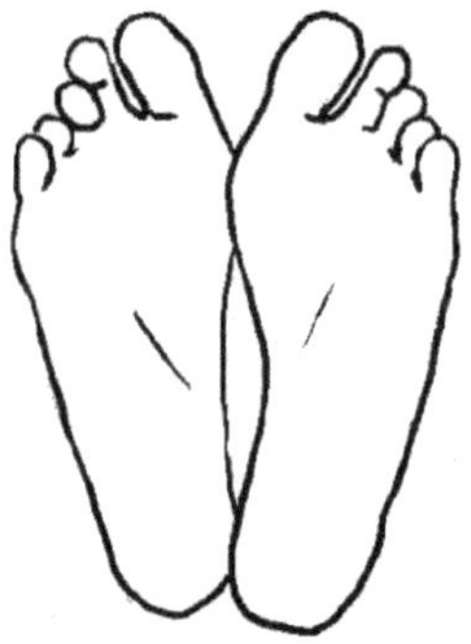

Functional Cognitive Activities
Therapist Resource

Communication
- Write thank-you cards.
- Complete written applications and medical forms.
- Use a calendar or day planner.
- Make and use a memory book.
- Use the white or yellow pages (print book or online).
- Use the phone for phone calls and/or texting.
- Use the computer and /or internet.
- Make a list of phone numbers.

Healthcare
- Schedule future healthcare visits.

Medication Management
- Set up medication schedule and pill box.

Leisure
- Play board games, card games, puzzles.
- Follow written directions for a craft or game.
- Read newspaper and magazines.
- Use the TV guide.

Meal Preparation
- Follow a recipe.
- Follow instructions on food box.
- Understand food labels.
- Plan meals

Money Management
- Use money to pay for goods.
- Pay bills online or write a check.
- Manage bank accounts.
- Place an order from a take-out menu.
- Place an order from a catalog or online.

Shopping
- Clip coupons.
- Write a grocery list.
- Write a budget.
- Estimate cost of items.

Community Tasks
- Shop at a store
- Arrange for transportation.
- Follow a map.
- Keep an appointment.

Good Posture

Using good posture will limit stress on your back.

Lying Posture

- Stretch your back muscles. Lie on your stomach for 20 minutes every day.
- Sleep on a firm mattress. A king or queen size bed allows room to move.
- Use only one pillow under your head. If you need to raise your head, use a foam wedge.
- The best posture for sleeping is on your side. Bend knees slightly with a pillow in between.
- Place pillows under your calves when lying on your back.
- Use a log roll to get out of bed. Keep your back straight. Log roll to one side and sit up. Use your arms to help.

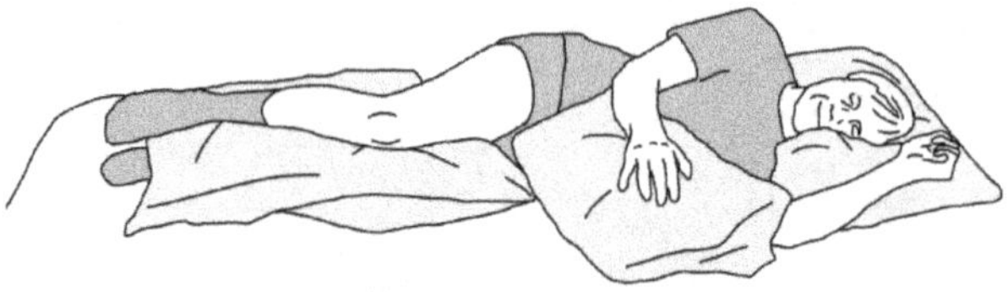

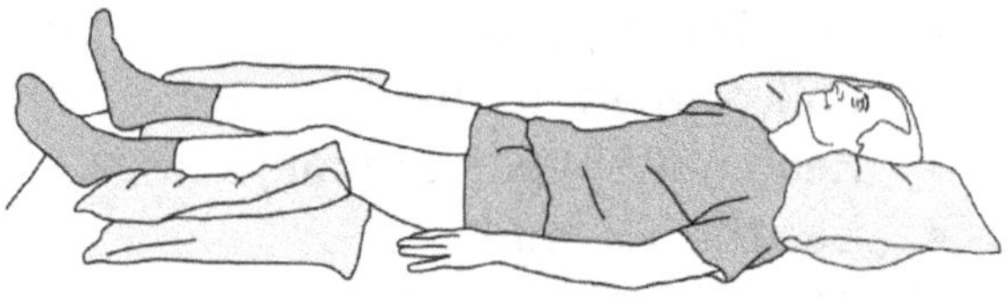

Standing Posture

- Stand up tall. Hold your head straight and tuck in your chin. Bring your shoulders back and down. Tighten your stomach muscles. Tuck in your tailbone.
- Check your posture by standing with your back against a wall.
- Keep tasks at a relaxed height. If you have to bend over, raise the height of the task.
- To wash dishes or iron, put one foot on a small stepstool or inside the cupboard. This will reduce the strain on your low back.
- Do not stand for more than 20-30 minutes. Walk around or do some stretches.

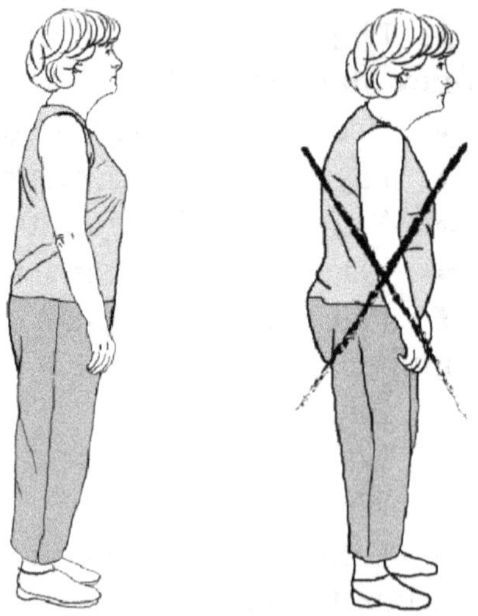

Good Posture

Sitting Posture

- Choose a chair that allows you to rest both feet flat on the floor.
- Your knees should be at the same height, or a bit higher, than your hips
- Place your bottom toward the back of the chair. Use a lumbar support or a rolled towel to support your lower back.
- Use padded armrests to support the weight of your arms. This allows your neck and shoulders to relax.
- Keep your upper back and neck straight.
- Do not sit for more than 20-30 minutes. Stand up, walk around or do some stretches.
- At a desk, prop materials up so your head does not tilt down.
- When reading or knitting, put a pillow on your lap to raise the items. This will help keep your back straight.
- If you use a computer, place the screen at or slightly below eye level.
- Use a headset or the phone speaker when you use the phone.

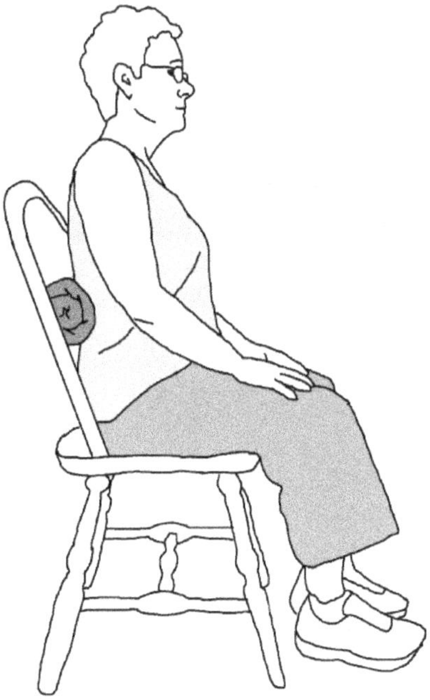

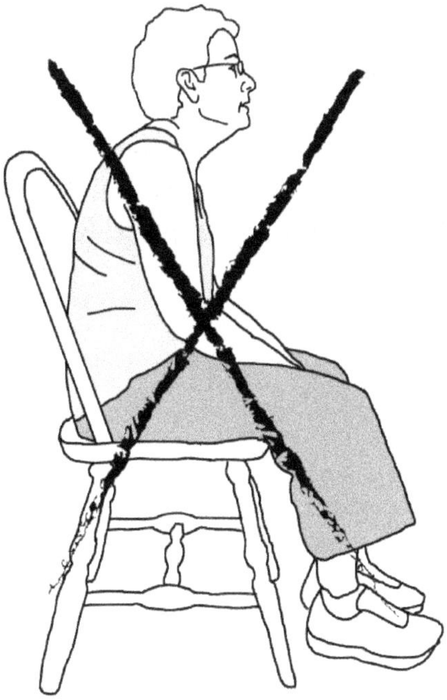

Good Sleep Habits

Daily Habits

- Spend time in the sunlight every day.
- Get regular exercise. Do not work out within four hours of bedtime.
- Do not have caffeine after lunch (coffee, tea and sodas, or chocolate).
- Try not to take a daytime nap. If you do, limit the time to 20 minutes.
- Stick to a set bedtime and wake time.
- If frequent trips to the toilet are a problem, try not drinking too much before bedtime. Go to bed with an empty bladder.
- Do not drink liquor in the evening. It might help you fall asleep, but you will wake in the night.
- Do not smoke close to bedtime.
- Do not eat within 2 hours of bedtime.

Sleeping Room

- Keep the room cool.
- Block out noise, and reduce as much light as you can.
- Reserve the bed for sleep and intimacy.
- Do not watch TV or use tablets and cell phones in bed.

Getting Ready For Bed

- Do not take worries to bed.
- Have a bedtime routine to help you relax. Take a warm bath, read, or stretch.
- Do not lie in bed for a long time trying to go to sleep. After 30 minutes, get up and do something quiet. Read or listen to quiet music. Then try again to fall asleep.

Handwriting - Component Exercises

Circles - both ways

Lines

Loops

Hills and points

Handwriting - Cursive Exercises

Wave shapes

c a d g o q

Point shapes

t i j p u w y

Loop shapes

l e b k h f

Hill shapes

n m v x z

Other shapes

r s

Handwriting - Pangrams

A pangram is a sentence that has all the letters of the alphabet.

The job requires extra pluck and zeal from every young wage earner. (54 letters)

A quart jar of oil mixed with zinc oxide makes a very bright paint. (53 letters)

The quick brown fox jumps over a lazy dog. (33 letters)

The five boxing wizards jump quickly. (31 letters)

Hip Dislocation Precautions - Posterior Approach

Follow precautions for 6-12 weeks after surgery or until the doctor tells you to stop.

DO NOT Bend Your Trunk Forward More Than 90°
DO NOT Lift Your Knee on Your Affected Side Higher Than Your Hip

- Do not sit down in the bathtub. Use a shower chair.
- Do not lean forward past your knees to put on clothing or wash your feet. Use long-handled dressing tools. Do not pick up something from the floor or reach for the walker.
- Do not bring your knee up to your chest.
- Be careful when getting up and down. Keep your affected leg out front.
- Do not sit on a low chair or sofa. Raise height by adding pillows.
- Do not sit on a standard toilet. Use a raised toilet seat
- Do not sit in chairs without armrests.

DO NOT Bring Your Affected Leg Past the Center of Your Body

- Do not cross your legs or ankles.
- Always keep your knees apart.
- When sitting or lying down, keep a pillow or wedge between your knees.
- Keep your legs apart and pivot your whole body when getting out and in bed.
- Do not lie on your affected hip without talking to your doctor.

DO NOT Rotate or Twist Your Affected Leg Inward

- Do not twist to your side to reach for objects.
- Do not pivot on your affected leg. To turn or reach, take small steps.
- Do not point your toes inward. Keep your toes pointed forward. Use a pillow or wedge between your knees.

Occupational Therapy TOOLKIT

Home Safety and Performance Assessment
Therapist Resource

Name: Date:

Address: Phone:

Who was present during the home safety assessment:

Type of dwelling:	☐ Own	☐ Apartment/condo	☐ One floor
	☐ Rent	☐ Town/row house	☐ Two floor
	☐	☐ Single Family	☐ Three floor

Lives with: (include pets)

Have there been any falls in the past 6 months? Describe setting, activity, what happened, result.

What safety needs, concerns and goals do the client and/or others have?

Assistive device used to access the home

☐ none ☐ cane ☐ walker ☐ rollator ☐ standard wheelchair ☐ scooter or electric w/c

Personal fall risk factors

☐ Low vision	☐ Orthostatic hypotension
☐ Uses walking device	☐ Fear of falling
☐ Risk taking behavior	☐ Takes high-risk medications
☐ Takes 4 or more medications	☐ Prior falls
☐ Foot problems	☐
☐ Chronic illnesses	☐
☐ Walking and balance problems	☐

Home Safety and Performance Assessment
Therapist Resource

Exterior and Access to the Home

Lighting on stairs/ramp/sidewalk/porch/driveway is good	Yes	No
Pathways are in safe condition and not slick or uneven (cracks in sidewalk, moss covered)	Yes	No
Pathways are free of hazards (debris, leaves, garden hose, newspapers, overhanging plants/scrubs, doormat)	Yes	No
Handrails installed on both sides of the stairs/steps	Yes	No
Handrails are secure and easy to grip (less than 6.25 inches/13 cm diameter).	Yes	No
All exterior doors are wide enough to allow walker/wheelchair	Yes	No
All thresholds for the exterior doors are low and beveled	Yes	No
House numbers visible on the home	Yes	No
Client safely ascends and descends the outside stairs/steps	Yes	No
Client locks/unlocks, opens/closes, door/screen door/sliding door	Yes	No
Client carries items into house	Yes	No
Client obtains the mail and newspaper	Yes	No
Client uses elevator safely and manages controls (if applicable)	Yes	No

Foyer and Hallways

Lighting in the foyer and hallways is good.	Yes	No
Nightlight present in the hallway.	Yes	No
Throw rugs, mats, runners are non-slip and out of traffic areas.	Yes	No
Throw rugs are not located on top of carpeting.	Yes	No
Flooring or carpeting is in safe condition (not curled or wrinkled, no loose areas or holes)	Yes	No
Foyer and hallways is clear of tripping hazards and furniture (shoes, mail, cords, newspapers, umbrellas)	Yes	No
All interior doors and pathways are wide enough for walker or wheelchair	Yes	No
All thresholds for the interior doors are low and beveled	Yes	No
Client opens/closes all doors and closets.	Yes	No
Client turns on lights before entering a room.	Yes	No
Client manages lamp switches and is able to changes light bulbs.	Yes	No

Kitchen

Lighting in the kitchen is good	Yes	No
Flooring is in safe condition and is non-slip	Yes	No
Floor is free of tripping hazards (food storage, pet bowls, trash)	Yes	No
The workspace near the cooking area is tidy	Yes	No
There is a low-pile, non-slip mat in front of the sink	Yes	No
Often-used items are stored between eye and knee level	Yes	No
Client can pick up items and clean spills from the floor	Yes	No
Client operates the faucets and garbage disposer	Yes	No

Home Safety and Performance Assessment
Therapist Resource

Kitchen (continued)

Client reaches items on upper shelves without using a stepstool	Yes	No
Client reaches items on lower shelves	Yes	No
Client retrieves items from refrigerator and freezer	Yes	No
Client operates stove, oven, microwave	Yes	No
Client safely moves hot items from stove, oven, microwave	Yes	No
Client carries meal items from kitchen to table	Yes	No
Client empties and disposes of trash	Yes	No
Client uses dining table and chair	Yes	No

Living Areas

Lighting in the living areas is good	Yes	No
Flooring and carpeting is in safe condition (not curled or wrinkled, no loose areas or holes)	Yes	No
All throw rugs are non-slip and are not on top of carpeting	Yes	No
All pathways are clear of tripping hazards (pillows, blankets, shoes, books, newspaper, low furniture, phone and electric cords)	Yes	No
All furniture is sturdy and secure (no wheels)	Yes	No
Client transfers to and from upholstered chair/sofa	Yes	No
Client opens and closes the windows	Yes	No
Client opens and closes the blinds/curtains/shades	Yes	No
Client can access and operate the thermostat and air conditioner	Yes	No

Interior Stairways or Steps

Lighting on the stairs and steps is good	Yes	No
Stairs, steps and landings are free of clutter, on both sides	Yes	No
Carpet and other floor covering is in good condition (not curled or wrinkled, no loose areas or holes)	Yes	No
Handrails are present on both sides of the stairs and steps	Yes	No
Handrails are secure and easy to grip (less than 6.25 in/13 cm in diameter)	Yes	No
Handrails extend beyond the top and bottom steps	Yes	No
Client descends and ascends stairs and steps safely	Yes	No
Client safely carries items up and down stairs safely	Yes	No
Client uses the stair-chair lift safely (if applicable)	Yes	No

Bedroom

Lighting in the bedroom is good	Yes	No
Lights can be turned on before entering the bedroom	Yes	No
There is a lamp next to the bed	Yes	No
The path to the bathroom is clear of hazards and well lit	Yes	No
All throw rugs are non-slip and not on top of carpeting	Yes	No

Home Safety and Performance Assessment
Therapist Resource

Bedroom (continued)

Flooring or carpeting is in safe condition (not curled or wrinkled, no loose areas or holes)	Yes	No
Floor free of tripping hazards (shoes, dirty clothes, bed coverings)	Yes	No
All pathways are free of furniture	Yes	No
The bed is stable and of appropriate height and firmness	Yes	No
There is a chair with armrests to use for dressing	Yes	No
Client transfers in and out of bed safely	Yes	No
Client able to manage the bed covers	Yes	No
Client able to carry clothes to dressing area	Yes	No
Client opens/closes the dresser drawers/doors	Yes	No
Client opens/closes the windows	Yes	No
Client opens/closes the blinds/curtains/shades	Yes	No

All Closets

Shelves and clothes poles are easy to reach	Yes	No
Closets organized so items are easy to find	Yes	No
Client able to remove and return items to closet rods/shelves	Yes	No

Bathroom

Lighting in the bathroom is good	Yes	No
There is a nightlight in the bathroom	Yes	No
All area rugs are non-slip and low pile	Yes	No
Flooring or carpeting is in safe condition (not curled or wrinkled, no loose areas or holes)	Yes	No
The floor is free of tripping hazards (supplies, towels, dirty clothes)	Yes	No
Grab bars installed in the tub/shower	Yes	No
There is a non-slip mat or other non-slip surface on the tub/shower floor	Yes	No
Supplies within the tub/shower can be reached	Yes	No
The water heater thermostat is set below 120°F/49°C	Yes	No
Client transfers to the toilet safely	Yes	No
Client transfers to the tub/shower safely	Yes	No
Towel bars not used for support	Yes	No
Client manages the shower/tub faucet and sets water temperature	Yes	No
Client reaches the toilet paper and flushes toilet	Yes	No
Client reaches items in the cupboards	Yes	No
Client does not rush to the bathroom	Yes	No

Other/Basement/Laundry Area

Lighting is good in all areas.	Yes	No

Home Safety and Performance Assessment
Therapist Resource

Other/Basement/Laundry Area (continued)

All throw rugs are non-slip and are not on top of carpeting	Yes	No
All pathways are clear of tripping hazards	Yes	No
Flooring or carpeting is in safe condition. (not curled or wrinkled, no loose areas or holes)	Yes	No
Client is able to transport clothes to and from laundry area	Yes	No
Laundry supplies can be reached easily and safely	Yes	No
Client able to get clothes in and out of the washer and dryer	Yes	No
Client able to access and operate machines	Yes	No
Client able to hand wash and hang clothes to dry	Yes	No
Client manages the ironing board and can iron clothes	Yes	No

Telephone

Phones are located on each level and in the bedroom (if applicable)	Yes	No
Phones reached from the floor (if applicable)	Yes	No
Emergency numbers posted by each telephone (if applicable)	Yes	No
Client has cell phone, carries easily, can operate	Yes	No
Client answers the phone without rushing	Yes	No
Client has a personal emergency response system and wears all the time	Yes	No

Fire Safety

There is a fire escape plan and emergency plan	Yes	No
Smoke detectors in working order, batteries changed every 12 months	Yes	No
Flammables are stored outside the oven or away from the stove	Yes	No
Fire sources (candles, heaters, smoking) are located away from upholstered furniture and bedding	Yes	No
Fire extinguishers current and easy to reach	Yes	No

Recommendations:

____

____

____

____

____

____

5 of 6

Home Safety and Performance Assessment
Therapist Resource

Recommendations:

6 of 6

How to Check Your Heart Rate

Turn your hand over. Place 2 fingers at the base of your thumb.

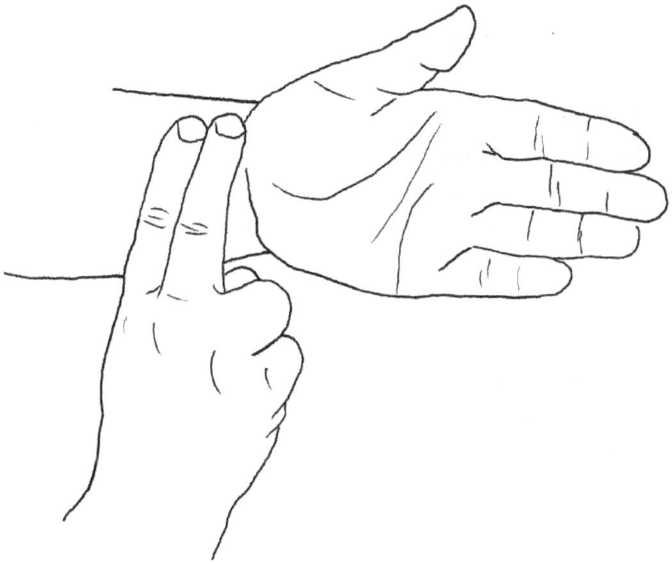

Feel your heart rate by pressing lightly in the little groove.

Watch a clock with a second hand. Count the beats for one minute. The number of times your heart beats in one minute is your heart rate. Write down the number of beats per minute (BPM).

Joint Protection and Energy Conservation for Wheelchair Users

Respect Pain
- Avoid or change the tasks that cause pain.
- Use the arm that is not painful.
- Ask for help with tasks that cause pain.

Balance Rest and Tasks
- Take frequent breaks or change the task.
- Do not hold your arms in one place for a long time.
- Plan the day. Switch between light and heavy tasks.
- Allow yourself enough time.

Maintain Strength and Range of Motion
- Exercise in a pain-free range.
- Do not push the wheelchair as an exercise.
- Move every day in a pain-free range.

Use Good Posture and Body Mechanics
- Use good posture.
- Use good skills with transfers.
- Keep objects within easy reach.
- Carry objects close to your body.
- Avoid reaching over your head.

Reduce the Effort Needed to Do the Job
- Use long, smooth strokes to push the wheelchair.
- Use a transfer assist devices. Sliding board, patient lifts, and power seat lifts. Ask for help with transfer.
- Do level transfers when you can.
- Switch between using a power wheelchair or power-assist device and a non-power wheelchair.
- Make sure the tires on a non-power wheelchair have enough air.

Avoid Needless Motion and Tasks
- Limit the number of transfers you do each day.
- Use other ways to relieve pressure. Push-ups, lean forward, and lean to your side.
- Limit pushing up inclines or over rough surfaces.

Joint Protection for Arthritis

Respect Pain
- Avoid or change tasks that cause pain.
- Wear splints and/or braces.

Balance Rest and Activity
- Take frequent breaks or change the task.
- Rest before you get tired.
- Avoid staying in one position for a long time.
- Allow extra time for tasks. Do not rush.
- Plan the day. Switch between light and heavy tasks.

Use Your Stronger, Larger Muscles and Joints
- Push open a door using your body weight rather than your fingers.
- Lift objects by scooping them with both hands, palms up.
- Instead of using a pinch, use a grip.
- Instead of lifting objects, slide them.
- Place a loop on the refrigerator door and use your elbow to open.
- Close doors using the palm of your hand.
- Close drawers with the side of your hand or your hip.

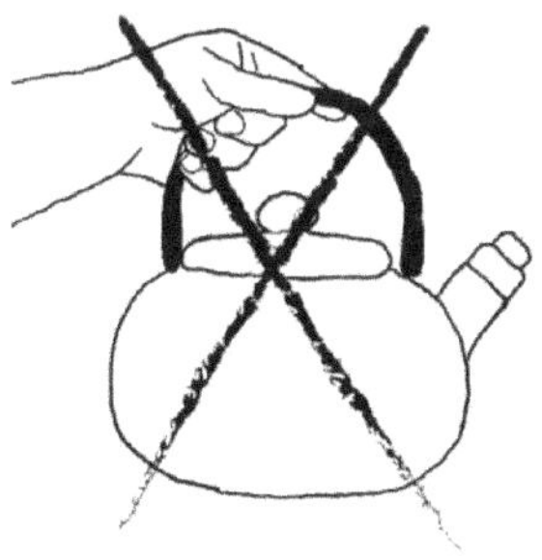

Maintain Strength and Range of Motion
- Doing self-care tasks will help maintain your range of motion.
- Move every day in a pain-free range.
- Practice exercises given by your health care team.

Reduce the Effort Needed to Do the Job
- Ask for help
- Sit to bathe on a shower chair.
- Use long-handled dressing tools.
- Use a turntable to keep desks and counters clear and tools within easy reach.
- Use electric devices (toothbrush, razor, kitchen tools).
- Use prepared foods and freeze extra food for an easy meal.

Joint Protection for Arthritis

Use Good Body Mechanics

- To pick up items from the floor, stoop down; sit in a chair and bend at your hips; or use a reacher.
- Carry heavy objects close to your body.
- Use good posture.

Do Not Use a Tight Grip

- Hold items no tighter than needed.
- Do not carry heavy handbags, pails, and bags with your hands.
- Use built-up handles on pens, spoons, forks, pot handles and tools.
- Use tools such as a jar opener.
- Instead of wringing out a washcloth, press out the water with your palms.

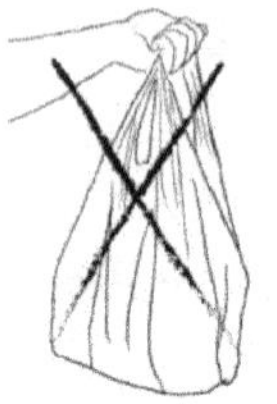

Do Not Push Your Fingers toward Your Little Finger

- Finger motions should move towards your thumb.
- Do not rest your chin on the side of your fingers.
- Add levers to keys, handles, and knobs.
- Hold toothbrush and hairbrush straight across your palm.

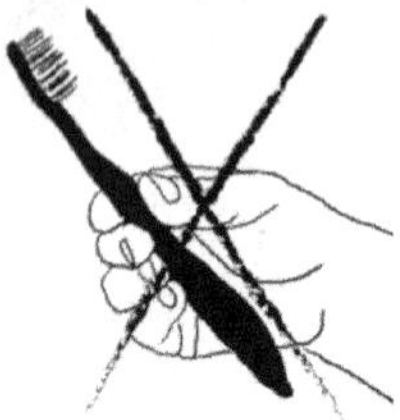

Do Not Pinch Items between Your Thumb and Your Fingers

- Hold a book, plate or mug in the palms of your hands.
- If you are reading for a long time, use a book holder.
- Instead of a clutch-style purse, select one with a shoulder strap.
- Squeeze out toothpaste using your palms.

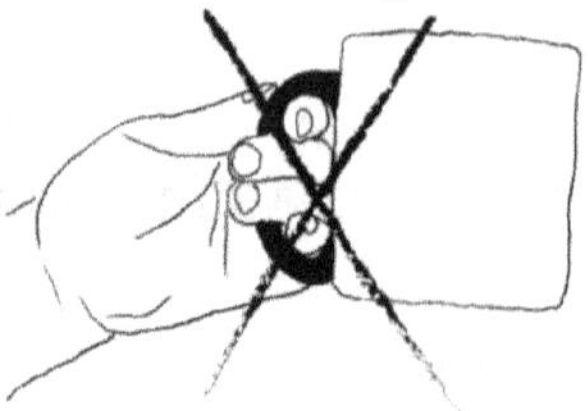
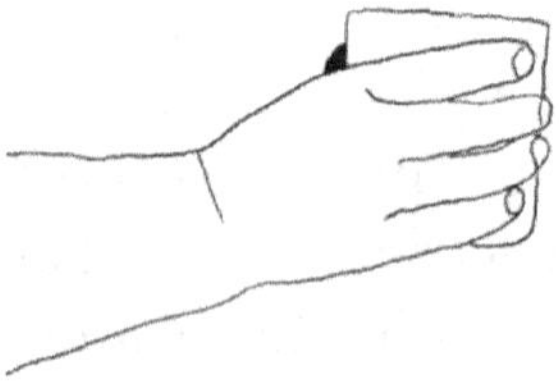

Occupational Therapy TOOLKIT

Leg Measurements

Date	**Upper leg ______ cm above knee crease**		**Knee crease**		**Calf ______ cm below knee crease**		**Ankle**		**Mid-foot**	
	Left	Right	Left	Right	Left	Right	Left	Right	Left	Right

Record measurements in centimeters.

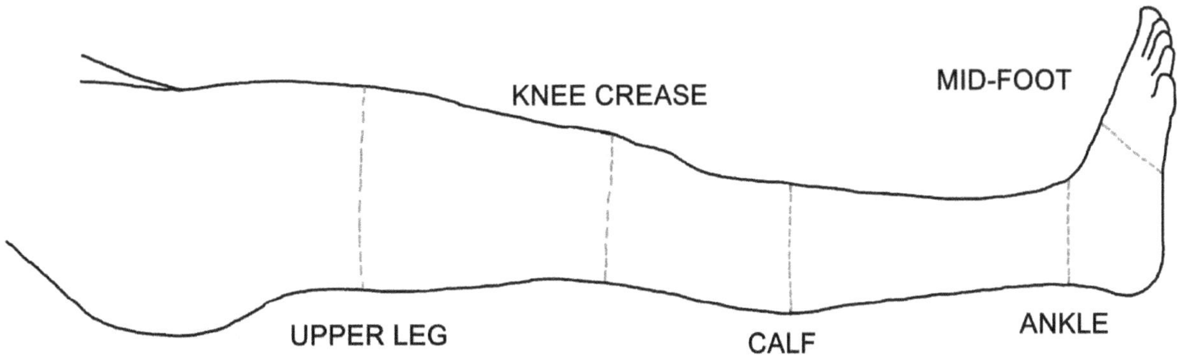

Leisure Activities

Food Prep

Make lemonade, fruit salad.

Crafts and Hobbies

String beads, collect trading cards, stamps or coins, color pictures, make a scrapbook, knit, crochet, draw, paint, woodwork, quilt, leatherwork, needlework, mosaics, ceramics, weaving, latch hook, macramé, car repair, build models, woodcarving, photography, genealogy.

Education

Adult education classes, foreign languages, history, politics, science, lectures, museums, art galleries.

Exercise and Physical Activities

Ball toss, balloon volley, exercise videos, walk a dog, horseshoes, swimming, yoga, Tai Chi, bike, walk at mall, swim, aerobics, community exercise programs.

Garden Activities

Rake, mow, sweep, water, weed, prune.

Household Chores

Empty dishwasher, fold laundry, wipe counters, sweep floor, wash windows, vacuum, and set the table.

Music and Dancing

Play CDs, tapes, or records. Sing or dance to well-known songs. Play a musical instrument or play musical games like 'Name That Tune.'

Out and About / Entertainment

Bingo, cinema, concerts, theatre, take a drive, shop, travel, attend festivals.

Outdoor Activities

Bird watch, fish, hike, boat.

Pets

Care for, feed, groom and exercise a pet.

Quiet Activities

Listen to books and news on tape, watch TV or videos, read aloud, reminisce, look at photo albums, meditate, pray.

Social

Card games, eat out, community centers, attend church, bible study, book clubs, current events groups, visit friends and family, volunteer.

Sports (active or spectator)

Bowl, golf, miniature golf, team sports, tennis.

Tabletop Activities

Clip coupons, write letters or cards, play games (dominoes, card games, board games), jigsaw puzzles, computer games, use the internet.

Low Vision - Eating

Eating Tips

- Use the "clock" method to find items on the table and the plate of food.

- Slide hands across table to find dishes.

- Push the food against a piece of bread or a plate guard.

- To pour liquids, put one finger in the cup and pour until you feel the liquid.

- Use dishes and drinkware that do not break.

- Push food from the edge of the plate to the center.

Low Vision - Functional Reading
Therapist Resource

Reading Task	Font Size	Visual Acuity Notation	Classification of Visual Impairment
Footnotes	4-point type	20/20 - 20/25	Range of normal vision
Newsprint	8-point type	20/30 - 20/60	Near normal vision
Large Print	16-point type	20/80 - 20/160	Moderate impairment
Headlines	40-point type	20/200 - 20/400	Severe impairment (20/200 = legal blindness)
Ad Copy	> 80-point type	20/500 - 20/1000	Profound impairment

Low Vision - Functional Vision
Therapist Resource

Harder to see

Use the telephone book.
Drive at night.
Read a newspaper, medication label, mail.
Match clothes.
Recognize faces and expressions.
Write a check.
Shop for groceries or clothes.
Tell time on a watch.
Manage housework.
Identify coins.
Read street signs.
See steps, stairs or curbs.
Notice objects off to the side while walking.
Read labels on food and sundries.
Find something on a crowded shelf.
Read newspaper headlines.
Pour liquids.
Play board or card games.
Use appliances.
Use a telephone.
Prepare meals.
Manage medication.
Groom (shave, style hair, apply makeup).
Watch TV.
Drive during the day.
Read large print books.
Take part in sports (bowling, golf, walks).
Watch a movie, a play or sports event.
Dress, bathe, and eat.

Easier to see

Low Vision - Improve Your Other Senses

Improve Your Sense of Touch

- Feel textures like wool, silk, cotton, plastic.
- Identify small objects or coins.
- Sort sizes of screws and nuts.
- Practice using power cords and outlets.
- Peel and slice fruits.
- Identify changes in floor surfaces.

Improve Your Sense of Hearing

- Learn people by their voice and walk.
- Learn the sounds in your home and the location and distance of the sounds.
- Find the location of dropped items.

1 of 2

Low Vision - Improve Your Other Senses

Improve Your Sense of Taste

- Recognize items by taste, like salt, spices, sugar, and coffee.

Improve Your Sense of Smell

- Recognize common spices and foods.
- Recognize perfume, soaps, and shampoo.
- Learn the scents of the stores you visit.

Improve Your Memory Skills

- Learn phone numbers and birthdays.
- Play games that require the recall of letters, numbers, or music notes.
- Practice math problems in your head.
- Recall stories, current events.

Low Vision - Kitchen Tasks

Arrange

- Put away items in the same place.
- Arrange drawers with a method that makes sense to you (forks on the left, spoons to the right).
- Arrange foods so that every type has its own place.

Cut and Chop

- Use cutting boards in colors that contrast with the food. Use a white cutting board for peppers and carrots. Use a dark cutting board for onions and apples.

Measure

- To measure boiling water, measure the water before heating.
- Use a large print measuring cup.

Low Vision - Kitchen Tasks

Cookbooks and Recipes

- Use cookbooks in Braille and large print.
- Type and print recipes or write them using large bold print.

Pour, Drain, and Mix

- Place a tray or cookie sheet under the bowl while pouring and mixing.
- Mix and pour in the sink to catch spills.
- Use a tray to carry items that might spill.

Use the Stove and Oven

- Place food in a pan, and the pan on a burner. Turn the heat on.
- Use long-sleeve oven mitt.

Low Vision - Mark and Label Items

Mark Devices

- Use raised plastic dots to mark the settings on devices, computers and keyboards.

Label Clothes

- Use safety pins for different colors. Put a safety pin on the inside label of clothes. A pin pointing to the side is red. A safety pin pointing up is brown. No pin is blue.

- Use a colored marker on the clothing tags.

- Remove the labels from some clothes and not the others.

- Hang clothes that match on one hanger.

- Learn to identify clothes by the feel, style, buttons or other features.

Low Vision - Mark and Label Items

Label Food

- Use a rubber band around milk carton to tell it from juice carton.

- Place labels marked with bold writing or color-coded labels.

- Arrange food items in a certain order and place.

- Use rubber bands to tell one can from the other. Use two bands for fruit and three bands for beans.

- Use ABC magnets on canned goods.

2 of 2

Low Vision - Leisure

Leisure

- Use large print playing cards.
- Play games such as checkers, chess, bingo, or Braille Scrabble.
- Listen to the radio, TV, or music.
- Enjoy books and magazines in large print, recorded, or in Braille. Order them from the National Library Service for the Blind and Physically Handicapped.
- Take part in senior programs like weekly meals.
- Bowl, swim, hike, fish, tandem bike ride or dance.
- Learn a new craft, such as clay, tile or mosaics.

Low Vision - Lighting

Lighting Tips

- People with glaucoma and macular degeneration may see better with higher light levels.
- Less light may work better for those with central cataracts.

Basic Lighting

- Use a few lamps to light a room and create even light levels. Consider the type and strength of the light bulb and the placement of lights in the room.
- Make sure you have enough lighting at night.
- Use tall table lamps with light-colored shades and wide brims at the bottom.
- Use floor lamps that direct light toward the ceiling.
- Install motion-sensor lighting.

Low Vision - Lighting

Task Lighting

- Try different types of light bulbs.
- Place the lamp to your side and aim the light source below eye level.
- Try a gooseneck lamp. Direct the light where you need it.
- Use a flashlight for task lighting. A flashlight is useful when using devices and in dark areas of cupboards and closets.
- Use good lighting at the top and bottom of the stairs.

Low Vision - Medication

Medication Tips

- Have the pharmacy put large-print labels on the pill bottles.

- Use a weekly or daily pillbox.

- Use a dark-colored tray or box lid when filling the pillbox. The tray's raised edge prevents pills from rolling onto the floor.

- Store medications in the same place you take them. Put the pill bottles you take at night on the nightstand. Put the pill bottles you take with meals on the kitchen table. Use child proof caps for safety. Keep all medications out of reach from children and pets.

- Use a magnifying glass to read labels. Keep one with medications.

Medication Tips

- Write the first letter of the medicine in bold marker or Hi-Marks on the lid.
- The size and shape of containers can help you tell them apart.
- Medications may have a unique shape, size, texture or smell.
- Use rubber bands to tell pill bottles apart or to mark the dosage.
- For persons with diabetes use a talking glucometer, needle magnifier and large print blood sugar log.
- Use a talking scale and talking blood pressure meter.

2 of 2

Low Vision - Money

Identify Money

- Coins - Focus on the size, edge, and thickness. The dime is the smallest, and the half-dollar is the largest. The penny and nickel have a smooth edge. The dime, quarter, and half-dollar have a ridged edge. The nickel is the thickest coin.

- Bills - Fold bills in different ways. Leave $1 bills unfolded. Fold $5 lengthwise. Fold $10 in half. Fold $20 lengthwise and then in half.

Manage Bank Account

- Statements come in large print.

- Use large-print checks and registers.

- Calculators come with large buttons.

Pay Bills

- Ask for help.

- Pay bills with online banking or by phone.

Low Vision - Moving Around

Moving Around

- Count the steps it takes to walk from one area to another.

- To protect yourself when walking, extend one arm out front. Keep your elbow bent a little and hold your fingers straight.

- When you drop an object, use sound to figure out where the object fell. Stoop down and use your hand in a fan-like motion.

- Ask a sighted people to describe the room.

- Ask a sighted people to guide you around the room to get an idea of the size.

- Ask a sighted person to draw on your back. They can use a finger to make a picture of the objects in the room.

Low Vision - Reading, Writing, Phone Use

Reading

- Use eccentric viewing, page-orientation skills and scanning.
- Use a magnifying glass.
- Use a yellow overlay.
- Get large-print items like books, monthly bills, magazines, checks and registers.
- Listen to audio books.

Writing

- Increase task lighting.
- Use contrast.
  - Black or navy ink on cream paper is best (bright white paper may cause glare).
  - Place paper on a dark colored mat so you do not write off the page.

1 of 2

Low Vision - Reading, Writing, Phone Use

Writing

- Use writing guides, bold-line or raised-line paper and bold-line pens.
- Use screen magnifiers on the computer, screen reading software, video magnifiers.

Phone Use

To make it easy to dial:

- Get a large button phone.
- Mark the buttons with raised dots.
- Increase font size and visibility on cell phone.

Keep a list of phone numbers.

- Use a large print address book.
- Make a large print list of phone numbers.
- Store numbers on the phone, use voice dial.

2 of 2

Low Vision - Reduce Glare

Reduce Glare

- Hang sheer curtains, blinds, or shades that allow light through, but reduce glare.

- Use shades on all lamps.

- When outdoors, wear a visor or a hat with a wide brim. Wear sunglasses.

Low Vision - Safety

Tips

- Set up and maintain a safe layout of furniture and other items.
- Keep items in the same place.
- Keep doors open all the way.
- Keep chairs up against table.
- Keep cupboard drawers and cupboard doors closed.
- Remove throw rugs or secure with backing.
- Keep hallways and stairs free and clear of hazards.
- Attach sand paper to the ends of the handrail to warn you.
- Install a gate or door on open stairways.

Occupational Therapy TOOLKIT

Low Vision - Use Contrast

Use Color

- Choose solid colors instead of patterns.

- In the bathroom, select a toilet seat cover that contrasts with the floor. Use a colored tub mat for a white tub. Place one on the bottom of the tub and drape one over the edge. Use soap and shampoo in colors that contrast with the tub and sink.

- Choose a bright bedspread that contrasts with the floor. Place bright colored pillows on chair and sofa.

- Use a light cutting board for dark foods and a dark one for light foods.

- Outline the edges with colored tape. Counters, steps, coffee tables, doorways, doorsills, switch plates and bathtubs.

Pain Journal

Date: _______________

What time did your pain start? _______________

How long did your pain last? _______________

Where was your pain?

____

On a scale of 1-10, rate your level of pain.

1	2	3	4	5	6	7	8	9	10

none extreme

Describe your pain.

____

____

____

What caused your pain or increase in pain?

____

____

____

How did your pain affect you being able to do tasks or relate to others?

____

____

____

What did you do to reduce your pain? What was the result?

____

____

____

What could you have done differently?

____

____

____

Phantom Limb Pain

- Keep a pain journal. This can help you see patterns.
- Relax using deep (diaphragmatic) breathing and other tools.
- Distract yourself with TV, video games, or music.
- Soak in a warm bath or use a shower massage on your limb.
- Wrap your limb in a warm blanket or towel.
- Exercise your limb to increase blood flow. Tighten the muscles in your limb, then slowly release.
- Do not stay in one place for more than 20 minutes. Move around
- Massage, tap or apply vibration to your limb.
- Increase the pressure around your limb by using a wrap or shrinker sock. If you use a prosthesis, put it on and take a short walk.
- Decrease the pressure around your limb by taking off the prosthesis for a few minutes.

Position in Bed - Left Side Weakness

Lying on the Back
Place a pillow under the person's left shoulder. Place their left arm out to their side. Rest it on the pillow. Place a folded towel under their left hip.

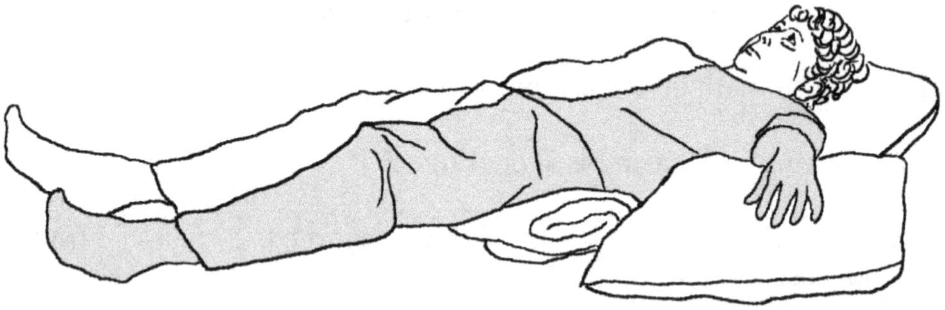

Side Lying on the Right Side
Place the person's left arm on a pillow. Pull their shoulder forward. Roll their left hip forward. Place their left knee and ankle on a pillow.

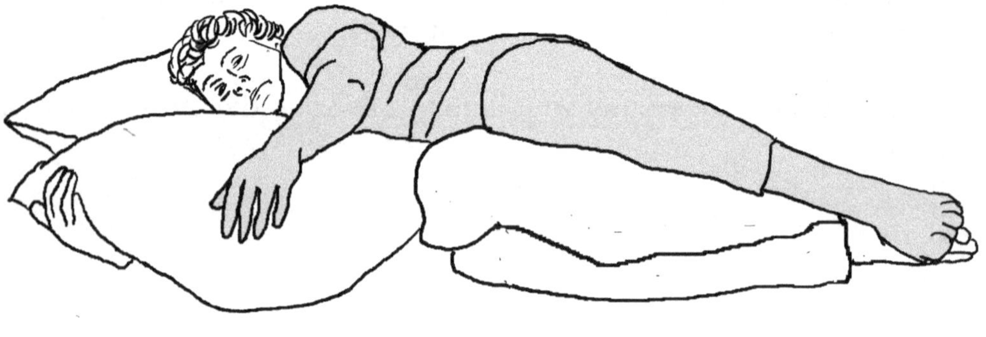

Side Lying on the Left Side
Protract the person's left shoulder. Extend their arm out to the side. Support their right leg on a pillow.

Position in Bed - Right Side Weakness

Lying on the Back
Place a pillow under the person's right shoulder. Place their right arm out to the side. Rest it on the pillow. Place a folded towel under their right hip.

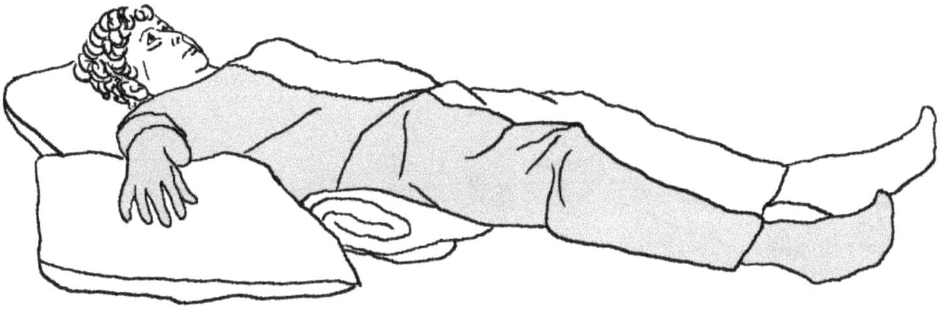

Side Lying on the Left Side
Place the person's right arm on a pillow. Pull their shoulder forward. Roll their right hip forward. Place their right knee and ankle on a pillow.

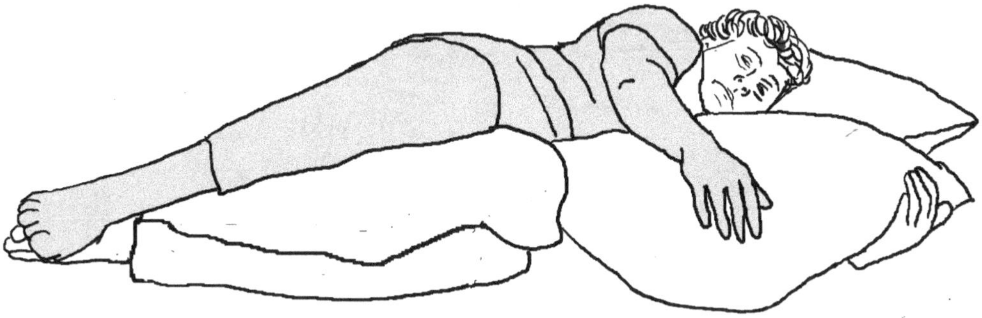

Side Lying on the Right Side
Protract the person's right shoulder. Extend their arm out to the side. Support their left leg on a pillow.

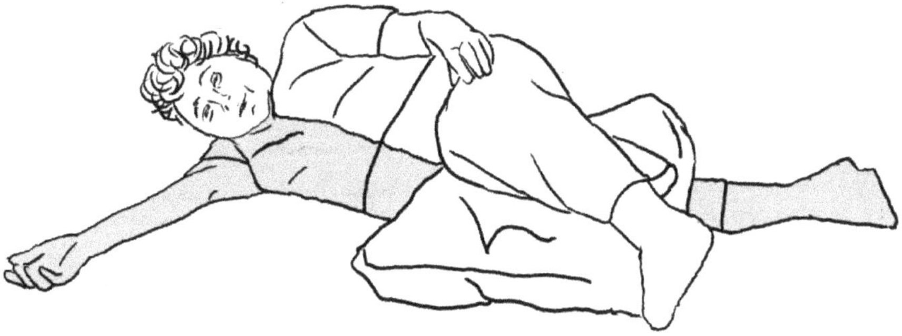

Position in Bed to Reduce Pressure

Use pillows to help keep bony areas from touching. Change position every _____ hours.

Keep the bottom sheet, pads and clothing free from wrinkles. Keep the bed free of food crumbs and other items.

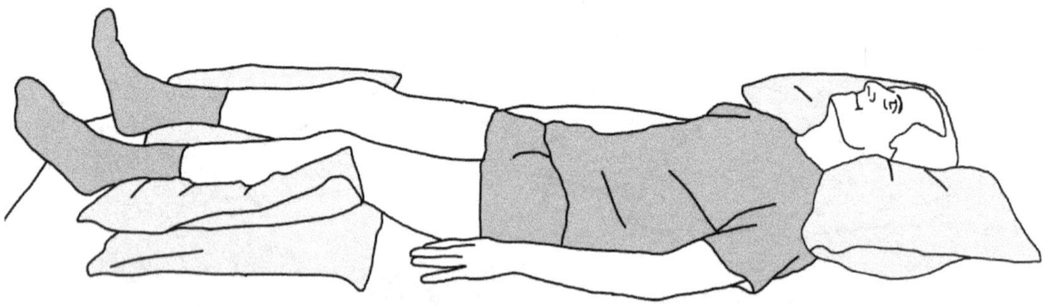

Back - Place a pillow under the person's lower legs. Keep their heels up off the bed.

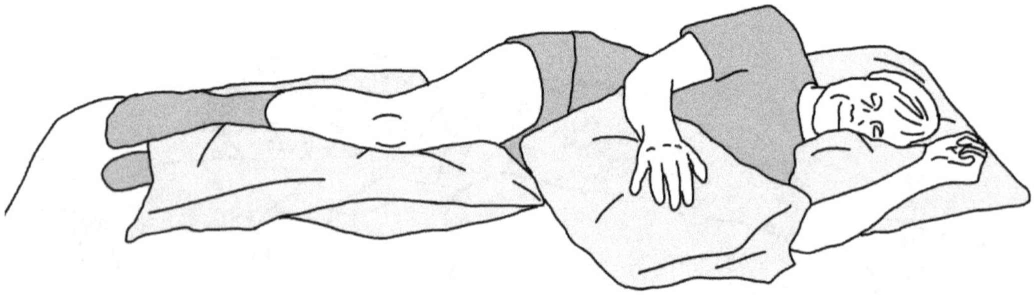

Side - Place a pillow between the person's knees and ankles. Support their arm on a pillow.

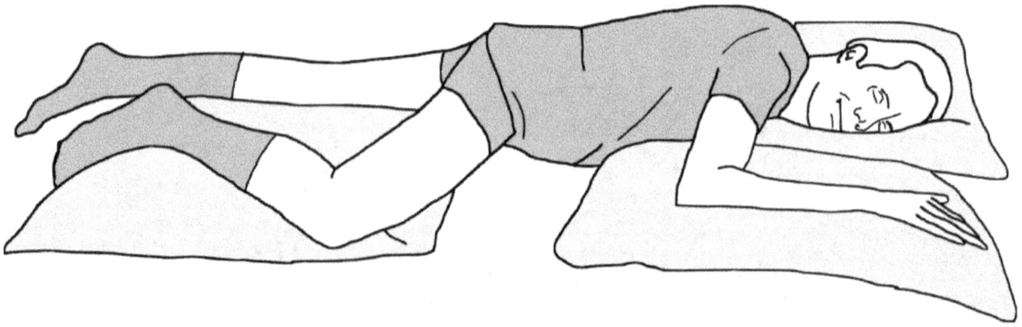

Stomach - Place a pillow under the person's one knee and one arm as shown.

Position Your Arm - Left Side Weakness

Sitting in a Wheelchair

Sit in the middle of the wheelchair with your hips back into the chair. Use your right leg to move the wheelchair.

Support your left arm on an arm trough (see picture) or a lap tray.

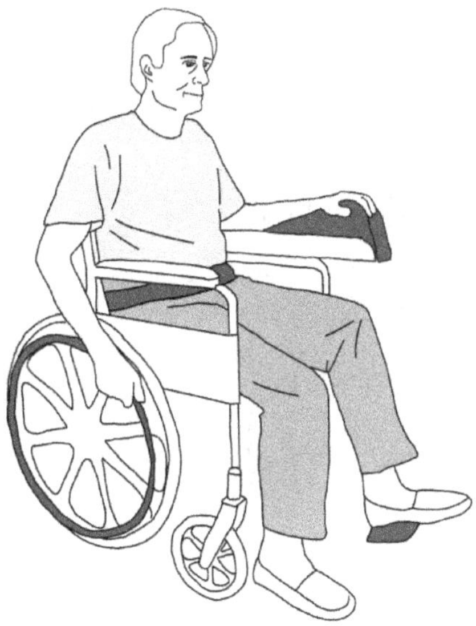

Sitting Up in Bed

Raise the head of the bed. Place a small pillow behind your elbow. Bring your left arm forward. Place your forearm and hand on a pillow placed on your lap.

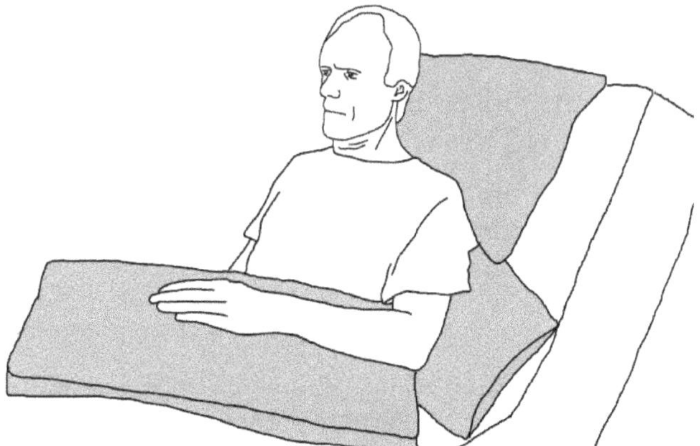

Position Your Arm - Right Side Weakness

Sitting in a Wheelchair

Sit in the middle of the wheelchair with your hips back into the chair. Use your left leg to move the wheelchair.

Support your right arm on an arm trough (see picture) or a lap tray.

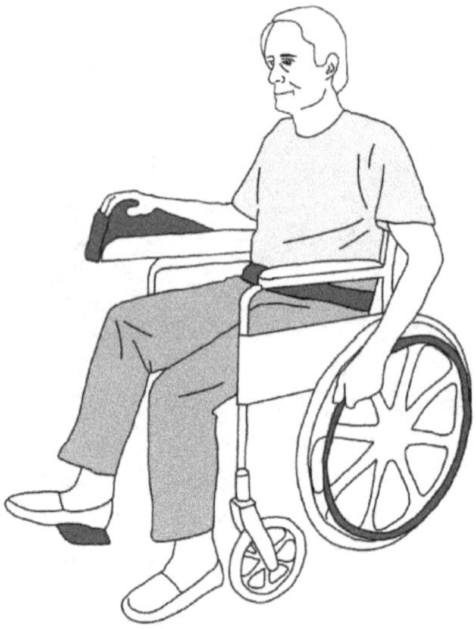

Sitting Up in Bed

Raise the head of the bed. Place a small pillow behind your elbow. Bring your right arm forward. Place your forearm and hand on a pillow placed on your lap.

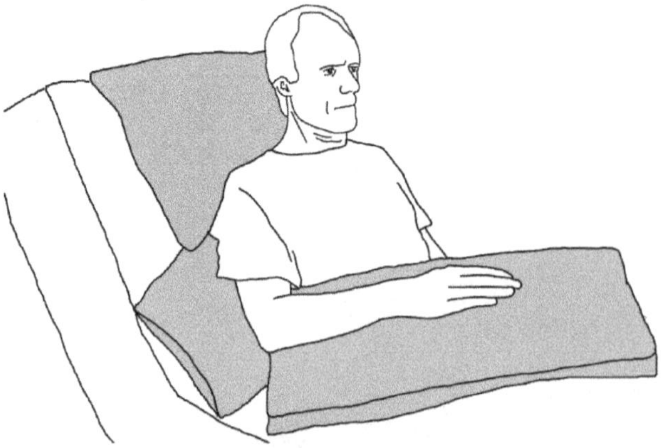

Position Your Residual Limb - Above Knee Amputation

Position your residual limb to prevent tightness in your hip joint. Tightness of your hip joint may prevent you from with wearing a prosthesis.

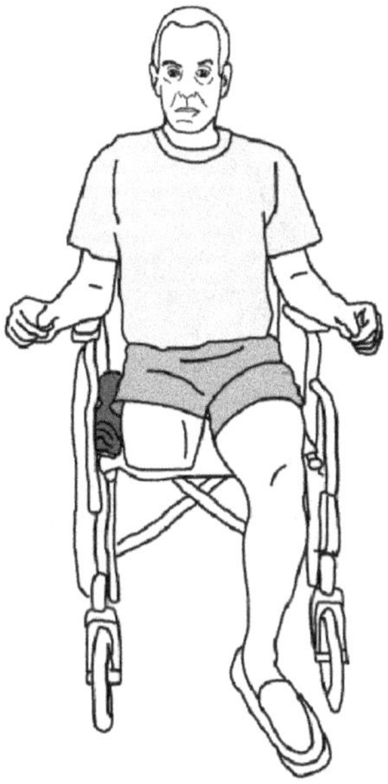

Keep your residual limb from rolling outward. Use a rolled towel placed to the outside of your residual limb.

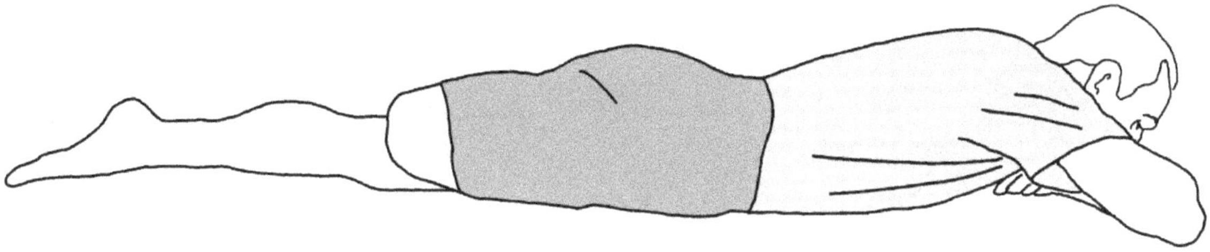

Lie on your stomach _____ times a day, for _____ minutes each time. Do **not** put a pillow under your stomach or hip.

Notes: ____

____

____

____

____

Occupational Therapy TOOLKIT

Position Your Residual Limb - Below Knee Amputation

Position your residual limb to prevent tightness in your hip and knee joint. Tightness of your hip and/or knee joint may prevent you from with wearing a prosthesis.

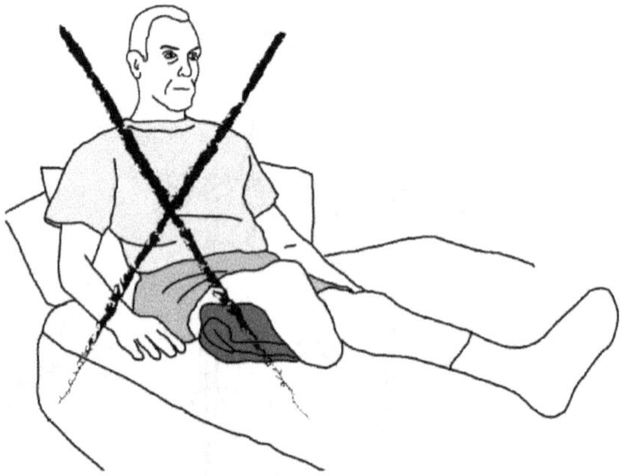

Keep your residual knee straight. Do not use pillows under your residual limb.

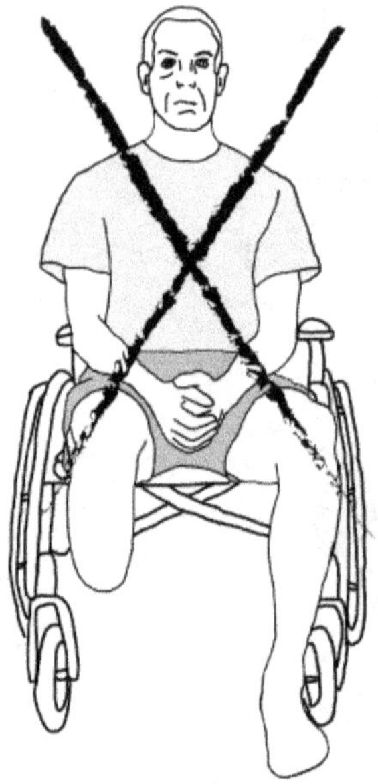

Do not hang your residual limb off the edge of a chair or bed. Use a kneeboard or a side chair to support your residual limb.

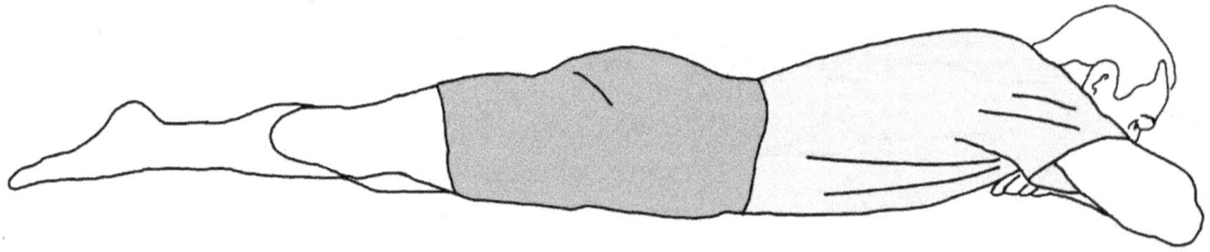

Lie on your stomach _____ times a day, for _____ minutes each time. Do **not** put a pillow under your stomach or hip.

Notes: ____

____

____

____

____

Postural Drainage Positions

Use postures alone or with chest percussion.
Do not do postural drainage soon after a meal.

Lie on your back with your knees bent, Put 2-3 pillows under your hips. Your chest should be lower than your hips. Breathe using deep (diaphragmatic) breathing.

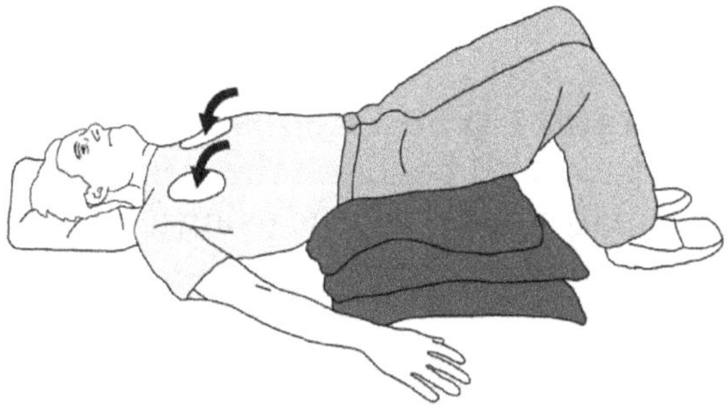

Stay in this posture for _____ minutes.

Lie on your side. Put 2-3 pillows under your hips. Your chest should be lower than your hips. Use a small pillow under your head. Breathe using deep (diaphragmatic) breathing.

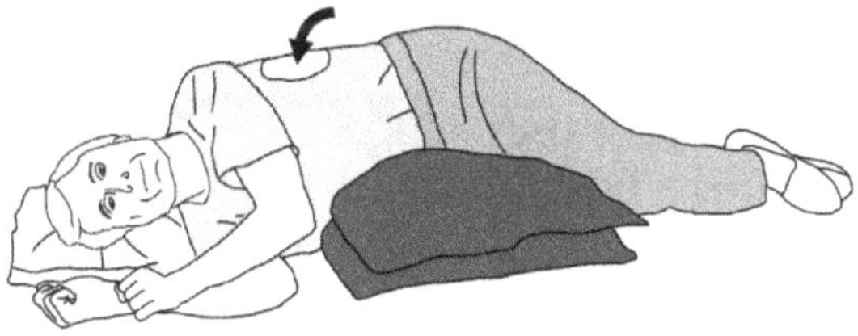

Stay in this posture for _____ minutes on each side.

Switch to your other side.

Lie on your stomach. Place 2-3 pillows under your hips. Your chest should be lower than your hips. Use a small pillow under your head. Breathe using deep (diaphragmatic) breathing.

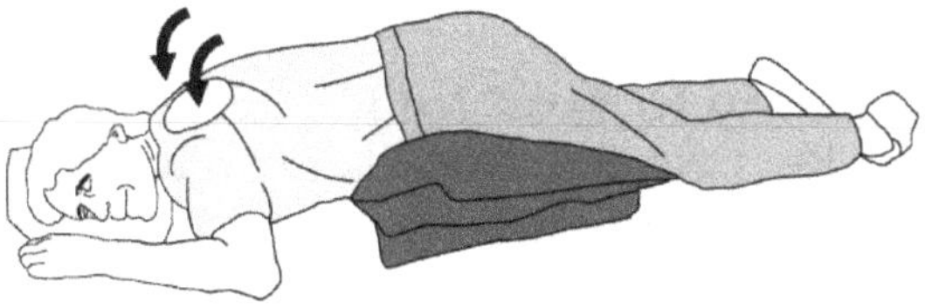

Stay in this posture for _____ minutes.

Pressure Relief

Relieve pressure off your bottom every _____ minutes/hours.

Lock the wheelchair brakes. Lift the footrests and place both feet flat on the floor.

☐ **Stand Up and Reposition**
Place both hands on the armrests. Push up to stand. Balance using a walker or counter.

Hold this position for a count of _____.

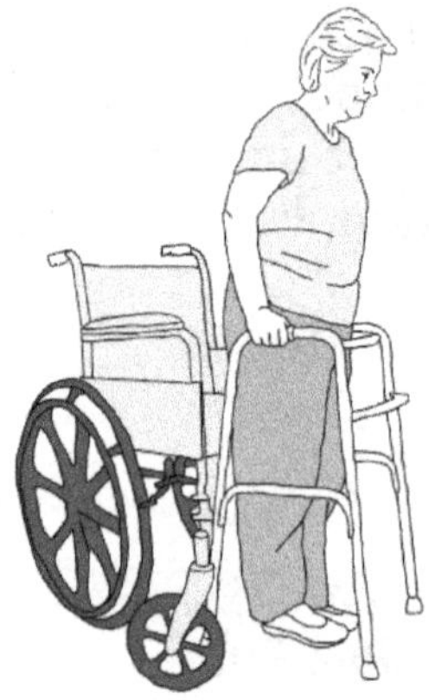

☐ **Chair Push-Up**
Place both hands on the armrests and push up. Take the weight off your bottom.

Hold this position for a count of _____.

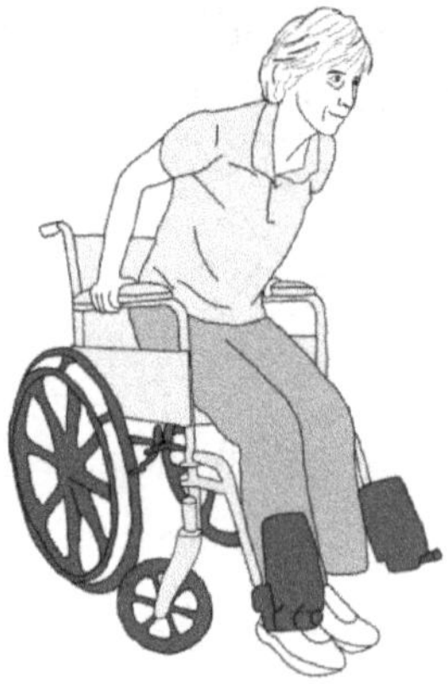

☐ **Lean to Your Side**
Remove one armrest. Lean to your side onto a bed or table. Take the weight off the other side of your bottom.

Hold this position for a count of _____.
Repeat to your other side.

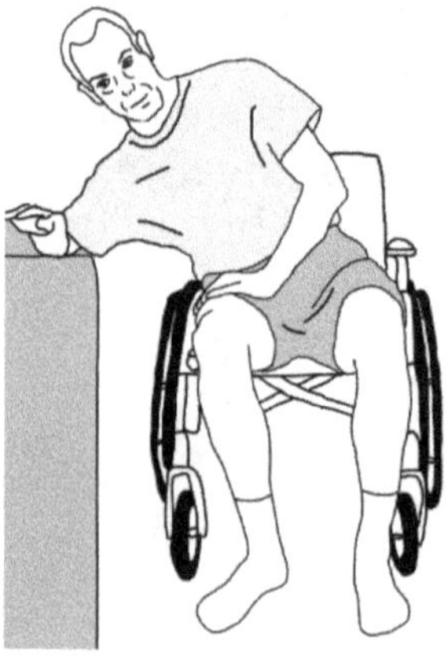

Pressure Relief

Relieve pressure off your bottom every _____ minutes/hours.

Lock the wheelchair brakes. Lift the footrests and place both feet flat on the floor.

☐ **Lean Forward with Support**
Lean forward onto a sturdy bench or bed. Take the weight off your bottom.

Hold this position for a count of _____.

☐ **Cross Legs**
Cross one leg over your other leg, hold your knee in place. Lean to your side. Take the weight off the other side of your bottom.

Hold this position for a count of _____.
Repeat to your other side.

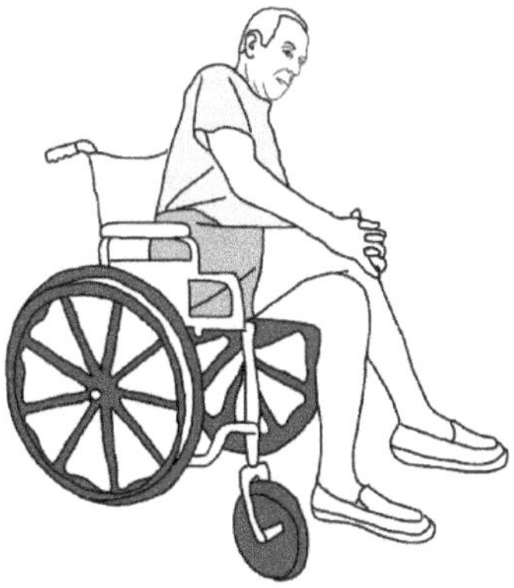

Protect the Arm - Left Side Weakness

Protect the Arm During Assisted Transfers

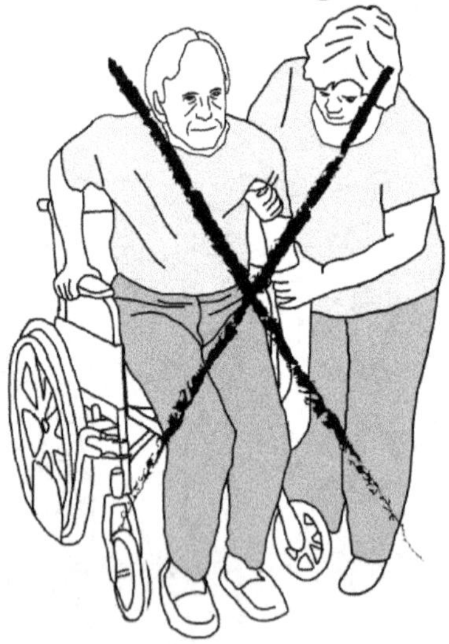

Do not pull on the person's left arm.

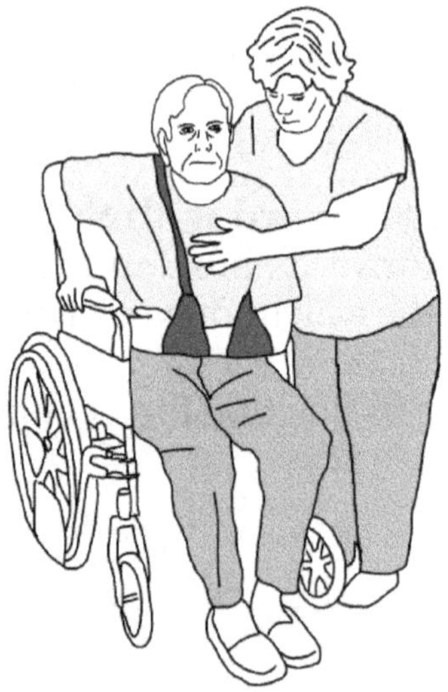

Use a sling on their left arm. Put one hand on the person's chest. Hold the transfer belt with your other hand.

Protect the Arm when Walking

Do not hold the person under their left arm.

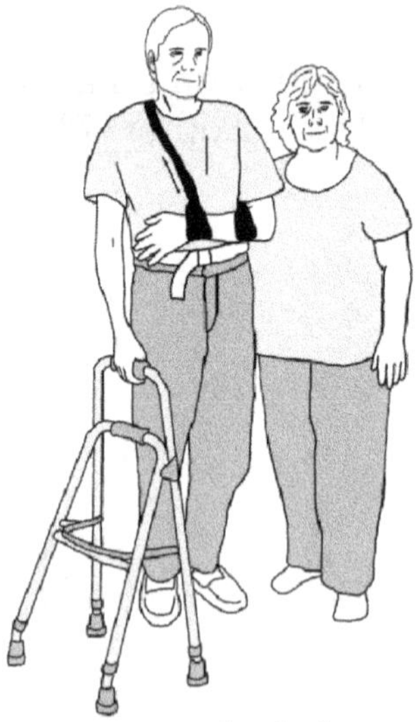

Use a sling to support the left arm. Hold the transfer belt with your other hand.

Protect the Arm - Right Side Weakness

Protect the Arm During Assisted Transfers

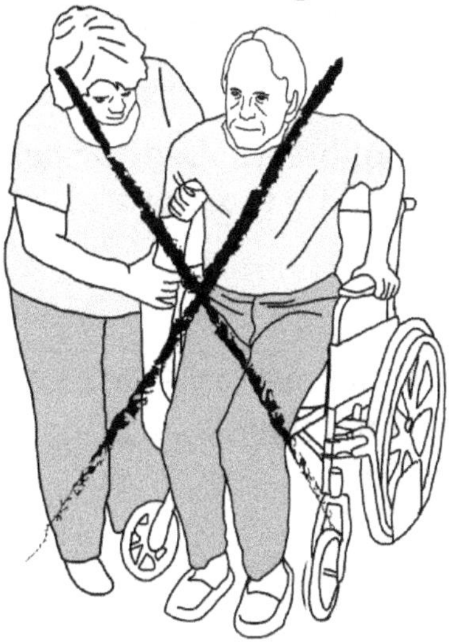

Do not pull on the person's right arm.

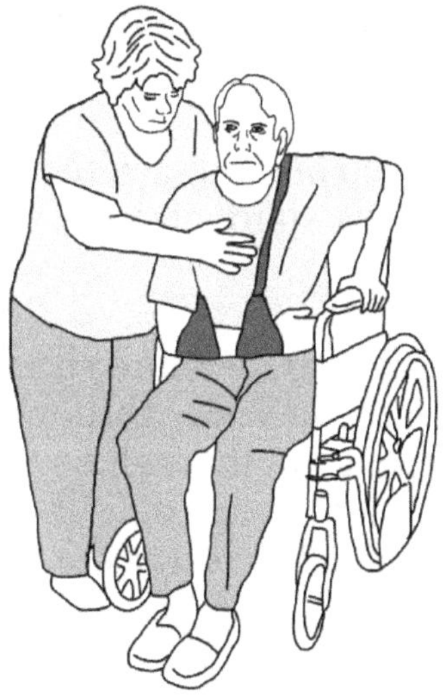

Use a sling on their right arm. Put one hand on the person's chest. Hold the transfer belt with your other hand.

Protect the Arm when Walking

Do not hold the person under their right arm.

Use a sling to support their right arm. Hold the transfer belt with your other hand.

Pursed Lip Breathing

Pursed lip breathing helps you control your breathing. Breathing into your nose warms, filters, and moistens the air. Blowing out through pursed lips slows down your breathing and allows your lungs to use more oxygen.

Use pursed lip breathing with tasks that make you short of breath. Use during exercise, showers, or for stairs. If you are short of breath, use pursed lip breathing to control your breathing.

1. Relax your neck and shoulder muscles.
2. Breathe in slowly through your nose, like smelling a flower.
3. Breathe out through pursed lips, like cooling off a hot liquid. Do not force the air out. Breathe out with ease.
4. You should breathe out twice as long as you breathe in.

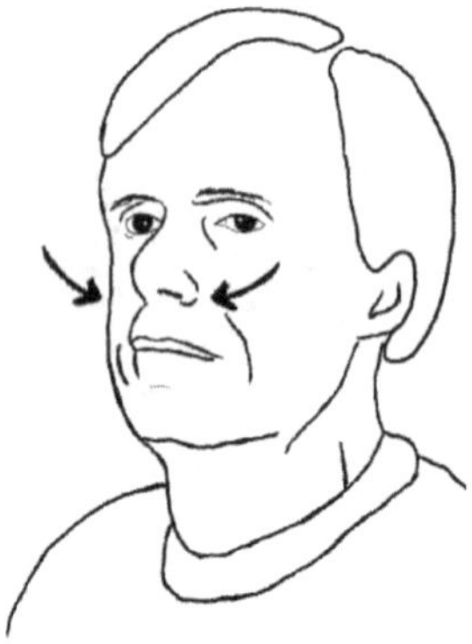

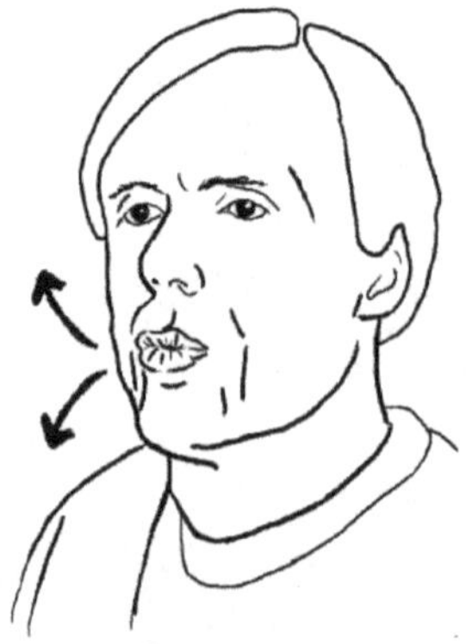

Occupational Therapy TOOLKIT

Scar Massage

Before you massage the scar, apply moist heat for _____ minutes.

Use the tips of your fingers. Add a small amount of lotion on the scar. Massage the scar and the tissue around the scar with light to medium pressure. Scar massage should not be painful. You will need to massage the scar for _____ months.

Start by using one or two fingers. Make small circles. Move over the length of the scar and the skin around the scar.

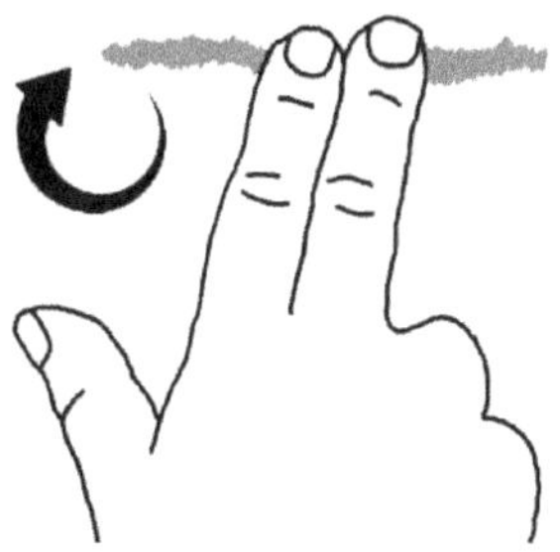

Next, massage the scar up and down. Move over the length of the scar and the skin around the scar.

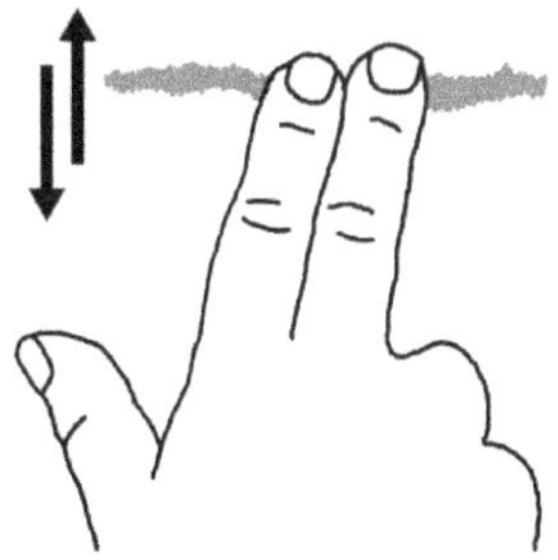

Next, massage the scar side-to-side. Move over the length of the scar and the skin around the scar.

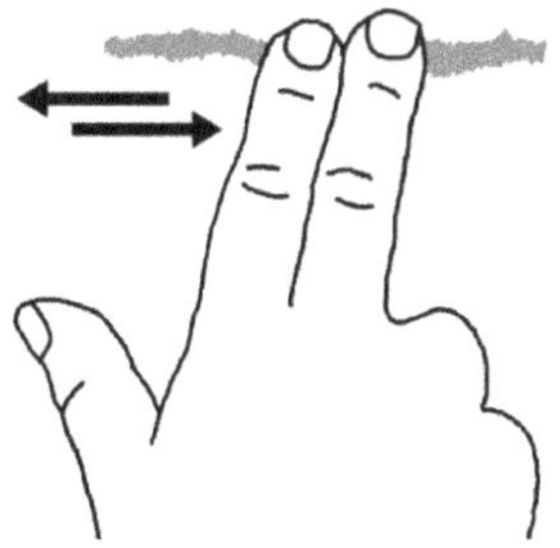

Massage the scar for _____ minutes. Repeat _____ times a day.

Stop scar massage if you notice any problems: more pain, the scar feels warmer than the skin around it, the scar bleeds, the scar blisters. Contact the therapist or doctor.

SMART Goals

Start by writing a goal. Think of something you would like to achieve.

Now, make your goal SMART. Think about these questions.

S Specific	How will you achieve your goal?
M Measurable	How will you measure your progress?
A Achievable	Is your goal easy to reach?
R Relevant	Is your goal important to you? Are you able to do what it takes?
T Timely	When do you want to finish your goal?

Write your SMART goal here:

Occupational Therapy TOOLKIT

SMART Goals - Action Plan

Copy your SMART goal here: ____

What steps you will take?

1.
2.
3.
4.
5.

What might keep you from meeting your SMART goal?

How can you overcome these?

Who can give you support? How can they support you?

On a scale of 1-10, how sure you are of meeting your SMART goal.

1	2	3	4	5	6	7	8	9	10

not sure — extremely sure

On a scale of 1-10, rate how committed you are to meeting your SMART goal.

1	2	3	4	5	6	7	8	9	10

not committed — extremely committed

Spinal Surgery Precautions

Follow these precautions until the doctor tells you it is okay to stop. You will follow them for 6-12 weeks after surgery.

You may have to wear a brace. Wear this brace when out of bed to limit movement of your spine. For comfort, wear a t-shirt under the brace.

If your doctor's advice differs from those listed here, *always follow your doctor's orders*.

- No Bending
  Do not bend at your waist.

- No Lifting
  Do not lift items that weigh more than ______ lb/kg.

- No Twisting or Turning
  After cervical surgery, do not twist or turn your neck.
  Keep your head straight.
  Keep your ears and shoulders lined up.

  After lumbar surgery, do not twist or turn your trunk.
  Keep your shoulders and hips lined up.

- No Pulling
  Do not pull yourself out of bed
  Do not allow someone to pull you up.
  Use a log roll to get out of bed.
  Do not pull on the handrail to climb the stairs.

- Change your position often.

- Limit sitting upright to less than 20 minutes at a time. You can sit reclined as long as you like.

Splint/Brace Instructions

If you have any questions, please call ____________________ at ________________.

Type of splint/brace:

____

The purpose of the splint/brace:

____

____

When to wear the splint/brace:

____

____

When to remove the splint/brace:

____

____

How to wear the splint/brace:

____

____

How to care for the splint/brace:

____

____

____

Stop wearing the splint/brace and contact the therapist if you have:

- Increased pain or soreness
- More swelling or stiffness
- Numbness
- Skin irritation
- Red areas

Notes: ____

____

____

____

Sternal (Breastbone) Precautions

It will take time for your breastbone to heal. To prevent strain or pressure, follow these precautions until your doctor instructs you to stop.

If your doctor's advice differs from those listed here, *always follow your doctor's orders.*

Do not drive. Do not sit in front of an airbag.

Do not strain or hold your breath during exercises, tasks, or when using the toilet.

Do not lift
- Do not lift above shoulder level.
- Do not lift more than _____ lb/kg.

Do not push
- Do not push up in bed. Cross your arms and use your trunk to sit up.
- Do not push up from a chair. Cross your arms and use your legs to stand.
- Do not push down on the walker when walking. Use it only to balance yourself.
- Do not push open a heavy door. Use your hip to push it open.
- Do not push open or close a sliding glass door.
- Do not push items like chairs, footstools, and bedside tables.

Do not pull
- Do not use a trapeze over the bed.
- Do not let others pull on your arms.
- Do not pull on the handrail to climb the stairs. Use it only to balance yourself.
- Do not pull open a heavy door.
- Do not pull open a sliding glass door.
- Do not pull items like chairs, footstools, and bedside tables.

Do not reach back
- Do not reach back for the arms of a chair. Feel for the chair with the back of your legs. Cross your arms and use your legs to sit.
- Do not reach back to clean after using the toilet. Use a long-handled device.

Occupational Therapy TOOLKIT

Stress Management

What Are the Causes of Stress?

- Major life events: death of a spouse, divorce, separation, death of close family, personal injury or illness, marriage, job loss, retirement.

- Daily life events: conflicts, waiting for others, not sleeping well, meeting new people, being late, feeling bored, having too much to do.

Find the Causes of Your Stress

- Keep a journal for two weeks. Write down the stressful events that occur.

How Stress Affects You

- Physical signs: feeling tired, tightness of your neck and shoulder muscles, headaches, high blood pressure, chest pain, heart skips a beat.

- Mental signs: memory problems, trouble with choices, poor judgment, not able to focus, negative thinking, racing thoughts.

- Emotional signs: restless, anxious, depressed, apathetic, angry, overwhelmed.

- Behavioral signs: eating more or eating less, sleeping too much or too little, nervous habits (e.g. nail biting, pacing), teeth grinding or jaw clenching, losing your temper, overreacting to problems.

How to Cope with Stress

- Prevent or avoid the event.
- Change as much of the event as you can.
- Change your response to the event.
  - Talk about how you are feeling.
  - Take one thing at a time.
  - Learn to accept what you cannot change.

Take Care of Yourself, So You Can Handle Stress Better

- Eat a well-balanced diet.
- Engage in a workout that includes stretch, strength and cardio exercises.
- Get enough sleep.
- Balance self-care and work with fun.
- Talk to someone about your feelings.
- Do something nice for yourself every day.

Stress Management - Relaxation Tools

Learn to Relax

- Choose a relaxation tool.
    - Deep (diaphragmatic) breathing
    - Focused breathing
    - Progressive muscle relaxation
    - Guided imagery or visualization
    - Self-hypnosis
    - Mindfulness
    - Meditation
    - Prayer, chanting, readings from spiritual texts
    - Tai Chi
    - Yoga
- Practice on a regular basis.
- Practice during stressful events.
- Add some sensory activities to your day.
    - Sight - Look at something that relaxes you or makes you smile.
    - Sound - Listen to music, listen to nature sounds, sing a song.
    - Smell - Smell flowers, perfume, citrus fruit, essential oils, fresh coffee.
    - Taste - Eat or drink. Savor each bite.
    - Touch - Give yourself a hand massage, groom a pet, wrap in a soft blanket.
    - Movement -Walk, stretch, dance, rock in a rocking chair, knead bread dough.

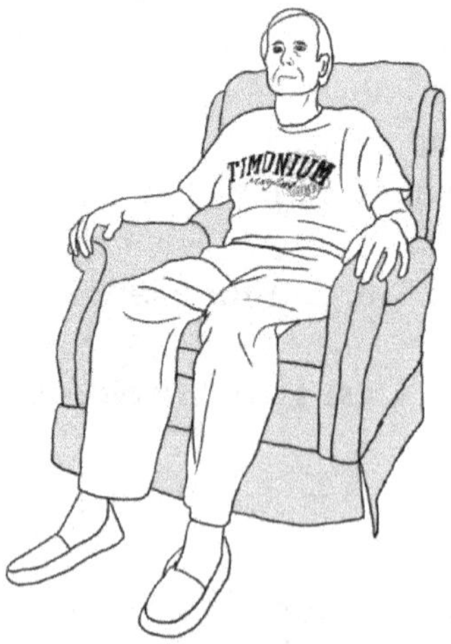

Stress Management - Stress Journal

Date and time: ____

On a scale of 1-10, rate your level of stress.

1	2	3	4	5	6	7	8	9	10

none extreme

Why did your stress increase? What happened? Who was involved?

____

____

____

____

____

What was your reaction? Describe your thoughts, feelings and actions.

____

____

____

____

____

What did you do to reduce your stress and what was the result?

____

____

____

____

____

What could you have done differently?

____

____

____

____

Occupational Therapy TOOLKIT

Superficial Cold

Use superficial cold for acute pain and swelling. Cold is also good for arthritis and post-exercise soreness.

Apply cold to ________________________ for _____ minutes _____ times a day.

☐ **Crushed ice in a plastic bag** - Use a towel between the bag of crushed ice and your skin.

☐ **Cold gel pack** - Use a towel between the cold gel pack and your skin.

☐ **Frozen bag of peas** - Place a towel between the bag of frozen peas and your skin. Mark the bag "for therapy" and do not eat.

☐ **Ice blocks** - Freeze water in a paper cups. Peel off the top. Quickly move the ice block over the painful area. Do not hold the ice block in one spot.

☐ **Contrast bath** - Dip your ________________ in hot water 100°F (38°C) for 3 minutes. Follow with by 1 minute in cold water 65°F (18°C). Repeat 4-5 times, always end with cold water.

Cautions

- Never use cold on any area of the body for more than 20 minutes.
- Do not use cold if you have poor circulation or trouble feeling cold.
- Cold decreases flexibility, so warm up the area for 20 minutes before exercising or activity.

Occupational Therapy TOOLKIT

Superficial Heat

Use superficial heat for chronic pain and to warm muscles before exercise. Heat will increase circulation, reduce stiff joints and relax your muscles.

Apply heat to ________________________ for _____ minutes _____ times a day.

- ☐ **Warm bath or shower**
- ☐ **Heating pads -** Place a towel between the heating pad and your skin. Do not sit or lie on a heating pad. Do not use the heating pad if you think you might fall asleep. Limit the use of a heating pad to 20 minutes on the low setting.
- ☐ **Electric blanket or mattress pad**
- ☐ **Hot water bottle -** Place a towel between the hot water bottle and your skin.
- ☐ **Paraffin bath -** Help with arthritis pain.
- ☐ **Warm water soaks**
- ☐ **Gel mitts -** Heat in the microwave.
- ☐ **Disposable heat wraps**
- ☐ **Swimming pool -** Heated to at least 85°F (30°C).

Cautions

- Never use heat for more than 20 minutes.
- Do not apply heat to an acute injury or swelling.
- Do not apply heat if you have trouble feeling heat.
- If you use a menthol gel, always remove it before using heat.

Occupational Therapy TOOLKIT

Tips to Conserve Energy

Pace Yourself

- Allow yourself enough time to complete a task without having to rush.
- Do not schedule too many tasks in one day.
- Spread heavy and light tasks during the day and week.

Plan Ahead

- Gather all items you will need before you start a task.
- Arrange items and keep within easy reach.

Make Tasks Easy

- Do the tasks that matter to you.
- Ask for help.
- Use tools when needed.
- Use devices to do the work for you.

Do Not Get Tired

- Do not wait until you are tired before you stop and rest.
- Plan to take a rest break every hour.
- Sit when you can.
- Do not plan tasks right after a meal.
- Get a good night's sleep.

Avoid Needless Motion and Tasks

- Limit the need to bend, reach and twist.
- Limit using your arms above your shoulders.
- Support both elbows on the counter.

Use Good Posture

- Sit and stand straight.

Use Good Body Motions

- Stand close to the object you want to move.
- Push or pull items when you can. Slide objects along the counter.
- Limit the need to bend, reach and twist.
- Carry items close to your body. Keep your back straight
- Use your legs muscles to lift. Do not use your back.

Tips to Conserve Energy with Meal and Home Tasks

Pace yourself and rest often.

Cooking

- Gather all items before starting.
- Prepare part of the meal ahead of time.
- Sit to prepare and mix food, and wash dishes.
- Use recipes that are quick and easy.

After Meal Clean Up

- Let the dishes soak to limit scrubbing.
- Let the dishes air dry.
- Eat on paper plates a few times a week.
- Limit the amount of trash. Use a garbage grinder. Empty the trash often.

Shopping and Meal Planning

- Write the shopping list to follow the store aisles.
- Shop when the store is not busy.
- Get help reaching for high and low items and for heavy items.
- Use the store's scooter to shop.
- Ask the clerk to bag the items lightly. Put cold and frozen food in the same bag.
- Make many trips to bring the bags into the house. Bring the cold and frozen foods first. After you have rested, return for the other items.
- Shop online for home delivery.

Laundry

- Sit to iron, sort clothes, pre-treat stains and fold laundry.
- Transfer wet clothes into dryer a few items at a time.
- Get help to fold large items such as sheets.

House Cleaning

- Divide each room into smaller areas. Clean an area at a time.
- Divide chores over the whole week; do a little each day.
- Use long-handled dusters and cleaning wands.
- Pick up items off the floor using a reacher.
- Use paper towels to limit laundry.

Bed Making

- Make half the bed while you are still lying in it. Pull the top sheet and blanket up on one side and smooth out. Exit from the unmade side and finish.

Tips to Conserve Energy with Self Care Tasks

Pace yourself and rest often.

Eating

- Eat slowly and fully chew food.
- Eat six small meals a day instead of three big meals.
- Do not eat gas-forming food. They can bloat your stomach and make it harder to breathe. These include peas, melons, turnips, onions, cauliflower, apples, corn, broccoli, cucumbers, cabbage, beans, and Brussels sprouts.

Grooming

- Sit to shave, comb your hair and brush your teeth.
- Support your elbows on the counter while grooming or shaving.
- Use an electric toothbrush and an electric razor.
- Wash your hair in the shower. Keep your elbows low and your chin tucked.

Bathing and Showering

- If you use oxygen during exercise, then use it when you take a shower.
- Allow plenty of time.
- Gather all the items you will need.
- Sit to bathe and dry. Use a bath chair in the shower.
- Limit bending. Use a long brush to wash your back and feet. Use a hand-held shower to rinse.
- Use a shower caddy and soap on a rope. Place soap in a nylon stocking tied to the shower seat or soap dish.
- Have a towel or robe nearby. Use hand towels because they are not as heavy. Put on a terry cloth robe to dry off.

Dressing

- Allow plenty of time.
- Gather all the items you will need.
- Sit to dress and undress.
- Limit bending. Put your foot on your other knee or use long-handled tools to put on pants, shoes and socks.
- Wear clothes that are easy to put on. Try slip-on shoes, stretch waistbands, and one size larger.
- Do not wear tight clothes like belts, ties, tight socks, girdles and bras.

Occupational Therapy TOOLKIT

Tips to Improve Attention

What is Attention?
Attention means being able to focus on a task or a thought.

Take Care of Yourself

- Get a good night's sleep.
- Take slow, deep breaths.
- Exercise on most days.
- Eat a good diet.
- Drink water.
- Reduce stress.
- Wear your glasses.
- Wear your hearing aids.

Do Not Get Tired

- Plan tasks when you have the most energy.
- Take breaks.

Arrange Your Home and Work

- Arrange all items in consistent places.
- Return items when done using them.
- Schedule a weekly time to clean and organize the activity areas.

Limit Distractions

- Focus on one thing at a time.
- Find a quiet place.
- Close the curtains.
- Turn off the TV, cell phone, and computer.
- In a busy place, sit facing away from the noise.

Practice Paying Attention

- Remind yourself to focus.
- Take notes.
- Say the steps aloud while you do the task.
- If thoughts get in the way, jot them down on a notepad.
- When talking to others, ask them to speak slowly and clearly. When they have finished, repeat the main ideas back.

Tips to Improve Figure Ground

What is Figure Ground?

Figure ground is being able to pick an object out from the background. You may have trouble finding an item in a cluttered drawer, a white sock on a white counter, the brakes on the wheelchair or food on the table.

How Others Can Help

- They can help you sort and arrange your items.
- They can look at photos and name items for you to find.

Changes to Make in Your Home

- Keep items in the same place so you always know where to find them. Return items to their place when you are finished.
- Keep items that look alike apart from each other. For instance, do not put white socks with white t-shirts.
- Label the contents of drawers and cupboards.
- Label items using a bold tip marker. Use large print for easy reading.
- Use lights that lessen shadows in the home.
- Limit clutter. Have only a few items in the closet or on the table.
- Add color and contrast to help find objects. Use colored labels, colored tape on doorknobs, light switches or stove controls.

Tasks to Try

- Use a ruler to help you stay on the line when writing or reading.
- Sort the laundry, spoons and forks, or coins.
- Find objects in a cluttered room or drawer.
- Look for hidden pictures like "Where's Waldo".
- Cut out shapes or coupons outlined with a red marker.

Tips to Improve Form Constancy

What is Form Constancy?
Form constancy is picking out one object from other objects by its shape. You can so it even when the object is smaller, larger or turned. You may have trouble finding an object if turned on the side. You might confuse items of like shapes, such as a vase and a glass.

Changes to Make in Your Home

- Keep items upright, with the label showing.
- Keep items in the same place so you always know where to find them. Return items to their place when you are finished.
- Keep items that look alike apart from each other. For instance, do not put white socks with white t-shirts.
- Label the contents of drawers and cupboards.
- Label items using a bold tip marker. Use large print for easy reading.
- Use lights that lessen shadows in the home.
- Limit clutter. Have only a few items in the closet or on the table.
- Add color and contrast to help find objects. Use colored labels, colored tape on doorknobs, light switches or stove controls.

Tasks to Try

- Build block designs using a picture or a model.
- Build puzzles.
- Use your sense of touch to find objects.

Tips to Improve Left Side Awareness

Daily Living Tasks

- Place grooming items on your left side. Someone can guide your hand and help you find and use these items.
- Place clothes on your left side. Turn your body to find the clothing.
- During mealtime, place your left arm on the table. Use a brightly colored placemat to help you find the borders around your meal.
- Place the nightstand on your left side. Put the phone, remote control, water and other items on it. Keep the call light or other alert system on your right side.
- Have others sit or stand on your left side when helping you.

Scanning Tasks

- Use brightly colored tape or Velcro to outline the work area. Trace around the edge with your finger.
- Ask someone to write or draw on the right side of a dry erase board. You can copy them onto the left side of the board. Then clean off the board using your left hand.
- Play board games and card games. Work crossword and word find puzzles.
- Practice reading and writing the newspaper headlines. Use a ruler to keep track of each line when reading.
- Look for pictures in a magazine, describe what you see.
- Name all the items in your room.
- On your left wrist, wear a bell or a watch with a timer. Set it to beep, to remind you to attend to your left side.

Use Your Left Arm and Hand

- Tap the fingers of your left hand or squeeze a soft rubber ball.
- Pick objects out of a basket. Place them on the table using your left hand.

Tips to Improve Left Side Awareness

Use a Mental Image
Imagine a lighthouse or look at a drawing of a lighthouse to remind you to sweep your vision to the left side. Color the light beams with a yellow marker.

"Imagine you are a lighthouse like this one. Imagine your eyes are like the lights inside the top. Sweep all the way to the left and right of the horizon to guide the ships at sea to safety. Use your 'lighthouse beam' to sweep. Scan across the tabletop, book, newspaper and around the room. Remember to sweep your beam and scan to the left side." (Niemeier JP (1998) The Lighthouse Strategy)

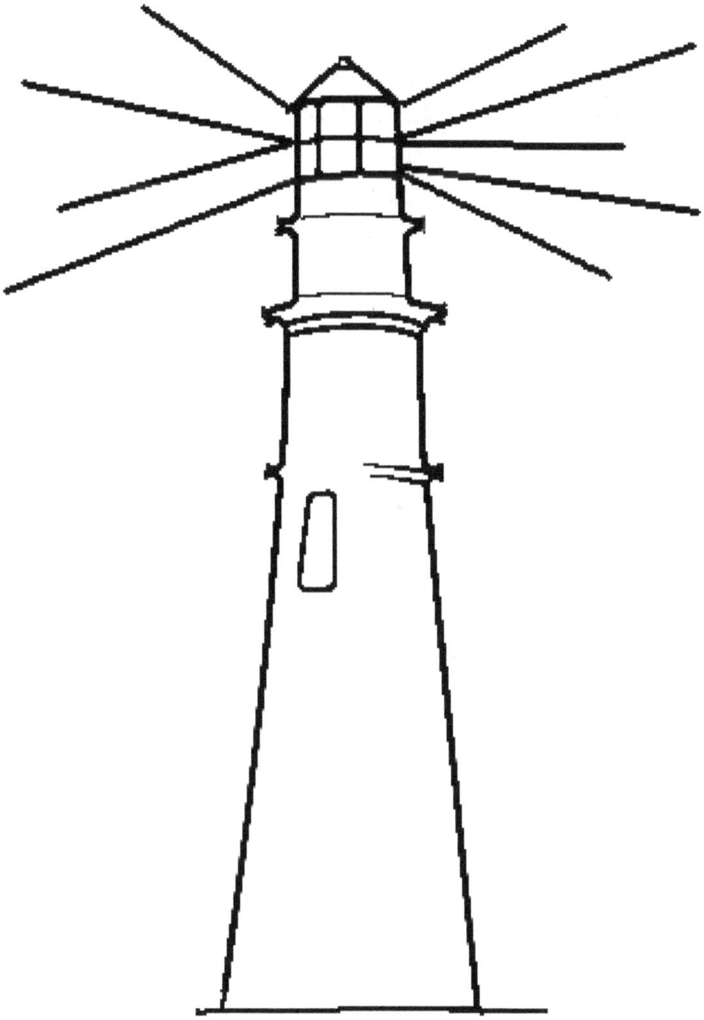

Tips to Improve Memory

What is Memory?
Memory is the ability to take in, store, retrieve, and use knowledge.

Take Care of Yourself
- Get a good night's sleep.
- Take slow, deep breaths.
- Exercise most days.
- Eat a balanced diet.
- Drink water.
- Reduce your stress.

Exercise Your Memory
- Play word puzzles: crosswords, logic, and word find.
- Play word games: Boggle, Scrabble, and Wheel of Fortune.
- Play number games: Sudoku and math puzzles.
- Play card games: Bridge, rummy, and canasta.
- Read often and read a variety of books.
- Repeat and recall groups of words, like a grocery list.
- Learn new words.
- Learn a new language.
- Use your other hand.

Make Changes to Your Home
- Keep a notepad by the phone for phone messages.
- Put vital items on a corkboard.
- Find a special place for items like keys, wallet, and glasses. Always put them back in the same place.
- Attach items to your person. Put reading glasses on a neck cord or the phone in a pocket.
- Label cupboards and drawers.
- Label doors so you know which room is which.

Tips to Improve Memory - External Memory Aids

Follow a Routine

- Follow a routine. Try to do the same activities at the same time every day. Make a chart of events using pictures or photos.
- Set a day for each chore. For instance, laundry on Monday, shop on Tuesday, and clean on Friday.
- Keep a daily journal. Look at your schedule often, so you do not forget to do things. Set a time each day to focus on planning the next day.

Use Reminders

- Write down the things you need to recall. Use a dry erase board.
- Use a large calendar. Keep it where you will see it.
- Keep a daily journal to write down ideas and thoughts you have. Keep it with you all the time and try to write in it every day
- Place photos of your contacts near the phone. Label the photos with names and phone numbers.
- Have step-by-step directions on how to use devices, like the coffee maker or washing machine.
- Use your cell phone to take a picture of something you need to remember.

Let Others Help

- Set up online bill paying.
- Set an alarm to remind you when it is time to take medications. Use a pillbox with a built-in timer.
- Have others take notes during meetings with the doctor.
- Use phones that autodial.
- Use voice assistants such as Google Home, Apple's Siri and Amazon's Alexa.

Tips to Improve Memory - Internal Memory Aids

Tips

- Focus on what you want to recall.
- Break down new learning into small parts. Learn the small parts instead of trying to learn it all at one time.
- Repeat the new learning back in your own words.
- Find out how you learn best. Is it by seeing, by hearing or by doing? To improve your memory, use all these learning styles. For instance, learn how to get to a new store. Look at a map to the store (seeing). Describe the route aloud (hearing). Have someone go with you the first time (doing).

Use Aids

- Repeat information. When you meet a new person, repeat their name a few times during the visit.
- Say the ABC's to think of words or names you want to recall.
- Connect what you want to recall with something you already know. Connect the house number of 1960 with the year you were born. Connect someone you just met with a friend with the same name.
- Form a visual image. If you park on level 3B, think of three bees buzzing around your car. The more vivid and colorful the images, the easier they will be to recall.
- Group information. Arrange a long list in smaller lists. Write a grocery list by store aisle.

Tips to Improve Motor Planning

What is Motor Planning?
Motor planning is thinking of, planning and carrying out the steps to complete a task. Problems with motor planning can affect your ability to complete tasks. You may have trouble getting dressed, tying shoes, throwing a ball, using a comb, or using a spoon.

How Others Can Help

- They can encourage you to work slowly and safely.
- They can show you a task by sitting next to you instead of in front of you.
- They can guide your hands to help you do a task.
- They can encourage you to tell you what you are doing for each step.
- They can make a list in words or pictures that you can follow.
- They can help you practice tasks that are part of your daily routine.

Tips to Improve Right Side Awareness

Daily Living Tasks

- Place grooming items on your right side. Someone can guide your hand to help you find and use these items.
- Place clothes on your right side. Turn your body to find the clothing.
- During mealtime, place your right arm on the table. Use a brightly colored placemat to help you find the borders around the meal.
- Place the nightstand on your right side. Place the phone, remote control, water and other items on it. Keep the call light or other alert system on your left side.
- Have someone sit or stand on your right side when providing help.

Scanning Tasks

- Use brightly colored tape or Velcro to outline the work area. Trace around the edge with your finger.
- Ask someone to write or draw on the left side of a dry erase board. You can copy them onto the right side of the board. Then clean off the board using your right hand.
- Play board games and card games. Work crossword and word find puzzles.
- Practice reading and writing the newspaper headlines. Use a ruler to keep track of each line when reading.
- Look for pictures in a magazine, describe what you see.
- Find and name all the items in your room.
- On your right wrist, wear a bell or a watch with a timer. Set it to beep, to remind you to attend to your right side.

Use Your Right Arm and Hand

- Tap the fingers of your right hand or squeeze a soft rubber ball.
- Pick objects out of a basket. Place them on the table using your right hand.

Tips to Improve Right Side Awareness

Use a Mental Image
Imagine a lighthouse or look at a drawing of a lighthouse to remind you to sweep your vision to the right side. Color the light beams with a yellow marker.

"Imagine you are a lighthouse like this one. Imagine your eyes are like the lights inside the top. Sweep all the way to the right and left of the horizon to guide the ships at sea to safety. Use your 'lighthouse beam' to sweep. Scan across the tabletop, book, newspaper and around the room. Remember to sweep your beam and scan to the right side." (Niemeier JP (1998) The Lighthouse Strategy)

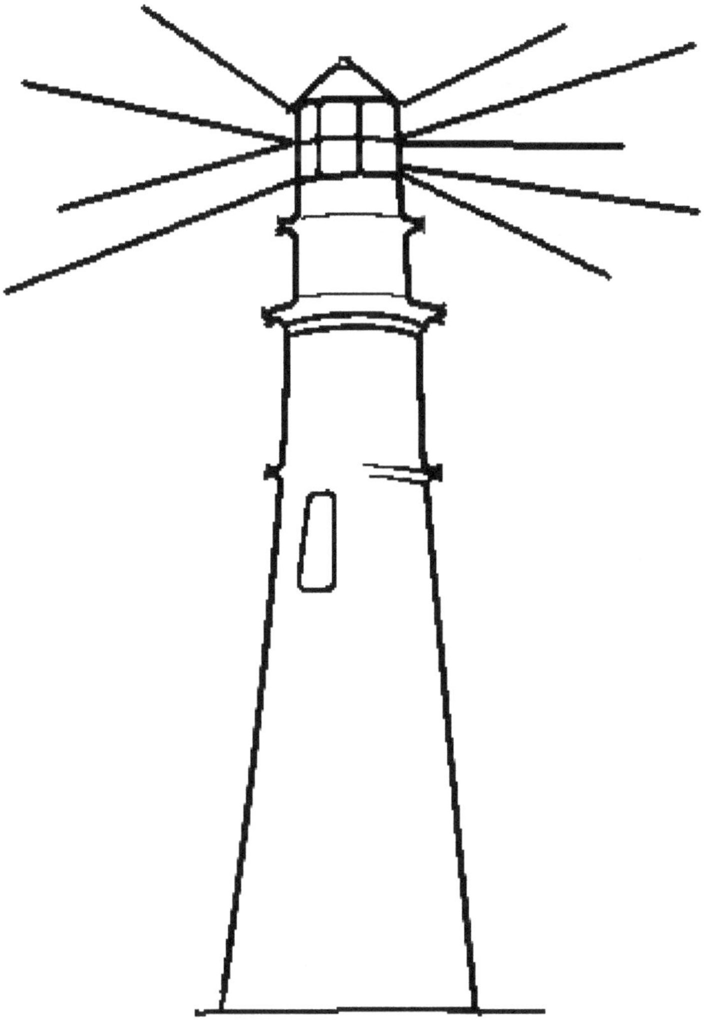

Tips to Improve Thinking Skills

Take Care of Yourself

- Get a good night's sleep.
- Take slow, deep breaths.
- Exercise on most days.
- Eat a balanced diet
- Drink water.
- Reduce your stress.

Do Not Get Tired

- Plan tasks when you have the most energy.
- Take breaks.

Limit Distractions

- Focus on one thing at a time
- Find a quiet place.
- Close the curtains.
- Turn off the TV, cell phone and computer.

Get Organized

- Arrange all items in consistent places.
- Return items to their place when you are finished.
- Store items used at the same time next to each other.
- Schedule a weekly time to clean and arrange.
- Allow yourself plenty of time to plan tasks and record your plans. Use aids such as calendars, journals, smart phones or computers.

Ask for Help

- Set a timer or alarm to remind you of things to do in the day.
- Have others remind you to start tasks.
- Ask others to give you clear, step-by-step directions including pictures.
- Use step-by-step checklists of tasks for your morning routine or making a meal.
- Discuss your plans with others. They can remind you if needed.

Follow a Routine

- Keep a daily journal
- Look at your schedule often, so you do not forget to do things.
- Check off each activity when you finish.
- Set a time each day to plan and organize for the next day.
- Set a day for each chore like laundry on Monday, shop on Tuesday
- Make a chart of events using pictures or photos.

Tips to Improve Vision

Low Vision

- See a vision specialist for corrective lenses.
- Wear eyeglasses during tasks.
- Make changes to your home and tasks. Use large print items; a magnifying glass; increase lighting; use contrast; decrease clutter.
- Improve your other senses (hearing, touch, smell, taste).

Visual Field Loss

- See a vision specialist for prism lenses and eye (ocular) exercises.
- Make up for the loss of visual field by turning your head.
- Outline work areas. Use a colored mat under your plate. A ribbon can mark the edge of a book. Use tape to outline the counter edge.
- Add color and contrast to doorways and furniture.
- When writing, fix your vision on the tip of the pen.
- Play board games and card games. Work crossword and word find puzzles.
- Read and copy the newspaper headlines. Use a ruler to keep track of each line when reading.
- Avoid crowds or busy places.

Double Vision

- See a vision specialist for patching, prism lenses, and eye (ocular) exercises.

Occupational Therapy TOOLKIT

Tips to Improve Visual-Motor Integration

What is Visual-Motor Integration?
Visual-motor integration also called eye-hand coordination, eye-foot coordination and eye-body coordination.

Activities to Try

- String beads.
- Use salad or bread tongs to pick up small objects.
- Practice dialing a phone.
- Sort various small objects (coins, buttons).
- Sew, knit and crochet.
- Play catch with a soft ball, or rolled-up socks.
- Play balloon or beach ball volley.
- Toss rolled-up socks into a laundry basket.
- Trace or cut out shapes or pictures from a magazine.
- Cut out coupons.
- Measure out pasta, flour, beans, rice, sugar or spices.
- Lace shoes and tie shoes. Button, zip, or snap.
- Play games. Jenga, cribbage and Scrabble
- Craft projects: paint-by-number, coloring books, origami.
- Kick a beach ball back and forth.
- Tap your feet and clap your hands in time with music.
- Move through an obstacle course.

Tips to Improve Visual Spatial Relations

What are Visual Spatial Relations?
Visual spatial relations help you understand what is around you and where.

- You in relation to other people
- You in relation to other objects
- Objects in relation to other objects

You may have trouble with turning clothes the right way for dressing; putting paste onto the toothbrush or walking through doorways.

How Others Can Help

- Do not use words that describe the position of things (up, down, over, under, above, below, behind, in front, in, out, on, next to, left and right).

Changes to Make in the Home

- Decide on a special place to keep objects like keys, wallets or glasses. Always put them back in the same place.
- Have only a few items on the counter, in the closet or on the table.
- Add color and contrast to help you to find items. Use colored labels and colored tape on doorknobs, light switches or stove controls.

Tasks to Try

- Move around the furniture and through doorways.
- Copy 3-D block designs.
- Use graph paper to help space the letters when writing.
- Use your sense of touch to find items.
- Reach for cans in the cupboard.
- Set the table.
- Water the plants.

Tips to Manage Action Tremors

Take Care of Yourself

- Get a good night's sleep.
- Exercise most days.
- Manage your stress.
- Reduce or do away with caffeine.
- Take medication as prescribed.

Brace Your Arm

- Brace your arm against the wall.
- Brace your elbows against your body.
- Support your arms on the table or counter.
- Support your wrist with your other hand.

Use Weighted Items

- Use ______ lb/kg wrist weights during tasks.
- Use weighted spoons and forks or heavy glasses.
- Use weighted large pens.

Change the Way You Do Things

- Complete activities when tremors are less severe.
- Change the task. For example, drink soup or cereal from a mug.
- Place non-slip mats under dishes to keep them from moving.
- Use a plate guard to push food onto a spoon.
- To shave, wash your face, or brush your teeth, move your head instead of your arm.
- Use an electric razor and an electric toothbrush.
- Use a computer or voice recorder instead of writing.
- Change the computer accessibility functions.
- Buy a special computer mouse that filters out hand shaking.

Tips to Prevent Lower Body Lymphedema

Check all areas of your leg every day for signs of problems. Report concerns to the doctor.

Know the Signs of Edema (swelling)

Your foot, leg, stomach and/or groin will feel tight or heavy.
Shoes and clothing will feel tight.
Your leg measurement may be larger than your base level.

Know the Signs of Cellulitis (infection of the skin and tissues under the skin)

The signs include redness, swelling, tenderness, pain, warmth, fever

Protect Your Leg

Keep your legs and feet clean. Wash with a mild soap and water. Dry gently include skin folds and between your toes. See a foot doctor for nail care.

Skin care

- Use lotion to keep your skin from getting dry or cracked.
- Use sunscreen and bug spray when going outside.
- Use an electric razor to shave your legs.
- Avoid extreme hot or cold such as ice packs, heating pads and hot tubs.
- Do not walk without shoes or slippers.

Do not stand, sit or cross your legs for a long period.

Try to keep your leg above the level of your heart when you can.

Avoid needles (injections, blood draws, acupuncture) or blood pressure cuff on your leg.

Do not wear clothes that have tight bands at your waist or ankles. Do not wear tight shoes.

Try to maintain a healthy weight. Being overweight can increase the chances of swelling. Limit eating foods high in salt and fat.

Wear a lymphedema alert bracelet.

Tips to Prevent Upper Body Lymphedema

Check all areas of your arm every day for signs of problems. Report concerns to the doctor.

Know the Signs of Edema (swelling)

Your hand, arm, armpit and/or chest will feel tight and heavy.
Jewelry and clothing will feel tight.
Your arm measurement may be larger than your base level.

Know the Signs of Cellulitis (infection of the skin and tissues under the skin)

The signs include redness, swelling, tenderness, pain, warmth, fever

Protect Your Arm

Keep your arm, hand, and nails clean. Wash with a mild soap and water. Dry gently.

Skin care

- Use lotion to keep your skin from getting dry or cracked.
- Use sunscreen and bug spray when going outside.
- Use an electric razor if you shave under your arm.
- Avoid extreme hot or cold such as ice packs, heating pads and hot tubs.
- Wear gloves when gardening, doing housework, or using the oven.

Do not overtire your arm.

- Do not use forceful motions like scrubbing.
- Do not pull on your arm.
- Do not lift or carry more than _____ lb/kg.

Try to keep your arm above the level of your heart when you can.

Wear clothes and jewelry that are not tight around your wrist. Women should wear well-fitted bras. Bra straps should not be too tight.

Avoid needles (injections, blood draws, acupuncture) or blood pressure cuff on your arm.

Try to maintain a healthy weight. Being overweight can increase the chances of swelling. Limit eating foods high in salt and fat.

Wear a lymphedema alert bracelet.

Occupational Therapy TOOLKIT

Using a Front Wheel Walker (2 wheels)

Safety Tips

- Always keep the walker close.
- Wear well-fitted shoes. Do not wear clothes that drag. They can get caught in the walker
- Have the walker repaired if the rubber tips or the wheels show signs of wear.

Safe Pathways

- Keep pathways clear of throw rugs, clutter and cords. They could catch on the walker and cause a fall.
- Arrange the furniture to allow room to move with the walker.
- Do not walk on a rug that is on top of the carpet.
- Place the walker wheels to the inside so they will not catch on doorframes.

Walking

- Walk in the center of the walker.
- Walk slowly and with good posture. Keep your back straight.
- Look forward when you are walking, not down at your feet.
- Push the walker to move forward. Keep it an arm's length in front of you. You may lose your balance if you step too far forward.

Sitting Down

- Do not start to sit while you are still turning.
- Stand in front of the chair, with the backs of your legs touching the chair.
- Reach behind for the chair with both hands
- Do not lean on the walker when sitting down, because it could tip over.
- Slowly lower yourself into the chair.

Standing Up

- Place the walker in front.
- Move forward to the edge of the chair.
- Place both hands on the chair arms. Do not pull up on the walker because it could tip over.
- Lean forward with "nose over toes."
- Push yourself up to standing.
- Make sure you have your balance before walking.

Using a Front Wheel Walker (2 wheels)

How to Carry Items

- Keep both hands on the walker for balance. Carry items using pockets, a small purse or bag hung over one side, or use a basket, bag, or tray made for a walker.

Reaching

- To reach for an item in front, get close or use a reacher.

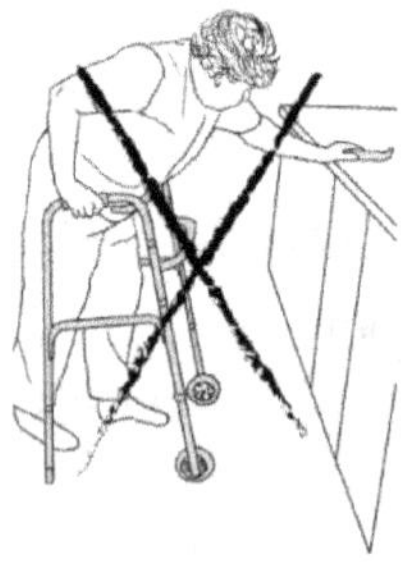

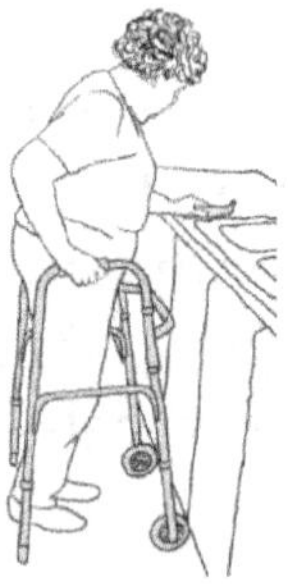

- Do not reach to the side of the walker. Turn the walker and face the item you need to reach.

- Do not bend over to pick up an item from the floor. Use a reacher.

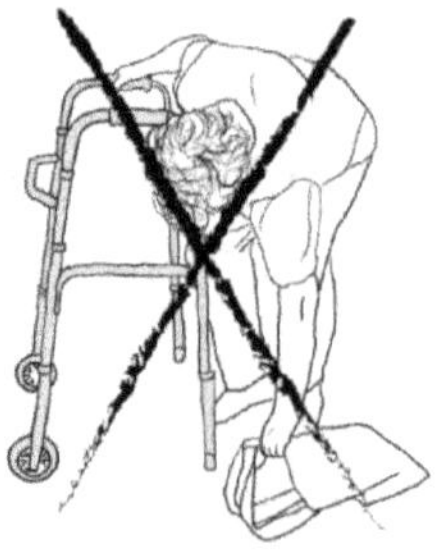

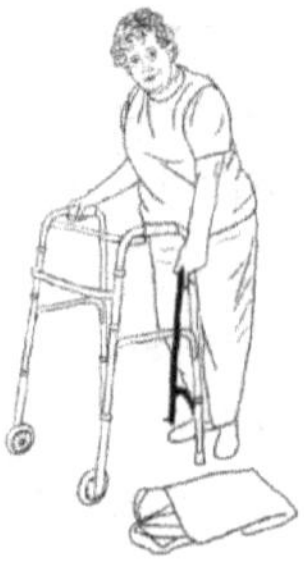

Using a Rollator (3 or 4 wheels)

Safety Tips

- Always keep the rollator close.
- Wear well-fitted shoes. Do not wear clothes that drag. They can get caught in the walker.
- Repair the rollator if the brakes do not hold tightly or the wheels show wear.

Safe Pathways

- Keep the pathways clear of throw rugs, clutter and cords. They could catch on the rollator and cause a fall.
- Arrange the furniture to allow room to move with the rollator.
- Do not walk on a rug that is on top of the carpet.

Walking

- Walk in the center of the rollator.
- Walk slowly and with good posture. Keep your back straight.
- Look forward when you walk, not down at your feet.
- Push the rollator to move forward. Keep it an arm's length in front of you. You may lose your balance if you step too far forward.

Using the Rollator Seat

- Lock the brakes by pressing down on the brake handles. When locking the brakes, you will hear a click or snap.
- Turn around holding the handles of the rollator.
- Feel the seat at the back of your legs and sit down.
- Leave the brakes on while seated.
- Do not let someone push the rollator while you are sitting on it.

Sitting Down in a Chair

- Do not start to sit while you are still turning.
- Stand in front of the chair, with the backs of your legs touching the chair.
- Lock the brakes by pressing down on the brake handles. When locking the brakes, you will hear a click or snap.
- Reach behind for the chair with both hands.
- Do not lean on the rollator when sitting down, because it could tip over.
- Slowly lower yourself into the chair.

Using a Rollator (3 or 4 wheels)

Standing Up

- Place the rollator in front.
- Lock the brakes by pressing down on the brake handles. When locking the brakes, you will hear a click or snap.
- Move forward to the edge of the chair.
- Place both hands on the chair arms. Do not pull up on the rollator, because it could tip over.
- Lean forward with "nose over toes."
- Push up to standing.
- Unlock the brakes.
- Make sure you have your balance before walking.

How to Carry Items

- Keep both hands on the rollator for balance. Carry items using pockets, a small purse or bag hung over one side, or use a basket, bag, or tray made for a rollator.

Reaching

- To reach for an item in front, get close as you and lock the brakes.
- Do not reach to the side of the rollator. Turn the rollator, lock the brakes and face the item you need to reach.
- Do not bend over to pick up an item from the floor. Lock the rollator brakes and use a reacher.

Occupational Therapy TOOLKIT

Using a Standard Walker (no wheels)

Safety Tips

- Always keep the walker close.
- Wear well-fitted shoes. Do not wear clothes that drag. They can get caught in the walker.
- Have the walker repaired if the rubber tips show signs of wear.

Safe Pathways

- Keep the pathways clear of throw rugs, clutter and cords. They could catch on the walker and cause a fall.
- Arrange the furniture to allow room to move with the walker.
- Do not walk on a rug that is on top of the carpet.

Walking

- Walk in the center of the walker.
- Walk slowly and with good posture. Keep your back straight.
- Look forward when you walk, not down at your feet.
- Sequence for using a standard, non-wheeled walker:
    1. Pick up and place the walker.
    2. All four legs of the walker should be on the ground before stepping.
    3. Step with one foot.
    4. Step with your other foot.
    5. Pick up and place the walker again.

Sitting Down

- Do not start to sit while you are still turning.
- Stand in front of the chair, with the backs of your legs touching the chair.
- Reach behind for the chair with both hands.
- Do not lean on the walker when sitting down, it could tip over.
- Slowly lower yourself into the chair.

Standing Up

- Place the walker in front.
- Move forward to the edge of the chair.
- Place both hands on the chair arms. Do not pull on the walker it could tip over.
- Lean forward with "nose over toes."
- Push yourself up to standing.
- Make sure you have your balance before walking.

Using a Standard Walker (no wheels)

How to Carry Items

- Keep both hands on the walker for balance. Carry items using pockets, a small purse or bag hung over one side, or use a basket, bag, or tray made for a walker.

Reaching

- To reach for an item in front, get close or use a reacher.

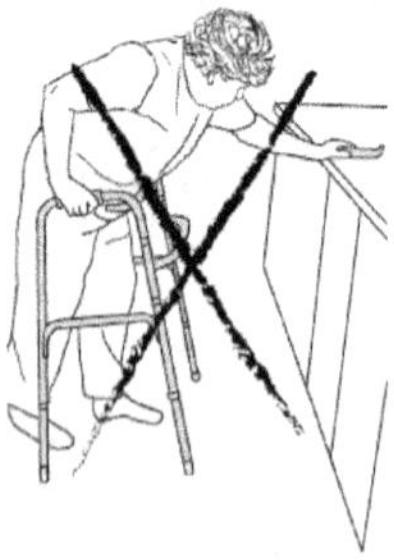

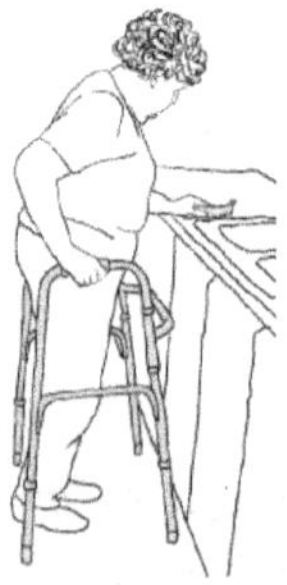

- Do not reach to the side of the walker. Turn the walker and face the item you need to reach.

- Do not bend over to pick up an item from the floor. Use a reacher.

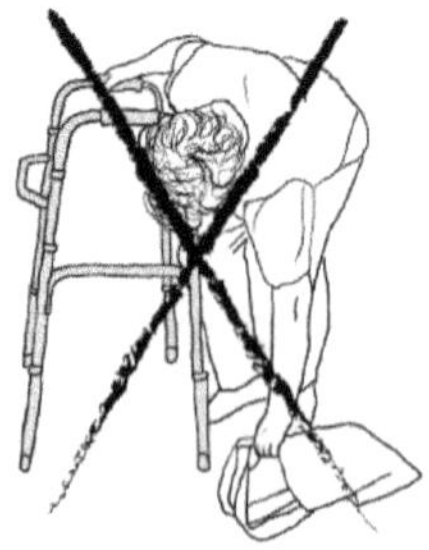

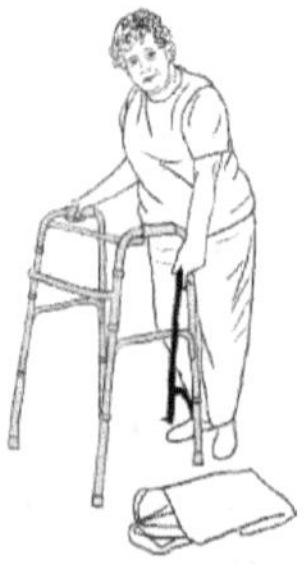

Using a Wheelchair

Safety Tips

- Keep the brakes on when sitting in the wheelchair. Apply the brakes before you transfer. If the brakes are hard to lock, use a brake extension. If the brakes are not holding, get them repaired.

- Wear the seatbelt when sitting in the wheelchair.

- Before you transfer or stand up, move the footrest to the side. Do not just flip up the footplate, you could trip.

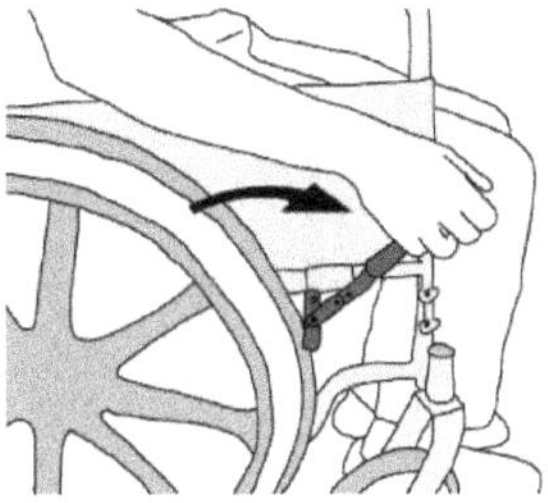

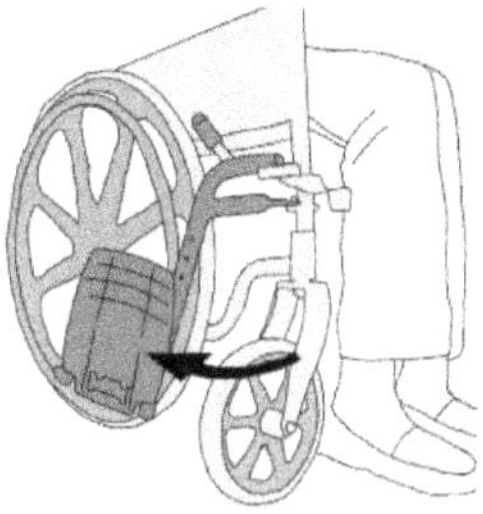

Safe Pathways

- Keep pathways clear of throw rugs, clutter and cords. Arrange the furniture to allow room to move in the wheelchair.

How to Carry Items

- Tuck a purse at your side or buy a wheelchair bag.

- Keep loose objects or lap cover away from the wheels.

- Do not put heavy loads on the back of the wheelchair. The wheelchair could tip over when you stand up.

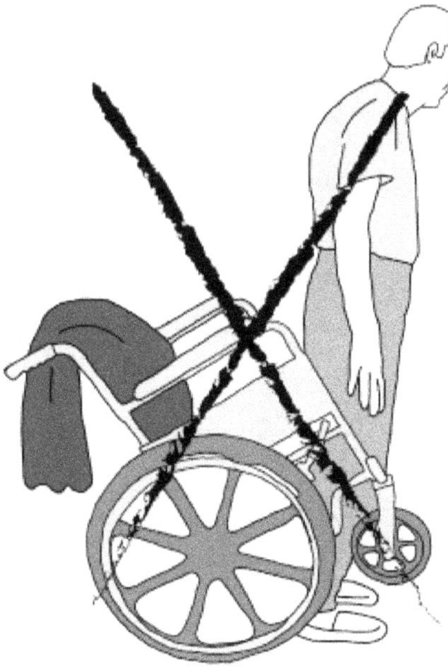

Using a Wheelchair

How to Reach Safely

- Move the wheelchair close to the item. Lock the brakes and place the front wheels forward. Reach only as far as you can without moving from the seat.

- Never reach between your knees to pick up an item from the floor. Do not lean over the back of the wheelchair. Use a reacher to pick up objects from the floor.

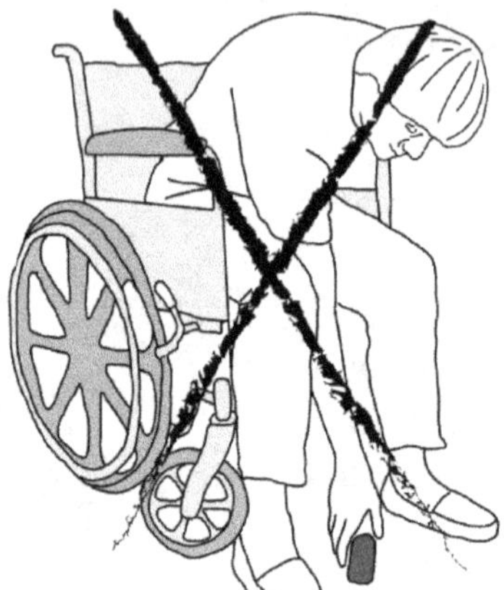

Writing Tips for Parkinson's

Writing Tools

- Try different pens and pen grips (thick, thin, with or without textured or non-slip surfaces, weighted, fine point, easy-flow, roller ball, ballpoint or felt tip).
- Hold the pen in a new way. Try placing it between your index and middle finger and hold it with your thumb.

Prepare

- Allow yourself plenty of time.
- Limit distractions, turn off the TV and avoid talking.
- Sit with your elbow and wrist on the table.
- Use good lighting.

Writing

- Use lined paper or graph paper.
- Play music to help get a rhythm for writing. Find one that works best for you, like a march or a smooth waltz.
- Think about making "big and slow" strokes.
- Imagine writing big letters in your mind.
- Print instead of cursive writing

Writing Options

- Use the speaker on the phone when taking a message. This will free up your hands for writing.
- Get a signature stamp for writing checks
- Use a computer for writing.
- Use a speech to text program.
- Use a voice recorder.

Occupational Therapy TOOLKIT

Ankle and Foot Active Range of Motion

Do the checked exercises _____ times per day, _____ days a week.

☐ **Pull Foot Back**
Sit in a chair. Pull your foot toward your knee.

Do _____ sets of _____.
Repeat with your other foot.

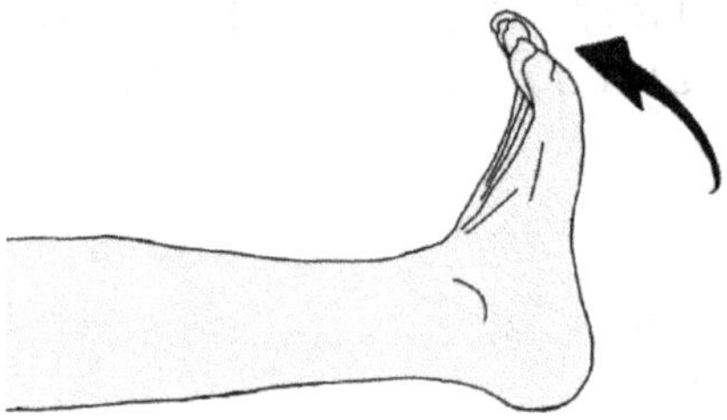

☐ **Point Foot**
Sit in a chair. Point your toes.

Do _____ sets of _____.
Repeat with your other foot.

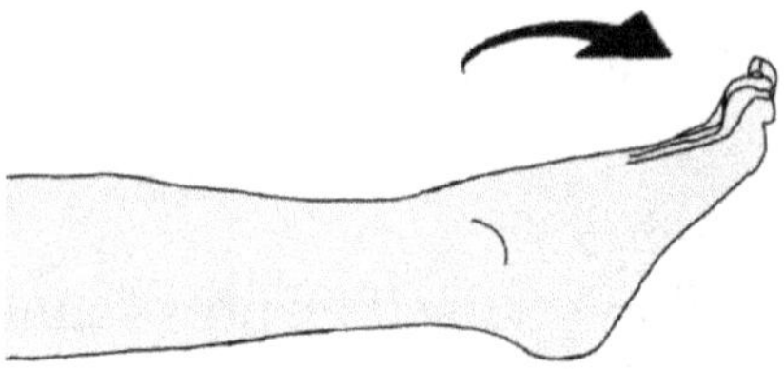

☐ **Turn Foot In**
Sit in a chair. Point your toes up. Turn your foot inward.

Do _____ sets of _____.
Repeat with your other foot.

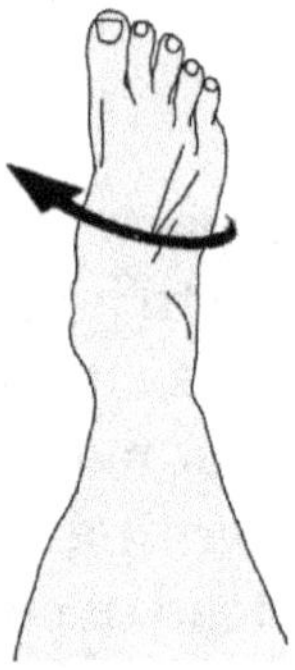

☐ **Turn Foot Out**
Sit in a chair. Point your toes up. Turn your foot outward.

Do _____ sets of _____.
Repeat with your other foot.

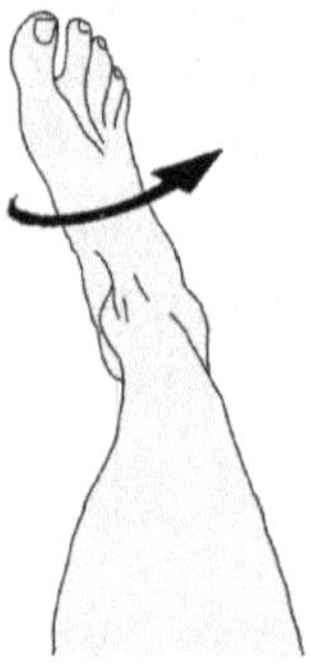

Occupational Therapy TOOLKIT

Ankle and Foot Active Range of Motion

Do the checked exercises _____ times per day, _____ days a week.

☐ **Ankle Circles**
Sit in a chair. Make circles with your foot. Move one way and then the other.

Do _____ sets of _____.
Repeat with your other foot.

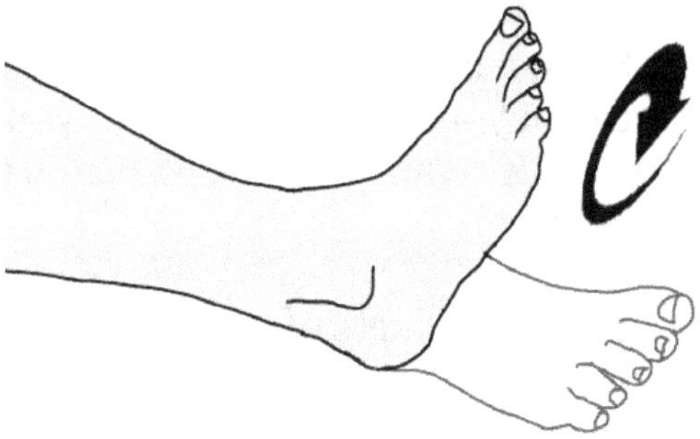

☐ **Toe Curls**
Sit in a chair. Keep your ankle in neutral. Curl your toes down.

Do _____ sets of _____.
Repeat with your other foot.

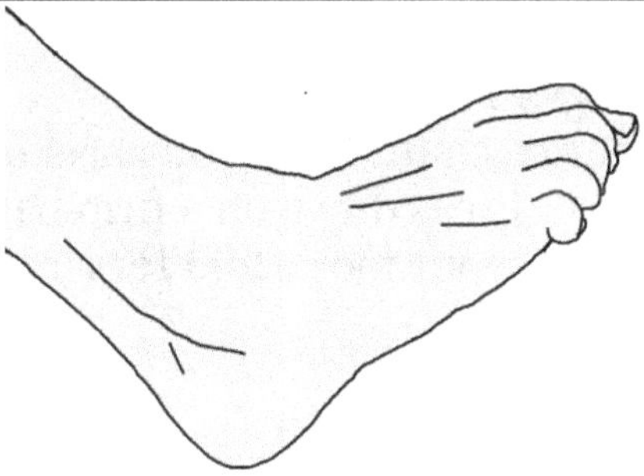

☐ **Pull Toes Back**
Sit in a chair. Keep your ankle in neutral. Pull your toes back.

Do _____ sets of _____.
Repeat with your other foot.

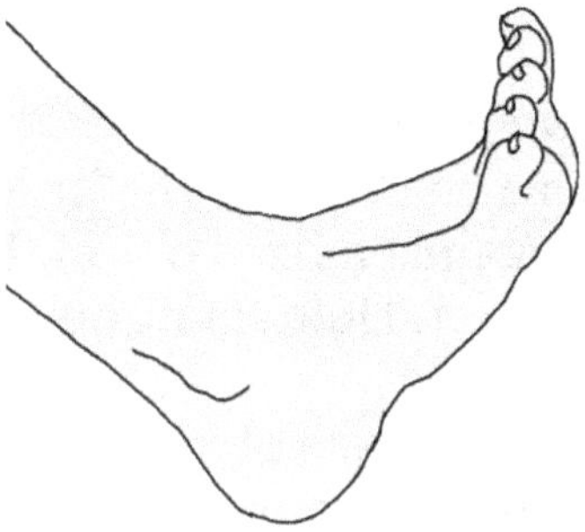

☐ **ABC's**
Sit in a chair. Point your toes. Trace the letters of the ABC's in the air.

Do _____ sets of _____.
Repeat with your other foot.

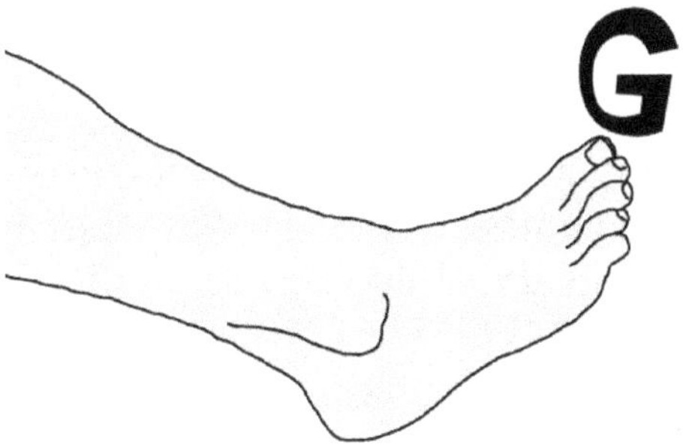

Occupational Therapy TOOLKIT

Ankle and Foot Isometric Exercises

Do the checked exercises _____ times per day, _____ days a week.

☐ **Press Foot Up**
Sit in a chair. Place your stronger foot on top of your weaker foot. Lift your weaker foot up against the resistance. Hold for a count of _____.

Do _____ sets of _____.
Repeat with your other foot.

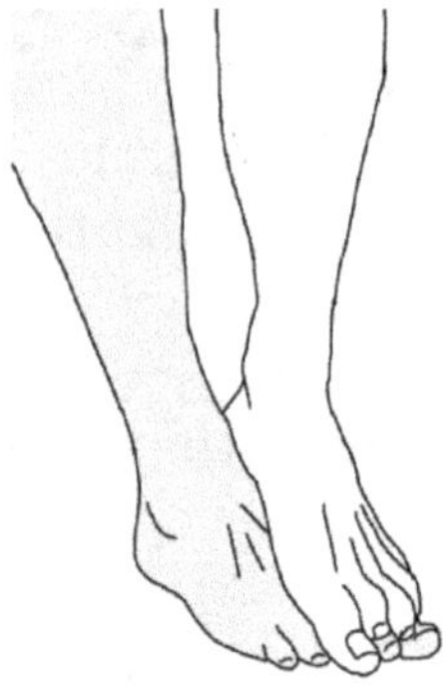

☐ **Press Foot Down**
Sit in a chair. Keep your heel on the floor. Press down on a firm ball with the ball of your foot. Hold for a count of _____.

Do _____ sets of _____.
Repeat with your other foot.

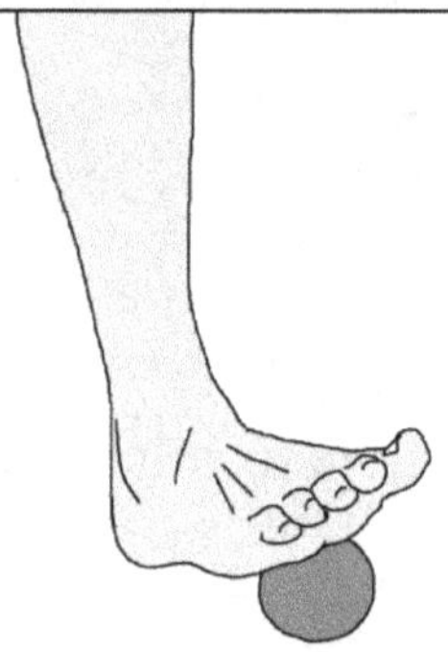

☐ **Press Foot Inward**
Sit in a chair. Place the inside of your foot against a fixed object. Push against the object. Hold for a count of _____.

Do _____ sets of _____.
Repeat with your other foot.

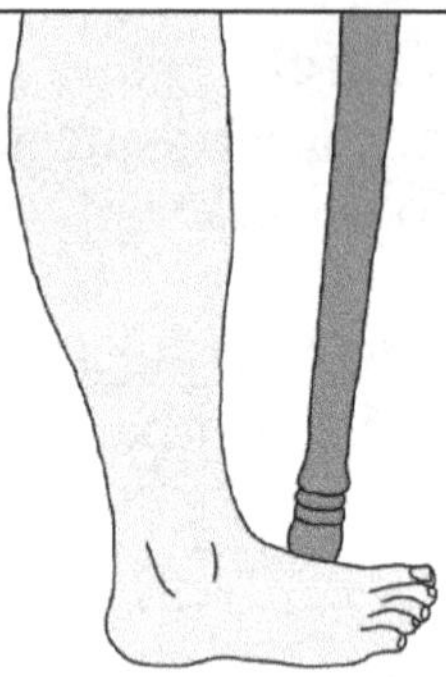

☐ **Press Foot Outward**
Sit in a chair. Place the outside of your foot against a fixed object. Push against the object. Hold for a count of _____.

Do _____ sets of _____.
Repeat with your other foot.

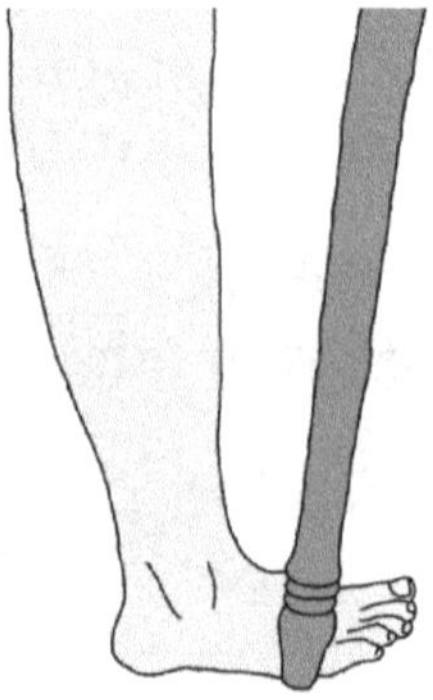

Ankle and Foot Strength Exercises

Do the checked exercises _____ times per day, _____ days a week.

☐ **Towel Sweep Out**
Sit in a chair. Place your heel on the floor and the front of your foot on a towel. Place a _____ lb/kg weight on the towel. Push the towel outward with a sweeping motion.

Do _____ sets of _____.
Repeat with your other foot.

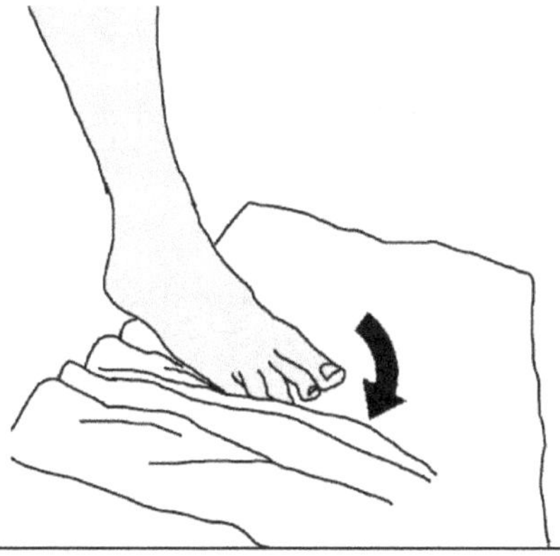

☐ **Towel Sweep In**
Sit in a chair. Place your heel on the floor and the front of your foot on a towel. Place a _____ lb/kg weight on the towel. Push the towel inward with a sweeping motion.

Do _____ sets of _____.
Repeat with your other foot.

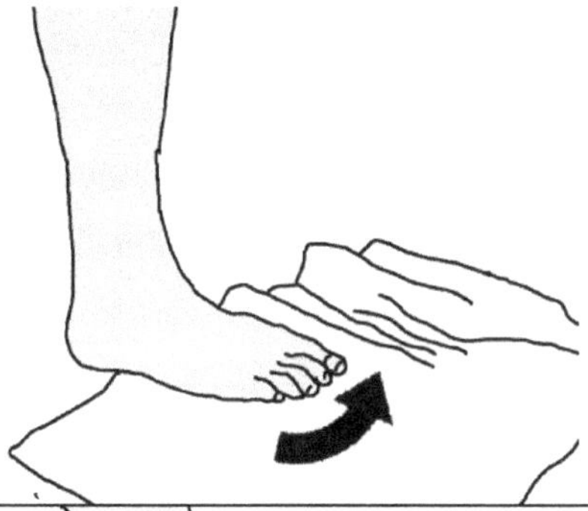

☐ **Towel Scrunch**
Sit in a chair. Place your heel on the floor and the front of your foot on a towel. Place a _____ lb/kg weight on the towel. Curl your toes to pull the towel toward you.

Do _____ sets of _____.
Repeat with your other foot.

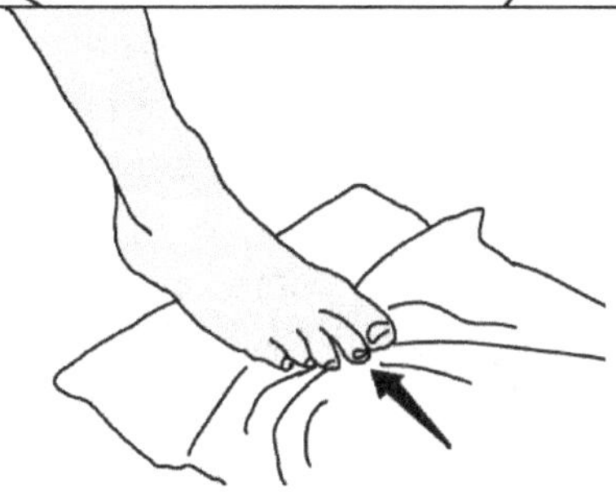

☐ **Marbles**
Sit in a chair. Pick up marbles or small smooth rocks using your toes.

Do _____ sets of _____.
Repeat with your other foot.

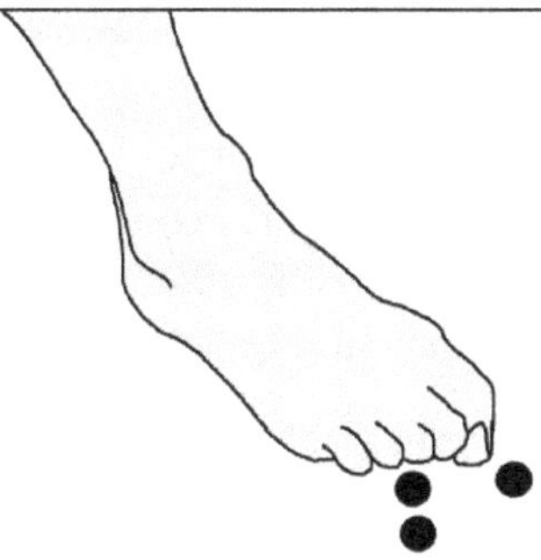

Occupational Therapy TOOLKIT

Ankle and Foot Strength Exercises

Do the checked exercises _____ times per day, _____ days a week.

☐ **Heel Raises**
Hold onto a stable object. Raise your heels off the floor

Do _____ sets of _____.

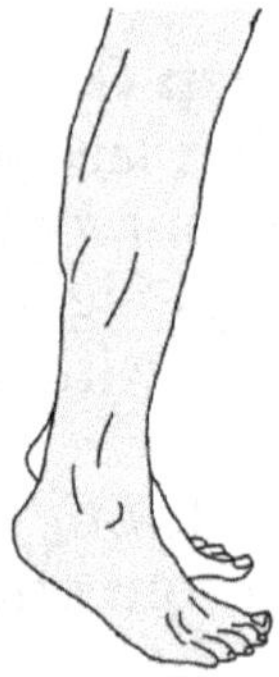

☐ **Toe Raises**
Hold onto a stable object. Raise your toes off the floor.

Do _____ sets of _____.

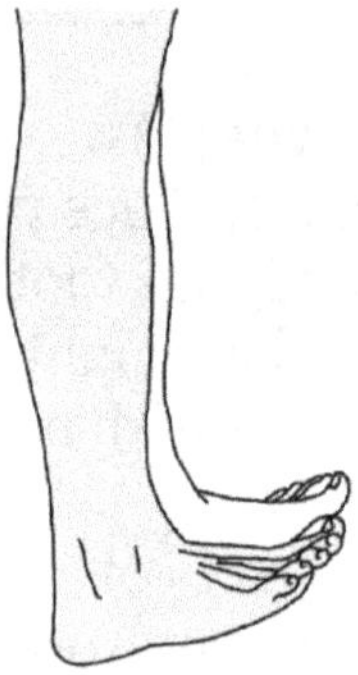

☐ **Single Leg Balance**
Hold onto a stable object. Stand on one foot. Hold for a count of _____.

Do _____ sets of _____.
Repeat with your other leg.

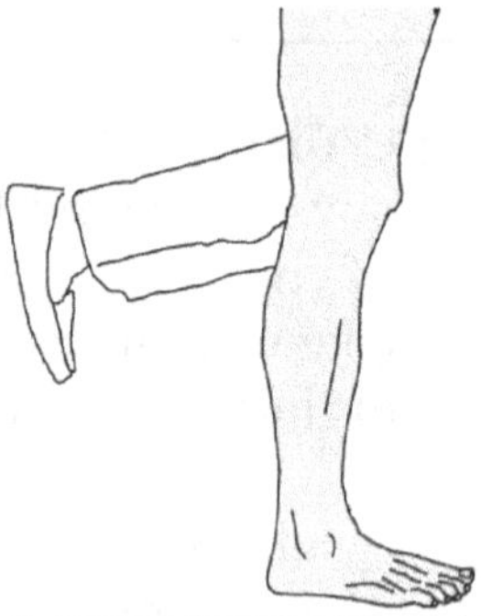

☐ **Single Leg Balance on a Towel**
Place a folded towel on the floor. Hold onto a stable object. Stand on the towel with one foot. Hold for a count of _____.

Do _____ sets of _____
Repeat with your other leg.

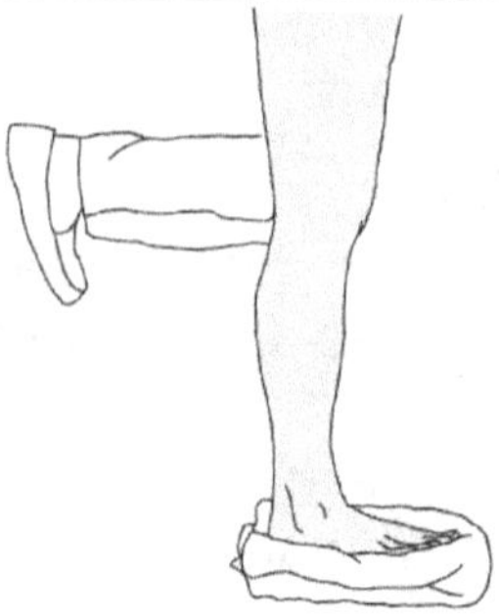

Ankle and Foot Stretches

Do the checked exercises ______ times per day, ______ days a week.

☐ **Calf Stretch**
Stand an arm's length from the wall. Place one foot in front of the other. Put your hands on the wall. Bend the forward knee. Lean forward until you feel a stretch. Hold for a count of ______.

Do ______ sets of ______.
Repeat with your other leg.

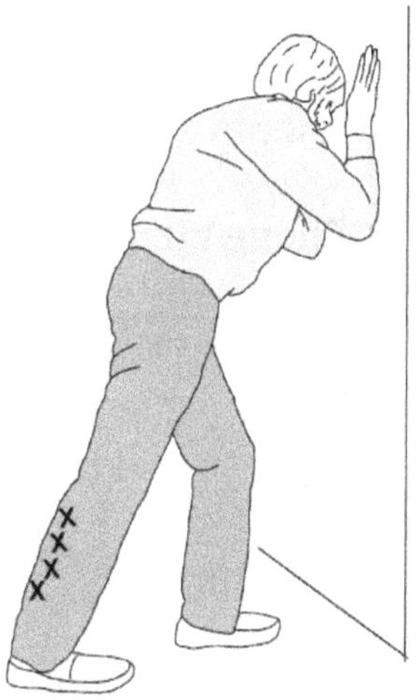

☐ **Heel Stretch**
Place a strap around the ball of your foot. Keep your knee straight. Pull the strap until you feel a stretch in the back of your calf. Hold for a count of ______.

Do ______ sets of ______.
Repeat with your other leg.

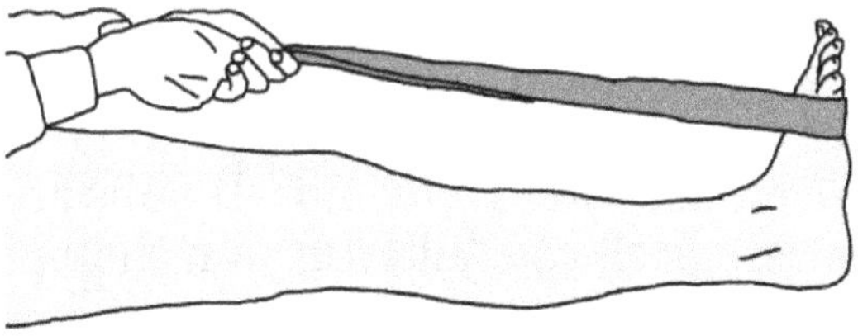

☐ **Stair Stretch**
Hold the rail. Stand on a step with your heels off the edge. Lower your heels down until you feel a stretch in the back of your calf. Hold for a count of ______.

Do ______ sets of ______.

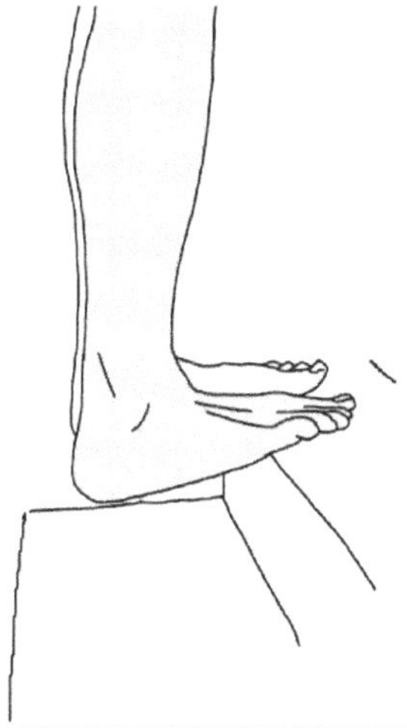

Occupational Therapy TOOLKIT

Arm Cycle

Name: ________________________________

Date: ________________________________

Therapist: ________________________________

Phone number: (_____)______________________

Use the arm cycle _____ times a week for _____ minutes.

Drink water as needed.

Use good posture. Keep your stomach muscles tight and your back straight.

Begin cycling slowly. Increase to a moderate level, 5 to 6 on a 10-point scale. You should be able to talk.

Sore muscles lasting a few days and feeling tired are normal after exercise. Exhaustion, sore joints, and painful muscle pulls are not normal. If you have these symptoms, do not exercise until you talk with your therapist.

If you have chest tightness or pain, shortness of breath, feel dizzy, faint, or sick to your stomach, stop and call emergency services at _____.

Occupational Therapy TOOLKIT

Balance Exercise Guidelines

Name: ___________________________________

Date: ____________________________________

Therapist: _________________________________

Phone number: (_____)______________________

Do the checked exercises _____ times per day, _____ days a week.

Use good posture. Keep your stomach muscles tight and your back straight.

Practice your balance throughout the day. Stand on one foot or stand with one foot in front of the other. Do this when you are brushing your teeth, washing the dishes or waiting in line. You can also stand up and sit down from a chair without using your arms.

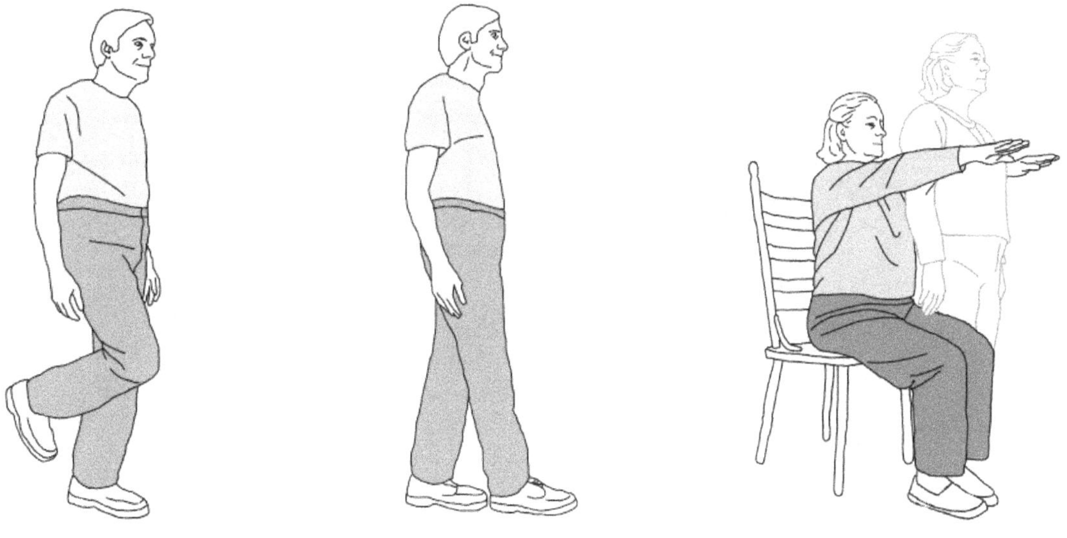

Sore muscles lasting a few days and feeling tired are normal after exercise. Exhaustion, sore joints, and painful muscle pulls are not normal. If you have these symptoms, do not exercise until you talk with your therapist.

If you have chest tightness or pain, shortness of breath, feel dizzy, faint, or sick to your stomach, stop and call emergency services at _____.

Occupational Therapy TOOLKIT

Balance Exercises - Sitting

Have someone sit next to you to help you keep your balance. Reach for objects placed around you.

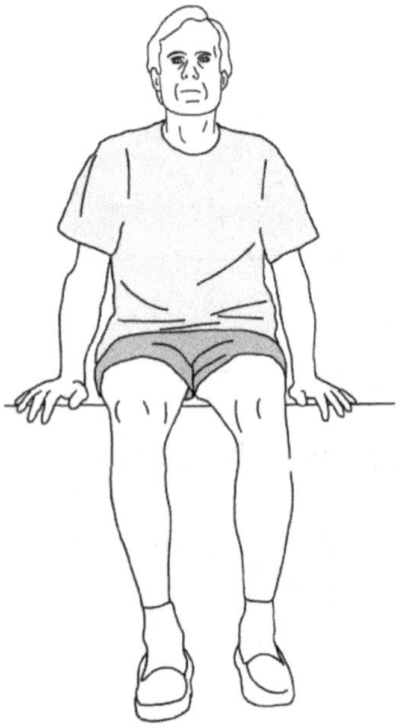

Sit at the edge of the bed or on a sofa. Your feet should be flat on the floor.

Reach forward at shoulder level.

Reach to the same side at shoulder level.

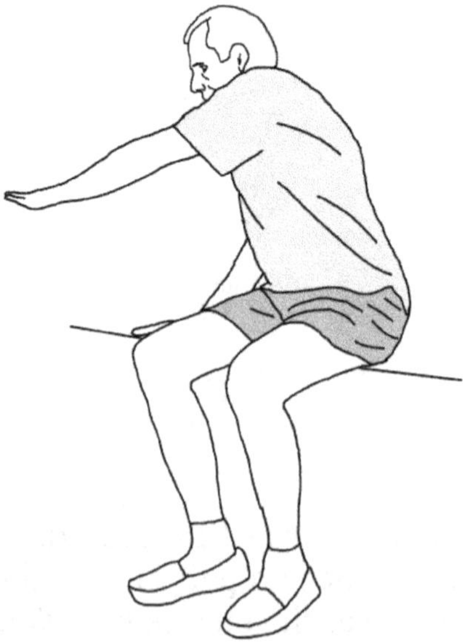

Reach to the other side.

Balance Exercises - Sitting

Have someone sit next to you to help you keep your balance. Reach for objects placed around you.

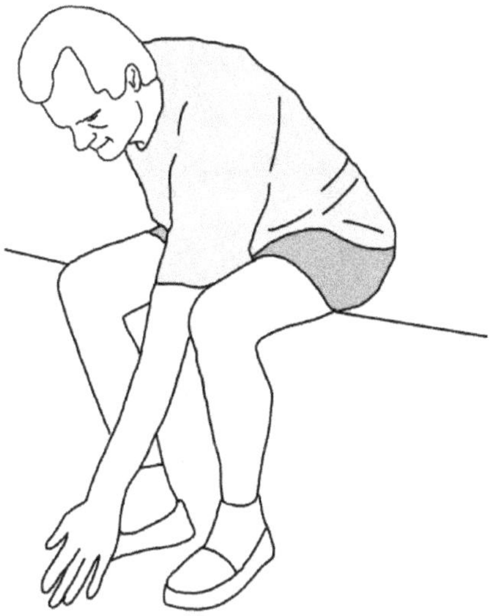

Reach to the floor between your feet.

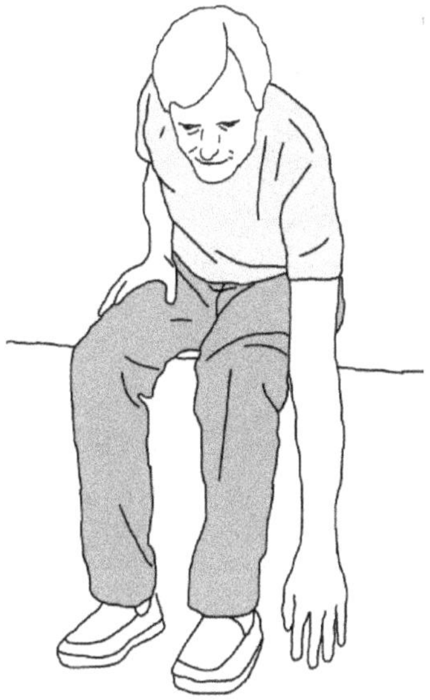

Reach to the floor.

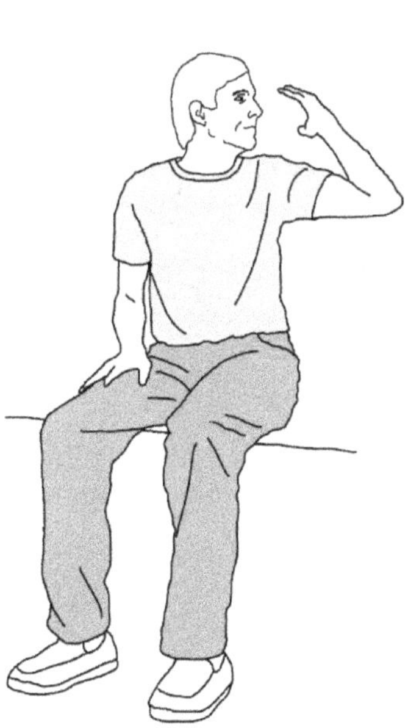

Reach behind and over the same shoulder.

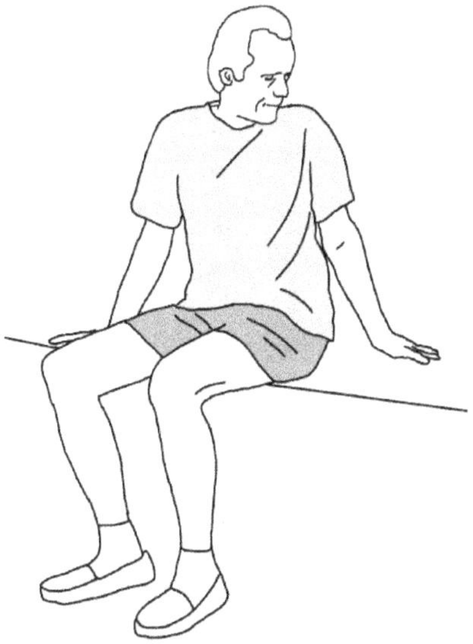

Reach behind.

Balance Exercises - Sitting

Have someone sit next to you to help you keep your balance.

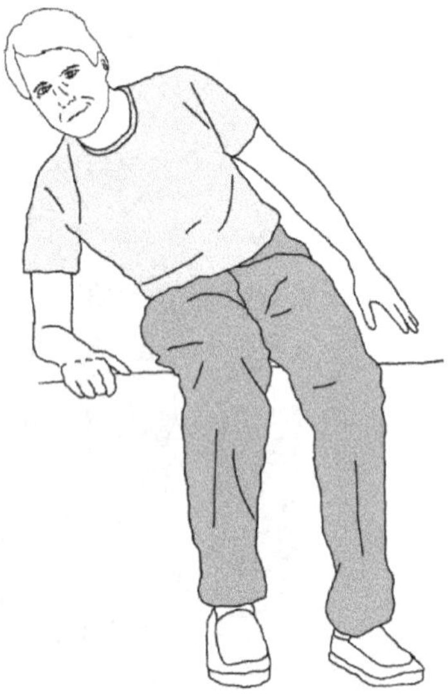

Lower onto your right elbow.

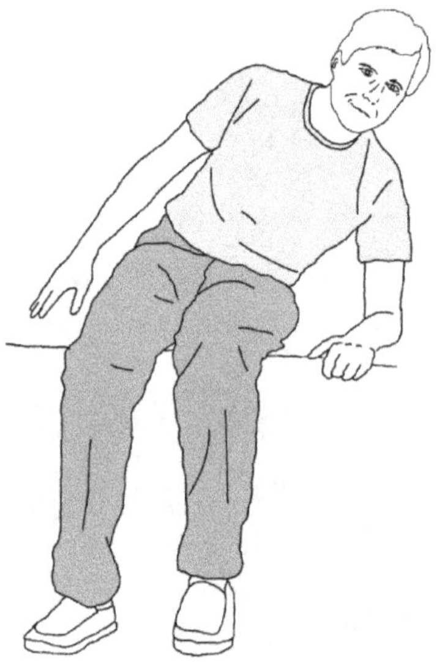

Lower onto your left elbow.

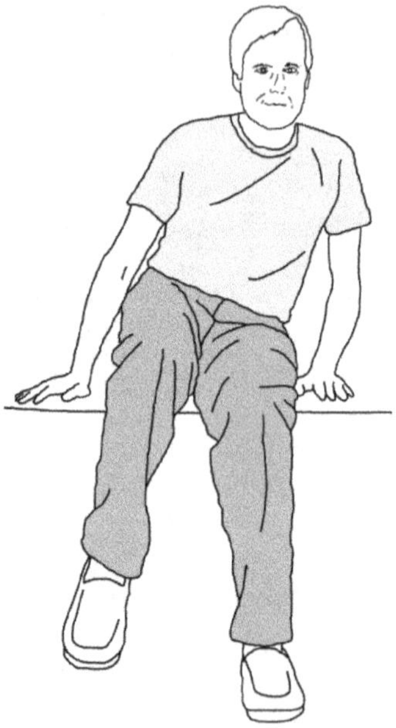

Hike up your right hip.

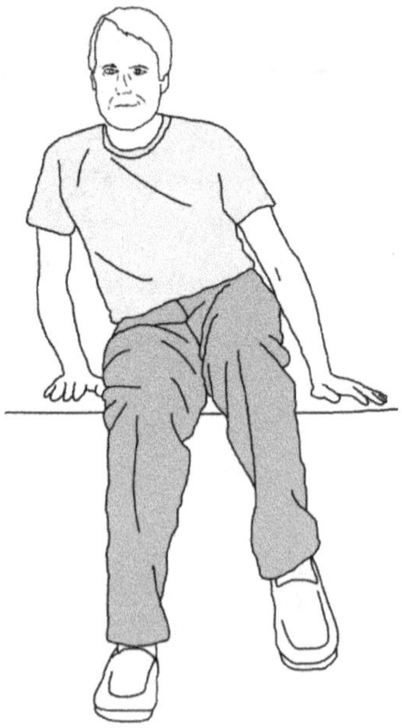

Hike up your left hip.

Balance Exercises - Standing

Do these exercises while holding (circle one)

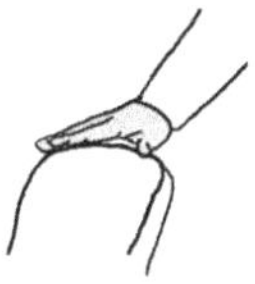

a stable object.

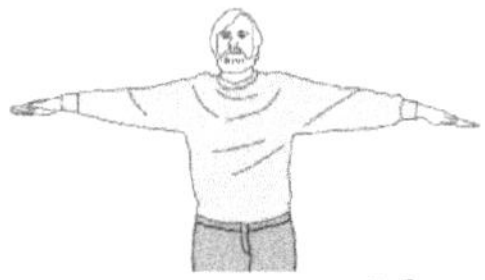

arms out to sides.

arms across chest.

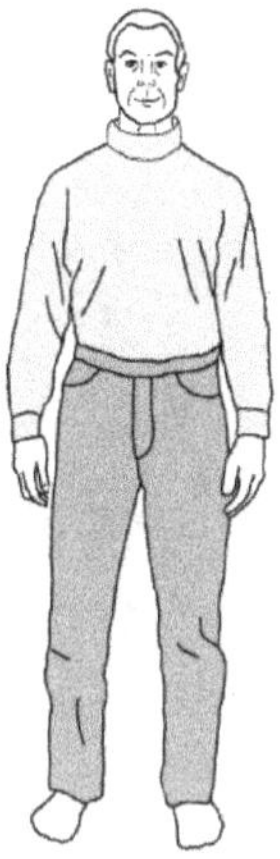

☐ Stand with your feet shoulder width apart. Shift your weight side to side, then forward and back.
Practice for ____________.

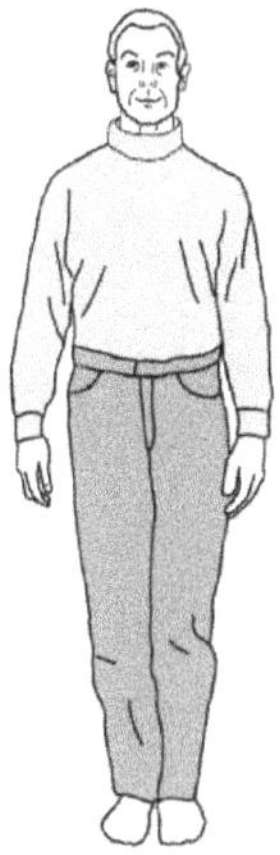

☐ Stand with your feet together. Shift your weight side to side, then forward and back.
Practice for ___________.

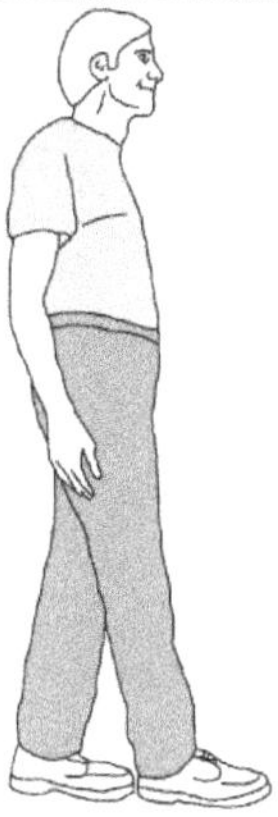

☐ Stand with one foot in front of the other. Shift your weight side to side, then forward and back.
Practice for ______________.

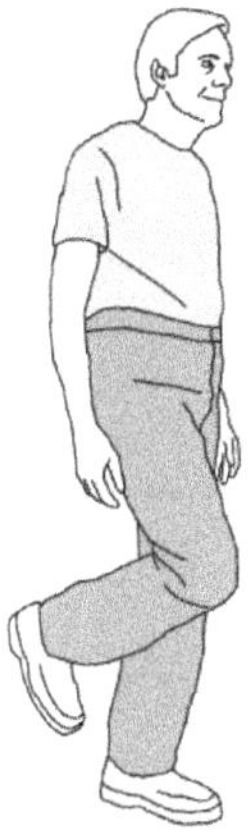

☐ Stand on one leg. Hold for a count of _______ on each leg.

Occupational Therapy TOOLKIT

Balance Exercises - Standing

Do these exercises while holding (circle one)

a stable object.

arms out to sides.

arms across chest.

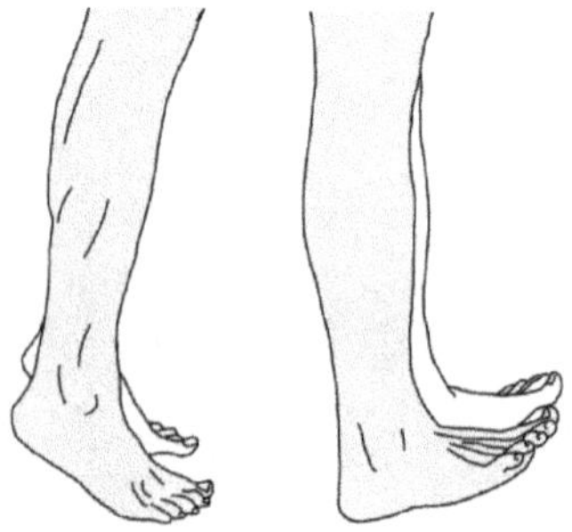

☐ Rise onto your toes then roll back onto your heels.

Do ______ sets of ______.

☐ Bend your knees slightly and then straighten back up.

Do ______ sets of ______.

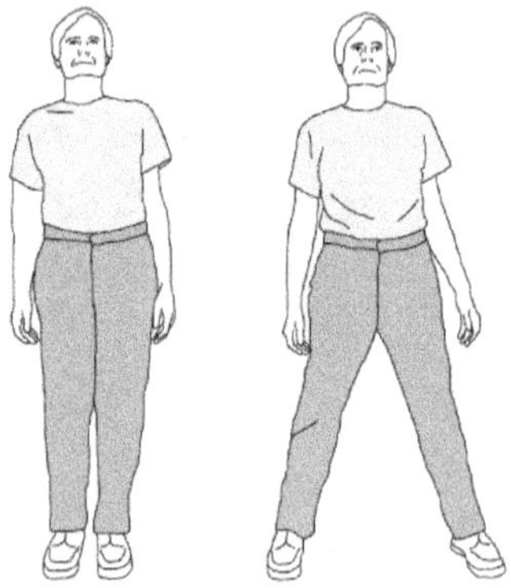

☐ Side step to the right, then side step back to the left.

Practice for ________________.

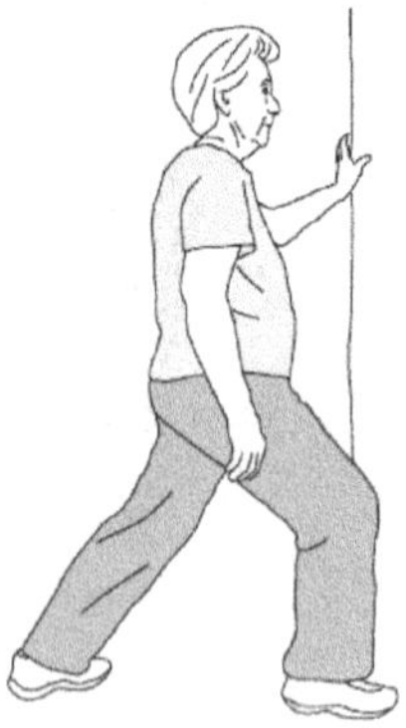

☐ Lunge forward.

Do ______ sets of ______ with each leg.

Balance Exercises - Standing

Do these exercises while holding (circle one)

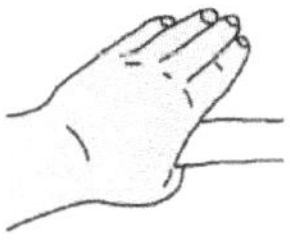
a counter or wall.

arms out to sides.

arms across chest.

☐ Turn in a half-circle to the right. Then turn in a half-circle to the left.

Practice for _______________.

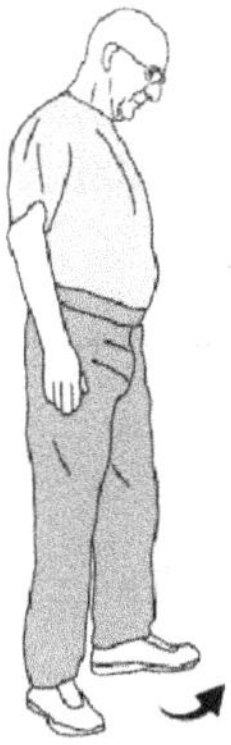

☐ Walk forward heel to toe, then walk backwards toe to heel.

Practice for _______________.

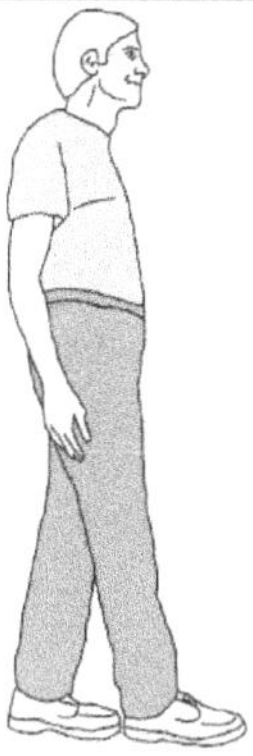

☐ Cross your right foot in front of your left foot. Step out with your left foot. Cross your right foot behind your left foot.

Practice for _______________.

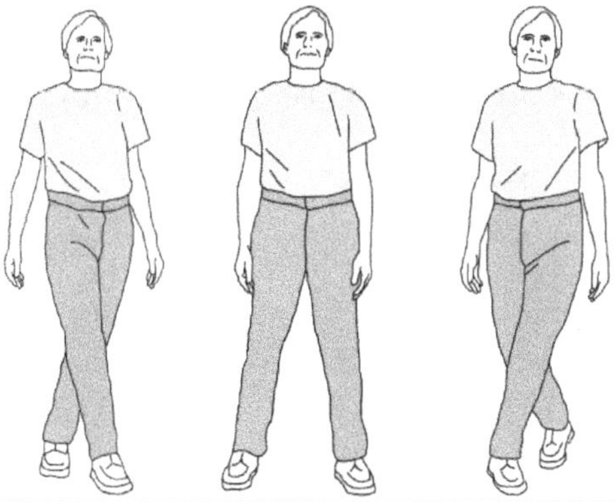

Balance Exercises - Standing

Do these exercises while holding (circle one)

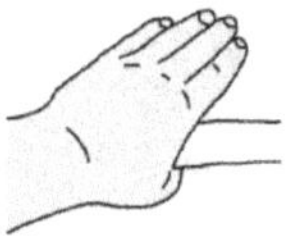
a counter or wall.

arms out to sides.

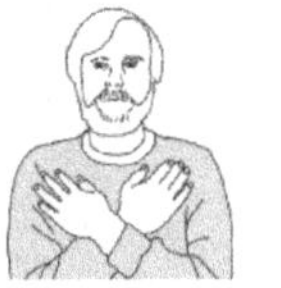
arms across chest.

☐ Step up and over an aerobic step.
Turn around and repeat.

Practice for ______________.

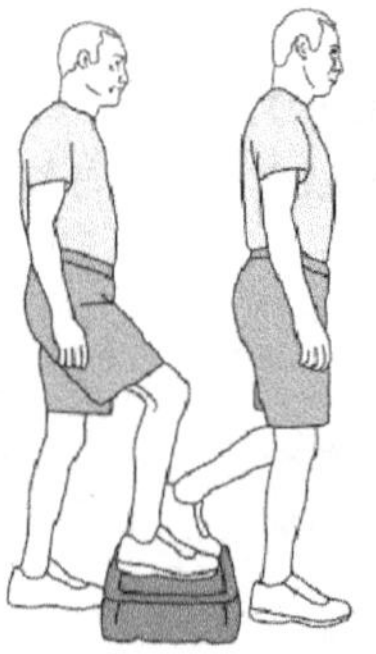

Place six paper cups on the floor, space them about 16 inches/40 cm apart.

☐ Step forward over each paper cup.

Practice for ______________.

☐ Step to the side over each paper cup.

Practice for ______________.

Pick the paper cups up from the floor.

Occupational Therapy TOOLKIT

Burn Injury Stretches - Guidelines

Name: ______________________________

Date: ______________________________

Therapist: ______________________________

Phone number: (_____)____________________

Do the checked stretches _____ times a day, every day.

Stretch slowly and smoothly. Stretch to the point of tension, not pain. Do not jerk or bouncing when stretching

Do not hold your breath during exercise. Count aloud if needed.

Use good posture. Keep your stomach muscles tight and your back straight.

Sore muscles lasting a few days and feeling tired are normal after exercise. Exhaustion, sore joints, and painful muscle pulls are not normal. If you have these symptoms, do not exercise until you talk with your therapist.

If you have chest tightness or pain, shortness of breath, feel dizzy, faint, or sick to your stomach, stop and call emergency services at _____.

Notes:

____

____

____

____

____

____

____

____

Burn Injury Stretches - Face

Do the checked stretches _____ times a day, every day.

☐ **Eyebrows**
Raise your eyebrows, and then frown.
Hold each stretch for a count of _____.

Do _____ sets of _____.

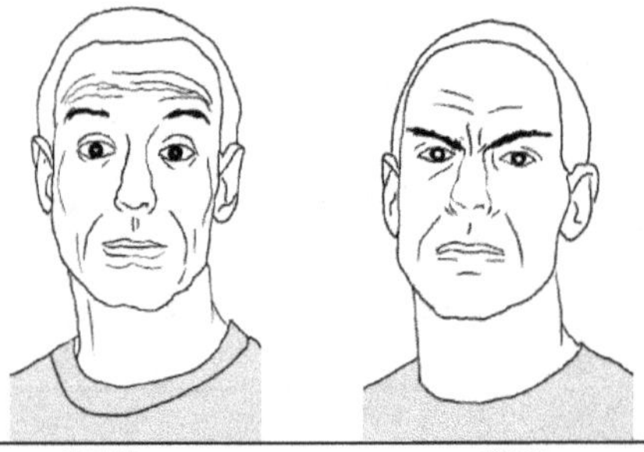

☐ **Eyes**
Close your eyes tight, and then open wide. Hold each stretch for a count of _____.

Do _____ sets of _____.

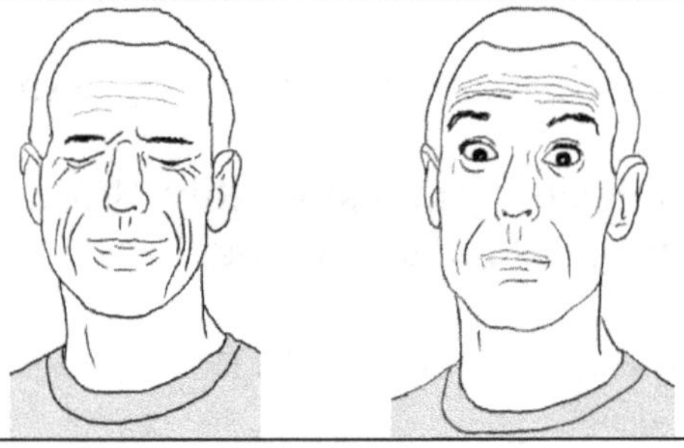

☐ **Mouth**
Smile, and then pucker your lips. Hold each stretch for a count of _____.

Do _____ sets of _____.

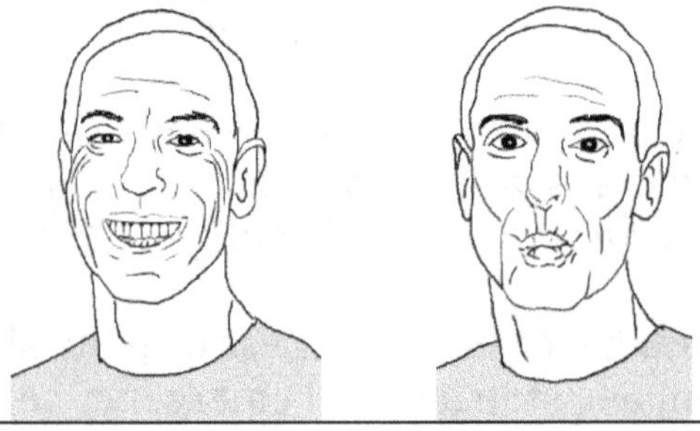

☐ **Mouth**
Open your mouth wide, and then close.
Hold each stretch for a count of _____.

Do _____ sets of _____.

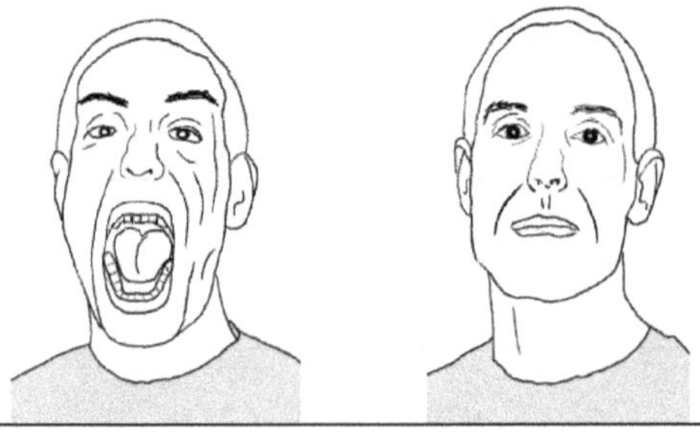

☐ **Mouth**
Say each letter of the ABC's clearly.

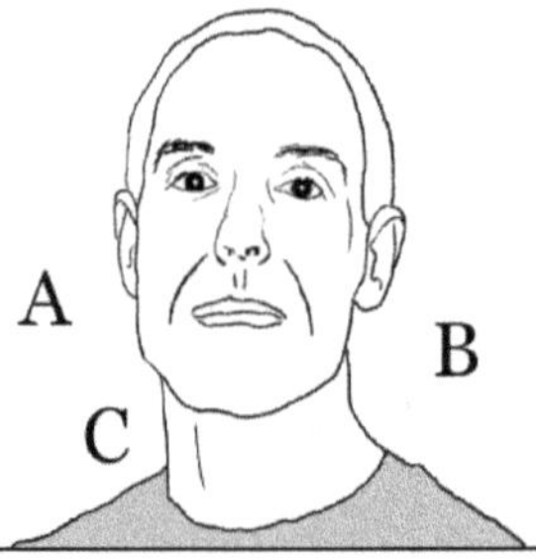

Occupational Therapy TOOLKIT

Burn Injury Stretches - Neck

Do the checked stretches _____ times a day, every day.

☐ **Back of Neck** (cervical flexion)
Bend your head forward. Keep your chin tucked. Hold for a count of _______.

Do ______ sets of ______.

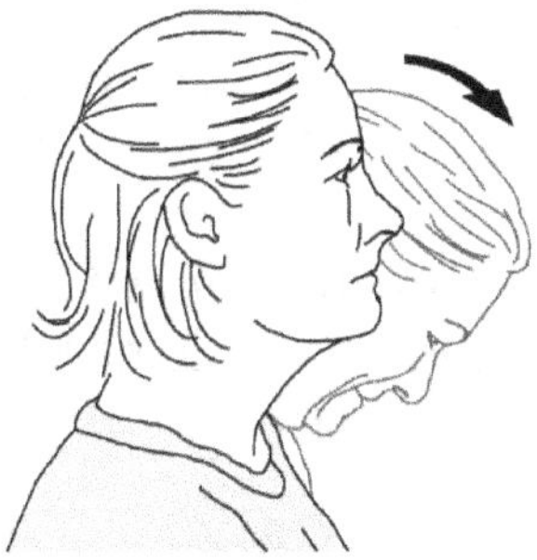

☐ **Throat Area** (cervical extension)
Look up. Hold for a count of _______.

Do ______ sets of ______.

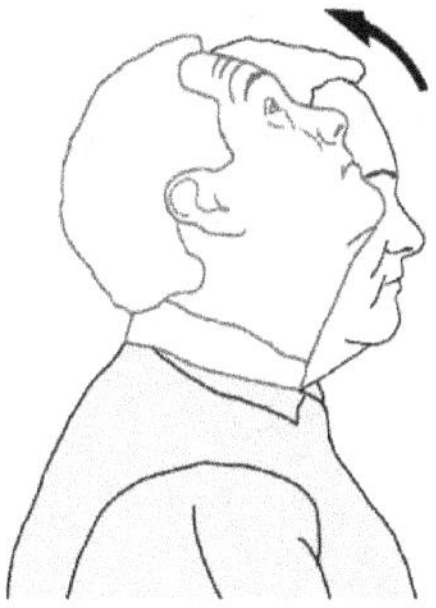

☐ **Side of Neck** (lateral flexion)
Bend your head to one side. Bend to the other side. Hold each side for a count of _______.

Do ______ sets of ______.

☐ **Side of Neck** (lateral rotation)
Turn your head to look over your shoulder. Turn to the other side. Hold each side for a count of _______.

Do ______ sets of ______.

Burn Injury Stretches - Trunk

Do the checked stretches _____ times a day, every day.

☐ **Chest and Stomach** (deep breathing)
Inhale deeply in through your nose and allow the hand on your stomach to rise. Exhale slowly through pursed lips while gently pushing in with the hand that is on the stomach. The hand on your chest should be still.

Do ______ sets of ______.

☐ **Chest and Stomach** (spinal extension)
Place hands behind you on a stable object. Lean back. Hold for a count of ______.

Do ______ sets of ______.

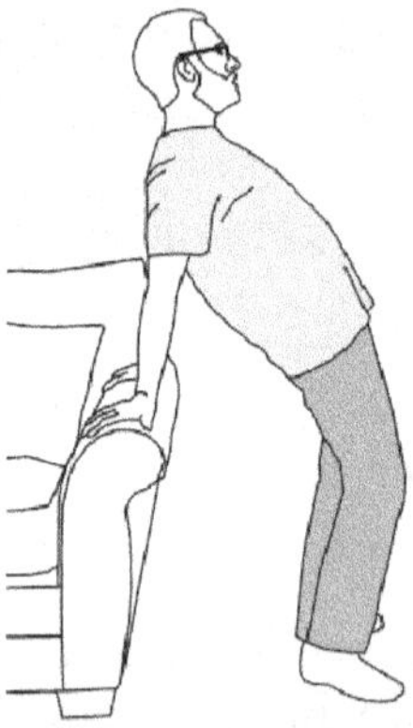

☐ **Chest and Stomach** (spinal extension)
Lie over some folded towels or a cushion. Hold for a count of ______.

Do ______ sets of ______.

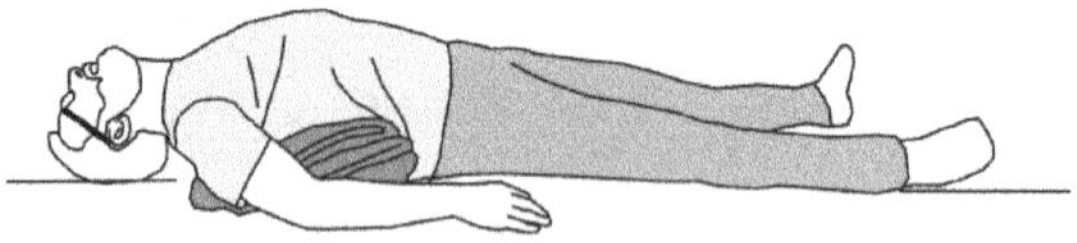

☐ **Back** (spinal flexion)
Bend forward, reach to the floor. Hold for a count of ______.

Do ______ sets of ______.

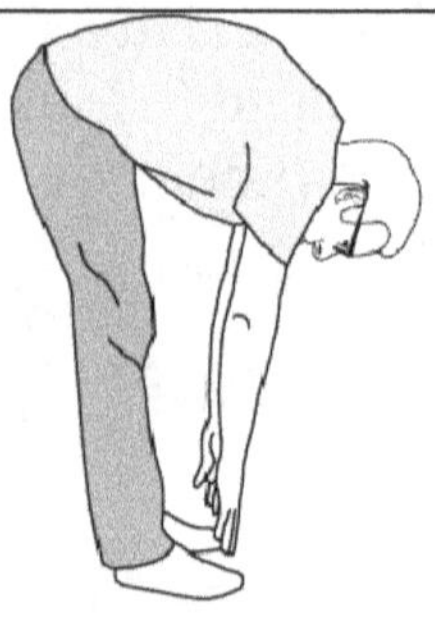

Occupational Therapy TOOLKIT

Burn Injury Stretches - Trunk

Do the checked stretches _____ times a day, every day.

☐ **Back** (spinal flexion)
Sit with your leg out straight. Bend forward, reach to your toes.
Hold for a count of ______.

Do ______ sets of ______.

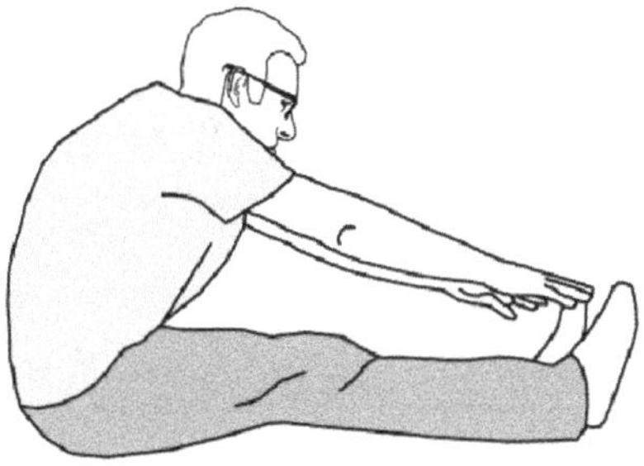

☐ **Side of Trunk** (rotation)
Turn to one side. Turn to the other side.
Hold each side for a count of _______.

Do ______ sets of ______.

☐ **Side of Trunk** (rotation)
Lie on your back with legs straight and arms out to the side. Draw up your right knee and rotate it over to the left side. Repeat to the other side. Hold each side for a count of ______.

Do ______ sets of ______ on each side.

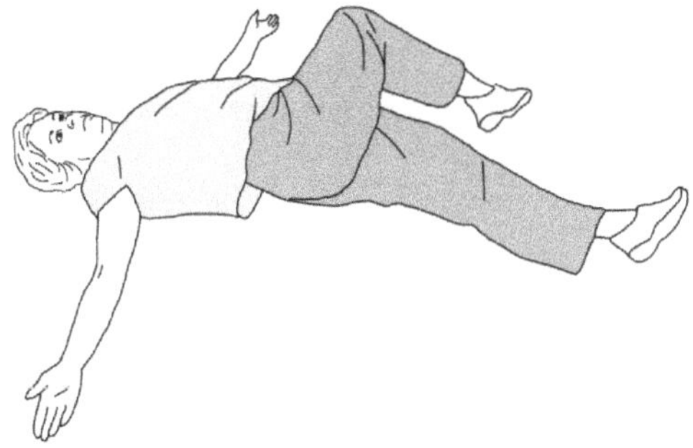

☐ **Side of Trunk** (lateral flexion)
Raise arm overhead. Bend over to one side. Repeat on the other side. Hold each side for a count of ______.

Do ______ sets of ______.

Burn Injury Stretches - Shoulder

Do the checked stretches _____ times a day, every day.

☐ **Armpit** (shoulder flexion)
Stand facing the wall. Walk your fingers up the wall until you feel the stretch. Hold for a count of _____.

Do _____ sets of _____ with each arm.

☐ **Armpit** (shoulder abduction)
Stand with your side next to a wall. Walk your fingers up the wall, until you feel the stretch. Hold for a count of _____.

Do _____ sets of _____ with each arm.

☐ **Front of Shoulder** (shoulder extension)
Sit with your arms propped behind. Hold for a count of _____.

Do _____ sets of _____.

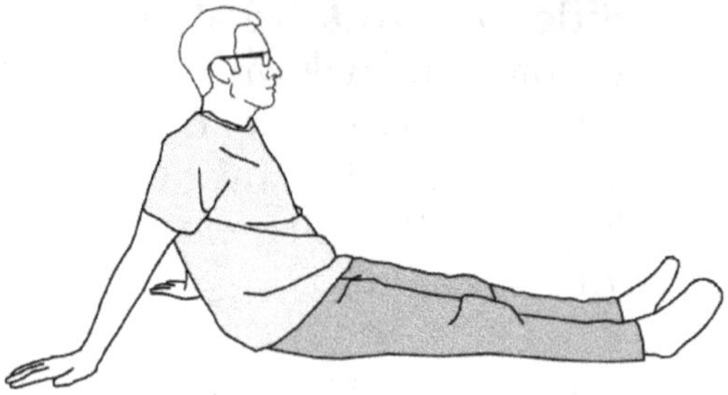

☐ **Corner Stretch** (horizontal abduction)
Stand facing a corner. Raise your arms to shoulder height. Press your chest into the corner. Hold for a count of _____.

Do _____ sets of _____.

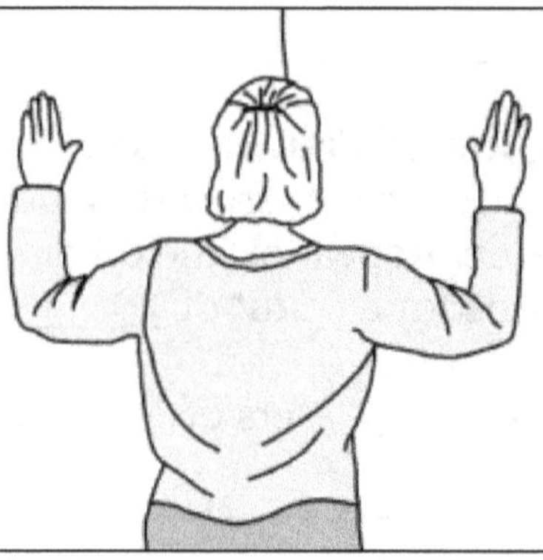

Burn Injury Stretches - Shoulder

Do the checked stretches ______ times a day, every day.

☐ **Back of Shoulder** (horizontal adduction)
Raise arms out front. Use one arm to pull the other arm across your body. Hold for a count of ______.

Do ______ sets of ______ with each arm.

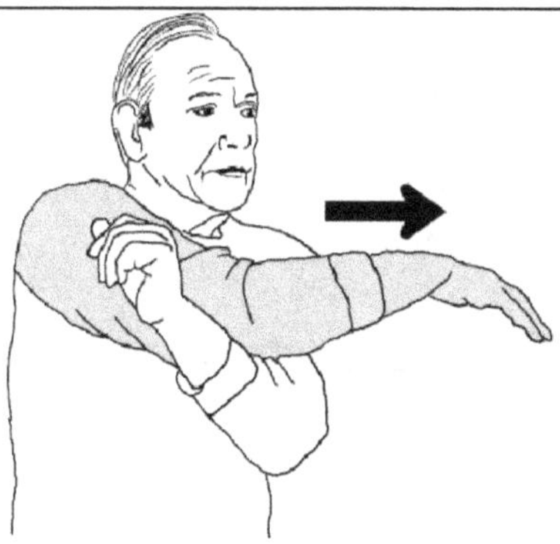

☐ **Around Shoulder** (internal rotation)
Place your hand behind your back. Use your other hand, to move it toward your shoulder blade. Hold for a count of ______.

Do ______ sets of ______ with each arm.

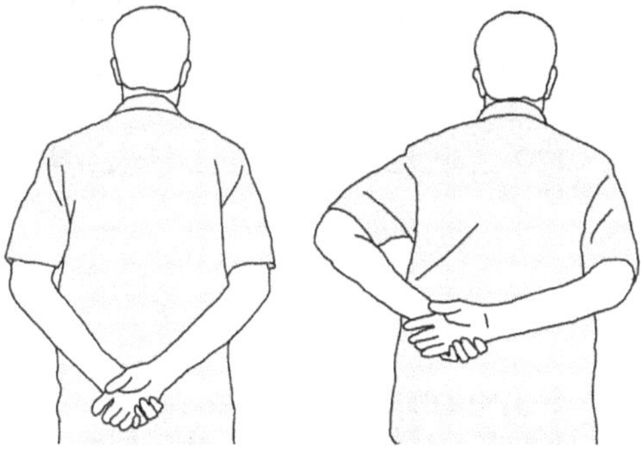

☐ **Around Shoulder** (external rotation)
Keep your arm at a 90-degree angle to your body and your elbow bent at a 90-degree angle. Use a dowel to rotate your arm back toward the head of the bed. Hold for a count of _______.

Do ______ sets of ______ with each arm.

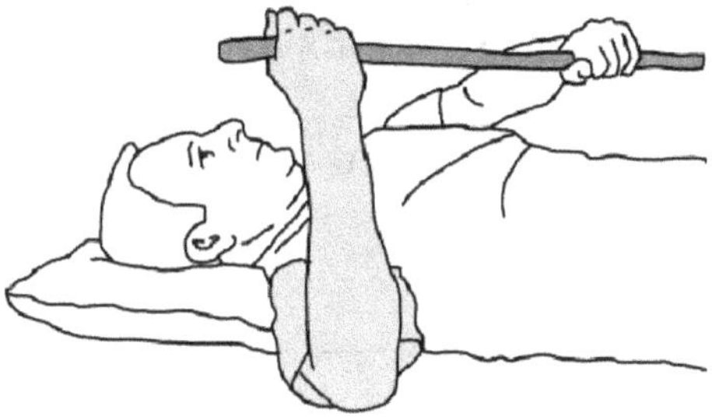

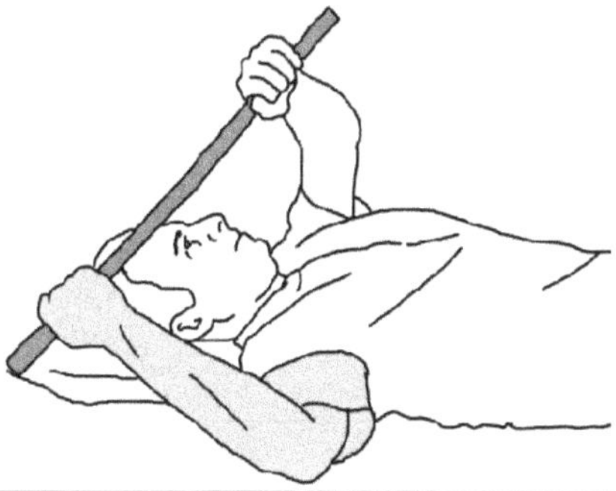

Burn Injury Stretches - Elbow, Forearm, Wrist

Do the checked stretches _____ times a day, every day.

☐ **Elbow** (elbow flexion)
Hold your wrist. Bend your elbow, move your hand toward your shoulder. Hold for a count of _____.

Do _____ sets of _____ with each arm.

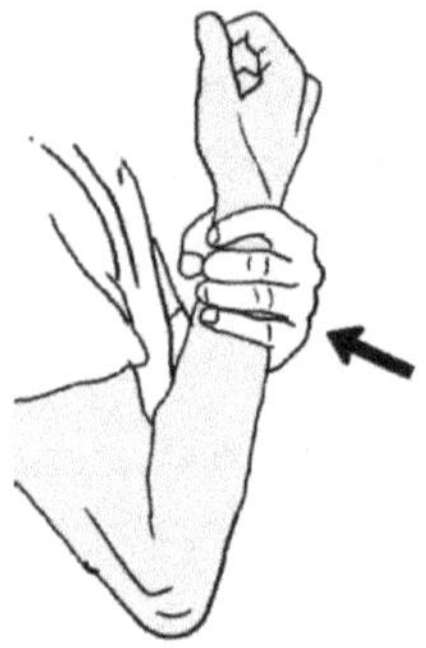

☐ **Inside Elbow** (elbow extension)
Hold your wrist. Straighten your arm. Hold for a count of _____.

Do _____ sets of _____ with each arm.

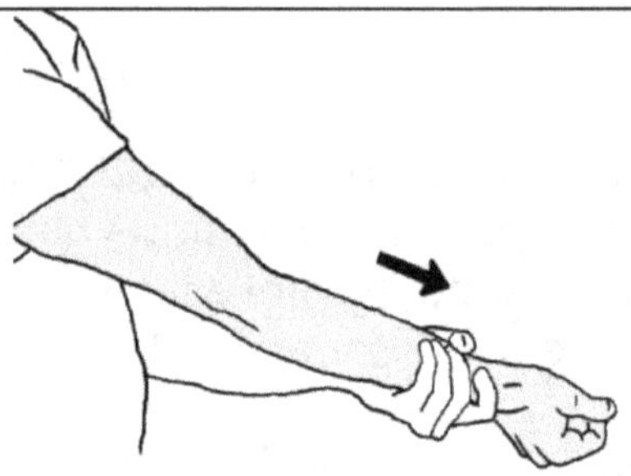

☐ **Forearm** (forearm supination)
Keep your elbow tucked into your side. Turn your hand palm up using your other hand. Hold for a count of _____.

Do _____ sets of _____ with each arm.

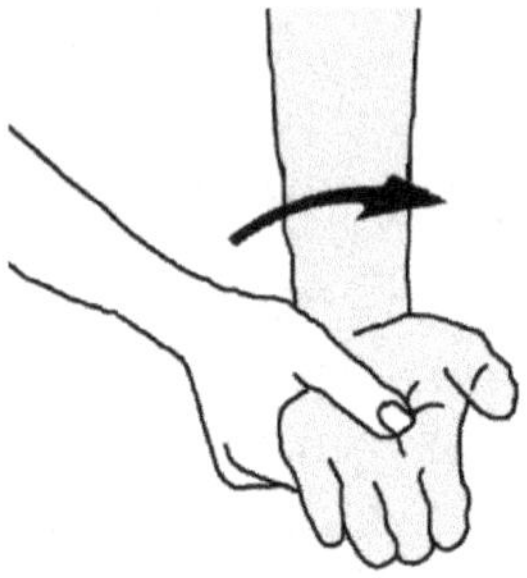

☐ **Forearm** (forearm pronation)
Keep your elbow tucked into your side. Turn your hand palm down using your other hand. Hold for a count of _____.

Do _____ sets of _____ with each arm.

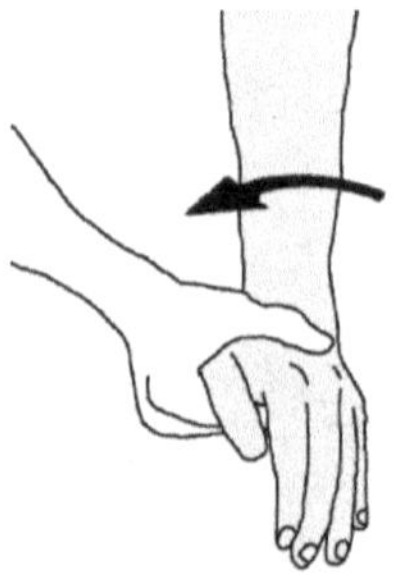

Burn Injury Stretches - Elbow, Forearm, Wrist

Do the checked stretches _____ times a day, every day.

☐ **Back of Wrist** (wrist flexion)
Hold your arm out in front. Keep your elbow straight and your palm down. Use your other hand to stretch your wrist. To increase the stretch, close your fingers into a fist. Turn your arm toward your little finger. Hold for a count of ______.

Do _____ sets of _____ with each hand.

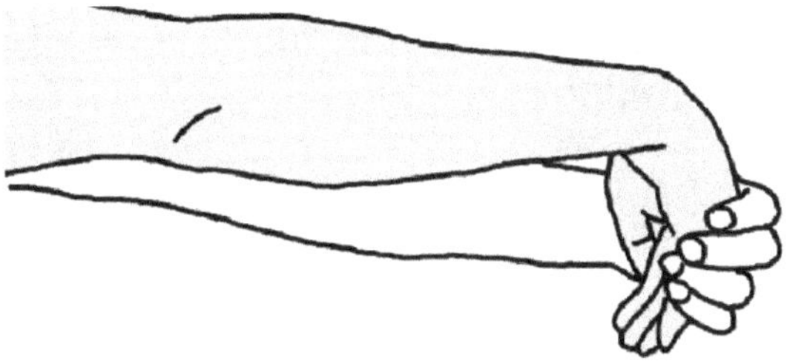

☐ **Inside of Wrist** (wrist extension)
Hold your arm out in front. Keep your elbow straight and your palm up. Use your other hand to stretch your wrist. To increase the stretch, use your other hand to straighten your fingers and turn your arm toward your thumb. Hold for a count of ______.

Do _____ sets of _____ with each hand.

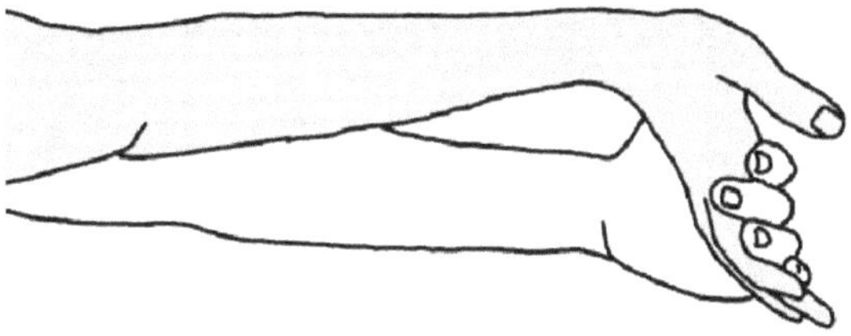

☐ **Side of Wrists** (radial/ulnar deviation)
Place one hand flat on the table. Use your other hand to move your wrist toward your thumb (radial). Hold for a count of _____.

Use your other hand to move your wrist toward your little finger (ulnar). Hold for a count of _____.

Do _____ sets of _____ with each hand.

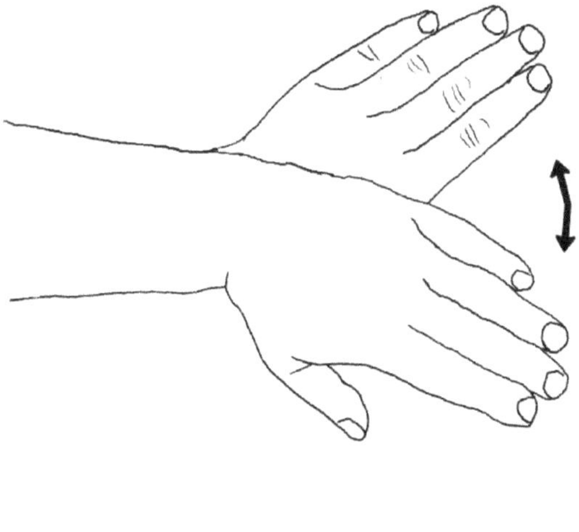

Burn Injury Stretches - Left Hand

Do the checked stretches ______ times a day, every day.

☐ **Back of Hand and Fingers** (composite fist)
Close your hand into a fist, use your other hand to press your fingers into a tighter fist. Hold for a count of ______.

Do ______ sets of ______.

☐ **Palm of Hand and Fingers** (extension)
Place your hand flat on a stable surface, use your other hand to press your fingers and palm flat. Hold for a count of ______.

Do ______ sets of ______.

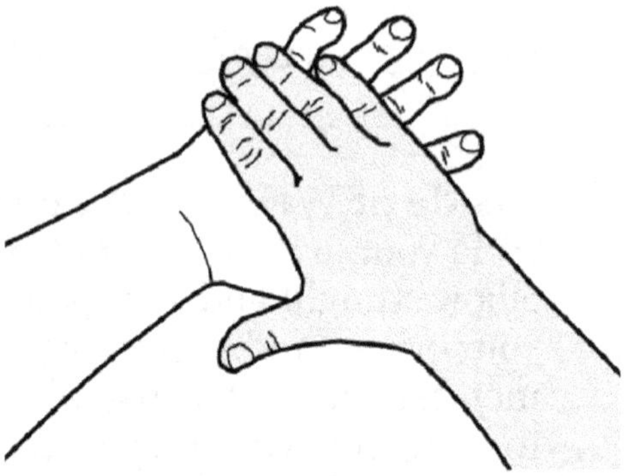

☐ **Between Fingers** (digit abduction)
Lace your fingers. Press to stretch in between each finger. Hold for a count of ______.

Do ______ sets of ______.

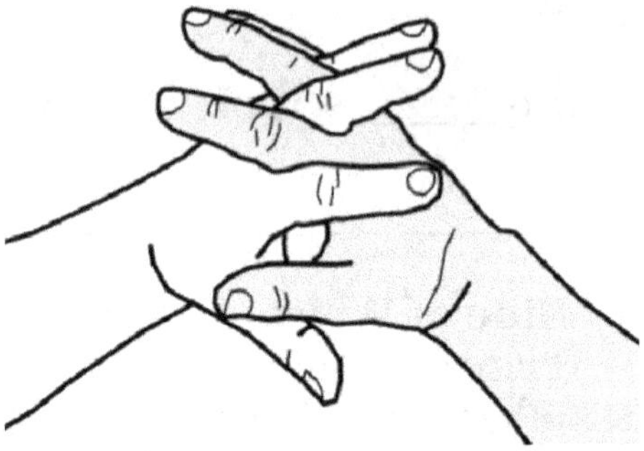

☐ **Fingers** (intrinsic plus)
Keep your fingers straight. Bend at the knuckles. Hold for a count of ______.

Do ______ sets of ______.

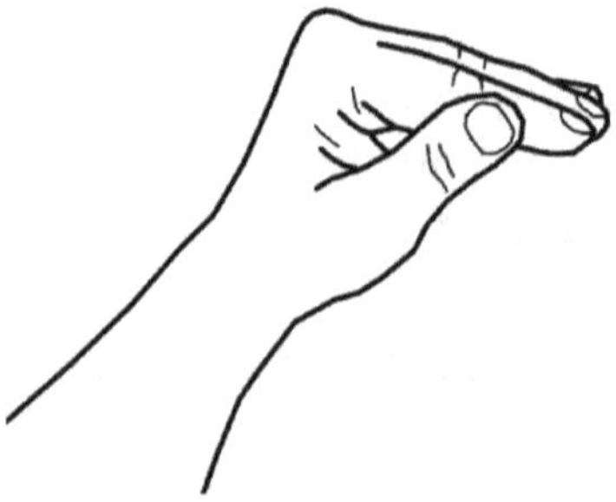

Burn Injury Stretches - Left Hand

Do the checked stretches _____ times a day, every day.

☐ **Fingers** (intrinsic minus)
Keep your knuckles straight and bend the two finger joints. Use your other hands to apply pressure against your fingers. Hold for a count of _____.

Do _____ sets of _____.

☐ **Thumb** (thumb opposition)
Stretch your thumb out to the side and then over to the base of your little finger. Hold for a count of _____.

Do _____ sets of _____.

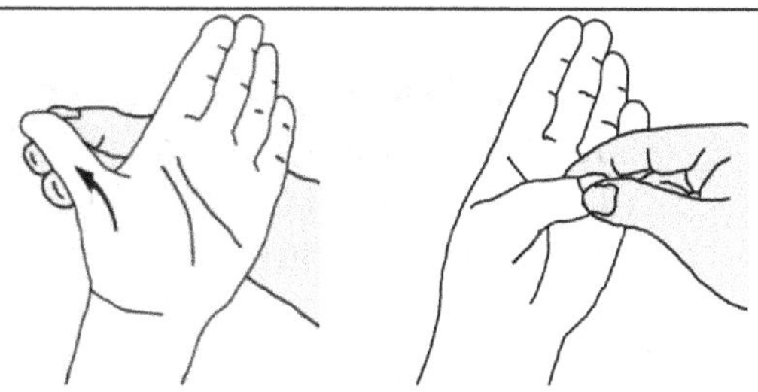

☐ **Thumb** (thumb abduction)
Place your hand flat. Hold your thumb at the base and stretch it away from your fingers. Hold for a count of _____.

Do _____ sets of _____.

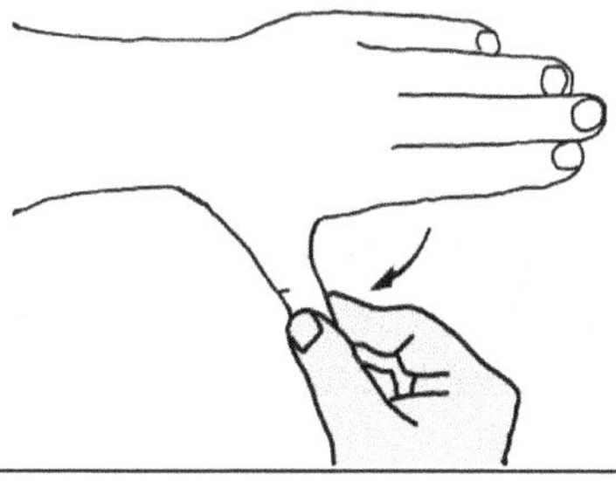

☐ **Thumb** (thumb web space)
Apply pressure on web space. Hold for a count of _____.

Do _____ sets of _____.

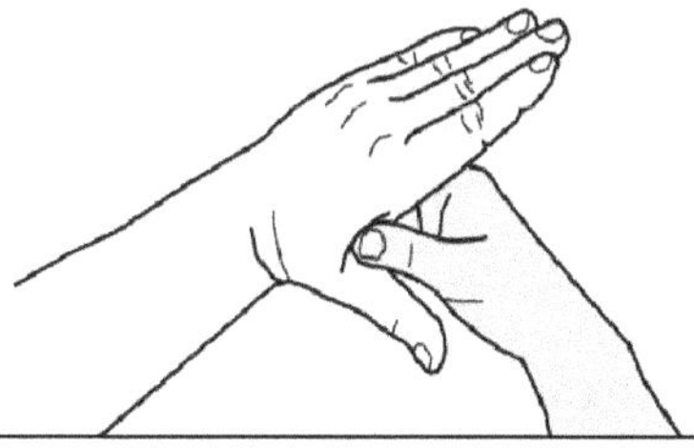

☐ **Thumb** (thumb flexion)
Hold your thumb at the tip. Bend the two thumb joints. Hold for a count of _____.

Do _____ sets of _____.

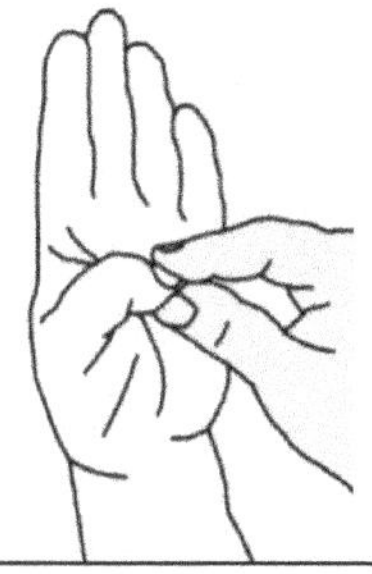

Burn Injury Stretches - Right Hand

Do the checked stretches _____ times a day, every day.

☐ **Back of Hand and Fingers** (composite fist)
Close your hand into a fist, use your other hand to press your fingers into a tighter fist. Hold for a count of _____.

Do _____ sets of _____.

☐ **Palm of Hand and Fingers** (extension)
Place your hand flat on a stable surface, use your other hand to press your fingers and palm flat. Hold for a count of _____.

Do _____ sets of _____.

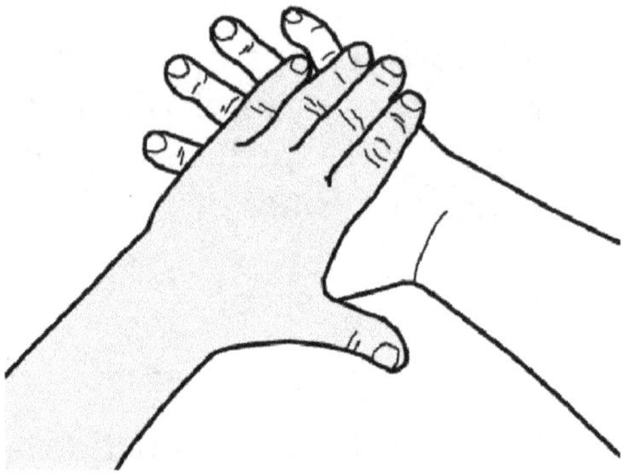

☐ **Between Fingers** (digit abduction)
Lace your fingers. Press to stretch in between each finger. Hold for a count of _____.

Do _____ sets of _____.

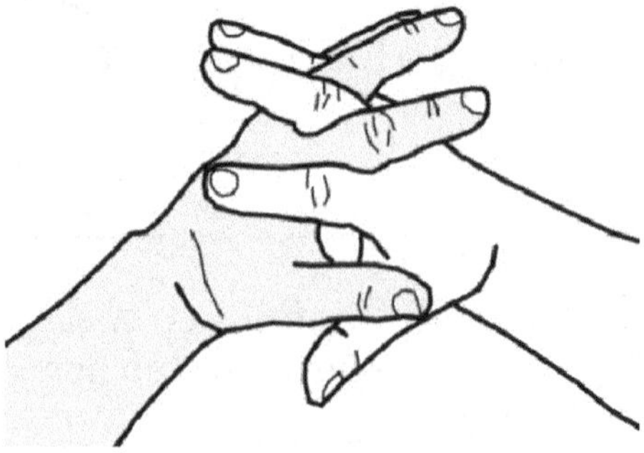

☐ **Fingers** (intrinsic plus)
Keep all your fingers straight. Bend your hand at the knuckles. Hold for a count of _____.

Do _____ sets of _____.

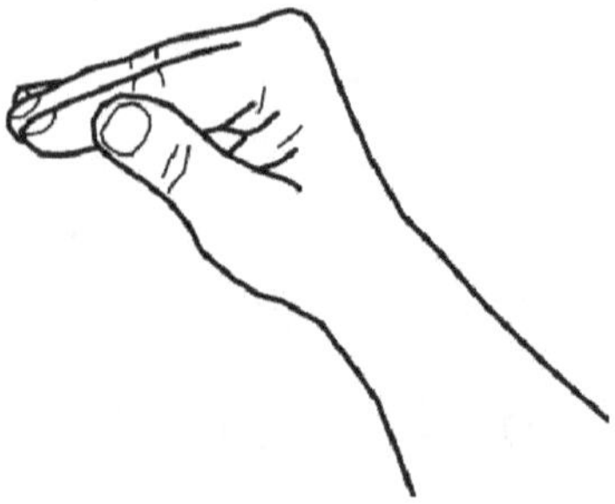

Burn Injury Stretches - Right Hand

Do the checked stretches _____ times a day, every day.

☐ **Fingers** (intrinsic minus)
Keep the knuckles straight and bend the two finger joints. Use your other hand to apply pressure against your fingers. Hold for a count of _____.

Do _____ sets of _____.

☐ **Thumb** (thumb opposition)
Stretch your thumb out to the side and then over to the base of your little finger. Hold for a count of _____.

Do _____ sets of _____.

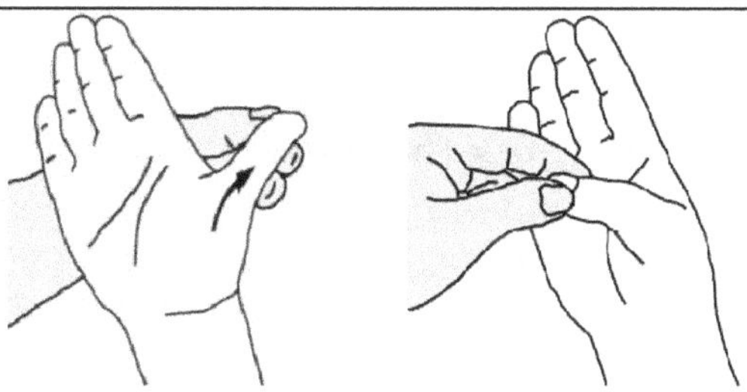

☐ **Thumb** (thumb abduction)
Place your hand flat. Hold your thumb at the base and stretch it away from your fingers. Hold for a count of _____.

Do _____ sets of _____.

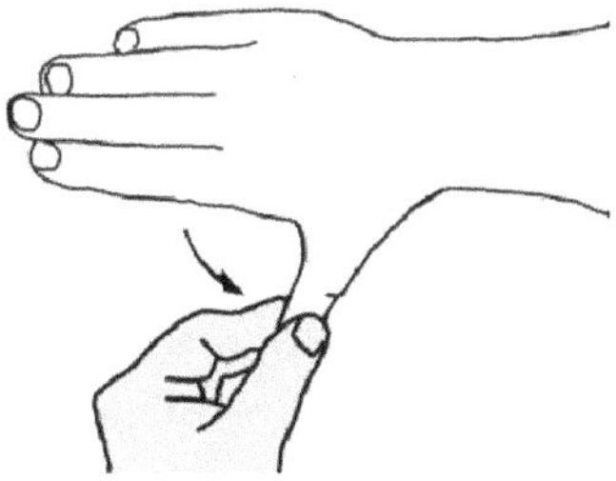

☐ **Thumb** (thumb web space)
Press on the web space. Hold for a count of _____.

Do _____ sets of _____.

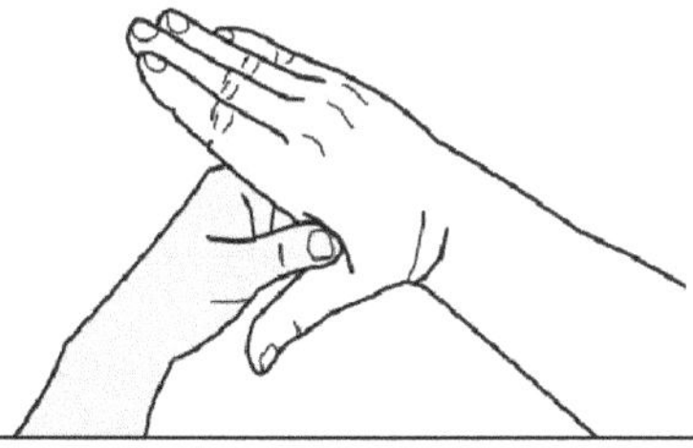

☐ **Thumb** (thumb flexion)
Hold your thumb at the tip. Bend the two thumb joints. Hold for a count of _____.

Do _____ sets of _____.

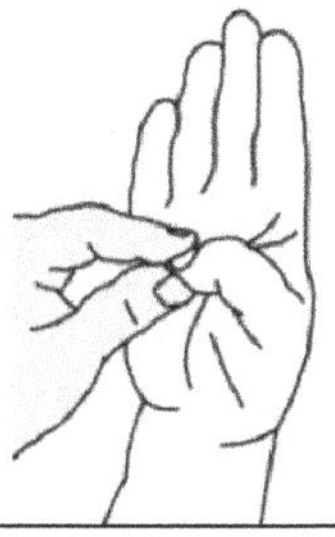

Burn Injury Stretches - Hip and Knee

Do the checked stretches _____ times a day, every day.

☐ **Buttocks** (hip flexion)
Bend forward onto the bed or a table.
Hold for a count of _____.

Do _____ sets of _____.

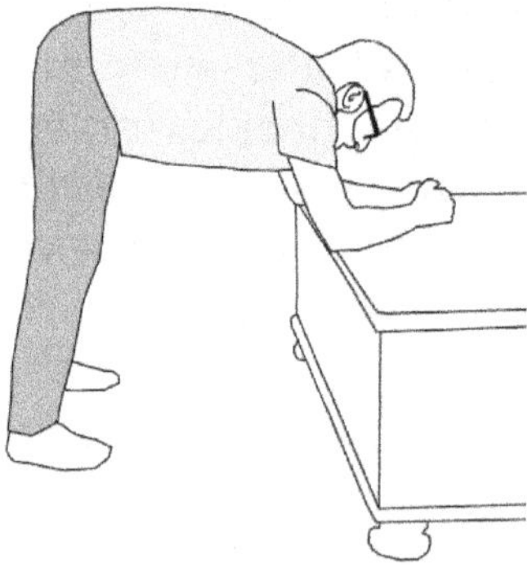

☐ **Buttock** (hip flexion)
Lie on your back with both knees bent. Bring one knee up to your chest. Hold for a count of _____.

Do _____ sets of _____ with each leg.

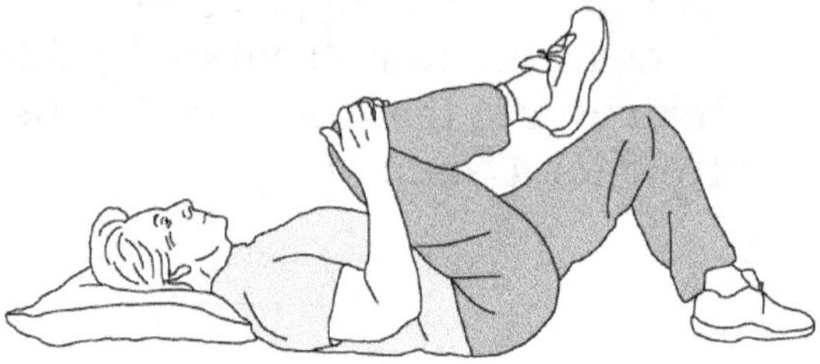

☐ **Front of Hip** (hip extension)
Stand at the bottom of the stairs. Hold onto the rail. Place one foot up onto the second step. Lean into the steps.
Hold for a count of _____.

Do _____ sets of _____ with each leg.

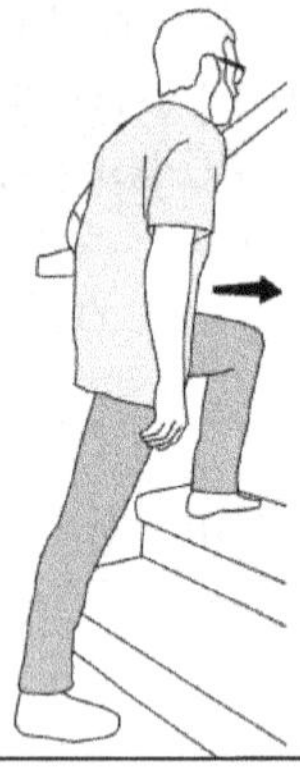

☐ **Front of Hip** (hip extension)
Sit on the end of the bed. Lie back. Bring one leg up toward your chest. Allow your other leg to hang off the end of the bed.
Hold for a count of _____.

Do _____ sets of _____ with each leg.

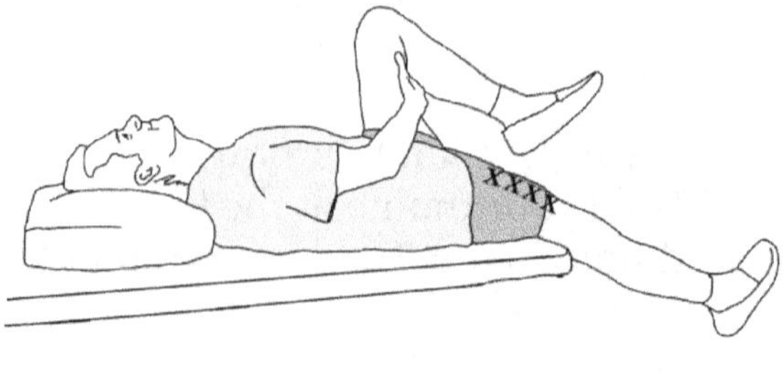

Burn Injury Stretches - Hip and Knee

Do the checked stretches ______ times a day, every day.

☐ **Side of Hip** (hip adduction)
Lie on your back. Cross one leg over the other. Place your hand on your thigh and pull your leg across. Do not roll to the side. Hold for a count of ______.

Do ______ sets of ______ with each leg.

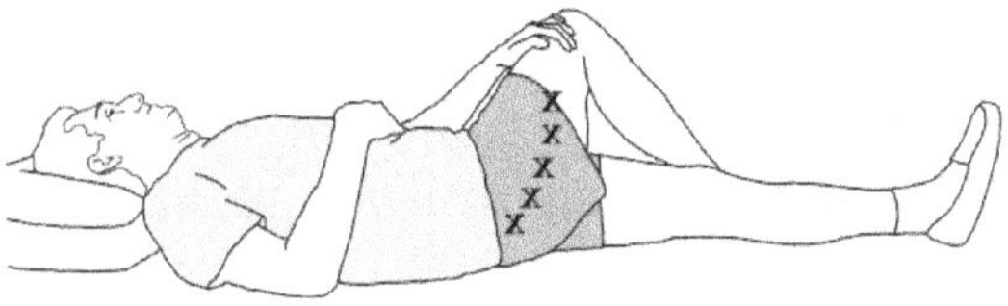

☐ **Between Thighs** (hip abduction)
Sit with the soles of your feet touching. Hold for a count of ______.

Do ______ sets of ______.

☐ **Front of Knee** (knee flexion)
Sit with your legs straight. Place a towel around the bottom of your foot. Pull your knee in toward your chest. Hold for a count of ______.

Do ______ sets of ______ with each leg.

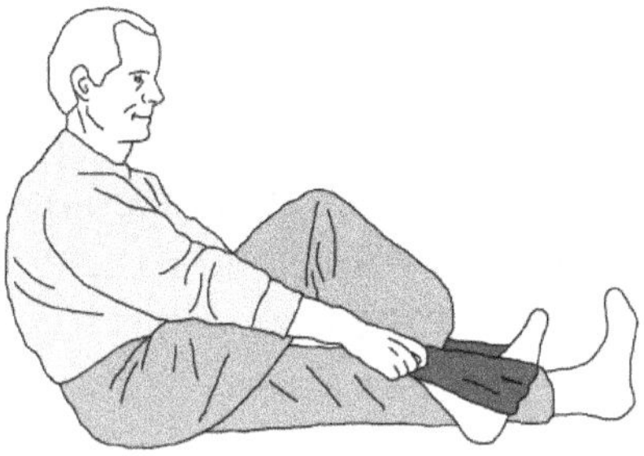

☐ **Back of Knee** (knee extension)
Sit with your legs straight. Place a folded towel under one ankle. Press down on your knee. Hold for a count of ______.

Do ______ sets of ______ with each leg.

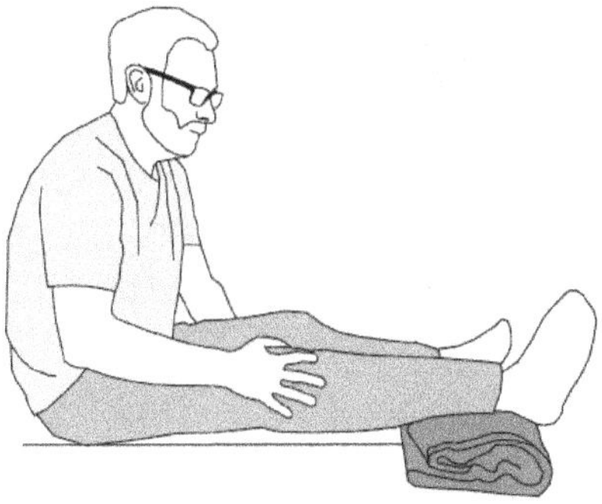

Burn Injury Stretches - Ankle and Toes

Do the checked stretches _____ times a day, every day.

☐ **Back of Ankle and Heel** (dorsiflexion)
Stand an arm's length from the wall. Place one foot in front of the other. Put your hands on the wall. Bend the forward knee. Lean forward until you feel a stretch. Hold for a count of _____.

Do _____ sets of _____ with each leg.

☐ **Back of Ankle and Heel** (dorsiflexion)
Place a strap around your foot. Keep your knee straight. Pull the strap until you feel a stretch. Hold for a count of _____.

Do _____ sets of _____ with each leg.

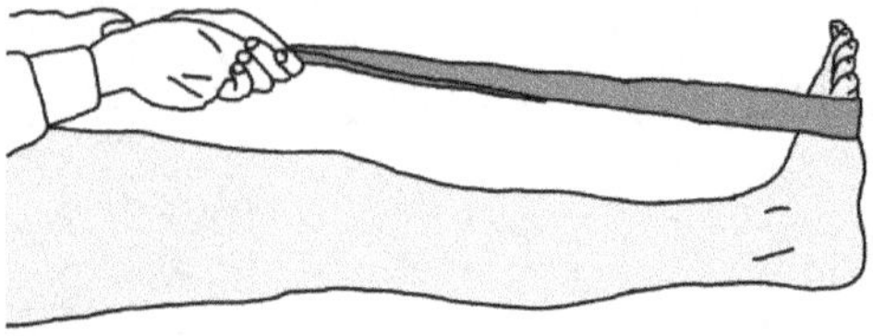

☐ **Front of Ankle** (plantar flexion)
Sit with your foot crossed over your other knee. Use your hand to stretch your ankle and point the toes. Hold for a count of _____.

Do _____ sets of _____ with each foot.

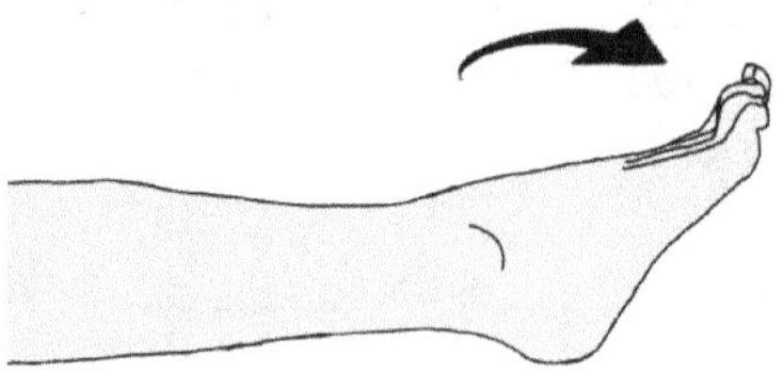

☐ **Side of Ankle** (inversion and eversion)
Sit with your foot on your other knee. Use your hand to move your ankle inward. Next, use your hand to move your ankle outward. Hold each stretch for a count of _____.

Do _____ sets of _____ with each foot.

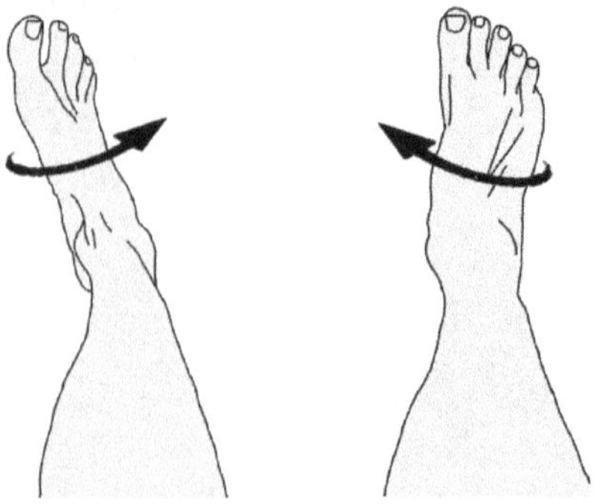

Burn Injury Stretches - Ankle and Toes

Do the checked stretches ______ times a day, every day.

☐ **Bottom of Foot and Toes** (extension)
Sit with your foot on your other knee. Grab your toes and pull them back toward your leg. Hold for a count of ______.

Do ______ sets of ______ with each foot.

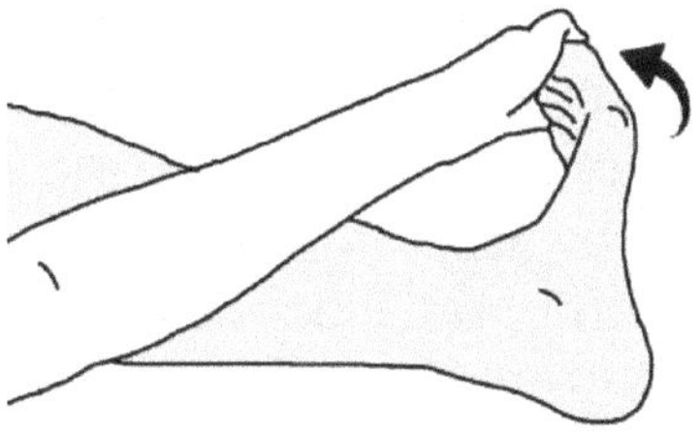

☐ **Bottom of Foot and Toes** (extension)
Stand and hold onto a stable surface. Rise onto your toes. Hold for a count of ______.

Do ______ sets of ______.

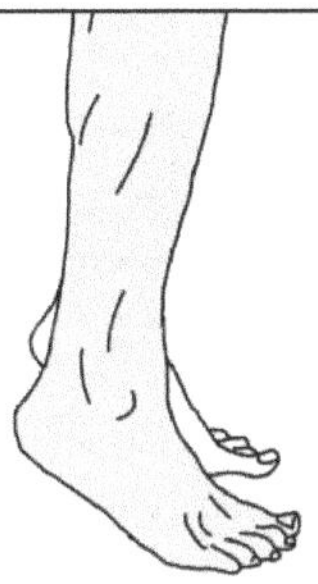

☐ **Top of Foot and Toes** (toe flexion)
Sit with your foot on your other knee. Grab your toes and curl them. Hold for a count of ______.

Do ______ sets of ______ with each foot.

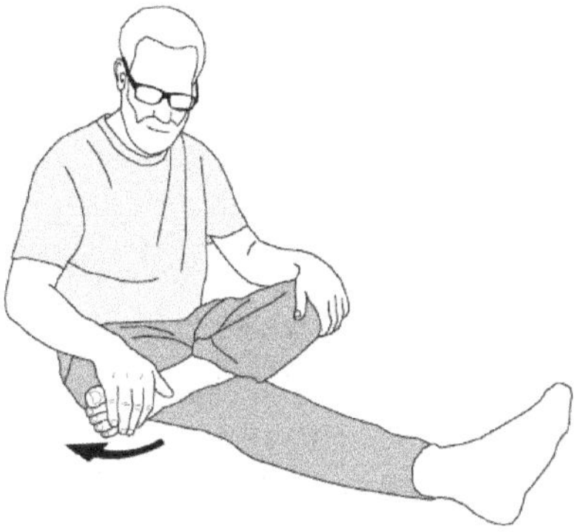

☐ **In Between Toes** (toe abduction)
Sit with your foot on your other knee. Use your fingers to spread each toe apart. Hold for a count of ______.

Do ______ sets of ______ with each toe.

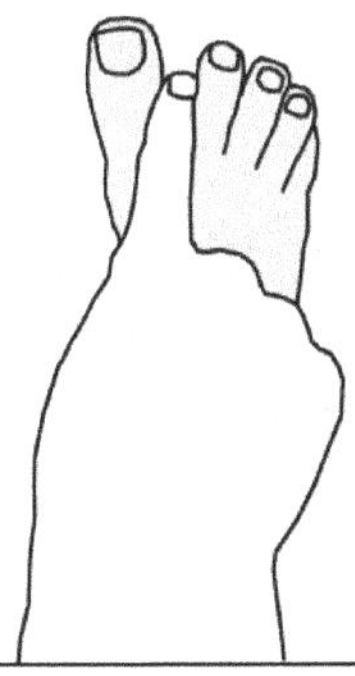

Cool-Down Stretches

Do the checked stretches _____ times a day, every day.

☐ **Front of Leg**
Hold onto a stable object. Reach back and hold one foot. Stand up straight. Pull your foot toward your bottom. You will feel the stretch in the front of your thigh. Hold to a count of ______.

Do ______ sets of ______ with each leg.

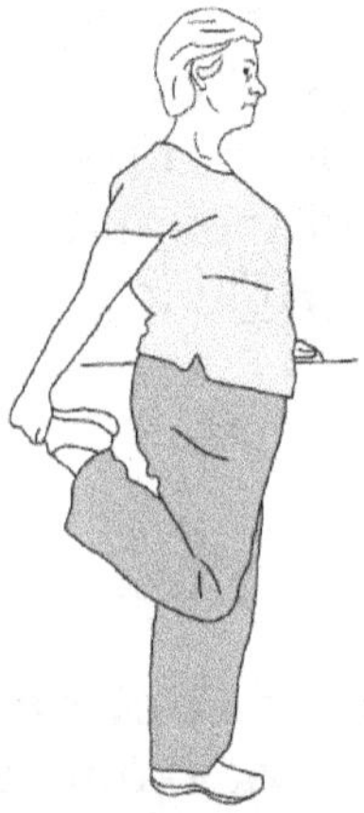

☐ **Back of Leg**
Sit in chair and extend one leg forward. Keep your knee straight. Lean forward and reach toward your toes. Hold to a count of ______.

Do ______ sets of ______ with each leg.
.

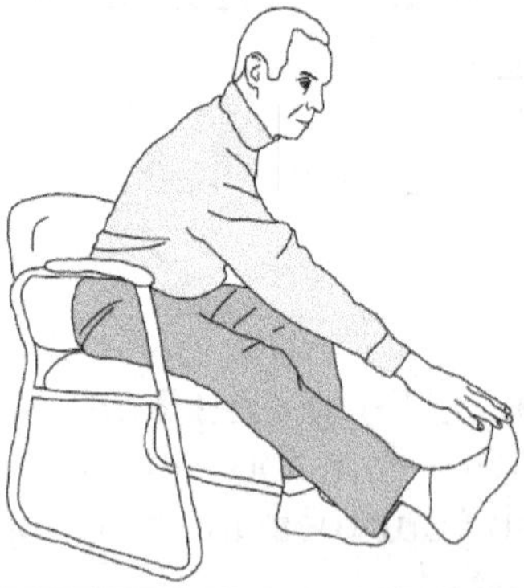

☐ **Overhead Stretch**
Interlace your fingers. Lift arms above head. Turn the palms facing up. Stretch your arms up. Hold to a count of ______.

Do ______ sets of ______.

☐ **Shoulder Stretch**
Raise your arms out front. Pull your elbow across toward your other shoulder. Hold to a count of ______.

Do ______ sets of ______ with each arm.

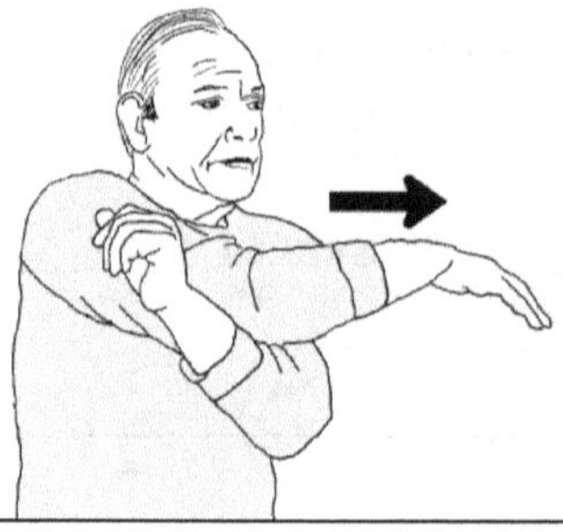

Occupational Therapy TOOLKIT

Core Exercise Guidelines

Name: ________________________________

Date: ________________________________

Therapist: ________________________________

Phone number: (_____)_______________________

Do the checked exercises _____ times per day, _____ days a week.

Exercise slowly and smoothly.

Do not hold your breath during exercise. Count aloud if needed.

Use good posture. Keep your stomach muscles tight and your back straight. These exercises should not cause back pain.

Sore muscles lasting a few days and feeling tired are normal after exercise. Exhaustion, sore joints, and painful muscle pulls are not normal. If you have these symptoms, do not exercise until you talk with your therapist.

If you have chest tightness or pain, shortness of breath, feel dizzy, faint, or sick to your stomach, stop and call emergency services at _____.

Notes:

____

____

____

____

____

____

____

____

Core Exercises - Back Muscles

Do the checked exercises _____ times per day, _____ days a week.

☐ **Bridge**
Bend both knees and place feet flat. Squeeze your hip muscles and lift your hips up from the bed. Hold for a count of _____.

Do _____ sets of _____.

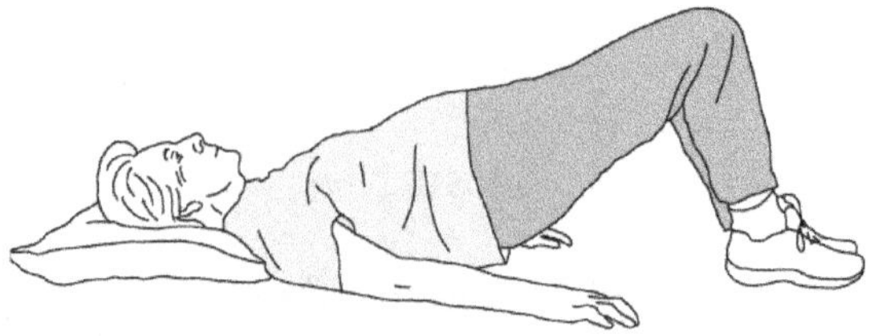

☐ **Bridge with Hip Rotation**
Bend both knees and place feet flat. Squeeze your hip muscles and lift your hips up from the bed. Spread your knees apart and then bring them back together.

Do _____ sets of _____.

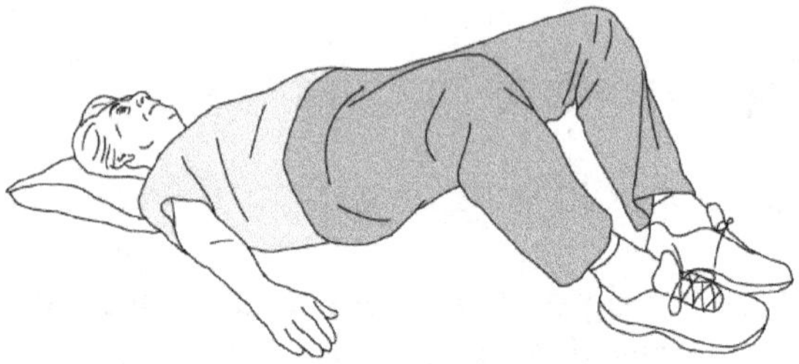

☐ **Bridge with Marching**
Bend both knees and place feet flat. Squeeze your hip muscles and lift your hips up from the bed. Lift your feet up and down.

Do _____ sets of _____.

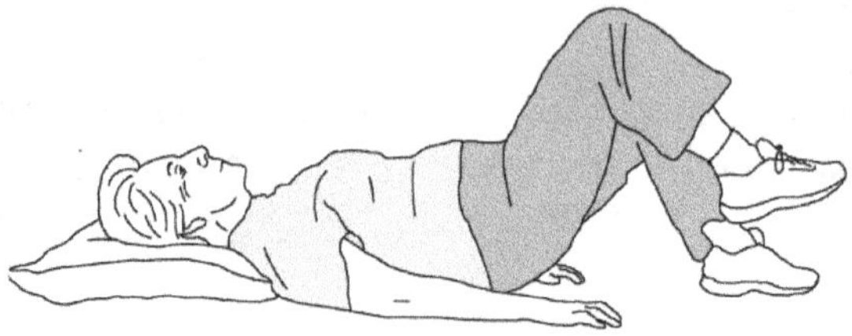

☐ **Bridge with Straight Leg Raise**
Bend both knees and place feet flat. Squeeze your hip muscles and lift your hips up from the bed. Straighten your right leg. Hold for a count of _______. Lower and straighten your left leg.

Do _____ sets of _____ on each leg.

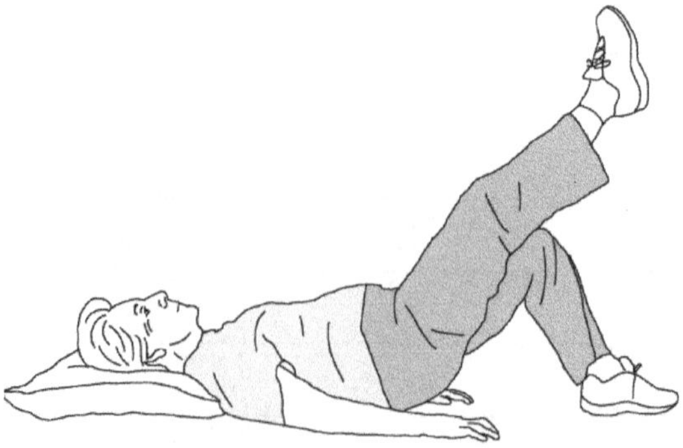

Core Exercises - Back Muscles

Do the checked exercises _____ times per day, _____ days a week.

☐ **Weight Shift**
Shift your weight forward onto your arms. Shift your weight back onto your knees.

Do _____ sets of _____.

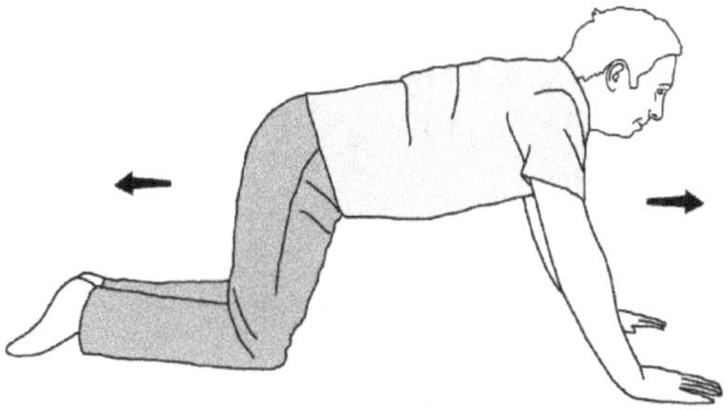

☐ **Arm Raises**
Raise your right arm. Return to all fours. Raise your left arm. Return to all fours.

Do _____ sets of _____.

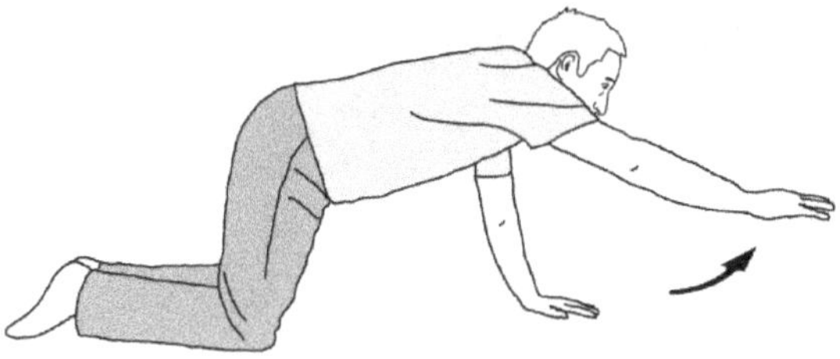

☐ **Leg Raises**
Raise your right leg. Return to all fours. Raise your left leg. Return to all fours.

Do _____ sets of _____.

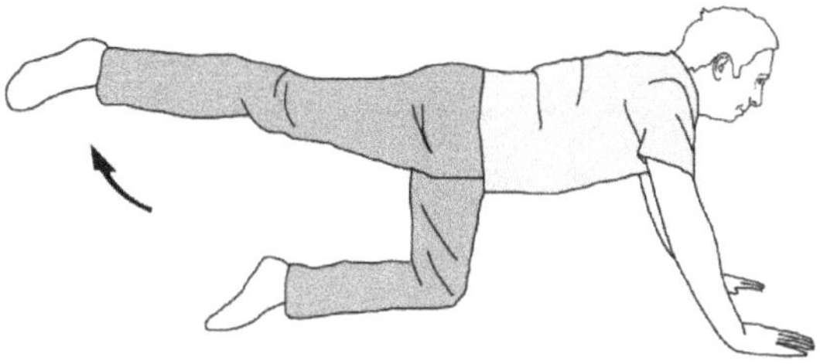

☐ **Arm and Leg Raises**
Raise your right arm and left leg at the same time. Return to all fours. Raise your left arm and right leg. Return to all fours.

Do _____ sets of _____.

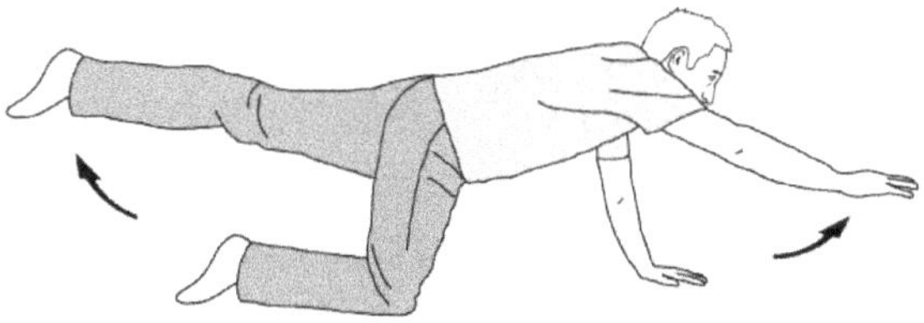

Core Exercises - Back Muscles

Do the checked exercises _____ times per day, _____ days a week.

☐ **One Arm Raises**
Raise your right arm up, then lower. Raise your left arm up, then lower.

Do _____ sets of _____.

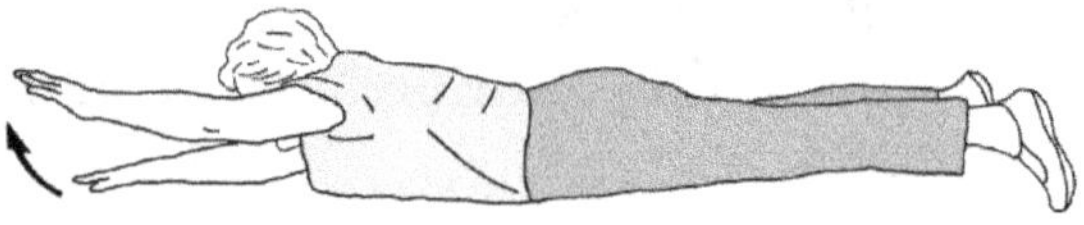

☐ **Both Arm Raises**
Raise both your arms up, then lower.

Do _____ sets of _____.

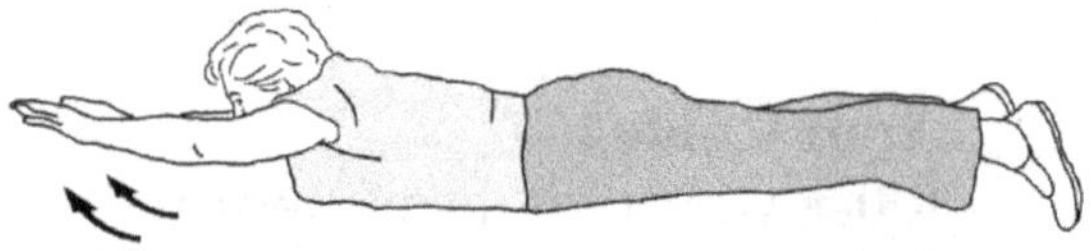

☐ **One Leg Raises**
Raise your right leg up, then lower. Raise your left leg up, then lower.

Do _____ sets of _____.

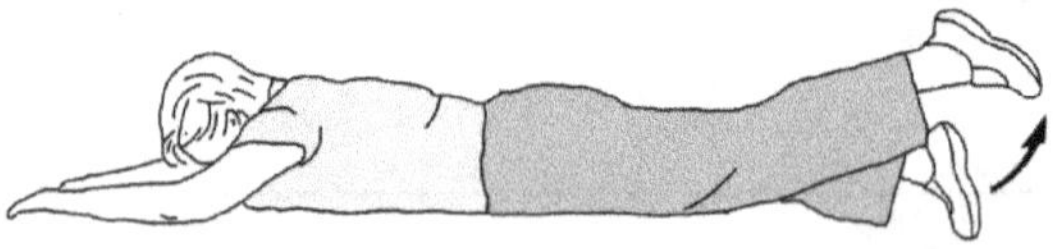

☐ **Both Leg Raises**
Lift both legs up, then lower.

Do _____ sets of _____.

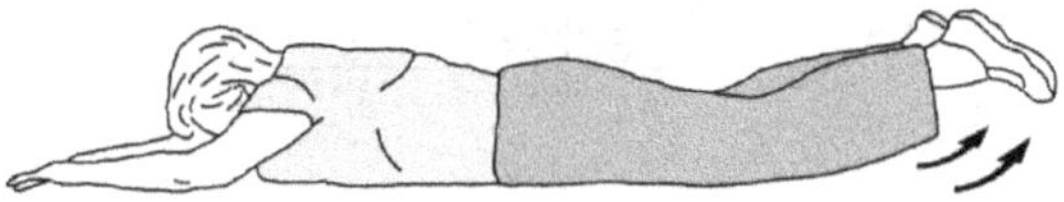

☐ **Arm and Leg Raises**
Raise your right arm and left leg up at the same time, then lower. Raise your left arm and right leg up at the same time, then lower.

Do _____ sets of _____.

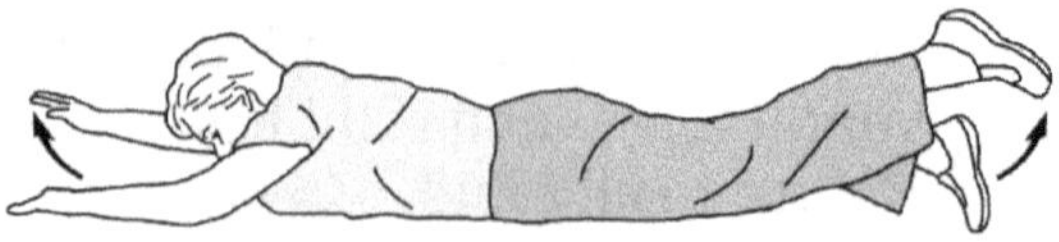

Occupational Therapy TOOLKIT

Core Exercises - Pelvic Muscles

Do the checked exercises _____ times per day, _____ days a week.

☐ **Pelvic Tilt**
Lie on your back with knees bent. Flatten your back into the mat by tightening the muscles of your stomach and bottom. Hold for a count of ______.

Do ______ sets of ______.

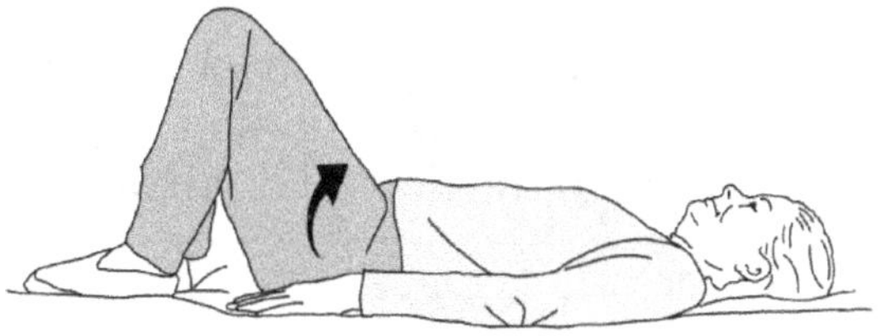

☐ **Pelvic Tilt - Arm Raise**
Do a pelvic tilt. Hold arms straight out from your body. Raise one arm over your head. Repeat on the other side.

Do ______ sets of ______.

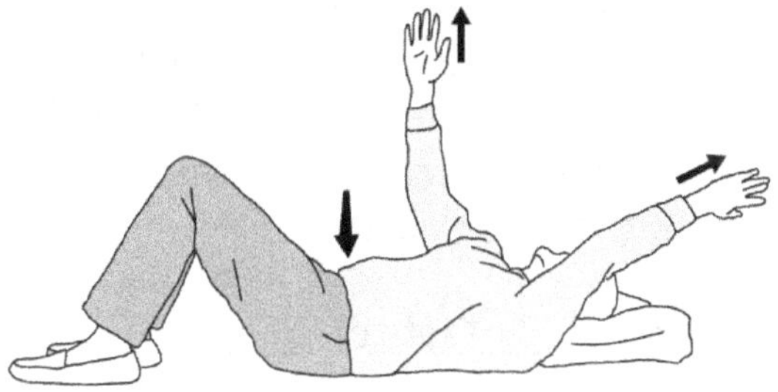

☐ **Pelvic Tilt - Leg Raise**
Do a pelvic tilt. Lift one foot off the floor. Repeat on the other side.

Do ______ sets of ______.

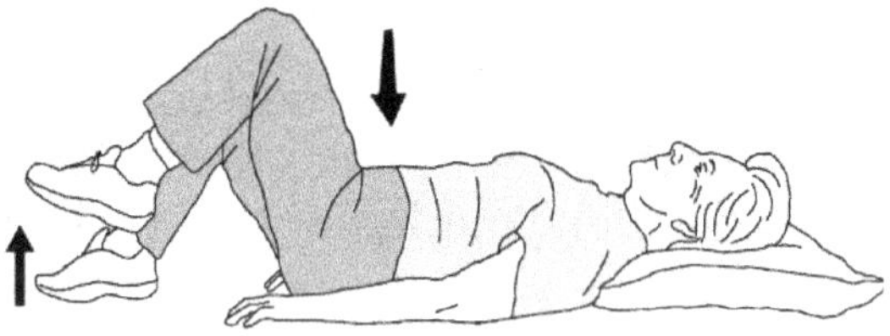

☐ **Pelvic Tilt - Arm and Leg Raise**
Do a pelvic tilt. Lift one foot off the floor and raise your other arm over your head at the same time. Return. Repeat with the other leg and arm.

Do ______ sets of ______.

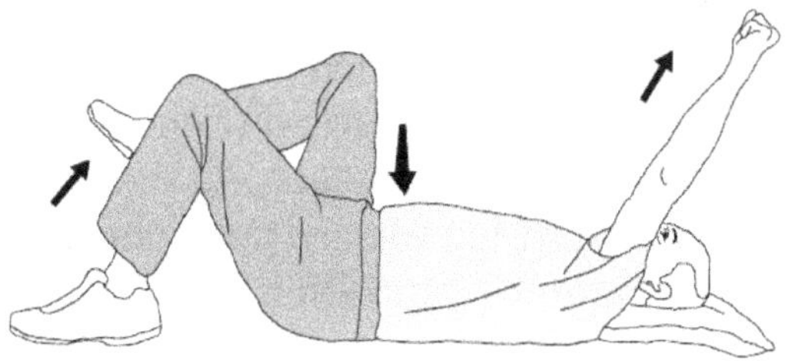

Core Exercises - Stomach Muscles

Do the checked exercises _____ times per day, _____ days a week.

☐ **Crunches**
Bend your knees. Cross arms over your chest, lift your upper back off the mat, exhale. Hold for a count of _____. Return to the floor and inhale.

Do _____ sets of _____.

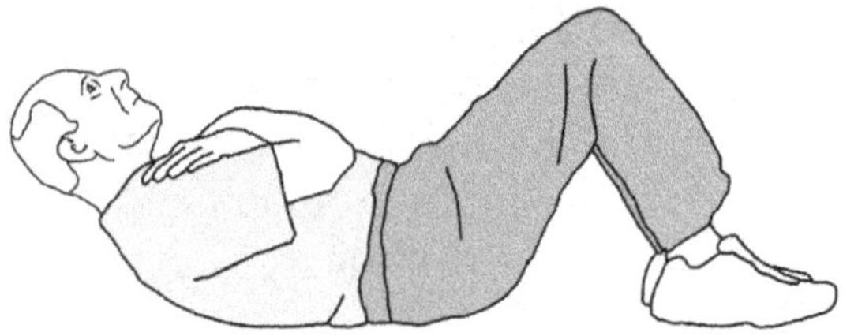

☐ **Diagonal Crunches**
Extend your arms and reach to one side, lift your upper back off the mat and exhale. Return to floor and inhale. Repeat to the other side.

Do _____ sets of _____.

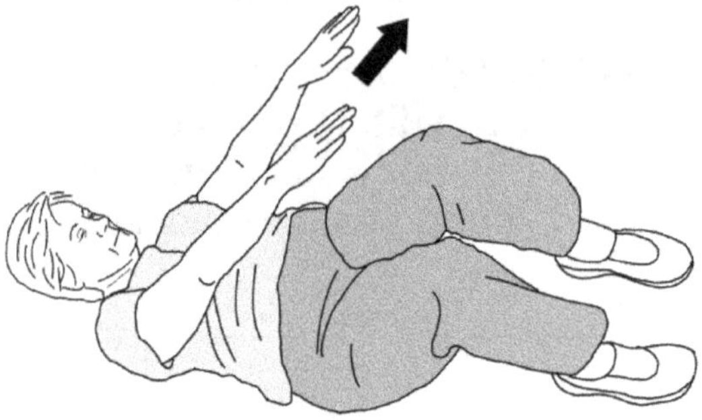

☐ **Double Knee Lift**
Bring your knees toward your chest. Keep your stomach muscles tight. Then straighten your legs without touching the mat.

Do _____ sets of _____.

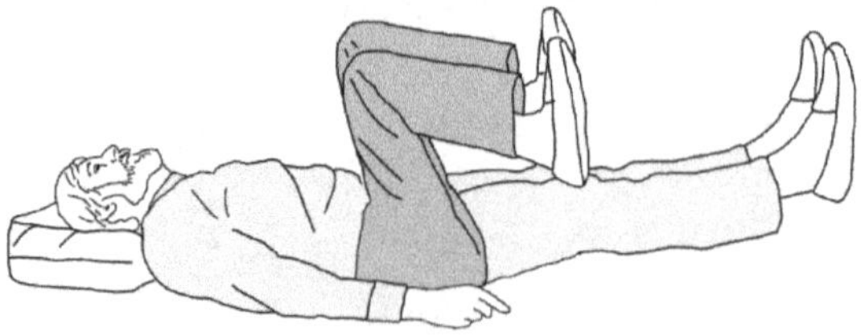

☐ **Straight Leg Raise**
Keep your stomach muscles tight. Bring both knees toward your chest. Straighten one leg without touching the mat. Bring your first leg toward your chest while you straighten your other leg.

Do _____ sets of _____.

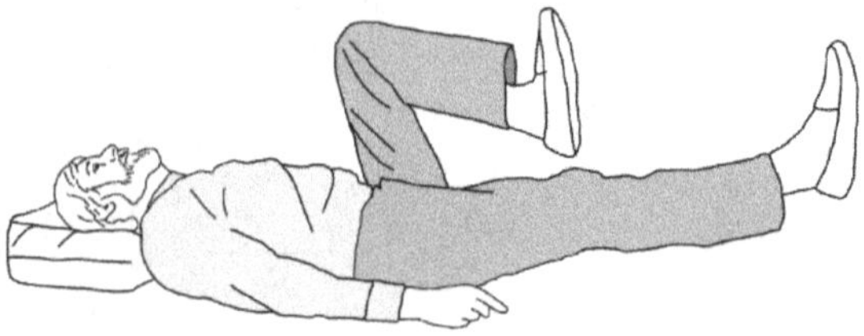

Dowel Exercises - Supine

Do the checked exercises _____ times per day, _____ days a week.

☐ Lie down. Hold dowel shoulder width apart with palms facing up. Keep your elbows straight. Raise the dowel over your head.

Do _____ sets of _____.

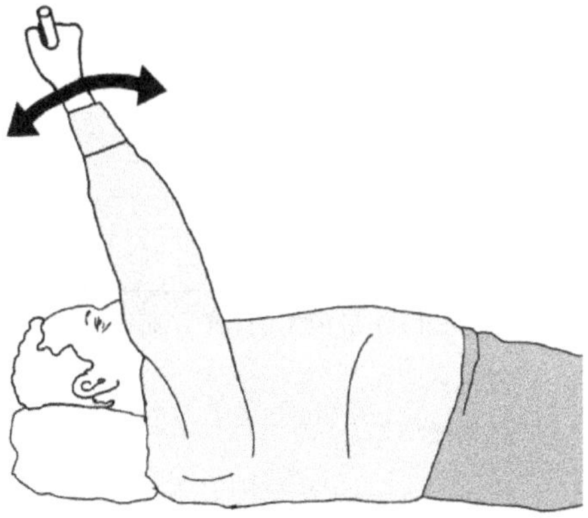

☐ Lie down. Hold dowel shoulder width apart with palms facing down. Push the dowel up from your chest.

Do _____ sets of _____.

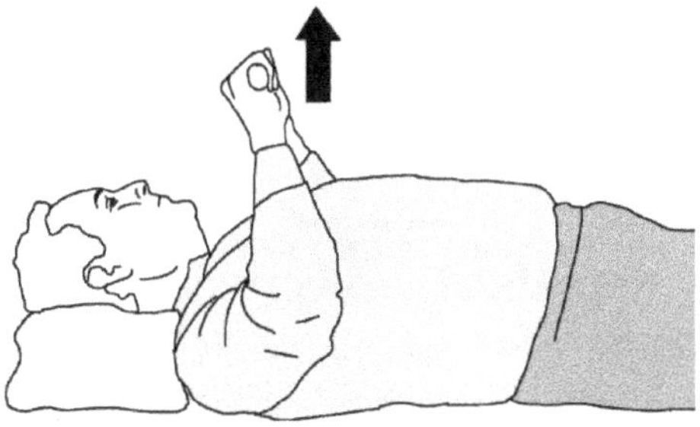

☐ Lie down. Hold dowel shoulder width apart with palms facing down. Hold your arms at shoulder height. Move the dowel side to side.

Do _____ sets of _____.

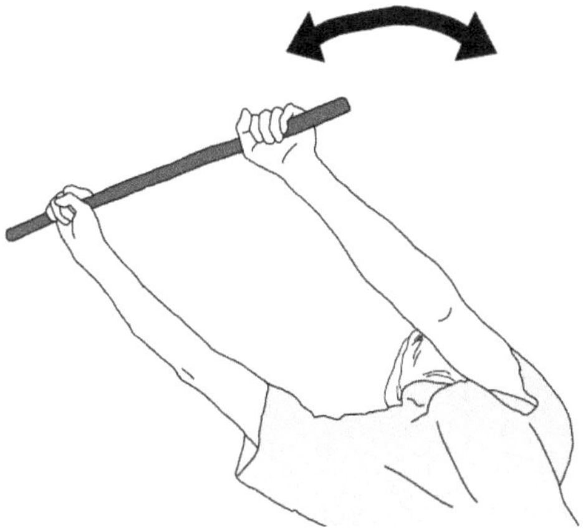

Dowel Exercises - Supine

Do the checked exercises _____ times per day, _____ days a week.

☐ Lie down. Hold dowel as shown. Hold your elbows into your sides. Use the dowel to rotate your right arm out to the side.

Do _____ sets of _____.
Repeat to the other side.

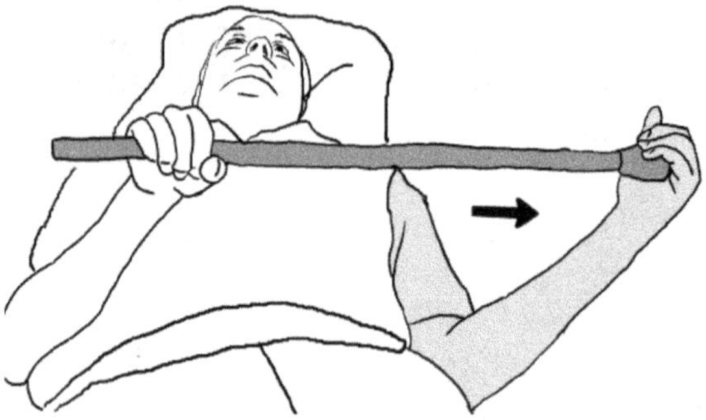

☐ Lie down. Hold dowel as shown. Hold your elbow straight with your arm to your side. Use the dowel to move your arm away from your side.

Do _____ sets of _____.
Repeat to the other side.

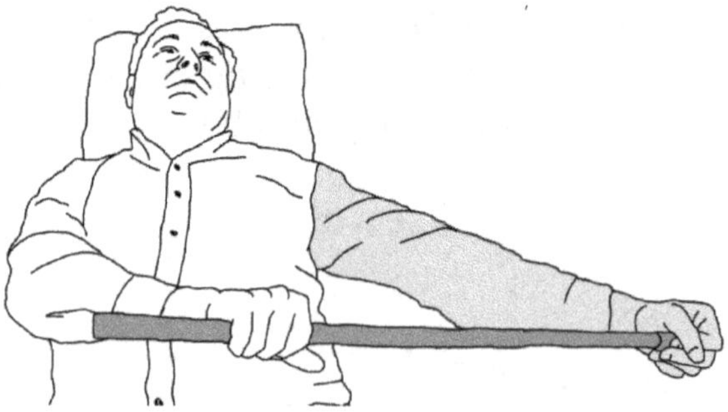

☐ Sit on the edge of the bed. Hold dowel behind your back. Move the dowel up your back.

Do _____ sets of _____.

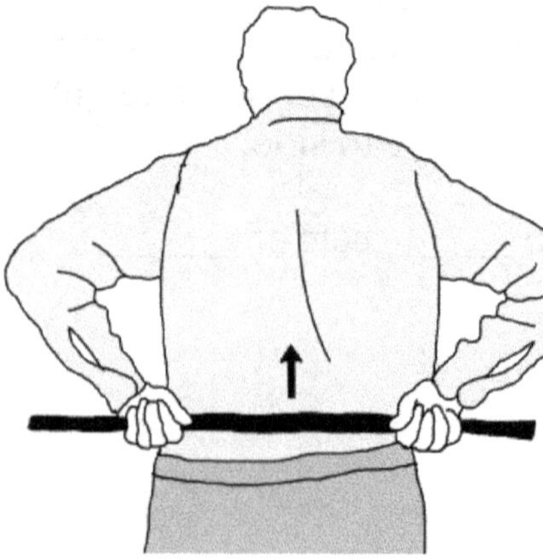

Dowel Exercises - Upright

Do the checked exercises ______ times per day, ______ days a week.

☐ Hold dowel shoulder width apart with palms facing up. Keep your elbows straight. Raise the dowel over your head.

Do ______ sets of ______.

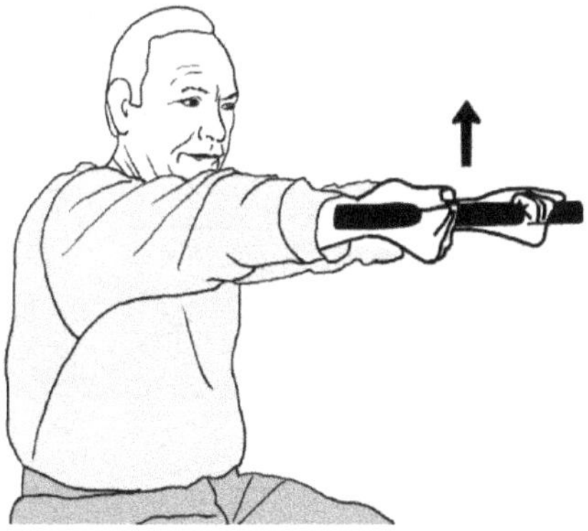

☐ Hold dowel shoulder width apart with palms facing down. Keep your arms at shoulder height. Move the dowel side to side.

Do ______ sets of ______.

☐ Hold dowel, shoulder width apart. Hold with your right palm facing up and left palm facing down. Lift the dowel up to your right side.

Do ______ sets of ______.
Repeat to the left side.

Dowel Exercises - Upright

Do the checked exercises _____ times per day, _____ days a week.

☐ Hold dowel behind your back. Keep your elbows straight. Lift the dowel away from your body.

Do _____ sets of _____.

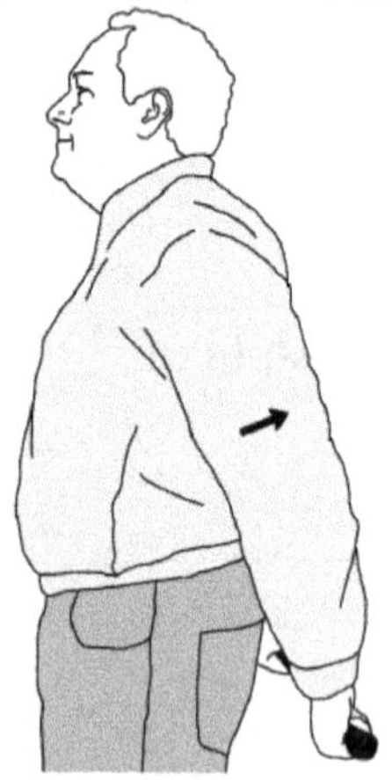

☐ Hold dowel behind your back. Move the dowel up your back.

Do _____ sets of _____.

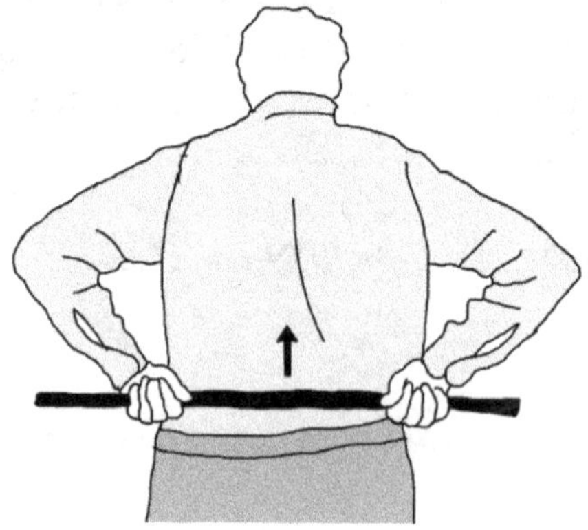

☐ Hold your elbows into your sides. Hold the dowel with your right palm facing up and left palm facing down. Use the dowel to rotate your right arm out to the side.

Do _____ sets of _____.
Repeat to the left side.

Elbow, Forearm and Wrist Active Range of Motion

Do the checked exercises with **left** **right** **both** arms.
Do the checked exercises _____ times per day, _____ days a week.

☐ Hold your arm at your side with your palm facing up. Bend and straighten your elbow.

Do _____ sets of _____.

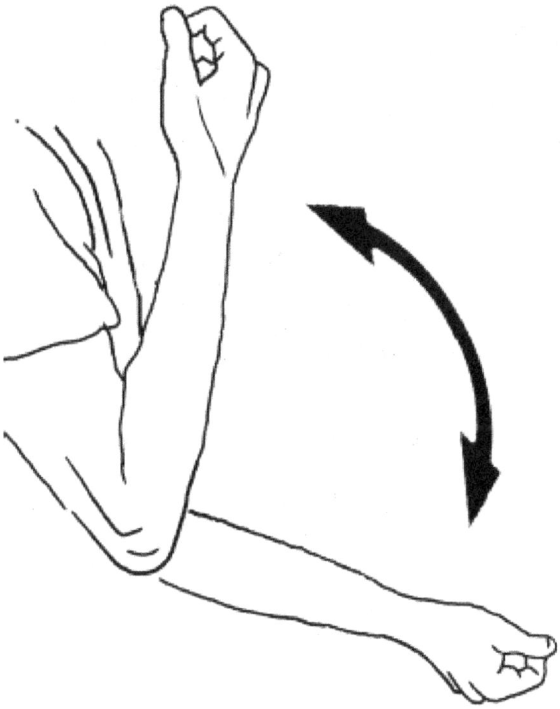

☐ Keep your elbows tucked into your sides. Make a loose fist. Turn your palm up and turn your palm down.

Do _____ sets of _____.

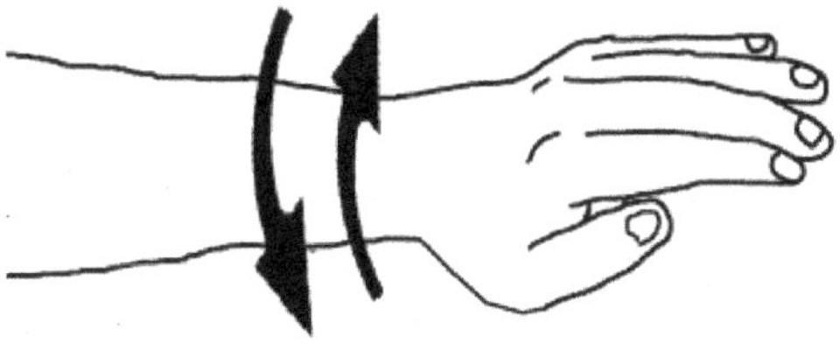

Elbow, Forearm and Wrist Active Range of Motion

Do the checked exercises with **left** **right** **both** arms.
Do the checked exercises _____ times per day, _____ days a week.

☐ Let your hand hang over the edge of a table. Bend your wrist, raise and lower your hand.

Do _____ sets of _____.

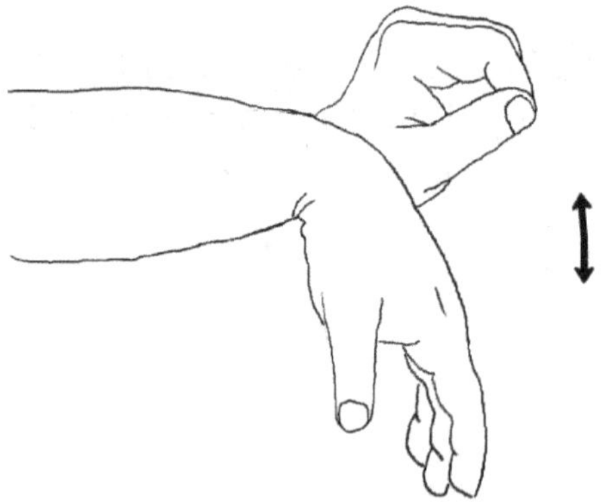

☐ Place your hand flat on the table. Move your hand side to side.

Do _____ sets of _____.

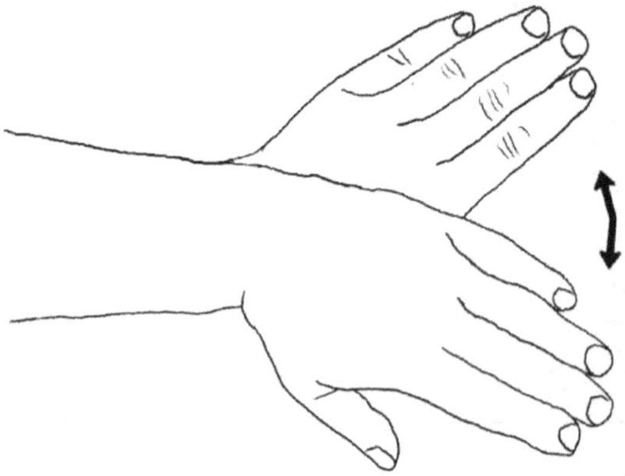

☐ Make circles with your hand. Move one way and then the other.

Do _____ sets of _____.

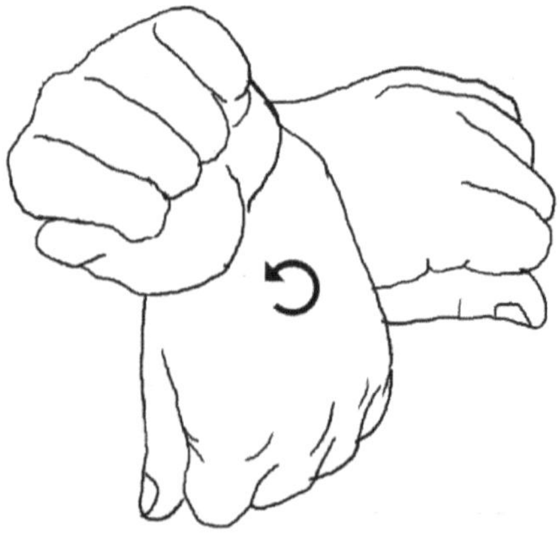

Occupational Therapy TOOLKIT

Elbow, Forearm and Wrist Strength Exercises

Do the checked exercises with **left** **right** **both** arms.
Do the checked exercises ______ times per day, ______ days a week.

☐ Hold a ______ lb/kg weight.
Hold your arm at your side with your palm facing forward. Bend and straighten your elbow.

Do ______ sets of ______.

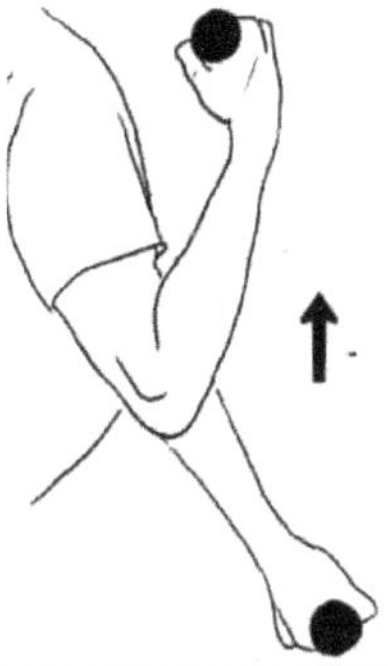

☐ Hold a ______ lb/kg weight.
Hold your arm at your side with your palm facing back. Bend and straighten your elbow.

Do ______ sets of ______.

☐ Hold a ______ lb/kg weight.
Hold the weight behind your head. Straighten your arm over your head.

Do ______ sets of ______.

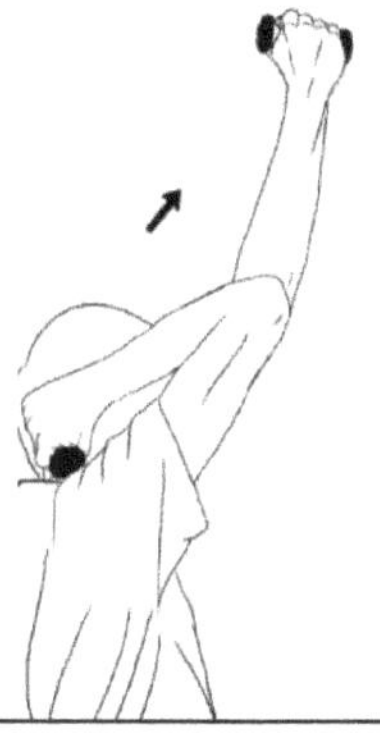

☐ Hold a ______ lb/kg weight.
Bend your elbows. Tuck them into your sides. Turn your palms up and down.

Do ______ sets of ______.

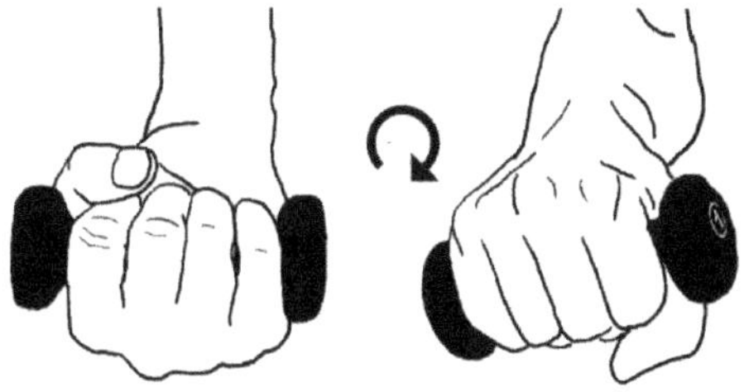

Occupational Therapy TOOLKIT

Elbow, Forearm and Wrist Strength Exercises

Do the checked exercises with **left** **right** **both** arms.
Do the checked exercises _____ times per day, _____ days a week.

☐ Hold a _____ lb/kg weight.
Let your hand hang over the edge of a table, palm facing down. Raise and lower the weight, bending at your wrist.

Do _____ sets of _____.

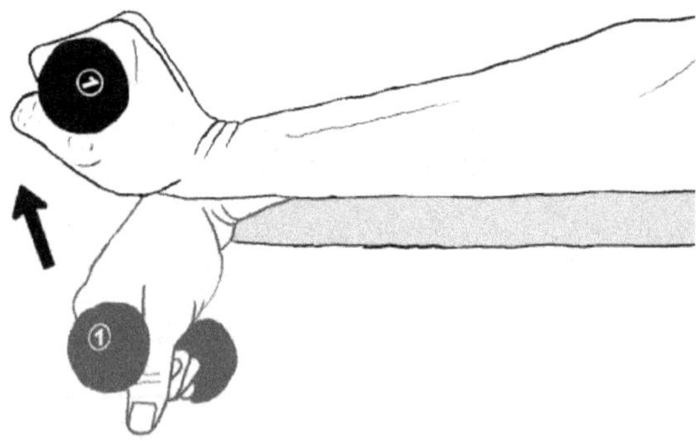

☐ Hold a _____ lb/kg weight.
Let your hand hang over the edge of a table, palm facing up. Raise and lower the weight, bending at your wrist.

Do _____ sets of _____.

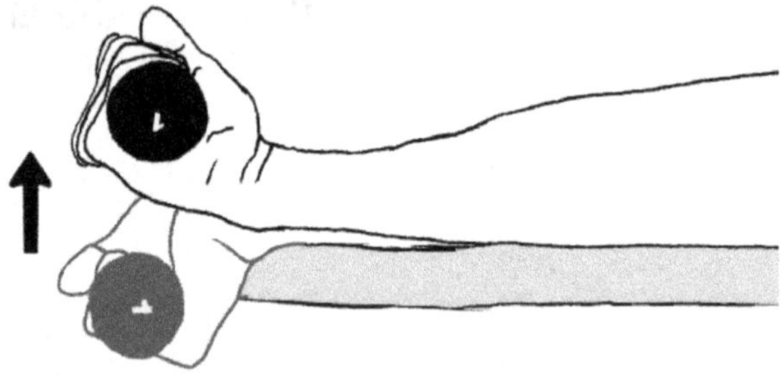

☐ Hold a _____ lb/kg weight.
Let your hand hang over the edge of a table, with your thumb pointing up. Move your hand up then down, bending at your wrist.

Do _____ sets of _____.

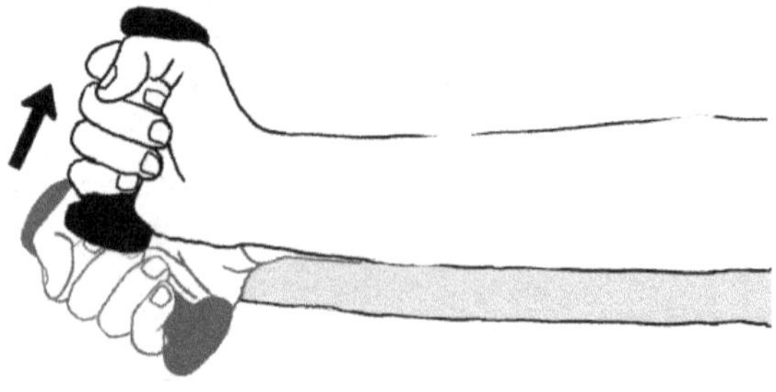

Elbow, Forearm and Wrist Stretches

Do the checked exercises with **left** **right** **both** arms.
Do the checked exercises _____ times per day, _____ days a week.

☐ Hold your arm at your side with your palm facing forward. Grasp your wrist and bend your elbow. Hold for a count of ______.

Do _____ sets of _____.

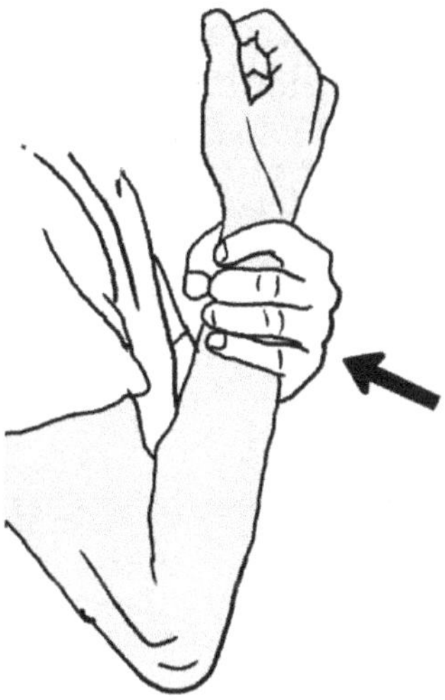

☐ Hold your arm at your side with your palm facing forward. Grasp your wrist and straighten your arm. Hold for a count of ______.

Do _____ sets of _____.

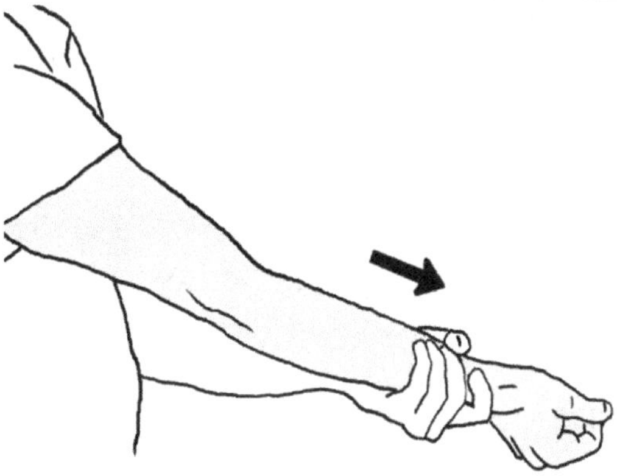

☐ Keep your elbows tucked into your sides. Grasp your hand and turn your palm up. Hold for a count of ______. Grasp your hand and turn your palm down. Hold for a count of ______.

Do _____ sets of _____.

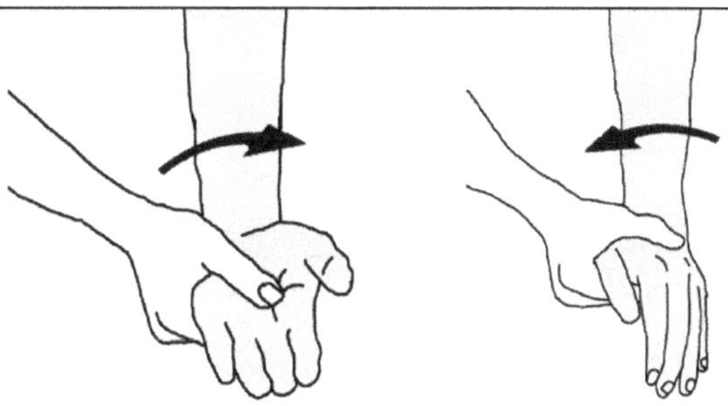

Elbow, Forearm and Wrist Stretches

Do the checked exercises with **left** **right** **both** arms.
Do the checked exercises _____ times per day, _____ days a week.

☐ Hold your arm out in front. Keep your elbow straight and your palm down. Use your other hand to stretch your wrist. To increase the stretch, close your fingers into a fist. Turn your arm toward your little finger. Hold for a count of ______.

Do _____ sets of _____.

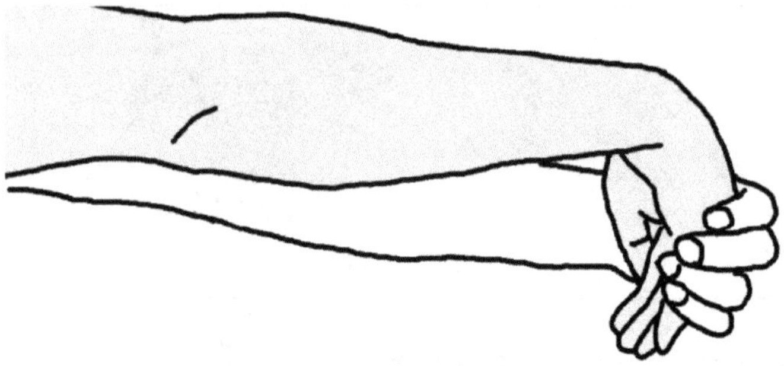

☐ Hold your arm out in front. Keep your elbow straight and your palm up. Use your other hand to stretch your wrist. To increase the stretch, use your other hand to straighten your fingers and turn your arm toward your thumb. Hold for a count of ______.

Do _____ sets of _____.

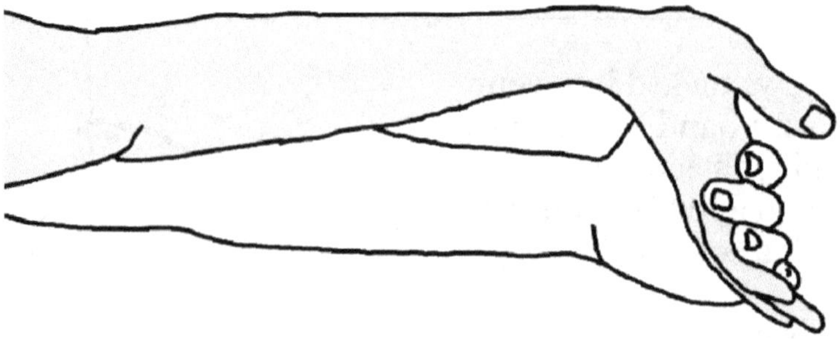

Occupational Therapy TOOLKIT

Elbow, Forearm and Wrist Stretches

Do the checked exercises _____ times per day, _____ days a week.

☐ Place your palms together. Lower both hands to increase stretch. Hold for a count of ______.

Do _____ sets of _____.

☐ Place the back of your hands together. Raise both hands to increase the stretch. Hold for a count of ______.

Do _____ sets of _____.

☐ Place the backs of your hands together. Make a full fist. Raise both hands to increase the stretch. Hold for a count of ______.

Do _____ sets of _____.

Elbow Stretches for Below Elbow Amputation

Perform the stretches _____ times per day, _____ days a week

☐ **Elbow Flexion**
Place a rolled towel under your residual limb. Bend your elbow as far as you can. Use your hand to put pressure on the back of your residual limb until you feel a stretch. Hold for _____ seconds.

Do _____ sets of _____.

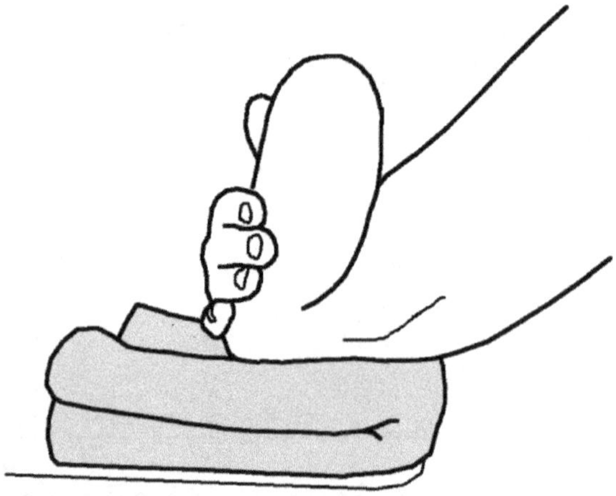

☐ **Elbow Extension**
Place a rolled towel under your residual limb. Straighten your elbow as far as you can. Use your hand to push down on the end of your residual limb until you feel a stretch. Hold for _____ seconds.

Do _____ sets of _____.

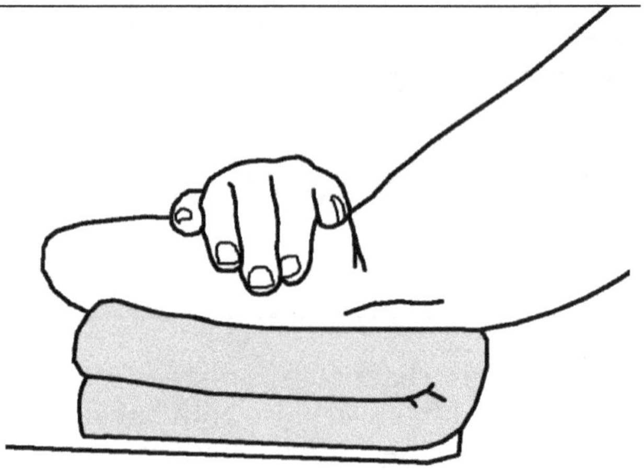

Occupational Therapy TOOLKIT

Elbow, Wrist and Hand Active Exercises

Do _____ sets of _____ of each exercise.

☐ Bend and straighten your elbow

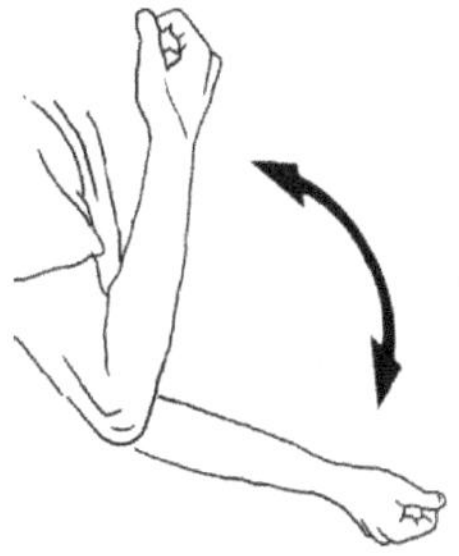

☐ Turn your palm up and dow

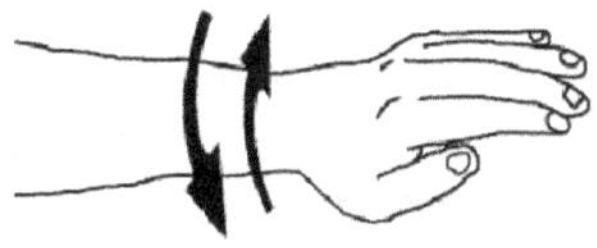

☐ Bend your wrist up and down

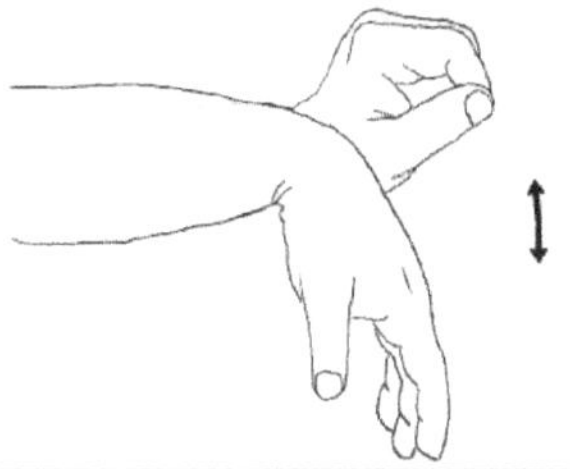

☐ Move your hand side to side

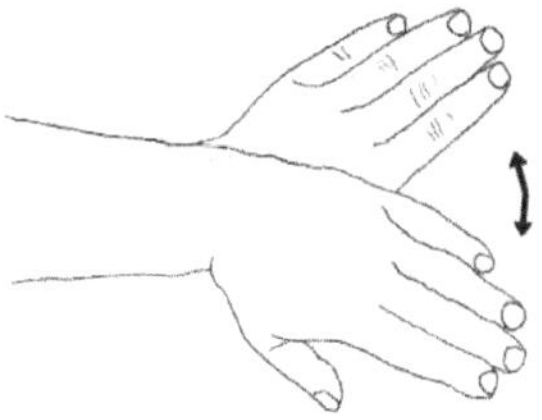

☐ Move your hand in a circle

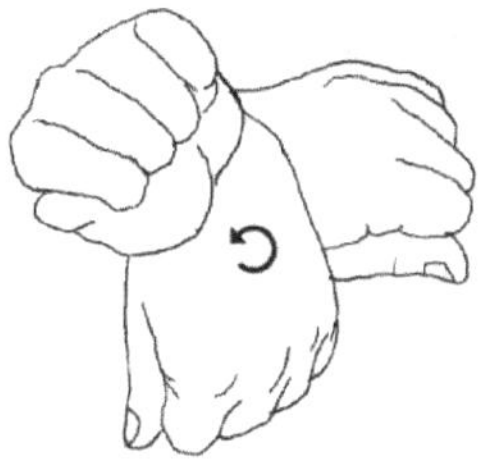

☐ Open and close your hand

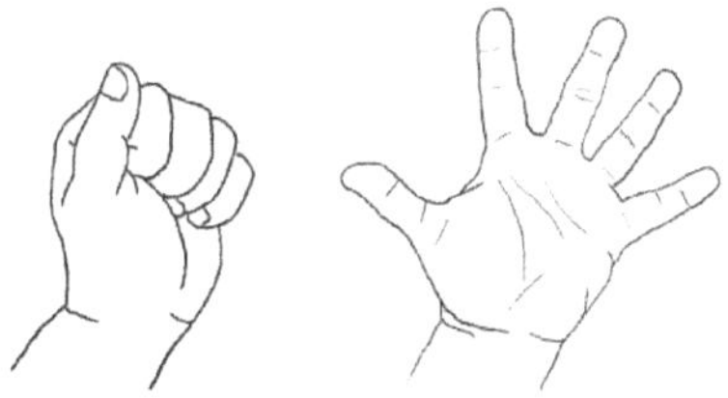

☐ Bend your thumb over toward the base of your pinkie finger.

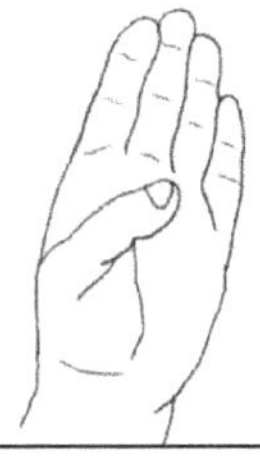

☐ Squeeze a soft ball

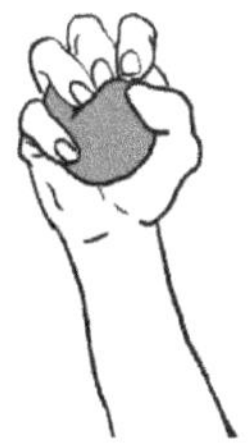

Occupational Therapy TOOLKIT

Exercise Ball Guidelines

Name: ____________________________________

Date: ______________________________________

Therapist: __________________________________

Phone number: (_____)______________________

Do the checked exercises _____ times per day, _____ days a week.

Exercise slowly and smoothly.

Do not hold your breath during exercise. Count aloud if needed.

Use good posture. Keep your stomach muscles tight and your back straight.

The correct ball size: 45-cm 55-cm 65-cm 75-cm 85-cm (circle one)

Inflate the exercise ball so your feet rest on the floor when seated. Your knees should be even or just above your hips.

Sore muscles lasting a few days and feeling tired are normal after exercise. Exhaustion, sore joints, and painful muscle pulls are not normal. If you have these symptoms, do not exercise until you talk with your therapist.

If you have chest tightness or pain, shortness of breath, feel dizzy, faint, or sick to your stomach, stop and call emergency services at _____.

Notes:

____

____

____

____

Exercise Ball - Back Muscles

☐ **Bridge**
Lie on the floor with both legs on the exercise ball. Keep your stomach muscles tight. Lift your hips up off the floor. Hold for a count of _____.

Do _____ sets of _____.

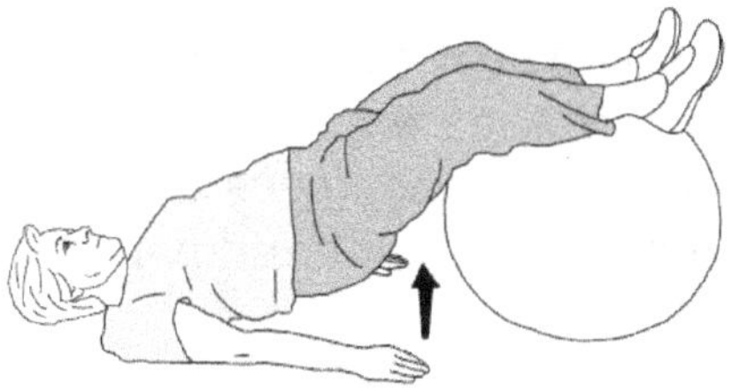

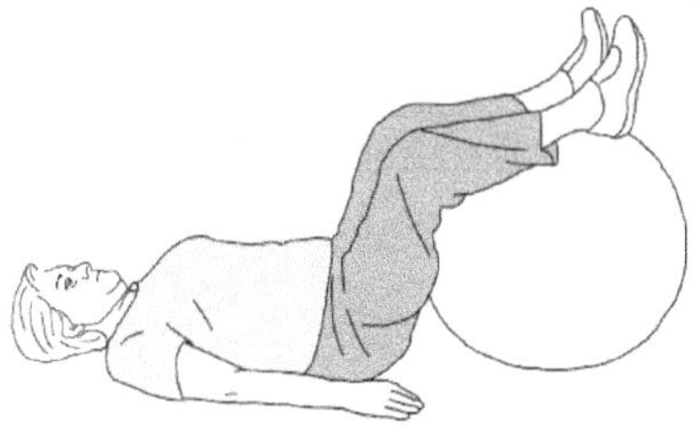

☐ **Bridge with Leg Lift**
Lie on the floor with both legs on the exercise ball. Keep your stomach muscles tight. Lift your hips up off the floor. Lift your right leg off the ball. Repeat with your left leg.

Do _____ sets of _____.

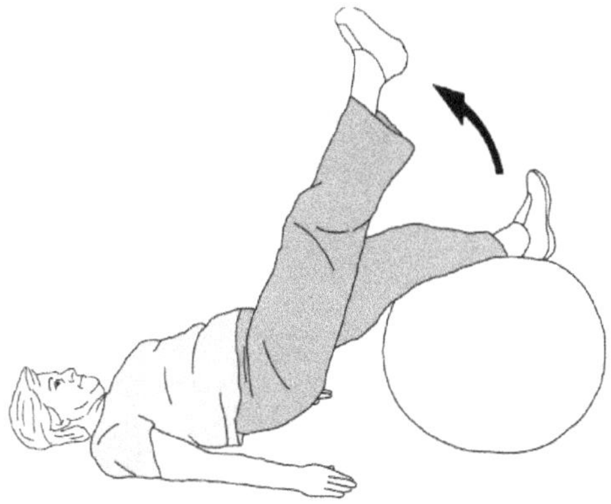

☐ **Bridge with Leg and Arm Lift**
Lie on the floor with both legs on the exercise ball. Lift your hips up off the floor. Keep your stomach muscles tight. Lift the right leg off the ball and raise your left arm over your head. Repeat with your left leg and right arm.

Do _____ sets of _____.

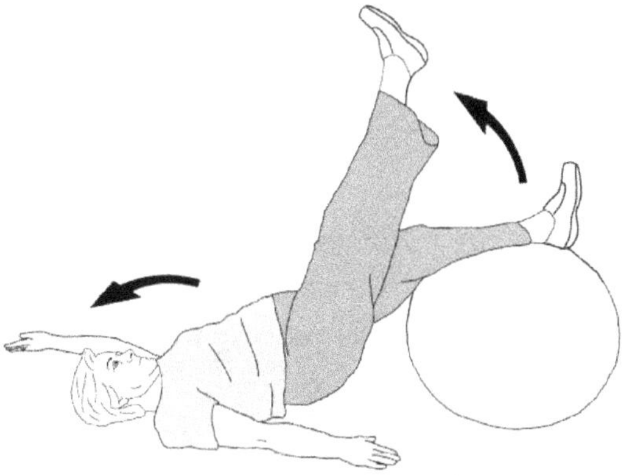

Exercise Ball - Back Muscles

Position for all exercises
Lie with the exercise ball under your stomach. Your hands and knees are on the floor. Keep your back straight and pain-free.

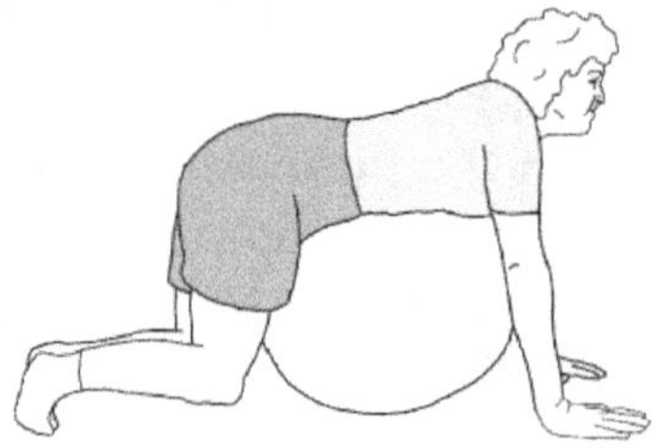

☐ **Arm Raise**
Raise both arms off the floor to shoulder level. Hold to a count of ______.

Do ______ sets of ______.

☐ **Leg Raise**
Lift both legs off the floor. Balance on your arms. Hold for a count of ______.

Do ______ sets of ______.

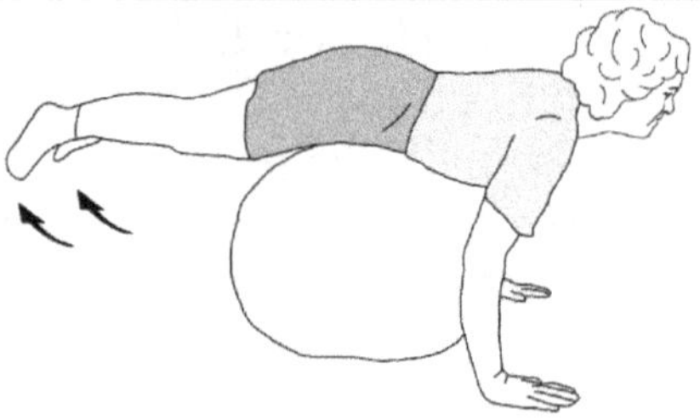

☐ **Arm and Leg Raise**
Raise your right arm and left leg off the floor. Hold for a count of ______. Repeat with your left arm and right leg. Hold for a count of ______.

Do ______ sets of ______ on each side.

☐ **Walk Out**
Support your weight with your hands. Walk your hands forward away from the ball until your thighs are resting on the ball. Hold for a count of ______. Walk your hands back until your feet are on the floor.

Do ______ sets of ______.

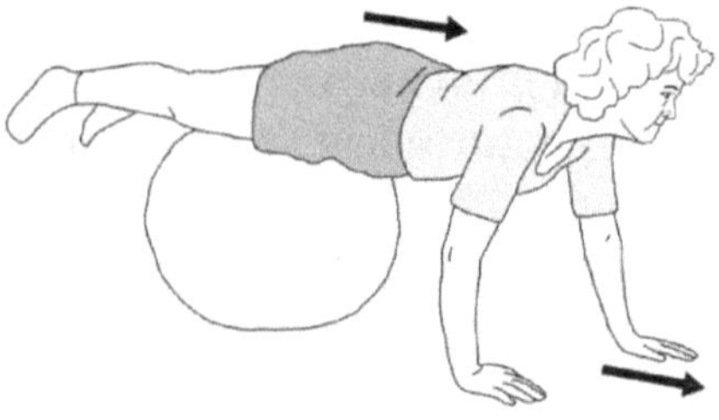

Exercise Ball - Pelvic Muscles

Position for all exercises
Sit in the center of the exercise ball with both your feet on the floor. Sit up straight.

☐ **Side to Side**
Move your hips from side to side.

Do ______ sets of ______.

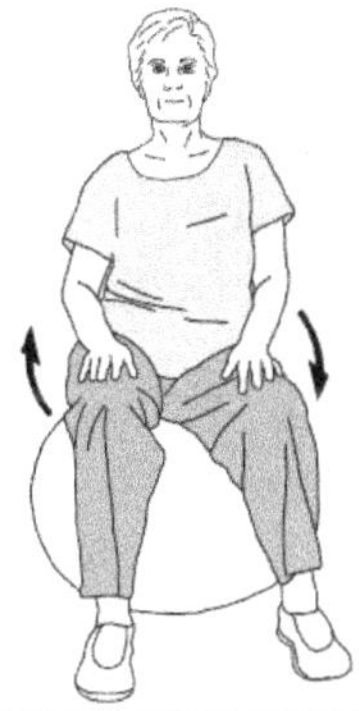

☐ **Forward and Back**
Roll your hips forward and back.

Do ______ sets of ______.

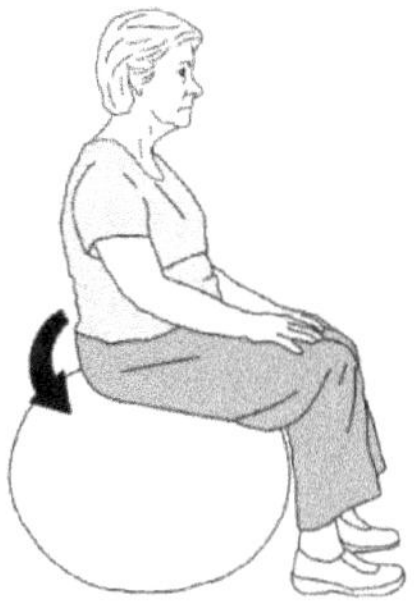

☐ **Circles**
Shift your weight around in a circle.

Do ______ sets of ______.

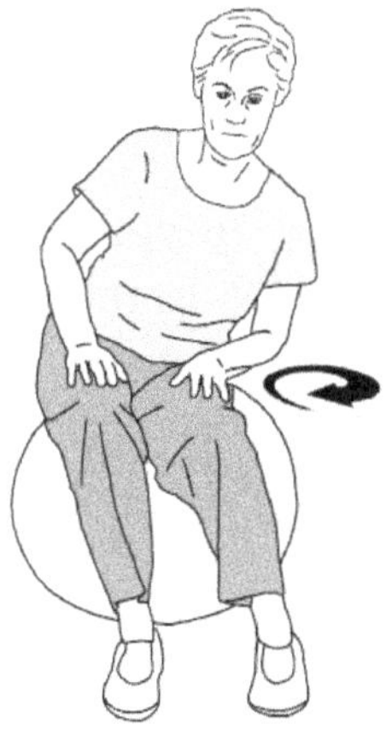

Exercise Ball - Pelvic Muscles

Position for all exercises
Sit in the center of the exercise ball with both your feet on the floor. Sit up straight.

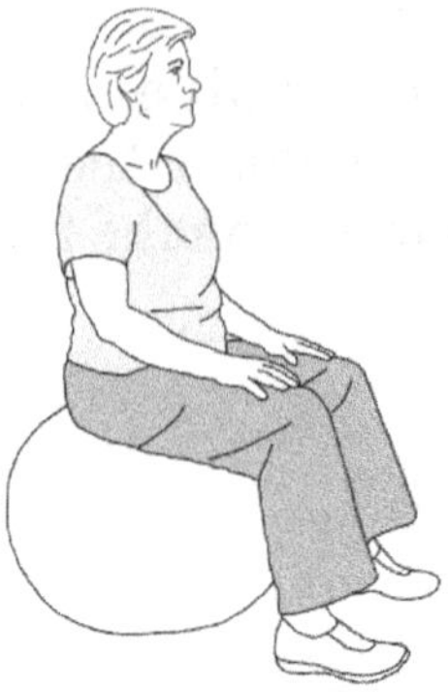

☐ **March in Place**
Raise and lower your right foot, then raise and lower your left foot.

Do ______ sets of ______.

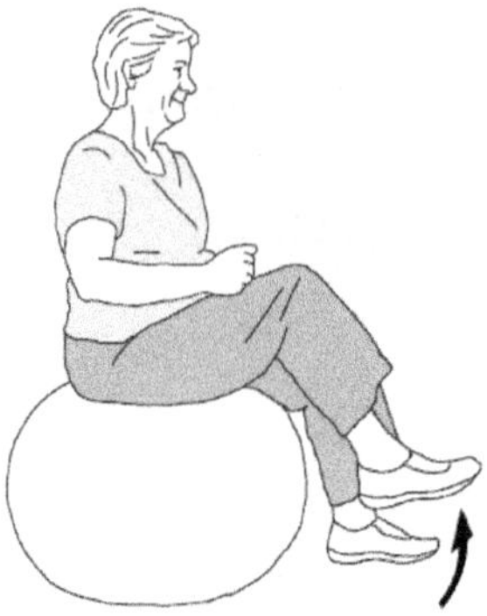

☐ **March in Place and Move Arms**
Raise and lower your right foot and left arm at the same time. Repeat with your left foot and right arm.

Do ______ sets of ______.

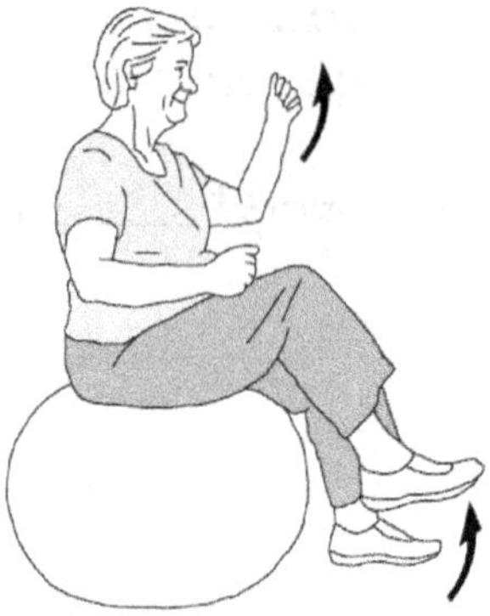

☐ **Trunk Turns**
Turn and reach to the right and then turn and reach to the left.

Do ______ sets of ______.

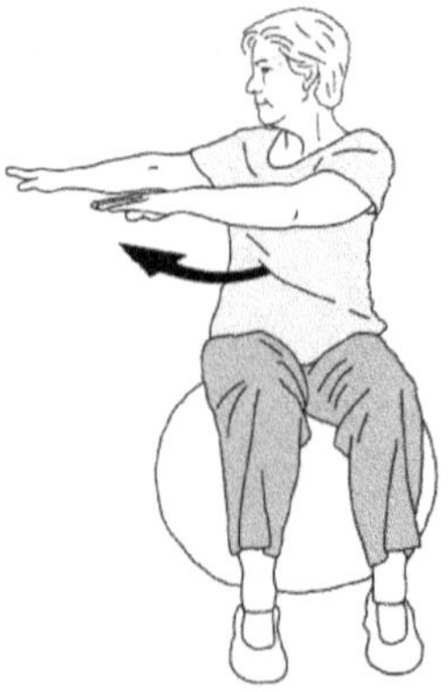

Exercise Ball - Stomach Muscles

☐ **Crunch**
Sit on exercise ball with your arms crossed. Lean back half way, keep your back straight and bend at your hips. Use your stomach muscles to sit up. Hold to a count of ______.

Do ______ sets of ______.

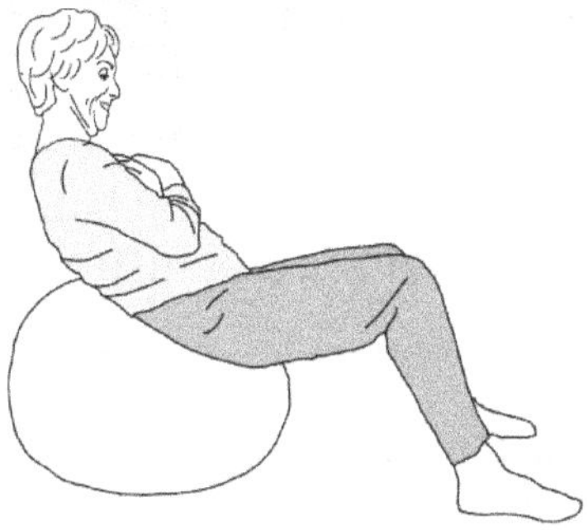

☐ **Diagonal Crunch**
Sit on exercise ball with your hands behind your head. Lean back half way, keep your back straight and bend at your hips. Use your stomach muscles to sit up and twist to the right. Hold to a count of ______. Repeat to the left side.

Do ______ sets of ______.

☐ **Reverse Curl**
Lie on your back with your legs bent and resting on the ball. Squeeze the ball between your calves and thighs. Bend at your hips and use your stomach muscles to lift the ball off the floor. Hold to a count of ______.

Do ______ sets of ______.

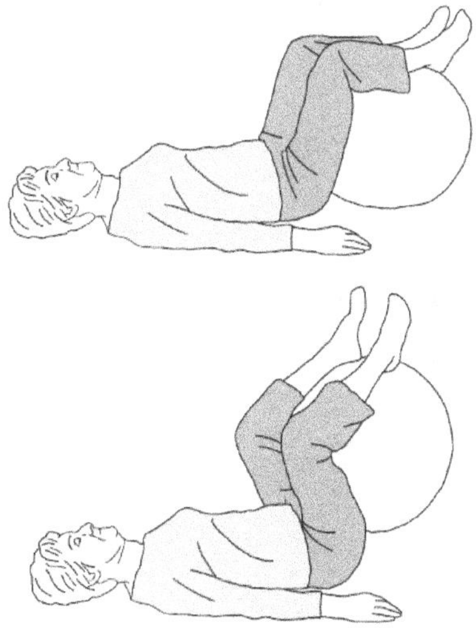

Exercise Ball - Stomach Muscles

Position for all exercises
Sit on the ball. Walk your legs away from the ball until your shoulders and upper back are resting on the ball. Keep your back straight in a pain-free position.

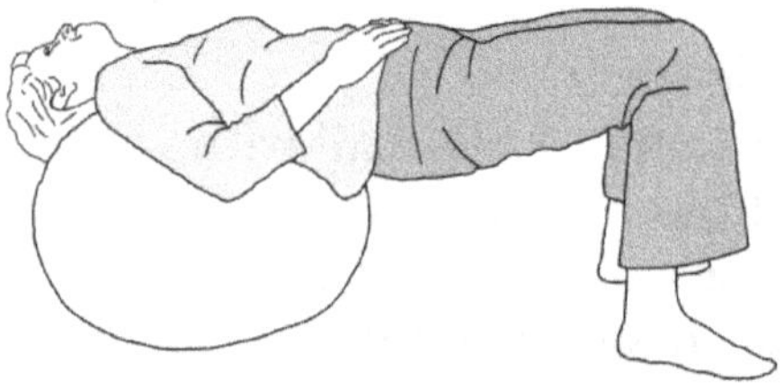

☐ **Arm Raise**
Raise both arms over your head. Keep your elbows straight. Hold to a count of _______.

Do ______ sets of ______.

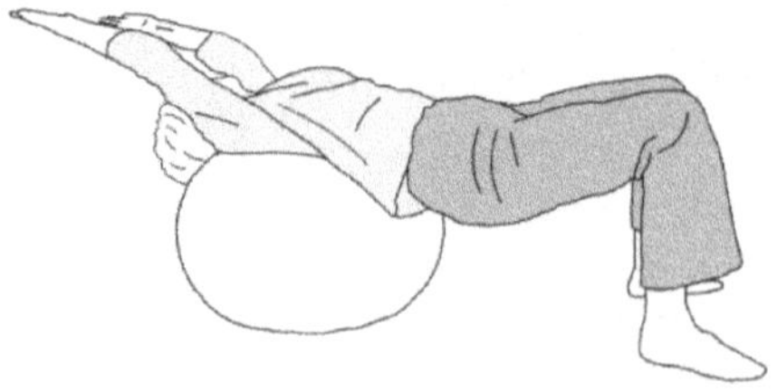

☐ **Arm Spread**
Move your arms out from your sides at shoulder level, Keep your elbows straight and bring your hands together.

Do ______ sets of ______.

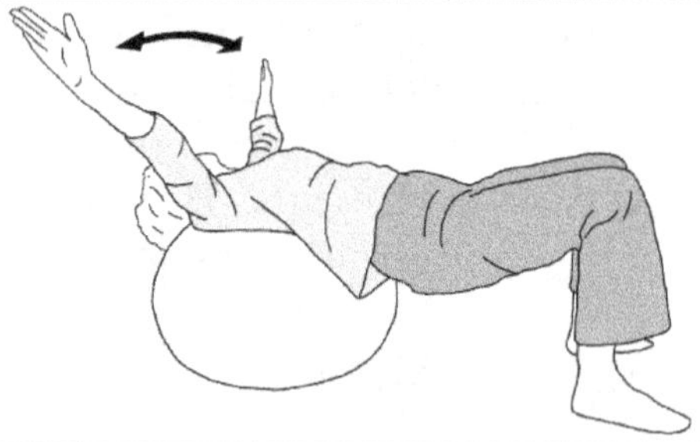

☐ **Knee Squeeze**
Squeeze your knees. Hold to a count of _______.

Do ______ sets of ______.

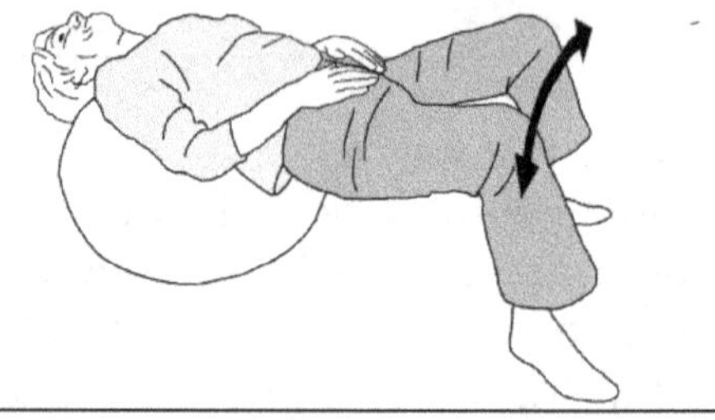

☐ **Bottom Tuck**
Raise and lower your bottom.

Do ______ sets of ______.

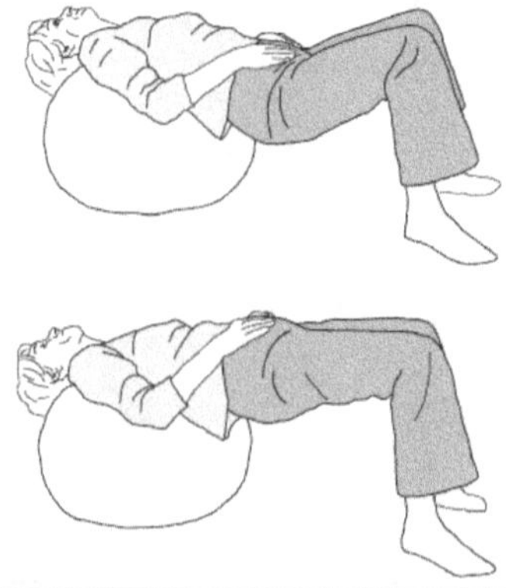

Exercise Tips for Amyotrophic Lateral Sclerosis

Name: ______________________________

Date: ______________________________

Therapist: ______________________________

Phone number: (_____)______________________

Do the checked exercises _____ times a day, _____ days a week.

Exercise slowly and smoothly. Avoid getting tired. Stop and rest as often as needed.

Do not hold your breath during exercise. Count aloud if needed.

Use good posture. Keep your stomach muscles tight and your back straight.

If exercise causes sore muscles or feeling tired that lasts longer than half an hour after exercise, it is too hard. Do not exercise until you talk with your therapist.

If you have chest tightness or pain, shortness of breath, feel dizzy, faint, or sick to your stomach, stop and call emergency services at _____.

Notes:

____

____

____

____

____

____

____

____

Occupational Therapy TOOLKIT

Exercise Tips for Arthritis

Name: ______________________________

Date: ______________________________

Therapist: ______________________________

Phone number: (______)______________________

Choose the Best Time:

- When you have the least amount of pain and stiffness.
- When you are not tired.
- When your medication is having the most effect.

Prepare Yourself:

- Warm up for 5-10 minutes. Do some gentle stretching and march in place.
- Massage your joints.

Tips

- Do the checked exercises _____ times a day, _____ days a week,
- Exercise slowly and smoothly.
- Use good posture. Keep your stomach muscles tight and your back straight.
- Do not hold your breath during exercise. Count aloud if needed.
- Do not overdo it. If you have pain two hours after exercising or your symptoms are worse the next day, then you have done too much. Talk to your therapist about changes the next time by reducing the repetitions or resistance.

Cautions:

- If you have chest tightness or pain, shortness of breath, feel dizzy, faint, or sick to your stomach, stop and call emergency services at _____.
- Follow the precautions given to you about exercises to avoid because of hip replacements, compression fractures, or osteoporosis.

Notes:

____

____

____

Exercise Tips for Diabetes

Name: ______________________________

Date: ______________________________

Therapist: ______________________________

Phone number: (_____)______________________

Do the checked exercises _____ times a day, _____ days a week.

Exercise slowly and smoothly.

Use good posture. Keep your stomach muscles tight and your back straight.

Check your blood sugar levels before, during and after exercise. Avoid exercise if blood sugar levels are above 250 mg/dL or under 100 mg/dL.

Have a small carbohydrate snack with you in case of low blood sugar during or after exercise.

Do not hold your breath during exercise. Count aloud if needed.

Sore muscles lasting a few days and feeling tired are normal after exercise. Exhaustion, sore joints, and painful muscle pulls are not normal. If you have these symptoms, do not exercise until you talk with your therapist.

If you have chest tightness or pain, shortness of breath, feel dizzy, faint, or sick to your stomach, stop and call emergency services at _____.

Notes:

____

____

____

____

Exercise Tips for Guillain-Barré Syndrome

Name: ________________________________

Date: ________________________________

Therapist: ____________________________

Phone number: (_____)____________________

Do the checked exercises _____ times a day, _____ days a week.

Exercise slowly and smoothly. Use low repetitions and low resistance. Take frequent rest breaks.

Use good posture. Keep your stomach muscles tight and your back straight.

Do not hold your breath during exercise. Count aloud if needed.

Sore muscles lasting a few days and feeling tired are normal after exercise. Exhaustion, sore joints, and painful muscle pulls are not normal. If you have these symptoms, do not exercise until you talk with your therapist.

If you have chest tightness or pain, shortness of breath, feel dizzy, faint, or sick to your stomach, stop and call emergency services at _____.

Notes:

____

____

____

____

____

____

Exercise Tips for Multiple Sclerosis

Name: ______________________________

Date: ______________________________

Therapist: ______________________________

Phone number: (_____)____________________

Do the checked exercises _____ times a day, _____ days a week.

Exercise slowly and smoothly. Avoid getting tired. Stop and rest as often as you need to.

Use good posture. Keep your stomach muscles tight and your back straight.

Do not hold your breath during exercise. Count aloud if needed.

Avoid increasing your core body temperature. Do not exercise during the hottest time of the day, and drink plenty of cool fluids. If you notice any symptoms that you didn't have before you began exercising, slow down or stop exercising until you cool down.

Sore muscles lasting a few days and feeling tired are normal after exercise. Exhaustion, sore joints, and painful muscle pulls are not normal. If you have these symptoms, do not exercise until you talk with your therapist.

If you have chest tightness or pain, shortness of breath, feel dizzy, faint, or sick to your stomach, stop and call emergency services at _____.

Notes:

____

____

____

____

____

Occupational Therapy TOOLKIT

Exercise Tips for Myasthenia Gravis

Name: ______________________________

Date: ______________________________

Therapist: ______________________________

Phone number: (_____)____________________

Do the checked exercises _____ times a day, _____ days a week.

Exercise slowly and smoothly. Exercise at a low to moderate intensity. Avoid getting tired.

Use good posture. Keep your stomach muscles tight and your back straight.

Do not hold your breath during exercise. Count aloud if needed.

Avoid increasing your core body temperature. Do not exercise during the hottest time of the day, and drink plenty of cool fluids. If you notice any symptoms that you didn't have before you began exercising, slow down or stop exercising until you cool down.

Sore muscles lasting a few days and feeling tired are normal after exercise. Exhaustion, sore joints, and painful muscle pulls are not normal. If you have these symptoms, do not exercise until you talk with your therapist.

If you have chest tightness or pain, shortness of breath, feel dizzy, faint, or sick to your stomach, stop and call emergency services at _____.

Notes:

____

____

____

____

Exercise Tips for Orthopedic Conditions

Name: ______________________________

Date: ______________________________

Therapist: ______________________________

Phone number: (_____)____________________

Do the checked exercises _____ times per day, _____ days a week.

Before exercise, apply a heat pack to your __________ for _____ minutes.

After exercise, apply a cold pack to your __________ for _____ minutes.

Exercise slowly and smoothly. Stretch to the point of tension, not pain. Do not jerk or bounce when stretching.

Use good posture. Keep your stomach muscles tight and your back straight.

Do not hold your breath during exercise. Count aloud if needed.

Sore muscles lasting a few days and feeling tired are normal after exercise. Exhaustion, sore joints, and painful muscle pulls are not normal. If you have these symptoms, do not exercise until you talk with your therapist.

If you have chest tightness or pain, shortness of breath, feel dizzy, faint, or sick to your stomach, stop and call emergency services at _____.

Notes:

____

____

____

____

Exercise Tips for Post-Poliomyelitis Syndrome

Name: ________________________________

Date: ________________________________

Therapist: ________________________________

Phone number: (_____)________________________

Do the checked exercises _____ times a day, _____ days a week.

Exercise slowly and smoothly.

Use good posture. Keep your stomach muscles tight and your back straight.

Do not hold your breath during exercise. Count aloud if needed.

Do not exercise to the point of muscle fatigue. Rest in between exercises and allow enough time for your muscles to recover.

Sore muscles lasting a few days and feeling tired are normal after exercise. Exhaustion, sore joints, and painful muscle pulls are not normal. If you have these symptoms, do not exercise until you talk with your therapist.

If you have chest tightness or pain, shortness of breath, feel dizzy, faint, or sick to your stomach, stop and call emergency services at _____.

Notes:

____

____

____

____

____

Occupational Therapy TOOLKIT

Exercise Tips for Renal Conditions

Name: ______________________________________

Date: ______________________________________

Therapist: ___________________________________

Phone number: (______)________________________

Do the checked exercises ______ times a day, ______ days a week.

Exercise slowly and smoothly.

Use good posture. Keep your stomach muscles tight and your back straight.

Do not hold your breath during exercise. Count aloud if needed.

Do not exercise if you have a fever, or if you have missed dialysis. Exercise on your non-dialysis days, or before dialysis. Your blood pressure may be too low after dialysis to exercise.

Sore muscles lasting a few days and feeling tired are normal after exercise. Exhaustion, sore joints, and painful muscle pulls are not normal. If you have these symptoms, do not exercise until you talk with your therapist.

If you have chest tightness or pain, shortness of breath, feel dizzy, faint, or sick to your stomach, stop and call emergency services at ______.

Notes:

____

____

____

____

____

Occupational Therapy TOOLKIT

Face and Neck Active Range of Motion

Do the checked exercises _____ times per day, _____ days a week.

☐ Raise both eyebrows and frown.

Do ______ sets of ______.

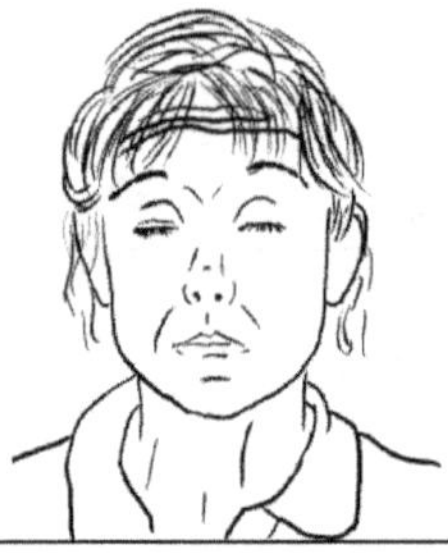

☐ Close both eyes tightly, and open eyes wide.

Do ______ sets of ______.

☐ Smile without showing your teeth, and pucker.

Do ______ sets of ______.

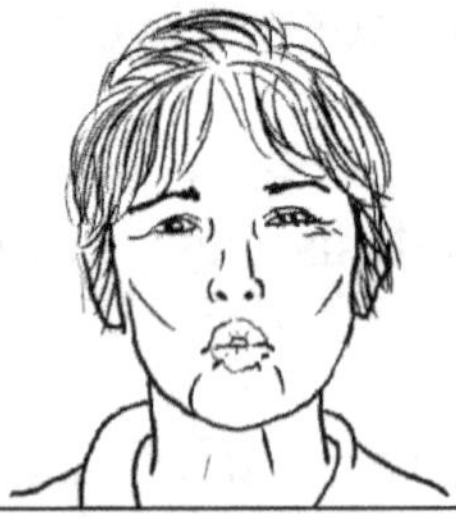

☐ Stick out your tongue.
Move your tongue side to side.
Move your tongue up and down.

Do ______ sets of ______ for each movement.

☐ Open your mouth wide, and close.

Do ______ sets of ______.

Face and Neck Active Range of Motion

Do the checked exercises _____ times per day, _____ days a week.

☐ Push your bottom jaw forward, and pull it back.

Do _____ sets of _____.

☐ Move your jaw side to side.

Do _____ sets of _____.

☐ Turn your head from one side to the other side.

Do _____ sets of _____.

☐ Tilt your head from one side to the other.

Do _____ sets of _____.

☐ Look up and look down.

Do _____ sets of _____.

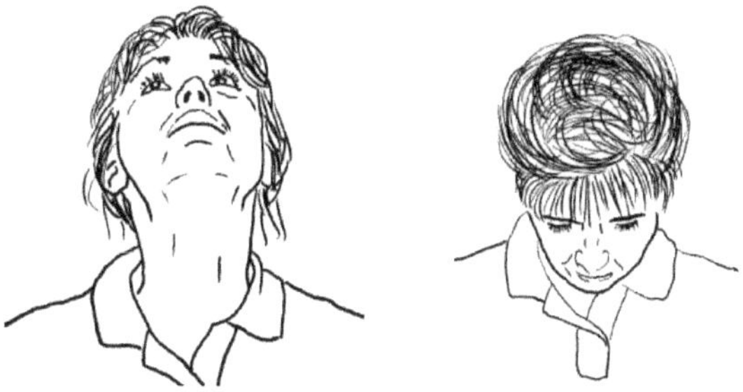

Fine Motor Activities

Pinch and grip

- ☐ Clip clothespins.
- ☐ Practice opening cans, bottles, storage bags.
- ☐ Do craft projects: copper tooling, basket weaving, polymer clay, using hand tools.
- ☐ Do putty exercises.
- ☐ Cut out coupons.
- ☐ Do kitchen activities: cake decorating, kneading bread dough, squeezing citrus fruit for juice, peeling and grating.

Fine motor

- ☐ Pick up beans, buttons and nails.
- ☐ Screw and unscrew nuts and bolts.
- ☐ Tie and untie a length of rope.
- ☐ String beads.
- ☐ Lace shoes.
- ☐ Use the computer keyboard for games and email.
- ☐ Practice using buttons, laces, zippers, buckles and snaps.
- ☐ Trace around a stencil.
- ☐ Do craft projects: paint-by-number, color pictures, origami, mosaic tile.
- ☐ Play leisure games: cribbage, Connect Four, dominos, Scrabble, HiQ, play cards.
- ☐ Practice needlework, crochet, knitting, macramé, sewing, plastic canvas.
- ☐ Flip a pencil from tip to eraser.
- ☐ Hold pencil near the eraser, move your fingers down the pencil to the tip.
- ☐ Roll a pencil with the tips of your fingers.

Move items in your hand

- ☐ Pick up coins, beans or buttons. Hold as many as you can in your hand.
- ☐ Rotate objects (dice, balls) in your hand.

Occupational Therapy TOOLKIT

Finger and Thumb Strength Exercises - Left

Name: ______________________________

Date: ______________________________

Therapist: ______________________________

Phone number: (_____)____________________

Do the checked exercises _____ times per day, _____ days a week.

Before exercise, apply a heat pack to your __________ for _____ minutes.

After exercise, apply a cold pack to your __________ for _____ minutes.

Exercise slowly and smoothly.

Do not hold your breath during exercise. Count aloud if needed.

Use good posture. Keep your stomach muscles tight and your back straight.

Sore muscles lasting a few days and feeling tired are normal after exercise. Exhaustion, sore joints, and painful muscle pulls are not normal. If you have these symptoms, do not exercise until you talk with your therapist.

If you have chest tightness or pain, shortness of breath, feel dizzy, faint, or sick to your stomach, stop and call emergency services at _____.

Notes:

____

____

____

____

____

Occupational Therapy TOOLKIT

Finger and Thumb Strength Exercises - Left

Do the checked exercises _____ times per day, _____ days a week.

☐ **Finger Pull** (finger flexors)
Hook your fingers together. Pull apart.

Do _____ sets of _____.

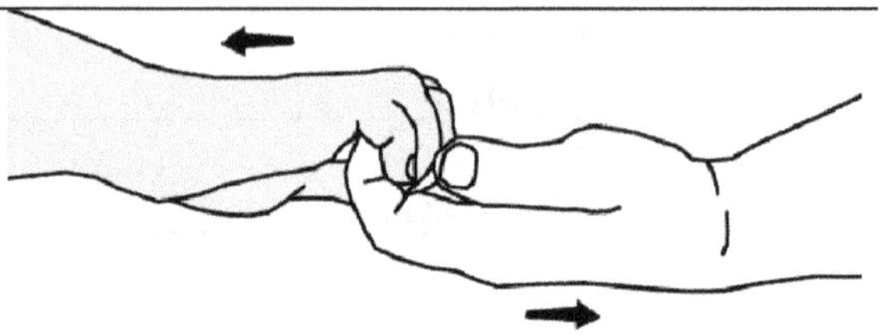

☐ **Table Press** (finger extensors)
Place your hand over the edge of a table.
Resist straightening at your knuckles.

Do _____ sets of _____.

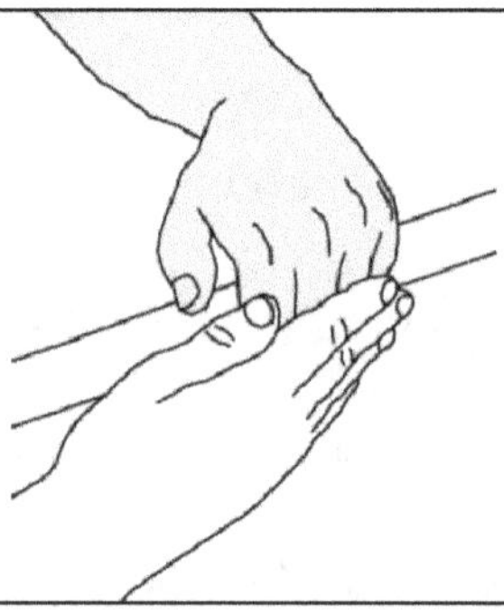

☐ **Lace Fingers** (digit adduction)
Lace your fingers. Press to stretch in between each finger.

Do _____ sets of _____.

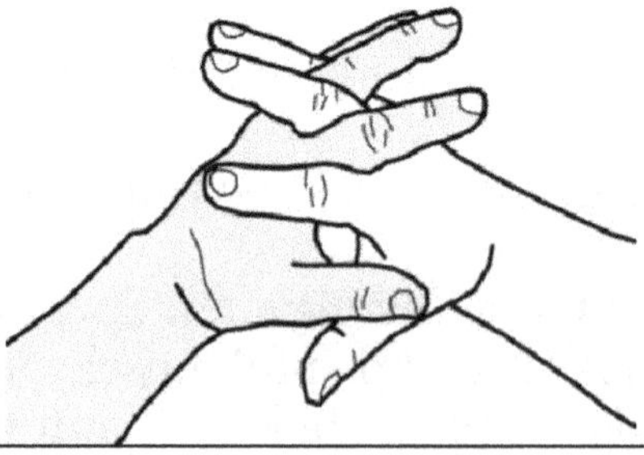

☐ **Rubber Band** (digit abduction)
Place a rubber band around the base of your fingers. Spread your fingers apart.

Do _____ sets of _____.

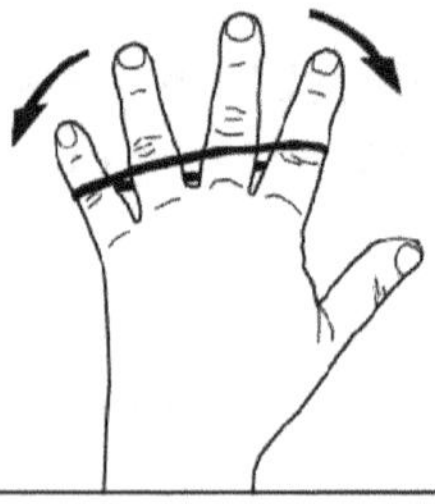

☐ **Crumple Newspaper**

Do _____ sets of _____.

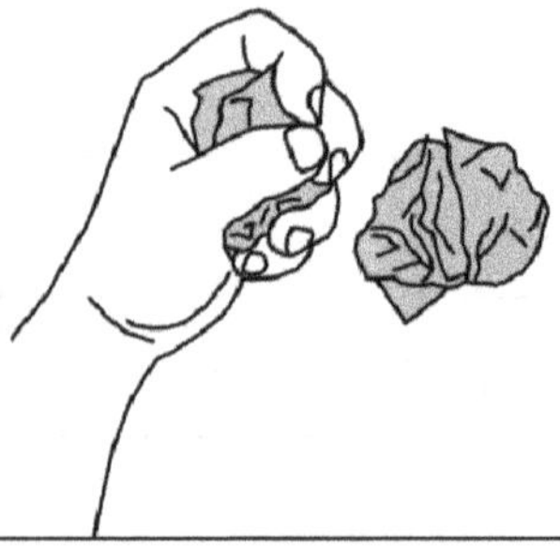

Occupational Therapy TOOLKIT

Finger and Thumb Strength Exercises - Left

Do the checked exercises _____ times per day, _____ days a week.

☐ **Thumb (**CM radial abduction**)**
Place your hand flat on a table. Loop a rubber band around your hand. Move your thumb out to form an "L".

Do ______ sets of ______.

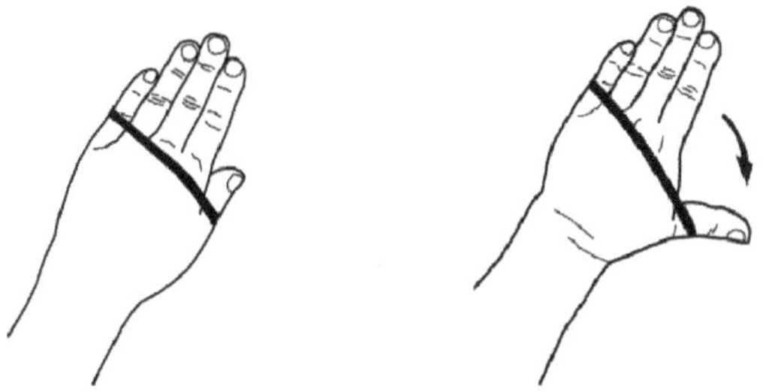

☐ **Thumb** (CM radial adduction)
Place your hand flat on a table. Hold your thumb to form an "L". Loop a rubber band around your thumb and hold with your other hand as shown. Move your thumb in toward your fingers.

Do ______ sets of ______.

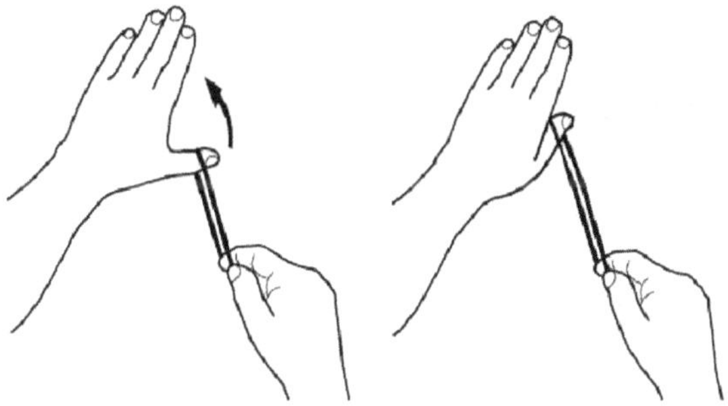

☐ **Thumb** (CM palmar abduction)
Place the pinky side of your hand on the table. Loop a rubber band around your thumb and hold with your other hand as shown. Move your thumb out to form an "L".

Do ______ sets of ______.

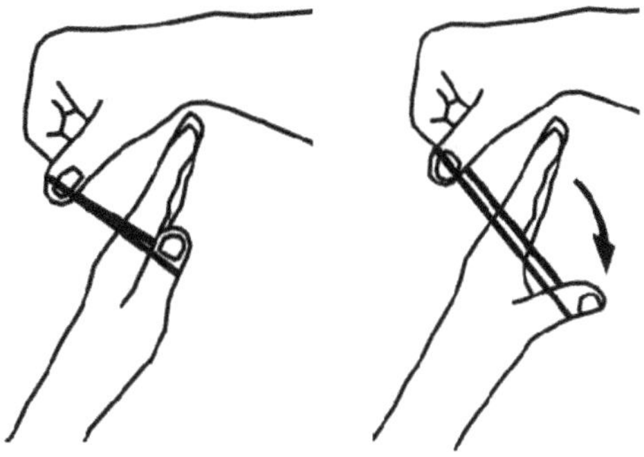

☐ **Thumb** (CM palmar adduction)
Place the pinky side of your hand on the table. Hold your thumb to form an "L". Loop a rubber band around your thumb and hold with your other hand as shown. Move your thumb in toward your fingers.

Do ______ sets of ______.

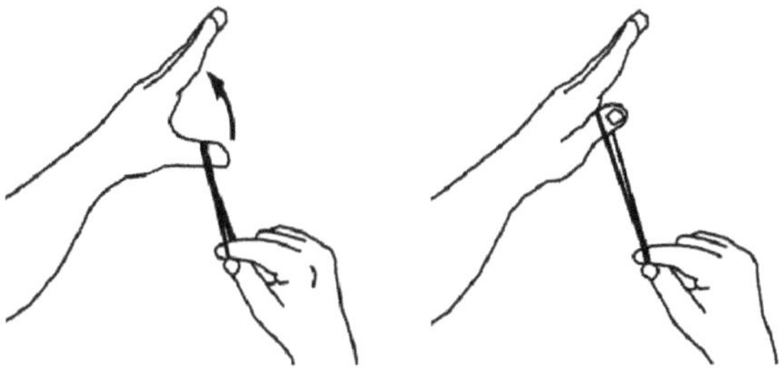

Finger and Thumb Strength Exercises - Right

Name: ________________________________

Date: ________________________________

Therapist: ____________________________

Phone number: (_____)_____________________

Do the checked exercises _____ times per day, _____ days a week.

Before exercise, apply a heat pack to your __________ for _____ minutes.

After exercise, apply a cold pack to your __________ for _____ minutes.

Exercise slowly and smoothly.

Do not hold your breath during exercise. Count aloud if needed.

Use good posture. Keep your stomach muscles tight and your back straight.

Sore muscles lasting a few days and feeling tired are normal after exercise. Exhaustion, sore joints, and painful muscle pulls are not normal. If you have these symptoms, do not exercise until you talk with your therapist.

If you have chest tightness or pain, shortness of breath, feel dizzy, faint, or sick to your stomach, stop and call emergency services at _____.

Notes:

____

____

____

____

____

Finger and Thumb Strength Exercises - Right

Do the checked exercises ______ times per day, ______ days a week.

☐ **Finger Pull** (finger flexors)
Hook your fingers together. Pull apart.

Do ______ sets of ______.

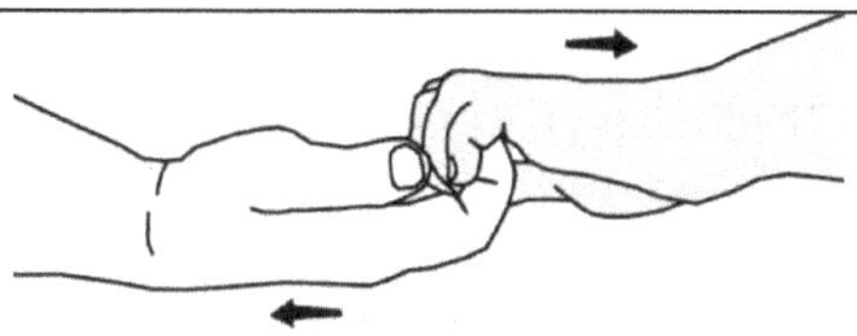

☐ **Table Edge** (finger extensors)
Place your hand over the edge of a table.
Resist straightening at your knuckles.

Do ______ sets of ______.

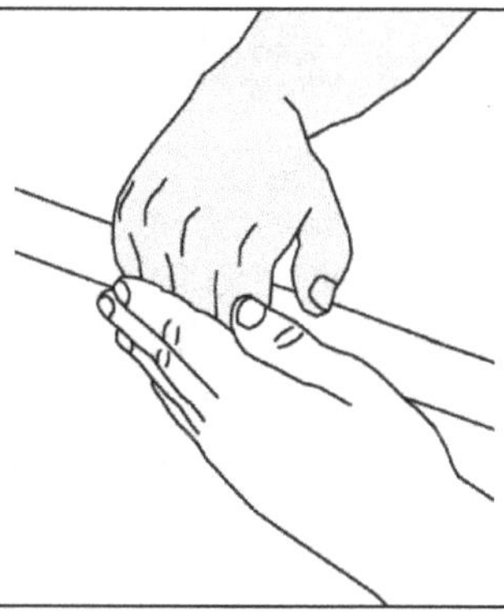

☐ **Lace Fingers** (digit adduction)
Lace your fingers. Press to stretch in between each finger

Do ______ sets of ______.

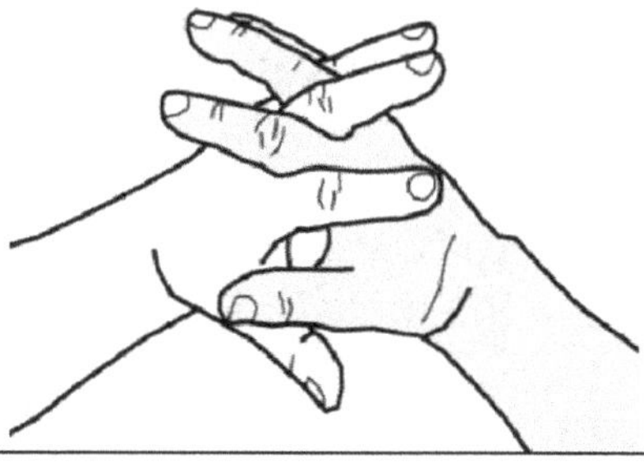

☐ **Rubber Band** (digit abduction)
Place a rubber band around the base of your fingers. Spread your fingers apart

Do ______ sets of ______.

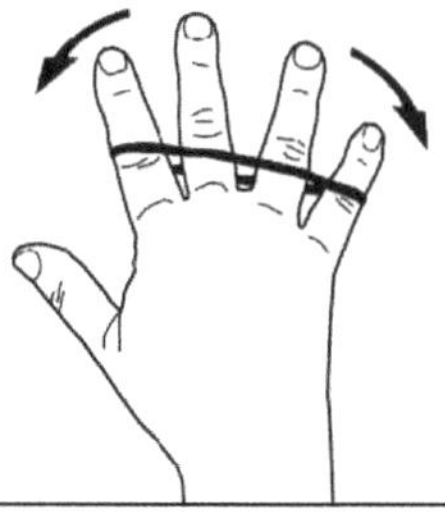

☐ **Crumple Newspaper**

Do ______ sets of ______.

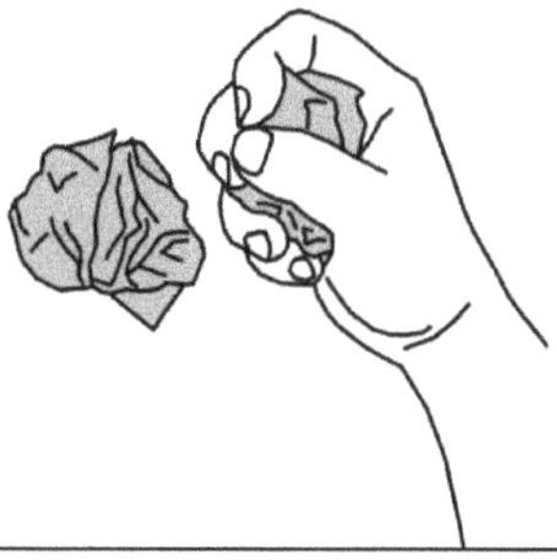

Occupational Therapy TOOLKIT

Finger and Thumb Strength Exercises - Right

Do the checked exercises _____ times per day, _____ days a week.

☐ **Thumb** (CM radial abduction)
Place your hand flat on a table. Loop a rubber band around your hand. Move your thumb out to form an "L".

Do ______ sets of ______.

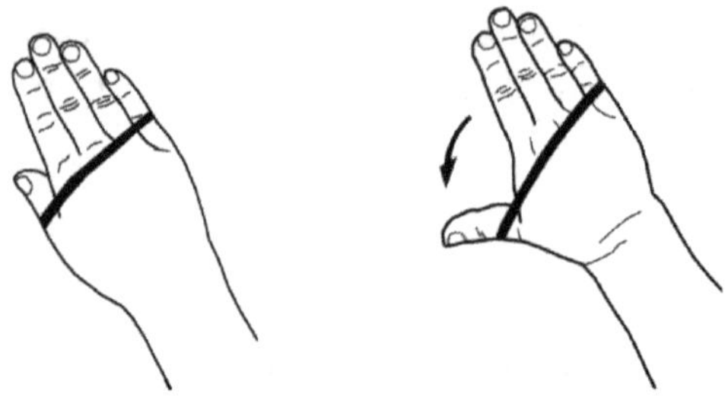

☐ **Thumb** (CM radial adduction)
Place your hand flat on a table. Hold your thumb to form an "L". Loop a rubber band around your thumb and hold with your other hand as shown. Move your thumb in toward your fingers.

Do ______ sets of ______.

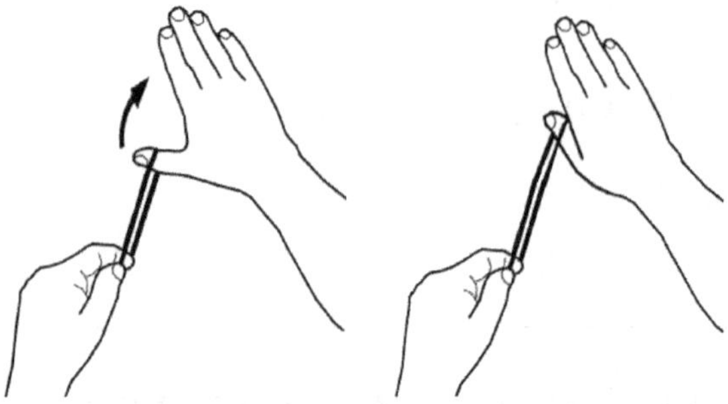

☐ **Thumb** (CM palmar abduction)
Place the pinky side of your hand on the table. Loop a rubber band around your thumb and hold with your other hand as shown. Move your thumb out to form an "L".

Do ______ sets of ______.

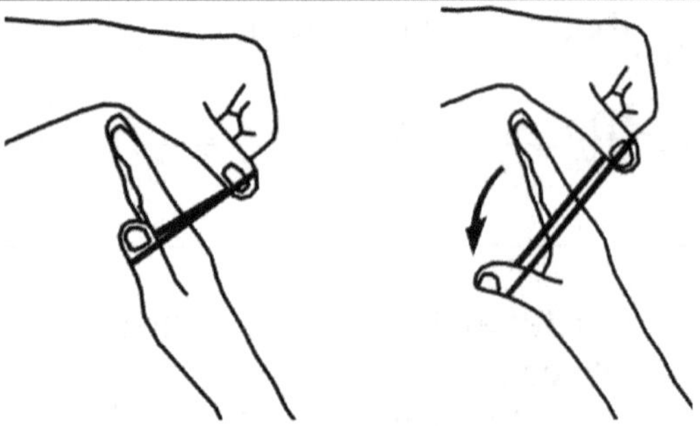

☐ **Thumb** (CM palmar adduction)
Place the pinky side of your hand on the table. Hold your thumb to form an "L". Loop a rubber band around your thumb and hold with your other hand as shown. Move your thumb in toward your fingers.

Do ______ sets of ______.

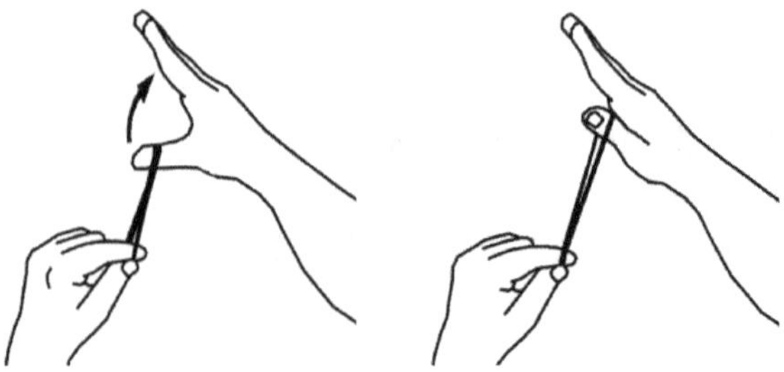

Occupational Therapy TOOLKIT

Finger and Thumb Stretches and Active Range of Motion - Left

Name: ______________________________

Date: ______________________________

Therapist: ______________________________

Phone number: (_____)______________________

Do the checked exercises _____ times per day, _____ days a week.

Before exercise, apply a heat pack to your __________ for _____ minutes.

After exercise, apply a cold pack to your __________ for _____ minutes.

Exercise slowly and smoothly.

Stretch to the point of tension, not pain. Do not jerk or bouncing when stretching

Do not hold your breath during exercise. Count aloud if needed.

Use good posture. Keep your stomach muscles tight and your back straight.

Sore muscles lasting a few days and feeling tired are normal after exercise. Exhaustion, sore joints, and painful muscle pulls are not normal. If you have these symptoms, do not exercise until you talk with your therapist.

If you have chest tightness or pain, shortness of breath, feel dizzy, faint, or sick to your stomach, stop and call emergency services at _____.

Notes:

____

____

____

____

Finger and Thumb Stretches and Active Range of Motion
Hand Anatomy

Finger Joints

First	DIP	Distal Inter Phalangeal
Middle	PIP	Proximal Inter Phalangeal
Base	MP	Metacarpal Phalangeal

Thumb Joints

First	IP	Inter Phalangeal
Middle	MP	Metacarpal Phalangeal
Base	CM	Carpo Metacarpal

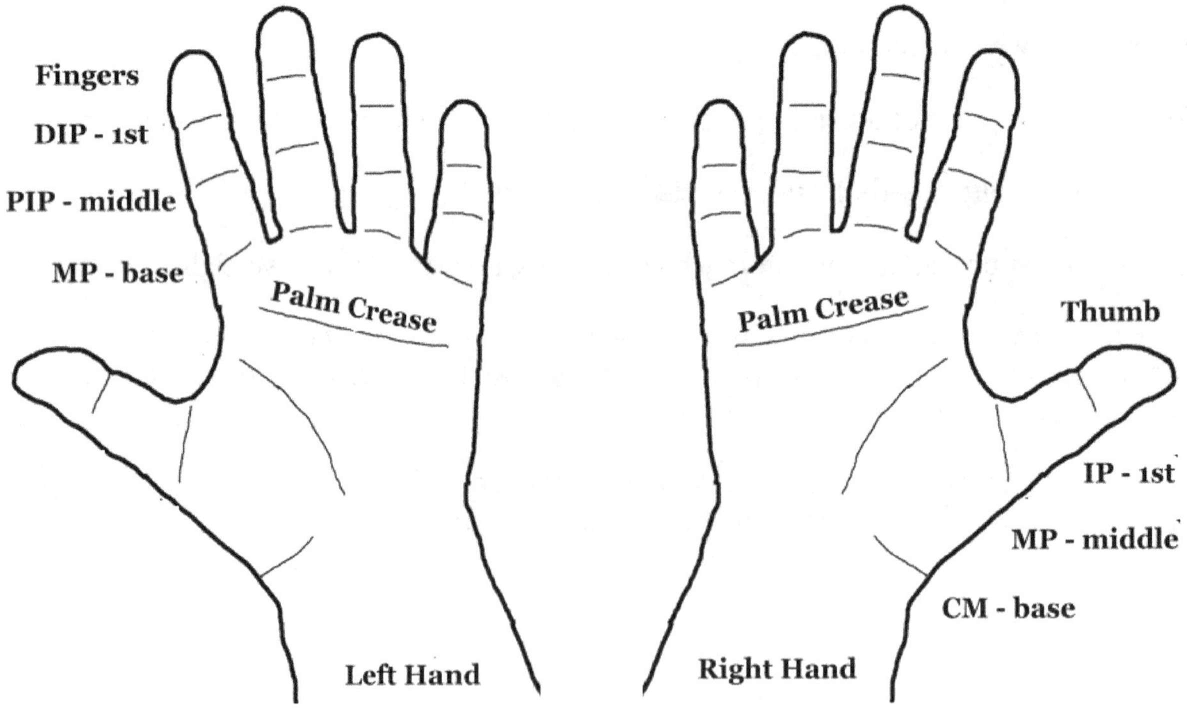

Finger and Thumb Stretches and Active Range of Motion - Left

Stretching

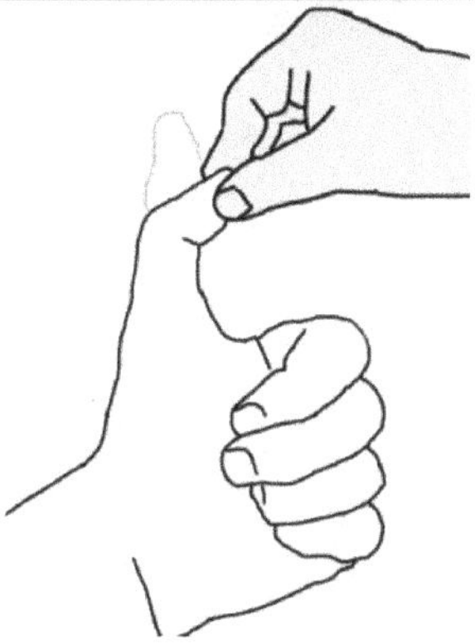

☐ **Thumb IP Flexion & Extension**
Hold the tip of your thumb. Bend the first (IP) joint. Hold for a count of ______. Straighten the first (IP) joint. Hold for a count of ______.

Do ______ sets of ______.

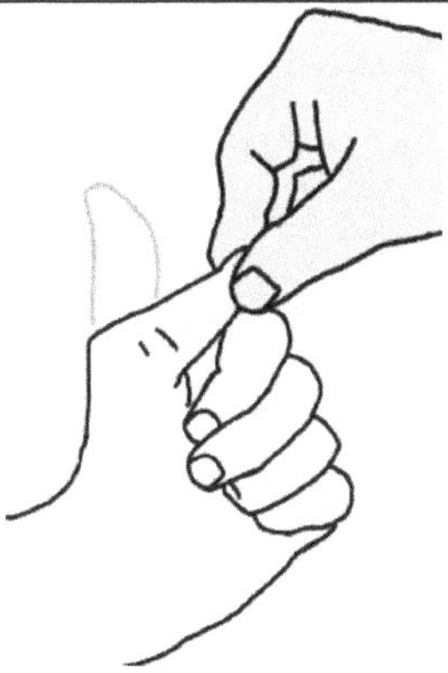

☐ **Thumb MP Flexion & Extension**
Hold your thumb at the first (IP) joint. Bend the middle (MP) joint. Hold for a count of ______. Straighten the middle (MP) joint. Hold for a count of ______.

Do ______ sets of ______.

Active Range of Motion

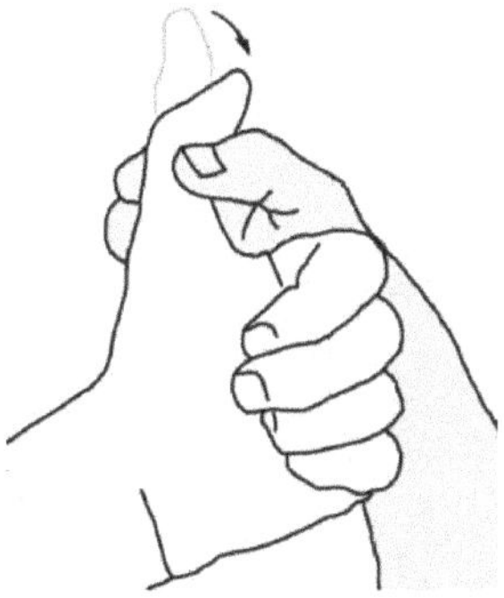

☐ **Thumb IP Flexion & Extension**
Support your thumb below the first (IP) joint. Actively bend and straighten the first joint.

Do ______ sets of ______.

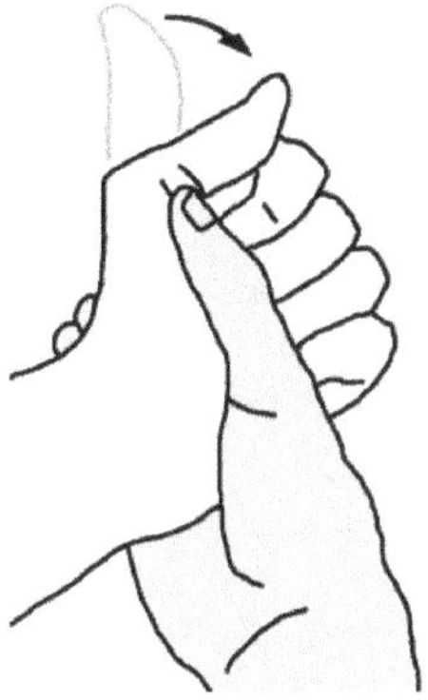

☐ **Thumb MP Flexion & Extension**
Support your thumb below the middle (MP) joint. Actively bend and straighten the middle (MP) joint.

Do ______ sets of ______.

Finger and Thumb Stretches and Active Range of Motion - Left

Stretching

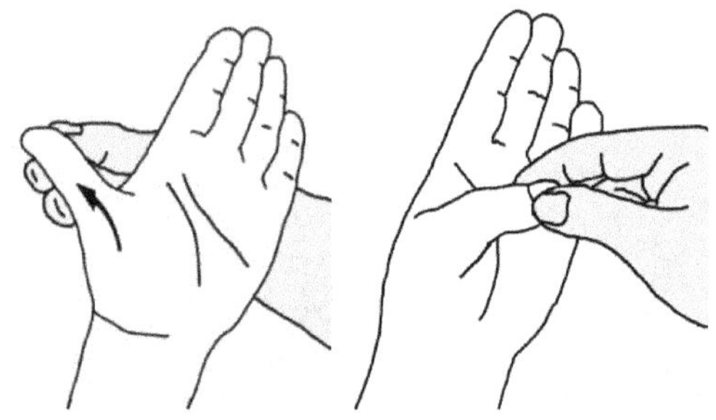

☐ **Thumb CM Flexion & Extension**
Hold your thumb. Bend the (CM) joint at the base of your thumb. Hold for a count of ______. Extend the (CM) joint. Hold for a count of ______.

Do ______ sets of ______.

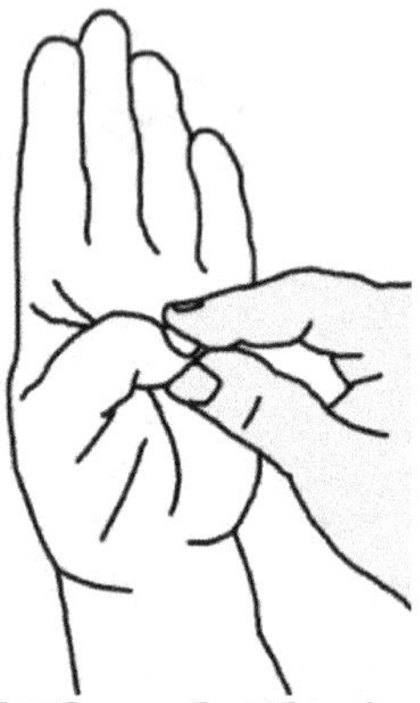

☐ **Combined Thumb Flexion**
Hold your thumb. Bend your thumb so the tip is touching your palm. Hold for a count of ______.

Do ______ sets of ______.

Active Range of Motion

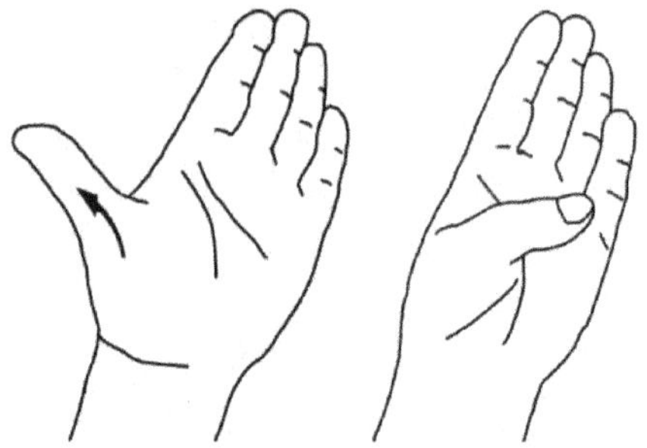

☐ **Thumb CM Flexion & Extension**
Actively bend and straighten the base (CM) joint.

Do ______ sets of ______.

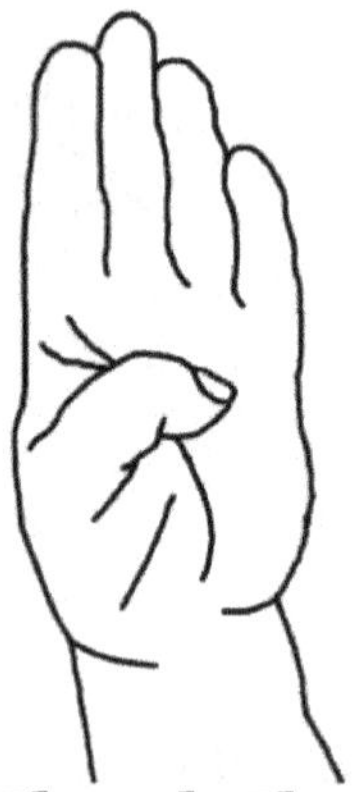

☐ **Combined Thumb Flexion**
Actively bend your thumb so the tip is touching your palm.

Do ______ sets of ______.

Occupational Therapy TOOLKIT

Finger and Thumb Stretches and Active Range of Motion - Left

Stretching	Active Range of Motion
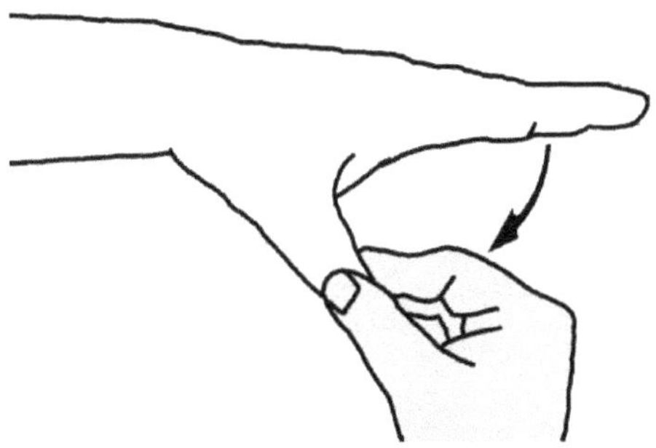	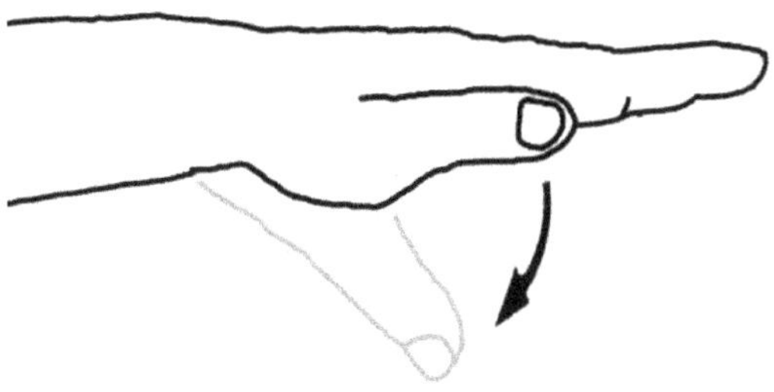
☐ **Thumb CM Palmar Abduction** Place your hand on the end of the table with your thumb over the side. Stretch your thumb downward, pointing to the floor. Hold for a count of _______. Do ______ sets of ______.	☐ **Thumb CM Palmar Abduction** Place your hand on the end of the table with your thumb over the side. Actively move your thumb downward, pointing to the floor. Do ______ sets of ______.
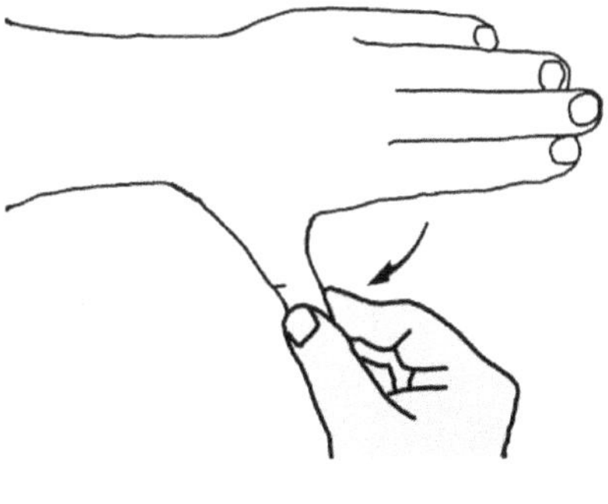	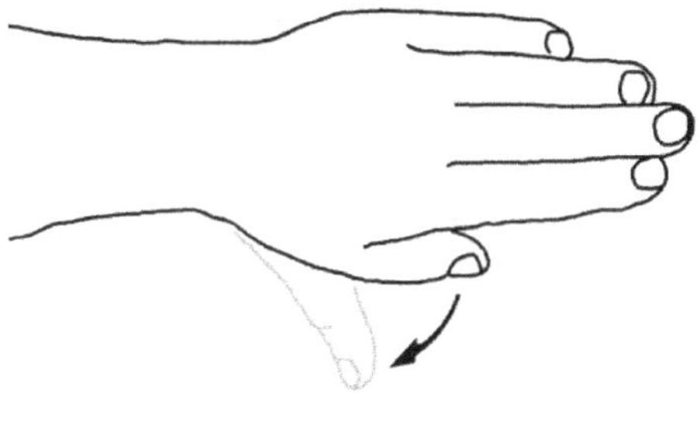
☐ **Thumb CM Radial Abduction** Place your hand flat on the table. Stretch your thumb away from your hand. Hold for a count of _______. Do ______ sets of ______.	☐ **Thumb CM Radial Abduction** Place your hand flat on the table. Actively move your thumb away from your hand. Do ______ sets of ______.

Occupational Therapy TOOLKIT

Finger and Thumb Stretches and Active Range of Motion - Left

Stretching	Active Range of Motion
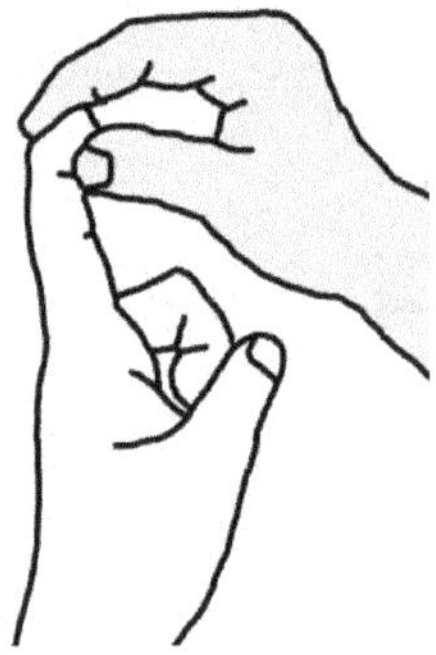	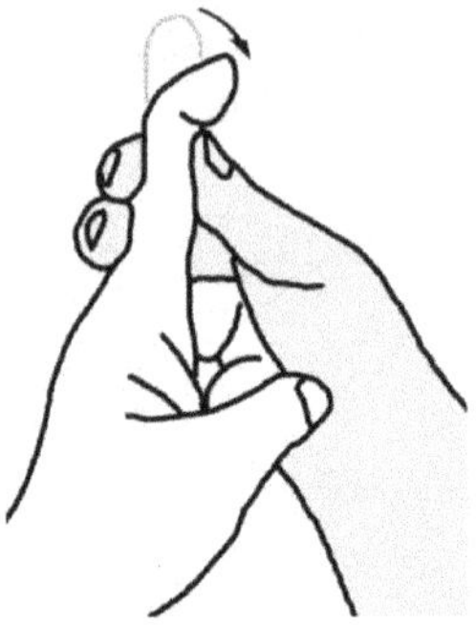
☐ **Finger DIP Flexion & Extension** Hold the tip of your finger. Bend the first (DIP) joint. Hold for a count of ______. Straighten the first (DIP) joint. Hold for a count of _______. Do ______ sets of ______ with each finger.	☐ **Finger DIP Flexion & Extension** Support your finger below the first (DIP) joint. Actively bend and straighten the first (DIP) joint. Do ______ sets of ______ with each finger.
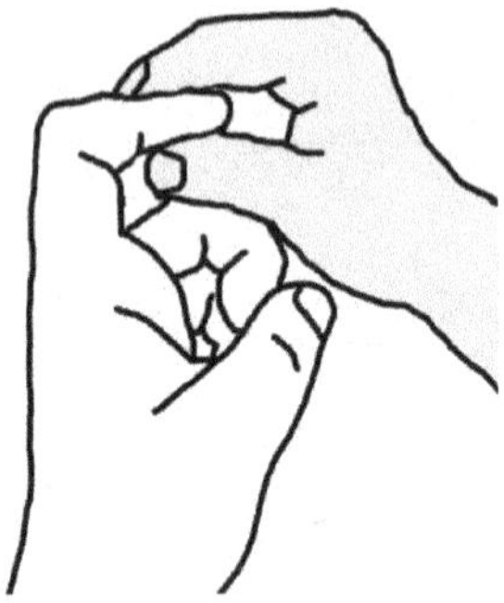	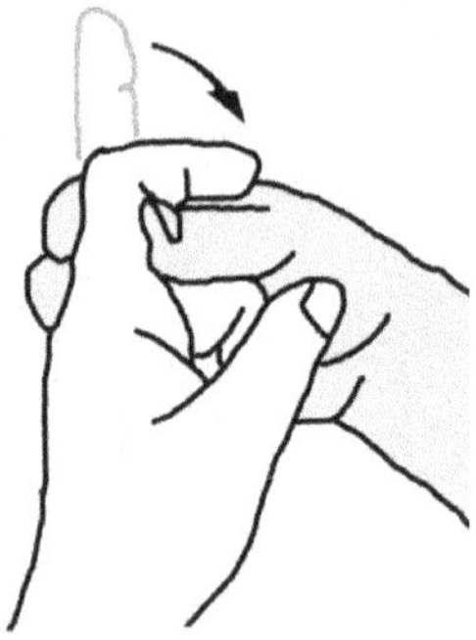
☐ **Finger PIP Flexion & Extension** Hold your finger at the first (DIP) joint. Bend the middle (PIP) joint. Hold for a count of ______. Straighten the middle (PIP) joint. Hold for a count of _______. Do ______ sets of ______ with each finger.	☐ **Finger PIP Flexion & Extension** Support your finger below the middle (PIP) joint. Actively bend and straighten the middle (PIP) joint. Do ______ sets of ______ with each finger.

Occupational Therapy TOOLKIT

Finger and Thumb Stretches and Active Range of Motion - Left

Stretching

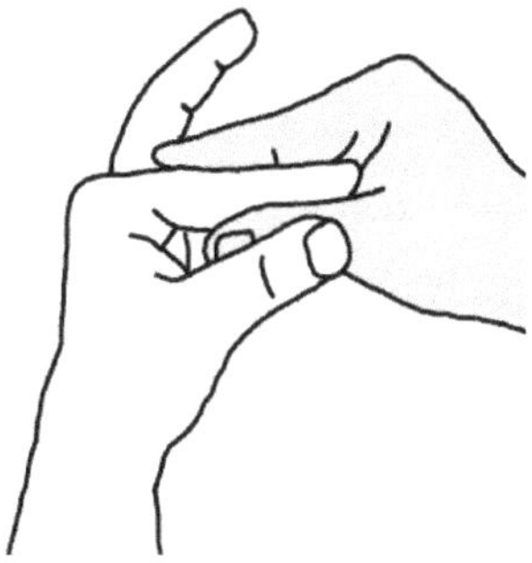

☐ **Finger MP Flexion**
Hold your finger straight at the first (DIP) and middle (PIP) joints. Bend the base (MP) joint to form a 90-degree angle. Hold for a count of ______.

Do _____ sets of _____ with each finger.

Active Range of Motion

☐ **Finger MP Flexion**
Hold your finger straight at the first (DIP) and middle (PIP) joints. Actively bend the base (MP) joint to form a 90-degree angle.

Do _____ sets of _____ with each finger.

Stretching

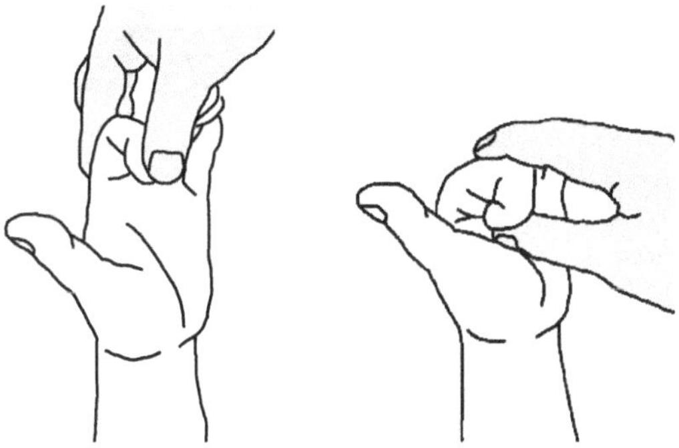

☐ **Combined Finger Flexion**
Bend your finger at the first (DIP) and middle (PIP) joints. Now bend the base (MP) joint to form a box. Hold for a count of ______.

Do _____ sets of _____ with each finger.

Active Range of Motion

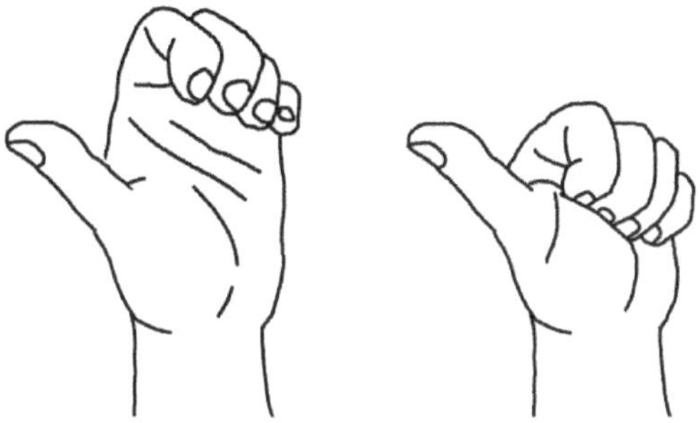

☐ **Combined Finger Flexion**
Actively bend your finger at the first (DIP) and middle (PIP) joints. Now bend the base (MP) joint to form a box.

Do _____ sets of _____ with all fingers.

Finger and Thumb Stretches and Active Range of Motion - Left

Stretching	Active Range of Motion
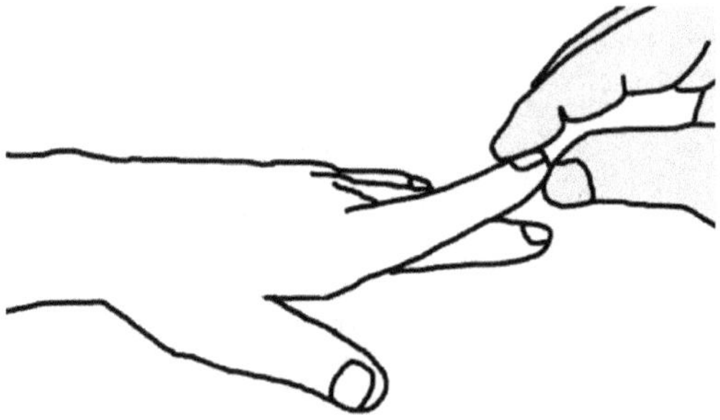	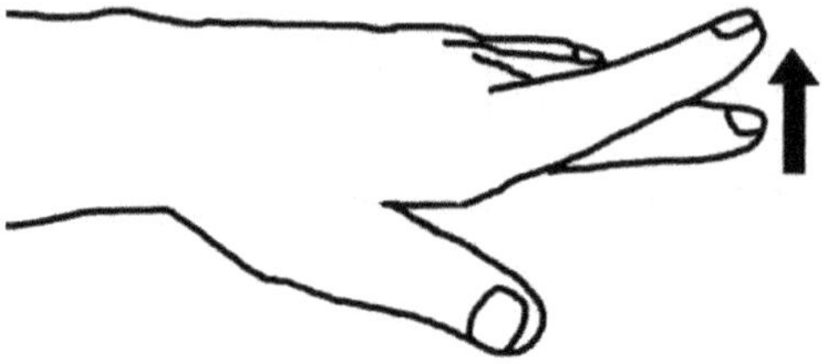
☐ **Finger MP Extension** Place your hand flat on the table. Hold the tip of your finger. Lift your finger off the table. Hold for a count of ______. Do ______ sets of ______ with each finger.	☐ **Finger MP Extension** Place your hand flat on the table. Actively lift your finger off the table. Do ______ sets of ______ with each finger.
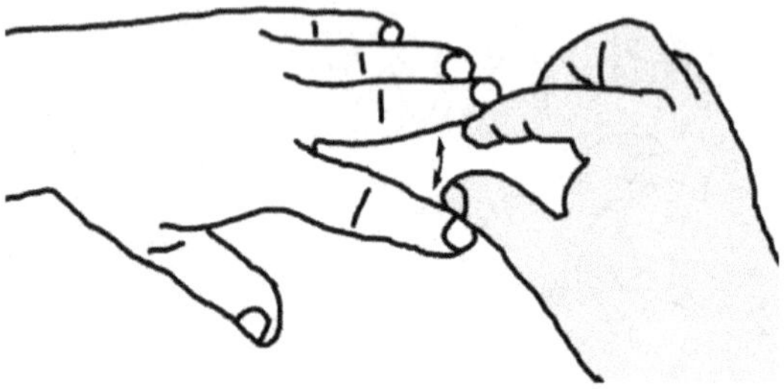	
☐ **Finger MP Abduction** Place your hand flat on the table. Spread two fingers apart. Hold for a count of ______. Do ______ sets of ______ with each finger.	☐ **Finger MP Abduction** Place your hand flat on the table. Actively spread two fingers apart. Do ______ sets of ______ with each finger.

Occupational Therapy TOOLKIT

Finger and Thumb Stretches and Active Range of Motion - Right

Name: ____________________________________

Date: ____________________________________

Therapist: ________________________________

Phone number: (______)_______________________

Do the checked exercises ______ times per day, ______ days a week.

Before exercise, apply a heat pack to your ___________ for _____ minutes.

After exercise, apply a cold pack to your ___________ for _____ minutes.

Exercise slowly and smoothly.

Stretch to the point of tension, not pain. Do not jerk or bouncing when stretching

Do not hold your breath during exercise. Count aloud if needed.

Use good posture. Keep your stomach muscles tight and your back straight.

Sore muscles lasting a few days and feeling tired are normal after exercise. Exhaustion, sore joints, and painful muscle pulls are not normal. If you have these symptoms, do not exercise until you talk with your therapist.

If you have chest tightness or pain, shortness of breath, feel dizzy, faint, or sick to your stomach, stop and call emergency services at ______.

Notes:

____

____

____

____

Finger and Thumb Stretches and Active Range of Motion
Hand Anatomy

Finger Joints

First	DIP	Distal Inter Phalangeal Joint
Middle	PIP	Proximal Inter Phalangeal Joint
Base	MP	Metacarpal Phalangeal Joint

Thumb Joints

First	IP	Inter Phalangeal Joint
Middle	MP	Metacarpal Phalangeal Joint
Base	CM	Carpometacarpal Joint

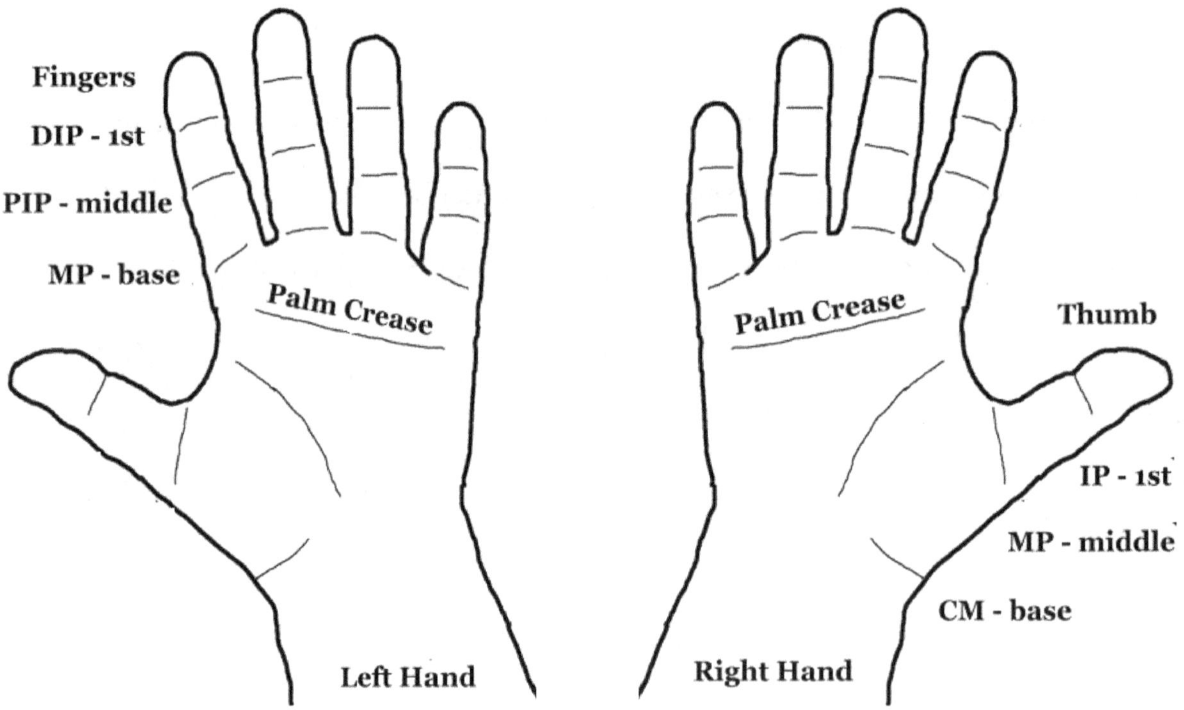

Occupational Therapy TOOLKIT

Finger and Thumb Stretches and Active Range of Motion - Right

Stretching

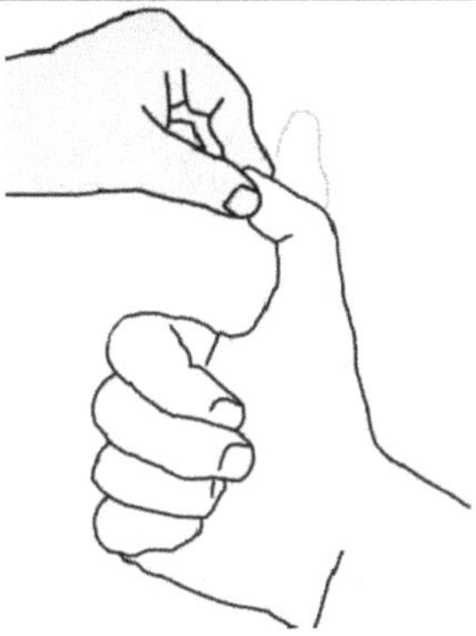

☐ **Thumb IP Flexion & Extension**
Hold the tip of your thumb. Bend the first (IP) joint. Hold for a count of ______. Straighten the first (IP) joint. Hold for a count of _______.

Do ______ sets of ______.

☐ **Thumb MP Flexion & Extension**
Hold your thumb at the first (IP) joint. Bend the middle (MP) joint. Hold for a count of ______. Straighten the middle (MP) joint. Hold for a count of _______.

Do ______ sets of ______.

Active Range of Motion

☐ **Thumb IP Flexion & Extension**
Support your thumb below the first (IP) joint. Actively bend and straighten.

Do ______ sets of ______.

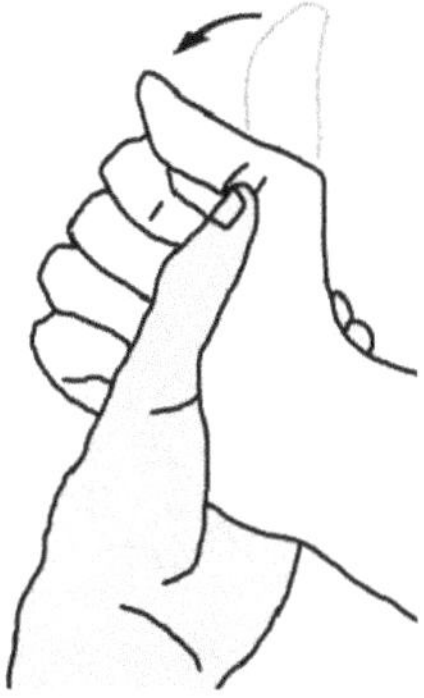

☐ **Thumb MP Flexion & Extension**
Support your thumb below the middle (MP) joint. Actively bend and straighten the middle (MP) joint.

Do ______ sets of ______.

Occupational Therapy TOOLKIT

Finger and Thumb Stretches and Active Range of Motion - Right

Stretching

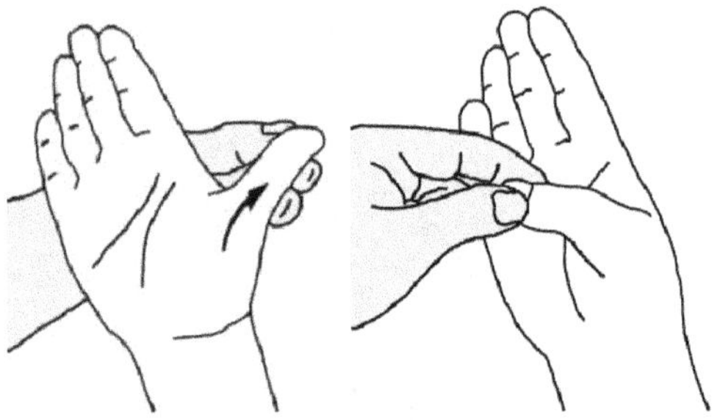

☐ **Thumb CM Flexion & Extension**
Hold your thumb. Bend the (CM) joint at the base of your thumb. Hold for a count of ______. Extend the (CM) joint. Hold for a count of _______.

Do ______ sets of ______.

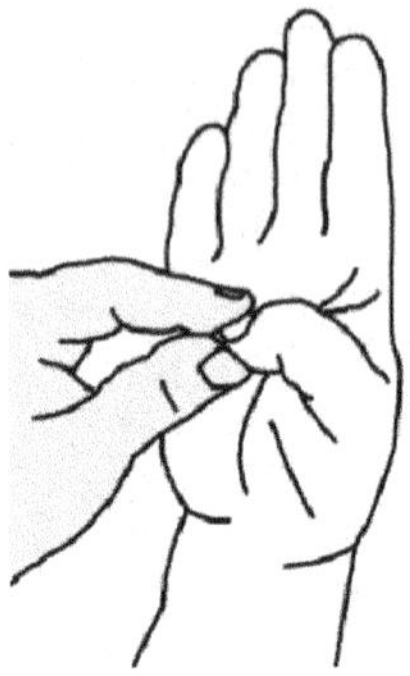

☐ **Combined Thumb Flexion**
Hold your thumb. Bend your thumb so the tip is touching your palm. Hold for a count of _______.

Do ______ sets of ______.

Active Range of Motion

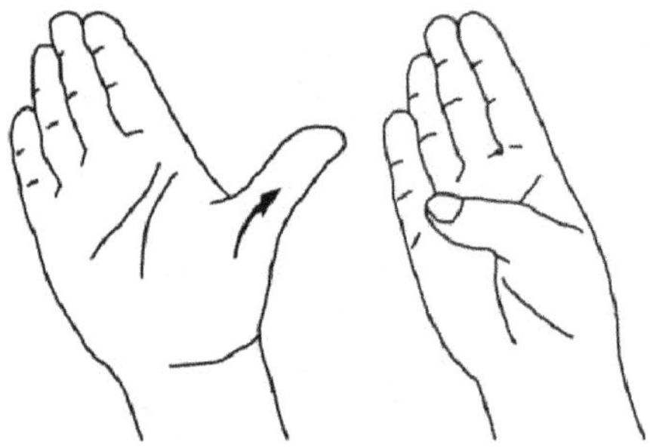

☐ **Thumb CM Flexion & Extension**
Actively bend and straighten the base (CM) joint.

Do ______ sets of ______.

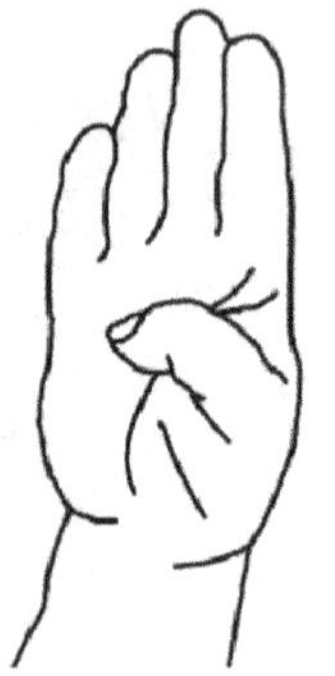

☐ **Combined Thumb Flexion**
Actively bend your thumb so the tip is touching your palm.

Do ______ sets of ______.

Occupational Therapy TOOLKIT

Finger and Thumb Stretches and Active Range of Motion - Right

Stretching

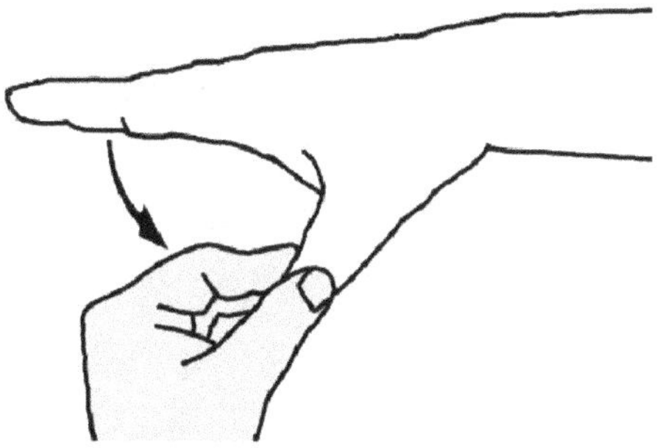

☐ **Thumb CM Palmar Abduction**
Place your hand on the end of the table with your thumb over the side. Stretch your thumb downward, pointing to the floor. Hold for a count of ______.

Do _____ sets of _____.

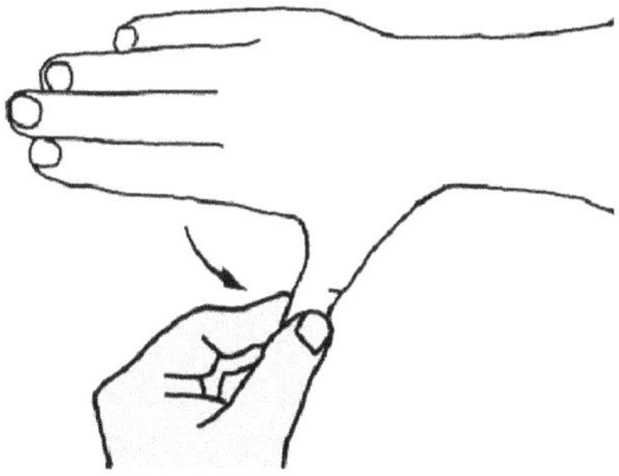

☐ **Thumb CM Radial Abduction**
Place your hand flat on the table. Stretch the thumb away from your hand. Hold for a count of ______.

Do _____ sets of _____.

Active Range of Motion

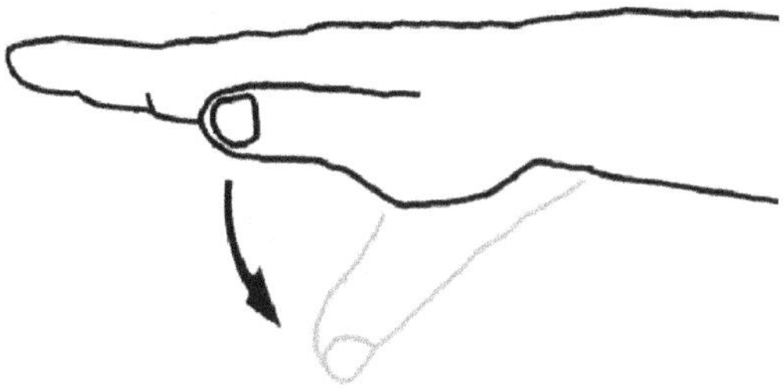

☐ **Thumb CM Palmar Abduction**
Place your hand on the end of the table with your thumb over the side. Actively move your thumb downward, pointing to the floor.

Do _____ sets of _____.

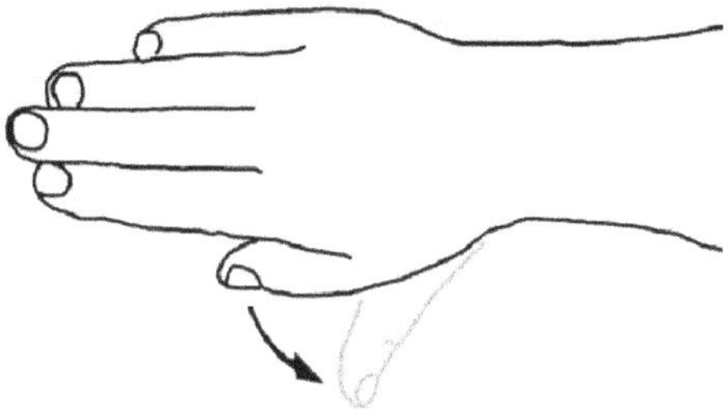

☐ **Thumb CM Radial Abduction**
Place your hand flat on the table. Actively move your thumb away from your hand.

Do _____ sets of _____.

Occupational Therapy TOOLKIT

Finger and Thumb Stretches and Active Range of Motion - Right

Stretching

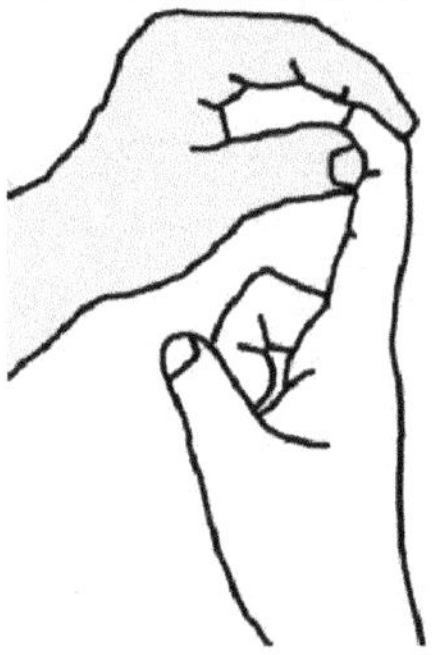

☐ **Finger DIP Flexion & Extension**
Hold the tip of your finger. Bend the first (DIP) joint. Hold for a count of ______. Straighten the first (DIP) joint. Hold for a count of _______.

Do ______ sets of ______ with each finger.

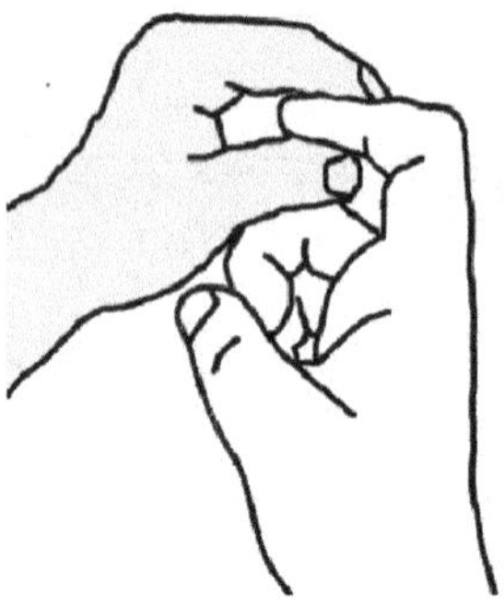

☐ **Finger PIP Flexion & Extension**
Hold your finger at the first (DIP) joint. Bend the middle (PIP) joint. Hold for a count of ______. Straighten the middle (PIP) joint. Hold for a count of _______.

Do ______ sets of ______ with each finger.

Active Range of Motion

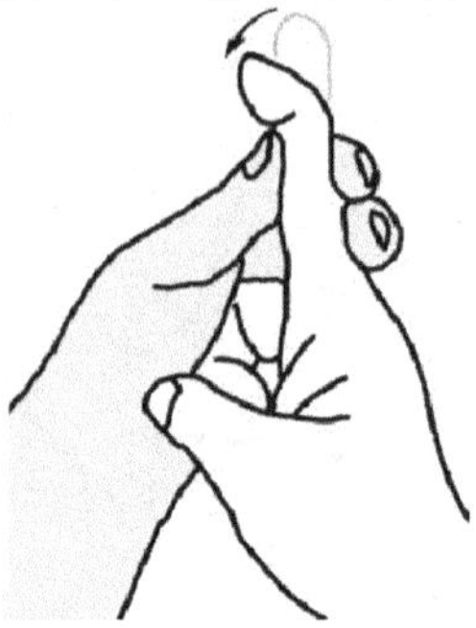

☐ **Finger DIP Flexion & Extension**
Support your finger below the first (DIP) joint. Actively bend and straighten the first (DIP) joint.

Do ______ sets of ______ with each finger.

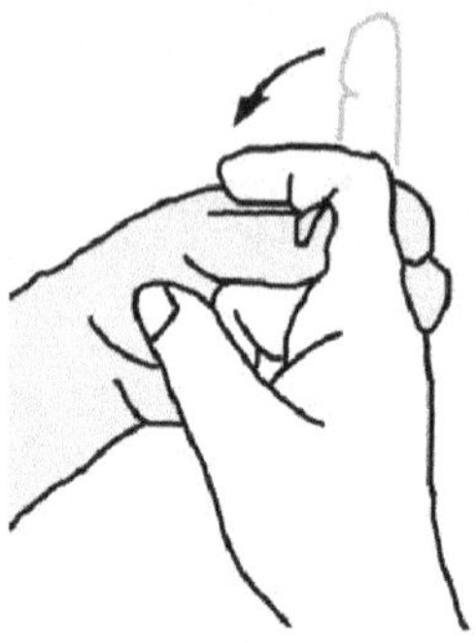

☐ **Finger PIP Flexion & Extension**
Support your finger below the middle (PIP) joint. Actively bend and straighten the middle (PIP) joint.

Do ______ sets of ______ with each finger.

Occupational Therapy TOOLKIT

Finger and Thumb Stretches and Active Range of Motion - Right

Stretching	Active Range of Motion
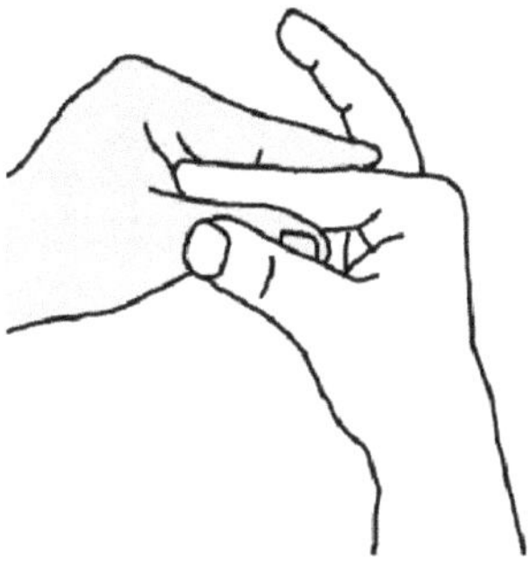	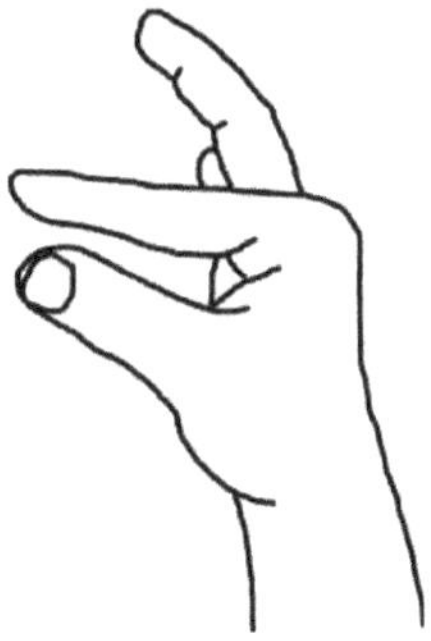
☐ **Finger MP Flexion** Hold your finger straight at the first (DIP) and middle (PIP) joints. Bend the base (MP) joint to form a 90-degree angle. Hold for a count of ______. Do _____ sets of _____ with each finger.	☐ **Finger MP Flexion** Hold your finger straight at the first (DIP) and middle (PIP) joints. Actively bend the base (MP) joint to form a 90-degree angle. Do _____ sets of _____ with each finger.
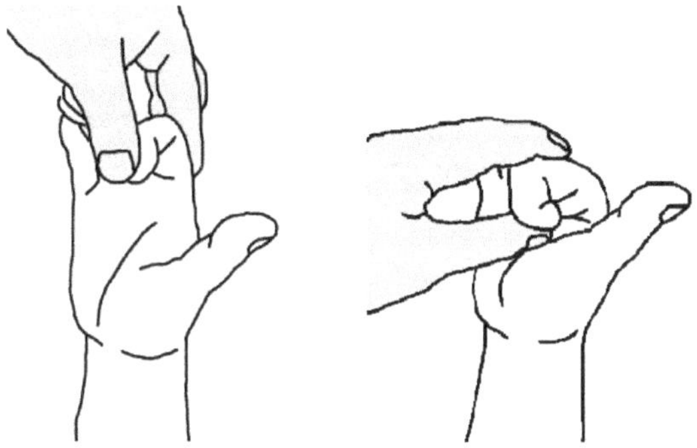	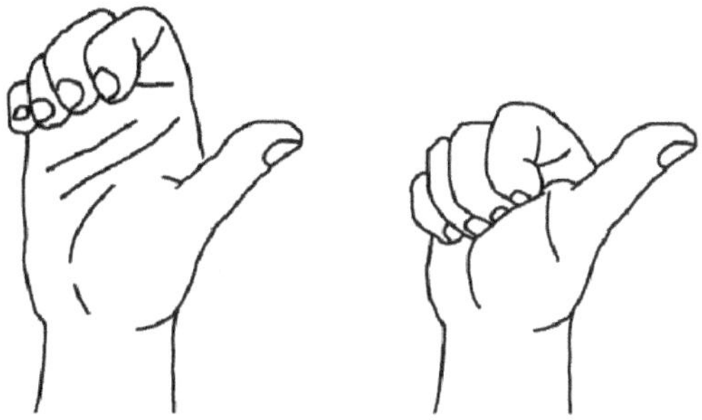
☐ **Combined Finger Flexion** Bend your finger at the first (DIP) and middle (PIP) joints. Now bend the base (MP) joint to form a box. Hold for a count of ______. Do _____ sets of _____ with each finger.	☐ **Combined Finger Flexion** Actively bend your finger at the first (DIP) and middle (PIP) joints. Now bend the base (MP) joint to form a box. Do _____ sets of _____ with all fingers.

Occupational Therapy TOOLKIT

Finger and Thumb Stretches and Active Range of Motion - Right

Stretching	Active Range of Motion
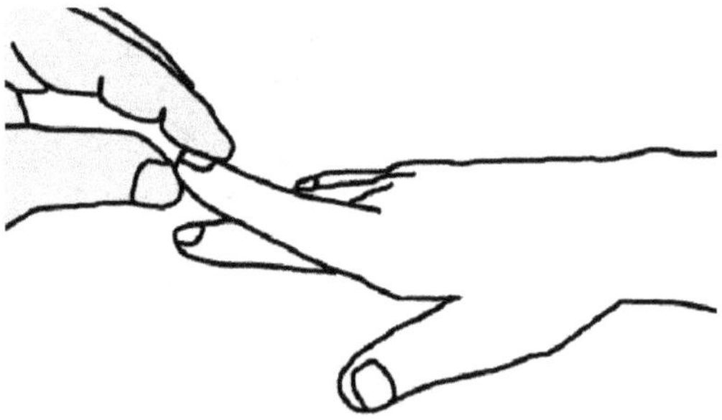	
☐ **Finger MP Extension** Place your hand flat on the table. Hold the tip of your finger. Lift your finger off the table. Hold for a count of ______. Do _____ sets of _____ with each finger.	☐ **Finger MP Extension** Place your hand flat on the table. Actively lift your finger off the table. Hold for a count of ______. Do _____ sets of _____ with each finger.
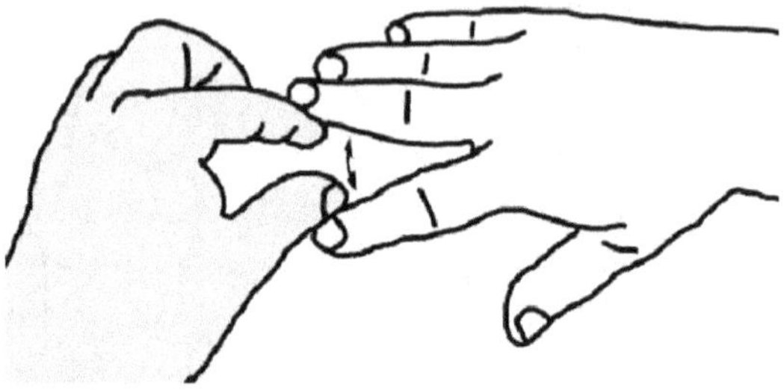	
☐ **Finger MP Abduction** Place your hand flat on the table. Spread two fingers apart. Hold for a count of ______. Do _____ sets of _____ with each finger.	☐ **Finger MP Abduction** Place your hand flat on the table. Actively spread two fingers apart. Hold for a count of ______. Do _____ sets of _____ with each finger.

Flexor Tendon Glides

Do each movement in order _____ times per day, _____ days a week.

Hold your wrist straight. Straighten your fingers and stretch your thumb to the side. Hold for a count of _______.

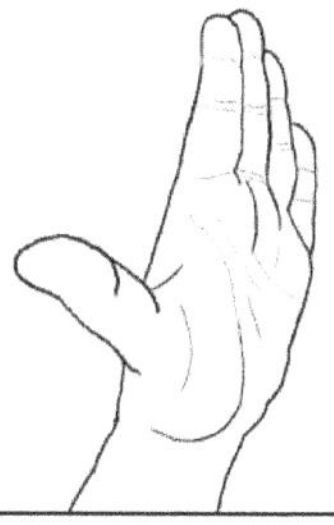

Hold your wrist straight. Keep your knuckles straight and bend your finger joints down. Hold for a count of _______.

Hold your wrist straight. Make a fist with your thumb wrapped over the front of your fingers. Hold for a count of _______.

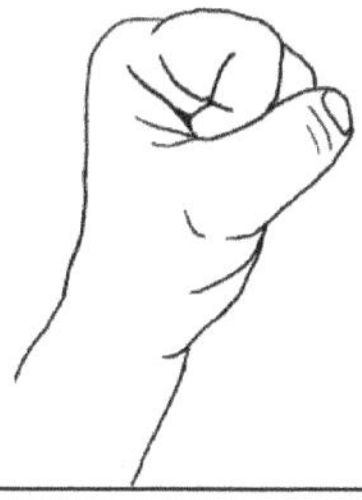

Hold your wrist straight. Keep your knuckles bent and straighten your fingers. Hold for a count of _______.

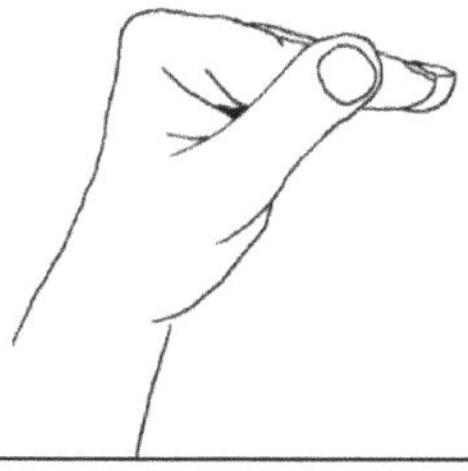

Hold your wrist straight. Reach the tips of your fingers down toward your wrist and stretch your thumb back. Hold for a count of _______.

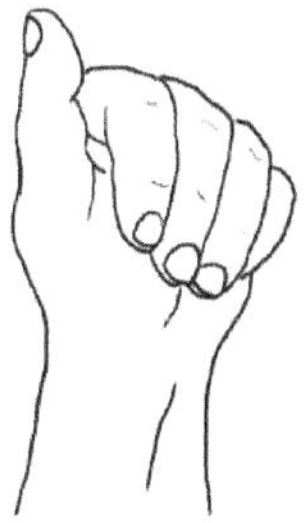

Occupational Therapy TOOLKIT

Forearm and Wrist Active Range of Motion

Do the checked exercises with **left** **right** **both** arms.
Do the checked exercises _____ times per day, _____ days a week.

☐ Bend your elbows. Tuck them into your sides. Turn your palms up and down.

Do _____ sets of _____.

☐ Let your hand hang over the edge of a table. Raise and lower your hand from the wrist.

Do _____ sets of _____.

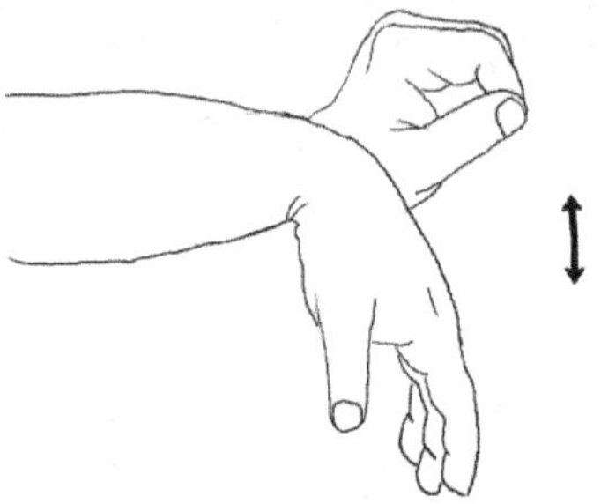

☐ Place your hand flat on the table. Move your hand side to side bending at your wrist.

Do _____ sets of _____.

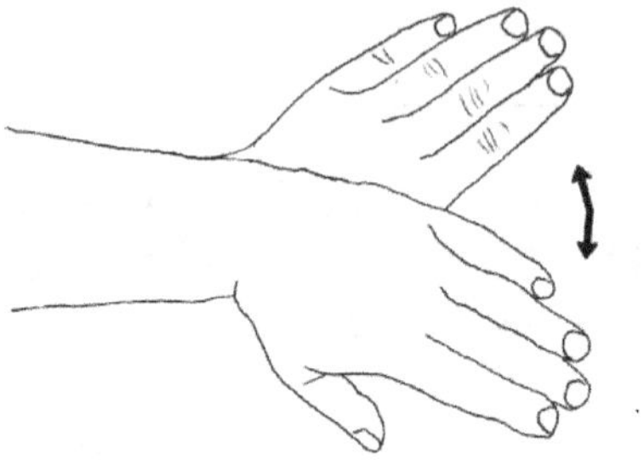

☐ Make circles with your hand. Move one way and then the other.

Do _____ sets of _____.

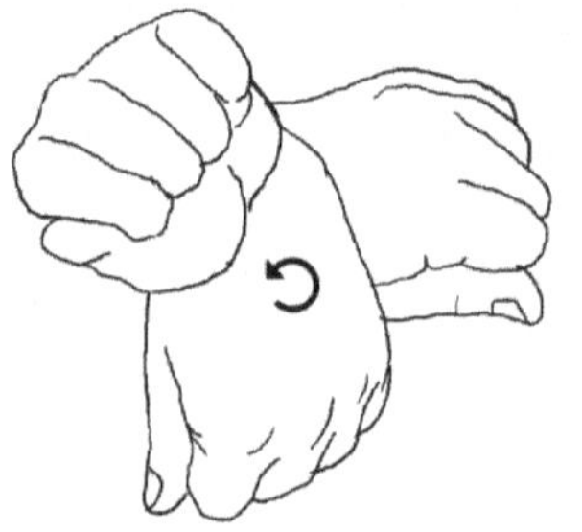

Occupational Therapy TOOLKIT

Forearm and Wrist Strength Exercises

Do the checked exercises with **left** **right** **both** arms.
Do the checked exercises _____ times per day, _____ days a week.

☐ Hold a _____ lb/kg weight. Bend your elbows. Tuck them into your sides. Turn your palms up and down.

Do _____ sets of _____.

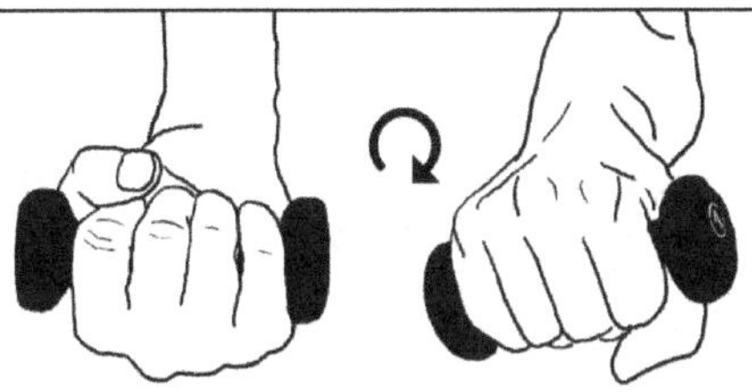

☐ Hold a _____ lb/kg weight. Let your hand hang over the edge of a table with your palm face down. Raise and lower your hand bending at your wrist.

Do _____ sets of _____.

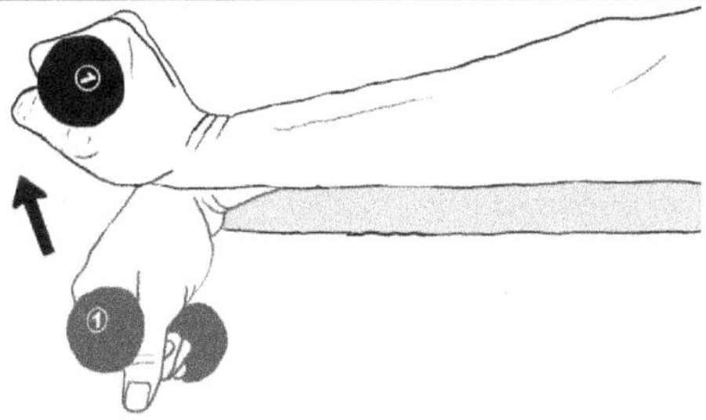

☐ Hold a _____ lb/kg weight. Let your hand hang over the edge of a table with your palm face up. Raise and lower your hand bending at your wrist.

Do _____ sets of _____.

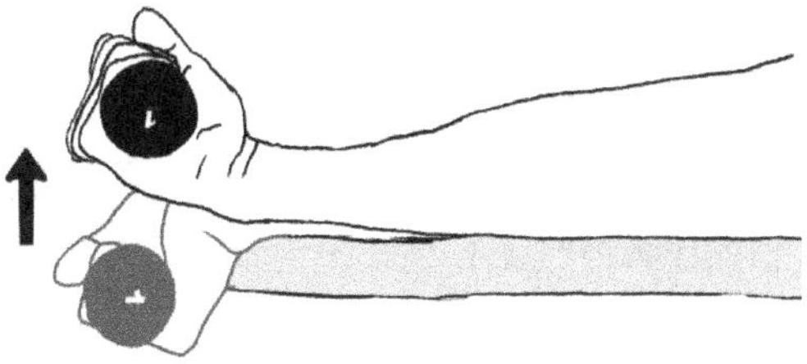

☐ Hold a _____ lb/kg weight. Let your hand hang over the edge of a table with your thumb pointing up. Move your hand up then down bending at your wrist.

Do _____ sets of _____.

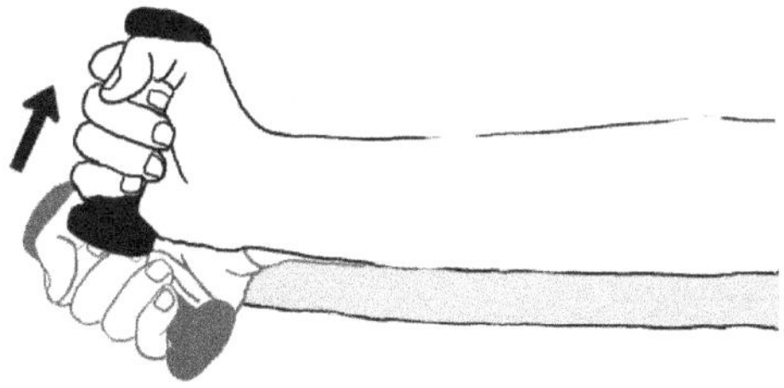

Occupational Therapy TOOLKIT

Forearm and Wrist Stretches

Do the checked exercises with **left** **right** **both** arms.
Do the checked exercises _____ times per day, _____ days a week.

☐ Keep your elbows tucked into your sides. Grasp hand. Turn your hand palm up and palm down. Hold for a count of _______.

Do ______ sets of ______.

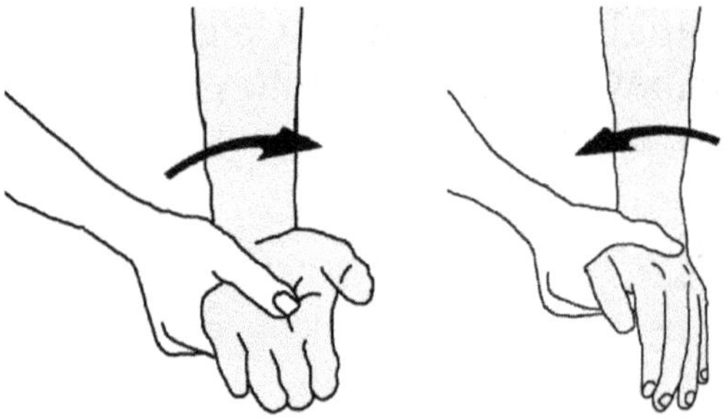

☐ Hold your arm out in front. Keep your elbow straight and your palm down. Use your other hand to stretch your wrist. To increase the stretch, close your fingers into a fist. Turn your arm toward your little finger. Hold for a count of _______.

Do ______ sets of ______.

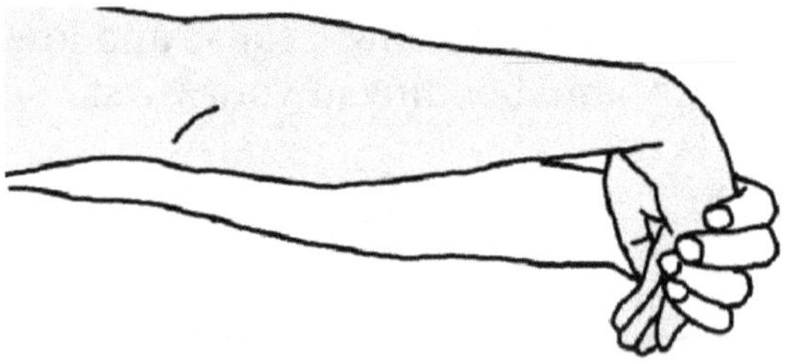

☐ Hold your arm out in front. Keep your elbow straight and your palm up. Use your other hand to stretch your wrist. To increase the stretch, use your other hand to straighten your finger and turn your arm toward your thumb. Hold for a count of _______.

Do ______ sets of ______.

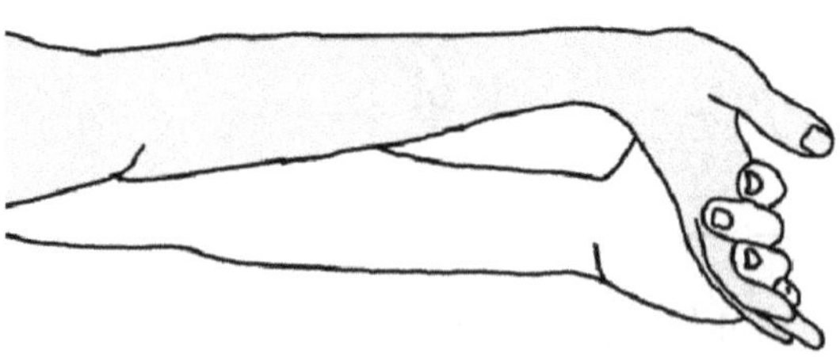

Occupational Therapy TOOLKIT

Forearm and Wrist Stretches

Do the checked exercises _____ times per day, _____ days a week.

☐ Place your palms together. Lower both hands to increase stretch. Hold for a count of ______.

Do _____ sets of _____.

☐ Place the back of your hands together. Raise both hands to increase the stretch. Hold for a count of ______.

Do _____ sets of _____.

☐ Place the backs of your hands together. Make a full fist. Raise both hands to increase the stretch. Hold for a count of ______.

Do _____ sets of _____.

General Exercise Tips

Name: ______________________________

Date: ______________________________

Therapist: ______________________________

Phone number: (_____)______________________

Do the checked exercises _____ times per day, _____ days a week.

Exercise slowly and smoothly.

Do not hold your breath during exercise. Count aloud if needed.

Use good posture. Keep your stomach muscles tight and your back straight.

Sore muscles lasting a few days and feeling tired are normal after exercise. Exhaustion, sore joints, and painful muscle pulls are not normal. If you have these symptoms, do not exercise until you talk with your therapist.

If you have chest tightness or pain, shortness of breath, feel dizzy, faint, or sick to your stomach, stop and call emergency services at _____.

Notes:

____

____

____

____

____

____

Gross Motor Tasks

Use your weaker arm to practice the checked tasks.

- ☐ Push up from an armchair
- ☐ Throw a ball.
- ☐ Toss a balloon.
- ☐ Drink from mug.
- ☐ Eat with a built-up spoon.
- ☐ Wash your other arm and face.
- ☐ Apply body lotion to your other arm.
- ☐ Brush your hair.
- ☐ Help with getting dressing.
- ☐ Help with kitchen tasks: kneading, stirring, rolling, whisking.
- ☐ Reach into the cupboard.
- ☐ Wipe down the table.
- ☐ Wring out a rag or sponge.
- ☐ Hold a dish while your stronger hand washes.
- ☐ Stack paper cups.
- ☐ Hold the phone.
- ☐ Fold laundry.
- ☐ Clean mirrors and windows.

Hip and Knee Exercises - Lying

Do the checked exercises _____ times per day, _____ days a week.

☐ **Heel Slides**
Lie on your back with your knees straight. Bend your right knee and slide your heel toward your bottom.

Do _____ sets of _____.
Repeat with your left leg.

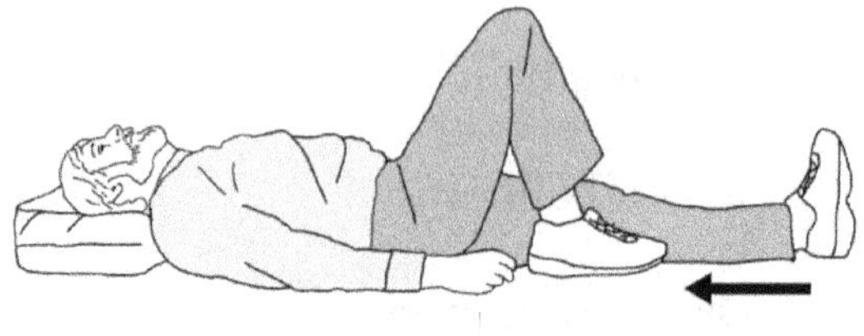

☐ **Knee Bend**
Lie on your stomach. Bend your right leg and bring your heel toward your bottom.

Do _____ sets of _____.
Repeat with your left leg.

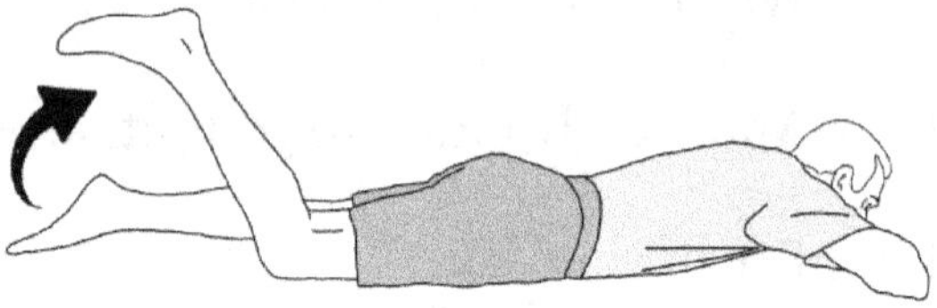

☐ **Quad Sets**
Lie on your back with your legs straight. Tighten your thigh muscles and press your knees into the bed. Hold for a count of _____.

Do _____ sets of _____.

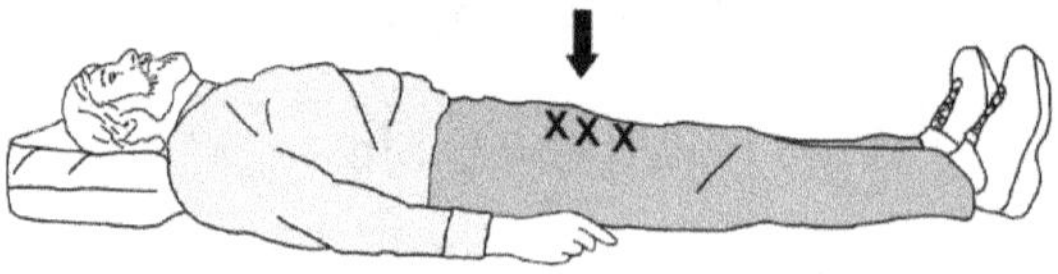

☐ **Short Arc Quads**
Lie on your back with your knees straight. Place a large coffee can or towel roll under your right knee. Straighten your knee. Hold for a count of _____.

Do _____ sets of _____.
Repeat with your left leg.

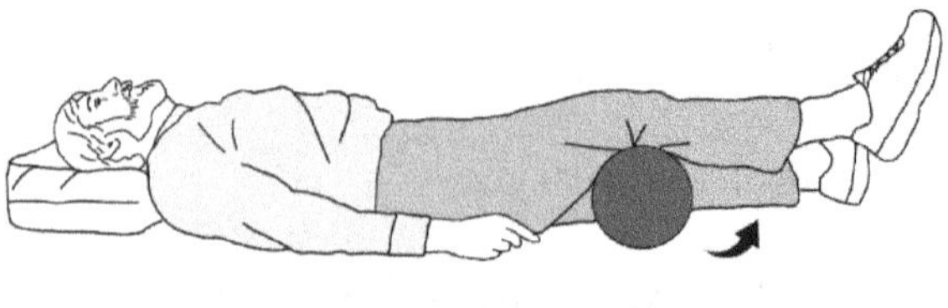

Hip and Knee Exercises - Lying

Do the checked exercises _____ times per day, _____ days a week.

☐ **Hip Flexion**
Lie on your back with your legs straight. Bring your right knee up to your chest.

Do _____ sets of _____.
Repeat with your left leg.

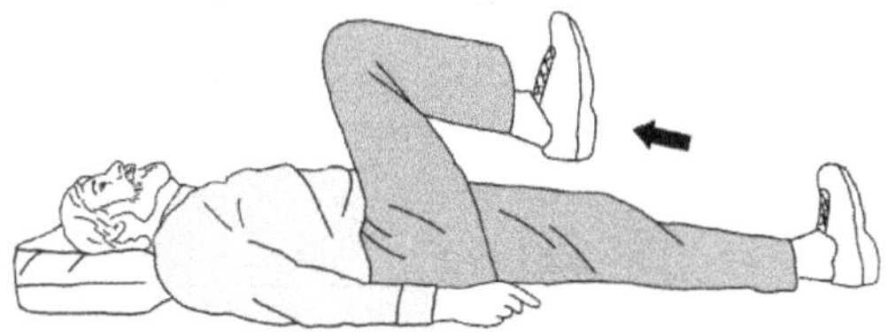

☐ **Straight Leg Raise**
Lie on your back with your left leg bent. Keep your right knee straight and raise your leg up to a 45-degree angle.

Do _____ sets of _____.
Repeat with your left leg.

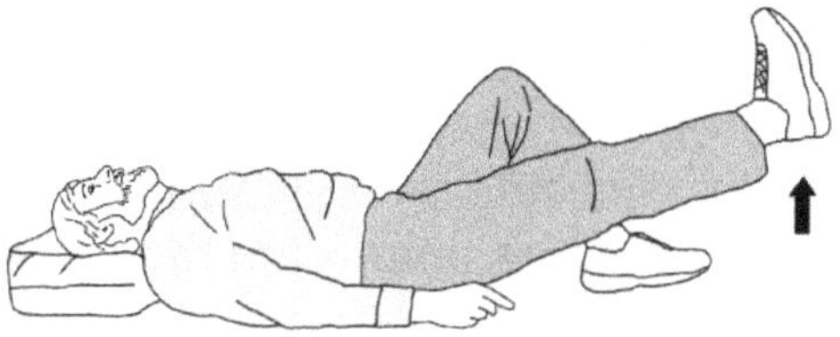

☐ **Glut Sets**
Lie on your back with your legs straight. Squeeze your bottom. Hold for a count of _____.

Do _____ sets of _____.

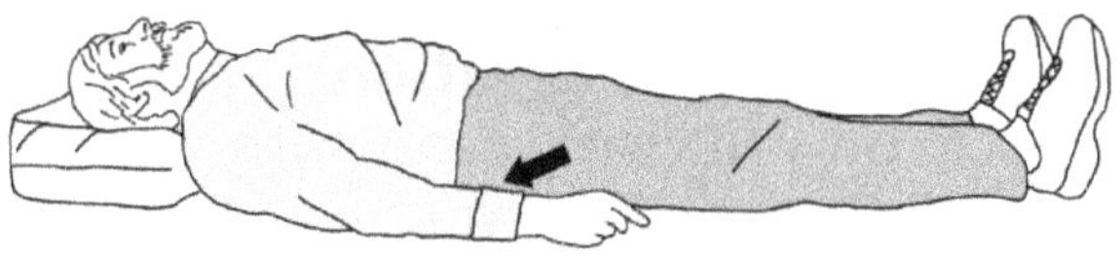

☐ **Hip Extension**
Lie on your stomach. Keep your leg straight. Lift your right leg off the bed. Do not arch your back.

Do _____ sets of _____.
Repeat with your left leg.

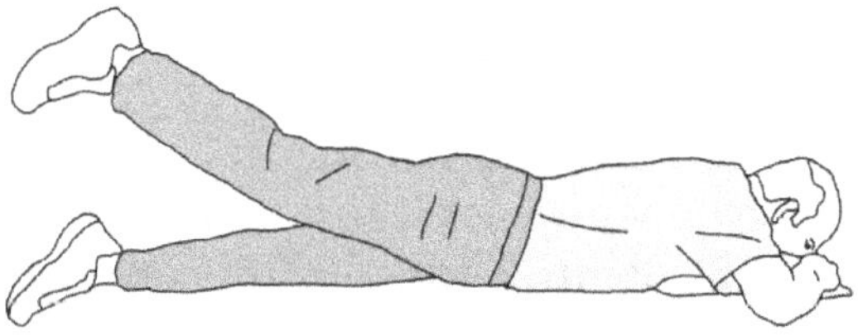

Hip and Knee Exercises - Lying

Do the checked exercises _____ times per day, _____ days a week.

☐ **Hip Adduction**
Lie on your back. Place a towel roll between your thighs. Squeeze the towel roll. Hold for a count of _____.

Do _____ sets of _____.

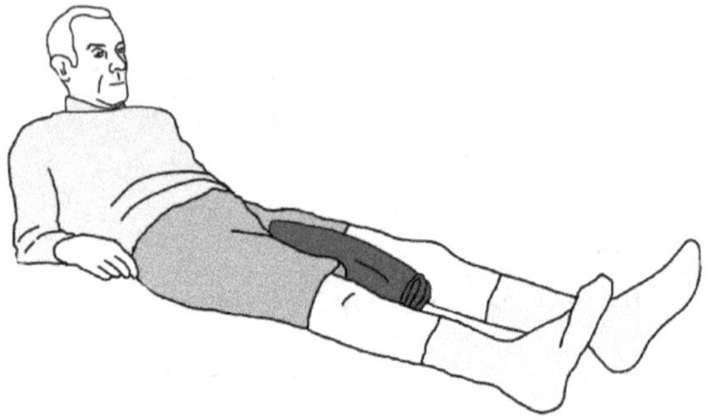

☐ **Hip Abduction**
Lie on your back. Move your right leg out to the side. Keep your knee straight and your toes pointed to the ceiling.

Do _____ sets of _____.
Repeat with your left leg.

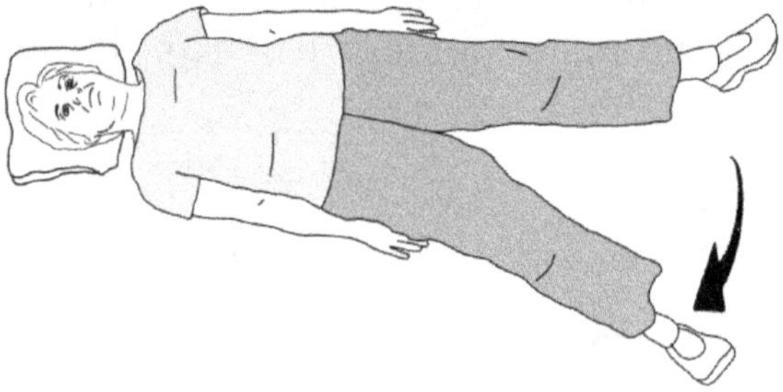

☐ **Hip Internal Rotation**
Lie on your back. Start with your toes pointing up. Turn your legs in, so your toes touch.

Do _____ sets of _____.

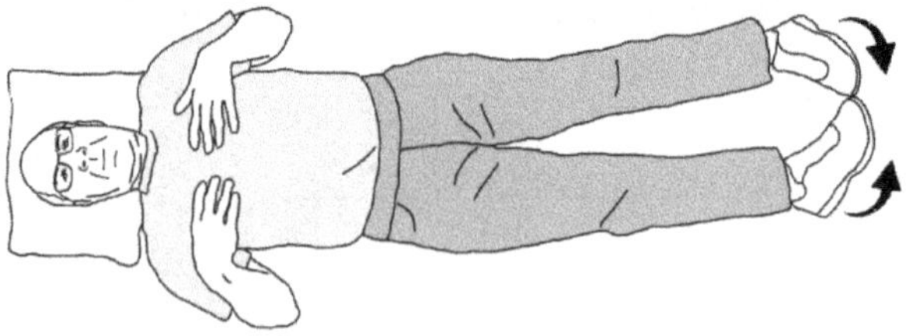

☐ **Hip External Rotation**
Lie on your back. Start with your toes pointing up. Turn your legs out, so your toes point apart.

Do _____ sets of _____.

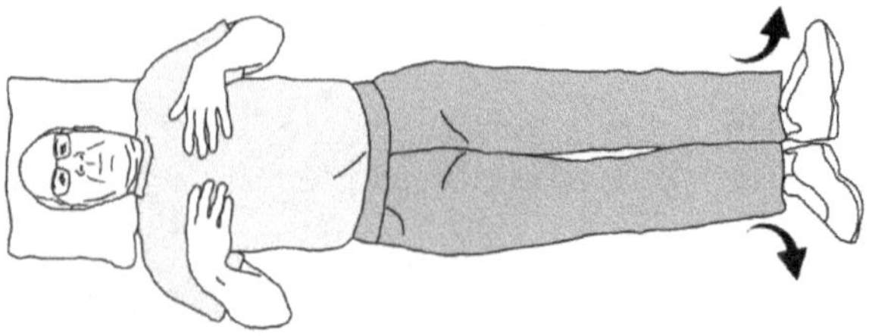

Occupational Therapy TOOLKIT

Hip and Knee Exercises - Seated

Use a ______ lb/kg weight on your right ankle, a ______ lb/kg weight on your left ankle.

Do the checked exercises ______ times per day, ______ days a week.

☐ **Knee Flexion**
Sit with feet flat on floor. Extend your right leg out in front. Slide your foot back.

Do ______ sets of ______.
Repeat with your left leg.

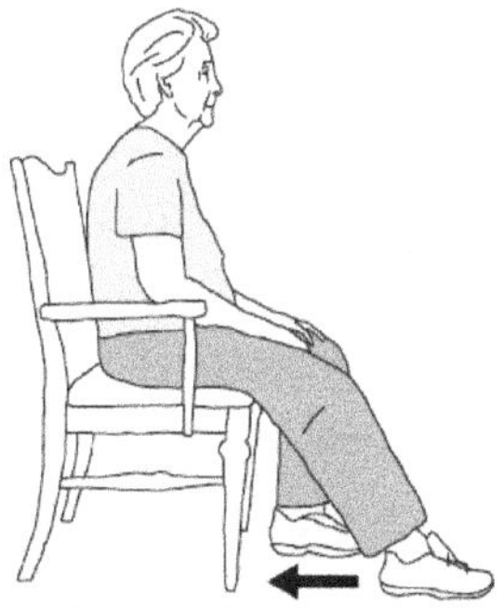

☐ **Knee Extension**
Sit with both feet on the floor. Straighten your right leg by tightening your thigh muscles. Hold for a count of ______.

Do ______ sets of ______.
Repeat with your left leg.

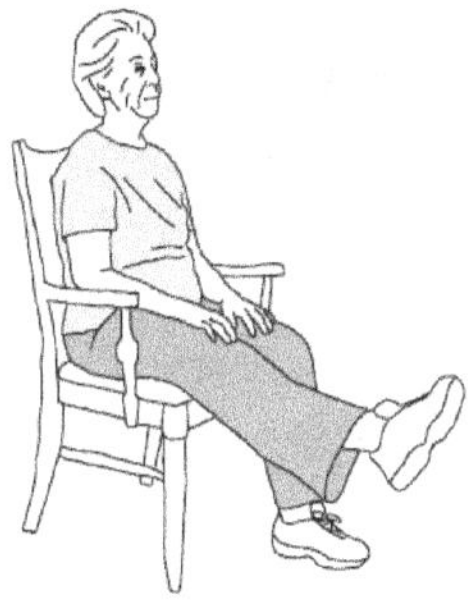

☐ **Hip Flexion**
Sit with feet flat on floor. Lift your right knee up, then lower and lift your left knee.

Do ______ sets of ______.

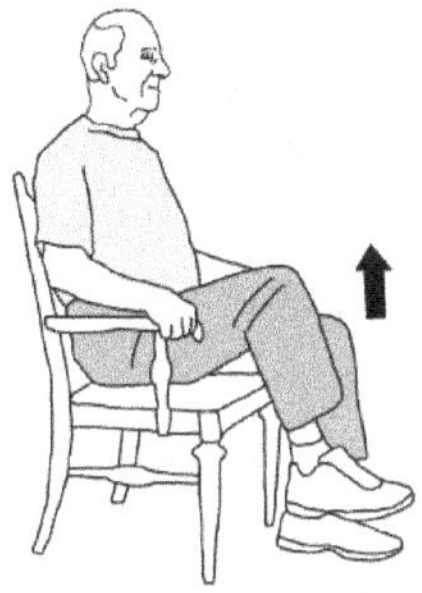

☐ **Buttocks Squeeze**
Sit with feet flat on floor. Squeeze the muscles in your hips and bottom. Hold for a count of ______.

Do ______ sets of ______.

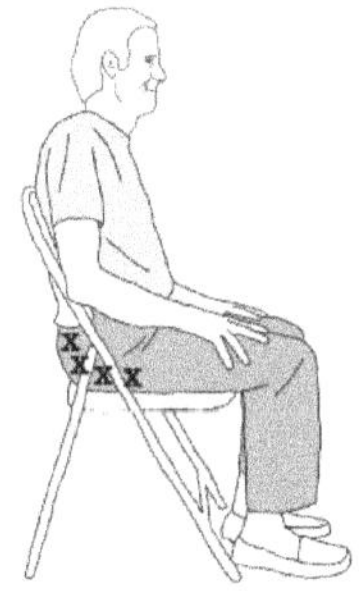

Hip and Knee Exercises - Seated

Use a _____ lb/kg weight on your right ankle, a _____ lb/kg weight on your left ankle.

Do the checked exercises _____ times per day, _____ days a week.

☐ **Hip Internal Rotation**
Sit with feet flat on floor. Rotate your right hip inward.

Do _____ sets of _____.
Repeat with your left leg.

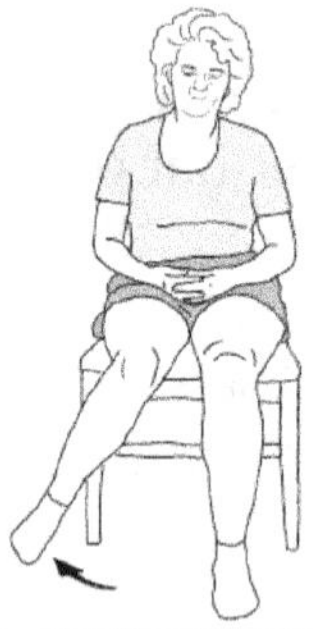

☐ **Hip External Rotation**
Sit with feet flat on floor. Rotate your right hip outward.

Do _____ sets of _____.
Repeat with your left leg.

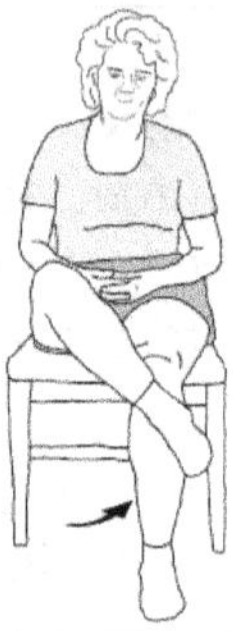

☐ **Hip Adduction**
Sit with feet flat on floor. Place a ball between your knees. Squeeze the ball. Hold for a count of _____.

Do _____ sets of _____.

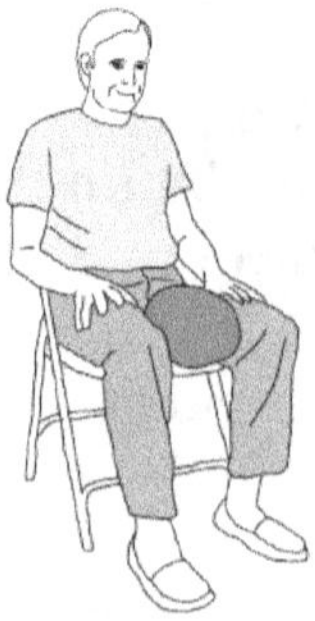

☐ **Hip Abduction**
Sit with feet flat on floor. Spread your knees apart and then bring them back.

Do _____ sets of _____.

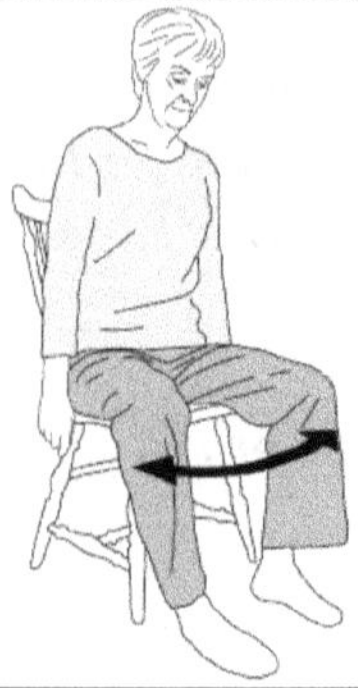

Hip and Knee Exercises - Standing

Use a ______ lb/kg weight on your right ankle, a ______ lb/kg weight on your left ankle.

Do the checked exercises ______ times per day, ______ days a week.

☐ **Knee Flexion**
Hold onto a stable object. Bend your right knee up behind you.

Do ______ sets of ______.
Repeat with your left leg.

☐ **Quarter Squat**
Hold onto a stable object. Bend your knees slightly and then straighten back up.

Do ______ sets of ______.

☐ **Hip Flexion with Knee Bent**
Hold onto a stable object. Lift your right knee.

Do ______ sets of ______.
Repeat with your left leg.

☐ **Hip Flexion with Straight Leg**
Hold onto a stable object. Keep your leg straight. Raise your right leg forward.

Do ______ sets of ______.
Repeat with your left leg.

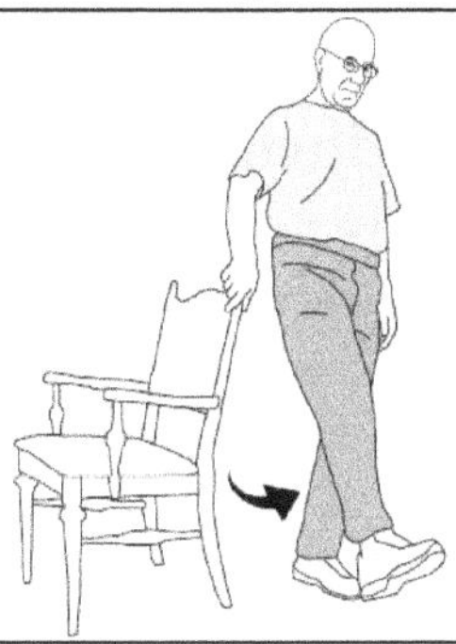

Occupational Therapy TOOLKIT

Hip and Knee Exercises - Standing

Use a _____ lb/kg weight on your right ankle, a _____ lb/kg weight on your left ankle.

Do the checked exercises _____ times per day, _____ days a week.

☐ **Stand Up and Sit Down**
Keep your back straight and your arms out in front. Stand up and sit down without using your arms.

Do _____ sets of _____.

☐ **Hip Extension**
Hold onto a stable object. Keep your leg straight. Lift your right leg back. Do not lean forward.

Do _____ sets of _____.
Repeat with your left leg.

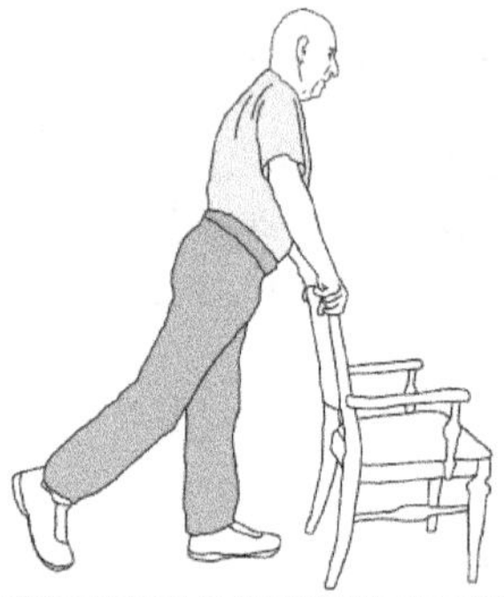

☐ **Hip Adduction**
Hold onto a stable object with your right hand. Keep your knee straight. Cross your right leg in front of the left leg.

Do _____ sets of _____.
Repeat with your left leg.

☐ **Hip Abduction**
Hold onto a stable object. Keep your knee straight. Lift your right leg out to the side.

Do _____ sets of _____.
Repeat with your left leg.

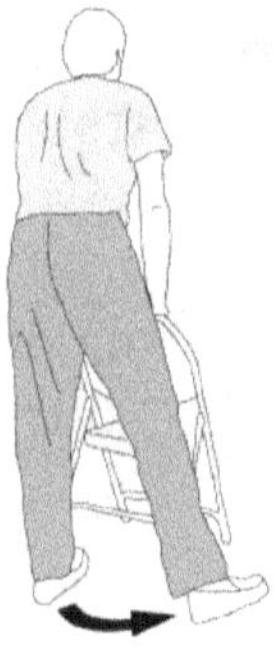

Hip and Knee Exercises - Standing

Use a _____ lb/kg weight on your right ankle, a _____ lb/kg weight on your left ankle.

Do the checked exercises _____ times per day, _____ days a week.

☐ **Hip Internal Rotation**
Hold onto a stable object with your left hand. Hold your right leg up and rotate your hip out to the side.

Do _____ sets of _____.
Repeat with your left leg.

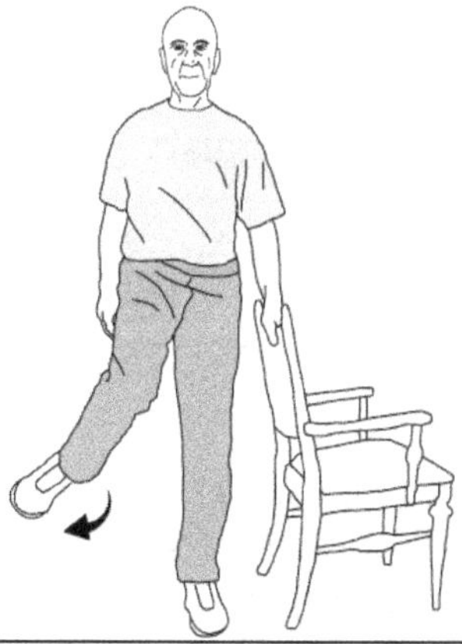

☐ **Hip External Rotation**
Hold onto a stable object with your left hand. Move your right foot up toward your left knee

Do _____ sets of _____.
Repeat with your left leg.

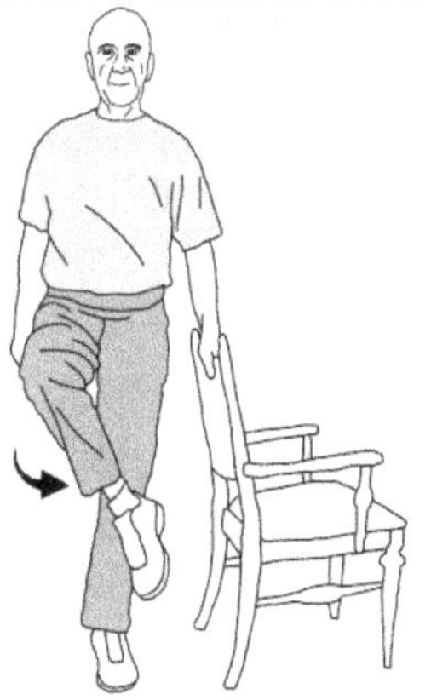

Occupational Therapy TOOLKIT

Level 1 Activities
Help Your Weaker Arm Move

Name: ______________________________

Date: ______________________________

Therapist: ______________________________

Phone number: (_____)______________________

This packet includes the checked handouts:
- ☐ Passive Range of Motion
- ☐ Position in Bed
- ☐ Position Your Arm
- ☐ Protect the Arm
- ☐ Self Range of Motion
- ☐ Use Your Arm with Assisted Guiding
- ☐ Weight Bearing Exercises

These activities and exercises will help protect your arm from injury. They may help your arm start moving again.

Ask your family or friends to help you with your program.

The exercises should not cause any pain, if they do, stop and contact your therapist.

Occupational Therapy TOOLKIT

Level 2 Activities
Use Your Weaker Arm to Passively Hold

Name: ______________________________

Date: ______________________________

Therapist: ______________________________

Phone number: (_____)____________________

This packet includes the checked handouts:

☐ Position in Bed
☐ Position Your Arm
☐ Protect the Arm
☐ Passive Range of Motion
☐ Self Range of Motion
☐ Use Your Arm with Assisted Guiding
☐ Use Your Arm with Self-Guiding
☐ Use Your Arm to Passively Hold
☐ Weight Bearing Exercises

These exercises will help strengthen your weaker arm, so you can use your arm with daily tasks.

Ask your family or friends to help you with your program.

Try to do these exercises throughout the day, every day.

Exercise slowly and smoothly.

Do not hold your breath during exercise. Count aloud if needed.

Sore muscles lasting a few days and feeling tired are normal after exercising. Exhaustion, sore joints, and painful muscle pulls are not normal. If you have these symptoms, do not exercise until you talk with your therapist.

Occupational Therapy TOOLKIT

Level 3 Activities
Use Your Weaker Arm to Actively Move and Hold

Name: ______________________________

Date: ______________________________

Therapist: ______________________________

Phone number: (_____)______________________

This packet includes the checked handouts:

- ☐ Self Range of Motion
- ☐ Scapular Mobility and Strength Exercises
- ☐ Use Your Arm to Actively Hold
- ☐ Use Your Arm with Self-Guiding
- ☐ Use Your Arm with Assisted Guiding
- ☐ Weight Bearing Exercises

These exercises will help strengthen your weaker arm, so you can use your arm with daily tasks.

Ask your family or friends to help you with your program.

Try to do these exercises throughout the day, every day.

Exercise slowly and smoothly.

Do not hold your breath during exercise. Count aloud if needed.

Sore muscles lasting a few days and feeling tired are normal after exercising. Exhaustion, sore joints, and painful muscle pulls are not normal. If you have these symptoms, do not exercise until you talk with your therapist.

Occupational Therapy TOOLKIT

Level 4 Activities
Use Your Weaker Arm with Gross Motor Activities

Name: ______________________________

Date: ______________________________

Therapist: ______________________________

Phone number: (_____)____________________

This packet includes the checked handouts:
- ☐ Upper Body Exercises - Using a Ball
- ☐ Gross Motor Activities
- ☐ Hand Strength Exercises
- ☐ Scapular Mobility and Strength Exercises
- ☐ Arm Exercises
- ☐ Use Your Arm with Gross Motor Activities
- ☐ Weight Bearing Exercises

You will also need:
- ☐ Wrist weights _____ pound
- ☐ Exercise putty ___________ color
- ☐ 12-inch ball
- ☐ Cups to stack
- ☐ Inflated balloon

These exercises will help strengthen your weaker arm, so you can use your arm with daily tasks.

Ask your family or friends to help you with your program.

Try to do these exercises throughout the day, every day.

Exercise slowly and smoothly.

Do not hold your breath during exercise. Count aloud if needed.

Sore muscles lasting a few days and feeling tired are normal after exercising. Exhaustion, sore joints, and painful muscle pulls are not normal. If you have these symptoms, do not exercise until you talk with your therapist.

Occupational Therapy TOOLKIT

Level 5 Activities
Use Your Weaker Arm with Fine Motor Activities

Name: ______________________________

Date: ______________________________

Therapist: ______________________________

Phone number: (_____)______________________

This packet includes the checked handouts:
- ☐ Fine Motor Activities
- ☐ Putty Exercises
- ☐ Upper Body Strength Activities
- ☐ Upper Body Exercises - Hand Weights

You will also need:
- ☐ Wrist weights _____ pound
- ☐ Exercise putty ___________ color
- ☐ Fine motor box

These exercises will help strengthen your weaker arm, so you can use your arm with daily tasks.

Ask your family or friends to help you with your program.

Try to do these exercises throughout the day, every day.

Exercise slowly and smoothly.

Do not hold your breath during exercise. Count aloud if needed.

Sore muscles lasting a few days and feeling tired are normal after exercising. Exhaustion, sore joints, and painful muscle pulls are not normal. If you have these symptoms, do not exercise until you talk with your therapist.

Low Back Stretches

Do the checked exercises _____ times per day, _____ days a week.

☐ **Single Knee to Chest**
Lie on back with both feet on the floor. Bring your right knee up to your chest. Hold for a count of _____. Lower your leg. Bring your left knee up to your chest. Hold for a count of ______. Lower your leg.

Do _____ set(s) of _____.

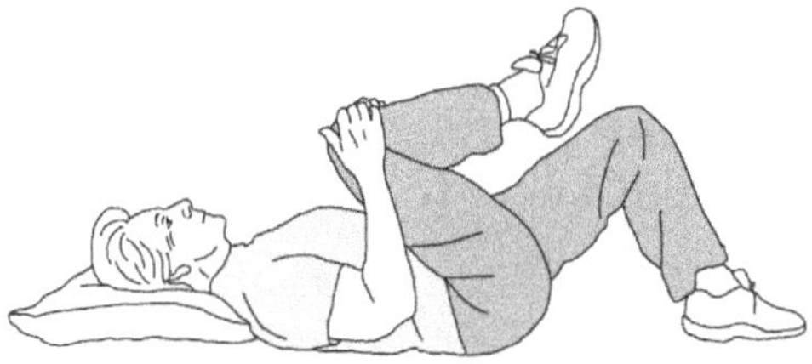

☐ **Double Knee to Chest**
Lie on back with both feet on the floor. Bring both knees to your chest. Hold for a count of ______. Lower your legs.

Do _____ set(s) of _____.

☐ **Glut Stretch**
Lie on your back. Pull your knee of your right leg toward your left shoulder.
Hold for a count of ______.

Do _____ set(s) of _____.
Repeat with your left leg.

☐ **Hamstring Stretch**
Lie on back with your legs straight. Place both hand behind your right knee. Straighten your knee until you feel a stretch. Hold for a count of ______.

Do _____ set(s) of _____.
Repeat with your left leg.

Low Back Stretches

Do the checked exercises _____ times per day, _____ days a week.

☐ **Back Stretch**
Lie on your back, knees bent and feet flat. Place your hands behind your head. Roll your knees to your right side. Hold for a count of _______.

Do ______ set(s) of ______.
Repeat to your left side.

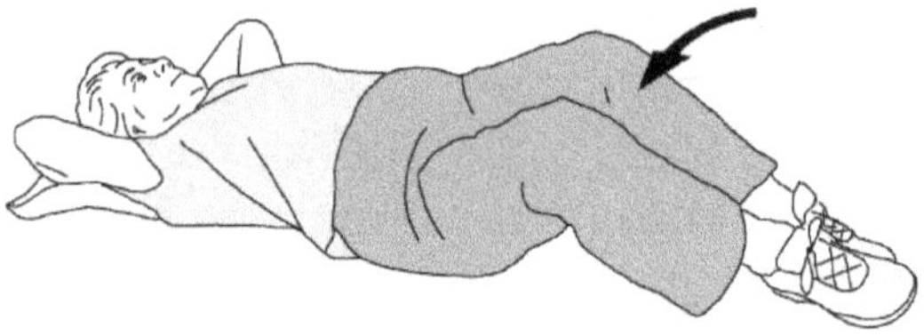

☐ **Rotation Stretch**
Lie on your back, legs straight and arms out to the sides. Draw up your right knee and rotate over to the left side. Hold for a count of _______.

Do ______ set(s) of ______.
Repeat with your left leg.

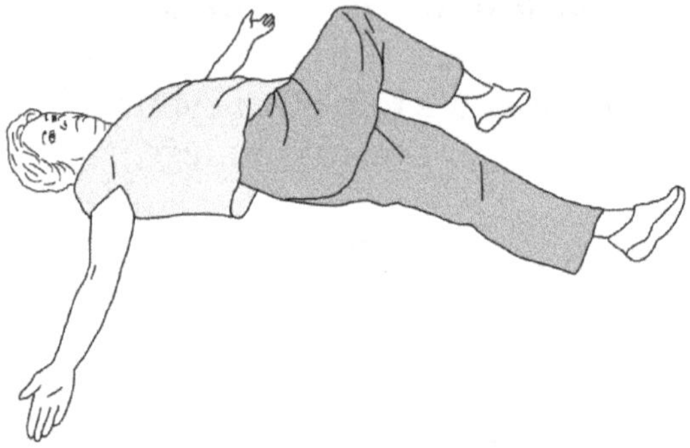

☐ **Cat Stretch**
Get on your hands and knees. Let your back and stomach sag toward the floor. Then arch your back, as if you are pulling your stomach up toward the ceiling. Hold for a count of _______.

Do ______ set(s) of ______.

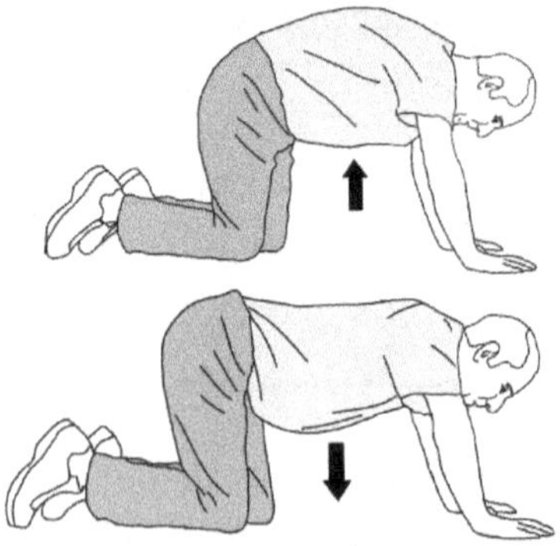

☐ **Prone Extension**
Lie on your stomach. Prop up on your elbows. Hold for a count of _______

Do ______ set(s) of ______.

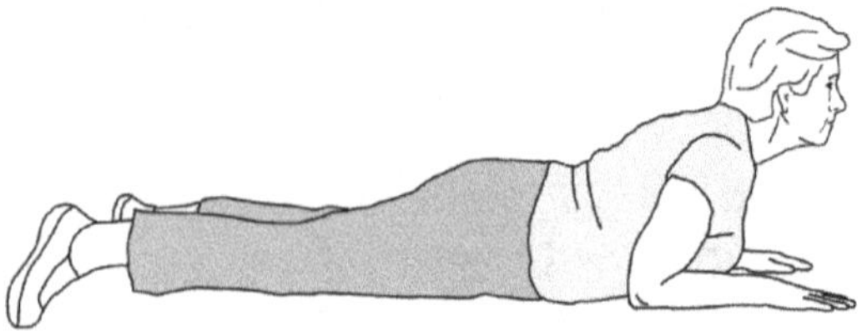

Occupational Therapy TOOLKIT

Mastectomy Exercises

Name: ______________________________

Date: ______________________________

Therapist: ______________________________

Phone number: (_____)______________________

Do the checked exercises _____ times per day, _____ days a week.

Exercise slowly and smoothly.

Use deep (diaphragmatic) breathing during each exercise.

Use good posture. Keep your stomach muscles tight and your back straight. Relax your shoulders during the exercises.

These exercises should not cause pain. If you have pain, stop and consult your therapist or doctor.

If you have chest tightness or pain, shortness of breath, feel dizzy, faint, or sick to your stomach, stop and call emergency services at _____.

Notes:

Mastectomy Exercises Phase 1

☐ **Head Tilt**
Tilt your head toward your shoulder. Tilt to the other side.

Do ______ sets of ______.

☐ **Head Turns**
Look over your shoulder to one side. Look to the other side.

Do ______ sets of ______.

☐ **Shoulder Shrug**
Shrug your shoulders.

Do ______ sets of ______.

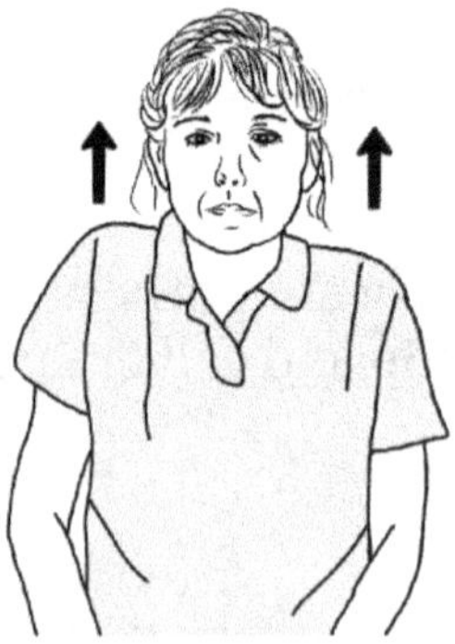

☐ **Shoulder Rolls**
Roll your shoulders.

Do ______ sets of ______.

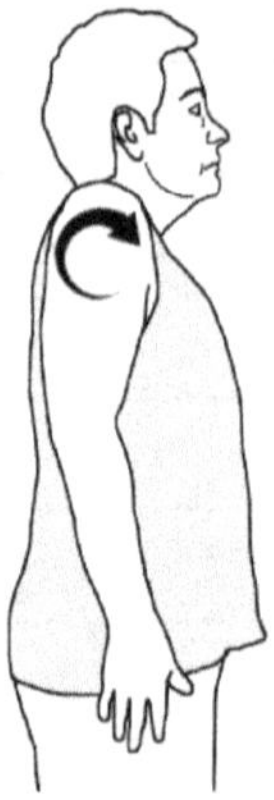

Mastectomy Exercises Phase 1

☐ **Back Stretch**
Hold your hands behind your back. Squeeze your shoulder blades.

Do ______ sets of ______.

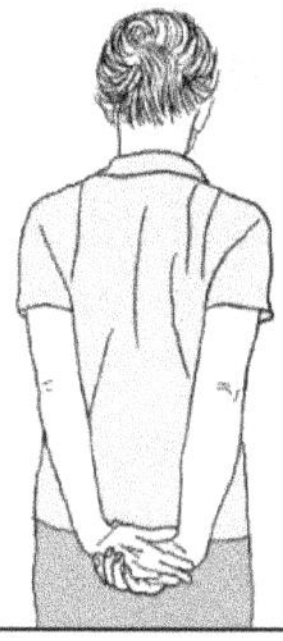

☐ **Pendulum**
Hold onto a stable object. Lean forward. Relax your shoulder muscles. Use your body to swing your arm. Repeat with your other arm.

- Swing your arm in a small circle to the right ______ times.
- Swing your arm in a small circle to the left ______ times.
- Swing your arm side-to-side ______ times.
- Swing your arm forward and back ______ times.

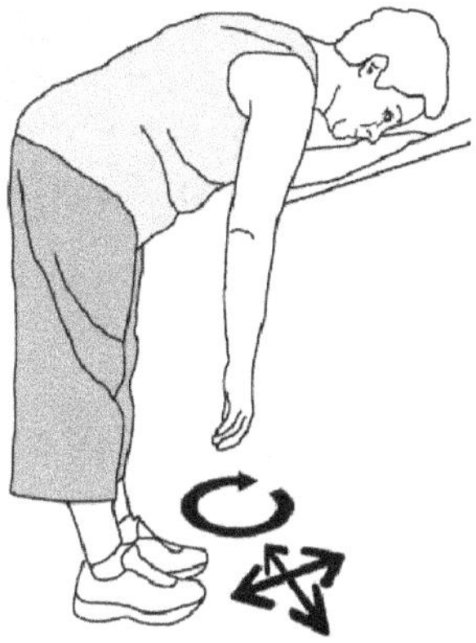

☐ **Punch**
Lift both arms out in front. Move only from your shoulder. Punch your arms forward and then pull them back.

Do ______ sets of ______.

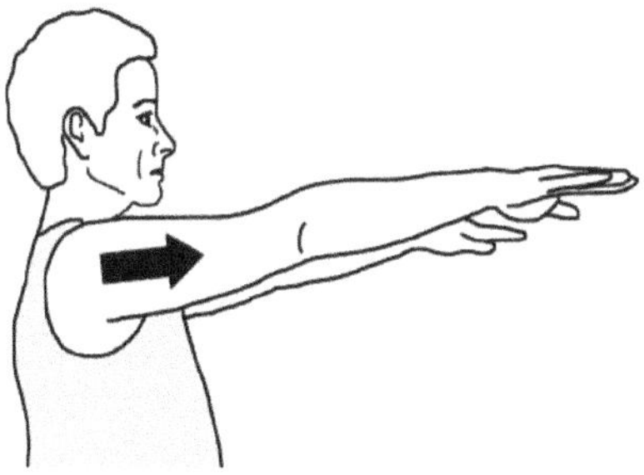

☐ **Ball Squeeze**
Squeeze a soft ball.

Do ______ sets of ______with each hand.

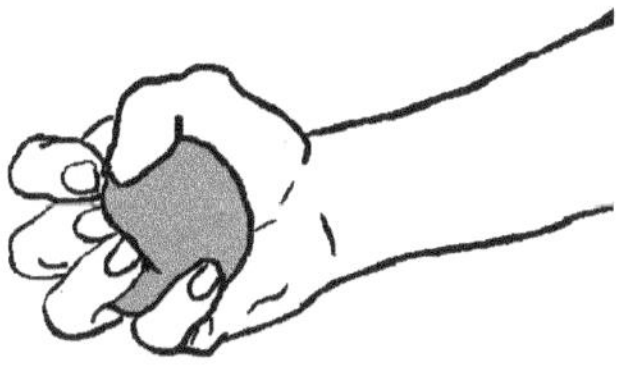

Mastectomy Exercises Phase 2

☐ **Corner Stretch**
Stand facing a corner. Raise your arms to shoulder height. Press your chest into the corner. Hold for a count of _____.

Do _____ sets of _____.

☐ **Wall Walk**
Stand facing the wall. Walk your fingers up the wall.

Do _____ sets of _____.
Repeat with your other arm.

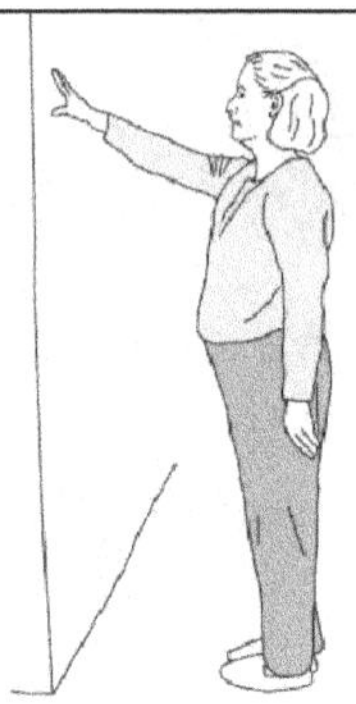

☐ **Elbow Spread**
Clasp your hands behind your neck. Bring your elbows together and then spread your elbows apart.

Do _____ sets of _____.

☐ **Side Bends**
Cradle your arms and then lift them over your head. Bend to one side then bend to the other side.

Do _____ sets of _____.

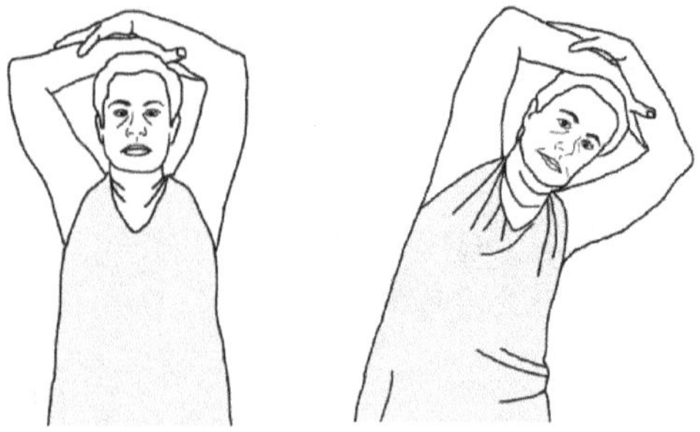

Mastectomy Exercises Phase 2

☐ **Dowel Front Lift**
Hold a dowel with your hands shoulder width apart. Lift the dowel up in front as high as you can.

Do ______ sets of ______.

☐ **Dowel Side Lift**
Hold a dowel with your hands shoulder width apart. Lift the dowel up to the side as high as you can. Repeat to other side.

Do ______ sets of ______.

☐ **Dowel Back Lift**
Hold the dowel behind you. Keep your elbows straight. Lift the dowel away from your body.

Do ______ sets of ______.

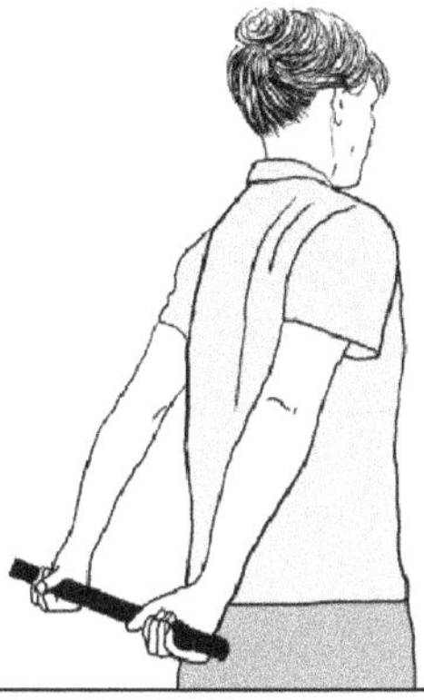

☐ **Towel Stretch**
Hold one end of a towel and drape it over the same shoulder. Reach back and hold the other end with your other hand. Gently pull the towel upward over your head.

Do ______ sets of ______.
Repeat with your other arm.

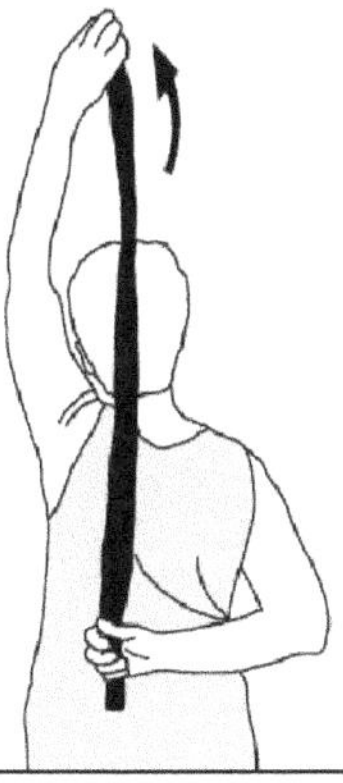

Occupational Therapy TOOLKIT

Median Nerve Glides

Do each movement in order _____ times per day, _____ days a week.

Hold your wrist straight and your fingers and thumb in a loose fist. Hold to a count of _____.

Straighten your fingers. Keep your thumb next to your index finger and your wrist straight. Hold to a count of _____.

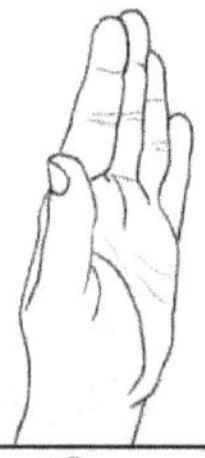

Bend your wrist and fingers back. Keep your thumb next to your index finger. Hold to a count of _____.

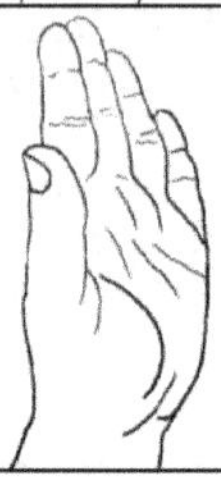

Move your thumb away from your fingers. Hold to a count of _____.

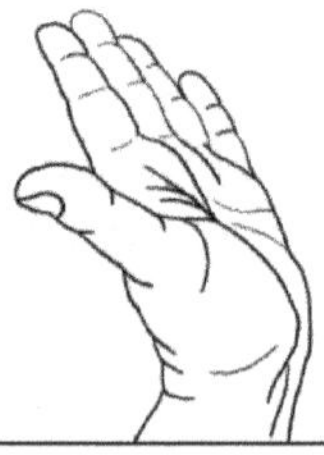

Spread your fingers apart. Hold to a count of _____.

Reach under your outstretched hand with your other hand and gently pull your thumb to turn your palm up. Hold to a count of _____.

Neck Active Range of Motion

Do the checked exercises _____ times per day, _____ days a week.

☐ Bend your head forward. Keep your chin tucked.

Do ______ sets of ______.

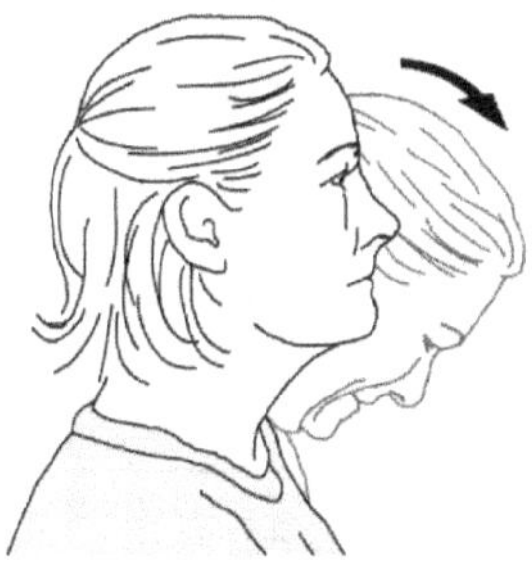

☐ Bend your head back.

Do ______ sets of ______.

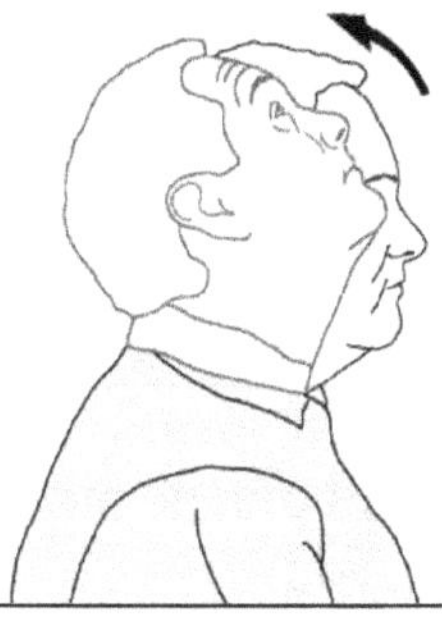

☐ Bend your head to the side. Keep looking forward. Repeat to your other side.

Do ______ sets of ______ to each side.

☐ Turn your head to look over your shoulder. Repeat to your other side.

Do ______ sets of ______ to each side.

Neck Isometric Exercises

Do the checked exercises _____ times per day, _____ days a week.

☐ Place your hand on your forehead. Resist bending your head forward. Hold for a count of ______.

Do _____ sets of _____.

☐ Place your hands at the back of your head. Resist bending your head back. Hold for a count of ______.

Do _____ sets of _____.

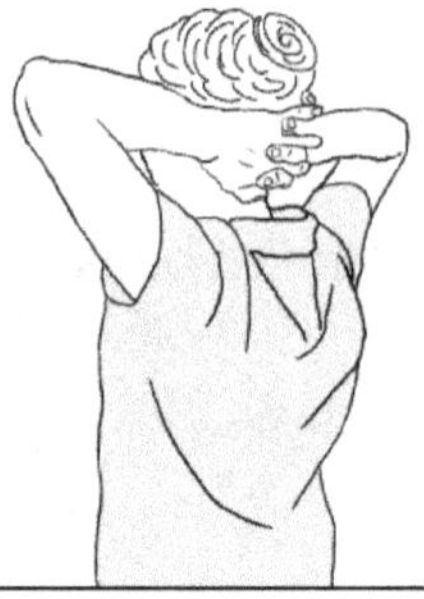

☐ Place one hand on the side of your head. Resist tilting your head to the side. Hold for a count of ______.

Do _____ sets of _____.
Repeat on your other side.

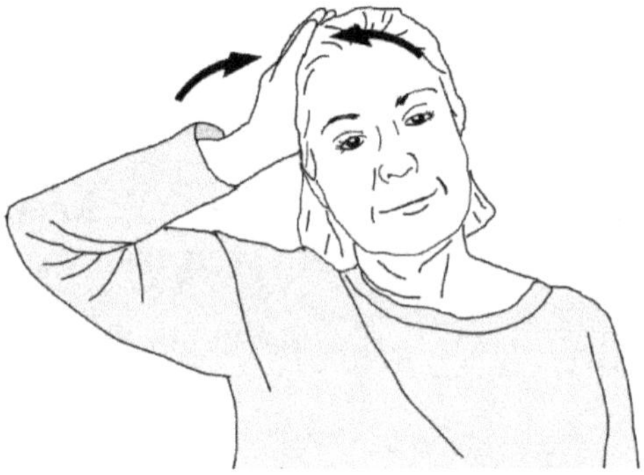

☐ Place your hand on your cheek. Resist turning your head to the side. Hold for a count of ______.

Do _____ sets of _____.
Repeat on your other side.

Neck Strength Exercises

Do the checked exercises _____ times per day, _____ days a week.

☐ Get onto your hands and knees. Tighten your stomach muscles. Lower and raise your head.

Do _____ sets of _____.

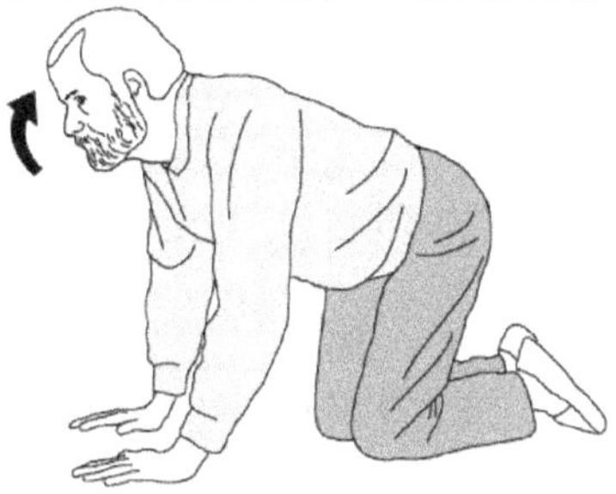

☐ Lie on your back. Lift your head, and curl your chin to your chest.

Do _____ sets of _____.

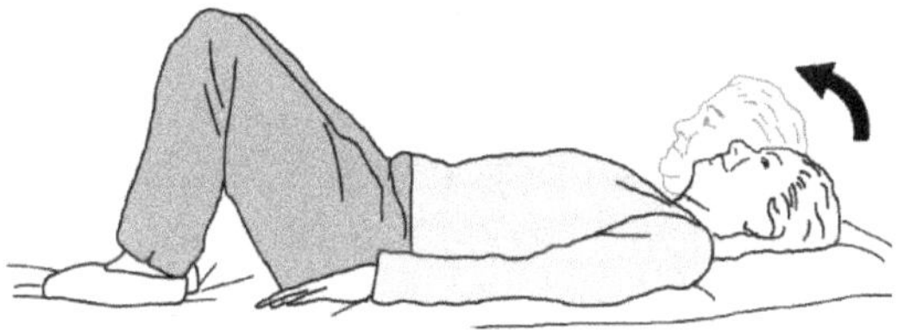

☐ Lie on your side with your arm over your head. Rest your head on the out-stretched arm. Lift your head.

Do _____ sets of _____.
Repeat on your other side.

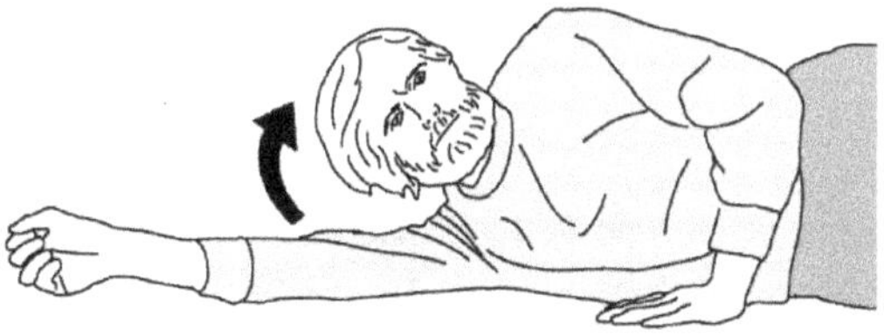

☐ Get onto your hands and knees. Tighten your stomach muscles. Keep your head and neck straight.

Raise your right arm straight ahead.
Raise your right arm to the side.
Raise your right arm to the back.

Do _____ sets of _____.
Repeat on your other side.

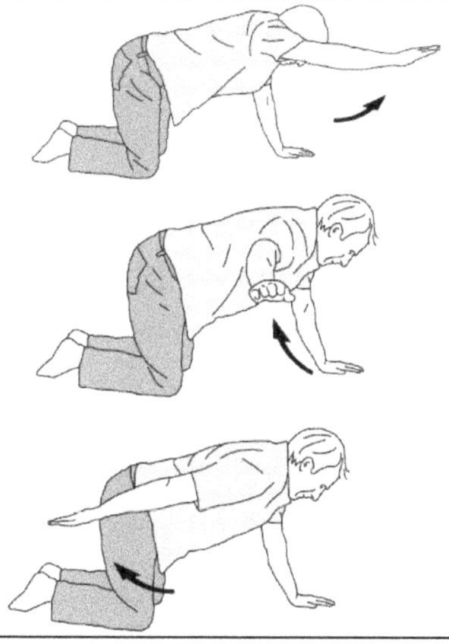

Neck Stretches

Do the checked exercises _____ times per day, _____ days a week.

☐ Place your arm behind your back. Turn your head toward the other side. Hold for a count of ______.

Do _____ sets of _____.
Repeat on your other side.

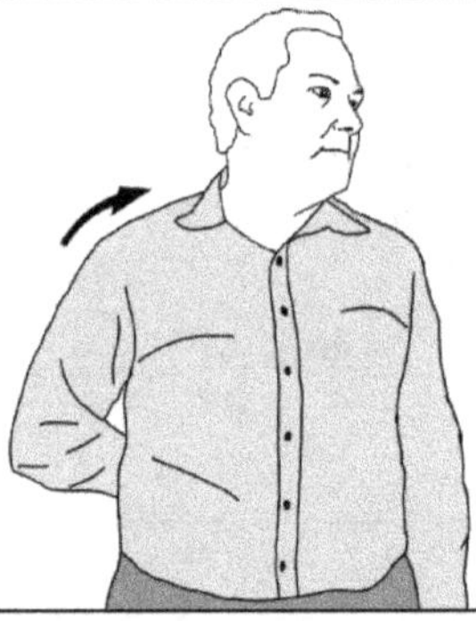

☐ Place your hand on top of your head. Gently bring your ear toward your shoulder. Hold for a count of ______.

Do _____ sets of _____.
Repeat on your other side.

☐ Squeeze your shoulder blades. Hold for a count of ______.

Do _____ sets of _____.

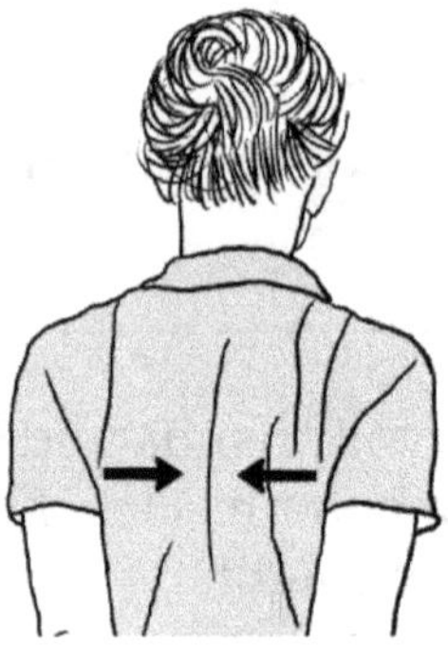

☐ Pull your chin straight back. Hold for a count of ______.

Do _____ sets of _____.

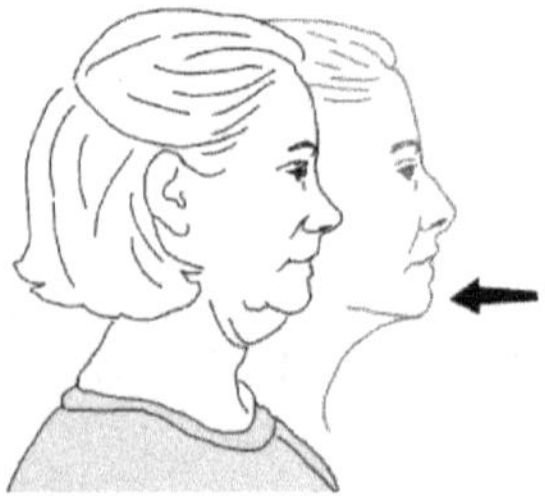

Occupational Therapy TOOLKIT

Nerve Flossing - Median

Do the sequence _____ times per day, _____ days a week.

Do the exercise with **left** **right** **both** arms.

Starting Position
Raise your affected arm out to the side. Turn your palm face up. Bend your wrist back. Tilt your head to the unaffected side. Maintain this position.

Movement 1
Slowly bend your elbow.

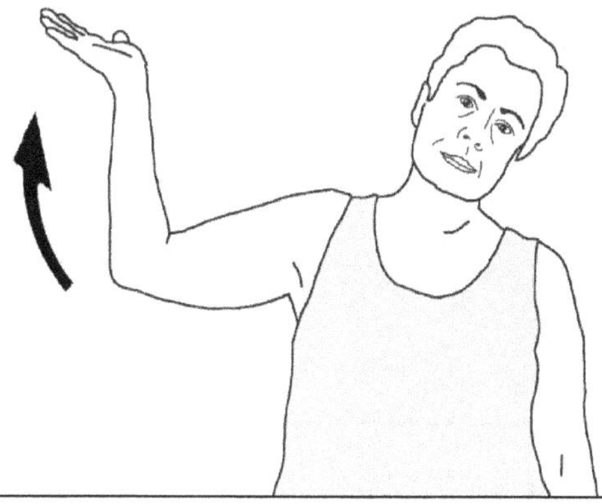

Movement 2
Slowly straighten your arm.

Repeat _____ times.

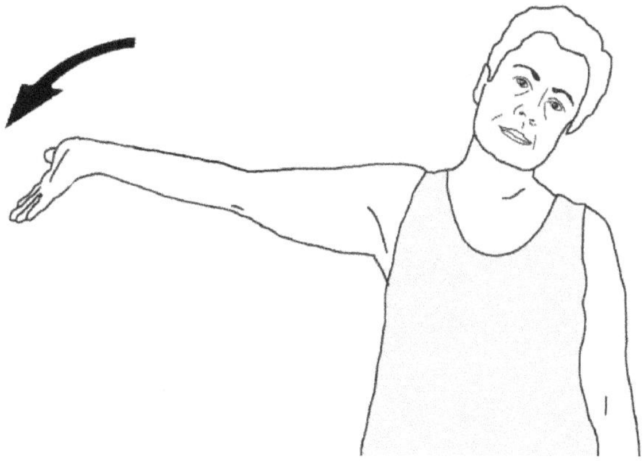

Occupational Therapy TOOLKIT

Nerve Flossing - Radial

Do the sequence _____ times per day, _____ days a week.

Do the exercise with **left** **right** **both** arms.

Starting Position
Hold your affected arm at your side. Bend your wrist. Point your fingers forward. Tilt your head to the unaffected side. Maintain this position.

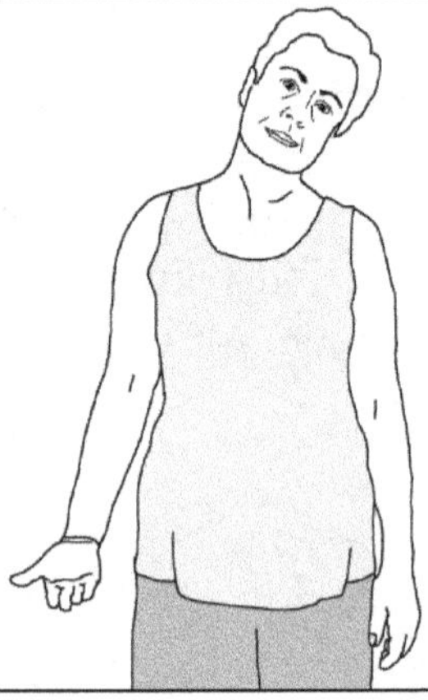

Movement 1
Slowly lift your arm away from your side. Lift to about 18 inches/45 cm.

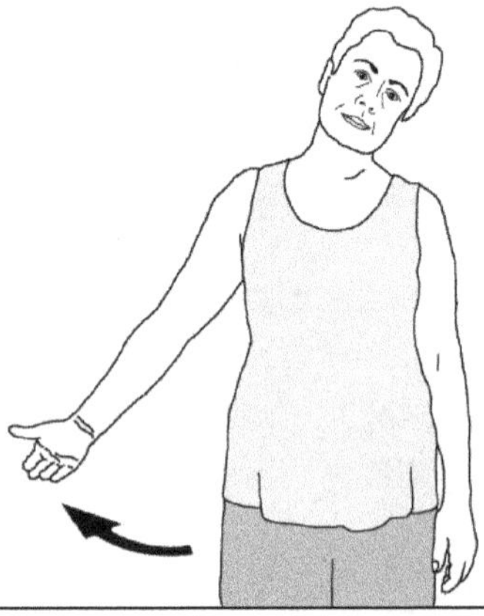

Movement 2
Lower your arm to the side.

Repeat _____ times.

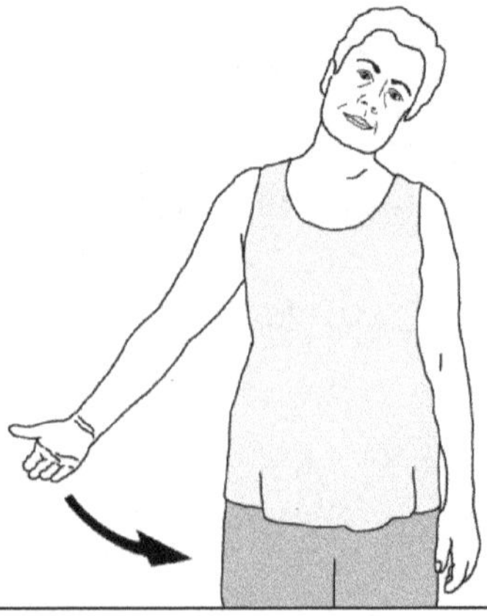

Nerve Flossing - Ulnar

Do the sequence _____ times per day, _____ days a week.

Do the exercise with **left** **right** **both** arms.

Starting Position
Raise your affected arm out to the side. Turn your palm facing up. Make a circle with your thumb and index finger. Tilt your head to the unaffected side. Maintain this position.

Movement 1
Keep your head tilted to the side. Bend your elbow and hook your three fingers under your chin.

Movement 2
Place your thumb and index finger "circle" over your eye.

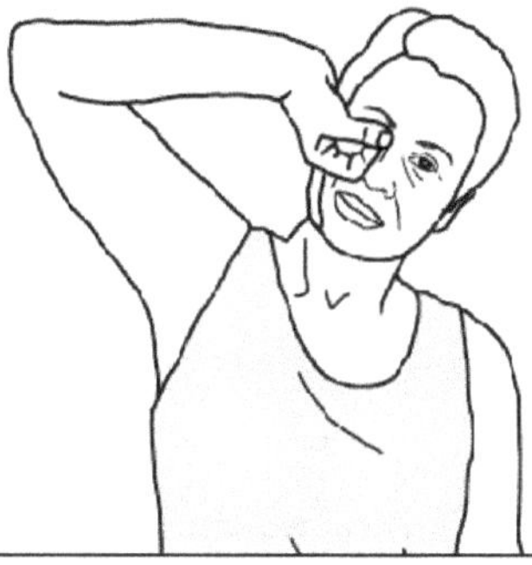

Movement 3
Return your arm out to the side with your palm facing up and your thumb and index finger making a circle.

Repeat _____ times.

Osteoporosis Extension Exercises

Name: ______________________________

Date: ______________________________

Therapist: ______________________________

Phone number: (_____)______________________

Do the checked exercises _____ times per day, _____ days a week.

Exercise slowly and smoothly.

Use good posture with each exercise. Keep your stomach muscles tight and your neck and back straight.

Do not hold your breath during exercise. Count aloud if needed.

Sore muscles lasting a few days and feeling tired are normal after exercise. Exhaustion, sore joints, and painful muscle pulls are not normal. If you have these symptoms, do not exercise until you talk with your therapist.

If you have chest tightness or pain, shortness of breath, feel dizzy, faint, or sick to your stomach, stop and call emergency services at _____.

Notes:

____

____

____

____

____

____

____

____

Occupational Therapy TOOLKIT

Osteoporosis Extension Exercises

During the exercises, keep your back and neck straight and your stomach muscles tight.

☐ **Mini Wall Squat**
Stand with your back to the wall. Do a small squat. Hold for a count of ______. Return to standing.

Do ______ sets of ______.

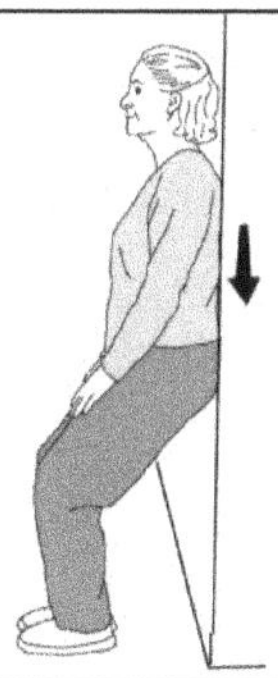

☐ **Wall Stretch**
Place your palms flat on the wall at shoulder height. Place your feet 6 inches/13 cm from the wall. Slide your hands up the wall. Hold this stretch for a count of ______.

Do ______ sets of ______.

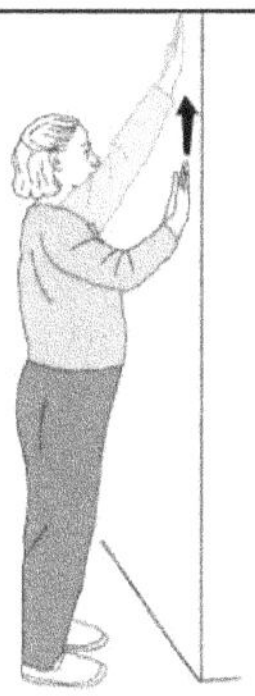

☐ **Calf Stretch**
Hold onto a stable object. Slide your affected foot back. Keep the heel on the floor. Lean forward onto your bent front knee. Hold for a count of ______.

Do ______ sets of ______.
Repeat on your other side.

☐ **Lift Back**
Hold onto a stable object. Hold a ______ lb/kg weight. Raise your arm up back.

Do ______ sets of ______.
Repeat on your other side.

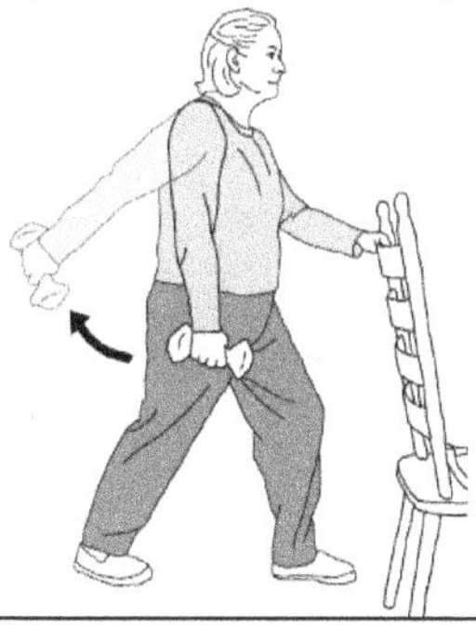

Osteoporosis Extension Exercises

During the exercises, keep your back and neck straight and your stomach muscles tight.

☐ **Chin Tuck**
Pull your chin straight back.

Do ______ sets of ______.

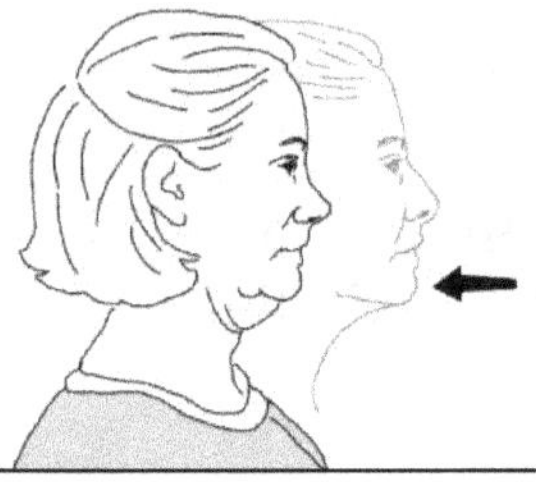

☐ **Upper Back Stretch**
Pull your elbows back and squeeze your shoulder blades. Hold for a count of _______.

Do ______ sets of ______.

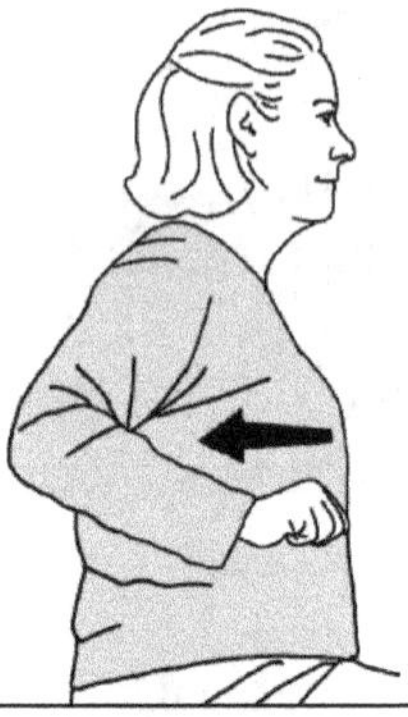

☐ **Chest Stretch**
Place your hands behind your neck. Slowly spread your elbows apart. Hold for a count of _______.

Do ______ sets of ______.

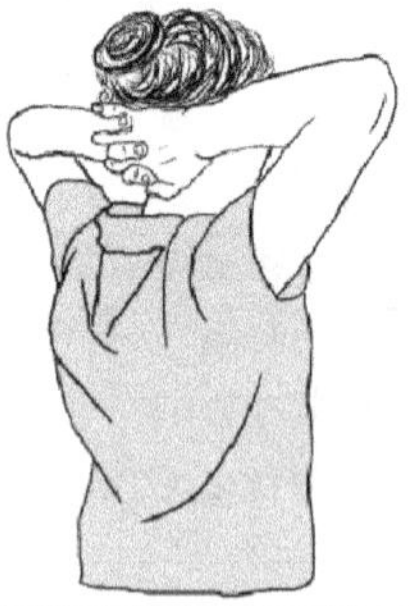

☐ **Stand Up and Sit Down**
Keep your back straight and your arms out in front. Stand up and sit down without using your arms.

Do ______ sets of ______.

Osteoporosis Extension Exercises

During the exercises, keep your back and neck straight and your stomach muscles tight.

☐ **Pelvic Tilt**
Lie on your back with knees bent. Flatten your back into the mat by tightening the muscles of your stomach and bottom. Hold for a count of ______.

Do _____ sets of _____.

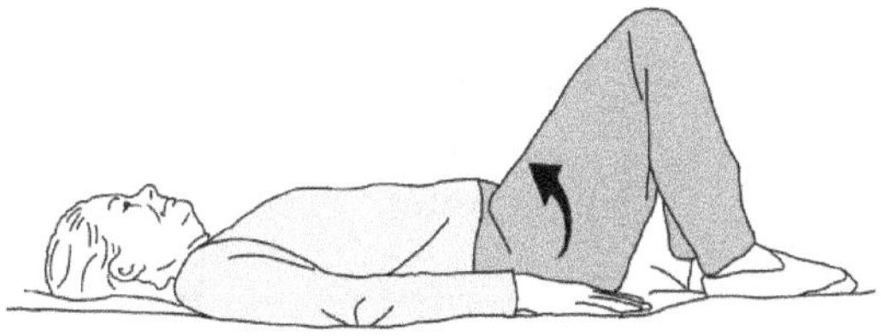

☐ **Stomach Bracing**
Lie on your back. Bend your knees. Draw your belly button in, then bear down and tighten your stomach muscles. Hold for a count of ______.

Do _____ sets of _____.

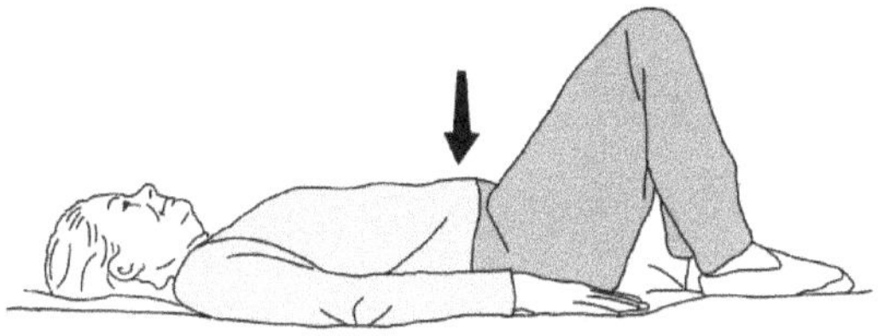

☐ **Back and Shoulder Stretch**
Lie on your back. Bend your knees. Tighten your stomach muscles and slowly stretch your arms above your head.

Do _____ sets of _____.

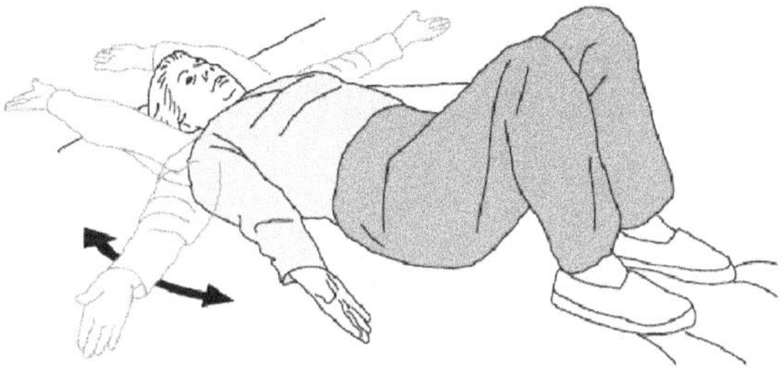

☐ **Bridge**
Bend both knees and place feet flat. Squeeze your hip muscles and lift your hips up from the bed. Hold for a count of _____.

Do _____ sets of _____.

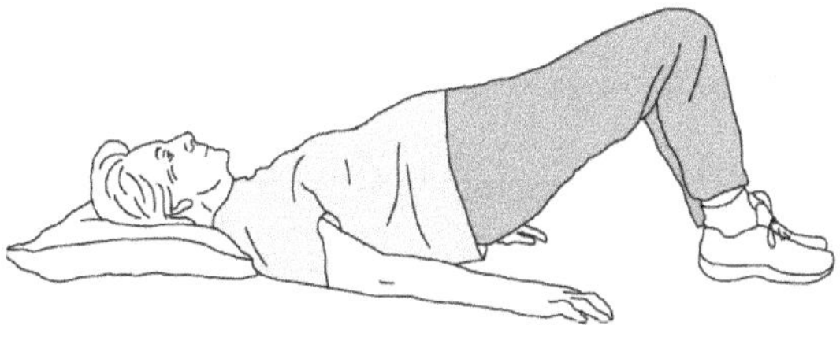

Occupational Therapy TOOLKIT

Parkinson's Disease Exercises

Name: ________________________________

Date: ________________________________

Therapist: ____________________________

Phone number: (_____)______________________

Do the checked exercises _____ times per day, _____ days a week.

Exercise slowly and smoothly.

Use good posture. Keep your stomach muscles tight and your back straight.

Do not hold your breath during exercise. Count aloud if needed.

Sore muscles lasting a few days and feeling tired are normal after exercise. Exhaustion, sore joints, and painful muscle pulls are not normal. If you have these symptoms, do not exercise until you talk with your therapist.

If you have chest tightness or pain, shortness of breath, feel dizzy, faint, or sick to your stomach, stop and call emergency services at _____.

Notes:

Parkinson's Disease Exercises

☐ Raise your eyebrows, and then frown.

Do ______ sets of ______.

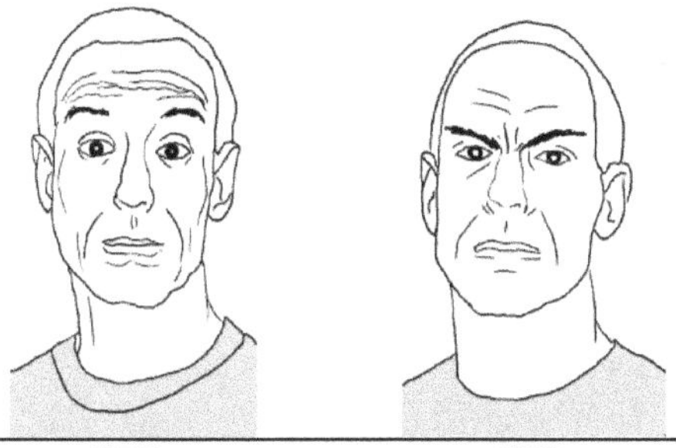

☐ Close your eyes tight, and then open wide.

Do ______ sets of ______.

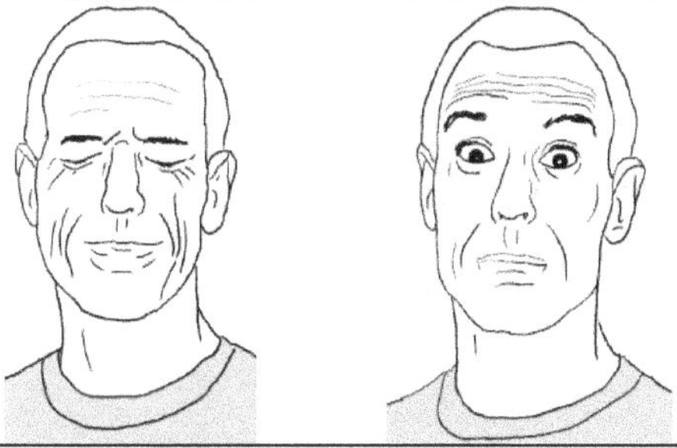

☐ Smile, and then pucker your lips.

Do ______ sets of ______.

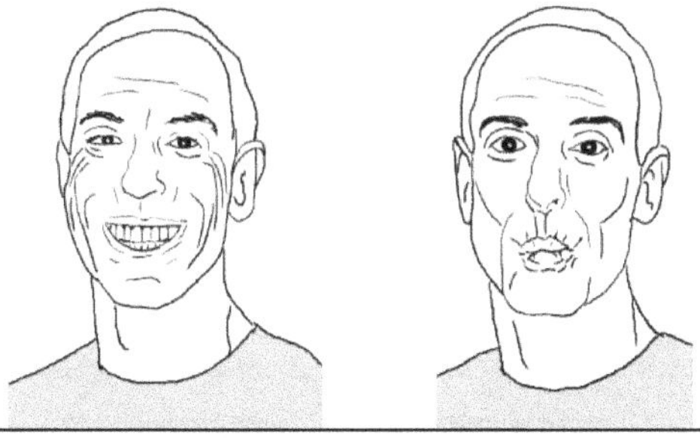

☐ Open your mouth wide, and then close.

Do ______ sets of ______.

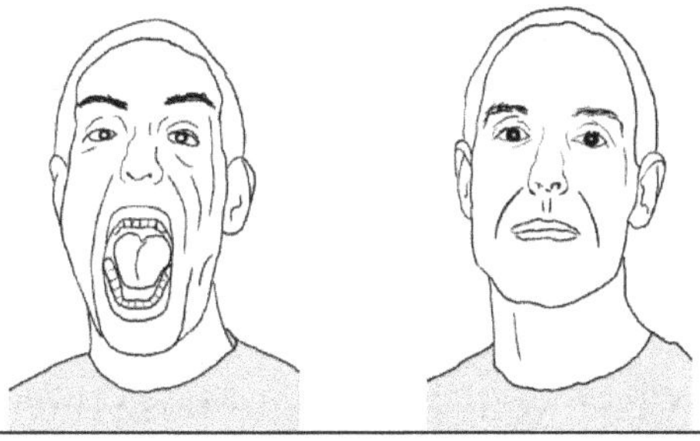

☐ Lick your lips.

Do ______ sets of ______.

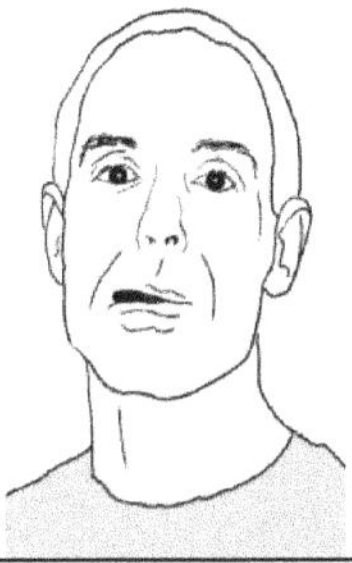

Parkinson's Disease Exercises

☐ Turn your head side to side.

Do ______ sets of ______.

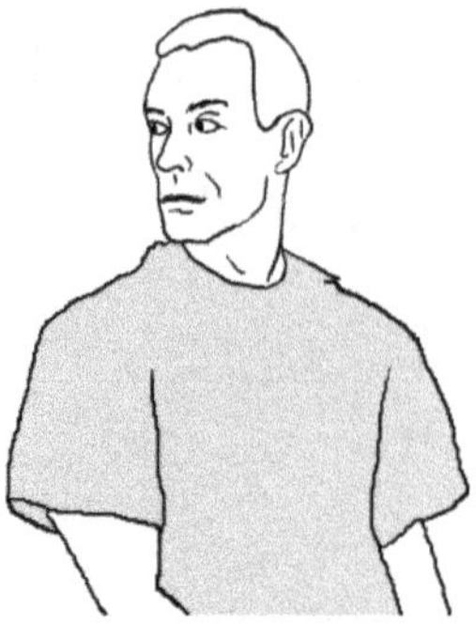

☐ Look up and then look forward.

Do ______ sets of ______.

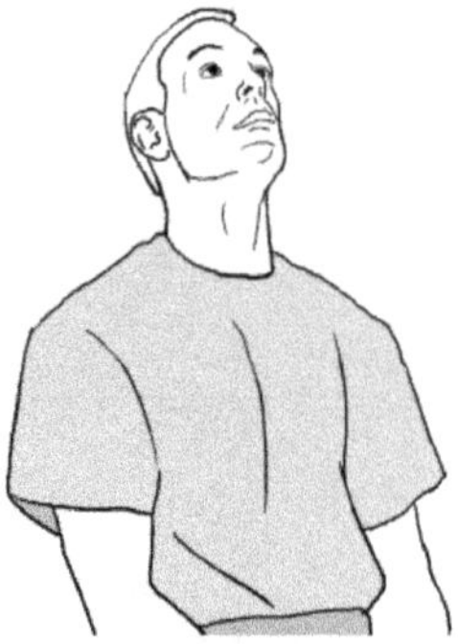

☐ Pull your shoulders back.

Do ______ sets of ______.

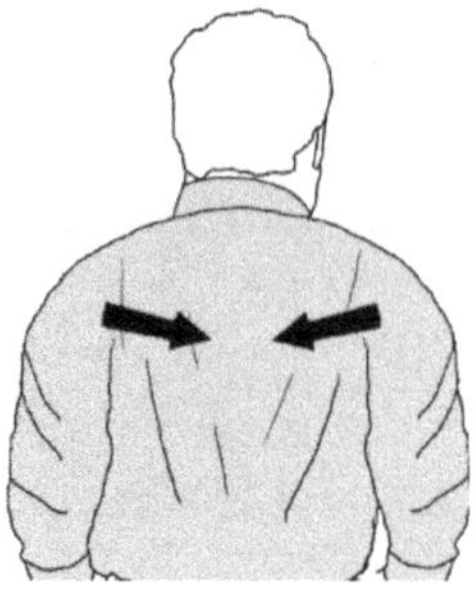

☐ Clasp your hands and raise them over your head.

Do ______ sets of ______.

Parkinson's Disease Exercises

☐ Turn one hand palm up and the other palm down.

Do ______ sets of ______.

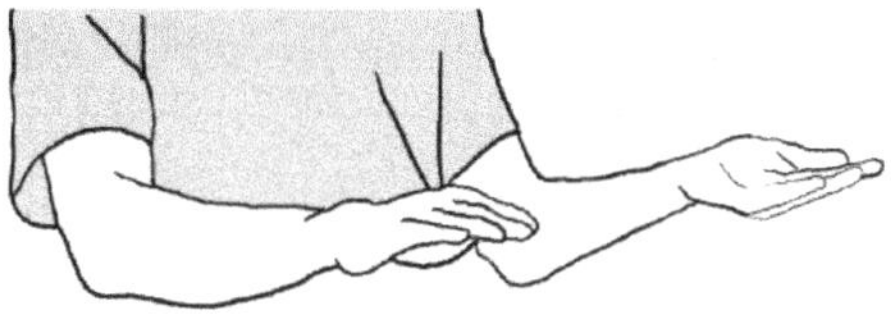

☐ Make circles with your hands. Move one way and then the other.

Do ______ sets of ______.

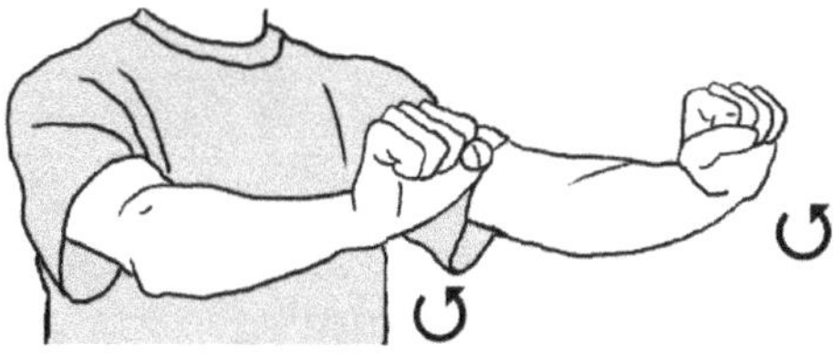

☐ Bend one hand up toward the ceiling and the other down toward the floor.

Do ______ sets of ______.

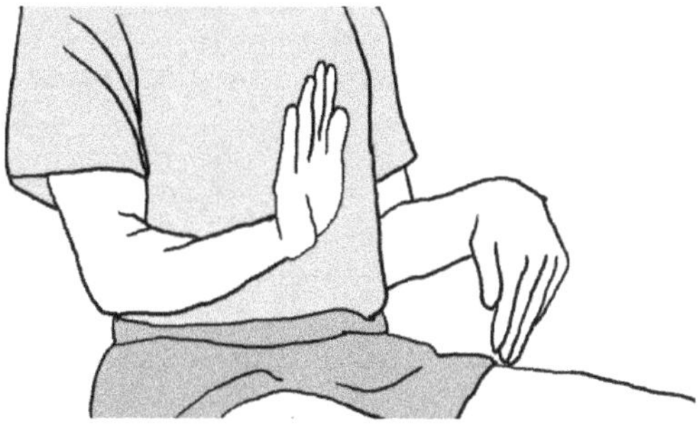

☐ Open one hand. Make a fist with the other hand.

Do ______ sets of ______.

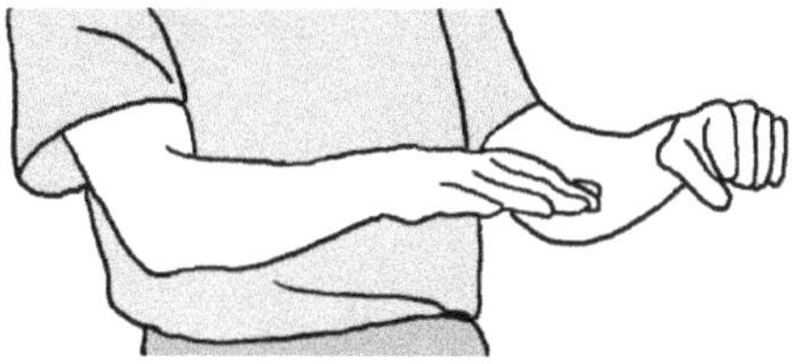

*

☐ Touch your thumb to each finger, one at a time.

Do ______ sets of ______.

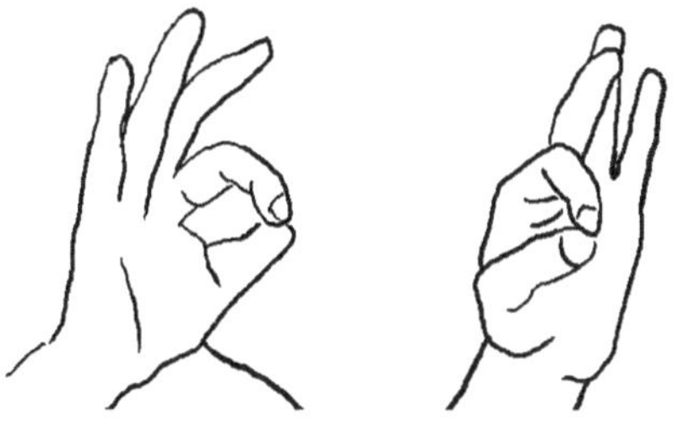

Parkinson's Disease Exercises

☐ Sit with both feet on floor. Cross your arms and raise them to shoulder height. Twist to the right. Hold to a count of ______. Twist to the left. Hold to a count of ______.

Do ______ sets of ______.

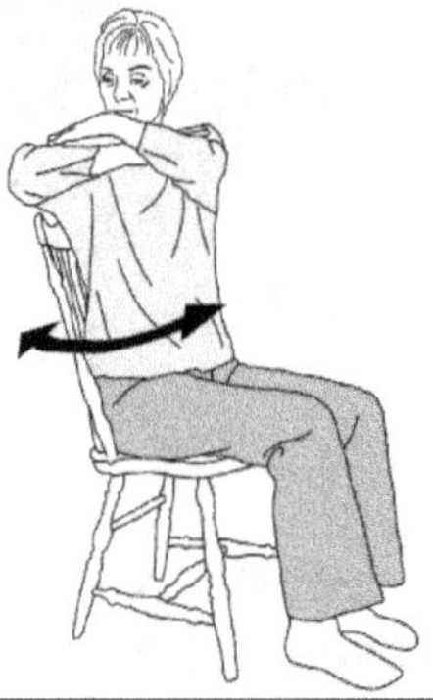

☐ Sit with both feet on floor. Bend to the side. Hold to a count of ______.

Do ______ sets of ______.
Repeat to the other side.

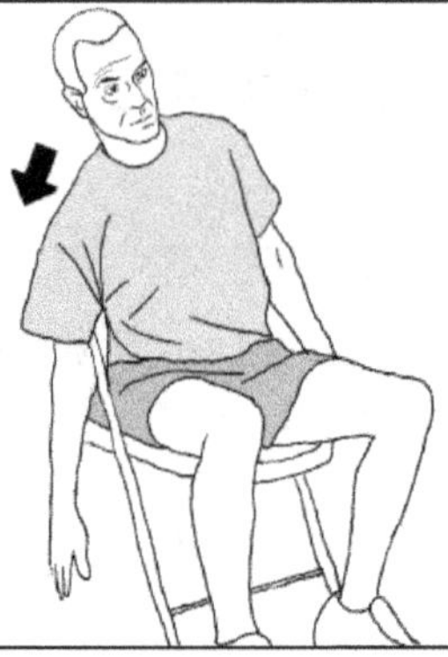

☐ Sit in chair and extend your right leg forward. Keep knee straight and gently lean forward toward your toes. Hold to a count of ______.

Do ______ sets of ______.
Repeat with your left leg.

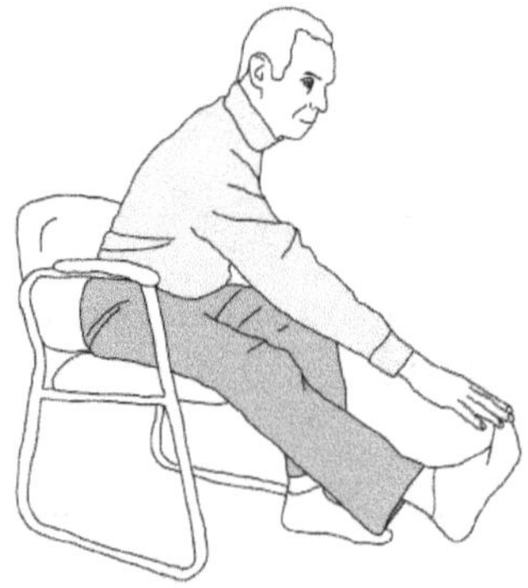

☐ Sit with both feet on floor. Bring the right leg up to your left knee. Hold to a count of ______.

Do ______ sets of ______.
Repeat with your left leg.

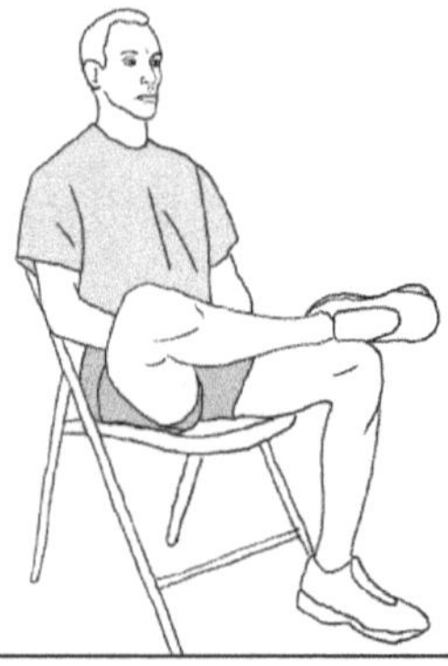

Parkinson's Disease Exercises

☐ Sit in chair and extend your right leg forward. Make circles with your right foot. Move one way and then the other.

Do _____ sets of _____.
Repeat with your left foot.

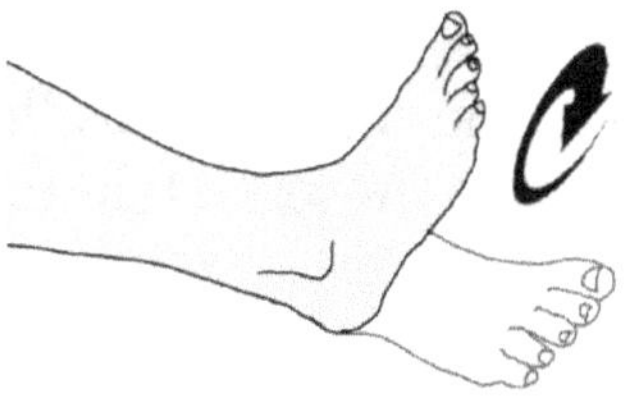

☐ Sit with feet flat on the floor and hands on the armrests of a sturdy chair. Straighten elbows to lift bottom off the chair. Keep most of your body weight on your arms. Hold to a count of _____.

Do _____ sets of _____.

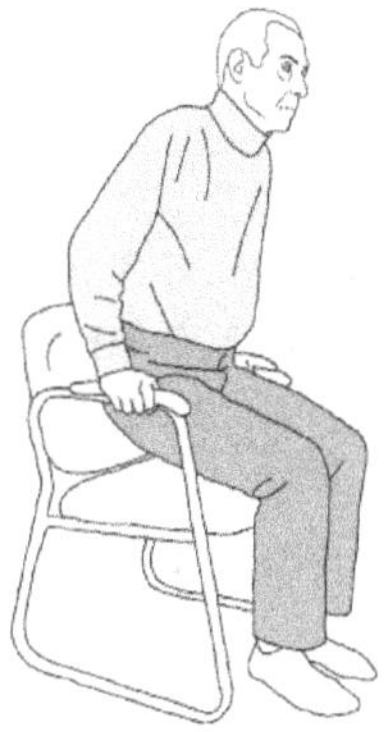

☐ Hold onto a stable object. Slide one foot back until your back leg is straight. Lean your weight forward onto your bent front knee. Hold for a count of _____.

Do _____ sets of _____.
Repeat on your other side.

☐ Hold onto a stable object. Rise onto your toes, lifting your heels off the floor. Then rock back onto your heels, lifting your toes off the floor.

Do _____ sets of _____.

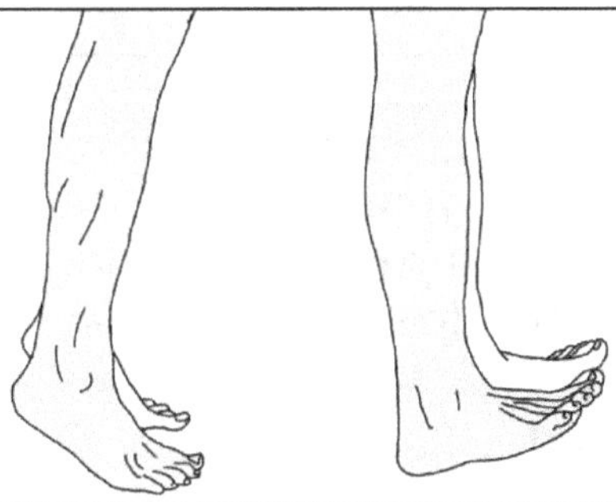

Occupational Therapy TOOLKIT

Parkinson's Disease Exercises

☐ Lie on your back with your knees bent. Place arms out to your sides. Turn your head to the right as you allow both legs to fall over to the left. Hold for a count of _______.

Do ______ sets of ______.
Repeat to the other side

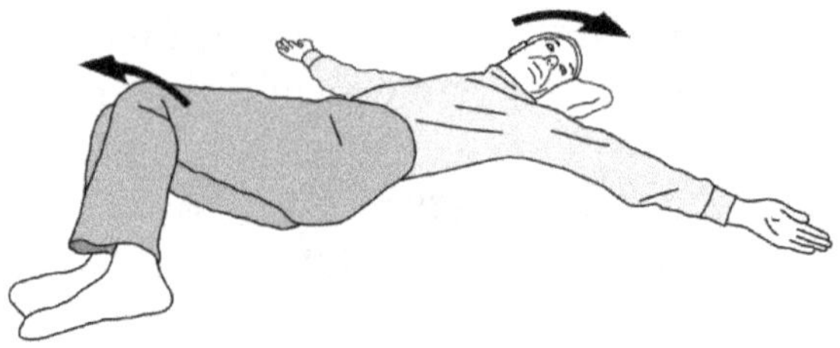

☐ Bend both knees and place feet flat. Tighten stomach muscles and raise your hips. Hold for a count of _______.

Do ______ sets of ______.

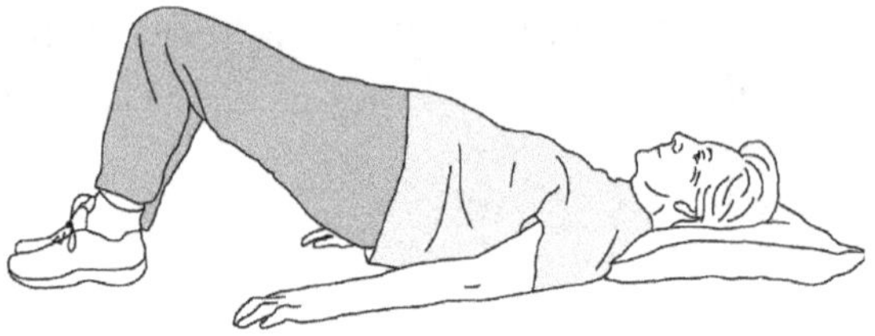

☐ Lie on your back with your knees bent. Allow your knees to fall out to the sides, and then bring them back together.

Do ______ sets of ______.

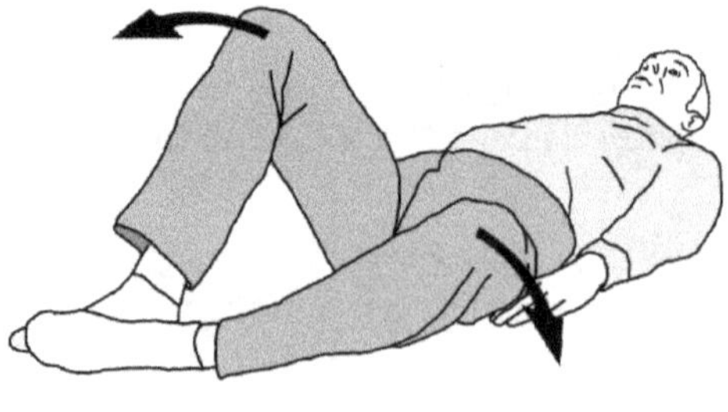

☐ Lie on your back with your knees bent. Bring your left knee to your chest and extend your right leg down toward the bed. Hold for a count of _______.

Do ______ sets of ______.
Repeat on your other side.

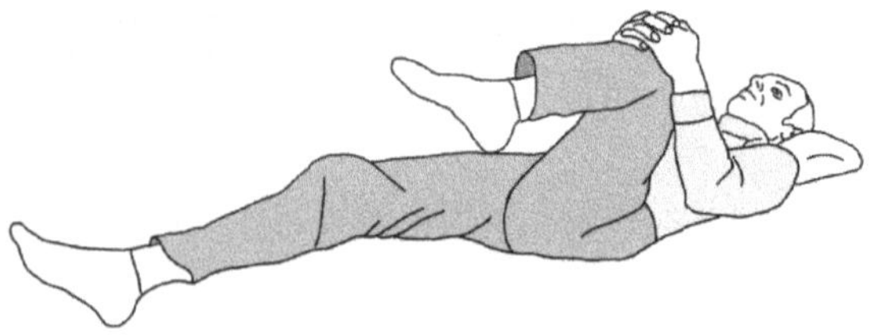

Passive Range of Motion

Name: ______________________________

Date: ______________________________

Therapist: ______________________________

Phone number: (_____)____________________

Do the checked exercises _____ times per day, _____ days a week.

Do the exercises smoothly and gently. Never force, jerk, or over stretch a muscle.

Do all exercises in order.

Make these exercises a part of the person's daily routine. Do the exercises at the same time every day. Do the exercises when you bath the person or while they are watching TV. This will make the time go faster and help the person relax. You may want to break the exercises into two or three sessions.

Stop the exercises if the person feels pain. Sore muscles lasting a few days and feeling tired are normal after exercise. Exhaustion, sore joints, and painful muscle pulls are not normal. If the person has these symptoms, do not exercise until you talk with the therapist

If the person has chest tightness or pain, shortness of breath, feel dizzy, faint, or sick to their stomach, stop and call emergency services at _____.

Notes:

____

____

____

____

____

Passive Range of Motion - Neck and Back

☐ **Chin to Chest**
Gently move the chin toward the chest.

Repeat ______ times.

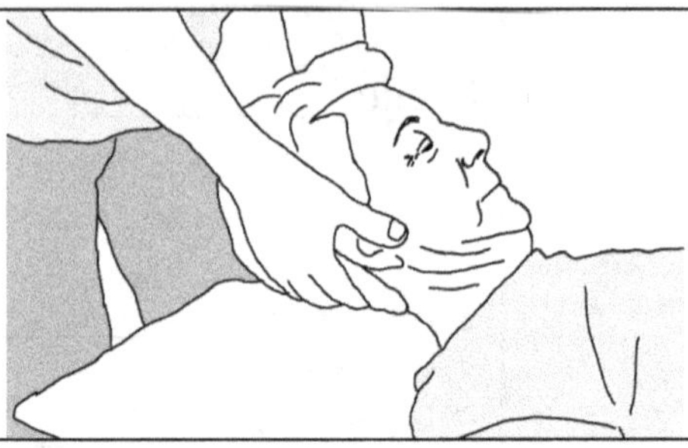

☐ **Head Turns**
Gently turn the head side to side.

Repeat ______ times.

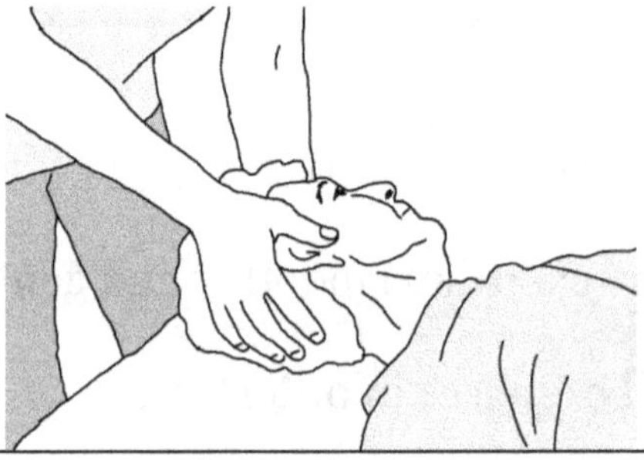

☐ **Low Back Stretch**
Bend the knees and lift both legs. Gently move both legs toward the chest.

Repeat ______ times.

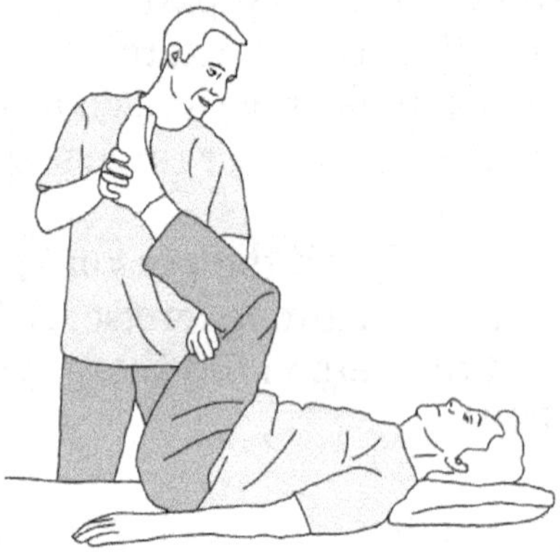

☐ **Back Rotation**
Bend the knees, place one hand on the shoulder and one hand on the knees. Keep the shoulder on the bed. Gently rotate the knees to one side.

Repeat ______ times on each side.

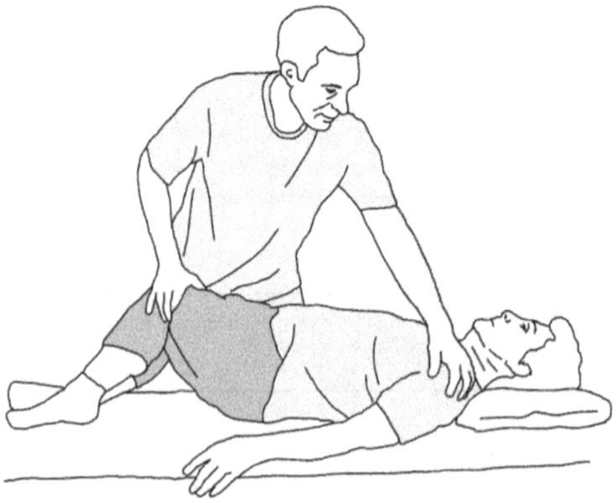

Occupational Therapy TOOLKIT

Passive Range of Motion - Shoulder

☐ **Shoulder Blade**
Roll the person onto the side. Place one hand on the shoulder and the other on the shoulder blade. Gently move the shoulder blade up and down and back and forth. Repeat on the other side.

Repeat _____ times on each side.

☐ **Front Raise**
Straighten the arm to the side. Turn the palm in toward the body. The thumb should point toward the head of the bed. Gently move the arm up toward the ceiling to shoulder level. Repeat with the other side.

Repeat _____ times on each side.

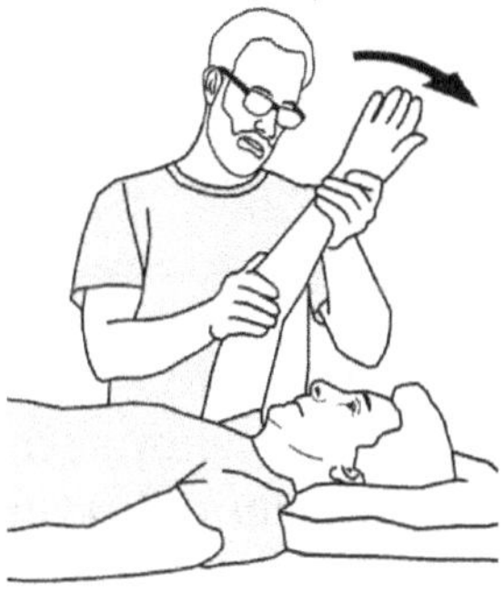

☐ **Side Raise**
Bring the arm out to the side. Gently move it out from the body to shoulder level. Repeat with the other side.

Repeat _____ times on each side.

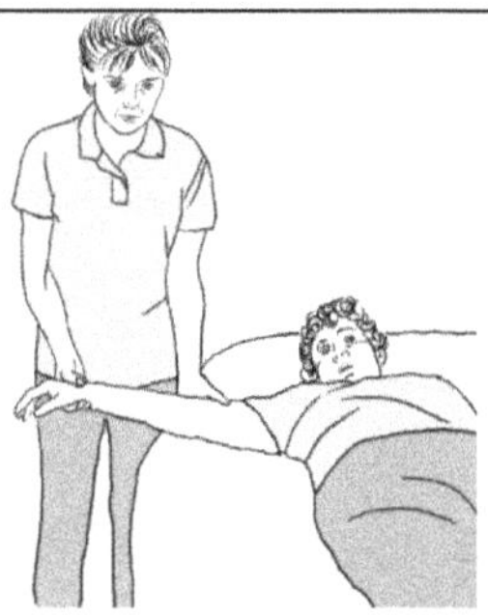

☐ **Arm Turns**
Bring the arm out to the side. Bend the elbow so the fingers point up. Gently rotate the arm so the fingers point down toward the toes. Then rotate the arm so the fingers point up toward the head of the bed. Repeat with the other side.

Repeat _____ times on each side.

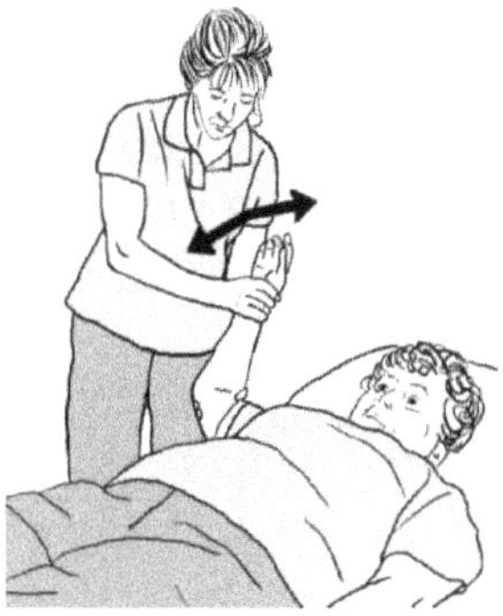

Passive Range of Motion - Elbow, Forearm and Wrist

☐ **Elbow Bend**
Hold the arm at the side. Gently bend and straighten the elbow. Repeat with the other side.

Repeat ______ times on each side.

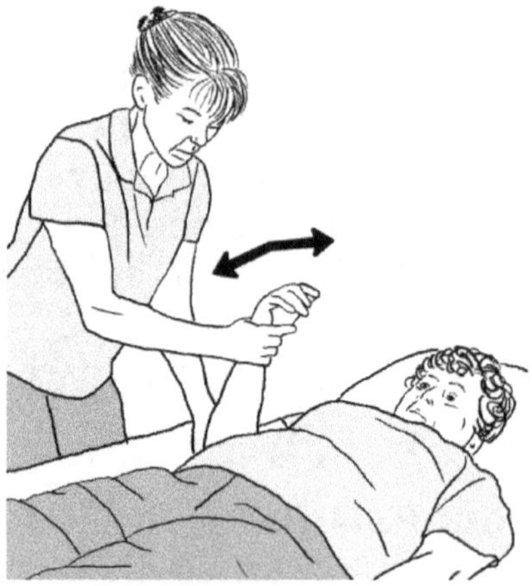

☐ **Forearm Turns**
Hold the elbow against the side. Gently turn the forearm palm up and down. Repeat with the other side.

Repeat ______ times on each side.

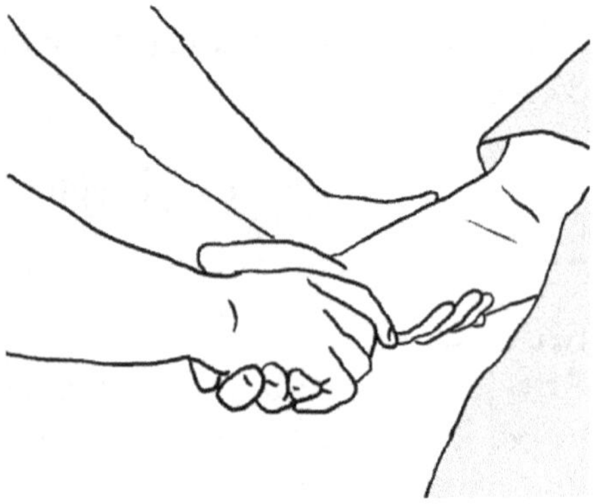

☐ **Wrist Turns**
Gently bend the wrist back and forth.
Gently move the hand side to side.
Gently rotate the hand in a circle.
Repeat with the other side.

Repeat ______ times on each side.

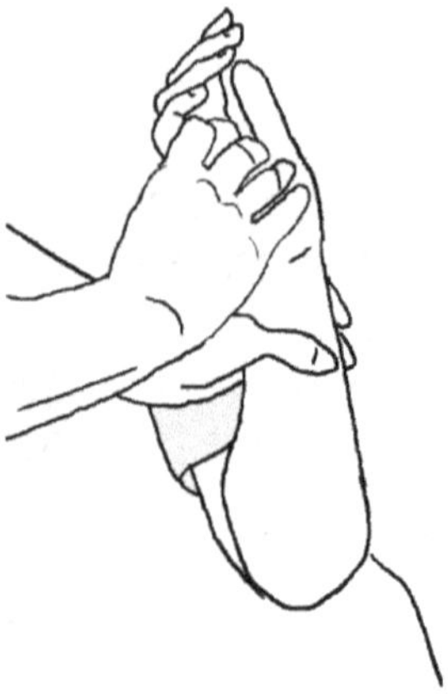

Passive Range of Motion - Fingers and Thumb

☐ **Make a Fist**
Gently bend the hand into a fist and straighten. Repeat with the other side.

Repeat ______ times on each side.

☐ **Finger Spread**
Gently spread each finger apart. Repeat with the other side.

Repeat ______ times on each side.

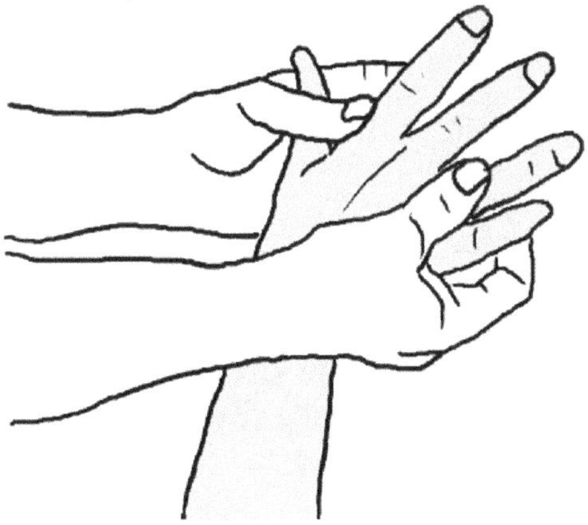

☐ **Thumb Across**
Gently move the thumb across the palm and back. Repeat with the other side.

Repeat ______ times on each side.

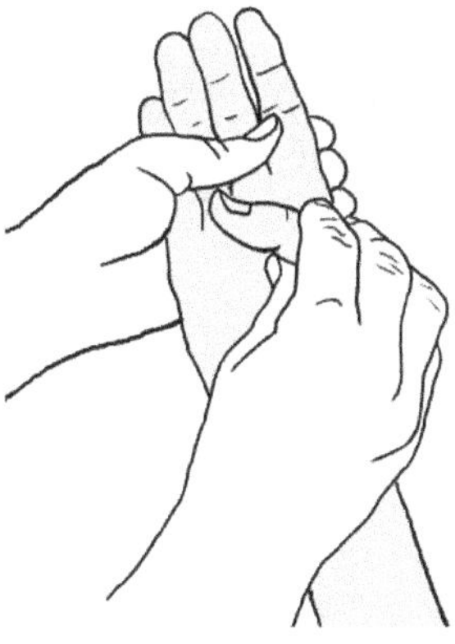

Occupational Therapy TOOLKIT

Passive Range of Motion - Hip and Knee

☐ **Leg Bend**
Gently bend the hip and knee up toward the chest. Repeat with the other side.

Repeat ______ times on each side.

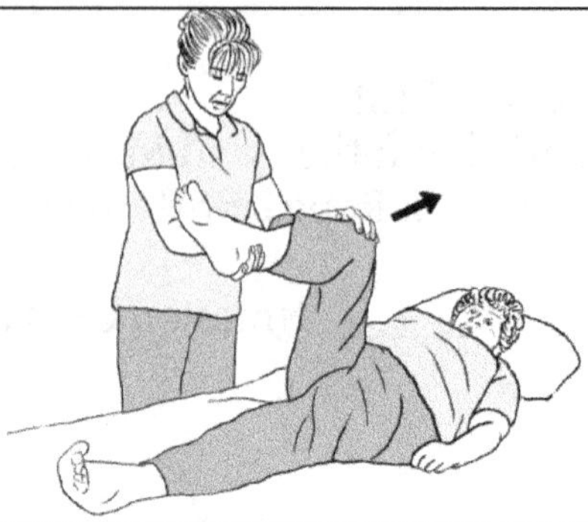

☐ **Side Raise**
Gently move the leg out to the side. Repeat with the other side.

Repeat ______ times on each side.

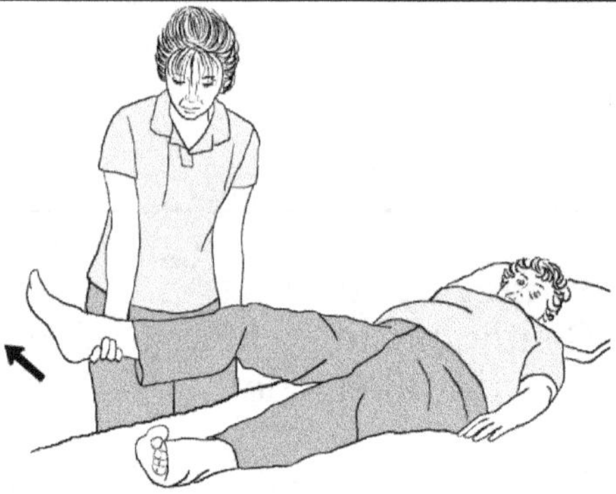

☐ **Hip Turns**
Gently bend the knee and cross the leg over the other leg. Repeat with the other side.

Repeat ______ times on each side.

☐ **Back of Leg Stretch**
Raise the leg. Gently stretch the back of the knee Repeat with the other side.

Repeat ______ times on each side.

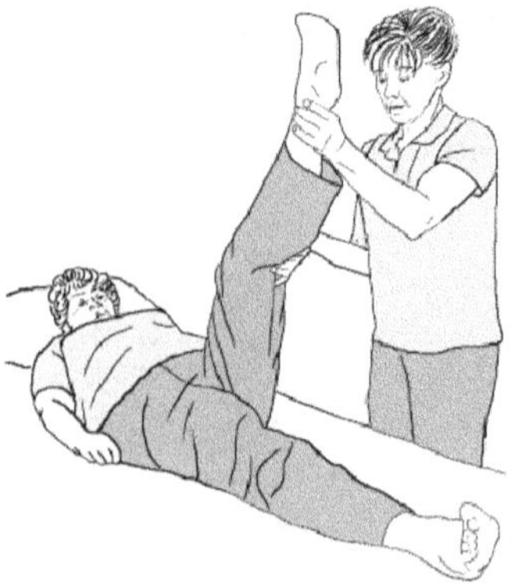

Occupational Therapy TOOLKIT

Passive Range of Motion - Ankle and Foot

☐ **Ankle Bends**
Gently move the ankle back and forth. Repeat with the other side.

Repeat ______ times on each side.

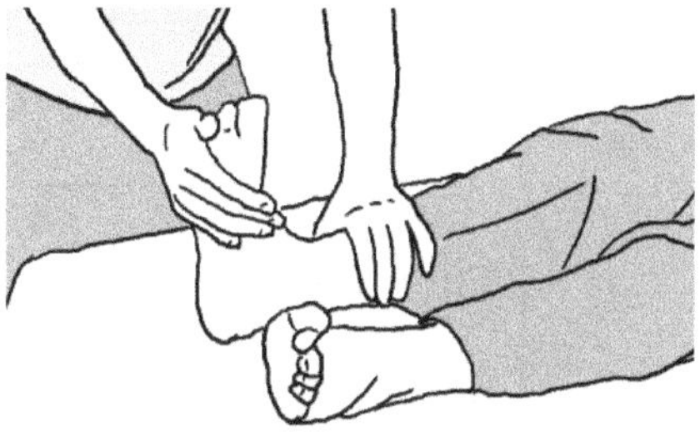

☐ **Ankle Turns**
Gently turn the foot and ankle in a circle. Repeat with the other side.

Repeat ______ times on each side.

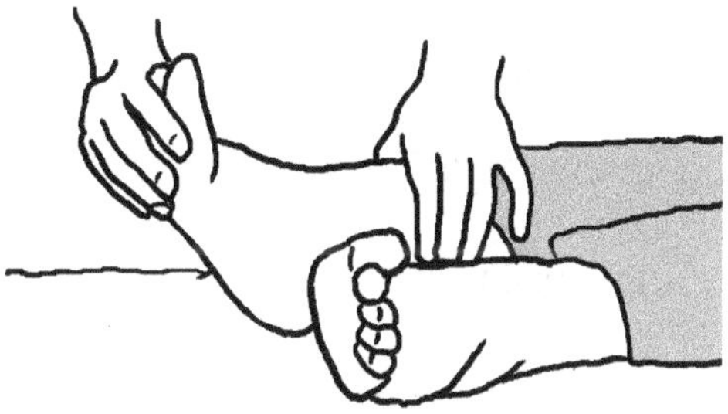

☐ **Toe Curls**
Gently curl the toes. Repeat with the other side.

Repeat ______ times on each side.

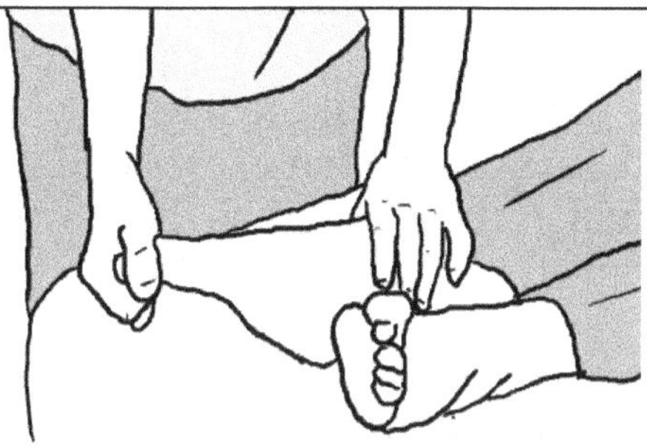

☐ **Toe Spread**
Gently spread each toe apart. Repeat with the other side.

Repeat ______ times on each side.

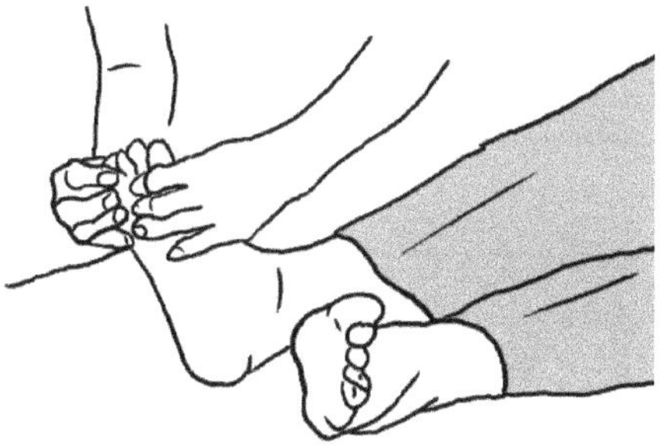

Passive Range of Motion - Left Side Weakness

Name: ______________________________

Date: ______________________________

Therapist: ______________________________

Phone number: (_____)______________________

Do the checked exercises _____ times per day, _____ days a week.

Do the exercises smoothly and gently. Never force, jerk, or over stretch a muscle.

Do all exercises in order.

Make these exercises a part of the person's daily routine. Do the exercises at the same time every day. Do the exercises when you bath the person or while they are watching TV. This will make the time go faster and help the person relax. You may want to break the exercises into two or three sessions.

Stop the exercises if the person feels pain. Sore muscles lasting a few days and feeling tired are normal after exercise. Exhaustion, sore joints, and painful muscle pulls are not normal. If the person has these symptoms, do not exercise until you talk with the therapist

If the person has chest tightness or pain, shortness of breath, feel dizzy, faint, or sick to their stomach, stop and call emergency services at _____.

Notes:

____

____

____

____

____

Passive Range of Motion - Left Side Weakness
Neck and Back

☐ **Chin to Chest**
Gently move the chin toward the chest.

Repeat ______ times.

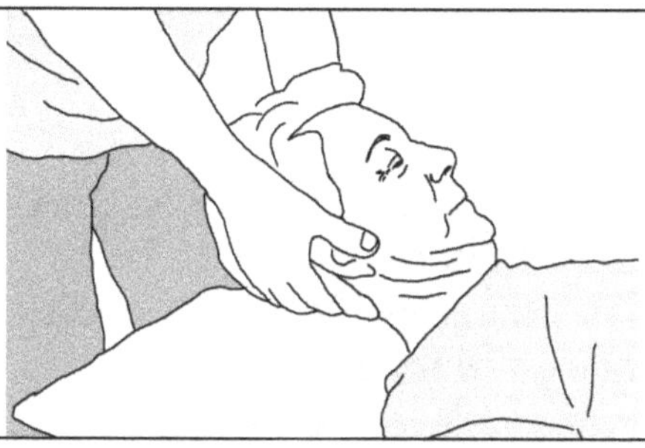

☐ **Head Turns**
Gently turn the head side to side.

Repeat ______ times on each side.

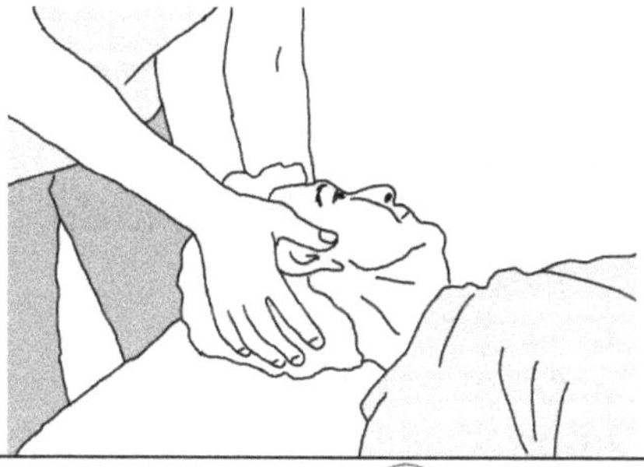

☐ **Low Back Flexion**
Bend the knees and lift both legs. Gently move both legs toward the chest.

Repeat ______ times.

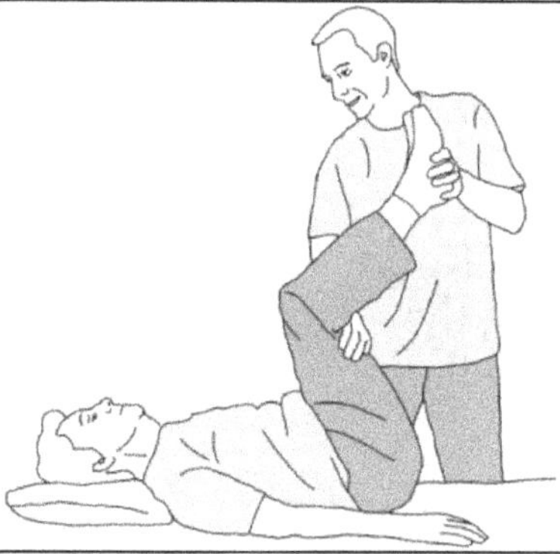

☐ **Back Rotation**
Bend the knees, place one hand on the shoulder and one hand on the knees. Keep the shoulder on the bed. Gently rotate the knees to one side.

Repeat ______ times on each side

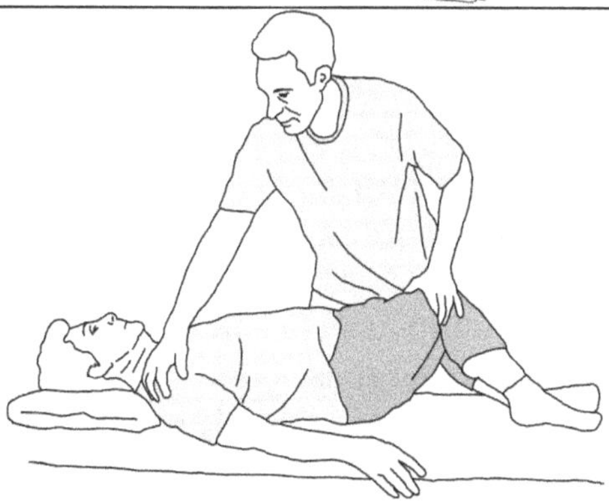

Passive Range of Motion - Left Side Weakness
Shoulder

☐ **Shoulder Blade**
Roll the person onto the right side. Place one hand on the shoulder and the other on the shoulder blade. Gently move the left shoulder blade up and down and back and forth.

Repeat ______ times.

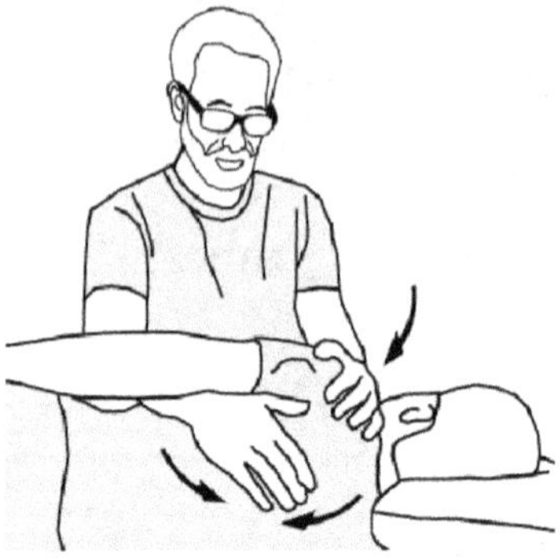

☐ **Front Raise**
Straighten the left arm to the side. Turn the palm in toward the body. The thumb should point toward the head of the bed. Gently move the arm up toward the ceiling to shoulder level.

Repeat ______ times.

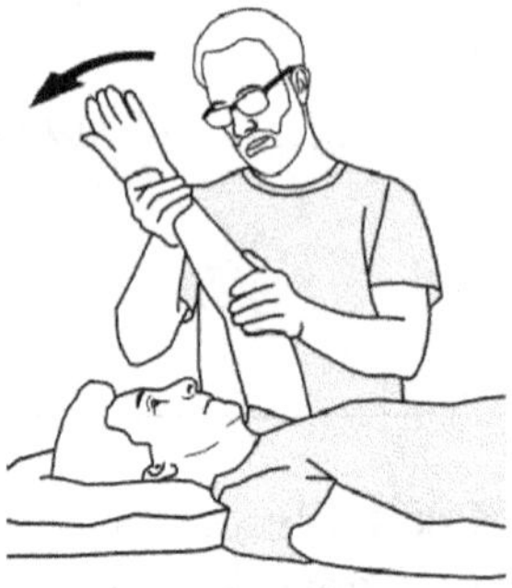

☐ **Side Raise**
Bring the left arm out to the side. Gently move it out from body to shoulder level.

Repeat ______ times.

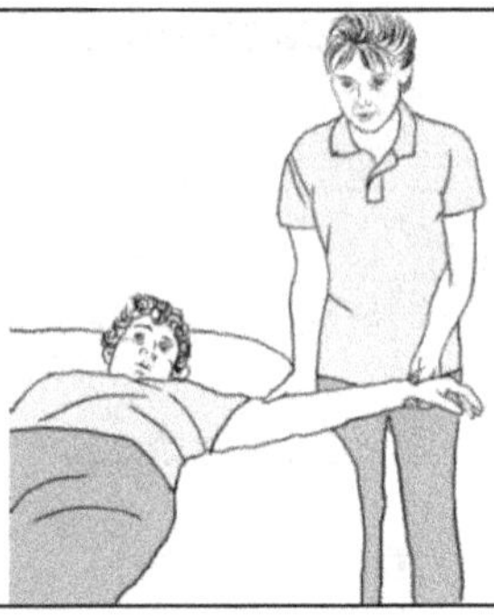

☐ **Arm Turns**
Bring the left arm out to the side. Bend the elbow so the fingers point up. Gently rotate the arm so the fingers point down toward the toes. Then rotate the arm so the fingers point up toward the head of the bed.

Repeat ______ times.

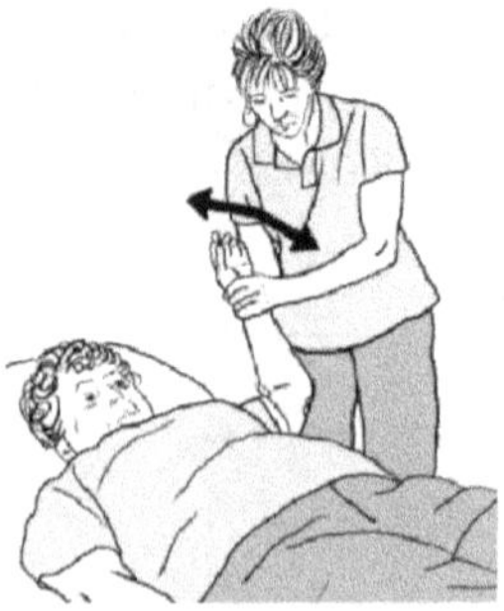

Occupational Therapy TOOLKIT

Passive Range of Motion - Left Side Weakness
Elbow, Forearm and Wrist

☐ **Elbow Bend**
Hold the left arm at the side. Gently bend and straighten the elbow.

Repeat ______ times.

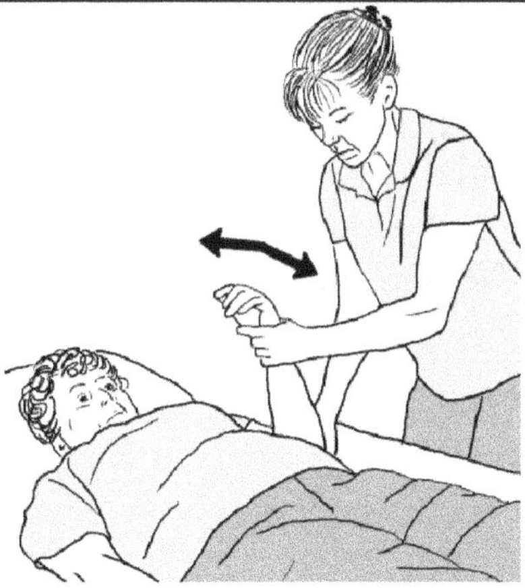

☐ **Forearm Turns**
Hold the left elbow against the side. Gently turn the forearm palm up and down.

Repeat ______ times.

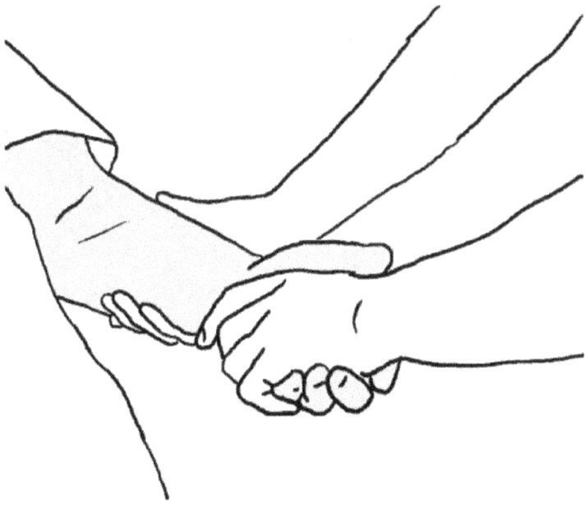

☐ **Wrist Turns**
Gently bend the left wrist back and forth.
Gently move the left wrist side to side.
Gently rotate the left wrist in a circle.

Repeat ______ times.

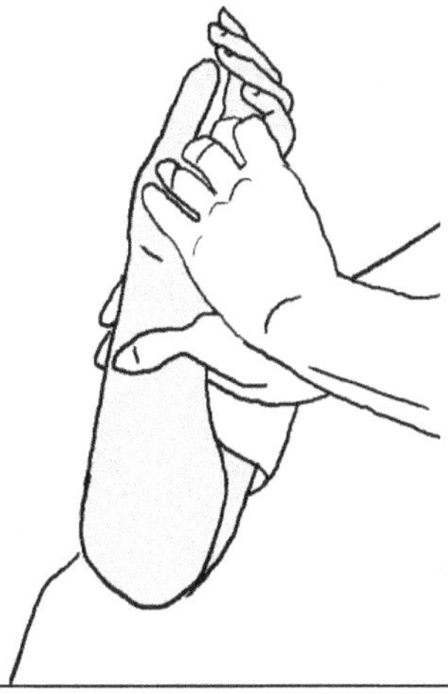

Passive Range of Motion - Left Side Weakness
Fingers and Thumb

☐ **Make a Fist**
Gently bend the left hand into a fist and straighten.

Repeat ______ times.

☐ **Finger Spread**
Gently spread each finger apart.

Repeat ______ times.

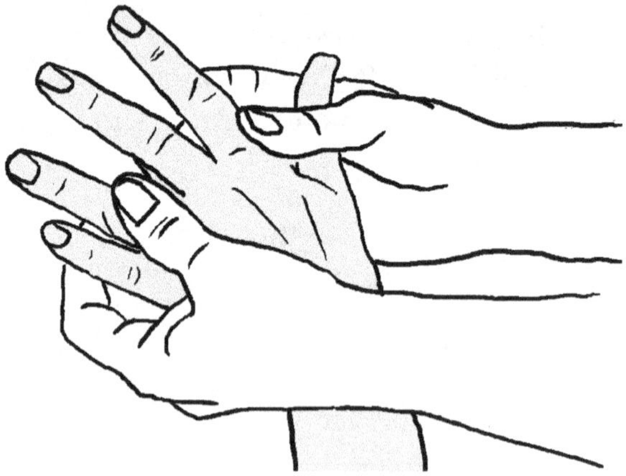

☐ **Thumb Across**
Move the left thumb across the palm and back.

Repeat ______ times.

Passive Range of Motion - Left Side Weakness
Hip and Knee

☐ **Leg Bend**
Gently bend the left hip and knee up toward their chest.

Repeat ______ times.

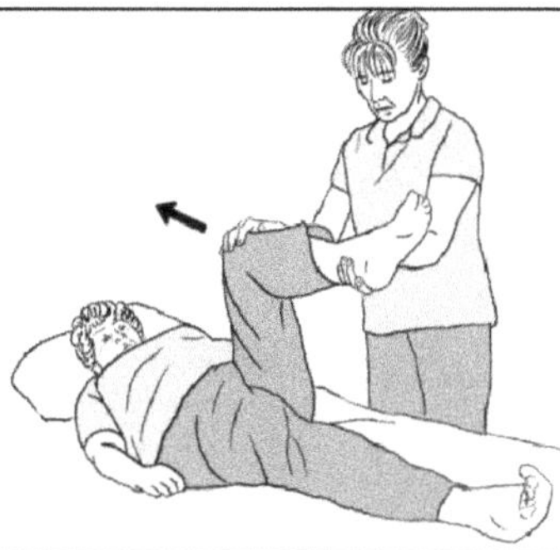

☐ **Side Raise**
Gently move the left leg out to the side.

Repeat ______ times.

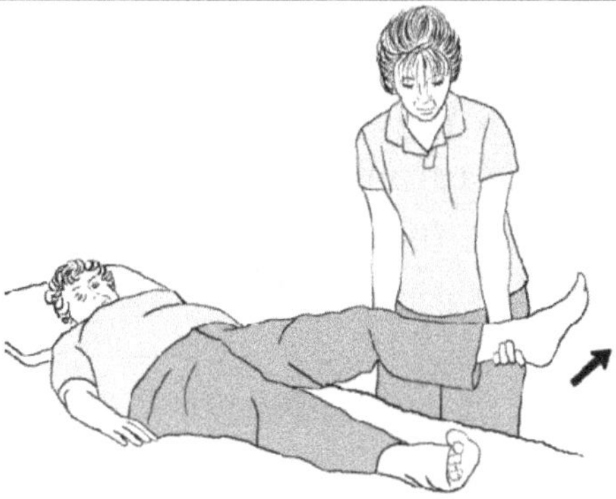

☐ **Hip Turns**
Gently bend the left knee and cross the leg over the other leg.

Repeat ______ times.

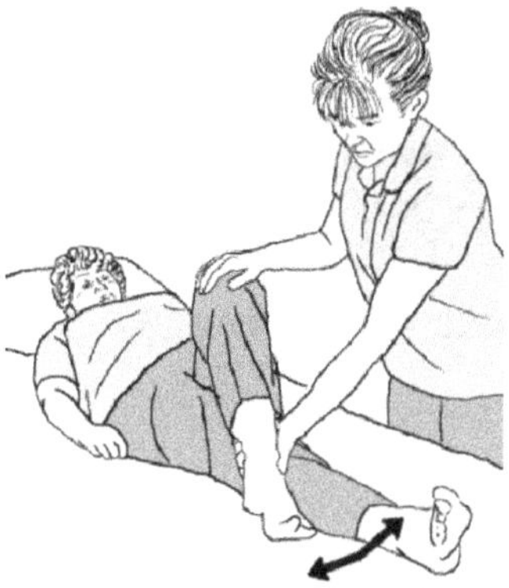

☐ **Back of Leg Stretch**
Raise the left leg. Gently stretch the back of the knee.

Repeat ______ times.

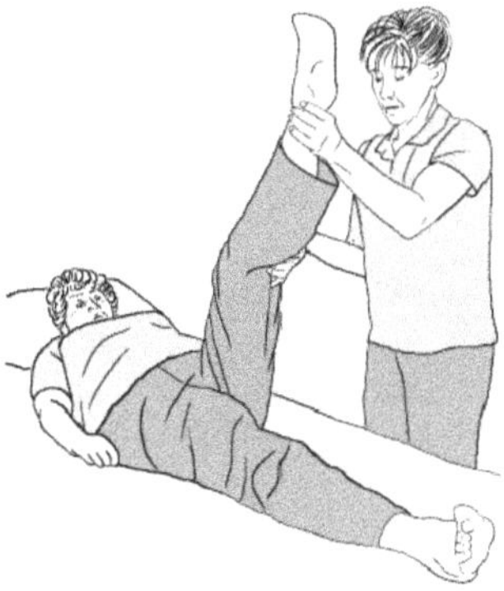

Passive Range of Motion - Left Side Weakness
Ankle and Foot

☐ **Ankle Bends**
Gently bend the left ankle back and forth.

Repeat ______ times.

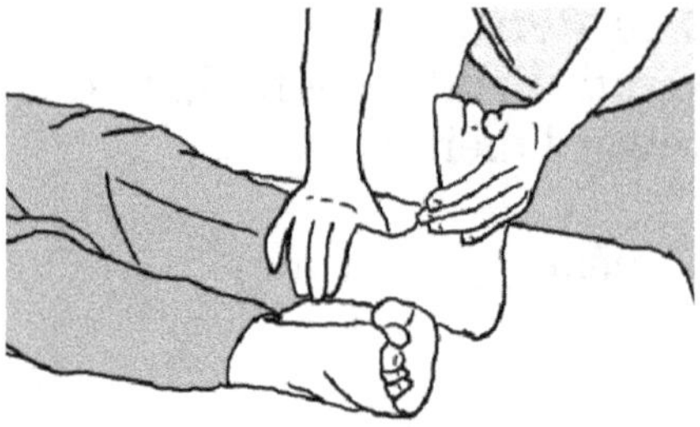

☐ **Ankle Turns**
Gently turn the left ankle in a circle.

Repeat ______ times.

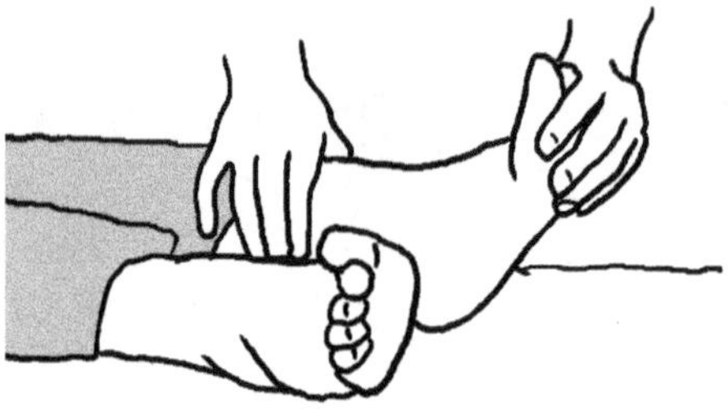

☐ **Toe Curls**
Gently curl the toes of the left foot.

Repeat ______ times.

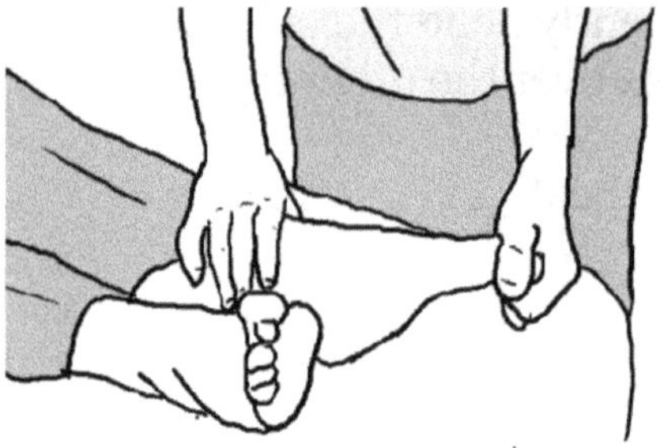

☐ **Toe Spread**
Gently spread each toe of the left foot.

Repeat ______ times.

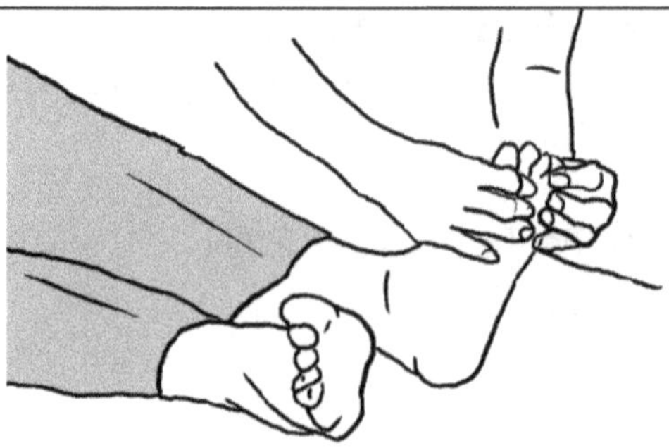

Occupational Therapy TOOLKIT

Passive Range of Motion - Right Side Weakness

Name: ______________________________

Date: ______________________________

Therapist: ______________________________

Phone number: (_____)____________________

Do the checked exercises _____ times per day, _____ days a week.

Do the exercises smoothly and gently. Never force, jerk, or over stretch a muscle.

Do all exercises in order.

Make these exercises a part of the person's daily routine. Do the exercises at the same time every day. Do the exercises when you bath the person or while they are watching TV. This will make the time go faster and help the person relax. You may want to break the exercises into two or three sessions.

Stop the exercises if the person feels pain. Sore muscles lasting a few days and feeling tired are normal after exercise. Exhaustion, sore joints, and painful muscle pulls are not normal. If the person has these symptoms, do not exercise until you talk with the therapist

If the person has chest tightness or pain, shortness of breath, feel dizzy, faint, or sick to their stomach, stop and call emergency services at _____.

Notes:

____

____

____

____

____

Occupational Therapy TOOLKIT

Passive Range of Motion - Right Side Weakness
Neck and Back

☐ **Chin to Chest**
Gently move the chin toward the chest.

Repeat ______ times.

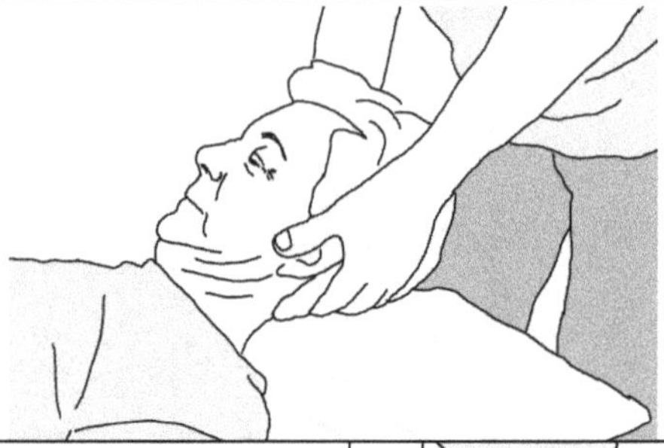

☐ **Head Turns**
Gently turn the head side to side.

Repeat ______ times on each side.

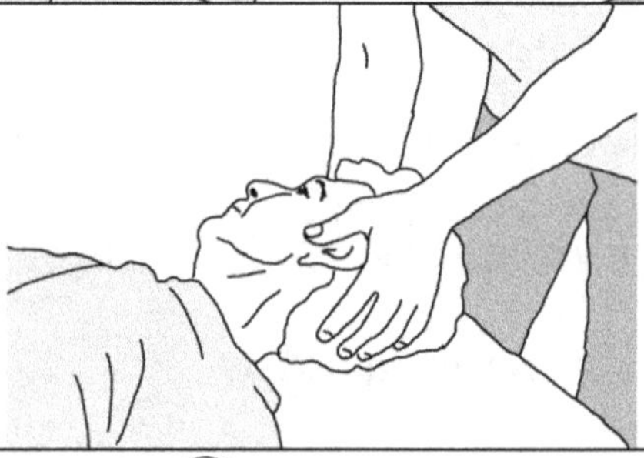

☐ **Low Back Flexion**
Bend the knees and lift both legs. Gently move both legs toward the chest.

Repeat ______ times.

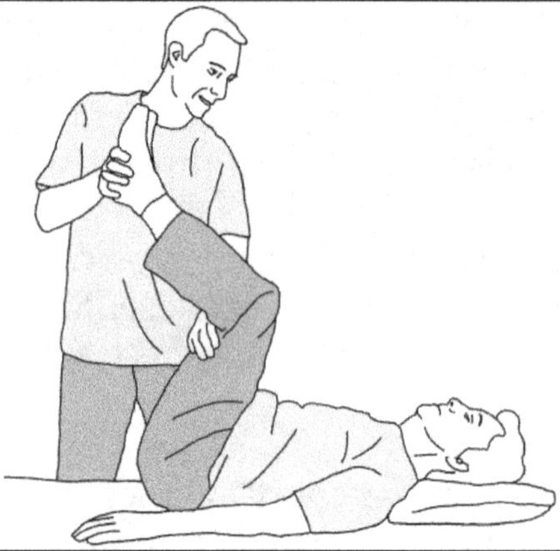

☐ **Back Rotation**
Bend the knees, place one hand on the shoulder and one hand on the knees. Keep the shoulder on the bed. Gently rotate the knees to one side.

Repeat ______ times on each side

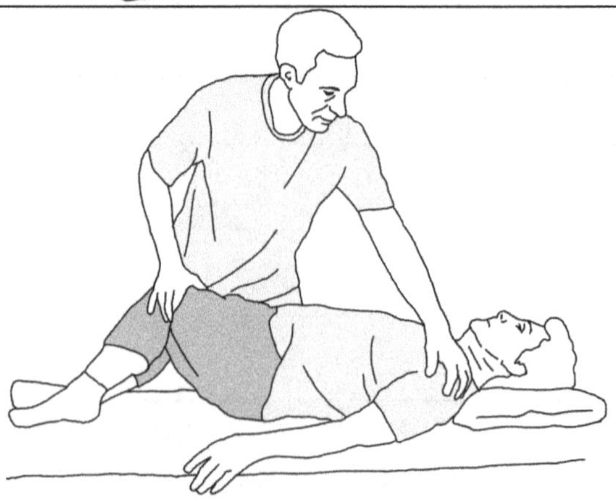

Passive Range of Motion - Right Side Weakness
Shoulder

☐ **Shoulder Blade**
Roll the person onto the left side. Place one hand on the shoulder and the other on the shoulder blade. Gently move the right shoulder blade up and down and back and forth.

Repeat ______ times.

☐ **Front Raise**
Straighten the right arm to the side. Turn the palm in toward the body. The thumb should point toward the head of the bed. Gently move the arm up toward the ceiling to shoulder level.

Repeat ______ times.

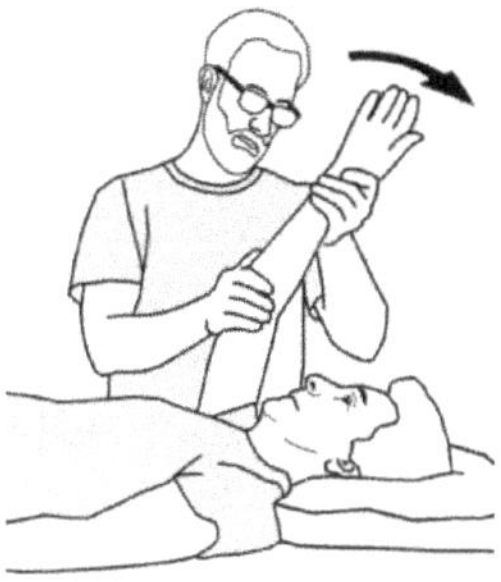

☐ **Side Raise**
Bring the right arm out to the side. Gently move it out from the body to shoulder level.

Repeat ______ times.

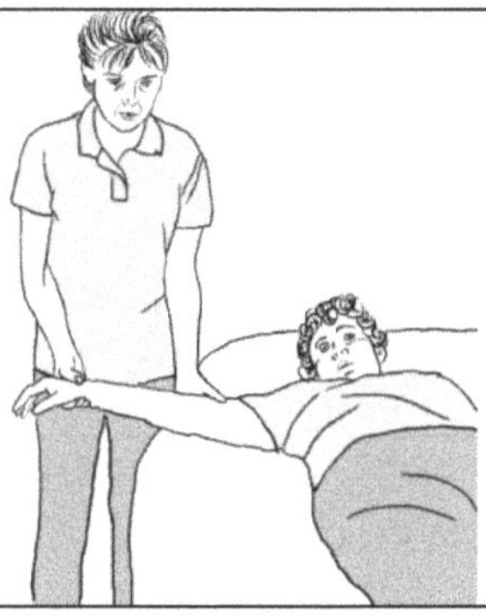

☐ **Arm Turns**
Bring the right arm out to the side. Bend the elbow so the fingers point up. Gently rotate the arm so the fingers point down toward the toes. Then rotate the arm so the fingers point up toward the head of the bed.

Repeat ______ times.

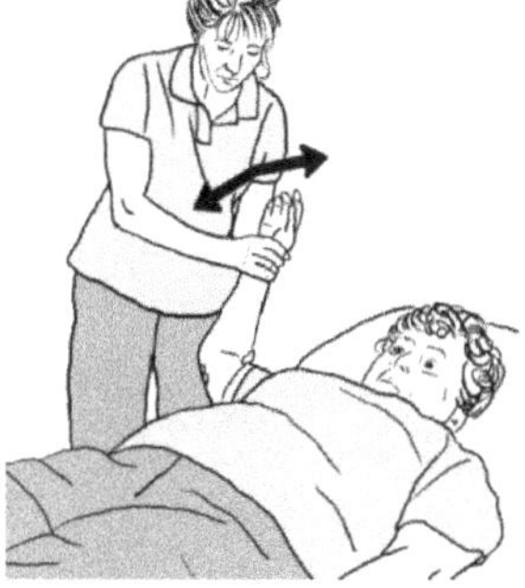

Passive Range of Motion - Right Side Weakness
Elbow, Forearm and Wrist

☐ **Elbow Bend**
Hold the right arm at the side. Gently bend and straighten the elbow.

Repeat ______ times.

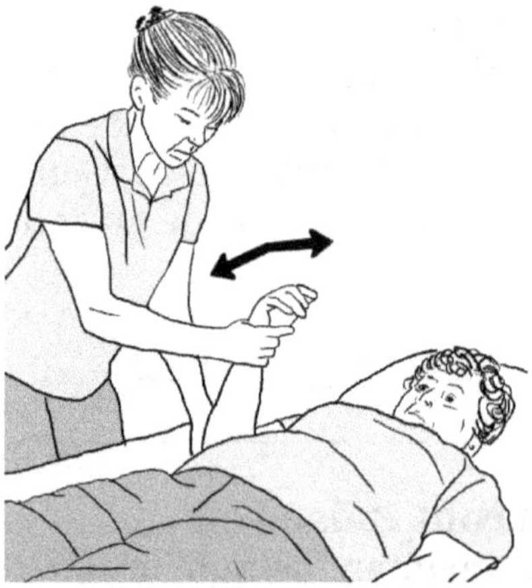

☐ **Forearm Turns**
Hold the right elbow against the side. Gently turn the forearm palm up and down.

Repeat ______ times.

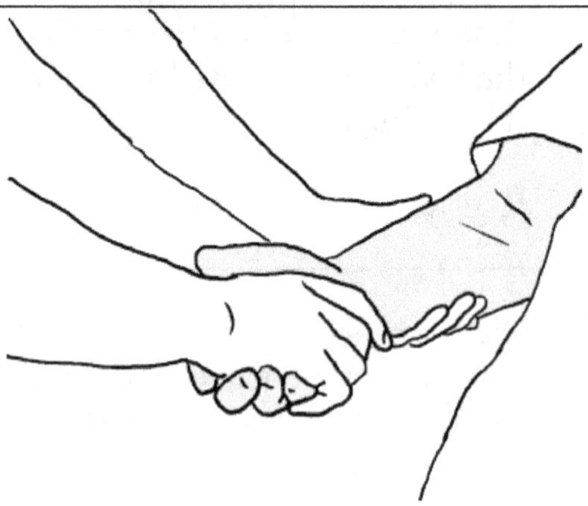

☐ **Wrist Turns**
Gently bend the right wrist back and forth.
Gently move the right wrist side to side.
Gently rotate the right wrist in a circle.

Repeat ______ times.

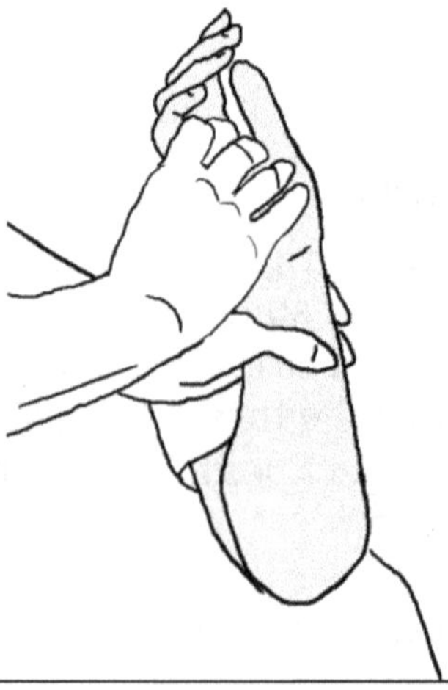

Passive Range of Motion - Right Side Weakness
Fingers and Thumb

☐ **Make a Fist**
Gently bend the right hand into a fist and straighten.

Repeat ______ times.

☐ **Finger Spread**
Gently spread each finger apart.

Repeat ______ times.

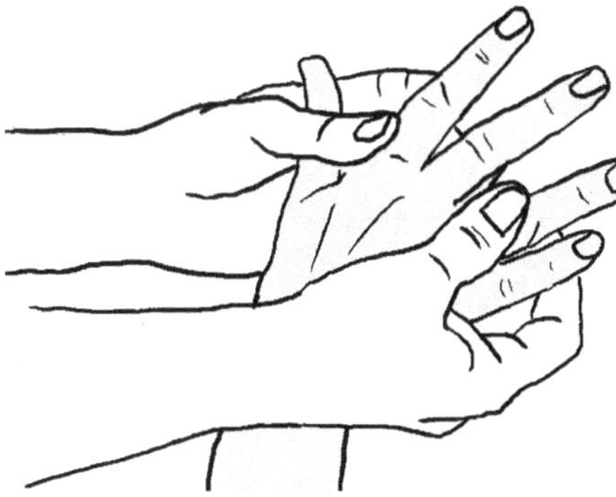

☐ **Thumb Across**
Move the right thumb across the palm and back.

Repeat ______ times.

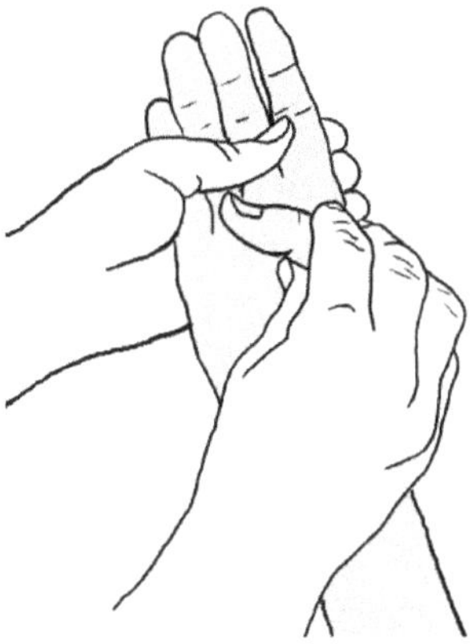

Occupational Therapy TOOLKIT

Passive Range of Motion - Right Side Weakness
Hip and Knee

☐ **Leg Bend**
Gently bend the right hip and knee up toward their chest.

Repeat ______ times.

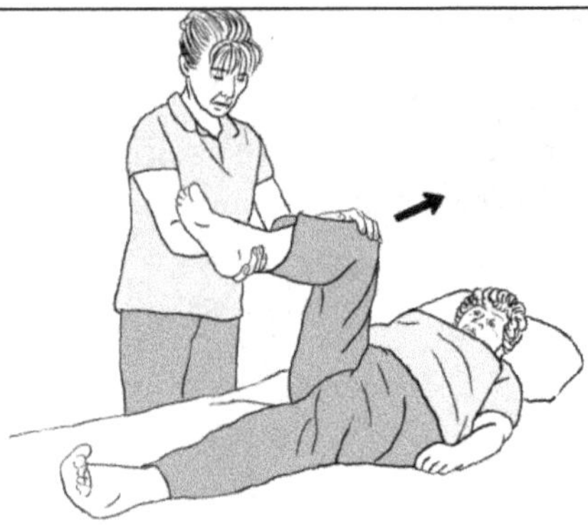

☐ **Side Raise**
Gently move the right leg out to the side.

Repeat ______ times.

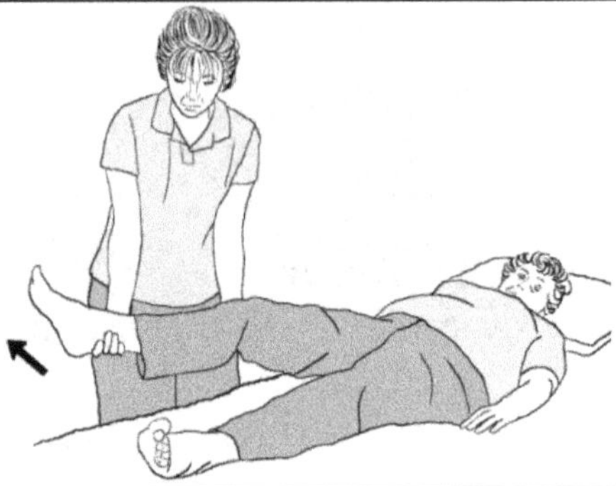

☐ **Hip Turns**
Gently bend the right knee and cross the leg over the other leg.

Repeat ______ times.

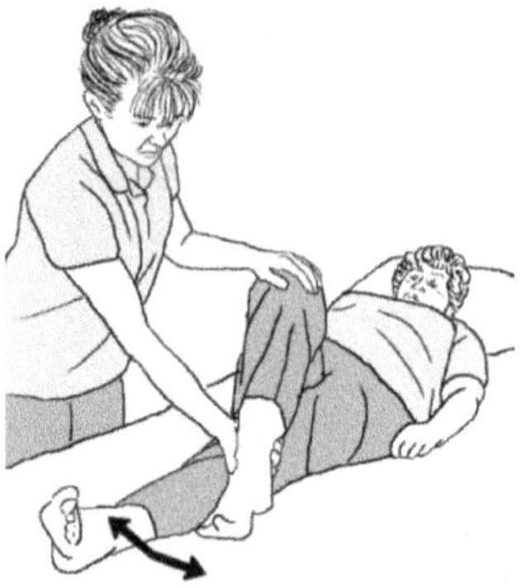

☐ **Back of Leg Stretch**
Raise the right leg. Gently stretch the back of the knee

Repeat ______ times.

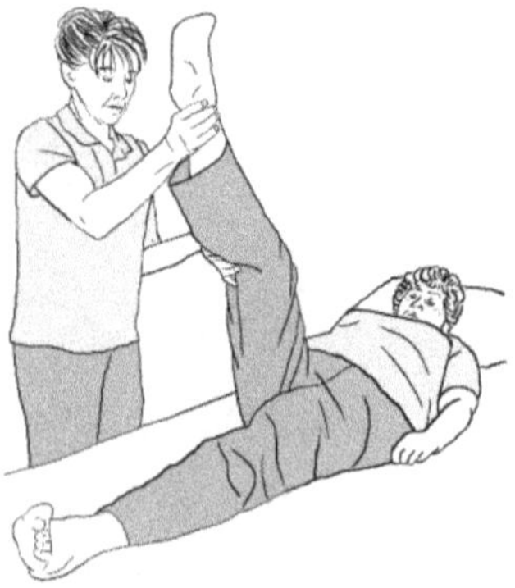

Passive Range of Motion - Right Side Weakness
Ankle and Foot

☐ **Ankle Bends**
Gently bend the right ankle back and forth.

Repeat ______ times.

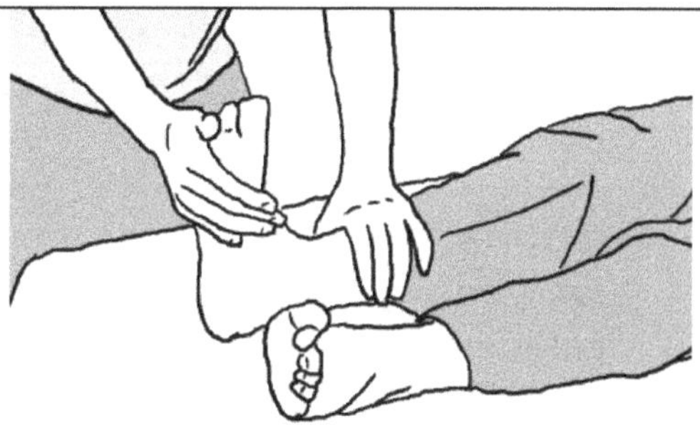

☐ **Ankle Turns**
Gently turn the right ankle in a circle.

Repeat ______ times.

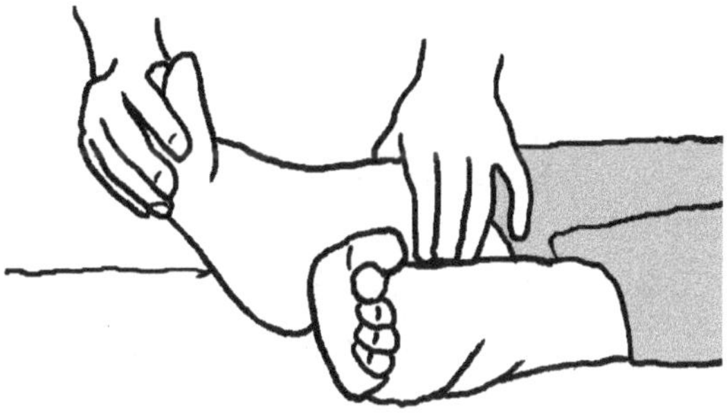

☐ **Toe Curls**
Gently curl the toes of the right foot.

Repeat ______ times.

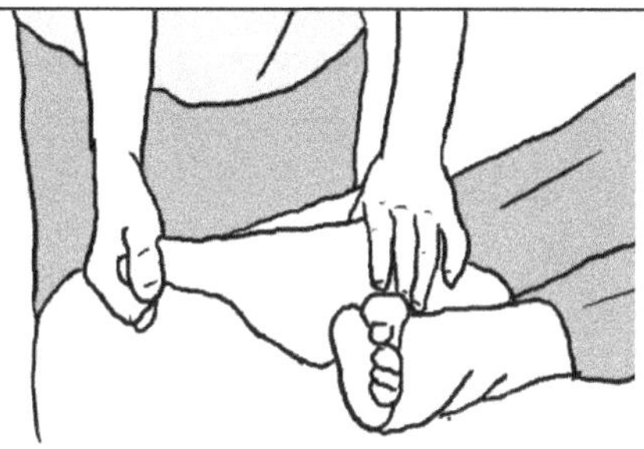

☐ **Toe Spread**
Gently spread each toe of the right foot.

Repeat ______ times.

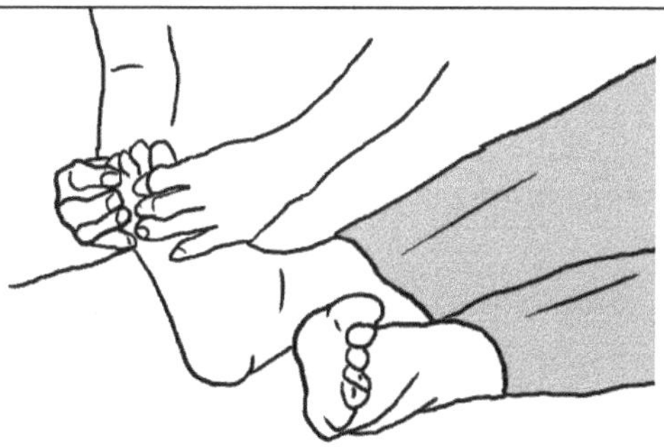

Pelvic Floor (Kegel) Exercise

Do these exercises _____ times per day, _____ days a week

Practice these exercises anywhere and at any time. Practice while watching TV, waiting at a red light, washing the dishes or standing in line.

Instructions:

- Locate the pelvic floor muscles by squeezing the rectum. Like you are holding the passage of gas.
- Relax your stomach muscles and breathe with ease during the exercise.
- One pelvic floor (Kegel) exercise consists of squeezing and holding, then fully relaxing the muscles. Lift these muscles in and up.
- Start by squeezing and holding the pelvic floor muscles for 10 seconds then fully relax the muscles for 10 seconds. Do _____ sets of _____.
- Next squeeze and hold the pelvic floor muscles for 2 seconds then fully relax the muscles for 2 seconds. Do _____ sets of _____.

Pendulum Exercises - Left

Do the checked exercise _____ times per day, _____ days a week

Hold onto a stable object. Lean forward. Relax your shoulder muscles. Use your body to swing your left arm.

- ☐ Swing your arm in a small circle to the right _____ times.
- ☐ Swing your arm in a small circle to the left _____ times.
- ☐ Swing your arm side-to-side _____ times.
- ☐ Swing your arm forward and back _____ times.

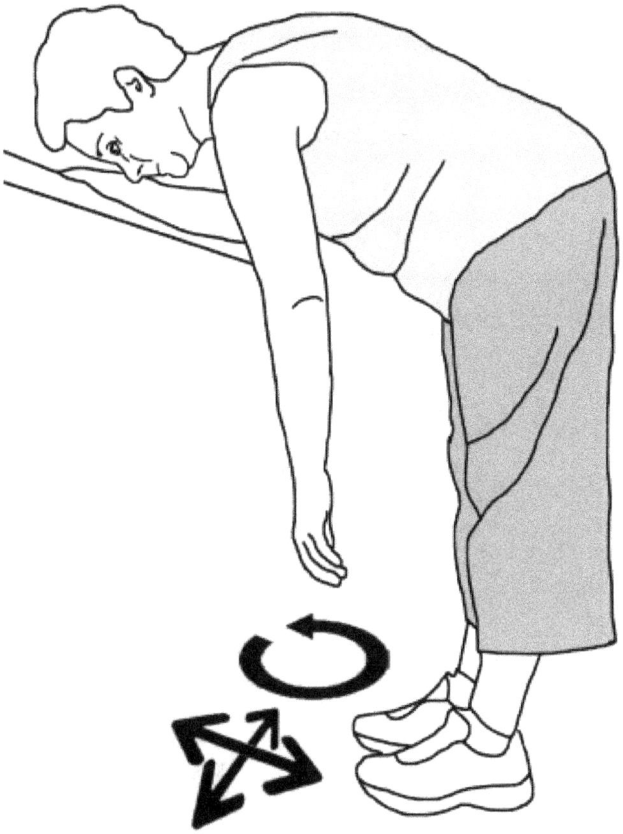

Occupational Therapy TOOLKIT

Pendulum Exercises - Right

Do this exercise _____ times per day, _____ days a week

Hold onto a stable object. Lean forward. Relax your shoulder muscles. Use your body to swing your right arm.

- ☐ Swing your arm in a small circle to the right _____ times.
- ☐ Swing your arm in a small circle to the left _____ times.
- ☐ Swing your arm side-to-side _____ times.
- ☐ Swing your arm forward and back _____ times.

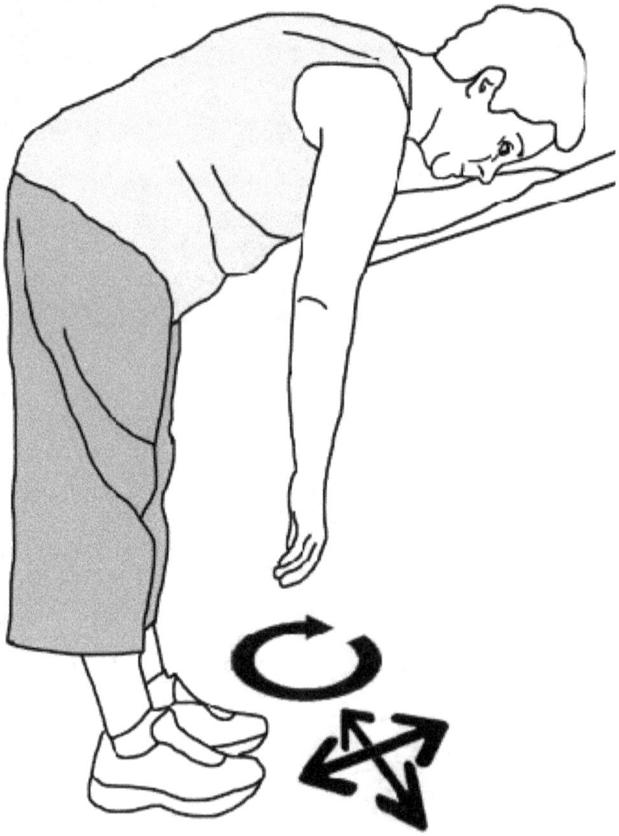

Physical Activity Plan

Name: ______________________________

Date: ______________________________

Therapist: ______________________________

Phone number: (_____)____________________

My Goals: ____

Aerobic

Aerobic activities I enjoy ______________________________
Do _____ times a week, _____ minutes per day.
Warm up for 5 minutes before aerobic activity. Cool down for 5 minutes after.
Exercise at a moderate intensity, 5-6 on a 10-point scale. You should be able to talk.

Strength

Do the exercises _____ times per day, _____ days a week.
Do _____ sets of _____ for each muscle group.
Inhale before lifting. Exhale during the lift. Inhale to return to the start position.

Stretch

Do after aerobic and strength exercises.
Stretch each muscle group two or three times. Hold for 20 to 30 seconds.

Balance

Add balance exercises into your exercise routine.

Activity	Sun	Mon	Tue	Wed	Thu	Fri	Sat
Aerobic							
Strength							
Stretch							
Balance							

Posture Exercises

Do the checked exercises _____ times per day, _____ days a week.

☐ **Chin Tuck**
Pull your chin straight back. Hold for a count of _____.

Do _____ sets of _____.

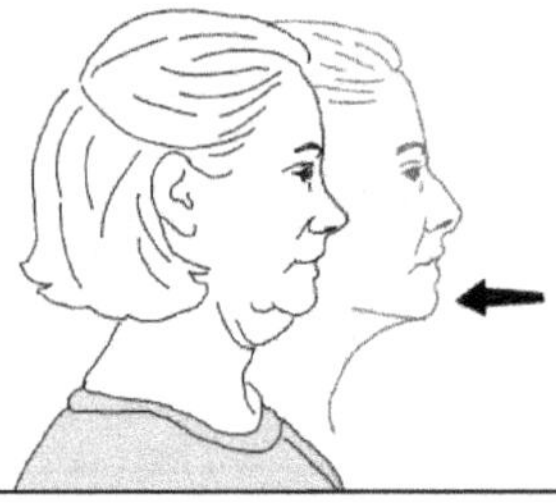

☐ **Overhead Stretch**
Clasp your hands and raise them up over your head. Hold for a count of _____.

Do _____ sets of _____.

☐ **Chest Stretch**
Place your hands behind your neck. Slowly spread your elbows apart. Hold for a count of _____.

Do _____ sets of _____.

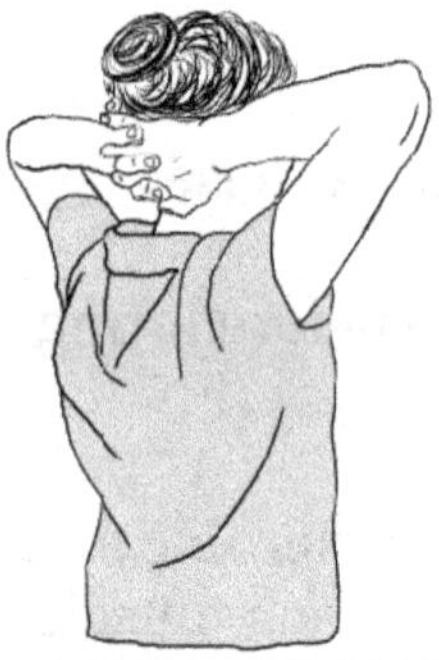

☐ **Upper Back Stretch**
Pull your elbows back and squeeze your shoulder blades. Hold for a count of _____.

Do _____ sets of _____.

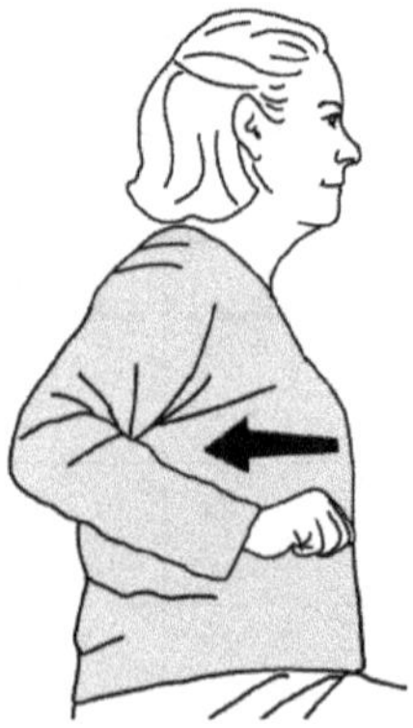

Posture Exercises

Do the checked exercises _____ times per day, _____ days a week.

☐ **Row**
Secure the stretch band at elbow height. For safety, be sure the door opens away from you. Stand facing the door. Pull your right elbow back. Hold for a count of _____.

Do _____ sets of _____.
Repeat on the left side.

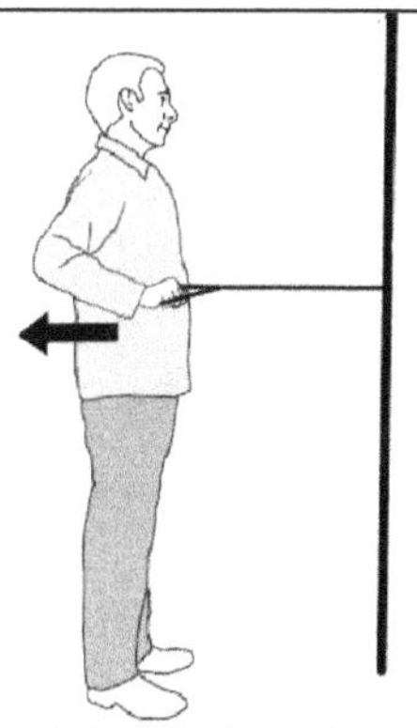

☐ **Pull Apart**
Hold a _____ stretch band between your hands. Raise your arms to shoulder level. Pull the stretch band across your chest. Hold for a count of _____.

Do _____ sets of _____.

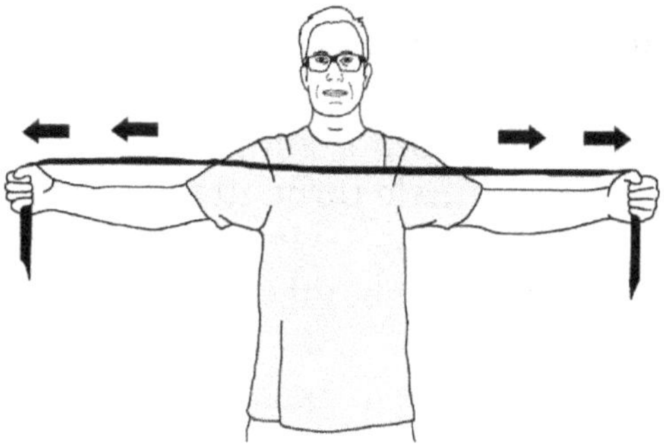

☐ **Shoulder Shrugs**
Hold a _____ lb/kg weight in each hand. Shrug your shoulders.

Do _____ sets of _____.

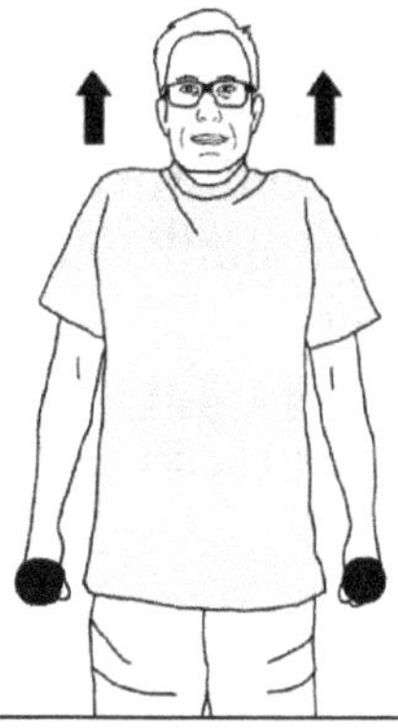

☐ **Upright Row**
Hold a _____ lb/kg weight in each hand. Hold your hands in front of thighs, palms facing in. Lift the weights to chest level.

Do _____ sets of _____.

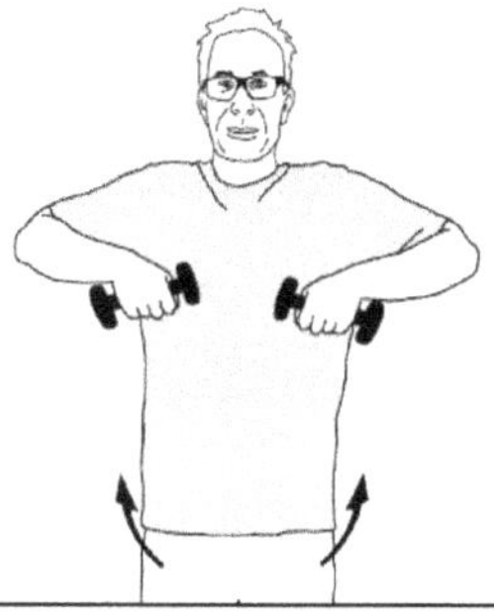

Pulmonary Exercises

Name: ___________________________________

Date: ___________________________________

Therapist: ________________________________

Phone number: (_____)______________________

Do the checked exercises _____ times a day, _____ days a week.

Exercise slowly and smoothly.

Do not hold your breath. Count aloud if needed. Use the pursed lip breathing during the exercises. Inhale through your nose and exhale through pursed lips.

If you use oxygen, then you should use it during exercise.

Do not exercise if you are not feeling well or if you have a fever.

Use good posture. Keep your stomach muscles tight and your back straight.

Sore muscles lasting a few days and feeling tired are normal after exercise. Exhaustion, sore joints, and painful muscle pulls are not normal. If you have these symptoms, do not exercise until you talk with your therapist.

If you have chest tightness or pain, shortness of breath, feel dizzy, faint, or sick to your stomach, stop and call emergency services at _____.

Notes:

____

____

____

____

____

____

Pulmonary Exercises

☐ **Head Circles**
Roll your head slowly from side to side. Do not roll your head back. Breathe in through your nose and out through pursed lips.

Do ______ sets of ______.

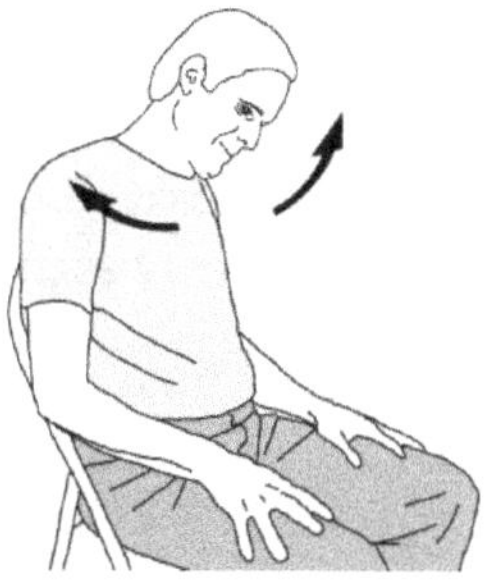

☐ **Elbow Breathing**
Lift your elbows to shoulder level, and touch your hands in front of your chest. Inhale through your nose as you pull your elbows back. Exhale through pursed lips as you relax.

Do ______ sets of ______.

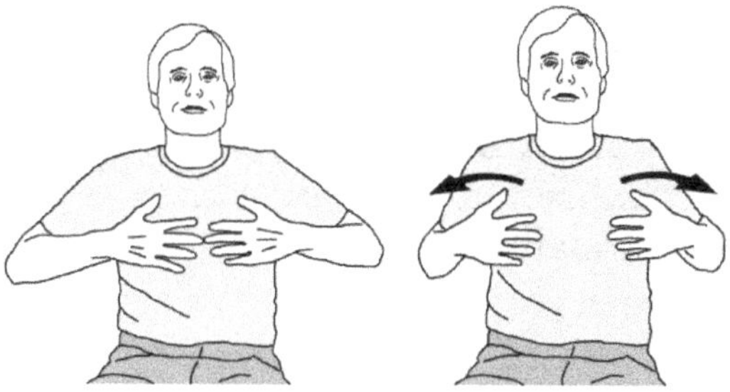

☐ **Shoulder Shrugs**
Inhale through your nose as you shrug your shoulders. Exhale through pursed lips as you press your shoulders down.

Do ______ sets of ______.

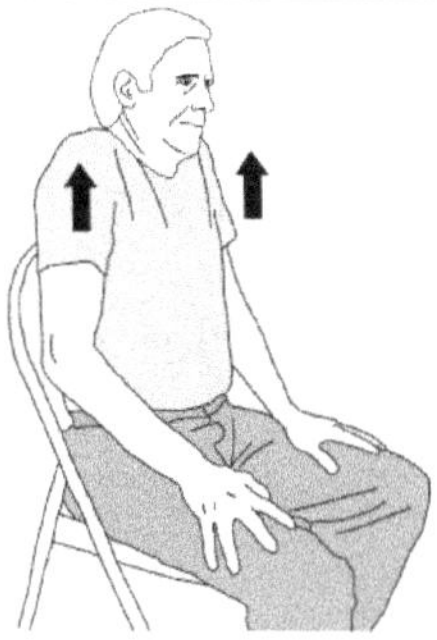

☐ **Elbow Spread**
Place your hands behind your neck. Inhale through your nose as your spread your elbows apart. Exhale as you bring your elbows together and roll your neck and upper back forward.

Do ______ sets of ______.

Pulmonary Exercises

☐ **Arm Raise**
Inhale through your nose as you raise your arms up in front. Exhale through pursed lips as you return your arms to your side.

Do ______ sets of ______.

☐ **Arm Curls**
Inhale through your nose as you bend both arms to touch your shoulders. Exhale through pursed lips as you straighten them.

Do ______ sets of ______.

☐ **Side Twist**
Exhale through pursed lips as you reach across your body to the right. Inhale through your nose as you return to center. Repeat to your left side.

Do ______ sets of ______.

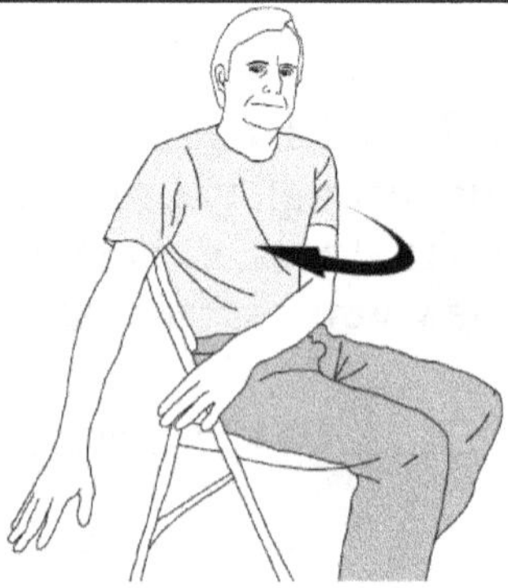

☐ **Side Bend**
Exhale through pursed lips as you bend over to the right side. Inhale through your nose as you return upright. Repeat to your left side.

Do ______ sets of ______.

Pulmonary Exercises

☐ **Chair Push-Ups**
Sit with feet flat on the floor and hands on the armrests. Exhale through pursed lips as you push up from the chair. Inhale through your nose as you lower back down.

Do ______ sets of ______.

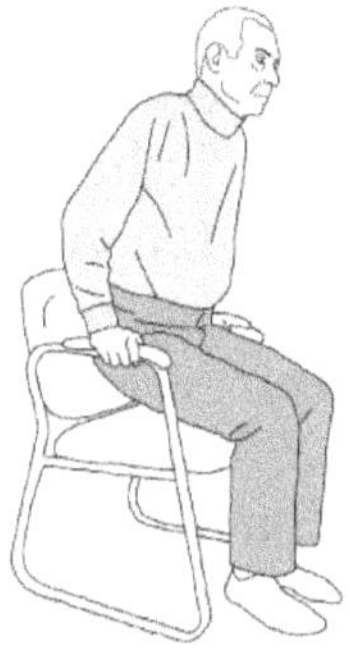

☐ **Stand Up and Sit Down**
Keep your back straight and your arms out in front. Exhale through pursed lips as you stand up. Inhale through your nose as you sit down.

Do ______ sets of ______.

☐ **Wall Push-Up**
Place your hands on the wall. Inhale through your nose as you lower your body toward the wall. Exhale through pursed lips as you push out from the wall.

Do ______ sets of ______.

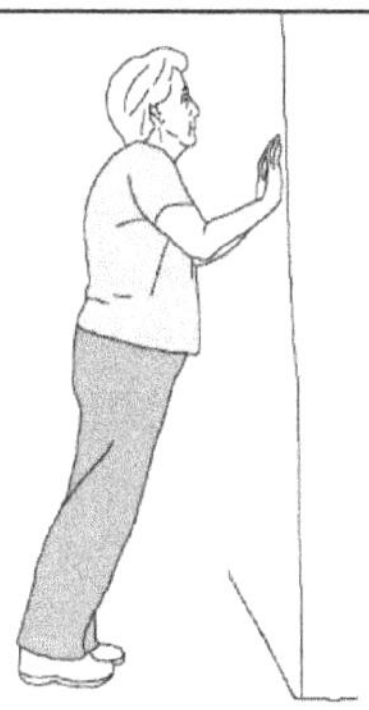

☐ **Quarter Squat**
Hold onto a stable object. Exhale through pursed lips as you slightly bend your knees and lower down. Inhale through your nose as you straighten up.

Do ______ sets of ______.

Pulmonary Exercises

☐ **Straight Knee**
Sit in a chair. Exhale through pursed lips as you straighten your right knee by tightening your thigh muscles. Inhale through your nose as you lower your leg.

Do _____ sets of _____.
Repeat with your left leg.

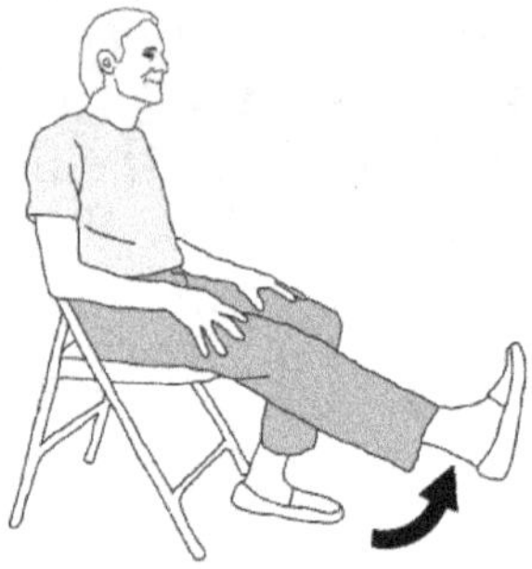

☐ **Knee Curl**
Hold onto a stable object. Exhale through pursed lips as you bend your right knee up behind you. Inhale through your nose as you lower your leg

Do _____ sets of _____.
Repeat with your left leg.

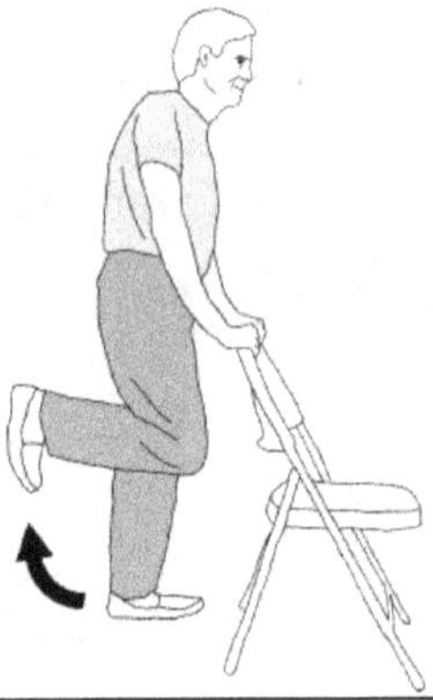

☐ **Side Raise**
Hold onto a stable object. Exhale through pursed lips as you lift your right leg out to the side. Inhale through your nose as you lower your leg.

Do _____ sets of _____.
Repeat with your left leg.

☐ **Toe Raise**
Hold onto a stable object. Exhale through pursed lips as you rise onto your toes. Inhale through your nose as you lower down.

Do _____ sets of _____.

Putty Exercises

Do the checked exercises _____ times per day, _____ days a week.

☐ Shape the putty into a ball. Squeeze the putty with all your fingers.

Do ______ sets of ______.

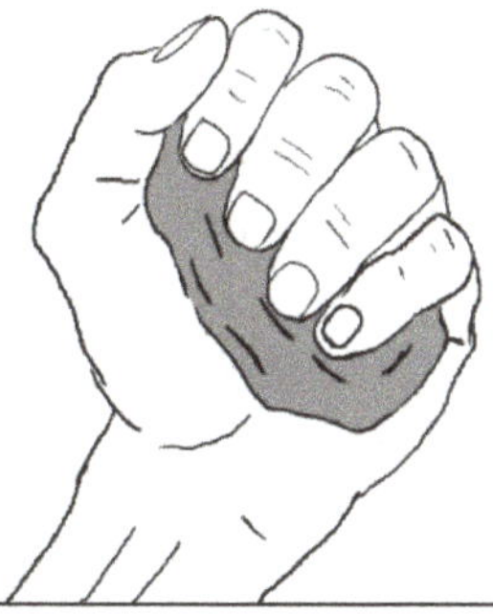

☐ Shape the putty into a ball. Hold the putty in your hand. Press your thumb into the putty.

Do ______ sets of ______.

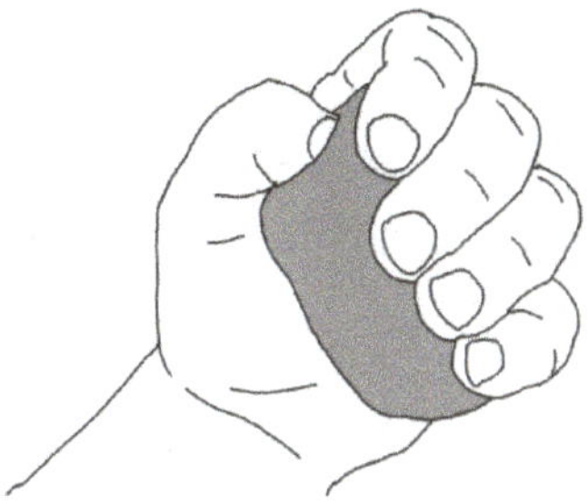

☐ Shape the putty into a ball. Pinch the putty between your thumb and the side of your index finger.

Do ______ sets of ______.

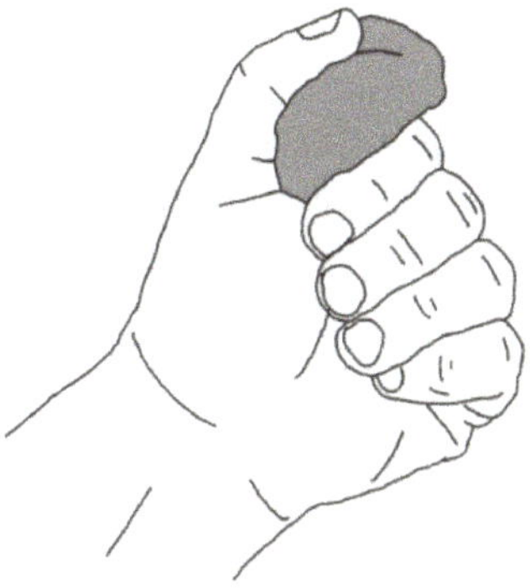

☐ Shape the putty into a ball. Hold your fingers straight and your knuckles bent. Squeeze the putty between your fingers and thumb.

Do ______ sets of ______.

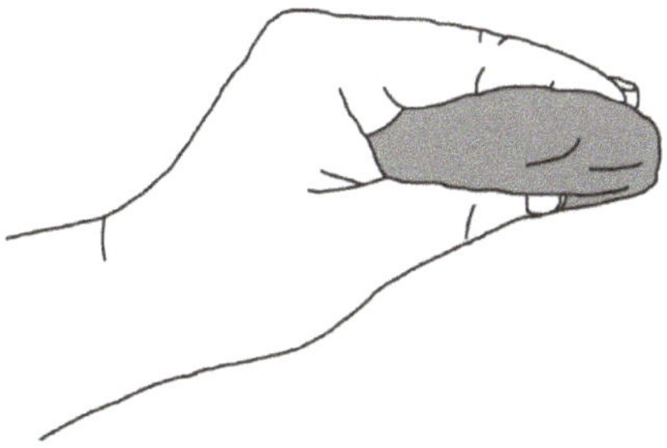

Occupational Therapy TOOLKiT

Putty Exercises

Do the checked exercises _____ times per day, _____ days a week.

☐ Flatten the putty into a pancake. Place your fingers into the center of the putty and spread the putty outward.

Do _____ sets of _____.

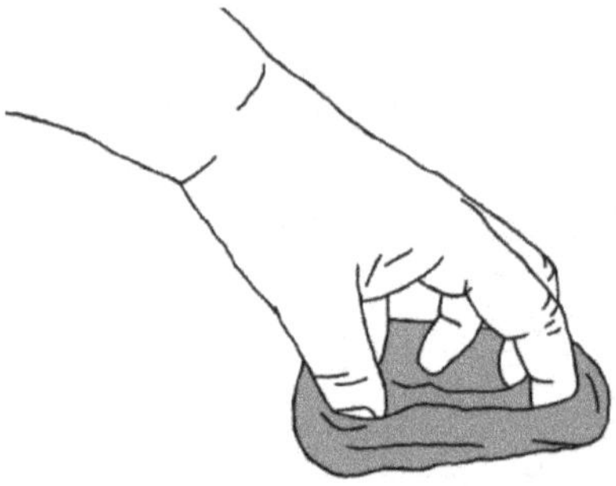

☐ Flatten the putty into a pancake. Spread the putty apart using two fingers at a time.

Do _____ sets of _____.

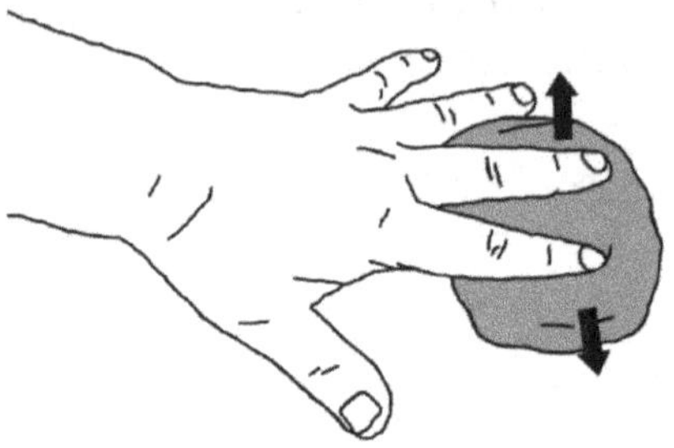

☐ Shape the putty into a sausage. Squeeze the putty between your fingers.

Do _____ sets of _____.

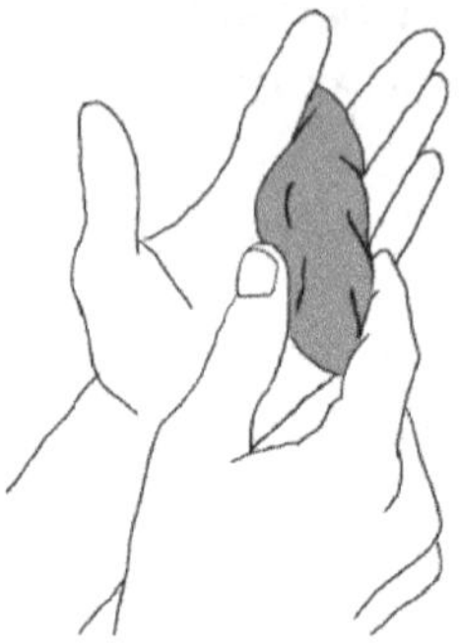

☐ Shape the putty into a sausage. Pinch the putty between your thumb and each finger.

Do _____ sets of _____.

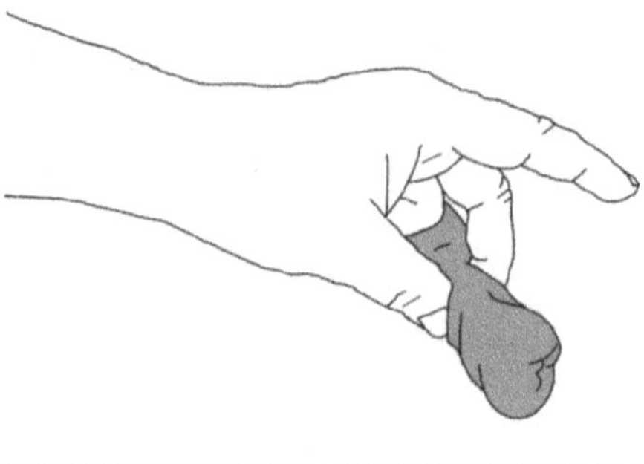

Scapular Mobility and Strength Exercises - Left Side Weakness

Name: ______________________________

Date: ______________________________

Therapist: ______________________________

Phone number: (_____)____________________

These exercises will improve the mobility and strength of your shoulder blade.

Do the checked exercises _____ times a day, _____ days a week.

Exercise slowly and smoothly.

These exercises should not cause pain. Sore muscles lasting a few days and feeling tired are normal after exercise. Exhaustion, sore joints, and painful muscle pulls are not normal. If you have these symptoms, do not exercise until you talk with your therapist

If you have chest tightness or pain, shortness of breath, feel dizzy, faint, or sick to your stomach, stop and call emergency services at _____.

Notes:

____

____

____

____

____

____

Scapular Mobility and Strength Exercises - Left Side Weakness

Your caregiver will support the weight of your left arm by cradling it in their left arm.

Your caregiver will place their right hand on the lower boarder of your left shoulder blade (scapula).

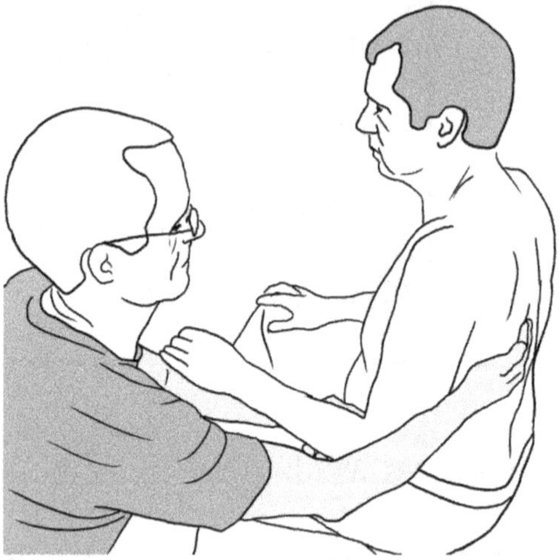

☐ Your caregiver will glide your left shoulder blade and shoulder up.

Do ______ sets of ______.

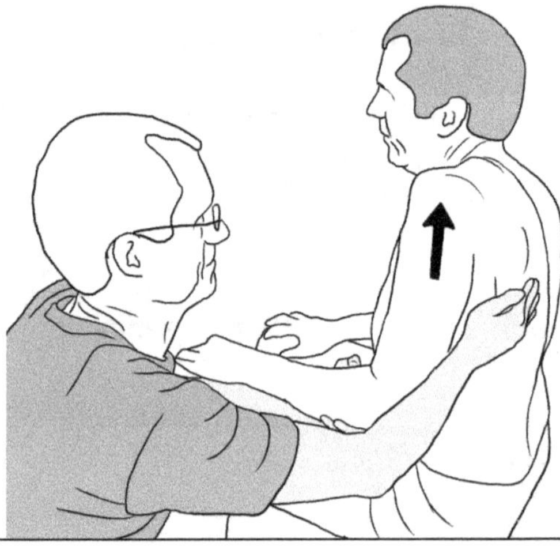

☐ Your caregiver will glide your left shoulder blade forward into protraction.

Do ______ sets of ______.

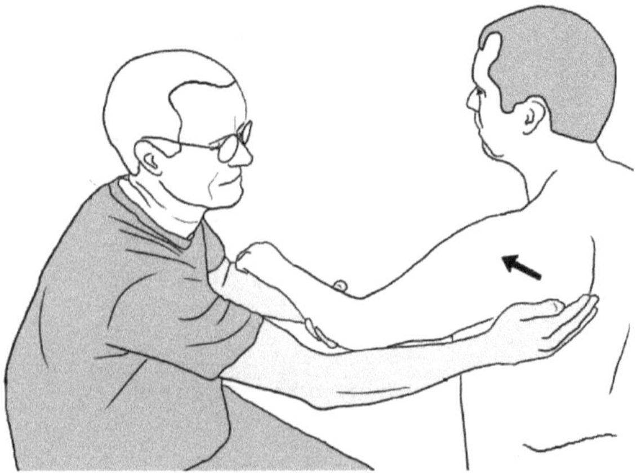

Scapular Mobility and Strength Exercises - Left Side Weakness

☐ With your left palm facing up, your caregiver will lift your left arm while gliding your shoulder blade into protraction.

Do ______ sets of ______.

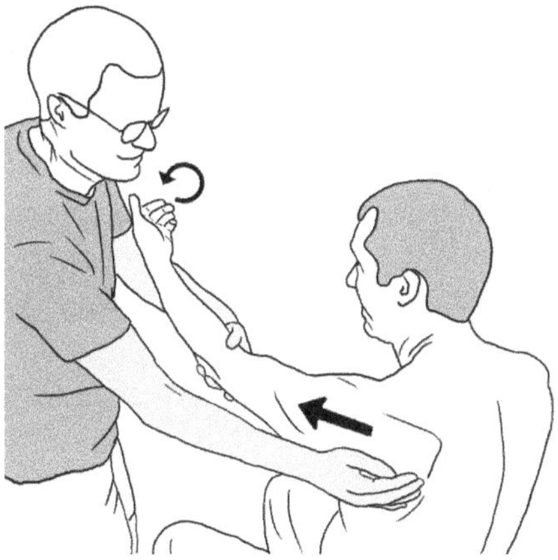

☐ Shrug your left shoulder.

Do ______ sets of ______.

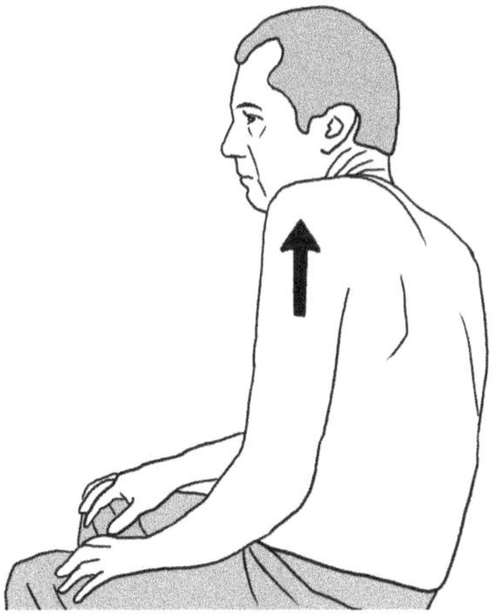

☐ Roll your left shoulder. Move your shoulder forward, up, back and then down.

Do ______ sets of ______.

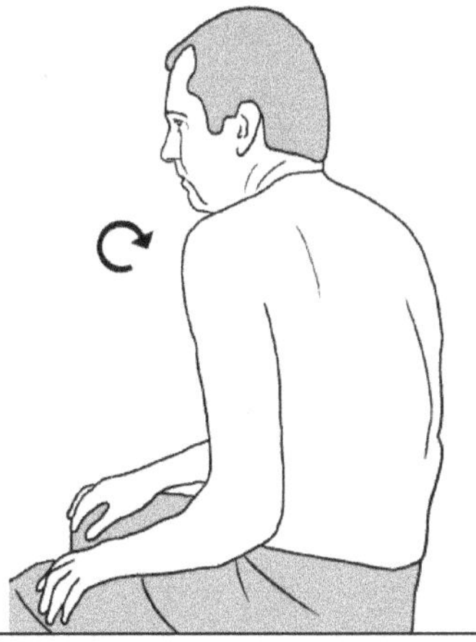

Scapular Mobility and Strength Exercises - Left Side Weakness

☐ Hold your left arm pointing up to the ceiling. Your caregiver will support the weight of your arm. Actively push your arm up toward the ceiling.

Do ______ sets of ______.

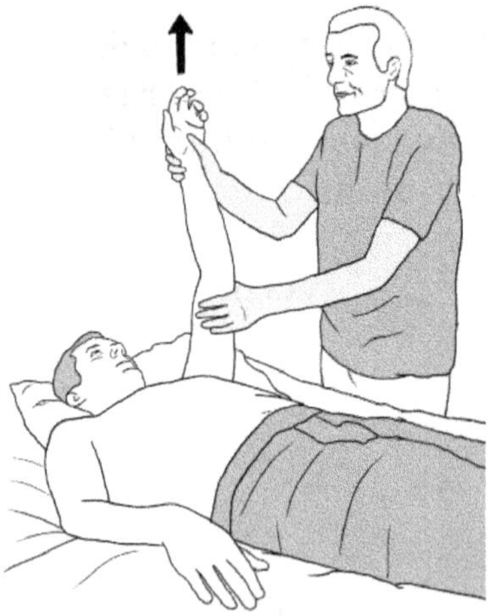

☐ Sit facing the table. Place your left arm out in front with your hand on a 6 inch/15 cm ball.

Roll the ball from side to side.
Do ______ sets of ______.

Roll the ball toward you then away.
Do ______ sets of ______.

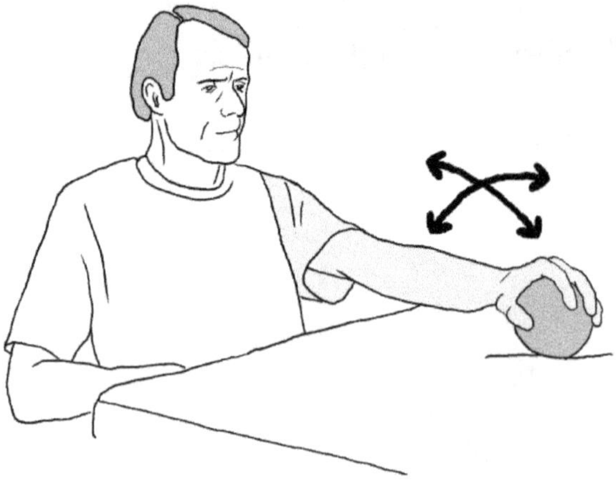

☐ Sit with the table to your left side. Place your left arm out to the side with your hand on a 6 inch/15 cm ball.

Roll the ball from side to side.
Do ______ sets of ______.

Roll the ball toward you then away.
Do ______ sets of ______.

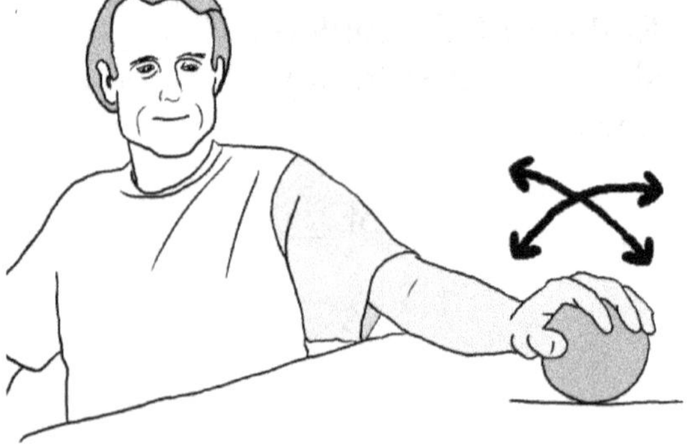

Occupational Therapy TOOLKIT

Scapular Mobility and Strength Exercises - Right Side Weakness

Name: ____

Date: ____

Therapist: _____________________________________

Phone number: (______)__________________________

These exercises will improve the mobility and strength of your shoulder blade.

Do the checked exercises ______ times a day, ______ days a week.

Exercise slowly and smoothly.

These exercises should not cause pain. Sore muscles lasting a few days and feeling tired are normal after exercise. Exhaustion, sore joints, and painful muscle pulls are not normal. If you have these symptoms, do not exercise until you talk with your therapist

If you have chest tightness or pain, shortness of breath, feel dizzy, faint, or sick to your stomach, stop and call emergency services at ______.

Notes:

____

____

____

____

____

____

Scapular Mobility and Strength Exercises - Right Side Weakness

Your caregiver will support the weight of your right arm by cradling it in their right arm.

Your caregiver will place their left hand on the lower boarder of your right shoulder blade (scapula).

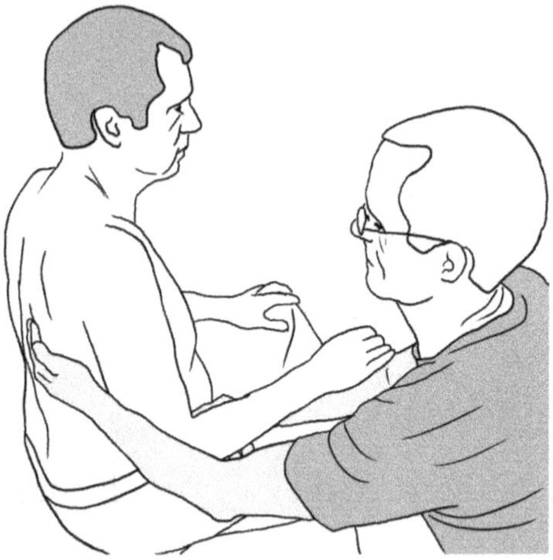

☐ Your caregiver will glide your right shoulder blade and shoulder up.

Do ______ sets of ______.

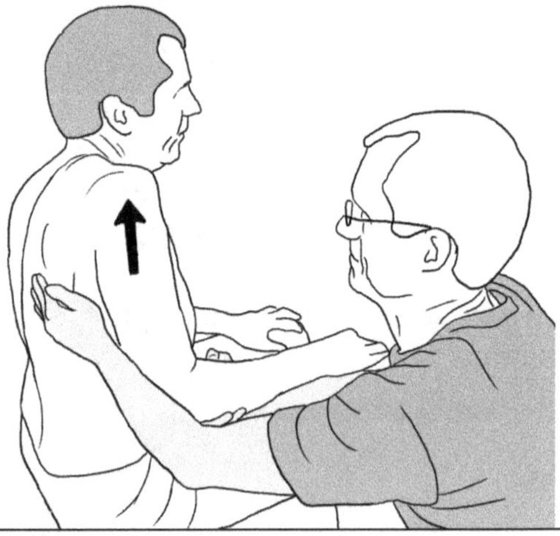

☐ Your caregiver will glide your right shoulder blade forward into protraction.

Do ______ sets of ______.

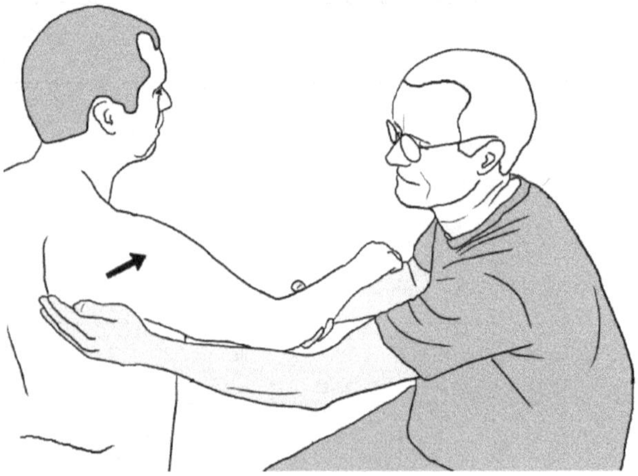

Occupational Therapy TOOLKIT

Scapular Mobility and Strength Exercises - Right Side Weakness

☐ With your palm facing up, your caregiver will lift your right arm while gliding your shoulder blade into protraction.

Do ______ sets of ______.

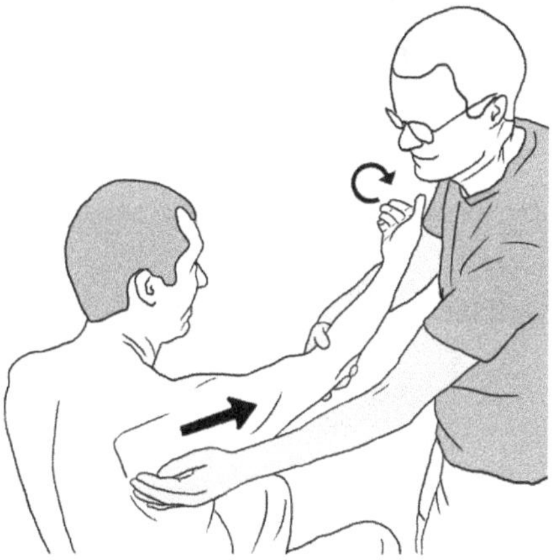

☐ Shrug your right shoulder.

Do ______ sets of ______.

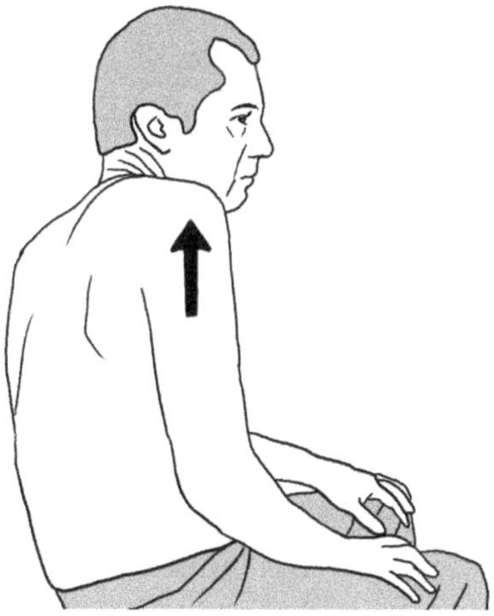

☐ Roll your right shoulder. Move your shoulder forward, up, back and then down.

Do ______ sets of ______.

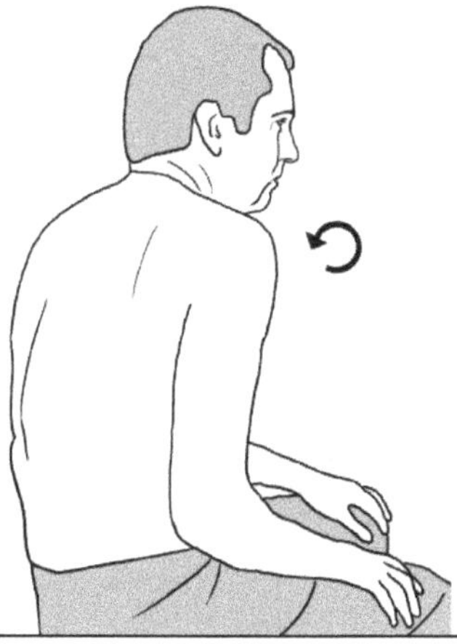

Occupational Therapy TOOLKIT

Scapular Mobility and Strength Exercises - Right Side Weakness

- ☐ Hold your left arm pointing up to the ceiling. Your caregiver will support the weight of your arm. Actively push your arm up toward the ceiling.

  Do ______ sets of ______.

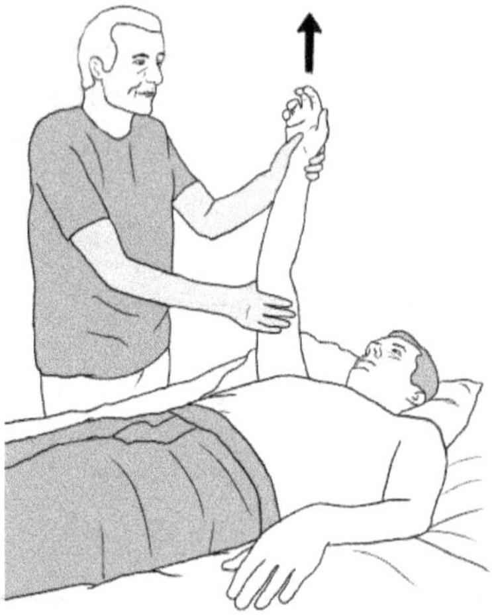

- ☐ Sit facing the table. Place your right arm out in front with your hand on a 6 inch/15 cm ball.

  Roll the ball from side to side.
  Do ______ sets of ______.

  Roll the ball toward you then away.
  Do ______ sets of ______.

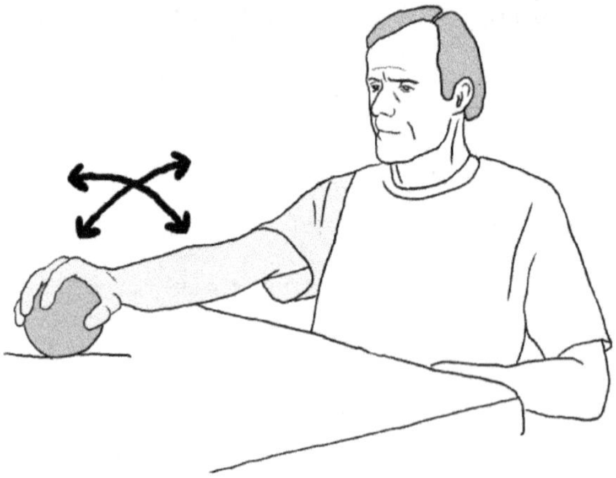

- ☐ Sit with the table to your right side. Place your right arm out to the side with your hand on a 6 inch/15 cm ball.

  Roll the ball from side to side.
  Do ______ sets of ______.

  Roll the ball toward you then away.
  Do ______ sets of ______.

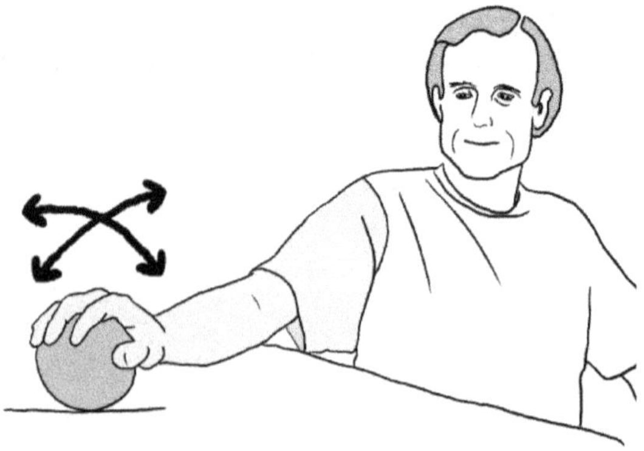

Self Range of Motion - Left Side Weakness

Name: ______________________________________

Date: ______________________________________

Therapist: __________________________________

Phone number: (_____)________________________

Do the checked exercises _____ times per day, _____ days a week.

Exercise slowly and smoothly. These exercises should not cause pain.

Do not hold your breath during exercises. Count aloud if needed.

Use good posture. Keep your stomach muscles tight and your back straight.

Sore muscles lasting a few days and feeling tired are normal after exercise. Exhaustion, sore joints, and painful muscle pulls are not normal. If you have these symptoms, do not exercise until you talk with your therapist

If you have chest tightness or pain, shortness of breath, feel dizzy, faint, or sick to your stomach, stop and call emergency services at _____.

Notes:

____

____

____

____

____

____

Self Range of Motion - Left Side Weakness

☐ Clasp your hands. Stretch your arms forward on the table. Return to sitting upright.

Do ______ sets of ______.

☐ Place both hans on a towel, on the table. Place your right hand on top of your left hand. Polish the table by making large circles to the right and then large circles to the left.

Do ______ sets of ______.

☐ Cradle your left arm with your right arm. Push your left shoulder up.

Do ______ sets of ______.

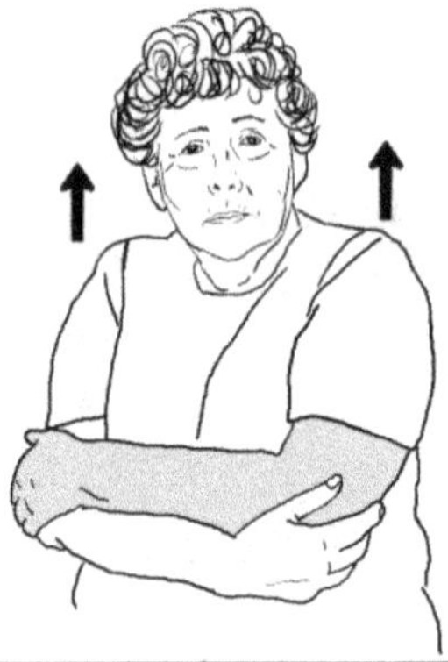

☐ Cradle your left arm in your right arm Lift both arms to chest level, then move both arms side to side.

Do ______ sets of ______.

Self Range of Motion - Left Side Weakness

☐ Hold your left forearm. Lift your left arm up as high as you can.

Do _____ sets of _____.

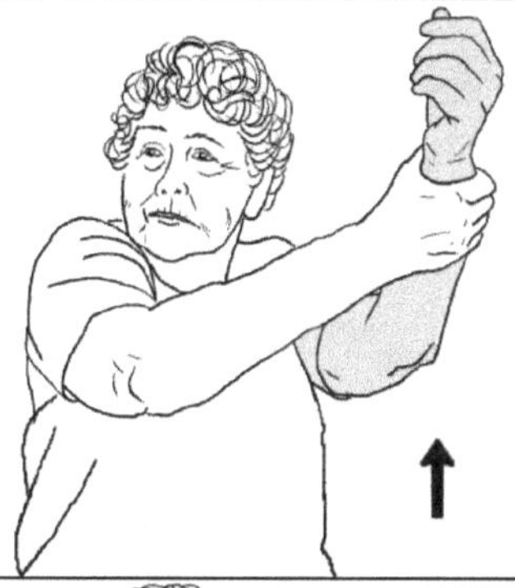

☐ Hold your left forearm. Straighten and bend your elbow.

Do _____ sets of _____.

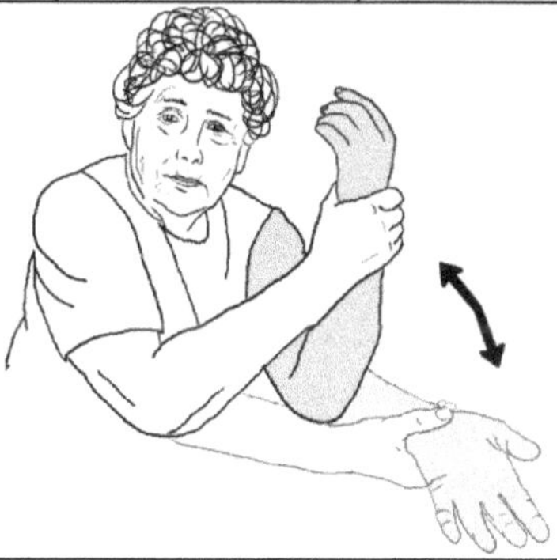

☐ Be certain your chair is not going to move. Lock the brakes if you are sitting in a wheelchair.

Hold your left wrist with your right hand. Lean forward and dangle your arms in front, between your legs.

Do _____ sets of _____.

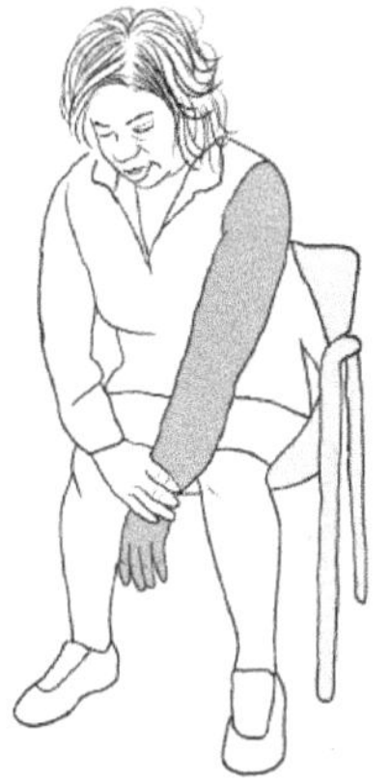

☐ Hold your left forearm. Turn your left palm facing up and then turn your palm over.

Do _____ sets of _____.

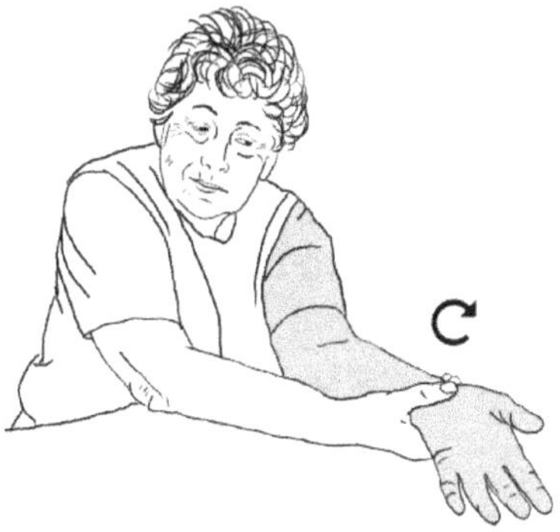

 | www.ottoolkit.com

Occupational Therapy TOOLKIT

Self Range of Motion - Left Side Weakness

☐ Hold your left hand using your right hand. Bend your wrist back. Then move your wrist from side to side.

Do ______ sets of ______.

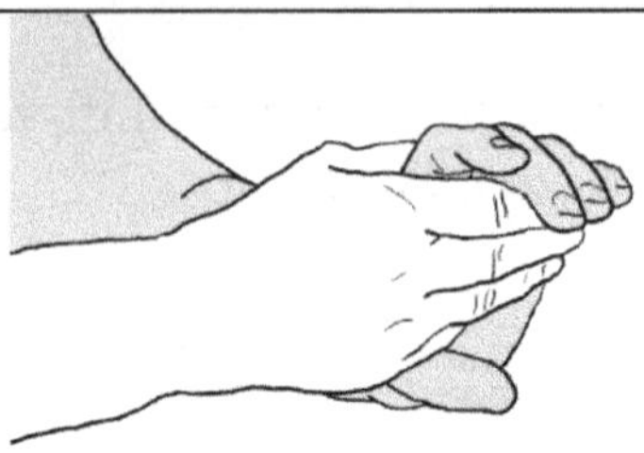

☐ With your right hand, bend each finger and your thumb down into the palm of your left hand, and then straighten.

Do ______ sets of ______.

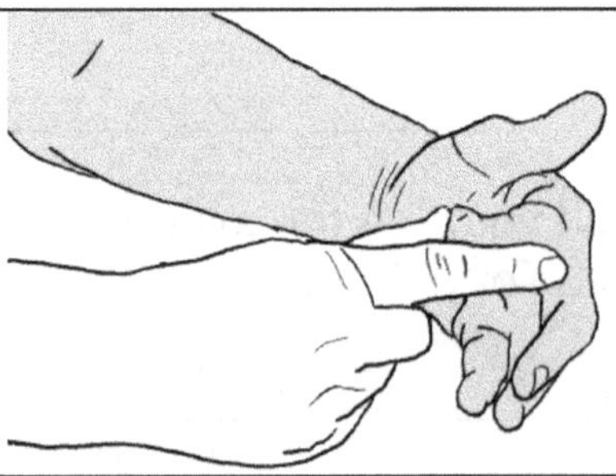

☐ With your right hand, spread the space between your thumb and first finger of your left hand.

Do ______ sets of ______.

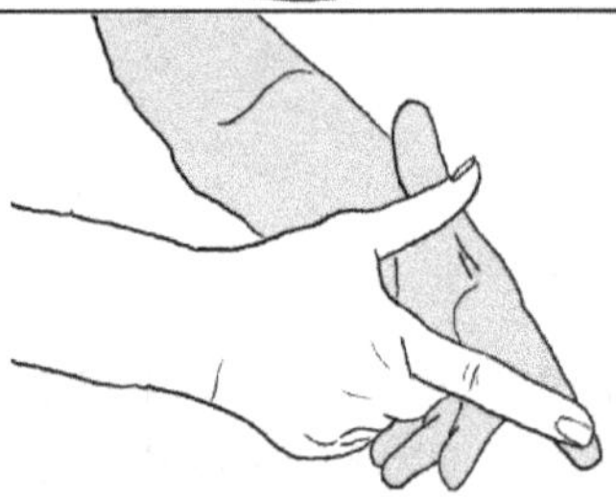

☐ While lying down, extend your left arm out to the side. Gently roll onto your left side.

Do ______ sets of ______.

☐ While lying down, clasp your hands and place them behind your neck, relax your elbows down to the pillow.

Do ______ sets of ______.

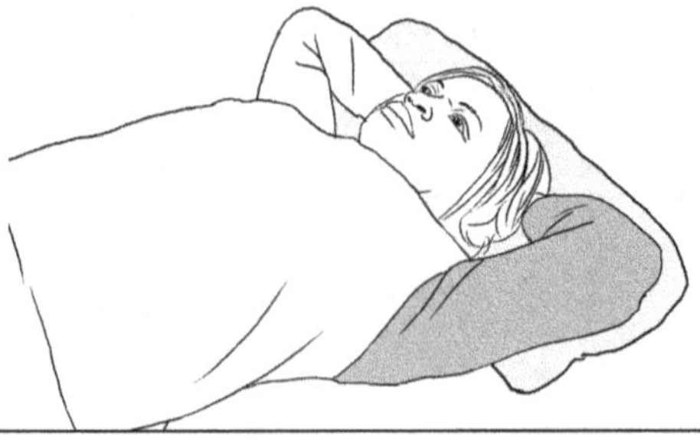

Occupational Therapy TOOLKIT

Self Range of Motion - Right Side Weakness

Name: ______________________________

Date: ______________________________

Therapist: ______________________________

Phone number: (_____)____________________

Do the checked exercises _____ times per day, _____ days a week.

Exercise slowly and smoothly. These exercises should not cause pain.

Do not hold your breath during exercise. Count aloud if needed.

Use good posture. Keep your stomach muscles tight and your back straight.

Sore muscles lasting a few days and feeling tired are normal after exercise. Exhaustion, sore joints, and painful muscle pulls are not normal. If you have these symptoms, do not exercise until you talk with your therapist

If you have chest tightness or pain, shortness of breath, feel dizzy, faint, or sick to your stomach, stop and call emergency services at _____.

Notes:

____

____

____

____

____

____

Occupational Therapy TOOLKIT

Self Range of Motion - Right Side Weakness

☐ Clasp your hands. Stretch your arms forward on the table. Return to sitting upright.

Do ______ sets of ______.

☐ Place both hands on a towel, on the table. Place your left hand on top of your right hand. Polish the table by making large circles to the right and then large circles to the left.

Do ______ sets of ______.

☐ Cradle your right arm with your left arm. Push your right shoulder up.

Do ______ sets of ______.

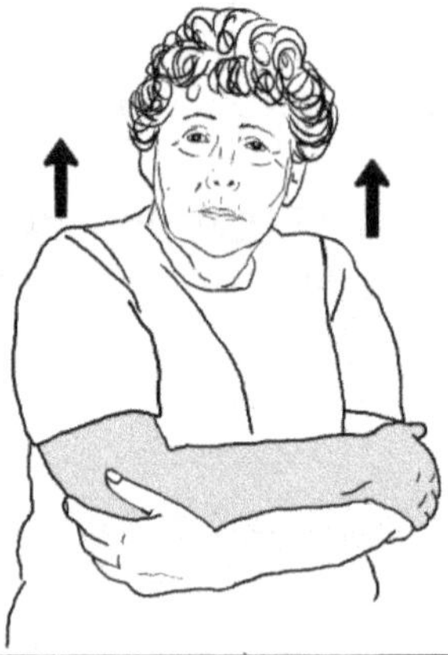

☐ Cradle your right arm in your left arm Lift both arms to chest level, then move both arms side to side.

Do ______ sets of ______.

Self Range of Motion - Right Side Weakness

☐ Hold your right forearm. Lift your right arm up as high as you can.

Do ______ sets of ______.

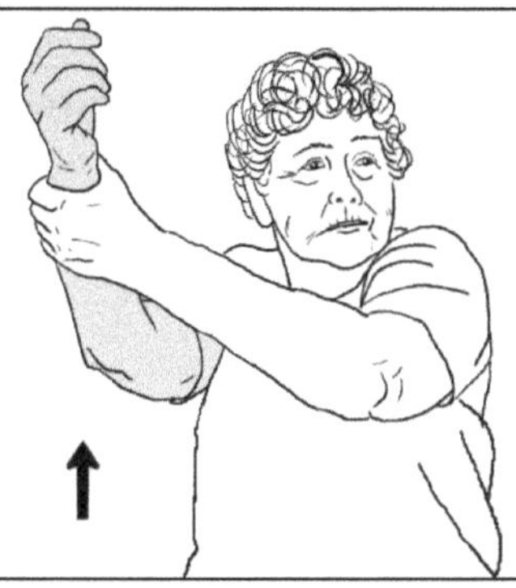

☐ Hold your right forearm. Straighten and bend your elbow.

Do ______ sets of ______.

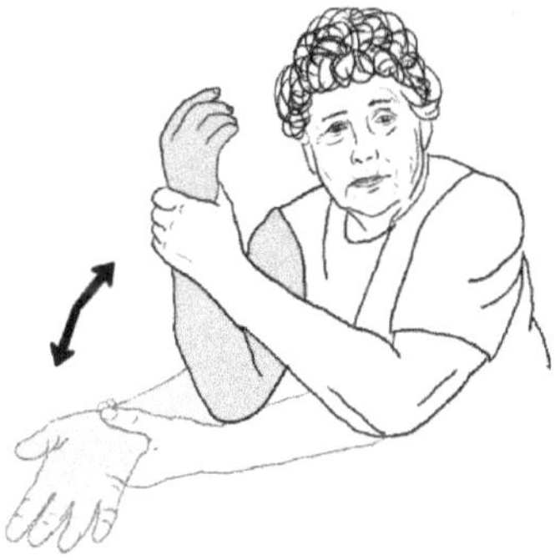

☐ Be certain your chair is not going to move. Lock the brakes if you are sitting in a wheelchair.

Hold your right wrist with your left hand. Lean forward and dangle your arms in front, between your legs.

Do ______ sets of ______.

☐ Hold your right forearm. Turn your right palm facing up and then turn your palm over.

Do ______ sets of ______.

Occupational Therapy TOOLKIT

Self Range of Motion - Right Side Weakness

☐ Hold your right hand using your left hand. Bend your wrist back.

Do ______ sets of ______.

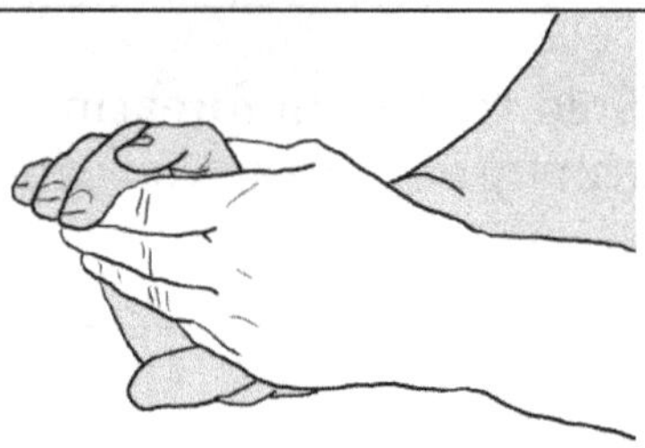

☐ With your left hand, bend each finger and thumb down into the palm of your right hand, then straighten.

Do ______ sets of ______.

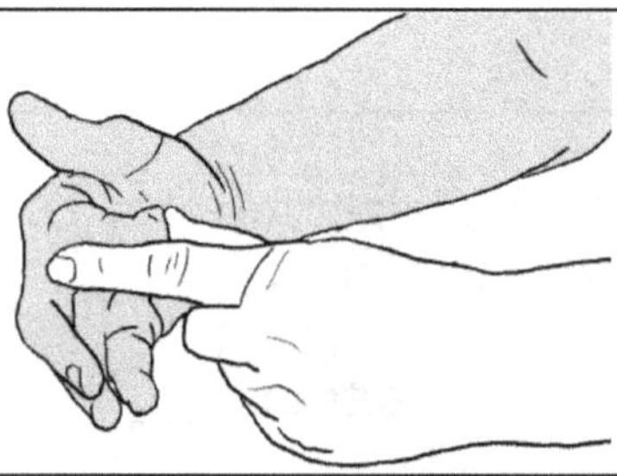

☐ With your left hand, spread the space between your thumb and first finger of your right hand.

Do ______ sets of ______.

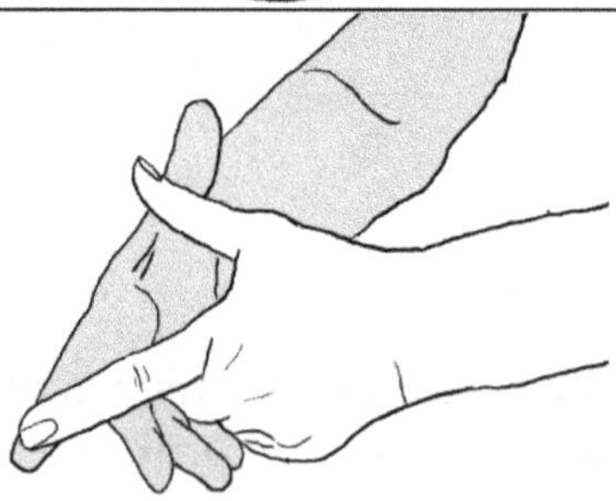

☐ While lying down, extend your right arm out to the side. Gently roll onto your right side.

Do ______ sets of ______.

☐ While lying down, clasp your hands and place them behind your neck, relax your elbows down to the pillow.

Do ______ sets of ______.

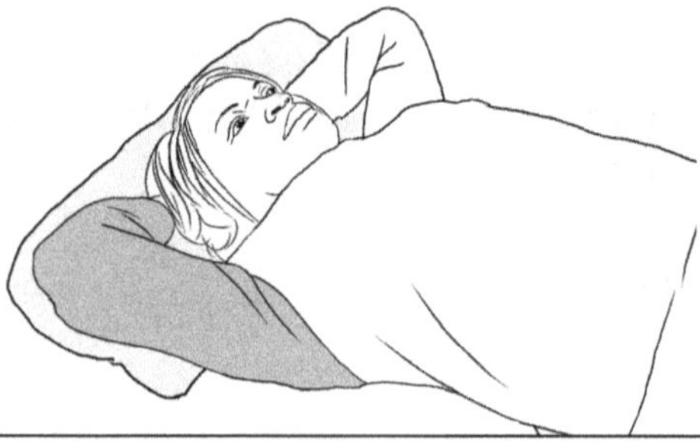

Shoulder Active Range of Motion

Do the checked exercises _____ times per day, _____ days a week.

☐ Raise your arms up in front, as high as you can.

Do _____ sets of _____.

☐ Raise your arms up from your sides.

Do _____ sets of _____.

☐ Lift your arms back.

Do _____ sets of _____.

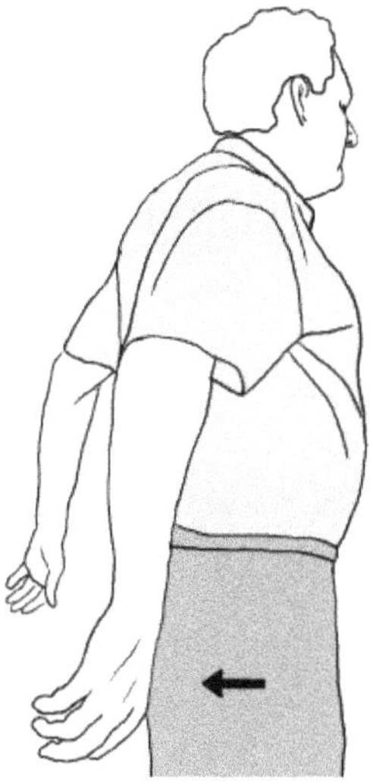

Occupational Therapy TOOLKIT

Shoulder Active Range of Motion

Do the checked exercises _____ times per day, _____ days a week.

☐ Place your hands behind your lower back and reach up your spine.

Do _____ sets of _____.

☐ Reach your hands behind your neck and reach down your spine.

Do _____ sets of _____.

☐ Keep your arms at shoulder level. Cross your arms in front and then spread your arms apart.

Do _____ sets of _____.

Occupational Therapy TOOLKIT

Shoulder and Hand Active Exercises

Do _____ sets of _____ of each exercise.
Do the checked exercises _____ times per day, _____ days a week.

☐ Roll your shoulder.

☐ Reach over your head.

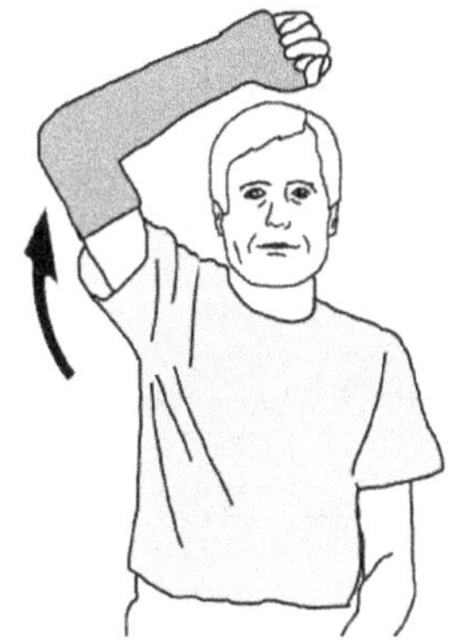

☐ Reach back.

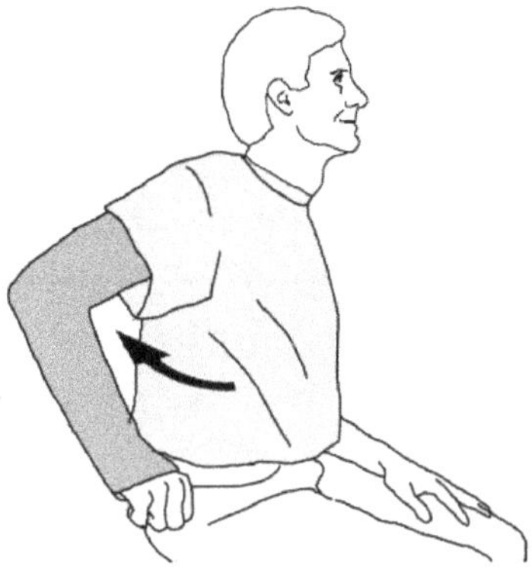

☐ Reach across to other shoulder.

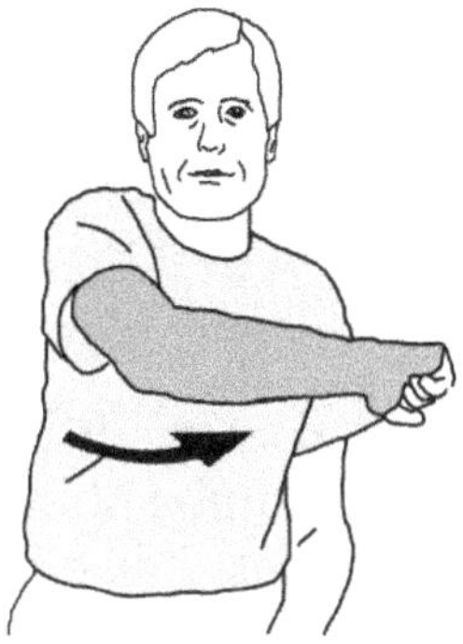

☐ Open and close your hand.

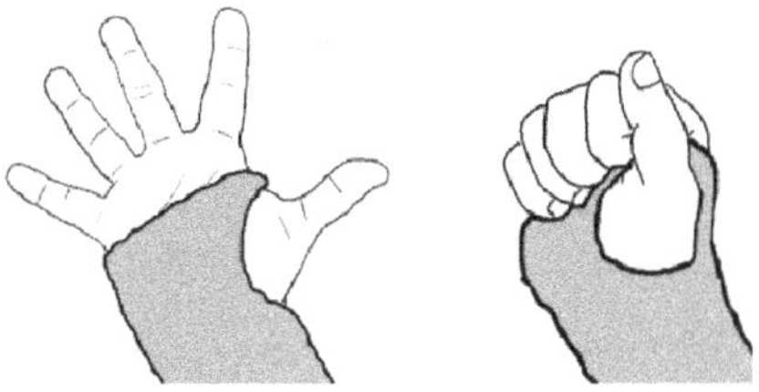

☐ Squeeze a soft ball.

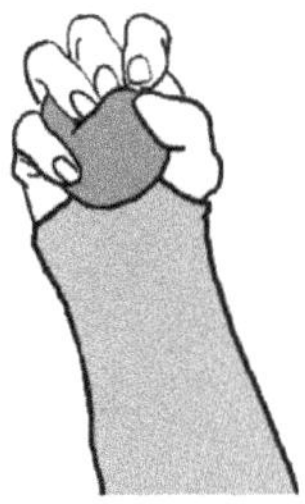

Occupational Therapy TOOLKIT

Shoulder and Rotator Cuff Active Exercises - Left

Do the checked exercises _____ times per day, _____ days a week.

☐ **Forward Raise** (flexion)
Keep your thumbs pointing up and your elbows straight. Raise both arms forward to shoulder level.

Do _____ sets of _____.

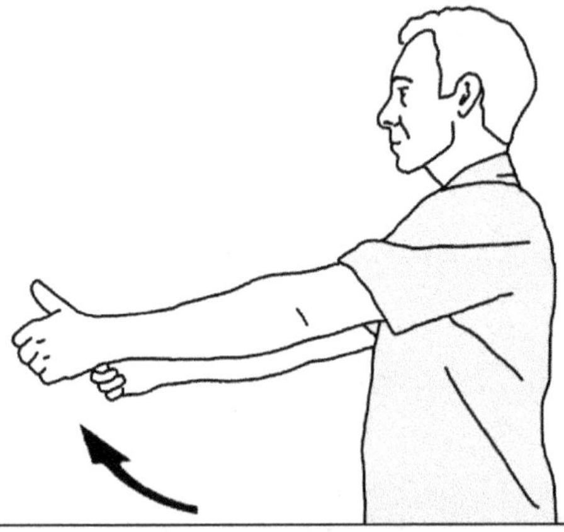

☐ **Side Raise** (abduction)
Keep your thumbs pointing up and your elbows straight. Raise both arms up from the sides to shoulder level.

Do _____ sets of _____.

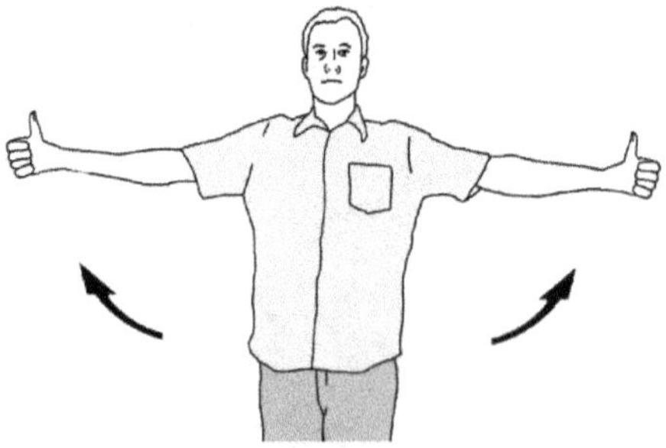

☐ **Corner Raise** (scaption)
Keep your thumbs pointing up and your elbows straight. Raise both arms forward and up at a 45° angle. Raise both arms to shoulder level.

Do _____ sets of _____.

Shoulder and Rotator Cuff Active Exercises - Left

☐ **Punch**
Lie on your back. Lift your left arm. Move only from your shoulder. Punch your arm up.

Do ______ sets of ______.

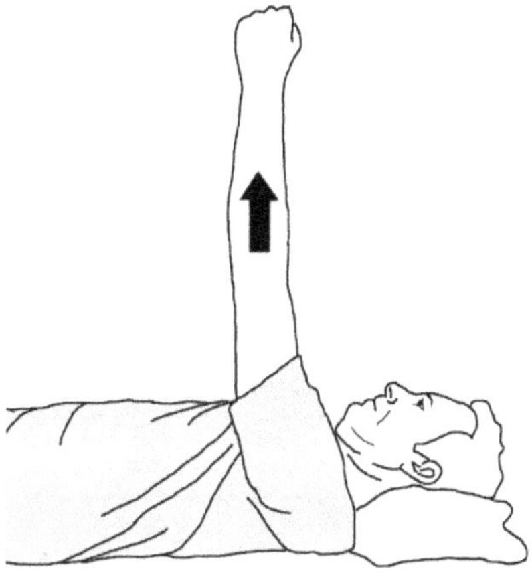

☐ **External Rotation**
Lie on your right side and place a folded hand towel under your left elbow. Bend your elbow and rest it on your stomach. Rotate at your shoulder and raise your hand up toward the ceiling.

Do ______ sets of ______.

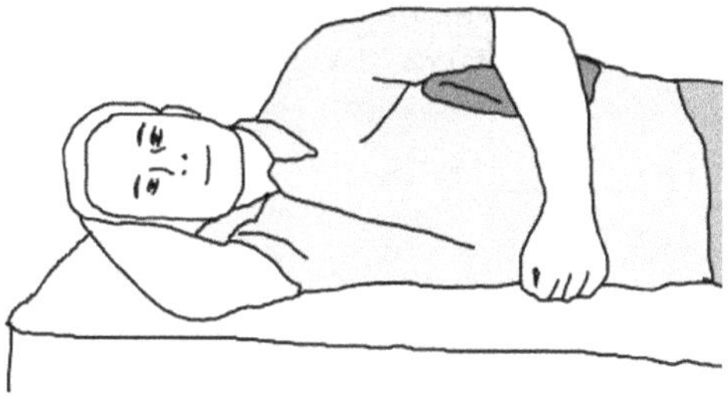

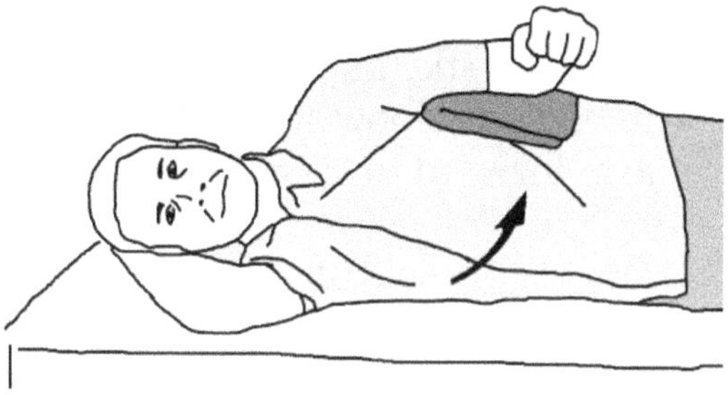

☐ **Internal Rotation**
Lie on your left side. Tuck your arm against your body with your elbow bent. Rotate at your shoulder and bring your arm into your chest.

Do ______ sets of ______.

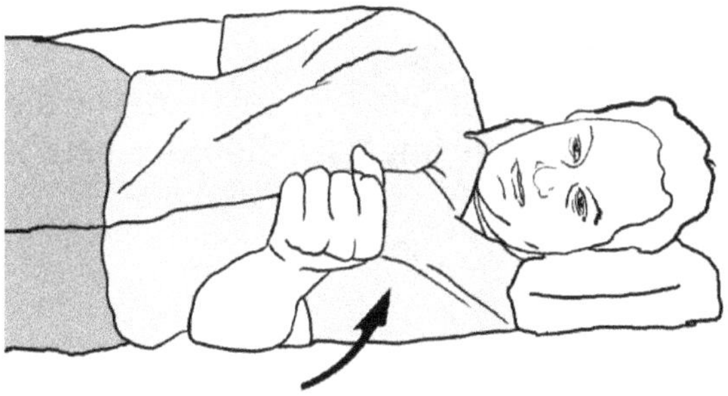

Shoulder and Rotator Cuff Active Exercises - Left

Lie on your stomach with your left arm hanging over the side.

☐ **Shoulder Blade Retraction**
Keep your elbow straight. Squeeze your left shoulder blade. Do not shrug your shoulder toward your ear.

Do ______ sets of ______.

☐ **Letter I** (flexion)
Keep your elbow straight. Raise your left arm forward to shoulder height.

Do ______ sets of ______.

☐ **Letter Y** (scaption)
Raise your left arm up from the side at a 45-degree angle to shoulder height.

Do ______ sets of ______.

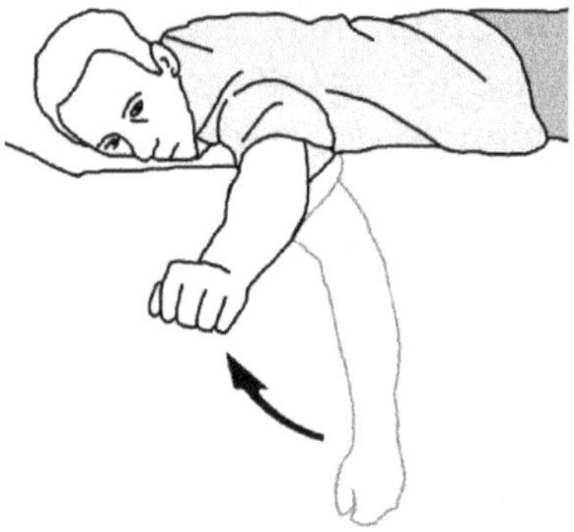

Occupational Therapy TOOLKIT

Shoulder and Rotator Cuff Active Exercises - Left

☐ **Letter T** (horizontal abduction)
Raise your left arm up to the side to shoulder height.

Do ______ sets of ______.

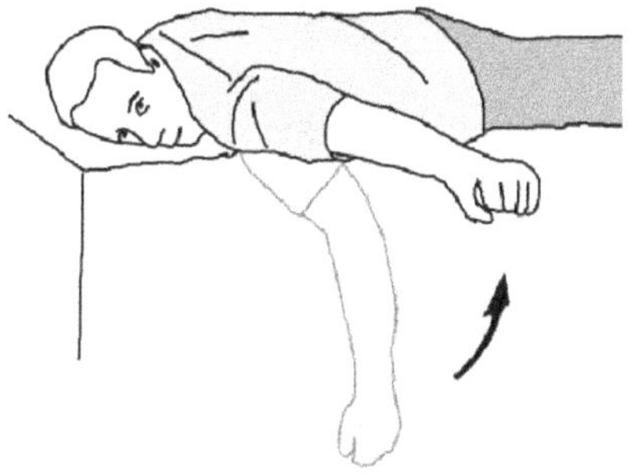

☐ **Letter A** (extension)
Raise your left arm backward to the level of your hip

Do ______ sets of ______.

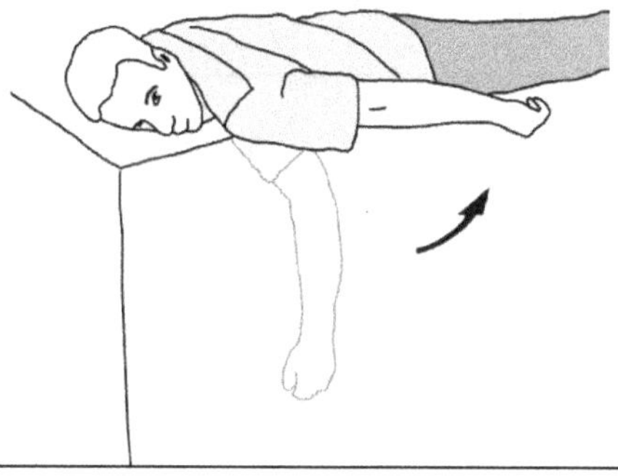

☐ **Rowing**
Lift your left elbow up toward the ceiling.

Do ______ sets of ______.

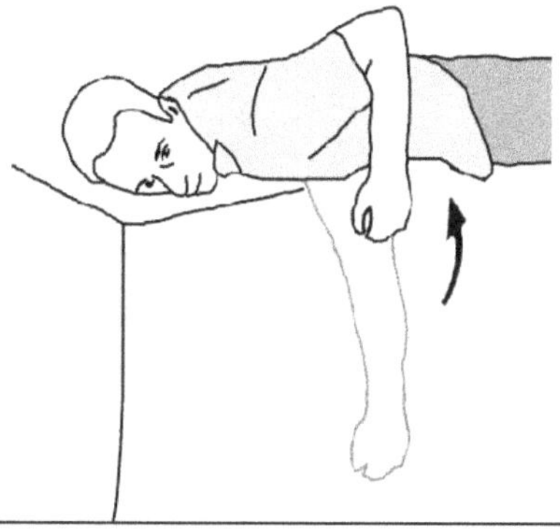

☐ **Rotation**
Raise your left arm to shoulder height with your elbows at a 90-degree angle. Rotate your hand upward, until your hand is even with the bed.

Do ______ sets of ______.

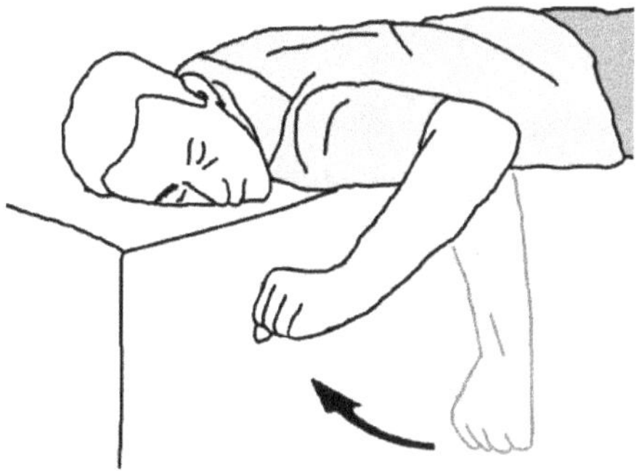

Shoulder and Rotator Cuff Active Exercises - Right

Do the checked exercises _____ times per day, _____ days a week.

☐ **Forward Raise** (flexion)
Keep your thumbs pointing up and your elbows straight. Raise both arms forward to shoulder level.

Do _____ sets of _____.

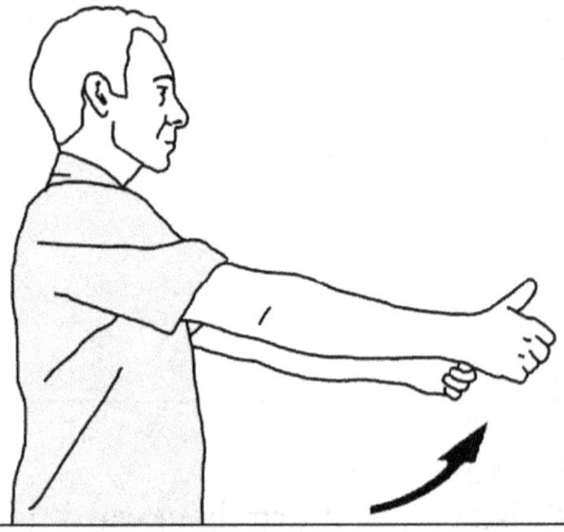

☐ **Side Raise** (abduction)
Keep your thumbs pointing up and your elbows straight. Raise both arms up from the sides to shoulder level.

Do _____ sets of _____.

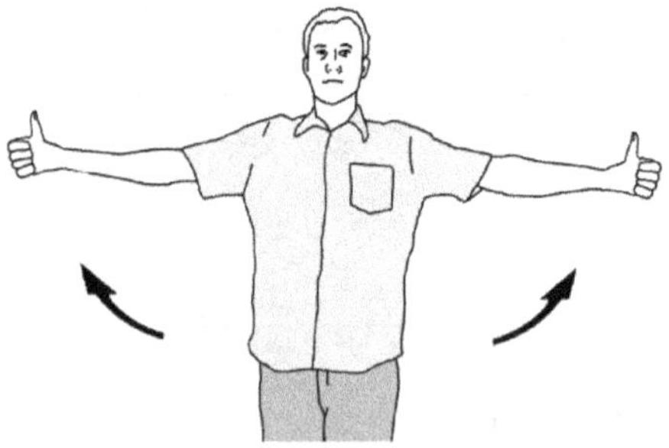

☐ **Corner Raise** (scaption)
Keep your thumbs pointing up and your elbows straight. Raise both arms forward and up at a 45° angle. Raise both arms to shoulder level.

Do _____ sets of _____.

Shoulder and Rotator Cuff Active Exercises - Right

☐ **Punch**
Lie on your back. Lift your right arm. Move only from your shoulder. Punch your arm up.

Do ______ sets of ______.

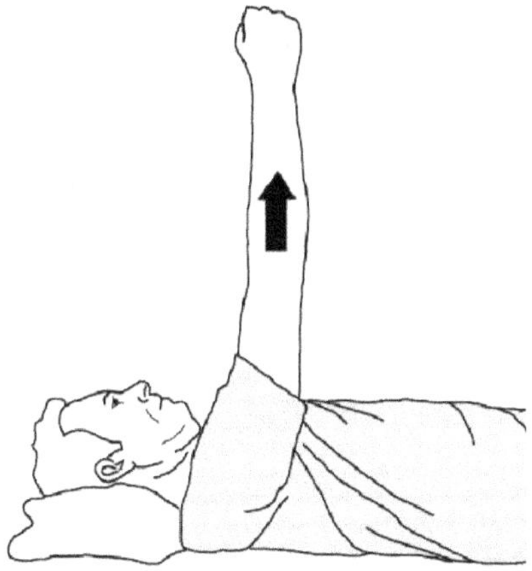

☐ **External Rotation**
Lie on your left side and place a folded hand towel under your right elbow. Bend your elbow and rest it on your stomach. Rotate at your shoulder and raise your hand up toward the ceiling.

Do ______ sets of ______.

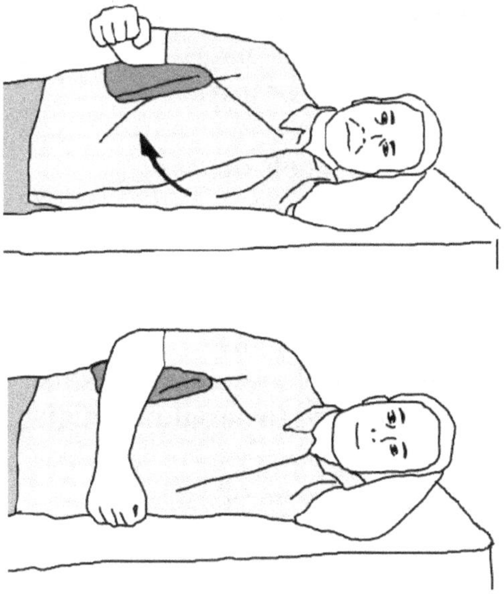

☐ **Internal Rotation**
Lie on your right side. Tuck your arm against your body with your elbow bent. Rotate at your shoulder and bring your arm into your chest.

Do ______ sets of ______.

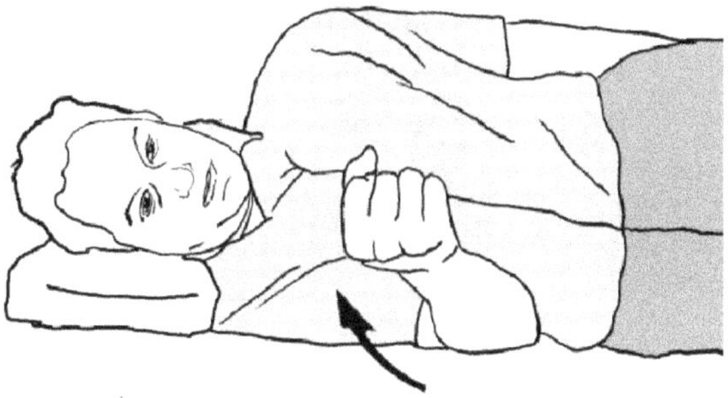

Shoulder and Rotator Cuff Active Exercises - Right

Lie on your stomach with your right arm hanging over the side.

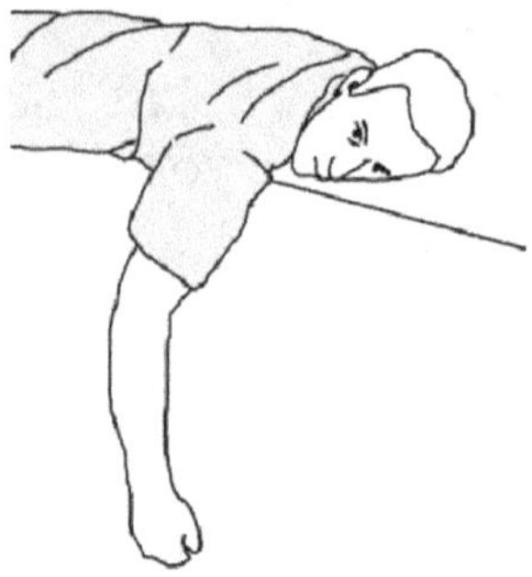

☐ **Shoulder Blade Retraction**
Keep your elbow straight. Squeeze your right shoulder blade. Do not shrug your shoulder toward your ear.

Do _____ sets of _____.

☐ **Letter I** (flexion)
Keep your elbow straight. Raise your right arm forward to shoulder height.

Do _____ sets of _____.

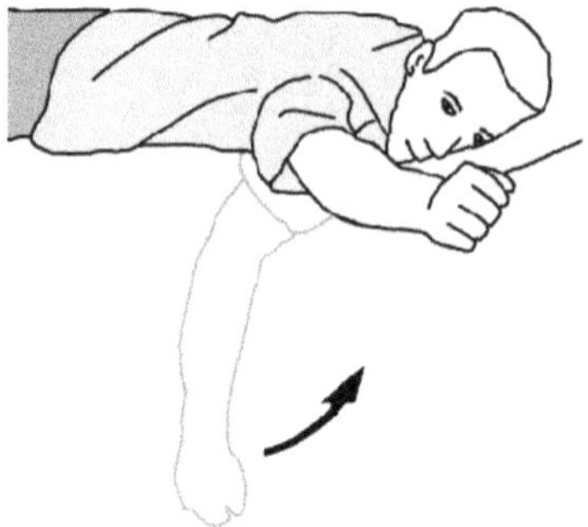

☐ **Letter Y** (scaption)
Raise your right arm up from the side at a 45-degree angle to shoulder height.

Do _____ sets of _____.

Shoulder and Rotator Cuff Active Exercises - Right

☐ **Letter T** (horizontal abduction)
Raise your right arm up to the side to shoulder height.

Do ______ sets of ______.

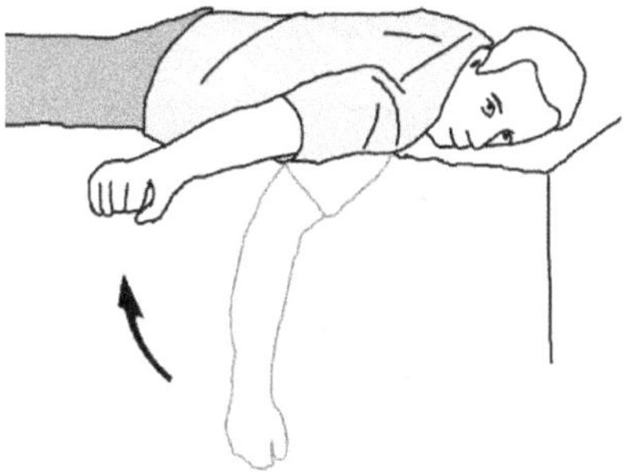

☐ **Letter A** (extension)
Raise your right arm backward to the level of your hip

Do ______ sets of ______.

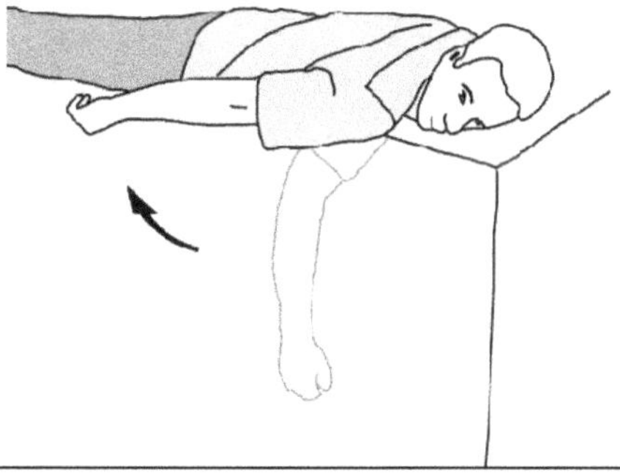

☐ **Rowing**
Lift your right elbow up toward the ceiling.

Do ______ sets of ______.

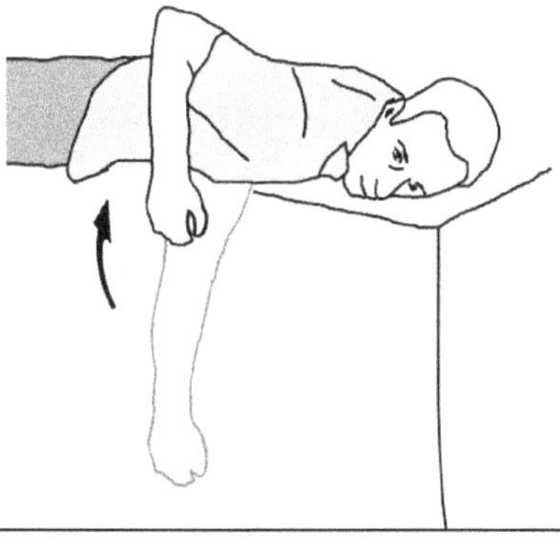

☐ **Rotation**
Raise your right arm to shoulder height with the elbow at a 90-degree angle. Rotate your hand upward, until your hand is even with the bed.

Do ______ sets of ______.

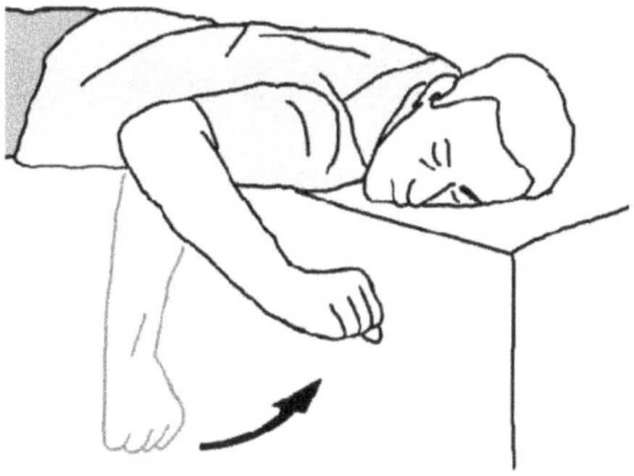

Occupational Therapy TOOLKIT

Shoulder and Rotator Cuff Exercises
Free Weight - Left

Do the checked exercises _____ times per day, _____ days a week.

☐ **Forward Raise** (flexion)
Hold a ______ lb/kg weight in each hand. Keep your thumbs pointing up and your elbows straight. Raise both arms forward.

Do ______ sets of ______.

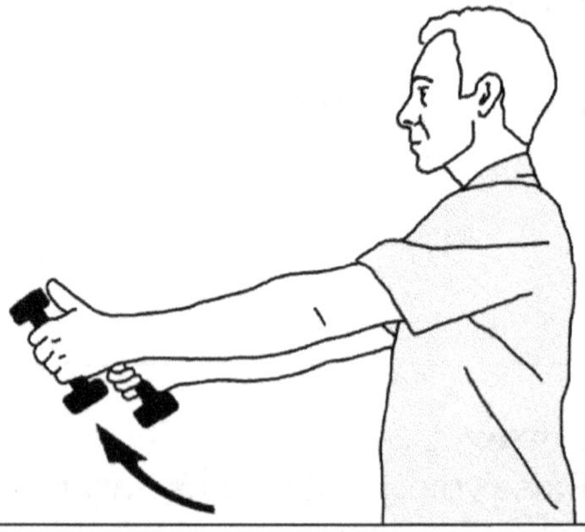

☐ **Side Raise** (abduction)
Hold a ______ lb/kg weight in each hand. Keep your thumbs up and your elbows straight. Raise both arms up from the sides to shoulder level.

Do ______ sets of ______.

☐ **Corner Raise** (scaption)
Hold a ______ lb/kg weight in each hand. Keep your thumbs up and your elbows straight. Raise both arms forward at a 45° angle. Raise both arms to shoulder level.

Do ______ sets of ______.

Occupational Therapy TOOLKIT

Shoulder and Rotator Cuff Exercises
Free Weight - Left

☐ **Punch**
Lie on your back. Hold a ______ lb/kg weight in your left hand. Lift your left arm. Move only from your shoulder. Punch your arm up.

Do ______ sets of ______.

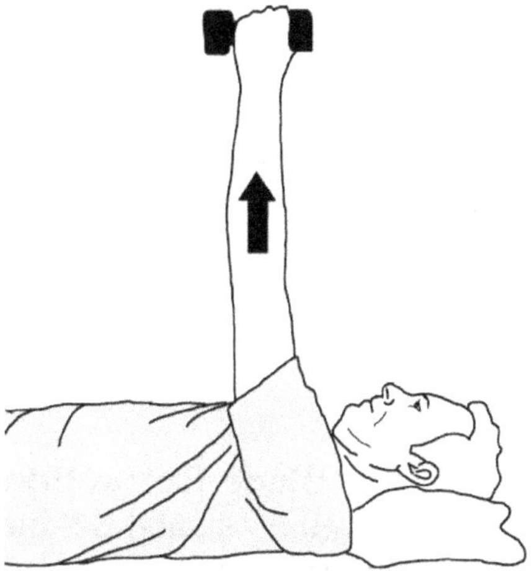

☐ **External Rotation**
Lie on your right side and place a folded hand towel under your left elbow. Bend your elbow and rest it on your stomach. Hold a ______ lb/kg weight in your left hand. Rotate at your shoulder and raise your hand up, toward the ceiling.

Do ______ sets of ______.

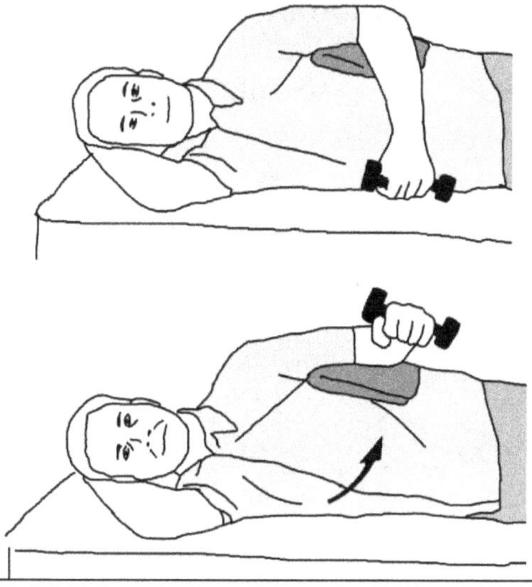

☐ **Internal Rotation**
Lie on your left side. Tuck your arm against your body with your elbow bent. Hold a ______ lb/kg weight in your left hand. Rotate at your shoulder and bring your arm into your chest.

Do ______ sets of ______.

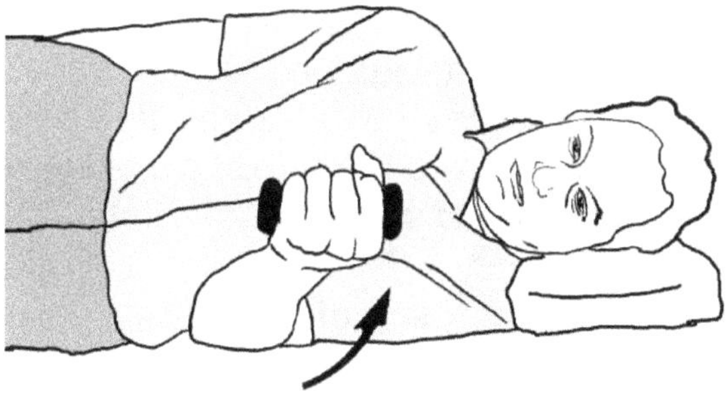

Shoulder and Rotator Cuff Exercises
Free Weight - Left

Lie on your stomach with your left arm hanging over the side.

Hold a ______ lb/kg weight in your left hand.

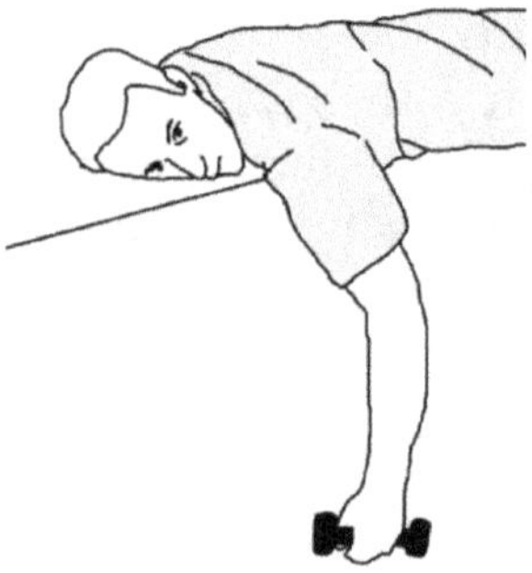

☐ **Shoulder Blade Retraction**
Keep your elbow straight. Squeeze your left shoulder blade. Do not shrug your shoulder toward your ear.

Do ______ sets of ______.

☐ **Letter I** (flexion)
Keep your elbow straight. Raise your left arm forward to shoulder height.

Do ______ sets of ______.

☐ **Letter Y** (scaption)
Keep your elbow straight. Raise your left arm up from the side at a 45-degree angle to shoulder height.

Do ______ sets of ______.

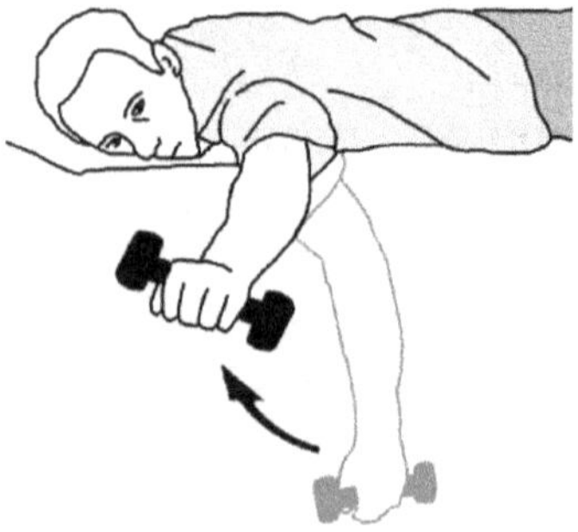

Occupational Therapy TOOLKIT

Shoulder and Rotator Cuff Exercises
Free Weight - Left

☐ **Letter T** (horizontal abduction)
Keep your elbow straight. Raise your left arm up to the side, to shoulder height.

Do ______ sets of ______.

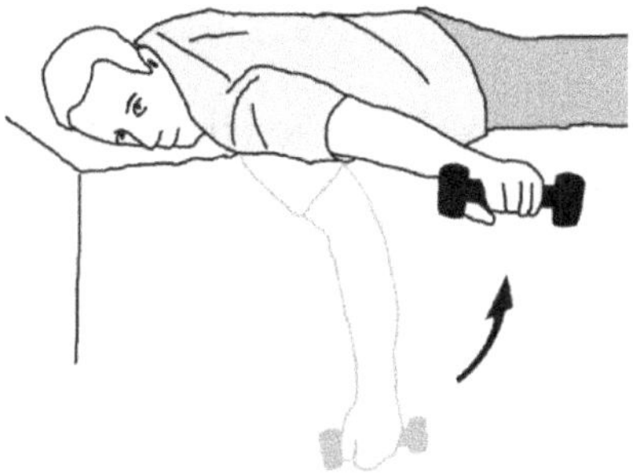

☐ **Letter A** (extension)
Keep your elbow straight. Raise your left arm back to the level of your hip

Do ______ sets of ______.

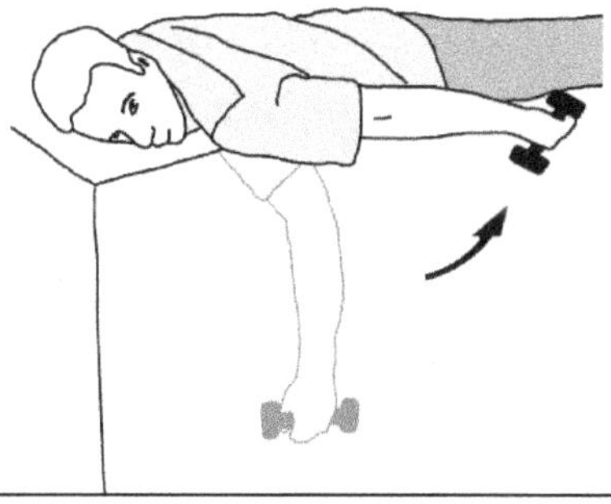

☐ **Rowing**
Lift your left elbow up toward the ceiling.

Do ______ sets of ______.

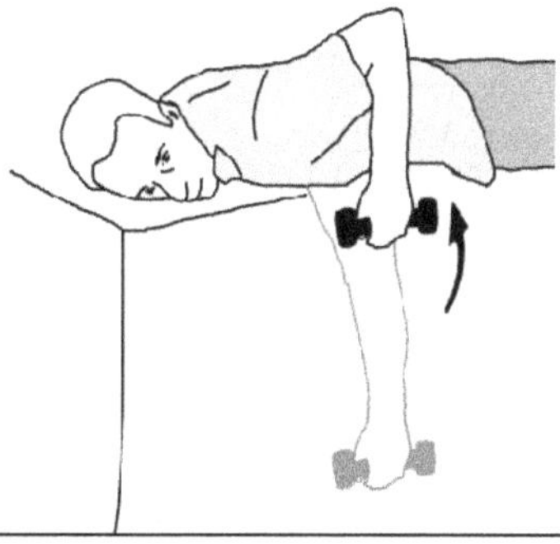

☐ **Rotation**
Raise your left arm to shoulder height with your elbow at a 90-degree angle. Rotate your hand upward, until your hand is even with the bed.

Do ______ sets of ______.

Occupational Therapy TOOLKIT

Shoulder and Rotator Cuff Exercises
Free Weight - Right

Do the checked exercises _____ times per day, _____ days a week.

☐ **Forward Raise** (flexion)
Hold a _____ lb/kg weight in each hand. Keep your thumbs pointing up and your elbows straight. Raise both arms forward.

Do _____ sets of _____.

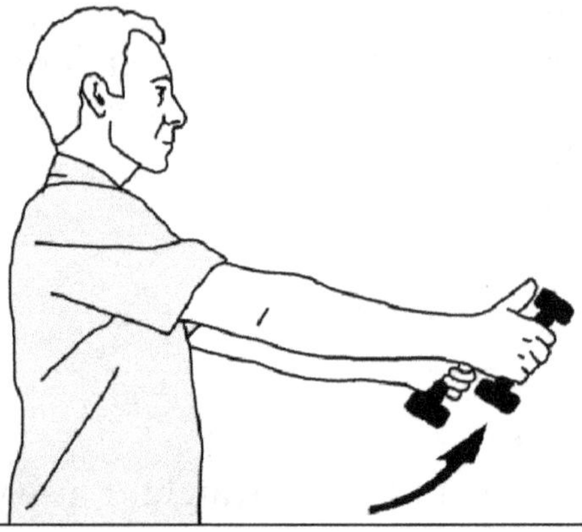

☐ **Side Raise** (abduction)
Hold a _____ lb/kg weight in each hand. Keep your thumbs up and your elbows straight. Raise both arms up from the sides to shoulder level.

Do _____ sets of _____.

☐ **Corner Raise** (scaption)
Hold a _____ lb/kg weight in each hand. Keep your thumbs up and your elbows straight. Raise both arms forward at a 45° angle. Raise both arms to shoulder level.

Do _____ sets of _____.

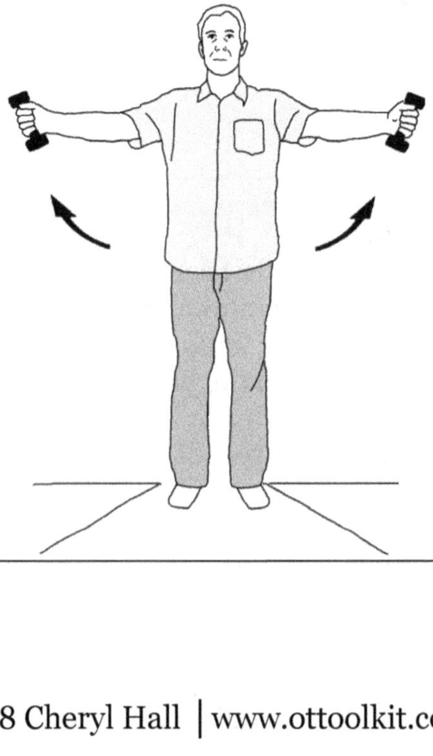

Occupational Therapy TOOLKIT

Shoulder and Rotator Cuff Exercises
Free Weight - Right

☐ **Punch**
Lie on your back. Hold a ______ lb/kg weight in your right hand. Lift your right arm. Move only from your shoulder. Punch your arm up.

Do ______ sets of ______.

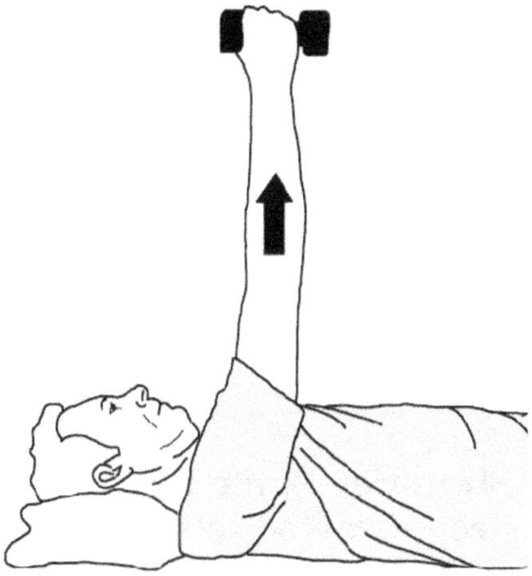

☐ **External Rotation**
Lie on your left side and place a folded hand towel under your right elbow. Bend your elbow and rest it on your stomach. Hold a ______ lb/kg weight in your right hand. Rotate at your shoulder and raise your hand up, toward the ceiling.

Do ______ sets of ______.

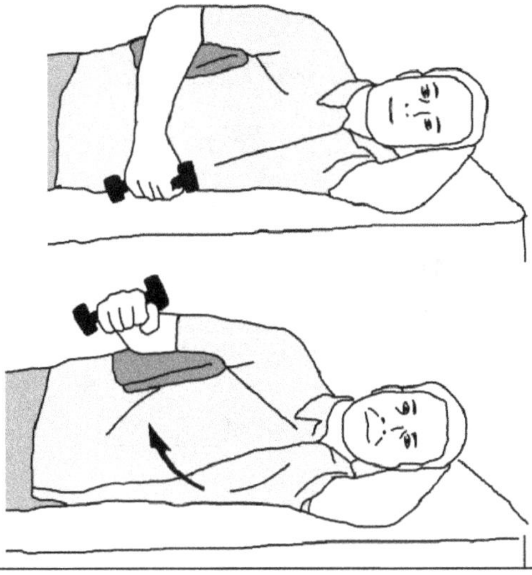

☐ **Internal Rotation**
Lie on your right side. Tuck your arm against your body with your elbow bent. Hold a ______ lb/kg weight in your right hand. Rotate at your shoulder and bring your arm into your chest.

Do ______ sets of ______.

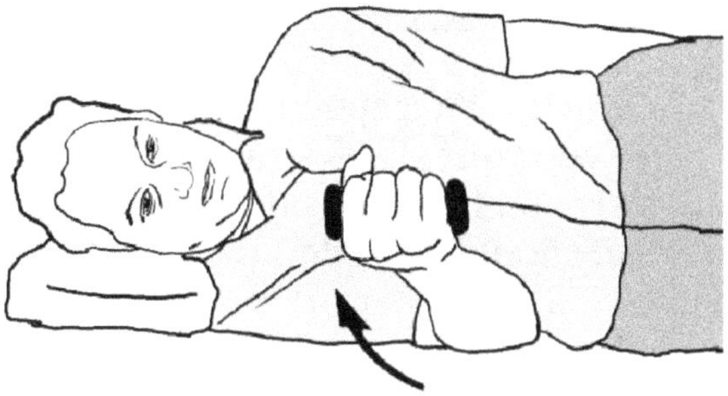

Shoulder and Rotator Cuff Exercises
Free Weight - Right

Lie on your stomach with your right arm hanging over the side.

Hold a ______ lb/kg weight in your right hand.

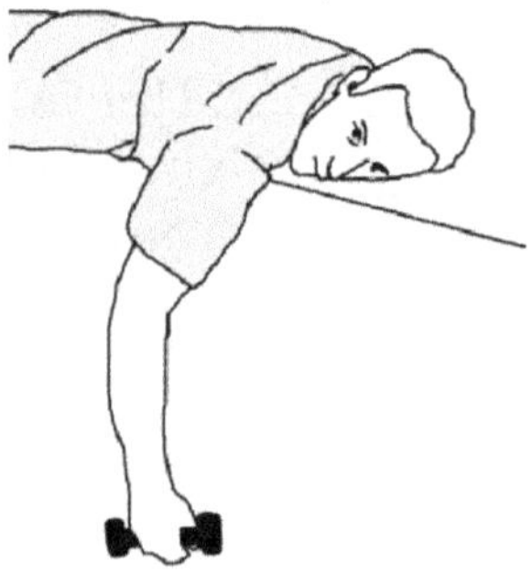

☐ **Shoulder Blade Retraction**
Keep your elbow straight. Squeeze your right shoulder blade. Do not shrug your shoulder toward your ear.

Do ______ sets of ______.

☐ **Letter I** (flexion)
Keep your elbow straight. Raise your right arm forward to shoulder height.

Do ______ sets of ______.

☐ **Letter Y** (scaption)
Keep your elbow straight. Raise your right arm up from the side at a 45-degree angle, to shoulder height.

Do ______ sets of ______.

Occupational Therapy TOOLKIT

Shoulder and Rotator Cuff Exercises
Free Weight - Right

☐ **Letter T** (horizontal abduction)
Keep your elbow straight. Raise your right arm up to the side, to shoulder height.

Do ______ sets of ______.

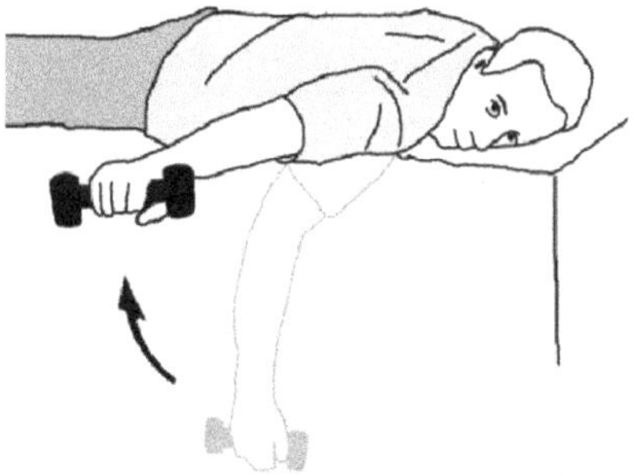

☐ **Letter A** (extension)
Keep your elbow straight. Raise your right arm back to the level of your hip

Do ______ sets of ______.

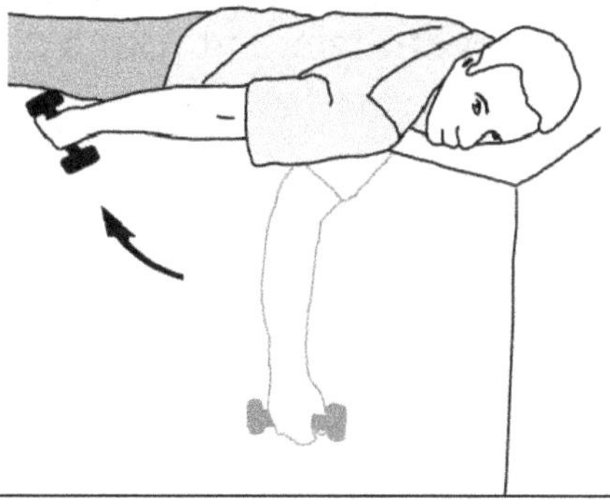

☐ **Rowing**
Lift your right elbow up toward the ceiling.

Do ______ sets of ______.

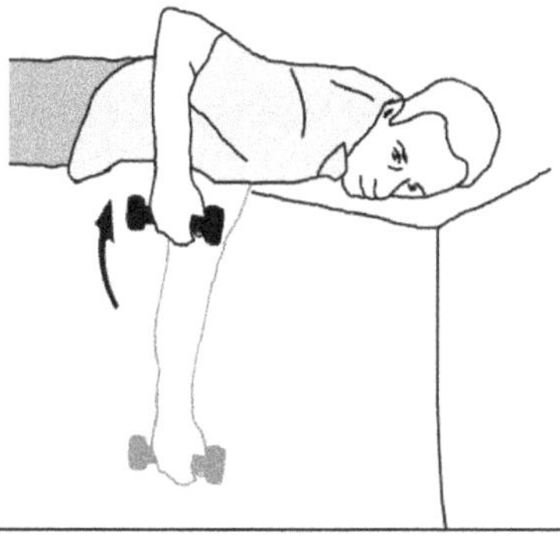

☐ **Rotation**
Raise your right arm to shoulder height with your elbow bent at a 90-degree angle. Rotate your hand upward, until your hand is even with the bed.

Do ______ sets of ______.

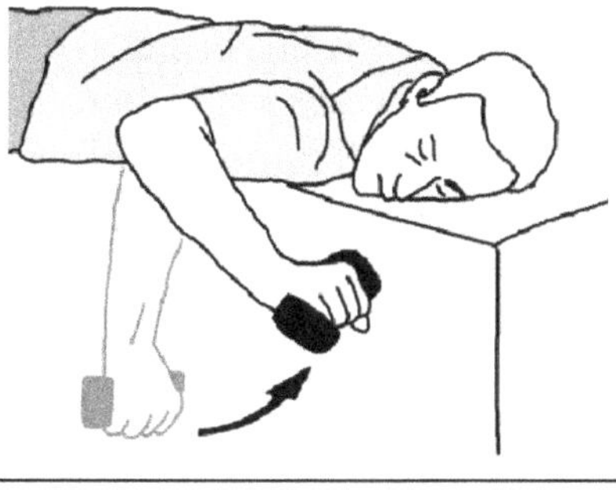

Shoulder and Rotator Cuff Exercises
Stretch Band - Left

Do the checked exercises _____ times per day, _____ days a week.

Take a length of _____ stretch band and knot the loose ends. For safety, be sure the door opens away from you. Secure the stretch band between the door and the door jam. The knot end is on the other side of the closed door.

☐ **Forward Raise** (flexion)
Secure the stretch band at mid-calf height. Stand with your back to the door. Turn your palm up. Keep your elbow straight. Lift your left arm up in front.

Do _____ sets of _____.

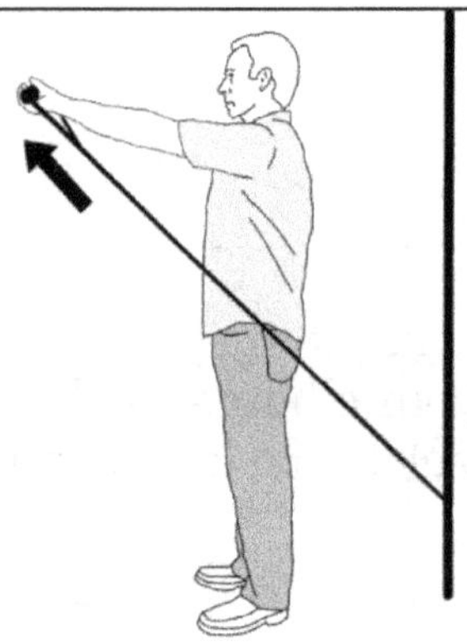

☐ **Side Raise** (abduction)
Secure the stretch band at mid-calf height. Stand with your right side to the door. Keep your elbow straight and your thumb pointed up. Raise your left arm up from your side.

Do _____ sets of _____.

☐ **Internal Rotation**
Secure the stretch band at elbow height. Stand with your left side to the door. Place a folded hand towel under your left arm. Rotate your left arm across your chest. Do not twist your body.

Do _____ sets of _____.

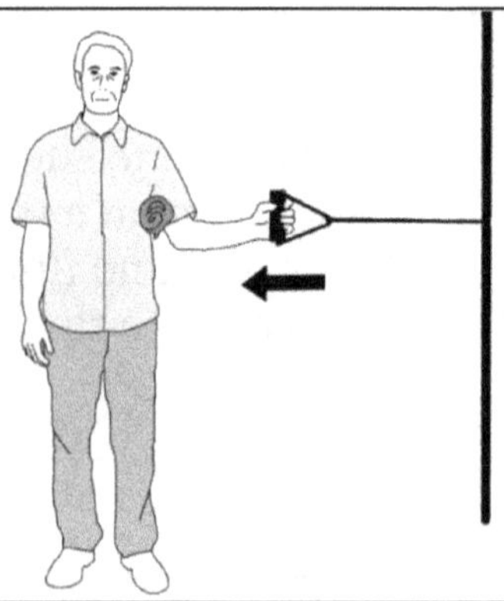

Shoulder and Rotator Cuff Strength Exercises
Stretch Band - Left

☐ **External Rotation**
Secure the stretch band at elbow height. Stand with your right side to the door. Place a folded hand towel under your left arm. Rotate your left shoulder out to the side. Don't twist your body

Do ______ sets of ______.

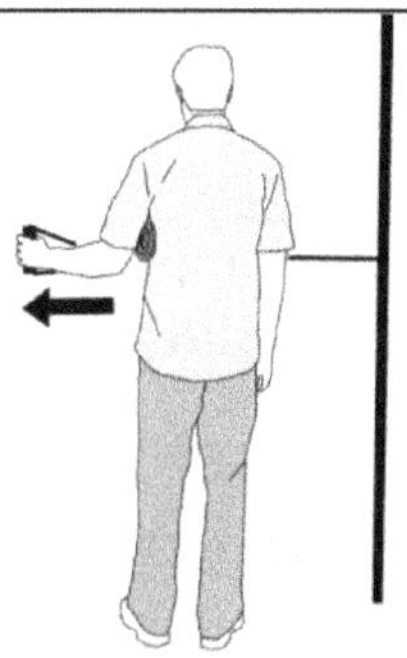

☐ **Rows**
Secure the stretch band at elbow height. Stand facing the door. Pull your left elbow back.

Do ______ sets of ______.

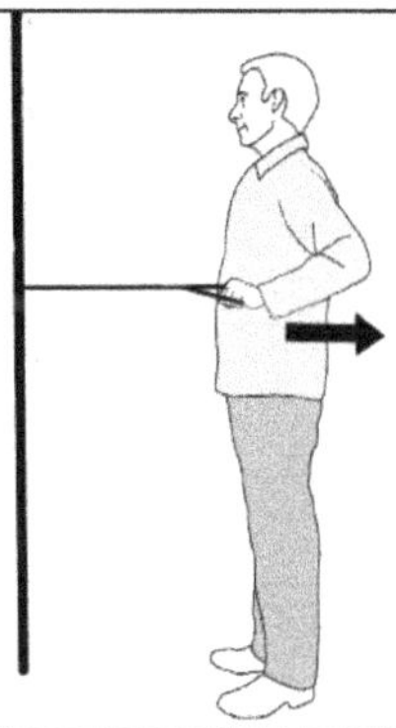

☐ **Pull Down** (adduction)
Secure the stretch band at the top of the door. Stand with your left side to the door. Pull your left arm to your side.

Do ______ sets of ______.

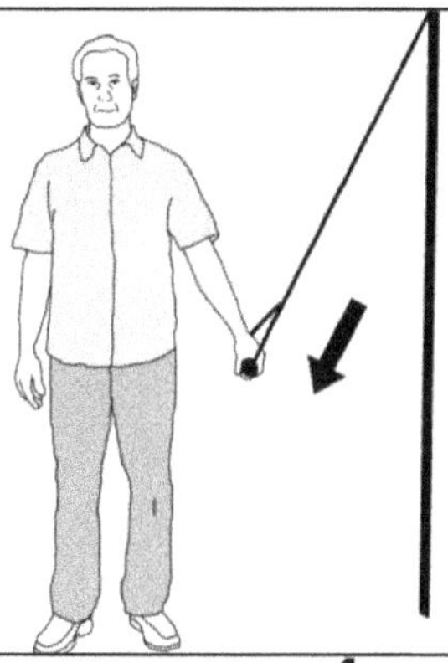

☐ **Pull Back** (extension)
Secure the stretch band at the top of the door. Stand facing the door. Pull your left arm back, a little past your body.

Do ______ sets of ______.

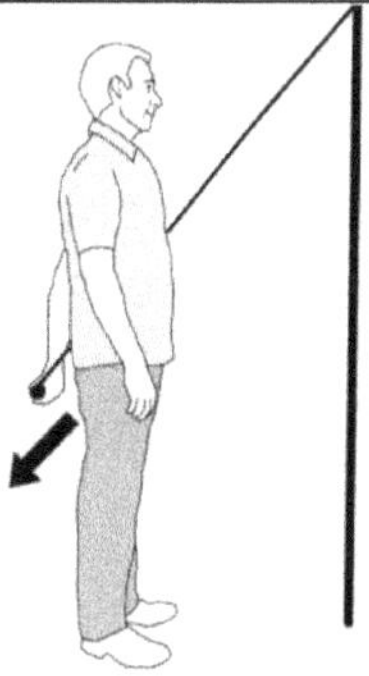

Shoulder and Rotator Cuff Strength Exercises
Stretch Band - Right

Do the checked exercises _____ times per day, _____ days a week.

Take a length of _____ stretch band and knot the loose ends. For safety, be sure the door opens away from you. Secure the stretch band between the door and the door jam. The knot end is on the other side of the closed door.

☐ **Forward Raise** (flexion)
Secure the stretch band at mid-calf height. Stand with your back to the door. Turn your palm up. Keep your elbow straight. Lift your right arm up in front.

Do _____ sets of _____.

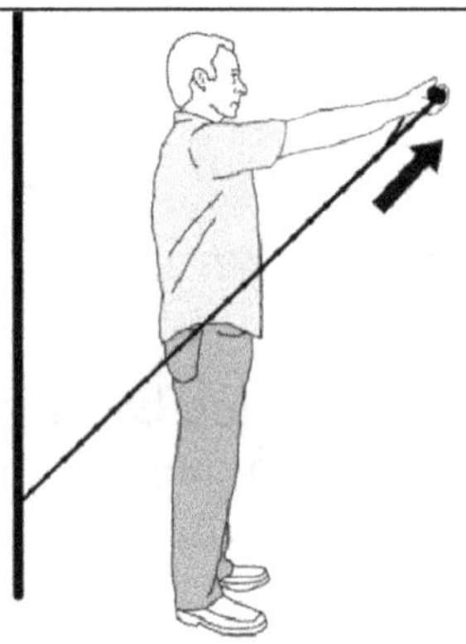

☐ **Side Raise** (abduction)
Secure the stretch band at mid-calf height. Stand with your left side to the door. Keep your elbow straight and your thumb pointed up. Raise your right arm up from your side.

Do _____ sets of _____.

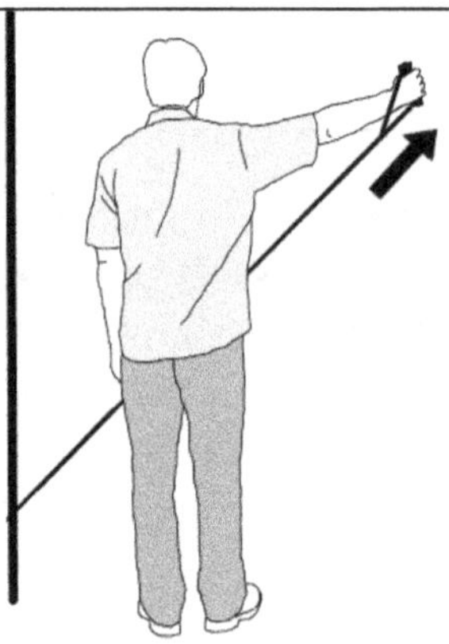

☐ **Internal Rotation**
Secure the stretch band at elbow height. Stand with your right side to the door. Place a folded hand towel under your right arm. Rotate your right arm across your chest. Do not twist your body.

Do _____ sets of _____.

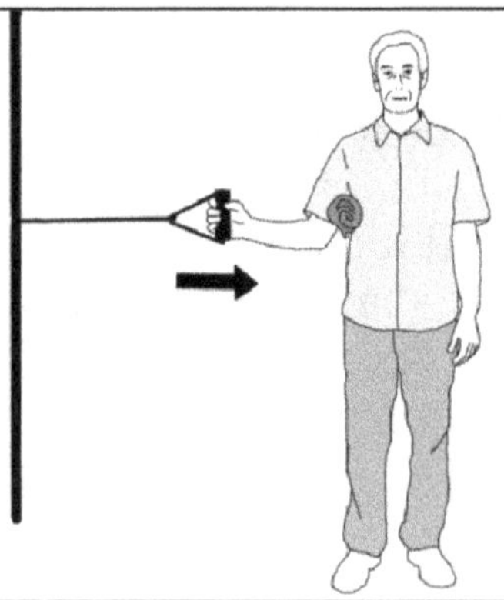

Shoulder and Rotator Cuff Strength Exercises
Stretch Band - Right

☐ **External Rotation**
Secure the stretch band at elbow height. Stand with your left side to the door. Place a folded hand towel under your right arm. Rotate your right shoulder out to the side. Don't twist your body

Do ______ sets of ______.

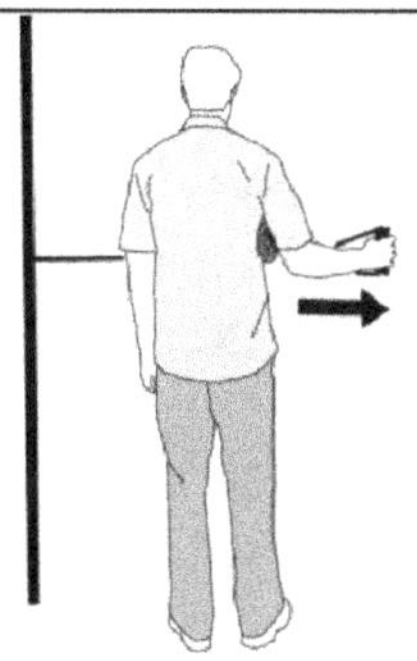

☐ **Rows**
Secure the stretch band at elbow height. Stand facing the door. Pull your right elbow back.

Do ______ sets of ______.

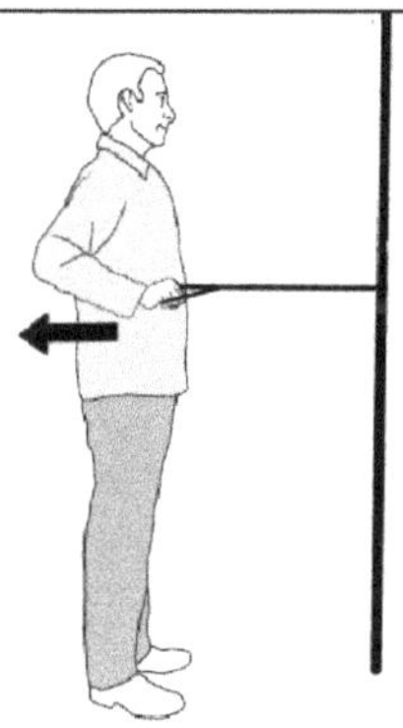

☐ **Pull Down** (adduction)
Secure the stretch band at the top of the door. Stand with your right side to the door. Pull your right arm to your side.

Do ______ sets of ______.

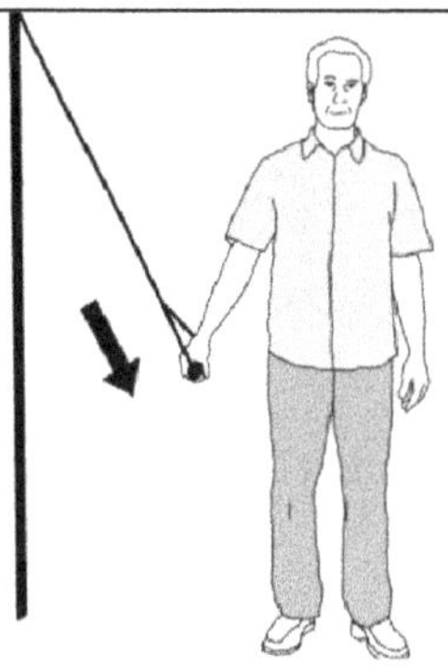

☐ **Pull Back** (extension)
Secure the stretch band at the top of the door. Stand facing the door. Pull your right arm back, a little past your body.

Do ______ sets of ______.

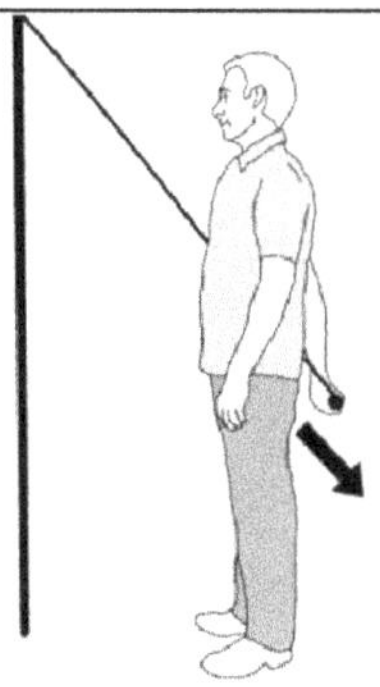

Occupational Therapy TOOLKIT

Shoulder Blade Exercises

Do the checked exercises _____ times per day, _____ days a week.

☐ **Stretch Across**
Pull your right arm across your body.
Hold for a count of _____.

Do _____ sets of _____.
Repeat on your left side.

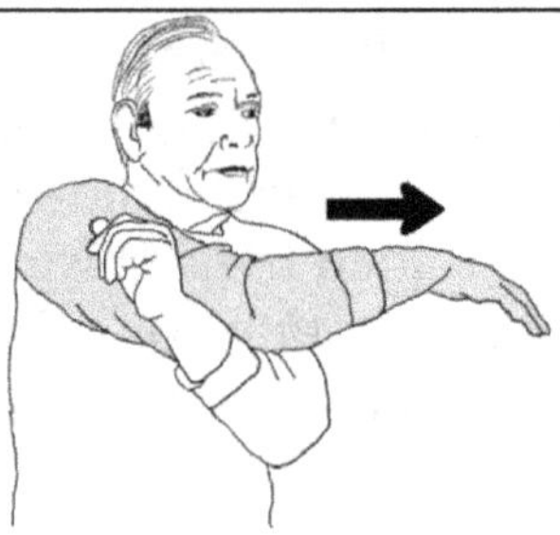

☐ **Corner Stretch**
Stand facing a corner. Raise your arms to shoulder height. Press your chest into the corner. Hold for a count of _____.

Do _____ sets of _____.

☐ **Shoulder Shrugs**
Shrug your shoulders. Hold for a count of _____.

Do _____ sets of _____.

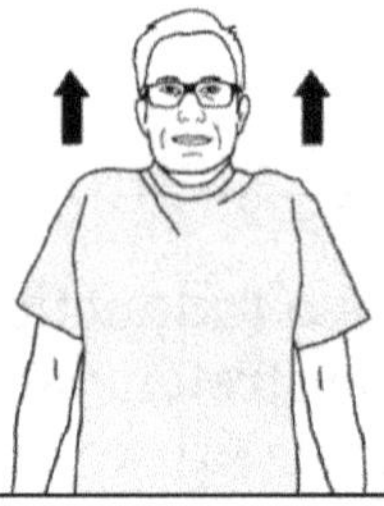

☐ **Rolls**
Roll your shoulders back.

Do _____ sets of _____.

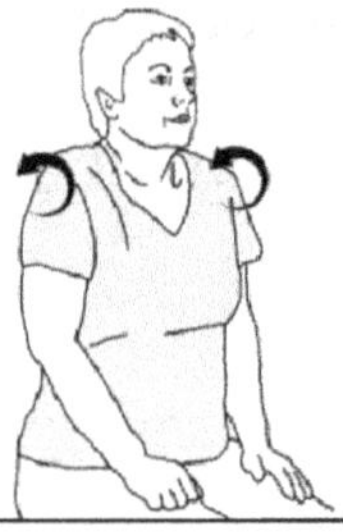

☐ **Upper Back Stretch**
Pull your elbows back. Squeeze your shoulder blades. Hold for a count of _____.

Do _____ sets of _____.

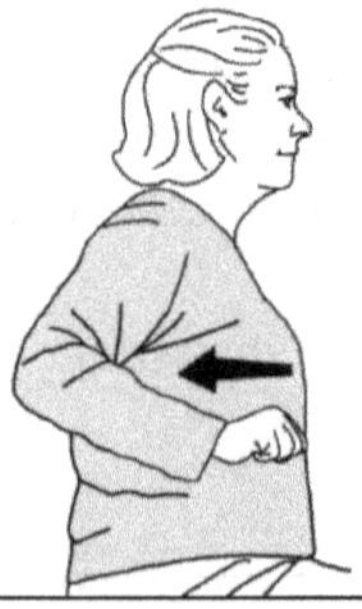

Occupational Therapy TOOLKIT

Shoulder Blade Exercises

Do the checked exercises ______ times per day, ______ days a week.

☐ **Punch**
Lie on your back. Lift your right arm straight up. Punch up with your arm. Hold for a count of ______.

Do ______ sets of ______.
Repeat on the left side.

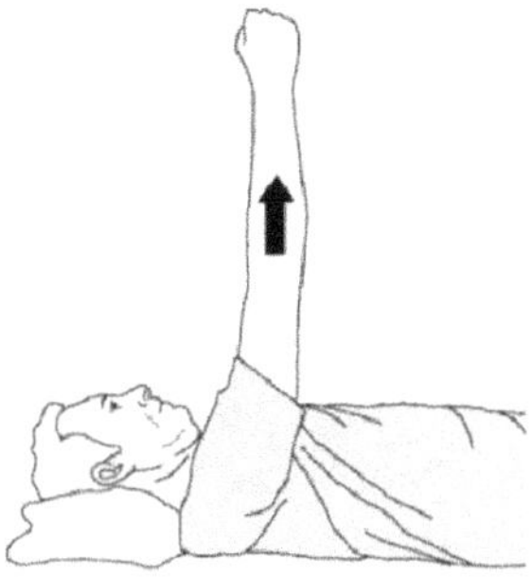

☐ **Chair Push-Ups**
Sit with feet flat on the floor and hands on the armrests. Push up from the armrest and lift your hips off the chair. Hold for a count of ______.

Do ______ sets of ______.

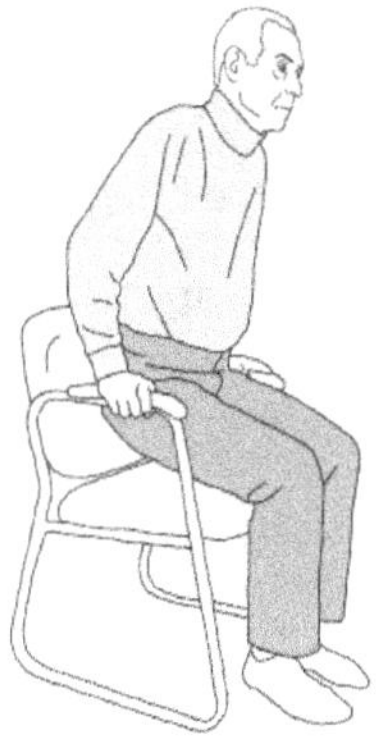

☐ **Pull Apart**
Hold a ______ stretch band between your hands. Raise your arms to shoulder level. Pull the stretch band across your chest. Hold for a count of ______.

Do ______ sets of ______.

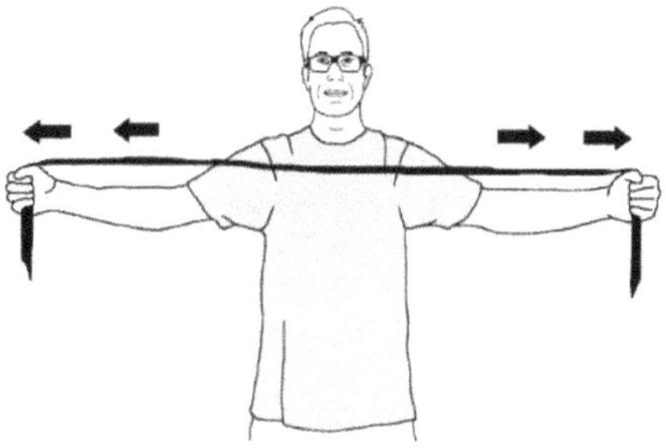

☐ **Row**
Secure the stretch band at elbow height. For safety, be sure the door opens away from you. Stand facing the door. Pull your right elbow back. Hold for a count of ______.

Do ______ sets of ______.
Repeat on the left side.

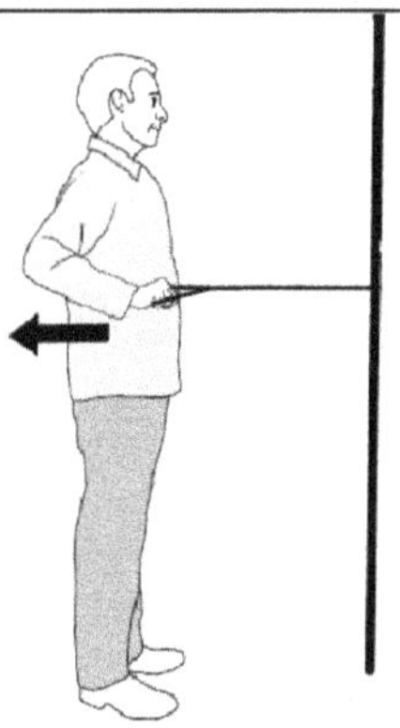

Occupational Therapy TOOLKIT

Shoulder, Elbow, and Hand Active Exercises

Do _____ sets of _____ of each exercise.

Do the checked exercises _____ times per day, _____ days a week.

☐ Roll your shoulder.

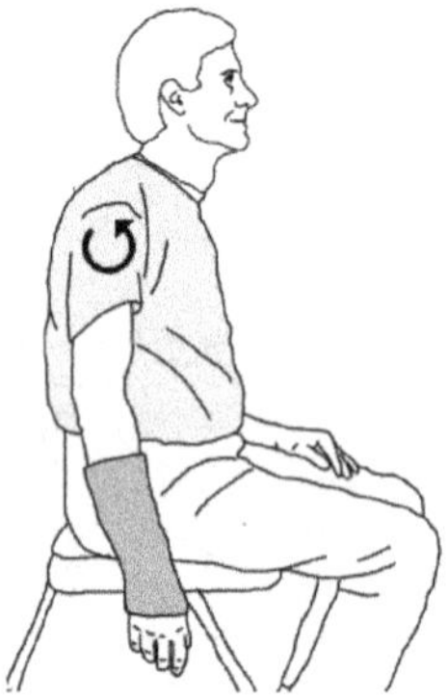

☐ Reach behind your neck.

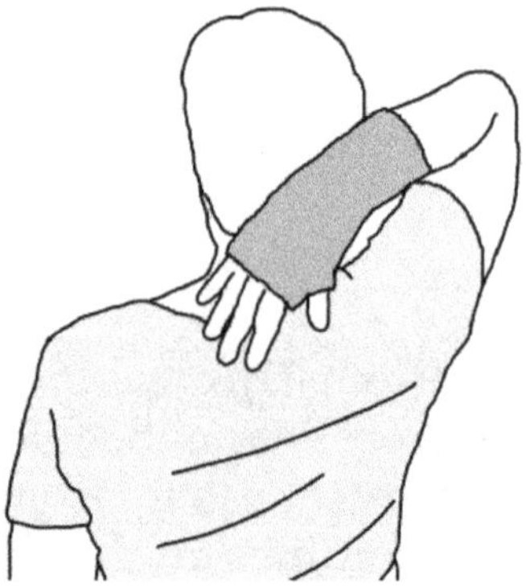

☐ Reach behind your low back.

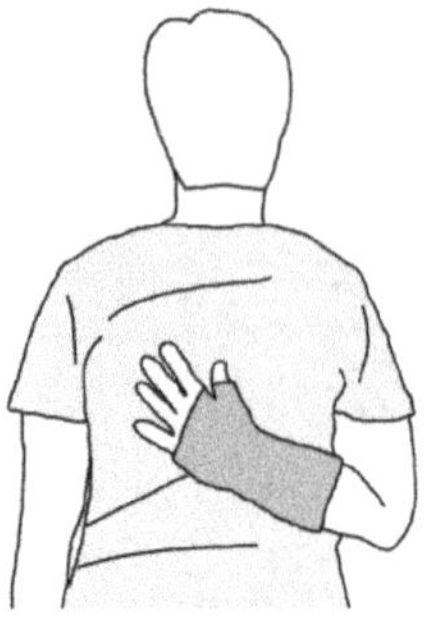

☐ Bend and straighten your elbow.

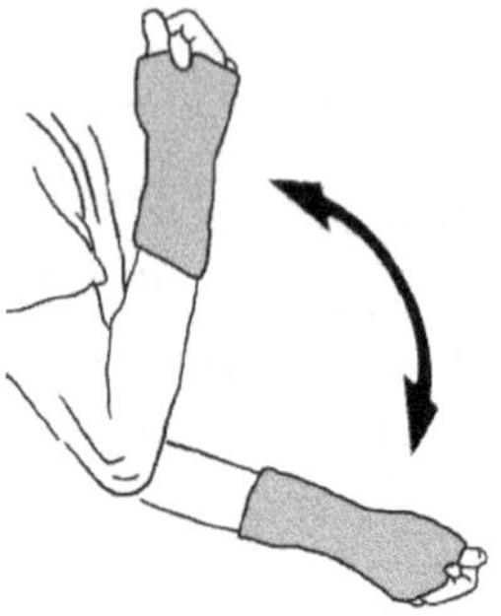

☐ Open and close your hand.

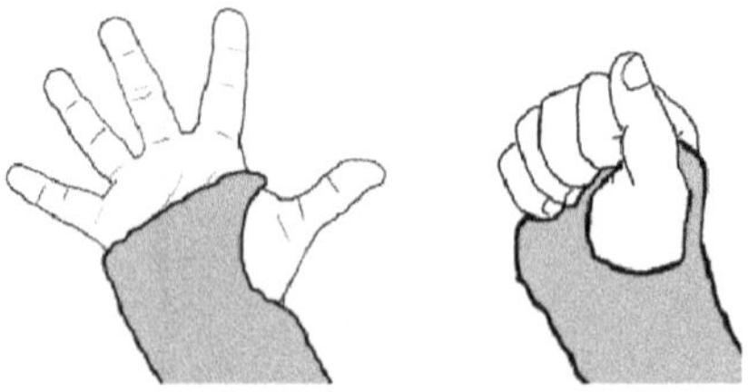

☐ Squeeze a soft ball.

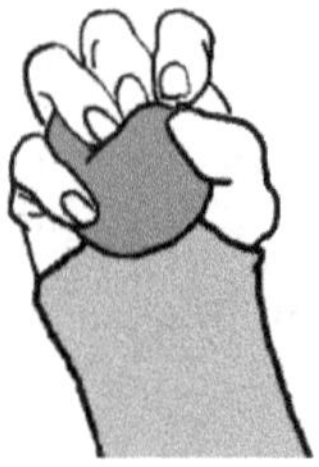

Occupational Therapy TOOLKIT

Shoulder Isometric Left - Seated

Name: ___________________________________

Date: ____________________________________

Therapist: ________________________________

Phone number: (_____)______________________

Do the checked exercises _____ times per day, _____ days a week.

These are isometric exercises; you will not be moving the joint, only contracting the muscles against light resistance.

Sit in an upholstered chair or sofa with the armrest next to your left arm.

Use good posture. Keep your stomach muscles tight and your back straight.

Do not hold your breath during exercise. Count aloud if needed.

Sore muscles lasting a few days and feeling tired are normal after exercise. Exhaustion, sore joints, and painful muscle pulls are not normal. If you have these symptoms, do not exercise until you talk with your therapist.

If you have chest tightness or pain, shortness of breath, feel dizzy, faint, or sick to your stomach, stop and call emergency services at _____.

Notes:

____

____

____

____

____

____

Shoulder Isometric Left - Seated

☐ **Shoulder Flexion**
Hold your left arm at your side with your elbow bent. Use your right hand to resist your left arm from moving forward. Hold for a count of ______.

Do ______ sets of ______.

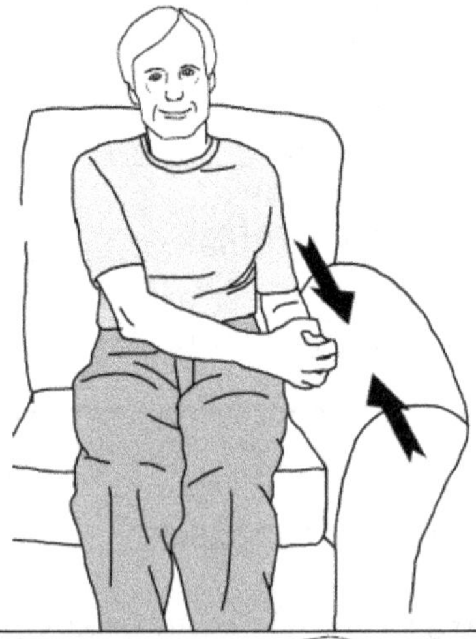

☐ **Shoulder Extension**
Hold your left arm at your side with your elbow bent. Use the chair back to resist your left arm from moving back. Hold for a count of ______.

Do ______ sets of ______.

☐ **Shoulder Abduction**
Hold your left arm at your side with your elbow bent. Use the chair arm to resist your left arm lifting to the side. Hold for a count of ______.

Do ______ sets of ______.

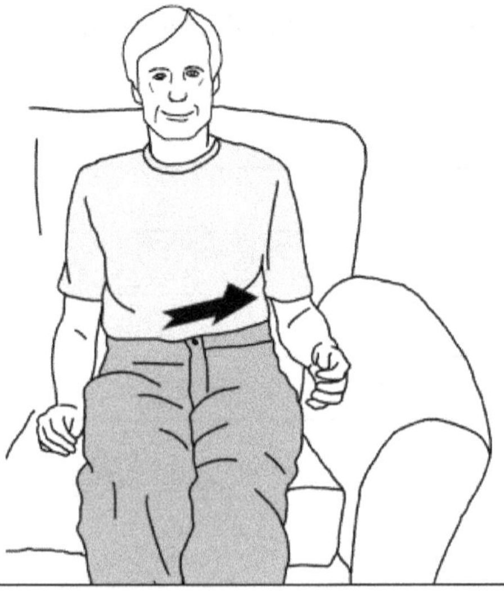

Shoulder Isometric Left - Seated

☐ **Shoulder Adduction**
Hold your left arm at your side with your elbow bent. Press your left elbow into your body. Hold for a count of _______.

Do ______ sets of ______.

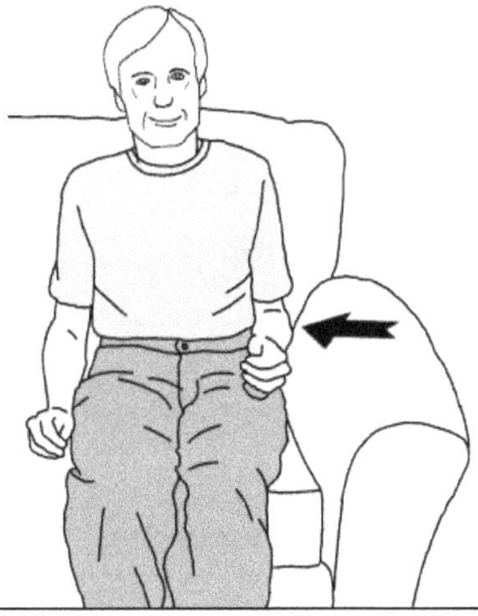

☐ **External Rotation**
Hold your left arm at your side with your elbow bent. Use the chair arm to resist your left arm from rotating to the side. Hold for a count of _______.

Do ______ sets of ______.

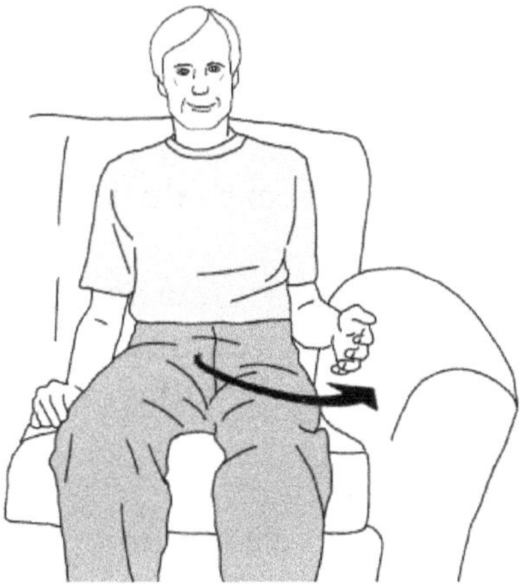

☐ **Internal Rotation**
Hold your left arm at your side with your elbow bent. Use your right hand to resist your left arm from rotating into your body. Hold for a count of _______.

Do ______ sets of ______.

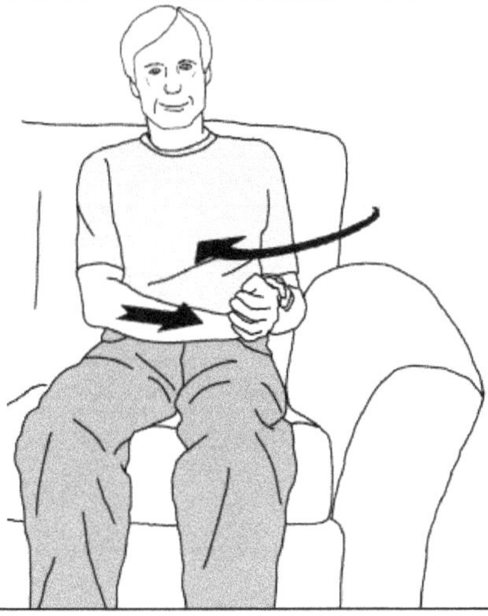

Occupational Therapy TOOLKIT

Shoulder Isometric Left - Standing

Name: ________________________________

Date: ________________________________

Therapist: ________________________________

Phone number: (______)________________________

Do the checked exercises ______ times per day, ______ days a week.

These are isometric exercises; you will not be moving the joint, only contracting the muscles against light resistance.

Use good posture. Keep your stomach muscles tight and your back straight.

Do not hold your breath during exercise. Count aloud if needed.

Sore muscles lasting a few days and feeling tired are normal after exercise. Exhaustion, sore joints, and painful muscle pulls are not normal. If you have these symptoms, do not exercise until you talk with your therapist.

If you have chest tightness or pain, shortness of breath, feel dizzy, faint, or sick to your stomach, stop and call emergency services at ______.

Notes:

____

____

____

____

____

____

____

____

Shoulder Isometric Left - Standing

☐ **Shoulder Flexion**
Stand facing the wall. Make a fist with your left hand. Place a pillow between the wall and your fist. Use the wall to resist moving your arm forward. Hold for a count of ______.

Do ______ sets of ______.

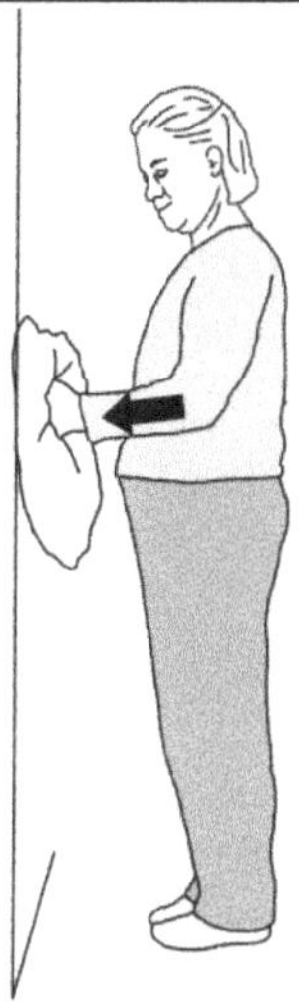

☐ **Shoulder Extension**
Stand with your back against the wall. Place the pillow between the wall and your left elbow. Use the wall to resist moving your arm back. Hold for a count of ______.

Do ______ sets of ______.

☐ **Shoulder Abduction**
Stand with your left side toward the wall. Place the pillow between the wall and your left elbow. Hold your elbow bent or straight. Use the wall to resist moving your arm up from the side. Hold for a count of ______.

Do ______ sets of ______.

Shoulder Isometric Left - Standing

☐ **Shoulder Adduction**
Hold the pillow under your left arm. Use the pillow to resist moving your arm into your side. Hold for a count of ______.

Do _____ sets of _____.

☐ **Shoulder External Rotation**
Stand with your left side toward the wall. Place the pillow between the wall and your left elbow. Use the wall to resist rotating your left arm out. Hold for a count of ______.

Do _____ sets of _____.

☐ **Shoulder Internal Rotation**
Stand to the side of a wall corner. Place a pillow between the outer edge of the corner and your left hand. Use the wall to resist rotating your left arm in. Hold for a count of ______.

Do _____ sets of _____.

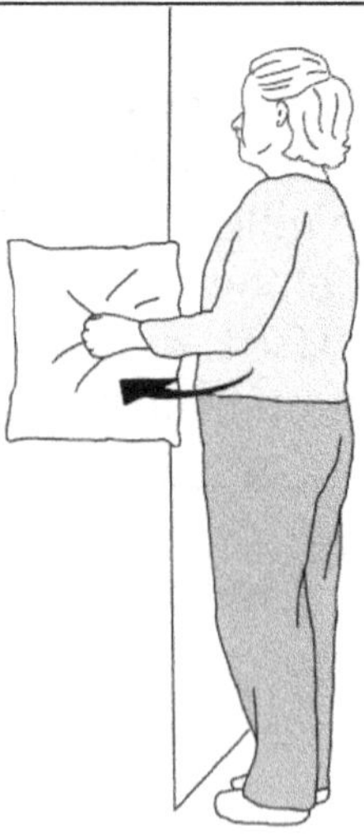

Shoulder Isometric Right - Seated

Name: ________________________________

Date: ________________________________

Therapist: ________________________________

Phone number: (_____)______________________

Do the checked exercises _____ times per day, _____ days a week.

These are isometric exercises; you will not be moving the joint, only contracting the muscles against light resistance.

Sit in an upholstered chair or sofa with the armrest next to your right arm.

Use good posture. Keep your stomach muscles tight and your back straight.

Do not hold your breath during exercise. Count aloud if needed.

Sore muscles lasting a few days and feeling tired are normal after exercise. Exhaustion, sore joints, and painful muscle pulls are not normal. If you have these symptoms, do not exercise until you talk with your therapist.

If you have chest tightness or pain, shortness of breath, feel dizzy, faint, or sick to your stomach, stop and call emergency services at _____.

Notes:

____

____

____

____

____

____

Shoulder Isometric Right - Seated

☐ **Shoulder Flexion**
Hold your right arm at your side with your elbow bent. Use your left hand to resist your right arm from moving forward. Hold for a count of ______.

Do ______ sets of ______.

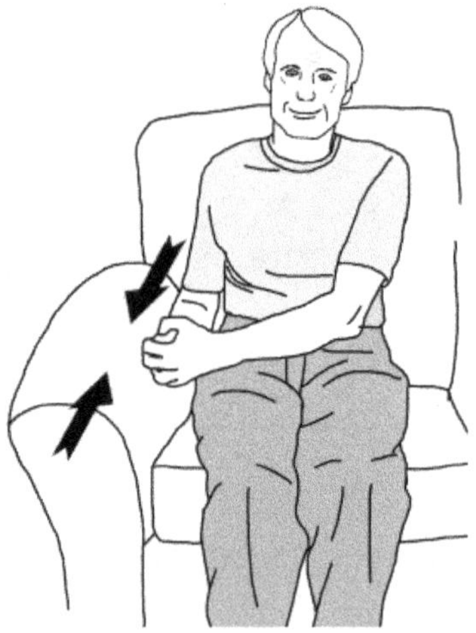

☐ **Shoulder Extension**
Hold your right arm at your side with your elbow bent. Use the chair back to resist your right arm from moving back. Hold for a count of ______.

Do ______ sets of ______.

☐ **Shoulder Abduction**
Hold your right arm at your side with your elbow bent. Use the chair arm to resist your right arm lifting to the side. Hold for a count of ______.

Do ______ sets of ______.

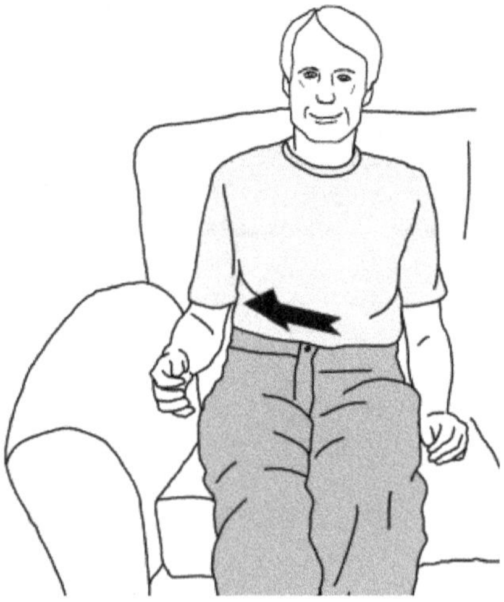

Occupational Therapy TOOLKIT

Shoulder Isometric Right - Seated

☐ **Shoulder Adduction**
Hold your right arm at your side with your elbow bent. Press your right elbow into your body. Hold for a count of ______.

Do _____ sets of _____.

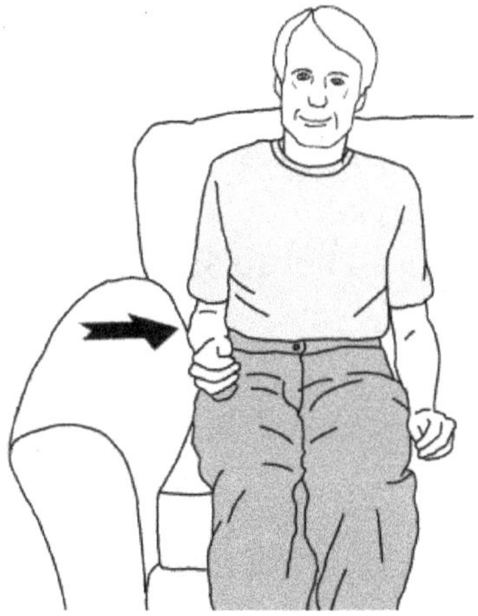

☐ **External Rotation**
Hold your right arm at your side with your elbow bent. Use the chair arm to resist your right arm from rotating to the side. Hold for a count of ______.

Do _____ sets of _____.

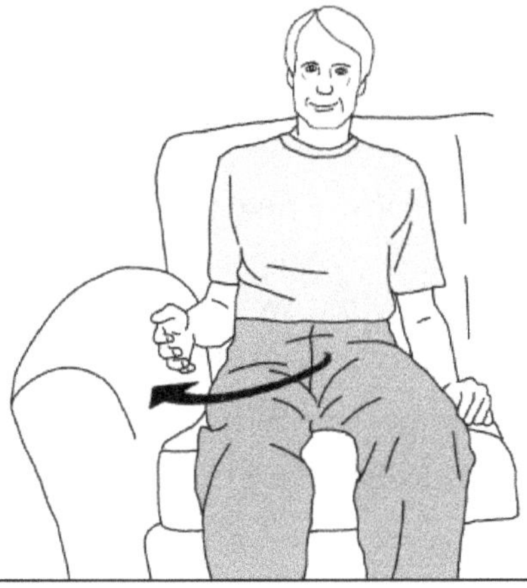

☐ **Internal Rotation**
Hold your right arm at your side with your elbow bent. Use your left hand to resist your right arm from rotating into your body. Hold for a count of ______.

Do _____ sets of _____.

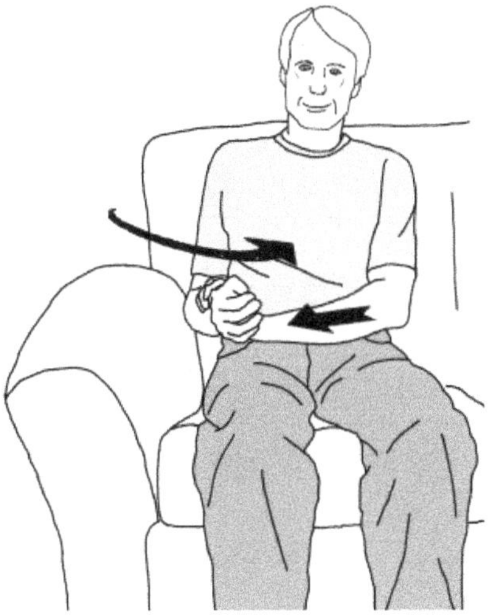

Occupational Therapy TOOLKIT

Shoulder Isometric Right - Standing

Name: ________________________________

Date: ________________________________

Therapist: ________________________________

Phone number: (_____)________________________

Do the checked exercises _____ times per day, _____ days a week.

These are isometric exercises; you will not be moving the joint, only contracting the muscles against light resistance.

Use good posture. Keep your stomach muscles tight and your back straight.

Do not hold your breath during exercise. Count aloud if needed.

Sore muscles lasting a few days and feeling tired are normal after exercise. Exhaustion, sore joints, and painful muscle pulls are not normal. If you have these symptoms, do not exercise until you talk with your therapist.

If you have chest tightness or pain, shortness of breath, feel dizzy, faint, or sick to your stomach, stop and call emergency services at _____.

Notes:

____

____

____

____

____

____

____

____

Shoulder Isometric Right - Standing

☐ **Shoulder Flexion**
Stand facing the wall. Make a fist with your right hand. Place a pillow between the wall and your fist. Use the wall to resist moving your arm forward. Hold for a count of _______.

Do ______ sets of ______.

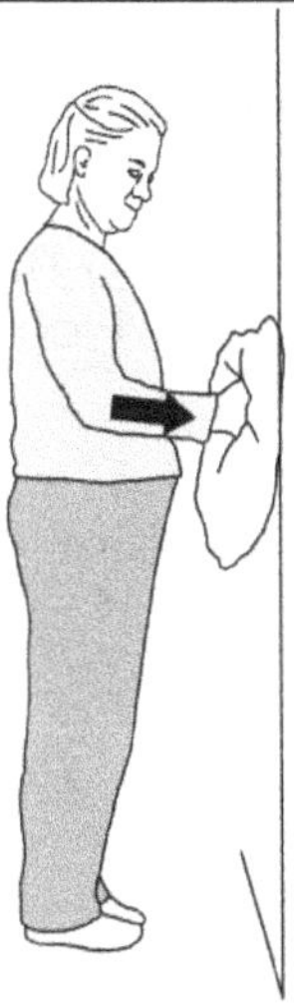

☐ **Shoulder Extension**
Stand with your back against the wall. Place the pillow between the wall and your right elbow. Use the wall to resist moving your arm back. Hold for a count of _______.

Do ______ sets of ______.

☐ **Shoulder Abduction**
Stand with your right side toward the wall. Place the pillow between the wall and your right elbow. Hold your elbow bent or straight. Use the wall to resist moving your arm up from the side. Hold for a count of _______.

Do ______ sets of ______.

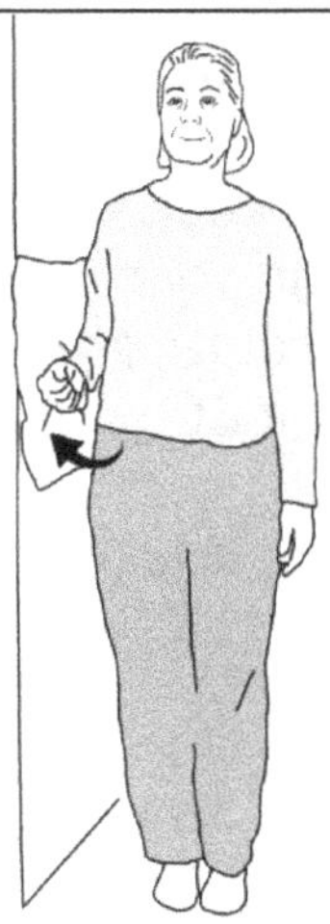

Occupational Therapy TOOLKIT

Shoulder Isometric Right - Standing

☐ **Shoulder Adduction**
Hold the pillow under your right arm. Use the pillow to resist moving your arm into your side. Hold for a count of ______.

Do _____ sets of _____.

☐ **Shoulder External Rotation**
Stand with your right side toward the wall. Place the pillow between the wall and your right elbow. Use the wall to resist rotating your right arm out. Hold for a count of ______.

Do _____ sets of _____.

☐ **Shoulder Internal Rotation**
Stand to the side of a wall corner. Place a pillow between the outer edge of the corner and your right hand. Use the wall to resist rotating your right arm in. Hold for a count of ______.

Do _____ sets of _____.

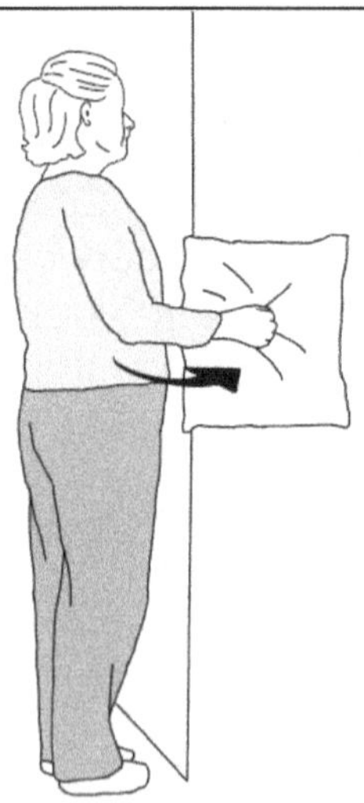

Shoulder Passive and Active-Assisted Range of Motion - Left

Do the checked exercises ______ times per day, ______ days a week.

☐ **Pendulum**
Hold onto a stable object. Lean forward. Relax your shoulder muscles. Use your body to swing your left arm.

- ☐ Small circle to the right______ times.
- ☐ Small circle to the left ______ times.
- ☐ Side-to-side ______ times.
- ☐ Forward and back ______ times.

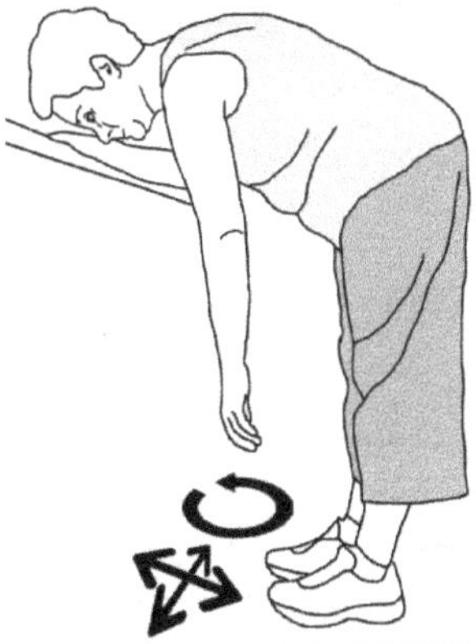

☐ **Ball Squeeze**
Squeeze a soft ball.

Do ______ sets of ______.

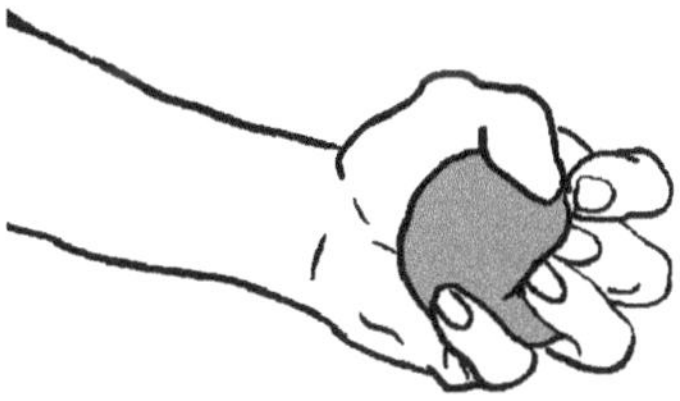

☐ **Shoulder Flexion**
Keep your left arm in line with your body. Hold your left arm at your wrist. Help to lift your left arm up. Raise arm to ______ degrees.

Do ______ sets of ______.

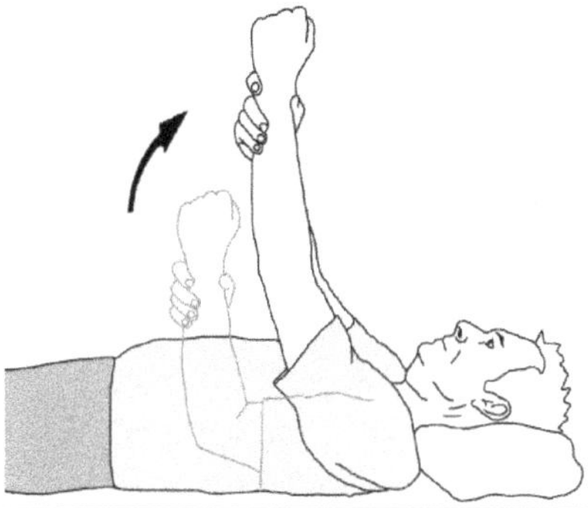

☐ **Shoulder External Rotation**
Keep your left arm against your body. Hold a dowel as shown. Use your right arm to rotate your left arm away from your body. Rotate arm to ______ degrees.

Do ______ sets of ______.

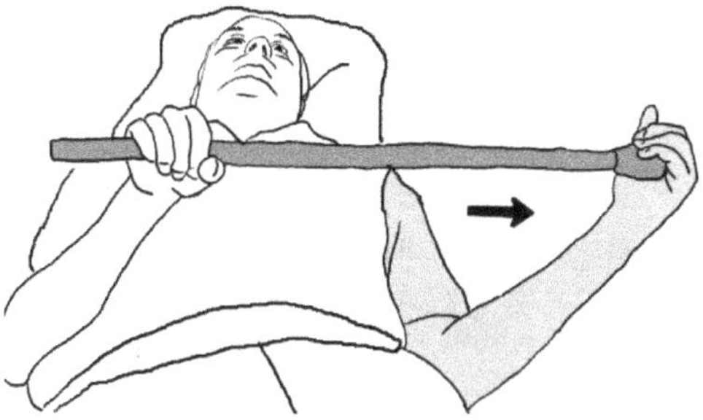

Shoulder Passive and Active-Assisted Range of Motion - Left

☐ **Shoulder Shrug**
Shrug your shoulders.

Do ______ sets of ______.

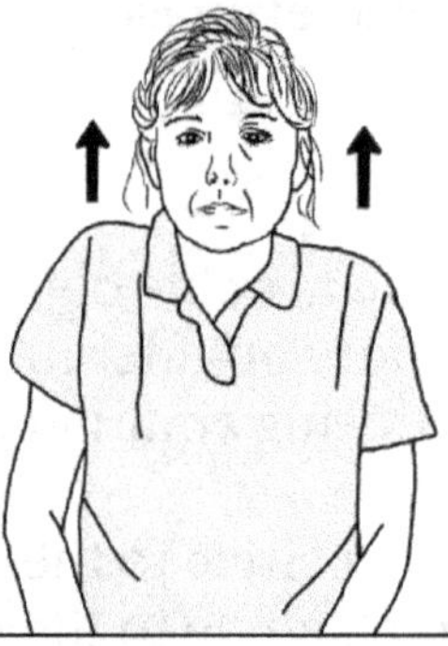

☐ **Shoulder Retraction**
Pull your shoulders back and down.

Do ______ sets of ______.

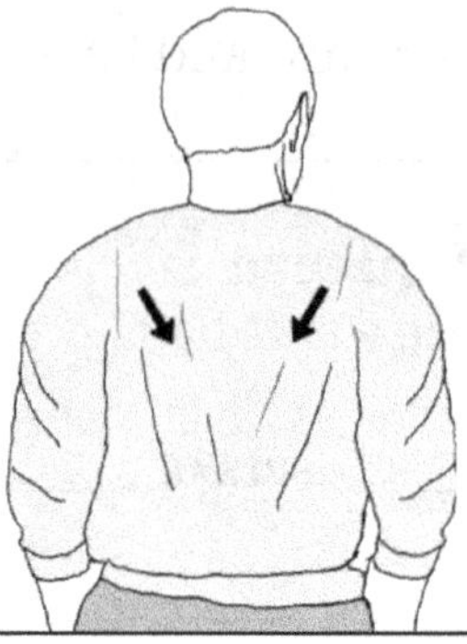

☐ **Behind-the-Back Internal Rotation**
Start the 3rd week after surgery. Place your left hand behind your back. Use your right hand, to lift your left hand toward your shoulder blade.

Do ______ sets of ______.

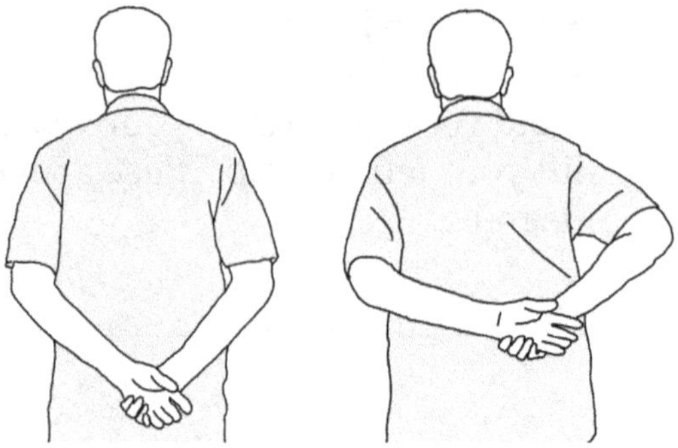

☐ **Side Raise with Cane**
Place your left hand over one end of cane. Push the cane with your right hand, bringing left arm out to side and upwards. Keep elbow of your left arm straight.

Do ______ sets of ______.

Occupational Therapy TOOLKIT

Shoulder Passive and Active-Assisted Range of Motion - Right

Do the checked exercises _____ times per day, _____ days a week.

☐ **Pendulum**
Hold onto a stable object. Lean forward. Relax your shoulder muscles. Use your body to swing your right arm.

- ☐ Small circle to the right_____ times.
- ☐ Small circle to the left _____ times.
- ☐ Side-to-side _____ times.
- ☐ Forward and back _____ times.

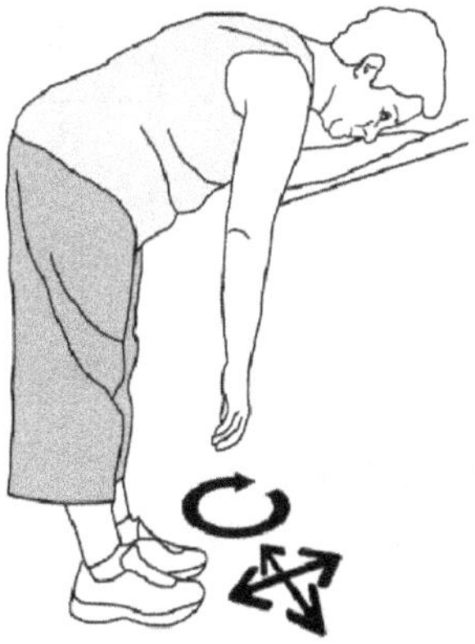

☐ **Ball Squeeze**
Squeeze a soft ball.

Do _____ sets of _____.

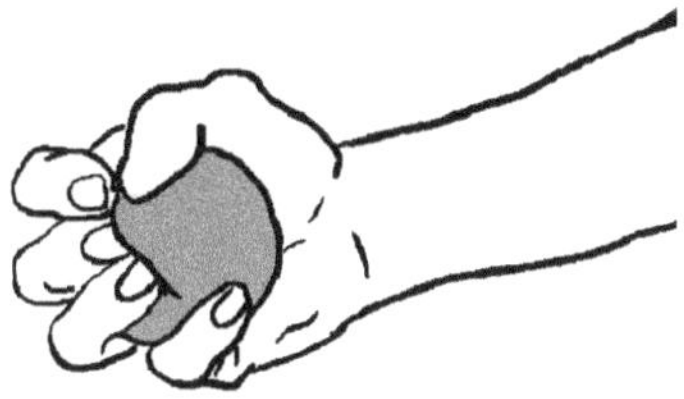

☐ **Shoulder Flexion**
Keep your right arm in line with your body. Hold your right arm at your wrist. Lift your right arm up.

Do _____ sets of _____.

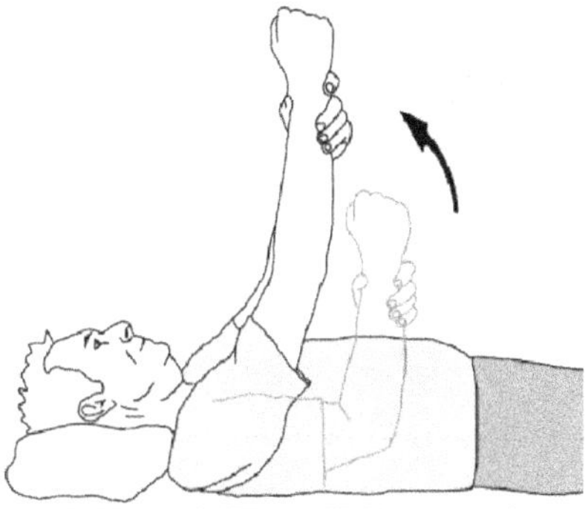

☐ **Shoulder External Rotation**
Keep your right arm against your body. Hold a cane or dowel as shown. Use your left arm to rotate your right arm away from your body.

Do _____ sets of _____.

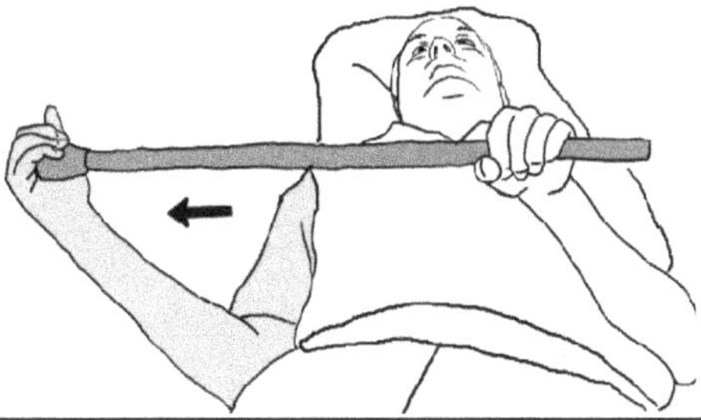

Shoulder Passive and Active-Assisted Range of Motion - Right

☐ **Shoulder Shrug**
Shrug your shoulders up.

Do _____ sets of _____.

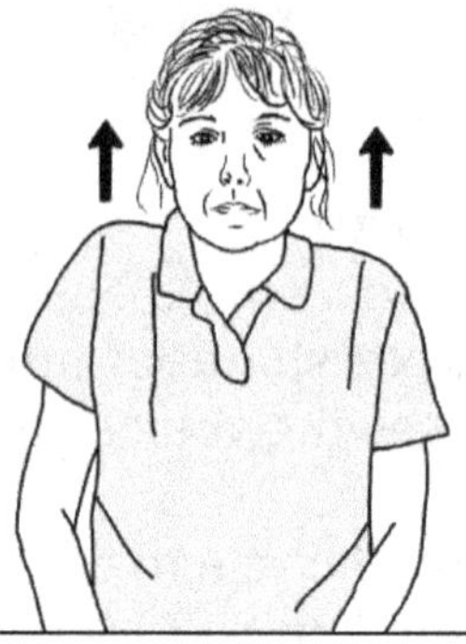

☐ **Shoulder Pull**
Pull your shoulders back and down.

Do _____ sets of _____.

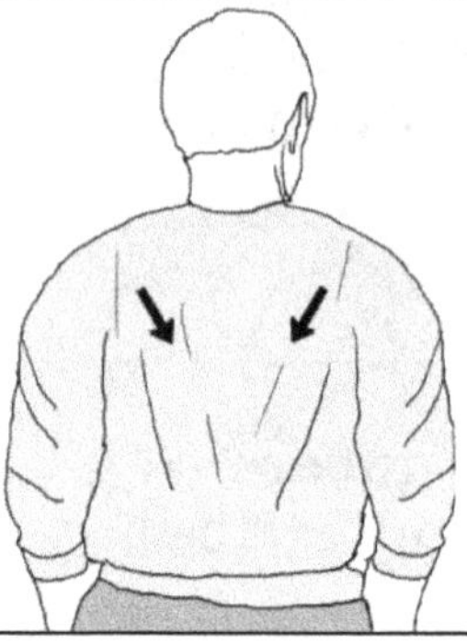

☐ **Behind-the-Back Internal Rotation**
Start the 3rd week after surgery. Place your right hand behind your back. Use your left hand, to lift your right hand toward your shoulder blade.

Do _____ sets of _____.

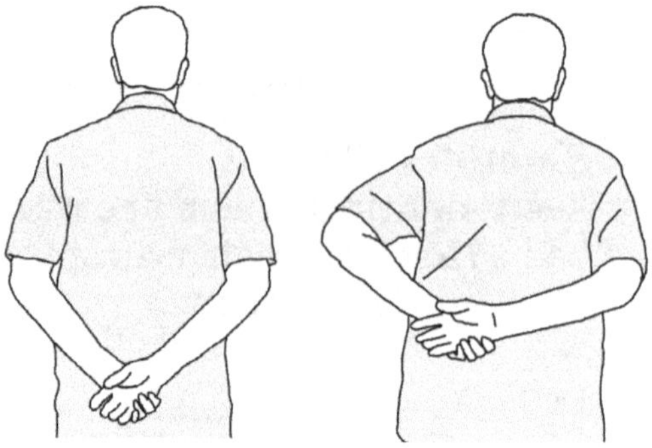

☐ **Side Raise with Cane**
Place your right hand over one end of cane. Push the cane with your left hand, bringing right arm out to side and upwards. Keep elbow of your right arm straight.

Do _____ sets of _____.

Shoulder Pulley Exercises - Left

Attach the pulley to the top of the door. For safety, be sure the door opens away from you.
Do the checked exercises _____ times per day, _____ days a week.

☐ Sit with your back to the door. Hold the pulley handles. Point your thumbs up. Gently use your right arm to pull your left arm up. Hold for the count of _____.

Do _____ sets of _____.

☐ Sit with your back to the door. Hold the pulley handles. Point your thumbs up. Gently use your right arm to pull your left arm up to the side. Hold for the count of _____.

Do _____ sets of _____.

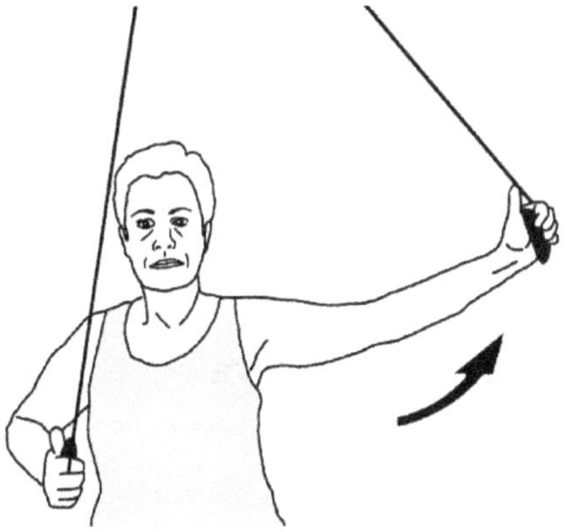

☐ Stand with your right arm next to the door. Hold the pulley handle with your right hand in front of your chest. Hold the other handle with your left hand behind your back. Gently pull your right hand down in front to raise your left arm up in back. Hold for the count of _____.

Do _____ sets of _____.

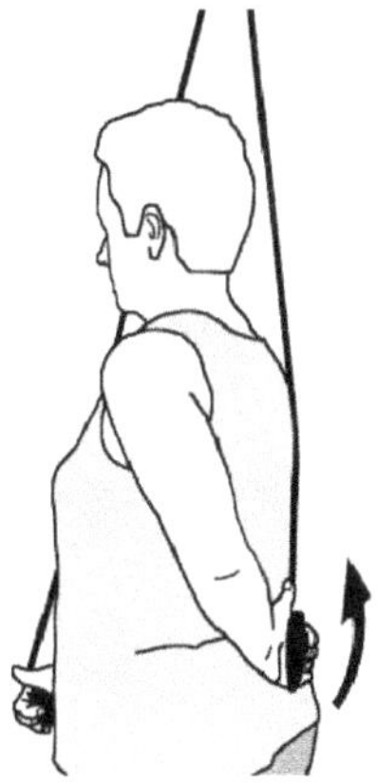

Shoulder Pulley Exercises - Right

Attach the pulley to the top of the door. For safety, be sure the door opens away from you.
Do the checked exercises _____ times per day, _____ days a week.

☐ Sit with your back to the door. Hold the pulley handles. Point your thumbs up. Gently use your left arm to pull your right arm up. Hold for the count of _____.

Do _____ sets of _____.

☐ Sit with your back to the door. Hold the pulley handles. Point your thumbs up. Gently use your left arm to pull your right arm up to the side. Hold for the count of _____.

Do _____ sets of _____.

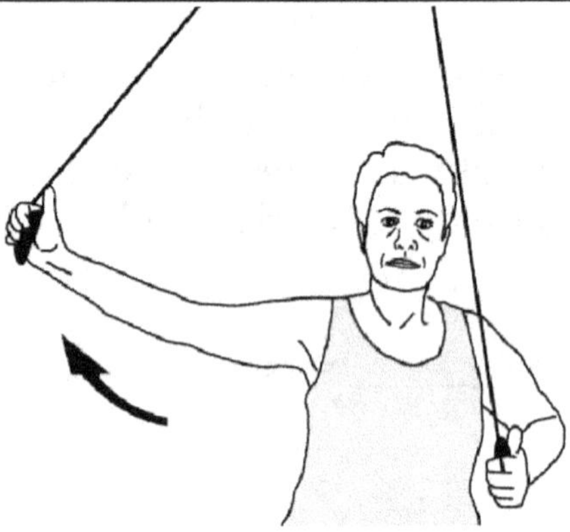

☐ Stand with your left arm next to the door. Hold the pulley handle with your left hand in front of your chest. Hold the other handle with your right hand behind your back. Gently pull your left hand down in front to raise your right arm up in back. Hold for the count of _____.

Do _____ sets of _____.

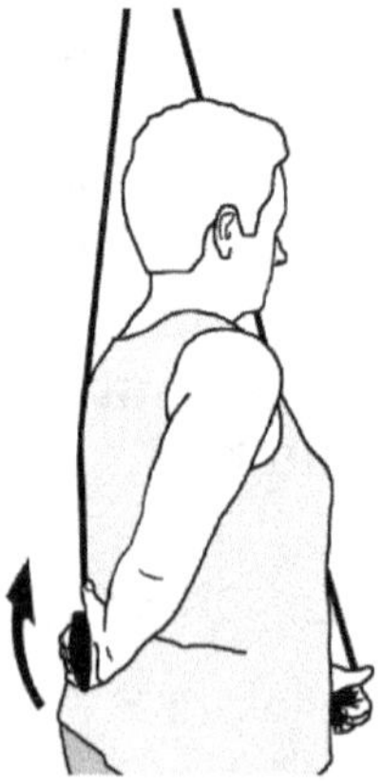

Shoulder Stretches - Left

Do the checked exercises _____ times a day, _____ days a week.

☐ **Weighted Pendulum**
Hold a _____ lb/kg weight in your left hand. Hold onto a stable object. Lean forward. Relax your shoulder muscles. Use your body to swing your left arm.

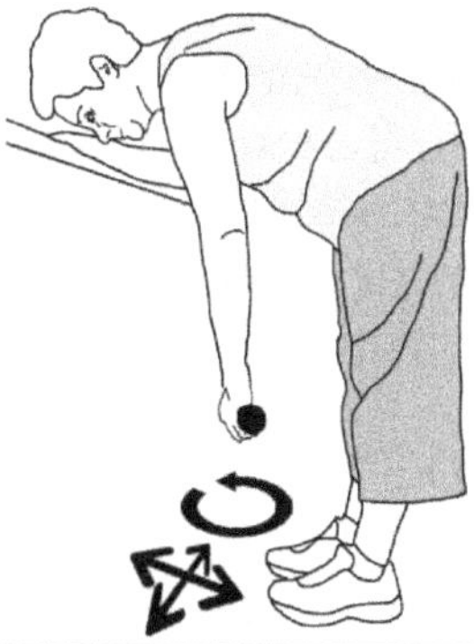

- ☐ Small circle to the right_____ times.
- ☐ Small circle to the left _____ times.
- ☐ Side-to-side _____ times.
- ☐ Forward and back _____ times.

☐ **Forward Stretch on Tabletop**
Sit with a table to your left side. Place your arm on the table. Relax your shoulder muscles. Lean forward at your waist. Slide your left hand forward. Hold for a count of _____.

Do _____ sets of _____.

☐ **Towel Stretch**
Place a towel over your right shoulder; grab the end from behind with your left hand. Pull the towel up as shown. Hold for a count of _____.

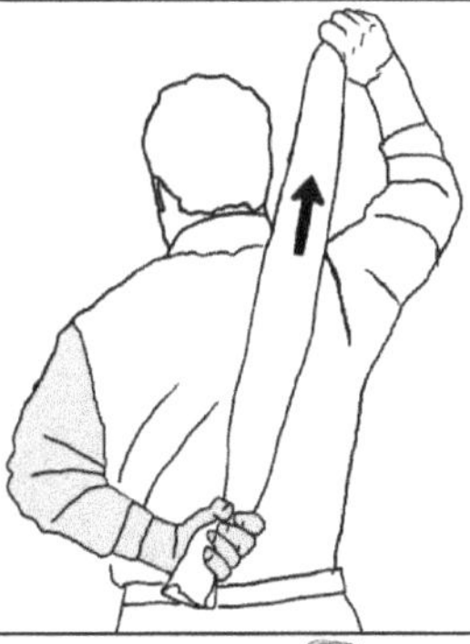

Do _____ sets of _____.

☐ **Stretch Across Body**
Pull your left arm across your body, using your right arm. Hold for a count of _____.

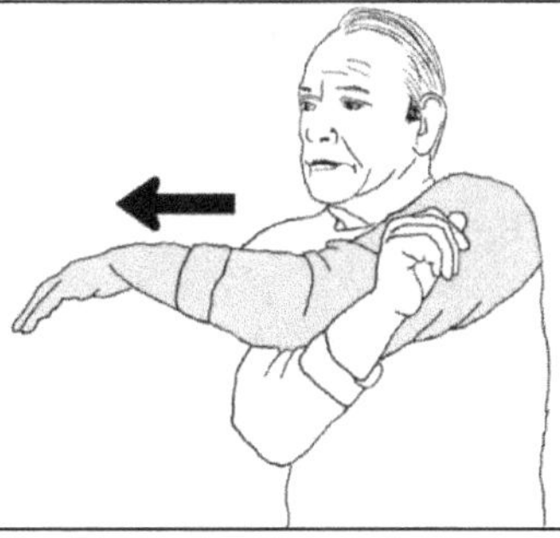

Do _____ sets of _____.

Shoulder Stretches - Left

Do the checked exercises _____ times a day, _____ days a week.

☐ **Sleeper Stretch**
Roll onto your left side with your arm outstretched and elbow bent. Gently push your left arm down toward the bed. Hold for a count of _____.

Do _____ sets of _____.

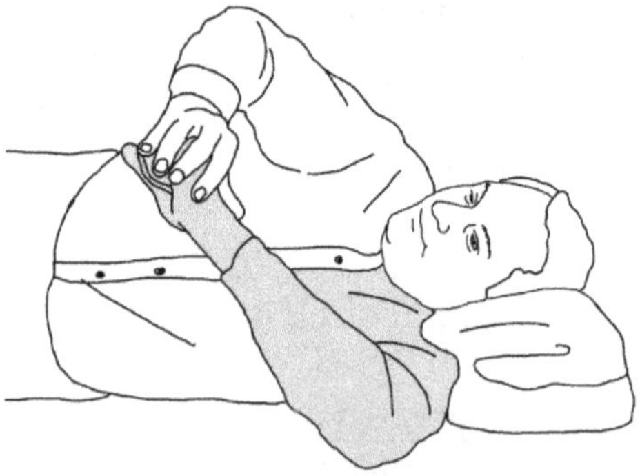

☐ **External Rotation @ 90° Abduction**
Keep your left arm at a 90-degree angle to your body and your elbow bent at a 90-degree angle. Use a dowel to rotate your left arm back toward the head of the bed. Hold for a count of _____.

Do _____ sets of _____.

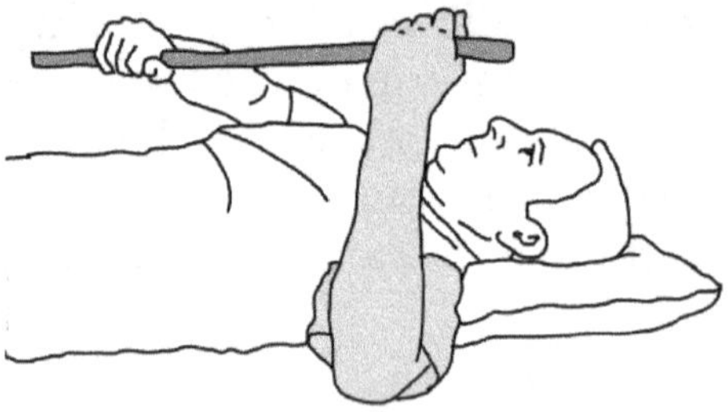

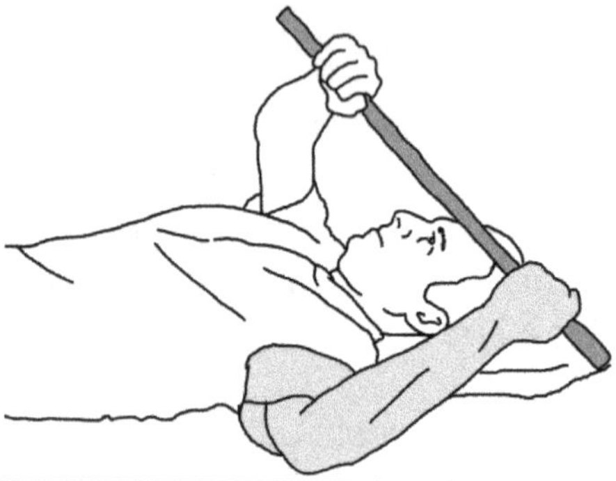

☐ **Hands-Behind-the-Head Stretch**
Clasp your hands behind your head. Slowly lower your elbows to the side. Hold for a count of _____.

Do _____ sets of _____.

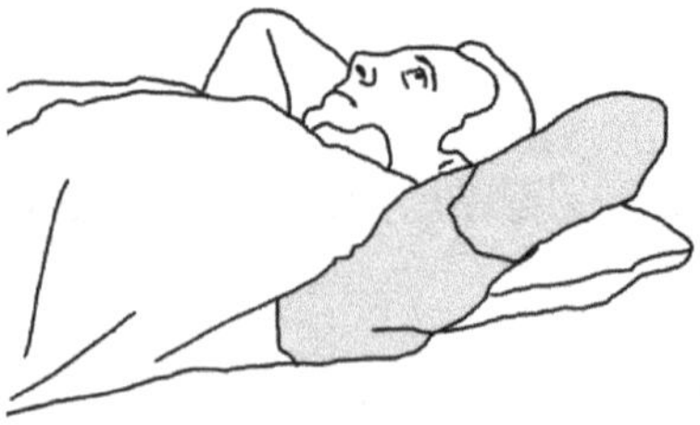

Occupational Therapy TOOLKIT

Shoulder Stretches - Right

Do the checked exercises _____ times a day, _____ days a week.

☐ **Weighted Pendulum**
Hold a _____ lb/kg weight in your right hand. Hold onto a stable object. Lean forward. Relax your shoulder muscles. Use your body to swing your right arm.

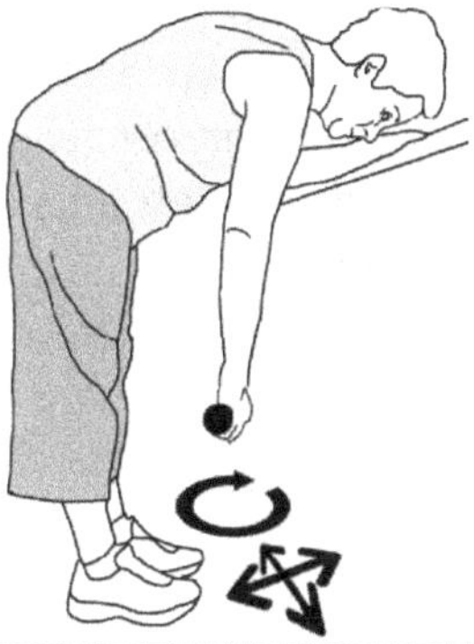

- ☐ Small circle to the right_____ times.
- ☐ Small circle to the left _____ times.
- ☐ Side-to-side _____ times.
- ☐ Forward and back _____ times.

☐ **Forward Stretch on Tabletop**
Sit with a table to your right side. Place your arm on the table. Relax your shoulder muscles. Lean forward at your waist. Slide your right hand forward. Hold for a count of _____.

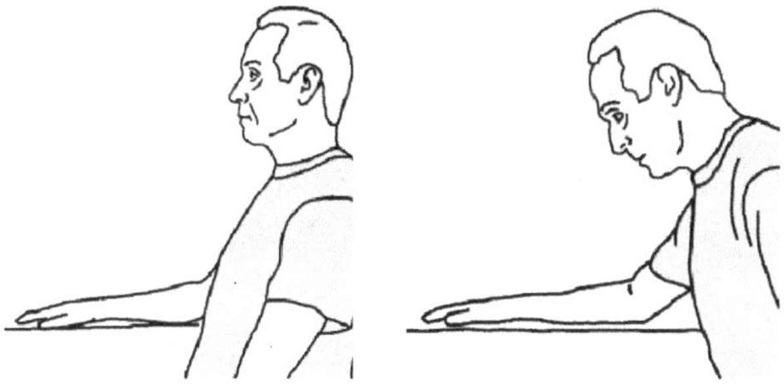

Do _____ sets of _____.

☐ **Towel Stretch**
Place a towel over your left shoulder; grab the end from behind with your right hand. Pull the towel up as shown. Hold for a count of _____.

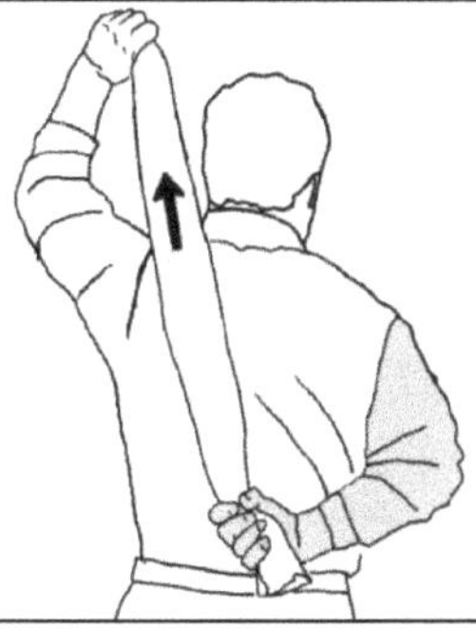

Do _____ sets of _____.

☐ **Stretch Across Body**
Pull your right arm across your body, using your left arm. Hold for a count of _____.

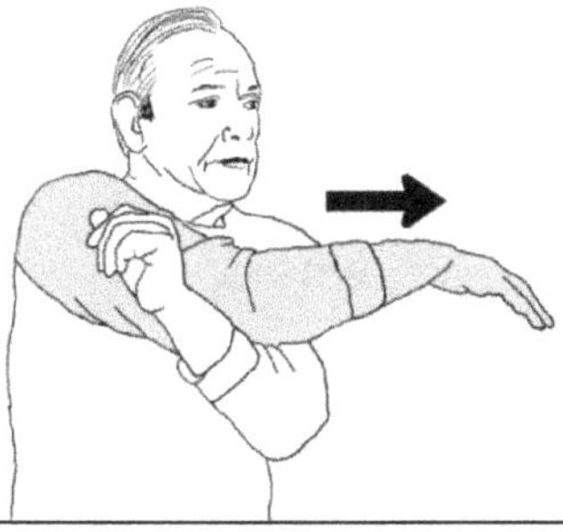

Do _____ sets of _____.

Shoulder Stretches - Right

Do the checked exercises _____ times a day, _____ days a week.

☐ **Sleeper Stretch**
Roll onto your right side with your arm outstretched and elbow bent. Gently push your right arm down toward the bed. Hold for a count of _____.

Do _____ sets of _____.

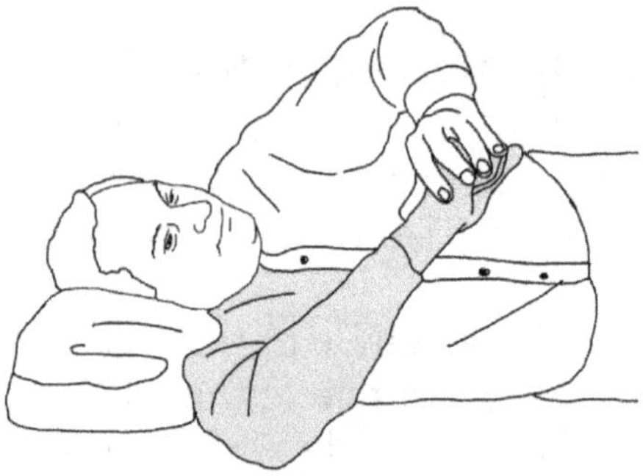

☐ **External Rotation @ 90° Abduction**
Keep your right arm at a 90-degree angle to your body and your elbow bent at a 90-degree angle. Use a dowel to rotate your right arm back toward the head of the bed. Hold for a count of _____.

Do _____ sets of _____.

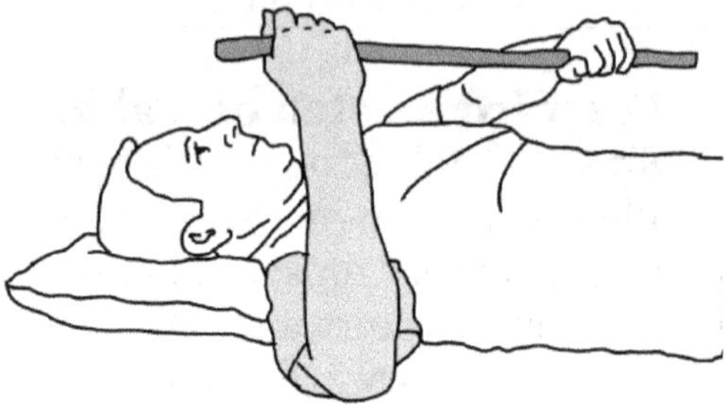

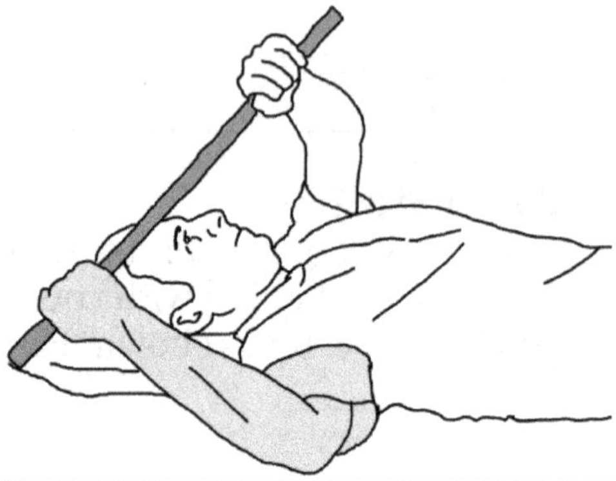

☐ **Hands-Behind-the-Head Stretch**
Clasp your hands behind your head. Slowly lower your elbows to the side. Hold for a count of _____.

Do _____ sets of _____.

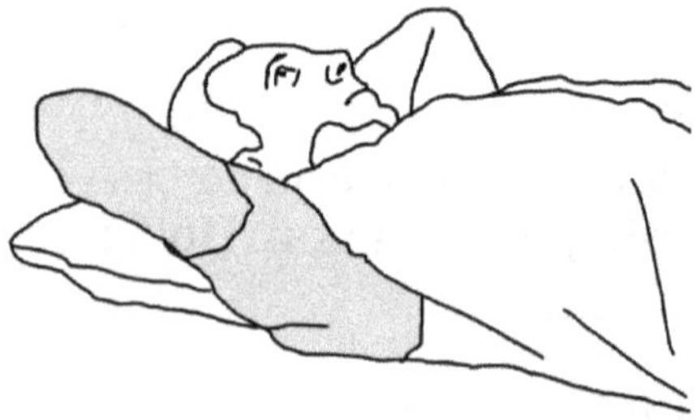

Stretch Band Exercises - Arms

Name: ______________________________

Date: ______________________________

Therapist: ______________________________

Phone number: (_____)______________________

Do the checked exercises _____ times per day, _____ days a week

Use a __________ stretch band.

Exercise slowly and smoothly. Do not allow the stretch band to snap back.

Use good posture. Keep your stomach muscles tight and your back straight.

Do not hold your breath during exercise. Count aloud if needed.

Sore muscles lasting a few days and feeling tired are normal after exercise. Exhaustion, sore joints, and painful muscle pulls are not normal. If you have these symptoms, do not exercise until you talk with your therapist.

If you have chest tightness or pain, shortness of breath, feel dizzy, faint, or sick to your stomach, stop and call emergency services at _____.

Caring for the Stretch Bands:
Before use, look at the stretch band for small nicks, tears, or punctures that may cause it to break. Replace if you find any flaws.

Keep the stretch band away from the sun and other heat sources.

If the stretch band becomes sticky, clean with mild soap and water, dry flat, and then dust with talc powder.

Notes:

____

____

Occupational Therapy TOOLKIT

Stretch Band Exercises - Arms

☐ **Arm Raise**
Hold the stretch band with both hands, about _____ inches/cm apart. Secure the stretch band using your left hand on your right knee. Keep your right elbow straight and your thumb pointed up. Raise your right arm up.

Do _____ sets of _____.
Repeat with your left arm

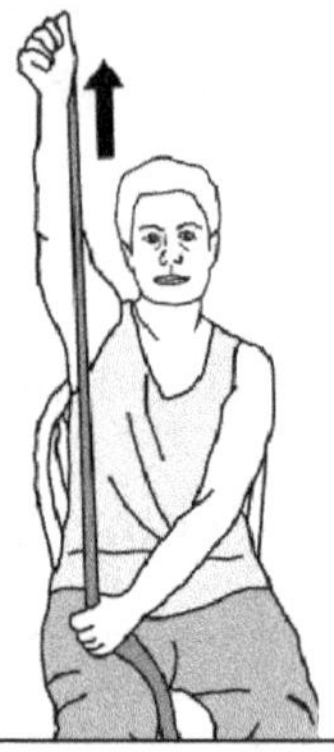

☐ **Arm Back**
Hold the stretch band with both hands, about _____ inches/cm apart. Secure the stretch band using your left hand on your right knee. Keep your right elbow straight. Pull your right arm back.

Do _____ sets of _____.
Repeat with your left arm

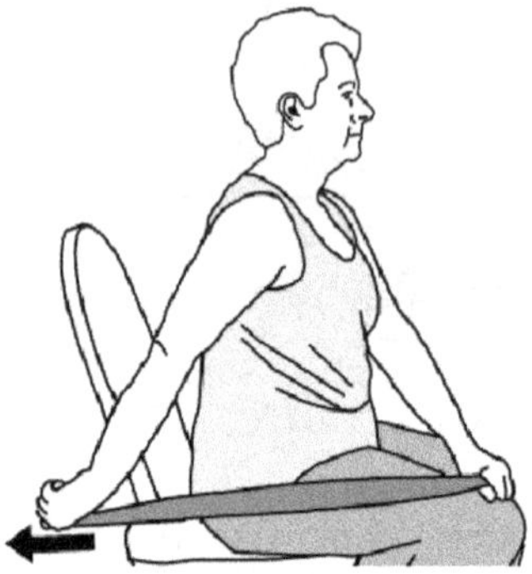

☐ **Arm Up to the Side**
Hold the stretch band with both hands, about _____ inches/cm apart. Secure the stretch band using your left hand on your right hip. Keep your right elbow straight and your thumb pointed up. Raise your right arm up to the side.

Do _____ sets of _____.
Repeat on your left side

☐ **Pull Apart**
Hold the stretch band with both hands, about _____ inches/cm apart. Raise your arms to shoulder level. Pull the stretch band across your chest. Hold for a count of _____.

Do _____ sets of _____.

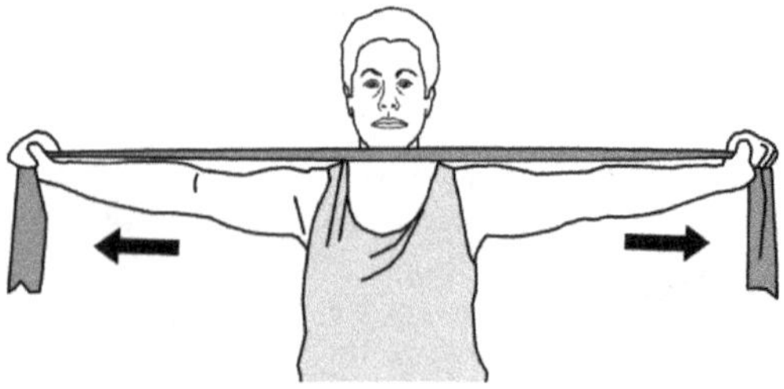

Occupational Therapy TOOLKIT

Stretch Band Exercises - Arms

☐ **Diagonal Up**
Hold the stretch band with both hands, about _____ inches/cm apart. Hold your left arm down to your side. Pull the stretch band with your right arm up across your body.

Do _____ sets of _____.
Repeat with your left arm.

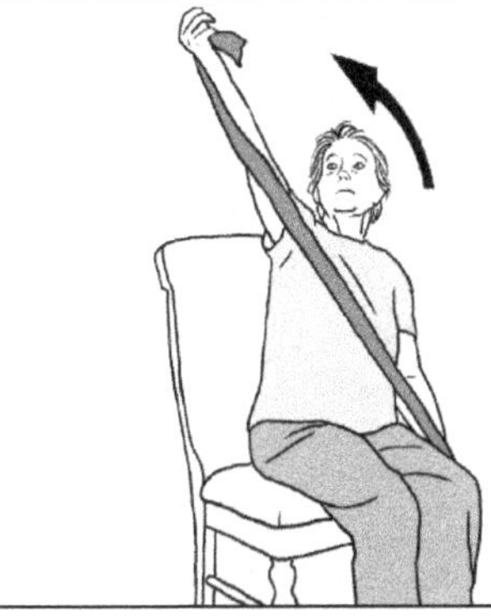

☐ **Diagonal Down**
Hold the stretch band with both hands, about _____ inches/cm apart. Hold the stretch band with your left hand at the left shoulder. Pull the stretch band with your right arm down across your body.

Do _____ sets of _____.
Repeat with your left arm.

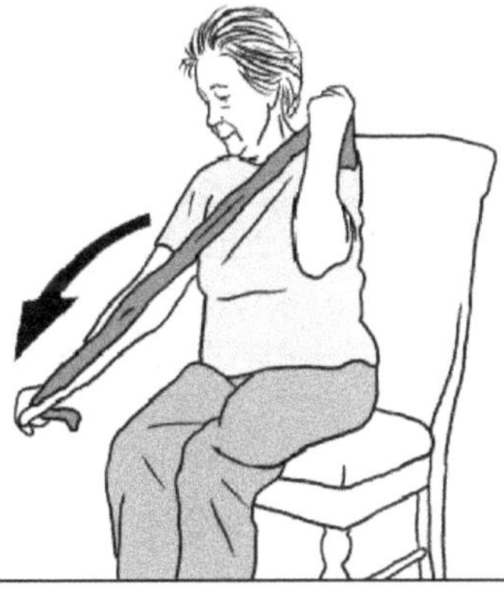

☐ **Bend Elbow**
Hold the stretch band with both hands, about _____ inches/cm apart. Secure the stretch band using your left hand on your right hip. Keep your right arm held next to your side. Bend and straighten your right elbow.

Do _____ sets of _____.
Repeat with your left arm.

☐ **Straighten Elbow**
Hold the stretch band with both hands, about _____ inches/cm apart. Secure the stretch band using your left hand on your right shoulder. Straighten your right arm, up over your head.

Do _____ sets of _____.
Repeat with your left arm.

Stretch Band Exercises - Arms

☐ **Wrist Lifts**

Place the stretch band under your right foot. Rest your right forearm on your right knee with your palm turned down. Hold the stretch band and lift your right wrist up.

Do _____ sets of _____.
Repeat with your left arm.

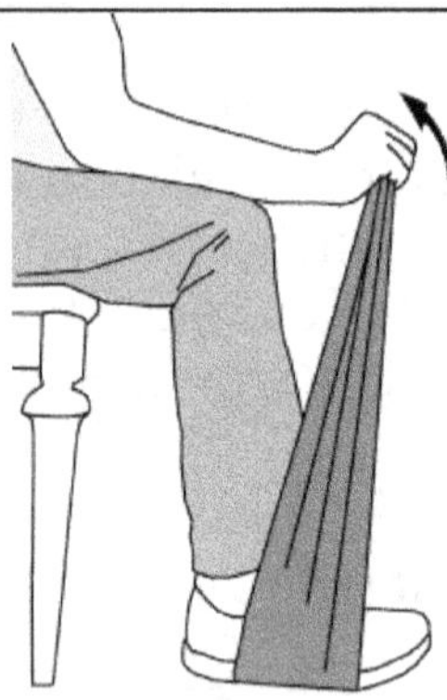

☐ **Wrist Curls**

Place the stretch band under your right foot. Rest your right forearm on your right knee with your palm turned up. Hold the stretch band and curl your wrist up.

Do _____ sets of _____.
Repeat with your left arm.

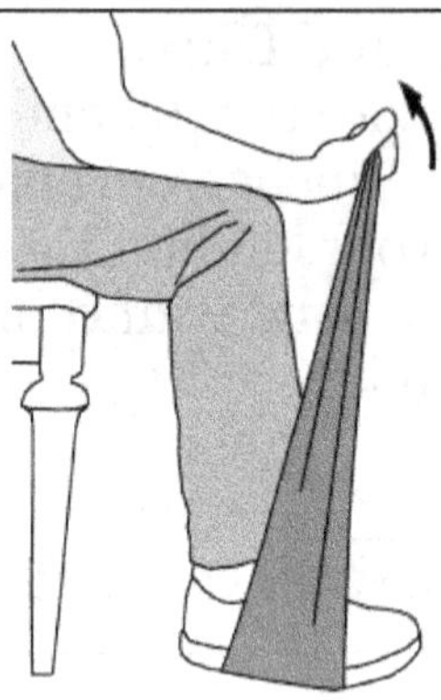

Stretch Band Exercises - Legs

Name: ______________________________

Date: ______________________________

Therapist: ______________________________

Phone number: (_____)____________________

Do the checked exercises _____ times per day, _____ days a week

Use a __________ stretch band.

Exercise slowly and smoothly. Do not allow the stretch band to snap back.

Use good posture. Keep your stomach muscles tight and your back straight.

Do not hold your breath during exercise. Count aloud if needed.

Sore muscles lasting a few days and feeling tired are normal after exercise. Exhaustion, sore joints, and painful muscle pulls are not normal. If you have these symptoms, do not exercise until you talk with your therapist.

If you have chest tightness or pain, shortness of breath, feel dizzy, faint, or sick to your stomach, stop and call emergency services at _____.

Caring for the Stretch Bands:
Before use, look at the stretch band for small nicks, tears, or punctures that may cause it to break. Replace if you find any flaws.

Keep the stretch band away from the sun and other heat sources.

If the stretch band becomes sticky, clean with mild soap and water, dry flat, and then dust with talc powder.

Notes:

____

____

Stretch Band Exercises - Hip and Knee

☐ **Squat**
Place the looped stretch band under both feet. Keep your back straight. Squat down. Tighten up on the stretch band and stand up.

Do ______ sets of ______.

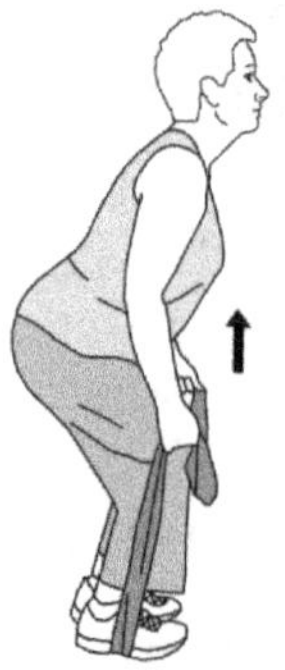

☐ **Leg Press**
Place the looped stretch band under your right foot. Bend your knee and hip toward your chest. Press your leg out straight.

Do ______ sets of ______.
Repeat with your left leg.

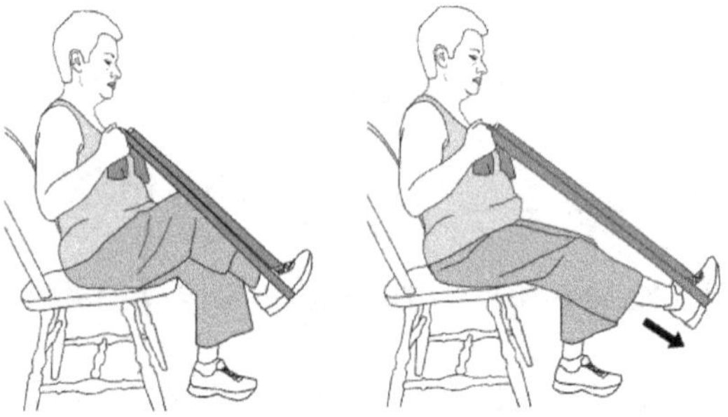

☐ **Knee Spread**
Place the stretch band under both thighs. Cross the band over your lap. Hold the stretch band tight. Spread your legs apart.

Do ______ sets of ______.

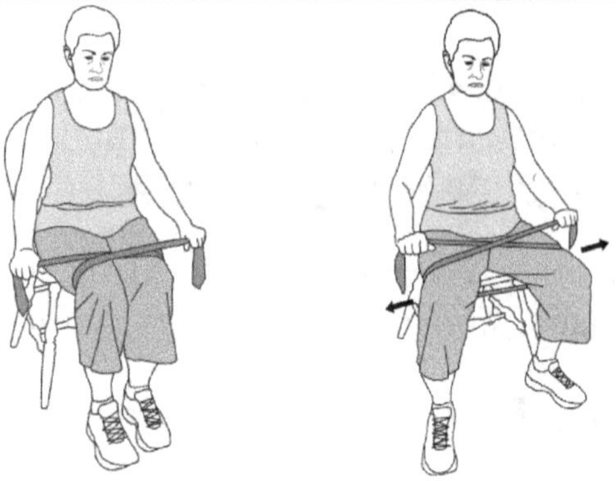

☐ **Knee Lift**
Place the stretch band under both thighs. Cross the band over your lap. Hold the stretch band tight. Lift your right knee up.

Do ______ sets of ______.
Repeat with your left knee.

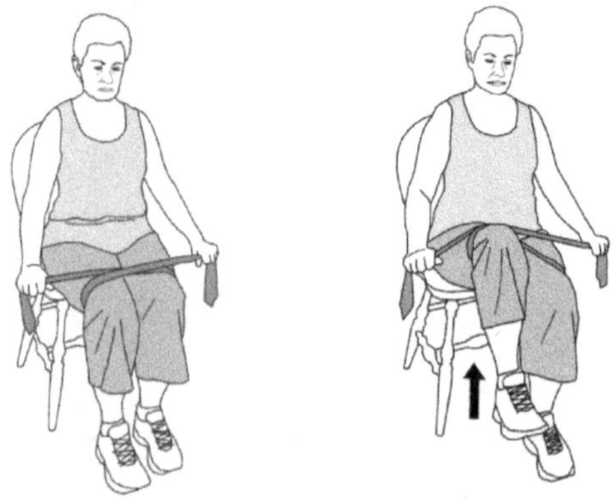

Stretch Band Exercises - Hip and Knee

☐ **Swing Leg Out**
Secure the looped stretch band to a stable object placed to the left. Put the stretch band around your right ankle. Rotate your right hip out to the side.

Do ______ sets of ______.
Repeat with your left leg.

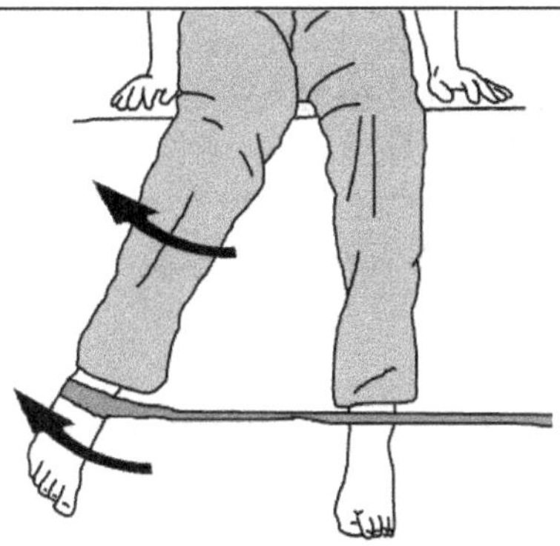

☐ **Swing Leg In**
Secure the looped stretch band to a stable object placed to the right. Put the stretch band around your right ankle. Rotate your right hip in.

Do ______ sets of ______.
Repeat with your left leg.

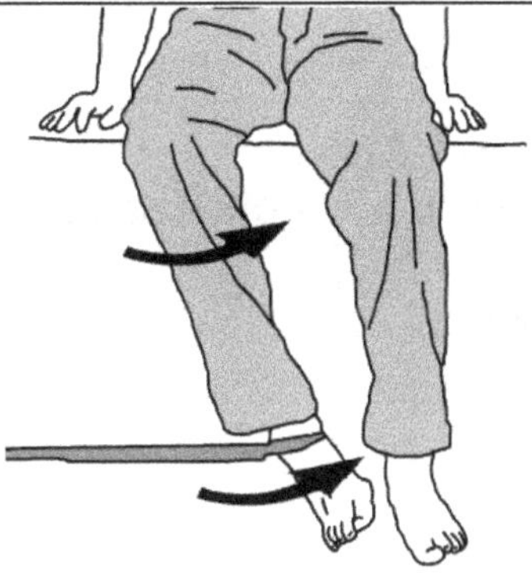

☐ **Bend Knee**
Loop the stretch band around your right ankle. Place the stretch band under your left foot and hold the ends with your left hand. Pull your right foot back, under the chair.

Do ______ sets of ______.
Repeat with your left leg.

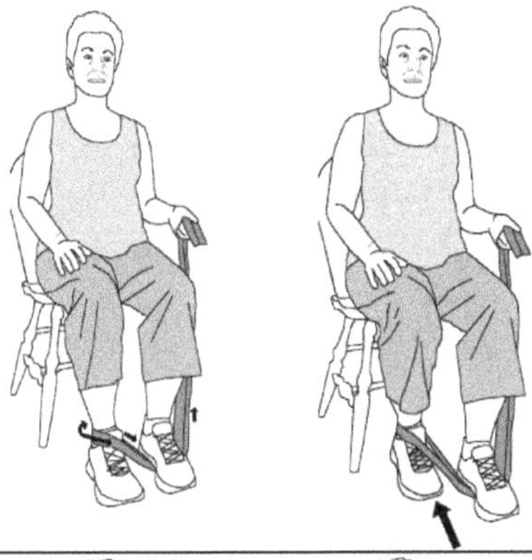

☐ **Straighten Knee**
Loop the stretch band around your right ankle. Place the stretch band under your left foot. Hold the ends with your left hand. Kick your right leg out.

Do ______ sets of ______.
Repeat with your left leg.

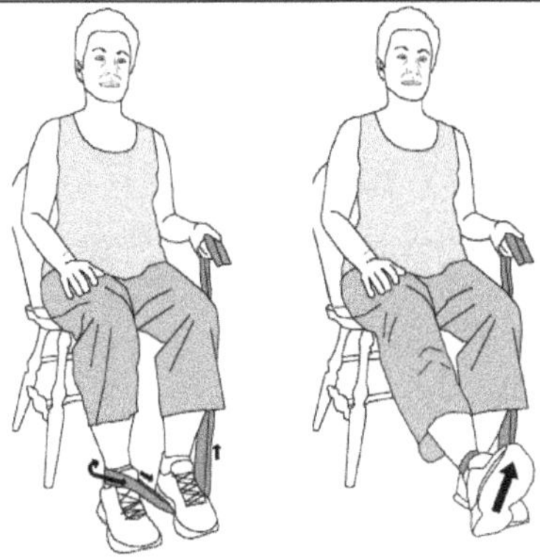

Stretch Band Exercises - Ankle

☐ **Point Toes**
Place the length of stretch band under your right foot. Hold your leg out straight. Point your toes.

Do ______ sets of ______.
Repeat with your left leg.

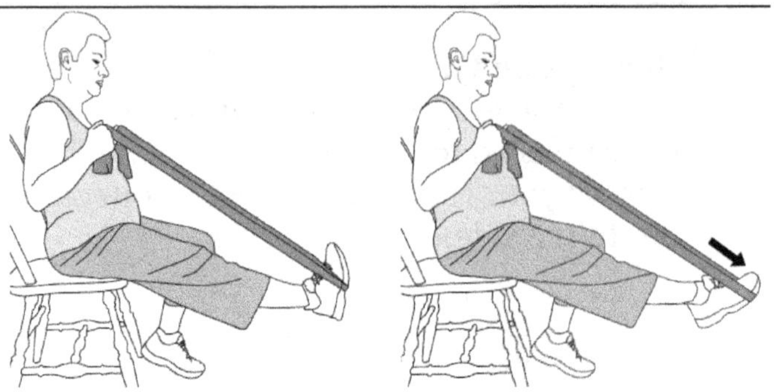

☐ **Bend Ankle**
Secure the looped stretch band to a stable object to the front. Put the stretch band around your right foot. Pull your toes toward you.

Do ______ sets of ______.
Repeat with your left leg.

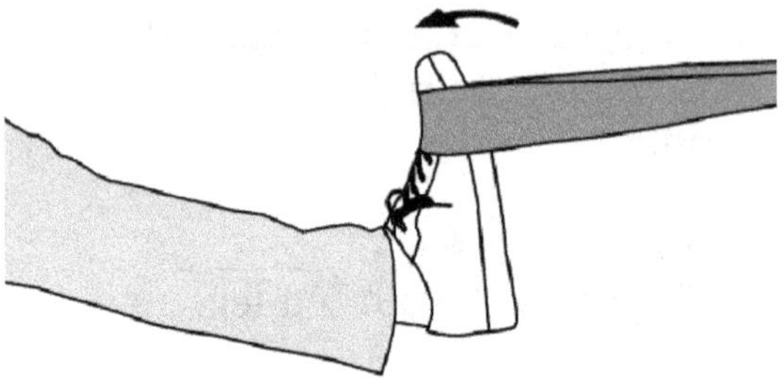

☐ **Turn Foot Inward**
Place the stretch band under your right foot. Wrap the stretch band around the inside of your leg, behind your knee. Turn your foot inward.

Do ______ sets of ______.
Repeat with your left leg.

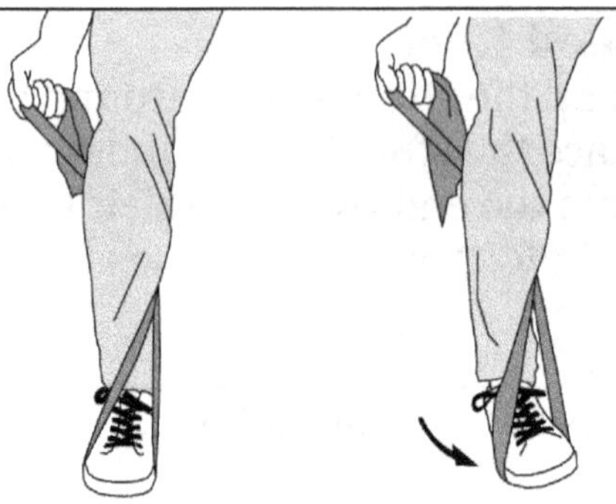

☐ **Turn Foot Outward**
Place the stretch band under your right foot. Wrap the stretch band around the outside of your leg, behind your knee. Turn your foot outward.

Do ______ sets of ______.
Repeat with your left leg.

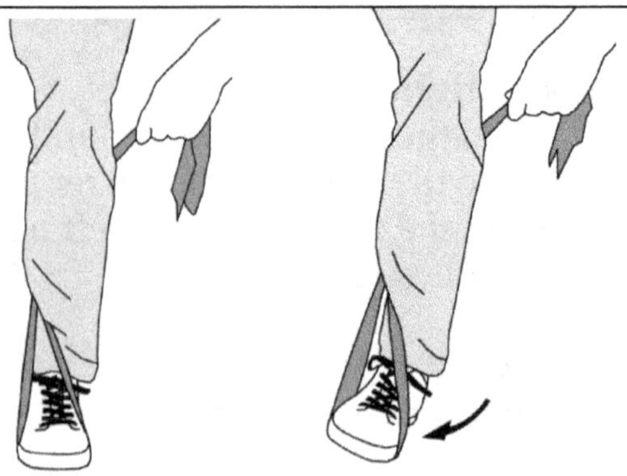

Thigh Stretches

Do the checked stretches ______ times per day, ______ days a week.

☐ **Back of Thigh**
Place both hands behind your knee. Straighten your leg until you feel a stretch. Hold for a count of ______.

Do ______ sets of ______.
Repeat on your other side.

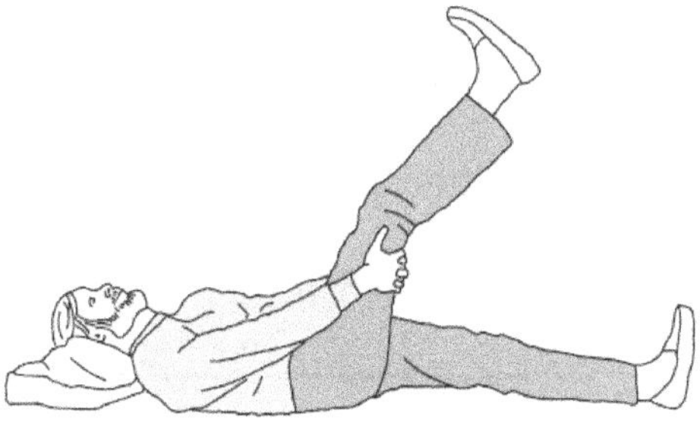

☐ **Back of Thigh**
Sit in a chair with your leg straight. Reach toward your toes. Hold for a count of ______.

Do ______ sets of ______.
Repeat on your other side.

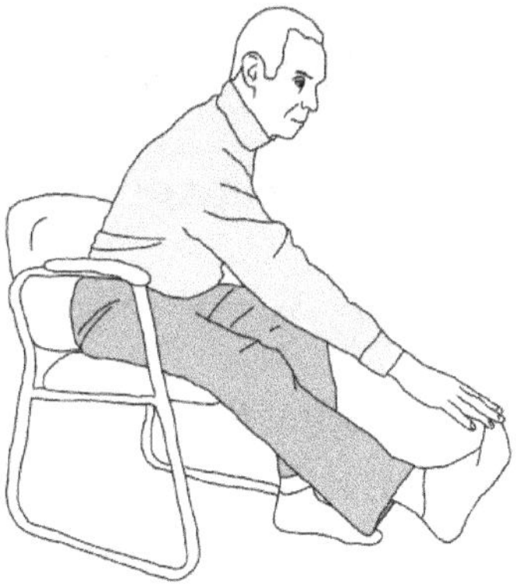

☐ **Front of Thigh**
Lie on your side. Bend your leg back and hold your foot with your hand. Pull your foot toward your bottom .
Hold for a count of ______.

Do ______ sets of ______.
Repeat on your other side.

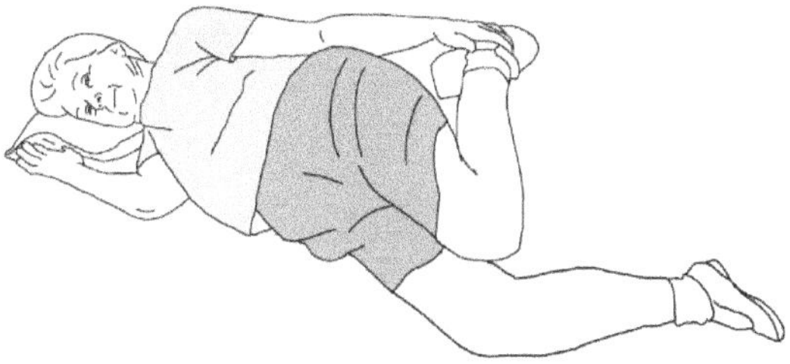

☐ **Knee Opening**
Lie on your back with your knees bent. Allow your knees to fall out to the sides. Hold for a count of ______.

Do ______ sets of ______.

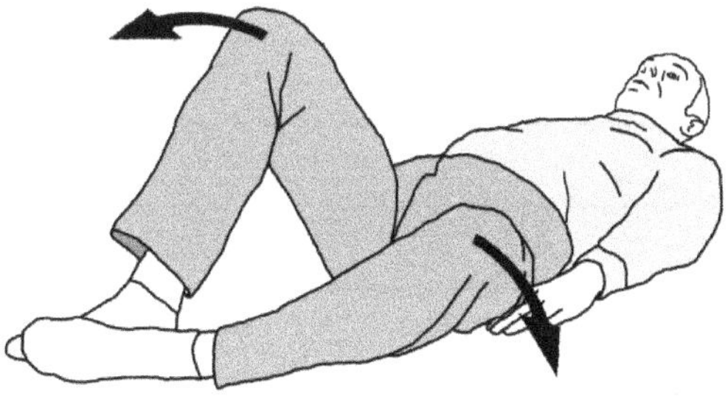

Upper Body Active Range of Motion

Name: ________________________________

Date: ________________________________

Therapist: ____________________________

Phone number: (_____)____________________

Do the checked exercises _____ times per day, _____ days a week.

Exercise slowly and smoothly.

Do not hold your breath during exercise. Count aloud if needed.

Use good posture. Keep your stomach muscles tight and your back straight.

Sore muscles lasting a few days and feeling tired are normal after exercise. Exhaustion, sore joints, and painful muscle pulls are not normal. If you have these symptoms, do not exercise until you talk with your therapist

If you have chest tightness or pain, shortness of breath, feel dizzy, faint, or sick to your stomach, stop and call emergency services at _____.

Notes:

____

____

____

____

____

____

____

____

Occupational Therapy TOOLKIT

Upper Body Active Range of Motion - Neck, Face and Jaw

☐ Bring your chin to your chest, and then look forward.

Do ______ sets of ______.

☐ Turn your head to look over your shoulder. Turn to the other side.

Do ______ sets of ______.

☐ Tilt your head to the side. Tilt to the other side.

Do ______ sets of ______.

☐ Open your mouth as wide as you can.

Do ______ sets of ______.

☐ Move your lower jaw forward.

Do ______ sets of ______.

☐ Move your lower jaw side to side.

Do ______ sets of ______.

Occupational Therapy TOOLKIT

Upper Body Active Range of Motion - Shoulders

☐ Shrug your shoulders.

Do ______ sets of ______.

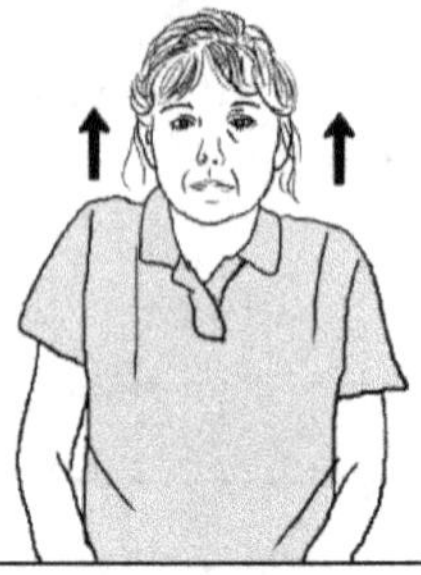

☐ Squeeze your shoulder blades.

Do ______ sets of ______.

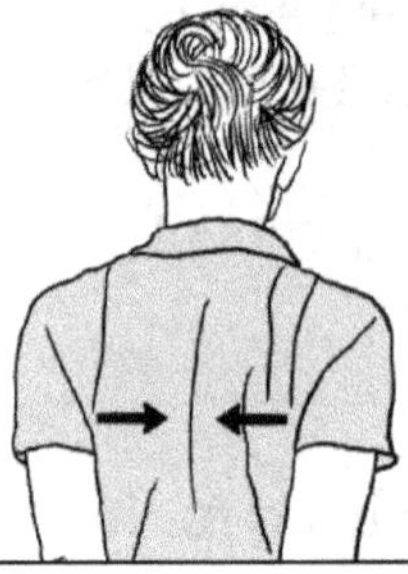

☐ Raise your arms over head.

Do ______ sets of ______.

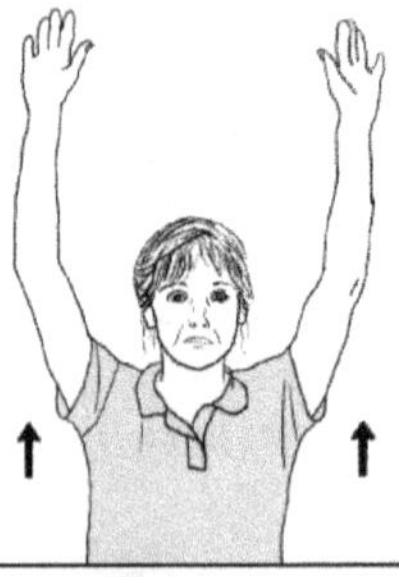

☐ Bring your arms back.

Do ______ sets of ______.

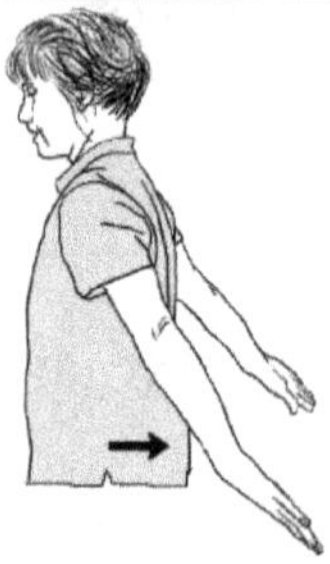

☐ Raise your arms up from the side.

Do ______ sets of ______.

Upper Body Active Range of Motion - Shoulders and Elbows

☐ Spread your arms open then cross in front.

Do ______ sets of ______.

☐ Place your hands on your lower back. Move up your spine.

Do ______ sets of ______.

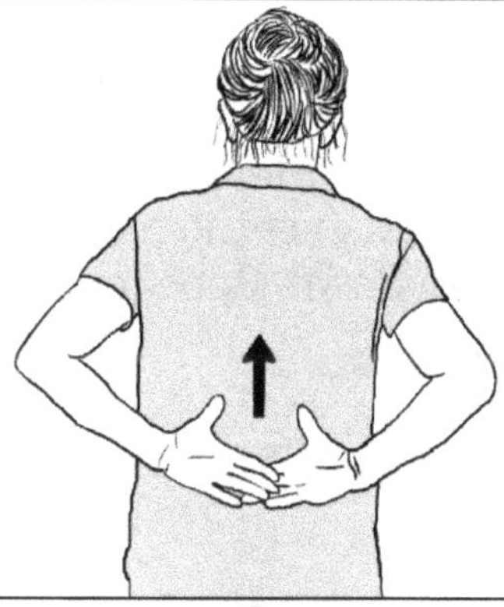

☐ Place your hands behind your neck. Reach down toward your shoulder blades.

Do ______ sets of ______.

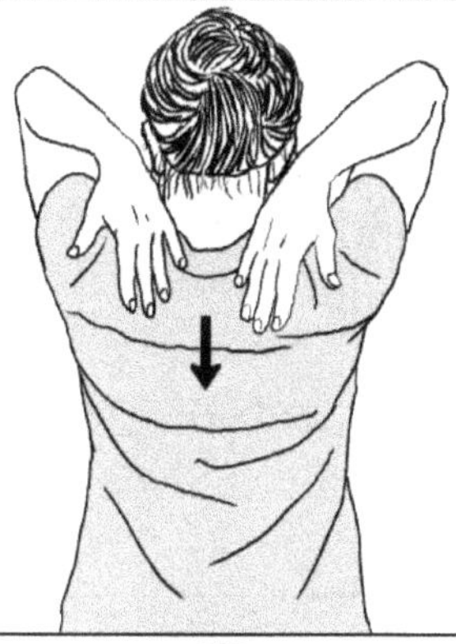

☐ Bend and straighten your arms.

Do ______ sets of ______.

Occupational Therapy TOOLKIT

Upper Body Active Range of Motion - Forearm and Wrist

☐ Bend your elbows. Hold them into your sides. Turn your palms up. Turn your palms down.

Do ______ sets of ______.

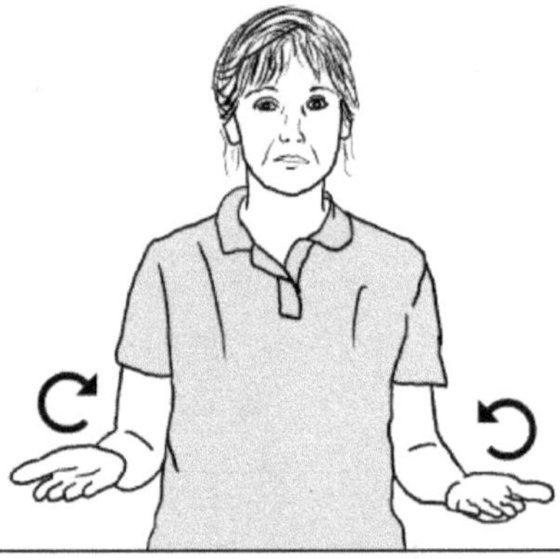

☐ Support your forearm on a table with your hand over the edge. Lift your hand up then down. Repeat with the other hand.

Do ______ sets of ______.

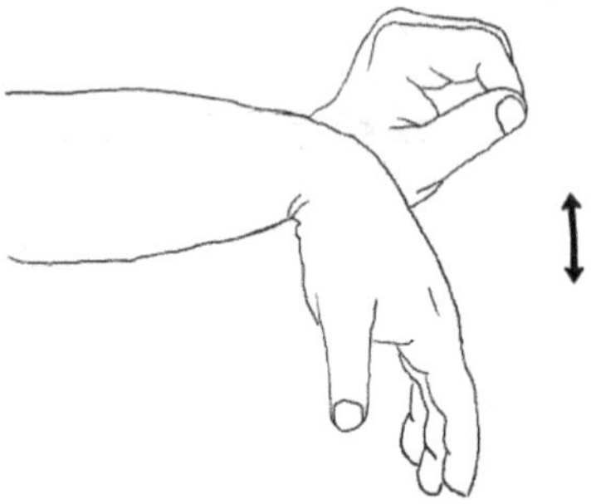

☐ Support your forearms on a table. Move your hand side to side. Repeat with the other hand.

Do ______ sets of ______.

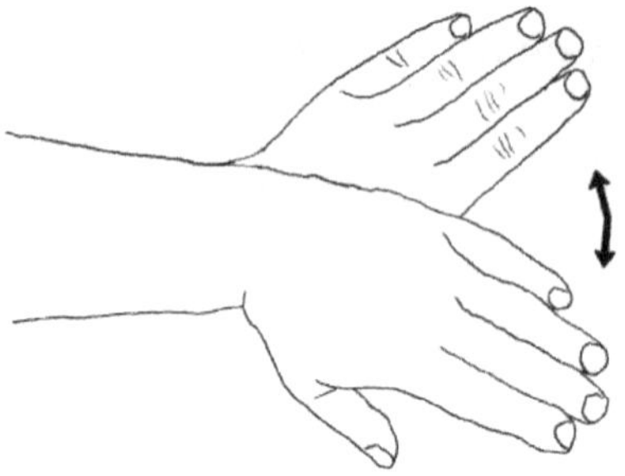

☐ Move your wrist in a circle. Repeat with your other hand.

Do ______ sets of ______.

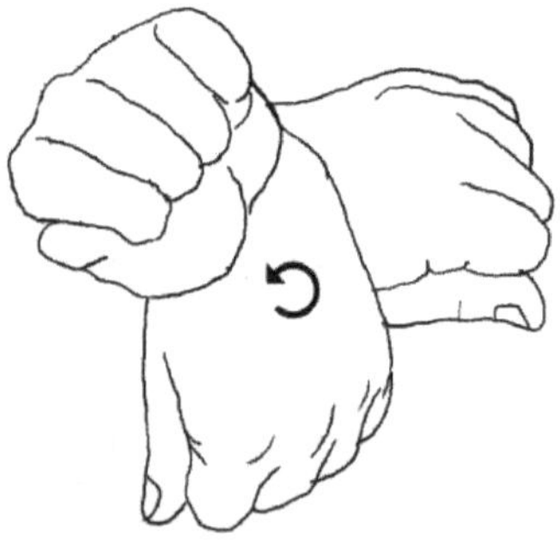

Occupational Therapy TOOLKIT

Upper Body Active Range of Motion - Finger and Thumb

☐ Bend your thumb over toward the base of your little finger, and then straighten. Repeat with the other hand.

Do ______ sets of ______.

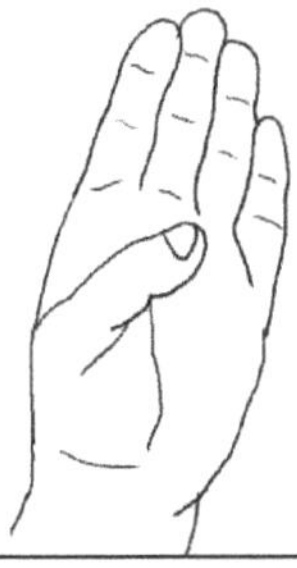

☐ Make a fist, and then spread your fingers apart. Repeat with the other hand.

Do ______ sets of ______.

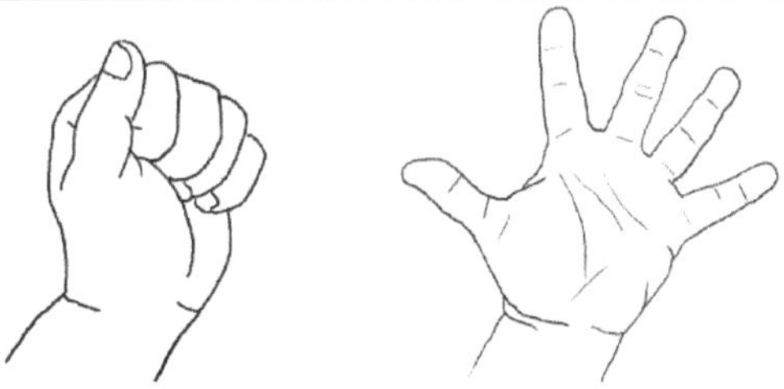

☐ Claw your fingers, and then straighten. Repeat with the other hand.

Do ______ sets of ______.

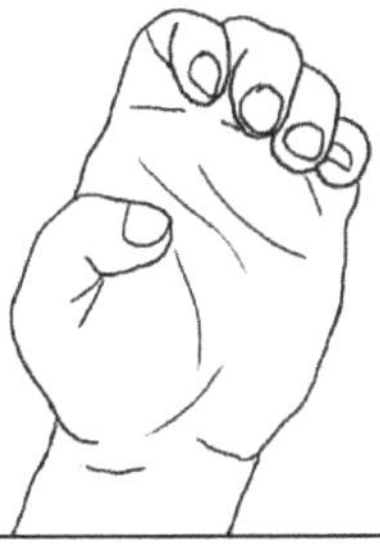

☐ Place your hand flat on the table and lift your fingers up. Repeat with the other hand.

Do ______ sets of ______.

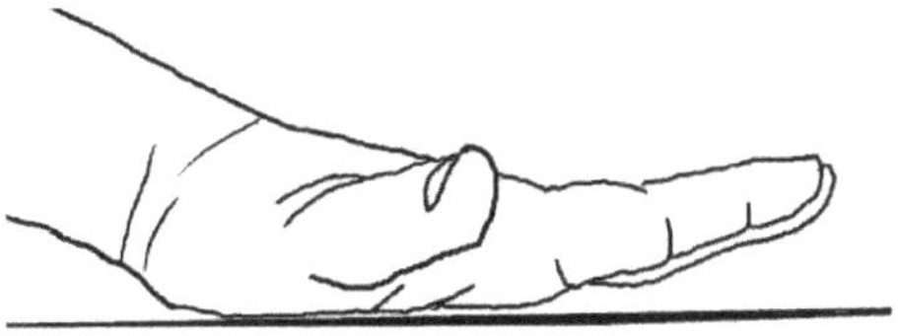

☐ Keep your fingers straight. Bend your knuckles. Repeat with the other hand.

Do ______ sets of ______.

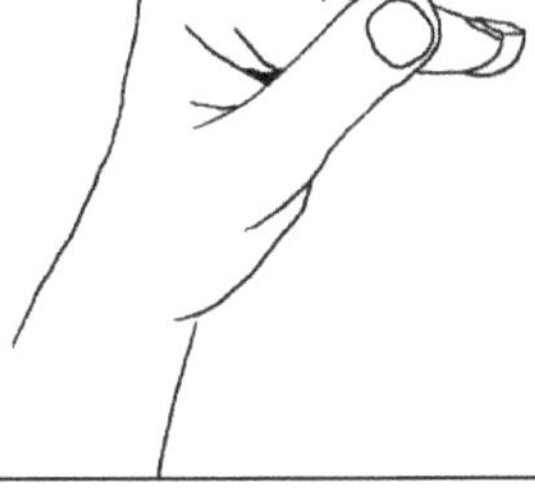

Occupational Therapy TOOLKIT

Upper Body Active Range of Motion - Trunk

☐ Raise one arm over your head. Bend to the side. Repeat to the other side.

Do ______ sets of ______.

☐ Sit. Keep your back straight. Lean forward from your hips. Reach toward your toes.

Do ______ sets of ______.

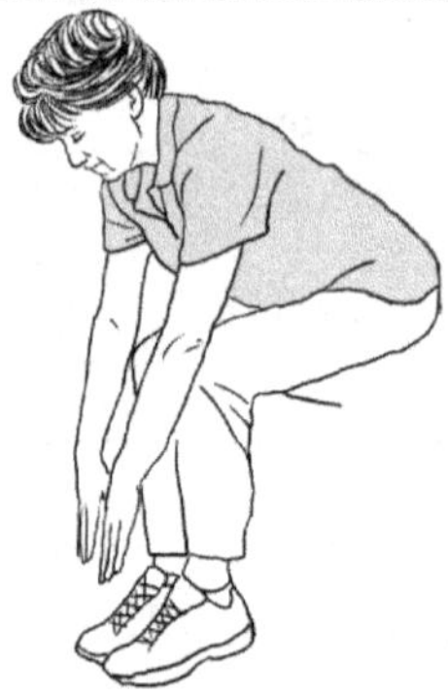

☐ Place your hands on your hips. Turn your body and look over your shoulder. Repeat on the other side.

Do ______ sets of ______.

☐ Lean backward slowly and arch your back.

Do ______ sets of ______.

Upper Body Exercises - Hand Weights

Name: ______________________________

Date: ______________________________

Therapist: ______________________________

Phone number: (_____)____________________

Exercise _____ times a day, _____ times a week.

Exercise slowly and smoothly.

Do the exercises while **sitting** **standing** (circle one).

Do not hold your breath during exercise. Count aloud if needed.

Sore muscles lasting a few days and feeling tired are normal after exercise. Exhaustion, sore joints, and painful muscle pulls are not normal. If you have these symptoms, do not exercise until you talk with your therapist.

If you have chest tightness or pain, shortness of breath, feel dizzy, faint, or sick to your stomach, stop and call emergency services at _____.

Notes:

____

____

____

____

____

____

____

____

Upper Body Exercises - Warm-Up

☐ Roll your shoulders in a circle

Do ______ sets of ______.

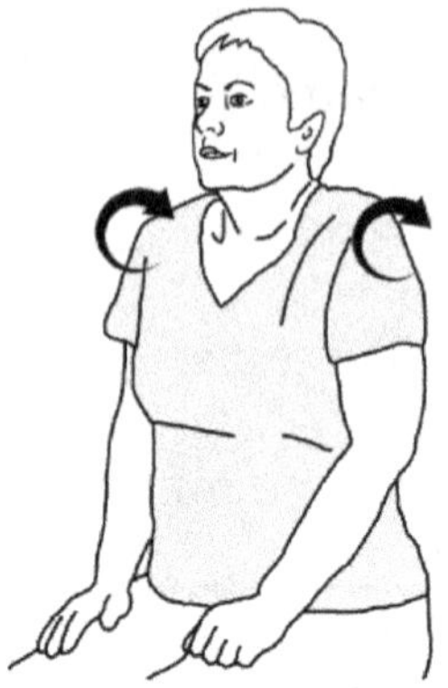

☐ Reach out in front and twist your arms.

Do ______ sets of ______.

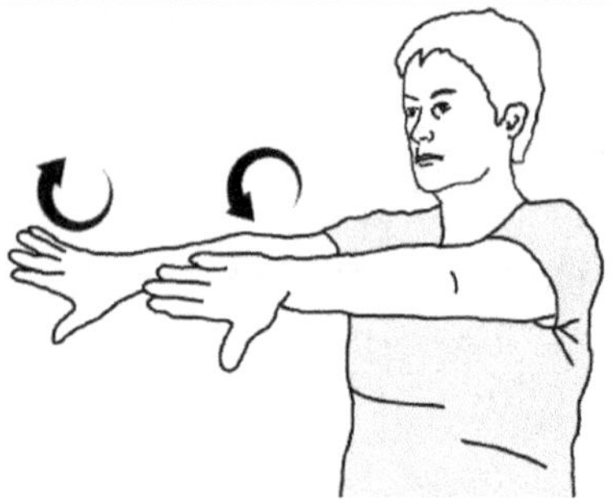

☐ Reach out in front and cross your arms back and forth.

Do ______ sets of ______.

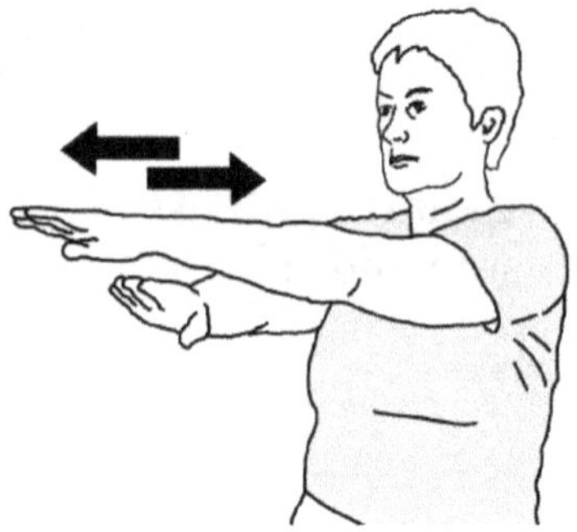

☐ Reach out in front and move your arms up and down.

Do ______ sets of ______.

Occupational Therapy TOOLKIT

Upper Body Exercises - Hand Weights

Hold a _____ weight in your right hand, and a _____ weight in your left hand

☐ **Press Up**
Press the weights up from your shoulders.

Do ______ sets of ______.

☐ **Forward Raise**
Hold your elbows straight and point your thumbs up. Lift the weights over your head.

Do ______ sets of ______.

☐ **Rotation**
Tuck your elbows into your sides. Rotate your arms out.

Do ______ sets of ______.

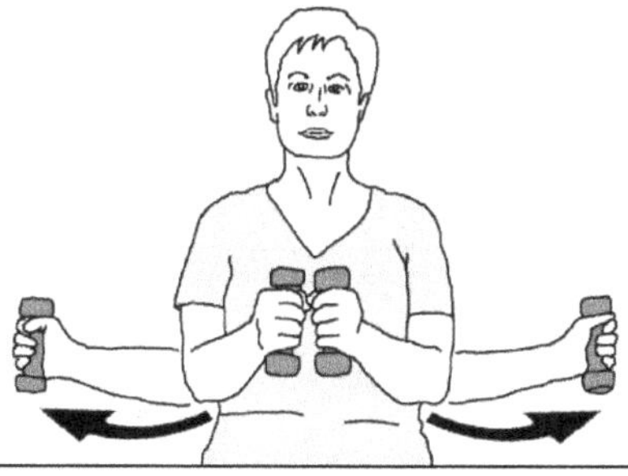

☐ **Side Raise**
Hold both arms out to the side with thumbs pointing up. Raise your arms up.

Do ______ sets of ______.

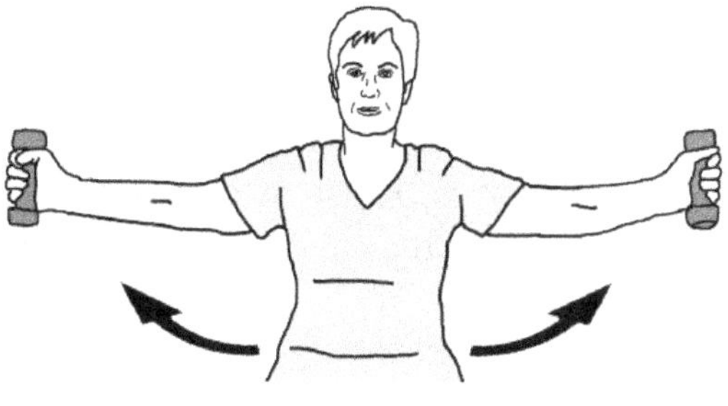

Occupational Therapy TOOLKIT

Upper Body Exercises - Hand Weights

Hold a _____ weight in your right hand, and a _____ weight in your left hand

---

☐ **Elbow Curls**
With your palms up, bend and straighten your elbows.

Do _____ sets of _____.

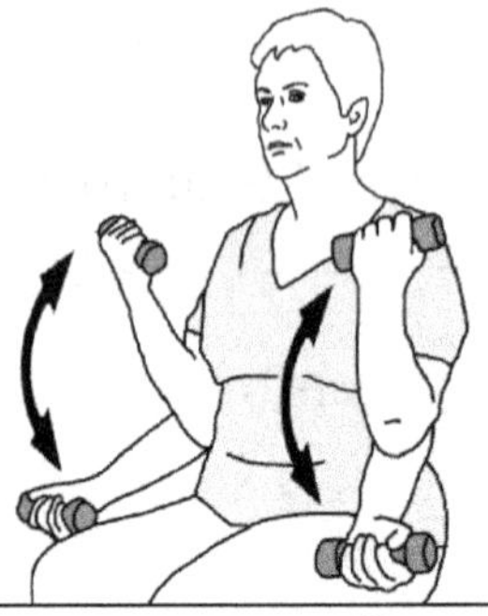

☐ **Elbow Extension**
Hold the weight behind your neck, and then straighten your arm above your head. Repeat on your other side.

Do _____ sets of _____.

☐ **Forearm Turns**
Bend your elbows. Hold them at your sides. Turn your palms up then turn your palms down.

Do _____ sets of _____.

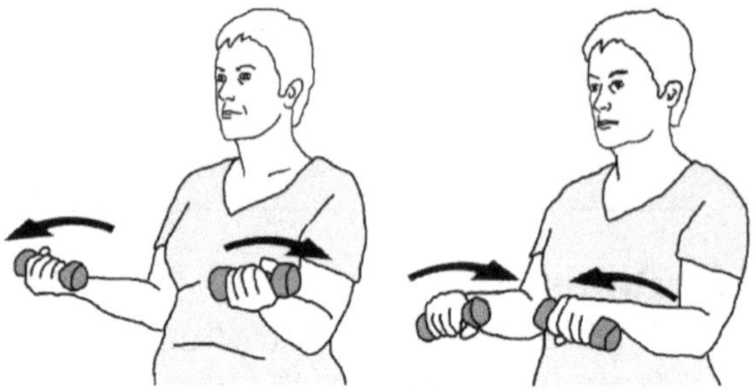

☐ **Wrist Bends**
Bend your elbows. Hold them at your sides with your palms up. Raise and lower your hands at your wrist.

Hold your elbows at your sides with your palms down. Raise and lower your hands at your wrist.

Do _____ sets of _____.

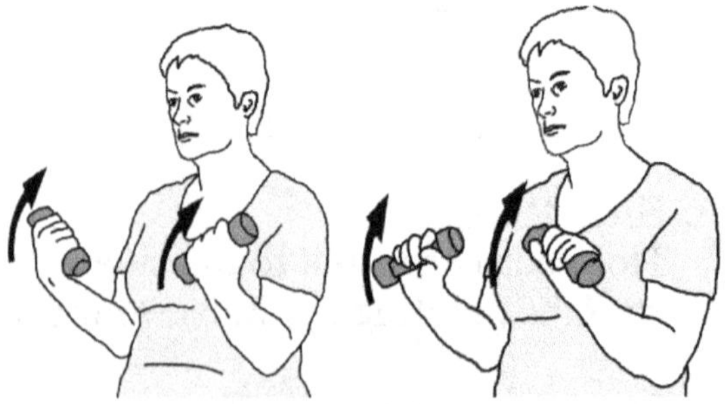

Upper Body Stretches - Cool Down

☐ Reach behind your neck. Hold for a count of ______.

Do _____ sets of _____.
Repeat on your other side.

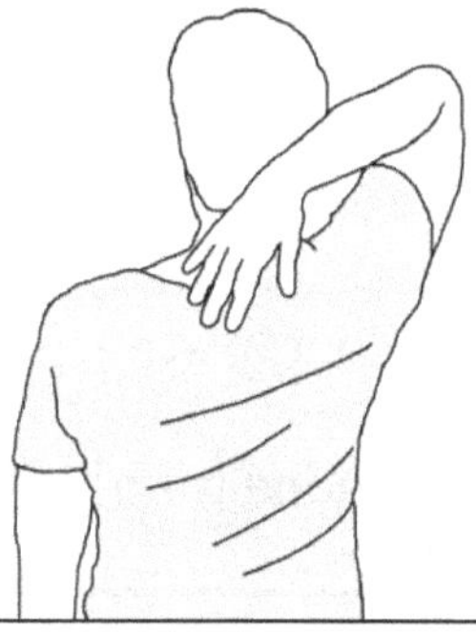

☐ Reach behind your lower back. Hold for a count of ______.

Do _____ sets of _____.
Repeat on your other side.

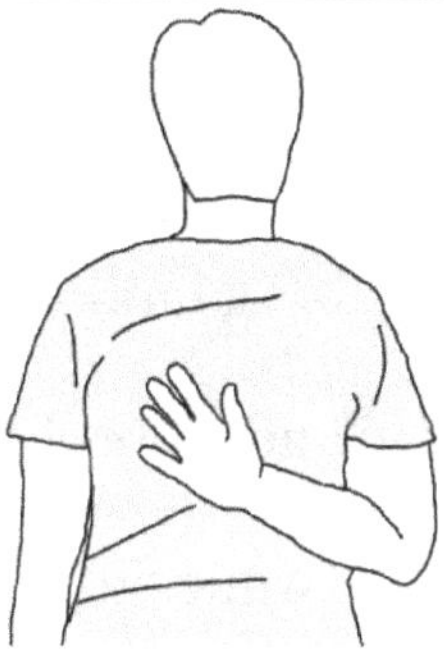

☐ Place one hand on your other shoulder. Use your other hand to push your elbow. Hold for a count of ______.

Do _____ sets of _____.
Repeat on your other side.

☐ Lace your fingers and reach up. Hold for a count of ______.

Do _____ sets of _____.

Occupational Therapy TOOLKIT

Upper Body Exercises - Using a Ball

Name: ___________________________________

Date: ___________________________________

Therapist: ________________________________

Phone number: (_____)______________________

Exercise _____ times a day, _____ times a week.

Hold a _____ lb/kg ball.

Exercise slowly and smoothly.

Do the exercises while sitting   standing (circle one).

Do not hold your breath during exercise. Count aloud if needed.

Sore muscles lasting a few days and feeling tired are normal after exercise. Exhaustion, sore joints, and painful muscle pulls are not normal. If you have these symptoms, do not exercise until you talk with your therapist.

If you have chest tightness or pain, shortness of breath, feel dizzy, faint, or sick to your stomach, stop and call emergency services at _____.

Notes:

____

____

____

____

____

____

____

____

Upper Body Exercises - Using a Ball

☐ Raise the ball over head.

Do ______ sets of ______.

☐ Push the ball out from your chest.

Do ______ sets of ______.

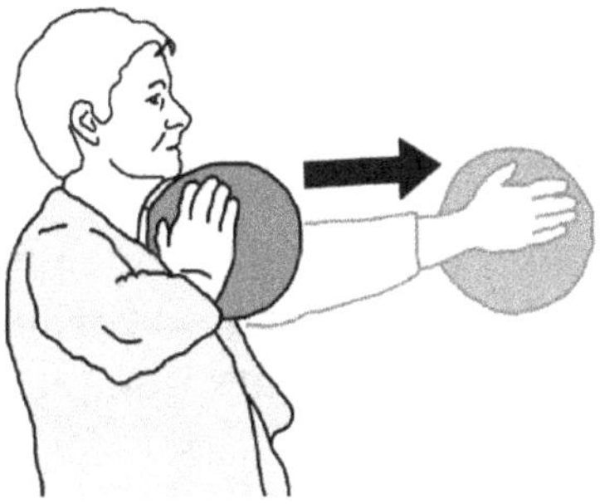

☐ Reach with the ball from side to side.

Do ______ sets of ______.

☐ Circle the ball in front of you.

Do ______ sets of ______.

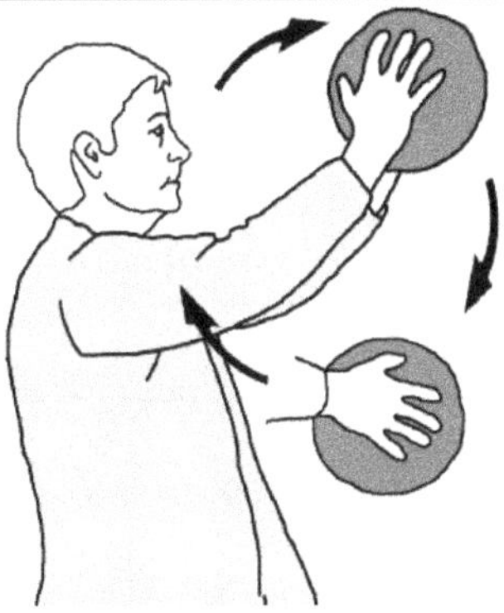

Upper Body Exercises - Using a Ball

☐ Sit. Move the ball from your chin to your right knee, then from your chin to your left knee.

Do ______ sets of ______.

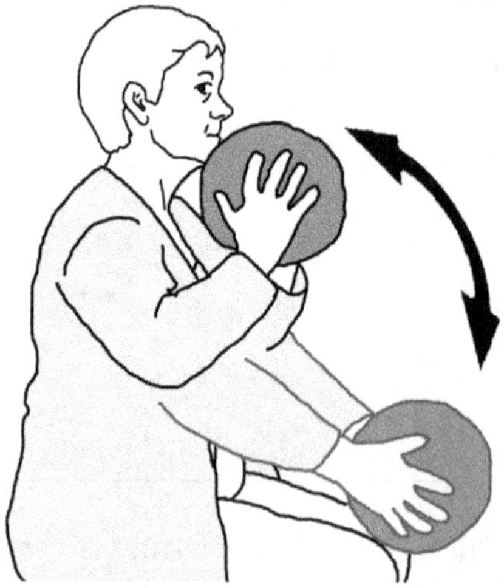

☐ Hold the ball with your right hand on top, and your left hand on the bottom. Turn the ball so your left hand is on top.

Do ______ sets of ______.

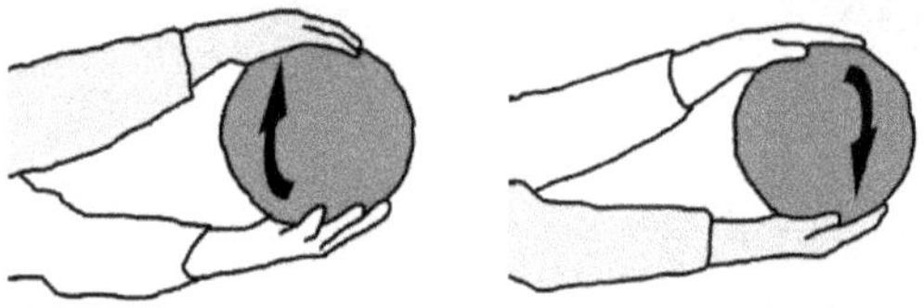

☐ Hold the ball between your hands and bend your wrists side to side

Do ______ sets of ______.

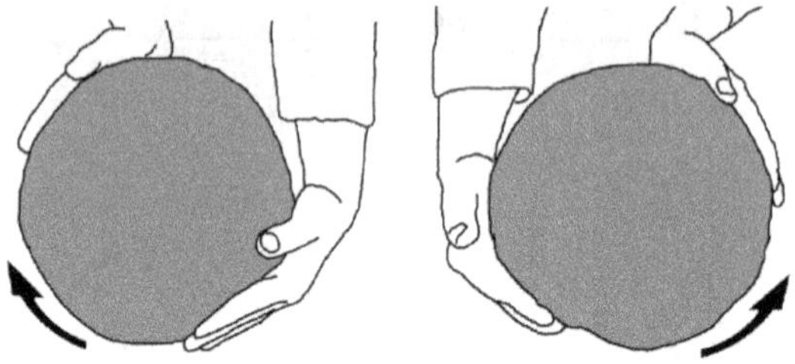

☐ Hold the ball between your hands and bend your wrists up and down

Do ______ sets of ______.

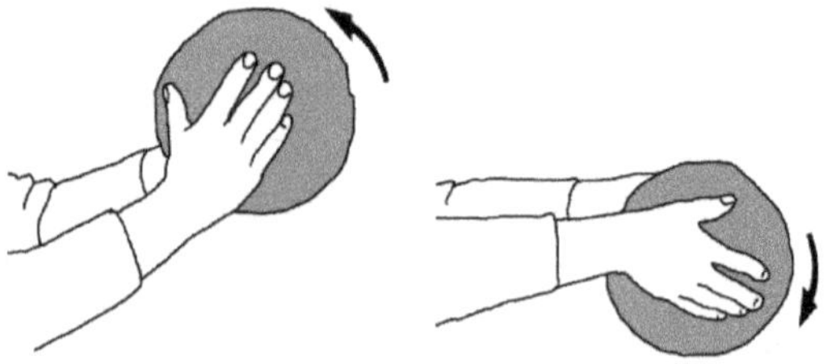

Upper Body Strength Activities

Do armchair push-ups.

Throw a ball or darts.

Play balloon volley.

Wash mirrors and windows.

Mop and sweep.

Vacuum and dust.

Make beds.

Hang clothes.

Put items on shelf.

Do cooking tasks: kneading, stirring, rolling, whisking.

Wash and dry dishes.

Fold clothes.

Rake leaves.

Drive nails with hammer.

Wash the car.

Paint a wall.

Occupational Therapy TOOLKIT

Use Your Left Arm to Actively Move and Hold

Use your left arm as much as you can during the day. Here are a few ideas.

Move your left arm out of the way when dressing and bathing.

Use your left hand to hold a dish while you wash it with your right hand.

Carry a piece of clothing under your left arm.

Use your left arm to help with bed mobility.

Use Your Left Arm to Passively Hold

Use your left arm as much as you can during the day. Here are a few ideas.

Use your left hand to hold your plate while eating.

Hold a sheet of paper with your left hand while writing with your right hand.

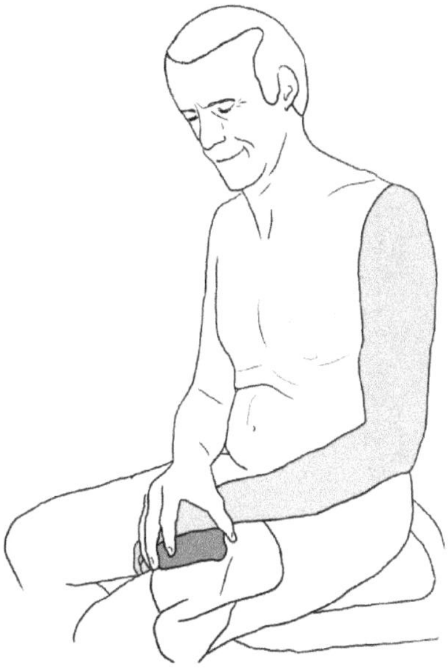

Hold a washcloth with your left hand and apply soap with your right hand.

Hold your toothbrush with your left hand and apply toothpaste with your right hand.

Use Your Left Arm with Assisted Guiding

Use your left arm as much as you can during the day. Here are a few ideas.

Your caregiver will place their hand over your left hand to help you hold the glass. Pour the drink with your right hand.

Your caregiver will place their hand over your left hand to help you hold the hairbrush.

Your caregiver will place their hand over your left hand to help you fold the laundry.

Your caregiver will place their hand over your left hand to help you hold the spoon.

Occupational Therapy TOOLKIT

Use Your Left Arm with Gross Motor Activities

Use your left arm as much as you can during the day. Here are a few ideas. You may need to support your left arm in an overhead sling or on the table.

Use your left hand to stack cups and put them in the cupboard.

Use your left hand to hold a built-up spoon during meals.

Use your left hand to use a built-up hairbrush.

Use your left hand to apply lotion to your right arm.

Use Your Left Arm with Self-Guiding

Use your left arm as much as you can during the day. Here are a few ideas.

Place your left hand on a washcloth. Use your right hand to guide the washcloth on the counter.

Place a cracker, cookie or other finger food in your left hand. Use your right hand to guide the food up to your mouth.

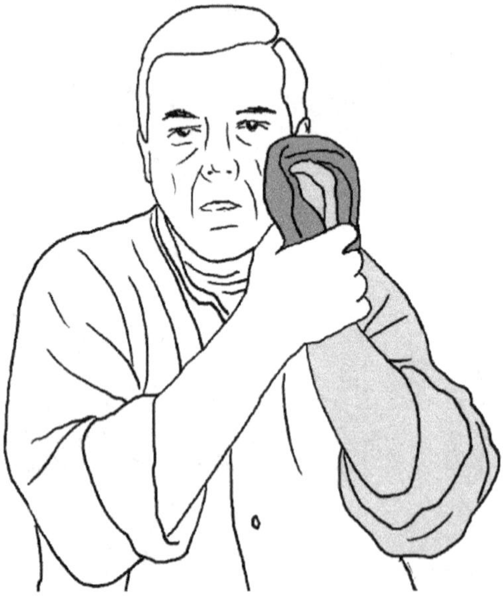

Place a washcloth in your left hand. Use your right hand to guide the washcloth to wash your face.

Place an electric razor in your left hand. Use your right hand to guide the razor to your face.

Occupational Therapy TOOLKIT

Use Your Right Arm to Actively Move and Hold

Use your right arm as much as you can during the day. Here are a few ideas.

Move your right arm out of the way when dressing and bathing.

Use your right hand to hold a dish while you wash it with your left hand.

Carry a piece of clothing under your right arm.

Use your right arm to help with bed mobility.

Use Your Right Arm to Passively Hold

Use your right arm as much as you can during the day. Here are a few ideas.

Use your right hand to hold your plate while eating.

Hold a sheet of paper with your right hand while writing.

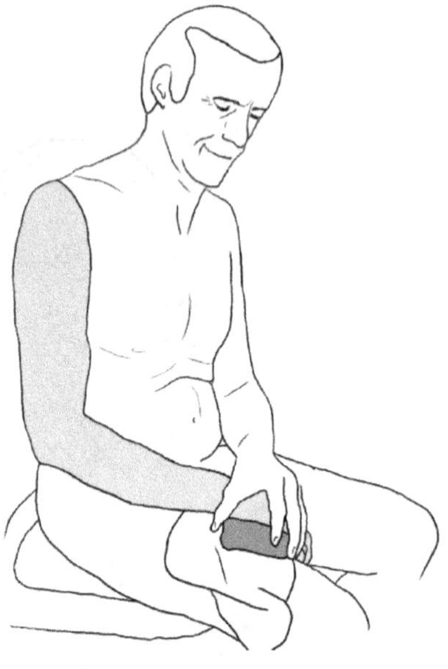

Hold a washcloth with your right hand and apply soap with your left hand.

Hold your toothbrush with your right hand and apply the toothpaste with your left hand.

Occupational Therapy TOOLKIT

Use Your Right Arm with Assisted Guiding

Use your right arm as much as you can during the day. Here are a few ideas.

Your caregiver will place their hand over your right hand to help you hold the glass. Pour the drink with your left hand.

Your caregiver will place their hand over your right hand to help you hold the hairbrush.

Your caregiver will place their hand over your right hand to help you fold the laundry.

Your caregiver will place their hand over your right hand to help you hold the spoon.

Use Your Right Arm with Gross Motor Activities

Use your right arm as much as you can during the day. Here are a few ideas. You may need to support your right arm in an overhead sling or on the table.

Use your right hand to stack cups and put them in the cupboard.

Use your right hand to hold a built-up spoon during meals.

Use your right hand to use a built-up hairbrush.

Use your right hand to apply lotion to your left arm.

Occupational Therapy TOOLKIT

Use Your Right Arm with Self-Guiding

Use your right arm as much as you can during the day. Here are a few ideas.

Place your right hand on a washcloth. Use your left hand to guide the washcloth over the counter.

Place a cracker, cookie or other finger food in your right hand. Use your left hand to guide the food up to your mouth.

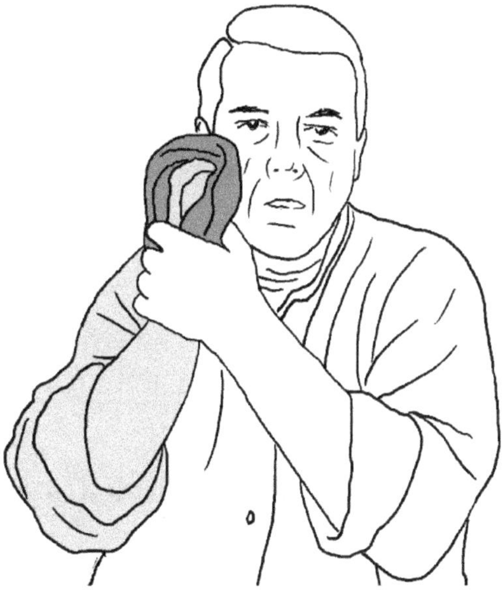

Place a washcloth in your right hand. Use your left hand to guide the washcloth to wash your face.

Place an electric razor in your right hand. Use your left hand to guide the razor to your face.

Occupational Therapy TOOLKIT

Walking Guidelines

Name: ________________________________

Date: ________________________________

Therapist: ________________________________

Phone number: (_____)________________________

Walk for _____ minutes _____ times per day. Walk _____ days a week

Wear comfortable clothing and walking shoes. Take a bottle of water and your phone.

Walk using a ___________________________.

Use good posture:

- Hold your head up. Keep your back and neck straight.
- Tighten your stomach muscles.
- Let your shoulders and arms move freely and with ease.

Before starting each walk, spend some time warming up your muscles.

Begin walking slowly and increase to a moderate intensity (5 to 6 on a 10-point scale). You should be able to talk while walking.

When your walk is over, do some stretching exercises.

Sore muscles lasting a few days and feeling tired are normal after exercise. Exhaustion, sore joints, and painful muscle pulls are not normal. If you have these symptoms, do not exercise until you talk with your therapist

If you have chest tightness or pain, shortness of breath, feel dizzy, faint, or sick to your stomach, stop and call emergency services at _____.

Notes:

____

____

____

Warm-Up Exercises

☐ **Arm Circles**
Hold out your arms and rotate them in a circle.

Circle your arms for a count of ______.

☐ **Boxing**
Punch forward with your right fist and then your left fist.

Box for a count of ______.

☐ **Arm Swings**
Swing your arms at your sides.

Swing your arms for a count of ______.

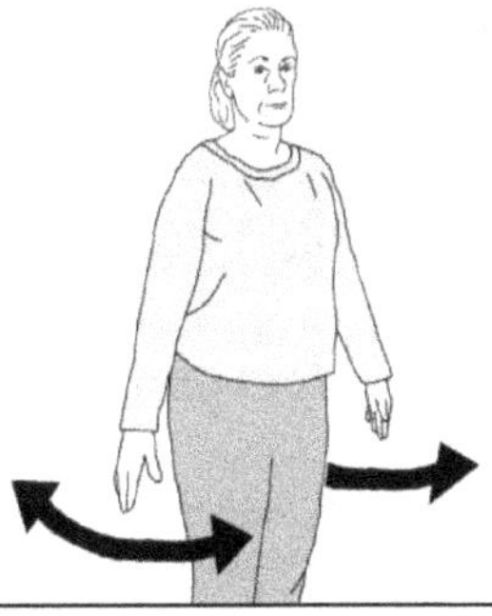

☐ **March in Place**
Step up and down; bring your knees as high as you can.

March in place for a count of ______.

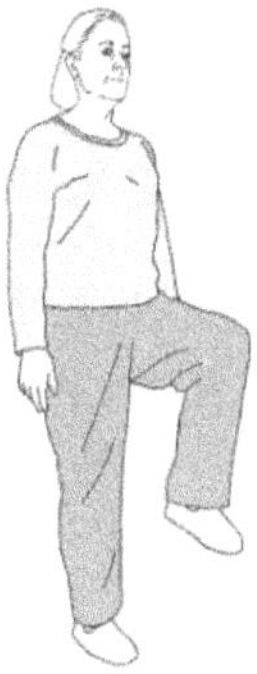

☐ **Grip Strength**
Squeeze a soft ball.

Do ______ sets of ______ with each hand.

Weight Bearing Exercises - Left Side Weakness

Do the checked exercises _____ times a day, _____ days a week.

☐ Sit at the table. Clasp your hands. Stretch your arms forward. Roll onto your left shoulder. Rest your head on your left shoulder. Hold for a count of _____.

Do _____ sets of _____.

☐ Stand at the table. Bend forward and place both arms on the table with your hands flat. Lean your weight into your left arm. Hold for a count of _____.

Do _____ sets of _____.

☐ Stand at the table. Place your left hand flat on the table. Keep your elbow straight. You may need someone to help you with this. Lean your weight into your left arm. Hold for a count of _____.

Do _____ sets of _____.

Occupational Therapy TOOLKIT

Weight Bearing Exercises - Right Side Weakness

Do the checked exercises _____ times a day, _____ days a week.

☐ Sit at the table. Clasp your hands. Stretch your arms forward. Roll onto your right shoulder. Rest your head on your right shoulder. Hold for a count of _____.

Do _____ sets of _____.

☐ Stand at the table. Lean forward and place both arms on the table with your hands flat. Lean your weight into your right arm. Hold for a count of _____.

Do _____ sets of _____.

☐ Stand at the table. Place your right hand flat on the table. Keep your elbow straight. You may need someone to help you with this. Lean your weight into your right arm. Hold for a count of _____.

Do _____ sets of _____.

Occupational Therapy TOOLKIT

Bibliography

Action Tremors

Duthie EH (1998) Practice of Geriatrics, 3rd ed., Philadelphia, W. B. Saunders Company

International Essential Tremor Foundation www.essentialtremor.org/index.php

Movement Disorders Society www.movementdisorders.org

National Institute of Neurological Disorders and Stroke (2016) Tremor Fact Sheet Accessed from https://www.ninds.nih.gov/Disorders/Patient-Caregiver-Education/Fact-Sheets/Tremor-Fact-Sheet

Plumb M (2000) Essential Tremor: The Facts. Oxford University Press

Wagle Shukla A, Vedam-Mai V, Vaillancourt DE, Okun MS, Warren L (2014) Cooling of limbs: A cool therapy for treatment of essential tremor Movement Disorders 29 Suppl 1:1162

Wagle Shukla A (2014) What is Essential Tremor, how is it evaluated and how is it treated? Diann Shaddox Foundation

Worldwide Education and Awareness For Movement Disorders www.wemove.org

Wynn P, (2012) Holding Steady, Today in OT

Activities of Daily Living Training

AARP website www.aarp.org/health/rx_drugs/usingmeds/

ABLEDATA www.abledata.com

Addressing Sexuality with Adult Burn Survivors Guidelines for Staff Phoenix Society. Retrieved from https://www.phoenixsociety.org/resources/entry/addressingsexualityguidelines

Alessi CA, Yoon EJ, Schnelle JF, (1999). A randomized trial of a combined physical activity and environmental intervention in nursing home residents: do sleep and agitation improve?. J Am Geriatr Soc.

American Automobile Association. (n.d.) The AAA roadwise review: A tool to help seniors drive safely longer. retrieved from http://seniordriving.aaa.com/evaluate-your-driving-ability/interactive-driving-evaluation

American Occupational Therapy Association (2014) Occupational therapy practice framework: Domain and process, 3rd Ed. Amer J Occup Ther

American Occupational Therapy Association: (2002) Occupational therapy practice framework: domain and process, Am J Occup Ther

American Occupational Therapy Association Commission on Practice (1998) Standards of practice for occupational therapy, Bethesda, MD, 1998, AOTA.

American Occupational Therapy Association. (2007). Specialized knowledge and skills in eating and feeding for occupational therapy practice. American Journal of Occupational Therapy, 61 (November, December)

Ancoli-Israel S, Ayalon. (2006) Diagnosis and treatment of sleep disorders in older adults. Am J Geriatr Psychiatry.

The complete 108-page bibliography is available at http://www.ottoolkit.com/pdfs/bibliography.pdf

CPSIA information can be obtained
at www.ICGtesting.com
Printed in the USA
JSHW021021070920
7664JS00004B/8

9 781948 72600